The Longman Anthology of British Literature

✦—✦═◈═✦—✦

VOLUME 2B

David Damrosch
COLUMBIA UNIVERSITY

Kevin J. H. Dettmar
SOUTHERN ILLINOIS UNIVERSITY

Christopher Baswell
UNIVERSITY OF CALIFORNIA, LOS ANGELES

Clare Carroll
QUEENS COLLEGE, CITY UNIVERSITY OF NEW YORK

Heather Henderson

Constance Jordan
CLAREMONT GRADUATE UNIVERSITY

Peter J. Manning
STATE UNIVERSITY OF NEW YORK, STONY BROOK

Anne Howland Schotter
WAGNER COLLEGE

William Chapman Sharpe
BARNARD COLLEGE

Stuart Sherman
FORDHAM UNIVERSITY

Jennifer Wicke
UNIVERSITY OF VIRGINIA

Susan J. Wolfson
PRINCETON UNIVERSITY

The Longman Anthology of British Literature
Third Edition

David Damrosch and Kevin J. H. Dettmar
General Editors

VOLUME 2B

THE VICTORIAN AGE
Heather Henderson *and* William Sharpe

PEARSON
Longman

New York   San Francisco   Boston
London   Toronto   Sydney   Tokyo   Singapore   Madrid
Mexico City   Munich   Paris   Cape Town   Hong Kong   Montreal

Vice President and Editor-in-Chief: *Joseph Terry*
Senior Development Editor: *Mikola De Roo*
Director of Development: *Mary Ellen Curley*
Executive Marketing Manager: *Ann Stypuloski*
Supplements Editor: *Donna Campion*
Media Supplements Editor: *Jenna Egan*
Production Manager: *Ellen MacElree*
Project Coordination, Text Design, and Page Makeup: *Elm Street Publishing Services, Inc.*
Cover Design Manager: *Nancy Danahy*
On the Cover: *The Baleful Head c. 1876 (gouache) by Sir Edward Burne-Jones (1833–1898),*
Southampton City Art Gallery, Hampshire, UK/Bridgeman Art Library.
Photo Researcher: *Julie Tesser*
Manufacturing Buyer: *Al Dorsey*
Printer and Binder: *Quebecor-World/Taunton*
Cover Printer: *The Lehigh Press, Inc.*

For permission to use copyrighted material, grateful acknowledgment is made to the copyright
holders on pages xxxiv–xxxv, which are hereby made part of this copyright page.

Library of Congress Cataloging-in-Publication Data
The Longman anthology of British literature / David Damrosch, gerenal editor.——3rd ed.
   p. cm.
  Includes bibilographical references and index.
    ISBN 0-321-33397-7 (vol. 1: alk. paper)——ISBN 0-321-33398-5 (vol. 2:alk. paper)
  1. English literature. 2. Great Britain——Literary collections. I. Damrosch, David.
PR1109 L69 2006
820.8——dc22

                        2005030799

Please visit our website at http://www.ablongman.com/damrosch.

ISBN Single Volume Edition, Volume II: 0-321-33398-5
ISBN Volume 2A, The Romantics and Their Contemporaries: 0-321-33394-2
ISBN Volume 2B, The Victorian Age: 0-321-33395-0
ISBN Volume 2C, The Twentieth Century: 0-321-33396-9

1 2 3 4 5 6 7 8 9 0—QWT—08 07 06 05

CONTENTS

⇒ PERSPECTIVES ⇐
Aestheticism, Decadence, and the *Fin de Siècle*   2059

LIST OF ILLUSTRATIONS

The Victorian Age

ADDITIONAL AUDIO AND ONLINE RESOURCES

Voices of British Literature, Volume Two, ISBN 0-321-36475-9
An Audio CD to Accompany *The Longman Anthology of British Literature*, Volume Two   Throughout most of history, literature was written to be read, recited, or sung out loud. The selections on the above CD, which can be ordered/packaged with this anthology, present a range of the many voices of British literature from the nineteenth and twentieth centuries and open up a range of cultural contexts for student discussion and writing. Below is the list of selections in The Victorian Age Volume with corresponding CD audio tracks. The corresponding page numbers in this anthology are also listed below for easy cross-referencing.

Track in *Voices of British Literature*, Volume Two	Page in Text

Companion Website for *The Longman Anthology of British Literature*
<www.ablongman.com/damroschbritlit3e>

For additional resources on each period in British literature, including a timeline of the period, additional author and Web resources, and an Online Research Guide, go to <www.ablongman.com/damroschbritlit3e>. To make movement between the anthology and the Website easier, cross-references to the Website have also been added throughout the main text of the book.

PREFACE

Literature has a double life. Born in one time and place and read in another, literary works are at once products of their age and independent creations, able to live on long after their original world has disappeared. The goal of this anthology is to present a wealth of poetry, prose, and drama from the full sweep of the literary history of Great Britain and its empire, and to do so in ways that will bring out both the works' original cultural contexts and their lasting aesthetic power. These aspects are, in fact, closely related: Form and content, verbal music and social meanings, go hand in hand. This double life makes literature, as Aristotle said, "the most philosophical" of all the arts, intimately connected to ideas and to realities that the writer transforms into moving patterns of words. The challenge is to show these works in the contexts in which, and for which, they were written, while at the same time not trapping them within those contexts. The warm response this anthology has received from the hundreds of teachers who have adopted it in its first two editions reflects the growing consensus that we do not have to accept an "either/or" choice between the literature's aesthetic and cultural dimensions. Our users' responses have now guided us in seeing how we can improve our anthology further, so as to be most pleasurable and stimulating to students, most useful to teachers, and most responsive to ongoing developments in literary studies. This preface can serve as a road map to the new phase in this book's life.

A GENEROUS REPRESENTATION OF MAJOR CLASSIC TEXTS

As in previous editions, major works in all three genres are included in their entirety—among them *Beowulf*, More's *Utopia*, Shakespeare's *The Tempest*, Dickens' *A Christmas Carol*, Stevenson's *The Strange Case of Dr Jekyll and Mr Hyde*, Wilde's *The Importance of Being Earnest*, Conrad's *Heart of Darkness*, and Shaw's *Pygmalion*. The book also continues to offer a wealth of significant poetry selections, from Chaucer, Spenser, and Milton to Blake, Keats, and Yeats—and beyond. In response to instructors' requests, several important works that are taught most frequently have been added to this edition, including:

- J. R. R. Tolkien's translation of *Sir Gawain and the Green Knight*
- the modern translation of Chaucer's General Prologue from *The Canterbury Tales* (appearing on facing pages from the Middle English)
- an expanded selection of poems from Sidney's *Astrophil and Stella*
- additional poems from Lady Mary Wroth

- the complete text of Milton's *Paradise Lost*

- chapters from the third voyage and the complete fourth voyage from Swift's *Gulliver's Travels*

- more poems from Blake's *Songs of Innocence and of Experience*

- more by Wordsworth, including an expanded selection of his Preface to *Lyrical Ballads*

- Keats' *Lamia*

- more World War I poems, including an expanded selection of women poets

- Beckett's *Endgame*

- more prose selections by Salman Rushdie

- a wider range of works touching on issues of post-colonialism by such authors as Chinua Achebe, Lorna Goodison, Hanif Kureishi, and Agha Shahid Ali.

LITERATURE IN ITS TIME—AND IN OURS

When we engage with a rich literary history that extends back over a thousand years, we often encounter writers who assume their readers know all sorts of things that are little known today: historical facts, social issues, literary and cultural references. Beyond specific information, these works will have come out of a very different literary culture than our own. Even the contemporary British Isles present a cultural situation—or a mix of cultures—very different from what North American readers encounter at home, and these differences only increase as we go farther back in time. A major emphasis of this anthology is to bring the works' original cultural moment to life: not because the works simply or naively reflect that moment of origin, but because they do refract it in fascinating ways. British literature is both a major heritage for modern North America and, in many ways, a very distinct culture; reading British literature will regularly give an experience both of connection and of difference. Great writers create imaginative worlds that have their own compelling internal logic, and a prime purpose of this anthology is to help readers to understand the formal means—whether of genre, rhetoric, or style—with which these writers have created works of haunting beauty. At the same time, as Virginia Woolf says in *A Room of One's Own*, the gossamer threads of the artist's web are joined to reality "with bands of steel." This anthology pursues a range of strategies to bring out both the beauty of these webs of words and their points of contact with reality.

The Longman Anthology brings related authors and works together in several ways:

☞ PERSPECTIVES: Broad groupings that illuminate underlying issues in a variety of the major works of a period.

☞ AND ITS TIME: A focused cluster that illuminates a specific cultural moment or a debate to which an author is responding.

☞ RESPONSES: One or more texts in which later authors in the tradition respond creatively to the challenging texts of their forebears.

These groupings provide a range of means of access to the literary culture of each period. The Perspectives sections do much more than record what major writers thought about an issue: they give a variety of views in a range of voices, to illustrate the wider culture within which the literature was being written. An attack on tobacco by King James the First; theological reflections by the pioneering scientist Isaac Newton; haunting testimony by Victorian child workers concerning their lives; these and many other vivid readings give rhetorical as well as social contexts for the poems, plays, and stories around them. Perspectives sections typically relate to several major authors of the period, as with a section on Government and Self-Government that relates broadly to Sir Thomas More's *Utopia*, to Spenser's *Faerie Queene*, and to Milton's *Paradise Lost*. Most of the writers included in Perspectives sections are important figures of the period who might be neglected if they were listed on their own with just a few pages each; grouping them together has proven to be useful pedagogically as well as intellectually. Perspectives sections may also include work by a major author whose primary listing appears elsewhere in the period; thus, a Perspective section on the abolition of slavery—a hotly debated issue in England from the 1790s through the 1830s—includes poems and essays on slavery by Wordsworth, Coleridge, and Barbauld, so as to give a rounded presentation of the issue in ways that can inform the reading of those authors in their individual sections.

When we present a major work "And Its Time," we give a cluster of related materials to suggest the context within which the work was written. Thus Sir Philip Sidney's great *Apology for Poetry* is accompanied by readings showing the controversy that was raging at the time concerning the nature and value of poetry. Some of the writers in these groupings and in our Perspectives sections have not traditionally been seen as literary figures, but all have produced lively and intriguing works, from medieval clerics writing about saints and sea monsters, to a polemical seventeenth-century tract giving *The Arraignment of Lewd, Idle, Froward, and Unconstant Women*, to rousing speeches by Winston Churchill as the British faced the Nazis during World War II.

Also, we include "Responses" to significant texts in the British literary tradition, demonstrating the sometimes far-reaching influence these works have had over the decades and centuries, and sometimes across oceans and continents. *Beowulf* and John Gardiner's *Grendel* are separated by the Atlantic oceans, perhaps eleven- or twelve hundred years—and, most notably, their attitude toward the poem's monster. The *Morte Darthur* is reinterpreted comically by the 1970s British comedy troupe Monty Python's Flying Circus; post–WWII poet Thom Gunn discusses the importance of the poetry of Ben Jonson; Judge John M. Woolsey, in the legal decision allowing the sale of James Joyce's *Ulysses* in the United States, succinctly makes the case for dangerous and unsettling art in the contemporary world.

CULTURAL EDITIONS

The publication of this edition of the *Longman Anthology* finds the first ten volumes of the Longman Cultural Editions now in print, which carry further the anthology's emphases by presenting major texts along with a generous selection of contextual material. Included in that first decade of volumes are frequently taught texts ranging from *Beowulf* and *Hamlet* to *Frankenstein* and *Northanger Abbey;* nearly three dozen new titles are currently being developed, bringing the list of available titles up to the early twentieth century. In some instances, dedicating a full, separate volume to major texts (like *Othello/Miriam* and *Frankenstein*)—available free, for course use, with the anthology itself—has helped to free up space for our many additions in this new edition. Taken together, our new edition and the Longman Cultural Editions offer an unparalleled set of materials for the enjoyment and study of British literary culture from its earliest beginnings to the present.

ILLUSTRATING VISUAL CULTURE

Another important context for literary production has been a different kind of culture: the visual. This edition includes a suite of color plates in each volume, along with one hundred black-and-white illustrations throughout the anthology, chosen to show artistic and cultural images that figured importantly for literary creation. Sometimes, a poem refers to a specific painting, or more generally emulates qualities of a school of visual art. At other times, more popular materials like advertisements may underlie scenes in Victorian or Modernist writing. In some cases, visual and literary creation have merged, as in Hogarth's series *A Rake's Progress*, included in Volume 1, or Blake's illustrated engravings of his *Songs of Innocence and of Experience*, several of whose plates are reproduced in color in Volume 2. A thumbnail portrait of major authors in each period marks the beginning of author introductions.

AIDS TO UNDERSTANDING

We have attempted to contextualize our selections in suggestive rather than exhaustive ways, trying to enhance rather than overwhelm the experience of reading the texts themselves. Thus, when difficult or archaic words need defining in poems, we use glosses in the margins, so as to disrupt the reader's eye as little as possible; footnotes are intended to be concise and informative, rather than massive or interpretive. Important literary and social terms are defined when they are used; for convenience of reference, there is also an extensive glossary of literary and cultural terms at the end of each volume, together with useful summaries of British political and religious organization, and of money, weights, and measures. For further reading, carefully selected, up-to-date bibliographies for each period and for each author can be found in each volume.

LOOKING—AND LISTENING—FURTHER

Beyond the boundaries of the anthology itself, we have incorporated a pair of CDs, one for each semester, giving a wide range of readings of texts in the anthology and of selections of music from each period. It is only in the past century or two that people usually began to read literature silently; most literature has been written in the expectation that it would be read aloud, or even sung in the case of lyric poetry ("lyric" itself means a work meant to be sung to the accompaniment of a lyre or other instruments). The aural power and beauty of these works is a crucial dimension of their experience. To make this resource easier to use, a list of selections with corresponding CD audio tracks appears after the main Table of Contents and List of Illustrations, under "Additional Audio and Online Resources." For further explorations, we have also expanded our Web site, available to all users at www.ablongman.com/damroschbritlit3e; this site gives a wealth of information, annotated links to related sites, and an archive of texts for further reading. Links to relevant pages are appended to anthology selections. For instructors, we have revised and expanded our popular companion volume, *Teaching British Literature*, written directly by the anthology editors, 600 pages in length, available free to everyone who adopts the anthology.

WHAT IS BRITISH LITERATURE?

Turning now to the book itself, let us begin by defining our basic terms: What is "British" literature? What is literature itself? And just what should an anthology of this material look like at the present time? The term "British" can mean many things, some of them contradictory, some of them even offensive to people on whom the name has been imposed. If the term "British" has no ultimate essence, it does have a history. The first British were Celtic people who inhabited the British Isles and the northern coast of France (still called Brittany) before various Germanic tribes of Angles and Saxons moved onto the islands in the fifth and sixth centuries. Gradually the Angles and Saxons amalgamated into the Anglo-Saxon culture that became dominant in the southern and eastern regions of Britain and then spread outward; the old British people were pushed west, toward what became known as Cornwall, Wales, and Ireland, which remained independent kingdoms for centuries, as did Celtic Scotland to the north. By an ironic twist of linguistic fate, the Anglo-Saxons began to appropriate the term British from the Britons they had displaced, and they took as a national hero the early, semi-mythic Welsh King Arthur. By the seventeenth century, English monarchs had extended their sway over Wales, Ireland, and Scotland, and they began to refer to their holdings as "Great Britain." Today, Great Britain includes England, Wales, Scotland, and Northern Ireland, but does not include the Republic of Ireland, which has been independent from England since 1922.

This anthology uses "British" in a broad sense, as a geographical term encompassing the whole of the British Isles. For all its fraught history, it seems a more satisfactory term than to speak simply of "English" literature, for two reasons. First: most speakers of English live in countries that are not the focus of this anthology; second, while the English language and its literature have long been dominant in the British Isles, other cultures in the region have always used other languages and have produced great literature in these languages. Important works by Irish, Welsh, and Scots writers appear regularly in the body of this anthology, some of them written directly in their languages and presented here in translation, and others written in an English inflected by the rhythms, habits of thought, and modes of expression characteristic of these other languages and the people who use them.

We use the term "literature" in a similarly capacious sense, to refer to a range of artistically shaped works written in a charged language, appealing to the imagination at least as much as to discursive reasoning. It is only relatively recently that creative writers have been able to make a living composing poems, plays, and novels, and only in the past hundred years or so has creating "belles lettres" or high literary art been thought of as a sharply separate sphere of activity from other sorts of writing that the same authors would regularly produce. Sometimes, Romantic poets wrote sonnets to explore the deepest mysteries of individual perception and memory; at other times, they wrote sonnets the way a person might now write an Op-Ed piece, and such a sonnet would be published and read along with parliamentary debates and letters to the editor on the most pressing contemporary issues.

WOMEN'S WRITING, AND MEN'S

Literary culture has always involved an interplay between central and marginal regions, groupings, and individuals. A major emphasis in literary study in recent years has been the recovery of writing by women writers, some of them little read until recently, others major figures in their time. The first two editions of this anthology included more women, and more writing by the women we included, than any other anthology had ever done or does even today. This edition increases the presence of women writers still more, with newly augmented selections for writers like Lady Mary Wroth, Mary Leapor, and Eliza Haywood, as well as by including new voices like Frances Burney, the contemporary Welsh poet Gwyneth Lewis, and a cluster of women poets writing out of their response to World War I. Attending to these voices gives us a new variety of compelling works, and helps us rethink the entire periods in which they wrote. The first third of the nineteenth century, for example, can be defined more broadly than as a "Romantic Age" dominated by six male poets; looking closely at women's writing as well as at men's, we can deepen our understanding of the period as a whole, including the specific achievements of Blake, William Wordsworth, Coleridge, Keats, Percy Shelley, and Byron, all of whom continue to have a major presence in these pages as most of them did during the nineteenth century.

VARIETIES OF LITERARY EXPERIENCE

Above all, we have striven to give as full a presentation as possible to the varieties of great literature produced over the centuries in the British Isles, by women as well as by men, in outlying regions as well as in the metropolitan center of London, and in prose, drama, and verse alike. We have taken particular care to do justice to prose fiction: we include entire novels or novellas by Charles Dickens, Robert Louis Stevenson, Joseph Conrad, and Virginia Woolf, as well as a wealth of short fiction from the eighteenth century to the present. For the earlier periods, we include More's entire *Utopia,* and we give major space to narrative poetry by Chaucer and Spenser, and to Milton's *Paradise Lost* and Swift's *Gulliver's Travels,* among others. Drama appears throughout the anthology, from the medieval *Second Play of the Shepherds* and *Mankind* to a range of twentieth-century plays: George Bernard Shaw's *Pygmalion,* Samuel Beckett's *Endgame,* and Hanif Kureishi's play about sexual and ethnic tensions in postcolonial London, *My Beautiful Laundrette.* Finally, lyric poetry appears in profusion throughout the anthology, from early lyrics by anonymous Middle English poets and the trenchantly witty Dafydd ap Gwilym to the powerful contemporary voices of Philip Larkin, Seamus Heaney, Eavan Boland, and Derek Walcott—himself a product of colonial British education, heir of Shakespeare and James Joyce—who closes the anthology with poems about Englishness abroad and foreignness in Britain.

As topical as these contemporary writers are, we hope that this anthology will show that the great works of earlier centuries can also speak to us compellingly today, their value only increased by the resistance they offer to our views of ourselves and our world. To read and reread the full sweep of this literature is to be struck anew by the degree to which the most radically new works are rooted in centuries of prior innovation. Even this preface can close in no better way than by quoting the words written eighteen hundred years ago by Apuleius of Madaura—both a consummate artist and a kind of anthologist of extraordinary tales—when he concluded the prologue to his masterpiece *The Golden Ass:* Attend, reader, and pleasure is yours.

David Damrosch & Kevin Dettmar

ACKNOWLEDGMENTS

In planning and preparing the third edition of our anthology, the editors have been fortunate to have the support, advice, and assistance of many people. Our editor, Joe Terry, has been unwavering in his enthusiasm for the book and his commitment to it; he and his associates Roth Wilkofsky, Janet Lanphier, and Ann Stypuloski have supported us in every possible way throughout the process, ably assisted by Katy Needle, Christine Halsey, and Abby Lindquist. Our developmental editor Mika De Roo guided us and our manuscript from start to finish with unfailing acuity and Wildean wit. Our copyeditor marvelously integrated the work of a dozen editors. Jenna Egan, Mika De Roo, Teresa Ward, and Heidi Jacobs have devoted enormous energy and creativity to revising our Web site and audio CD. Caroline Gloodt cleared our many permissions, and Julie Tesser and Felicity Palmer tracked down and cleared our many new illustrations. Finally, Valerie Zaborski and Ellen MacElree oversaw the production with sunny good humor and kept the book successfully on track on a very challenging schedule, working closely with Karin Vonesh, Leah Strauss, and Eric Arima at Elm Street Publishing Services.

Our plans for the new edition have been shaped by comments and suggestions from many faculty who have used the book over the past four years. We are specifically grateful for the thoughtful advice of our reviewers for this edition, Arthur D. Barnes (Louisiana State University), Candace Barrington (Central Connecticut State University), Bruce Brandt (South Dakota State University), Philip Collington (Niagara University), Hilary Englert (New Jersey City University), Sandra C. Fowler (The University of Alabama), Leslie Graff (University at Buffalo), Natalie Grinnell (Wofford College), Noah Heringman (University of Missouri – Columbia), Romana Huk (University of Notre Dame), Mary Anne Hutchison (Utica College), Patricia Clare Ingham (Indiana University), Kim Jacobs (University of Cincinnati Clermont College), Carol Jamison (Armstrong Atlantic State University), Mary Susan Johnston (Minnesota State University), Eileen A. Joy (Southern Illinois University – Edwardsville), George Justice (University of Missouri), Leslie M. LaChance (University of Tennessee at Martin), Lisa Lampert (University of California, San Diego), Dallas Liddle (Augsburg College), Michael Mays (University of Southern Mississippi), James J. McKeown Jr. (McLennan Community College), Kathryn McKinley (Florida International University), Barry Milligan (Wright State University), James Najarian (Boston College), Deborah Craig Nester (Worcester State College), Daniel Novak (Tulane University), Laura E. Rutland (Berry College), Marcy L. Tanter (Tarleton State University), Jan Widmayer (Boise State University), and William A. Wilson (San Jose State University).

We remain grateful as well for the guidance of the many reviewers who advised us on the creation of the first two editions, the base on which this new edition has been built. In addition to the people named above, we would like to thank Lucien Agosta (California State University, Sacramento), Anne W. Astell (Purdue University), Derek Attridge (Rutgers University), Linda Austin (Oklahoma State University), Robert Barrett (University of Pennsylvania), Joseph Bartolomeo (University of Massachusetts, Amherst), Mary Been (Clovis Community College), Stephen Behrendt (University of Nebraska), Todd Bender (University of Wisconsin, Madison), Bruce Boehrer (Florida State University), Joel J. Brattin (Worcester Polytechnic Institute),

James Campbell (University of Central Florida), J. Douglas Canfield (University of Arizona), Paul A. Cantor (University of Virginia), George Allan Cate (University of Maryland, College Park), Linda McFerrin Cook (McLellan Community College), Eugene R. Cunnar (New Mexico State University), Earl Dachslager (University of Houston), Elizabeth Davis (University of California, Davis), Andrew Elfenbein (University of Minnesota), Margaret Ferguson (University of California, Davis), Sandra K. Fisher (State University of New York, Albany), Allen J. Frantzen (Loyola University, Chicago), Kate Gartner Frost (University of Texas), Kevin Gardner (Baylor University), Leon Gottfried (Purdue University), Mark L. Greenberg (Drexel University), Peter Greenfield (University of Puget Sound), Natalie Grinnell (Wofford College), James Hala (Drew University), Wayne Hall (University of Cincinnati), Donna Hamilton (University of Maryland), Wendell Harris (Pennsylvania State University), Richard H. Haswell (Washington State University), Susan Sage Heinzelman (University of Texas, Austin), Standish Henning (University of Wisconsin, Madison), Jack W. Herring (Baylor University), Carrie Hintz (Queens College), Maurice Hunt (Baylor University), Eric Johnson (Dakota State College), Colleen Juarretche (University of California, Los Angeles), Roxanne Kent-Drury (Northern Kentucky University), R. B. Kershner (University of Florida), Lisa Klein (Ohio State University), Adam Komisaruk (West Virginia University), Rita S. Kranidis (Radford University), John Laflin (Dakota State University), Paulino Lim (California State University, Long Beach), Elizabeth B. Loizeaux (University of Maryland), Ed Malone (Missouri Western State College), John J. Manning (University of Connecticut), William W. Matter (Richland College), Evan Matthews (Navarro College), Lawrence McCauley (College of New Jersey), Michael B. McDonald (Iowa State University), Peter E. Medine (University of Arizona), Celia Millward (Boston University), Charlotte Morse (Virginia Commonwealth University), Mary Morse (Rider University), Thomas C. Moser, Jr. (University of Maryland), Jude V. Nixon (Baylor University), Richard Nordquist (Armstrong Atlantic State University), John Ottenhoff (Alma College), Violet O'Valle (Tarrant County Junior College, Texas), Joyce Cornette Palmer (Texas Women's University), Leslie Palmer (University of North Texas), Richard Pearce (Wheaton College), Rebecca Phillips (West Virginia University), Renée Pigeon (California State University, San Bernardino), Tadeusz Pioro (Southern Methodist University), Deborah Preston (Dekalb College), William Rankin (Abilene Christian University), Sherry Rankin (Abilene Christian University), Luke Reinsma (Seattle Pacific University), Elizabeth Robertson (University of Colorado), Deborah Rogers (University of Maine), David Rollison (College of Marin), Brian Rosenberg (Allegheny College), Charles Ross (Purdue University), Kathryn Rummel (California Polytechnic), Harry Rusche (Emory University), Kenneth D. Shields (Southern Methodist University), R. G. Siemens (Malaspina University-College), Clare A. Simmons (Ohio State University), Sally Slocum (University of Akron), Phillip Snyder (Brigham Young University), Isabel Bonnyman Stanley (East Tennessee University), Brad Sullivan (Florida Gulf Coast University), Margaret Sullivan (University of California, Los Angeles), Herbert Sussmann (Northeastern University), Ronald R. Thomas (Trinity College), Theresa Tinkle (University of Michigan), William A. Ulmer (University of Alabama), Jennifer A. Wagner (University of Memphis), Anne D. Wallace (University of Southern Mississippi), Brett Wallen (Cleveland Community College), Jackie Walsh (McNeese State University, Louisiana), Daniel Watkins (Duquesne University), John Watkins (University of Minnesota), Martin Wechselblatt (University of Cincinnati), Arthur

Weitzman (Northeastern University), Bonnie Wheeler (Southern Methodist University), Dennis L. Williams (Central Texas College), Paula Woods (Baylor University), and Julia Wright (University of Waterloo).

Other colleagues brought our developing book into the classroom, teaching from portions of the work-in-progress. Our thanks go to Lisa Abney (Northwestern State University), Charles Lynn Batten (University of California, Los Angeles), Brenda Riffe Brown (College of the Mainland, Texas), John Brugaletta (California State University, Fullerton), Dan Butcher (Southeastern Louisiana University), Lynn Byrd (Southern University at New Orleans), David Cowles (Brigham Young University), Sheila Drain (John Carroll University), Lawrence Frank (University of Oklahoma), Leigh Garrison (Virginia Polytechnic Institute), David Griffin (New York University), Rita Harkness (Virginia Commonwealth University), Linda Kissler (Westmoreland County Community College, Pennsylvania), Brenda Lewis (Motlow State Community College, Tennessee), Paul Lizotte (River College), Wayne Luckman (Green River Community College, Washington), Arnold Markely (Pennsylvania State University, Delaware County), James McKusick (University of Maryland, Baltimore), Eva McManus (Ohio Northern University), Manuel Moyrao (Old Dominion University), Kate Palguta (Shawnee State University, Ohio), Paul Puccio (University of Central Florida), Sarah Polito (Cape Cod Community College), Meredith Poole (Virginia Western Community College), Tracy Seeley (University of San Francisco), Clare Simmons (Ohio State University), and Paul Yoder (University of Arkansas, Little Rock).

As if all this help weren't enough, the editors also drew directly on friends and colleagues in many ways, for advice, for information, sometimes for outright contributions to headnotes and footnotes, even (in a pinch) for aid in proofreading. In particular, we wish to thank David Ackiss, Marshall Brown, James Cain, Cathy Corder, Jeffrey Cox, Michael Coyle, Pat Denison, Tom Farrell, Andrew Fleck, Jane Freilich, Laurie Glover, Lisa Gordis, Joy Hayton, Ryan Hibbet, V. Lauryl Hicks, Nelson Hilton, Jean Howard, David Kastan, Stanislas Kemper, Andrew Krull, Ron Levao, Carol Levin, David Lipscomb, Denise MacNeil, Jackie Maslowski, Richard Matlak, Anne Mellor, James McKusick, Melanie Micir, Michael North, David Paroissien, Stephen M. Parrish, Peter Platt, Cary Plotkin, Desma Polydorou, Gina Renee, Alan Richardson, Esther Schor, Catherine Siemann, Glenn Simshaw, David Tresilian, Shasta Turner, Nicholas Watson, Michael Winckleman, Gillen Wood, and Sarah Zimmerman for all their guidance and assistance.

The pages on the Restoration and the eighteenth century are the work of many collaborators, diligent and generous. Michael F. Suarez, S. J. (Campion Hall, Oxford) edited the Swift and Pope sections; Mary Bly (Fordham University) edited Sheridan's *School for Scandal*; Michael Caldwell (University of Chicago) edited the portions of "Reading Papers" on *The Craftsman* and the South Sea Bubble. Steven N. Zwicker (Washington University) co-wrote the period introduction, and the headnotes for the Dryden section. Bruce Redford (Boston University) crafted the footnotes for Dryden, Gay, Johnson, and Boswell. Susan Brown, Christine Coch, Tara Czechowski, Paige Reynolds, and Andrew Tumminia helped with texts, footnotes, and other matters throughout; William Pritchard gathered texts, wrote notes, and prepared the bibliography. To all, abiding thanks.

It has been a pleasure to work with all of these colleagues in the ongoing collaborative process that has produced this book and brought it to this new stage of its life and use. This book exists for its readers, whose reactions and suggestions we warmly welcome, as these will in turn reshape this book for later users in the years to come.

POLITICAL AND RELIGIOUS ORDERS

One political order that cannot be ignored by readers of British literature and history is the monarchy, since it provides the terms by which historical periods are even today divided up. Thus much of the nineteenth century is often spoken of as the "Victorian" age or period, after Queen Victoria (reigned 1837–1901), and the writing of the period is given the name Victorian literature. By the same token, writing of the period 1559–1603 is often called "Elizabethan" after Elizabeth I, and that of 1901–1910 "Edwardian" after Edward VII. This system however is based more on convention than logic, since few would call the history (or literature) of late twentieth-century Britain "Elizabethan" any more than they would call the history and literature of the eighteenth century "Georgian," though four king Georges reigned between 1714 and 1820. Where other, better terms exist these are generally adopted.

As these notes suggest, however, it is still common to think of British history in terms of the dates of the reigning monarch, even though the political influence of the monarchy has been strictly limited since the seventeenth century. Thus, where an outstanding political figure has emerged it is he or she who tends to name the period of a decade or longer; for the British, for example, the 1980s was the decade of "Thatcherism" as for Americans it was the period of "Reaganomics." The monarchy, though, still provides a point of common reference and has up to now shown a remarkable historical persistence, transforming itself as occasion dictates to fit new social circumstances. Thus, while most of the other European monarchies disappeared early in the twentieth century, if they had not already done so, the British institution managed to transform itself from imperial monarchy, a role adopted in the nineteenth century, to become the head of a welfare state and member of the European Union. Few of the titles gathered by Queen Victoria, such as Empress of India, remain to Elizabeth II (reigns 1952–), whose responsibilities now extend only to the British Isles with some vestigial role in Australia, Canada, and New Zealand among other places.

The monarchy's political power, like that of the aristocracy, has been successively diminished over the past several centuries, with the result that today both monarch and aristocracy have only formal authority. This withered state of today's institutions, however, should not blind us to the very real power they wielded in earlier centuries. Though the medieval monarch King John had famously been obliged to recognize the rule of law by signing the Magna Carta ("Great Charter") in 1215, thus ending arbitrary rule, the sixteenth- and seventeenth-century English monarchs still officially ruled by "divine right" and were under no obligation to attend to the wishes of Parliament. Charles I in the 1630s reigned mostly without summoning a parliament, and the concept of a "constitutional monarchy," being one whose powers were formally bound by statute, was introduced only when King William agreed to the Declaration of Right in 1689. This document, together with the contemporaneous Bill of Rights, while recognizing that sovereignty still rests in the monarch, formally transferred executive and legislative powers to Parliament. Bills still have to receive Royal Assent, though this was last denied by Queen Anne in 1707; the monarch still holds "prerogative" powers, though these, which include the appointment of certain officials, the dissolution of Parliament and so on, are, in practice wielded by the prime minister. Further information on the political character of various historical periods can be found in the period introductions.

Political power in Britain is thus held by the prime minister and his or her cabinet, members of which are also members of the governing party in the House of Commons. As long as the government is able to command a majority in the House of Commons, sometimes by a coalition of several parties but more usually by the absolute majority of one, it both makes the laws and carries them out. The situation is therefore very different from the American doctrine of the "Separation of Powers," in which Congress is independent of the President and can even be controlled by the opposing party. The British state of affairs has led to the office of prime minister being compared to that of an "elected dictatorship" with surprising frequency over the past several hundred years.

British government is bicameral, having both an upper and a lower house. Unlike other bicameral systems, however, the upper house, the House of Lords, is not elected, its membership being largely hereditary. Membership can come about in four main ways: (1) by birth, (2) by appointment by the current prime minister often in consultation with the Leader of the Opposition, (3) by virtue of holding a senior position in the judiciary, and (4) by being a bishop of the Established Church (the Church of England). In the House of Commons, the lower house, the particular features of the British electoral system have meant that there are never more than two large parties, one of which is in power. These are, together, "Her Majesty's Government and Opposition." Local conditions in Northern Ireland and Scotland have meant that these areas sometimes send members to Parliament in London who are members neither of the Conservative nor of the Labour parties; in general, however, the only other group in the Commons is the small Liberal Party.

Taking these categories in turn, all members of the hereditary aristocracy (the "peerage") have a seat in the House of Lords. The British aristocracy, unlike those of other European countries, was never formally dispossessed of political power (for example by a revolution), and though their influence is now limited, nevertheless all holders of hereditary title—dukes, marquesses, earls, viscounts and barons, in that order of precedence—sit in the Lords. Some continue to do political work and may be members of the Government or of the Opposition, though today it would be considered unusual for a senior member of government to sit in the House of Lords. The presence of the hereditary element in the Lords tends to give the institution a conservative tone, though the presence of the other members ensures this is by no means always the case. Secondly there are "life peers," who are created by the monarch on the prime minister's recommendation under legislation dating from 1958. They are generally individuals who have distinguished themselves in one field or another; retiring senior politicians from the Commons are generally elevated to the Lords, for example, as are some senior civil servants, diplomats, business and trade union leaders, academics, figures in the arts, retiring archbishops, and members of the military. Some of these take on formal political responsibilities and others do not. Finally, senior members of the judiciary sit in the Lords as Law Lords, while senior members of the Church of England hierarchy also sit in the Lords and frequently intervene in political matters. It has been a matter of some controversy whether senior members of other religious denominations, or religions, should also sit in the House of Lords. Within the constitution (by the Parliament Act of 1911 and other acts) the powers of the House of Lords are limited mostly to the amendment and delay of legislation; from time to time the question of its reform or abolition is raised.

In addition, there are minor orders of nobility that should be mentioned. A baronet is a holder of a hereditary title, but he is not a member of the peerage; the style is Sir (followed by his first and last names), Baronet (usually abbreviated as Bart. or Bt.). A knight is a member of one of the various orders of British knighthood, the oldest of which dates back to the Middle Ages (the Order of the Garter), the majority to the eighteenth or nineteenth centuries (the Order of the Thistle, the Bath, Saint Michael, and Saint George, etc.). The title is nonhereditary and is given for various services; it is marked by various initials coming after the name. K.C.B., for example, stands for "Knight Commander of the Bath," and there are many others.

In the House of Commons itself, the outstanding feature is the dominance of the party system. Party labels, such as "Whigs" and "Tories," were first used from the late seventeenth century, when groups of members began to form opposing factions in a Parliament now freed of much of the power of the king. The "Tories," for example, a name now used to refer to the modern Conservative Party, were originally members of that faction that supported James II (exiled in 1689); the word "Tory" comes from the Irish (Gaelic) for outlaw or thief. The "Whigs," on the other hand, supported the constitutional reforms associated with the 1689

Glorious Revolution; the word "whig" is obscurely related to the idea of regicide. The Whig faction largely dominated the political history of the eighteenth century, though the electorate was too small, and politics too controlled by the patronage of the great aristocratic families, for much of a party system to develop. It was only in the middle decades of the nineteenth century that the familiar party system in parliament and the associated electioneering organization in the country at large came into being. The Whigs were replaced by the Liberal Party around the mid-century, as the Liberals were to be replaced by the Labour Party in the early decades of the twentieth century; the Tories had become firm Conservatives by the time of Lord Derby's administrations in the mid-nineteenth century.

The party system has always been fertile ground for a certain amount of parliamentary theater, and it has fostered the emergence of some powerful personalities. Whereas the eighteenth-century Whig prime minister Sir Robert Walpole owed his authority to a mixture of personal patronage and the power made available through the alliances of powerful families, nineteenth-century figures such as Benjamin Disraeli (Conservative prime minister 1868, 1874–1880) and William Ewart Gladstone (Liberal prime minister 1868–1874; 1880–1885; 1885; 1892–1894), were at the apex of their respective party machines. Disraeli, theatrical, personable and with a keen eye for publicity (he was, among other things, a close personal friend of Queen Viotoria), formed a great contrast to the massive moral appeals of his parliamentary opponent Gladstone. One earlier figure, William Pitt (1759–1806), prime minister at twenty-four and leader of the country during the French Revolution and earlier Napoleonic wars, stands comparison with these in the historical record; of twentieth-century political figures, David Lloyd-George, Liberal prime minister during World War I, and Winston Churchill, Conservative, during World War II, deserve special mention.

Though political power in the United Kingdom now rests with Parliament at Westminster in London, this has not always been the only case. Wales, which is now formally a principality within the political construction. "England and Wales," was conquered by the English toward the end of the thirteenth century—too early for indigenous representative institutions to have fallen into place. Scotland, on the other hand, which from 1603 was linked with England under a joint monarchy but only became part of the same political entity with the Act of Union in 1707, did develop discrete institutions. Recent votes in both Scotland and Wales are leading toward greater local legislative control over domestic issues in both Scotland and Wales. Many Scottish institutions—for example, the legal and educational systems—are substantially different from those of England, which is not true in the case of Wales. The Church of Scotland in particular has no link with the Church of England, having been separately established in 1690 on a Presbyterian basis; this means that authority in the Scottish church is vested in elected pastors and lay elders and not in an ecclesiastical hierarchy of priests and bishops. But the most vexed of the relationships within the union has undoubtedly been that between England and Ireland.

There has been an English presence in Ireland from the Middle Ages on, and this became dominant in the later sixteenth century when English policy was deliberately to conquer and colonize the rest of the country. The consequence of this policy, however, was that an Irish Protestant "Ascendancy" came to rule over a largely dispossessed Catholic Irish peasantry; in 1689 at the Battle of the Boyne this state of affairs was made permanent, as Irish Catholic support for the exiled and Catholic-sympathizing James II was routed by the invading troops of the new Protestant king, William III. An Irish parliament met in Dublin, but this was restricted to Protestants; the Church of Ireland was the established Protestant church in a country where most of the population was Catholic. Irish political representation was shifted to Westminster by Pitt in 1800 under the formal Act of Union with Ireland; the Church of Ireland was disestablished by Gladstone later in the century. In the twentieth century, continuing agitation in the Catholic south of the country first for Home Rule and subsequently for independence from Britain—agitation that had been a feature of almost the whole nineteenth century at greater or lesser levels of intensity—led to the establishment first of the Irish Free State

(1922) and later of the Republic (1948). In the Protestant North of the country, a local parliament met from 1922 within the common framework of the United Kingdom, but this was suspended in 1972 and representation returned to Westminster, as renewed violence in the province threatened local institutions. In Northern Ireland several hundred years of conflict between Protestants, who form the majority of the population in the province, and Catholics have led to continuing political problems.

Since the Reformation in the sixteenth century Britain has officially been a Protestant country with a national church headed by the monarch. This "Established Church," the Church of England or Anglican Church, has its own body of doctrine in the Thirty-Nine Articles and elsewhere, its own order of services in the Book of Common Prayer, and its own translation of the Bible (the "Authorized Version"), commissioned by James I (reigned 1603–1625) as Head of the Church. There is an extensive ecclesiastical hierarchy and a worldwide communion that includes the American Episcopalian Church.

The Reformation in England was not an easy business, and it has certain negative consequences even today. Some of these have been touched upon above in the case of Ireland. Those professing Roman Catholicism were excluded from political office and suffered other penalties until 1829, and a Catholic hierarchy parallel to that of the Church of England only came into being in Britain in the later nineteenth century. Though many of the restrictions on Roman Catholics enacted by Act of Parliament at the end of the seventeenth century were considerably softened in the course of the eighteenth, nevertheless they were very real.

English Protestantism, however, is far from being all of a piece. As early as the sixteenth century, many saw the substitution of the King's authority and that of the national ecclesiastical hierarchy for that of the Pope to be no genuine Protestant Reformation, which they thought demanded local autonomy and individual judgment. In the seventeenth century many "dissenting" or "Non-Conformist" Protestant sects thus grew up or gathered strength (many becoming "Puritans"), and these rejected the authority of the national church and its bishops and so the authority of the king. They had a brief moment of freedom during the Civil War and the Commonwealth (1649–1660) following the execution of Charles I, when there was a flowering of sects from Baptists and Quakers, which still exist today, to Ranters, Shakers, Anabaptists, Muggletonians, etc., which in the main do not (except for some sects in the United States). The monarchy and the Church were decisively reestablished in 1660, but subsequent legislation, most importantly the Act of Toleration (1689), suspended laws against dissenters on certain conditions.

Religious dissent or nonconformity remained powerful social movements over the following centuries and received new stimulus from the "New Dissenting" revivalist movements of the eighteenth century (particularly Methodism, though there was also a growth in the Congregationalist and Baptist churches). By the nineteenth century, the social character and geographical pattern of English dissent had been established: religious nonconformity was a feature of the new working classes brought into being by the Industrial Revolution in the towns of the Midlands and North of England. Anglicanism, which was associated with the pre-industrial traditional order, was rejected also by many among the rising bourgeoisie and lower middle classes; almost every major English novel of the mid-nineteenth century and beyond is written against a background of religious nonconformity or dissent, which had complex social and political meanings. Nonconformity was also a particular feature of Welsh society.

Under legislation enacted by Edward I in 1290, the Jews were expelled from England, and there were few of them in the country until the end of the seventeenth century, when well-established Jewish communities began to appear in London (the medieval legislation was repealed under the Commonwealth in the 1650s). Restrictions on Jews holding public office continued until the mid-nineteenth century, and at the end of the century large Jewish communities were formed in many English cities by refugees from Central and Eastern European anti-Semitism.

Britain today is a multicultural country and significant proportions of the population, many of whom came to Britain from former British Empire territories, profess Hinduism or Islam, among other religions. The United Kingdom has been a member of the European Union since the early 1970s, and this has further loosened ties between Britain and former empire territories or dominions, many of which are still linked to Britain by virtue of the fact that the British monarch is Head of the "Commonwealth," an organization to which many of them belong. In some cases, the British monarch is also Head of State. Most importantly, however, British membership of the European Union has meant that powers formerly held by the national parliament have been transferred either to the European Parliament in Strasbourg, France, or to the European Commission, the executive agency in Brussels, Belgium, or, in the case of judicial review and appeal, to the European Court of Justice. This process seems set to generate tensions in Britain for some years to come.

David Tresilian

ENGLISH MONARCHS

Before the Norman conquest (1066), these included:

Alfred the Great	871–899
Edmund I	940–946
Ethelred the Unready	948–1016
Edward the Confessor	1042–1066
Harold II	1066

The following monarchs are divided by the dynasty ("House") to which they belong:

Normandy

William I the Conqueror	1066–1087
William II, Rufus	1087–1100
Henry I	1100–1135

Blois

Stephen	1135–1154

Plantagenet

Henry II	1154–1189
Richard I "Coeur de Lion"	1189–1199
John	1199–1216
Henry III	1216–1272
Edward I	1272–1307
Edward II	1307–1327
Edward III	1327–1377
Richard II	1377–1399

Lancaster

Henry IV	1399–1413
Henry V	1413–1422
Henry VI	1422–1471

York

Edward IV	1461–1483
Edward V	1483
Richard III	1483–1485

Tudor

Henry VII	1485–1509
Henry VIII	1509–1547
Edward VI	1547–1553
Mary I	1553–1558
Elizabeth I	1558–1603

Kings of England and of Scotland:

Stuart

James I (James VI of Scotland)	1603–1625
Charles I	1625–1649
Commonwealth (Republic)	
Council of State	1649–1653
Oliver Cromwell, Lord Protector	1653–1658
Richard Cromwell	1658–1660

Stuart

Charles II	1660–1685
James II (Interregnum 1688–1689)	1685–1688
William III and Mary II	1685–1701 (Mary dies 1694)
Anne	1702–1714

Hanover

George I	1714–1727
George II	1727–1760
George III	1760–1820
George IV	1820–1830
William IV	1830–1837
Victoria	1837–1901

Saxe-Coburg and Gotha

Edward VII	1901–1910

Windsor

George V	1910–1936
Edward VIII	1936
George VI	1936–1952
Elizabeth II	1952–

CREDITS

COLOR PLATE CREDITS

The Victorian Age

＋·＝◆＝·＋

1832–1901

> Never since the beginning of Time was there, that we hear or read of, so intensely self-conscious a Society. Our whole relations to the Universe and to our fellow-man have become an Inquiry, a Doubt.
>
> —*Thomas Carlyle, 1831*

Nothing characterizes Victorian society so much as its quest for self-definition. The sixty-three years of Victoria's reign were marked by momentous and intimidating social changes, startling inventions, prodigious energies; the rapid succession of events produced wild prosperity and unthinkable poverty, humane reforms and flagrant exploitation, immense ambitions and devastating doubts. Between 1800 and 1850 the population doubled from nine to eighteen million, and Britain became the richest country on earth, the first urban industrial society in history. For some, it was a period of great achievement, deep faith, indisputable progress. For others, it was "an age of destruction," religious collapse, vicious profiteering. To almost everyone it was apparent that, as Sir Henry Holland put it in 1858, "we are living in *an age of transition.*"

But what Matthew Arnold called the "multitudinousness" of British culture overwhelmed all efforts to give the era a collective identity or a clear sense of purpose. Dazzled and dazed by their steam-powered printing presses, their railways and telegraphs, journalism and junk mail, Victorians suffered from both future shock and the information explosion. For the first time a nation had become self-consciously modern: people were sure only of their differences from previous generations, certain only that traditional ways of life were fast being transformed into something perilously unstable and astonishingly new. As the novelist William Makepeace Thackeray noted, "We are of the time of chivalry. . . . We are of the age of steam."

VICTORIA AND THE VICTORIANS

In an unpredictable, tumultuous era, the stern, staid figure of Queen Victoria came to represent stability and continuity. The adjective "Victorian" was first used in 1851 to celebrate the nation's mounting pride in its institutions and commercial success. That year, the global predominance of British industry had emerged incontestably at the original "world's fair" in London, the "Great Exhibition of the Works of Industry of All Nations," which Prince Albert helped organize. Arrayed for the world to see in a vast "Crystal Palace" of iron and glass, the marvels of British manufacture achieved a regal stature of their own and cast their allure upon the monarchy in turn. In the

Sunlight Soap advertisement commemorating the 1897 Jubilee of Victoria's reign.

congratulatory rhetoric that surrounded the event, the conservative, retiring queen emerged as the durable symbol of her dynamic, aggressively businesslike realm.

In succeeding decades, the official portraits of Queen Victoria, gradually aging, reflected her country's sense of its own maturation as a society and world power. Etched by conflict with her prime ministers, the birth of nine children, and the early death of her beloved Prince Albert, Victoria's once pretty face became deeply lined and heavily jowled. Represented as a fairy-tale teenaged queen at her coronation in 1837, she radiated a youthful enthusiasm that corresponded to the optimism of the earlier 1830s. It seemed a decade of new beginnings. Settling into the role of fertile matron-monarch, she offered a domestic image to match the booming productivity of the 1850s. Reclusive after Albert died in 1861, she eventually took on the austere role of the black-satined Empress of India, projecting a world-weary glumness that lent gravity to the imperial heyday of the 1870s. Finally, as the aged, venerated Widow of Windsor, she became a universal icon, prompting the nostalgic worldwide spectacles of the Golden and Diamond Jubilees in 1887 and 1897. When Victoria died in 1901, after the longest reign in English history, a newspaper wrote: "Few of us, perhaps, have realized till now how large a part she had in the life of everyone of us; how the thread of her life [bound] the warp of the nation's progress."

During the seven decades of her rule, Victoria's calm profile, stamped on currency and displayed in offices and outposts from London to Bombay, presided over the expansion of Britain into the world's greatest empire. Economically and politically, Britannia ruled not only the waves but more than a quarter of the globe's land-mass. Among its domains were Canada, Australia, New Zealand, South Africa, the Indian subcontinent and Ceylon, Malaya, Hong Kong, Singapore, Burma, Jamaica, Trinidad, British Guiana, Bermuda, the Bahamas, Rhodesia, Kenya, Uganda, and Nigeria. By the 1890s one out of every four people on earth was a "subject" of Queen Victoria.

Victoria stood not only for England and Empire, but also for Duty, Family, and, especially, Propriety. "We have come to regard the Crown as the head of our moral-ity" wrote the historian Walter Bagehot. As a description of behavior, "Victorian" signifies social conduct governed by strict rules, formal manners, and rigidly defined gender roles. Relations between the sexes were hedged about with sexual prudery and an intense concern for maintaining the appearance of propriety in public, whatever the private facts. But although she was presented as the ultimate role model, Victoria herself could not escape the contradictions of her era. The most powerful woman on earth, she denounced "this mad, wicked folly of Women's Rights." Her quiet reserve restored the dignity of the monarchy after the rakish ways of George IV, but she al-lowed advertisers to trade shamelessly on her image and product endorsements. Her face was universally known, featured on everything from postage stamps to tea trays, yet after Albert's death she lived in seclusion, rarely seeing either her ministers or the public. An icon of motherhood, she detested pregnancy, childbirth, and babies. As an emblem of Britain's greatness, Queen Victoria gave her subjects the public iden-tity and purpose that privately they—and she, in her diaries—recognized as an unful-filled ideal.

The Victorians have left us a contradictory picture of themselves. On the one hand, they were phenomenally energetic, dedicated to the Gospel of Work and driven by a solemn sense of duty to the Public Good. Popular authors like Dickens and Trollope churned out three-volume novels, engaged in numerous philan-thropic projects, devoured twelve-course dinners, took twenty-mile walks, and produced a voluminous correspondence. Explorers and missionaries such as Bur-ton, Speke, Stanley, and Livingston took enormous risks to map uncharted terri-tory or spread Christianity "in darkest Africa." Although an invalid, Florence Nightingale revamped the entire British military medical and supply system from her bedroom office. All this activity was sustained by belief in its implicit moral benefit. In matters of character Victorians prized respectability, earnestness, a sense of duty and public service; most would have regarded an industrious, pious conventionality as the best road not only to material recompense but to heavenly rewards as well.

Yet the fabled self-confidence of this overachieving society often rings hollow. Their literature conveys an uneasy sense that their obsession with work was in part a deliberate distraction, as if Victorians were discharging public responsibilities in order to ease nagging doubts about their religious faith, about changing gender roles, about the moral quandaries of class privilege and imperial rule. Much of the era's social con-servatism, such as its resistance to women's rights and to class mobility, may be traced to the fear of change. They struggled to dominate the present moment in order to keep an uncertain future at bay. Few questioned that tremendous advances were tak-ing place in science, public health, transportation, and the general standard of living, but each new idea or discovery seemed to have unexpected, distressing repercussions.

The critic J. A. Froude remarked in 1841 that "the very truths which have come forth have produced doubts . . . this dazzle has too often ended in darkness." Discoveries in geology, biology, and textual scholarship shattered belief in the literal truth of the Bible. The Industrial Revolution shifted power from the landed aristocracy toward an insecure, expanding middle class of businessmen and professionals, impoverishing millions of once rural laborers along the way. Strident, riotous campaigns to extend voting rights to males of the middle and working classes produced fears of armed insurrection. Coupled with the agitations for and against trade unions, women's equality, socialism, and the separation of church and state, the fitful transformation of Britain's political and economic structure often teetered on the brink of open class warfare. In the national clamor for reform, every sector of the population fought for its privileges and feared for its rights. The following pages introduce the Victorian period by looking at several key issues: the era's energy and invention, its doubts about religion and industrialism, its far-reaching social reforms, its conflicted fascination with Empire, the commercialization and expansion of the reading public, and the period's vigorous self-scrutiny in the mirror of literature.

THE AGE OF ENERGY AND INVENTION

The most salient characteristic of life in this latter portion of the 19th century is its SPEED.

—*W. R. Greg, Life at High Pressure, 1875*

The "newness" of Victorian society—its speed, progress, and triumphant ingenuity—was epitomized by the coming of the railway. Until the 1830s, the fastest ways to travel or transport goods were still the most ancient ones, by sail or horse. But on seeing the first train pass through the Rugby countryside in 1839, Thomas Arnold astutely remarked: "Feudality is gone forever." The earliest passenger railway line opened in 1830 between Liverpool and Manchester; by 1855, eight thousand miles of track had been laid. Speeds of fifty miles per hour were soon routine; the journey from London to Edinburgh that had taken two weeks in 1800 now took less than a day.

Carrying passengers, freight, newspapers, and mail, the railways helped create a national consciousness by linking once remote parts of the country into a single economy and culture. Networks of information, distribution, and services moved news, goods, and people from one end of Britain to the other to the rhythm of the railway timetable. The accelerating pace of life that railways introduced became one of the defining features of the age.

Moreover, the railway irrevocably altered the face of the landscape. Its bridges, tunnels, cuttings, crossings, viaducts, and embankments permanently scarred a rural landscape whose fields, hedgerows, and highways were rooted deep in history. In the cities, engineers and entrepreneurs carved room for vast railyards and stations by demolishing populous districts. Discharging commodities and crowds, the railways transformed town centers everywhere, bolstering local economies and stimulating construction as they arrived, but depriving once thriving coaching inns and former mail routes of traffic and trade. Underground trains restructured the experience of

Robert Howlett, *Portrait of Isambard Kingdom Brunel and Launching Chains of the Great Eastern,* 1857. Howlett's interest in contemporary subjects, ranging from steamships and Crimean War heroes to telescopic views of the moon, exemplified the belief that as a new medium itself, photography was supremely suited to capture "progress" in all its manifestations. In his portrait of Brunel, the audacious engineer who designed the Great Western Railway and the world's largest steamship, *The Great Eastern,* Howlett evoked both industrial might and Victorian self-confidence; the man of genius dominates the chains that dwarf him.

travel within the city as well: the world's first subway line opened in 1863 in London; a complete inner London system was operating by 1884. Finally, railway-sponsored mass tourism eroded the regional distinctiveness and insularity of individual places. The inventor of the organized excursion, Thomas Cook, saw his advertising slogan, "RAILWAYS FOR THE MILLIONS," turned into a simple statement of fact.

Optimistic social prophets envisioned all classes reaping the fruits of the Industrial Revolution. The widespread Victorian belief in Progress was sustained by many factors, including rising incomes, the greater availability of goods, the perception of surplus production, and the leading role of Britain in world affairs. Many people were awed by the sheer size of industrial achievement: the heaviest ships, the longest tunnels, the biggest warehouses, the most massive factory outputs ever known, all contributed to a sublimity of scale that staggered the public's imagination.

Every decade brought impressive innovations that transformed the rhythms of everyday life. The first regular Atlantic steamship crossings began in 1838, flouting the age-old dependence on wind and tide, importing tea from China, cotton from India or Alabama, beef from Australia, and exporting to world markets finished goods ranging from Sheffield cutlery and Manchester textiles to Pear's Soap and the latest Dickens novel.

Equally momentous in its own way was Henry Fox Talbot's discovery between 1839 and 1841 of how to produce and print a photographic negative. The technology of his "sun-pictures" revolutionized the entire visual culture and changed the human relationship to the past. A moment in time could now be "fixed" forever. Thus, more than a century later, we have photographic records of many subsequent innovations: the construction of the London sewer system; the laying of the transatlantic cable in 1865, putting London and New York in almost instantaneous contact via telegraph; the popularity in the 1890s of bicycles, gramophones, electric trams, and the first regular motion picture shows; and in the year of Victoria's death, 1901, Marconi's first transatlantic wireless radio message.

Capturing the public mood, Disraeli wrote in 1862: "It is a privilege to live in this age of rapid and brilliant events. What an error to consider it a utilitarian age. It is one of infinite romance." For the growing middle class there was an Aladdin-like sense of wonderment at the astounding abundance of *things*: an incredible hodge-podge of inventions, gimmicks, and gadgets began to make up the familiar paraphernalia of modern life, including chain stores, washing and sewing machines, postage stamps, canned foods, toothpaste, sidewalk newsstands, illustrated magazines and newspapers, typewriters, breakfast cereal, slide projectors, skin creams, diet pills, shampoo, ready-to-wear clothes, sneakers (called "plimsolls"), and even a cumbersome prototype computer, designed by Charles Babbage.

Victorian architecture, interior design, and clothing embodied the obsession with plenitude, presenting a bewildering variety of prefabricated, highly ornamented styles. A house might feature Gothic revival, neoclassical, Egyptian, Moorish, baronial, or Arts-and-Crafts motifs, every inch of its interior covered with wallpapers, etchings, draperies, carvings, lacework, and knickknacks. Though fashions varied, men and women were usually as well upholstered as their furniture, tightly buttoned from top to toe in sturdy fabrics, their clothes complexly layered on the outside (men's waistcoats, jackets, cravats, and watches) and inside (women's crinolines, petticoats, bustles, corsets, and drawers).

In a Protestant culture that linked industriousness with godliness, both capitalism and consumerism were fueled by prevailing religious attitudes. For Thomas Carlyle, work itself had a divine sanction: "Produce! Produce!" he wrote in *Sartor Resartus*: "Were it but the pitifullest infinitesimal fraction of a Product, produce it in God's name!" His compatriots obliged: by 1848 Britain's output of cotton cloth and iron was more than half of the world total, and the coal output two-thirds of world production. At the Great Exhibition of 1851, when Britain was dubbed "the workshop of the world," the display struck the Reverend Charles Kingsley as triumphant evidence of God's will: "If these forefathers of ours could rise from their graves this day they would be inclined to see in our hospitals, in our railroads, in the achievements of our physical science . . . proofs of the kingdom of God . . . vaster than any of which they had dreamed."

But for Karl Marx, laboring to write *Das Kapital* (1867) at a desk in the British Museum Reading Room, it was not enough to find God in the material world. He saw that through the hoopla of the marketplace, products had acquired a "mystical character" and "theological niceties" of their own. Yet Marx did not regard commodities as proof of God's existence; instead, he argued that they functioned as deities in their own right. An ignored subversive stationed at the heart of the empire, Marx perceived how status-filled objects seemed to take on lives that defined human social relations, even as they degraded the workers that produced them.

Looking around at the wonders of British industry, Marx decided that people had become, finally, less important than things. For him, it was the Age of Commodity Fetishism.

THE AGE OF DOUBT

It was the age of science, new knowledge, searching criticism, followed by multiplied doubts and shaken beliefs.

—*John Morley*

Despite their reverence for material accomplishment and the tenets of organized religion, the Victorians were deeply conflicted in their beliefs and intentions. In retrospect, the forces that shook the foundations of Victorian society might be summed up in two names, Marx and Darwin: though Marx was virtually unknown at the time, his radical critique of unbridled free enterprise brought to the most acute level contemporary analyses of economic injustice and the class system. Darwin's staggering evolutionary theories implied that biblical accounts of creation could not be literally true. But well before either had published a word, British thought was in crisis: "The Old has passed away," wrote Carlyle in 1831, "but, alas, the New appears not in its stead." In his 1851 novel *Yeast,* Charles Kingsley described how deluged the Victorians felt by challenges to their faith and social order: "The various stereotyped systems . . . received by tradition [are] breaking up under them like ice in a thaw," he wrote; "a thousand facts and notions, which they know not how to classify, [are] pouring in on them like a flood."

The Crisis of Faith

In the midst of this tumult, the Victorians were troubled by Time. On the one hand, there was not enough of it: the accelerated pace of change kept people too busy to assimilate the torrent of new ideas and technologies. In the 1880s the essayist F. R. Harrison contended that Victorians were experiencing "a life lived so full . . . that we have no time to reflect where we have been and whither we intend to go." On the other hand, there was too much time: well before Darwin, scientists were showing that vast eons of geological and cosmic development had preceded human history, itself suddenly lengthening due to such discoveries as the Neanderthal skeletons found in 1856.

Their sense of worth diminished by both time clocks and time lines, Victorians felt they had little opportunity for reflection and often took scant comfort in it. Matthew Arnold complained of "this strange disease of modern life with its sick hurry, its divided aims." Yet this climate of anxious uncertainty provoked intense religious fervor, and debates about church doctrine and the proper forms of Christian worship occupied the national consciousness throughout the century. "This is the age of experiment," wrote the historian E. P. Hood in 1850, regarding the constant testing of belief, "but the cheerful fact is, that almost all men are yearning after a faith."

The most influential group were the "Evangelicals," a term which covers not only "dissenting" or "nonconformist" Protestant sects outside the Church of England (such as Methodists, Presbyterians, Congregationalists, and Baptists), but also the Evangelical party or "Low Church" faction within the Church of England. Anti-Catholic,

Bible-oriented, concerned with humanitarian issues, and focused on the salvation of individual souls within a rigid framework of Christian conduct, Evangelicalism dominated the religious and often the social life of working- and middle-class Britons. Evangelicals practiced self-denial and frugality; they rejected most forms of entertainment as sinful or frivolous, and regarded any but the simplest church service as a "popish" throwback to Catholicism, which they abhorred on nationalistic as well as religious grounds. It was Evangelicalism that was largely responsible for the freeing of slaves in the British colonies in 1833, for the strictness of Victorian morality at home, and for British missionary zeal abroad.

At the other end of the spectrum were the Anglo-Catholics of the Tractarian or Oxford Movement, which flourished in the 1830s and 1840s. Through an appeal to early church history, they sought to revitalize the power and spiritual intensity of the Church of England, insisting on the authority of the Church hierarchy, and reaffirming the Church's traditional position as a grace-granting intermediary between Christians and their God. The movement collapsed when its leader, John Henry Newman, converted to Roman Catholicism in 1845. But the antirational, romantic spirit of this small group left a substantial legacy in the renewed ritualism of "High Church" practices. Gothic revival architecture, the burning of altar candles and incense, the resplendent vestments of the clergy—all these were aspects of a religious apprehension of sensuous beauty and mysticism that had not been seen in England since before the Reformation. This "High Church" aestheticism came into direct and ongoing conflict with "Low Church" sobriety.

The crisis of religious doubt occasioned by biblical scholarship and scientific discoveries hit Christian belief hard. But it prompted an array of coping strategies and new ideas about the position of human beings in the universe that remain significant to this day. Most Victorian authors and intellectuals found a way to reassert religious ideas. Thus George Eliot, for instance, maintained that an Evangelical sense of duty and ethics was essential as a social "glue" to prevent the disintegration of society in the absence of religious authority. That it was still an era which *wanted* to believe is evident from the huge success of Tennyson's *In Memoriam* (1850), in which the poet's hard-won religious faith finally triumphs over science-induced despair. Extending evolutionary theory to spiritual advantage, Tennyson hoped man might transcend animality by encouraging his divine soul to "Move upward, working out the beast, / And let the ape and tiger die." Even Darwin's defender Thomas Huxley, who coined the word "agnostic," also celebrated Auguste Comte's positivism and "the Religion of Humanity." Huxley spoke for many who had renounced organized religion but not spiritual impulses when he said that Carlyle's *Sartor Resartus* "led me to know that a deep sense of religion was compatible with the entire absence of theology." Finally, some artists and writers used Christian icons as an avant-garde protest against the secular direction of modern life. "The more materialistic science becomes," said the artist Edward Burne-Jones, "the more angels shall I paint."

The Industrial Catastrophe

In principle, the Victorian crisis of faith should at least have pleased the Utilitarians. The creed of these atheistic, rationalist followers of Jeremy Bentham was strictly practical: measure all human endeavor by its ability to produce "the greatest happiness for the greatest number." Sharing a committed, "can do" philosophy of social reform, Utilitarianism and Evangelicalism were the two dominant ideologies shaping early and mid-Victorian life. But despite the significant changes they effected in government and education during the 1820s and 1830s, even the Utilitarians ran out of self-assurance and moral steam in the morass of mid-Victorian cultural ferment.

A few energetic idealists dreamed of leveling age-old inequalities. "Glory to Man in the highest!" wrote Swinburne in 1869, "for Man is the master of things." But here too a form of evolutionary theory was undercutting the conventional pieties of social discourse. "Love thy neighbor" had no more moral authority for the "Social Darwinist" than it had historical accuracy for the textual scholar. Summed up in the phrase "survival of the fittest"—coined by the philosopher Herbert Spencer in 1852, seven years before *The Origin of Species* appeared—Social Darwinism viewed as dangerous any attempt to regulate the supposedly immutable laws of society. Evolutionary forces decreed that only the fittest should survive in capitalist competition as well as in nature. Applied to nations and races as well as individuals, this theory supported the apparent destiny of England to prosper and rule the world.

Social Darwinism was a brutal offshoot of the influential economic theory of laissez-faire capitalism. Drawing on Adam Smith's *The Wealth of Nations* (1776), businessmen argued that the unfettered pursuit of self-interest, in the form of unrestricted competition in a free market, would be best for society. This was an idea that Utilitarians and many Evangelicals rejected in favor of legislative regulation, since their view of the imperfections of humanity indicated that one person's self-interest was likely to mean another's exploitation. The desperate need to protect the poor and disadvantaged, and the difficulty of doing so, was cause for much soul-searching, particularly among those who had made a religion of social reform.

Concern about the fairness and efficacy of the social structure was exacerbated by the unprecedented rate of urbanization. "Our age is preeminently the age of great cities" declared historian Robert Vaughan in 1843. At the beginning of the nineteenth century only one-fifth of the British population lived in cities; by the end of the century, more than three-quarters did. Such vast numbers of people crowding into the cities created hideous problems of housing, sanitation, and disease. For the poor, living and working conditions were appalling, particularly in the 1830s and 1840s, when neither housing nor factories were regulated. Industrial workers labored six days a week, for as many as fourteen or sixteen hours a day, in stifling, deafening, dangerous workshops, then went home to unheated rooms they often shared with other families, six or seven people to a bed of rags. Drinking water often came from rivers filled with industrial pollution and human waste. Without job security, healthcare, or pensions, the injured, the sick, and the aged fell by the wayside. In manufacturing cities the competition for survival was indeed intense: the life expectancy among working people in Manchester in 1841 was about twenty years.

Foreign visitors in particular were struck with wonder and horror at the conjunction of so much misery and so much wealth. "From this filthy sewer pure gold flows," marveled the French historian Alexis de Tocqueville: "From this foul drain the greatest stream of human industry flows out to fertilize the whole world." Friedrich Engels spent a year in Manchester, producing the most detailed and shocking firsthand account of Victorian industrial life, *The Condition of the Working Class in England in 1844*. Karl Marx, who lived in England for thirty-four years, worked his observations into his famous

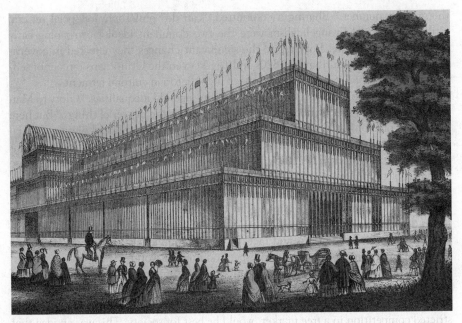

The Crystal Palace, site of the Great Exhibition of 1851, after its re-erection at Sydenham, c. 1855.

theory of "surplus labor value." Under the current system, he said, wretched factory hands would never receive adequate payment for the wealth they created by transforming raw materials into precious commodities. Like many people at the time, both liberal and conservative, Marx expected that violent class warfare was imminent.

On average real wages went up and prices went down in Victoria's reign, with per capita income doubling between 1800 and 1860. But the boom-and-bust cycles of free trade made for unsteady wages, seesaw prices, sudden layoffs, and volatile labor relations, as Britain made a lurching transition to an industrial and commercial economy. There were serious depressions or slowdowns almost every decade, but the worst took place during "the Hungry Forties." Scarce food, widespread unemployment, and general despair provoked riots and fears of revolution. The statesman Charles Greville noted in his diary in 1842, "There is an immense and continually increasing population, no adequate demand for labor . . . no confidence, but a universal alarm, disquietude, and discontent." An American observer of the industrial scene named Henry Coleman remarked, "Every day that I live I thank Heaven that I am not a poor man with a family in England." When the economy recovered, many fled. Between the years 1850 and 1880, three million emigrants left Britain, two-thirds for the United States.

THE AGE OF REFORM

The whole meaning of Victorian England is lost if it is thought of as a country of stuffy complacency and black top-hatted moral priggery. Its frowsty crinolines and dingy hansom cabs, its gas-lit houses and over-ornate draperies, concealed a people engaged in a tremendously exciting adventure—the daring experiment of fitting industrial man into a democratic society.

—*Historian David Thompson, 1950*

Despite crushing problems and the threat of social breakdown, the Victorian period can justly be called an age of reform. Each of the issues that threatened to bring the country into open conflict or destroy the social fabric was in the course of the century addressed peacefully through legislation: voting rights were extended, working conditions improved, and women's rights began to gain ground, without the bloody revolutions or insurrections that struck France in 1838, 1848, and 1870, and Germany in 1848. As fears of revolution receded, the subtler worries of Mill and Arnold, based on their observation of American democracy, seemed more to the point. How could liberty of thought be preserved in a mass culture dedicated to majority rule? How could the best ideas elevate, rather than succumb to, the lowest common denominator?

Politics and Class

The key to the century's relatively peaceful progress was the passage of legislation for political and social reform. The start of the Victorian era is often dated 1832, five years before Victoria's coronation, because in that year the First Reform Bill was enacted. It gave representation to the new industrial towns, such as Manchester, Birmingham, and Leeds, all cities of over 100,000 inhabitants that had lacked a single seat in Parliament. It also enlarged the electorate by about 50 percent, granting the vote to some propertied portions of the middle class. Still, only one in six adult males could vote, and the aristocracy retained parliamentary control. Agitation for reform continued, especially in the Chartist movement of 1838–1848. Taking its name from the People's Charter of 1838, it was a loose alliance of artisans and factory workers that called for sweeping reforms, including universal male suffrage, the secret ballot, equal electoral districts, and annual elections. Chartism was the world's first independent working-class movement, its membership swelling into the millions during the depressions of the 1840s. The Chartists presented giant petitions, signed by one to five million people, to Parliament in 1839, 1842, and 1848. But each time they were rejected, and the movement collapsed after a government show of force effectively defused the demonstrations accompanying the petition of 1848.

The lot of workers was to improve piecemeal, not through the grand political reorganization envisioned by Chartism, as Parliament grudgingly passed acts regulating food, factories, and the right to unionize. An important breakthrough came with the repeal of the Corn Laws in 1846. The laws levied tariffs on the importation of foreign grain; they were sponsored by the landed aristocracy to protect the high price of their home-grown grains (called "corn" in Britain). Therefore, as the poet Thomas Hood wrote in 1842, "bread was dear and flesh and blood were cheap." The new urban business interests fought the protectionist tariffs in the name of "Free Trade." They preferred a stable, better-fed workforce to one that rioted or starved in times of scarcity, but they also wanted cheap bread to keep their workers' wages down. Later, the Public Health acts of 1848 and 1869 improved the availability of tea, sugar, and beer. In the 1870s the importation of wheat from the United States and refrigerated meat and fruit from Australia and New Zealand meant a more varied diet for the working classes, who could by now also afford the new custom of having large bacon-and-egg breakfasts.

Beginning in 1833, a crucial series of Factory Acts slowly curtailed the horrors of industrial labor. The 1833 Act provided for safety inspections of machinery, prohibited the employment of children under nine, and limited the workweek to forty-eight hours for children under twelve. Though the law was poorly enforced, a trend had begun. The Ten Hours Act of 1847 limited the time women and children could work daily in textile factories, and ensuing acts gradually regulated safety and working conditions in other industries. Workers' political power increased when the Second Reform Bill (1867) doubled the electorate, including all male urban householders. During this period employers also felt increasing pressure from extralegal trade union movements, including miners, textile workers, and women garment workers. An uncomprehending middle class (including Dickens and Gaskell) often regarded unionists as anarchists and murderers. But trade unions were finally legalized in 1871, and the first working-class Members of Parliament were unionist miners elected in 1874. By the 1890s there were 1.5 million trade union members, many of them part of the growing Socialist movement, and the foundations of the modern Labour Party had been laid.

Thus the high hopes of Chartism had in a sense succeeded, many of its supposedly dangerous demands eventually met. As Engels noted, these changes also benefited the middle class who resisted them, as people realized the value—social as well as economic—of reduced hostilities and improved cooperation between classes. Everyone also gained from related reforms that reflected weakening class barriers and increasing social mobility. In 1870 the Education Act initiated nationally funded public education in England and Wales. In the 1880s, middle-class investigators and social workers spearheaded the "discovery of poverty" in London's East End, one of a range of efforts that brought better housing, nutrition, and education to the poor. Finally, the nation as a whole benefited from what historian Asa Briggs has called "the one great political invention in Victorian England"—a civil service staffed through open examinations rather than patronage.

By the last decades of the century, Britain had become a more democratic and pluralistic society; it enjoyed greater freedom in matters of religion, political views, and intellectual life than any other country. Overall, the middle class were the chief generators and beneficiaries of social change. Outsiders before 1832, they became key players in the Victorian period. Though they never dominated politics, which remained largely an aristocratic preserve, they set the tone and agenda for the era's socioeconomic evolution.

"The Woman Question"

Still, one group found almost all doors closed against it. Throughout much of Victoria's reign, women had few opportunities for higher education or satisfying employment: from scullery maids to governesses, female workers of all ranks were severely exploited, and prior to the 1870s married women had no legal rights. What contemporaries called "the Woman Question" was hotly debated in every decade, but only at the end of the century were the first women allowed to vote in local elections. Full female suffrage came only after World War I. Despite articulate champions such as

Harriet Martineau and John Stuart Mill, and the examples of successful women such as George Eliot, the Brontës, Florence Nightingale, and the Queen herself, proponents of women's rights made slow headway against prevailing norms. Though Victorians acknowledged the undeniable literary achievements of numerous women writers, many regarded this "brain-work" as a serious aberration that unfitted women for motherhood. The medical establishment backed the conventional view that women were physically and intellectually inferior, a "weaker sex" that would buckle under the weight of strong passion, serious thought, or vigorous exercise. Only in their much vaunted "femininity" did women have an edge, as nurturers of children and men's better instincts.

The ideal Victorian woman was supposed to be domestic and pure, selflessly motivated by the desire to serve others rather than fulfill her own needs. In particular, her duty was to soothe the savage beast her husband might become as he fought in the jungle of free trade. Her role prescribed by Coventry Patmore's wildly popular poem, *The Angel in the House* (1854–1862), the model woman would provide her family with an uplifting refuge from the moral squalor of the working world. Only a small portion of the nation's women could afford to remain at home, but the constant celebration of home and hearth by politicians, the press, and respected authors made conspicuous domesticity the expected role for well-born and well-married women. Many upper- and middle-class women spent their days paying social calls or acquiring "female accomplishments" such as needlework, sketching, or flower arranging. Though this leisure played an important part in generating new literary markets targeted at women, it provoked devastating satires of time-wasting females by Elizabeth Barrett Browning, Charles Dickens, and Florence Nightingale, among others. By the 1860s, with the birth of the department store and modern advertising, leisured women were also for the first time wooed as consumers and portrayed as smart shoppers.

Though their contribution was minimized, women were in fact heavily involved in the labor force, making up one-third of all workers, and 90 percent of the nation's largest labor category, household servants. For so-called "redundant" women who could not find husbands or work, the situation was especially grim. Low wages and unemployment drove tens of thousands of girls and women into prostitution, which, due to the growth of the military and repressive Victorian sexual mores, became one more "boom industry" whose workers reaped few rewards.

If a woman's life was economically precarious outside marriage, her existence was legally terminated within that bond. A woman lost the few civil rights she had as she became "one body" with her husband. Married women had, at the start of the era, no legal right to custody of their own children or to own property. The Divorce and Matrimonial Causes Act of 1857 established a civil divorce court in London, and subsequent acts created protection against assault, desertion, and cruelty, but only a wealthy few could afford legal proceedings. The Married Women's Property Acts of 1870 and 1882, however, gave women the right to possess wages they earned after marriage, as well as any property they owned before it.

Gradually, with the aid of male allies, women created educational opportunities for themselves. The first women's college opened in London in 1848, and the first women's colleges opened at Cambridge in 1869 and at Oxford in 1879—though women were not allowed to take Oxbridge degrees. Elizabeth Blackwell, the first woman M.D., became an accredited physician both in Britain and the United States in 1859; by 1895 there were 264 women doctors. In the 1890s, the much parodied image of the liberated "New Woman" began circulating in the press. By then many young women were braving a conservative backlash to take new positions in office work, the civil service, nursing, and teaching. They also enjoyed the social freedom that accompanied their expanding role in the economy. The novelist Walter Besant wrote admiringly in 1897 of the "personal independence that is the keynote of the situation. . . . The girls go off by themselves on their bicycles; they go about as they please. . . . For the first time in man's history it is regarded as a right and proper thing to trust a girl as a boy insists on being trusted."

The uphill battle that feminists faced is conveyed in the cautious motto of a national-market periodical for women. Published from 1890 to 1912, *Woman* magazine declared its mission: "Forward, but not too fast." Antisuffragists of both sexes found willing allies among those who regarded women as weak and unworldly, better equipped for housekeeping than speechmaking. As the nineteenth century waned, many women and most men would still have endorsed Dickens's parodic view of the public woman, Mrs Jellyby in *Bleak House:* she is so focused on missionary work in Africa that she cannot see the lamentable state of her family in the very next room.

THE AGE OF EMPIRE

I contend that we are the first race in the world, and the more of
the world we inhabit, the better it is for the human race.

—Cecil Rhodes

With the prime meridian conveniently located at Greenwich, just southeast of London, Victorians could measure all the world in relation to a British focal point, culturally as well as geographically. Abroad, as at home, it was an Englishman's duty to rule whatever childlike or womanly peoples he came across, for their own good. For Queen Victoria, the mission of empire was obvious: "to protect the poor natives and advance civilization." The conviction of innate superiority was reinforced by the implacable desire of British business to dominate world markets. The vast size of Britain's naval and commercial fleets and its head start in industrial production helped the cause, and Britain's military and commercial might was unsurpassed. Victorian advertising reveals the global realities and hopes of the emerging merchant empires. Tetley's tea ads depicted their plantations in Ceylon, as well as the ships, trains, and turbanned laborers that secured "the largest sale in the world." Pear's Soap advertising campaigns kept up with British expeditionary forces worldwide, finding potential customers in temporary adversaries such as the "Fuzzy-Wuzzies" of the Sudanese wars or the Boers of South Africa. One advertiser even challenged convention by speaking of "Brightest Africa"—because of the continent's vast market potential.

Yet the empire was hard to assemble and expensive—monetarily and morally—to maintain. Slavery was abolished in British dominions in 1833, but many fortunes still depended on the cheap production of sugar at West Indian plantations, as well as slave-produced cotton from the United States. Thus British implication in the slave trade remained a volatile issue. All Britain took sides in the Governor Eyre scandal of 1865, when the acting governor of Jamaica imposed severe martial law to put down a rebellion by plantation workers. Carlyle, Dickens, and Ruskin supported the executions and floggings, while John Stuart Mill sought to have Eyre tried for murder.

Closer to home, the perennial "Irish Question" resurfaced urgently during the potato famine of 1845–1847. Through the British government's callousness and ineptitude, a million and a half Irish died of starvation and disease and an equal number emigrated. In the wake of this disaster, the Irish engaged in rebellions, uprisings, and massive political efforts to gain parliamentary "Home Rule" for Ireland. But concern about the unity of the Empire, the safety of Protestants in the north of Ireland, and the supposed inability of the Irish to govern themselves led Parliament to defeat all efforts at Irish autonomy during Victoria's reign.

The Asian empire captured the popular imagination for the first time through the so-called "Indian Mutiny" of 1857–1859, a broad-based rebellion against the East India Company, the commercial entity that ruled most of India. The gory details of Indian atrocities, followed by equally bloody and more extensive British reprisals, filled the press and inflamed the public. The crown now took possession, and henceforth British policy was much more guarded, attempting to respect local institutions and practices. Later, as Rudyard Kipling recorded in his novel *Kim* (1901), India became an important setting for the "Great Game" of espionage to prevent foreign destabilization of British interests worldwide.

In the second half of the century, frequent and often bungled conflicts riveted public attention. The Crimean War of 1854–1856, in which Britain fought on the side of Turkey to prevent Russian expansion in the Middle East, cost 21,000 British lives but made little change in the European balance of power. "Some one had blunder'd," as Tennyson wrote in *The Charge of the Light Brigade*. The newspapers' exposure of the gross mismanagement of the war effort, however, led to improved supply systems, medical care, and weapons, and the rebuilding of the armed forces, all of which served Britain in ensuing colonial wars. A veteran of the Crimea, General George Gordon, rose to fame in 1860, capturing Peking and protecting far-flung Britons in the Second Opium War. But in 1884 he and several thousand others were massacred at Khartoum in the Sudan after a year's siege by religiously inspired rebels. Governmental dithering caused the British relief force to arrive two days too late. On another front, the Boer War of 1899–1902 stimulated war mania at home but tarnished Britain's image throughout the world. In pursuit of freer access to South African gold and diamond mines, the world's greatest military power bogged down in a guerilla war that ended only when British forces herded Afrikaner civilians into concentration camps, where 20,000 died.

Many viewed these conflicts as part of "the White Man's burden," as Kipling phrased it: the duty to spread British order and culture throughout the world. Yet imperialism had many opponents. In 1877 the Liberal leader William Gladstone argued that the Empire was a drain on the economy and population, serving only "to compromise British character in the judgment of the impartial world." Even Queen Victoria complained of the "overbearing and offensive behavior" of the Indian Civil Service for "trying to trample on the people and continually reminding them and making them feel that they are a conquered people." Like the growth of Victorian cities, the unplanned agglomeration of British colonies involved such a haphazard mixture of economic expansion, high-minded sentiment, crass exploitation, political

THE FORMULA OF BRITISH CONQUEST

PEARS' SOAP IS THE BEST

REGD COPYRIGHT

PEARS' SOAP IN THE SOUDAN.
"Even if our invasion of the Soudan has done nothing else it has at any rate left the Arab something to puzzle his fuzzy head over, for the legend
PEARS' SOAP IS THE BEST,
inscribed in huge white characters on the rock which marks the farthest point of our advance towards Berber, will tax all the wits of the Dervishes of the Desert to translate."—Phil Robinson, *War Correspondent (in the Soudan) of the Daily Telegraph in London*, 1884.

"The Formula of British Conquest," Pears' Soap advertisement from *Illustrated London News,* 27 August 1887.

expediency, and blatant racism that it apparently had no clear rationale. "We seem," said Cambridge historian J. R. Seeley in 1883, "to have conquered and peopled half the world in a fit of absence of mind."

Victorians did not only go to the ends of the earth; they saw the world's abundance come home to them. Britain and especially London became a magnet for all manner of people and things, a world within a world. There were many distinguished foreign sojourners at the center of empire. Among the artists, exiles, and expatriates who visited or stayed were the deposed French emperor Louis Napoleon, the painters Vincent Van Gogh and James McNeill Whistler, and the writers Arthur Rimbaud, Paul Verlaine, and Stephen Crane. Many of the era's great images and cultural moments came from outsiders: London was memorably painted by Claude Monet, anatomized by Henry James, serenaded by Frédéric Chopin and Franz Liszt, and entertained by Buffalo Bill. It received possibly its most searching critique from Karl Marx and Friedrich Engels, who drafted the *Communist Manifesto* there in 1847. Not only the country's prosperity and cultural prestige attracted people, but also its tolerance and democracy. Despite the wage slavery and imperialist ideology that he saw only too clearly, Engels was forced to admit: "England is unquestionably the freest—that is, the least unfree—country in the world, North America not excepted."

THE AGE OF READING

> Even idleness is eager now,—eager for amusement; prone to excur-
> sion-trains, art-museums, periodical literature, and exciting novels.
>
> —*George Eliot*

Publishing was a major industry in the Victorian period. Magazines, newspapers, novels, poetry, histories, travel narratives, sporting news, scandal sheets, and penny cyclopedias kept people entertained and informed as never before. A thriving commercial literary culture was built on rising literacy rates, with as many as 97 percent of both sexes able to read by 1900. The expansion of the reading public went hand-in-hand with new print technologies, including steam-powered presses, the introduction of cheaper wood-pulp (instead of rag-based) paper, and, eventually, mechanized typesetting. Illustrations were widely used, notably in serialized fiction, where they helped unpracticed readers to follow the story. After 1875 wood engravings gave way to photogravure, and in the 1880s halftone printing enabled photographs to replace hand-drawn works as the primary means of visual communication. Colored illustrations were handtinted at first, often by poor women and children working at home; later chromolithography made colored reproductions of artwork possible. British publishing gradually transformed itself into a modern industry with worldwide distribution and influence. Copies of *The Times* circulated in uncharted Africa; illustrations torn from magazines adorned bushmen's huts in the Great Karoo.

Readers' tastes varied according to class, income, and education. The well-educated but unintellectual upper class formed only a small portion of the Victorian reading public. As the historian Walter Bagehot noted at the time, "A great part of the 'best' English people keep their minds in a state of decorous dullness." At the other end of the social scale, working-class literacy rates were far below the general standard but increased as working hours diminished, housing improved, and public libraries spread. The appetite for cheap literature steadily grew, feeding on a diet of religious tracts, self-help manuals, reprints of classics, penny newspapers, and the expanding range of sensational entertainment: "penny dreadfuls and shilling shockers," serials, bawdy ballads, and police reports of lurid crimes.

It was the burgeoning middle class, however, that formed the largest audience for new prose and poetry and produced the authors to meet an increasing demand for books that would edify, instruct, and entertain. This was the golden age of the English novel, but poetry and serious nonfiction also did a brisk trade, as did "improving" works on religion, science, philosophy, and economics. But new books, especially fiction, were still a luxury in the earlier Victorian period. Publishers inflated prices so that readers would rent novels and narrative poems—just as people rent movies today—from commercial circulating libraries, which provided a larger and steadier income than individual sales. The collaboration between publishers and libraries required authors to produce "three deckers," long novels packaged in three separate volumes that thereby tripled rental fees and allowed three readers to peruse a single novel at one time. An economical alternative was to buy the successive "numbers" of a book as they appeared in individual, illustrated monthly installments. This form of publication became common with the tremendous success of Dickens's first novel, *Pickwick Papers,* which came out in parts in 1836 and 1837. By the 1860s most novels were serialized in weekly or monthly magazines, giving the reader a wealth of additional material for about the same price.

The serialization of novels had a significant impact on literary form. Most of the major novelists, including Dickens, Thackeray, Collins, Gaskell, Trollope, and Eliot, had to organize their work into enticing, coherent morsels that kept characters and story lines clear from month to month, and left readers eager to buy the next installment. Authors felt pressure to keep ahead of deadlines, often not knowing which turn a story might take. But they also enjoyed the opportunity to stay in the public eye, to weave in references to current events, or to make adjustments based on sales and reviews. For their part, readers experienced literature as an ongoing part of their lives. They had time to absorb and interpret their reading, and even to influence the outcome of literary events: throughout his career, Dickens was badgered by readers who wanted to see more of one character, less of another, or prevent the demise of a third.

The close relationship authors shared with their public had its drawbacks: writers had to censor their content to meet the prim standards of "circulating library morality." In keeping with the Evangelical temper of the times, middle-class Victorian recreation centered on the home, where one of the most sacred institutions was the family reading circle. Usually wives or daughters read aloud to the rest of the household. Any hint of impropriety, anything that might bring "a blush to the cheek of the Young Person"—as Dickens warily satirized the trend—was aggressively ferreted out by publishers and libraries. Even revered poets such as Tennyson and Barrett Browning found themselves edited by squeamish publishers.

A better testimony to the intelligence and perceptiveness of the Victorian reading public is the fact that so many of today's classics were best-sellers then, including the novels of the Brontës, Dickens, and George Eliot; the poetry of Tennyson, Elizabeth and Robert Browning, and Christina Rossetti; and the essays of Carlyle, Ruskin, and Arnold. These works were addressed to readers who had an impressive level of literary and general culture, kept up to snuff by the same magazines and reviews in which the best fiction, poetry, and prose appeared. Educated Victorians had an insatiable appetite for "serious" literature on religious issues, socioeconomic theory, scientific developments, and general information of all sorts. It was an era of outstanding, influential periodicals that combined entertaining writing with intellectual substance: politically oriented quarterlies such as the Whig *Edinburgh Review* and the Benthamite *Westminster Review;* more varied monthlies such as *Fraser's Magazine,* where Carlyle's *Sartor Resartus* first appeared, and *Cornhill,* which published works by Ruskin, Thackeray, Eliot, Trollope, and Hardy; the satirical weekly *Punch,* still published today; and Dickens's low-priced weeklies *Household Words* and *All the Year Round* for a more general readership. As a rule, the public had faith in the press, regarding it as a forum essential to the progress and management of democracy. At the same time, as political and cultural power broadened, the press took seriously its new role as creator, shaper, and transmitter of public opinion.

A NOVEL FACT.

Old-fashioned Party (with old-fashioned prejudices). "Ah! very Clever, I dare say. But I see it's Written by a Lady, and I want a Book that my Daughters may read. Give me Something else!"

Cartoon from *Punch* magazine, 1867.

Celebrated authors were hailed as heroes, regarded as public property, and respected as sages; they inspired a passionate adulation. Robert Browning first approached Elizabeth Barrett by writing her a fan letter. The public sought instruction and guidance from authors, who were alternately flattered and dismayed by the responsibilities thrust upon them. The critic Walter Houghton points out that "every writer had his congregation of devoted or would-be devoted disciples who read his work in much the spirit they had once read the Bible." Robert Browning lived to see an international proliferation of Browning Societies, dedicated to expounding his supposed moral teachings. Hero worship was yet another Victorian invention.

THE AGE OF SELF-SCRUTINY

The energy of Victorian literature is its most striking trait, and self-exploration is its favorite theme. Victorians produced a staggeringly large body of literature, renowned for its variety and plenitude. Their writing is distinguished by its particularity, eccentricity, long-windedness, earnestness, ornateness, fantasy, humor, experimentation, and self-consciousness. As befits a scientific age, most authors exhibited a willingness to experiment with new forms of representation, coupled with a penchant for realism, a love of closely observed detail: Tennyson was famous for his myopic descriptions of flowers; Browning transcribed tics of speech like a clinical psychologist; Eliot compared her scenes to Dutch genre paintings; and Dickens indignantly defended the accuracy of his characterization and the plausibility of his plots. Sustained labor was as important as keen observation: "lyric" poems ran to hundreds of lines, novels spanned a thousand pages, essayists constructed lengthy paragraphs with three or four generous sentences. One single book, alternately discredited and revered, underpinned the whole literary enterprise. The King James Version of the Bible shaped the cadences, supplied the imagery, and proposed the structures through which Victorians apprehended the universe; knowledge of it immensely deepens one's appreciation of the time.

Like the photographic close-ups invented by Julia Margaret Cameron, much Victorian literature tries to get at what Matthew Arnold called "the buried life" of individuals struggling for identity in a commercial, technocratic society. In the 1830s Carlyle was already alluding to "these autobiographical times of ours." Autobiography rapidly assumed new importance as a literary form, driven by the apparent necessity of each person working out a personal approach to the universe and a position within the culture. As Matthew Arnold announced in 1853, "the dialogue of the mind with itself has commenced."

Often written under intense emotional pressure, nonfiction prose on social or aesthetic issues turned into an art form as personal as lyric poetry, expressing the writers' interior lives as well as their ideas. Yet the very variety of disguised or semiautobiographical forms (such as the dramatic monologue) suggests that introspection produced its own moral perplexities. In a culture that stressed action, production, civic duty, and family responsibility, such apparently self-indulgent self-scrutiny might well seem unworthy: "I sometimes hold it half a sin / To put in words the grief I feel," said Tennyson about the loss of his best friend. Thus the guilty confessional impulse was forced underground to reemerge almost everywhere: in first-person narratives, devotional poems, travelogues, novels of religious or emotional crisis, intimate essays, dramatic lyrics, fictionalized memoirs, and recollections of famous people and places.

The Major Genres

Victorian literature is remarkable in that there were three great literary genres: nonfiction prose emerged as the artistic equal of poetry and fiction. Topical and influential in their day, the criticism and essays of such writers as Carlyle, Mill, Newman, Ruskin, Darwin, Arnold, Nightingale, Pater, and Wilde achieved classic status by virtue of their distinctive styles and force of intellect. In richly varied rhythms they record the process of original minds seeking to understand the relation of individuals to nature and culture in the new industrial world. Though their works might be categorized as religion, politics, aesthetics, or science, all these authors wrote revealingly of their intellectual development, and all explored the literary resources of the language, from simile and metaphor to fable and fantasy. Oscar Wilde argued for the supreme creativity of the autobiographical critic-as-artist: "That is what the highest criticism really is, the record of one's own soul." His teacher Walter Pater remarked simply that prose is "the special and opportune art of the modern world."

Poets struggled to refute this sentiment. Poetry commanded more respect than prose as a literary genre, but despite the immense success of Tennyson, it gradually lost ground in popularity. Whether this occurred because of, or in spite of, poetry's deliberate cultivation of a mass audience is difficult to say. But whereas Victorians regarded the Romantic poets as visionaries who opened dazzling new vistas onto the self and nature, they encouraged contemporary poets to keep their ideas down to earth, to offer practical advice about managing the vicissitudes of heart and soul in a workaday world. What was viewed, with some suspicion, as the Romantic emphasis on self-expression gave way to more qualified soul-searching with an eye toward moral content that the public could grasp and apply. Carlyle's famous admonition in *Sartor Resartus* set the tone for the period: "Close thy *Byron;* open thy *Goethe*." In other words, forget the tormented introspection and alienation associated with Byronic heroes; strive instead to improve society and practice greater artistic control; know your work and do it.

Whether they felt guilty, inspired, infuriated, or amused over their audience's thirst for instruction, Victorian poets took advantage of it to expand the resources of poetry in English. Though there are obvious lines of influence from the Romantics— Tennyson acknowledged Keats, Shelley was an early influence on Browning, and Arnold steeped himself in Wordsworth—the innovations are perhaps even more striking. Eclectic poets introduced their readers to a bewildering variety of rhythms, stanzas, topics, words, and ideas. Contemporary social concerns vied with—and sometimes merged into—Greek mythology and Arthurian legend as subject matter. Swinburne and Hopkins engaged in verbal pyrotechnics that produced new meters amid an ecstasy of sound; Elizabeth Barrett Browning unleashed stormy feminist lyrics marked by a dazzling intellect; Arnold captured readers with his startling emotional honesty; Christina Rossetti whittled her lines down to a thought-teasing purity; Arthur Symons and William Ernest Henley adapted French *vers libre* to create modern "free verse."

Perhaps the most important development was the rise of the dramatic monologue. Almost every poet found occasion to speak through characters apparently quite foreign in time, place, or social situation. Tennyson's liquid vowel sounds and Browning's clotted consonant clusters are trademarks of very different styles, but both poets use their distinctive music to probe the psychology of the speakers in their dramatic poems. Adapting the sound of their lines to fit the rhythms of their speakers' thoughts, poets acquired a more conversational tone and expanded the psychological range of their craft. While Browning was preoccupied with extreme psychological states, many poets shared his desire to represent a person or event from multiple perspectives, through shifting voices and unreliable narrators. These relativistic approaches also encouraged poets to experiment with new angles of vision suggested by the initially disorienting array of developments in visual culture. Photography, panoramas, stereopticons, impressionist painting, illustrated newspapers, and the mass reproduction of art images all left their mark on poetic practice. The ultimate effect was to engender poems whose ability to please or even communicate depended on the active participation of the reader.

Though nonfiction prose and poetry flourished, the Victorian era is still considered the great age of British fiction. Novelists strove to embody the character and genius of the time. The novel's triumphant adaptation of practically any material into "realistic" narrative and detail fueled an obsession with storytelling that spilled over into anecdotal painting, program music, and fictive or autobiographical frames for essays and histories. The novels themselves generally explored the relation between individuals and their society through the mechanism of a central love plot, around

which almost any subject could be investigated, including the quest for self-knowledge, religious crises, industrialism, education, women's roles, crime and punishment,
or the definition of gentlemanliness.

Convoluted by later standards, Victorian novels received their most famous assessment from Henry James, who regarded them as "loose baggy monsters." The English novel, he said, is "a treasure house of detail, but an indifferent whole." Shrewd as
the observation was, it overlooks the thematic density that unifies Dickens's sprawling three-deckers; the moral consciousness that registers every nuance of thought in
George Eliot's rural panoramas; the intricate narrative structures and ardent self-
questioning that propel the tormented romances of the Brontës. Their novels work
within an established social frame, focusing on the characters' freedom to act within
fairly narrow moral codes in an unpredictable universe; they deal with questions of
social responsibility and personal choice, the impulses of passion and the dictates of
conscience. Yet even as they portrayed familiar details of contemporary social life,
novelists challenged the confines of "realist" fiction, experimenting with multiple
perspectives, unreliable narrators, stories within stories, direct appeals to the reader,
and strange extremes of behavior.

The Role of Art in Society

"The past for poets, the present for pigs." This polemical statement by the painter
Samuel Palmer sums up much of the period's literary debate. Because Victorian
times seemed so thoroughly to break from the past, "modern" became a common
but often prejudicial word. Was there anything of lasting artistic value to be found
in ordinary everyday life? Many writers felt there was not; they preferred to indulge instead in what Tennyson called the "passion of the past." Most poetry
shunned the details of contemporary urban existence, and even the great novelists
like Dickens, Eliot, and Thackeray situated much of their work in the pre-Victo-
rian world of their parents. Some of this writing was escapist, but many authors
saw in earlier times a more ethically and aesthetically coherent world that could
serve as a model for Victorian social reform. The Pre-Raphaelite painters and their
literary allies sought out medieval models, while Matthew Arnold returned to the
Greco-Roman classics: "They, at any rate, knew what they wanted in art, and we
do not."

But another group vigorously disagreed; they stressed the importance of creating
an up-to-date art that would validate or at least grapple with the uniqueness of Victorian life. In *Aurora Leigh* Elizabeth Barrett Browning contended that "this live
throbbing age" should take precedence over all other topics: "if there's room for poets
in this world," she said, "Their sole work is to represent the age / Their age, not
Charlemagne's." In 1850 the critic F. G. Stephens argued that poets should empha-
size "the poetry of the things about us; our railways, factories, mines, roaring cities,
steam vessels, and the endless novelties and wonders produced every day." As the
century wore on, there was a broadening in social scope: the life of the working
classes became a serious literary topic, and in the 1870s and 1880s "naturalist" writers
probed the structures of everyday life at near-subsistence level. Thomas Hardy wrote
searching studies of rural life; George Gissing, whose first wife was a prostitute, docu-
mented in harsh detail "the nether world" of backstreet London.

Whether they favored the past or present as a literary landscape, whether they criticized or lauded the times they lived in, most Victorian writers felt at home in their era. Though they had their own interests, they did not act as alienated outcasts but addressed social needs and responded to the public desire for instruction and reassurance. They recognized the force of John Stuart Mill's remark: "Whatever we may think or affect to think of the present age, we cannot get out of it; we must suffer with its sufferings, and enjoy with its enjoyments; we must share in its lot."

Amid all this energetic literary production, a substantial portion of readers demanded to know if literature had any value at all. Utilitarians regarded art as a waste of time and energy, while Evangelicals were suspicious of art's appeal to the senses and emotions rather than the soul and the conscience. "All poetry is misrepresentation," said the founder of Utilitarianism, Jeremy Bentham, who could not see how fanciful words might be of service to humanity. Such was the temper of the time that writers strove mightily to prove that audiences could derive moral and religious benefit from impractical things like circuses or watercolors. Even secular critics sought to legitimize art's role in society by contending that if religion failed, literature would take its place as a guiding light. "Literature is but a branch of Religion," said Carlyle; "in our time, it is the only branch that still shows any greenness." "More and more," said Arnold, "mankind will discover that we have to turn to poetry to interpret life for us, to console us, to sustain us."

The great expectations most Victorians had for their literature inevitably produced reactions against such moral earnestness. In the theater, a huge variety of comedies, melodramas, pantomimes, and music-hall skits amused all classes; 150,000 people a day went to theaters in London during the 1860s. Yet in comparison to other literary forms, little of lasting value remains. Though leading authors such as Browning, Tennyson, and Henry James tried their hand at writing for the stage, it was not until the 1890s, with the sophisticated wit of Oscar Wilde, the subtle social inquiry of Arthur Wing Pinero, and the provocative "problem plays" of Bernard Shaw, that British theater offered more than light entertainment for the masses. The way for serious drama had been prepared by the wonderfully clever musicals of W. S. Gilbert and Arthur Sullivan, which satirized such topics as Aestheticism (*Patience*, 1881), the House of Lords (*Iolanthe*, 1882), and the struggle for sexual equality (*Princess Ida*, 1884). Victorian social drama came into its own late in the era, when it began directly to explore its own relevance, dissecting social and theatrical conventions even as it questioned whether art could—or should—teach anything at all.

Doubts about the mission of art to improve society culminated in the Aesthetic movement of the 1880s and 1890s, whose writers sought to show, in Oscar Wilde's words, that "there is no such thing as a moral or an immoral book. Books are well written or badly written. That is all." In an era of practicality, art declared its freedom by positing its sheer uselessness. Wilde argued that it is "through Art, and through Art only, that we can shield ourselves from the sordid perils of actual existence." Thus many authors at the end of the Victorian period renounced the values that characterize the age as a whole.

And yet the Aesthetes were still quintessentially Victorian in feeling that, as writers, they had to expose their inner being, whether uplifting or shocking, to the public gaze. In their thoughts and deeds, but especially in their words, writers were expected to harness their autobiographical impulses to society's need for guidance and amusement—or even outrage. "I never travel without my diary," one of Wilde's characters remarks: "One should always have something sensational to read in the train."

Every generalization about the Victorians comes with a ready-made contradiction: they were materialist but religious, self-confident but insecure, monstrous exploiters who devoted themselves to humane reforms; they were given to blanket pronouncements about the essential nature of sexes and races, the social order, and the Christian universe, but they relentlessly probed the foundations of their thought; they demanded a moral literature and thrilled to mindless page-turners. Yet in all these matters they were constantly concerned with rules, codes of duty and behavior, their places in a complex and often frustrating social order. Even the alienated rebels of the 1890s cared intensely (a favorite word) what people thought and how shocking their calculated transgressions might make them.

For a few decades after World War I, the Victorians' obsession with the tightly buttoned structures of everyday life seemed their only legacy, offering an easy target for Modernists who sought to declare their own free-thinking independence. "Queen Victoria was like a great paper-weight," wrote H. G. Wells, "that for half a century sat upon men's minds, and when she was removed their ideas began to blow about all over the place haphazardly." But the end of the Victorian period is now more than a century past, and the winds of change have blown many Victorian ideas back into favor. More and more readers delight to discover beneath the stiff manners and elaborate conventions of a bygone era an anxious, humorous, dynamic people very much like ourselves.

 For additional resources on the Victorians, including a timeline of the period, go to *The Longman Anthology of British Literature* Web site at www.ablongman.com/ damroschbritlit3e.

Thomas Carlyle
1795–1881

Thomas Carlyle was a difficult and cranky character whose imaginative, eccentric works of history and social criticism had an immense influence on his fellow Victorians. Mill, Tennyson, Browning, Dickens, Ruskin, and many others idolized him. George Eliot believed that even if all Carlyle's books were burnt, "it would be only like cutting down an oak after its acorns have sown a forest. For there is hardly a superior or active mind of this generation that has not been modified by Carlyle's writings; there has hardly been an English book written for the last ten or twelve years that would not have been different if Carlyle had not lived."

Carlyle was born in the small village of Ecclefechan in Scotland, the eldest son of a stonemason and his wife who gave their numerous children a strict Calvinist upbringing. From his devout and self-disciplined parents, Carlyle learned early the value of hard work, and he later preached the Gospel of Work to his generation. His parents recognized his exceptional abilities and sent him to the University of Edinburgh to study for the ministry.

Religious doubts, however, prevented him from seeking ordination; at nineteen he wrote, "I am growing daily and hourly more lukewarm about this preaching business." He tried schoolteaching instead, but hated it, and feared that his youth was "hurrying darkly and uselessly away." Tormented by ill health and his lack of a vocation, Carlyle gradually turned to a literary career. Inspired by German literature and philosophy, he began reviewing and translating.

In 1821 Carlyle met Jane Welsh. Middle-class, well-educated, and with literary aspirations of her own, Jane did not at first take Carlyle seriously as a suitor, but he was determined to marry her. Prophetically, he wrote to a friend that he expected their marriage to be "the most turbulent, incongruous thing on earth—a mixture of honey and wormwood" with "thunder and lightning and furious storms—all mingled together into the same season—and the sunshine always in the *smallest* quantity!" Despite this gloomy forecast, they married in 1826, embarking on one of the century's most famous, and most speculated about, marriages. Jane was sharp-tongued and high-strung, Thomas was perpetually irritable, depressed, and complaining, yet they stayed together for nearly forty years. Samuel Butler rather nastily remarked that "it was very good of God to let Carlyle and Mrs. Carlyle marry one another and so make only two people miserable instead of four, besides being very amusing."

In 1828 they left the social and intellectual pleasures of Edinburgh for six years of self-imposed exile in Craigenputtoch, a bleak, remote sheep farm. Here Carlyle wrote the essays that would begin to make his name, *Signs of the Times, On History*, and *Characteristics*, as well as his first book, *Sartor Resartus* (1833–1834). A symbolic autobiography, *Sartor* records Carlyle's struggle to find meaning in life after his loss of faith. A decade earlier, during a period of despair and spiritual crisis which he terms "The Everlasting No," Carlyle had experienced a kind of epiphany, a profound and lifelong conviction of the existence of a transcendent reality. *Sartor*, however, is a strange book, mixing metaphorical philosophy and narrative hijinks in the reconstruction of the odd life of its comic hero, Diogenes Teufelsdröckh. Carlyle had a long and discouraging struggle to find a publisher for it.

In 1834 the Carlyles moved to London, to a house in Chelsea where they spent the rest of their lives. The bustling city was a great contrast to the lonely farm, providing more access to stimulating books and friendships, but Carlyle continued to struggle with poverty, poor health, and insomnia. He set to work on his chronicle of *The French Revolution* (1837), the most dramatic and apocalyptic event in recent European history. In impassioned and impressionistic prose, he traced the downfall of an aristocracy of corrupt impostors, who had to be swept away to allow for the rebirth of a healthy society. In their destruction he read a warning

Julia Margaret Cameron, *Thomas Carlyle,* 1867. The greatest of Victorian portrait photographers, Cameron lived near Tennyson on the Isle of Wight, and by virtue of her irrepressible personality managed to get his many distinguished visitors to sit through grueling photo sessions in her drafty greenhouse. Tennyson once brought the American poet Longfellow to her, saying "You will have to do whatever she tells you. I will come back soon and see what is left of you." Cameron's portrait of Carlyle conveys not only his stern prophetic power but also her own sense of photography's ability to discover a transcendent energy in simple human features: "My mortal but yet divine! Art of photography."

for England, whose leaders seemed to be abandoning the country to democracy and laissez-faire capitalism.

After completing the first of three volumes, Carlyle suffered a catastrophic setback: he lent the manuscript to his friend John Stuart Mill, whose housemaid accidentally burned it in the fireplace. Carlyle was devastated, but he forced himself to begin again. Rewriting was torture: Carlyle called *The French Revolution* "a wild savage Book" that "has come out of my own soul; born in blackness, whirl-wind and sorrow."

Yet, to his own surprise, this was the book that finally brought him widespread public recognition and some relief from financial strain. He enjoyed the admiration, and savored his new role as Sage and Prophet—though he complained that nobody listened when he addressed his contemporaries on a variety of social issues. Invited to give a series of lectures, later published as *On Heroes and Hero-Worship* (1841), Carlyle offered historical examples of what he considered true leadership. Then, in *Past and Present* (1843), he contrasted the coherent social and religious fabric of life in the Middle Ages with the chaos of the modern world. Democracy, to Carlyle, meant the breakdown of political order, the "despair of finding any heroes to govern you." He urged the "Captains of Industry" to become modern heroes, as feudal lords had been in an idealized medieval past, and to reestablish a sense of human community in mechanized England.

Carlyle believed that strong leaders were the only hope for social reform. Turning to history once again for examples, he wrote about *Oliver Cromwell* (1845) and *Frederick the Great* (1858–1865). Six volumes long, *Frederick* was hailed as Carlyle's masterpiece, and Carlyle was elected Rector of Edinburgh University. While he was in Scotland delivering his inaugural speech in 1866, Jane Welsh Carlyle died. In his grief, Carlyle wrote a moving memoir of his wife, to which he added others, including portraits of his friend Edward Irving, and Wordsworth; these were published after his death as *Reminiscences* (1881).

Although Carlyle continued to have public honors heaped upon him in old age, a reaction against his authoritarianism had begun as early as 1850, when he published the *Latter-Day Pamphlets*, a jeremiad against democracy, and *Shooting Niagara, and After?* (1867), an attack on the Second Reform Bill. While he remained an important figure, admired and respected, he was frustrated at feeling, as the critic G. B. Tennyson has put it, "everywhere honored and nowhere heeded." Carlyle's lifelong insistence on divine purpose at work in the universe was deeply attractive to a society in the grip of social unrest and religious malaise—but few were willing to accept the tasks that Carlyle claimed God had set for them. Carlyle's reputation rests on his vigorous denunciation of a materialist society and his rousing calls for social reform. Like a biblical prophet, Carlyle exhorts his followers to mend their ways. In powerfully idiosyncratic language, he condemns laziness and greed, alienation and mechanization, and urges the necessity for spiritual rebirth.

 For additional resources on Carlyle, go to *The Longman Anthology of British Literature* Web site at www.ablongman.com/damroschbritlit3e.

from Past and Present[1]
Midas[2]
[THE CONDITION OF ENGLAND]

The condition of England, on which many pamphlets are now in the course of publication, and many thoughts unpublished are going on in every reflective head, is justly regarded as one of the most ominous, and withal one of the strangest, ever seen in this world. England is full of wealth, of multifarious produce, supply for human want in every kind; yet England is dying of inanition. With unabated bounty the land of England blooms and grows; waving with yellow harvests; thick-studded with workshops, industrial implements, with fifteen millions of workers, understood to be the strongest, the cunningest and the willingest our Earth ever had; these men are here; the work they have done, the fruit they have realised is here, abundant, exuberant on every hand of us: and behold, some baleful fiat as of Enchantment has gone forth, saying, "Touch it not, ye workers, ye master-workers, ye master-idlers; none of you can touch it, no man of you shall be the better for it; this is enchanted fruit!" On the poor workers such fiat falls first, in its rudest shape; but on the rich master-workers too it falls; neither can the rich master-idlers, nor any richest or highest man escape, but all are like to be brought low with it, and made "poor" enough, in the money sense or a far fataler one.

Of these successful skilful workers some two millions, it is now counted, sit in Workhouses, Poor-law Prisons;[3] or have "out-door relief"[4] flung over the wall to

1. *Past and Present* (1843) was Carlyle's response to the crisis of poverty and class estrangement during the Hungry Forties. Unemployment among industrial workers, combined with appalling conditions for the relief of the poor, had led to violent rioting. Even the Chartist movement's more peaceful attempts to address social and economic injustices through political reform aroused fears of revolution. Carlyle called for strong leaders to take charge. He contrasted the selfish indifference of laissez-faire industrialists and privileged aristocrats to the responsible paternalism of feudal lords and medieval monks. Medieval inequality and lack of personal freedom, he argued, were preferable to the modern "liberty to starve."
2. From Book 1, ch. 1. Midas was a legendary king who

was granted his wish that everything he touched might turn to gold; belatedly he realized he could not eat, for food became gold in his mouth.
3. Under the Poor Law Amendment Act of 1834, workhouses were established to provide relief to the poor. To deter loafers, the workhouses were made as unpleasant as possible: the standard of living was deliberately rendered worse than that of the lowest paid worker, and the inmates were expected to perform prison labor, such as picking oakum or breaking stones. Men and women were housed separately so that families were broken up.
4. Under the system of "outdoor relief," which existed prior to the Poor Law Amendment Act of 1834, each parish provided for its own poor through minimum allowances.

them,—the workhouse Bastille[5] being filled to bursting, and the strong Poor-law broken asunder by a stronger. They sit there, these many months now; their hope of deliverance as yet small. In workhouses, pleasantly so-named, because work cannot be
done in them. Twelve-hundred-thousand workers in England alone; their cunning
right-hand lamed, lying idle in their sorrowful bosom; their hopes, outlooks, share of
this fair world, shut-in by narrow walls. They sit there, pent up, as in a kind of horrid
enchantment; glad to be imprisoned and enchanted, that they may not perish
starved. The picturesque Tourist, in a sunny autumn day, through this bounteous
realm of England, descries the Union Workhouse on his path. "Passing by the Workhouse of St. Ives in Huntingdonshire, on a bright day last autumn," says the picturesque Tourist, "I saw sitting on wooden benches, in front of their Bastille and
within their ring-wall and its railings, some half-hundred or more of these men. Tall
robust figures, young mostly or of middle age; of honest countenance, many of them
thoughtful and even intelligent-looking men. They sat there, near by one another;
but in a kind of torpor, especially in a silence, which was very striking. In silence: for,
alas, what word was to be said? An Earth all lying round, crying, Come and till me,
come and reap me;—yet we here sit enchanted! In the eyes and brows of these men
hung the gloomiest expression, not of anger, but of grief and shame and manifold
inarticulate distress and weariness; they returned my glance with a glance that
seemed to say, "Do not look at us. We sit enchanted here, we know not why. The Sun
shines and the Earth calls; and, by the governing Powers and Impotences of this England, we are forbidden to obey. It is impossible, they tell us!" There was something
that reminded me of Dante's Hell in the look of all this; and I rode swiftly away."

So many hundred thousands sit in workhouses: and other hundred thousands
have not yet got even workhouses; and in thrifty Scotland itself, in Glasgow or Edinburgh City, in their dark lanes, hidden from all but the eye of God, and of rare
Benevolence the minister of God, there are scenes of woe and destitution and desolation, such as, one may hope, the Sun never saw before in the most barbarous regions
where men dwelt. Competent witnesses, the brave and humane Dr. Alison,[6] who
speaks what he knows, whose noble Healing Art in his charitable hands becomes
once more a truly sacred one, report these things for us: these things are not of this
year, or of last year, have no reference to our present state of commercial stagnation,
but only to the common state. Not in sharp fever-fits, but in chronic gangrene of this
kind is Scotland suffering. A Poor-law, any and every Poor-law, it may be observed, is
but a temporary measure; an anodyne, not a remedy: Rich and Poor, when once the
naked facts of their condition have come into collision, cannot long subsist together
on a mere Poor-law. True enough:—and yet, human beings cannot be left to die!
Scotland too, till something better come, must have a Poor-law, if Scotland is not to
be a byword among the nations. O, what a waste is there; of noble and thrice-noble
national virtues; peasant Stoicisms, Heroisms; valiant manful habits, soul of a Nation's worth,—which all the metal of Potosi[7] cannot purchase back; to which the
metal of Potosi, and all you can buy with *it,* is dross and dust!

Why dwell on this aspect of the matter? It is too indisputable, not doubtful now
to any one. Descend where you will into the lower class, in Town or Country, by

5. The Bastille was a Parisian prison and a symbol of oppression; the storming of the Bastille in 1789 marked the
opening of the French Revolution.
6. William Pulteney Alison, Scottish physican and au-

thor of *Observations on the Management of the Poor in Scotland* (1840).
7. Bolivian city noted for its silver, tin, lead, and copper
mines.

Color Plate 11 Stood Up. Sir John Everell Millais, *Mariana*, 1851. Millais based this painting on Tennyson's poem *Mariana* (page 1233). When first exhibited, the painting was accompanied by these lines: "She only said, 'My life is dreary, / He cometh not,' she said: / She said, 'I am aweary, aweary. / I would that I were dead!'" Millais's painting is typically Pre-Raphaelite in its use of bright colors, narrative details, and medieval trappings. The stained glass windows depict the Annunciation, suggesting an ironic contrast between the Virgin's fulfillment and Mariana's frustration. Not everyone was moved by this vision of anguished longing; the art critic John Ruskin snorted derisively that had Millais "depicted Mariana working in a meadowed grange, instead of idle in a moated one, it had been to better purpose."

Color Plate 12 Uplifting Art. William Holman Hunt, *The Awakening Conscience*, 1853. A "kept" woman (she wears no wedding ring) and her lover have been blithely singing at the piano when suddenly she has a spiritual revelation: she sees the light and realizes it is not too late to reform. The painting is full of symbolic details: the cat toying with the bird suggests the true nature of the gentleman's relationship with his mistress; the glove carelessly tossed aside hints at her probable future as a prostitute. Ruskin wrote, "the very hem of the poor girl's dress, at which the painter has laboured so closely, thread by thread, has a story in it, if we think how soon its pure whiteness may be soiled with dust and rain, her outcast feet failing in the street." The sunny garden reflected in the mirror symbolizes the possibility of redemption if she can escape the importuning arms that encircle her.

Color Plate 13   London Labor.   Ford Madox Brown, *Work*, 1852–1865. Inspired by the sight of men laying sewers in London, this Dickensian novel of a painting portrays work across the entire social spectrum. Brown called the young British excavator in the center "The outward and visible type of Work"—he is the hero, "the strong fully developed navvy who does his work and loves his beer." On horseback is a very rich gentleman, "probably a Colonel in the army, with a seat in Parliament, and fifteen thousand a year" and his daughter. Standing on the right are two influential intellectuals. Thomas Carlyle and the Reverend F. D. Maurice (who founded the Working Man's College where Brown taught art); they are "the brain workers, who seeming to be idle, work, and are the cause of well ordained work and happiness, in others." The beer seller, who grew up in the slums of Birmingham, is "humpbacked, dwarfish, and . . . vulgar," yet has prospered through energy and hard work: "in his way he also is a sort of hero." The flower seller is a "ragged wretch who has never been taught to work." The neglected children are motherless, as "the baby's black ribbons and their extreme dilapidation indicate," and "the care of the two little ones is an anxious charge for the elder girl."

Color Plates 14 and 15 Daughter of Eve. Augustus Egg, *Past and Present, No. 1* (above) and *Past and Present, No. 3* (below), 1858. *Past and Present* tells the story of an adulterous woman's downfall in three scenes. In the first, the distraught husband holds the letter that has just revealed his wife's infidelity; she lies prostrate with grief and shame, while the house of cards their children are building collapses (on the wall one picture depicts the expulsion of Adam and Eve from Eden: the other shows a shipwreck). The third scene takes place five years later; the mother is now a homeless outcast, huddled under a bridge with her illegiti-mate child (behind her a poster advertises two plays, *Victims* and *The Cure for Love*, while another describes "Pleasure Excursions to Paris"). Meanwhile, in the second scene (not illus-trated here) her two orphaned daughters gaze forlornly at the same moon as their mother, from whom they are forever separated. Egg's use of symbolic detail recalls Holman Hunt's *The Awakening Conscience* (Color Plate 12), another version of the theme of the "fallen woman."

Color Plate 16 Repining or Repenting? William Morris, *Guenevere*, or *La Belle Iseult*, 1858. Morris published his first book of poems, *The Defence of Guenevere*, in March 1858, and this painting was long believed to depict Guenevere, King Arthur's adulterous queen, standing beside her rumpled bed. Arthurian themes were enormously popular among the Victorians (Tennyson published his first *Idylls of the King* in 1858). But the picture is now thought to portray Queen Iseult grieving over the absence of her exiled lover, Sir Tristram. Either way, the brooding posture of the "fallen woman" is accentuated by the sensuous richness of her dress and surroundings: the illuminated missal, Turkish carpet, and elaborately patterned hangings and tapestries. The model was Jane Burden, whom Morris married the following year.

Color Plate 17   Unearthly Longing.   Dante Gabriel Rossetti, *The Blessed Damozel*,
1871–1879. Rossetti based this painting on his poem *The Blessed Damozel* (page 1713), written
before he was 20 years old. The Damozel, surrounded by angels, leans over the golden bar of
Heaven and gazes wistfully down toward her lover below on earth. The painting is split into two
parts—rather like a Renaissance altarpiece—emphasizing the separation of the lovers.

Color Plate 18   Fireworks in Court.   James McNeill Whistler, *Nocturne in Black and Gold: The Falling Rocket*, 1875. Working at the limit of representation, Whistler aggressively opposed the literary, anecdotal qualities of Pre-Raphaelite and mainstream Victorian art. This painting of fireworks exploding at the Cremome Gardens amusement park so riled the critic John Ruskin that he wrote. "I have seen, and heard, much of Cockney impudence before now; but never expected to hear a coxcomb ask two hundred guineas for flinging a pot of paint in the public's face." Whistler sued Ruskin for libel, and Whistler's brilliant defense of his work at the ensuing trial paved the way for the impressionist and abstract styles of the modern era. (For Whistler's manifesto of art for art's sake, see his "Ten O'Clock" lecture, page 2065.)

Color Plate 19 Death of a Female Artist. John Williams Waterhouse, *The Lady of Shalott*, 1888. Tennyson's poem *The Lady of Shalott* (page 1235) inspired many Victorian paintings, including one by Holman Hunt (page 1236). Hunt shows the lady imprisoned in her tower; Waterhouse depicts her floating "down the river's dim expanse / Like some bold seer in a trance" toward Camelot. The painting shows her loosening the boat's chain and "singing her last song," as in the poem, but Waterhouse has added the crucifix and candles.

Color Plate 20 Late Victorian Languor. Sir Edward Burne-Jones, *Love Among the Ruins*, 1894. The painting's title is taken from Robert Browning's poem (page 1425), but it is not so much an illustration of the poem as a romantic evocation of its subject. The languid poses and pale faces, sumptuous colors and flowing drapery, show how the Pre-Raphaelite influence continued late in the century. Unlike narrative paintings (such as *Mariana*, *The Awakening Conscience*, and *Past and Present*, Color Plates 11, 12, 14, and 15), there is no story to be "read" in the details. As Burne-Jones wrote, "I mean by a picture, a beautiful romantic dream of something that never was, never will be—in a better light than any light that ever shone— in a land that no-one can define or remember, only desire—and the forms divinely beautiful."

what avenue you will, by Factory Inquiries, Agricultural Inquiries, by Revenue Returns, by Mining-Labourer Committees, by opening your own eyes and looking, the same sorrowful result discloses itself: you have to admit that the working body of this rich English Nation has sunk or is fast sinking into a state, to which, all sides of it considered, there was literally never any parallel. At Stockport Assizes,—and this too has no reference to the present state of trade, being of date prior to that,—a Mother and a Father are arraigned and found guilty of poisoning three of their children, to defraud a "burial-society" of some 3*l*.8*s*. due on the death of each child: they are arraigned, found guilty; and the official authorities, it is whispered, hint that perhaps the case is not solitary, that perhaps you had better not probe farther into that department of things. This is in the autumn of 1841; the crime itself is of the previous year or season. "Brutal savages, degraded Irish," mutters the idle reader of Newspapers; hardly lingering on this incident. Yet it is an incident worth lingering on; the depravity, savagery and degraded Irishism being never so well admitted. In the British land, a human Mother and Father, of white skin and professing the Christian religion, had done this thing; they, with their Irishism and necessity and savagery, had been driven to do it. Such instances are like the highest mountain apex emerged into view; under which lies a whole mountain region and land, not yet emerged. A human Mother and Father had said to themselves, What shall we do to escape starvation? We are deep sunk here, in our dark cellar; and help is far.—Yes, in the Ugolino Hunger-tower stern things happen; best-loved little Gaddo fallen dead on his Father's knees![8]—The Stockport Mother and Father think and hint: Our poor little starveling Tom, who cries all day for victuals, who will see only evil and not good in this world: if he were out of misery at once; he well dead, and the rest of us perhaps kept alive? It is thought, and hinted; at last it is done. And now Tom being killed, and all spent and eaten, Is it poor little starveling Jack that must go, or poor little starveling Will?—What a committee of ways and means!

In starved sieged cities, in the uttermost doomed ruin of old Jerusalem fallen under the wrath of God, it was prophesied and said, "The hands of the pitiful women have sodden their own children."[9] The stern Hebrew imagination could conceive no blacker gulf of wretchedness; that was the ultimatum of degraded god-punished man. And we here, in modern England, exuberant with supply of all kinds, besieged by nothing if it be not by invisible Enchantments, are we reaching that?—How come these things? Wherefore are they, wherefore should they be?

Nor are they of the St. Ives workhouses, of the Glasgow lanes, and Stockport cellars, the only unblessed among us. This successful industry of England, with its plethoric wealth, has as yet made nobody rich; it is an enchanted wealth, and belongs yet to nobody. We might ask, Which of us has it enriched? We can spend thousands where we once spent hundreds; but can purchase nothing good with them. In Poor and Rich, instead of noble thrift and plenty, there is idle luxury alternating with mean scarcity and inability. We have sumptuous garnitures for our Life, but have forgotten to *live* in the middle of them. It is an enchanted wealth; no man of us can yet touch it. The class of men who feel that they are truly better off by means of it, let them give us their name!

---

8. Count Ugolino and his sons and grandsons were starved to death in a tower by his political opponents; in Canto 33 of the *Inferno* Dante implies that Ugolino, out of starvation and desperation, cannibalized his children's corpses.

9. Cf. Lamentations 4.10.

Many men eat finer cookery, drink dearer liquors,—with what advantage they can report, and their Doctors can: but in the heart of them, if we go out of the dyspeptic stomach, what increase of blessedness is there? Are they better, beautifuler, stronger, braver? Are they even what they call "happier"? Do they look with satisfaction on more things and human faces in this God's-Earth; do more things and human faces look with satisfaction on them? Not so. Human faces gloom discordantly, disloyally on one another. Things, if it be not mere cotton and iron things, are growing disobedient to man. The Master Worker is enchanted, for the present, like his Workhouse Workman; clamours, in vain hitherto, for a very simple sort of "Liberty": the liberty "to buy where he finds it cheapest, to sell where he finds it dearest." With guineas jingling in every pocket, he was no whit richer; but now, the very guineas threatening to vanish, he feels that he is poor indeed. Poor Master Worker! And the Master Unworker, is not he in a still fataler situation? Pausing amid his game-preserves, with awful eye,—as he well may! Coercing fifty-pound tenants;[1] coercing, bribing, cajoling; "doing what he likes with his own." His mouth full of loud futilities, and arguments to prove the excellence of his Corn-law;[2] and in his heart the blackest misgiving, a desperate half-consciousness that his excellent Corn-law is indefensible, that his loud arguments for it are of a kind to strike men too literally *dumb*.

To whom, then, is this wealth of England wealth? Who is it that it blesses; makes happier, wiser, beautifuler, in any way better? Who has got hold of it, to make it fetch and carry for him, like a true servant, not like a false mock-servant; to do him any real service whatsoever? As yet no one. We have more riches than any Nation ever had before; we have less good of them than any Nation ever had before. Our successful industry is hitherto unsuccessful; a strange success, if we stop here! In the midst of plethoric plenty, the people perish; with gold walls, and full barns, no man feels himself safe or satisfied. Workers, Master Workers, Unworkers, all men, come to a pause; stand fixed, and cannot farther. Fatal paralysis spreading inwards, from the extremities, in St. Ives workhouses, in Stockport cellars, through all limbs, as if towards the heart itself. Have we actually got enchanted, then; accursed by some god?—

Midas longed for gold, and insulted the Olympians. He got gold, so that whatsoever he touched became gold,—and he, with his long ears, was little the better for it. Midas had misjudged the celestial music-tones; Midas had insulted Apollo and the gods: the gods gave him his wish, and a pair of long ears, which also were a good appendage to it. What a truth in these old Fables!

from *Gospel of Mammonism*[3]
[THE IRISH WIDOW]

One of Dr. Alison's Scotch facts struck us much. A poor Irish Widow, her husband having died in one of the Lanes of Edinburgh, went forth with her three children, bare of all resource, to solicit help from the Charitable Establishments of that City. At this Charitable Establishment and then at that she was refused; referred from one to the other, helped by none;—till she had exhausted them all; till her strength and heart failed her: she sank down in typhus-fever; died, and infected her Lane with fever, so that "seventeen other persons" died of fever there in consequence. The hu-

---

1. The Reform Bill of 1832 enfranchised tenants who paid 50 pounds or more in annual rent.
2. The Corn Laws regulated the import of grain into Eng-
land. Intended to protect domestic agriculture, they also limited food supplies and raised food prices.
3. From Book 3, ch. 2.

mane Physician asks thereupon, as with a heart too full for speaking, Would it not have been *economy* to help this poor Widow? She took typhus-fever, and killed seventeen of you!—Very curious. The forlorn Irish Widow applies to her fellow-creatures, as if saying, "Behold I am sinking, bare of help: ye must help me! I am your sister, bone of your bone; one God made us: ye must help me!" They answer, "No, impossible; thou art no sister of ours." But she proves her sisterhood; her typhus-fever kills *them:* they actually were her brothers, though denying it! Had human creature ever to go lower for a proof?

For, as indeed was very natural in such case, all government of the Poor by the Rich has long ago been given over to Supply-and-demand, Laissez-faire and such-like,[4] and universally declared to be "impossible." "You are no sister of ours; what shadow of proof is there? Here are our parchments, our padlocks, proving indisputably our money-safes to be *ours,* and you to have no business with them. Depart! It is impossible!"—Nay, what wouldst thou thyself have us do? cry indignant readers. Nothing, my friends,—till you have got a soul for yourselves again. Till then all things are "impossible." Till then I cannot even bid you buy, as the old Spartans would have done, two-pence worth of powder and lead, and compendiously shoot to death this poor Irish Widow: even that is "impossible" for you. Nothing is left but that she prove her sisterhood by dying, and infecting you with typhus. Seventeen of you lying dead will not deny such proof that she *was* flesh of your flesh; and perhaps some of the living may lay it to heart.

from *Labour*[5]
[KNOW THY WORK]

For there is a perennial nobleness, and even sacredness, in Work. Were he never so benighted, forgetful of his high calling, there is always hope in a man that actually and earnestly works: in Idleness alone is there perpetual despair. Work, never so Mammonish,[6] mean, *is* in communication with Nature; the real desire to get Work done will itself lead one more and more to truth, to Nature's appointments and regulations, which are truth.

The latest Gospel in this world is, Know thy work and do it. "Know thyself": long enough has that poor "self" of thine tormented thee; thou wilt never get to "know" it, I believe! Think it not thy business, this of knowing thyself; thou art an unknowable individual: know what thou canst work at; and work at it, like a Hercules![7] That will be thy better plan.

It has been written, "an endless significance lies in Work"; a man perfects himself by working. Foul jungles are cleared away, fair seedfields rise instead, and stately cities; and withal the man himself first ceases to be a jungle and foul unwholesome desert thereby. Consider how, even in the meanest sorts of Labour, the whole soul of a man is composed into a kind of real harmony, the instant he sets himself to work! Doubt, Desire, Sorrow, Remorse, Indignation, Despair itself, all these like helldogs lie beleaguering the soul of the poor dayworker, as of every man: but he bends himself with free valour against his task, and all these are stilled, all these shrink murmuring far off into their caves. The man is now a man. The blessed glow of Labour in him, is

---

4. The free trade philosophy of British industrialists who believed in the market's ability to regulate itself and in the right to do business unhampered by government regulation.

5. From Book 3, ch. 9.
6. Mammon is the personification of material wealth. "Ye cannot serve God and mammon" (Matthew 7.24).
7. Hercules had to perform twelve labors.

it not as purifying fire, wherein all poison is burnt up, and of sour smoke itself there is made bright blessed flame!

Destiny, on the whole, has no other way of cultivating us. A formless Chaos, once set it *revolving*, grows round and ever rounder; ranges itself, by mere force of gravity, into strata, spherical courses; is no longer a Chaos, but a round compacted World. What would become of the Earth, did she cease to revolve? In the poor old Earth, so long as she revolves, all inequalities, irregularities disperse themselves; all irregularities are incessantly becoming regular. Hast thou looked on the Potter's wheel,—one of the venerablest objects; old as the Prophet Ezechiel and far older? Rude lumps of clay, how they spin themselves up, by mere quick whirling, into beautiful circular dishes. And fancy the most assiduous Potter, but without his wheel; reduced to make dishes, or rather amorphous botches, by mere kneading and baking! Even such a Potter were Destiny, with a human soul that would rest and lie at ease, that would not work and spin! Of an idle unrevolving man the kindest Destiny, like the most assiduous Potter without wheel, can bake and knead nothing other than a botch; let her spend on him what expensive colouring, what gilding and enamelling she will, he is but a botch. Not a dish; no, a bulging, kneaded, crooked, shambling, squint-cornered, amorphous botch,—a mere enamelled vessel of dishonour! Let the idle think of this.

Blessed is he who has found his work; let him ask no other blessedness. He has a work, a life-purpose; he has found it, and will follow it! How, as a free-flowing channel, dug and torn by noble force through the sour mud-swamp of one's existence, like an ever-deepening river there, it runs and flows;—draining-off the sour festering water, gradually from the root of the remotest grass-blade; making, instead of pestilential swamp, a green fruitful meadow with its clear-flowing stream. How blessed for the meadow itself, let the stream and *its* value be great or small! Labour is Life: from the inmost heart of the Worker rises his god-given Force, the sacred celestial Life-essence breathed into him by Almighty God; from his inmost heart awakens him to all nobleness,—to all knowledge, "self-knowledge" and much else, so soon as Work fitly begins. Knowledge? The knowledge that will hold good in working, cleave thou to that; for Nature herself accredits that, says Yea to that. Properly thou hast no other knowledge but what thou hast got by working: the rest is yet all a hypothesis of knowledge; a thing to be argued of in schools, a thing floating in the clouds, in endless logic-vortices, till we try it and fix it. "Doubt, of whatever kind, can be ended by Action alone."

from *Democracy*[8]
[LIBERTY TO DIE BY STARVATION]

Life was never a May-game for men: in all times the lot of the dumb millions born to toil was defaced with manifold sufferings, injustices, heavy burdens, avoidable and unavoidable; not play at all, but hard work that made the sinews sore and the heart sore. As bond-slaves, *villani, bordarii, sochemanni,* nay indeed as dukes, earls and kings, men were oftentimes made weary of their life; and had to say, in the sweat of their brow and of their soul, Behold, it is not sport, it is grim earnest, and our back can bear no more! Who knows not what massacrings and harryings there have been; grinding, long-continuing, unbearable injustices,—till the heart had to rise in madness, and

8. From Book 3, ch. 13.

some "*Eu Sachsen, nimith euer sachses,* You Saxons, out with your gully-knives, then!" You Saxons, some "arrestment," partial "arrestment of the Knaves and Dastards" has become indispensable!—The page of Dryasdust[9] is heavy with such details.

And yet I will venture to believe that in no time, since the beginnings of Society, was the lot of those same dumb millions of toilers so entirely unbearable as it is even in the days now passing over us. It is not to die, or even to die of hunger, that makes a man wretched; many men have died; all men must die,—the last exit of us all is in a Fire-Chariot of Pain.[1] But it is to live miserable we know not why; to work sore and yet gain nothing; to be heart-worn, weary, yet isolated, unrelated, girt-in with a cold universal Laissez-faire: it is to die slowly all our life long, imprisoned in a deaf, dead, Infinite Injustice, as in the accursed iron belly of a Phalaris' Bull![2] This is and remains forever intolerable to all men whom God has made. Do we wonder at French Revolutions, Chartisms, Revolts of Three Days? The times, if we will consider them, are really unexampled.

Never before did I hear of an Irish Widow reduced to "prove her sisterhood by dying of typhus-fever and infecting seventeen persons,"—saying in such undeniable way, "You *see* I was your sister!" Sisterhood, brotherhood, was often forgotten; but not till the rise of these ultimate Mammon and Shotbelt Gospels[3] did I ever see it so expressly denied. If no pious Lord or *Law-ward* would remember it, always some pious Lady ("*Hlaf-dig,*" Benefactress, "*Loaf-giveress,*" they say she is,—blessings on her beautiful heart!) was there, with mild mother-voice and hand, to remember it; some pious thoughtful *Elder,* what we now call "Prester," *Presbyter* or "Priest," was there to put all men in mind of it, in the name of the God who had made all.

Not even in Black Dahomey[4] was it ever, I think, forgotten to the typhus-fever length. Mungo Park,[5] resourceless, had sunk down to die under the Negro Village-Tree, a horrible White object in the eyes of all. But in the poor Black Woman, and her daughter who stood aghast at him, whose earthly wealth and funded capital consisted of one small calabash of rice, there lived a heart richer than *Laissez-faire:* they, with a royal munificence, boiled their rice for him; they sang all night to him, spinning assiduous on their cotton distaffs, as he lay to sleep: "Let us pity the poor white man; no mother has he to fetch him milk, no sister to grind him corn!" Thou poor black Noble One,—thou *Lady* too: did not a God make thee too; was there not in thee too something of a God!—

Gurth, born thrall of Cedric the Saxon,[6] has been greatly pitied by Dryasdust and others. Gurth, with the brass collar round his neck, tending Cedric's pigs in the glades of the wood, is not what I call an exemplar of human felicity: but Gurth, with the sky above him, with the free air and tinted boscage and umbrage[7] round him, and in him at least the certainty of supper and social lodging when he came home; Gurth to me seems happy, in comparison with many a Lancashire and Buckinghamshire man of these days, not born thrall of anybody! Gurth's brass collar did not gall him: Cedric *deserved* to be his master. The pigs were Cedric's, but Gurth too would get his

9. Sir Walter Scott's name for an imaginary historian who is a pedantic and dull scholar.
1. 2 Kings 2.11–12.
2. Phalaris was a Sicilian tyrant who killed his enemies by roasting them in the belly of a brass bull.
3. Carlyle is referring to the landed aristocracy's concern with maintaining their exclusive rights to shoot game.
4. A former French territory in West Africa where cannibalism was rumored to persist.
5. Scottish explorer of Africa, and author of *Travels in the Interior of Africa* (1799), Park was killed by Africans in 1806.
6. In Sir Walter Scott's novel *Ivanhoe* (1819), the swineherd Gurth is a serf belonging to the well-to-do farmer, Cedric.
7. Thickets and shade.

parings of them. Gurth had the inexpressible satisfaction of feeling himself related indissolubly, though in a rude brass-collar way, to his fellow-mortals in this Earth. He had superiors, inferiors, equals.—Gurth is now "emancipated" long since; has what we call "Liberty." Liberty, I am told, is a divine thing. Liberty when it becomes the "Liberty to die by starvation" is not so divine!

Liberty? The true liberty of a man, you would say, consisted in his finding out, or being forced to find out the right path, and to walk thereon. To learn, or to be taught, what work he actually was able for; and then by permission, persuasion, and even compulsion, to set about doing of the same! That is his true blessedness, honour, "liberty" and maximum of wellbeing: if liberty be not that, I for one have small care about liberty. You do not allow a palpable madman to leap over precipices; you violate his liberty, you that are wise; and keep him, were it in strait-waistcoats, away from the precipices! Every stupid, every cowardly and foolish man is but a less palpable madman: his true liberty were that a wiser man, that any and every wiser man, could, by brass collars, or in whatever milder or sharper way, lay hold of him when he was going wrong, and order and compel him to go a little righter. O, if thou really art my *Senior*, Seigneur, my *Elder*, Presbyter or Priest,—if thou art in very deed my *Wiser*, may a beneficent instinct lead and impel thee to "conquer" me, to command me! If thou do know better than I what is good and right, I conjure thee in the name of God, force me to do it; were it by never such brass collars, whips and handcuffs, leave me not to walk over precipices! That I have been called, by all the Newspapers, a "free man" will avail me little, if my pilgrimage have ended in death and wreck. O that the Newspapers had called me slave, coward, fool, or what it pleased their sweet voices to name me, and I had attained not death, but life!—Liberty requires new definitions.

Captains of Industry[8]

If I believed that Mammonism with its adjuncts was to continue henceforth the one serious principle of our existence, I should reckon it idle to solicit remedial measures from any Government, the disease being insusceptible of remedy. Government can do much, but it can in nowise do all. Government, as the most conspicuous object in Society, is called upon to give signal of what shall be done; and, in many ways, to preside over, further, and command the doing of it. But the Government cannot do, by all its signaling and commanding, what the Society is radically indisposed to do. In the long-run every Government is the exact symbol of its People, with their wisdom and unwisdom; we have to say, Like People like Government.—The main substance of this immense Problem of Organising Labour, and first of all of Managing the Working Classes, will, it is very clear, have to be solved by those who stand practically in the middle of it; by those who themselves work and preside over work. Of all that can be enacted by any Parliament in regard to it, the germs must already lie potentially extant in those two Classes, who are to obey such enactment. A Human Chaos *in* which there is no light, you vainly attempt to irradiate by light shed *on* it: order never can arise there.

But it is my firm conviction that the "Hell of England" will *cease* to be that of "not making money"; that we shall get a nobler Hell and a nobler Heaven! I anticipate light *in* the Human Chaos, glimmering, shining more and more; under manifold

---

8. From Book 4, ch. 4.

true signals from without That light shall shine. Our deity no longer being Mammon,—O Heavens, each man will then say to himself: "Why such deadly haste to make money? I shall not go to Hell, even if I do not make money! There is another Hell, I am told!" Competition, at railway-speed, in all branches of commerce and work will then abate:—good felt-hats for the head, in every sense, instead of seven-feet lath-and-plaster hats on wheels, will then be discoverable! Bubble-periods,[9] with their panics and commercial crises, will again become infrequent; steady modest industry will take the place of gambling speculation. To be a noble Master, among noble Workers, will again be the first ambition with some few; to be a rich Master only the second. How the Inventive Genius of England, with the whirr of its bobbins and billy-rollers[1] shoved somewhat into the backgrounds of the brain, will contrive and devise, not cheaper produce exclusively, but fairer distribution of the produce at its present cheapness! By degrees, we shall again have a Society with something of Heroism in it, something of Heaven's Blessing on it; we shall again have, as my German friend[2] asserts, "instead of Mammon-Feudalism with unsold cotton-shirts and Preservation of the Game, noble just Industrialism and Government by the Wisest!"

It is with the hope of awakening here and there a British man to know himself for a man and divine soul, that a few words of parting admonition, to all persons to whom the Heavenly Powers have lent power of any kind in this land, may now be addressed. And first to those same Master-Workers, Leaders of Industry; who stand nearest and in fact powerfulest, though not most prominent, being as yet in too many senses a Virtuality rather than an Actuality.

The Leaders of Industry, if Industry is ever to be led, are virtually the Captains of the World! if there be no nobleness in them, there will never be an Aristocracy more. But let the Captains of Industry consider: once again, are they born of other clay than the old Captains of Slaughter; doomed forever to be no Chivalry, but a mere gold-plated *Doggery*,—what the French well name *Canaille*, "Doggery" with more or less gold carrion at its disposal? Captains of Industry are the true Fighters, henceforth recognisable as the only true ones: Fighters against Chaos, Necessity and the Devils and Jötuns;[3] and lead on Mankind in that great, and alone true, and universal warfare; the stars in their courses fighting for them, and all Heaven and all Earth saying audibly, Well done! Let the Captains of Industry retire into their own hearts, and ask solemnly, If there is nothing but vulturous hunger, for fine wines, valet reputation and gilt carriages, discoverable there? Of hearts made by the Almighty God I will not believe such a thing. Deep-hidden under wretchedest god-forgetting Cants, Epicurisms, Dead-Sea Apisms;[4] forgotten as under foulest fat Lethe mud and weeds, there is yet, in all hearts born into this God's-World, a spark of the Godlike slumbering. Awake, O nightmare sleepers; awake, arise, or be forever fallen! This is not playhouse poetry; it is sober fact. Our England, our world cannot live as it is. It will connect itself with a God again, or go down with nameless throes and fire-consummation to the Devils. Thou who feelest aught of such a Godlike stirring in thee, any faintest intimation of it as through heavy-laden dreams, follow *it*, I conjure thee. Arise, save thyself, be one of those that save thy country.

Bucaniers, Chactaw Indians, whose supreme aim in fighting is that they may get the scalps, the money, that they may amass scalps and money: out of such came no

---

9. Ups and downs in the stock market.
1. Machines that prepare cotton or wool for spinning.
2. Teufelsdröckh, the central character in *Sartor Resartus*.
3. Giants in Norse mythology.

4. An Islamic myth held that a tribe living near the Dead Sea were turned into apes because they refused to heed the prophecies of Moses.

Chivalry, and never will! Out of such came only gore and wreck, infernal rage and misery; desperation quenched in annihilation. Behold it, I bid thee, behold there, and consider! What is it that thou have a hundred thousand-pound bills laid-up in thy strong-room, a hundred scalps hung-up in thy wigwam? I value not them or thee. Thy scalps and thy thousand-pound bills are as yet nothing, if no nobleness from within irradiate them; if no Chivalry, in action, or in embryo ever struggling towards birth and action, be there.

Love of men cannot be bought by cash-payment; and without love men cannot endure to be together. You cannot lead a Fighting World without having it regimented, chivalried: the thing, in a day, becomes impossible; all men in it, the highest at first, the very lowest at last, discern consciously, or by a noble instinct, this necessity. And can you any more continue to lead a Working World unregimented, anarchic? I answer, and the Heavens and Earth are now answering, No! The thing becomes not "in a day" impossible; but in some two generations it does. Yes, when fathers and mothers, in Stockport hunger-cellars, begin to eat their children, and Irish widows have to prove their relationship by dying of typhus-fever; and amid Governing "Corporations of the Best and Bravest," busy to preserve their game by "bushing," dark millions of God's human creatures start up in mad Chartisms, impracticable Sacred-Months, and Manchester Insurrections;[5]—and there is a virtual Industrial Aristocracy as yet only half-alive, spell-bound amid money-bags and ledgers; and an actual Idle Aristocracy seemingly near dead in somnolent delusions, in trespasses and double-barrels; "sliding," as on inclined-planes, which every new year they *soap* with new Hansard's-jargon[6] under God's sky, and so are "sliding," ever faster, towards a "scale" and balance-scale whereon is written *Thou art found Wanting:*—in such days, after a generation or two, I say, it does become, even to the low and simple, very palpably impossible! No Working World, any more than a Fighting World, can be led on without a noble Chivalry of Work, and laws and fixed rules which follow out of that,—far nobler than any Chivalry of Fighting was. As an anarchic multitude on mere Supply-and-demand, it is becoming inevitable that we dwindle in horrid suicidal convulsion and self-abrasion, frightful to the imagination, into *Chactaw* Workers. With wigwams and scalps,—with palaces and thousand-pound bills; with savagery, depopulation, chaotic desolation! Good Heavens, will not one French Revolution and Reign of Terror suffice us, but must there be two? There will be two if needed; there will be twenty if needed; there will be precisely as many as are needed. The Laws of Nature will have themselves fulfilled. That is a thing certain to me.

Your gallant battle-hosts and work-hosts, as the others did, will need to be made loyally yours; they must and will be regulated, methodically secured in their just share of conquest under you;—joined with you in veritable brotherhood, sonhood, by quite other and deeper ties than those of temporary day's wages! How would mere red-coated regiments, to say nothing of chivalries, fight for you, if you could discharge them on the evening of the battle, on payment of the stipulated shillings,—and they discharge you on the morning of it! Chelsea Hospitals,[7] Pensions, promotions, rigorous lasting covenant on the one side and on the other, are indispensable even for a hired fighter. The Feudal Baron, much more,—how could he subsist with mere tem-

5. Manchester was the site of Chartist agitation in 1838–1839. In 1819, the infamous "Peterloo Massacre" occurred there when charging cavalry killed a dozen people at an outdoor workers' meeting. See Shelley's The *Mask of Anarchy* (1819), written in response to the killing, page 824.
6. *Hansard* is the official record of Parliamentary debate.
7. A home and hospital for disabled soldiers.

porary mercenaries round him, at sixpence a day; ready to go over to the other side, if sevenpence were offered? He could not have subsisted;—and his noble instinct saved him from the necessity of even trying! The Feudal Baron had a Man's Soul in him; to which anarchy, mutiny, and the other fruits of temporary mercenaries, were intolerable: he had never been a Baron otherwise, but had continued a Chactaw and Bucanier. He felt it precious, and at last it became habitual, and his fruitful enlarged existence included it as a necessity, to have men round him who in heart loved him; whose life he watched over with rigour yet with love; who were prepared to give their life for him, if need came. It was beautiful; it was human! Man lives not otherwise, nor can live contented, anywhere or anywhen. Isolation is the sum-total of wretchedness to man. To be cut off, to be left solitary: to have a world alien, not your world; all a hostile camp for you; not a home at all, of hearts and faces who are yours, whose you are! It is the frightfulest enchantment; too truly a work of the Evil One. To have neither superior, nor inferior, nor equal, united manlike to you. Without father, without child, without brother. Man knows no sadder destiny. "How is each of us," exclaims Jean Paul,[8] "so lonely in the wide bosom of the All!" Encased each as in his transparent "ice-palace"; our brother visible in his, making signals and gesticulations to us;—visible, but forever unattainable: on his bosom we shall never rest, nor he on ours. It was not a God that did this; no!

Awake, ye noble Workers, warriors in the one true war: all this must be remedied. It is you who are already half-alive, whom I will welcome into life; whom I will conjure, in God's name, to shake off your enchanted sleep, and live wholly! Cease to count scalps, gold-purses; not in these lies your or our salvation. Even these, if you count only these, will not long be left. Let bucaniering be put far from you; alter, speedily abrogate all laws of the bucaniers, if you would gain any victory that shall endure. Let God's justice, let pity, nobleness and manly valour, with more gold-purses or with fewer, testify themselves in this your brief Life-transit to all the Eternities, the Gods and Silences. It is to you I call; for ye are not dead, ye are already half-alive: there is in you a sleepless dauntless energy, the prime-matter of all nobleness in man. Honour to you in your kind. It is to you I call: ye know at least this, That the mandate of God to His creature man is: Work! The future Epic of the World rests not with those that are near dead, but with those that are alive, and those that are coming into life.

Look around you. Your world-hosts are all in mutiny, in confusion, destitution; on the eve of fiery wreck and madness! They will not march farther for you, on the sixpence a day and supply-and-demand principle: they will not; nor ought they, nor can they. Ye shall reduce them to order, begin reducing them. To order, to just subordination; noble loyalty in return for noble guidance. Their souls are driven nigh mad; let yours be sane and ever saner. Not as a bewildered bewildering mob; but as a firm regimented mass, with real captains over them, will these men march any more. All human interests, combined human endeavours, and social growths in this world, have, at a certain stage of their development, required organising: and Work, the grandest of human interests, does now require it.

God knows, the task will be hard: but no noble task was ever easy. This task will wear away your lives, and the lives of your sons and grandsons: but for what purpose, if not for tasks like this, were lives given to men? Ye shall cease to count your thousand-pound scalps, the noble of you shall cease! Nay the very scalps, as I say, will not

8. Jean Paul Richter (1763–1825), German writer

long be left if you count only these. Ye shall cease wholly to be barbarous vulturous Chactaws, and become noble European Nineteenth-Century Men. Ye shall know that Mammon, in never such gigs[9] and flunky "respectabilities," is not the alone God; that of himself he is but a Devil, and even a Brute-god.

Difficult? Yes, it will be difficult. The short-fibre cotton; that too was difficult. The waste cotton-shrub, long useless, disobedient, as the thistle by the wayside,—have ye not conquered it: made it into beautiful bandana webs; white woven shirts for men; bright-tinted air-garments wherein flit goddesses? Ye have shivered mountains asunder, made the hard iron pliant to you as soft putty: the Forest-giants, Marsh-jötuns bear sheaves of golden-grain; Aegir the Sea-demon himself stretches his back for a sleek highway to you, and on Firehorses and Windhorses ye career. Ye are most strong. Thor red-bearded, with his blue sun-eyes, with his cheery heart and strong thunder-hammer, he and you have prevailed. Ye are most strong, ye Sons of the icy North, of the far East,—far marching from your rugged Eastern Wildernesses, hitherward from the gray Dawn of Time! Ye are Sons of the *Jötun*-land; the land of Difficulties Conquered. Difficult? You must try this thing. Once try it with the understanding that it will and shall have to be done. Try it as ye try the paltrier thing, making of money! I will bet on you once more, against all Jötuns, Tailor-gods, Double-barrelled Law-wards, and Denizens of Chaos whatsoever!

1843   1843

---

9. A two-wheeled, one-horse carriage.

drag us along the rails. She (for they make these curious little fire-horses all mares) consisted of a boiler, a stove, a small platform, a bench, and behind the bench a barrel containing enough water to prevent her being thirsty for fifteen miles,—the whole machine not bigger than a common fire-engine. She goes upon two wheels, which are her feet, and are moved by bright steel legs called pistons; these are propelled by steam, and in proportion as more steam is applied to the upper extremities (the hip-joints, I suppose) of these pistons, the faster they move the wheels; and when it is desirable to diminish the speed, the steam, which unless suffered to escape would burst the boiler, evaporates through a safety-valve into the air. The reins, bit, and bridle of this wonderful beast—a small steel handle, which applies or withdraws the steam from its legs or pistons, so that a child might manage it. The coals, which are its oats, were under the bench, and there was a small glass tube affixed to the boiler, with water in it, which indicates by its fulness or emptiness when the creature wants water, which is immediately conveyed to it from its reservoirs. There is a chimney to the stove, but as they burn coke there is none of the dreadful black smoke which accompanies the progress of a steam-vessel. This snorting little animal, which I felt rather inclined to pat, was then harnessed to our carriage, and, Mr. Stephenson having taken me on the bench of the engine with him, we started at about ten miles an hour. * * * You can't imagine how strange it seemed to be journeying on thus, without any visible cause of progress other than the magical machine, with its flying white breath and rhythmical, unvarying pace, between these rocky walls, which are already clothed with moss and ferns and grasses; and when I reflected that these great masses of stone had been cut asunder to allow our passage thus far below the surface of the earth, I felt as if no fairy tale was ever half so wonderful as what I saw. * * *

* * * He explained to me the whole construction of the steam-engine, and said he could soon make a famous engineer of me, which, considering the wonderful things he *has* achieved, I dare not say is impossible. * * * The engine having received its supply of water * * * set off at its utmost speed, thirty-five miles an hour, swifter than a bird flies (for they tried the experiment with a snipe). You cannot conceive what that sensation of cutting the air was; the motion is as smooth as possible, too. I could either have read or written. * * * When I closed my eyes this sensation of flying was quite delightful, and strange beyond description; yet, strange as it was, I had a perfect sense of security, and not the slightest fear * * * [as] this brave little she-dragon of ours flew on.

1830   1878

—• ❖ •—

Thomas Babington Macaulay
1800–1859

Not everyone deplored the high human cost of rapid industrialization: the historian Thomas Babington Macaulay saw it as evidence of social progress. He was a firm believer in "the natural tendency of society to improvement," and he took great pride in the material achievements of his age. He expressed his views forcefully in reviewing Robert Southey, whose *Colloquies on the Progress and Prospects of Society* (1829) had criticized industrialism and urged a return to a romanticized rural past. In reply, Macaulay argued that in the nineteenth century "people live longer because they are better fed, better lodged, better clothed, and better attended in sickness, and that these improvements are owing to that increase of national wealth which the manufacturing system has produced."

For more about Macaulay, see Perspectives: Religion and Science, page 1377.

from **A Review of Southey's Colloquies**
[THE NATURAL PROGRESS OF SOCIETY]

History is full of the signs of this natural progress of society. We see in almost every part of the annals of mankind how the industry of individuals, struggling up against wars, taxes, famines, conflagrations, mischievous prohibitions, and more mischievous protections, creates faster than governments can squander, and repairs whatever invaders can destroy. We see the wealth of nations increasing, and all the arts of life approaching nearer and nearer to perfection, in spite of the grossest corruption and the wildest profusion on the part of rulers.

The present moment is one of great distress. But how small will that distress appear when we think over the history of the last forty years; a war, compared with which all other wars sink into insignificance;[1] taxation, such as the most heavily taxed people of former times could not have conceived; a debt larger than all the public debts that ever existed in the world added together; the food of the people studiously rendered dear; the currency imprudently debased, and imprudently restored. Yet is the country poorer than in 1790? We firmly believe that, in spite of all the misgovernment of her rulers, she has been almost constantly becoming richer and richer. Now and then there has been a stoppage, now and then a short retrogression; but as to the general tendency there can be no doubt. A single breaker may recede; but the tide is evidently coming in.

If we were to prophesy that in the year 1930 a population of fifty millions, better fed, clad, and lodged than the English of our time, will cover these islands, that Sussex and Huntingdonshire will be wealthier than the wealthiest parts of the West Riding of Yorkshire now are, that cultivation, rich as that of a flower garden, will be carried up to the very tops of Ben Nevis and Helvelyn,[2] that machines constructed on principles yet undiscovered will be in every house, that there will be no highways but railroads, no traveling but by steam, that our debt, vast as it seems to us, will appear to our great-grandchildren a trifling encumbrance, which might easily be paid off in a year or two, many people would think us insane. We prophesy nothing; but this we say: If any person had told the Parliament which met in perplexity and terror after the crash in 1720 that in 1830 the wealth of England would surpass all their wildest dreams, that the annual revenue would equal the principal of that debt which they considered as an intolerable burden, that for one man of ten thousand pounds then living there would be five men of fifty thousand pounds, that London would be twice as large and twice as populous, and that nevertheless the rate of mortality would have diminished to one-half of what it then was, that the post office would bring more into the exchequer than the excise and customs had brought in together under Charles the Second,[3] that stage coaches would run from London to York in twenty-four hours, that men would be in the habit of sailing without wind, and would be beginning to ride without horses, our ancestors would have given as much credit to the prediction as they gave to *Gulliver's Travels*. Yet the prediction would have been true; and they would have perceived that it was not altogether absurd, if they had considered that the country was then raising every year a sum which

1. The Napoleonic Wars, which took place from 1792 until 1815.
2. Mountains in Scotland and the Lake District of England.

3. Reigned 1660–1685.

would have purchased the fee-simple[4] of the revenue of the Plantagenets, ten times what supported the Government of Elizabeth, three times what, in the time of Cromwell,[5] had been thought intolerably oppressive. To almost all men the state of things under which they have been used to live seems to be the necessary state of things. We have heard it said that five per cent is the natural interest of money, that twelve is the natural number of a jury, that forty shillings is the natural qualification of a county voter. Hence it is that, though in every age everybody knows that up to his own time progressive improvement has been taking place, nobody seems to reckon on any improvement during the next generation. We cannot absolutely prove that those are in error who tell us that society has reached a turning point, that we have seen our best days. But so said all who came before us, and with just as much apparent reason. "A million a year will beggar us," said the patriots of 1640. "Two millions a year will grind the country to powder," was the cry in 1660. "Six millions a year, and a debt of fifty millions!" exclaimed Swift, "the high allies have been the ruin of us." "A hundred and forty millions of debt!" said Junius;[6] "well may we say that we owe Lord Chatham more than we shall ever pay, if we owe him such a load as this." "Two hundred and forty millions of debt!" cried all the statesmen of 1783 in chorus; "what abilities, or what economy on the part of a minister, can save a country so burdened?" We know that if, since 1783, no fresh debt had been incurred, the increased resources of the country would have enabled us to defray that debt at which Pitt, Fox, and Burke[7] stood aghast, nay, to defray it over and over again, and that with much lighter taxation than what we have actually borne. On what principle is it that, when we see nothing but improvement behind us, we are to expect nothing but deterioration before us?

It is not by the intermeddling of Mr Southey's idol, the omniscient and omnipotent State, but by the prudence and energy of the people, that England has hitherto been carried forward in civilization; and it is to the same prudence and the same energy that we now look with comfort and good hope. Our rulers will best promote the improvement of the nation by strictly confining themselves to their own legitimate duties, by leaving capital to find its most lucrative course, commodities their fair price, industry and intelligence their natural reward, idleness and folly their natural punishment, by maintaining peace, by defending property, by diminishing the price of law, and by observing strict economy in every department of the State. Let the Government do this: the People will assuredly do the rest.

1830

Parliamentary Papers ("Blue Books")

Factories, mills, and mines all employed women and children as cheap labor. They often worked grueling hours under appalling conditions, for wages that barely enabled them to subsist. Their misery attracted the attention of various official fact-finding commissions, whose

4. Complete ownership of their estates. The Plantagenets ruled England from 1154 to 1399.
5. Elizabeth reigned from 1558 to 1603. Oliver Cromwell was Lord Protector from 1653 to 1658.
6. Pseudonym of a political commentator (active from 1769 to 1772) who supported William Pitt, Earl of Chatham. Pitt led the costly war against France.
7. William Pitt, Charles James Fox, and Edmund Burke were 18th-century statesmen.

horrifying reports, known as the "Blue Books," revealed that five-year-old children slaved in pitch-dark mines for twelve hours a day, and that pregnant and half-naked women crawled through mine shafts hauling heavy loads of coal. Such investigations helped bring about the 1833 and 1842 Factory Acts that prohibited the employment of children under nine and limited those under twelve to forty-eight hours of work per week. In the following passages young girls testify before parliamentary commissions about the circumstances of their lives.

Testimony of Hannah Goode, a Child Textile Worker

I work at Mr. Wilson's mill. I attend the drawing-head.[1] I get 5s. 9d. It is four or five years since we worked double hours. We only worked an hour over then. We got a penny for that. We went in the morning at six o'clock by the mill clock. It is about half past five by our clock at home when we go in, and we are about a quarter too fast by Nottingham. We come out at seven by the mill. The clock is in the engine-house. It goes like other clocks. I think the youngest child is about seven. There are only two males in the mill. I dare say there are twenty under nine years. They go in when we do and come out when we do. The smallest children work at the cards,[2] and doffing the spinning bobbins.[3] I work in that room. We never stop to take our meals, except at dinner. It has gone on so this six years and more. It is called an hour for dinner from coming out to going in. We have a full hour. Some stop in, if they have a mind. The men stop half an hour at dinner-time to clean the wheels. The children stop to clean their own work; that may take them five or ten minutes or so. That is taken out of the dinner-time. William Crookes is overlooker in our room; he is cross-tempered sometimes. He does not beat me; he beats the little children if they do not do their work right. They want beating now and then. He has a strap; he never beats them with any thing else, except his hand. The children are in a middling way as to goodness. I have sometimes seen the little children drop asleep or so, but not lately. If they are catched asleep they get the strap. They are always very tired at night. I have weakened[4] them sometimes to prevent Crookes seeing them; not very often, because they don't often go to sleep. Sometimes they play about the street when they come out; sometimes they go home. The girls often go home and sew. I sit up often till nine or ten o'clock at home, picking the spinners waste. I get 2$\frac{1}{2}$d. a pound for that. I can pick about half a pound a night, working very hard. I have known the people complain of their children getting beat. There is no rule about not beating the children. When the engine stops, all stops except the reeling. The reelers are all grown up. I can read a little; I can't write. I used to go to school before I went to the mill; I have [not] since. I am sixteen. We have heard nothing in our mill about not working so long.

1833

Testimony of Ann and Elizabeth Eggley, Child Mineworkers

Ann Eggley, eighteen years old.————I'm sure I don't know how to spell my name. We go at four in the morning, and sometimes at half-past four. We begin to work as

---

1. The drawing frame, a machine that drew out, or lengthened, the wool after it had been carded.
2. Work at the carding machine, which consisted of rollers studded with wires to comb the wool and remove

debris.
3. Removing the full bobbins or spindles of wool, and taking them to other machines to be made into thread.
4. Wakened.

soon as we get down. We get out after four, sometimes at five, in the evening. We work the whole time except an hour for dinner, and sometimes we haven't time to eat. I hurry[5] by myself, and have done so for long. I know the corves are very heavy they are the biggest corves anywhere about. The work is far too hard for me; the sweat runs off me all over sometimes. I am very tired at night. Sometimes when we get home at night we have not power to wash us, and then we go to bed. Sometimes we fall asleep in the chair. Father said last night it was both a shame and a disgrace for girls to work as we do, but there was nought else for us to do. I have tried to get winding[6] to do, but could not. I begun to hurry when I was seven and I have been hurrying ever since. I have been 11 years in the pit. The girls are always tired. I was poorly twice this winter; it was with headache. I hurry for Robert Wiggins; he is not akin to me. I riddle[7] for him. We all riddle for them except the littlest when there is two. We don't always get enough to eat and drink, but we get a good supper. I have known my father go at two in the morning to work when we worked at Twibell's, where there is a day-hole to the pit, and he didn't come out till four. I am quite sure that we work constantly 12 hours except on Saturdays. We wear trousers and our shifts[8] in the pit, and great big shoes clinkered and nailed. The girls never work naked to the waist in our pit. The men don't insult us in the pit. The conduct of the girls in the pit is good enough sometimes, and sometimes bad enough. I never went to a day-school. I went a little to a Sunday-school, but I soon gave it over. I thought it too bad to be confined both Sundays and week-days. I walk about and get the fresh air on Sundays. I have not learnt to read. I don't know my letters. I never learnt nought. I never go to church or chapel; there is no church or chapel at Gawber, there is none nearer than a mile. If I was married I would not go to the pits, but I know some married women that do. The men do not insult the girls with us, but I think they do in some. I have never heard that a good man came into the world who was God's Son to save sinners. I never heard of Christ at all. Nobody has ever told me about him, nor have my father and mother ever taught me to pray. I know no prayer: I never pray. I have been taught nothing about such things.

Elizabeth Eggley, sixteen years old.————I am sister to the last witness. I hurry in the same pit, and work for my father. I find my work very much too hard for me. I hurry alone. It tires me in my arms and back most. We go to work between four and five in the morning. If we are not there by half past five we are not allowed to go down at all. We come out at four, five, or six at night as it happens. We stop in generally 12 hours, and sometimes longer. We have to hurry only from the bank-face down to the horse-gate and back. I am sure it is very hard work and tires us very much; it is too hard for girls to do. We sometimes go to sleep before we get to bed. We haven't a very good house; we have but two rooms for all the family. I have never been to school except four times, and then I gave over because I could not get things to go in.[9] I cannot read: I do not know my letters. I don't know who Jesus Christ was. I never heard of Adam either. I never heard about them at all. I have often been obliged to stop in bed all Sunday to rest myself. I never go to church or chapel.

1842

---

5. A hurrier pushed carriages loaded with ore through the mine shafts. These handtrucks, called corves, weighed as much as 800 pounds.
6. Helping to hoist the coal up the shaft to the surface.

7. Sift the coal through a sieve.
8. Loose-fitting undergarments.
9. I.e., proper clothing.

⊷ ⧮◈⧯ ⊶

Charles Dickens
1812–1870

During the "railway mania" of the 1840s, nearly nine thousand miles of new track were laid across Britain. In 1842 the young Queen Victoria took her first railway journey, and was "quite charmed by it"—though she was also criticized for having risked her life. The railroads were a visible symbol of progress, but as Dickens dramatizes in his novel *Dombey and Son*, their construction brought about a vast demolition of neighborhoods and upheaval of the landscape. In the later novel *Hard Times*, Dickens portrays industrial Manchester as "Coketown" because of the coal residue that blackened the city. He emphasizes the dreary regimentation and the loss of personal identity produced by the mechanization of labor. The workers who tended the machines were called "hands," a term that aptly symbolized their dehumanization. But, as Dickens insists throughout *Hard Times*, oppressive working conditions were only part of the problem; the factory system also fostered alienation and hostility between classes, and the masters were apparently content for their workers to be deprived of education, religion, and even entertainment.

For more about Charles Dickens, see the principal listing on page 1462.

 For online resources on Dickens, go to *The Longman Anthology of British Literature* Web site at www.ablongman.com/damroschbritlit3e.

from Dombey and Son
[THE COMING OF THE RAILWAY]

The first shock of a great earthquake had, just at that period, rent the whole neighbourhood to its centre.[1] Traces of its course were visible on every side. Houses were knocked down; streets broken through and stopped; deep pits and trenches dug in the ground; enormous heaps of earth and clay thrown up; buildings that were undermined and shaking, propped by great beams of wood. Here, a chaos of carts, overthrown and jumbled together, lay topsy-turvy at the bottom of a steep unnatural hill; there, confused treasures of iron soaked and rusted in something that had accidentally become a pond. Everywhere were bridges that led nowhere; thoroughfares that were wholly impassable; Babel towers[2] of chimneys, wanting half their height; temporary wooden houses and enclosures, in the most unlikely situations; carcases of ragged tenements, and fragments of unfinished walls and arches, and piles of scaffolding, and wildernesses of bricks, and giant forms of cranes, and tripods straddling above nothing. There were a hundred thousand shapes and substances of incompleteness, wildly mingled out of their places, upside down, burrowing in the earth, aspiring in the air, mouldering in the water, and unintelligible as any dream. Hot springs and fiery eruptions, the usual attendants upon earthquakes, lent their contributions of confusion to the scene. Boiling water hissed and heaved within dilapidated walls; whence, also, the glare and roar of flames came issuing forth; and mounds of ashes blocked up rights of way, and wholly changed the law and custom of the neighbourhood.

1. Dickens is describing the construction of the London-Birmingham railway, which demolished many buildings in Camden Town, an area in London he knew as a boy. The line opened in 1838.
2. The tower of Babel was supposed to have been built high enough to reach heaven (Genesis 11).

In short, the yet unfinished and unopened Railroad was in progress; and, from the very core of all this dire disorder, trailed smoothly away, upon its mighty course of civilisation and improvement.

But as yet, the neighbourhood was shy to own the Railroad. One or two bold speculators had projected streets; and one had built a little, but had stopped among the mud and ashes to consider farther of it. A bran-new Tavern, redolent of fresh mortar and size, and fronting nothing at all, had taken for its sign The Railway Arms; but that might be rash enterprise—and then it hoped to sell drink to the workmen. So, the Excavators' House of Call had sprung up from a beer-shop; and the old-established Ham and Beef Shop had become the Railway Eating House, with a roast leg of pork daily, through interested motives of a similar immediate and popular description. Lodging-house keepers were favourable in like manner; and for the like reasons were not to be trusted. The general belief was very slow. There were frowzy fields, and cow-houses, and dunghills, and dustheaps, and ditches, and gardens, and summer-houses, and carpet-beating grounds, at the very door of the Railway. Little tumuli[3] of oyster shells in the oyster season, and of lobster shells in the lobster season, and of broken crockery and faded cabbage leaves in all seasons, encroached upon its high places. Posts, and rails, and old cautions to trespassers, and backs of mean houses, and patches of wretched vegetation, stared it out of countenance. Nothing was the better for it, or thought of being so. If the miserable waste ground lying near it could have laughed, it would have laughed it to scorn, like many of the miserable neighbours.

1846

from Hard Times
[COKETOWN]

Coketown, to which Messrs Bounderby and Gradgrind[1] now walked, was a triumph of fact; it had no greater taint of fancy in it than Mrs Gradgrind herself. Let us strike the key-note, Coketown, before pursuing our tune.

It was a town of red brick, or of brick that would have been red if the smoke and ashes had allowed it; but, as matters stood it was a town of unnatural red and black like the painted face of a savage. It was a town of machinery and tall chimneys, out of which interminable serpents of smoke trailed themselves for ever and ever, and never got uncoiled. It had a black canal in it, and a river that ran purple with ill-smelling dye, and vast piles of building full of windows where there was a rattling and a trembling all day long, and where the piston of the steam-engine worked monotonously up and down, like the head of an elephant in a state of melancholy madness. It contained several large streets all very like one another, and many small streets still more like one another, inhabited by people equally like one another, who all went in and out at the same hours, with the same sound upon the same pavements, to do the same work, and to whom every day was the same as yesterday and tomorrow, and every year the counterpart of the last and the next.

3. Artificial mounds. Oysters, a luxury today, were popular with poor people in Dickens's day; in *Pickwick Papers* Sam Weller says: "Poverty and oysters always seem to go together."

1. Bounderby is a mill owner; Gradgrind runs a school on Utilitarian principles.

These attributes of Coketown were in the main inseparable from the work by which it was sustained; against them were to be set off, comforts of life which found their way all over the world, and elegancies of life which made, we will not ask how much of the fine lady, who could scarcely bear to hear the place mentioned. The rest of its features were voluntary, and they were these.

You saw nothing in Coketown but what was severely workful. If the members of a religious persuasion built a chapel there—as the members of eighteen religious persuasions had done—they made it a pious warehouse of red brick, with sometimes (but this only in highly ornamented examples) a bell in a bird-cage on the top of it. The solitary exception was the New Church; a stuccoed edifice with a square steeple over the door, terminating in four short pinnacles like florid wooden legs. All the public inscriptions in the town were painted alike, in severe characters of black and white. The jail might have been the infirmary, the infirmary might have been the jail, the town-hall might have been either, or both, or anything else, for anything that appeared to the contrary in the graces of their construction. Fact, fact, fact, everywhere in the material aspect of the town; fact, fact, fact, everywhere in the immaterial. The M'Choakumchild school was all fact, and the school of design was all fact, and the relations between master and man were all fact, and everything was fact between the lying-in hospital and the cemetery, and what you couldn't state in figures, or show to be purchaseable in the cheapest market and saleable in the dearest, was not, and never should be, world without end, Amen.[2]

A town so sacred to fact, and so triumphant in its assertion, of course got on well? Why no, not quite well. No? Dear me!

No. Coketown did not come out of its own furnaces, in all respects like gold that had stood the fire. First, the perplexing mystery of the place was, Who belonged to the eighteen denominations? Because, whoever did, the labouring people did not. It was very strange to walk through the streets on a Sunday morning, and note how few of *them* the barbarous jangling of bells that was driving the sick and nervous mad, called away from their own quarter, from their own close rooms, from the corners of their own streets, where they lounged listlessly, gazing at all the church and chapel going, as at a thing with which they had no manner of concern. Nor was it merely the stranger who noticed this, because there was a native organization in Coketown itself, whose members were to be heard of in the House of Commons every session, indignantly petitioning for acts of parliament that should make these people religious by main force. Then, came the Teetotal Society, who complained that these same people *would* get drunk, and showed in tabular statements that they did get drunk, and proved at tea parties that no inducement, human or Divine (except a medal), would induce them to forego their custom of getting drunk. Then, came the chemist and druggist, with other tabular statements, showing that when they didn't get drunk, they took opium. Then, came the experienced chaplain of the jail, with more tabular statements, outdoing all the previous tabular statements, and showing that the same people *would* resort to low haunts, hidden from the public eye, where they heard low singing and saw low dancing, and mayhap joined in it; and where A. B., aged twenty-four next birthday, and committed for eighteen months' solitary, had himself said (not that he had ever shown himself particularly worthy of belief) his ruin began, as he was perfectly sure and confident that otherwise he would have been

2. The conclusion of the Anglican form of the Lord's Prayer.

a tip-top moral specimen. Then, came Mr Gradgrind and Mr Bounderby, the two gentlemen at this present moment walking through Coketown, and both eminently practical, who could, on occasion, furnish more tabular statements derived from their own personal experience, and illustrated by cases they had known and seen, from which it clearly appeared—in short it was the only clear thing in the case—that these same people were a bad lot altogether, gentlemen; that do what you would for them they were never thankful for it, gentlemen; that they were restless, gentlemen; that they never knew what they wanted; that they lived upon the best, and bought fresh butter, and insisted on Mocha coffee, and rejected all but prime parts of meat, and yet were eternally dissatisfied and unmanageable.

1854

━━◆━━

Benjamin Disraeli
1804–1881

The subtitle of Benjamin Disraeli's novel *Sybil*, "The Two Nations," encapsulates the Victorians' uneasy sense of being a divided society. The Hungry Forties were a time of unprecedented economic distress: Britain was the world's wealthiest nation, yet people were starving in the streets, and many feared that a revolution was in the offing. Thomas Carlyle had argued in *Past and Present* that "isolation is the sum-total of wretchedness to man." Here, Disraeli echoes his call for cooperation and benevolent paternalism to forge new relations between classes. Disraeli went on to become a Conservative Prime Minister, noted both for his nostalgic vision of aristocratic leadership and for the domestic social reforms that took place during his administration.

from Sybil
[THE TWO NATIONS]

"It is a community of purpose that constitutes society," continued the younger stranger; "without that, men may be drawn into contiguity, but they still continue virtually isolated."

"And is that their condition in cities?"

"It is their condition everywhere; but in cities that condition is aggravated. A density of population implies a severer struggle for existence, and a consequent repulsion of elements brought into too close contact. In great cities men are brought together by the desire of gain. They are not in a state of co-operation, but of isolation, as to the making of fortunes; and for all the rest they are careless of neighbours. Christianity teaches us to love our neighbour as ourself; modern society acknowledges no neighbour."

"Well, we live in strange times," said Egremont, struck by the observation of his companion, and relieving a perplexed spirit by an ordinary exclamation, which often denotes that the mind is more stirred than it cares to acknowledge, or at the moment is able to express.

"When the infant begins to walk, it also thinks that it lives in strange times," said his companion.

"Your inference?" asked Egremont.

"That society, still in its infancy, is beginning to feel its way."

"This is a new reign," said Egremont, "perhaps it is a new era."

"I think so," said the younger stranger.

"I hope so," said the elder one.

"Well, society may be in its infancy," said Egremont, slightly smiling; "but, say what you like, our Queen reigns over the greatest nation that ever existed."

"Which nation?" asked the younger stranger, "for she reigns over two."

The stranger paused; Egremont was silent, but looked inquiringly.

"Yes," resumed the younger stranger after a moment's interval. "Two nations; between whom there is no intercourse and no sympathy; who are as ignorant of each other's habits, thoughts, and feelings, as if they were dwellers in different zones, or inhabitants of different planets; who are formed by a different breeding, are fed by a different food, are ordered by different manners, and are not governed by the same laws."

"You speak of—" said Egremont, hesitatingly.

"The Rich and the Poor."

1845

✦

Friedrich Engels
1820–1895

In the manufacturing city of Manchester, whose size had increased more than tenfold between 1760 and 1830, the average life expectancy of working people in 1841 was only twenty years. Friedrich Engels, a German who had come to Manchester to study the cotton trade, was so appalled by his observations of the urban poor that he wrote an exposé of their degradation, stressing the "hypocritical town planning" that insulated the middle class from the sight of squalor and suffering. Engels's book was published in German in 1845; it became a socialist classic, and laid the groundwork for Engels's collaboration with Karl Marx. Lenin called the book "a terrible indictment of capitalism and of the middle classes." It was finally translated into English in 1892.

from The Condition of the Working Class in England in 1844
from *The Great Towns*

London is unique, because it is a city in which one can roam for hours without leaving the built-up area and without seeing the slightest sign of the approach of open country. This enormous agglomeration of population on a single spot has multiplied a hundred-fold the economic strength of the two and a half million inhabitants concentrated there. This great population has made London the commercial capital of the world and has created the gigantic docks in which are assembled the thousands of ships which always cover the River Thames. I know nothing more imposing than the view one obtains of the river when sailing from the sea up to London Bridge. Especially above Woolwich the houses and docks are packed tightly together on both banks of the river. The further one goes up the river the thicker becomes the concentration of ships lying at anchor, so that eventually only a narrow shipping lane is left free in mid-stream. Here hundreds of steamships dart rapidly to and fro. All this is so magnificent and impressive that one is lost in admiration. The traveller has good reason to marvel at England's greatness even before he steps on English soil.

It is only later that the traveller appreciates the human suffering which has made all this possible. He can only realise the price that has been paid for all this magnificence after he has tramped the pavements of the main streets of London for some days and has tired himself out by jostling his way through the crowds and by dodging the endless stream of coaches and carts which fills the streets. It is only when he has visited the slums of this great city that it dawns upon him that the inhabitants of modern London have had to sacrifice so much that is best in human nature in order to create those wonders of civilisation with which their city teems. The vast majority of Londoners have had to let so many of their potential creative faculties lie dormant, stunted and unused in order that a small, closely-knit group of their fellow citizens could develop to the full the qualities with which nature has endowed them. The restless and noisy activity of the crowded streets is highly distasteful, and it is surely abhorrent to human nature itself. Hundreds of thousands of men and women drawn from all classes and ranks of society pack the streets of London. Are they not all human beings with the same innate characteristics and potentialities? Are they not all equally interested in the pursuit of happiness? And do they not all aim at happiness by following similar methods? Yet they rush past each other as if they had nothing in common. They are tacitly agreed on one thing only—that everyone should keep to the right of the pavement so as not to collide with the stream of people moving in the opposite direction. No one even thinks of sparing a glance for his neighbour in the streets. The more that Londoners are packed into a tiny space, the more repulsive and disgraceful becomes the brutal indifference with which they ignore their neighbours and selfishly concentrate upon their private affairs. We know well enough that this isolation of the individual—this narrow-minded egotism—is everywhere the fundamental principle of modern society. But nowhere is this selfish egotism so blatantly evident as in the frantic bustle of the great city. The disintegration of society into individuals, each guided by his private principles and each pursuing his own aims has been pushed to its furthest limits in London. Here indeed human society has been split into its component atoms.

From this it follows that the social conflict—the war of all against all—is fought in the open. * * * Here men regard their fellows not as human beings, but as pawns in the struggle for existence. Everyone exploits his neighbour with the result that the stronger tramples the weaker under foot. The strongest of all, a tiny group of capitalists, monopolise everything, while the weakest, who are in the vast majority, succumb to the most abject poverty.

What is true of London, is true also of all the great towns, such as Manchester, Birmingham and Leeds. Everywhere one finds on the one hand the most barbarous indifference and selfish egotism and on the other the most distressing scenes of misery and poverty. Signs of social conflict are to be found everywhere. Everyone turns his house into a fortress to defend himself—under the protection of the law—from the depredations of his neighbours. Class warfare is so open and shameless that it has to be seen to be believed. The observer of such an appalling state of affairs must shudder at the consequences of such feverish activity and can only marvel that so crazy a social and economic structure should survive at all.

Capital is the all-important weapon in the class war. Power lies in the hands of those who own, directly or indirectly, foodstuffs and the means of production. The poor, having no capital, inevitably bear the consequences of defeat in the struggle. Nobody troubles about the poor as they struggle helplessly in the whirlpool of modern industrial life. The working man may be lucky enough to find employment, if by

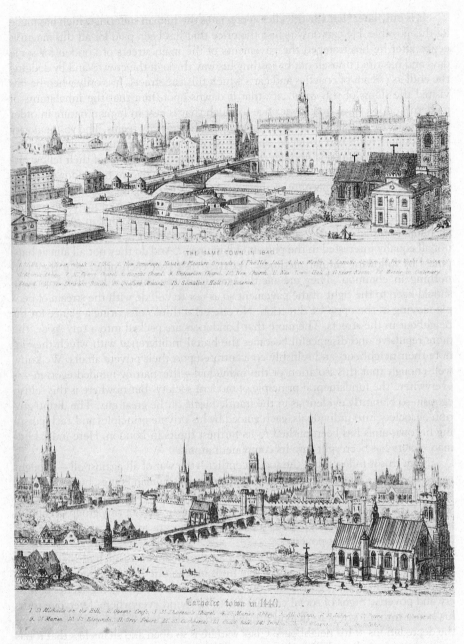

Augustus Welby Northmore Pugin, *Catholic Town in 1440 / Same Town in 1840,* from *Contrasts,*
1836. Pugin, an architect, anticipated Ruskin's belief that art is an index of spiritual values. He argued for a revival of Gothic architecture as a means of regenerating Victorian morality. In
Contrasts he juxtaposed medieval and Victorian scenes to display the superiority of Gothic styles,
institutions, and attitudes. Here, church spires have given way to smokestacks; trees and open
fields have been replaced by looming factories, a lunatic asylum, and an enormous panoptic jail;
the social and spiritual harmony of a preindustrial age has fragmented into a hodgepodge of com-
peting religious sects.

his labour he can enrich some member of the middle classes. But his wages are so low that they hardly keep body and soul together. If he cannot find work, he can steal, unless he is afraid of the police; or he can go hungry and then the police will see to it that he will die of hunger in such a way as not to disturb the equanimity of the middle classes. While I was in England at least twenty or thirty people died of hunger under the most scandalous circumstances, and yet when an inquest was held the jury seldom had the courage to bring in a verdict in accordance with the facts. However clear and unequivocal the evidence, the middle classes, from whom the juries were drawn, always found a loophole which enabled them to avoid a verdict of "death from starvation." In such circumstances the middle classes dare not tell the truth, because if they did so, they would be condemning themselves out of their own mouths.

* * *

Every great town has one or more slum areas into which the working classes are packed. Sometimes, of course, poverty is to be found hidden away in alleys close to the stately homes of the wealthy. Generally, however, the workers are segregated in separate districts where they struggle through life as best they can out of sight of the more fortunate classes of society. The slums of the English towns have much in common—the worst houses in a town being found in the worst districts. They are generally unplanned wildernesses of one- or two-storied terrace houses built of brick. Wherever possible these have cellars which are also used as dwellings. These little houses of three or four rooms and a kitchen are called cottages, and throughout England, except for some parts of London, are where the working classes normally live. The streets themselves are usually unpaved and full of holes. They are filthy and strewn with animal and vegetable refuse. Since they have neither gutters nor drains the refuse accumulates in stagnant, stinking puddles. Ventilation in the slums is inadequate owing to the hopelessly unplanned nature of these areas. A great many people live huddled together in a very small area, and so it is easy to imagine the nature of the air in these workers' quarters. However, in fine weather the streets are used for the drying of washing and clothes lines are stretched across the streets from house to house and wet garments are hung out on them.

We propose to describe some of these slums in detail. In London there is the well-known "rookery"[1] of St. Giles. * * * St. Giles is situated in the most densely-populated part of London and is surrounded by splendid wide streets which are used by the fashionable world. It is close to Oxford Street, Trafalgar Square and the Strand. It is a confused conglomeration of tall houses of three or four stories. The narrow, dirty streets are just as crowded as the main thoroughfares, but in St. Giles one sees only members of the working classes. The narrowness of the roads is accentuated by the presence of streetmarkets in which baskets of rotting and virtually uneatable vegetables and fruit are exposed for sale. The smell from these and from the butchers' stalls is appalling. The houses are packed from cellar to attic and they are as dirty inside as outside. No human being would willingly inhabit such dens. Yet even worse conditions are to be found in the houses which lie off the main road down narrow alleys leading to the courts. These dwellings are approached by covered passages between the houses. The extent to which these filthy passages are falling into decay beggars all description. There is hardly an unbroken windowpane to be seen, the walls are crumbling, the door posts and window frames are loose and rotten. The doors, where they exist, are made of old boards nailed together. In-

---

1. An overcrowded and deteriorating district of tenement dwellings.

deed in this nest of thieves doors are superfluous, because there is nothing worth stealing. Piles of refuse and ashes lie all over the place and the slops thrown out into the street collect in pools which emit a foul stench. Here live the poorest of the poor. Here the worst-paid workers rub shoulders with thieves, rogues and prostitutes. Most of them have come from Ireland or are of Irish extraction. Those who have not yet been entirely engulfed in the morass of iniquity by which they are surrounded are daily losing the power to resist the demoralising influences of poverty, dirt and low environment. * * *

However wretched may be the dwellings of some of the workers—who do at least have a roof over their heads—the situation of the homeless is even more tragic. Every morning fifty thousand Londoners wake up not knowing where they are going to sleep at night. The most fortunate are those who have a few pence in their pocket in the evening and can afford to go to one of the many lodging houses which exist in all the big cities. But these establishments only provide the most miserable accommodation. They are crammed full of beds from top to bottom—four, five and even six beds in a room—until there is no room for more. Each bed is filled to capacity and may contain as many as four, five or even six lodgers. The lodging house keeper allocates his accommodation to all his customers in rotation as they arrive. No attempt is made to segregate the sick and the healthy, the old and the young, the men and the women, the drunk and the sober. If these ill-assorted bed-fellows do not agree there are quarrels and fights which often lead to injuries. But if they do agree among themselves, it is even worse, for they are either planning burglaries or are engaged in practices of so bestial a nature that no words exist in a modern civilised tongue to describe them. Those who cannot afford a bed in a lodging house sleep where they can, in passages, arcades or any corner where the police and the owners are unlikely to disturb their slumbers. * * *

If we cross Blackstone Edge on foot or take the train we reach Manchester, the regional capital of South Lancashire, and enter the classic home of English industry. This is the masterpiece of the Industrial Revolution and at the same time the mainspring of all the workers' movements. Once more we are in a beautiful hilly countryside. The land slopes gently down towards the Irish Sea, intersected by the charming green valleys of the Ribble, the Irwell, the Mersey and their tributaries. A hundred years ago this region was to a great extent thinly populated marsh-land. Now it is covered with towns and villages and is the most densely-populated part of England. In Lancashire—particularly in Manchester—is to be found not only the origin but the heart of the industry of the United Kingdom. Manchester Exchange is the thermometer which records all the fluctuations of industrial and commercial activity. The evolution of the modern system of manufacture has reached its climax in Manchester. It was in the South Lancashire cotton industry that water and steam power first replaced hand machines. It was here that such machines as the power-loom and the self-acting mule replaced the old hand-loom and spinning wheel. It is here that the division of labour has been pushed to its furthest limits. These three factors are the essence of modern industry. In all three of them the cotton industry was the pioneer and remains ahead in all branches of industry. In the circumstances it is to be expected that it is in this region that the inevitable consequences of industrialisation in so far as they affect the working classes are most strikingly evident. Nowhere else can the life and conditions of the industrial proletariat be studied in all their aspects as in South Lancashire. Here can be seen most clearly the degradation into which the worker sinks owing to the introduction of steam power, machinery and the division of labour. Here, too, can be seen most the strenuous efforts of the proletariat to raise themselves from their degraded situation. I propose to examine conditions in Manchester in greater detail for two reasons. In the first place, Manchester is the classic type of modern industrial town. Secondly, I know Manchester as well as I know my native town and I know more about it than most of its inhabitants. * * *

* * * Owing to the curious lay-out of the town it is quite possible for someone to live for years in Manchester and to travel daily to and from his work without ever seeing a working-class quarter or coming into contact with an artisan. He who visits Manchester simply on business or for pleasure need never see the slums, mainly because the working-class districts and the middle-class districts are quite distinct. This division is due partly to deliberate policy and partly to instinctive and tacit agreement between the two social groups. In those areas where the two social groups happen to come into contact with each other the middle classes sanctimoniously ignore the existence of their less fortunate neighbours. In the centre of Manchester there is a fairly large commercial district, which is about half a mile long and half a mile broad. This district is almost entirely given over to offices and warehouses. Nearly the whole of this district has no permanent residents and is deserted at night, when only policemen patrol its dark, narrow thoroughfares with their bull's eye lanterns. This district is intersected by certain main streets which carry an enormous volume of traffic. The lower floors of the buildings are occupied by shops of dazzling splendour. A few of the upper stories on these premises are used as dwellings and the streets present a relatively busy appearance until late in the evening. Around this commercial quarter there is a belt of built up areas on the average one and a half miles in width, which is occupied entirely by working-class dwellings. This area of workers' houses includes all Manchester proper, except the centre. * * * The upper classes enjoy healthy country air and live in luxurious and comfortable dwellings which are linked to the centre of Manchester by omnibuses which run every fifteen or thirty minutes. To such an extent has the convenience of the rich been considered in the planning of Manchester that these plutocrats can travel from their houses to their places of business in the centre of the town by the shortest routes, which run entirely through working-class districts, without even realising how close they are to the misery and filth which lie on both sides of the road. This is because the main streets which run from the Exchange in all directions out of the town are occupied almost uninterruptedly on both sides by shops, which are kept by members of the lower middle classes. In their own interests these shopkeepers should keep the outsides of their shops in a clean and respectable condition, and in fact they do so. These shops have naturally been greatly influenced by the character of the population in the area which lies behind them. Those shops which are situated in the vicinity of commercial or middle class residential districts are more elegant than those which serve as a facade for the workers' grimy cottages. Nevertheless, even the less pretentious shops adequately serve their purpose of hiding from the eyes of wealthy ladies and gentlemen with strong stomachs and weak nerves the misery and squalor which are part and parcel of their own riches and luxury. * * *

I am quite aware of the fact that this hypocritical town-planning device is more or less common to all big cities. * * * But in my opinion Manchester is unique in the systematic way in which the working classes have been barred from the main streets. Nowhere else has such care been taken to avoid offending the tender susceptibilities of the eyes and the nerves of the middle classes. Yet Manchester is the very town in which building has taken place in a haphazard manner with little or no planning or interference from the authorities. When the middle classes zealously proclaim that all is well with the working classes, I cannot help feeling that the politically "progressive" industrialists, the Manchester "bigwigs," are not quite so innocent of this shameful piece of town planning as they pretend.

* * * I will now give a description of the working-class districts of Manchester. The first of them is the Old Town, which lies between the northern limit of the commercial quarter and the River Irk. * * * Here one is really and truly in a district which is quite obviously given over entirely to the working classes, because even the shop-keepers and the publicans[2] of Long Millgate make no effort to give their establishments a semblance of cleanliness. The condition of this street may be deplorable, but it is by no means as bad as the alleys and courts which lie behind it, and which can be approached only by covered passages so narrow that two people cannot pass. Anyone who has never visited these courts and alleys can have no idea of the fantastic way in which the houses have been packed together in disorderly confusion in impudent defiance of all reasonable principles of town planning. And the fault lies not merely in the survival of old property from earlier periods in Manchester's history. Only in quite modern times has the policy of cramming as many houses as possible on to such space as was not utilised in earlier periods reached its climax. The result is that today not an inch of space remains between the houses and any further building is now physically impossible. * * *

* * * To the right and left a number of covered passages from Long Millgate give access to several courts. On reaching them one meets with a degree of dirt and revolting filth, the like of which is not to be found elsewhere. The worst courts are those leading down to the Irk, which contain unquestionably the most dreadful dwellings I have ever seen. In one of these courts, just at the entrance where the covered passage ends there is a privy without a door. This privy is so dirty that the inhabitants of the court can only enter or leave the court if they are prepared to wade through puddles of stale urine and excrement. Anyone who wishes to confirm this description should go to the first court on the bank of the Irk above Ducie Bridge. Several tanneries are situated on the bank of the river and they fill the neighbourhood with the stench of animal putrefaction. The only way of getting to the courts below Ducie Bridge is by going down flights of narrow dirty steps and one can only reach the houses by treading over heaps of dirt and filth. * * * The view from this bridge, which is mercifully concealed by a high parapet from all but the tallest mortals, is quite characteristic of the whole district. At the bottom the Irk flows, or rather, stagnates. It is a narrow, coal-black, stinking river full of filth and rubbish which it deposits on the more low-lying right bank. In dry weather this bank presents the spectacle of a series of the most revolting blackish-green puddles of slime from the depths of which bubbles of miasmatic[3] gases constantly rise and create a stench which is unbearable even to those standing on the bridge forty or fifty feet above the level of the water. Moreover, the flow of the river is continually interrupted by numerous high weirs, behind which large quantities of slime and refuse collect and putrefy. Above Ducie Bridge there are some tall tannery buildings, and further up there are dye-works, bone mills and gasworks. All the filth, both liquid and solid, discharged by these works finds its way into the River Irk, which also receives the contents of the adjacent sewers and privies. The nature of the filth deposited by this river may well be imagined. If one looks at the heaps of garbage below Ducie Bridge one

---

2. Pub-keepers.   3. Heavy, vaporous, and possibly disease ridden.

can gauge the extent to which accumulated dirt, filth and decay permeates the courts on the steep left bank of the river. The houses are packed very closely together and since the bank of the river is very steep it is possible to see a part of every house. All of them have been blackened by soot, all of them are crumbling with age and all have broken window panes and window frames. * * * In the background one sees the paupers' cemetery, and the stations of the railways to Liverpool and Leeds. Behind these buildings is situated the workhouse, Manchester's "Poor Law Bastille."[4] The workhouse is built on a hill and from behind its high walls and battlements seems to threaten the whole adjacent working-class quarter like a fortress.

* * * The recently constructed extension of the Leeds railway which crosses the Irk at this point has swept away some of these courts and alleys, but it has thrown open to public gaze some of the others. So it comes about that there is to be found immediately under the railway bridge a court which is even filthier and more revolting than all the others. This is simply because it was formerly so hidden and secluded that it could only be reached with considerable difficulty, [but is now exposed to the human eye]. I thought I knew this district well, but even I would never have found it had not the railway viaduct made a breach in the slums at this point. One walks along a very rough path on the river bank, in between clothes-posts and washing lines to reach a chaotic group of little, one-storied, one-roomed cabins. Most of them have earth floors, and working, living and sleeping all take place in the one room. In such a hole, barely six feet long and five feet wide, I saw two beds—and what beds and bedding!—which filled the room, except for the fireplace and the doorstep. Several of these huts, as far as I could see, were completely empty, although the door was open and the inhabitants were leaning against the door posts. In front of the doors filth and garbage abounded. I could not see the pavement, but from time to time, I felt it was there because my feet scraped it. This whole collection of cattle sheds for human beings was surrounded on two sides by houses and a factory and on a third side by the river. * * *

Enough of this! All along the Irk slums of this type abound. There is an unplanned and chaotic conglomeration of houses, most of which are more or less unhabitable. The dirtiness of the interiors of these premises is fully in keeping with the filth that surrounds them. How can people dwelling in such places keep clean! There are not even adequate facilities for satisfying the most natural daily needs. There are so few privies that they are either filled up every day or are too far away for those who need to use them. How can these people wash when all that is available is the dirty water of the Irk? Pumps and piped water are to be found only in the better-class districts of the town. Indeed no one can blame these helots[5] of modern civilisation if their homes are no cleaner than the occasional pigsties which are a feature of these slums. * * *

This, then, is the Old Town of Manchester. On re-reading my description of the Old Town I must admit that, far from having exaggerated anything, I have not written vividly enough to impress the reader with the filth and dilapidation of a district which is quite unfit for human habitation. The shameful lay-out of the Old Town has made it impossible for the wretched inhabitants to enjoy cleanliness, fresh air, and good health. And such a district of at least twenty to thirty thousand inhabitants lies in the very centre of the second city in England, the most important factory town in

---

4. The Poor Laws of the 1830s established workhouses for the poor, where conditions were so appalling that they were likened to prisons such as the Bastille in Paris.
5. Serfs or slaves.

the world. It is here that one can see how little space human beings need to move about in, how little air—and what air!—they need to breathe in order to exist, and how few of the decencies of civilisation are really necessary in order to survive. It is true that this is the *Old Town* and Manchester people stress this when their attention is drawn to the revolting character of this hell upon earth. But that is no defence. Everything in this district that arouses our disgust and just indignation is of relatively recent origin and belongs to the industrial age. The two or three hundred houses which survive from the earlier period of Manchester's history have long ago been deserted by their original inhabitants. It is only industry which has crammed them full of the hordes of workers who now live there. It is only the modern industrial age which has built over every scrap of ground between these old houses to provide accommodation for the masses who have migrated from the country districts and from Ireland. It is only the industrial age that has made it possible for the owners of these shacks, fit only for the accommodation of cattle, to let them at high rents for human habitations. It is only modern industry which permits these owners to take advantage of the poverty of the workers, to undermine the health of thousands to enrich themselves. Only industry has made it possible for workers who have barely emerged from a state of serfdom to be again treated as chattels and not as human beings. The workers have been caged in dwellings which are so wretched that no one else will live in them, and they actually pay good money for the privilege of seeing these dilapidated hovels fall to pieces about their ears. Industry alone has been responsible for all this and yet this same industry could not flourish except by degrading and exploiting the workers.

1845

Henry Mayhew
1812–1887

In London, the most visible occupations of children were in the streets. They earned a precarious living hawking goods, begging, performing, and providing various services, from running errands to prostitution. Henry Mayhew interviewed hundreds of street people, gathering four volumes of testimony about the lives of this exploited and neglected underclass. With an extraordinary ear for slang and oddities of speech, he shaped each narrative into a kind of dramatic monologue. By publishing "the history of a people, from the lips of the people themselves ... in their own 'unvarnished' language," Mayhew gave voice to a multitude of forgotten workers. The critic John D. Rosenberg has described Mayhew's image of London as "a vast, ingeniously balanced mechanism in which each class subsists on the drippings and droppings of the stratum above, all the way from the rich, whom we scarcely glimpse, down to the deformed and starving, whom we see groping for bits of salvageable bone or decaying vegetables in the markets."

from London Labour and the London Poor
WATERCRESS GIRL

The little watercress girl who gave me the following statement, although only eight years of age, had entirely lost all childish ways, and was, indeed, in thoughts and manner, a woman. There was something cruelly pathetic in hearing this infant, so young that her features had scarcely formed themselves, talking of the bitterest struggles of life, with the calm earnestness of one who had endured them all. I did not know how to talk with her. At first I treated her as a child, speaking on childish subjects; so that I might, by being familiar with her, remove all shyness, and get her to narrate her life freely. I asked her about her toys and her games with her companions; but the look of amazement that answered me soon put an end to any attempt at fun on my part. I then talked to her about the parks, and whether she ever went to them. "The parks!" she replied in wonder, "where are they?" I explained to her, telling her that they were large open places with green grass and tall trees, where beautiful carriages drove about, and people walked for pleasure, and children played. Her eyes brightened up a little as I spoke; and she asked, half doubtingly, "Would they let such as me go there—just to look?" All her knowledge seemed to begin and end with water-cresses,[1] and what they fetched. She knew no more of London than that part she had seen on her rounds, and believed that no quarter of the town was handsomer or pleasanter than it was at Farringdon-market or at Clerkenwell, where she lived. Her little face, pale and thin with privation, was wrinkled where the dimples ought to have been, and she would sigh frequently. When some hot dinner was offered to her, she would not touch it, because, if she eat too much, "it made her sick," she said; "and she wasn't used to meat, only on a Sunday."

The poor child, although the weather was severe, was dressed in a thin cotton gown, with a threadbare shawl wrapped round her shoulders. She wore no covering to her head, and the long rusty hair stood out in all directions. When she walked she shuffled along, for fear that the large carpet slippers that served her for shoes should slip off her feet.

"I go about the streets with water-creases, crying, 'Four bunches a penny, water-creases.' I am just eight years old—that's all, and I've a big sister, and a brother and a sister younger than I am. On and off, I've been very near a twelve-month in the streets. Before that, I had to take care of a baby for my aunt. No, it wasn't heavy—it was only two months old; but I minded it for ever such a time—till it could walk. It was a very nice little baby, not a very pretty one; but, if I touched it under the chin, it would laugh. Before I had the baby, I used to help mother, who was in the fur trade; and, if there was any slits in the fur, I'd sew them up. My mother learned me to needle-work and to knit when I was about five. I used to go to school, too; but I wasn't there long. I've forgot all about it now, it's such a time ago; and mother took me away because the master whacked me, though the missus use'n't to never touch me. I didn't like him at all. What do you think? he hit me three times, ever so hard, across the face with his cane, and made me go dancing down stairs; and when mother saw the marks on my cheek, she went to blow him up,[2] but she couldn't see him—he was afraid. That's why I left school.

"The creases is so bad now, that I haven't been out with 'em for three days. They're so cold, people won't buy 'em; for when I goes up to them, they say, 'They'll freeze our bellies.' Besides, in the market, they won't sell a ha'penny handful now—they're ris to[3] a penny and tuppence. In summer there's lots, and 'most as cheap as dirt; but I have to be down at Farringdon-market between four and five, or else I can't get any creases, because everyone almost—especially the Irish—is selling them, and they're picked up so quick. Some of the saleswomen—we never calls 'em ladies—is

1. An herb whose leaves are used in salads and as garnishes.   3. Their price has risen to.
2. Scold him.

very kind to us children, and some of them altogether spiteful. The good one will give you a bunch for nothing, when they're cheap; but the others, cruel ones, if you try to bate them a farden less[4] than they ask you, will say, 'Go along with you, you're no good.' I used to go down to market along with another girl, as must be about fourteen, 'cos she does her back hair up. When we've bought a lot, we sits down on a door-step, and ties up the bunches. We never goes home to breakfast till we've sold out; but, if it's very late, then I buys a penn'orth of pudden, which is very nice with gravy. I don't know hardly one of the people, as goes to Farringdon, to talk to; they never speaks to me, so I don't speak to them. We children never play down there, 'cos we're thinking of our living. No; people never pities me in the street—excepting one gentleman, and he says, says he, 'What do you do out so soon in the morning?' but he gave me nothink—he only walked away.

"It's very cold before winter comes on reg'lar—specially getting up of a morning. I gets up in the dark by the light of the lamp in the court. When the snow is on the ground, there's no creases. I bears the cold—you must; so I puts my hands under my shawl, though it hurts 'em to take hold of the creases, especially when we takes 'em to the pump to wash 'em. No; I never see any children crying—it's no use.

"Sometimes I make a great deal of money. One day I took 1s. 6d., and the creases cost 6d.; but it isn't often I get such luck as that. I oftener makes 3d. or 4d. than 1s.; and then I'm at work, crying, 'Creases, four bunches a penny, creases!' from six in the morning to about ten. What do you mean by mechanics?—I don't know what they are. The shops buys most of me. Some of 'em says, 'Oh! I ain't a-goin' to give a penny for these;' and they want 'em at the same price as I buys 'em at.

"I always give mother my money, she's so very good to me. She don't often beat me; but, when she do, she don't play with me. She's very poor, and goes out cleaning rooms sometimes, now she don't work at the fur. I ain't got no father, he's a father-in-law. No; mother ain't married again—he's a father-in-law. He grinds scissors, and he's very good to me. No; I dont mean by that that he says kind things to me, for he never hardly speaks. When I gets home, after selling creases, I stops at home. I puts the room to rights: mother don't make me do it, I does it myself. I cleans the chairs, though there's only two to clean. I takes a tub and scrubbing-brush and flannel, and scrubs the floor—that's what I do three or four times a week.

"I don't have no dinner. Mother gives me two slices of bread-and-butter and a cup of tea for breakfast, and then I go till tea, and has the same. We has meat of a Sunday, and, of course, I should like to have it every day. Mother has just the same to eat as we has, but she takes more tea—three cups, sometimes. No; I never has no sweet-stuff; I never buy none—I don't like it. Sometimes we has a game of 'honey-pots' with the girls in the court, but not often. Me and Carry H— carries the little 'uns. We plays, too, at 'kiss-in-the-ring.' I knows a good many games, but I don't play at 'em, 'cos going out with creases tires me. On a Friday night, too, I goes to a Jew's house till eleven o'clock on Saturday night. All I has to do is to snuff the candles and poke the fire. You see they keep their Sabbath then, and they won't touch anything; so they gives me my wittals[5] and $1\frac{1}{2}d.$, and I does it for 'em. I have a reg'lar good lot to eat. Supper of Friday night, and tea after that, and fried fish of a Saturday morning, and meat for dinner, and tea, and supper, and I like it very well.

---

4. Give them a farthing (a quarter of a penny) less.   5. Victuals, food.

"Oh, yes; I've got some toys at home. I've a fire-place, and a box of toys, and a knife and fork, and two little chairs. The Jews gave 'em to me where I go to on a Friday, and that's why I said they was very kind to me. I never had no doll; but I misses little sister—she's only two years old. We don't sleep in the same room; for father and mother sleeps with little sister in the one pair, and me and brother and other sister sleeps in the top room. I always goes to bed at seven, 'cos I has to be up so early.

"I am a capital hand at bargaining—but only at buying watercreases. They can't take me in. If the woman tries to give me a small handful of creases, I says, 'I ain't a goin' to have that for a ha'porth,' and I go to the next basket, and so on, all round. I know the quantities very well. For a penny I ought to have a full market hand, or as much as I could carry in my arms at one time, without spilling. For 3*d*. I has a lap full, enough to earn about a shilling; and for 6*d*. I gets as many as crams my basket. I can't read or write, but I knows how many pennies goes to a shilling, why, twelve, of course, but I don't know how many ha'pence there is, though there's two to a penny. When I've bought 3*d*. of creases, I ties 'em up into as many little bundles as I can. They must look biggish, or the people won't buy them, some puffs them out as much as they'll go. All my money I earns I puts in a club and draws it out to buy clothes with. It's better than spending it in sweet-stuff, for them as has a living to earn. Besides it's like a child to care for sugar-sticks, and not like one who's got a living and vittals to earn. I ain't a child, and I shan't be a woman till I'm twenty, but I'm past eight, I am. I don't know nothing about what I earns during the year, I only know how many pennies goes to a shilling, and two ha'pence goes to a penny, and four fardens goes to a penny. I knows, too, how many fardens goes to tuppence—eight. That's as much as I wants to know for the markets."

[A Boy Crossing-Sweeper]

I found the lad who first gave me an insight into the proceedings of the associated crossing-sweepers crouched on the stone steps of a door in Adelaide-street, Strand; and when I spoke to him he was preparing to settle down in a corner and go to sleep—his legs and body being curled round almost as closely as those of a cat on a hearth.

The moment he heard my voice he was upon his feet, asking me to "give a halfpenny to poor little Jack."

He was a good-looking lad, with a pair of large mild eyes, which he took good care to turn up with an expression of supplication as he moaned for his halfpenny.

A cap, or more properly a stuff bag, covered a crop of hair which had matted itself into the form of so many paint-brushes, while his face, from its roundness of feature and the complexion of dirt, had an almost Indian look about it; the colour of his hands, too, was such that you could imagine he had been shelling walnuts.

He ran before me, treading cautiously with his naked feet, until I reached a convenient spot to take down his statement, which was as follows:—

"I've got no mother or father; mother has been dead for two years, and father's been gone more than that—more nigh five years—he died at Ipswich, in Suffolk. * * *

* * * "I used, when I was with mother, to go to school in the morning, and go at nine and come home at twelve to dinner, then go again at two and leave off at half-past four,—that is, if I behaved myself and did all my lessons right; for if I did not I was kept back till I *did* them so. Mother used to pay one shilling a-week, and extra for the copy-books and things. I can read and write—oh, yes, I mean read and write well—read anything, even old English; and I write pretty fair,—though I don't get

The Boy Crossing-Sweepers. After a daguerreotype by Richard Beard, from Henry Mayhew's *London Labour and the London Poor,* 1851.

much reading now, unless it's a penny paper—I've got one in my pocket now—it's the *London Journal*—there's a tale in it now about two brothers, and one of them steals the child away and puts another in his place, and then he gets found out, and all that, and he's just been falling off a bridge now. * * *

"After mother died, sister still kept on making nets,[6] and I lived with her for some time, until she told me she couldn't afford to keep me no longer, though she seemed to have a pretty good lot to do; but she would never let me go with her to the shops, though I could crochet, which she'd learned me, and used to run and get her all her silks and things what she wanted. But she was keeping company with a young man, and one day they went out, and came back and said they'd been and got married. It was him as got rid of me.

"He was kind to me for the first two or three months, while he was keeping her company; but before he was married he got a little cross, and after he was married he begun to get more cross, and used to send me to play in the streets, and tell me not to come home again till night. One day he hit me, and I said I wouldn't be hit about by him, and then at tea that night sister gave me three shillings, and told me I must go and get my own living. So I bought a box and brushes (they cost me just the money) and went cleaning boots, and I done pretty well with them, till my box was stole from me by a boy where I was lodging. He's in prison now—got six calendar for picking pockets.

6. Hairnets, which she sold to hairdressers.

"Sister kept all my clothes. When I asked her for 'em, she said they was disposed of along with all mother's goods; but she gave me some shirts and stockings, and such-like, and I had very good clothes, only they was all worn out. I saw sister after I left her, many times. I asked her many times to take me back, but she used to say, 'It was not her likes, but her husband's, or she'd have had me back;' and I think it was true, for until he came she was a kind-hearted girl; but he said he'd enough to do to look after his own living; he was a fancy-baker by trade.

"I was fifteen the 24th of last May, sir, and I've been sweeping crossings now near upon two years. There's a party of six of us, and we have the crossings from St. Martin's Church as far as Pall Mall. I always go along with them as lodges in the same place as I do. In the daytime, if it's dry, we do anythink what we can—open cabs, or anythink; but if it's wet, we separate, and I and another gets a crossing—those who gets on it first, keeps it,—and we stand on each side and take our chance.

"We do it in this way:—if I was to see two gentlemen coming, I should cry out, 'Two toffs!' and then they are mine; and whether they give me anythink or not they are mine, and my mate is bound not to follow them; for if he did he would get a hiding from the whole lot of us. If we both cry out together, then we share. If it's a lady and gentleman, then we cries, 'A toff and a doll!' Sometimes we are caught out in this way. Perhaps it is a lady and gentleman and a child; and if I was to see them, and only say, 'A toff and a doll,' and leave out the child, then my mate can add the child; and as he is right and I wrong, then it's his party.

"If there's a policeman close at hand we mustn't ask for money; but we are always on the look-out for the policemen, and if we see one, then we calls out 'Phillup!' for that's our signal. One of the policemen at St. Martin's Church—Bandy, we calls him—knows what Phillup means, for he's up to us; so we had to change the word. (At the request of the young crossing-sweeper the present signal is omitted.)

"Yesterday on the crossing I got threepence halfpenny, but when it's dry like to-day I do nothink, for I haven't got a penny yet. We never carries no pockets, for if the policemen find us we generally pass the money to our mates, for if money's found on us we have fourteen days in prison. * * *

"When we see the rain we say together, 'Oh! there's a jolly good rain! we'll have a good day to-morrow.' If a shower comes on, and we are at our room, which we general are about three o'clock, to get somethink to eat—besides, we general go there to see how much each other's taken in the day—why, out we run with our brooms. * * *

"When we gets home at half-past three in the morning, whoever cries out 'first wash' has it. First of all we washes our feet, and we all uses the same water. Then we washes our faces and hands, and necks, and whoever fetches the fresh water up has first wash; and if the second don't like to go and get fresh, why he uses the dirty. Whenever we come in the landlady makes us wash our feet. Very often the stones cuts our feet and makes them bleed; then we bind a bit of rag round them. * * *

"When there's snow on the ground we puts our money together, and goes and buys an old shovel, and then, about seven o'clock in the morning, we goes to the shops and asks them if we shall scrape the snow away. We general gets twopence every house, but some gives sixpence, for it's very hard to clean the snow away, particular when it's been on the ground some time. It's awful cold, and gives us chilblains on our feet; but we don't mind it when we're working, for we soon gets hot then.

1849–1850

1861–1862

John Stuart Mill

1806—1873

The name John Stuart Mill has become synonymous with genius. But for the Victorians it was also associated with outrageously radical views: Mill advocated sexual equality, the right to divorce, universal suffrage, free speech, and proportional representation. He first gained public attention as a social reformer, promoting the rationalist ideas of his godfather, Jeremy Bentham, founder of Utilitarianism. Mill went on to become the era's leading philosopher and political theorist, an outspoken member of Parliament, and Britain's most prestigious proponent of women's rights.

Mill's education is legendary: the Victorians were fond of social experiments, but few were stranger or more disturbing than James Mill's efforts to prove that a child could learn so much so early in life. He began teaching his son Greek at the age of three, making him memorize long lists of Greek words and their English translations. He also "home-schooled" his son in history, languages, calculus, logic, political economy, geography, psychology, and rhetoric. The boy's responsibilities included tutoring his younger siblings—eventually, eight of them— in these subjects. All this went on while his father, busy writing his multivolume *History of British India*, surveyed his children from the other end of the dining-room table.

As Mill's *Autobiography* shows, the human cost of the experiment was high. In an early draft he wrote that "I . . . grew up in the absence of love & in the presence of fear." His stern father denied Mill both pleasures and playmates, and so dominated the boy's mother that he interpreted her submissiveness as indifference to his existence. At fourteen, when his father declared his education finished, Mill had, by his own account, the knowledge of a man of forty—but he still could not brush his own hair.

Undaunted by such trivia, Mill decided he wanted to be "a reformer of the world." When he was seventeen, he founded the Utilitarian Society, which vigorously debated how to achieve the Utilitarian goal of bringing the greatest happiness to the greatest number of people. But at twenty he was plunged into depression when he realized that achieving all his goals would not satisfy him: "I seemed to have nothing left to live for." Overwork and the utter neglect of human emotion in his otherwise comprehensive education led Mill to a nervous breakdown in 1826.

Discovering that "the habit of analysis has a tendency to wear away the feelings," Mill gradually recovered by reading poetry, especially that of Wordsworth. The poet aroused his interest in "the common feelings and common destiny of human beings." Despite his assessment of himself as an "unpoetical nature," Mill became one of the most astute critics of his generation, recognizing before anyone else the unusual strengths and psychological motivations of both Tennyson and Browning. His essay *What is Poetry?* (1833) argues that true poetry expresses the passionate, solitary meditations of the author; it is not so much heard as "*overheard.*"

In 1823 Mill followed in his father's footsteps by taking a clerkship in the Examiner's Office of the East India Company, the commercial enterprise that, in effect, governed British India. He eventually headed the department, as his father had before him. The center of his professional life, however, was his own writing and political activism. His position allowed him time to become an energetic propagandist for radical causes and legal reform—he was even arrested at age seventeen, a few weeks after the job began, for distributing information on birth control. He also edited the *London and Westminster Review* (1836–1840), while writing important essays on Coleridge and Jeremy Bentham. His *System of Logic* (1843) and *Principles of Political Economy* (1848) immediately became standard works in the field; he followed these with influential books on philosophy, politics, and economics, including *Thoughts on Parliamentary Reform* (1859), *Utilitarianism* (1861), *Representative Government* (1861), and *Auguste Comte and Positivism* (1865).

The most significant event of Mill's adult life was meeting the brilliant and beautiful Harriet Taylor in 1830. She shared his radical views on women's rights, and they soon formed an intimate friendship. But she was married and the mother of three children, a fact which lent piquancy to their efforts to establish the legal right of divorce. They finally married in 1851, after the death of her husband. Mill claimed that she deserved equal credit for his works, calling them "joint productions" of their intellectual life together. "When two persons have their thoughts and speculations completely in common," he wrote in his *Autobiography*, "it is of little consequence . . . which of them holds the pen." After Harriet Taylor died in 1858, her daughter Helen became Mill's companion; she carried on their work in woman's rights into the twentieth century.

Mill retired from the East India Company in 1858 when the British government took over the company's affairs. Although he refused to seek votes or curry favor with any constituency, Mill was elected Member of Parliament for Westminster from 1865 to 1868, making memorable speeches on behalf of political reform, Irish freedom, and women's voting rights. A century ahead of mainstream Anglo-American lawmakers, he demanded nonsexist language for legislation, including a proposal that the Second Reform Bill (1867) be rewritten to replace the word "man" with the word "person." After his defeat in the election of 1868, Mill spent most of his remaining years in Avignon, France, where he died in 1873.

In the twentieth century, Mill's reputation has been sustained by the continuing relevance of his work. *On Liberty* (1859) has become the classic defense of the individual's right, in a modern society dominated by bureaucracy and mass culture, to resist the constraints of both government and public opinion. *The Subjection of Women* (1869) insists that men should grant "perfect equality" to women, demonstrating that "what is now called the nature of women is an eminently artificial thing—the result of forced repression in some directions, unnatural stimulation in others." Finally, the *Autobiography* (1873) poignantly applies these insights to the construction of the author's own identity, revealing how Mill's life was shaped by the forced repressions and stimulations of his unusual family environment.

These three works also embody Mill's distinctive qualities as a writer and thinker: he advances his arguments with exceptional clarity, anticipating objections and providing interesting examples to prove his points; he makes his appeals to the reader on the basis of reason, no matter how emotionally charged the topic may be; and he displays an underlying concern for what is good for the public at large. Never content merely to assert human rights or display moral outrage, Mill dedicated himself to convincing others that freedom of thought and action—for women as well as for men—is not simply right but beneficial to society as a whole.

 For additional resources on Mill, go to *The Longman Anthology of British Literature* Web site at www.ablongman.com/damroschbritlit3e.

from **On Liberty**
from *Chapter 2. Of the Liberty of Thought and Discussion*

The time, it is to be hoped, is gone by, when any defence would be necessary of the "liberty of the press" as one of the securities against corrupt or tyrannical government. * * * If all mankind minus one, were of one opinion, and only one person were of the contrary opinion, mankind would be no more justified in silencing that one person, than he, if he had the power, would be justified in silencing mankind. Were an opinion a personal possession of no value except to the owner; if to be obstructed in the enjoyment of it were simply a private injury, it would make some difference whether the injury was inflicted only on a few persons or on many. But the peculiar evil of silencing the expression of an opinion is, that it is robbing the human race; posterity as well as the existing generation; those who dissent from the opinion, still more than those who hold it. If the opinion is right, they are deprived of the opportunity of exchanging error for truth: if wrong, they lose, what is almost as great a benefit, the clearer perception and livelier impression of truth, produced by its collision with error.

   * * * The majority of the eminent men of every past generation held many opinions now known to be erroneous, and did or approved numerous things which no one will now justify. Why is it, then, that there is on the whole a preponderance among mankind of rational opinions and rational conduct? If there really is this preponderance—which there must be unless human affairs are, and have always been, in an almost desperate state—it is owing to a quality of the human mind, the source of everything respectable in man either as an intellectual or as a moral being, namely, that his errors are corrigible. He is capable of rectifying his mistakes, by discussion and experience. Not by experience alone. There must be discussion, to show how experience is to be interpreted. Wrong opinions and practices gradually yield to fact and argument: but facts and arguments, to produce any effect on the mind, must be brought before it. Very few facts are able to tell their own story, without comments to bring out their meaning. The whole strength and value, then, of human judgment, depending on the one property, that it can be set right when it is wrong, reliance can be placed on it only when the means of setting it right are kept constantly at hand. In the case of any person whose judgment is really deserving of confidence, how has it become so? Because he has kept his mind open to criticism of his opinions and conduct. Because it has been his practice to listen to all that could be said against him; to profit by as much of it as was just, and expound to himself, and upon occasion to others, the fallacy of what was fallacious. Because he has felt, that the only way in which a human being can make some approach to knowing the whole of a subject, is by hearing what can be said about it by persons of every variety of opinion, and studying all modes in which it can be looked at by every character of mind. No wise man ever acquired his wisdom in any mode but this. * * *

   In the present age—which has been described as "destitute of faith, but terrified at scepticism"[1]—in which people feel sure, not so much that their opinions are true, as that they should not know what to do without them—the claims of an opinion to be protected from public attack are rested not so much on its truth, as on its importance to society. There are, it is alleged, certain beliefs, so useful, not to say indispensable to well-being, that it is as much the duty of governments to uphold those beliefs, as to protect any other of the interests of society. In a case of such necessity, and so directly in the line of their duty, something less than infallibility may, it is maintained, warrant, and even bind, governments, to act on their own opinion, confirmed by the general opinion of mankind. It is also often argued, and still oftener thought, that none but bad men would desire to weaken these salutary beliefs; and there can be nothing wrong, it is thought, in restraining bad men, and prohibiting what only such men would wish to practise. This mode of thinking makes the justification of restraints on discussion not a question of the truth of doctrines, but of their usefulness; and flatters itself by that means to escape the responsibility of claiming to be an infallible judge of opinions. But those who thus satisfy themselves, do not perceive that the assumption of infallibility is merely shifted from one point to another. The usefulness of an opinion is itself matter of opinion: as disputable, as open to discussion, and requiring discussion as much, as the opinion itself. There is the same need of an infallible judge of opinions to decide an opinion to be noxious,

---

1. By Thomas Carlyle in *Memoirs of the Life of Scott* (1838).

as to decide it to be false, unless the opinion condemned has full opportunity of defending itself. And it will not do to say that the heretic may be allowed to maintain the utility or harmlessness of his opinion, though forbidden to maintain its truth. The truth of an opinion is part of its utility. If we would know whether or not it is desirable that a proposition should be believed, is it possible to exclude the consideration of whether or not it is true? * * *

We have now recognised the necessity to the mental well-being of mankind (on which all their other well-being depends) of freedom of opinion, and freedom of the expression of opinion, on four distinct grounds; which we will now briefly recapitulate.

First, if any opinion is compelled to silence, that opinion may, for aught we can certainly know, be true. To deny this is to assume our own infallibility.

Secondly, though the silenced opinion be an error, it may, and very commonly does, contain a portion of truth; and since the general or prevailing opinion on any subject is rarely or never the whole truth, it is only by the collision of adverse opinions that the remainder of the truth has any chance of being supplied.

Thirdly, even if the received opinion be not only true, but the whole truth; unless it is suffered to be, and actually is, vigorously and earnestly contested, it will, by most of those who receive it, be held in the manner of a prejudice, with little comprehension or feeling of its rational grounds. And not only this, but, fourthly, the meaning of the doctrine itself will be in danger of being lost, or enfeebled, and deprived of its vital effect on the character and conduct: the dogma becoming a mere formal profession, inefficacious for good, but cumbering the ground, and preventing the growth of any real and heartfelt conviction, from reason or personal experience.

Before quitting the subject of freedom of opinion, it is fit to take some notice of those who say, that the free expression of all opinions should be permitted, on condition that the manner be temperate, and do not pass the bounds of fair discussion. Much might be said on the impossibility of fixing where these supposed bounds are to be placed; for if the test be offence to those whose opinion is attacked, I think experience testifies that this offence is given whenever the attack is telling and powerful, and that every opponent who pushes them hard, and whom they find it difficult to answer, appears to them, if he shows any strong feeling on the subject, an intemperate opponent. But this, though an important consideration in a practical point of view, merges in a more fundamental objection. Undoubtedly the manner of asserting an opinion, even though it be a true one, may be very objectionable, and may justly incur severe censure. But the principal offences of the kind are such as it is mostly impossible, unless by accidental self-betrayal, to bring home to conviction. The gravest of them is, to argue sophistically,[2] to suppress facts or arguments, to misstate the elements of the case, or misrepresent the opposite opinion. But all this, even to the most aggravated degree, is so continually done in perfect good faith, by persons who are not considered, and in many other respects may not deserve to be considered, ignorant or incompetent, that it is rarely possible on adequate grounds conscientiously to stamp the misrepresentation as morally culpable; and still less could law presume to interfere with this kind of controversial misconduct. With regard to what is commonly meant by intemperate discussion, namely invective, sarcasm, personality, and the like, the denunciation of these weapons would deserve more sympathy if it were ever proposed to interdict them equally to both sides; but it

2. In a plausible but fallacious manner.

is only desired to restrain the employment of them against the prevailing opinion: against the unprevailing they may not only be used without general disapproval, but will be likely to obtain for him who uses them the praise of honest zeal and righteous indignation. Yet whatever mischief arises from their use, is greatest when they are employed against the comparatively defenceless; and whatever unfair advantage can be derived by any opinion from this mode of asserting it, accrues almost exclusively to received opinions. The worst offence of this kind which can be committed by a polemic, is to stigmatize those who hold the contrary opinion as bad and immoral men. To calumny of this sort, those who hold any unpopular opinion are peculiarly exposed, because they are in general few and uninfluential, and nobody but themselves feels much interested in seeing justice done them; but this weapon is, from the nature of the case, denied to those who attack a prevailing opinion: they can neither use it with safety to themselves, nor, if they could, would it do anything but recoil on their own cause. In general, opinions contrary to those commonly received can only obtain a hearing by studied moderation of language, and the most cautious avoidance of unnecessary offence, from which they hardly every deviate even in a slight degree without losing ground: while unmeasured vituperation employed on the side of the prevailing opinion, really does deter people from professing contrary opinions, and from listening to those who profess them. For the interest, therefore, of truth and justice, it is far more important to restrain this employment of vituperative language than the other; and, for example, if it were necessary to choose, there would be much more need to discourage offensive attacks on infidelity, than on religion. It is, however, obvious that law and authority have no business with restraining either, while opinion ought, in every instance, to determine its verdict by the circumstances of the individual case; condemning every one, on whichever side of the argument he places himself, in whose mode of advocacy either want of candour, or malignity, bigotry, or intolerance of feeling manifest themselves; but not inferring these vices from the side which a person takes, though it be the contrary side of the question to our own: and giving merited honour to every one, whatever opinion he may hold, who has calmness to see and honesty to state what his opponents and their opinions really are, exaggerating nothing to their discredit, keeping nothing back which tells or can be supposed to tell, in their favour. This is the real morality of public discussion: and if often violated, I am happy to think that there are many controversialists who to a great extent observe it, and a still greater number who conscientiously strive towards it.

from *Chapter 3. Of Individuality, as One of the Elements of Well-Being*

Such being the reasons which make it imperative that human beings should be free to form opinions, and to express their opinions without reserve; and such the baneful consequences to the intellectual, and through that to the moral nature of man, unless this liberty is either conceded, or asserted in spite of prohibition; let us next examine whether the same reasons do not require that men should be free to act upon their opinions—to carry these out in their lives, without hindrance, either physical or moral, from their fellow-men, so long as it is at their own risk and peril. This last proviso is of course indispensable. No one pretends that actions should be as free as opinions. On the contrary, even opinions lose their immunity, when the circumstances in which they are expressed are such as to constitute their expression a positive instigation to some mischievous act. An opinion that corn-dealers are starvers of the poor, or that private property is robbery, ought to be unmolested when simply circulated through the press, but may justly incur punishment when delivered orally to an excited mob assembled before the house of a corn-dealer, or when handed about among the same mob in the form of a placard. Acts, of whatever kind, which, without justifiable cause, do harm to others, may be, and in the more important cases absolutely require to be, controlled by the unfavourable sentiments, and, when needful, by the active interference of mankind. The liberty of the individual must be thus far limited; he must not make himself a nuisance to other people. But if he refrains from molesting others in what concerns them, and merely acts according to his own inclination and judgment in things which concern himself, the same reasons which show that opinion should be free, prove also that he should be allowed, without molestation, to carry his opinions into practice at his own cost. * * * As it is useful that while mankind are imperfect there should be different opinions, so is it that there should be different experiments of living; that free scope should be given to varieties of character, short of injury to others; and that the worth of different modes of life should be proved practically, when any one thinks fit to try them. It is desirable, in short, that in things which do not primarily concern others, individuality should assert itself. * * *

* * * The majority, being satisfied with the ways of mankind as they now are (for it is they who make them what they are), cannot comprehend why those ways should not be good enough for everybody; and what is more, spontaneity forms no part of the ideal of the majority of moral and social reformers, but is rather looked on with jealousy, as a troublesome and perhaps rebellious obstruction to the general acceptance of what these reformers, in their own judgment, think would be best for mankind. Few persons, out of Germany, even comprehend the meaning of the doctrine which Wilhelm Von Humboldt, so eminent both as a *savant* and as a politician, made the text of a treatise—that "the end of man, or that which is prescribed by the eternal or immutable dictates of reason, and not suggested by vague and transient desires, is the highest and most harmonious development of his powers to a complete and consistent whole;" that, therefore, the object "towards which every human being must ceaselessly direct his efforts, and on which especially those who design to influence their fellow-men must ever keep their eyes, is the individuality of power and development;" that for this there are two requisites, "freedom, and variety of situations;" and that from the union of these arise "individual vigour and manifold diversity," which combine themselves in "originality."[1]

Little, however, as people are accustomed to a doctrine like that of Von Humboldt, and surprising as it may be to them to find so high a value attached to individuality, the question, one must nevertheless think, can only be one of degree. No one's idea of excellence in conduct is that people should do absolutely nothing but copy one another. No one would assert that people ought not to put into their mode of life, and into the conduct of their concerns, any impress whatever of their own judgment, or of their own individual character. On the other hand, it would be absurd to pretend that people ought to live as if nothing whatever had been known in the world before they came into it; as if experience had as yet done nothing towards showing that one mode of existence, or of conduct, is preferable to another. Nobody denies that people should be so taught and trained in youth, as to know and

1. From *The Sphere and Duties of Government* by Baron Wilhelm von Humboldt. Although written in 1791, this treatise was not published until 1852; it was translated into English in 1854.

benefit by the ascertained results of human experience. But it is the privilege and proper condition of a human being, arrived at the maturity of his faculties, to use and interpret experience in his own way. It is for him to find out what part of recorded experience is properly applicable to his own circumstances and character. * * *

He who lets the world, or his own portion of it, choose his plan of life for him, has no need of any other faculty than the ape-like one of imitation. He who chooses his plan for himself, employs all his faculties. He must use observation to see, reasoning and judgment to foresee, activity to gather materials for decision, discrimination to decide, and when he has decided, firmness and self-control to hold to his deliberate decision. And these qualities he requires and exercises exactly in proportion as the part of his conduct which he determines according to his own judgment and feelings is a large one. It is possible that he might be guided in some good path, and kept out of harm's way, without any of these things. But what will be his comparative worth as a human being? It really is of importance, not only what men do, but also what manner of men they are that do it. Among the works of man, which human life is rightly employed in perfecting and beautifying, the first in importance surely is man himself. Supposing it were possible to get houses built, corn grown, battles fought, causes tried, and even churches erected and prayers said, by machinery—by automatons in human form—it would be a considerable loss to exchange for these automatons even the men and women who at present inhabit the more civilized parts of the world, and who assuredly are but starved specimens of what nature can and will produce. Human nature is not a machine to be built after a model, and set to do exactly the work prescribed for it, but a tree, which requires to grow and develop itself on all sides, according to the tendency of the inward forces which make it a living thing.

It will probably be conceded that it is desirable people should exercise their understandings, and that an intelligent following of custom, or even occasionally an intelligent deviation from custom, is better than a blind and simply mechanical adhesion to it. To a certain extent it is admitted, that our understanding should be our own: but there is not the same willingness to admit that our desires and impulses should be our own likewise; or that to possess impulses of our own, and of any strength, is anything but a peril and a snare. Yet desires and impulses are as much a part of a perfect human being, as beliefs and restraints: and strong impulses are only perilous when not properly balanced; when one set of aims and inclinations is developed into strength, while others, which ought to co-exist with them, remain weak and inactive. It is not because men's desires are strong that they act ill; it is because their consciences are weak. There is no natural connexion between strong impulses and a weak conscience. The natural connexion is the other way. * * * A person whose desires and impulses are his own—are the expression of his own nature, as it has been developed and modified by his own culture—is said to have a character. One whose desires and impulses are not his own, has no character, no more than a steam-engine has a character. If, in addition to being his own, his impulses are strong, and are under the government of a strong will, he has an energetic character. Whoever thinks that individuality of desires and impulses should not be encouraged to unfold itself, must maintain that society has no need of strong natures—is not the better for containing many persons who have much character—and that a high general average of energy is not desirable.

In some early states of society, these forces might be, and were, too much ahead of the power which society then possessed of disciplining and controlling them. There has been a time when the element of spontaneity and individuality was in excess, and the social principle had a hard struggle with it. The difficulty then was, to induce men of strong bodies or minds to pay obedience to any rules which required them to control their impulses. To overcome this difficulty, law and discipline, like the Popes struggling against the Emperors, asserted a power over the whole man, claiming to control all his life in order to control his character—which society had not found any other sufficient means of binding. But society has now fairly got the better of individuality; and the danger which threatens human nature is not the excess, but the deficiency, of personal impulses and preferences. Things are vastly changed, since the passions of those who were strong by station or by personal endowment were in a state of habitual rebellion against laws and ordinances, and required to be rigorously chained up to enable the persons within their reach to enjoy any particle of security. In our times, from the highest class of society down to the lowest, every one lives as under the eye of a hostile and dreaded censorship. Not only in what concerns others, but in what concerns only themselves, the individual or the family do not ask themselves—what do I prefer? or, what would suit my character and disposition? or, what would allow the best and highest in me to have fair play, and enable it to grow and thrive? They ask themselves, what is suitable to my position? what is usually done by persons of my station and pecuniary circumstances? or (worse still) what is usually done by persons of a station and circumstances superior to mine? I do not mean that they choose what is customary, in preference to what suits their own inclination. It does not occur to them to have any inclination, except for what is customary. Thus the mind itself is bowed to the yoke: even in what people do for pleasure, conformity is the first thing thought of; they like in crowds; they exercise choice only among things commonly done: peculiarity of taste, eccentricity of conduct, are shunned equally with crimes: until by dint of not following their own nature, they have no nature to follow: their human capacities are withered and starved: they become incapable of any strong wishes or native pleasures, and are generally without either opinions or feelings of home growth, or properly their own. Now is this, or is it not, the desirable condition of human nature?

    * * * Many persons, no doubt, sincerely think that human beings thus cramped and dwarfed, are as their Maker designed them to be; just as many have thought that trees are a much finer thing when clipped into pollards,[2] or cut out into figures of animals, than as nature made them. But if it be any part of religion to believe that man was made by a good Being, it is more consistent with that faith to believe, that this Being gave all human faculties that they might be cultivated and unfolded, not rooted out and consumed, and that he takes delight in every nearer approach made by his creatures to the ideal conception embodied in them, every increase in any of their capabilities of comprehension, of action, or of enjoyment. There is a different type of human excellence from the Calvinistic;[3] a conception of humanity as having its nature bestowed on it for other purposes than merely to be abnegated. "Pagan self-assertion" is one of the elements of human worth, as well as "Christian self-denial."[4] There is a Greek ideal of self-development, which the Platonic and Christian ideal of self-government blends with, but does not supersede. It may be better to be a John

2. Trees pruned severely to create a thick growth of branches and foliage overhead.
3. Followers of the French Protestant theologian, John Calvin (1509–1564), believed that human nature was depraved and sinful. Elsewhere in the essay, Mill says that the Calvinist idea is that "the one great offence of man is

self-will. All the good of which humanity is capable, is comprised in obedience. . . . Human nature being radically corrupt, there is no redemption for any one until human nature is killed within him."
4. From "Simonides" in John Sterling's *Essays* (1848).

Knox than an Alcibiades, but it is better to be a Pericles than either;[5] nor would a Pericles, if we had one in these days, be without anything good which belonged to John Knox.

It is not by wearing down into uniformity all that is individual in themselves, but by cultivating it and calling it forth, within the limits imposed by the rights and interests of others, that human beings become a noble and beautiful object of contemplation; and as the works partake the character of those who do them, by the same process human life also becomes rich, diversified, and animating, furnishing more abundant aliment[6] to high thoughts and elevating feelings, and strengthening the tie which binds every individual to the race, by making the race infinitely better worth belonging to. In proportion to the development of his individuality, each person becomes more valuable to himself, and is therefore capable of being more valuable to others. There is a greater fulness of life about his own existence, and when there is more life in the units there is more in the mass which is composed of them. As much compression as is necessary to prevent the stronger specimens of human nature from encroaching on the rights of others, cannot be dispensed with; but for this there is ample compensation even in the point of view of human development. The means of development which the individual loses by being prevented from gratifying his inclinations to the injury of others, are chiefly obtained at the expense of the development of other people. And even to himself there is a full equivalent in the better development of the social part of his nature, rendered possible by the restraint put upon the selfish part. To be held to rigid rules of justice for the sake of others, developes the feelings and capacities which have the good of others for their object. But to be restrained in things not affecting their good, by their mere displeasure, developes nothing valuable, except such force of character as may unfold itself in resisting the restraint. If acquiesced in, it dulls and blunts the whole nature. To give any fair play to the nature of each, it is essential that different persons should be allowed to lead different lives. In proportion as this latitude has been exercised in any age, has that age been noteworthy to posterity. Even despotism does not produce its worst effects, so long as individuality exists under it; and whatever crushes individuality is despotism, by whatever name it may be called, and whether it professes to be enforcing the will of God or the injunctions of men.

Having said that Individuality is the same thing with development, and that it is only the cultivation of individuality which produces, or can produce, well-developed human beings, I might here close the argument: for what more or better can be said of any condition of human affairs, than that it brings human beings themselves nearer to the best thing they can be? or what worse can be said of any obstruction to good, than that it prevents this? Doubtless, however, these considerations will not suffice to convince those who most need convincing; and it is necessary further to show, that these developed human beings are of some use to the undeveloped—to point out to those who do not desire liberty, and would not avail themselves of it, that they may be in some intelligible manner rewarded for allowing other people to make use of it without hindrance.

In the first place, then, I would suggest that they might possibly learn something from them. It will not be denied by anybody, that originality is a valuable element in

5. John Knox (1505–1572), Scottish Calvinist reformer; Alcibiades (450–404 B.C.), dissolute Athenian general; Pericles (500–429 B.C.), wise and virtuous Athenian statesman.
6. Nourishment.

human affairs. There is always need of persons not only to discover new truths, and point out when what were once truths are true no longer, but also to commence new practices, and set the example of more enlightened conduct, and better taste and sense in human life. * * * Persons of genius, it is true, are, and are always likely to be, a small minority; but in order to have them, it is necessary to preserve the soil in which they grow. Genius can only breathe freely in an *atmosphere* of freedom. Persons of genius are, *ex vi termini* [by definition], *more* individual than any other people—less capable, consequently, of fitting themselves, without hurtful compression, into any of the small number of moulds which society provides in order to save its members the trouble of forming their own character. If from timidity they consent to be forced into one of these moulds, and to let all that part of themselves which cannot expand under the pressure remain unexpanded, society will be little the better for their genius. If they are of a strong character, and break their fetters, they become a mark for the society which has not succeeded in reducing them to commonplace, to point at with solemn warning as "wild," "erratic," and the like; much as if one should complain of the Niagara river for not flowing smoothly between its banks like a Dutch canal.

I insist thus emphatically on the importance of genius, and the necessity of allowing it to unfold itself freely both in thought and in practice, being well aware that no one will deny the position in theory, but knowing also that almost every one, in reality, is totally indifferent to it. People think genius a fine thing if it enables a man to write an exciting poem, or paint a picture. But in its true sense, that of originality in thought and action, though no one says that it is not a thing to be admired, nearly all, at heart, think that they can do very well without it. Unhappily this is too natural to be wondered at. Originality is the one thing which unoriginal minds cannot feel the use of. They cannot see what it is to do for them: how should they? If they could see what it would do for them, it would not be originality. The first service which originality has to render them, is that of opening their eyes: which being once fully done, they would have a chance of being themselves original. Meanwhile, recollecting that nothing was ever yet done which some one was not the first to do, and that all good things which exist are the fruits of originality, let them be modest enough to believe that there is something still left for it to accomplish, and assure themselves that they are more in need of originality, the less they are conscious of the want.

In sober truth, whatever homage may be professed, or even paid, to real or supposed mental superiority, the general tendency of things throughout the world is to render mediocrity the ascendant power among mankind. In ancient history, in the middle ages, and in a diminishing degree through the long transition from feudality to the present time, the individual was a power in himself; and if he had either great talents or a high social position, he was a considerable power. At present individuals are lost in the crowd. In politics it is almost a triviality to say that public opinion now rules the world. The only power deserving the name is that of masses, and of governments while they make themselves the organ of the tendencies and instincts of masses. This is as true in the moral and social relations of private life as in public transactions. Those whose opinions go by the name of public opinion, are not always the same sort of public: in America they are the whole white population; in England, chiefly the middle class. But they are always a mass, that is to say, collective mediocrity. And what is a still greater novelty, the mass do not now take their opinions from dignitaries in Church or State, from ostensible leaders, or from books. Their thinking is done for them by men much like themselves, addressing them or speaking in their name, on the spur of the moment, through the newspapers. I am not complaining of all this. I do not assert that anything better is compatible, as a general rule, with the present low state of the human mind. But that does not hinder the government of mediocrity from being mediocre government. No government by a democracy or a numerous aristocracy, either in its political acts or in the opinions, qualities, and tone of mind which it fosters, ever did or could rise above mediocrity, except in so far as the sovereign Many have let themselves be guided (which in their best times they always have done) by the counsels and influence of a more highly gifted and instructed One or Few. The initiation of all wise or noble things, comes and must come from individuals; generally at first from some one individual. The honour and glory of the average man is that he is capable of following that initiative; that he can respond internally to wise and noble things, and be led to them with his eyes open. I am not countenancing the sort of "hero-worship" which applauds the strong man of genius for forcibly seizing on the government of the world and making it do his bidding in spite of itself.[7] All he can claim is, freedom to point out the way. The power of compelling others into it, is not only inconsistent with the freedom and development of all the rest, but corrupting to the strong man himself. It does seem, however, that when the opinions of masses of merely average men are everywhere become or becoming the dominant power, the counterpoise and corrective to that tendency would be, the more and more pronounced individuality of those who stand on the higher eminences of thought. It is in these circumstances most especially, that exceptional individuals, instead of being deterred, should be encouraged in acting differently from the mass. In other times there was no advantage in their doing so, unless they acted not only differently, but better. In this age, the mere example of nonconformity, the mere refusal to bend the knee to custom, is itself a service. Precisely because the tyranny of opinion is such as to make eccentricity a reproach, it is desirable, in order to break through that tyranny, that people should be eccentric. Eccentricity has always abounded when and where strength of character has abounded; and the amount of eccentricity in a society has generally been proportional to the amount of genius, mental vigour, and moral courage which it contained. That so few now dare to be eccentric, marks the chief danger of the time. * * *

There is one characteristic of the present direction of public opinion, peculiarly calculated to make it intolerant of any marked demonstration of individuality. The general average of mankind are not only moderate in intellect, but also moderate in inclinations: they have no tastes or wishes strong enough to incline them to do anything unusual, and they consequently do not understand those who have, and class all such with the wild and intemperate whom they are accustomed to look down upon. * * * These tendencies of the times cause the public to be more disposed than at most former periods to prescribe general rules of conduct, and endeavour to make every one conform to the approved standard. And that standard, express or tacit, is to desire nothing strongly. Its ideal of character is to be without any marked character; to maim by compression, like a Chinese lady's foot, every part of human nature which stands out prominently, and tends to make the person markedly dissimilar in outline to commonplace humanity.

As is usually the case with ideals which exclude one-half of what is desirable, the present standard of approbation produces only an inferior imitation of the other half.

---

7. Cf. Thomas Carlyle, *On Heroes and Hero-Worship* (1841).

Instead of great energies guided by vigorous reason, and strong feelings strongly controlled by a conscientious will, its result is weak feelings and weak energies, which therefore can be kept in outward conformity to rule without any strength either of will or of reason. Already energetic characters on any large scale are becoming merely traditional. There is now scarcely any outlet for energy in this country except business. The energy expended in this may still be regarded as considerable. What little is left from that employment, is expended on some hobby; which may be a useful, even a philanthropic hobby, but is always some one thing, and generally a thing of small dimensions. The greatness of England is now all collective: individually small, we only appear capable of anything great by our habit of combining; and with this our moral and religious philanthropists are perfectly contented. But it was men of another stamp than this that made England what it has been; and men of another stamp will be needed to prevent its decline.

The despotism of custom is everywhere the standing hindrance to human advancement, being in unceasing antagonism to that disposition to aim at something better than customary, which is called, according to circumstances, the spirit of liberty, or that of progress or improvement. The spirit of improvement is not always a spirit of liberty, for it may aim at forcing improvements on an unwilling people; and the spirit of liberty, in so far as it resists such attempts, may ally itself locally and temporarily with the opponents of improvement; but the only unfailing and permanent source of improvement is liberty, since by it there are as many possible independent centres of improvement as there are individuals. The progressive principle, however, in either shape, whether as the love of liberty or of improvement, is antagonistic to the sway of Custom, involving at least emancipation from that yoke; and the contest between the two constitutes the chief interest of the history of mankind. The greater part of the world has, properly speaking, no history, because the despotism of Custom is complete. This is the case over the whole East. Custom is there, in all things, the final appeal; justice and right mean conformity to custom; the argument of custom no one, unless some tyrant intoxicated with power, thinks of resisting. And we see the result. Those nations must once have had originality; they did not start out of the ground populous, lettered, and versed in many of the arts of life; they made themselves all this, and were then the greatest and most powerful nations of the world. What are they now? The subjects or dependents of tribes whose forefathers wandered in the forests when theirs had magnificent palaces and gorgeous temples, but over whom custom exercised only a divided rule with liberty and progress. A people, it appears, may be progressive for a certain length of time, and then stop: when does it stop? When it ceases to possess individuality. If a similar change should befall the nations of Europe, it will not be in exactly the same shape: the despotism of custom with which these nations are threatened is not precisely stationariness. It proscribes singularity, but it does not preclude change, provided all change together. We have discarded the fixed costumes of our forefathers; every one must still dress like other people, but the fashion may change once or twice a year. We thus take care that when there is change it shall be for change's sake, and not from any idea of beauty or convenience; for the same idea of beauty or convenience would not strike all the world at the same moment, and be simultaneously thrown aside by all at another moment. But we are progressive as well as changeable: we continually make new inventions in mechanical things, and keep them until they are again superseded by better; we are eager for improvement in politics, in education, even in morals, though in this last our idea of improvement chiefly consists in persuading or forcing other people to be as good as ourselves. It is not progress that we object to; on the contrary, we flatter ourselves that we are the most progressive people who ever lived. It is individuality that we war against: we should think we had done wonders if we had made ourselves all alike; forgetting that the unlikeness of one person to another is generally the first thing which draws the attention of either to the imperfection of his own type, and the superiority of another, or the possibility, by combining the advantages of both, of producing something better than either. We have a warning example in China—a nation of much talent, and, in some respects, even wisdom, owing to the rare good fortune of having been provided at an early period with a particularly good set of customs, the work, in some measure, of men to whom even the most enlightened European must accord, under certain limitations, the title of sages and philosophers. They are remarkable, too, in the excellence of their apparatus for impressing, as far as possible, the best wisdom they possess upon every mind in the community, and secur-ing that those who have appropriated most of it shall occupy the posts of honour and power. Surely the people who did this have discovered the secret of human progres-siveness, and must have kept themselves steadily at the head of the movement of the world. On the contrary, they have become stationary—have remained so for thousands of years; and if they are ever to be farther improved, it must be by foreign-ers. They have succeeded beyond all hope in what English philanthropists are so industriously working at—in making a people all alike, all governing their thoughts and conduct by the same maxims and rules; and these are the fruits. The modern *régime* of public opinion is, in an unorganized form, what the Chinese educational and political systems are in an organized; and unless individuality shall be able successfully to assert itself against this yoke, Europe, notwithstanding its noble antecedents and its professed Christianity, will tend to become another China.

1859

from The Subjection of Women[1]
from Chapter 1

The object of this essay is to explain as clearly as I am able, the grounds of an opinion which I have held from the very earliest period when I had formed any opinions at all on social or political matters, and which, instead of being weakened or modified, has been constantly growing stronger by the progress of reflection and the experience of life: That the principle which regulates the existing social relations between the two sexes—the legal subordination of one sex to the other—is wrong in itself, and now one of the chief hindrances to human improvement; and that it ought to be replaced by a principle of perfect equality, admitting no power or privilege on the one side, nor disability on the other. * * *

  * * * If the authority of men over women, when first established, had been the result of a conscientious comparison between different modes of constituting the government of society; if, after trying various other modes of social organization—the government of women over men, equality between the two, and such mixed and divided modes of government as might be invented—it had been decided, on the testimony of experience, that the mode in which women are wholly under the rule of men, having no share at all in public concerns, and each in private being under the

1. See Mary Wollstonecraft's A *Vindication of the Rights of Woman* (1792), page 281, and also Perspectives: The Wollstonecraft Controversy and the Rights of Women, page 319.

legal obligation of obedience to the man with whom she has associated her destiny, was the arrangement most conducive to the happiness and well being of both; its general adoption might then be fairly thought to be some evidence that, at the time when it was adopted, it was the best: though even then the considerations which recommended it may, like so many other primeval social facts of the greatest importance, have subsequently, in the course of ages, ceased to exist. But the state of the case is in every respect the reverse of this. In the first place, the opinion in favour of the present system, which entirely subordinates the weaker sex to the stronger, rests upon theory only; for there never has been trial made of any other: so that experience, in the sense in which it is vulgarly opposed to theory, cannot be pretended to have pronounced any verdict. And in the second place, the adoption of this system of inequality never was the result of deliberation, or forethought, or any social ideas, or any notion whatever of what conduced to the benefit of humanity or the good order of society. It arose simply from the fact that from the very earliest twilight of human society, every woman (owing to the value attached to her by men, combined with her inferiority in muscular strength) was found in a state of bondage to some man. * * *

Some will object, that a comparison cannot fairly be made between the government of the male sex and the forms of unjust power which I have adduced in illustration of it,[2] since these are arbitrary, and the effect of mere usurpation, while it on the contrary is natural. But was there ever any domination which did not appear natural to those who possessed it? There was a time when the division of mankind into two classes, a small one of masters and a numerous one of slaves, appeared, even to the most cultivated minds, to be a natural, and the only natural, condition of the human race. No less an intellect, and one which contributed no less to the progress of human thought, than Aristotle, held this opinion without doubt or misgiving; and rested it on the same premises on which the same assertion in regard to the dominion of men over women is usually based, namely that there are different natures among mankind, free natures, and slave natures; that the Greeks were of a free nature, the barbarian races of Thracians and Asiatics of a slave nature.[3] But why need I go back to Aristotle? Did not the slaveowners of the Southern United States maintain the same doctrine, with all the fanaticism with which men cling to the theories that justify their passions and legitimate their personal interests? Did they not call heaven and earth to witness that the dominion of the white man over the black is natural, that the black race is by nature incapable of freedom, and marked out for slavery?—some even going so far as to say that the freedom of manual labourers is an unnatural order of things anywhere. Again, the theorists of absolute monarchy have always affirmed it to be the only natural form of government; issuing from the patriarchal, which was the primitive and spontaneous form of society, framed on the model of the paternal, which is anterior to society itself, and, as they contend, the most natural authority of all. Nay, for that matter, the law of force itself, to those who could not plead any other, has always seemed the most natural of all grounds for the exercise of authority. Conquering races hold it to be Nature's own dictate that the conquered should obey the conquerors, or, as they euphoniously paraphrase it, that the feebler and more unwarlike races should submit to the braver and manlier. The smallest acquaintance

---

2. Mill has been describing slave owners' power over slaves, or tyrants' power over their subjects.
3. In *Politics* Aristotle asserts that it is as natural for free men to rule over slaves as for men to rule over women (sec. 1260a2–14).

with human life in the middle ages, shows how supremely natural the dominion of the feudal nobility over men of low condition appeared to the nobility themselves, and how unnatural the conception seemed, of a person of the inferior class claiming equality with them, or exercising authority over them. It hardly seemed less so to the class held in subjection. The emancipated serfs and burgesses,[4] even in their most vigorous struggles, never made any pretension to a share of authority; they only demanded more or less of limitation to the power of tyrannizing over them. So true is it that unnatural generally means only uncustomary, and that everything which is usual appears natural. The subjection of women to men being a universal custom, any departure from it quite naturally appears unnatural. But how entirely, even in this case, the feeling is dependent on custom, appears by ample experience. Nothing so much astonishes the people of distant parts of the world, when they first learn anything about England, as to be told that it is under a queen: the thing seems to them so unnatural as to be almost incredible. To Englishmen this does not seem in the least degree unnatural, because they are used to it; but they do feel it unnatural that women should be soldiers or members of Parliament. In the feudal ages, on the contrary, war and politics were not thought unnatural to women, because not unusual; it seemed natural that women of the privileged classes should be of manly character, inferior in nothing but bodily strength to their husbands and fathers. The independence of women seemed rather less unnatural to the Greeks than to other ancients, on account of the fabulous Amazons (whom they believed to be historical), and the partial example afforded by the Spartan women; who, though no less subordinate by law than in other Greek states, were more free in fact, and being trained to bodily exercises in the same manner with men, gave ample proof that they were not naturally disqualified for them. There can be little doubt that Spartan experience suggested to Plato, among many other of his doctrines, that of the social and political equality of the two sexes.[5]

But, it will be said, the rule of men over women differs from all these others in not being a rule of force: it is accepted voluntarily; women make no complaint, and are consenting parties to it. In the first place, a great number of women do not accept it. Ever since there have been women able to make their sentiments known by their writings (the only mode of publicity which society permits to them), an increasing number of them have recorded protests against their present social condition: and recently many thousands of them, headed by the most eminent women known to the public, have petitioned Parliament for their admission to the Parliamentary Suffrage.[6] The claim of women to be educated as solidly, and in the same branches of knowledge, as men, is urged with growing intensity, and with a great prospect of success; while the demand for their admission into professions and occupations hitherto closed against them, becomes every year more urgent. Though there are not in this country, as there are in the United States, periodical Conventions and an organized party to agitate for the Rights of Women, there is a numerous and active Society organized and managed by women, for the more limited object of obtaining the political franchise. Nor is it only in our own country and in America that women are

4. Serfs were legally bound to the land and to their feudal lord; burgesses were townspeople.
5. See The Republic, 5: "Then, if we are to set women to the same tasks as men, we must teach them the same things. They must have the same two branches of training for mind and body and also be taught the art of war,

and they must receive the same treatment" (trans. by F. M. Cornford).
6. This petition was presented in the House of Commons in 1866 by Mill himself; he was the first member of Parliament to advocate women's suffrage.

beginning to protest, more or less collectively, against the disabilities under which they labour. France, and Italy, and Switzerland, and Russia now afford examples of the same thing. How many more women there are who silently cherish similar aspirations, no one can possibly know; but there are abundant tokens how many *would* cherish them, were they not so strenuously taught to repress them as contrary to the proprieties of their sex. It must be remembered, also, that no enslaved class ever asked for complete liberty at once. When Simon de Montfort[7] called the deputies of the commons to sit for the first time in Parliament, did any of them dream of demanding that an assembly, elected by their constituents, should make and destroy ministries, and dictate to the king in affairs of state? No such thought entered into the imagination of the most ambitious of them. The nobility had already these pretensions; the commons pretended to nothing but to be exempt from arbitrary taxation, and from the gross individual oppression of the king's officers. It is a political law of nature that those who are under any power of ancient origin, never begin by complaining of the power itself, but only of its oppressive exercise. There is never any want of women who complain of ill usage by their husbands. There would be infinitely more, if complaint were not the greatest of all provocatives to a repetition and increase of the ill usage. It is this which frustrates all attempts to maintain the power but protect the woman against its abuses. In no other case (except that of a child) is the person who has been proved judicially to have suffered an injury, replaced under the physical power of the culprit who inflicted it. Accordingly wives, even in the most extreme and protracted cases of bodily ill usage, hardly ever dare avail themselves of the laws made for their protection: and if, in a moment of irrepressible indignation, or by the interference of neighbours, they are induced to do so, their whole effort afterwards is to disclose as little as they can, and to beg off their tyrant from his merited chastisement.

All causes, social and natural, combine to make it unlikely that women should be collectively rebellious to the power of men. They are so far in a position different from all other subject classes, that their masters require something more from them than actual service. Men do not want solely the obedience of women, they want their sentiments. All men, except the most brutish, desire to have, in the woman most nearly connected with them, not a forced slave but a willing one, not a slave merely, but a favourite. They have therefore put everything in practice to enslave their minds. The masters of all other slaves rely, for maintaining obedience, on fear; either fear of themselves, or religious fears. The masters of women wanted more than simple obedience, and they turned the whole force of education to effect their purpose. All women are brought up from the very earliest years in the belief that their ideal of character is the very opposite to that of men; not self-will, and government by self-control, but submission, and yielding to the control of others. All the moralities tell them that it is the duty of women, and all the current sentimentalities that it is their nature, to live for others; to make complete abnegation of themselves, and to have no life but in their affections. And by their affections are meant the only ones they are allowed to have—those to the men with whom they are connected, or to the children who constitute an additional and indefeasible tie between them and a man. When we put together three things—first, the natural attraction between opposite sexes; secondly, the wife's entire dependence on the husband, every privilege or

7. An English statesman and nobleman who in 1265 convened the first parliament to include representatives of the common people.

pleasure she has being either his gift, or depending entirely on his will; and lastly, that the principal object of human pursuit, consideration, and all objects of social ambition, can in general be sought or obtained by her only through him—it would be a miracle if the object of being attractive to men had not become the polar star of feminine education and formation of character. And, this great means of influence over the minds of women having been acquired, an instinct of selfishness made men avail themselves of it to the utmost as a means of holding women in subjection, by representing to them meekness, submissiveness, and resignation of all individual will into the hands of a man, as an essential part of sexual attractiveness. Can it be doubted that any of the other yokes which mankind have succeeded in breaking, would have subsisted till now if the same means had existed, and had been as sedulously used, to bow down their minds to it? If it had been made the object of the life of every young plebeian to find personal favour in the eyes of some patrician,[8] of every young serf with some seigneur; if domestication with him, and a share of his personal affections, had been held out as the prize which they all should look out for, the most gifted and aspiring being able to reckon on the most desirable prizes; and if, when this prize had been obtained, they had been shut out by a wall of brass from all interests not centering in him, all feelings and desires but those which he shared or inculcated; would not serfs and seigneurs, plebeians and patricians, have been as broadly distinguished at this day as men and women are? And would not all but a thinker here and there, have believed the distinction to be a fundamental and unalterable fact in human nature?

The preceding considerations are amply sufficient to show that custom, however universal it may be, affords in this case no presumption, and ought not to create any prejudice, in favour of the arrangements which place women in social and political subjection to men. But I may go farther, and maintain that the course of history, and the tendencies of progressive human society, afford not only no presumption in favour of this system of inequality of rights, but a strong one against it; and that, so far as the whole course of human improvement up to this time, the whole stream of modern tendencies, warrants any inference on the subject, it is, that this relic of the past is discordant with the future, and must necessarily disappear.

For, what is the peculiar character of the modern world—the difference which chiefly distinguishes modern institutions, modern social ideas, modern life itself, from those of times long past? It is, that human beings are no longer born to their place in life, and chained down by an inexorable bond to the place they are born to, but are free to employ their faculties, and such favourable chances as offer, to achieve the lot which may appear to them most desirable. * * *

The social subordination of women thus stands out an isolated fact in modern social institutions; a solitary breach of what has become their fundamental law; a single relic of an old world of thought and practice exploded in everything else, but retained in the one thing of most universal interest; as if a gigantic dolmen,[9] or a vast temple of Jupiter Olympius, occupied the site of St. Paul's and received daily worship, while the surrounding Christian churches were only resorted to on fasts and festivals. This entire discrepancy between one social fact and all those which accompany it, and the radical opposition between its nature and the progressive movement which is the boast of the modern world, and which has successively swept away everything

8. Plebeians were the commoners and patricians the aristocrats of ancient Rome.

9. Tablelike prehistoric monument of standing stones, associated with pagan religious rites.

else of an analogous character, surely affords, to a conscientious observer of human tendencies, serious matter for reflection. It raises a *prima facie* [immediate] presumption on the unfavourable side, far outweighing any which custom and usage could in such circumstances create on the favourable; and should at least suffice to make this, like the choice between republicanism and royalty, a balanced question.

The least that can be demanded is, that the question should not be considered as prejudged by existing fact and existing opinion, but open to discussion on its merits, as a question of justice and expediency: the decision on this, as on any of the other social arrangements of mankind, depending on what an enlightened estimate of tendencies and consequences may show to be most advantageous to humanity in general, without distinction of sex. And the discussion must be a real discussion, descending to foundations, and not resting satisfied with vague and general assertions. It will not do, for instance, to assert in general terms, that the experience of mankind has pronounced in favour of the existing system. Experience cannot possibly have decided between two courses, so long as there has only been experience of one. If it be said that the doctrine of the equality of the sexes rests only on theory, it must be remembered that the contrary doctrine also has only theory to rest upon. All that is proved in its favour by direct experience, is that mankind have been able to exist under it, and to attain the degree of improvement and prosperity which we now see; but whether that prosperity has been attained sooner, or is now greater, than it would have been under the other system, experience does not say. On the other hand, experience does say, that every step in improvement has been so invariably accompanied by a step made in raising the social position of women, that historians and philosophers have been led to adopt their elevation or debasement as on the whole the surest test and most correct measure of the civilization of a people or an age. Through all the progressive period of human history, the condition of women has been approaching nearer to equality with men. This does not of itself prove that the assimilation must go on to complete equality; but it assuredly affords some presumption that such is the case.

Neither does it avail anything to say that the *nature* of the two sexes adapts them to their present functions and position, and renders these appropriate to them. Standing on the ground of common sense and the constitution of the human mind, I deny that any one knows, or can know, the nature of the two sexes, as long as they have only been seen in their present relation to one another. If men had ever been found in society without women, or women without men, or if there had been a society of men and women in which the women were not under the control of the men, something might have been positively known about the mental and moral differences which may be inherent in the nature of each. What is now called the nature of women is an eminently artificial thing—the result of forced repression in some directions, unnatural stimulation in others. It may be asserted without scruple, that no other class of dependents have had their character so entirely distorted from its natural proportions by their relation with their masters; for, if conquered and slave races have been, in some respects, more forcibly repressed, whatever in them has not been crushed down by an iron heel has generally been let alone, and if left with any liberty of development, it has developed itself according to its own laws; but in the case of women, a hot-house and stove cultivation has always been carried on of some of the capabilities of their nature, for the benefit and pleasure of their masters. * * *

Hence, in regard to that most difficult question, what are the natural differences between the two sexes—a subject on which it is impossible in the present state of society to obtain complete and correct knowledge—while almost everybody dogmatizes upon it, almost all neglect and make light of the only means by which any partial insight can be obtained into it. This is, an analytic study of the most important department of psychology, the laws of the influence of circumstances on character. For, however great and apparently ineradicable the moral and intellectual differences between men and women might be, the evidence of their being natural differences could only be negative. Those only could be inferred to be natural which could not possibly be artificial—the residuum, after deducting every characteristic of either sex which can admit of being explained from education or external circumstances. The profoundest knowledge of the laws of the formation of character is indispensable to entitle any one to affirm even that there is any difference, much more what the difference is, between the two sexes considered as moral and rational beings; and since no one, as yet, has that knowledge (for there is hardly any subject which, in proportion to its importance, has been so little studied), no one is thus far entitled to any positive opinion on the subject. Conjectures are all that can at present be made; conjectures more or less probable, according as more or less authorized by such knowledge as we yet have of the laws of psychology, as applied to the formation of character.

Even the preliminary knowledge, what the differences between the sexes now are, apart from all question as to how they are made what they are, is still in the crudest and most incomplete state. Medical practitioners and physiologists have ascertained, to some extent, the differences in bodily constitution; and this is an important element to the psychologist: but hardly any medical practitioner is a psychologist. Respecting the mental characteristics of women; their observations are of no more worth than those of common men. It is a subject on which nothing final can be known, so long as those who alone can really know it, women themselves, have given but little testimony, and that little, mostly suborned. It is easy to know stupid women. Stupidity is much the same all the world over. A stupid person's notions and feelings may confidently be inferred from those which prevail in the circle by which the person is surrounded. Not so with those whose opinions and feelings are an emanation from their own nature and faculties. It is only a man here and there who has any tolerable knowledge of the character even of the women of his own family. I do not mean, of their capabilities; these nobody knows, not even themselves, because most of them have never been called out. I mean their actually existing thoughts and feelings. Many a man thinks he perfectly understands women, because he has had amatory relations with several, perhaps with many of them. If he is a good observer, and his experience extends to quality as well as quantity, he may have learnt something of one narrow department of their nature—an important department, no doubt. But of all the rest of it, few persons are generally more ignorant, because there are few from whom it is so carefully hidden. The most favourable case which a man can generally have for studying the character of a woman, is that of his own wife: for the opportunities are greater, and the cases of complete sympathy not so unspeakably rare. And in fact, this is the source from which any knowledge worth having on the subject has, I believe, generally come. But most men have not had the opportunity of studying in this way more than a single case: accordingly one can, to an almost laughable degree, infer what a man's wife is like, from his opinions about women in general. To make even this one case yield any result, the woman must be worth knowing, and the man not only a competent judge, but of a character so sympathetic in itself, and so well adapted to hers, that he can either read her mind by sympathetic intuition, or has nothing in himself which makes her shy of disclosing it. Hardly any-thing, I believe, can be more rare than this conjunction. It often happens that there is the most complete unity of feeling and community of interests as to all external things, yet the one has as little admission into the internal life of the other as if they were common acquaintance. Even with true affection, authority on the one side and subordination on the other prevent perfect confidence. Though nothing may be in-tentionally withheld, much is not shown. In the analogous relation of parent and child, the corresponding phenomenon must have been in the observation of every one. As between father and son, how many are the cases in which the father, in spite of real affection on both sides, obviously to all the world does not know, nor suspect, parts of the son's character familiar to his companions and equals. The truth is, that the position of looking up to another is extremely unpropitious to complete sincerity and openness with him. The fear of losing ground in his opinion or in his feelings is so strong, that even in an upright character, there is an unconscious tendency to show only the best side, or the side which, though not the best, is that which he most likes to see: and it may be confidently said that thorough knowledge of one another hardly ever exists, but between persons who, besides being intimates, are equals. How much more true, then, must all this be, when the one is not only under the authority of the other, but has it inculcated on her as a duty to reckon everything else subordi-nate to his comfort and pleasure, and to let him neither see nor feel anything coming from her, except what is agreeable to him. All these difficulties stand in the way of a man's obtaining any thorough knowledge even of the one woman whom alone, in general, he has sufficient opportunity of studying. When we further consider that to understand one woman is not necessarily to understand any other woman; that even if he could study many women of one rank, or of one country, he would not thereby understand women of other ranks or countries; and even if he did, they are still only the women of a single period of history; we may safely assert that the knowledge which men can acquire of women, even as they have been and are, without reference to what they might be, is wretchedly imperfect and superficial, and always will be so, until women themselves have told all that they have to tell.

And this time has not come; nor will it come otherwise than gradually. It is but of yesterday that women have either been qualified by literary accomplishments, or permitted by society, to tell anything to the general public. As yet very few of them dare tell anything, which men, on whom their literary success depends, are unwilling to hear. Let us remember in what manner, up to a very recent time, the expression, even by a male author, of uncustomary opinions, or what are deemed eccentric feel-ings, usually was, and in some degree still is, received; and we may form some faint conception under what impediments a woman, who is brought up to think custom and opinion her sovereign rule, attempts to express in books anything drawn from the depths of her own nature. The greatest woman who has left writings behind her sufficient to give her an eminent rank in the literature of her country, thought it nec-essary to prefix as a motto to her boldest work, "Un homme peut braver l'opinion; une femme doit s'y soumettre."[1] The greater part of what women write about women is mere sycophancy to men. In the case of unmarried women, much of it seems only intended to increase their chance of a husband. Many, both married and unmarried, overstep the mark, and inculcate a servility beyond what is desired or relished by any

1. From the title page of Madame de Staël's *Delphine* (1802): "A man can defy opinion; a woman must submit to it."

man, except the very vulgarest. But this is not so often the case as, even at a quite late period, it still was. Literary women are becoming more freespoken, and more willing to express their real sentiments. Unfortunately, in this country especially, they are themselves such artificial products, that their sentiments are compounded of a small element of individual observation and consciousness, and a very large one of acquired associations. This will be less and less the case, but it will remain true to a great extent, as long as social institutions do not admit the same free development of originality in women which is possible to men. When that time comes, and not before, we shall see, and not merely hear, as much as it is necessary to know of the nature of women, and the adaptation of other things to it. * * *

One thing we may be certain of—that what is contrary to women's nature to do, they never will be made to do by simply giving their nature free play. The anxiety of mankind to interfere in behalf of nature, for fear lest nature should not succeed in effecting its purpose, is an altogether unnecessary solicitude. What women by nature cannot do, it is quite superfluous to forbid them from doing. What they can do, but not so well as the men who are their competitors, competition suffices to exclude them from; since nobody asks for protective duties and bounties in favour of women; it is only asked that the present bounties and protective duties in favour of men should be recalled. If women have a greater natural inclination for some things than for others, there is no need of laws or social inculcation to make the majority of them do the former in preference to the latter. Whatever women's services are most wanted for, the free play of competition will hold out the strongest inducements to them to undertake. And, as the words imply, they are most wanted for the things for which they are most fit; by the apportionment of which to them, the collective faculties of the two sexes can be applied on the whole with the greatest sum of valuable result.

The general opinion of men is supposed to be, that the natural vocation of a woman is that of a wife and mother. I say, is supposed to be, because, judging from acts—from the whole of the present constitution of society—one might infer that their opinion was the direct contrary. They might be supposed to think that the alleged natural vocation of women was of all things the most repugnant to their nature; insomuch that if they are free to do anything else—if any other means of living, or occupation of their time and faculties, is open, which has any chance of appearing desirable to them—there will not be enough of them who will be willing to accept the condition said to be natural to them. If this is the real opinion of men in general, it would be well that it should be spoken out. I should like to hear somebody openly enunciating the doctrine (it is already implied in much that is written on the subject)—"It is necessary to society that women should marry and produce children. They will not do so unless they are compelled. Therefore it is necessary to compel them." The merits of the case would then be clearly defined. It would be exactly that of the slaveholders of South Carolina and Louisiana. "It is necessary that cotton and sugar should be grown. White men cannot produce them. Negroes will not, for any wages which we choose to give. *Ergo* they must be compelled." An illustration still closer to the point is that of impressment.[2] Sailors must absolutely be had to defend the country. It often happens that they will not voluntarily enlist. Therefore there must be the power of forcing them. How often has this logic been used! and, but for

2. The practice of seizing men and forcing them to serve as sailors in the navy.

one flaw in it, without doubt it would have been successful up to this day. But it is open to the retort—First pay the sailors the honest value of their labour. When you have made it as well worth their while to serve you, as to work for other employers, you will have no more difficulty than others have in obtaining their services. To this there is no logical answer except "I will not": and as people are now not only ashamed, but are not desirous, to rob the labourer of his hire,[3] impressment is no longer advocated. Those who attempt to force women into marriage by closing all other doors against them, lay themselves open to a similar retort. If they mean what they say, their opinion must evidently be, that men do not render the married condition so desirable to women, as to induce them to accept it for its own recommendations. It is not a sign of one's thinking the boon one offers very attractive, when one allows only Hobson's choice, "that or none." And here, I believe, is the clue to the feelings of those men, who have a real antipathy to the equal freedom of women. I believe they are afraid, not lest women should be unwilling to marry, for I do not think that any one in reality has that apprehension; but lest they should insist that marriage should be on equal conditions; lest all women of spirit and capacity should prefer doing almost anything else, not in their own eyes degrading, rather than marry, when marrying is giving themselves a master, and a master too of all their earthly possessions. And truly, if this consequence were necessarily incident to marriage, I think that the apprehension would be very well founded. I agree in thinking it probable that few women, capable of anything else, would, unless under an irresistible *entrainement* [enchantment], rendering them for the time insensible to anything but itself, choose such a lot, when any other means were open to them of filling a conventionally honourable place in life: and if men are determined that the law of marriage shall be a law of despotism, they are quite right, in point of mere policy, in leaving to women only Hobson's choice. But, in that case, all that has been done in the modern world to relax the chain on the minds of women, has been a mistake. They never should have been allowed to receive a literary education. Women who read, much more women who write, are, in the existing constitution of things, a contradiction and a disturbing element: and it was wrong to bring women up with any acquirements but those of an odalisque,[4] or of a domestic servant.

1860   1869

Statement Repudiating the Rights of Husbands[1]

6th March 1851

Being about, if I am so happy as to obtain her consent, to enter into the marriage relation with the only woman I have ever known, with whom I would have entered into that state; and the whole character of the marriage relation as constituted by law being such as both she and I entirely and conscientiously disapprove, for this among other reasons, that it confers upon one of the parties to the contract, legal power and control over the person, property, and freedom of action of the other party, independent of her own wishes and will; I, having no means of legally divesting myself of

---

3. Luke 10.7.
4. Concubine in a harem.
1. At the time Mill wrote this, shortly before his marriage to Harriet Taylor, married women occupied a peculiar position under British law. A woman, upon her marriage,

entered into a state called coverture. This meant she was subsumed into the legal personhood of her husband and could neither sign legal contracts nor own property. Cf. Caroline Norton's *Letter to the Queen* (1855) in Perspectives: Victorian Ladies and Gentlemen, page 1626.

these odious powers (as I most assuredly would do if an engagement to that effect could be made legally binding on me), feel it my duty to put on record a formal protest against the existing law of marriage, in so far as conferring such powers; and a solemn promise never in any case or under any circumstances to use them. And in the event of marriage between Mrs. Taylor and me I declare it to be my will and intention, and the condition of the engagement between us, that she retains in all respects whatever the same absolute freedom of action, and freedom of disposal of herself and of all that does or may at any time belong to her, as if no such marriage had taken place; and I absolutely disclaim and repudiate all pretence to have acquired any *rights* whatever by virtue of such marriage.

J. S. Mill

from **Autobiography**[1]
from *Chapter 1. Childhood, and Early Education*

It may be useful that there should be some record of an education which was unusual and remarkable, and which, whatever else it may have done, has proved how much more than is commonly supposed may be taught, and well taught, in those early years which, in the common modes of what is called instruction, are little better than wasted. * * *

I was born in London, on the 20th of May 1806, and was the eldest son of James Mill, the author of *The History of British India*.[2] My father, the son of a petty tradesman and (I believe) small farmer, at Northwater Bridge, in the county of Angus, was, when a boy, recommended by his abilities to the notice of Sir John Stuart, of Fettercairn, one of the Barons of the Exchequer in Scotland, and was, in consequence, sent to the University of Edinburgh at the expense of a fund established by Lady Jane Stuart (the wife of Sir John Stuart) and some other ladies for educating young men for the Scottish Church. He there went through the usual course of study, and was licensed as a Preacher, but never followed the profession; having satisfied himself that he could not believe the doctrines of that or any other Church. For a few years he was a private tutor in various families in Scotland, among others that of the Marquis of Tweeddale; but ended by taking up his residence in London, and devoting himself to authorship. Nor had he any other means of support until 1819, when he obtained an appointment in the India House.[3]

In this period of my father's life there are two things which it is impossible not to be struck with: one of them unfortunately a very common circumstance, the other a most uncommon one. The first is, that in his position, with no resource but the precarious one of writing in periodicals, he married and had a large family; conduct than which nothing could be more opposed, both as a matter of good sense and of duty, to the opinions which, at least at a later period of life, he strenuously upheld. The other circumstance, is the extraordinary energy which was required to lead the life he led, with the disadvantages under which he laboured from the first, and with those which he brought upon himself by his marriage. * * * But he, with these burthens on him, planned, commenced, and completed, the *History of India*; and this in the course of about ten years, a shorter time than has been occupied (even by writers who had no

1. Mill's autobiography was published posthumously, five months after his death.
2. Published in 1817, Mill's *History* was long regarded as

authoritative, and it earned him a post with the East India Company.
3. The offices of the East India Company.

other employment) in the production of almost any other historical work of equal bulk, and of anything approaching to the same amount of reading and research. And to this is to be added, that during the whole period, a considerable part of almost every day was employed in the instruction of his children: in the case of one of whom, myself, he exerted an amount of labour, care, and perseverance rarely, if ever, employed for a similar purpose, in endeavouring to give, according to his own conception, the highest order of intellectual education.

A man who, in his own practice, so vigorously acted up to the principle of losing no time, was likely to adhere to the same rule in the instruction of his pupil. I have no remembrance of the time when I began to learn Greek. I have been told that it was when I was three years old. My earliest recollection on the subject, is that of committing to memory what my father termed Vocables, being lists of common Greek words, with their signification in English, which he wrote out for me on cards. Of grammar, until some years later, I learnt no more than the inflexions of the nouns and verbs, but, after a course of vocables, proceeded at once to translation; and I faintly remember going through Aesop's *Fables*, the first Greek book which I read. The *Anabasis*,[4] which I remember better, was the second. I learnt no Latin until my eighth year. At that time I had read, under my father's tuition, a number of Greek prose authors, among whom I remember the whole of Herodotus,[5] and of Xenophon's *Cyropaedia*[6] and *Memorials of Socrates;* some of the lives of the philosophers by Diogenes Laertius; part of Lucian,[7] and Isocrates *Ad Demonicum* and *Ad Nicoclem.* I also read, in 1813, the first six dialogues (in the common arrangement) of Plato, from the *Euthyphron* to the *Theaetetus* inclusive: which last dialogue, I venture to think, would have been better omitted, as it was totally impossible I should understand it. But my father, in all his teaching, demanded of me not only the utmost that I could do, but much that I could by no possibility have done. What he was himself willing to undergo for the sake of my instruction, may be judged from the fact, that I went through the whole process of preparing my Greek lessons in the same room and at the same table at which he was writing: and as in those days Greek and English Lexicons were not, and I could make no more use of a Greek and Latin Lexicon than could be made without having yet begun to learn Latin, I was forced to have recourse to him for the meaning of every word which I did not know. This incessant interruption he, one of the most impatient of men, submitted to, and wrote under that interruption several volumes of his *History* and all else that he had to write during those years. ⁎ ⁎ ⁎

In my eighth year I commenced learning Latin, in conjunction with a younger sister, to whom I taught it as I went on, and who afterwards repeated the lessons to my father: and from this time, other sisters and brothers being successively added as pupils, a considerable part of my day's work consisted of this preparatory teaching. It was a part which I greatly disliked; the more so, as I was held responsible for the lessons of my pupils, in almost as full a sense as for my own: I however derived from this discipline the great advantage, of learning more thoroughly and retaining more lastingly the things which I was set to teach: perhaps, too, the practice it afforded in explaining difficulties to others, may even at that age have been useful. In other respects, the experience of my boyhood is not favorable to the plan of teaching children by means of one another. The teaching, I am sure, is very inefficient as

4. A work by Xenophon (c. 434–355 B.C.), Greek historian and soldier, describing a military expedition.
5. Greek historian of the 5th century B.C.

6. A fictionalized biography of Cyrus, King of Persia.
7. Greek satirist (c. A.D. 124–200).

teaching, and I well know that the relation between teacher and taught is not a good moral discipline to either. * * *

* * * I had read, up to this time, very little English poetry. Shakespeare my father had put into my hands, chiefly for the sake of the historical plays, from which however I went on to the others. My father never was a great admirer of Shakespeare, the English idolatry of whom he used to attack with some severity. He cared little for any English poetry except Milton (for whom he had the highest admiration), Goldsmith, Burns, and Gray's "Bard," which he preferred to his *Elegy:* perhaps I may add Cowper and Beattie. He had some value for Spenser, and I remember his reading to me (unlike his usual practice of making me read to him) the first book of *The Fairie Queene;* but I took little pleasure in it. The poetry of the present century he saw scarcely any merit in, and I hardly became acquainted with any of it till I was grown up to manhood, except the metrical romances of Walter Scott, which I read at his recommendation and was intensely delighted with; as I always was with animated narrative. * * *

In the course of instruction which I have partially retraced, the point most superficially apparent is the great effort to give, during the years of childhood, an amount of knowledge in what are considered the higher branches of education, which is seldom acquired (if acquired at all) until the age of manhood. The result of the experiment shews the ease with which this may be done, and places in a strong light the wretched waste of so many precious years as are spent in acquiring the modicum of Latin and Greek commonly taught to schoolboys; a waste, which has led so many educational reformers to entertain the ill-judged proposal of discarding those languages altogether from general education. If I had been by nature extremely quick of apprehension, or had possessed a very accurate and retentive memory, or were of a remarkably active and energetic character, the trial would not be conclusive; but in all these natural gifts I am rather below than above par. What I could do, could assuredly be done by any boy or girl of average capacity and healthy physical constitution: and if I have accomplished anything, I owe it, among other fortunate circumstances, to the fact that through the early training bestowed on me by my father, I started, I may fairly say, with an advantage of a quarter of a century over my contemporaries. * * *

It is evident that this, among many other of the purposes of my father's scheme of education, could not have been accomplished if he had not carefully kept me from having any great amount of intercourse with other boys. He was earnestly bent upon my escaping not only the ordinary corrupting influence which boys exercise over boys, but the contagion of vulgar modes of thought and feeling; and for this he was willing that I should pay the price of inferiority in the accomplishments which schoolboys in all countries chiefly cultivate. The deficiencies in my education were principally in the things which boys learn from being turned out to shift for themselves, and from being brought together in large numbers. From temperance and much walking, I grew up healthy and hardy, though not muscular; but I could do no feats of skill or physical strength, and knew none of the ordinary bodily exercises. It was not that play, or time for it, was refused me. Though no holidays were allowed, lest the habit of work should be broken, and a taste for idleness acquired, I had ample leisure in every day to amuse myself; but as I had no boy companions, and the animal need of physical activity was satisfied by walking, my amusements, which were mostly solitary, were in general of a quiet, if not a bookish turn, and gave little stimulus to any other kind even of mental activity than that which was already called forth by my studies. I consequently remained long, and in a less degree have always remained, inexpert in anything requiring manual dexterity. * * * My father was the extreme opposite in these particulars: his senses and mental faculties were always on the alert; he carried decision and energy of character in his whole manner, and into every action of life: and this, as much as his talents, contributed to the strong impression which he always made upon those with whom he came into personal contact. But the children of energetic parents, frequently grow up unenergetic, because they lean on their parents, and the parents are energetic for them. The education which my father gave me, was in itself much more fitted for training me to *know* than to *do*.

from *Chapter 5. A Crisis in My Mental History. One Stage Onward*

From the winter of 1821, when I first read Bentham,[1] and especially from the commencement of the *Westminster Review*,[2] I had what might truly be called an object in life; to be a reformer of the world. My conception of my own happiness was entirely identified with this object. The personal sympathies I wished for were those of fellow labourers in this enterprise. I endeavoured to pick up as many flowers as I could by the way; but as a serious and permanent personal satisfaction to rest upon, my whole reliance was placed on this: and I was accustomed to felicitate myself on the certainty of a happy life which I enjoyed, through placing my happiness in something durable and distant, in which some progress might be always making, while it could never be exhausted by complete attainment. This did very well for several years, during which the general improvement going on in the world and the idea of myself as engaged with others in struggling to promote it, seemed enough to fill up an interesting and animated existence. But the time came when I awakened from this as from a dream. It was in the autumn of 1826. I was in a dull state of nerves, such as everybody is occasionally liable to; unsusceptible to enjoyment or pleasurable excitement; one of those moods when what is pleasure at other times, becomes insipid or indifferent; the state, I should think, in which converts to Methodism usually are, when smitten by their first "conviction of sin." In this frame of mind it occurred to me to put the question directly to myself, "Suppose that all your objects in life were realized; that all the changes in institutions and opinions which you are looking forward to, could be completely effected at this very instant: would this be a great joy and happiness to you?" And an irrepressible self-consciousness distinctly answered, "No!" At this my heart sank within me: the whole foundation on which my life was constructed fell down. All my happiness was to have been found in the continual pursuit of this end. The end had ceased to charm, and how could there ever again be any interest in the means? I seemed to have nothing left to live for.

At first I hoped that the cloud would pass away of itself; but it did not. A night's sleep, the sovereign remedy for the smaller vexations of life, had no effect on it. I awoke to a renewed consciousness of the woeful fact. I carried it with me into all companies, into all occupations. Hardly anything had power to cause me even a few minutes oblivion of it. For some months the cloud seemed to grow thicker and

---

1. Jeremy Bentham (1748–1832), political and economic philosopher and founder of utilitarianism.
2. Political and philosophical journal established in 1824 by Bentham, with the assistance of James Mill, which served as the mouthpiece of the Radicals. Both James and John Stuart Mill contributed regularly until 1828.

thicker. The lines in Coleridge's "Dejection"—I was not then acquainted with them—exactly describe my case:

> A grief without a pang, void, dark and drear,
> A drowsy, stifled, unimpassioned grief,
> Which finds no natural outlet or relief
> In word, or sigh, or tear.[3]

In vain I sought relief from my favourite books; those memorials of past nobleness and greatness, from which I had always hitherto drawn strength and animation. I read them now without feeling, or with the accustomed feeling *minus* all its charm; and I became persuaded, that my love of mankind, and of excellence for its own sake, had worn itself out. I sought no comfort by speaking to others of what I felt. If I had loved any one sufficiently to make confiding my griefs a necessity, I should not have been in the condition I was. I felt, too, that mine was not an interesting, or in any way respectable distress. There was nothing in it to attract sympathy. Advice, if I had known where to seek it, would have been most precious. The words of Macbeth to the physician often occurred to my thoughts.[4] But there was no one on whom I could build the faintest hope of such assistance. My father, to whom it would have been natural to me to have recourse in any practical difficulties, was the last person to whom, in such a case as this, I looked for help. Everything convinced me that he had no knowledge of any such mental state as I was suffering from, and that even if he could be made to understand it, he was not the physician who could heal it. My education, which was wholly his work, had been conducted without any regard to the possibility of its ending in this result; and I saw no use in giving him the pain of thinking that his plans had failed, when the failure was probably irremediable, and at all events, beyond the power of *his* remedies. Of other friends, I had at that time none to whom I had any hope of making my condition intelligible. It was however abundantly intelligible to myself; and the more I dwelt upon it, the more hopeless it appeared.

My course of study had led me to believe, that all mental and moral feelings and qualities, whether of a good or of a bad kind, were the results of association; that we love one thing and hate another, take pleasure in one sort of action or contemplation, and pain in another sort, through the clinging of pleasurable or painful ideas to those things, from the effect of education or of experience. As a corollary from this, I had always heard it maintained by my father, and was myself convinced, that the object of education should be to form the strongest possible associations of the salutary class; associations of pleasure with all things beneficial to the great whole, and of pain with all things hurtful to it. This doctrine appeared inexpugnable; but it now seemed to me on retrospect, that my teachers had occupied themselves but superficially with the means of forming and keeping up these salutary associations. They seemed to have trusted altogether to the old familiar instruments, praise and blame, reward and punishment. Now I did not doubt that by these means, begun early and applied unremittingly, intense

3. *Dejection, an Ode*, 11.21–24.
4. "Canst thou not minister to a mind diseas'd, / Pluck out from the memory a rooted sorrow, / Raze out the written troubles of the brain, / And with some sweet oblivious antidote / Cleanse the stuff'd bosom of that perilous stuff / Which weighs upon the heart" (*Macbeth* 5.3.40–45).

associations of pain and pleasure, especially of pain, might be created, and might produce desires and aversions capable of lasting undiminished to the end of life. But there must always be something artificial and casual in associations thus produced. The pains and pleasures thus forcibly associated with things, are not connected with them by any natural tie; and it is therefore, I thought, essential to the durability of these associations, that they should have become so intense and inveterate as to be practically indissoluble, before the habitual exercise of the power of analysis had commenced. For I now saw, or thought I saw, what I had always before received with incredulity—that the habit of analysis has a tendency to wear away the feelings: as indeed it has when no other mental habit is cultivated, and the analysing spirit remains without its natural complements and correctives. The very excellence of analysis (I argued) is that it tends to weaken and undermine whatever is the result of prejudice; that it enables us mentally to separate ideas which have only casually clung together: and no associations whatever could ultimately resist this dissolving force, were it not that we owe to analysis our clearest knowledge of the permanent sequences in nature; the real connexions between Things, not dependent on our will and feelings; natural laws, by virtue of which, in many cases, one thing is inseparable from another in fact; which laws, in proportion as they are clearly perceived and imaginatively realized, cause our ideas of things which are always joined together in Nature, to cohere more and more closely in our thoughts. Analytic habits may thus even strengthen the associations between causes and effects, means and ends, but tend altogether to weaken those which are, to speak familiarly, a *mere* matter of feeling. They are therefore (I thought) favourable to prudence and clearsightedness, but a perpetual worm at the root both of the passions and of the virtues; and above all, fearfully undermine all desires, and all pleasures, which are the effects of association, that is, according to the theory I held, all except the purely physical and organic; of the entire insufficiency of which to make life desirable, no one had a stronger conviction than I had. These were the laws of human nature by which, as it seemed to me, I had been brought to my present state. All those to whom I looked up, were of opinion that the pleasure of sympathy with human beings, and the feelings which made the good of others, and especially of mankind on a large scale, the object of existence, were the greatest and surest sources of happiness. Of the truth of this I was convinced, but to know that a feeling would make me happy if I had it, did not give me the feeling. My education, I thought, had failed to create these feelings in sufficient strength to resist the dissolving influence of analysis, while the whole course of my intellectual cultivation had made precocious and premature analysis the inveterate habit of my mind. I was thus, as I said to myself, left stranded at the commencement of my voyage, with a well equipped ship and a rudder, but no sail; without any real desire for the ends which I had been so carefully fitted out to work for: no delight in virtue or the general good, but also just as little in anything else. The fountains of vanity and ambition seemed to have dried up within me, as completely as those of benevolence. I had had (as I reflected) some gratification of vanity at too early an age: I had obtained some distinction, and felt myself of some importance, before the desire of distinction and of importance had grown into a passion: and little as it was which I had attained, yet having been attained too early, like all pleasures enjoyed too soon, it had made me *blasé* and indifferent to the pursuit. Thus neither selfish nor unselfish pleasures were pleasures to me. And there seemed no power in nature sufficient to begin the formation of my character anew, and create in a mind now irretrievably analytic, fresh associations of pleasure with any of the objects of human desire.

These were the thoughts which mingled with the dry heavy dejection of the melancholy winter of 1826–7. During this time I was not incapable of my usual occupations. I went on with them mechanically, by the mere force of habit. I had been so drilled in a certain sort of mental exercise, that I could still carry it on when all the spirit had gone out of it. I even composed and spoke several speeches at the debating society, how, or with what degree of success I know not. Of four years continual speaking at that society, this is the only year of which I remember next to nothing. Two lines of Coleridge, in whom alone of all writers I have found a true description of what I felt, were often in my thoughts, not at this time (for I had never read them), but in a later period of the same mental malady:

> Work without hope draws nectar in a sieve,
> And hope without an object cannot live.[5]

In all probability my case was by no means so peculiar as I fancied it, and I doubt not that many others have passed through a similar state; but the idiosyncracies of my education had given to the general phenomenon a special character, which made it seem the natural effect of causes that it was hardly possible for time to remove. I frequently asked myself, if I could, or if I was bound to go on living, when life must be passed in this manner. I generally answered to myself, that I did not think I could possibly bear it beyond a year. When, however, not more than half that duration of time had elapsed, a small ray of light broke in upon my gloom. I was reading, accidentally, Marmontel's *Mémoires*,[6] and came to the passage which relates his father's death, the distressed position of the family, and the sudden inspiration by which he, then a mere boy, felt and made them feel that he would be everything to them—would supply the place of all that they had lost. A vivid conception of the scene and its feelings came over me, and I was moved to tears. From this moment my burthen grew lighter. The oppression of the thought that all feeling was dead within me, was gone. I was no longer hopeless: I was not a stock or a stone. I had still, it seemed, some of the material out of which all worth of character, and all capacity for happiness, are made. Relieved from my ever present sense of irremediable wretchedness, I gradually found that the ordinary incidents of life could again give me some pleasure; that I could again find enjoyment, not intense, but sufficient for cheerfulness, in sunshine and sky, in books, in conversation, in public affairs; and that there was, once more, excitement, though of a moderate kind, in exerting myself for my opinions, and for the public good. Thus the cloud gradually drew off, and I again enjoyed life: and though I had several relapses, some of which lasted many months, I never again was as miserable as I had been.

The experiences of this period had two very marked effects on my opinions and character. In the first place, they led me to adopt a theory of life, very unlike that on which I had before acted, and having much in common with what at that time I

---

5. The last lines of Coleridge's poem *Work Without Hope*, page 625.

6. *Mémoires d'un père* (1804; English trans. 1805), by Jean François Marmontel.

certainly had never heard of, the anti-self-consciousness theory of Carlyle.[7] I never, indeed, wavered in the conviction that happiness is the test of all rules of conduct, and the end of life. But I now thought that this end was only to be attained by not making it the direct end. Those only are happy (I thought) who have their minds fixed on some object other than their own happiness; on the happiness of others, on the improvement of mankind, even on some art or pursuit, followed not as a means, but as itself an ideal end. Aiming thus at something else, they find happiness by the way. The enjoyments of life (such was now my theory) are sufficient to make it a pleasant thing, when they are taken *en passant* [in passing], without being made a principal object. Once make them so, and they are immediately felt to be insufficient. They will not bear a scrutinizing examination. Ask yourself whether you are happy, and you cease to be so. The only chance is to treat, not happiness, but some end external to it, as the purpose of life. Let your self-consciousness, your scrutiny, your self-interrogation, exhaust themselves on that; and if otherwise fortunately circumstanced you will inhale happiness with the air you breathe, without dwelling on it or thinking about it, without either forestalling it in imagination, or putting it to flight by fatal questioning. This theory now became the basis of my philosophy of life. And I still hold to it as the best theory for all those who have but a moderate degree of sensibility and of capacity for enjoyment, that is, for the great majority of mankind.

The other important change which my opinions at this time underwent, was that I, for the first time, gave its proper place, among the prime necessities of human well-being, to the internal culture of the individual. I ceased to attach almost exclusive importance to the ordering of outward circumstances, and the training of the human being for speculation and for action. I had now learnt by experience that the passive susceptibilities needed to be cultivated as well as the active capacities, and required to be nourished and enriched as well as guided. I did not, for an instant, lose sight of, or undervalue, that part of the truth which I had seen before; I never turned recreant to intellectual culture, or ceased to consider the power and practice of analysis as an essential condition both of individual and of social improvement. But I thought that it had consequences which required to be corrected, by joining other kinds of cultivation with it. The maintenance of a due balance among the faculties, now seemed to me of primary importance. The cultivation of the feelings became one of the cardinal points in my ethical and philosophical creed. And my thoughts and inclinations turned in an increasing degree towards whatever seemed capable of being instrumental to that object.

I now began to find meaning in the things which I had read or heard about the importance of poetry and art as instruments of human culture. But it was some time longer before I began to know this by personal experience. The only one of the imaginative arts in which I had from childhood taken great pleasure, was music; the best effect of which (and in this it surpasses perhaps every other art) consists in exciting enthusiasm; in winding up to a high pitch those feelings of an elevated kind which are already in the character, but to which this excitement gives a glow and a fervour, which though transitory at its utmost height, is precious for sustaining them at other times. This effect of music I had often experienced; but, like all my pleasurable

---

7. The theory Mill refers to is set forth in Carlyle's essay, *Characteristics* (1831), and in Book 2, ch. 9, of *Sartor Resartus* (1833–1834), "The Everlasting Yea."

susceptibilities, it was suspended during the gloomy period. I had sought relief again and again from this quarter, but found none. After the tide had turned, and I was in process of recovery, I had been helped forward by music, but in a much less elevated manner. I at this time first became acquainted with Weber's *Oberon*,[8] and the extreme pleasure which I drew from its delicious melodies did me good, by shewing me a source of pleasure to which I was as susceptible as ever. The good however was much impaired by the thought, that the pleasure of music (as is quite true of such pleasure as this was, that of mere tune) fades with familiarity, and requires either to be revived by intermittence, or fed by continual novelty. And it is very characteristic both of my then state, and of the general tone of my mind at this period of my life, that I was seriously tormented by the thought of the exhaustibility of musical combinations. The octave consists only of five tones and two semitones, which can be put together in only a limited number of ways, of which but a small proportion are beautiful: most of these, it seemed to me, must have been already discovered, and there could not be room for a long succession of Mozarts and Webers, to strike out as these had done, entirely new and surpassingly rich veins of musical beauty. This source of anxiety may perhaps be thought to resemble that of the philosophers of Laputa,[9] who feared lest the sun should be burnt out. It was, however, connected with the best feature in my character, and the only good point to be found in my very unromantic and in no way honorable distress. For though my dejection, honestly looked at, could not be called other than egotistical, produced by the ruin, as I thought, of my fabric of happiness, yet the destiny of mankind in general was ever in my thoughts, and could not be separated from my own. I felt that the flaw in my life, must be a flaw in life itself; that the question was, whether, if the reformers of society and government could succeed in their objects, and every person in the community were free and in a state of physical comfort, the pleasures of life, being no longer kept up by struggle and privation, would cease to be pleasures. And I felt that unless I could see my way to some better hope than this for human happiness in general, my dejection must continue; but that if I could see such an outlet, I should then look on the world with pleasure; content as far as I was myself concerned, with any fair share of the general lot.

This state of my thoughts and feelings made the fact of my reading Wordsworth for the first time (in the autumn of 1828) an important event in my life. I took up the collection of his poems from curiosity, with no expectation of mental relief from it, though I had before resorted to poetry with that hope. In the worst period of my depression I had read through the whole of Byron (then new to me) to try whether a poet, whose peculiar department was supposed to be that of the intenser feelings, could rouse any feeling in me. As might be expected, I got no good from this reading, but the reverse. The poet's state of mind was too like my own. His was the lament of a man who had worn out all pleasures, and who seemed to think that life, to all who possess the good things of it, must necessarily be the vapid uninteresting thing which I found it. His Harold and Manfred had the same burthen on them which I had; and I was not in a frame of mind to derive any comfort from the vehement sensual passion of his Giaours, or the sullenness of his Laras.[1] But while Byron was exactly what did not suit my condi-

---

8. *Oberon, or the Elf-King's Oath*, a romantic opera by Carl Maria von Weber (1786–1826).
9. See *Gulliver's Travels*, Part 3, by Jonathan Swift (1667–1745).

1. References to Byron's *Childe Harold's Pilgrimage* (1812–1818), *Manfred* (1817), *The Giaour* (1813), and *Lara* (1814), poems with brooding, self-involved heroes.

tion, Wordsworth was exactly what did. I had looked into *The Excursion*[2] two or three years before, and found little in it; and should probably have found as little, had I read it at this time. But the miscellaneous poems, in the two-volume edition of 1815 (to which little of value was added in the latter part of the author's life), proved to be the precise thing for my mental wants at that particular juncture.

In the first place, these poems addressed themselves powerfully to one of the strongest of my pleasurable susceptibilities, the love of rural objects and natural scenery; to which I had been indebted not only for much of the pleasure of my life, but quite recently for relief from one of my longest relapses into depression. In this power of rural beauty over me, there was a foundation laid for taking pleasure in Wordsworth's poetry; the more so, as his scenery lies mostly among mountains, which, owing to my early Pyrenean excursion,[3] were my ideal of natural beauty. But Wordsworth would never have had any great effect on me, if he had merely placed before me beautiful pictures of natural scenery. Scott does this still better than Wordsworth, and a very second-rate landscape does it more effectually than any poet. What made Wordsworth's poems a medicine for my state of mind, was that they expressed, not mere outward beauty, but states of feeling, and of thought coloured by feeling, under the excitement of beauty.[4] They seemed to be the very culture of the feelings, which I was in quest of. In them I seemed to draw from a source of inward joy, of sympathetic and imaginative pleasure, which could be shared in by all human beings; which had no connexion with struggle or imperfection, but would be made richer by every improvement in the physical or social condition of mankind. From them I seemed to learn what would be the perennial sources of happiness, when all the greater evils of life shall have been removed. And I felt myself at once better and happier as I came under their influence. There have certainly been, even in our own age, greater poets than Wordsworth; but poetry of deeper and loftier feeling could not have done for me at that time what his did. I needed to be made to feel that there was real, permanent happiness in tranquil contemplation. Wordsworth taught me this, not only without turning away from, but with a greatly increased interest in, the common feelings and common destiny of human beings. And the delight which these poems gave me, proved that with culture of this sort, there was nothing to dread from the most confirmed habit of analysis. At the conclusion of the Poems came the famous "Ode," falsely called Platonic, "Intimations of Immortality": in which, along with more than his usual sweetness of melody and rhythm, and along with the two passages of grand imagery but bad philosophy so often quoted, I found that he too had had similar experience to mine; that he also had felt that the first freshness of youthful enjoyment of life was not lasting; but that he had sought for compensation, and found it, in the way in which he was now teaching me to find it. The result was that I gradually, but completely, emerged from my habitual depression, and was never again subject to it. I long continued to value Wordsworth less according to his intrinsic merits, than by the measure of what he had done for me. Compared with the greatest poets, he may be said to be the poet of unpoetical natures, possessed of quiet and contemplative tastes. But unpoetical natures are precisely those which require poetic cultivation. This cultivation Wordsworth is much more fitted to give, than poets who are intrinsically far more poets than he.

1873

---

2. Wordsworth's *The Excursion* (1814) is a long meditative poem.
3. In 1820, at the age of 15, Mill had traveled in the Spanish Pyrenees and been strongly impressed by the experience.
4. See Wordsworth's Preface to *Lyrical Ballads* (1800), pages 408–20.

—•— ✖◆✖ —•—

Elizabeth Barrett Browning
1806–1861

Elizabeth Barrett Browning was the most celebrated woman poet of the Victorian era. She was admired by contemporaries as varied as William Wordsworth, Queen Victoria, Edgar Allan Poe (who introduced an American edition of her work), Christina Rossetti, and John Ruskin (who proclaimed *Aurora Leigh* the greatest poem in English). Her popularity was especially remarkable because she interspersed her ardent love lyrics with hard-hitting poems on radical political causes and feminist themes. In the United States, she influenced not only sequestered writers like Emily Dickinson but also political activists like Susan B. Anthony.

The eldest of eleven children, Elizabeth Barrett grew up in a country manor house called Hope End in Hertfordshire. The Barretts were a wealthy family whose fortune derived from a slave plantation in Jamaica. While her submissive mother, Mary Clark, encouraged her to write, it was her protective but authoritarian father, Edward Moulton-Barrett, who dominated her affections and received laudatory poems on his birthdays. From an early age Barrett envisioned herself combining male and female attributes to become "the feminine of Homer." As the critic Dorothy Mermin has pointed out, the ambitious child-poet was already imaginatively inhabiting two gender roles, the imprisoned female muse and the active male quester: "At five I supposed myself a heroine and in my day dreams of bliss I constantly imaged to myself a forlorn damsel in distress rescued by some noble knight."

Barrett took advantage of her family's resources to give herself an exceptional education, unusual for a woman of her day. Her passion for Greek poetry led her to translate Aeschylus's *Prometheus Bound* (1833). Two earlier works also reflected her wide reading: at twelve she wrote a four-book epic, *The Battle of Marathon*, which her father had privately printed, and at twenty she anonymously published a long philosophical poem, *An Essay on Mind, with Other Poems* (1826). But her intellectual development was offset by an illness that broke her health at the age of fifteen. Thereafter, her bold aspirations and mental energy were at odds with her semi-invalid state. Her sense of isolation increased in 1828 when her mother died, and again when declining family fortunes led her father to move the family from the home she loved, first to Sidmouth, Devon, in 1832 and then to London in 1835, where they eventually settled at 50 Wimpole Street.

It was here that Barrett became almost a recluse. Disliking the dirty, foggy city, she hardly left the house, but she corresponded avidly with a circle of literary and public figures. In 1838 chronic lung disease weakened her further; she already had developed what would be a lifelong dependence on morphine as a painkiller. Her doctors insisted that she go to Mediterranean climes, but the farthest her father would allow was Torquay, on the south coast of England. She lived there for three years, returning prostrate with grief after her brother Edward died in a boating accident. For the next several years, her spirits sustained only by her poetry, she worked, slept, and received visitors on a couch in a room sealed against the London air. Often exhausted, she was unable to see the aged Wordsworth when he came to pay his respects.

As she and her small circle of friends were quick to realize, Elizabeth Barrett had become like Tennyson's Lady of Shalott, having no other life but to weave her poetic web in solitude. *The Seraphim and Other Poems* (1838) established her reputation, and the two volumes of *Poems* (1844) consolidated her position as the era's finest "poetess." The latter book included *A Drama of Exile*, a sequel to Milton's *Paradise Lost* in which Eve emerges as a heroine, and also *The Cry of the Children*, condemning child labor in factories. Despite her oppositional politics, the suppleness of her thought and her passionate voice were so highly regarded by critics and public alike that she was mentioned as a candidate for Poet Laureate when Wordsworth died in 1850.

But by then she had utterly transformed her life. In 1845 she began corresponding with Robert Browning—she was nearly forty, and famous; he was thirty-three and his only reputation was for obscurity. Their literary friendship rapidly blossomed into romance, which they had to hide from her father, who had tacitly forbidden his children to marry. After a secret marriage in London in 1846, the couple eloped to Italy, where they settled in Florence at Casa Guidi. There, the fairy tale continued: happily married and living in a warm climate, she recovered much of her health, wrote her best work, gained the love of the Italians with her nationalistic verse, and gave birth to a son, Robert Weidemann Browning ("Pen"), in 1849. She had prophetically written to Browning, in the last letter before their elopement: "I begin to think that none are so bold as the timid, when they are fairly roused."

Her union with Robert Browning was responsible for two works that have since formed the cornerstone of her reputation. The first is their justly famous correspondence. The story of their courtship was widely known, but its intimate details were not revealed until the publication of their letters in 1899. Second, as their relationship developed she wrote a series of love poems to Browning. She finished the last poem two days before their wedding, and the collection was published in 1850, under the deliberately misleading title *Sonnets from the Portuguese*. Among the most significant sonnet sequences since those of Shakespeare and Sidney, these poems revived the form in Victorian England and revised in brilliant new ways what had hitherto been a primarily masculine poetic tradition. Casting the male recipient of her sonnets in the role of sexual object, yet also allowing for his reciprocal passion and poetic drive, Barrett Browning records the interplay of gifted lovers whose desire is inseparable from their quest for verbal mastery.

In her final years Barrett Browning's career continued to flourish. She and her husband enjoyed a wide circle of friends, including Tennyson, Ruskin, Carlyle, Rossetti, and Margaret Fuller. They traveled a great deal, to Rome, Paris, and several times back to London where they were warmly received by both their families—with the exception of her father, who refused to forgive or even see her again. In 1851 she published *Casa Guidi Windows*, which promoted the cause of Italian independence from Austria. *Poems Before Congress* (1860) stirred controversy in England over its volatile and "unwomanly" political views, particularly its scathing attack on American slavery. But her health was failing, and after recurrent illnesses, she died in Florence in her husband's arms. *Last Poems* appeared posthumously in 1862.

Her greatest achievement, however, lies in her verse novel, *Aurora Leigh* (1856), a daring combination of epic, romance, and *bildungsroman*. The first major poem in English in which the heroine, like the author, is a woman writer, *Aurora Leigh* rewrites Wordsworth's *The Prelude* from a female point of view. With its Miltonic echoes, the blank-verse format claims epic importance not only for the growth of the woman poet, but also for a woman's struggle to achieve artistic and economic independence in modern society. The poem blends these themes, moreover, with a witty, Byronic treatment of Victorian manners and social issues, and an emotionally charged love plot that recalls Charlotte Brontë's *Jane Eyre*. The story of how the aspiring poet Aurora Leigh overcomes the prejudices of both a masculine audience and the man she loves, in order to find fame and happiness in Italy, closely mirrors Barrett Browning's own. The poem was an overwhelming success, even though many contemporary readers were scandalized by its radical revision of Victorian ideals of femininity and its picture of how the two sexes might work together so that each could achieve its fullest human potential. Scorning to measure herself against any but the greatest male authors, Elizabeth Barrett Browning was the first to show English readers the enormous possibilities of a poetic tradition in which women participated on equal terms.

To George Sand[1]
A Desire

Thou large-brained woman and large-hearted man,
Self-called George Sand! whose soul, amid the lions
Of thy tumultuous senses, moans defiance
And answers roar for roar, as spirits can:
5   I would some mild miraculous thunder ran
Above the applauded circus,[2] in appliance
Of thine own nobler nature's strength and science,
Drawing two pinions,° white as wings of swan,   *wings*
From thy strong shoulders, to amaze the place
10   With holier light! that thou to woman's claim
And man's, mightst join beside the angel's grace
Of a pure genius sanctified from blame,
Till child and maiden pressed to thine embrace
To kiss upon thy lips a stainless fame.

                                             1844

To George Sand
A Recognition

True genius, but true woman! dost deny
The woman's nature with a manly scorn,
And break away the gauds° and armlets worn   *jewelry*
By weaker women in captivity?
5   Ah, vain denial! that revolted cry
Is sobbed in by a woman's voice forlorn,—
Thy woman's hair, my sister, all unshorn
Floats back dishevelled strength in agony,
Disproving thy man's name: and while before
10   The world thou burnest in a poet-fire,
We see thy woman-heart beat evermore
Through the large flame. Beat purer, heart, and higher,
Till God unsex thee on the heavenly shore
Where unincarnate spirits purely aspire!

                                             1844

1. George Sand was the pseudonym of Aurore Dudevant (1804–1876), a French Romantic novelist noted for her free and unconventional ways, including the adoption of male dress. Barrett Browning admired Sand's genius, and defended her against those critical of her morality.
2. Roman arena where Christians were thrown to the lions.

A Year's Spinning

1

He listened at the porch that day,
    To hear the wheel go on, and on;
And then it stopped, ran back away,
    While through the door he brought the sun:
5   But now my spinning is all done.

2

He sat beside me, with an oath
    That love ne'er ended, once begun;
I smiled—believing for us both,
    What was the truth for only one:
10   And now my spinning is all done.

3

My mother cursed me that I heard
    A young man's wooing as I spun:
Thanks, cruel mother, for that word,—
    For I have, since, a harder known!
15   And now my spinning is all done.

4

I thought—O God!—my first-born's cry
    Both voices to mine ear would drown:
I listened in mine agony—
    It was the *silence* made me groan!
20   And now my spinning is all done.

5

Bury me 'twixt my mother's grave,
    (Who cursed me on her death-bed lone)
And my dead baby's (God it save!)
    Who, not to bless me, would not moan.
25   And now my spinning is all done.

6

A stone upon my heart and head,
    But no name written on the stone!
Sweet neighbours, whisper low instead,
    "This sinner was a loving one—
30   And now her spinning is all done."

7

And let the door ajar remain,
    In case he should pass by anon;
And leave the wheel out very plain,—
    That HE, when passing in the sun,
35   May see the spinning is all done.

1850

from **Sonnets from the Portuguese**[1]

1

I thought once how Theocritus had sung
Of the sweet years, the dear and wished-for years,
Who each one in a gracious hand appears
To bear a gift for mortals, old or young:[2]
5   And, as I mused it in his antique tongue,[3]
I saw, in gradual vision through my tears,
The sweet, sad years, the melancholy years,
Those of my own life, who by turns had flung
A shadow across me. Straightway I was 'ware,
10   So weeping, how a mystic Shape did move
Behind me, and drew me backward by the hair;
And a voice said in mastery, while I strove,—
"Guess now who holds thee?"—"Death," I said. But, there,
The silver answer rang,—"Not Death, but Love."

13

And wilt thou have me fashion into speech
The love I bear thee, finding words enough,
And hold the torch out, while the winds are rough,
Between our faces, to cast light on each?—
5   I drop it at thy feet. I cannot teach
My hand to hold my spirit so far off
From myself—me—that I should bring thee proof
In words, of love hid in me out of reach.
Nay, let the silence of my womanhood
10   Commend my woman-love to thy belief,—
Seeing that I stand unwon, however wooed,
And rend the garment of my life, in brief,
By a most dauntless, voiceless fortitude,
Lest one touch of this heart convey its grief.

14

If thou must love me, let it be for nought
Except for love's sake only. Do not say
"I love her for her smile—her look—her way
Of speaking gently,—for a trick of thought
5   That falls in well with mine, and certes brought
A sense of pleasant ease on such a day"—

---

1. These very personal poems chronicle Elizabeth Barrett's courtship with Robert Browning. She did not show them to him until after they were married, when he pronounced them "the finest sonnets written in any language since Shakespeare's." He overcame her reluctance to publish them by proposing the somewhat cryptic title implying that they are merely translations.

2. In *Idylls* 15, Theocritus, a Greek pastoral poet of the 3rd century B.C., tells how "the dainty-footed Hours" brought Adonis to Aphrodite. The song celebrates the return of spring, the season when Elizabeth Barrett first met Robert Browning.

3. I.e., Greek.

For these things in themselves, Belovèd, may
Be changed, or change for thee,—and love, so wrought,
May be unwrought so. Neither love me for
10 Thine own dear pity's wiping my cheeks dry,—
A creature might forget to weep, who bore
Thy comfort long, and lose thy love thereby!
But love me for love's sake, that evermore
Thou mayst love on, through love's eternity.

21

Say over again, and yet once over again,
That thou dost love me. Though the word repeated
Should seem "a cuckoo-song,"[4] as thou dost treat it,
Remember, never to the hill or plain,
5 Valley and wood, without her cuckoo-strain
Comes the fresh Spring in all her green completed.
Belovèd, I, amid the darkness greeted
By a doubtful spirit-voice, in that doubt's pain
Cry, "Speak once more—thou lovest!" Who can fear
10 Too many stars, though each in heaven shall roll,
Too many flowers, though each shall crown the year?
Say thou dost love me, love me, love me—toll
The silver iterance!°—only minding, Dear,   repetition
To love me also in silence with thy soul.

22

When our two souls stand up erect and strong,
Face to face, silent, drawing nigh and nigher,
Until the lengthening wings break into fire
At either curvèd point,—what bitter wrong
5 Can the earth do to us, that we should not long
Be here contented? Think. In mounting higher,
The angels would press on us and aspire
To drop some golden orb of perfect song
Into our deep, dear silence. Let us stay
10 Rather on earth, Belovèd,—where the unfit
Contrarious moods of men recoil away
And isolate pure spirits, and permit
A place to stand and love in for a day,
With darkness and the death-hour rounding it.

24

Let the world's sharpness, like a clasping knife,
Shut in upon itself and do no harm
In this close hand of Love, now soft and warm,

4. Repetitious, like the cuckoo's song.

And let us hear no sound of human strife
5   After the click of the shutting. Life to life—
I lean upon thee, Dear, without alarm,
And feel as safe as guarded by a charm
Against the stab of worldlings, who if rife
Are weak to injure.[5] Very whitely still
10 The lilies of our lives may reassure
Their blossoms from their roots, accessible
Alone to heavenly dews that drop not fewer,
Growing straight, out of man's reach, on the hill.
God only, who made us rich, can make us poor.

28

My letters! all dead paper, mute and white!
And yet they seem alive and quivering
Against my tremulous hands which loose the string
And let them drop down on my knee to-night.
5   This said,—he wished to have me in his sight
Once, as a friend: this fixed a day in spring[6]
To come and touch my hand . . . a simple thing,
Yet I wept for it!—this, . . . the paper's light . . .
Said, *Dear, I love thee*; and I sank and quailed
10 As if God's future thundered on my past.
This said, *I am thine*—and so its ink has paled
With lying at my heart that beat too fast.
And this . . . O Love, thy words have ill availed
If, what this said, I dared repeat at last!

32

The first time that the sun rose on thine oath
To love me, I looked forward to the moon
To slacken all those bonds which seemed too soon
And quickly tied to make a lasting troth.
5   Quick-loving hearts, I thought, may quickly loathe;
And, looking on myself, I seemed not one
For such man's love!—more like an out-of-tune
Worn viol, a good singer would be wroth
To spoil his song with, and which, snatched in haste,
10 Is laid down at the first ill-sounding note.
I did not wrong myself so, but I placed
A wrong on *thee*. For perfect strains may float
'Neath master-hands, from instruments defaced,—
And great souls, at one stroke, may do and doat.

5. I.e., against the stabs of worldly people, who may be numerous but have little power to harm us.   6. On 17 May 1845, Robert Browning wrote to arrange their first meeting: "I will call at two on Tuesday."

38

First time he kissed me, he but only kissed
The fingers of this hand wherewith I write;
And ever since, it grew more clean and white,
Slow to world-greetings, quick with its "Oh, list,"°   *listen*
5   When the angels speak. A ring of amethyst
I could not wear here, plainer to my sight,
Than that first kiss. The second passed in height
The first, and sought the forehead, and half missed,
Half falling on the hair. O beyond meed!°   *deserving*
10   That was the chrism[7] of love, which love's own crown,
With sanctifying sweetness, did precede.
The third upon my lips was folded down
In perfect, purple state; since when, indeed,
I have been proud and said, "My love, my own."

43

How do I love thee? Let me count the ways.
I love thee to the depth and breadth and height
My soul can reach, when feeling out of sight
For the ends of Being and ideal Grace.
5   I love thee to the level of everyday's
Most quiet need, by sun and candle-light.
I love thee freely, as men strive for Right;
I love thee purely, as they turn from Praise.
I love thee with the passion put to use
10   In my old griefs, and with my childhood's faith.
I love thee with a love I seemed to lose
With my lost saints,—I love with the breath,
Smiles, tears, of all my life!—and, if God choose,
I shall but love thee better after death.

1845–1847   1850

from **Aurora Leigh**[1]
from *Book 1*
[SELF-PORTRAIT]

Of writing many books there is no end;
And I who have written much in prose and verse
For others' uses, will write now for mine,—
Will write my story for my better self,
5   As when you paint your portrait for a friend,
Who keeps it in a drawer and looks at it
Long after he has ceased to love you, just
To hold together what he was and is.

7. Consecrated oil used to anoint during a coronation.
1. Barrett Browning called *Aurora Leigh*, a poem in nine books, a "verse novel." It portrays the struggles of a young poet to find her artistic voice and pursue her vocation despite the obstacles confronting a woman writer.

Elizabeth Barrett Browning, from the frontispiece of the fourth edition of *Aurora Leigh* (1859). This etched portrait of Barrett Browning—with the disheveled hair, frank gaze, and bohemian-looking jacket—signals to the reader that the author has a lot in common with her heroine, the feminist poet Aurora Leigh. During this period Barrett Browning was living in Florence and at the height of her fame, passionately involved in denouncing the slave trade in America and demanding independence for her adoptive country, Italy.

I, writing thus, am still what men call young;
10   I have not so far left the coasts of life
To travel inward, that I cannot hear
That murmur of the outer Infinite
Which unweaned babies smile at in their sleep
When wondered at for smiling; not so far,
15   But still I catch my mother at her post
Beside the nursery door, with finger up,
"Hush, hush—here's too much noise!" while her sweet eyes
Leap forward, taking part against her word
In the child's riot. Still I sit and feel
20   My father's slow hand, when she had left us both,
Stroke out my childish curls across his knee,
And hear Assunta's daily jest (she knew
He liked it better than a better jest)
Inquire how many golden scudi[2] went
25   To make such ringlets. O my father's hand,
Stroke heavily, heavily the poor hair down,
Draw, press the child's head closer to thy knee!
I'm still too young, too young, to sit alone.

2. Italian coins; Assunta was Aurora's nurse.

I write. My mother was a Florentine,
30 Whose rare blue eyes were shut from seeing me
When scarcely I was four years old, my life
A poor spark snatched up from a failing lamp
Which went out therefore. She was weak and frail;
She could not bear the joy of giving life,
35 The mother's rapture slew her. If her kiss
Had left a longer weight upon my lips
It might have steadied the uneasy breath,
And reconciled and fraternised my soul
With the new order. As it was, indeed,
40 I felt a mother-want about the world,
And still went seeking, like a bleating lamb
Left out at night in shutting up the fold,—
As restless as a nest-deserted bird
Grown chill through something being away, though what
45 It knows not. I, Aurora Leigh, was born
To make my father sadder, and myself
Not overjoyous, truly. Women know
The way to rear up children (to be just),
They know a simple, merry, tender knack
50 Of tying sashes, fitting baby-shoes,
And stringing pretty words that make no sense,
And kissing full sense into empty words,
Which things are corals to cut life upon,
Although such trifles: children learn by such,
55 Love's holy earnest in a pretty play
And get not over-early solemnised,
But seeing, as in a rose-bush, Love's Divine
Which burns and hurts not,—not a single bloom,—
Become aware and unafraid of Love.
60 Such good do mothers. Fathers love as well
—Mine did, I know,—but still with heavier brains,
And wills more consciously responsible,
And not as wisely, since less foolishly;
So mothers have God's license to be missed.

65 My father was an austere Englishman,
Who, after a dry lifetime spent at home
In college-learning, law, and parish talk,
Was flooded with a passion unaware,
His whole provisioned and complacent past
70 Drowned out from him that moment. As he stood
In Florence, where he had come to spend a month
And note the secret of Da Vinci's drains,[3]
He musing somewhat absently perhaps
Some English question . . . whether men should pay

3. Leonardo da Vinci (1452–1519) was an architect and engineer, as well as an artist; he designed the aqueduct that supplied Milan's water.

75 The unpopular but necessary tax
    With left or right hand—in the alien sun
    In that great square of the Santissima[4]
    There drifted past him (scarcely marked enough
    To move his comfortable island scorn)
80 A train of priestly banners, cross and psalm,
    The white-veiled rose-crowned maidens holding up
    Tall tapers, weighty for such wrists, aslant
    To the blue luminous tremor of the air,
    And letting drop the white wax as they went
85 To eat the bishop's wafer[5] at the church;
    From which long trail of chanting priests and girls,
    A face flashed like a cymbal on his face
    And shook with silent clangour brain and heart,
    Transfiguring him to music. Thus, even thus,
90 He too received his sacramental gift
    With eucharistic meanings; for he loved.

[HER MOTHER'S PORTRAIT]

                        And as I grew
    In years, I mixed, confused, unconsciously,
    Whatever I last read or heard or dreamed,
    Abhorrent, admirable, beautiful,
150 Pathetical, or ghastly, or grotesque,
    With still that face . . . which did not therefore change,
    But kept the mystic level of all forms,
    Hates, fears, and admirations, was by turns
    Ghost, fiend, and angel, fairy, witch, and sprite,
155 A dauntless Muse who eyes a dreadful Fate,
    A loving Psyche who loses sight of Love,[6]
    A still Medusa[7] with mild milky brows
    All curdled and all clothed upon with snakes
    Whose slime falls fast as sweat will; or anon
160 Our Lady of the Passion, stabbed with swords
    Where the Babe sucked; or Lamia[8] in her first
    Moonlighted pallor, ere she shrunk and blinked
    And shuddering wriggled down to the unclean;
    Or my own mother, leaving her last smile
165 In her last kiss upon the baby-mouth
    My father pushed down on the bed for that,—
    Or my dead mother, without smile or kiss,

---

4. The Florentine church of the Santissima Annunziata,
or Holy Annunciation.
5. To take Holy Communion.
6. Psyche was beloved of Cupid (or Eros), whom she had
never seen because he always came to her after dark; one
night she lit her lamp to look at him as he slept, where-

upon he left her.
7. A gorgon, a female monster with serpents for hair, the
sight of whom turned people to stone.
8. A monster with the head and upper body of a maiden,
and lower body of a serpent.

Buried at Florence. All which images,
Concentred on the picture, glassed themselves
170 Before my meditative childhood, as
The incoherencies of change and death
Are represented fully, mixed and merged,
In the smooth fair mystery of perpetual Life.

[AURORA'S EDUCATION]

Then, land!—then, England! oh, the frosty cliffs[9]
Looked cold upon me. Could I find a home
Among those mean red houses through the fog?
And when I heard my father's language first
255 From alien lips which had no kiss for mine
I wept aloud, then laughed, then wept, then wept,
And some one near me said the child was mad
Through much sea-sickness. The train swept us on:
Was this my father's England? the great isle?
260 The ground seemed cut up from the fellowship
Of verdure, field from field,[1] as man from man;
The skies themselves looked low and positive,
As almost you could touch them with a hand,
And dared to do it they were so far off
265 From God's celestial crystals;[2] all things blurred
And dull and vague. Did Shakespeare and his mates
Absorb the light here?—not a hill or stone
With heart to strike a radiant colour up
Or active outline on the indifferent air.

270 I think I see my father's sister stand
Upon the hall-step of her country-house
To give me welcome. She stood straight and calm,
Her somewhat narrow forehead braided tight
As if for taming accidental thoughts
275 From possible pulses;[3] brown hair pricked with gray
By frigid use of life (she was not old,
Although my father's elder by a year),
A nose drawn sharply, yet in delicate lines;
A close mild mouth, a little soured about
280 The ends, through speaking unrequited loves
Or peradventure niggardly half-truths;
Eyes of no colour,—once they might have smiled,
But never, never have forgot themselves
In smiling; cheeks, in which was yet a rose
285 Of perished summers, like a rose in a book,

---

9. The white chalk cliffs of Dover.
1. English fields are divided by hedgerows.
2. The stars, or perhaps the crystalline sphere the ancients believed lay beyond them.
3. Pulsations of strong emotion.

Kept more for ruth° than pleasure,—if past bloom,   *remorse*
Past fading also.

             She had lived, we'll say,
A harmless life, she called a virtuous life,
A quiet life, which was not life at all
290   (But that, she had not lived enough to know),
Between the vicar and the country squires,
The lord-lieutenant looking down sometimes
From the empyrean to assure their souls
Against chance vulgarisms, and, in the abyss,
295   The apothecary, looked on once a year
To prove their soundness of humility.
The poor-club exercised her Christian gifts
Of knitting stockings, stitching petticoats,
Because we are of one flesh, after all,
300   And need one flannel° (with a proper sense   *petticoat*
Of difference in the quality)—and still
The book-club, guarded from your modern trick
Of shaking dangerous questions from the crease,[4]
Preserved her intellectual. She had lived
305   A sort of cage-bird life, born in a cage,
Accounting that to leap from perch to perch
Was act and joy enough for any bird.
Dear heaven, how silly are the things that live
In thickets, and eat berries!

             I, alas,
310   A wild bird scarcely fledged, was brought to her cage,
And she was there to meet me. Very kind.
Bring the clean water, give out the fresh seed.

             * * *
             So it was.
385   I broke the copious curls upon my head
In braids, because she liked smooth-ordered hair.
I left off saying my sweet Tuscan words
Which still at any stirring of the heart
Came up to float across the English phrase
390   As lilies (*Bene* or *Che che*[5]), because
She liked my father's child to speak his tongue.
I learnt the collects and the catechism,
The creeds, from Athanasius back to Nice,
The Articles,[6] the Tracts *against* the times[7]

---

4. Books were sold with their pages uncut; one had to cut the folds, or creases, to open the pages and read the book.
5. "Good" and "no, indeed" (Italian).
6. The Thirty-nine Articles are the principles of Angli-can faith; collects are Anglican prayers.
7. An ironic reference to the High Church movement's *Tracts for the Times*, written by Newman, Keble, and Pusey; thus, the aunt is Low Church.

395   (By no means Buonaventure's "Prick of Love"⁸),
       And various popular synopses of
       Inhuman doctrines never taught by John,⁹
       Because she liked instructed piety.
       I learnt my complement of classic French
400   (Kept pure of Balzac and neologism¹)
       And German also, since she liked a range
       Of liberal education,—tongues, not books.
       I learnt a little algebra, a little
       Of the mathematics,—brushed with extreme flounce
405   The circle of the sciences, because
       She misliked women who are frivolous.
       I learnt the royal genealogies
       Of Oviedo, the internal laws
       Of the Burmese empire,—by how many feet
410   Mount Chimborazo outsoars Teneriffe.
       What navigable river joins itself
       To Lara, and what census of the year five
       Was taken at Klagenfurt,—because she liked
       A general insight into useful facts.
415   I learnt much music,—such as would have been
       As quite impossible in Johnson's day²
       As still it might be wished—fine sleights of hand
       And unimagined fingering, shuffling off
       The hearer's soul through hurricanes of notes
420   To a noisy Tophet;° and I drew . . . costumes   Hell
       From French engravings, nereids neatly draped
       (With smirks of simmering godship): I washed in°   water-colored
       Landscapes from nature (rather say, washed out).
       I danced the polka and Cellarius,
425   Spun glass, stuffed birds, and modelled flowers in wax,
       Because she liked accomplishments in girls.
       I read a score of books on womanhood
       To prove, if women do not think at all,
       They may teach thinking (to a maiden aunt
430   Or else the author),—books that boldly assert
       Their right of comprehending husband's talk
       When not too deep, and even of answering
       With pretty "may it please you," or "so it is,"—
       Their rapid insight and fine aptitude,
435   Particular worth and general missionariness,
       As long as they keep quiet by the fire

8. Saint Buonaventure (1221–1274) wrote of ecstatic, mystical Christian experiences; he believed in the power of love over the power of reason.
9. The author of the gospel.
1. Honoré de Balzac (1799–1850), French realist novelist who described things considered unpleasant or immoral,
hence unsuitable reading for young ladies. A neologism is a newly coined word.
2. When informed that a piece of music being played by a young lady was extremely difficult, Samuel Johnson responded, "Would that it had been impossible."

And never say "no" when the world says "ay,"
For that is fatal,—their angelic reach
Of virtue, chiefly used to sit and darn,
440 And fatten household sinners,—their, in brief,
Potential faculty in everything
Of abdicating power in it: she owned
She liked a woman to be womanly,
And English women, she thanked God and sighed
445 (Some people always sigh in thanking God)
Were models to the universe. And last
I learnt cross-stitch, because she did not like
To see me wear the night with empty hands
A-doing nothing. So, my shepherdess
450 Was something after all (the pastoral saints
Be praised for't), leaning lovelorn with pink eyes
To match her shoes, when I mistook the silks;
Her head uncrushed by that round weight of hat
So strangely similar to the tortoise-shell
455 Which slew the tragic poet.[3]
                              By the way,
The works of women are symbolical.
We sew, sew, prick our fingers, dull our sight,
Producing what? A pair of slippers, sir,
To put on when you're weary—or a stool
460 To stumble over and vex you . . . "curse that stool!"
Or else at best, a cushion, where you lean
And sleep, and dream of something we are not
But would be for your sake. Alas, alas!
This hurts most, this—that, after all, we are paid
465 The worth of our work, perhaps.

                              In looking down
Those years of education (to return)
I wonder if Brinvilliers suffered more
In the water-torture[4] . . . flood succeeding flood
To drench the incapable throat and split the veins . . .
470 Than I did. Certain of your feebler souls
Go out in such a process; many pine
To a sick, inodorous light; my own endured:
I had relations in the Unseen, and drew
The elemental nutriment and heat
475 From nature, as earth feels the sun at nights,
Or as a babe sucks surely in the dark.
I kept the life thrust on me, on the outside
Of the inner life with all its ample room

3. The Greek playwright Aeschylus was supposed to have been killed when an eagle, mistaking his bald head for a stone, dropped a tortoise on it to break the shell.

4. In 1676 Marie Marguerite, Marquise de Brinvilliers, was tortured by having water forced down her throat, then executed.

For heart and lungs, for will and intellect,
480   Inviolable by conventions. God,
I thank thee for that grace of thine!

[DISCOVERY OF POETRY]

815   The cygnet finds the water, but the man
Is born in ignorance of his element
And feels out blind at first, disorganised
By sin i' the blood,—his spirit-insight dulled
And crossed by his sensations. Presently
820   He feels it quicken in the dark sometimes,
When, mark, be reverent, be obedient,
For such dumb motions of imperfect life
Are oracles of vital Deity
Attesting the Hereafter. Let who says
825   "The soul's a clean white paper," rather say,
A palimpsest,[5] a prophet's holograph
Defiled, erased and covered by a monk's,—
The apocalypse, by a Longus![6] poring on
Which obscene text, we may discern perhaps
830   Some fair, fine trace of what was written once,
Some upstroke of an alpha and omega
Expressing the old scripture.
                              Books, books, books!
I had found the secret of a garret-room
Piled high with cases in my father's name,
835   Piled high, packed large,—where, creeping in and out
Among the giant fossils of my past,
Like some small nimble mouse between the ribs
Of a mastodon, I nibbled here and there
At this or that box, pulling through the gap,
840   In heats of terror, haste, victorious joy,
The first book first. And how I felt it beat
Under my pillow, in the morning's dark,
An hour before the sun would let me read!
My books! At last because the time was ripe,
845   I chanced upon the poets.

                      As the earth
Plunges in fury, when the internal fires
Have reached and pricked her heart, and, throwing flat
The marts and temples, the triumphal gates
And towers of observation, clears herself
850   To elemental freedom—thus, my soul,
At poetry's divine first finger-touch,

---

5. Parchment where the original writing has been scraped off so it can be reused.
6. I.e., imagine that the words of the apocalyse have been erased and written over by Longus, a Greek writer of romances.

Let go conventions and sprang up surprised,
Convicted of the great eternities
Before two worlds.

               What's this, Aurora Leigh,
855   You write so of the poets, and not laugh?
Those virtuous liars, dreamers after dark,
Exaggerators of the sun and moon,
And soothsayers in a tea-cup?

               I write so
Of the only truth-tellers now left to God,
860   The only speakers of essential truth,
Opposed to relative, comparative,
And temporal truths; the only holders by
His sun-skirts, through conventional gray glooms;
The only teachers who instruct mankind
865   From just a shadow on a charnel-wall[7]
To find man's veritable stature out
Erect, sublime,—the measure of a man,
And that's the measure of an angel, says
The apostle. Ay, and while your common men
870   Lay telegraphs, gauge railroads, reign, reap, dine,
And dust the flaunty carpets of the world
For kings to walk on, or our president,
The poet suddenly will catch them up
With his voice like a thunder,—"This is soul,
875   This is life, this word is being said in heaven,
Here's God down on us! what are you about?"
How all those workers start amid their work,
Look round, look up, and feel, a moment's space,
That carpet-dusting, though a pretty trade,
880   Is not the imperative labour after all.

from *Book 2*
[WOMAN AND ARTIST]

Times followed one another. Came a morn
I stood upon the brink of twenty years,
And looked before and after, as I stood
Woman and artist,—either incomplete,
5   Both credulous of completion. There I held
The whole creation in my little cup,
And smiled with thirsty lips before I drank
"Good health to you and me, sweet neighbor mine,
And all these peoples."

7. Wall of a building where bodies or bones are deposited.

I was glad, that day;
10   The June was in me, with its multitudes
Of nightingales all singing in the dark,
And rosebuds reddening where the calyx[1] split.
I felt so young, so strong, so sure of God!
So glad, I could not choose be very wise!
15   And, old at twenty, was inclined to pull
My childhood backward in a childish jest
To see the face of't once more, and farewell!
In which fantastic mood I bounded forth
At early morning,—would not wait so long
20   As even to snatch my bonnet by the strings,
But, brushing a green trail across the lawn
With my gown in the dew, took will and away
Among the acacias of the shrubberies,
To fly my fancies in the open air
25   And keep my birthday, till my aunt awoke
To stop good dreams. Meanwhile I murmured on
As honeyed bees keep humming to themselves,
"The worthiest poets have remained uncrowned
Till death has bleached their foreheads to the bone;
30   And so with me it must be unless I prove
Unworthy of the grand adversity,
And certainly I would not fail so much.
What, therefore, if I crown myself to-day
In sport, not pride, to learn the feel of it,
35   Before my brows be numbed as Dante's own
To all the tender pricking of such leaves?
Such leaves! what leaves?"
                  I pulled the branches down
To choose from.
              "Not the bay![2] I choose no bay
(The fates deny us if we are overbold),
40   Nor myrtle—which means chiefly love; and love
Is something awful which one dares not touch
So early o' mornings. This verbena strains
The point of passionate fragrance; and hard by,
This guelder-rose, at far too slight a beck
45   Of the wind, will toss about her flower-apples.
Ah—there's my choice,—that ivy on the wall,
That headlong ivy! not a leaf will grow
But thinking of a wreath. Large leaves, smooth leaves,
Serrated like my vines, and half as green.
50   I like such ivy, bold to leap a height
'Twas strong to climb; as good to grow on graves
As twist about a thyrsus;[3] pretty too

1. The green outer leaves which protect a flowerbud.
2. Laurel; Apollo, the god of poetry, wore a wreath of
laurel leaves.
3. Ivy-covered staff carried by the Greek god Dionysus.

(And that's not ill) when twisted round a comb."
Thus speaking to myself, half singing it,
55   Because some thoughts are fashioned like a bell
To ring with once being touched, I drew a wreath
Drenched, blinding me with dew, across my brow,
And fastening it behind so, turning faced
... My public!—cousin Romney—with a mouth
60   Twice graver than his eyes.

                I stood there fixed,—
My arms up, like the caryatid,[4] sole
Of some abolished temple, helplessly
Persistent in a gesture which derides
A former purpose. Yet my blush was flame,
65   As if from flax, not stone.

                    "Aurora Leigh,
The earliest of Auroras!"[5]

                    Hand stretched out
I clasped, as shipwrecked men will clasp a hand,
Indifferent to the sort of palm. The tide
Had caught me at my pastime, writing down
70   My foolish name too near upon the sea
Which drowned me with a blush as foolish. "You,
My cousin!"
                The smile died out in his eyes
And dropped upon his lips, a cold dead weight,
For just a moment, "Here's a book I found!
75   No name writ on it—poems, by the form;
Some Greek upon the margin,—lady's Greek
Without the accents. Read it? Not a word.
I saw at once the thing had witchcraft in't,
Whereof the reading calls up dangerous spirits:
80   I rather bring it to the witch."

                  "My book.
You found it" ...

                "In the hollow by the stream
That beech leans down into—of which you said
The Oread in it has a Naiad's heart
And pines for waters."[6]

                "Thank you."
                    "Thanks to *you*

85   My cousin! that I have seen you not too much
Witch, scholar, poet, dreamer, and the rest,
To be a woman also."

4. Female figure with upraised arms, used as a supporting architectural column.

5. Aurora, the goddess of the dawn.
6. An Oread is a tree nymph; a Naiad is a water nymph.

With a glance
The smile rose in his eyes again and touched
The ivy on my forehead, light as air.
90   I answered gravely "Poets needs must be
Or men or women—more's the pity."

                              "Ah,
But men, and still less women, happily,
Scarce need be poets. Keep to the green wreath,
Since even dreaming of the stone and bronze
95   Brings headaches, pretty cousin, and defiles
The clean white morning dresses."

                          "So you judge!
Because I love the beautiful I must
Love pleasure chiefly, and be overcharged
For ease and whiteness! well, you know the world,
100 And only miss your cousin, 'tis not much.
But learn this; I would rather take my part
With God's Dead, who afford to walk in white
Yet spread His glory, than keep quiet here
And gather up my feet from even a step
105 For fear to soil my gown in so much dust.
I choose to walk at all risks.—Here, if heads
That hold a rhythmic thought, much ache perforce,
For my part I choose headaches,—and to-day's
My birthday."
              "Dear Aurora, choose instead
110 To cure them. You have balsams."

                          "I perceive.
The headache is too noble for my sex.
You think the heartache would sound decenter,
Since that's the woman's special, proper ache,
And altogether tolerable, except
115 To a woman."

                    [NO FEMALE CHRIST]

                          "There it is!—
180 You play beside a death-bed like a child,
Yet measure to yourself a prophet's place
To teach the living. None of all these things
Can women understand. You generalise
Oh, nothing,—not even grief! Your quick-breathed hearts,
185 So sympathetic to the personal pang,
Close on each separate knife-stroke, yielding up
A whole life at each wound, incapable
Of deepening, widening a large lap of life
To hold the world-full woe. The human race
190 To you means, such a child, or such a man,
You saw one morning waiting in the cold,

Beside that gate, perhaps. You gather up
A few such cases, and when strong sometimes
Will write of factories and of slaves, as if
195   Your father were a negro, and your son
A spinner in the mills. All's yours and you,
All, coloured with your blood, or otherwise
Just nothing to you. Why, I call you hard
To general suffering. Here's the world half-blind
200   With intellectual light, half-brutalised
With civilisation, having caught the plague
In silks from Tarsus,[7] shrieking east and west
Along a thousand railroads, mad with pain
And sin too! . . . does one woman of you all
205   (You who weep easily) grow pale to see
This tiger shake his cage?—does one of you
Stand still from dancing, stop from stringing pearls,
And pine and die because of the great sum
Of universal anguish?—Show me a tear
210   Wet as Cordelia's,[8] in eyes bright as yours,
Because the world is mad. You cannot count,
That you should weep for this account, not you!
You weep for what you know. A red-haired child
Sick in a fever, if you touch him once,
215   Though but so little as with a finger-tip,
Will set you weeping; but a million sick . . .
You could as soon weep for the rule of three
Or compound fractions. Therefore, this same world,
Uncomprehended by you, must remain
220   Uninfluenced by you.—Women as you are,
Mere women, personal and passionate,
You give us doating mothers, and perfect wives,
Sublime Madonnas, and enduring saints!
We get no Christ from you,—and verily
225   We shall not get a poet, in my mind."

[AURORA'S REJECTION OF ROMNEY]

There he glowed on me
With all his face and eyes. "No other help?"
345   Said he—"no more than so?"[9]

---

7. I.e., with civilized luxuries come evils, just as the trading ships bringing silks from Tarsus—a wealthy center of trade in the ancient Middle East—might also have brought rats that spread the plague.
8. Cordelia weeps when she is reunited with her father (King Lear, 4.7.71); her feelings are entirely personal. Romney mentions Cordelia to bolster his argument that women cannot play any role in world affairs because they are incapable of taking a broad view of human suffering.
9. Romney wants to alleviate the misery of the poor through social reform. Aurora has offered her approval of his plans, but he asks if she can offer him another kind of help—i.e., to be his wife or "helpmate" (line 402 below).

                "What help?" I asked.
"You'd scorn my help,—as Nature's self, you say,
Has scorned to put her music in my mouth
Because a woman's. Do you now turn round
And ask for what a woman cannot give?"

350   "For what she only can, I turn and ask,"
He answered, catching up my hands in his,
And dropping on me from his high-eaved brow
The full weight of his soul,—"I ask for love,
And that, she can; for life in fellowship
355   Through bitter duties—that, I know she can;
For wifehood—will she?"

                "Now," I said, "may God
Be witness 'twixt us two!" and with the word,
Meseemed I floated into a sudden light
Above his stature,—"am I proved too weak
360   To stand alone, yet strong enough to bear
Such leaners on my shoulder? poor to think,
Yet rich enough to sympathise with thought?
Incompetent to sing, as blackbirds can,
Yet competent to love, like HIM?"

                    I paused;
365   Perhaps I darkened, as the lighthouse will
That turns upon the sea. "It's always so.
Anything does for a wife."

                "Aurora, dear,
And dearly honoured,"—he pressed in at once
With eager utterance,—"you translate me ill.
370   I do not contradict my thought of you
Which is most reverent, with another thought
Found less so. If your sex is weak for art
(And I, who said so, did but honour you
By using truth in courtship), it is strong
375   For life and duty. Place your fecund heart
In mine, and let us blossom for the world
That wants love's colour in the grey of time.
My talk, meanwhile, is arid to you, ay,
Since all my talk can only set you where
380   You look down coldly on the arena-heaps
Of headless bodies, shapeless, indistinct!
The Judgment-Angel scarce would find his way
Through such a heap of generalised distress
To the individual man with lips and eyes,
385   Much less Aurora. Ah, my sweet, come down,
And hand in hand we'll go where yours shall touch
These victims, one by one! till, one by one,
The formless, nameless trunk of every man

Shall seem to wear a head with hair you know,
390   And every woman catch your mother's face
To melt you into passion."

                      "I am a girl,"
I answered slowly; "you do well to name
My mother's face. Though far too early, alas,
God's hand did interpose 'twixt it and me,
395   I know so much of love as used to shine
In that face and another. Just so much;
No more indeed at all. I have not seen
So much love since, I pray you pardon me,
As answers even to make a marriage with
400   In this cold land of England. What you love
Is not a woman, Romney, but a cause:
You want a helpmate, not a mistress, sir,
A wife to help your ends,—in her no end.
Your cause is noble, your ends excellent,
405   But I, being most unworthy of these and that,
Do otherwise conceive of love. Farewell."

"Farewell, Aurora? you reject me thus?"
He said.

           "Sir, you were married long ago.
You have a wife already whom you love,
410   Your social theory. Bless you both, I say.
For my part, I am scarcely meek enough
To be the handmaid of a lawful spouse.
Do I look a Hagar,[1] think you?"

                      "So you jest."
"Nay, so, I speak in earnest," I replied.
415   "You treat of marriage too much like, at least,
A chief apostle: you would bear with you
A wife . . . a sister . . . shall we speak it out?
A sister of charity."

              "Then, must it be
Indeed farewell? And was I so far wrong
420   In hope and in illusion, when I took
The woman to be nobler than the man,
Yourself the noblest woman, in the use
And comprehension of what love is,—love,
That generates the likeness of itself
425   Through all heroic duties? so far wrong,
In saying bluntly, venturing truth on love,
'Come, human creature, love and work with me,'—

1. In Genesis 16, Hagar was the handmaiden of Abraham's lawful wife, Sarah; Hagar bore Abraham a son, Ishmael, when it appeared that Sarah was barren.

Instead of 'Lady, thou art wondrous fair,
And, where the Graces walk before, the Muse
430 Will follow at the lightning of their eyes,
And where the Muse walks, lovers need to creep:
Turn round and love me, or I die of love.'"

With quiet indignation I broke in.
"You misconceive the question like a man,
435 Who sees a woman as the complement
Of his sex merely. You forget too much
That every creature, female as the male,
Stands single in responsible act and thought
As also in birth and death. Whoever says
440 To a loyal woman, 'Love and work with me,'
Will get fair answers if the work and love,
Being good themselves, are good for her—the best
She was born for. Women of a softer mood,
Surprised by men when scarcely awake to life,
445 Will sometimes only hear the first word, love,
And catch up with it any kind of work,
Indifferent, so that dear love go with it.
I do not blame such women, though, for love,
They pick much oakum;[2] earth's fanatics make
450 Too frequently heaven's saints. But *me* your work
Is not the best for,—nor your love the best,
Nor able to commend the kind of work
For love's sake merely. Ah, you force me, sir,
To be overbold in speaking of myself:
455 I too have my vocation,—work to do,
The heavens and earth have set me since I changed
My father's face for theirs, and, though your world
Were twice as wretched as you represent,
Most serious work, most necessary work
460 As any of the economists'. Reform,
Make trade a Christian possibility,
And individual right no general wrong;
Wipe out earth's furrows of the Thine and Mine,
And leave one green for men to play at bowls,[3]
465 With innings for them all! . . . What then, indeed,
If mortals are not greater by the head
Than any of their prosperities? what then,
Unless the artist keep up open roads
Betwixt the seen and unseen,—bursting through
470 The best of your conventions with his best,
The speakable, imaginable best
God bids him speak, to prove what lies beyond

---

2. Prisoners and paupers in workhouses were forced to pick oakum (untwist strands of old rope); it was tedious and humble labor.
3. Lawn bowling.

Both speech and imagination? A starved man
Exceeds a fat beast: we'll not barter, sir,
475 The beautiful for barley.—And, even so,
I hold you will not compass your poor ends
Of barley-feeding and material ease,
Without a poet's individualism
To work your universal. It takes a soul,
480 To move a body: it takes a high-souled man,
To move the masses, even to a cleaner stye:
It takes the ideal, to blow a hair's-breadth off
The dust of the actual.—Ah, your Fouriers[4] failed,
Because not poets enough to understand
485 That life develops from within.—For me,
Perhaps I am not worthy, as you say,
Of work like this: perhaps a woman's soul
Aspires, and not creates: yet we aspire,
And yet I'll try out your perhapses, sir,
490 And if I fail . . . why, burn me up my straw[5]
Like other false works—I'll not ask for grace;
Your scorn is better, cousin Romney. I
Who love my art, would never wish it lower
To suit my stature. I may love my art.
495 You'll grant that even a woman may love art,
Seeing that to waste true love on anything
Is womanly, past question."

                                I retain
The very last word which I said that day,
As you the creaking of the door, years past,
500 Which let upon you such disabling news
You ever after have been graver. He,
His eyes, the motions in his silent mouth,
Were fiery points on which my words were caught,
Transfixed for ever in my memory
505 For his sake, not their own. And yet I know
I did not love him . . . nor he me . . . that's sure . . .
And what I said is unrepented of,
As truth is always. Yet . . . a princely man!—
If hard to me, heroic for himself!
510 He bears down on me through the slanting years,
The stronger for the distance. If he had loved,
Ay, loved me, with that retributive face,. . .
I might have been a common woman now
And happier, less known and less left alone,
515 Perhaps a better woman after all,
With chubby children hanging on my neck

4. François Marie Charles Fourier (1772–1837), a French
social theorist who advocated communal property.

5. I.e., destroy my poetry.

To keep me low and wise. Ah me, the vines
That bear such fruit are proud to stoop with it.
The palm stands upright in a realm of sand.
520 And I, who spoke the truth then, stand upright,
Still worthy of having spoken out the truth,
By being content I spoke it though it set
Him there, me here.—O woman's vile remorse,
To hanker after a mere name, a show,
525 A supposition, a potential love!
Does every man who names love in our lives
Become a power for that?

from *Book 3*
[THE WOMAN WRITER IN LONDON]

Why what a pettish, petty thing I grow,—
A mere mere woman, a mere flaccid nerve,
A kerchief left out all night in the rain,
Turned soft so,—overtasked and overstrained
40 And overlived in this close London life!
And yet I should be stronger.

                Never burn
Your letters, poor Aurora! for they·stare
With red seals from the table, saying each,
"Here's something that you know not." Out, alas,
45 'Tis scarcely that the world's more good and wise
Or even straighter and more consequent
Since yesterday at this time—yet, again,
If but one angel spoke from Ararat[1]
I should be very sorry not to hear:
50 So open all the letters! let me read:
Blanche Ord, the writer in the "Lady's Fan,"
Requests my judgment on . . . that, afterwards.
Kate Ward desires the model of my cloak,
And signs "Elisha to you."[2] Pringle Sharpe
55 Presents his work on "Social Conduct," craves
A little money for his pressing debts. . .
From me, who scarce have money for my needs;
Art's fiery chariot which we journey in
Being apt to singe our singing-robes to holes,
60 Although you ask me for my cloak, Kate Ward!
Here's Rudgely knows it,—editor and scribe;
He's "forced to marry where his heart is not,
Because the purse lacks where he lost his heart."
Ah,——lost it because no one picked it up;

---

1. The mountain where Noah's ark rested after the Flood
and where God spoke to Noah (Genesis 8).
2. When the prophet Elijah was carried to heaven in a
chariot of fire, his cloak fell to earth and was taken up by
his successor Elisha (2 Kings 2.1–15); Kate Ward means
that she wants to copy Aurora's cloak.

65   That's really loss,—(and passable impudence).
        My critic Hammond flatters prettily,
        And wants another volume like the last.
        My critic Belfair wants another book
        Entirely different, which will sell (and live?),
70   A striking book, yet not a startling book,
        The public blames originalities
        (You must not pump spring-water unawares
        Upon a gracious public full of nerves):
        Good things, not subtle, new yet orthodox,
75   As easy reading as the dog-eared page
        That's fingered by said public fifty years,
        Since first taught spelling by its grandmother,
        And yet a revelation in some sort:
        That's hard, my critic Belfair. So—what next?
80   My critic Stokes objects to abstract thoughts;
        "Call a man John, a woman Joan," says he,
        "And do not prate so of *humanities:*"
        Whereat I call my critic simply, Stokes.
        My critic Jobson recommends more mirth
85   Because a cheerful genius suits the times,
        And all true poets laugh unquenchably
        Like Shakespeare and the gods. That's very hard.
        The gods may laugh, and Shakespeare; Dante smiled
        With such a needy heart on two pale lips,
90   We cry "Weep rather, Dante." Poems are
        Men, if true poems: and who dares exclaim
        At any man's door, "Here, 'tis understood
        The thunder fell last week and killed a wife
        And scared a sickly husband—what of that?
95   Get up, be merry, shout and clap your hands,
        Because a cheerful genius suits the times—"?
        None says so to the man, and why indeed
        Should any to the poem? A ninth seal;[3]
        The apocalypse is drawing to a close.
100   Ha,—this from Vincent Carrington,—"Dear friend,
        I want good counsel. Will you lend me wings
        To raise me to the subject, in a sketch
        I'll bring to-morrow—may I? at eleven?
        A poet's only born to turn to use:
105   So save you! for the world . . . and Carrington."
        "(Writ after.) Have you heard of Romney Leigh,
        Beyond what's said of him in newspapers,
        His phalansteries[4] there, his speeches here,

---

3. In Revelation 5.1 there is a book closed with seven seals, the opening of which will herald the Apocalypse. The reference to a ninth seal satirically suggests some-thing more extreme than the Apocalypse itself.
4. The communes advocated by the socialist Fourier.

His pamphlets, pleas, and statements, everywhere?
110   He dropped *me* long ago, but no one drops
A golden apple—though indeed one day
You hinted that, but jested. Well, at least
You know Lord Howe who sees him . . . whom he sees
And *you* see and I hate to see,—for Howe
115   Stands high upon the brink of theories,
Observes the swimmers and cries 'Very fine,'
But keeps dry linen equally,—unlike
That gallant breaster, Romney. Strange it is,
Such sudden madness seizing a young man
120   To make earth over again,—while I'm content
To make the pictures. Let me bring the sketch.
A tiptoe Danae,[5] overbold and hot,
Both arms a-flame to meet her wishing Jove
Halfway, and burn him faster down; the face
125   And breasts upturned and straining, the loose locks
All glowing with the anticipated gold.
Or here's another on the self-same theme.[6]
She lies here—flat upon her prison-floor,
The long hair swathed about her to the heel
130   Like wet seaweed. You dimly see her through
The glittering haze of that prodigious rain,
Half blotted out of nature by a love
As heavy as fate. I'll bring you either sketch.
I think, myself, the second indicates
More passion."

135   Surely. Self is put away,
And calm with abdication. She is Jove,
And no more Danae—greater thus. Perhaps
The painter symbolises unaware
Two states of the recipient artist-soul,
140   One, forward, personal, wanting reverence,
Because aspiring only. We'll be calm,
And know that, when indeed our Joves come down,
We all turn stiller than we have ever been.
                    * * *
Serene and unafraid of solitude,
170   I worked the short days out,—and watched the sun
On lurid morns or monstrous afternoons
(Like some Druidic idol's fiery brass
With fixed unflickering outline of dead heat,
From which the blood of wretches pent inside
175   Seems oozing forth to incarnadine the air[7])

5. Carrington has sketched Danae, the beloved of Zeus, whom Zeus visited in a shower of gold.
6. I.e., the second picture is also of Danae and the golden
shower ("prodigious rain") that is Zeus.
7. It was believed that ancient Celtic druids performed human sacrifices.

Push out through fog with his dilated disk,
And startle the slant roofs and chimney-pots
With splashes of fierce colour. Or I saw
Fog only, the great tawny weltering fog,
180   Involve the passive city, strangle it
Alive, and draw it off into the void,
Spires, bridges, streets, and squares, as if a sponge
Had wiped out London,—or as noon and night
Had clapped together and utterly struck out
185   The intermediate time, undoing themselves
In the act. Your city poets see such things
Not despicable. Mountains of the south,
When drunk and mad with elemental wines
They rend the seamless mist and stand up bare,
190   Make fewer singers, haply. No one sings,
Descending Sinai: on Parnassus mount[8]
You take a mule to climb and not a muse
Except in fable and figure: forests chant
Their anthems to themselves, and leave you dumb.
195   But sit in London at the day's decline,
And view the city perish in the mist
Like Pharaoh's armaments in the deep Red Sea,[9]
The chariots, horsemen, footmen, all the host,
Sucked down and choked to silence—then, surprised
200   By a sudden sense of vision and of tune,
You feel as conquerors though you did not fight,
And you and Israel's other singing girls,
Ay, Miriam[1] with them, sing the song you choose.

from *Book 5*
[EPIC ART AND MODERN LIFE]

The critics say that epics have died out
140   With Agamemnon and the goat-nursed gods;[1]
I'll not believe it. I could never deem,
As Payne Knight[2] did (the mythic mountaineer
Who travelled higher than he was born to live,
And showed sometimes the goitre in his throat[3]
145   Discoursing of an image seen through fog),
That Homer's heroes measured twelve feet high.

8. Sinai is the mountain where God gave the Commandments to Moses; Parnassus is the mountain where the
Muses, the Greek goddesses of the arts and of knowledge,
dwelled. The idea is that neither biblical nor classical
sources can provide poetic inspiration for the modern
poet; only the city can do so.
9. In Exodus 14.21–30, God parts the Red Sea so the Israelites can escape from Egypt but drowns Pharaoh's pursuing armies.
1. Miriam, the sister of Moses and Aaron, led the women
of Israel in singing to celebrate the drowning of the
Egyptian army (Exodus 15.19–21).
1. Agamemnon led the Greeks in the Trojan War, as
chronicled in Homer's epic, the *Iliad*; Zeus was nursed by
a goat.
2. Richard Payne Knight (1750–1824), a classical scholar
who speculated about Homer and the Elgin marbles.
3. A swelling of the throat (caused by lack of iodine in
the water at high altitudes), symbolizing the foolishness
of Payne Knight's utterances.

They were but men:—his Helen's hair turned grey
Like any plain Miss Smith's who wears a front;[4]
And Hector's infant whimpered at a plume[5]
150 As yours last Friday at a turkey-cock.
All actual heroes are essential men,
And all men possible heroes: every age,
Heroic in proportions, double-faced,
Looks backward and before, expects a morn
155 And claims an epos.°   *epic poem*

          Ay, but every age
Appears to souls who live in't (ask Carlyle[6])
Most unheroic. Ours, for instance, ours:
The thinkers scout it, and the poets abound
Who scorn to touch it with a finger-tip:
160 A pewter age,[7]—mixed metal, silver-washed;
An age of scum, spooned off the richer past,
An age of patches for old gaberdines,°   *overcoats*
An age of mere transition,[8] meaning nought
Except that what succeeds must shame it quite
165 If God please. That's wrong thinking, to my mind,
And wrong thoughts make poor poems.

                        Every age,
Through being beheld too close, is ill-discerned
By those who have not lived past it. We'll suppose
Mount Athos carved, as Alexander schemed,
170 To some colossal statue of a man.[9]
The peasants, gathering brushwood in his ear,
Had guessed as little as the browsing goats
Of form or feature of humanity
Up there,—in fact, had travelled five miles off
175 Or ere the giant image broke on them,
Full human profile, nose and chin distinct,
Mouth, muttering rhythms of silence up the sky
And fed at evening with the blood of suns;
Grand torso,—hand, that flung perpetually
180 The largesse of a silver river down
To all the country pastures. 'Tis even thus
With times we live in,—evermore too great
To be apprehended near.

---

4. Hairpiece worn over the forehead; artificial bangs.
5. When the Trojan warrior Hector tried to embrace his infant son before going into battle, the baby was terrified of his father's plumed helmet.
6. In *On Heroes and Hero Worship* (1841) Thomas Carlyle urges a renewal of the idea of the heroic.
7. Inferior to the Golden, the Silver, or even the Bronze Age; Hesiod proposed that history is a constant process of decline.

8. In *The Spirit of the Age* (1831) John Stuart Mill says the present era is "an age of transition."
9. Alexander the Great thought of having Mount Athos carved in the form of a gigantic statue of a conqueror, with a basin in one hand to collect water for the pastures below.

But poets should
Exert a double vision; should have eyes
185   To see near things as comprehensively
As if afar they took their point of sight,
And distant things as intimately deep
As if they touched them. Let us strive for this.
I do distrust the poet who discerns
190   No character or glory in his times,
And trundles back his soul five hundred years,
Past moat and drawbridge, into a castle-court,
To sing—oh, not of lizard or of toad
Alive i' the ditch there,—'twere excusable,
195   But of some black chief, half knight, half sheep-lifter,
Some beauteous dame, half chattel and half queen,
As dead as must be, for the greater part,
The poems made on their chivalric bones;
And that's no wonder: death inherits death.

200   Nay, if there's room for poets in this world
A little overgrown (I think there is),
Their sole work is to represent the age,
Their age, not Charlemagne's,[1]—this live, throbbing age,
That brawls, cheats, maddens, calculates, aspires,
205   And spends more passion, more heroic heat,
Betwixt the mirrors of its drawing-rooms,
Than Roland with his knights at Roncesvalles.[2]
To flinch from modern varnish, coat or flounce,
Cry out for togas and the picturesque,
210   Is fatal,—foolish too. King Arthur's self
Was commonplace to Lady Guenever;
And Camelot to minstrels seemed as flat
As Fleet Street to our poets.[3]

Never flinch,
But still, unscrupulously epic, catch
215   Upon the burning lava of a song
The full-veined, heaving, double-breasted Age:
That, when the next shall come, the men of that
May touch the impress with reverent hand, and say
"Behold,—behold the paps we all have sucked!
220   This bosom seems to beat still, or at least
It sets ours beating: this is living art,
Which thus presents and thus records true life."

1853–1856   1856

1. Charlemagne was king of the Franks (768–814) and emperor of the West, laying the foundation for the Holy Roman Empire.
2. Legendary hero whose defeat at Roncesvalles (in the Spanish Pyrenees) was disastrous for Charlemagne's forces; his exploits are the subject of a medieval epic poem, Le Chanson de Roland.
3. I.e., to his wife Guenevere, even the glorious King Arthur was ordinary, and his kingdom was no more a subject for the poets of his own time than Fleet Street—location of London publishers and newspaper offices—is for the poets of the 19th century.

from **A Curse for a Nation**[1]
Prologue

I heard an angel speak last night,
    And he said "Write!
Write a Nation's curse for me,
And send it over the Western Sea."

5   I faltered, taking up the word:
    "Not so, my lord!
If curses must be, choose another
To send thy curse against my brother.

"For I am bound by gratitude,
10   By love and blood,
To brothers of mine across the sea,
Who stretch out kindly hands to me."

"Therefore," the voice said, "shalt thou write
    My curse to-night.
15   From the summits of love a curse is driven,
As lightning is from the tops of heaven."

"Not so," I answered. "Evermore
    My heart is sore
For my own land's sins: for little feet
20   Of children bleeding along the street:

"For parked-up honours that gainsay
    The right of way:
For almsgiving through a door that is
Not open enough for two friends to kiss:

25   "For love of freedom which abates
    Beyond the Straits:
For patriot virtue starved to vice on
Self-praise, self-interest, and suspicion:

"For an oligarchic parliament,
30   And bribes well-meant.
What curse to another land assign,
When heavy-souled for the sins of mine?"

"Therefore," the voice said, "shalt thou write
    My curse to-night.
35   Because thou hast strength to see and hate
A foul thing done *within* thy gate."

"Not so," I answered once again.
    "To curse, choose men.

---

1. The United States, which claimed to represent freedom yet permitted slavery.

For I, a woman, have only known
40   How the heart melts and the tears run down."

"Therefore," the voice said, "shalt thou write
      My curse to-night.
Some women weep and curse, I say
(And no one marvels), night and day.

45   "And thou shalt take their part to-night,
      Weep and write.
A curse from the depths of womanhood
Is very salt, and bitter, and good."

So thus I wrote, and mourned indeed,
50   What all may read.
And thus, as was enjoined on me,
I send it over the Western Sea.

                                  1860

A Musical Instrument

1

What was he doing, the great god Pan,[1]
    Down in the reeds by the river?
Spreading ruin and scattering ban,°   *curses*
Splashing and paddling with hoofs of a goat,
5   And breaking the golden lilies afloat
    With the dragon-fly on the river.

2

He tore out a reed, the great god Pan,
    From the deep cool bed of the river:
The limpid water turbidly ran,
10   And the broken lilies a-dying lay,
And the dragon-fly had fled away,
    Ere he brought it out of the river.

3

High on the shore sat the great god Pan
    While turbidly flowed the river;
15   And hacked and hewed as a great god can,
With his hard bleak steel at the patient reed,
Till there was not a sign of the leaf indeed
    To prove it fresh from the river.

---

1. Pan was the god of woods and fields; he had a human head and torso but goat's ears, legs, and tail. He was enamored of the beautiful nymph Syrinx who fled to a river for protection and was transformed into reeds on the riverbank. Pan fashioned some of the reeds into a musical instrument called the panpipe, or syrinx.

4

He cut it short, did the great god Pan,
20   (How tall it stood in the river!)
Then drew the pith, like the heart of a man,
Steadily from the outside ring,
And notched the poor dry empty thing
      In holes, as he sat by the river.

5

25   "This is the way," laughed the great god Pan
      (Laughed while he sat by the river),
"The only way, since gods began
To make sweet music, they could succeed."
Then, dropping his mouth to a hole in the reed,
30   He blew in power by the river.

6

Sweet, sweet, sweet, O Pan!
      Piercing sweet by the river!
Blinding sweet, O great god Pan!
The sun on the hill forgot to die,
35   And the lilies revived, and the dragon-fly
      Came back to dream on the river.

7

Yet half a beast is the great god Pan,
      To laugh as he sits by the river,
Making a poet out of a man:
40   The true gods sigh for the cost and pain,—
For the reed which grows nevermore again
      As a reed with the reeds in the river.

1860   1860

The Best Thing in the World

What's the best thing in the world?
June-rose, by May-dew impearled;
Sweet south-wind, that means no rain;
Truth, not cruel to a friend;
5   Pleasure, not in haste to end;
Beauty, not self-decked and curled

Till its pride is over-plain;
Light, that never makes you wink;
Memory, that gives no pain;
10   Love, when, so, you're loved again.
What's the best thing in the world?
—Something out of it, I think.

1862

—⊷ ⊱◈⊰ ⊷—

Alfred, Lord Tennyson
1809–1892

"There, that is the first money you have ever earned by your poetry, and, take my word for it, it will be the last." These were the words of Tennyson's crusty grandfather, as he doled out ten shillings for the teenager's ode on the death of his grandmother. The pen proved mightier than the prediction, however, as Tennyson went on to become the most celebrated poet of the age. His books sold tens of thousands of copies; the Queen and Parliament named him Poet Laureate, then Lord, and finally Baron Tennyson; his annual income surpassed ten thousand pounds a year; and he was widely regarded as something more than a poet—a prophet, a sage, and an infallible moneymaker. A New York publisher once offered him a thousand pounds for any three-stanza poem he cared to write.

It is often said that Tennyson's greatness lay in eloquently presenting the anxieties and aspirations of his era. In poems such as *Ulysses, In Memoriam,* and *Idylls of the King,* he expressed the energy, resolve, faith, and idealism of an industrious society that was nonetheless racked by deep doubts about its materialism, the truth of the Bible, and the possibility of achieving a truly Christian society. But Tennyson was not just a mouthpiece for his age: in the early and mid-Victorian period Tennyson was one of its most progressive voices, espousing views that were all the more daring for a shy and sensitive man struggling to realize his dream of becoming "a *popular* poet." His assertion in *The Princess* (1847) that "the woman's cause is man's" anticipates Mill's *The Subjection of Women* by more than twenty years; in the course of writing *In Memoriam* (1850) he lucidly formulated some of the main principles of evolutionary theory well before Darwin's *Origin of Species* (1859); he called public attention to the industrialized misery and revolutionary anger of the poor during the 1840s while the contemporaneous works of Marx and Engels were virtually unknown; and in *Locksley Hall* (1842) he evoked the technological promise of the future as compellingly as any science fiction writer.

One key to Tennyson's poetic success was his prosaic devotion to the Victorian gospel of hard work. He labored patiently, in poverty and without recognition, to overcome his troubled background. Born in Somersby, Lincolnshire, Tennyson was the third surviving son in a close-knit but emotionally unstable family of eleven children, two of whom suffered lifelong mental illness, while two more were addicted to drugs and alcohol. The poet's father, George, was an awkward, tormented man whose ill temper was aggravated into alcoholism and violence when he was disinherited in favor of his younger brother and then forced to accept a position as village rector. It seems that the entire family was prone to epilepsy. Well into maturity, Alfred was haunted by fear of "the black blood of the Tennysons."

Tennyson's grim childhood was brightened by his mother's warmth and affection, his father's extensive library, and both parents' love of poetry. The rectory was surrounded by large gardens and open countryside, and as a child Tennyson composed nature poetry in the manner of James Thomson's *Seasons*. Early years at a brutally strict grammar school, followed by intensive tutoring from his erudite father, gave Tennyson a solid grounding in Greek, Latin, English, and modern languages by the time he went to Cambridge University in 1827. He had already mastered the styles of poets ranging from Horace and Virgil to Shakespeare, Milton, Scott, and Byron, and earlier that year he published his first book, *Poems by Two Brothers*. It was written with his brother Charles, with whom he used to exchange lines on their country walks, shouting them out across the hedges. The habit of building poems around a series of sonorous individual lines would remain with Tennyson all his life.

At Cambridge the timid country boy began gradually to assume the artistic persona that would be revered throughout the empire. Tall, ruggedly handsome, and with a faraway look in his eyes that was actually due to myopia, Tennyson fit everyone's idea of how a poet should look. He distinguished himself by the quality of his talk, his humorous storytelling, and his acting ability. In 1829 he received the Chancellor's Medal for *Timbuctoo*, the first poem in blank verse ever to win. The same year he and his best friend Arthur Henry Hallam joined "The Apostles," a select group of undergraduates who met to discuss social, philosophical, and literary issues. Members became lifelong friends, and their admiration of his early work helped convince the reticent Tennyson to publish *Poems, Chiefly Lyrical* in 1830. The book received mixed reviews.

In 1831 his father died, and Tennyson had to return home without a degree. Yet Tennyson persevered, issuing in 1832 a new volume, *Poems*. This time, the reviews were actively hostile. Tennyson's morale was sustained only by the visits to Somersby of Hallam, who by now was engaged to Tennyson's sister Emily. Then in 1833 Hallam died suddenly of a cerebral hemorrhage while on a trip to Vienna, and Tennyson's life changed forever.

Within a week of hearing the news, Tennyson began work on his greatest poem, though he did not know then that the brief lyric passages of love, loss, and doubt that he composed to assuage his grief would eventually become *In Memoriam*, an epic meditation on mortality, evolution, and the hard-won consolations of inner faith. He was already proficient, like his early hero Byron, in turning his own private misery into virtuoso evocations of emotionally charged landscapes. As John Stuart Mill wrote in 1835, Tennyson excelled in "the power of *creating* scenery, in keeping with some state of human feeling, so fitted to it as to be the embodied symbol of it, and to summon up the state of feeling itself, with a force not to be surpassed by anything but reality." Quoting *Mariana* as an example, Mill concluded that "words surely never created a more vivid feeling of physical and spiritual dreariness."

Outwardly Tennyson was calm, actively reading, writing, and socializing, but in his poetry he pictured himself as a weeping widower who mourned "a loss forever new." In 1842 he reluctantly published a two-volume edition of *Poems*, improving earlier works and introducing new ones, most notably *Ulysses* and *Morte d'Arthur*. Although his reputation was now rising, the poet was at a low ebb. He was so poor and hampered by responsibilities to his unraveling family that he was forced to postpone indefinitely his marriage to Emily Sellwood, to whom he had become engaged in 1838.

At this point Tennyson lost all his money in a scheme for carving wood by machinery. His friends feared he was on the verge of suicide. Here, as at other dark times in his life, he relied on sheer willpower to follow the advice he once offered to a depressed friend: "Just go grimly on." Eventually travel, hydropathic cures, new acquaintances, and improving finances assuaged his melancholia. Publication of *The Princess* in 1847 finally gave him the popular notice he had long sought.

But it was not until 1850 that Tennyson triumphed in life and art. In May, after seventeen years' brooding, he published *In Memoriam* to great acclaim; on June 13 he married Emily; and by the end of June one reviewer was calling him "the greatest living poet." The sentiment was timely, since Wordsworth had died in April, and by November Tennyson was named Poet Laureate. In 1852 his first son, Hallam, was born, and in 1853 the Tennysons moved to a neo-Gothic country estate called Farringford on the Isle of Wight.

His experimental "monodrama" *Maud* (1855) sold well though it baffled the critics, one of whom remarked that there was one vowel too many, no matter which, in the title. But the combined sales of his works enabled him to buy Farringford, where he could work in peace amid wreaths of tobacco smoke, adored by Emily and protected from his fans by a large staff. There he entertained great personages of the day, from Prince Albert and Garibaldi to his neighbor Julia Margaret Cameron, who badgered him into photographic immortality. Henceforth, whenever he visited London, he was sought after in society and mobbed by admirers.

The stability of his new life enabled Tennyson to pursue many longer projects, including the best-selling narrative poem *Enoch Arden* (1864) and several successful plays. Most of his

Max Beerbohm, *Tennyson Reading "In Memoriam" to his Sovereign*, 1904.

energies were taken up, however, with the great work of his later life, *Idylls of the King*. A trip to Wales helped fuel his interest in Arthurian legends, and he published groups of *Idylls* in 1859 and 1869. As with *In Memoriam* and *Maud*, the poet gradually felt his way, as he composed the parts, toward a larger design for the whole. All the while he held before him the image of "my lost Arthur," until recollections of his actual friend Arthur Hallam blended with the two literary Arthurs of *In Memoriam* and *Idylls of the King*. He rounded out his tale to an epic twelve books, not producing a final version until 1888, just a few years before his death.

In the *Idylls* as in much of his earlier poetry, Tennyson is a poet of deferment. His most memorable characters—Mariana, the Lotos Eaters, Ulysses, Tithonus, and the speakers of *In Memoriam* and *Maud*, among them—long for reunions and releases that are ever yet to come, as distant as the return of King Arthur from Avalon. In old age Tennyson remembered of his youth that even before he could read, "the words 'far, far away' always had a strange charm for me."

After Tennyson's death in 1892 and his burial with great pomp in Westminster Abbey, his reputation suffered a decline that lasted till the end of the Modernist period around 1945. But Tennyson's lyric genius was admired by poets as various as the Pre-Raphaelites and Whitman, Poe, and Hopkins. Auden and Eliot were in rare agreement that he had "the finest ear of any English poet since Milton." Critics continue to dispute whether the sense of Tennyson's poetry is equal to its magnificent sound, but any close reading of his work will reveal Tennyson's deep ambivalence about the world of which he gradually became both oracle and icon. Often beneath his harmonies we hear echoes of his favorite childhood sound, "voices crying in the wind." As Eliot observed, Tennyson was "the most instinctive rebel against the society in which he was the most perfect conformist."

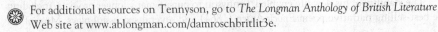 For additional resources on Tennyson, go to *The Longman Anthology of British Literature* Web site at www.ablongman.com/damroschbritlit3e.

The Kraken[1]

Below the thunders of the upper deep;
Far, far beneath in the abysmal sea,
His ancient, dreamless, uninvaded sleep
The Kraken sleepeth: faintest sunlights flee
5   About his shadowy sides: above him swell
Huge sponges of millennial growth and height;
And far away into the sickly light,
From many a wondrous grot° and secret cell   grotto, cave
Unnumber'd and enormous polypi°   octopuses
10   Winnow with giant arms the slumbering green.
There hath he lain for ages and will lie
Battening upon huge seaworms in his sleep,
Until the latter fire[2] shall heat the deep;
Then once by man and angels to be seen,
15   In roaring he shall rise and on the surface die.

1830

Mariana

"Mariana in the moated grange."[1]

Measure for Measure

With blackest moss the flower-plots
    Were thickly crusted, one and all:
The rusted nails fell from the knots
    That held the pear to the gable-wall.
5   The broken sheds look'd sad and strange:
        Unlifted was the clinking latch;
        Weeded and worn the ancient thatch
    Upon the lonely moated grange.
        She only said, "My life is dreary,
10   He cometh not," she said;
        She said, "I am aweary, aweary,
            I would that I were dead!"

    Her tears fell with the dews at even;
        Her tears fell ere the dews were dried;
15   She could not look on the sweet heaven.
        Either at morn or eventide.
    After the flitting of the bats,
        When thickest dark did trance° the sky,   traverse
        She drew her casement-curtain by,
20   And glanced athwart the glooming flats.

1. Giant mythical sea monster.
2. The fire of Judgment Day, which will consume the world.
1. The *moated grange* was no particular grange, but one which rose to the music of Shakespeare's words: "There, at the moated grange, resides this dejected Mariana" (*Measure for Measure* Act 3. Sc. 1) [Tennyson's note]. In Shakespeare's play, Angelo refuses to marry Mariana after her brother and her dowry are lost in a shipwreck. See Sir John Everett Millais's painting *Mariana* (Color Plate 11).

She only said, "The night is dreary,
   He cometh not," she said;
She said, "I am aweary, aweary,
   I would that I were dead!"

25   Upon the middle of the night,
   Waking she heard the night-fowl crow:
The cock sung out an hour ere light:
   From the dark fen the oxen's low
Came to her: without hope of change,
30   In sleep she seem'd to walk forlorn,
   Till cold winds woke the gray-eyed morn
About the lonely moated grange.
   She only said, "The day is dreary,
     He cometh not," she said;
35   She said, "I am aweary, aweary,
     I would that I were dead!"

About a stone-cast from the wall
   A sluice with blacken'd waters slept,
And o'er it many, round and small,
40   The cluster'd marish-mosses[2] crept.
Hard by a poplar shook alway,
   All silver-green with gnarled bark:
   For leagues no other tree did mark
The level waste, the rounding gray.
45   She only said, "My life is dreary,
     He cometh not," she said;
   She said, "I am aweary, aweary,
     I would that I were dead!"

And ever when the moon was low,
50   And the shrill winds were up and away,
In the white curtain, to and fro,
   She saw the gusty shadow sway.
But when the moon was very low,
   And wild winds bound within their cell,[3]
55   The shadow of the poplar fell
Upon her bed, across her brow.
   She only said, "The night is dreary,
     He cometh not," she said;
   She said, "I am aweary, aweary,
60   I would that I were dead!"

All day within the dreamy house,
   The doors upon their hinges creak'd;
The blue fly sung in the pane; the mouse

---

2. The little marsh-moss lumps that float on the surface of water [Tennyson's note].

3. The cave of Aeolus, god of the winds.

Behind the mouldering wainscot shriek'd,
65 Or from the crevice peer'd about.
Old faces glimmer'd thro' the doors,
Old footsteps trod the upper floors,
Old voices called her from without.
She only said, "My life is dreary,
70   He cometh not," she said;
She said, "I am aweary, aweary,
I would that I were dead!"

The sparrow's chirrup on the roof,
The slow clock ticking, and the sound
75 Which to the wooing wind aloof
The poplar made, did all confound
Her sense; but most she loathed the hour
When the thick-moted sunbeam lay
Athwart the chambers, and the day
80 Was sloping toward his western bower.
Then, said she, "I am very dreary,
He will not come," she said;
She wept, "I am aweary, aweary,
Oh God, that I were dead!"

1830

The Lady of Shalott[1]
Part 1

On either side the river lie
Long fields of barley and of rye,
That clothe the wold° and meet the sky;   *rolling uplands*
And thro' the field the road runs by
5   To many-tower'd Camelot;
And up and down the people go,
Gazing where the lilies blow°   *bloom*
Round an island there below,
The island of Shalott.

10 Willows whiten, aspens quiver,
Little breezes dusk and shiver
Thro' the wave that runs for ever
By the island in the river
Flowing down to Camelot.
15 Four gray walls, and four gray towers,
Overlook a space of flowers,
And the silent isle imbowers
The Lady of Shalott.

---

1. The Lady of Shalott is evidently the Elaine of the *Morte d'Arthur*, but I do not think that I had ever heard of the latter when I wrote the former [Tennyson's note]. In Malory, Elaine dies of grief for love of Lancelot, but the curse, the weaving, and the mirror are all Tennyson's inventions.

William Holman Hunt, *The Lady of Shalott,* from the Moxon edition of Tennyson's poems, 1857. This edition was a high point in Victorian book illustration, including drawings by Rossetti and Millais as well as Hunt. Tennyson, however, complained about this illustration because it depicts the lady entangled in the threads of her tapestry, making her unable to leave the loom, as she does in his poem. Hunt responded: "I had only half a page on which to convey the impression of weird fate, whereas you use about fifteen pages to give expression to the complete idea." See also *The Lady of Shalott* by John Williams Waterhouse (Color Plate 19).

> By the margin, willow-veil'd,
> Slide the heavy barges trail'd
> By slow horses; and unhail'd
> The shallop° flitteth silken-sail'd   *small boat*
>   Skimming down to Camelot:
> But who hath seen her wave her hand?
> Or at the casement seen her stand?
> Or is she known in all the land,
>   The Lady of Shalott?
>
> Only reapers, reaping early
> In among the bearded barley,
> Hear a song that echoes cheerly
> From the river winding clearly,
>   Down to tower'd Camelot:
> And by the moon the reaper weary,
> Piling sheaves in uplands airy,
> Listening, whispers "Tis the fairy
>   Lady of Shalott.'"

Part 2

> There she weaves by night and day
> A magic web with colours gay.
> She has heard a whisper say,
> A curse is on her if she stay
>   To look down to Camelot.

Line numbers: 20, 25, 30, 35, 40

She knows not what the curse may be,
And so she weaveth steadily,
And little other care hath she,
45   The Lady of Shalott.

And moving thro' a mirror clear[2]
That hangs before her all the year,
Shadows of the world appear.
There she sees the highway near
50   Winding down to Camelot:
There the river eddy whirls,
And there the surly village-churls,°   peasants
And the red cloaks of market girls,
            Pass onward from Shalott.

55   Sometimes a troop of damsels glad,
An abbot on an ambling pad,°   horse
Sometimes a curly shepherd-lad,
Or long-hair'd page in crimson clad,
            Goes by to tower'd Camelot;
60   And sometimes thro' the mirror blue
The knights come riding two and two:
She hath no loyal knight and true,
            The Lady of Shalott.

But in her web she still delights
65   To weave the mirror's magic sights,
For often thro' the silent nights
A funeral, with plumes and lights
            And music, went to Camelot:
Or when the moon was overhead,
70   Came two young lovers lately wed;
"I am half sick of shadows," said
            The Lady of Shalott.

Part 3

A bow-shot from her bower-eaves,
He rode between the barley-sheaves,
75   The sun came dazzling thro' the leaves,
And flamed upon the brazen greaves°   leg armor
            Of bold Sir Lancelot.[3]
A red-cross knight for ever kneel'd
To a lady in his shield,[4]
80   That sparkled on the yellow field,
            Beside remote Shalott.

2. Working from the back of their tapestries, weavers placed mirrors on the other side to see the effect of their work.
3. The greatest of King Arthur's knights, Lancelot was in love with Queen Guinevere.
4. Lancelot's shield depicts the Redcrosse Knight—a character in Spenser's *Faerie Queene* who champions holiness—kneeling in homage to his lady.

The gemmy bridle glitter'd free,
Like to some branch of stars we see
Hung in the golden Galaxy.
85   The bridle bells rang merrily
   As he rode down to Camelot:
And from his blazon'd baldric° slung   *ornamented belt*
A mighty silver bugle hung,
And as he rode his armour rung,
90   Beside remote Shalott.

All in the blue unclouded weather
Thick-jewell'd shone the saddle-leather,
The helmet and the helmet-feather
Burn'd like one burning flame together,
95   As he rode down to Camelot.
As often thro' the purple night,
Below the starry clusters bright,
Some bearded meteor, trailing light,
   Moves over still Shalott.

100   His broad clear brow in sunlight glow'd;
On burnish'd hooves his war-horse trode;
From underneath his helmet flow'd
His coal-black curls as on he rode,
   As he rode down to Camelot.
105   From the bank and from the river
He flash'd into the crystal mirror,
"Tirra lirra," by the river
   Sang Sir Lancelot.

She left the web, she left the loom,
110   She made three paces thro' the room,
She saw the water-lily bloom,
She saw the helmet and the plume,
   She look'd down to Camelot.
Out flew the web and floated wide;
115   The mirror crack'd from side to side;
"The curse is come upon me," cried
   The Lady of Shalott.

Part 4

In the stormy east-wind straining,
The pale yellow woods were waning,
120   The broad stream in his banks complaining,
Heavily the low sky raining
   Over tower'd Camelot;
Down she came and found a boat
Beneath a willow left afloat,
125   And round about the prow she wrote
   The Lady of Shalott.

And down the river's dim expanse
Like some bold seër in a trance,
Seeing all his own mischance—
130   With a glassy countenance
        Did she look to Camelot.
And at the closing of the day
She loosed the chain, and down she lay;
The broad stream bore her far away,
135   The Lady of Shalott.

Lying, robed in snowy white
That loosely flew to left and right—
The leaves upon her falling light—
Thro' the noises of the night
140   She floated down to Camelot:
And as the boat-head wound along
The willowy hills and fields among,
They heard her singing her last song,
        The Lady of Shalott.

145   Heard a carol, mournful, holy,
Chanted loudly, chanted lowly,
Till her blood was frozen slowly,
And her eyes were darken'd wholly,
        Turn'd to tower'd Camelot.
150   For ere she reach'd upon the tide
The first house by the water-side,
Singing in her song she died,
        The Lady of Shalott.

Under tower and balcony,
155   By garden-wall and gallery,
A gleaming shape she floated by,
Dead-pale between the houses high,
        Silent into Camelot.
Out upon the wharfs they came;
160   Knight and burgher, lord and dame,
And round the prow they read her name,
        The Lady of Shalott.

Who is this? and what is here?
And in the lighted palace near
165   Died the sound of royal cheer;
And they cross'd themselves for fear,
        All the knights at Camelot:
But Lancelot mused a little space;
He said, "She has a lovely face;
170   God in his mercy lend her grace,
        The Lady of Shalott."

1832, 1842

The Lotos-Eaters[1]

"Courage!" he[2] said, and pointed toward the land,
"This mounting wave will roll us shoreward soon."
In the afternoon they came unto a land[3]
In which it seemed always afternoon.
5   All round the coast the languid air did swoon,
Breathing like one that hath a weary dream.
Full-faced above the valley stood the moon;
And like a downward smoke, the slender stream[4]
Along the cliff to fall and pause and fall did seem.

10   A land of streams! some, like a downward smoke,
Slow-dropping veils of thinnest lawn,[5] did go;
And some thro' wavering lights and shadows broke,
Rolling a slumbrous sheet of foam below.
They saw the gleaming river seaward flow
15   From the inner land: far off, three mountain-tops,
Three silent pinnacles of aged snow,
Stood sunset-flush'd: and, dew'd with showery drops,
Up-clomb the shadowy pine above the woven copse.

The charmèd sunset linger'd low adown
20   In the red West: thro' mountain clefts the dale
Was seen far inland, and the yellow down°   *upland plain*
Border'd with palm, and many a winding vale
And meadow, set with slender galingale;°   *an aromatic herb*
A land where all things always seem'd the same!
25   And round about the keel with faces pale,
Dark faces pale against that rosy flame,
The mild-eyed melancholy Lotos-eaters came.

Branches they bore of that enchanted stem,
Laden with flower and fruit, whereof they gave
30   To each, but whoso did receive of them,
And taste, to him the gushing of the wave
Far far away did seem to mourn and rave
On alien shores; and if his fellow spake,
His voice was thin, as voices from the grave;
35   And deep-asleep he seem'd, yet all awake,
And music in his ears his beating heart did make.

They sat them down upon the yellow sand,
Between the sun and moon upon the shore;

---

1. In Homer's *Odyssey*, Book 9, Odysseus (Ulysses) and his men, returning home from the Trojan War, are tempted to stay forever in the land of the Lotus-eaters. (Tennyson used the Greek spelling, "lotos," from "lotophagi," or lotos-eaters.) Anyone who ate the sweet fruit of the lotus would lose all desire to return home.
2. Odysseus.

3. "The strand" was, I think, my first reading, but the no rhyme of "land" and "land" was lazier [Tennyson's note].
4. Taken from the waterfall at Gavarnie, in the Pyrenees, when I was 20 or 21 [Tennyson's note].
5. Sheer linen fabric, used in theaters to suggest a waterfall.

And sweet it was to dream of Fatherland,
40   Of child, and wife, and slave; but evermore
Most weary seem'd the sea, weary the oar,
Weary the wandering fields of barren foam.
Then some one said, "We will return no more;"
And all at once they sang, "Our island home[6]
45   Is far beyond the wave; we will no longer roam."

Choric Song[7]

1

There is sweet music here that softer falls
Than petals from blown roses on the grass,
Or night-dews on still waters between walls
Of shadowy granite, in a gleaming pass;
50   Music that gentlier on the spirit lies,
Than tir'd eyelids upon tir'd eyes;[8]
Music that brings sweet sleep down from the blissful skies.
Here are cool mosses deep,
And thro' the moss the ivies creep,
55   And in the stream the long-leaved flowers weep,
And from the craggy ledge the poppy hangs in sleep.

2

Why are we weigh'd upon with heaviness,
And utterly consumed with sharp distress,
While all things else have rest from weariness?
60   All things have rest: why should we toil alone,
We only toil, who are the first of things,
And make perpetual moan,
Still from one sorrow to another thrown:
Nor ever fold our wings,
65   And cease from wanderings,
Nor steep our brows in slumber's holy balm;
Nor harken what the inner spirit sings,
"There is no joy but calm!"
Why should we only toil, the roof and crown of things?

3

70   Lo! in the middle of the wood,
The folded leaf is woo'd from out the bud
With winds upon the branch, and there
Grows green and broad, and takes no care,
Sun-steep'd at noon, and in the moon
75   Nightly dew-fed; and turning yellow

---

6. Ithaca, off the west coast of Greece.
7. What follows is sung by Odysseus's men.
8. I printed, contrary to my custom, "tir'd," not "tired,"
for fear that readers might pronounce the word "tirèd"
[Tennyson's note]. Tennyson wished to make "the word
neither monosyllable or disyllabic, but a dreamy child of
the two."

Falls, and floats adown the air.
Lo! sweeten'd with the summer light,
The full-juiced apple, waxing over-mellow,
Drops in a silent autumn night.
80   All its allotted length of days,
The flower ripens in its place,
Ripens and fades, and falls, and hath no toil,
Fast-rooted in the fruitful soil.

4

Hateful is the dark-blue sky,
85   Vaulted o'er the dark-blue sea.
Death is the end of life; ah, why
Should life all labour be?
Let us alone. Time driveth onward fast,
And in a little while our lips are dumb.
90   Let us alone. What is it that will last?
All things are taken from us, and become
Portions and parcels of the dreadful Past.
Let us alone. What pleasure can we have
To war with evil? Is there any peace
95   In ever climbing up the climbing wave?
All things have rest, and ripen toward the grave
In silence; ripen, fall and cease:
Give us long rest or death, dark death, or dreamful ease.

5

How sweet it were, hearing the downward stream,
100   With half-shut eyes ever to seem
Falling asleep in a half-dream!
To dream and dream, like yonder amber light,
Which will not leave the myrrh-bush on the height;
To hear each other's whisper'd speech;
105   Eating the Lotos day by day,
To watch the crisping ripples on the beach,
And tender curving lines of creamy spray;
To lend our hearts and spirits wholly
To the influence of mild-minded melancholy;
110   To muse and brood and live again in memory,
With those old faces of our infancy
Heap'd over with a mound of grass,
Two handfuls of white dust, shut in an urn of brass!

6

Dear is the memory of our wedded lives,
115   And dear the last embraces of our wives
And their warm tears: but all hath suffer'd change:
For surely now our household hearths are cold:
Our sons inherit us: our looks are strange:
And we should come like ghosts to trouble joy.

120   Or else the island princes[9] over-bold
       Have eat our substance, and the minstrel sings
       Before them of the ten years' war in Troy,[1]
       And our great deeds, as half-forgotten things.
       Is there confusion in the little isle?
125   Let what is broken so remain.
       The Gods are hard to reconcile:
       'Tis hard to settle order once again.
       There *is* confusion worse than death,
       Trouble on trouble, pain on pain,
130   Long labour unto aged breath,
       Sore task to hearts worn out by many wars
       And eyes grown dim with gazing on the pilot-stars.

                              7
       But, propt on beds of amaranth and moly,[2]
       How sweet (while warm airs lull us, blowing lowly)
135   With half-dropt eyelid still,
       Beneath a heaven dark and holy,
       To watch the long bright river drawing slowly
       His waters from the purple hill—
       To hear the dewy echoes calling
140   From cave to cave thro' the thick-twined vine—
       To watch the emerald-colour'd water falling
       Thro' many a wov'n acanthus-wreath[3] divine!
       Only to hear and see the far-off sparkling brine,
       Only to hear were sweet, stretch'd out beneath the pine.

                              8
145   The Lotos blooms below the barren peak:
       The Lotos blows by every winding creek:
       All day the wind breathes low with mellower tone:
       Thro' every hollow cave and alley lone
       Round and round the spicy downs the yellow Lotos-dust is blown.
150   We have had enough of action, and of motion we,
       Roll'd to starboard, roll'd to larboard, when the surge was seething free,
       Where the wallowing monster spouted his foam-fountains in the sea.
       Let us swear an oath, and keep it with an equal mind,
       In the hollow Lotos-land to live and lie reclined
155   On the hills like Gods together, careless of mankind.
       For they lie beside their nectar, and the bolts[4] are hurl'd
       Far below them in the valleys, and the clouds are lightly curl'd
       Round their golden houses, girdled with the gleaming world:

9. The suitors of Penelope, Odysseus's wife and presumed widow.
1. The Trojan War, from which Odysseus and his men are returning.
2. *Amaranth*, the immortal flower of legend; *moly*, the sacred herb of mystical power, used as a charm by Odysseus against Circe [Tennyson's note].
3. The plant seen in the capitals of Corinthian pillars [Tennyson's note].
4. Nectar is the food of the gods, and thunderbolts their weapons.

Where they smile in secret, looking over wasted lands,
160   Blight and famine, plague and earthquake, roaring deeps and fiery sands,
Clanging fights, and flaming towns, and sinking ships, and praying hands.
But they smile, they find a music centred in a doleful song
Steaming up, a lamentation and an ancient tale of wrong,
Like a tale of little meaning tho' the words are strong;
165   Chanted from an ill-used race of men that cleave the soil,
Sow the seed, and reap the harvest with enduring toil,
Storing yearly little dues of wheat, and wine and oil;
Till they perish and they suffer—some, 'tis whisper'd—down in hell
Suffer endless anguish, others in Elysian[5] valleys dwell,
170   Resting weary limbs at last on beds of asphodel.[6]
Surely, surely, slumber is more sweet than toil, the shore
Than labour in the deep mid-ocean, wind and wave and oar;
Oh rest ye, brother mariners, we will not wander more.

                                                    1832, 1842

Ulysses[1]

It little profits that an idle king,
By this still hearth, among these barren crags,
Match'd with an aged wife, I mete and dole
Unequal laws unto a savage race,
5   That hoard, and sleep, and feed, and know not me.

I cannot rest from travel: I will drink
Life to the lees: all times I have enjoy'd
Greatly, have suffer'd greatly, both with those
That loved me, and alone; on shore, and when
10   Thro' scudding drifts the rainy Hyades[2]
Vext the dim sea: I am become a name;
For always roaming with a hungry heart
Much have I seen and known; cities of men
And manners, climates, councils, governments,
15   Myself not least, but honour'd of them all;
And drunk delight of battle with my peers,
Far on the ringing plains of windy Troy.
I am a part of all that I have met;
Yet all experience is an arch wherethro'
20   Gleams that untravell'd world, whose margin fades

5. Paradisical; Elysium was the part of the underworld where the blessed dwelled after death.
6. Flowering plant of the lily family, said to grow in the Elysian fields.
1. The poem was written soon after Arthur Hallam's death, and it gives the feeling about the need of going further and braving the struggle of life perhaps more simply than anything in In Memoriam [Tennyson's note]. In Homer's Odyssey, Ulysses returns home to Ithaca, after ten years of wandering following the fall of Troy, and slays the suitors who have been harassing his wife Pene-

lope. "My father," wrote Tennyson's son, "takes up the story of further wanderings at the end of the Odyssey. Ulysses has lived in Ithaca for a long while before the craving for fresh travel seizes him. The comrades he addresses are of the same heroic mould as his old comrades." Dante also has Ulysses set off on another voyage, this time westward through the Strait of Gibraltar (Inferno 26).
2. The Hyades were a constellation of seven stars whose rising was believed to bring rain.

For ever and for ever when I move.
How dull it is to pause, to make an end,
To rust unburnish'd, not to shine in use!
As tho' to breathe were life. Life piled on life
25 Were all too little, and of one to me
Little remains: but every hour is saved
From that eternal silence, something more,
A bringer of new things; and vile it were
For some three suns to store and hoard myself,
30 And this gray spirit yearning in desire
To follow knowledge like a sinking star,
Beyond the utmost bound of human thought.

This is my son, mine own Telemachus,
To whom I leave the sceptre and the isle—
35 Well-loved of me, discerning to fulfil
This labour, by slow prudence to make mild
A rugged people, and thro' soft degrees
Subdue them to the useful and the good.
Most blameless is he, centred in the sphere
40 Of common duties, decent not to fail
In offices of tenderness, and pay
Meet adoration to my household gods,
When I am gone. He works his work, I mine.

There lies the port; the vessel puffs her sail:
45 There gloom the dark broad seas. My mariners,
Souls that have toil'd, and wrought, and thought with me—
That ever with a frolic welcome took
The thunder and the sunshine, and opposed
Free hearts, free foreheads—you and I are old;
50 Old age hath yet his honour and his toil;
Death closes all: but something ere the end,
Some work of noble note, may yet be done,
Not unbecoming men that strove with Gods.
The lights begin to twinkle from the rocks:
55 The long day wanes: the slow moon climbs: the deep
Moans round with many voices. Come, my friends,
'Tis not too late to seek a newer world.
Push off, and sitting well in order smite
The sounding furrows; for my purpose holds
60 To sail beyond the sunset, and the baths
Of all the western stars,[3] until I die.
It may be that the gulfs will wash us down:
It may be we shall touch the Happy Isles,[4]

3. The Greeks believed that the flat earth was encircled by an ocean into which the stars dipped at times.
4. The Islands of the Blessed were a land of perpetual summer thought to lie in the western ocean beyond the Pillars of Hercules (the Straits of Gibraltar). Great heroes—such as Achilles, the Greek warrior who killed the Trojan prince, Hector—were sent by the gods to live there as immortals.

And see the great Achilles, whom we knew.
65 Tho' much is taken, much abides; and tho'
We are not now that strength which in old days
Moved earth and heaven; that which we are, we are;
One equal temper of heroic hearts,
Made weak by time and fate, but strong in will
70 To strive, to seek, to find, and not to yield.

1833   1842

Tithonus[1]

The woods decay, the woods decay and fall,
The vapours weep their burthen to the ground,
Man comes and tills the field and lies beneath,
And after many a summer dies the swan.[2]
5   Me only cruel immortality
Consumes: I wither slowly in thine arms,[3]
Here at the quiet limit of the world,
A white-hair'd shadow roaming like a dream
The ever-silent spaces of the East,
10 Far-folded mists, and gleaming halls of morn.

        Alas! for this gray shadow, once a man—
So glorious in his beauty and thy choice,
Who madest him thy chosen, that he seem'd
To his great heart none other than a God!
15 I ask'd thee, "Give me immortality."
Then didst thou grant mine asking with a smile,
Like wealthy men who care not how they give.
But thy strong Hours indignant work'd their wills,
And beat me down and marr'd and wasted me,
20 And tho' they could not end me, left me maim'd
To dwell in presence of immortal youth,
Immortal age beside immortal youth,
And all I was, in ashes. Can thy love,
Thy beauty, make amends, tho' even now,
25 Close over us, the silver star,[4] thy guide,
Shines in those tremulous eyes that fill with tears
To hear me? Let me go: take back thy gift:
Why should a man desire in any way
To vary from the kindly race of men,
30 Or pass beyond the goal of ordinance[5]
Where all should pause, as is most meet for all?

1. Beloved by Aurora, who gave him eternal life but not eternal youth. He grew old and infirm, and as he could not die, according to the legend, was turned into a grasshopper [Tennyson's note]. Aurora was the goddess of the dawn.
2. Swans can live as many as 50 years.
3. Tithonus ages in Aurora's arms.
4. Venus, the morning star, is Aurora's guide because it shines just before the dawn.
5. Appointed limit [Tennyson's note]; i.e., to exceed the ordained length of ordinary human life.

A soft air fans the cloud apart; there comes
A glimpse of that dark world where I was born.
Once more the old mysterious glimmer steals

35 From thy pure brows, and from thy shoulders pure,
And bosom beating with a heart renew'd.
Thy cheek begins to redden thro' the gloom,
Thy sweet eyes brighten slowly close to mine,
Ere yet they blind the stars, and the wild team[6]

40 Which love thee, yearning for thy yoke, arise,
And shake the darkness from their loosen'd manes,
And beat the twilight into flakes of fire.

Lo! ever thus thou growest beautiful
In silence, then before thine answer given

45 Departest, and thy tears are on my cheek.

Why wilt thou ever scare me with thy tears,
And make me tremble lest a saying learnt,
In days far-off, on that dark earth, be true?
"The Gods themselves cannot recall their gifts."

50 Ay me! ay me! with what another heart
In days far-off, and with what other eyes
I used to watch—if I be he that watch'd—
The lucid outline forming round thee; saw
The dim curls kindle into sunny rings;

55 Changed with thy mystic change, and felt my blood
Glow with the glow that slowly crimson'd all
Thy presence and thy portals, while I lay,
Mouth, forehead, eyelids, growing dewy-warm
With kisses balmier than half-opening buds

60 Of April, and could hear the lips that kiss'd
Whispering I knew not what of wild and sweet,
Like that strange song I heard Apollo sing,
While Ilion like a mist rose into towers.[7]

Yet hold me not for ever in thine East:

65 How can my nature longer mix with thine?
Coldly thy rosy shadows bathe me, cold
Are all thy lights, and cold my wrinkled feet
Upon thy glimmering thresholds, when the steam
Floats up from those dim fields about the homes

70 Of happy men that have the power to die,
And grassy barrows of the happier dead.
Release me, and restore me to the ground;
Thou seëst all things, thou wilt see my grave:
Thou wilt renew thy beauty morn by morn;

6. The horses of dawn, who pull Aurora's chariot into the sky each morning.

7. Apollo built the walls of Ilion (Troy) with the music of his lyre.

75   I earth in earth forget these empty courts,
        And thee returning on thy silver wheels.
1833, 1859   1860

Break, Break, Break[1]

Break, break, break,
    On thy cold gray stones, O Sea!
And I would that my tongue could utter
    The thoughts that arise in me.

5   O well for the fisherman's boy,
        That he shouts with his sister at play!
    O well for the sailor lad,
        That he sings in his boat on the bay!

    And the stately ships go on
10   To their haven under the hill;
    But O for the touch of a vanish'd hand,
        And the sound of a voice that is still!

    Break, break, break
        At the foot of thy crags, O Sea!
15 But the tender grace of a day that is dead
        Will never come back to me.
1834   1842

The Epic [Morte d'Arthur][1]

At Francis Allen's on the Christmas-eve,—
The game of forfeits[2] done—the girls all kiss'd
Beneath the sacred bush° and past away—   *mistletoe*
The parson Holmes, the poet Everard Hall,
5   The host, and I sat round the wassail-bowl,°   *punch bowl*
Then half-way ebb'd: and there we held a talk,
How all the old honour had from Christmas gone,
Or gone, or dwindled down to some odd games
In some odd nooks like this; till I, tired out
10 With cutting eights that day upon the pond,
Where, three times slipping from the outer edge,
I bump'd the ice into three several stars,
Fell in a doze; and half-awake I heard
The parson taking wide and wider sweeps,
15 Now harping on the church-commissioners,[3]

1. Inspired by the death of the poet's friend, Arthur Hallam. Cf. *In Memoriam*, page 1261.
1. One of Tennyson's lifelong projects was an epic poem about King Arthur, which ultimately became *Idylls of the King*. The last poem in the sequence, describing the death of Arthur, was actually written first: it was begun in 1833, when Arthur Hallam died, and was called *Morte d'Arthur*. Tennyson framed the poem with *The Epic*, a description of contemporary (i.e., 19th century) Christmas Eve festivities, during which the poet—here called Everard Hall—was encouraged to read *Morte d'Arthur* aloud.
2. A party game where players have to forfeit an item, then redeem it by performing a silly task.
3. In 1835 the government set up a system of commissioners to oversee the finances of the Anglican Church.

Now hawking at Geology and schism;[4]
Until I woke, and found him settled down
Upon the general decay of faith
Right thro' the world, "at home was little left,
20   And none abroad: there was no anchor, none,
To hold by." Francis, laughing, clapt his hand
On Everard's shoulder, with "I hold by him."
"And I," quoth Everard, "by the wassail-bowl."
"Why yes," I said, "we knew your gift that way
25   At college: but another which you had,
I mean of verse (for so we held it then),
What came of that?" "You know," said Frank, "he burnt
His epic, his King Arthur, some twelve books"—
And then to me demanding why? "Oh, sir,
30   He thought that nothing new was said, or else
Something so said 'twas nothing—that a truth
Looks freshest in the fashion of the day;
God knows: he has a mint of reasons: ask.
It pleased *me* well enough." "Nay, nay," said Hall,
35   "Why take the style of those heroic times?
For nature brings not back the Mastodon,
Nor we those times; and why should any man
Remodel models? these twelve books of mine
Were faint Homeric echoes,[5] nothing-worth,
40   Mere chaff and draff, much better burnt." "But I,"
Said Francis, "pick'd the eleventh from this hearth
And have it: keep a thing, its use will come.
I hoard it as a sugar-plum for Holmes."
He laugh'd, and I, tho' sleepy, like a horse
45   That hears the corn-bin open, prick'd my ears;
For I remember'd Everard's college fame
When we were Freshmen: then at my request
He brought it; and the poet little urged,
But with some prelude of disparagement,
50   Read, mouthing out his hollow oes and aes,
Deep-chested music, and to this result.[6]

* * *

Here ended Hall, and our last light, that long
325   Had wink'd and threaten'd darkness, flared and fell:
At which the Parson, sent to sleep with sound,
And waked with silence, grunted "Good!" but we
Sat rapt: it was the tone with which he read—
Perhaps some modern touches here and there

---

4. A reference to current scientific and religious controversies.
5. I.e., Hall claims his poems merely echoed the great epics of Homer. He may have been fishing for a compliment: when the poet Walter Savage Landor read Tennyson's *Morte d'Arthur* in manuscript, he declared, "it is more Homeric than any poem of our time, and rivals some of the noblest parts of the Odyssey."
6. At this point Hall reads aloud *Morte d'Arthur*. (See lines 170–440 of *The Passing of Arthur*, pages 1320–26.)

330   Redeem'd it from the charge of nothingness—
       Or else we loved the man, and prized his work;
       I know not: but we sitting, as I said,
       The cock crew loud; as at that time of year
       The lusty bird takes every hour for dawn:
335   Then Francis, muttering, like a man ill-used,
       "There now—that's nothing!" drew a little back,
       And drove his heel into the smoulder'd log,
       That sent a blast of sparkles up the flue:
       And so to bed; where yet in sleep I seem'd
340   To sail with Arthur under looming shores,
       Point after point; till on to dawn, when dreams
       Begin to feel the truth and stir of day,
       To me, methought, who waited with a crowd,
       There came a bark that, blowing forward, bore
345   King Arthur, like a modern gentleman
       Of stateliest port;° and all the people cried,   bearing
       "Arthur is come again: he cannot die."[7]
       Then those that stood upon the hills behind
       Repeated—"Come again, and thrice as fair;"
350   And, further inland, voices echo'd—"Come
       With all good things, and war shall be no more."
       At this a hundred bells began to peal,
       That with the sound I woke, and heard indeed
       The clear church-bells ring in the Christmas-morn.

1833–1838   1842

The Eagle: A Fragment

He clasps the crag with crooked hands;
Close to the sun in lonely lands,
Ring'd with the azure world, he stands.

The wrinkled sea beneath him crawls;
He watches from his mountain walls.
And like a thunderbolt he falls.

1833   1851

Locksley Hall[1]

Comrades, leave me here a little, while as yet 'tis early morn:
Leave me here, and when you want me, sound upon the bugle-horn.

'Tis the place, and all around it, as of old, the curlews call,
Dreary gleams about the moorland flying over Locksley Hall;

7. There is a legend that King Arthur will return once
more to lead his people.
1. An imaginary place and an imaginary hero [Tennyson's
note]. Despite this claim, critics have wondered whether
the poem was inspired by Tennyson's thwarted courtship of
Rosa Baring, who rejected him for a wealthier man, or by
the experience of his brother Frederick, whose courtship of
their cousin Julia was equally fruitless.

5   Locksley Hall, that in the distance overlooks the sandy tracts,
     And the hollow ocean-ridges roaring into cataracts.

     Many a night from yonder ivied casement, ere I went to rest,
     Did I look on great Orion sloping slowly to the West.

     Many a night I saw the Pleiads,[2] rising thro' the mellow shade,
10   Glitter like a swarm of fire-flies tangled in a silver braid.

     Here about the beach I wander'd, nourishing a youth sublime
     With the fairy tales of science, and the long result of Time;

     When the centuries behind me like a fruitful land reposed;
     When I clung to all the present for the promise that it closed:°   *enclosed*

15   When I dipt into the future far as human eye could see;
     Saw the Vision of the world, and all the wonder that would be.——

     In the Spring a fuller crimson comes upon the robin's breast;
     In the Spring the wanton lapwing gets himself another crest;

     In the Spring a livelier iris changes on the burnish'd dove;[3]
20   In the Spring a young man's fancy lightly turns to thoughts of love.

     Then her cheek was pale and thinner than should be for one so young,
     And her eyes on all my motions with a mute observance hung.

     And I said, "My cousin Amy, speak, and speak the truth to me,
     Trust me, cousin, all the current of my being sets to thee."

25   On her pallid cheek and forehead came a colour and a light,
     As I have seen the rosy red flushing in the northern night.

     And she turn'd—her bosom shaken with a sudden storm of sighs—
     All the spirit deeply dawning in the dark of hazel eyes—

     Saying, "I have hid my feelings, fearing they should do me wrong;"
30   Saying, "Dost thou love me, cousin?" weeping, "I have loved thee long."

     Love took up the glass of Time, and turn'd it in his glowing hands;
     Every moment, lightly shaken, ran itself in golden sands.

     Love took up the harp of Life, and smote on all the chords with might;
     Smote the chord of Self, that, trembling, pass'd in music out of sight.

35   Many a morning on the moorland did we hear the copses ring,
     And her whisper throng'd my pulses with the fulness of the Spring.

     Many an evening by the waters did we watch the stately ships,
     And our spirits rush'd together at the touching of the lips.

     O my cousin, shallow-hearted! O my Amy, mine no more!
40   O the dreary, dreary moorland! O the barren, barren shore!

2. A constellation, as is Orion (previous line).   season, as does the robin's and the lapwing's in the
3. The plumage of the dove brightens during mating   preceding lines.

Falser than all fancy fathoms, falser than all songs have sung,
Puppet to a father's threat, and servile to a shrewish tongue!

Is it well to wish thee happy?—having known me—to decline
On a range of lower feelings and a narrower heart than mine!

45   Yet it shall be: thou shalt lower to his level day by day,
What is fine within thee growing coarse to sympathise with clay.

As the husband is, the wife is: thou art mated with a clown,°   boor
And the grossness of his nature will have weight to drag thee down.

He will hold thee, when his passion shall have spent its novel force,
50   Something better than his dog, a little dearer than his horse.

What is this? his eyes are heavy: think not they are glazed with wine.
Go to him: it is thy duty: kiss him: take his hand in thine.

It may be my lord is weary, that his brain is over-wrought:
Soothe him with thy finer fancies, touch him with thy lighter thought.

55   He will answer to the purpose, easy things to understand—
Better thou wert dead before me, tho' I slew thee with my hand!

Better thou and I were lying, hidden from the heart's disgrace,
Roll'd in one another's arms, and silent in a last embrace.

Cursed be the social wants that sin against the strength of youth!
60   Cursed be the social lies that warp us from the living truth!

Cursed be the sickly forms that err from honest Nature's rule!
Cursed be the gold that gilds the straiten'd° forehead of the fool!   narrowed

Well—'tis well that I should bluster!—Hadst thou less unworthy proved—
Would to God—for I had loved thee more than ever wife was loved.

65   Am I mad, that I should cherish that which bears but bitter fruit?
I will pluck it from my bosom, tho' my heart be at the root.

Never, tho' my mortal summers to such length of years should come
As the many-winter'd crow⁴ that leads the clanging rookery home.

Where is comfort? in division of the records of the mind?
70   Can I part her from herself, and love her, as I knew her, kind?

I remember one that perish'd: sweetly did she speak and move:
Such a one do I remember, whom to look at was to love.

Can I think of her as dead, and love her for the love she bore?
No—she never loved me truly: love is love for evermore.

75   Comfort? comfort scorn'd of devils! this is truth the poet sings,
That a sorrow's crown of sorrow is remembering happier things.⁵

4. Crows (or rooks) are known for their long lifespans.
5. Dante writes that there is no greater pain than to recall happy times in the midst of misery (*Inferno*
5.121–23).

Drug thy memories, lest thou learn it, lest thy heart be put to proof,
In the dead unhappy night, and when the rain is on the roof.

80   Like a dog, he hunts in dreams, and thou are staring at the wall,
Where the dying night-lamp flickers, and the shadows rise and fall.

Then a hand shall pass before thee, pointing to his drunken sleep,
To thy widow'd[6] marriage-pillows, to the tears that thou wilt weep.

Thou shalt hear the "Never, never," whisper'd by the phantom years,
And a song from out the distance in the ringing of thine ears;

85   And an eye shall vex thee, looking ancient kindness on thy pain.
Turn thee, turn thee on thy pillow: get thee to thy rest again.

Nay, but Nature brings thee solace; for a tender voice will cry.
'Tis a purer life than thine; a lip to drain thy trouble dry.

Baby lips will laugh me down: my latest rival brings thee rest.
90   Baby fingers, waxen touches, press me from the mother's breast.

O, the child too clothes the father with a dearness not his due.
Half is thine and half is his: it will be worthy of the two.

O, I see thee old and formal, fitted to thy petty part,
With a little hoard of maxims preaching down a daughter's heart.

95   "They were dangerous guides the feelings—she herself was not exempt—
Truly, she herself had suffer'd"—Perish in thy self-contempt!

Overlive it—lower yet—be happy! wherefore should I care?
I myself must mix with action, lest I wither by despair.

What is that which I should turn to, lighting upon days like these?
100 Every door is barr'd with gold, and opens but to golden keys.

Every gate is throng'd with suitors, all the markets overflow.
I have but an angry fancy: what is that which I should do?

I had been content to perish, falling on the foeman's ground,
When the ranks are roll'd in vapour, and the winds are laid with sound.[7]

105 But the jingling of the guinea helps the hurt that Honour feels,
And the nations do but murmur, snarling at each other's heels.

Can I but relive in sadness? I will turn that earlier page.
Hide me from my deep emotion, O thou wondrous Mother-Age![8]

Make me feel the wild pulsation that I felt before the strife,
110 When I heard my days before me, and the tumult of my life;

Yearning for the large excitement that the coming years would yield,
Eager-hearted as a boy when first he leaves his father's field,

6. Not literally, but in the sense that her marriage is no
true partnership.

7. I.e., the winds are stilled by the noise of firing artillery.
8. The time, early in life, when everything seems possible.

And at night along the dusky highway near and nearer drawn,
Sees in heaven the light of London flaring like a dreary dawn;

115 And his spirit leaps within him to be gone before him then,
Underneath the light he looks at, in among the throngs of men:

Men, my brothers, men the workers, ever reaping something new:
That which they have done but earnest of the things that they shall do:

For I dipt into the future, far as human eye could see,
120 Saw the Vision of the world, and all the wonder that would be;

Saw the heavens fill with commerce, argosies of magic sails,[9]
Pilots of the purple twilight, dropping down with costly bales;

Heard the heavens fill with shouting, and there rain'd a ghastly dew
From the nations' airy navies grappling in the central blue;

125 Far along the world-wide whisper of the south-wind rushing warm,
With the standards of the peoples plunging thro' the thunder-storm;

Till the war-drum throbb'd no longer, and the battle-flags were furl'd
In the Parliament of man, the Federation of the world.

There the common sense of most shall hold a fretful realm in awe,
130 And the kindly earth shall slumber, lapt in universal law.

So I triumph'd ere my passion sweeping thro' me left me dry,
Left me with the palsied heart, and left me with the jaundiced eye;

Eye, to which all order festers, all things here are out of joint:
Science moves, but slowly slowly, creeping on from point to point:

135 Slowly comes a hungry people, as a lion creeping nigher,
Glares at one that nods and winks behind a slowly-dying fire.

Yet I doubt not thro' the ages one increasing purpose runs,
And the thoughts of men are widen'd with the process of the suns.[1]

What is that to him that reaps not harvest of his youthful joys,
140 Tho' the deep heart of existence beat for ever like a boy's?

Knowledge comes, but wisdom lingers, and I linger on the shore,
And the individual withers, and the world is more and more.

Knowledge comes, but wisdom lingers, and he bears a laden breast,
Full of sad experience, moving toward the stillness of his rest.

145 Hark, my merry comrades call me, sounding on the bugle-horn,
They to whom my foolish passion were a target for their scorn:

Shall it not be scorn to me to harp on such a moulder'd string?
I am shamed thro' all my nature to have loved so slight a thing.

Weakness to be wroth with weakness! woman's pleasure, woman's pain—
150 Nature made them blinder motions bounded in a shallower brain:

9. Perhaps hot-air balloons, or other futuristic airships.   1. The passage of time.

Woman is the lesser man, and all thy passions, match'd with mine,
Are as moonlight unto sunlight, and as water unto wine—

Here at least, where nature sickens, nothing. Ah, for some retreat
Deep in yonder shining Orient, where my life began to beat;

155 Where in wild Mahratta-battle[2] fell my father evil-starr'd;—
I was left a trampled orphan, and a selfish uncle's ward.

Or to burst all links of habit—there to wander far away,
On from island unto island at the gateways of the day.

Larger constellations burning, mellow moons and happy skies,
160 Breadths of tropic shade and palms in cluster, knots of Paradise.

Never comes the trader, never floats an European flag,
Slides the bird o'er lustrous woodland, swings the trailer[3] from the crag;

Droops the heavy-blossom'd bower, hangs the heavy-fruited tree—
Summer isles of Eden lying in dark-purple spheres of sea.

165 There methinks would be enjoyment more than in this march of mind,
In the steamship, in the railway, in the thoughts that shake mankind.

There the passions cramp'd no longer shall have scope and breathing space;
I will take some savage woman, she shall rear my dusky race.

Iron jointed, supple-sinew'd, they shall dive, and they shall run,
170 Catch the wild goat by the hair, and hurl their lances in the sun;

Whistle back the parrot's call, and leap the rainbows of the brooks,
Not with blinded eyesight poring over miserable books—

Fool, again the dream, the fancy! but I *know* my words are wild,
But I count the gray barbarian lower than the Christian child.

175 I, to herd with narrow foreheads, vacant of our glorious gains,
Like a beast with lower pleasures, like a beast with lower pains!

Mated with a squalid savage—what to me were sun or clime?
I the heir of all the ages, in the foremost files of time—

I that rather held it better men should perish one by one,
180 Than that earth should stand at gaze like Joshua's moon in Ajalon![4]

Not in vain the distance beacons. Forward, forward let us range,
Let the great world spin for ever down the ringing grooves of change.[5]

Thro' the shadow of the globe we sweep into the younger day:
Better fifty years of Europe than a cycle of Cathay.[6]

---

2. Battles fought by a Hindu people, the Mahrattas, against the British in India, in 1803 and 1817.
3. Vine.
4. Joshua commanded the sun and the moon to stand still until the Israelites defeated their enemies in the valley of Ajalon (Joshua 10.12–13).

5. When I went by the first train from Liverpool to Manchester (1830) I thought that the wheels ran in a groove. It was a black night, and there was such a vast crowd round the train at the station that we could not see the wheels. Then I made this line [Tennyson's note].
6. China, regarded as backward by 19th-century Europeans.

185   Mother-Age (for mine I knew not) help me as when life begun:
       Rift the hills, and roll the waters, flash the lightnings, weigh the Sun.

       O, I see the crescent promise of my spirit hath not set.
       Ancient founts of inspiration well thro' all my fancy yet.

       Howsoever these things be, a long farewell to Locksley Hall!
190   Now for me the woods may wither, now for me the roof-tree fall.

       Comes a vapour from the margin, blackening over heath and holt,
       Cramming all the blast before it, in its breast a thunderbolt.

       Let it fall on Locksley Hall, with rain or hail, or fire or snow;
       For the mighty wind arises, roaring seaward, and I go.

1837–1838   1842

from THE PRINCESS[1]
Sweet and Low

Sweet and low, sweet and low,
    Wind of the western sea,
Low, low, breathe and blow,
    Wind of the western sea!
5   Over the rolling waters go,
    Come from the dying moon, and blow,
        Blow him again to me;
    While my little one, while my pretty one, sleeps.

    Sleep and rest, sleep and rest,
10   Father will come to thee soon;
    Rest, rest, on mother's breast,
        Father will come to thee soon;
    Father will come to his babe in the nest,
    Silver sails all out of the west
15   Under the silver moon:
    Sleep, my little one, sleep, my pretty one, sleep.

The Splendour Falls

The splendour falls on castle walls
    And snowy summits old in story:
The long light shakes across the lakes,
    And the wild cataract° leaps in glory.   waterfall
5   Blow, bugle, blow, set the wild echoes flying,
    Blow, bugle; answer, echoes, dying, dying, dying.

    O hark, O hear! how thin and clear,
        And thinner, clearer, farther going!

---

1. *The Princess* (1847) is a long narrative poem, set in a fairy-tale realm, about the effort to found a women's college. (The first British institution for the higher education of women, Queen's College, London, opened the next year.) The story is interspersed with brief "songs" or lyrics—some of them added later—whose musicality and depth of emotion soon won them admiration as independent works of art.

O sweet and far from cliff and scar°   *precipice*
10   The horns of Elfland faintly blowing!
Blow, let us hear the purple glens replying:
Blow, bugle; answer, echoes, dying, dying, dying.

O love, they die in yon rich sky,
      They faint on hill or field or river:
15 Our echoes roll from soul to soul,
      And grow for ever and for ever.
Blow, bugle, blow, set the wild echoes flying,
And answer, echoes, answer, dying, dying, dying.

Tears, Idle Tears[1]

Tears, idle tears, I know not what they mean,
Tears from the depth of some divine despair
Rise in the heart, and gather to the eyes,
In looking on the happy Autumn-fields,
5 And thinking of the days that are no more.

     Fresh as the first beam glittering on a sail,
That brings our friends up from the underworld,
Sad as the last which reddens over one
That sinks with all we love below the verge;
10 So sad, so fresh, the days that are no more.

     Ah, sad and strange as in dark summer dawns
The earliest pipe of half-awaken'd birds
To dying ears, when unto dying eyes
The casement° slowly grows a glimmering square;   *window*
15 So sad, so strange, the days that are no more.

     Dear as remember'd kisses after death,
And sweet as those by hopeless fancy feign'd
On lips that are for others; deep as love,
Deep as first love, and wild with all regret;
20   O Death in Life, the days that are no more.

Now Sleeps the Crimson Petal

Now sleeps the crimson petal, now the white;
Nor waves the cypress in the palace walk;
Nor winks the gold fin in the porphyry° font: *purple stone*
The fire-fly wakens: waken thou with me.

5   Now droops the milkwhite peacock like a ghost,
And like a ghost she glimmers on to me.

---

1. This song came to me on the yellowing autumn-tide at Tintern Abbey, full for me of its bygone memories [Tennyson's note]. The poet would remember not only Wordsworth's poem *Lines Written a Few Miles above Tintern Abbey*, but also his dead friend Hallam, buried not far away.

Now lies the Earth all Danaë[1] to the stars,
And all thy heart lies open unto me.

Now slides the silent meteor on, and leaves
10   A shining furrow, as thy thoughts in me.

Now folds the lily all her sweetness up,
And slips into the bosom of the lake:
So fold thyself, my dearest, thou, and slip
Into my bosom and be lost in me.

Come Down, O Maid[1]

Come down, O maid, from yonder mountain height:
What pleasure lives in height (the shepherd sang)
In height and cold, the splendour of the hills?
But cease to move so near the Heavens, and cease
5   To glide a sunbeam by the blasted Pine,
To sit a star upon the sparkling spire;
And come, for Love is of the valley, come,
For Love is of the valley, come thou down
And find him; by the happy threshold, he,
10   Or hand in hand with Plenty in the maize,
Or red with spirted purple of the vats,
Or foxlike in the vine; nor cares to walk
With Death and Morning on the silver horns,[2]
Nor wilt thou snare him in the white ravine,
15   Nor find him dropt upon the firths of ice,°   glaciers
That huddling slant in furrow-cloven falls
To roll the torrent out of dusky doors:[3]
But follow; let the torrent dance thee down
To find him in the valley; let the wild
20   Lean-headed Eagles yelp alone, and leave
The monstrous ledges there to slope, and spill
Their thousand wreaths of dangling water-smoke,
That like a broken purpose waste in air:
So waste not thou; but come; for all the vales
25   Await thee; azure pillars of the hearth[4]
Arise to thee; the children call, and I
Thy shepherd pipe, and sweet is every sound,
Sweeter thy voice, but every sound is sweet;
Myriads of rivulets hurrying thro' the lawn,

1. Danaë had been imprisoned by her father to keep
suitors away, but Zeus came to her in a shower of gold.
1. Written in Switzerland in 1846 after Tennyson had seen
the Jungfrau (German for "Maiden"), a mountain peak near
the villages of Lauterbrunnen and Grindelwald.
2. Death is the lifelessness on the high snow peaks

[Tennyson's note]. The silver horns are mountain peaks;
the Silberhorn is a spur of the Jungfrau.
3. The opening of the gorge is called dusky as a contrast
with the snows all about [Tennyson's note].
4. Smoke rising from the chimneys of cottages in the
valley.

30   The moan of doves in immemorial elms,
      And murmuring of innumerable bees.

["THE WOMAN'S CAUSE IS MAN'S"][1]

       "Blame not thyself too much," I said, "nor blame
240   Too much the sons of men and barbarous laws;
       These were the rough ways of the world till now.
       Henceforth thou hast a helper, me, that know
       The woman's cause is man's: they rise or sink
       Together, dwarf'd or godlike, bond or free:
245   For she that out of Lethe[2] scales with man
       The shining steps of Nature, shares with man
       His nights, his days, moves with him to one goal,
       Stays all the fair young planet in her hands[3]—
       If she be small, slight-natured, miserable,
250   How shall men grow? but work no more alone!
       Our place is much: as far as in us lies
       We two will serve them both in aiding her—
       Will clear away the parasitic forms
       That seem to keep her up but drag her down—
255   Will leave her space to burgeon out of all
       Within her—let her make herself her own
       To give or keep, to live and learn and be
       All that not harms distinctive womanhood.
       For woman is not undevelopt man,
260   But diverse: could we make her as the man,
       Sweet Love were slain: his dearest bond is this,
       Not like to like, but like in difference.
       Yet in the long years liker must they grow;
       The man be more of woman, she of man;
265   He gain in sweetness and in moral height,
       Nor lose the wrestling thews° that throw the world;   muscles
       She mental breadth, nor fail in childward care,
       Nor lose the childlike in the larger mind;
       Till at the last she set herself to man,
270   Like perfect music unto noble words;
       And so these twain, upon the skirts of Time,
       Sit side by side, full-summ'd in all their powers,

1. Princess Ida, the heroine of *The Princess*, founds a women's college, and swears she will never marry. But through various exploits—including masquerading as a woman to attend her college—Prince Florian convinces her that her feminist experiment is futile. She turns her college into a hospital and agrees to marry him. In this, his concluding speech (from Book 7), Florian envisions a future in which men and women will be more alike, and the relations between them will be improved.
2. The waters of forgetfulness, here implying a new beginning.
3. Hallam Tennyson notes: "Cf. Ross Wallace's lines:

'The hand that rocks the cradle is the hand that rules the world.' My father felt that woman must train herself more earnestly than heretofore to do the large work that lies before her, even though she may not be destined to be wife or mother, cultivating her understanding not her memory only, her imagination in its highest phases, her inborn spirituality and her sympathy with all that is pure, noble and beautiful, rather than mere social accomplishments; and that then and then only will she further the progress of humanity, then and then only men will continue to hold her in reverence."

Dispensing harvest, sowing the To-be,
Self-reverent each and reverencing each,
275   Distinct in individualities,
But like each other ev'n as those who love.
Then comes the statelier Eden back to men:
Then reign the world's great bridals, chaste and calm:
Then springs the crowning race of humankind.
280   May these things be!"
                                        Sighing she spoke "I fear
They will not."
                    "Dear, but let us type them now
In our own lives, and this proud watchword rest
Of equal; seeing either sex alone
Is half itself, and in true marriage lies
285   Nor equal, nor unequal: each fulfils
Defect in each, and always thought in thought,
Purpose in purpose, will in will, they grow,
The single pure and perfect animal,
The two-cell'd heart beating, with one full stroke,
290   Life."
                    And again sighing she spoke: "A dream
That once was mine! what woman taught you this?"

1839–1847   1847

In Memoriam A. H. H.   When Tennyson was twenty-four, his closest friend Arthur Henry Hallam died suddenly in Vienna. Regarded by all who knew him as the most promising intellect of his generation, Hallam had been Tennyson's confidante, best critic, and strongest supporter. It was Hallam who encouraged Tennyson to publish, helped him get his work through the press, and sustained him amidst criticism, self-doubt, and family crises. His perceptive review of the early poems remains among the best essays ever written on Tennyson. The poet learned of Hallam's death on 1 October 1833, and soon began composing short lyrics exploring the dark questions raised by so devastating an event. "I did not write them with any view of weaving them into a whole," Tennyson later said, "or for publication, until I found I had written so many."

The 131 sections of In Memoriam, produced over sixteen years, constitute a new type of elegy, what T. S. Eliot called "the concentrated diary" of a man confessing his love, sorrow, and doubts about the immortality of the soul. Tennyson drew on many sources, ranging from Greek pastoral elegy and Horace's Odes, to the sonnet sequences of Petrarch and Shakespeare. As in traditional elegy, the death of a friend blights joy in all living things, until the poet asserts his omnipresence in nature. But Tennyson expands his personal loss into the potential death of the human species, questioning the direction of evolution, science's challenges to Christian belief, and the ultimate destiny of the human spirit. The result is an intensely private autobiography of grief that nonetheless registers the troubled spiritual condition of Victorian England.

Presented as a broken narrative of the poet's fitful progress from despair to solace, In Memoriam covers a three-year period, from the death of Hallam in the autumn of 1833 to the spring of 1836. Sections 9–15 describe the return of Hallam's body to England by sea; section 19, its burial. The structural heart of the poem is the succession of three Christmases (sections 28–30, 78, 104–106), whose celebration of Christian rebirth gradually rings less hollow, more convincing. The poet's acceptance of his loss also deepens over the three springs that follow (sections 39, 86, and 115); the timeless renewal of nature eventually reawakens the poet to life. Yet for many readers, the bleak evidence of blindly predatory Nature at the poem's emotional nadir (sections 54, 55, and 56) nearly overshadows the brighter hopes of later sections. As Eliot remarked, In Memoriam triumphs not "because of the quality of its faith, but because of the quality of its doubt."

The form of the poem is justly famous. At the time he was writing Tennyson mistakenly thought he had created a new stanza—iambic tetrameter quatrains, rhyming *abba*—unaware that Sidney and Jonson had preceded him. But Tennyson's brilliant, sustained use of the quatrains was so well adapted to his material that the form has come to be called "the In Memoriam stanza." The first line-ending lingers in the memory while the central couplet pushes other sounds to the fore, then the rhyme is completed across that divide just as the stanza ends. This aural pattern of separation and completion parallels the intellectual and emotional progress of the poem: sound and substance combine in a verbal embrace of Tennyson's loss.

from In Memoriam A. H. H.
Obiit MDCCCXXXIII[1]

Strong Son of God, immortal Love,
   Whom we, that have not seen thy face,
   By faith, and faith alone, embrace,
Believing where we cannot prove;

5   Thine are these orbs of light and shade;[2]
   Thou madest Life in man and brute;
   Thou madest Death; and lo, thy foot
Is on the skull which thou hast made.

Thou wilt not leave us in the dust:
10   Thou madest man, he knows not why,
   He thinks he was not made to die;
And thou hast made him: thou art just.

Thou seemest human and divine,
   The highest, holiest manhood, thou:
15   Our wills are ours, we know not how,
Our wills are ours, to make them thine.

Our little systems have their day;[3]
   They have their day and cease to be:
   They are but broken lights of thee,
20   And thou, O Lord, art more than they.

We have but faith: we cannot know;
   For knowledge is of things we see;
   And yet we trust it comes from thee,
A beam in darkness: let it grow.

---

1. Died 1833. Tennyson wrote the introductory stanzas below, addressed to Christ, in 1849 after he had completed the poem.

2. Sun and moon [Tennyson's note].
3. Current notions of religion and philosophy.

25   Let knowledge grow from more to more,
            But more of reverence in us dwell;
            That mind and soul, according well,
        May make one music as before,[4]

        But vaster. We are fools and slight;
30   We mock thee when we do not fear:
            But help thy foolish ones to bear;
        Help thy vain worlds to bear thy light.

        Forgive what seem'd my sin in me;
            What seem'd my worth since I began;
35   For merit lives from man to man,
        And not from man, O Lord, to thee.

        Forgive my grief for one removed,
            Thy creature, whom I found so fair.
            I trust he lives in thee, and there
40   I find him worthier to be loved.

        Forgive these wild and wandering cries,
            Confusions of a wasted° youth;   ruined
            Forgive them where they fail in truth,
        And in thy wisdom make me wise.

                                    1
        I held it truth, with him who sings
            To one clear harp in divers tones,[5]
            That men may rise on stepping-stones
        Of their dead selves to higher things.

5   But who shall so forecast the years
            And find in loss a gain to match?
            Or reach a hand thro' time to catch
        The far-off interest of tears?[6]

        Let Love clasp Grief lest both be drown'd,
10   Let darkness keep her raven gloss:
            Ah, sweeter to be drunk with loss,
        To dance with death, to beat the ground,

        Than that the victor Hours should scorn
            The long result of love, and boast,
15   "Behold the man that loved and lost,
        But all he was is overworn."

                                    2
        Old Yew, which graspest at the stones
            That name the under-lying dead,

---

4. As in the ages of faith [Tennyson's note].
5. Goethe, according to Tennyson.

6. The good that grows for us out of grief [Tennyson's note].

Thy fibres net the dreamless head,
Thy roots are wrapt about the bones.

5   The seasons bring the flower again,
       And bring the firstling to the flock;
       And in the dusk of thee, the clock
Beats out the little lives of men.

O not for thee the glow, the bloom,
10   Who changest not in any gale,
       Nor branding summer suns avail
To touch thy thousand years of gloom:[7]

And gazing on thee, sullen tree,
       Sick° for thy stubborn hardihood,   *envious*
15   I seem to fail from out my blood
And grow incorporate into thee.

3

O Sorrow, cruel fellowship,
       O Priestess in the vaults of Death,
       O sweet and bitter in a breath,
What whispers from thy lying lip?

5   "The stars," she whispers, "blindly run;
       A web is wov'n across the sky;
       From out waste places comes a cry,
And murmurs from the dying sun:

"And all the phantom, Nature, stands—
10   With all the music in her tone,
       A hollow echo of my own,—
A hollow form with empty hands."

And shall I take a thing so blind,[8]
       Embrace her as my natural good;
15   Or crush her, like a vice of blood,
Upon the threshold of the mind?

4

To Sleep I give my powers away;
       My will is bondsman to the dark;
       I sit within a helmless bark,
And with my heart I muse and say:

5   O heart, how fares it with thee now,
       That thou should'st fail from thy desire,
       Who scarcely darest to inquire,
"What is it makes me beat so low?"

7. Hallam Tennyson says: "No autumn tints ever change   8. The blind thing is sorrow.
the green gloom of the yew."

Something it is which thou hast lost,
 Some pleasure from thine early years.
 Break, thou deep vase of chilling tears,
That grief hath shaken into frost!⁹

Such clouds of nameless trouble cross
 All night below the darken'd eyes;
 With morning wakes the will, and cries,
"Thou shalt not be the fool of loss."

5

I sometimes hold it half a sin
 To put in words the grief I feel;
 For words, like Nature, half reveal
And half conceal the Soul within.

But, for the unquiet heart and brain,
 A use in measured language lies;
 The sad mechanic exercise,
Like dull narcotics, numbing pain.

In words, like weeds,° I'll wrap me o'er,   *mourning clothes*
 Like coarsest clothes against the cold:
 But that large grief which these enfold
Is given in outline and no more.

6

One writes, that "Other friends remain,"
 That "Loss is common to the race"—
 And common is the commonplace,
And vacant chaff well meant for grain.

That loss is common would not make
 My own less bitter, rather more:
 Too common! Never morning wore
To evening, but some heart did break.

O father, wheresoe'er thou be,
 Who pledgest° now thy gallant son;   *toasts*
 A shot, ere half thy draught be done,
Hath still'd the life that beat from thee.

O mother, praying God will save
 Thy sailor,—while thy head is bow'd,
 His heavy-shotted hammock-shroud¹
Drops in his vast and wandering grave.

Ye know no more than I who wrought
 At that last hour to please him well;²

Who mused on all I had to tell,
20   And something written, something thought;

Expecting still his advent home;
    And ever met him on his way
    With wishes, thinking, "here to-day,"
Or "here to-morrow will he come."

25   O somewhere, meek, unconscious dove,
    That sittest ranging³ golden hair;
    And glad to find thyself so fair,
Poor child, that waitest for thy love!

For now her father's chimney glows
30   In expectation of a guest;
    And thinking "this will please him best,"
She takes a riband or a rose;

For he will see them on to-night;
    And with the thought her colour burns;
35   And, having left the glass, she turns
Once more to set a ringlet right;

And, even when she turn'd, the curse
    Had fallen, and her future Lord
    Was drown'd in passing thro' the ford,
40   Or kill'd in falling from his horse.

O what to her shall be the end?
    And what to me remains of good?
    To her, perpetual maidenhood,
And unto me no second friend.

7

Dark house, by which once more I stand
    Here in the long unlovely street,⁴
    Doors, where my heart was used to beat
So quickly, waiting for a hand,

5   A hand that can be clasp'd no more—
    Behold me, for I cannot sleep,
    And like a guilty thing I creep
At earliest morning to the door.

He is not here;⁵ but far away
10   The noise of life begins again,
    And ghastly thro' the drizzling rain
On the bald street breaks the blank day.

---

3. Arranging; the "meek, unconscious dove" was
Tennyson's sister Emily, who had been engaged to marry
Hallam.

4. Hallam's house at 67 Wimpole Street in London.
5. "He is not here, but is risen," said the angel at Jesus'
tomb (Luke 24.6).

8

A happy lover who has come
   To look on her that loves him well,
   Who 'lights and rings the gateway bell,
And learns her gone and far from home;

5   He saddens, all the magic light
   Dies off at once from bower and hall,
   And all the place is dark, and all
The chambers emptied of delight:

So find I every pleasant spot
10   In which we two were wont to meet,
   The field, the chamber and the street,
For all is dark where thou art not.

Yet as that other, wandering there
   In those deserted walks, may find
15   A flower beat with rain and wind,
Which once she foster'd up with care;

So seems it in my deep regret,
   O my forsaken heart, with thee
   And this poor flower of poesy
20   Which little cared for fades not yet.

But since it pleased a vanish'd eye,
   I go to plant it on his tomb,
   That if it can it there may bloom,
Or dying, there at least may die.

9

Fair ship, that from the Italian shore
   Sailest the placid ocean-plains
   With my lost Arthur's loved remains,
Spread thy full wings, and waft him o'er.

5   So draw him home to those that mourn
   In vain; a favourable speed
   Ruffle thy mirror'd mast, and lead
Thro' prosperous floods his holy urn.

All night no ruder air perplex
10   Thy sliding keel, till Phosphor,[6] bright
   As our pure love, thro' early light
Shall glimmer on the dewy decks.

Sphere all your lights around, above;
   Sleep, gentle heavens, before the prow;
15   Sleep, gentle winds, as he sleeps now,
My friend, the brother of my love;

6. The morning star.

My Arthur, whom I shall not see
   Till all my widow'd race be run;
   Dear as the mother to the son,
20   More than my brothers are to me.

10

I hear the noise about thy keel;
   I hear the bell struck in the night:
   I see the cabin-window bright;
I see the sailor at the wheel.

5   Thou bring'st the sailor to his wife,
   And travell'd men from foreign lands;
   And letters unto trembling hands;
And, thy dark freight, a vanish'd life.

So bring him: we have idle dreams:
10   This look of quiet flatters thus
   Our home-bred fancies: O to us,
The fools of habit, sweeter seems

To rest beneath the clover sod,
   That takes the sunshine and the rains,
15   Or where the kneeling hamlet drains
The chalice of the grapes of God;[7]

Than if with thee the roaring wells
   Should gulf him fathom-deep in brine;
   And hands so often clasp'd in mine,
20   Should toss with tangle° and with shells.   *seaweed*

11

Calm is the morn without a sound,
   Calm as to suit a calmer grief,
   And only thro' the faded leaf
The chestnut pattering to the ground:

5   Calm and deep peace on this high wold,[8]
   And on these dews that drench the furze,°   *heath shrubs*
   And all the silvery gossamers
That twinkle into green and gold:

Calm and still light on yon great plain
10   That sweeps with all its autumn bowers,
   And crowded farms and lessening towers,
To mingle with the bounding main:

Calm and deep peace in this wide air,
   These leaves that redden to the fall;
15   And in my heart, if calm at all,
If any calm, a calm despair:

---

7. A burial in England, either inside the church itself, near the area where people take communion, or outdoors, "beneath the clover sod," is preferable to burial at sea.

8. A Lincolnshire wold or upland from which the whole range of marsh to the sea is visible [Tennyson's note].

Calm on the seas, and silver sleep,
   And waves that sway themselves in rest,
   And dead calm in that noble breast
20 Which heaves but with the heaving deep.[9]

12

Lo, as a dove when up she springs
   To bear thro' Heaven a tale of woe,
   Some dolorous message knit below
The wild pulsation of her wings;

5 Like her I go; I cannot stay;
   I leave this mortal ark behind,[1]
   A weight of nerves without a mind,
And leave the cliffs, and haste away

O'er ocean-mirrors rounded large,
10 And reach the glow of southern skies,
   And see the sails at distance rise,
And linger weeping on the marge,

And saying; "Comes he thus, my friend?
   Is this the end of all my care?"
15 And circle moaning in the air:
"Is this the end? Is this the end?"

And forward dart again, and play
   About the prow, and back return
   To where the body sits, and learn
20 That I have been an hour away.

13

Tears of the widower, when he sees
   A late-lost form that sleep reveals,
   And moves his doubtful arms, and feels
Her place is empty, fall like these;

5 Which weep a loss for ever new,
   A void where heart on heart reposed;
   And, where warm hands have prest and closed,
Silence, till I be silent too.

Which weep the comrade of my choice,
10 An awful thought, a life removed,
   The human-hearted man I loved,
A Spirit, not a breathing voice.

Come Time, and teach me,[2] many years,
   I do not suffer in a dream;

9. The poet imagines Hallam's body being transported home by ship in autumn 1833, shortly after he died; the actual voyage took place later that winter.
1. My spirit flies out from my material self [Tennyson's note]. Cf. Genesis 8.8–12, where Noah sends out a dove from the ark to see if the Flood has abated.
2. Hallam Tennyson remarks: "Time will teach him the full reality of his loss, whereas now he scarce believes in it, and is like one who between sleeping and waking can weep and has dream-fancies."

15   For now so strange do these things seem,
          Mine eyes have leisure for their tears;

       My fancies time to rise on wing,
          And glance about the approaching sails,
          As tho' they brought but merchants' bales,
20   And not the burthen that they bring.

14

If one should bring me this report,
      That thou° hadst touch'd the land to-day,   *the ship*
      And I went down unto the quay,
And found thee lying in the port;

5   And standing, muffled round with woe,
      Should see thy passengers in rank
      Come stepping lightly down the plank,
And beckoning unto those they know;

And if along with these should come
10   The man I held as half-divine;
      Should strike a sudden hand in mine,
And ask a thousand things of home;

And I should tell him all my pain,
      And how my life had droop'd of late,
15   And he should sorrow o'er my state
And marvel what possess'd my brain;

And I perceived no touch of change,
      No hint of death in all his frame,
      But found him all in all the same,
20   I should not feel it to be strange.

15

To-night the winds begin to rise
      And roar from yonder dropping day:[3]
      The last red leaf is whirl'd away,
The rooks are blown about the skies;

5   The forest crack'd, the waters curl'd,
      The cattle huddled on the lea;
      And wildly dash'd on tower and tree
The sunbeam strikes along the world:

And but for fancies, which aver
10   That all thy motions gently pass
      Athwart a plane of molten glass,[4]
I scarce could brook the strain and stir

That makes the barren branches loud;
      And but for fear it is not so,

---

3. From the west, the direction of sunset.   4. A calm sea [Tennyson's note].

15   The wild unrest that lives in woe
            Would dote and pore on yonder cloud

            That rises upward always higher,
                And onward drags a labouring breast,
                And topples round the dreary west,
20   A looming bastion fringed with fire.

* * *

19

            The Danube to the Severn⁵ gave
                The darken'd heart that beat no more;
                They laid him by the pleasant shore,
            And in the hearing of the wave.

5   There twice a day the Severn fills;
                The salt sea-water passes by,
                And hushes half the babbling Wye,⁶
            And makes a silence in the hills.

            The Wye is hush'd nor moved along,
10   And hush'd my deepest grief of all,
                When fill'd with tears that cannot fall,
            I brim with sorrow drowning song.

            The tide flows down, the wave again
                Is vocal in its wooded walls;
15   My deeper anguish also falls,
            And I can speak a little then.

* * *

24

            And was the day of my delight
                As pure and perfect as I say?
                The very source and fount of Day
            Is dash'd with wandering isles of night.⁷

5   If all was good and fair we met,
                This earth had been the Paradise
                It never look'd to human eyes
            Since our first Sun arose and set.

            And is it that the haze of grief
10   Makes former gladness loom so great?
                The lowness of the present state,
            That sets the past in this relief?

            Or that the past will always win
                A glory from its being far;

5. Arthur Hallam died in Vienna, which is on the
Danube, and was buried at Clevedon, near the Severn
River in southwest England.
6. Taken from my own observation—the rapids of the

Wye are stilled by the incoming sea [Tennyson's note].
The Wye is a tributary of the Severn, a tidal river.
7. Moving sunspots.

15   And orb into the perfect star
         We saw not, when we moved therein?[8]

                    * * *

                    27
         I envy not in any moods
             The captive void of noble rage,
             The linnet° born within the cage,   *finch*
         That never knew the summer woods:

5   I envy not the beast that takes
             His license in the field of time,
             Unfetter'd by the sense of crime,
         To whom a conscience never wakes;

         Nor, what may count itself as blest,
10   The heart that never plighted troth
             But stagnates in the weeds of sloth;
         Nor any want-begotten rest.[9]

         I hold it true, whate'er befall;
             I feel it, when I sorrow most;
15   'Tis better to have loved and lost
         Than never to have loved at all.

                    28
         The time draws near the birth of Christ:[1]
             The moon is hid; the night is still;
             The Christmas bells from hill to hill
         Answer each other in the mist.

5   Four voices of four hamlets round,
             From far and near, on mead and moor,
             Swell out and fail, as if a door
         Were shut between me and the sound:

         Each voice four changes[2] on the wind,
10   That now dilate, and now decrease,
             Peace and goodwill, goodwill and peace,
         Peace and goodwill, to all mankind.

         This year I slept and woke with pain,
             I almost wish'd no more to wake,
15   And that my hold on life would break
         Before I heard those bells again:

         But they my troubled spirit rule,
             For they controll'd me when a boy;
             They bring me sorrow touch'd with joy,
20   The merry merry bells of Yule.

                    * * *

8. From a distance the earth would look like a perfect orb.   1. The first Christmas after Hallam's death.
9. Peace of mind owing to lack or "want" of having made   2. Arrangements of church bell ringing.
commitments.

30

With trembling fingers did we weave
    The holly round the Christmas hearth;
    A rainy cloud possess'd the earth,
And sadly fell our Christmas-eve.

5   At our old pastimes in the hall
    We gambol'd, making vain pretence
    Of gladness, with an awful sense
Of one mute Shadow watching all.

We paused: the winds were in the beech:
10   We heard them sweep the winter land;
    And in a circle hand-in-hand
Sat silent, looking each at each.

Then echo-like our voices rang;
    We sung, tho' every eye was dim,
15   A merry song we sang with him
Last year: impetuously we sang:

We ceased: a gentler feeling crept
    Upon us: surely rest is meet:°   *fitting*
    "They rest," we said, "their sleep is sweet,"
20   And silence follow'd, and we wept.

Our voices took a higher range;
    Once more we sang: "They do not die
    Nor lose their mortal sympathy,
Nor change to us, although they change;

25   "Rapt° from the fickle and the frail   *carried away*
    With gather'd power, yet the same,
    Pierces the keen seraphic flame
From orb° to orb, from veil to veil."   *star*

Rise, happy morn, rise, holy morn,
30   Draw forth the cheerful day from night:
    O Father, touch the east, and light
The light that shone when Hope was born.

* * *

34

My own dim life should teach me this,
    That life shall live for evermore,
    Else earth is darkness at the core,
And dust and ashes all that is;

5   This round of green, this orb of flame,[3]
    Fantastic beauty; such as lurks
    In some wild Poet, when he works
Without a conscience or an aim.

3. The earth; the sun.

What then were God to such as I?
10   'Twere hardly worth my while to choose
      Of things all mortal, or to use
A little patience ere I die;

'Twere best at once to sink to peace,
     Like birds the charming serpent draws,[4]
15   To drop head-foremost in the jaws
Of vacant darkness and to cease.

* * *

39

Old warder[5] of these buried bones,
     And answering now my random stroke
      With fruitful cloud and living smoke,[6]
Dark yew, that graspest at the stones

5 And dippest toward the dreamless head,
     To thee too comes the golden hour
      When flower is feeling after flower;
But Sorrow—fixt upon the dead,

And darkening the dark graves of men,—
10   What whisper'd from her lying lips?
      Thy gloom is kindled at the tips,[7]
And passes into gloom again.

* * *

50

Be near me when my light is low,
     When the blood creeps, and the nerves prick
      And tingle; and the heart is sick,
And all the wheels of Being slow.

5 Be near me when the sensuous frame
     Is rack'd with pangs that conquer trust;
      And Time, a maniac scattering dust,
And Life, a Fury slinging flame.[8]

Be near me when my faith is dry,
10   And men the flies of latter spring,
      That lay their eggs, and sting and sing
And weave their petty cells and die.

Be near me when I fade away,
     To point the term of human strife,
15   And on the low dark verge of life
The twilight of eternal day.

* * *

---

4. Some snakes were believed to hypnotize their prey.
5. The yew tree that stands by Hallam's grave; cf. Section 2. This section was written and added in 1868.
6. The yew, when flowering, in a wind or if struck sends up its pollen like smoke [Tennyson's note].
7. The tips of the yew branches are in flower.
8. The Furies—avengers of crime—carry torches.

54

Oh yet we trust that somehow good
   Will be the final goal of ill,
   To pangs of nature, sins of will,
Defects of doubt, and taints of blood;

5   That nothing walks with aimless feet;
   That not one life shall be destroy'd,
   Or cast as rubbish to the void,
When God hath made the pile complete;

That not a worm is cloven in vain;
10   That not a moth with vain desire
   Is shrivell'd in a fruitless fire,
Or but subserves another's gain.

Behold, we know not anything;
   I can but trust that good shall fall
15   At last—far off—at last, to all,
And every winter change to spring.

So runs my dream: but what am I?
   An infant crying in the night:
   An infant crying for the light:
20   And with no language but a cry.

55

The wish, that of the living whole
   No life may fail beyond the grave,
   Derives it not from what we have
The likest God within the soul?[9]

5   Are God and Nature then at strife,
   That Nature lends such evil dreams?
   So careful of the type[1] she seems,
So careless of the single life;

That I, considering everywhere
10   Her secret meaning in her deeds,
   And finding that of fifty seeds
She often brings but one to bear,

I falter where I firmly trod,
   And falling with my weight of cares
15   Upon the great world's altar-stairs
That slope thro' darkness up to God,

I stretch lame hands of faith, and grope,
   And gather dust and chaff, and call

---

9. The inner consciousness—the divine in man [Tennyson's note].

1. Species; i.e., Nature ensures the preservation of the species but is indifferent to the fate of the individual.

To what I feel is Lord of all,
20   And faintly trust the larger hope.[2]

56

"So careful of the type?" but no.
    From scarpèd[3] cliff and quarried stone
    She° cries, "A thousand types are gone: *Nature*
I care for nothing, all shall go."

5   "Thou makest thine appeal to me:
    I bring to life, I bring to death:
    The spirit does but mean the breath:
I know no more." And he, shall he,

Man, her last work, who seem'd so fair,
10   Such splendid purpose in his eyes,
    Who roll'd the psalm to wintry skies,
Who built him fanes° of fruitless prayer,   *temples*

Who trusted God was love indeed
    And love Creation's final law—
15   Tho' Nature, red in tooth and claw
With ravine, shriek'd against his creed—

Who loved, who suffer'd countless ills,
    Who battled for the True, the Just,
    Be blown about the desert dust,
20   Or seal'd° within the iron hills?   *fossilized*

No more? A monster then, a dream,
    A discord. Dragons of the prime,
    That tare° each other in their slime,[4]   *tore*
Were mellow music match'd° with him.   *compared*

25   O life as futile, then, as frail!
    O for thy voice to soothe and bless!
    What hope of answer, or redress?
Behind the veil, behind the veil.

* * *

59

O Sorrow,[5] wilt thou live with me
    No casual mistress, but a wife,
    My bosom-friend and half of life;
As I confess it needs must be;

5   O Sorrow, wilt thou rule my blood,
    Be sometimes lovely like a bride,

---

2. Hallam Tennyson notes: "My father means by 'the larger hope' that the whole human race would through, perhaps, ages of suffering, be at length purified and saved."

3. Steep cut-away cliffs with the strata exposed.
4. The geologic monsters of the early ages [Tennyson's note].
5. Cf. Section 3. Tennyson added this section in 1851.

And put thy harsher moods aside,
  If thou wilt have me wise and good.

My centred passion cannot move,
10   Nor will it lessen from to-day;
      But I'll have leave at times to play
  As with the creature of my love;

And set thee forth, for thou art mine,
      With so much hope for years to come,
15   That, howsoe'er I know thee, some
  Could hardly tell what name were thine.

* * *

67

When on my bed the moonlight falls,
  I know that in thy place of rest
  By that broad water of the west,[6]
There comes a glory on the walls;

5   Thy marble bright in dark appears,
      As slowly steals a silver flame
      Along the letters of thy name,
  And o'er the number of thy years.

The mystic glory swims away;
10   From off my bed the moonlight dies;
      And closing eaves of wearied eyes
  I sleep till dusk is dipt in gray:

And then I know the mist is drawn
      A lucid veil from coast to coast,
15   And in the dark church like a ghost
  Thy tablet glimmers to the dawn.

* * *

72

Risest thou thus, dim dawn, again,[7]
      And howlest, issuing out of night,
      With blasts that blow the poplar white,
  And lash with storm the streaming pane?

5   Day, when my crown'd estate° begun   *happiness*
      To pine in that reverse of doom,[8]
      Which sicken'd every living bloom,
  And blurr'd the splendour of the sun;

  Who usherest in the dolorous hour
10   With thy quick tears that make the rose

---

6. The Severn, near which Hallam was buried at Clevedon.
7. It is 15 September 1834, the first anniversary of
Hallam's death.

8. I.e., the disastrous reversal of fortune brought about by
doom, in the form of Hallam's death.

Pull sideways, and the daisy close
    Her crimson fringes to the shower;

Who might'st have heaved a windless flame
    Up the deep East, or, whispering, play'd
15   A chequer-work of beam and shade
Along the hills, yet look'd the same.

As wan, as chill, as wild as now;
    Day, mark'd as with some hideous crime,
    When the dark hand struck down thro' time,
20   And cancell'd nature's best: but thou,

Lift as thou may'st thy burthen'd brows
    Thro' clouds that drench the morning star,
    And whirl the ungarner'd sheaf afar,
And sow the sky with flying boughs,

25   And up thy vault with roaring sound
    Climb thy thick noon, disastrous day;
    Touch thy dull goal of joyless gray,[9]
And hide thy shame beneath the ground.

* * *

78

Again at Christmas[1] did we weave
    The holly round the Christmas hearth;
    The silent snow possess'd the earth,
And calmly fell our Christmas-eve:

5   The yule-clog° sparkled keen with frost,   *log*
    No wing of wind the region swept,
    But over all things brooding slept
The quiet sense of something lost.

As in the winters left behind,
10   Again our ancient games had place,
    The mimic picture's breathing grace,[2]
And dance and song and hoodman-blind.°   *blindman's bluff*

Who show'd a token of distress?
    No single tear, no mark of pain:
15   O sorrow, then can sorrow wane?
O grief, can grief be changed to less?

O last regret, regret can die!
    No—mixt with all this mystic frame,
    Her° deep relations are the same,   *sorrow's*
20   But with long use her tears are dry.

* * *

9. The dull sunset.
1. The second Christmas after Hallam's death.

2. Tableaux-vivants, an entertainment in which performers reenact a well-known work of art or historical event.

80

If any vague desire should rise,
 That holy Death ere Arthur died
 Had moved me kindly from his side,
And dropt the dust on tearless eyes;

5 Then fancy shapes, as fancy can,
 The grief my loss in him had wrought,
 A grief as deep as life or thought,
But stay'd in peace with God and man.

I make a picture in the brain;
10 I hear the sentence that he speaks;
 He bears the burthen of the weeks
But turns his burthen into gain.

His credit thus shall set me free;
 And, influence rich to soothe and save,
15 Unused example from the grave
Reach out dead hands to comfort me.

* * *

86

Sweet after showers, ambrosial air,
 That rollest from the gorgeous gloom
 Of evening over brake and bloom
And meadow, slowly breathing bare

5 The round of space, and rapt below
 Thro' all the dewy-tassell'd wood,
 And shadowing down the hornèd flood[3]
In ripples, fan my brows and blow

The fever from my cheek, and sigh
10 The full new life that feeds thy breath
 Throughout my frame, till Doubt and Death,
Ill brethren, let the fancy fly

From belt to belt of crimson seas
 On leagues of odour streaming far,
15 To where in yonder orient star
A hundred spirits whisper "Peace."

* * *

89

Witch-elms that counterchange[4] the floor
 Of this flat lawn with dusk and bright;
 And thou, with all thy breadth and height
Of foliage, towering sycamore;

---

3. Between two promontories [Tennyson's note].   4. The shadows cast by the elm tree checkered the lawn.

5　　　How often, hither wandering down,
　　　　　My Arthur found your shadows fair,
　　　　　And shook to all the liberal air
　　　The dust and din and steam of town:

　　　He brought an eye for all he saw;
10　　　　He mixt in all our simple sports;
　　　　　They pleased him, fresh from brawling courts
　　　And dusty purlieus of the law.[5]

　　　O joy to him in this retreat,
　　　　　Immantled in ambrosial dark,
15　　　　To drink the cooler air, and mark
　　　The landscape winking thro' the heat:

　　　O sound to rout the brood of cares,
　　　　　The sweep of scythe in morning dew,
　　　　　The gust that round the garden flew,
20　　　And tumbled half the mellowing pears!

　　　O bliss, when all in circle drawn
　　　　　About him, heart and ear were fed
　　　　　To hear him, as he lay and read
　　　The Tuscan poets[6] on the lawn:

25　　　Or in the all-golden afternoon
　　　　　A guest, or happy sister, sung,
　　　　　Or here she brought the harp and flung
　　　A ballad to the brightening moon:

　　　Nor less it pleased in livelier moods,
30　　　　Beyond the bounding hill to stray,
　　　　　And break the livelong summer day
　　　With banquet in the distant woods;

　　　Whereat we glanced from theme to theme,
　　　　　Discuss'd the books to love or hate,
35　　　　Or touch'd the changes of the state,
　　　Or threaded some Socratic dream;

　　　But if I praised the busy town,
　　　　　He loved to rail against it still,
　　　　　For "ground in yonder social mill
40　　　We rub each other's angles down,

　　　"And merge," he said, "in form and gloss
　　　　　The picturesque of man and man."
　　　　　We talk'd: the stream beneath us ran,
　　　The wine-flask lying couch'd in moss,

---

5. Hallam had been a law student.　　　　　6. Petrarch and Dante.

45 Or cool'd within the glooming wave;
        And last, returning from afar,
        Before the crimson-circled star
    Had fall'n into her father's grave,

    And brushing ankle-deep in flowers,
50   We heard behind the woodbine veil
        The milk that bubbled in the pail,
    And buzzings of the honied hours.

                    * * *

                    93
    I shall not see thee. Dare I say
        No spirit ever brake the band
        That stays him from the native land
    Where first he walk'd when claspt in clay?[7]

5   No visual shade of some one lost,
        But he, the Spirit himself, may come
        Where all the nerve of sense is numb;
    Spirit to Spirit, Ghost to Ghost.

    O, therefore from thy sightless° range   *invisible*
10   With gods in unconjectured bliss,
        O, from the distance of the abyss
    Of tenfold-complicated change,

    Descend, and touch, and enter; hear
        The wish too strong for words to name;
15   That in this blindness of the frame
    My Ghost may feel that thine is near.

                    94
    How pure at heart and sound in head,
        With what divine affections bold
        Should be the man whose thought would hold
    An hour's communion with the dead.

5   In vain shalt thou, or any, call
        The spirits from their golden day,
        Except, like them, thou too canst say,
    My spirit is at peace with all.

    They haunt the silence of the breast,
10   Imaginations calm and fair,
        The memory like a cloudless air,
    The conscience as a sea at rest:

    But when the heart is full of din,
        And doubt beside the portal waits,
15   They can but listen at the gates,
    And hear the household jar within.

7. Flesh; in other words, when he was alive.

95

By night we linger'd on the lawn,
    For underfoot the herb was dry;
    And genial warmth; and o'er the sky
The silvery haze of summer drawn;

5   And calm that let the tapers burn
    Unwavering: not a cricket chirr'd:
    The brook alone far-off was heard,
And on the board the fluttering urn:[8]

And bats went round in fragrant skies,
10   And wheel'd or lit the filmy shapes°   *moths*
    That haunt the dusk, with ermine capes
And woolly breasts and beaded eyes;

While now we sang old songs that peal'd
    From knoll to knoll, where, couch'd at ease,
15   The white kine° glimmer'd, and the trees   *cows*
Laid their dark arms about the field.

But when those others, one by one,
    Withdrew themselves from me and night,
    And in the house light after light
20 Went out, and I was all alone,

A hunger seized my heart; I read
    Of that glad year which once had been,
    In those fall'n leaves which kept their green,
The noble letters of the dead:

25 And strangely on the silence broke
    The silent-speaking words, and strange
    Was love's dumb cry defying change
To test his worth; and strangely spoke

The faith, the vigour, bold to dwell
30   On doubts that drive the coward back,
    And keen thro' wordy snares to track
Suggestion to her inmost cell.

So word by word, and line by line,
    The dead man touch'd me from the past.
35   And all at once it seem'd at last
The living soul[9] was flash'd on mine,

And mine in this was wound, and whirl'd
    About empyreal heights of thought,
    And came on that which is, and caught
40 The deep pulsations of the world,

8. Hot-water urn for making tea or coffee, heated by a fluttering flame.
9. "His living soul" in the first edition; the next line originally read "And mine in his was wound." Tennyson said that the first version "troubled me, as perhaps giving a wrong impression."

Aeonian music[1] measuring out
    The steps of Time—the shocks of Chance—
    The blows of Death. At length my trance
Was cancell'd, stricken thro' with doubt.[2]

45   Vague words! but ah, how hard to frame
    In matter-moulded forms of speech,
    Or ev'n for intellect to reach
Thro' memory that which I became:

Till now the doubtful dusk reveal'd
50   The knolls once more where, couch'd at ease,
    The white kine glimmer'd, and the trees
Laid their dark arms about the field:

And suck'd from out the distant gloom
    A breeze began to tremble o'er
55   The large leaves of the sycamore,
And fluctuate all the still perfume,

And gathering freshlier overhead,
    Rock'd the full-foliaged elms, and swung
    The heavy-folded rose, and flung
60   The lilies to and fro, and said

"The dawn, the dawn," and died away;
    And East and West, without a breath,
    Mixt their dim lights, like life and death,
To broaden into boundless day.

96

You say, but with no touch of scorn,
    Sweet-hearted, you, whose light-blue eyes
    Are tender over drowning flies,
You tell me, doubt is Devil-born.

5   I know not: one[3] indeed I knew
    In many a subtle question versed,
    Who touch'd a jarring lyre at first,
But ever strove to make it true:

Perplext in faith, but pure in deeds,
10   At last he beat his music out.
    There lives more faith in honest doubt,
Believe me, than in half the creeds.

He fought his doubts and gather'd strength,
    He would not make his judgment blind,
15   He faced the spectres of the mind
And laid them: thus he came at length

1. The music of the aeons.
2. The trance came to an end in a moment of critical doubt, but the doubt was dispelled by the glory of the dawn of the "boundless day" [Tennyson's note].
3. Arthur Hallam.

To find a stronger faith his own;
   And Power was with him in the night,
   Which makes the darkness and the light,
20   And dwells not in the light alone,

But in the darkness and the cloud,
   As over Sinaï's peaks of old,[4]
   While Israel made their gods of gold,
Altho' the trumpet blew so loud.

* * *

99

Risest thou thus, dim dawn, again,[5]
   So loud with voices of the birds,
   So thick with lowings of the herds,
Day, when I lost the flower of men;

5   Who tremblest thro' thy darkling red
   On yon swoll'n brook that bubbles fast
   By meadows breathing of the past,
And woodlands holy to the dead;

Who murmurest in the foliaged eaves
10   A song that slights the coming care,[6]
   And Autumn laying here and there
A fiery finger on the leaves;

Who wakenest with thy balmy breath
   To myriads on the genial earth,
15   Memories of bridal, or of birth,
And unto myriads more, of death.

O wheresoever those[7] may be,
   Betwixt the slumber of the poles,[8]
   To-day they count as kindred souls;
20   They know me not, but mourn with me.

* * *

104

The time draws near the birth of Christ;[9]
   The moon is hid, the night is still;
   A single church below the hill
Is pealing, folded in the mist.

5   A single peal of bells below,
   That wakens at this hour of rest
   A single murmur in the breast,
That these are not the bells I know.

---

4. In Exodus (19.16) God speaks to Moses after sending a dark cloud of smoke to cloak Mount Sinai.
5. It is now 15 September 1835, the second anniversary of Hallam's death.
6. The approach of winter.

7. The "myriads" who have memories of death.
8. The ends of the axis of the earth, which move so slowly that they seem not to move, but slumber [Tennyson's note].
9. It is now the third Christmas since Hallam's death.

Like strangers' voices here they sound,
10   In lands where not a memory strays,
        Nor landmark breathes of other days,
But all is new unhallow'd ground.

105

To-night ungather'd let us leave
    This laurel, let this holly stand:
    We live within the stranger's land,[1]
And strangely falls our Christmas-eve.

5   Our father's dust is left alone
        And silent under other snows:
        There in due time the woodbine blows,
    The violet comes, but we are gone.

    No more shall wayward grief abuse
10   The genial hour with mask and mime;
        For change of place, like growth of time,
    Has broke the bond of dying use.

    Let cares that petty shadows cast,
        By which our lives are chiefly proved,
15   A little spare the night I loved,
    And hold it solemn to the past.

    But let no footstep beat the floor,
        Nor bowl of wassail mantle warm;
        For who would keep an ancient form
20 Thro' which the spirit breathes no more?

    Be neither song, nor game, nor feast;
        Nor harp be touch'd, nor flute be blown;
        No dance, no motion, save alone
    What lightens in the lucid east

25 Of rising worlds° by yonder wood.   *stars*
        Long sleeps the summer in the seed;
        Run out your measured arcs, and lead
    The closing cycle rich in good.

106

Ring out, wild bells, to the wild sky,
    The flying cloud, the frosty light:
    The year is dying in the night;
Ring out, wild bells, and let him die.

5   Ring out the old, ring in the new,
        Ring, happy bells, across the snow:

---

1. The Tennyson family have moved away from their old home in Lincolnshire and can no longer bring themselves to observe their former festive customs, such as gathering holly for Christmas or dancing and drinking hot punch (the "bowl of wassail" in line 18).

The year is going, let him go;
    Ring out the false, ring in the true.

Ring out the grief that saps the mind,
    For those that here we see no more;
    Ring out the feud of rich and poor,
Ring in redress to all mankind.

Ring out a slowly dying cause,
    And ancient forms of party strife;
    Ring in the nobler modes of life,
With sweeter manners, purer laws.

Ring out the want, the care, the sin,
    The faithless coldness of the times;
    Ring out, ring out my mournful rhymes,
But ring the fuller minstrel in.

Ring out false pride in place and blood,
    The civic slander and the spite;
    Ring in the love of truth and right,
Ring in the common love of good.

Ring out old shapes of foul disease;
    Ring out the narrowing lust of gold;
    Ring out the thousand wars of old,
Ring in the thousand years of peace.

Ring in the valiant man and free,
    The larger heart, the kindlier hand;
    Ring out the darkness of the land,
Ring in the Christ that is to be.

        107

It is the day when he was born,[2]
    A bitter day that early sank
    Behind a purple-frosty bank
Of vapour, leaving night forlorn.

The time admits not flowers or leaves
    To deck the banquet. Fiercely flies
    The blast of North and East, and ice
Makes daggers at the sharpen'd eaves,

And bristles all the brakes and thorns
    To yon hard crescent, as she hangs
    Above the wood which grides° and clangs   *grinds*
Its leafless ribs and iron horns

2. Hallam's birthday was 1 February 1811.

Together, in the drifts, that pass
   To darken on the rolling brine
15   That breaks the coast. But fetch the wine,
Arrange the board and brim the glass;

Bring in great logs and let them lie,
   To make a solid core of heat;
   Be cheerful-minded, talk and treat
20 Of all things ev'n as he were by;

We keep the day. With festal cheer,
   With books and music, surely we
   Will drink to him, whate'er he be,
And sing the songs he loved to hear.

108

I will not shut me from my kind,
   And, lest I stiffen into stone,
   I will not eat my heart alone,
Nor feed with sighs a passing wind:

5 What profit lies in barren faith,
   And vacant yearning, tho' with might
   To scale the heaven's highest height,
Or dive below the wells of Death?

What find I in the highest place,
10   But mine own phantom chanting hymns?
   And on the depths of death there swims
The reflex of a human face.[3]

I'll rather take what fruit may be
   Of sorrow under human skies:
15   'Tis held that sorrow makes us wise,
Whatever wisdom sleep with thee.

* * *

115

Now fades the last long streak of snow,
   Now burgeons every maze of quick[4]
   About the flowering squares, and thick
By ashen roots the violets blow.

5 Now rings the woodland loud and long,
   The distance takes a lovelier hue,
   And drown'd in yonder living blue
The lark becomes a sightless song.

Now dance the lights on lawn and lea,
10   The flocks are whiter down the vale,

3. The reflection of his own face.
4. Hawthorn hedges are budding; the "flowering squares" in the next line are fields.

And milkier every milky sail
On winding stream or distant sea;

Where now the seamew pipes, or dives
In yonder greening gleam, and fly
15   The happy birds, that change their sky
To build and brood; that live their lives

From land to land; and in my breast
Spring wakens too; and my regret
Becomes an April violet,
20   And buds and blossoms like the rest.

* * *

117

O days and hours, your work is this
To hold me from my proper place,
A little while from his embrace,
For fuller gain of after bliss:

5   That out of distance might ensue
Desire of nearness doubly sweet;
And unto meeting when we meet,
Delight a hundredfold accrue,

For every grain of sand that runs,[5]
10   And every span of shade[6] that steals,
And every kiss of toothed wheels,[7]
And all the courses of the suns.

118

Contemplate all this work of Time,
The giant labouring in his youth;
Nor dream of human love and truth,
As dying Nature's earth and lime;

5   But trust that those we call the dead
Are breathers of an ampler day
For ever nobler ends. They° say,   *scientists*
The solid earth whereon we tread

In tracts of fluent heat began,
10   And grew to seeming-random forms,
The seeming prey of cyclic storms,
Till at the last arose the man;

Who throve and branch'd from clime to clime,
The herald of a higher race,
15   And of himself in higher place,
If so he type[8] this work of time

5. Through an hourglass.
6. On a sundial.

7. In the works of a clock.
8. Typifies or prefigures.

Within himself, from more to more;
  Or, crown'd with attributes of woe
  Like glories, move his course, and show
20 That life is not as idle ore,

But iron dug from central gloom,
  And heated hot with burning fears,
  And dipt in baths of hissing tears,
And batter'd with the shocks of doom

25 To shape and use. Arise and fly
  The reeling Faun, the sensual feast;
  Move upward, working out the beast,
And let the ape and tiger die.

                    119

Doors, where my heart was used to beat
  So quickly, not as one that weeps
  I come once more;[9] the city sleeps;
I smell the meadow in the street;

5 I hear a chirp of birds; I see
  Betwixt the black fronts long-withdrawn
  A light-blue lane of early dawn,
And think of early days and thee,

And bless thee, for thy lips are bland,
10   And bright the friendship of thine eye;
  And in my thoughts with scarce a sigh
I take the pressure of thine hand.

                    120

I trust I have not wasted breath:
  I think we are not wholly brain,
  Magnetic mockeries;° not in vain,   *automatons*
Like Paul with beasts,[1] I fought with Death;

5 Not only cunning casts in clay:
  Let Science prove we are, and then
  What matters Science unto men,
At least to me? I would not stay.

Let him, the wiser man who springs
10   Hereafter, up from childhood shape
  His action like the greater ape,[2]
But I was *born* to other things.

                    * * *

9. Tennyson has returned to Hallam's house in London;
see Section 7, page 1265.
1. St. Paul said: "If after the manner of men I have fought
with beasts at Ephesus, what advantageth it me, if the
dead rise not" (1 Corinthians 15.32).
2. Spoken ironically against mere materialism, not
against evolution [Tennyson's note].

123

There rolls the deep where grew the tree.
   O earth, what changes hast thou seen!
   There where the long street roars, hath been
The stillness of the central sea.

5   The hills are shadows, and they flow
   From form to form, and nothing stands;
   They melt like mist, the solid lands,
Like clouds they shape themselves and go.

But in my spirit will I dwell,
10   And dream my dream, and hold it true;
   For tho' my lips may breathe adieu,
I cannot think the thing farewell.

124

That which we dare invoke to bless;
   Our dearest faith; our ghastliest doubt;
   He, They, One, All; within, without;
The Power in darkness whom we guess;

5   I found Him not in world or sun,
   Or eagle's wing, or insect's eye;[3]
   Nor thro' the questions men may try,
The petty cobwebs we have spun:

If e'er when faith had fall'n asleep,
10   I heard a voice "believe no more"
   And heard an ever-breaking shore
That tumbled in the Godless deep;

A warmth within the breast would melt
   The freezing reason's colder part,
15   And like a man in wrath the heart
Stood up and answer'd "I have felt."

No, like a child in doubt and fear:
   But that blind clamour made me wise;
   Then was I as a child that cries,
20 But, crying, knows his father near;

And what I am beheld again
   What is, and no man understands;
   And out of darkness came the hands
That reach thro' nature, moulding men.

* * *

---

3. Tennyson rejects the argument that God's existence can be inferred from Nature—i.e., that the design of the universe is so orderly and complex that there must have been a designer.

130

Thy voice is on the rolling air;
   I hear thee where the waters run;
   Thou standest in the rising sun,
And in the setting thou art fair.

5   What art thou then? I cannot guess;
   But tho' I seem in star and flower
   To feel thee some diffusive power,
I do not therefore love thee less:

My love involves the love before;
10   My love is vaster passion now;
   Tho' mix'd with God and Nature thou,
I seem to love thee more and more.

Far off thou art, but ever nigh;
   I have thee still, and I rejoice;
15   I prosper, circled with thy voice;
I shall not lose thee tho' I die.

131

O living will[4] that shalt endure
   When all that seems shall suffer shock,
   Rise in the spiritual rock,[5]
Flow thro' our deeds and make them pure,

5   That we may lift from out of dust
   A voice as unto him that hears,
   A cry above the conquer'd years
To one that with us works, and trust,

With faith that comes of self-control,
10   The truths that never can be proved
   Until we close with all we loved,
And all we flow from, soul in soul.

* * *

from *Epilogue*[6]

And rise, O moon, from yonder down,
110   Till over down and over dale
   All night the shining vapour sail
And pass the silent-lighted town,

---

4. That which we know as Free-will in man [Tennyson's note].
5. "And did all drink the same spiritual drink: for they drank of that spiritual Rock that followed them: and that Rock was Christ" (1 Corinthians 10.4).
6. The *Epilogue* opens with a description of the marriage of Cecilia Tennyson, the poet's sister, to Edmund

Lushington on 10 October 1842. Tennyson said *In Memoriam* "begins with a funeral and ends with a marriage—begins with death and ends in promise of a new life—a sort of Divine Comedy, cheerful at the close." The last nine stanzas take place after the wedding is over, as the poet, leaving the reception, looks out over the darkened countryside.

The white-faced halls, the glancing rills,
    And catch at every mountain head,
115   And o'er the friths° that branch and spread   *estuaries*
Their sleeping silver thro' the hills;

And touch with shade the bridal doors,
    With tender gloom the roof, the wall;
    And breaking let the splendour fall
120 To spangle all the happy shores

By which they rest, and ocean sounds,
    And, star and system rolling past,
    A soul shall draw from out the vast
And strike his being into bounds,[7]

125 And, moved thro' life of lower phase,
    Result in man, be born and think,
    And act and love, a closer link
Betwixt us and the crowning race

Of those that, eye to eye, shall look
130   On knowledge; under whose command
    Is Earth and Earth's, and in their hand
Is Nature like an open book;

No longer half-akin to brute,
    For all we thought and loved and did,
135   And hoped, and suffer'd, is but seed
Of what in them is flower and fruit;

Whereof the man, that with me trod
    This planet, was a noble type
    Appearing ere the times were ripe,
140 That friend of mine who lives in God,

That God, which ever lives and loves,
    One God, one law, one element,
    And one far-off divine event,
To which the whole creation moves.
1833–1850   1850

The Charge of the Light Brigade[1]

1

Half a league, half a league,
Half a league onward,
All in the valley of Death

---

7. The poet anticipates the conception of a child, who will pass through various stages of embryonic development to "result in man" (line 126). His development will correspond to the stages of human evolution, perhaps even looking forward to the emergence of a higher form of life, of which Hallam was a precursor, "a noble type" (line 138).

1. In 1854, during the Crimean War, a misunderstood order caused a brigade of 600 British cavalry to make a foolhardy charge upon the batteries of Russian artillery at Balaclava, near Sebastopol. More than 400 soldiers were killed.

              Rode the six hundred.
5   "Forward, the Light Brigade!
          Charge for the guns!" he said:
          Into the valley of Death
              Rode the six hundred.[2]

                            2
          "Forward, the Light Brigade!"
10   Was there a man dismay'd?
          Not tho' the soldier knew
              Some one had blunder'd:
          Their's not to make reply,
          Their's not to reason why,
15   Their's but to do and die:
          Into the valley of Death
              Rode the six hundred.

                            3
          Cannon to right of them,
          Cannon to left of them,
20   Cannon in front of them
              Volley'd and thunder'd;
          Storm'd at with shot and shell,
          Boldly they rode and well,
          Into the jaws of Death,
25   Into the mouth of Hell
              Rode the six hundred.

                            4
          Flash'd all their sabres bare,
          Flash'd as they turn'd in air
          Sabring the gunners there,
30   Charging an army, while
              All the world wonder'd:
          Plunged in the battery-smoke
          Right thro' the line they broke;
          Cossack and Russian
35   Reel'd from the sabre-stroke
              Shatter'd and sunder'd.
          Then they rode back, but not
              Not the six hundred.

                            5
          Cannon to right of them,
40   Cannon to left of them,
          Cannon behind them
              Volley'd and thunder'd;
          Storm'd at with shot and shell,

---

2. In his Lincolnshire accent, Tennyson apparently pronounced "hundred" as "hunderd"—thus making it an exact rhyme
with "blundered" and "thundered."

While horse and hero fell,
45   They that had fought so well
Came thro' the jaws of Death,
Back from the mouth of Hell,
All that was left of them,
    Left of six hundred.

        6
50   When can their glory fade?
O the wild charge they made!
    All the world wonder'd.
Honour the charge they made!
Honour the Light Brigade,
55   Noble six hundred!
1854
                                                        1854

IDYLLS OF THE KING   An "idyll" typically describes picturesque and harmonious scenes of rustic life. Tennyson's idylls, in contrast, are glorious but also bitter and bloody tapestries of love, lust, deceit, and betrayal. He composed the twelve books of *Idylls of the King* over the course of fifty-three years (1833–1885), drawing not only on Thomas Malory's fifteenth-century *Morte D'Arthur*, his major source, but on many other ancient tales, including the Welsh *Mabinogion*. Some contemporaries thought that the effort could have been better spent dealing with current social problems: Carlyle sarcastically called the first four idylls "lollipops." But Tennyson intended an "allegorical or . . . parabolic drift in the poem," and many readers soon perceived the metaphoric parallels between Camelot and Victorian Britain—their virtues, vices, and moral vulnerability.

    The poet arranged the tales to create a mythic portrayal of a civilization's aspiration and decline. The story of the Round Table's creation and dissolution follows the seasons of the year, from Arthur and Guinevere's union in the springtime, when they redeem the wasted land, to Arthur's vanishing at the winter solstice. Throughout, Tennyson focuses on the human potential for either moral evolution or regression. Poised "between the man and beast" at the coming of Arthur, his people rise under the influence of the mysterious and almost supernatural king to become fully human and spiritually motivated. But as the knights of the Round Table fail to keep their vows, the "realm / Reels back into the beast." The adulterous love of Guinevere and Lancelot eventually provokes treachery and disillusion, and the fellowship of the Round Table perishes. *Pelleas and Ettarre* is a pivotal tale showing the disastrous encounter of youthful idealism with the poisonous hypocrisy and sexual indulgence that eat away at the heart of Arthur's dream. Finally, *The Passing of Arthur* describes the apocalyptic battle "where all of high and holy dies away" except the faint hope that, Christlike, Arthur may come again.

from Idylls of the King
The Coming of Arthur

Leodogran, the King of Cameliard,[1]
Had one fair daughter, and none other child;
And she was fairest of all flesh on earth,
Guinevere, and in her his one delight.

---

1. Tradition situates the realms of Leodogran and Arthur somewhere in the west of England or southern Wales. Tennyson uses the geographic imprecision of Arthurian legend for imaginative effect: both the wasteland and Camelot could be anywhere, more states of mind than actual places. Tennyson hints at this in the second Idyll, *Gareth and Lynette*, when a character marvels at Camelot's shimmering towers, saying "there is no such city anywhere, but all a vision."

5 For many a petty king ere Arthur came
 Ruled in this isle, and ever waging war
 Each upon other, wasted all the land;
 And still from time to time the heathen host[2]
 Swarm'd overseas, and harried what was left.
10 And so there grew great tracts of wilderness,
 Wherein the beast was ever more and more,
 But man was less and less, till Arthur came.
 For first Aurelius lived and fought and died,
 And after him King Uther[3] fought and died,
15 But either fail'd to make the kingdom one.
 And after these King Arthur for a space,
 And thro' the puissance of his Table Round,
 Drew all their petty princedoms under him,
 Their king and head, and made a realm, and reign'd.

20 And thus the land of Cameliard was waste,
 Thick with wet woods, and many a beast therein,
 And none or few to scare or chase the beast;
 So that wild dog, and wolf and boar and bear
 Came night and day, and rooted in the fields,
25 And wallow'd in the gardens of the King.
 And ever and anon the wolf would steal
 The children and devour, but now and then,
 Her own brood lost or dead, lent her fierce teat
 To human sucklings; and the children, housed
30 In her foul den, there at their meat would growl,
 And mock their foster-mother on four feet,
 Till, straighten'd, they grew up to wolf-like men,
 Worse than the wolves. And King Leodogran
 Groan'd for the Roman legions here again,
35 And Caesar's eagle:[4] then his brother king,
 Urien,[5] assail'd him: last a heathen horde,
 Reddening the sun with smoke and earth with blood,
 And on the spike that split the mother's heart
 Spitting the child, brake on him,[6] till, amazed,
40 He knew not whither he should turn for aid.

  But—for he heard of Arthur newly crown'd,
 Tho' not without an uproar made by those

---

2. Pagan Germanic tribes—Angles, Jutes, and Saxons—invaded the British isles periodically during the 5th century, further weakening what remained of Romanized British civilization. Arthur apparently rose to power as Roman influence declined, but since Malory, writers have set the events of Arthurian legend in an idealized era of medieval chivalry, which creates certain historical anachronisms.

3. Arthur's father, but Arthur was brought up as the foster son of a knight, unaware of his true identity until adulthood. Aurelius was Uther's brother.

4. Caesar's eagle—the regimental standard of the Roman legions—was a symbol of imperial power. The Roman conquest of Britain began with the invasion of Julius Caesar in 55–54 B.C.; by the 5th century, the Roman Empire was disintegrating and could no longer administer such distant possessions. Leodogran longs for the protection and orderly rule of the Romans.

5. King of North Wales.

6. The heathen horde assaulted Leodogran like a breaking wave, with pikes that figuratively pierced mothers' hearts by impaling their children.

Who cried, "He is not Uther's son"—the King
Sent to him, saying, "Arise, and help us thou!
45   For here between the man and beast we die."

        And Arthur yet had done no deed of arms,
But heard the call, and came: and Guinevere
Stood by the castle walls to watch him pass;
But since he neither wore on helm or shield
50   The golden symbol of his kinglihood,
But rode a simple knight among his knights,
And many of these in richer arms than he,
She saw him not, or mark'd not, if she saw,
One among many, tho' his face was bare.
55   But Arthur, looking downward as he past,
Felt the light of her eyes into his life
Smite on the sudden, yet rode on, and pitch'd
His tents beside the forest. Then he drave
The heathen; after, slew the beast, and fell'd
60   The forest, letting in the sun, and made
Broad pathways for the hunter and the knight
And so return'd.

                    For while he linger'd there,
A doubt that ever smoulder'd in the hearts
Of those great Lords and Barons of his realm
65   Flash'd forth and into war: for most of these,
Colleaguing with a score of petty kings,
Made head against him, crying, "Who is he
That he should rule us? who hath proven him
King Uther's son? for lo! we look at him,
70   And find nor face nor bearing, limbs nor voice,
Are like to those of Uther whom we knew.
This is the son of Gorloïs,[7] not the King;
This is the son of Anton,[8] not the King."

        And Arthur, passing thence to battle, felt
75   Travail, and throes and agonies of the life,
Desiring to be join'd with Guinevere;
And thinking as he rode, "Her father said
That there between the man and beast they die.
Shall I not lift her from this land of beasts
80   Up to my throne, and side by side with me?
What happiness to reign a lonely king,
Vext—O ye stars that shudder over me,
O earth that soundest hollow under me,
Vext with waste dreams? for saving I be join'd
85   To her that is the fairest under heaven,
I seem as nothing in the mighty world,

7. King of Cornwall and husband of Arthur's mother,   8. The knight who brought up Arthur.
Ygerne.

And cannot will my will, nor work my work
Wholly, nor make myself in mine own realm
Victor and lord. But were I join'd with her,
90   Then might we live together as one life,
And reigning with one will in everything
Have power on this dark land to lighten it,
And power on this dead world to make it live."

Thereafter—as he speaks who tells the tale—
95   When Arthur reach'd a field-of-battle bright
With pitch'd pavilions of his foe, the world
Was all so clear about him, that he saw
The smallest rock far on the faintest hill,
And even in high day the morning star.
100   So when the King had set his banner broad,
At once from either side, with trumpet-blast,
And shouts, and clarions shrilling unto blood,
The long-lanced battle let their horses run.
And now the Barons and the kings prevail'd,
105   And now the King, as here and there that war
Went swaying; but the Powers who walk the world
Made lightnings and great thunders over him,
And dazed all eyes, till Arthur by main might,
And mightier of his hands with every blow,
110   And leading all his knighthood threw the kings
Carádos, Urien, Cradlemont of Wales,
Claudias, and Clariance of Northumberland,
The King Brandagoras of Latangor,
With Anguisant of Erin, Morganore,
115   And Lot of Orkney. Then, before a voice
As dreadful as the shout of one who sees
To one who sins, and deems himself alone
And all the world asleep, they swerved and brake
Flying, and Arthur call'd to stay the brands
120   That hack'd among the flyers,[9] "Ho! they yield!"
So like a painted battle the war stood
Silenced, the living quiet as the dead,
And in the heart of Arthur joy was lord.
He laugh'd upon his warrior whom he loved
125   And honour'd most.[1] "Thou dost not doubt me King,
So well thine arm hath wrought for me to-day."
"Sir and my liege," he cried, "the fire of God
Descends upon thee in the battle-field:
I know thee for my King!" Whereat the two,
130   For each had warded either in the fight,
Sware on the field of death a deathless love.
And Arthur said, "Man's word is God in man:
Let chance what will, I trust thee to the death."

9. I.e., Arthur commanded his men to stop hacking their   1. Sir Lancelot.
retreating enemies with their swords (brands).

Then quickly from the foughten field he sent
135   Ulfius, and Brastias, and Bedivere,
His new-made knights, to King Leodogran,
Saying, "If I in aught have served thee well,
Give me thy daughter Guinevere to wife."

Whom when he heard, Leodogran in heart
140   Debating—"How should I that am a king,
However much he holp me at my need,
Give my one daughter saving to a king,
And a king's son?"—lifted his voice, and call'd
A hoary man, his chamberlain, to whom
145   He trusted all things, and of him required
His counsel: "Knowest thou aught of Arthur's birth?"

Then spake the hoary chamberlain and said,
"Sir King, there be but two old men that know:
And each is twice as old as I; and one
150   Is Merlin, the wise man that ever served
King Uther thro' his magic art; and one
Is Merlin's master (so they call him) Bleys,
Who taught him magic; but the scholar ran
Before the master, and so far, that Bleys
155   Laid magic by, and sat him down, and wrote
All things and whatsoever Merlin did
In one great annal-book, where after-years
Will learn the secret of our Arthur's birth."

To whom the King Leodogran replied,
160   "O friend, had I been holpen half as well
By this King Arthur as by thee to-day,
Then beast and man had had their share of me:
But summon here before us yet once more
Ulfius, and Brastias, and Bedivere."

165   Then, when they came before him, the King said,
"I have seen the cuckoo chased by lesser fowl,
And reason in the chase: but wherefore now
Do these your lords stir up the heat of war,
Some calling Arthur born of Gorloïs,
170   Others of Anton? Tell me, ye yourselves,
Hold ye this Arthur for King Uther's son?"

And Ulfius and Brastias answer'd, "Ay."
Then Bedivere, the first of all his knights
Knighted by Arthur at his crowning, spake—
175   For bold in heart and act and word was he,
Whenever slander breathed against the King—

"Sir, there be many rumours on this head:
For there be those who hate him in their hearts,
Call him baseborn, and since his ways are sweet,
180   And theirs are bestial, hold him less than man:

And there be those who deem him more than man,
And dream he dropt from heaven: but my belief
In all this matter—so ye care to learn—
Sir, for ye know that in King Uther's time
185 The prince and warrior Gorloïs, he that held
Tintagil castle by the Cornish sea,
Was wedded with a winsome wife, Ygerne:
And daughters had she borne him,—one whereof,
Lot's wife, the Queen of Orkney, Bellicent,
190 Hath ever like a loyal sister cleaved
To Arthur,—but a son she had not borne.
And Uther cast upon her eyes of love:
But she, a stainless wife to Gorloïs,
So loathed the bright dishonour of his love,
195 That Gorloïs and King Uther went to war:
And overthrown was Gorloïs and slain.
Then Uther in his wrath and heat besieged
Ygerne within Tintagil, where her men,
Seeing the mighty swarm about their walls,
200 Left her and fled, and Uther enter'd in,
And there was none to call to but himself.
So, compass'd by the power of the King,
Enforced she was to wed him in her tears,
And with a shameful swiftness: afterward,
205 Not many moons, King Uther died himself,
Moaning and wailing for an heir to rule
After him, lest the realm should go to wrack.
And that same night, the night of the new year,
By reason of the bitterness and grief
210 That vext his mother, all before his time
Was Arthur born, and all as soon as born
Deliver'd at a secret postern-gate
To Merlin, to be holden far apart
Until his hour should come; because the lords
215 Of that fierce day were as the lords of this,
Wild beasts, and surely would have torn the child
Piecemeal among them, had they known; for each
But sought to rule for his own self and hand,
And many hated Uther for the sake
220 Of Gorloïs. Wherefore Merlin took the child,
And gave him to Sir Anton, an old knight
And ancient friend of Uther; and his wife
Nursed the young prince, and rear'd him with her own;
And no man knew. And ever since the lords
225 Have foughten like wild beasts among themselves,
So that the realm has gone to wrack: but now,
This year, when Merlin (for his hour had come)
Brought Arthur forth, and set him in the hall,
Proclaiming, 'Here is Uther's heir, your king,'

230   A hundred voices cried, 'Away with him!
No king of ours! a son of Gorloïs he,
Or else the child of Anton, and no king,
Or else baseborn.' Yet Merlin thro' his craft,
And while the people clamour'd for a king,
235   Had Arthur crown'd; but after, the great lords
Banded, and so brake out in open war."

    Then while the King debated with himself
If Arthur were the child of shamefulness,
Or born the son of Gorloïs, after death,
240   Or Uther's son, and born before his time,
Or whether there were truth in anything
Said by these three, there came to Cameliard,
With Gawain and young Modred, her two sons,
Lot's wife, the Queen of Orkney, Bellicent;[2]
245   Whom as he could, not as he would, the King
Made feast for, saying, as they sat at meat,

    "A doubtful throne is ice on summer seas.
Ye come from Arthur's court. Victor his men
Report him! Yea, but ye—think ye this king—
250   So many those that hate him, and so strong,
So few his knights, however brave they be—
Hath body enow to hold his foemen down?"

    "O King," she cried, "and I will tell thee: few,
Few, but all brave, all of one mind with him;
255   For I was near him when the savage yells
Of Uther's peerage died, and Arthur sat
Crown'd on the daïs, and his warriors cried,
'Be thou the king, and we will work thy will
Who love thee.' Then the King in low deep tones,
260   And simple words of great authority,
Bound them by so strait° vows to his own self,   *strict*
That when they rose, knighted from kneeling, some
Were pale as at the passing of a ghost,
Some flush'd, and others dazed, as one who wakes
265   Half-blinded at the coming of a light.

    "But when he spake and cheer'd his Table Round
With large, divine, and comfortable words,
Beyond my tongue to tell thee—I beheld
From eye to eye thro' all their Order flash
270   A momentary likeness of the King:
And ere it left their faces, thro' the cross
And those around it and the Crucified,

---

2. The daughter of Gorloïs and Ygerne, Bellicent is Arthur's older half-sister. Her sons are Arthur's nephews: Gawain becomes one of Arthur's knights, but Modred eventually leads the rebellion against him.

Down from the casement over Arthur, smote
Flame-colour, vert and azure,[3] in three rays,
275   One falling upon each of three fair queens,
Who stood in silence near his throne, the friends
Of Arthur, gazing on him, tall, with bright
Sweet faces, who will help him at his need.

    "And there I saw mage Merlin, whose vast wit
280   And hundred winters are but as the hands
Of loyal vassals toiling for their liege.

    "And near him stood the Lady of the Lake,[4]
Who knows a subtler magic than his own—
Clothed in white samite,[5] mystic, wonderful.
285   She gave the King his huge cross-hilted sword,
Whereby to drive the heathen out: a mist
Of incense curl'd about her, and her face
Wellnigh was hidden in the minster° gloom;   *cathedral*
But there was heard among the holy hymns
290   A voice as of the waters, for she dwells
Down in a deep; calm, whatsoever storms
May shake the world, and when the surface rolls,
Hath power to walk the waters like our Lord.

    "There likewise I beheld Excalibur[6]
295   Before him at his crowning borne, the sword
That rose from out the bosom of the lake,
And Arthur row'd across and took it—rich
With jewels, elfin Urim,[7] on the hilt,
Bewildering heart and eye—the blade so bright
300   That men are blinded by it—on one side,
Graven in the oldest tongue of all this world,
'Take me,' but turn the blade and ye shall see,
And written in the speech ye speak yourself,
'Cast me away!' And sad was Arthur's face
305   Taking it, but old Merlin counsell'd him,
'Take thou and strike! the time to cast away
Is yet far-off.' So this great brand the king
Took, and by this will beat his foemen down."

    Thereat Leodogran rejoiced, but thought
310   To sift his doubtings to the last, and ask'd,

---

3. Red, green and blue; presumably the cross is part of a stained glass window set in the wall above Arthur. In *Morte D'Arthur* Malory said of the three queens: "one was king Arthur's sister Morgan le Fay; the other was the queene of Northgalis; and the third was the queene of the wast lands." In *The Passing of Arthur* they reappear to take Arthur to Avalon. Tennyson also identified them with Faith, Hope, and Charity.

4. The Lady of the Lake in the old Legends is the Church [Tennyson's note].
5. A rich silk stuff inwrought with gold and silver threads [Tennyson's note].
6. Arthur's legendary sword.
7. Cf. Exodus 28.30: "And thou shalt put in the breastplate of judgment the Urim and the Thummim," objects used for casting lots to determine God's will.

Fixing full eyes of question on her face,
"The swallow and the swift are near akin,
But thou art closer to this noble prince,
Being his own dear sister;" and she said,
315 "Daughter of Gorloïs and Ygerne am I;"
"And therefore Arthur's sister?" ask'd the King
She answer'd, "These be secret things," and sign'd
To those two sons to pass, and let them be.
And Gawain went, and breaking into song
320 Sprang out, and follow'd by his flying hair
Ran like a colt, and leapt at all he saw:
But Modred laid his ear beside the doors,
And there half-heard;[8] the same that afterward
Struck for the throne, and striking found his doom.

[Queen Bellicent tells Leodogran that, while she doesn't know if Arthur
is her brother, both Bleys and Merlin had confirmed her presentiment
that Arthur would become a great king.]

    She spake and King Leodogran rejoiced,
425 But musing "Shall I answer yea or nay?"
Doubted, and drowsed, nodded and slept, and saw,
Dreaming, a slope of land that ever grew,
Field after field, up to a height, the peak
Haze-hidden, and thereon a phantom king,
430 Now looming, and now lost; and on the slope
The sword rose, the hind fell, the herd was driven,
Fire glimpsed; and all the land from roof and rick,
In drifts of smoke before a rolling wind,
Stream'd to the peak, and mingled with the haze
435 And made it thicker; while the phantom king
Sent out at times a voice; and here or there
Stood one who pointed toward the voice, the rest
Slew on and burnt, crying, "No king of ours,
No son of Uther, and no king of ours;"
440 Till with a wink his dream was changed, the haze
Descended, and the solid earth became
As nothing, but the King stood out in heaven,
Crown'd. And Leodogran awoke, and sent
Ulfius, and Brastias and Bedivere,
445 Back to the court of Arthur answering yea.

    Then Arthur charged his warrior whom he loved
And honour'd most, Sir Lancelot, to ride forth
And bring the Queen;[9]—and watch'd him from the gates:
And Lancelot past away among the flowers,

8. Bellicent sends her sons away so they will not hear her discuss the mystery surrounding Arthur's birth, but Modred eavesdrops.
9. Although Arthur told Lancelot "I trust thee to the death" (line 133 above), subsequent Idylls reveal that Lancelot betrayed this trust by falling in love with Guinevere when he was sent to escort her to her wedding.

450   (For then was latter April) and return'd
       Among the flowers, in May, with Guinevere.
       To whom arrived, by Dubric the high saint,[1]
       Chief of the church in Britain, and before
       The stateliest of her altar-shrines, the King
455   That morn was married, while in stainless white,
       The fair beginners of a nobler time,
       And glorying in their vows and him, his knights
       Stood round him, and rejoicing in his joy.
       Far shone the fields of May thro' open door,
460   The sacred altar blossom'd white with May,
       The Sun of May descended on their King,
       They gazed on all earth's beauty in their Queen,
       Roll'd incense, and there past along the hymns
       A voice as of the waters, while the two
465   Sware at the shrine of Christ a deathless love:
       And Arthur said, "Behold, thy doom is mine.
       Let chance what will, I love thee to the death!"
       To whom the Queen replied with drooping eyes,
       "King and my lord, I love thee to the death!"
470   And holy Dubric spread his hands and spake,
       "Reign ye, and live and love, and make the world
       Other, and may thy Queen be one with thee,
       And all this Order of thy Table Round
       Fulfil the boundless purpose of their King!"

                          * * *

       There at the banquet those great Lords from Rome,[2]
       The slowly-fading mistress of the world,
505   Strode in, and claim'd their tribute as of yore.
       But Arthur spake, "Behold, for these have sworn
       To wage my wars, and worship me their King;
       The old order changeth, yielding place to new;
       And we that fight for our fair father Christ,
510   Seeing that ye be grown too weak and old
       To drive the heathen from your Roman wall,
       No tribute will we pay": so those great lords
       Drew back in wrath, and Arthur strove with Rome.

       And Arthur and his knighthood for a space
515   Were all one will, and thro' that strength the King
       Drew in the petty princedoms under him,
       Fought, and in twelve great battles overcame
       The heathen hordes, and made a realm and reign'd.

1868–1869   1869

---

1. Archbishop of Caerleon.
2. Emissaries from Rome, which still claimed tribute from
Britain as part of the Roman Empire. In lines 506–512

Arthur asserts his independence and refuses to pay, arguing that Rome had grown too weak to defend Britain
from other invaders.

Pelleas and Ettarre[1]

King Arthur made new knights to fill the gap
Left by the Holy Quest;[2] and as he sat
In hall at old Caerleon,[3] the high doors
Were softly sunder'd, and thro' these a youth,
5 Pelleas, and the sweet smell of the fields
Past, and the sunshine came along with him.

"Make me thy knight, because I know, Sir King,
All that belongs to knighthood, and I love."
Such was his cry: for having heard the King
10 Had let proclaim a tournament—the prize
A golden circlet and a knightly sword,
Full fain° had Pelleas for his lady won   *gladly*
The golden circlet, for himself the sword:
And there were those who knew him near the King,
15 And promised for him: and Arthur made him knight.

And this new knight, Sir Pelleas of the isles—
But lately come to his inheritance,
And lord of many a barren isle was he—
Riding at noon, a day or twain before,
20 Across the forest call'd of Dean, to find
Caerleon and the King, had felt the sun
Beat like a strong knight on his helm, and reel'd
Almost to falling from his horse; but saw
Near him a mound of even-sloping side,
25 Whereon a hundred stately beeches grew,
And here and there great hollies under them;
But for a mile all round was open space,
And fern and heath: and slowly Pelleas drew
To that dim day, then binding his good horse
30 To a tree, cast himself down; and as he lay
At random looking over the brown earth
Thro' that green-glooming twilight of the grove,
It seem'd to Pelleas that the fern without
Burnt as a living fire of emeralds,
35 So that his eyes were dazzled looking at it.
Then o'er it crost the dimness of a cloud
Floating, and once the shadow of a bird
Flying, and then a fawn; and his eyes closed.
And since he loved all maidens, but no maid
40 In special, half-awake he whisper'd, "Where?

1. Tennyson called this, the ninth book, "Almost the saddest of the Idylls. The breaking of the storm." The events are based on Malory's *Morte D'Arthur*, although Tennyson has changed the ending.
2. The quest for the Holy Grail, which began in the pre-
vious Idyll, has led to the departure of many of the knights of the Round Table.
3. A place in southeastern Wales where Arthur held court.

O where? I love thee, tho' I know thee not.
For fair thou art and pure as Guinevere,
And I will make thee with my spear and sword
As famous—O my Queen, my Guinevere,
45   For I will be thine Arthur when we meet."

    Suddenly waken'd with a sound of talk
And laughter at the limit of the wood,
And glancing thro' the hoary boles, he saw,
Strange as to some old prophet might have seem'd
50   A vision hovering on a sea of fire,
Damsels in divers colours like the cloud
Of sunset and sunrise, and all of them
On horses, and the horses richly trapt[4]
Breast-high in that bright line of bracken stood:
55   And all the damsels talk'd confusedly,
And one was pointing this way, and one that,
Because the way was lost.

             And Pelleas rose,
And loosed his horse, and led him to the light.
There she that seem'd the chief among them said,
60   "In happy time behold our pilot-star!
Youth, we are damsels-errant, and we ride,
Arm'd as ye see, to tilt against the knights
There at Caerleon, but have lost our way:
To right? to left? straight forward? back again?
65   Which? tell us quickly."

               Pelleas gazing thought,
"Is Guinevere herself so beautiful?"
For large her violet eyes look'd, and her bloom
A rosy dawn kindled in stainless heavens,
And round her limbs, mature in womanhood;
70   And slender was her hand and small her shape;
And but for those large eyes, the haunts of scorn,
She might have seem'd a toy to trifle with,
And pass and care no more. But while he gazed
The beauty of her flesh abash'd the boy,
75   As tho' it were the beauty of her soul:
For as the base man, judging of the good,
Puts his own baseness in him by default
Of will and nature, so did Pelleas lend
All the young beauty of his own soul to hers,
80   Believing her; and when she spake to him,
Stammer'd, and could not make her a reply.
For out of the waste islands had he come,

4. Adorned with rich cloths.

Where saving° his own sisters he had known   *except for*
Scarce any but the women of his isles,
85 Rough wives, that laugh'd and scream'd against the gulls,
Makers of nets, and living from the sea.

Then with a slow smile turn'd the lady round
And look'd upon her people; and as when
A stone is flung into some sleeping tarn,°   *pond*
90 The circle widens till it lip the marge,
Spread the slow smile thro' all her company.
Three knights were thereamong; and they too smiled,
Scorning him; for the lady was Ettarre,
And she was a great lady in her land.

95 Again she said, "O wild and of the woods,
Knowest thou not the fashion of our speech?
Or have the Heavens but given thee a fair face,
Lacking a tongue?"

"O damsel," answer'd he,
"I woke from dreams; and coming out of gloom
100 Was dazzled by the sudden light, and crave
Pardon: but will ye to Caerleon? I
Go likewise: shall I lead you to the King?"

"Lead then," she said; and thro' the woods they went.
And while they rode, the meaning in his eyes,
105 His tenderness of manner, and chaste awe,
His broken utterances and bashfulness,
Were all a burthen to her, and in her heart
She mutter'd, "I have lighted on a fool,
Raw, yet so stale!" But since her mind was bent
110 On hearing, after trumpet blown, her name
And title, "Queen of Beauty," in the lists
Cried—and beholding him so strong, she thought
That peradventure he will fight for me,
And win the circlet: therefore flatter'd him,
115 Being so gracious, that he wellnigh deem'd
His wish by hers was echo'd; and her knights
And all her damsels too were gracious to him,
For she was a great lady.

And when they reach'd
Caerleon, ere they past to lodging, she,
120 Taking his hand, "O the strong hand," she said,
"See! look at mine! but wilt thou fight for me,
And win me this fine circlet, Pelleas,
That I may love thee?"

Then his helpless heart
Leapt, and he cried, "Ay! wilt thou if I win?"

125   "Ay, that will I," she answer'd, and she laugh'd,
      And straitly nipt the hand, and flung it from her;
      Then glanced askew at those three knights of hers,
      Till all her ladies laugh'd along with her.

         "O happy world," thought Pelleas, "all, meseems,
130   Are happy; I the happiest of them all."
      Nor slept that night for pleasure in his blood,
      And green wood-ways, and eyes among the leaves;
      Then being on the morrow knighted, sware
      To love one only. And as he came away,
135   The men who met him rounded on their heels
      And wonder'd after him, because his face
      Shone like the countenance of a priest of old
      Against the flame about a sacrifice
      Kindled by fire from heaven: so glad was he.

140   Then Arthur made vast banquets, and strange knights
      From the four winds came in: and each one sat,
      Tho' served with choice from air, land, stream, and sea,
      Oft in mid-banquet measuring with his eyes
      His neighbour's make and might: and Pelleas look'd
145   Noble among the noble, for he dream'd
      His lady loved him, and he knew himself
      Loved of the King: and him his new-made knight
      Worshipt, whose lightest whisper moved him more
      Than all the ranged reasons of the world.

150   Then blush'd and brake the morning of the jousts,
      And this was call'd "The Tournament of Youth:"
      For Arthur, loving his young knight, withheld
      His older and his mightier from the lists,
      That Pelleas might obtain his lady's love,
155   According to her promise, and remain
      Lord of the tourney. And Arthur had the jousts
      Down in the flat field by the shore of Usk[5]
      Holden: the gilded parapets were crown'd
      With faces, and the great tower fill'd with eyes
160   Up to the summit, and the trumpets blew.
      There all day long Sir Pelleas kept the field
      With honour: so by that strong hand of his
      The sword and golden circlet were achieved.

         Then rang the shout his lady loved: the heat
165   Of pride and glory fired her face; her eye
      Sparkled; she caught the circlet from his lance,
      And there before the people crown'd herself:
      So for the last time she was gracious to him.

5. River near Caerleon.

Then at Caerleon for a space—her look
170   Bright for all others, cloudier on her knight—
Linger'd Ettarre: and seeing Pelleas droop,
Said Guinevere, "We marvel at thee much,
O damsel, wearing this unsunny face
To him who won thee glory!" And she said,
175   "Had ye not held your Lancelot in your bower,
My Queen, he had not won." Whereat the Queen,
As one whose foot is bitten by an ant,
Glanced down upon her, turn'd and went her way.

But after, when her damsels, and herself,
180   And those three knights all set their faces home,
Sir Pelleas follow'd. She that saw him cried,
"Damsels—and yet I should be shamed to say it—
I cannot bide Sir Baby. Keep him back
Among yourselves. Would rather that we had
185   Some rough old knight who knew the worldly way,
Albeit grizzlier than a bear, to ride
And jest with: take him to you, keep him off,
And pamper him with papmeat,° if ye will,   *infants' food*
Old milky fables of the wolf and sheep,
190   Such as the wholesome mothers tell their boys.
Nay, should ye try him with a merry one
To find his mettle, good: and if he fly us,
Small matter! let him." This her damsels heard,
And mindful of her small and cruel hand,
195   They, closing round him thro' the journey home,
Acted her hest,° and always from her side   *command*
Restrain'd him with all manner of device,
So that he could not come to speech with her.
And when she gain'd her castle, upsprang the bridge,
200   Down rang the grate of iron thro' the groove,
And he was left alone in open field.

"These be the ways of ladies," Pelleas thought,
"To those who love them, trials of our faith.
Yea, let her prove me to the uttermost,
205   For loyal to the uttermost am I."
So made his moan; and, darkness falling, sought
A priory not far off, there lodged, but rose
With morning every day, and, moist or dry,
Full-arm'd upon his charger all day long
210   Sat by the walls, and no one open'd to him.

And this persistence turn'd her scorn to wrath.
Then calling her three knights, she charged them, "Out!
And drive him from the walls." And out they came,
But Pelleas overthrew them as they dash'd
215   Against him one by one; and these return'd,

But still he kept his watch beneath the wall.

    Thereon her wrath became a hate; and once,
A week beyond, while walking on the walls
With her three knights, she pointed downward, "Look,
220   He haunts me—I cannot breathe—besieges me;
Down! strike him! put my hate into your strokes,
And drive him from my walls." And down they went,
And Pelleas overthrew them one by one;
And from the tower above him cried Ettarre,
225   "Bind him, and bring him in."

                       He heard her voice;
Then let the strong hand, which had overthrown
Her minion-knights, by those he overthrew
Be bounden straight, and so they brought him in.

    Then when he came before Ettarre, the sight
230   Of her rich beauty made him at one glance
More bondsman in his heart than in his bonds.
Yet with good cheer he spake, "Behold me, Lady,
A prisoner, and the vassal of thy will;
And if thou keep me in thy donjon here,
235   Content am I so that I see thy face
But once a day: for I have sworn my vows,
And thou hast given thy promise, and I know
That all these pains are trials of my faith,
And that thyself, when thou hast seen me strain'd
240   And sifted to the utmost, wilt at length
Yield me thy love and know me for thy knight."

    Then she began to rail so bitterly,
With all her damsels, he was stricken mute;
But when she mock'd his vows and the great King,
245   Lighted on words: "For pity of thine own self,
Peace, Lady, peace: is he not thine and mine?"
"Thou fool," she said, "I never heard his voice
But long'd to break away. Unbind him now,
And thrust him out of doors; for save he be
250   Fool to the midmost marrow of his bones,
He will return no more." And those, her three,
Laugh'd, and unbound, and thrust him from the gate.

    And after this, a week beyond, again
She call'd them, saying, "There he watches yet,
255   There like a dog before his master's door!
Kick'd, he returns: do ye not hate him, ye?
Ye know yourselves: how can ye bide at peace,
Affronted with his fulsome innocence?
Are ye but creatures of the board and bed,
260   No men to strike? Fall on him all at once,

And if ye slay him I reck not: if ye fail,
Give ye the slave mine order to be bound,
Bind him as heretofore, and bring him in:
It may be ye shall slay him in his bonds."

265   She spake; and at her will they couch'd their spears,
Three against one: and Gawain[6] passing by,
Bound upon solitary adventure, saw
Low down beneath the shadow of those towers
A villainy, three to one: and thro' his heart
270   The fire of honour and all noble deeds
Flash'd, and he call'd, "I strike upon thy side—
The caitiffs!"° "Nay," said Pelleas, "but forbear;   cowards
He needs no aid who doth his lady's will."

So Gawain, looking at the villainy done,
275   Forbore, but in his heat and eagerness
Trembled and quiver'd, as the dog, withheld
A moment from the vermin that he sees
Before him, shivers, ere he springs and kills.

And Pelleas overthrew them, one to three;
280   And they rose up, and bound, and brought him in.
Then first her anger, leaving Pelleas, burn'd
Full on her knights in many an evil name
Of craven, weakling, and thrice-beaten hound:
"Yet, take him, ye that scarce are fit to touch,
285   Far less to bind, your victor, and thrust him out,
And let who will release him from his bonds.
And if he comes again"—there she brake short;
And Pelleas answer'd, "Lady, for indeed
I loved you and I deem'd you beautiful,
290   I cannot brook to see your beauty marr'd
Thro' evil spite: and if ye love me not,
I cannot bear to dream you so forsworn:
I had liefer° ye were worthy of my love,   rather
Than to be loved again of you—farewell;
295   And tho' ye kill my hope, not yet my love,
Vex not yourself: ye will not see me more."

While thus he spake, she gazed upon the man
Of princely bearing, tho' in bonds, and thought,
"Why have I push'd him from me? this man loves,
300   If love there be: yet him I loved not. Why?
I deem'd him fool? yea, so? or that in him
A something—was it nobler than myself?—
Seem'd my reproach? He is not of my kind.
He could not love me, did he know me well.

6. King Arthur's nephew, and a Knight of the Round Table.

305   Nay, let him go—and quickly." And her knights
    Laugh'd not, but thrust him bounden out of door.

       Forth sprang Gawain, and loosed him from his bonds,
    And flung them o'er the walls; and afterward,
    Shaking his hands, as from a lazar's° rag,   *leper's*
310   "Faith of my body," he said, "and art thou not—
    Yea thou art he, whom late our Arthur made
    Knight of his table; yea and he that won
    The circlet? wherefore hast thou so defamed
    Thy brotherhood in me and all the rest,
315   As let these caitiffs on thee work their will?"

       And Pelleas answer'd, "O, their wills are hers
    For whom I won the circlet; and mine, hers,
    Thus to be bounden, so to see her face,
    Marr'd tho' it be with spite and mockery now,
320   Other than when I found her in the woods;
    And tho' she hath me bounden but in spite,
    And all to flout me, when they bring me in,
    Let me be bounden, I shall see her face;
    Else must I die thro' mine unhappiness."

325   And Gawain answer'd kindly tho' in scorn,
    "Why, let my lady bind me if she will,
    And let my lady beat me if she will:
    But an° she send her delegate to thrall   *if*
    These fighting hands of mine—Christ kill me then
330   But I will slice him handless by the wrist,
    And let my lady sear the stump for him,
    Howl as he may. But hold me for your friend:
    Come, ye know nothing: here I pledge my troth,
    Yea, by the honour of the Table Round,
335   I will be leal° to thee and work thy work,   *loyal*
    And tame thy jailing princess to thine hand.
    Lend me thine horse and arms, and I will say
    That I have slain thee. She will let me in
    To hear the manner of thy fight and fall;
340   Then, when I come within her counsels, then
    From prime to vespers[7] will I chant thy praise
    As prowest° knight and truest lover, more   *noblest*
    Than any have sung thee living, till she long
    To have thee back in lusty life again,
345   Not to be bound, save by white bonds and warm,
    Dearer than freedom. Wherefore now thy horse
    And armour: let me go: be comforted:
    Give me three days to melt her fancy, and hope
    The third night hence will bring thee news of gold."

---

7. From sunrise to sunset. Prime is the morning daily office of the church; vespers is evening prayer.

350   Then Pelleas lent his horse and all his arms,
       Saving the goodly sword, his prize, and took
       Gawain's, and said, "Betray me not, but help—
       Art thou not he whom men call light-of-love?"

          "Ay," said Gawain, "for women be so light."°   *fickle*
355   Then bounded forward to the castle walls,
       And raised a bugle hanging from his neck,
       And winded it, and that so musically
       That all the old echoes hidden in the wall
       Rang out like hollow woods at hunting-tide.

360   Up ran a score of damsels to the tower;
       "Avaunt,"° they cried, "our lady loves thee not."   *depart*
       But Gawain lifting up his vizor said,
       "Gawain am I, Gawain of Arthur's court,
       And I have slain this Pelleas whom ye hate:
365   Behold his horse and armour. Open gates,
       And I will make you merry."

                                And down they ran,
       Her damsels, crying to their lady, "Lo!
       Pelleas is dead—he told us—he that hath
       His horse and armour: will ye let him in?
370   He slew him! Gawain, Gawain of the court,
       Sir Gawain—there he waits below the wall,
       Blowing his bugle as who should say him nay."

          And so, leave given, straight on thro' open door
       Rode Gawain, whom she greeted courteously.
375   "Dead, is it so?" she ask'd. "Ay, ay," said he,
       "And oft in dying cried upon your name."
       "Pity on him," she answer'd, "a good knight,
       But never let me bide one hour at peace."
       "Ay," thought Gawain, "and you be fair enow:
380   But I to your dead man have given my troth,
       That whom ye loathe, him will I make you love."

          So those three days, aimless about the land,
       Lost in a doubt, Pelleas wandering
       Waited, until the third night brought a moon
385   With promise of large light on woods and ways.
       Hot was the night and silent; but a sound
       Of Gawain ever coming, and this lay°—   *ballad*
       Which Pelleas had heard sung before the Queen,
       And seen her sadden listening—vext his heart,
390   And marr'd his rest—"A worm within the rose."
       "A rose, but one, none other rose had I,
       A rose, one rose, and this was wondrous fair,
       One rose, a rose that gladden'd earth and sky,
       One rose, my rose, that sweeten'd all mine air—
395   I cared not for the thorns; the thorns were there.

"One rose, a rose to gather by and by,
One rose, a rose, to gather and to wear,
No rose but one—what other rose had I?
One rose, my rose; a rose that will not die,—
He dies who loves it,—if the worm be there."

    This tender rhyme, and evermore the doubt,
"Why lingers Gawain with his golden news?"
So shook him that he could not rest, but rode
Ere midnight to her walls, and bound his horse
Hard by the gates. Wide open were the gates,
And no watch kept; and in thro' these he past,
And heard but his own steps, and his own heart
Beating, for nothing moved but his own self,
And his own shadow. Then he crost the court,
And spied not any light in hall or bower,
But saw the postern portal also wide
Yawning; and up a slope of garden, all
Of roses white and red, and brambles mixt
And overgrowing them, went on, and found,
Here too, all hush'd below the mellow moon,
Save that one rivulet from a tiny cave
Came lightening downward, and so spilt itself
Among the roses, and was lost again.

    Then was he ware of three pavilions rear'd
Above the bushes, gilden-peakt: in one,
Red after revel, droned her lurdane[8] knights
Slumbering, and their three squires across their feet:
In one, their malice on the placid lip
Froz'n by sweet sleep, four of her damsels lay:
And in the third, the circlet of the jousts
Bound on her brow, were Gawain and Ettarre.

    Back, as a hand that pushes thro' the leaf
To find a nest and feels a snake, he drew:
Back, as a coward slinks from what he fears
To cope with, or a traitor proven, or hound
Beaten, did Pelleas in an utter shame
Creep with his shadow thro' the court again,
Fingering at his sword-handle until he stood
There on the castle-bridge once more, and thought,
"I will go back, and slay them where they lie."

    And so went back, and seeing them yet in sleep
Said, "Ye, that so dishallow the holy sleep,
Your sleep is death," and drew the sword, and thought,
"What! slay a sleeping knight? the King hath bound

395

400

405

410

415

420

425

430

435

8. From old French "lourdin," heavy [Tennyson's note].

440   And sworn me to this brotherhood;" again,
"Alas that ever a knight should be so false."
Then turn'd, and so return'd, and groaning laid
The naked sword athwart their naked throats,
There left it, and them sleeping; and she lay,
445   The circlet of the tourney round her brows,
And the sword of the tourney across her throat.

       And forth he past, and mounting on his horse
Stared at her towers that, larger than themselves
In their own darkness, throng'd into the moon.
450   Then crush'd the saddle with his thighs, and clench'd
His hands, and madden'd with himself and moan'd:

       "Would they have risen against me in their blood
At the last day?[9] I might have answer'd them
Even before high God. O towers so strong,
455   Huge, solid, would that even while I gaze
The crack of earthquake shivering to your base
Split you, and Hell burst up your harlot roofs
Bellowing, and charr'd you thro' and thro' within,
Black as the harlot's heart—hollow as a skull!
460   Let the fierce east scream thro' your eyelet-holes,
And whirl the dust of harlots round and round
In dung and nettles! hiss, snake—I saw him there—
Let the fox bark, let the wolf yell. Who yells
Here in the still sweet summer night, but I—
465   I, the poor Pelleas whom she call'd her fool?
Fool, beast—he, she, or I? myself most fool;
Beast too, as lacking human wit—disgraced,
Dishonour'd all for trial of true love—
Love?—we be all alike: only the King
470   Hath made us fools and liars. O noble vows!
O great and sane and simple race of brutes
That own° no lust because they have no law!   *admit*
For why should I have loved her to my shame?
I loathe her, as I loved her to my shame.
475   I never loved her, I but lusted for her—
Away—"
           He dash'd the rowel° into his horse,   *spur*
And bounded forth and vanish'd thro' the night.

       Then she, that felt the cold touch on her throat,
Awaking knew the sword, and turn'd herself
480   To Gawain: "Liar, for thou hast not slain
This Pelleas! here he stood, and might have slain
Me and thyself." And he that tells the tale

---

9. Pelleas wonders whether, if he had slain them, the corpses of Gawain and Ettarre would have risen to accuse him on Judgment Day.

Says that her ever-veering fancy turn'd
To Pelleas, as the one true knight on earth,
485 And only lover; and thro' her love her life
Wasted and pined, desiring him in vain.

But he by wild and way, for half the night,
And over hard and soft, striking the sod
From out the soft, the spark from off the hard,
490 Rode till the star above the wakening sun,
Beside that tower where Percivale was cowl'd,[1]
Glanced from the rosy forehead of the dawn.
For so the words were flash'd into his heart
He knew not whence or wherefore: "O sweet star,
495 Pure on the virgin forehead of the dawn!"
And there he would have wept, but felt his eyes
Harder and drier than a fountain bed
In summer: thither came the village girls
And linger'd talking, and they come no more
500 Till the sweet heavens have fill'd it from the heights
Again with living waters in the change
Of seasons: hard his eyes; harder his heart
Seem'd; but so weary were his limbs, that he,
Gasping, "Of Arthur's hall am I, but here,
505 Here let me rest and die," cast himself down,
And gulf'd his griefs in inmost sleep; so lay,
Till shaken by a dream, that Gawain fired
The hall of Merlin, and the morning star
Reel'd in the smoke, brake into flame, and fell.

510 He woke, and being ware of some one nigh,
Sent hands upon him, as to tear him, crying,
"False! and I held thee pure as Guinevere."

But Percivale stood near him and replied,
"Am I but false as Guinevere is pure?
515 Or art thou mazed° with dreams? or being one   bewildered
Of our free-spoken Table hast not heard
That Lancelot"—there he check'd himself and paused.

Then fared it with Sir Pelleas as with one
Who gets a wound in battle, and the sword
520 That made it plunges thro' the wound again,
And pricks it deeper: and he shrank and wail'd,
"Is the Queen false?" and Percivale was mute.
"Have any of our Round Table held their vows?"
And Percivale made answer not a word.
525 "Is the King true?" "The King!" said Percivale.

---

1. Sir Percivale, a devout knight of the Round Table, had become a monk.

"Why then let men couple at once with wolves.[2]
What! art thou mad?"

But Pelleas, leaping up,
Ran thro' the doors and vaulted on his horse
And fled: small pity upon his horse had he,
530 Or on himself, or any, and when he met
A cripple, one that held a hand for alms—
Hunch'd as he was, and like an old dwarf-elm
That turns its back on the salt blast, the boy
Paused not, but overrode him, shouting, "False,
535 And false with Gawain!" and so left him bruised
And batter'd, and fled on, and hill and wood
Went ever streaming by him till the gloom,
That follows on the turning of the world,
Darken'd the common path: he twitch'd the reins,
540 And made his beast that better knew it, swerve
Now off it and now on; but when he saw
High up in heaven the hall that Merlin built,
Blackening against the dead-green stripes of even,
"Black nest of rats," he groan'd, "ye build too high."

545 Not long thereafter from the city gates
Issued Sir Lancelot riding airily,
Warm with a gracious parting from the Queen,
Peace at his heart, and gazing at a star
And marvelling what it was: on whom the boy,

550 Across the silent seeded mellow-grass
Borne, clash'd: and Lancelot, saying, "What name hast thou
That ridest here so blindly and so hard?"
"No name, no name," he shouted, "a scourge am I
To lash the treasons of the Table Round."
555 "Yea, but thy name?" "I have many names," he cried:
"I am wrath and shame and hate and evil fame,
And like a poisonous wind I pass to blast
And blaze the crime of Lancelot and the Queen."
"First over me," said Lancelot, "shalt thou pass."
560 "Fight therefore," yell'd the youth, and either knight
Drew back a space, and when they closed, at once
The weary steed of Pelleas floundering flung
His rider, who call'd out from the dark field,
"Thou art false as Hell: slay me: I have no sword."[3]
565 Then Lancelot, "Yea, between thy lips—and sharp;
But here will I disedge it by thy death."[4]
"Slay then," he shriek'd, "my will is to be slain,"

2. The noble ideals of Arthur hold the kingdom together; thus, if he were untrue, the realm would disintegrate in barbaric savagery.

3. Because he has left it lying across the throats of Gawain and Ettarre.
4. I.e., blunt your sharp tongue by killing you.

And Lancelot, with his heel upon the fall'n,
Rolling his eyes, a moment stood, then spake:
570   "Rise, weakling; I am Lancelot; say thy say."

    And Lancelot slowly rode his warhorse back
To Camelot, and Sir Pelleas in brief while
Caught his unbroken limbs from the dark field,
And follow'd to the city. It chanced that both
575   Brake into hall together, worn and pale.
There with her knights and dames was Guinevere.
Full wonderingly she gazed on Lancelot
So soon return'd, and then on Pelleas, him
Who had not greeted her, but cast himself
580   Down on a bench, hard-breathing. "Have ye fought?"
She ask'd of Lancelot. "Ay, my Queen," he said.
"And thou hast overthrown him?" "Ay, my Queen."
Then she, turning to Pelleas, "O young knight,
Hath the great heart of knighthood in thee fail'd
585   So far thou canst not bide, unfrowardly,°   *good-naturedly*
A fall from *him?*" Then, for he answer'd not,
"Or hast thou other griefs? If I, the Queen,
May help them, loose thy tongue, and let me know."
But Pelleas lifted up an eye so fierce
590   She quail'd; and he, hissing "I have no sword,"
Sprang from the door into the dark.[5] The Queen
Look'd hard upon her lover, he on her;
And each foresaw the dolorous day to be:
And all talk died, as in a grove all song
595   Beneath the shadow of some bird of prey;
Then a long silence came upon the hall,
And Modred[6] thought, "The time is hard at hand."

The Passing of Arthur[1]

That story which the bold Sir Bedivere,[2]
First made and latest left of all the knights,
Told, when the man was no more than a voice
In the white winter of his age, to those
5   With whom he dwelt, new faces, other minds.

    For on their march to westward, Bedivere,
Who slowly paced among the slumbering host,
Heard in his tent the moanings of the King:

5. Although Malory gives Pelleas a happy ending, in the form of another damsel to love, Tennyson does not. In the next Idyll, *The Last Tournament*, Pelleas is so disenchanted by his discovery of corruption that he sets up a mock court of drunkenness and debauchery.
6. Arthur's nephew, who will lead the revolt against him.
1. The twelfth and final Idyll depicts the downfall of Camelot and the death of King Arthur. He and his nephew Gawain have been in France fighting against Lancelot, who had fled with Guinevere. They return to England to an insurrection led by Arthur's nephew Modred, and upon landing, Gawain is killed. Tennyson described the themes as "the temporary triumph of evil, the confusion of moral order, closing in the Great Battle of the West."
2. The first man Arthur knighted after being crowned, and the last one with him at the end. See *The Coming of Arthur*, lines 173–176, page 1297.

"I found Him in the shining of the stars,
10   I mark'd Him in the flowering of His fields,
But in His ways with men I find Him not.
I waged His wars, and now I pass and die.
O me! for why is all around us here
As if some lesser god had made the world,
15   But had not force to shape it as he would,
Till the High God behold it from beyond,
And enter it, and make it beautiful?
Or else as if the world were wholly fair,
But that these eyes of men are dense and dim,
20   And have not power to see it as it is:
Perchance, because we see not to the close;—
For I, being simple, thought to work His will,
And have but stricken with the sword in vain;
And all whereon I lean'd in wife and friend
25   Is traitor to my peace, and all my realm
Reels back into the beast, and is no more.
My God, thou hast forgotten me in my death:[3]
Nay—God my Christ—I pass but shall not die."

Then, ere that last weird battle in the west,
30   There came on Arthur sleeping, Gawain kill'd
In Lancelot's war, the ghost of Gawain blown
Along a wandering wind, and past his ear
Went shrilling, "Hollow, hollow all delight!
Hail, King! to-morrow thou shalt pass away.
35   Farewell! there is an isle of rest for thee.
And I am blown along a wandering wind,
And hollow, hollow, hollow all delight."
And fainter onward, like wild birds that change
Their season in the night and wail their way
40   From cloud to cloud, down the long wind the dream
Shrill'd; but in going mingled with dim cries
Far in the moonlit haze among the hills,
As of some lonely city sack'd by night,
When all is lost, and wife and child with wail
45   Pass to new lords; and Arthur woke and call'd,
"Who spake? A dream. O light upon the wind,
Thine, Gawain, was the voice—are these dim cries
Thine? or doth all that haunts the waste and wild
Mourn, knowing it will go along with me?"

50   This heard the bold Sir Bedivere and spake:
"O me, my King, let pass whatever will,

---

3. Arthur echoes the words of Christ on the cross, "My God, my God, why hast thou forsaken me?" (Matthew 27.46).

Elves, and the harmless glamour of the field;[4]
But in their stead thy name and glory cling
To all high places like a golden cloud
55 For ever: but as yet thou shalt not pass.
Light was Gawain in life, and light in death
Is Gawain, for the ghost is as the man;
And care not thou for dreams from him, but rise—
I hear the steps of Modred in the west,
60 And with him many of thy people, and knights
Once thine, whom thou hast loved, but grosser grown
Than heathen, spitting at their vows and thee.
Right well in heart they know thee for the King.
Arise, go forth and conquer as of old."

65   Then spake King Arthur to Sir Bedivere:
"Far other is this battle in the west
Whereto we move, than when we strove in youth,
And brake the petty kings, and fought with Rome,
Or thrust the heathen from the Roman wall,
70 And shook him thro' the north. Ill doom is mine
To war against my people and my knights.
The king who fights his people fights himself.
And they my knights, who loved me once, the stroke
That strikes them dead is as my death to me.
75 Yet let us hence, and find or feel a way
Thro' this blind haze, which ever since I saw
One lying in the dust at Almesbury,[5]
Hath folded in the passes of the world."

    Then rose the King and moved his host by night
80 And ever push'd Sir Modred, league by league,
Back to the sunset bound of Lyonnesse[6]—
A land of old upheaven from the abyss
By fire, to sink into the abyss again;
Where fragments of forgotten peoples dwelt,
85 And the long mountains ended in a coast
Of ever-shifting sand, and far away
The phantom circle of a moaning sea.
There the pursuer could pursue no more,
And he that fled no further fly the King;
90 And there, that day when the great light of heaven
Burn'd at his lowest in the rolling year,[7]
On the waste sand by the waste sea they closed.
Nor ever yet had Arthur fought a fight

---

4. The legends which cluster round the King's name [Tennyson's note]. One legend was that the elves bestowed gifts on Arthur as a child.
5. In the previous Idyll, *Guinevere*, Arthur visited his Queen in the convent at Almesbury, where she had taken refuge; she lay in the dust at his feet in remorse.
6. Mythical kingdom off the coast of Cornwall, which sank, Atlantis-like, under the sea.
7. The winter solstice [Tennyson's note].

Like this last, dim, weird battle of the west.
95   A deathwhite mist slept over sand and sea:
Whereof the chill, to him who breathed it, drew
Down with his blood, till all his heart was cold
With formless fear; and ev'n on Arthur fell
Confusion, since he saw not whom he fought.
100 For friend and foe were shadows in the mist,
And friend slew friend not knowing whom he slew;
And some had visions out of golden youth,
And some beheld the faces of old ghosts
Look in upon the battle; and in the mist
105 Was many a noble deed, many a base,
And chance and craft and strength in single fights,
And ever and anon with host to host
Shocks, and the splintering spear, the hard mail hewn,
Shield-breakings, and the clash of brands, the crash
110 Of battleaxes on shatter'd helms, and shrieks
After the Christ, of those who falling down
Look'd up for heaven, and only saw the mist;
And shouts of heathen and the traitor knights,
Oaths, insult, filth, and monstrous blasphemies,
115 Sweat, writhings, anguish, labouring of the lungs
In that close mist, and cryings for the light,
Moans of the dying, and voices of the dead.

Last, as by some one deathbed after wail
Of suffering, silence follows, or thro' death
120 Or deathlike swoon, thus over all that shore,
Save for some whisper of the seething seas,
A dead hush fell; but when the dolorous day
Grew drearier toward twilight falling, came
A bitter wind, clear from the North, and blew
125 The mist aside, and with that wind the tide
Rose, and the pale King glanced across the field
Of battle: but no man was moving there;
Nor any cry of Christian heard thereon,
Nor yet of heathen; only the wan wave
130 Brake in among dead faces, to and fro
Swaying the helpless hands, and up and down
Tumbling the hollow helmets of the fallen,
And shiver'd brands that once had fought with Rome,
And rolling far along the gloomy shores
135 The voice of days of old and days to be.

Then spake King Arthur to Sir Bedivere,
And whiter than the mist that all day long
Had held the field of battle was the King:

"Hearest thou this great voice that shakes the world,
140 And wastes the narrow realm whereon we move,

And beats upon the faces of the dead,
My dead, as tho' they had not died for me?—
O Bedivere, for on my heart hath fall'n
Confusion, till I know not what I am,
145   Nor whence I am, nor whether I be King.
Behold, I seem but King among the dead."

Then spake the bold Sir Bedivere: "My King,
King everywhere! and so the dead have kings,
There also will I worship thee as King.
150   Yet still thy life is whole, and still I live
Who love thee; but who hates thee, he that brought
The heathen back among us, yonder stands,
Modred, unharm'd, the traitor of thine house."

Then spake the King: "My house hath been my doom.
155   But call not thou this traitor of my house
Who hath but dwelt beneath one roof with me.
My house are rather they who sware my vows,
Yea, even while they brake them, own'd me King.
And well for thee, saying in my dark hour,
160   When all the purport of my throne hath fail'd,
That quick or dead thou holdest me for King.
King am I, whatsoever be their cry;
And one last act of kinghood shalt thou see
Yet, ere I pass." And uttering this the King
165   Made at the man: then Modred smote his liege
Hard on that helm which many a heathen sword
Had beaten thin; while Arthur at one blow,
Striking the last stroke with Excalibur,
Slew him, and all but slain himself, he fell.

170   So all day long the noise of battle roll'd
Among the mountains by the winter sea;
Until King Arthur's Table, man by man,
Had fall'n in Lyonnesse about their lord,
King Arthur. Then, because his wound was deep,
175   The bold Sir Bedivere uplifted him,
And bore him to a chapel nigh the field,
A broken chancel with a broken cross,
That stood on a dark strait of barren land:
On one side lay the Ocean, and on one
180   Lay a great water, and the moon was full.

Then spake King Arthur to Sir Bedivere:
"The sequel of to-day unsolders all
The goodliest fellowship of famous knights
Whereof this world holds record. Such a sleep
185   They sleep—the men I loved. I think that we
Shall never more, at any future time,

Delight our souls with talk of knightly deeds,
Walking about the gardens and the halls
Of Camelot, as in the days that were.
190 I perish by this people which I made,—
Tho' Merlin sware that I should come again
To rule once more;[8] but, let what will be, be,
I am so deeply smitten thro' the helm
That without help I cannot last till morn.
195 Thou therefore take my brand Excalibur,
Which was my pride: for thou rememberest how
In those old days, one summer noon, an arm
Rose up from out the bosom of the lake,
Clothed in white samite,[9] mystic, wonderful,
200 Holding the sword—and how I row'd across
And took it, and have worn it, like a king;
And, wheresoever I am sung or told
In aftertime, this also shall be known:
But now delay not: take Excalibur,
205 And fling him far into the middle mere:[1]
Watch what thou seëst, and lightly° bring me word."   *quickly*

    To him replied the bold Sir Bedivere:
"It is not meet, Sir King, to leave thee thus,
Aidless, alone, and smitten thro' the helm—
210 A little thing may harm a wounded man;
Yet I thy hest will all perform at full,
Watch what I see, and lightly bring thee word."

    So saying, from the ruin'd shrine he stept,
And in the moon athwart the place of tombs,
215 Where lay the mighty bones of ancient men,
Old knights, and over them the sea-wind sang
Shrill, chill, with flakes of foam. He, stepping down
By zigzag paths, and juts of pointed rock,
Came on the shining levels of the lake.

220   There drew he forth the brand Excalibur,
And o'er him, drawing it, the winter moon,
Brightening the skirts of a long cloud, ran forth
And sparkled keen with frost against the hilt:
For all the haft twinkled with diamond sparks,
225 Myriads of topaz-lights, and jacinth[2]-work
Of subtlest jewellery. He gazed so long
That both his eyes were dazzled as he stood,
This way and that dividing the swift mind,

8. According to legend, Arthur did not die but went to a mystical land from whence he will return to rule England again at the hour of its greatest need. [Tennyson's note].
9. A rich silk stuff inwrought with gold and silver threads

[Tennyson's note].
1. Middle of the lake.
2. Jacinth is the hyacinth stone, blue and purple [Tennyson's note].

In act to throw: but at the last it seem'd
230   Better to leave Excalibur conceal'd
There in the many-knotted waterflags,°   *yellow irises*
That whistled stiff and dry about the marge.
So strode he back slow to the wounded King.

    Then spake King Arthur to Sir Bedivere:
235   "Hast thou perform'd my mission which I gave?
What is it thou hast seen? or what hast heard?"

    And answer made the bold Sir Bedivere:
"I heard the ripple washing in the reeds,
And the wild water lapping on the crag."

240   To whom replied King Arthur, faint and pale:
"Thou hast betray'd thy nature and thy name,
Not rendering true answer, as beseem'd
Thy fealty, nor like a noble knight:
For surer sign had follow'd, either hand,
245   Or voice, or else a motion of the mere.
This is a shameful thing for men to lie.
Yet now, I charge thee, quickly go again,
As thou art lief° and dear, and do the thing   *beloved*
I bad thee, watch, and lightly bring me word."

250   Then went Sir Bedivere the second time
Across the ridge, and paced beside the mere,
Counting the dewy pebbles, fix'd in thought;
But when he saw the wonder of the hilt,
How curiously and strangely chased,° he smote   *ornamented*
255   His palms together, and he cried aloud:

    "And if indeed I cast the brand away,
Surely a precious thing, one worthy note,
Should thus be lost for ever from the earth,
Which might have pleased the eyes of many men.
260   What good should follow this, if this were done?
What harm, undone? Deep harm to disobey,
Seeing obedience is the bond of rule.
Were it well to obey then, if a king demand
An act unprofitable, against himself?
265   The King is sick, and knows not what he does.
What record, or what relic of my lord
Should be to aftertime, but empty breath
And rumours of a doubt? But were this kept,
Stored in some treasure-house of mighty kings,
270   Some one might show it at a joust of arms,
Saying, 'King Arthur's sword, Excalibur,
Wrought by the lonely maiden of the Lake.
Nine years she wrought it, sitting in the deeps
Upon the hidden bases of the hills.'

275   So might some old man speak in the aftertime
            To all the people, winning reverence.
            But now much honour and much fame were lost."

              So spake he, clouded with his own conceit,°   *foolish ideas*
            And hid Excalibur the second time,
280   And so strode back slow to the wounded King.

              Then spoke King Arthur, breathing heavily:
            "What is it thou hast seen? or what hast heard?"

              And answer made the bold Sir Bedivere:
            "I heard the water lapping on the crag,
285   And the long ripple washing in the reeds."

              To whom replied King Arthur, much in wrath:
            "Ah, miserable and unkind, untrue,
            Unknightly, traitor-hearted! Woe is me!
            Authority forgets a dying king,
290   Laid widow'd of the power in his eye
            That bow'd the will. I see thee what thou art,
            For thou, the latest-left of all my knights,
            In whom should meet the offices of all,
            Thou wouldst betray me for the precious hilt;
295   Either from lust of gold, or like a girl
            Valuing the giddy pleasure of the eyes.
            Yet, for a man may fail in duty twice,
            And the third time may prosper, get thee hence:
            But, if thou spare to fling Excalibur,
300   I will arise and slay thee with my hands."

              Then quickly rose Sir Bedivere, and ran,
            And, leaping down the ridges lightly, plunged
            Among the bulrush beds, and clutch'd the sword,
            And strongly wheel'd and threw it. The great brand
305   Made lightnings in the splendour of the moon,
            And flashing round and round, and whirl'd in an arch,
            Shot like a streamer of the northern morn,[3]
            Seen where the moving isles of winter shock[4]
            By night, with noises of the Northern Sea.
310   So flash'd and fell the brand Excalibur:
            But ere he dipt the surface, rose an arm
            Clothed in white samite, mystic, wonderful,
            And caught him by the hilt, and brandish'd him
            Three times, and drew him under in the mere,
315   And lightly went the other to the King.

---

3. The aurora borealis, or northern lights.   4. Where icebergs collide.

Then spoke King Arthur, drawing thicker breath
"Now see I by thine eyes that this is done.
Speak out: what is it thou hast heard, or seen?"

And answer made the bold Sir Bedivere:
320 "Sir King, I closed mine eyelids, lest the gems
Should blind my purpose, for I never saw,
Nor shall see, here or elsewhere, till I die,
Not tho' I live three lives of mortal men,
So great a miracle as yonder hilt.
325 Then with both hands I flung him, wheeling him;
But when I look'd again, behold an arm,
Clothed in white samite, mystic, wonderful,
That caught him by the hilt, and brandish'd him
Three times, and drew him under in the mere."

330 And answer made King Arthur, breathing hard:
"My end draws nigh; 'tis time that I were gone.
Make broad thy shoulders to receive my weight,
And bear me to the margin; yet I fear
My wound hath taken cold, and I shall die."

335 So saying, from the pavement he half rose,
Slowly, with pain, reclining on his arm,
And looking wistfully with wide blue eyes
As in a picture. Him Sir Bedivere
Remorsefully regarded thro' his tears,
340 And would have spoken, but he found not words;
Then took with care, and kneeling on one knee,
O'er both his shoulders drew the languid hands,
And rising bore him thro' the place of tombs.

But, as he walk'd, King Arthur panted hard,
345 Like one that feels a nightmare on his bed
When all the house is mute. So sigh'd the King,
Muttering and murmuring at his ear, "Quick, quick!
I fear it is too late, and I shall die."
But the other swiftly strode from ridge to ridge,
350 Clothed with his breath, and looking, as he walk'd,
Larger than human on the frozen hills.
He heard the deep behind him, and a cry
Before. His own thought drove him like a goad.
Dry clash'd his harness in the icy caves
355 And barren chasms, and all to left and right
The bare black cliff clang'd round him, as he based
His feet on juts of slippery crag that rang
Sharp-smitten with the dint of armed heels—
And on a sudden, lo! the level lake,
360 And the long glories of the winter moon.

Then saw they how there hove a dusky barge,
Dark as a funeral scarf from stem to stern,

Beneath them; and descending they were ware
That all the decks were dense with stately forms.
365 Black-stoled, black-hooded, like a dream—by these
Three Queens with crowns of gold:[5] and from them rose
A cry that shiver'd to the tingling stars,
And, as it were one voice, an agony
Of lamentation, like a wind that shrills
370 All night in a waste land, where no one comes,
Or hath come, since the making of the world.

    Then murmur'd Arthur, "Place me in the barge."
So to the barge they came. There those three Queens
Put forth their hands, and took the King, and wept.
375 But she, that rose the tallest of them all
And fairest, laid his head upon her lap,
And loosed the shatter'd casque,° and chafed his hands,   *helmet*
And call'd him by his name, complaining loud,
And dropping bitter tears against a brow
380 Striped with dark blood: for all his face was white
And colourless, and like the wither'd moon
Smote by the fresh beam of the springing east;
And all his greaves and cuisses° dash'd with drops   *leg armor*
Of onset;° and the light and lustrous curls—   *blood*
385 That made his forehead like a rising sun
High from the dais-throne—were parch'd with dust;
Or, clotted into points and hanging loose,
Mix'd with the knightly growth that fringed his lips.
So like a shatter'd column lay the King;
390 Not like that Arthur who, with lance in rest,
From spur to plume a star of tournament,
Shot thro' the lists at Camelot, and charged
Before the eyes of ladies and of kings.

    Then loudly cried the bold Sir Bedivere:
395 "Ah! my Lord Arthur, whither shall I go?
Where shall I hide my forehead and my eyes?
For now I see the true old times are dead,
When every morning brought a noble chance,
And every chance brought out a noble knight.
400 Such times have been not since the light that led
The holy Elders with the gift of myrrh.[6]
But now the whole Round Table is dissolved
Which was an image of the mighty world,
And I, the last, go forth companionless,

5. In the original *Morte D'Arthur* one was King Arthur's sister, Queen Morgan le Fay; the other was the Queen of Northgalis; the third was the Queen of the Waste Lands. Some say that the three Queens are Faith, Hope, and Charity [Tennyson's note]. The three queens heralded the beginning of Arthur's reign in *The Coming of Arthur*.
6. The Three Wise Men who came bearing gifts to the infant Jesus. Myrrh, used in embalming, foreshadowed Jesus' death.

405 And the days darken round me, and the years,
Among new men, strange faces, other minds."

And slowly answer'd Arthur from the barge:
"The old order changeth, yielding place to new,
And God fulfils himself in many ways,
410 Lest one good custom should corrupt the world.
Comfort thyself: what comfort is in me?
I have lived my life, and that which I have done
May He within himself make pure! but thou,
If thou shouldst never see my face again,
415 Pray for my soul. More things are wrought by prayer
Than this world dreams of. Wherefore, let thy voice
Rise like a fountain for me night and day.
For what are men better than sheep or goats
That nourish a blind life within the brain,
420 If, knowing God, they lift not hands of prayer
Both for themselves and those who call them friend?
For so the whole round earth is every way
Bound by gold chains about the feet of God.
But now farewell. I am going a long way
425 With these thou seëst—if indeed I go
(For all my mind is clouded with a doubt)—
To the island-valley of Avilion;[7]
Where falls not hail, or rain, or any snow,
Nor ever wind blows loudly; but it lies
430 Deep-meadow'd, happy, fair with orchard lawns
And bowery hollows crown'd with summer sea,
Where I will heal me of my grievous wound."

So said he, and the barge with oar and sail
Moved from the brink, like some full-breasted swan
435 That, fluting a wild carol ere her death,
Ruffles her pure cold plume, and takes the flood
With swarthy webs. Long stood Sir Bedivere
Revolving many memories, till the hull
Look'd one black dot against the verge of dawn,
440 And on the mere the wailing died away.

But when that moan had past for evermore,
The stillness of the dead world's winter dawn
Amazed him, and he groan'd, "The King is gone."
And therewithal came on him the weird rhyme,[8]
445 "From the great deep to the great deep he goes."

7. Avalon, "the island to which Arthur is borne in the barge and from which he will some day return—the Isle of the Blest" [Tennyson's note].
8. The rhyme is Merlin's riddle concerning Arthur's mys-
terious birth and death: "Sun, rain, and sun! and where is he who knows? From the great deep to the great deep he goes" (The Coming of Arthur, 409–10).

Whereat he slowly turn'd and slowly clomb
The last hard footstep of that iron crag;
Thence mark'd the black hull moving yet, and cried,
"He passes to be King among the dead,
450 And after healing of his grievous wound
He comes again; but—if he come no more—
O me, be yon dark Queens in yon black boat,
Who shriek'd and wail'd, the three whereat we gazed
On that high day, when, clothed with living light,
455 They stood before his throne in silence, friends
Of Arthur, who should help him at his need?"[9]

Then from the dawn it seem'd there came, but faint
As from beyond the limit of the world,
Like the last echo born of a great cry,
460 Sounds, as if some fair city were one voice
Around a king returning from his wars.

Thereat once more he moved about, and clomb
Ev'n to the highest he could climb, and saw,
Straining his eyes beneath an arch of hand,
465 Or thought he saw, the speck that bare the King,
Down that long water opening on the deep
Somewhere far off, pass on and on, and go
From less to less and vanish into light.
And the new sun rose bringing the new year.

1833–1869   1842, 1869

The Higher Pantheism[1]

The sun, the moon, the stars, the seas, the hills and the plains—
Are not these, O Soul, the Vision of Him who reigns?

Is not the Vision He? tho' He be not that which He seems?
Dreams are true while they last, and do we not live in dreams?

5 Earth, these solid stars, this weight of body and limb,
Are they not sign and symbol of thy division from Him?

Dark is the world to thee: thyself art the reason why;
For is He not all but that which has power to feel "I am I"?

Glory about thee, without thee; and thou fulfillest thy doom
10 Making Him broken gleams, and a stifled splendour and gloom.

Speak to Him thou for He hears, and Spirit with Spirit can meet—
Closer is He than breathing, and nearer than hands and feet.

9. See *The Coming of Arthur*, lines 274–78, page 1300.
1. Tennyson's son noted that this was written for the Metaphysical Society in 1869. Pantheism views God as coexistent with nature and its laws; the "higher pantheism" proposed by Tennyson sees nature not as God, but as merely a visible sign of a distinct and all-pervading Spirit that is beyond the power of imperfect human senses to grasp. Tennyson's paradoxes inspired Swinburne to produce a brutal but hilarious parody (see Response on next page).

God is law, say the wise; O Soul, and let us rejoice,
For if He thunder by law the thunder is yet His voice.

15   Law is God, say some: no God at all, says the fool;
For all we have power to see is a straight staff bent in a pool;

And the ear of man cannot hear, and the eye of man cannot see;
But if we could see and hear, this Vision—were it not He?

1869

RESPONSE
Algernon Charles Swinburne: The Higher Pantheism in a Nutshell[1]

One, who is not, we see: but one, whom we see not, is:
Surely this is not that: but that is assuredly this.

What, and wherefore, and whence? for under is over and under:
If thunder could be without lightning, lightning could be without thunder.

5   Doubt is faith in the main: but faith, on the whole, is doubt:
We cannot believe by proof: but could we believe without?

Why, and whither, and how? for barley and rye are not clover:
Neither are straight lines curves: yet over is under and over.

Two and two may be four: but four and four are not eight:
10   Fate and God may be twain: but God is the same thing as fate.

Ask a man what he thinks, and get from a man what he feels:
God, once caught in the fact, shows you a fair pair of heels.

Body and spirit are twins: God only knows which is which:
The soul squats down in the flesh, like a tinker drunk in a ditch.

15   More is the whole than a part: but half is more than the whole:
Clearly, the soul is the body: but is not the body the soul?

One and two are not one: but one and nothing is two:
Truth can hardly be false, if falsehood cannot be true.

Once the mastodon was: pterodactyls were common as cocks:
20   Then the mammoth was God: now is He a prize ox.

Parallels all things are: yet many of these are askew:
You are certainly I: but certainly I am not you.

Springs the rock from the plain, shoots the stream from the rock:
Cocks exist for the hen: but hens exist for the cock.

---

1. A parody of Tennyson's *The Higher Pantheism*. Swinburne's poem appeared in his anonymously published *Heptalogia, or The Seven Against Sense* (1880), which also included parodies of Browning, Patmore, Owen Meredith, Whitman, Rossetti, and Swinburne himself.

25   God, whom we see not, is: and God, who is not, we see:
        Fiddle, we know, is diddle: and diddle, we take it, is dee.

                                                                    1880

                              ⌒∞⌒

Flower in the Crannied Wall

        Flower in the crannied wall,
        I pluck you out of the crannies,
        I hold you here, root and all, in my hand,
        Little flower—but *if* I could understand
        What you are, root and all, and all in all,
        I should know what God and man is.

                                                                    1869

Crossing the Bar[1]

        Sunset and evening star,
            And one clear call for me!
        And may there be no moaning of the bar,[2]
            When I put out to sea,

5   But such a tide as moving seems asleep,
            Too full for sound and foam,
        When that which drew from out the boundless deep
            Turns again home.

        Twilight and evening bell,
10   And after that the dark!
        And may there be no sadness of farewell,
            When I embark;

        For tho' from out our bourne° of Time and Place   *boundary*
            The flood may bear me far,
15   I hope to see my Pilot face to face[3]
            When I have crost the bar.

1889   1889

---

1. Tennyson instructed that this poem should appear at
the end of every collection of his work, though it was not
in fact the last poem he wrote. The poem, he said, "came
in a moment" while he was crossing the Solent to return
home to Farringford on the Isle of Wight.
2. The sandbank that forms at the mouth of a harbor.
The "moaning" may be the sound of the river and the

sea meeting.
3. The pilot has been on board all the while, but in the
dark I have not seen him [Tennyson's note]. Cf. 1
Corinthians 13.12: "For now we see through a glass,
darkly; but then face to face: now I know in part; but
then shall I know even as also I am known."

Edward FitzGerald

1809–1883

"A Jug of Wine, a Loaf of Bread—and Thou": of the famous lines in Victorian literature, this carefree slogan is one of the most surprising. Its author was a retiring country gentleman of temperate habits, its audience a sober reading public that often regarded drink, sex, and idleness as paths to certain ruin. But Edward FitzGerald's creative translation of *The Rubáiyát of Omar Khayyám*, a twelfth-century Persian text, struck a responsive chord in Victorian hearts and minds. Published in 1859, the same year as Darwin's *The Origin of Species*, the poem gradually acquired enormous popularity in Britain and the United States. "The quaint mixture of farce and solemnity, passion and playfulness," said the late Victorian critic George Saintsbury, "make the poem actually, though not original or English, one of the greatest of English poems." It offered an alternate philosophy to those whose faith was shaken by the scientific erosion of the Bible's literal truth. The poem's hedonism springs from beautifully rendered expressions of doubt about life's meaning and religion's value. "O threats of Hell and Hopes of Paradise! / One thing at least is certain—*This* Life flies." Given how little humans know, given the brevity of life, one must live in the moment: "Drink! for you know not whence you came, nor why: / Drink! for you know not why you go, nor where."

A conservative man of independent means, FitzGerald spent most of his life in the Suffolk countryside, reading, studying, and translating. While he occasionally published his free adaptations of Greek, Persian, and Spanish classics, he never made any effort to become a professional writer, resolutely keeping his name off the title pages of his books. But he wrote wonderful letters: "I count myself a good correspondent," he admitted, adding with characteristic modesty, "but then I am an idle man." His addressees included some of the most important literary figures of the time, among them Thackeray, Tennyson, Carlyle, and the American critic Charles Eliot Norton. It was Norton who in 1869 wrote the first substantial review of the anonymously published *Rubáiyát* and then in 1872 traveled to England to unravel—successfully—the mystery of the poem's authorship.

"*Rubáiyát*" is not the name of an attitude or event but rather the plural for a type of short, epigrammatic poem written in Persian, a *rubái*. The original author of these four-line poems, Omar Khayyám (or, "Omar the Tentmaker"—probably his father's occupation), was an astronomer, mathematician, and poet born in Nishapur in what is now Iran. FitzGerald's imaginative version of his work might more accurately be called, "Selected Quatrains of Omar Khayyám, Much Revised." In 1856 FitzGerald's friend Edward Byles Cowell, a specialist in ancient languages who was departing for India, gave FitzGerald a going-away present: a transcript of the quatrains, then virtually unknown in England, that Cowell had made in Oxford. Upon his arrival in Calcutta, Cowell transcribed another Khayyám manuscript for FitzGerald. In May 1857 FitzGerald, who had had a series of personal setbacks—the death of his parents, the absence of Cowell, a brief, disastrous marriage—began translating the *Rubáiyát* "as a sort of Consolation."

There is no thematic order to Omar's stanzas in the original manuscripts, which FitzGerald described as "a strange succession of Grave and Gay." To give his translation narrative shape, FitzGerald created his own structure, the dawn-to-dusk musings of the aging Omar on a spring day. Of the 101 stanzas in FitzGerald's final version, published here, about half are close paraphrases of single, original quatrains, while the rest are composites and condensations of several *rubáiyát*. "Many Quatrains are mashed together," he acknowledged. Yet in making the poem less grand but more personal, FitzGerald ensured its literary vitality. As he reasoned in a letter to Cowell, "Better a live Sparrow than a stuffed Eagle."

The unusual stanza form that FitzGerald invented, which gives a single rhyme to all but the third line, may be the key to the poem's success. FitzGerald explained that "the penultimate line seems to lift and suspend the Wave that falls over in the last"—suggesting the brief interval of life before death inevitably ends it. When Dante Gabriel Rossetti happened upon the poem in 1861, he was caught by the music of Omar's ideas and immediately spread remaindered copies around the Pre-Raphaelite circle, starting the poem's slow rise to fame. Swinburne was so struck that he started his scandalous *Laus Veneris* in imitation that same evening.

If, as FitzGerald claimed, the poem "sang . . . of what all men feel in their hearts," in 1859 few dared to express their feelings so openly. But sentiments that would have shocked Victorians coming from a contemporary Englishman (as Pater and Wilde found out) seemed harmless enough in the voice of Omar the Tentmaker. Relocating Victorian skepticism and suppressed desires to twelfth-century Islamic Persia, the *Rubáiyát* was a highly effective piece of "orientalism"; it projected the Middle East as a land of indolence and pleasure where Westerners could pretend that the seductive views and vices they encountered were not their own. In stanzas 77 to 81, for example, the poem challenges the Judeo-Christian religious tradition, leading to the poem's most striking and parodic passage, what FitzGerald called the "Book of Pots" (stanzas 82–90). Here, empty wine jars speculate on the reason for their existence, until all is forgotten when the porter arrives to fill them.

"I / Was never deep in anything but—Wine." What is the reader to think of Omar's thirst? While this sensuous frankness risked upsetting his audience, FitzGerald argued for a sympathetic reading of Omar's plight, suggesting the universal role that he has, in fact, come to play in Anglo-American literature, a sort of Persian/Victorian Everyman: "Vainly endeavoring . . . to catch some authentic Glimpse of *Tomorrow*," FitzGerald concluded, Omar "fell back upon *Today* . . . as the only Ground he's got to stand upon, however momentarily slipping from under his Feet."

The Rubáiyát of Omar Khayyám of Naishápúr

1

Wake! For the Sun, who scatter'd into flight
The Stars before him from the Field of Night,
    Drives Night along with them from Heav'n, and strikes
The Sultán's Turret with a Shaft of Light.

2

5   Before the phantom of False morning[1] died,
Methought a Voice within the Tavern cried,
    "When all the Temple is prepared within,
Why nods the drowsy Worshiper outside?"

3

And, as the Cock crew, those who stood before
10 The Tavern shouted—"Open then the Door!
    You know how little while we have to stay,
And, once departed, may return no more."

4

Now the New Year reviving old Desires,[2]
The thoughtful Soul to Solitude retires,

1. A transient Light on the Horizon about an hour before the . . . True Dawn; a well-known phenomenon in the East [FitzGerald's note].

2. Spring; in Persia the new year began with the vernal equinox.

15   Where the WHITE HAND OF MOSES on the Bough
          Puts out, and Jesus from the Ground suspires.³°   *breathes*

                                    5

          Iram⁴ indeed is gone with all his Rose,
          And Jamshyd's Sev'n-ring'd Cup⁵ where no one knows;
                But still a Ruby kindles in the Vine,
20   And many a Garden by the Water blows.

                                    6

          And David's lips are lockt; but in divine
          High-piping Pehleví,⁶ with "Wine! Wine! Wine!
                Red Wine!"—the Nightingale cries to the Rose
          That sallow cheek of hers to incarnadine.

                                    7

25   Come, fill the Cup, and in the fire of Spring
          Your Winter-garment of Repentance fling:
                The Bird of Time has but a little way
          To flutter—and the Bird is on the Wing.

                                    8

          Whether at Naishápúr⁷ or Babylon,
30   Whether the Cup with sweet or bitter run,
                The Wine of Life keeps oozing drop by drop,
          The Leaves of Life keep falling one by one.

                                    9

          Each Morn a thousand Roses brings, you say;
          Yes, but where leaves the Rose of Yesterday?
35   And this first Summer month that brings the Rose
          Shall take Jamshyd and Kaikobád⁸ away.

                                    10

          Well, let it take them! What have we to do
          With Kaikobád the Great, or Kaikhosrú?
                Let Zál and Rustum bluster as they will,
40   Or Hátim call to Supper—heed not you.⁹

3. Exodus iv. 6; where Moses draws forth his Hand—not, according to the Persians, "leprous as Snow",—but white, as our May-blossom in Spring perhaps. According to them also the Healing Power of Jesus resided in his Breath [FitzGerald's note].
4. A royal Garden now sunk somewhere in the Sands of Arabia [FitzGerald's note].
5. FitzGerald notes that the cup of legendary king Jamshyd "was typical of the 7 Heavens, 7 Planets, 7 Seas, &c., and was a *Divining Cup*."
6. Pehleví, the old Heroic Sanskrit of Persia [FitzGerald's note].
7. The village in Persia where Omar was born.
8. Kaikobád was the founder of an ancient Persian dynasty.
9. Kaikhosrú, Zál, and Rustum were famous heroes; Hátim is "a type of Oriental generosity" [FitzGerald's note].

11

With me along the strip of Herbage strown
That just divides the desert from the sown,
    Where name of Slave and Sultán is forgot—
And Peace to Mahmúd[1] on his golden Throne!

12

45   A Book of Verses underneath the Bough,
A Jug of Wine, a Loaf of Bread—and Thou
    Beside me singing in the Wilderness—
Oh, Wilderness were Paradise enow!

13

Some for the Glories of This World; and some
50   Sigh for the Prophet's° Paradise to come;   *Muhammad's*
    Ah, take the Cash, and let the Credit go,
Nor heed the rumble of a distant Drum!

14

Look to the blowing Rose about us—"Lo,
Laughing," she says, "into the world I blow,
55   At once the silken tassel of my Purse
Tear, and its Treasure on the Garden throw."

15

And those who husbanded the Golden Grain,
And those who flung it to the winds like Rain,
    Alike to no such aureate° Earth are turn'd   *golden*
60   As, buried once, Men want dug up again.

16

The Worldly Hope men set their Hearts upon
Turns Ashes—or it prospers; and anon,
    Like Snow upon the Desert's dusty Face,
Lighting a little hour or two—is gone.

17

65   Think, in this battered Caravanserai°   *inn*
Whose Portals are alternate Night and Day,
    How Sultán after Sultán with his Pomp
Abode his destined Hour, and went his way.

18

They say the Lion and the Lizard keep
70   The Courts where Jamshyd gloried and drank deep:

1. Mahmúd the Great (c. 970–1030), conqueror of India.

And Bahrám,[2] that great Hunter—the Wild Ass
Stamps o'er his Head, but cannot break his Sleep.

19

I sometimes think that never blows so red
The Rose as where some buried Caesar bled;
75   That every Hyacinth[3] the Garden wears
Dropt in her Lap from some once lovely Head.

20

And this reviving Herb whose tender Green
Fledges the River-Lip on which we lean—
        Ah, lean upon it lightly! for who knows
80   From what once lovely Lip it springs unseen!

21

Ah, my Belovéd, fill the Cup that clears
TO-DAY of past Regret and future Fears:
        To-morrow!—why, To-morrow I may be
Myself with Yesterday's Sev'n thousand Years.[4]

22

85   For some we loved, the loveliest and the best
That from his Vintage rolling Time hath prest,
        Have drunk their Cup a Round or two before,
And one by one crept silently to rest.

23

And we, that now make merry in the Room
90   They left, and Summer dresses in new bloom,
        Ourselves must we beneath the Couch of Earth
Descend—ourselves to make a Couch—for whom?

24

Ah, make the most of what we yet may spend,
Before we too into the Dust descend;
95   Dust into Dust, and under Dust to lie,
Sans° Wine, sans Song, sans Singer, and—sans End!   *without*

25

Alike for those who for TO-DAY prepare,
And those that after some TO-MORROW stare,
        A Muezzín[5] from the Tower of Darkness cries,
100   "Fools! your Reward is neither Here nor There."

2. A Persian ruler who lost his life pursuing a wild ass.
3. In classical myth, hyacinths sprang up from the drops
of blood fallen from the beautiful youth Hyacinthus, accidentally killed by Apollo.

4. In Persian computation, the time from the creation of
Adam to Doomsday.
5. One who calls Muslims to prayer from the tower of a
mosque.

26

Why, all the Saints and Sages who discuss'd
Of the Two Worlds so wisely—they are thrust
   Like foolish Prophets forth; their Words to Scorn
Are scatter'd, and their Mouths are stopt with Dust.

27

105   Myself when young did eagerly frequent
Doctor and Saint, and heard great argument
   About it and about: but evermore
Came out by the same door where in I went.

28

With them the seed of Wisdom did I sow,
110   And with mine own hand wrought to make it grow;
   And this was all the Harvest that I reaped—
"I came like Water, and like Wind I go."

29

Into this Universe, and *Why* not knowing
Nor *Whence*, like Water willy-nilly flowing;
115   And out of it, as Wind along the Waste,
I know not *Whither*, willy-nilly blowing.

30

What, without asking, hither hurried *Whence?*
And, without asking, *Whither* hurried hence!
   Oh, many a Cup of this forbidden Wine[6]
120   Must drown the memory of that insolence!

31

Up from Earth's Centre through the Seventh Gate
I rose, and on the Throne of Saturn sate,[7]
   And many a Knot unravell'd by the Road;
But not the Master-knot of Human Fate.

32

125   There was the Door to which I found no Key;
There was the Veil through which I might not see:
   Some little talk awhile of ME and THEE[8]
There was—and then no more of THEE and ME.

---

6. Wine is prohibited in Islamic law.
7. In early cosmology, the sphere of Saturn, or Seventh Heaven, was the furthest of the concentric circles surrounding the earth; thus, at the limit of human knowledge.
8. Some dividual Existence or Personality distinct from the Whole [FitzGerald's note].

33

Earth could not answer; nor the Seas that mourn
130   In flowing Purple, of their Lord forlorn;
    Nor rolling Heaven, with all his Signs reveal'd
    And hidden by the sleeve of Night and Morn.

34

Then of the THEE IN ME who works behind
The Veil, I lifted up my hands to find
135   A Lamp amid the Darkness; and I heard,
    As from Without—"THE ME WITHIN THEE BLIND!"

35

Then to the Lip of this poor earthen Urn
I lean'd, the Secret of my Life to learn:
    And Lip to Lip it murmur'd—"While you live,
140   Drink!—for, once dead, you never shall return."

36

I think the Vessel, that with fugitive
Articulation answer'd, once did live,
    And drink; and Ah! the passive Lip I kiss'd,
    How many Kisses might it take—and give!⁹

37

145   For I remember stopping by the way
    To watch a Potter thumping his wet Clay:
        And with its all-obliterated Tongue
    It murmur'd—"Gently, Brother, gently, pray!"

38

And has not such a Story from of Old
150   Down Man's successive generations roll'd
        Of such a clod of saturated Earth
    Cast by the Maker into Human mould?

39

And not a drop that from our Cups we throw
For Earth to drink of, but may steal below
155   To quench the fire of Anguish in some Eye
    There hidden—far beneath, and long ago.¹

9. An allusion, according to FitzGerald, to an old Persian tale wherein a thirsty traveler is surprised to find formerly sweet water taste bitter: "a Voice—from Heaven, I think—tells him the clay from which the Bowl is made was once Man; and, into whatever shape renewed, can never lose the bitter flavour of Mortality" [FitzGerald's note].
1. According to custom, some wine was spilled before drinking: "The precious Liquor is not lost, but sinks into the ground to refesh the dust of some poor Wine-worshipper foregone" [FitzGerald's note].

40

As then the Tulip for her morning sup,
Of Heav'nly Vintage from the soil looks up
   Do you devoutly do the like, till Heav'n
160   To Earth invert you—like an empty Cup.

41

Perplext no more with Human or Divine,
To-morrow's tangle to the winds resign,
   And lose your fingers in the tresses of
The Cypress-slender Minister of Wine.[2]

42

165   And if the Wine you drink, the Lip you press,
End in what All begins and ends in—Yes;
   Think then you are TO-DAY what YESTERDAY
You were—TO-MORROW you shall not be less.

43

So when that Angel of the darker Drink
170 At last shall find you by the river-brink,
   And, offering his Cup, invite your Soul
Forth to your Lips to quaff—you shall not shrink.

44

Why, if the Soul can fling the Dust aside,
And naked on the Air of Heaven ride,
175   Were't not a Shame—were't not a Shame for him
In this clay carcase crippled to abide?

45

'Tis but a Tent where takes his one day's rest
A Sultán to the realm of Death addrest;
   The Sultán rises, and the dark Ferrásh[3]
180 Strikes, and prepares it for another Guest.

46

And fear not lest Existence closing your
Account, and mine, should know the like no more;
   The Eternal Sákí from that Bowl has pour'd
Millions of Bubbles like us, and will pour.

47

185   When You and I behind the Veil are past,
Oh, but the long, long while the World shall last,
   Which of our Coming and Departure heeds
As the Sea's self should heed a pebble-cast.

---

2. The servant who pours the wine, later called Sákí (stanza 46).   3. A servant who sets up and takes down ("strikes") tents.

48

A Moment's Halt—a momentary taste
190   Of BEING from the Well amid the Waste—
　　　And Lo!—the phantom Caravan has reach'd
　　The NOTHING it set out from—Oh, make haste!

49

Would you that spangle of Existence spend
About THE SECRET—quick about it, Friend!
195   　　A Hair perhaps divides the False and True—
　　And upon what, prithee, may life depend?

50

A Hair perhaps divides the False and True;
Yes; and a single Alif[4] were the clue—
　　　Could you but find it—to the Treasure-house,
200   And peradventure to THE MASTER too;

51

Whose secret Presence, through Creation's veins
Running Quicksilver-like eludes your pains;
　　　Taking all shapes from Máh to Máhi;[5] and
They change and perish all—but He remains;

52

205   A moment guess'd—then back behind the Fold
Immerst of Darkness round the Drama roll'd
　　　Which, for the Pastime of Eternity,
He doth Himself contrive, enact, behold.

53

But if in vain, down on the stubborn floor
210   Of Earth, and up to Heav'n's unopening Door,
　　　You gaze TO-DAY, while You are You—how then
TO-MORROW, You when shall be You no more?

54

Waste not your Hour, nor in the vain pursuit
Of This and That endeavour and dispute;
215   　　Better be jocund with the fruitful Grape
Than sadden after none, or bitter, Fruit.

55

You know, my Friends, with what a brave Carouse
I made a Second Marriage in my house;

---

4. First letter of the Arabic alphabet, drawn with a single vertical stroke.

5. From Fish to Moon [FitzGerald's note]; i.e., from lowest to highest.

Divorced old barren Reason from my Bed,
220   And took the Daughter of the Vine to Spouse.

56

For "Is" and "Is-not" though with Rule and Line,
And "Up-and-down" by Logic I define,
    Of all that one should care to fathom, I
Was never deep in anything but—Wine.

57

225   Ah, but my Computations, People say,
Reduced the Year to better reckoning?[6]—Nay,
    'Twas only striking from the Calendar
Unborn To-morrow, and dead Yesterday.

58

And lately, by the Tavern Door agape,
230   Came shining through the Dusk an Angel Shape
    Bearing a Vessel on his Shoulder; and
He bid me taste of it; and 'twas—the Grape!

59

The Grape that can with Logic absolute
The Two-and-Seventy jarring Sects confute:[7]
235   The sovereign Alchemist that in a trice
Life's leaden metal into Gold transmute:

60

The mighty Mahmúd, Allah-breathing Lord,
That all the misbelieving and black Horde
    Of Fears and Sorrows that infest the Soul
240   Scatters before him with his whirlwind Sword.[8]

61

Why, be this Juice the growth of God, who dare
Blaspheme the twisted tendril as a Snare?
    A Blessing, we should use it, should we not?
And if a Curse—why, then, who set it there?

62

245   I must abjure the Balm of Life, I must,
Scared by some After-reckoning ta'en on trust,

---

6. An outstanding mathematician and astronomer, Omar Khayyám helped revise the calendar in 1079, creating the Jalai era calendar, a measure of the solar year accurate to the fifth decimal place.

7. The Seventy-two Religions supposed to divide the World [FitzGerald's note].
8. Alluding to Sultan Mahmúd's Conquest of India and its dark people [FitzGerald's note].

Or lured with Hope of some Diviner Drink,
To fill the Cup—when crumbled into Dust!

63

O threats of Hell and Hopes of Paradise!
250   One thing at least is certain—*This* Life flies;
One thing is certain and the rest is Lies;
The Flower that once has blown for ever dies.

64

Strange, is it not? that of the myriads who
Before us pass'd the door of Darkness through
255   Not one returns to tell us of the Road,
Which to discover we must travel too.

65

The Revelations of Devout and Learn'd
Who rose before us, and as Prophets burn'd,
Are all but Stories, which, awoke from Sleep,
260   They told their comrades, and to Sleep return'd.

66

I sent my Soul through the Invisible,
Some letter of that After-life to spell:
And by and by my Soul return'd to me,
And answer'd, "I Myself am Heav'n and Hell":

67

265   Heav'n but the Vision of fulfill'd Desire,
And Hell the Shadow from a Soul on fire,
Cast on the Darkness into which Ourselves,
So late emerged from, shall so soon expire.

68

We are no other than a moving row
270   Of Magic Shadow-shapes that come and go
Round with the Sun-illumined Lantern held
In Midnight by the Master of the Show;[9]

69

But helpless Pieces of the Game He plays
Upon this Chequer-board of Nights and Days;
275   Hither and thither moves, and checks, and slays,
And one by one back in the Closet lays.

70

The Ball[1] no question makes of Ayes and Noes,
But Here or There as strikes the Player goes;

9. Fánúsi khiyál, a Magic-lantern still used in India; the cylindrical Interior being painted with various Figures, and so lightly poised and ventilated as to revolve round the lighted Candle within [FitzGerald's note].
1. Polo ball; the Persians invented the game of polo.

And He that toss'd you down into the Field,
280   *He* knows about it all—HE knows—HE knows!

71

The Moving Finger writes; and, having writ,
Moves on: nor all your Piety nor Wit
    Shall lure it back to cancel half a Line,
Nor all your Tears wash out a Word of it.

72

285   And that inverted Bowl they call the Sky,
Whereunder crawling coop'd we live and die,
    Lift not your hands to *It* for help—for It
As impotently moves as you or I.

73

With Earth's first Clay They did the Last Man knead,
290   And there of the Last Harvest sowed the Seed:
    And the first Morning of Creation wrote
What the Last Dawn of Reckoning shall read.

74

YESTERDAY *This* Day's Madness did prepare;
TO-MORROW's Silence, Triumph, or Despair:
295   Drink! for you know not whence you came, nor why:
Drink! for you know not why you go, nor where.

75

I tell you this—When, started from the Goal,
Over the flaming shoulders of the Foal
    Of Heav'n Parwín and Mushtarí they flung,
300   In my predestined Plot of Dust and Soul[2]

76

The Vine had struck a fibre: which about
If clings my Being—let the Dervish[3] flout;
    Of my Base metal may be filed a Key,
That shall unlock the Door he howls without.

77

305   And this I know: whether the one True Light
Kindle to Love, or Wrath consume me quite,
    One Flash of It within the Tavern caught
Better than in the Temple lost outright.

---

2. Omar's horoscope: when he was born, the gods flung the Pleiades (Parwín) and the planet Jupiter (Mushtarí) over the constellation Equelleus or "Little Horse" (Foal) with the result that Omar loves wine.

3. A Muslim ascetic who chooses to live in poverty and austerity. Omar is saying, "let the ascetic contemptuously insult ('flout') my using wine to find ('unlock') the truths he cannot know."

78

What! out of senseless Nothing to provoke
310   A conscious Something to resent the yoke
         Of unpermitted Pleasure, under pain
Of Everlasting Penalties, if broke!

79

What! from his helpless Creature be repaid
Pure Gold for what he lent him dross-allay'd—
315   Sue for a Debt he never did contract,
And cannot answer—Oh the sorry trade!

80

O Thou, who didst with pitfall and with gin°   *a trap*
Beset the Road I was to wander in,
         Thou wilt not with Predestined Evil round
320   Enmesh, and then impute my Fall to Sin!

81

O Thou, who Man of baser Earth didst make,
And ev'n with Paradise devise the Snake:
         For all the Sin wherewith the Face of Man
Is blacken'd—Man's forgiveness give—and take!

* * * * *

82

325   As under cover of departing Day
Slunk hunger-stricken Ramazán[4] away,
         Once more within the Potter's house alone
I stood, surrounded by the Shapes of Clay.

83

Shapes of all Sorts and Sizes, great and small,
330   That stood along the floor and by the wall;
         And some loquacious Vessels were; and some
Listen'd perhaps, but never talk'd at all.

84

Said one among them—"Surely not in vain
My substance of the common Earth was ta'en
335   And to this Figure moulded, to be broke,
Or trampled back to shapeless Earth again."

85

Then said a Second—"Ne'er a peevish Boy
Would break the Bowl from which he drank in joy;
         And He that with his hand the Vessel made
340   Will surely not in after Wrath destroy."

4. Ramadan, the month during which Muslims fast from sunrise to sunset.

86

After a momentary silence spake
Some Vessel of a more ungainly Make;
  "They sneer at me for leaning all awry:
What! did the Hand then of the Potter shake?"

87

345   Whereat some one of the loquacious Lot—
      I think a Súfi° pipkin°—waxing hot—   *Persian mystic / small pot*
        "All this of Pot and Potter—Tell me then,
      Who is the Potter, pray, and who the Pot?"

88

      "Why," said another, "Some there are who tell
350   Of one who threatens he will toss to Hell
        The luckless Pots he marr'd in making—Pish!
      He's a Good Fellow, and 'twill all be well."

89

      "Well," murmur'd one, "Let whoso make or buy,
      My Clay with long Oblivion is gone dry:
355   But fill me with the old familiar Juice,
      Methinks I might recover by and by."

90

      So while the Vessels one by one were speaking,
      The little Moon look'd in that all were seeking:
        And then they jogg'd each other, "Brother! Brother!
360   Now for the Porter's shoulder-knot a-creaking."⁵

                    * * * * *

91

      Ah, with the Grape my fading Life provide,
      And wash the Body whence the Life has died,
        And lay me, shrouded in the living Leaf,
      By some not unfrequented Garden-side.

92

365   That ev'n my buried Ashes such a snare
      Of Vintage shall fling up into the Air
        As not a True-believer passing by
      But shall be overtaken unaware.

---

5. At the Close of the Fasting Month, Ramazán [sic] . . . the first Glimpse of the New Moon . . . is looked for with the utmost Anxiety, and hailed with Acclamation. Then it is that the Porter's Knot may be heard—toward the *Cellar* [FitzGerald's note]. The shoulder knot is the strap on which the wine jars are carried.

93

Indeed the Idols I have loved so long
370   Have done my credit in this World much wrong:
     Have drown'd my Glory in a shallow Cup,
And sold my Reputation for a Song.

94

Indeed, indeed, Repentance oft before
I swore—but was I sober when I swore?
375   And then and then came Spring, and Rose-in-hand
My thread-bare Penitence apieces tore.

95

And much as Wine has play'd the Infidel,
And robb'd me of my Robe of Honour—Well,
     I wonder often what the Vintners buy
380   One half so precious as the stuff they sell.

96

Yet Ah, that Spring should vanish with the Rose!
That Youth's sweet-scented manuscript should close!
     The Nightingale that in the branches sang,
Ah whence, and whither flown again, who knows!

97

385   Would but the Desert of the Fountain yield
One glimpse—if dimly, yet indeed, reveal'd,
     To which the fainting Traveller might spring,
As springs the trampled herbage of the field!

98

Would but some wingéd Angel ere too late
390   Arrest the yet unfolded Roll of Fate,
     And make the stern Recorder otherwise
Enregister, or quite obliterate!

99

Ah Love! could you and I with Him conspire
To grasp this sorry Scheme of Things entire,
395   Would not we shatter it to bits—and then
Re-mould it nearer to the Heart's Desire!

* * * * *

100

Yon rising Moon that looks for us again—
How oft hereafter will she wax and wane;
     How oft hereafter rising look for us
400   Through this same Garden—and for *one* in vain!

101

And when like her, oh Sákí, you shall pass
Among the Guests Star-scatter'd on the Grass,

And in your joyous errand reach the spot
Where I made One—turn down an empty Glass!

TAMAM[6]

1859, 1868, 1872, 1879, 1889

⊶ ⊨✦≣ ⊷

Charles Darwin
1809–1882

Charles Darwin's five-year excursion on the *Beagle* has become the stuff of legend. No voyage since that of Columbus has had such a profound impact on the world. Darwin's ideas concerning evolution and natural selection brought about a revolution in human thought; they radically transformed our sense of our place in the universe. Yet *The Voyage of the Beagle* is a modestly written account of the meticulous observations of a young naturalist, as interested in ordinary beetles and coral formations as in the weirdly monstrous creatures he saw on the Galapagos Islands.

Nothing in Darwin's youth suggested a great man in the making. His father once warned him, "You care for nothing but shooting, dogs, and rat-catching, and you will be a disgrace to yourself and all your family." Darwin's father was a prosperous doctor, and he sent his son to Edinburgh University for two years to study medicine, but Darwin detested the subject and neglected his studies. Casting about for an occupation for this unpromising son, his father proposed the undemanding career of a country clergyman. Darwin agreed and spent the next three years at Cambridge where, according to his autobiography, he did little except collect beetles.

Although he considered his formal education a complete waste, Darwin was busy educating himself in natural history. The turning point in his life was an invitation to become the ship's naturalist on the H.M.S. *Beagle*'s surveying expedition. Knowing the ship would be away for years, Darwin's father initially refused permission to accept. At a time when the word "scientist" did not even exist, he could not see how such an undertaking could lead to any respectable profession. But he left a loophole, telling his son, "If you can find any man of common sense, who advises you to go, I will give my consent." Fortunately, Darwin's uncle supported the idea, and in 1831 the *Beagle* sailed for South America with the twenty-two-year-old Darwin aboard.

Darwin had to put up with cramped quarters, seasickness, and the captain's volatile temper, but he accomplished an extraordinary amount of work. He collected specimens, filled eighteen notebooks with scientific observations, and spent long periods ashore studying plants and animals, fossils, and indigenous cultures. He also kept a diary that eventually became the basis of *The Voyage of the Beagle* (1839, rev. 1845), one of the great classics of travel literature. Out of these investigations, particularly in the volcanic Galapagos Islands off the coast of South America, grew the theory of evolution.

Yet it is a myth that Darwin had a sudden insight concerning the origin of species while examining the strange tortoises, lizards, and finches in the Galapagos. Though he had read with interest the evolutionary speculations of his grandfather, Erasmus Darwin, he had remained a creationist: during the voyage he continued to believe that species were fixed forever at the moment

6. It is ended.

Linley Sambourne, *Man is But a Worm*, from *Punch's Almanack for 1882* (published December 1881). In 1881, Darwin, who had studied earthworms for forty years, published *The Formation of Vegetable Mould through the Action of Worms with Observations on their Habits*. Darwin justified his interest in the lowly worm by pointing out that "All the fertile areas of this planet have at least once passed through the bodies of earthworms." But it was his conclusion that sparked public attention, causing many to link worms with Darwin's evolutionary theory: "Worms," wrote Darwin, "although standing low in the scale of organization, possess some degree of intelligence." *Punch's* Linley Sambourne (1844–1910), one of the great Victorian caricaturists, depicted the ape-browed scientist sitting like Michelangelo's Adam as depicted on the Sistine Chapel ceiling. Mixing Creationism and Evolution, the Adamic Darwin retrospectively bestows life and consciousness on his ancestors, an evolving chain of monkeys that have sprung from worms. Emerging from CHAOS at the lower left, the creatures spin around "Time's Meter" until they arrive at the modern Victorian gentleman who doffs his hat to Darwin.

of their creation, as described in the Bible. Only back in England, working through his huge volume of notes, did he become convinced of the mutability of species.

Within a few months of his return home in 1836, Darwin had accepted evolution as the explanation for the natural phenomena he had observed. But he was in no hurry to publish his findings. In fact, twenty years went by before he learned in 1858 that a young naturalist, Alfred Russel Wallace, had arrived independently at the theory of natural selection. A joint paper of their findings was presented to the Linnaean Society, and Darwin at long last rushed to compile and publish *On the Origin of Species by Means of Natural Selection* (1859). Darwin realized that most living organisms produce far more offspring than can survive: not every acorn becomes an oak. Certain genetically favored individuals have a competitive edge in the struggle for life. Nature thus ensures the "survival of the fittest," and eventually their descendants evolve into new and better-adapted species.

The book created an immediate sensation. The original edition sold out the day it was published. Darwin was not the first to propose a theory of evolution, but he was the first to offer a persuasive account of the means by which evolution works. Geologists such as Charles Lyell had already shown that the earth was immensely older than six thousand years, the traditional estimate based on biblical chronology. In further undermining the biblical account of creation, Darwin shook the faith of his contemporaries.

Darwin was not eager to offend people, nor did he enjoy controversy. Thus in *The Origin of Species* he tactfully avoided any discussion of human origins, although he was already confident that evolution applied to human beings as well. In *The Descent of Man* (1871) he finally made his position clear: man is an animal. Darwin's ideas were profoundly unsettling. No longer sure of belonging to an ordered world overseen by a beneficent Creator, many people felt they had been set adrift in an indifferent cosmos. Tennyson's memorable phrase, "Nature, red in tooth and claw," expressed the Victorians' collective horror at Darwin's vision of nature as a cruel and violent battlefield.

Darwin's theories were earthshaking, but his private life was not. When the *Beagle* voyage ended, he debated the pros and cons of marriage, telling himself that a wife would provide an "object to be beloved and played with—better than a dog anyhow." Despite these unromantic musings, his marriage to his cousin Emma Wedgwood was long and happy. They settled down in a country house and had many children. For the rest of his life Darwin suffered from mysterious illnesses; they prevented his going into society, but they did not stop him working and writing. He never traveled again.

from The Voyage of the Beagle
from Chapter 10. Tierra Del Fuego[1]

December 17th, 1832.—Having now finished with Patagonia[2] and the Falkland Islands, I will describe our first arrival in Tierra del Fuego. A little after noon we doubled Cape St. Diego, and entered the famous strait of Le Maire. We kept close to the Fuegian shore, but the outline of the rugged, inhospitable Staten-land was visible amidst the clouds. In the afternoon we anchored in the Bay of Good Success. While entering we were saluted in a manner becoming the inhabitants of this savage land. A group of Fuegians partly concealed by the entangled forest, were perched on a wild point overhanging the sea; and as we passed by, they sprang up and waving their tattered cloaks sent forth a loud and sonorous shout. The savages followed the ship, and just before

---

1. A group of islands off the southern tip of South America.   2. The southernmost region of South America.

Thomas Landseer, after a drawing by C. Martens, A *Fuegian at Portrait Cove*, 1839. This illustration appeared in the *Narrative of the Surveying Voyages of His Majesty's Ships Adventure and Beagle, between the Years 1826 and 1836* (1839); Darwin's part of this report became *The Voyage of the Beagle*.

dark we saw their fire, and again heard their wild cry. The harbour consists of a fine piece of water half surrounded by low rounded mountains of clay-slate, which are covered to the water's edge by one dense gloomy forest. A single glance at the landscape was sufficient to show me how widely different it was from any thing I had ever beheld. At night it blew a gale of wind, and heavy squalls from the mountains swept past us. It would have been a bad time out at sea, and we, as well as others, may call this Good Success Bay.

In the morning the Captain sent a party to communicate with the Fuegians. When we came within hail, one of the four natives who were present advanced to receive us, and began to shout most vehemently, wishing to direct us where to land. When we were on shore the party looked rather alarmed, but continued talking and making gestures with great rapidity. It was without exception the most curious and interesting spectacle I ever beheld: I could not have believed how wide was the difference between savage and civilized man: it is greater than between a wild and domesticated animal, inasmuch as in man there is a greater power of improvement. The chief spokesman was old, and appeared to be the head of the family; the three others were powerful young men, about six feet high. The women and children had been sent away. These Fuegians are a very different race from the stunted, miserable wretches farther westward; and they seem closely allied to the famous Patagonians of the Strait of Magellan. Their only garment consists of a mantle made of guanaco[3] skin, with the wool outside; this they wear just thrown over their shoulders, leaving their persons as often exposed as covered. Their skin is of a dirty copper red colour.

The old man had a fillet[4] of white feathers tied round his head, which partly confined his black, coarse, and entangled hair. His face was crossed by two broad transverse bars; one, painted bright red, reached from ear to ear and included the upper lip; the other, white like chalk, extended above and parallel to the first, so that even his eyelids were thus coloured. The other two men were ornamented by streaks of black powder, made of charcoal. The party altogether closely resembled the devils which come on the stage in plays like Der Freischutz.[5]

Their very attitudes were abject, and the expression of their countenances distrustful, surprised, and startled. After we had presented them with some scarlet cloth, which they immediately tied round their necks, they became good friends. This was shown by the old man patting our breasts, and making a chuckling kind of noise, as people do when feeding chickens. I walked with the old man, and this demonstration of friendship was repeated several times; it was concluded by three hard slaps, which were given me on the breast and back at the same time. He then bared his bosom for me to return the compliment, which being done, he seemed highly pleased. The language of these people, according to our notions, scarcely deserves to be called articulate. Captain Cook has compared it to a man clearing his throat, but certainly no European ever cleared his throat with so many hoarse, guttural, and clicking sounds.

They are excellent mimics: as often as we coughed or yawned, or made any odd motion, they immediately imitated us. Some of our party began to squint and look awry; but one of the young Fuegians (whose whole face was painted black, excepting a white band across his eyes) succeeded in making far more hideous grimaces. They could repeat with perfect correctness each word in any sentence we addressed them, and they remembered such words for some time. Yet we Europeans all know how difficult it is to distinguish apart the sounds in a foreign language. Which of us, for instance, could follow an American Indian through a sentence of more than three words? All savages appear to possess, to an uncommon degree, this power of mimicry. I was told, almost in the same words, of the same ludicrous habit among the Caffres:[6] the Australians, likewise, have long been notorious for being able to imitate and describe the gait of any man, so that he may be recognized. How can this faculty be explained? is it a consequence of the more practised habits of perception and keener senses, common to all men in a savage state, as compared with those long civilized?

When a song was struck up by our party, I thought the Fuegians would have fallen down with astonishment. With equal surprise they viewed our dancing; but

3. A South American mammal with fawn-colored fur.
4. A headband.
5. An 1817 opera by Carl Maria von Weber (1786–1826), first performed in London in 1824. The

story concerns Max, a forester who nearly sells his soul to the devil.
6. Kaffirs are a Bantu-speaking African people.

one of the young men, when asked, had no objection to a little waltzing. Little accustomed to Europeans as they appeared to be, yet they knew and dreaded our fire-arms; nothing would tempt them to take a gun in their hands. They begged for knives, calling them by the Spanish word "cuchilla." They explained also what they wanted, by acting as if they had a piece of blubber in their mouth, and then pretending to cut instead of tear it.

I have not as yet noticed the Fuegians whom we had on board. During the former voyage of the *Adventure* and *Beagle* in 1826 to 1830, Captain Fitz Roy[7] seized on a party of natives, as hostages for the loss of a boat, which had been stolen, to the great jeopardy of a party employed on the survey; and some of these natives, as well as a child whom he bought for a pearl-button, he took with him to England, determining to educate them and instruct them in religion at his own expense. To settle these natives in their own country, was one chief inducement to Captain Fitz Roy to undertake our present voyage; and before the Admiralty had resolved to send out this expedition, Captain Fitz Roy had generously chartered a vessel, and would himself have taken them back. The natives were accompanied by a missionary, R. Matthews; of whom and of the natives, Captain Fitz Roy has published a full and excellent account. Two men, one of whom died in England of the smallpox, a boy and a little girl, were originally taken; and we had now on board, York Minster, Jemmy Button (whose name expresses his purchase-money), and Fuegia Basket. York Minster was a full-grown, short, thick, powerful man: his disposition was reserved, taciturn, morose, and when excited violently passionate; his affections were very strong towards a few friends on board; his intellect good. Jemmy Button was a universal favourite, but likewise passionate; the expression of his face at once showed his nice disposition. He was merry and often laughed, and was remarkably sympathetic with any one in pain: when the water was rough, I was often a little seasick, and he used to come to me and say in a plaintive voice, "Poor, poor fellow!" but the notion, after his aquatic life, of a man being sea-sick, was too ludicrous, and he was generally obliged to turn on one side to hide a smile or laugh, and then he would repeat his "Poor, poor fellow!" He was of a patriotic disposition; and he liked to praise his own tribe and country, in which he truly said there were "plenty of trees," and he abused all the other tribes: he stoutly declared that there was no Devil in his land. Jemmy was short, thick, and fat, but vain of his personal appearance; he used to wear gloves, his hair was neatly cut, and he was distressed if his well-polished shoes were dirtied. He was fond of admiring himself in a looking-glass; and a merry-faced little Indian boy from the Rio Negro, whom we had for some months on board, soon perceived this, and used to mock him: Jemmy, who was always rather jealous of the attention paid to this little boy, did not at all like this, and used to say, with rather a contemptuous twist of his head, "Too much skylark." It seems yet wonderful to me, when I think over all his many good qualities, that he should have been of the same race, and doubtless partaken of the same character, with the miserable, degraded savages whom we first met here. Lastly, Fuegia Basket was a nice, modest, reserved young girl, with a rather pleasing but sometimes sullen expression, and very quick in learning anything, especially languages. This she showed in picking up some Portuguese and Spanish, when left on shore for only a short time at Rio de Janeiro and Monte Video, and in her knowledge

---

7. Robert Fitz Roy (1805–1865) was the captain of the *Beagle*; he and Darwin had a sometimes difficult relationship.

of English. York Minster was very jealous of any attention paid to her; for it was clear he determined to marry her as soon as they were settled on shore. * * *

It was interesting to watch the conduct of the savages, when we landed, towards Jemmy Button: they immediately perceived the difference between him and ourselves, and held much conversation one with another on the subject. The old man addressed a long harangue to Jemmy, which it seems was to invite him to stay with them. But Jemmy understood very little of their language, and was, moreover, thoroughly ashamed of his countrymen. When York Minster afterwards came on shore, they noticed him in the same way, and told him he ought to shave; yet he had not twenty dwarf hairs on his face, whilst we all wore our untrimmed beards. They examined the colour of his skin, and compared it with ours. One of our arms being bared, they expressed the liveliest surprise and admiration at its whiteness, just in the same way in which I have seen the ourang-outang do at the Zoological Gardens. We thought that they mistook two or three of the officers, who were rather shorter and fairer, though adorned with large beards, for the ladies of our party. The tallest among the Fuegians was evidently much pleased at his height being noticed. When placed back to back with the tallest of the boat's crew, he tried his best to edge on higher ground, and to stand on tiptoe. He opened his mouth to show his teeth, and turned his face for a side view; and all this was done with such alacrity, that I dare say he thought himself the handsomest man in Tierra del Fuego. After our first feeling of grave astonishment was over, nothing could be more ludicrous than the odd mixture of surprise and imitation which these savages every moment exhibited. * * *

December 25th, 1832.— * * * While going one day on shore near Wollaston Island, we pulled alongside a canoe with six Fuegians. These were the most abject and miserable creatures I anywhere beheld. On the east coast the natives, as we have seen, have guanaco cloaks, and on the west, they possess seal-skins. Amongst these central tribes the men generally have an otter-skin, or some small scrap about as large as a pocket-handkerchief, which is barely sufficient to cover their backs as low down as their loins. It is laced across the breast by strings, and according as the wind blows, it is shifted from side to side. But these Fuegians in the canoe were quite naked, and even one full-grown woman was absolutely so. It was raining heavily, and the fresh water, together with the spray, trickled down her body. In another harbour not far distant, a woman, who was suckling a recently-born child, came one day alongside the vessel, and remained there out of mere curiosity, whilst the sleet fell and thawed on her naked bosom, and on the skin of her naked baby! These poor wretches were stunted in their growth, their hideous faces bedaubed with white paint, their skins filthy and greasy, their hair entangled, their voices discordant, and their gestures violent. Viewing such men, one can hardly make oneself believe that they are fellow-creatures, and inhabitants of the same world. It is a common subject of conjecture what pleasure in life some of the lower animals can enjoy: how much more reasonably the same question may be asked with respect to these barbarians! At night, five or six human beings, naked and scarcely protected from the wind and rain of this tempestuous climate, sleep on the wet ground coiled up like animals. Whenever it is low water, winter or summer, night or day, they must rise to pick shellfish from the rocks; and the women either dive to collect sea-eggs, or sit patiently in their canoes, and with a baited hairline without any hook, jerk out little fish. If a seal is killed, or the floating carcass of a putrid whale discovered, it is a feast; and such miserable food is assisted by a few tasteless berries and fungi. * * *

The different tribes have no government or chief; yet each is surrounded by other hostile tribes, speaking different dialects, and separated from each other only by a deserted border or neutral territory: the cause of their warfare appears to be the means of subsistence. Their country is a broken mass of wild rocks, lofty hills, and useless forests: and these are viewed through mists and endless storms. The habitable land is reduced to the stones on the beach; in search of food they are compelled unceasingly to wander from spot to spot, and so steep is the coast, that they can only move about in their wretched canoes. They cannot know the feeling of having a home, and still less that of domestic affection; for the husband is to the wife a brutal master to a laborious slave. Was a more horrid deed ever perpetrated, than that witnessed on the west coast by Byron, who saw a wretched mother pick up her bleeding dying infant-boy, whom her husband had mercilessly dashed on the stones for dropping a basket of sea-eggs! How little can the higher powers of the mind be brought into play: what is there for imagination to picture, for reason to compare, for judgment to decide upon? to knock a limpet from the rock does not require even cunning, that lowest power of the mind. Their skill in some respects may be compared to the instinct of animals; for it is not improved by experience: the canoe, their most ingenious work, poor as it is, has remained the same, as we know from Drake, for the last two hundred and fifty years.

Whilst beholding these savages, one asks, whence have they come? What could have tempted, or what change compelled a tribe of men, to leave the fine regions of the north, to travel down the Cordillera[8] or backbone of America, to invent and build canoes, which are not used by the tribes of Chile, Peru, and Brazil, and then to enter on one of the most inhospitable countries within the limits of the globe? Although such reflections must at first seize on the mind, yet we may feel sure that they are partly erroneous. There is no reason to believe that the Fuegians decrease in number; therefore we must suppose that they enjoy a sufficient share of happiness, of whatever kind it may be, to render life worth having. Nature by making habit omnipotent, and its effects hereditary, has fitted the Fuegian to the climate and the productions of his miserable country. * * *

January 15th, 1833.—The *Beagle* anchored in Goeree Roads. Captain Fitz Roy having resolved to settle the Fuegians, according to their wishes, in Ponsonby Sound, four boats were equipped to carry them there through the Beagle Channel. * * *

19th.—Three whale-boats and the yawl, with a party of twenty-eight, started under the command of Captain Fitz Roy. In the afternoon we entered the eastern mouth of the channel, and shortly afterwards found a snug little cove concealed by some surrounding islets. Here we pitched our tents and lighted our fires. * * *

Few if any of these natives could ever have seen a white man; certainly nothing could exceed their astonishment at the apparition of the four boats. Fires were lighted on every point (hence the name of Tierra del Fuego, or the land of fire), both to attract our attention and to spread far and wide the news. Some of the men ran for miles along the shore. I shall never forget how wild and savage one group appeared: suddenly four or five men came to the edge of an overhanging cliff; they were absolutely naked, and their long hair streamed about their faces; they held rugged staffs in their hands, and, springing from the ground, they waved their arms round their heads, and sent forth the most hideous yells. * * *

8. Andean mountain range.

22nd.— * * * At night we slept close to the junction of Ponsonby Sound with the Beagle Channel. A small family of Fuegians, who were living in the cove, were quiet and inoffensive, and soon joined our party round a blazing fire. We were well clothed, and though sitting close to the fire were far from too warm; yet these naked savages, though further off, were observed, to our great surprise, to be streaming with perspiration at undergoing such a roasting. They seemed, however, very well pleased, and all joined in the chorus of the seamen's songs: but the manner in which they were invariably a little behindhand was quite ludicrous. * * *

The next morning after our arrival (the 24th) the Fuegians began to pour in, and Jemmy's mother and brothers arrived. Jemmy recognized the stentorian voice of one of his brothers at a prodigious distance. The meeting was less interesting than that between a horse, turned out into a field, when he joins an old companion. There was no demonstration of affection; they simply stared for a short time at each other; and the mother immediately went to look after her canoe. We heard, however, through York, that the mother had been inconsolable for the loss of Jemmy, and had searched everywhere for him, thinking that he might have been left after having been taken in the boat. The women took much notice of and were very kind to Fuegia. We had already perceived that Jemmy had almost forgotten his own language. I should think there was scarcely another human being with so small a stock of language, for his English was very imperfect. It was laughable, but almost pitiable, to hear him speak to his wild brother in English, and then ask him in Spanish ("no sabe?") whether he did not understand him. * * *

February 6th.— * * * It was quite melancholy leaving the three Fuegians with their savage countrymen; but it was a great comfort that they had no personal fears. York, being a powerful resolute man, was pretty sure to get on well, together with his wife Fuegia. Poor Jemmy looked rather disconsolate, and would then, I have little doubt, have been glad to have returned with us. His own brother had stolen many things from him; and as he remarked, "what fashion call that?" He abused his countrymen, "all bad men, no sabe (know) nothing," and, though I never heard him swear before, "damned fools." Our three Fuegians, though they had been only three years with civilized men, would, I am sure, have been glad to have retained their new habits; but this was obviously impossible. I fear it is more than doubtful, whether their visit will have been of any use to them. * * *

On the 5th of March, we anchored in the cove at Woollya, but we saw not a soul there. We were alarmed at this, for the natives in Ponsonby Sound showed by gestures, that there had been fighting; and we afterwards heard that the dreaded Oens men had made a descent. Soon a canoe, with a little flag flying, was seen approaching, with one of the men in it washing the paint off his face. This man was poor Jemmy,—now a thin haggard savage, with long disordered hair, and naked, except a bit of a blanket round his waist. We did not recognize him till he was close to us; for he was ashamed of himself, and turned his back to the ship. We had left him plump, fat, clean, and well dressed;—I never saw so complete and grievous a change. As soon however as he was clothed, and the first flurry was over, things wore a good appearance. He dined with Captain Fitz Roy, and ate his dinner as tidily as formerly. He told us he had "too much" (meaning enough) to eat, that he was not cold, that his relations were very good people, and that he did not wish to go back to England: in the evening we found out the cause of this great change in Jemmy's feelings, in the arrival of his young and nice-looking wife. With his usual good feeling, he brought two beautiful otter-skins for two of his best friends, and some spear-heads and arrows made with his own hands for the Captain. He said he had built a canoe for himself, and he boasted that he could talk a little of his own language! But it is a most singular fact, that he appears to have taught all his tribe some English: an old man spontaneously announced "Jemmy Button's wife." Jemmy had lost all his property. He told us that York Minster had built a large canoe, and with his wife Fuegia, had several months since gone to his own country, and had taken farewell by an act of consummate villainy; he persuaded Jemmy and his mother to come with him, and then on the way deserted them by night, stealing every article of their property.

Jemmy went to sleep on shore, and in the morning returned, and remained on board till the ship got under weigh, which frightened his wife, who continued crying violently till he got into his canoe. He returned loaded with valuable property. Every soul on board was heartily sorry to shake hands with him for the last time. I do not now doubt that he will be as happy as, perhaps happier than, if he had never left his own country. Every one must sincerely hope that Captain Fitz Roy's noble hope may be fulfilled, of being rewarded for the many generous sacrifices which he made for these Fuegians, by some shipwrecked sailor being protected by the descendants of Jemmy Button and his tribe! When Jemmy reached the shore, he lighted a signal fire, and the smoke curled up, bidding us a last and long farewell, as the ship stood on her course into the open sea.

from *Chapter 17. Galapagos Archipelago*[1]

In the morning (17th)[2] we landed on Chatham Island, which, like the others, rises with a tame and rounded outline, broken here and there by scattered hillocks, the remains of former craters. Nothing could be less inviting than the first appearance. A broken field of black basaltic lava, thrown into the most rugged waves, and crossed by great fissures, is every where covered by stunted, sunburnt brushwood, which shows little signs of life. The dry and parched surface, being heated by the noonday sun, gave to the air a close and sultry feeling, like that from a stove: we fancied even that the bushes smelt unpleasantly. Although I diligently tried to collect as many plants as possible, I succeeded in getting very few; and such wretched-looking little weeds would have better become an arctic than an equatorial Flora. The brushwood appears, from a short distance, as leafless as our trees during winter; and it was some time before I discovered that not only almost every plant was now in full leaf, but that the greater number were in flower. * * *

The *Beagle* sailed round Chatham Island, and anchored in several bays. One night I slept on shore on a part of the island, where black truncated cones were extraordinarily numerous: from one small eminence I counted sixty of them, all surmounted by craters more or less perfect. The greater number consisted merely of a ring of red scoriae[3] or slags, cemented together: and their height above the plain of lava was not more than from fifty to a hundred feet: none had been very lately active. The entire surface of this part of the island seems to have been permeated, like a sieve, by the subterranean vapours: here and there the lava, whilst soft, has been blown into great bubbles; and in other parts, the tops of caverns similarly formed have fallen in, leaving circular pits with steep sides. From the regular form of the many craters, they gave to the country an artificial appearance, which vividly

1. A group of islands located 400 miles off the coast of Ecuador.   2. Of September 1835.
3. Lava.

reminded me of those parts of Staffordshire, where the great iron-foundries are most numerous. The day was glowing hot, and the scrambling over the rough surface and through the intricate thickets, was very fatiguing; but I was well repaid by the strange Cyclopean[4] scene. As I was walking along I met two large tortoises, each of which must have weighed at least two hundred pounds: one was eating a piece of cactus, and as I approached, it stared at me and slowly stalked away; the other gave a deep hiss, and drew in its head. These huge reptiles, surrounded by the black lava, the leafless shrubs, and large cacti, seemed to my fancy like some antediluvian[5] animals. The few dull-coloured birds cared no more for me, than they did for the great tortoises. * * *

The natural history of these islands is eminently curious, and well deserves attention. Most of the organic productions are aboriginal creations, found nowhere else; there is even a difference between the inhabitants of the different islands; yet all show a marked relationship with those of America, though separated from that continent by an open space of ocean, between 500 and 600 miles in width. The archipelago is a little world within itself, or rather a satellite attached to America, whence it has derived a few stray colonists, and has received the general character of its indigenous productions. Considering the small size of these islands, we feel the more astonished at the number of their aboriginal beings, and at their confined range. Seeing every height crowned with its crater, and the boundaries of most of the lava-streams still distinct, we are led to believe that within a period, geologically recent, the unbroken ocean was here spread out. Hence, both in space and time, we seem to be brought somewhat near to that great fact—that mystery of mysteries—the first appearance of new beings on this earth. * * *

The tortoises, when purposely moving towards any point, travel by night and day, and arrive at their journey's end much sooner than would be expected. The inhabitants, from observing marked individuals, consider that they travel a distance of about eight miles in two or three days. One large tortoise, which I watched, walked at the rate of sixty yards in ten minutes, that is 360 yards in the hour, or four miles a day,— allowing a little time for it to eat on the road. During the breeding season, when the male and female are together, the male utters a hoarse roar or bellowing, which, it is said, can be heard at the distance of more than a hundred yards. The female never uses her voice, and the male only at these times; so that when the people hear this noise, they know that the two are together. They were at this time (October) laying their eggs. The female, where the soil is sandy, deposits them together, and covers them up with sand; but where the ground is rocky she drops them indiscriminately in any hole: Mr. Bynoe[6] found seven placed in a fissure. The egg is white and spherical; one which I measured was seven inches and three-eighths in circumference, and therefore larger than a hen's egg. The young tortoises, as soon as they are hatched, fall a prey in great numbers to the carrion-feeding buzzard. The old ones seem generally to die from accidents, as from falling down precipices: at least, several of the inhabitants told me, that they had never found one dead without some evident cause.

The inhabitants believe that these animals are absolutely deaf; certainly they do not overhear a person walking close behind them. I was always amused when overtaking one of these great monsters, as it was quietly pacing along, to see how suddenly, the instant I passed, it would draw in its head and legs, and uttering a deep

4. Darwin may mean that the landscape is savage and wild, like that inhabited by the Cyclopes in Homer's *Odyssey*.

5. Ancient; literally, before the Flood.
6. Naval surgeon aboard the *Beagle*.

hiss fall to the ground with a heavy sound, as if struck dead. I frequently got on their backs, and then giving a few raps on the hinder part of their shells, they would rise up and walk away;—but I found it very difficult to keep my balance. The flesh of this animal is largely employed, both fresh and salted; and a beautifully clear oil is prepared from the fat. * * *

There can be little doubt that this tortoise is an aboriginal inhabitant of the Galapagos; for it is found on all, or nearly all, the islands, even on some of the smaller ones where there is no water; had it been an imported species, this would hardly have been the case in a group which has been so little frequented. * * *

I have not as yet noticed by far the most remarkable feature in the natural history of this archipelago; it is, that the different islands to a considerable extent are inhabited by a different set of beings. My attention was first called to this fact by the Vice-Governor, Mr. Lawson, declaring that the tortoises differed from the different islands, and that he could with certainty tell from which island any one was brought. I did not for some time pay sufficient attention to this statement, and I had already partially mingled together the collections from two of the islands. I never dreamed that islands, about fifty or sixty miles apart, and most of them in sight of each other, formed of precisely the same rocks, placed under a quite similar climate, rising to a nearly equal height, would have been differently tenanted; but we shall soon see that this is the case. It is the fate of most voyagers, no sooner to discover what is most interesting in any locality, than they are hurried from it; but I ought, perhaps, to be thankful that I obtained sufficient material to establish this most remarkable fact in the distribution of organic beings. * * *

If we now turn to the Flora, we shall find the aboriginal plants of the different islands wonderfully different. * * *

Hence we have the truly wonderful fact, that in James Island, of the thirty-eight Galapageian plants, or those found in no other part of the world, thirty are exclusively confined to this one island; and in Albemarle Island, of the twenty-six aboriginal Galapageian plants, twenty-two are confined to this one island, that is, only four are at present known to grow in the other islands of the archipelago; and so on. * * *

The distribution of the tenants of this archipelago would not be nearly so wonderful, if, for instance, one island had a mocking-thrush, and a second island some other quite distinct genus;—if one island had its genus of lizard, and a second island another distinct genus, or none whatever; * * * But it is the circumstance, that several of the islands possess their own species of the tortoise, mocking-thrush, finches, and numerous plants, these species having the same general habits, occupying analogous situations, and obviously filling the same place in the natural economy of this archipelago, that strikes me with wonder. * * * I must repeat, that neither the nature of the soil, nor height of the land, nor the climate, nor the general character of the associated beings, and therefore their action one on another, can differ much in the different islands. * * *

The only light which I can throw on this remarkable difference in the inhabitants of the different islands, is, that very strong currents of the sea running in a westerly and W.N.W. direction must separate, as far as transportal by the sea is concerned, the southern islands from the northern ones; and between these northern islands a strong N.W. current was observed, which must effectually separate James and Albemarle Islands. As the archipelago is free to a most remarkable degree from gales of wind, neither the birds, insects, nor lighter seeds, would be blown from island to island. And lastly, the profound depth of the ocean between the islands, and their apparently recent (in a geological sense) volcanic origin, render it highly unlikely that they were ever united; and this, probably, is a far more important consideration than any other, with respect to the geographical distribution of their inhabitants. Reviewing the facts here given, one is astonished at the amount of creative force, if such an expression may be used, displayed on these small, barren, and rocky islands; and still more so, at its diverse yet analogous action on points so near each other. I have said that the Galapagos Archipelago might be called a satellite attached to America, but it should rather be called a group of satellites, physically similar, organically distinct, yet intimately related to each other, and all related in a marked, though much lesser degree, to the great American continent.

I will conclude my description of the natural history of these islands, by giving an account of the extreme tameness of the birds.

This disposition is common to all the terrestrial species; namely, to the mocking-thrushes, the finches, wrens, tyrant-fly-catchers, the dove, and carrion-buzzard. All of them often approached sufficiently near to be killed with a switch, and sometimes, as I myself tried, with a cap or hat. A gun is here almost superfluous; for with the muzzle I pushed a hawk off the branch of a tree. One day, whilst lying down, a mocking-thrush alighted on the edge of a pitcher, made of the shell of a tortoise, which I held in my hand, and began very quietly to sip the water; it allowed me to lift it from the ground whilst seated on the vessel: I often tried, and very nearly succeeded, in catching these birds by their legs. * * *

From these several facts we may, I think, conclude, first, that the wildness of birds with regard to man, is a particular instinct directed against *him*, and not dependent on any general degree of caution arising from other sources of danger; secondly, that it is not acquired by individual birds in a short time, even when much persecuted; but that in the course of successive generations it becomes hereditary. With domesticated animals we are accustomed to see new mental habits or instincts acquired and rendered hereditary; but with animals in a state of nature, it must always be most difficult to discover instances of acquired hereditary knowledge. In regard to the wildness of birds towards man, there is no way of accounting for it, except as an inherited habit: comparatively few young birds, in any one year, have been injured by man in England, yet almost all, even nestlings, are afraid of him; many individuals, on the other hand, both at the Galapagos and at the Falklands, have been pursued and injured by man, but yet have not learned a salutary dread of him. We may infer from these facts, what havoc the introduction of any new beast of prey must cause in a country, before the instincts of the indigenous inhabitants have become adapted to the stranger's craft or power.

1839, 1845

from **On the Origin of Species by Means of Natural Selection**
or
The Preservation of Favoured Races in the Struggle for Life
from *Chapter 3. Struggle for Existence*

Before entering on the subject of this chapter, I must make a few preliminary remarks, to show how the struggle for existence bears on Natural Selection. * * * The mere existence of individual variability and of some few well-marked varieties, though necessary as the foundation for the work, helps us but little in understanding how species arise in nature. How have all those exquisite adaptations of one part of the organisation to another part, and to the conditions of life, and of one distinct organic being to another being, been perfected? We see these beautiful co-adaptations most plainly in the woodpecker and missletoe; and only a little less plainly in the humblest parasite which clings to the hairs of a quadruped or feathers of a bird; in the structure of the beetle which dives through the water; in the plumed seed which is wafted by the gentlest breeze; in short, we see beautiful adaptations everywhere and in every part of the organic world.

Again, it may be asked, how is it that varieties which I have called incipient species, become ultimately converted into good and distinct species, which in most cases obviously differ from each other far more than do the varieties of the same species? How do those groups of species, which constitute what are called distinct genera,[1] and which differ from each other more than do the species of the same genus, arise? All these results, as we shall more fully see in the next chapter, follow inevitably from the struggle for life. Owing to this struggle for life, any variation, however slight and from whatever cause proceeding, if it be in any degree profitable to an individual of any species, in its infinitely complex relations to other organic beings and to external nature, will tend to the preservation of that individual, and will generally be inherited by its offspring. The offspring, also, will thus have a better chance of surviving, for, of the many individuals of any species which are periodically born, but a small number can survive. I have called this principle, by which each slight variation, if useful, is preserved, by the term of Natural Selection, in order to mark its relation to man's power of selection. We have seen that man by selection can certainly produce great results, and can adapt organic beings to his own uses, through the accumulation of slight but useful variations, given to him by the hand of Nature. But Natural Selection, as we shall hereafter see, is a power incessantly ready for action, and is as immeasurably superior to man's feeble efforts, as the works of Nature are to those of Art.

We will now discuss in a little more detail the struggle for existence. * * * Nothing is easier than to admit in words the truth of the universal struggle for life, or more difficult—at least I have found it so—than constantly to bear this conclusion in mind. Yet unless it be thoroughly engrained in the mind, I am convinced that the whole economy of nature, with every fact on distribution, rarity, abundance, extinction, and variation, will be dimly seen or quite misunderstood. We behold the face of nature bright with gladness, we often see superabundance of food; we do not see, or we forget, that the birds which are idly singing round us mostly live on insects or seeds, and are thus constantly destroying life; or we forget how largely these songsters, or their eggs, or their nestlings, are destroyed by birds and beasts of prey; we do not always bear in mind, that though food may be now superabundant, it is not so at all seasons of each recurring year.

I should premise that I use the term Struggle for Existence in a large and metaphorical sense, including dependence of one being on another, and including (which is more important) not only the life of the individual, but success in leaving progeny. Two canine animals in a time of dearth, may be truly said to struggle with each other which shall get food and live. But a plant on the edge of a desert is said to struggle for life against the drought, though more properly it should be said to be dependent on the moisture. A plant which annually produces a thousand seeds, of

1. Plural of genus, a class of species with common characteristics.

which on an average only one comes to maturity, may be more truly said to struggle with the plants of the same and other kinds which already clothe the ground. The missletoe is dependent on the apple and a few other trees, but can only in a far-fetched sense be said to struggle with these trees, for if too many of these parasites grow on the same tree, it will languish and die. But several seedling missletoes, growing close together on the same branch, may more truly be said to struggle with each other. As the missletoe is disseminated by birds, its existence depends on birds; and it may metaphorically be said to struggle with other fruit-bearing plants, in order to tempt birds to devour and thus disseminate its seeds rather than those of other plants. In these several senses, which pass into each other, I use for convenience sake the general term of struggle for existence.

A struggle for existence inevitably follows from the high rate at which all organic beings tend to increase. Every being, which during its natural lifetime produces several eggs or seeds, must suffer destruction during some period of its life, and during some season or occasional year, otherwise, on the principle of geometrical increase, its numbers would quickly become so inordinately great that no country could support the product. Hence, as more individuals are produced than can possibly survive, there must in every case be a struggle for existence, either one individual with another of the same species, or with the individuals of distinct species or with the physical conditions of life. It is the doctrine of Malthus[2] applied with manifold force to the whole animal and vegetable kingdoms; for in this case there can be no artificial increase of food, and no prudential restraint from marriage. Although some species may be now increasing, more or less rapidly, in numbers, all cannot do so, for the world would not hold them.

There is no exception to the rule that every organic being naturally increases at so high a rate, that if not destroyed, the earth would soon be covered by the progeny of a single pair. Even slow-breeding man has doubled in twenty-five years, and at this rate, in a few thousand years, there would literally not be standing room for his prog-eny. Linnaeus[3] has calculated that if an annual plant produced only two seeds—and there is no plant so unproductive as this—and their seedlings next year produced two, and so on, then in twenty years there would be a million plants. The elephant is reckoned to be the slowest breeder of all known animals, and I have taken some pains to estimate its probable minimum rate of natural increase: it will be under the mark to assume that it breeds when thirty years old, and goes on breeding till ninety years old, bringing forth three pairs of young in this interval; if this be so, at the end of the fifth century there would be alive fifteen million elephants, descended from the first pair.

But we have better evidence on this subject than mere theoretical calculations, namely, the numerous recorded cases of the astonishingly rapid increase of various animals in a state of nature, when circumstances have been favourable to them during two or three following seasons. Still more striking is the evidence from our domestic animals of many kinds which have run wild in several parts of the world: if the statements of the rate of increase of slow-breeding cattle and horses in South America, and latterly in Australia, had not been well authenticated, they would have

2. In his *Essay on the Principle of Population* (1803), English economist Thomas Malthus argued that unchecked population growth would threaten the food supply; he proposed "moral restraint" as a partial solution.
3. Carl von Linné (1707–1778), Swedish botanist and founder of scientific classification systems.

been quite incredible. So it is with plants: cases could be given of introduced plants which have become common throughout whole islands in a period of less than ten years. * * *

In looking at Nature, it is most necessary to keep the foregoing considerations always in mind—never to forget that every single organic being around us may be said to be striving to the utmost to increase in numbers; that each lives by a struggle at some period of its life; that heavy destruction inevitably falls either on the young or old, during each generation or at recurrent intervals. Lighten any check, mitigate the destruction ever so little, and the number of the species will almost instantaneously increase to any amount. The face of Nature may be compared to a yielding surface, with ten thousand sharp wedges packed close together and driven inwards by incessant blows, sometimes one wedge being struck, and then another with greater force. * * *

The amount of food for each species of course gives the extreme limit to which each can increase; but very frequently it is not the obtaining food, but the serving as prey to other animals, which determines the average numbers of a species. Thus, there seems to be little doubt that the stock of partridges, grouse, and hares on any large estate depends chiefly on the destruction of vermin. If not one head of game were shot during the next twenty years in England, and, at the same time, if no vermin were destroyed, there would, in all probability, be less game than at present, although hundreds of thousands of game animals are now annually killed. On the other hand, in some cases, as with the elephant and rhinoceros, none are destroyed by beasts of prey: even the tiger in India most rarely dares to attack a young elephant protected by its dam.

Climate plays an important part in determining the average numbers of a species, and periodical seasons of extreme cold or drought, I believe to be the most effective of all checks. I estimated that the winter of 1854–55 destroyed four-fifths of the birds in my own grounds; and this is a tremendous destruction, when we remember that ten per cent. is an extraordinarily severe mortality from epidemics with man. The action of climate seems at first sight to be quite independent of the struggle for existence; but in so far as climate chiefly acts in reducing food, it brings on the most severe struggle between the individuals, whether of the same or of distinct species, which subsist on the same kind of food. Even when climate, for instance extreme cold, acts directly, it will be the least vigorous, or those which have got least food through the advancing winter, which will suffer most. When we travel from south to north, or from a damp region to a dry, we invariably see some species gradually getting rarer and rarer, and finally disappearing; and the change of climate being conspicuous, we are tempted to attribute the whole effect to its direct action. But this is a very false view: we forget that each species, even where it most abounds, is constantly suffering enormous destruction at some period of its life, from enemies or from competitors for the same place and food; and if these enemies or competitors be in the least degree favoured by any slight change of climate, they will increase in numbers, and, as each area is already fully stocked with inhabitants, the other species will decrease. * * *

That climate acts in main part indirectly by favouring other species, we may clearly see in the prodigious number of plants in our gardens which can perfectly well endure our climate, but which never become naturalised, for they cannot compete with our native plants, nor resist destruction by our native animals. * * *

Many cases are on record showing how complex and unexpected are the checks and relations between organic beings, which have to struggle together in the same country. I will give only a single instance, which, though a simple one, has interested me. In Staffordshire, on the estate of a relation where I had ample means of investigation, there was a large and extremely barren heath, which had never been touched by the hand of man; but several hundred acres of exactly the same nature had been enclosed twenty-five years previously and planted with Scotch fir. The change in the native vegetation of the planted part of the heath was most remarkable, more than is generally seen in passing from one quite different soil to another: not only the proportional numbers of the heath-plants were wholly changed, but twelve species of plants (not counting grasses and carices) flourished in the plantations, which could not be found on the heath. The effect on the insects must have been still greater, for six insectivorous birds were very common in the plantations, which were not to be seen on the heath; and the heath was frequented by two or three distinct insectivorous birds. Here we see how potent has been the effect of the introduction of a single tree, nothing whatever else having been done, with the exception that the land had been enclosed, so that cattle could not enter. * * *

A corollary of the highest importance may be deduced from the foregoing remarks, namely, that the structure of every organic being is related, in the most essential yet often hidden manner, to that of all other organic beings, with which it comes into competition for food or residence, or from which it has to escape, or on which it preys. This is obvious in the structure of the teeth and talons of the tiger; and in that of the legs and claws of the parasite which clings to the hair on the tiger's body. But in the beautifully plumed seed of the dandelion, and in the flattened and fringed legs of the water-beetle, the relation seems at first confined to the elements of air and water. Yet the advantage of plumed seeds no doubt stands in the closest relation to the land being already thickly clothed by other plants; so that the seeds may be widely distributed and fall on unoccupied ground. In the water-beetle, the structure of its legs, so well adapted for diving, allows it to compete with other aquatic insects, to hunt for its own prey, and to escape serving as prey to other animals.

The store of nutriment laid up within the seeds of many plants seems at first sight to have no sort of relation to other plants. But from the strong growth of young plants produced from such seeds (as peas and beans), when sown in the midst of long grass, I suspect that the chief use of the nutriment in the seed is to favour the growth of the young seedling, whilst struggling with other plants growing vigorously all around.

Look at a plant in the midst of its range, why does it not double or quadruple its numbers? We know that it can perfectly well withstand a little more heat or cold, dampness or dryness, for elsewhere it ranges into slightly hotter or colder, damper or drier districts. In this case we can clearly see that if we wished in imagination to give the plant the power of increasing in number, we should have to give it some advantage over its competitors, or over the animals which preyed on it. On the confines of its geographical range, a change of constitution with respect to climate would clearly be an advantage to our plant; but we have reason to believe that only a few plants or animals range so far, that they are destroyed by the rigour of the climate alone. Not until we reach the extreme confines of life, in the arctic regions or on the borders of an utter desert, will competition cease. The land may be extremely cold or dry, yet there will be competition between some few species, or between the individuals of the same species, for the warmest or dampest spots.

Hence, also, we can see that when a plant or animal is placed in a new country amongst new competitors, though the climate may be exactly the same as in its former home, yet the conditions of its life will generally be changed in an essential manner. If we wished to increase its average numbers in its new home, we should have to modify it in a different way to what we should have done in its native country; for we should have to give it some advantage over a different set of competitors or enemies.

It is good thus to try in our imagination to give any form some advantage over another. Probably in no single instance should we know what to do, so as to succeed. It will convince us of our ignorance on the mutual relations of all organic beings; a conviction as necessary, as it seems to be difficult to acquire. All that we can do, is to keep steadily in mind that each organic being is striving to increase at a geometrical ratio; that each at some period of its life, during some season of the year, during each generation or at intervals, has to struggle for life, and to suffer great destruction. When we reflect on this struggle, we may console ourselves with the full belief, that the war of nature is not incessant, that no fear is felt, that death is generally prompt, and that the vigorous, the healthy, and the happy survive and multiply.

1859

from The Descent of Man
from *Chapter 21. General Summary and Conclusion*
[NATURAL SELECTION AND SEXUAL SELECTION]

A brief summary will here be sufficient to recall to the reader's mind the more salient points in this work. Many of the views which have been advanced are highly speculative, and some no doubt will prove erroneous; but I have in every case given the reasons which have led me to one view rather than to another. It seemed worth while to try how far the principle of evolution would throw light on some of the more complex problems in the natural history of man. False facts are highly injurious to the progress of science, for they often long endure; but false views, if supported by some evidence, do little harm, as every one takes a salutary pleasure in proving their falseness; and when this is done, one path towards error is closed and the road to truth is often at the same time opened.

The main conclusion arrived at in this work, and now held by many naturalists who are well competent to form a sound judgment, is that man is descended from some less highly organised form. The grounds upon which this conclusion rests will never be shaken, for the close similarity between man and the lower animals in embryonic development, as well as in innumerable points of structure and constitution, both of high and of the most trifling importance,—the rudiments which he retains, and the abnormal reversions to which he is occasionally liable,—are facts which cannot be disputed. They have long been known, but until recently they told us nothing with respect to the origin of man. Now when viewed by the light of our knowledge of the whole organic world, their meaning is unmistakeable. The great principle of evolution stands up clear and firm, when these groups of facts are considered in connection with others, such as the mutual affinities of the members of the same group, their geographical distribution in past and present times, and their geological succession. It is incredible that all these facts should speak falsely. He who is not content to look, like a savage, at the phenomena of nature as disconnected, cannot any longer believe that man is the work of a separate act of creation. He will be forced to admit that the close resemblance of the embryo of man to that, for instance, of a dog—the construction of his skull, limbs, and whole frame, independently of the uses to which the parts may be put, on the same plan with that of other mammals—the occasional reappearance of various structures, for instance of several distinct muscles, which man does not normally possess, but which are common to the Quadrumana[1]— and a crowd of analogous facts—all point in the plainest manner to the conclusion that man is the co-descendant with other mammals of a common progenitor. * * *

It must not be supposed that the divergence of each race from the other races, and of all the races from a common stock, can be traced back to any one pair of progenitors. On the contrary, at every stage in the process of modification, all the individuals which were in any way best fitted for their conditions of life, though in different degrees, would have survived in greater numbers than the less well fitted. The process would have been like that followed by man, when he does not intentionally select particular individuals, but breeds from all the superior and neglects all the inferior individuals. He thus slowly but surely modifies his stock, and unconsciously forms a new strain. So with respect to modifications, acquired independently of selection, and due to variations arising from the nature of the organism and the action of the surrounding conditions, or from changed habits of life, no single pair will have been modified in a much greater degree than the other pairs which inhabit the same country, for all will have been continually blended through free intercrossing.

By considering the embryological structure of man,—the homologies[2] which he presents with the lower animals,—the rudiments which he retains,—and the reversions to which he is liable, we can partly recall in imagination the former condition of our early progenitors; and can approximately place them in their proper position in the zo-ological series. We thus learn that man is descended from a hairy quadruped, furnished with a tail and pointed ears, probably arboreal[3] in its habits, and an inhabitant of the Old World. This creature, if its whole structure had been examined by a naturalist, would have been classed amongst the Quadrumana, as surely as would the common and still more ancient progenitor of the Old and New World monkeys. The Quadrumana and all the higher mammals are probably derived from an ancient marsupial[4] animal, and this through a long line of diversified forms, either from some reptile-like or some amphibian-like creature, and this again from some fish-like animal. In the dim obscurity of the past we can see that the early progenitor of all the Vertebrata[5] must have been an aquatic animal, provided with branchiae,[6] with the two sexes united in the same individual, and with the most important organs of the body (such as the brain and heart) imperfectly developed. This animal seems to have been more like the larvae of our existing marine Ascidians[7] than any other known form.

The greatest difficulty which presents itself, when we are driven to the above conclusion on the origin of man, is the high standard of intellectual power and of moral disposition which he has attained. But every one who admits the general principle of evolution, must see that the mental powers of the higher animals, which are the same in kind with those of mankind, though so different in degree, are capable of advancement. Thus the interval between the mental powers of one of the higher apes and of a fish, or between those of an ant and scale-insect, is immense. The development of these powers in animals does not offer any special difficulty; for with our domesticated animals, the mental faculties are certainly variable, and the

1. "Four-handed"—i.e., those animals, such as monkeys and apes, which can use all four feet as hands.
2. Similarities due to common origin.
3. Tree-dwelling.
4. Animals with an external pouch for incubating and nurturing their young; today found primarily in Australia.
5. Vertebrates; animals with a segmented spine; commonly called the "higher animals."
6. Gills.
7. A group of marine animals, also known as "sea squirts."

variations are inherited. No one doubts that these faculties are of the utmost importance to animals in a state of nature. Therefore the conditions are favourable for their development through natural selection. The same conclusion may be extended to man; the intellect must have been all-important to him, even at a very remote period, enabling him to use language, to invent and make weapons, tools, traps, &c.; by which means, in combination with his social habits, he long ago became the most dominant of all living creatures. * * *

* * * The higher intellectual powers of man, such as those of ratiocination, abstraction, self-consciousness, &c., will have followed from the continued improvement of other mental faculties; but without considerable culture of the mind, both in the race and in the individual, it is doubtful whether these high powers would be exercised, and thus fully attained.

The development of the moral qualities is a more interesting and difficult problem. Their foundation lies in the social instincts, including in this term the family ties. These instincts are of a highly complex nature, and in the case of the lower animals give special tendencies towards certain definite actions; but the more important elements for us are love, and the distinct emotion of sympathy. Animals endowed with the social instincts take pleasure in each other's company, warn each other of danger, defend and aid each other in many ways. These instincts are not extended to all the individuals of the species, but only to those of the same community. As they are highly beneficial to the species, they have in all probability been acquired through natural selection.

A moral being is one who is capable of comparing his past and future actions and motives,—of approving of some and disapproving of others; and the fact that man is the one being who with certainty can be thus designated makes the greatest of all distinctions between him and the lower animals. But in our third chapter I have endeavoured to shew that the moral sense follows, firstly, from the enduring and always present nature of the social instincts, in which respect man agrees with the lower animals; and secondly, from his mental faculties being highly active and his impressions of past events extremely vivid, in which respects he differs from the lower animals. Owing to this condition of mind, man cannot avoid looking backwards and comparing the impressions of past events and actions. He also continually looks forward. Hence after some temporary desire or passion has mastered his social instincts, he will reflect and compare the now weakened impression of such past impulses, with the ever present social instinct; and he will then feel that sense of dissatisfaction which all unsatisfied instincts leave behind them. Consequently he resolves to act differently for the future—and this is conscience. Any instinct which is permanently stronger or more enduring than another, gives rise to a feeling which we express by saying that it ought to be obeyed. A pointer dog, if able to reflect on his past conduct, would say to himself, I ought (as indeed we say of him) to have pointed at that hare and not have yielded to the passing temptation of hunting it. * * *

The belief in God has often been advanced as not only the greatest, but the most complete of all the distinctions between man and the lower animals. It is however impossible, as we have seen, to maintain that this belief is innate or instinctive in man. On the other hand a belief in all-pervading spiritual agencies seems to be universal; and apparently follows from a considerable advance in the reasoning powers of man, and from a still greater advance in his faculties of imagination, curiosity and wonder. I am aware that the assumed instinctive belief in God has been used by many persons as an argument for His existence. But this is a rash argument, as we should thus be compelled to believe in the existence of many cruel and malignant spirits, possessing only a little more power than man; for the belief in them is far more general than of a beneficent Deity. The idea of a universal and beneficent Creator of the universe does not seem to arise in the mind of man, until he has been elevated by long-continued culture.

He who believes in the advancement of man from some lowly-organised form, will naturally ask how does this bear on the belief in the immortality of the soul. * * * Few persons feel any anxiety from the impossibility of determining at what precise period in the development of the individual, from the first trace of the minute germinal vesicle to the child either before or after birth, man becomes an immortal being; and there is no greater cause for anxiety because the period in the gradually ascending organic scale cannot possibly be determined.

I am aware that the conclusions arrived at in this work will be denounced by some as highly irreligious; but he who thus denounces them is bound to shew why it is more irreligious to explain the origin of man as a distinct species by descent from some lower form, through the laws of variation and natural selection, than to explain the birth of the individual through the laws of ordinary reproduction. The birth both of the species and of the individual are equally parts of that grand sequence of events, which our minds refuse to accept as the result of blind chance. The understanding revolts at such a conclusion, whether or not we are able to believe that every slight variation of structure,—the union of each pair in marriage,—the dissemination of each seed,—and other such events, have all been ordained for some special purpose.

Sexual selection has been treated at great length in these volumes; for, as I have attempted to shew, it has played an important part in the history of the organic world. * * *

Sexual selection depends on the success of certain individuals over others of the same sex in relation to the propagation of the species; whilst natural selection depends on the success of both sexes, at all ages, in relation to the general conditions of life. The sexual struggle is of two kinds; in the one it is between the individuals of the same sex, generally the male sex, in order to drive away or kill their rivals, the females remaining passive; whilst in the other, the struggle is likewise between the individuals of the same sex, in order to excite or charm those of the opposite sex, generally the females, which no longer remain passive, but select the more agreeable partners. This latter kind of selection is closely analogous to that which man unintentionally, yet effectually, brings to bear on his domesticated productions, when he continues for a long time choosing the most pleasing or useful individuals, without any wish to modify the breed. * * *

The belief in the power of sexual selection rests chiefly on the following considerations. The characters which we have the best reason for supposing to have been thus acquired are confined to one sex; and this alone renders it probable that they are in some way connected with the act of reproduction. These characters in innumerable instances are fully developed only at maturity; and often during only a part of the year, which is always the breeding-season. The males (passing over a few exceptional cases) are the most active in courtship; they are the best armed, and are rendered the most attractive in various ways. It is to be especially observed that the males display their attractions with elaborate care in the presence of the females; and that they rarely or never display them excepting during the season of love. It is incredible that all this display should be purposeless. Lastly we have distinct evidence with some quadrupeds and birds that the individuals of the one sex are capable of feeling a strong antipathy or preference for certain individuals of the opposite sex.

Bearing these facts in mind, and not forgetting the marked results of man's unconscious selection, it seems to me almost certain that if the individuals of one sex were during a long series of generations to prefer pairing with certain individuals of the other sex, characterised in some peculiar manner, the offspring would slowly but surely become modified in this same manner. I have not attempted to conceal that, excepting when the males are more numerous than the females, or when polygamy prevails, it is doubtful how the more attractive males succeed in leaving a larger number of offspring to inherit their superiority in ornaments or other charms than the less attractive males; but I have shewn that this would probably follow from the females,—especially the more vigorous females which would be the first to breed, preferring not only the more attractive but at the same time the more vigorous and victorious males.

Although we have some positive evidence that birds appreciate bright and beautiful objects, as with the Bower-birds of Australia, and although they certainly appreciate the power of song, yet I fully admit that it is an astonishing fact that the females of many birds and some mammals should be endowed with sufficient taste for what has apparently been effected through sexual selection; and this is even more astonishing in the case of reptiles, fish, and insects. But we really know very little about the minds of the lower animals. It cannot be supposed that male Birds of Paradise or Peacocks, for instance, should take so much pains in erecting, spreading, and vibrating their beautiful plumes before the females for no purpose. We should remember the fact given on excellent authority in a former chapter, namely that several peahens, when debarred from an admired male, remained widows during a whole season rather than pair with another bird.

Nevertheless I know of no fact in natural history more wonderful than that the female Argus pheasant should be able to appreciate the exquisite shading of the ball-and-socket ornaments and the elegant patterns on the wing-feathers of the male. He who thinks that the male was created as he now exists must admit that the great plumes, which prevent the wings from being used for flight, and which, as well as the primary feathers, are displayed in a manner quite peculiar to this one species during the act of courtship, and at no other time, were given to him as an ornament. If so, he must like-wise admit that the female was created and endowed with the capacity of appreciating such ornaments. I differ only in the conviction that the male Argus pheasant acquired his beauty gradually, through the females having preferred during many generations the more highly ornamented males; the aesthetic capacity of the females having been advanced through exercise or habit in the same manner as our own taste is gradually improved. In the male, through the fortunate chance of a few feathers not having been modified, we can distinctly see how simple spots with a little fulvous[8] shading on one side might have been developed by small and graduated steps into the wonderful ball-and-socket ornaments; and it is probable that they were actually thus developed.

Everyone who admits the principle of evolution, and yet feels great difficulty in admitting that female mammals, birds, reptiles, and fish, could have acquired the high standard of taste which is implied by the beauty of the males, and which generally coincides with our own standard, should reflect that in each member of the

8. Brownish-yellow.

vertebrate series the nerve-cells of the brain are the direct offshoots of those possessed by the common progenitor of the whole group. It thus becomes intelligible that the brain and mental faculties should be capable under similar conditions of nearly the same course of development, and consequently of performing nearly the same functions. * * *

He who admits the principle of sexual selection will be led to the remarkable conclusion that the cerebral system not only regulates most of the existing functions of the body, but has indirectly influenced the progressive development of various bodily structures and of certain mental qualities. Courage, pugnacity, perseverance, strength and size of body, weapons of all kinds, musical organs, both vocal and instrumental, bright colours, stripes and marks, and ornamental appendages, have all been indirectly gained by the one sex or the other, through the influence of love and jealousy, through the appreciation of the beautiful in sound, colour or form, and through the exertion of a choice; and these powers of the mind manifestly depend on the development of the cerebral system.

Man scans with scrupulous care the character and pedigree of his horses, cattle, and dogs before he matches them; but when he comes to his own marriage he rarely, or never, takes any such care. He is impelled by nearly the same motives as are the lower animals when left to their own free choice, though he is in so far superior to them that he highly values mental charms and virtues. On the other hand he is strongly attracted by mere wealth or rank. Yet he might by selection do something not only for the bodily constitution and frame of his offspring, but for their intellectual and moral qualities. Both sexes ought to refrain from marriage if in any marked degree inferior in body or mind; but such hopes are Utopian and will never be even partially realised until the laws of inheritance are thoroughly known. All do good service who aid towards this end. When the principles of breeding and of inheritance are better understood, we shall not hear ignorant members of our legislature rejecting with scorn a plan for ascertaining by an easy method whether or not consanguineous marriages[9] are injurious to man.

The advancement of the welfare of mankind is a most intricate problem: all ought to refrain from marriage who cannot avoid abject poverty for their children; for poverty is not only a great evil, but tends to its own increase by leading to recklessness in marriage. On the other hand * * * if the prudent avoid marriage, whilst the reckless marry, the inferior members will tend to supplant the better members of society. Man, like every other animal, has no doubt advanced to his present high condition through a struggle for existence consequent on his rapid multiplication; and if he is to advance still higher he must remain subject to a severe struggle. Otherwise he would soon sink into indolence, and the more highly-gifted men would not be more successful in the battle of life than the less gifted. Hence our natural rate of increase, though leading to many and obvious evils, must not be greatly diminished by any means. There should be open competition for all men; and the most able should not be prevented by laws or customs from succeeding best and rearing the largest number of offspring. Important as the struggle for existence has been and even still is, yet as far as the highest part of man's nature is concerned there are other agencies more important. For the moral qualities are advanced, either directly or indirectly, much more through the effects

9. Marriages between relatives.

of habit, the reasoning powers, instruction, religion, &c., than through natural selection; though to this latter agency the social instincts, which afforded the basis for the development of the moral sense, may be safely attributed.

The main conclusion arrived at in this work, namely that man is descended from some lowly-organised form, will, I regret to think, be highly distasteful to many persons. But there can hardly be a doubt that we are descended from barbarians. The astonishment which I felt on first seeing a party of Fuegians[1] on a wild and broken shore will never be forgotten by me, for the reflection at once rushed into my mind— such were our ancestors. These men were absolutely naked and bedaubed with paint, their long hair was tangled, their mouths frothed with excitement, and their expression was wild, startled, and distrustful. They possessed hardly any arts, and like wild animals lived on what they could catch; they had no government, and were merciless to every one not of their own small tribe. He who has seen a savage in his native land will not feel much shame, if forced to acknowledge that the blood of some more humble creature flows in his veins. For my own part I would as soon be descended from that heroic little monkey, who braved his dreaded enemy in order to save the life of his keeper; or from that old baboon, who, descending from the mountains, carried away in triumph his young comrade from a crowd of astonished dogs— as from a savage who delights to torture his enemies, offers up bloody sacrifices, practises infanticide without remorse, treats his wives like slaves, knows no decency, and is haunted by the grossest superstitions.

Man may be excused for feeling some pride at having risen, though not through his own exertions, to the very summit of the organic scale; and the fact of his having thus risen, instead of having been aboriginally placed there, may give him hopes for a still higher destiny in the distant future. But we are not here concerned with hopes or fears, only with the truth as far as our reason allows us to discover it. I have given the evidence to the best of my ability; and we must acknowledge, as it seems to me, that man with all his noble qualities, with sympathy which feels for the most debased, with benevolence which extends not only to other men but to the humblest living creature, with his god-like intellect which has penetrated into the movements and constitution of the solar system—with all these exalted powers—Man still bears in his bodily frame the indelible stamp of his lowly origin.

1871

from Autobiography
[A PASSION FOR COLLECTING]

A German Editor having written to me to ask for an account of the development of my mind and character with some sketch of my autobiography, I have thought that the attempt would amuse me, and might possibly interest my children or their children. I know that it would have interested me greatly to have read even so short and dull a sketch of the mind of my grandfather written by himself, and what he thought and did and how he worked. I have attempted to write the following account of myself, as if I were a dead man in another world looking back at my own life. * * *

By the time I went to * * * day-school my taste for natural history, and more especially for collecting, was well developed. I tried to make out the names of plants,

---

1. Inhabitants of Tierra del Fuego, which Darwin visited in 1832 during the voyage of the *Beagle*. See pages 1347–57.

and collected all sorts of things, shells, seals, franks, coins, and minerals. The passion for collecting, which leads a man to be a systematic naturalist, a virtuoso or a miser, was very strong in me, and was clearly innate, as none of my sisters or brother ever had this taste.

One little event during this year [1817] has fixed itself very firmly in my mind, and I hope that it has done so from my conscience having been afterwards sorely troubled by it; it is curious as showing that apparently I was interested at this early age in the variability of plants! I told another little boy * * * that I could produce variously coloured Polyanthuses and Primroses by watering them with certain coloured fluids, which was of course a monstrous fable, and had never been tried by me. * * *

I can say in my own favour that I was as a boy humane, but I owed this entirely to the instruction and example of my sisters. I doubt indeed whether humanity is a natural or innate quality. I was very fond of collecting eggs, but I never took more than a single egg out of a bird's nest, except on one single occasion, when I took all, not for their value, but from a sort of bravado. * * *

Looking back as well as I can at my character during my school life, the only qualities which at this period promised well for the future, were, that I had strong and diversified tastes, much zeal for whatever interested me, and a keen pleasure in understanding any complex subject or thing. I was taught Euclid by a private tutor, and I distinctly remember the intense satisfaction which the clear geometrical proofs gave me. I remember with equal distinctness the delight which my uncle gave me * * * by explaining the principle of the vernier[1] of a barometer. With respect to diversified tastes, independently of science, I was fond of reading various books, and I used to sit for hours reading the historical plays of Shakespeare, generally in an old window in the thick walls of the school. I read also other poetry, such as the recently published poems of Byron, Scott, and Thomson's *Seasons*.[2] I mention this because later in life I wholly lost, to my great regret, all pleasure from poetry of any kind, including Shakespeare. In connection with pleasure from poetry I may add that in 1822 a vivid delight in scenery was first awakened in my mind, during a riding tour on the borders of Wales, and which has lasted longer than any other aesthetic pleasure.

Early in my school-days a boy had a copy of the *Wonders of the World*, which I often read and disputed with other boys about the veracity of some of the statements; and I believe this book first gave me a wish to travel in remote countries, which was ultimately fulfilled by the voyage of the *Beagle*. * * *

With respect to science, I continued collecting minerals with much zeal, but quite unscientifically—all that I cared for was a new *named* mineral, and I hardly attempted to classify them. I must have observed insects with some little care, for when ten years old (1819) I went for three weeks to Plas Edwards on the sea-coast in Wales, I was very much interested and surprised at seeing a large black and scarlet Hemipterous insect, many moths (Zygaena) and a Cicindela,[3] which are not found in Shropshire. I almost made up my mind to begin collecting all the insects which I could find dead, for on consulting my sister, I concluded that it was not right to kill insects for the sake of making a collection. From reading White's *Selborne*[4] I took much pleasure in watching the habits of birds, and even made notes on the subject.

1. A scale indicating the divisions of a scientific instrument.
2. James Thomson, a Scottish poet, published *The Seasons* in 1726–1730.
3. Tiger beetle.

4. Gilbert White, a clergyman and naturalist, made a detailed study of his birthplace and lifelong residence, entitled *Natural History and Antiquities of Selborne* (1788).

In my simplicity I remember wondering why every gentleman did not become an ornithologist. * * *

* * * [In 1827] my father perceived or he heard from my sisters, that I did not like the thought of being a physician, so he proposed that I should become a clergyman. He was very properly vehement against my turning an idle sporting man, which then seemed my probable destination. I asked for some time to consider, as from what little I had heard and thought on the subject I had scruples about declaring my belief in all the dogmas of the Church of England; though otherwise I liked the thought of being a country clergyman. Accordingly I read with care *Pearson on the Creed* and a few other books on divinity; and as I did not then in the least doubt the strict and literal truth of every word in the Bible, I soon persuaded myself that our Creed must be fully accepted. It never struck me how illogical it was to say that I believed in what I could not understand and what is in fact unintelligible. I might have said with entire truth that I had no wish to dispute any dogma; but I never was such a fool as to feel and say "credo quia incredibile."[5]

Considering how fiercely I have been attacked by the orthodox it seems ludicrous that I once intended to be a clergyman. Nor was this intention and my father's wish ever formally given up, but died a natural death when on leaving Cambridge I joined the *Beagle* as Naturalist. * * *

* * * No pursuit at Cambridge was followed with nearly so much eagerness or gave me so much pleasure as collecting beetles. It was the mere passion for collecting, for I did not dissect them and rarely compared their external characters with published descriptions, but got them named anyhow. I will give a proof of my zeal: one day, on tearing off some old bark, I saw two rare beetles and seized one in each hand; then I saw a third and new kind, which I could not bear to lose, so that I popped the one which I held in my right hand into my mouth. Alas it ejected some intensely acrid fluid, which burnt my tongue so that I was forced to spit the beetle out, which was lost, as well as the third one. * * *

A short conversation with [Professor Sedgwick[6]] produced a strong impression on my mind. Whilst examining an old gravel-pit near Shrewsbury a labourer told me that he had found in it a large worn tropical Volute shell, such as may be seen on the chimney-pieces of cottages; and as he would not sell the shell I was convinced that he had really found it in the pit. I told Sedgwick of the fact, and he at once said (no doubt truly) that it must have been thrown away by someone into the pit; but then added, if really embedded there it would be the greatest misfortune to geology, as it would overthrow all that we know about the superficial deposits of the midland counties. These gravel-beds belonged in fact to the glacial period, and in after years I found in them broken arctic shells. But I was then utterly astonished at Sedgwick not being delighted at so wonderful a fact as a tropical shell being found near the surface in the middle of England. Nothing before had ever made me thoroughly realise, though I had read various scientific books, that science consists in grouping facts so that general laws or conclusions may be drawn from them.

Next morning we started for Llangollen, Conway, Bangor, and Capel Curig.[7] This tour was of decided use in teaching me a little how to make out the geology of a country. Sedgwick often sent me on a line parallel to his, telling me to bring back

---

5. I believe because it is unbelievable (Latin): a famous profession of religious faith.
6. Adam Sedgwick (1785–1873), professor of geology at

Cambridge and Darwin's mentor on his upcoming geological field trip to Wales.
7. Places in northern Wales.

specimens of the rocks and to mark the stratification on a map. I have little doubt that he did this for my good, as I was too ignorant to have aided him. On this tour I had a striking instance how easy it is to overlook phenomena, however conspicuous, before they have been observed by anyone. We spent many hours in Cwm Idwal, examining all the rocks with extreme care, as Sedgwick was anxious to find fossils in them; but neither of us saw a trace of the wonderful glacial phenomena all around us; we did not notice the plainly scored rocks, the perched boulders, the lateral and terminal moraines. Yet these phenomena are so conspicuous that, as I declared in a paper published many years afterwards in the *Philosophical Magazine*, a house burnt down by fire did not tell its story more plainly than did this valley. If it had still been filled by a glacier, the phenomena would have been less distinct than they now are.

* * *

On returning home from my short geological tour in N. Wales, I found a letter from Henslow,[8] informing me that Captain Fitz-Roy was willing to give up part of his own cabin to any young man who would volunteer to go with him without pay as naturalist to the Voyage of the *Beagle*. * * * I was instantly eager to accept the offer, but my father strongly objected, adding the words fortunate for me,—"If you can find any man of common sense, who advises you to go, I will give my consent." So I wrote that evening and refused the offer. On the next morning I went to Maer to be ready for September 1st, and whilst out shooting, my uncle sent for me, offering to drive me over to Shrewsbury and talk with my father. As my uncle thought it would be wise in me to accept the offer, and as my father always maintained that he was one of the most sensible men in the world, he at once consented in the kindest manner. I had been rather extravagant at Cambridge and to console my father said, "that I should be deuced clever to spend more than my allowance whilst on board the *Beagle*"; but he answered with a smile, "But they all tell me you are very clever."

Next day I started for Cambridge to see Henslow, and thence to London to see Fitz-Roy, and all was soon arranged. Afterwards on becoming very intimate with Fitz-Roy, I heard that I had run a very narrow risk of being rejected, on account of the shape of my nose! He was an ardent disciple of Lavater,[9] and was convinced that he could judge a man's character by the outline of his features; and he doubted whether anyone with my nose could possess sufficient energy and determination for the voyage. But I think he was afterwards well-satisfied that my nose had spoken falsely.

* * *

The voyage of the *Beagle* has been by far the most important event in my life and has determined my whole career; yet it depended on so small a circumstance as my uncle offering to drive me 30 miles to Shrewsbury, which few uncles would have done, and on such a trifle as the shape of my nose. I have always felt that I owe to the voyage the first real training or education of my mind. I was led to attend closely to several branches of natural history, and thus my powers of observation were improved, though they were already fairly developed.

The investigation of the geology of all the places visited was far more important, as reasoning here comes into play. On first examining a new district nothing can appear more hopeless than the chaos of rocks; but by recording the stratification and nature of the rocks and fossils at many points, always reasoning and predicting what

8. John Stevens Henslow (1796–1861), professor of botany at Cambridge.
9. Johann Kaspar Lavater (1741–1801), founder of the pseudoscience of phrenology, the theory that character can be read by studying the shape of the head.

will be found elsewhere, light soon begins to dawn on the district, and the structure of the whole becomes more or less intelligible. * * *

Looking backwards, I can now perceive how my love for science gradually preponderated over every other taste. * * * I discovered, though unconsciously and insensibly, that the pleasure of observing and reasoning was a much higher one than that of skill and sport. The primeval instincts of the barbarian slowly yielded to the acquired tastes of the civilized man. That my mind became developed through my pursuits during the voyage, is rendered probable by a remark made by my father, who was the most acute observer whom I ever saw, of a sceptical disposition, and far from being a believer in phrenology; for on first seeing me after the voyage, he turned round to my sisters and exclaimed, "Why, the shape of his head is quite altered." * * *

I need not here refer to the events of the voyage—where we went and what we did—as I have given a sufficiently full account in my published Journal. The glories of the vegetation of the Tropics rise before my mind at the present time more vividly than anything else. Though the sense of sublimity, which the great deserts of Patagonia and the forest-clad mountains of Tierra del Fuego excited in me, has left an indelible impression on my mind. The sight of a naked savage in his native land is an event which can never be forgotten. Many of my excursions on horseback through wild countries, or in the boats, some of which lasted several weeks, were deeply interesting; their discomfort and some degree of danger were at that time hardly a drawback and none at all afterwards. I also reflect with high satisfaction on some of my scientific work, such as solving the problem of coral-islands, and making out the geological structure of certain islands, for instance, St Helena.[1] Nor must I pass over the discovery of the singular relations of the animals and plants inhabiting the several islands of the Galapagos archipelago, and of all of them to the inhabitants of South America.

As far as I can judge of myself I worked to the utmost during the voyage from the mere pleasure of investigation, and from my strong desire to add a few facts to the great mass of facts in natural science. But I was also ambitious to take a fair place among scientific men. * * *

During these two years[2] I was led to think much about religion. Whilst on board the *Beagle* I was quite orthodox, and I remember being heartily laughed at by several of the officers (though themselves orthodox) for quoting the Bible as an unanswerable authority on some point of morality. I suppose it was the novelty of the argument that amused them. But I had gradually come, by this time, to see that the Old Testament from its manifestly false history of the world, with the Tower of Babel, the rainbow as a sign, etc., etc., and from its attributing to God the feelings of a revengeful tyrant, was no more to be trusted than the sacred books of the Hindoos, or the beliefs of any barbarian. * * *

By further reflecting that the clearest evidence would be requisite to make any sane man believe in the miracles by which Christianity is supported,—that the more we know of the fixed laws of nature the more incredible do miracles become,—that the men at that time were ignorant and credulous to a degree almost incomprehensible by us,—that the Gospels cannot be proved to have been written simultaneously with the events,—that they differ in many important details, far too important as it seemed to me to be admitted as the usual inaccuracies of eyewitnesses;—by such reflections as

---

1. Island in the southern Atlantic.   2. October 1836 to January 1839.

these, which I give not as having the least novelty or value, but as they influenced me, I gradually came to disbelieve in Christianity as a divine revelation. The fact that many false religions have spread over large portions of the earth like wild-fire had some weight with me. Beautiful as is the morality of the New Testament, it can hardly be denied that its perfection depends in part on the interpretation which we now put on metaphors and allegories.

But I was very unwilling to give up my belief;—I feel sure of this for I can well remember often and often inventing day-dreams of old letters between distinguished Romans and manuscripts being discovered at Pompeii or elsewhere which confirmed in the most striking manner all that was written in the Gospels. But I found it more and more difficult, with free scope given to my imagination, to invent evidence which would suffice to convince me. Thus disbelief crept over me at a very slow rate, but was at last complete. The rate was so slow that I felt no distress, and have never since doubted even for a single second that my conclusion was correct. I can indeed hardly see how anyone ought to wish Christianity to be true; for if so the plain language of the text seems to show that the men who do not believe, and this would include my Father, Brother and almost all my best friends, will be everlastingly punished.

And this is a damnable doctrine.

Although I did not think much about the existence of a personal God until a considerably later period of my life, I will here give the vague conclusions to which I have been driven. The old argument of design in nature, as given by Paley,[3] which formerly seemed to me so conclusive, fails, now that the law of natural selection has been discovered. We can no longer argue that, for instance, the beautiful hinge of a bivalve shell must have been made by an intelligent being, like the hinge of a door by man. There seems to be no more design in the variability of organic beings and in the action of natural selection, than in the course which the wind blows. Everything in nature is the result of fixed laws. * * *

But passing over the endless beautiful adaptations which we everywhere meet with, it may be asked how can the generally beneficent arrangement of the world be accounted for? Some writers indeed are so much impressed with the amount of suffering in the world, that they doubt if we look to all sentient beings, whether there is more of misery or of happiness;—whether the world as a whole is a good or a bad one. According to my judgment happiness decidedly prevails, though this would be very difficult to prove. If the truth of this conclusion be granted, it harmonises well with the effects which we might expect from natural selection. If all the individuals of any species were habitually to suffer to an extreme degree they would neglect to propagate their kind; but we have no reason to believe that this has ever or at least often occurred. Some other considerations, moreover, lead to the belief that all sentient beings have been formed so as to enjoy, as a general rule, happiness.

Every one who believes, as I do, that all the corporeal and mental organs (excepting those which are neither advantageous or disadvantageous to the possessor) of all beings have been developed through natural selection, or the survival of the fittest, together with use or habit, will admit that these organs have been formed so that their possessors may compete successfully with other beings, and thus increase in number. Now an animal may be led to pursue that course of action which is the

---

3. In *Natural Theology* (1802), William Paley argued that the beauty and harmony of nature prove the existence of a divine creator.

most beneficial to the species by suffering, such as pain, hunger, thirst, and fear,—or by pleasure, as in eating and drinking and in the propagation of the species, &c. or by both means combined, as in the search for food. But pain or suffering of any kind, if long continued, causes depression and lessens the power of action; yet is well adapted to make a creature guard itself against any great or sudden evil. Pleasurable sensations, on the other hand, may be long continued without any depressing effect; on the contrary they stimulate the whole system to increased action. Hence it has come to pass that most or all sentient beings have been developed in such a manner through natural selection, that pleasurable sensations serve as their habitual guides. We see this in the pleasure from exertion, even occasionally from great exertion of the body or mind,—in the pleasure of our daily meals, and especially in the pleasure derived from sociability and from loving our families. The sum of such pleasures as these, which are habitual or frequently recurrent, give, as I can hardly doubt, to most sentient beings an excess of happiness over misery, although many occasionally suffer much. Such suffering, is quite compatible with the belief in Natural Selection, which is not perfect in its action, but tends only to render each species as successful as possible in the battle for life with other species, in wonderfully complex and changing circumstances. * * *

With respect to immortality, nothing shows me how strong and almost instinctive a belief it is, as the consideration of the view now held by most physicists, namely that the sun with all the planets will in time grow too cold for life, unless indeed some great body dashes into the sun and thus gives it fresh life.—Believing as I do that man in the distant future will be a far more perfect creature than he now is, it is an intolerable thought that he and all other sentient beings are doomed to complete annihilation after such long-continued slow progress. To those who fully admit the immortality of the human soul, the destruction of our world will not appear so dreadful.

Another source of conviction in the existence of God, connected with the reason and not with the feelings, impresses me as having much more weight. This follows from the extreme difficulty or rather impossibility of conceiving this immense and wonderful universe, including man with his capacity of looking far backwards and far into futurity, as the result of blind chance or necessity. When thus reflecting I feel compelled to look to a First Cause having an intelligent mind in some degree analogous to that of man; and I deserve to be called a Theist.

This conclusion was strong in my mind about the time, as far as I can remember, when I wrote The Origin of Species; and it is since that time that it has very gradually with many fluctuations become weaker. But then arises the doubt—can the mind of man, which has, as I fully believe, been developed from a mind as low as that possessed by the lowest animal, be trusted when it draws such grand conclusions? May not these be the result of the connection between cause and effect which strikes us as a necessary one, but probably depends merely on inherited experience? Nor must we overlook the probability of the constant inculcation in a belief in God on the minds of children producing so strong and perhaps an inherited effect on their brains not yet fully developed, that it would be as difficult for them to throw off their belief in God, as for a monkey to throw off its instinctive fear and hatred of a snake.

I cannot pretend to throw the least light on such abstruse problems. The mystery of the beginning of all things is insoluble by us; and I for one must be content to remain an Agnostic. * * *

1876–1882   1887, 1958

"This is the Question"[4]

MARRY	NOT MARRY
Children—(if it please God)—constant companion, (friend in old age) who will feel interested in one, object to be beloved and played with—better than a dog anyhow—Home, and someone to take care of house—Charms of music and female chit-chat. These things good for one's health. Forced to visit and receive relations *but terrible loss of time*.	No children, (no second life) no one to care for one in old age.—What is the use of working without sympathy from near and dear friends—who are near and dear friends to the old except relatives.
My God, it is intolerable to think of spending one's whole life, like a neuter bee, working, working and nothing after all.—No, no won't do.—	Freedom to go where one liked—Choice of Society *and little of it*. Conversation of clever men at clubs.—
Imagine living all one's day solitarily in smoky dirty London House.—Only picture to yourself a nice soft wife on a sofa with good fire, and books and music perhaps—compare this vision with the dingy reality of Grt Marlboro' St. Marry—Marry—Marry Q.E.D.[5]	Not forced to visit relatives, and to bend in every trifle—to have the expense and anxiety of children—perhaps quarrelling.
	Loss of time—cannot read in the evenings—fatness and idleness—anxiety and responsibility—less money for books etc—if many children forced to gain one's bread.—(But then it is very bad for one's health to work too much)
	Perhaps my wife won't like London; then the sentence is banishment and degradation with indolent idle fool—

[On the reverse side of the page Darwin adds:]

It being proved necessary to marry—When? Soon or Late. The Governor says soon for otherwise bad if one has children—one's character is more flexible—one's feelings more lively, and if one does not marry soon, one misses so much good pure happiness.—

But then if I married tomorrow: there would be an infinity of trouble and expense in getting and furnishing a house,—fighting about no Society—morning calls—awkwardness—loss of time every day—(without one's wife was an angel and made one keep industrious)—Then how should I manage all my business if I were obliged to go every day walking with my wife.—Eheu!! I never should know French,—or see the Continent,—or go to America, or go up in a Balloon, or take solitary trip in Wales—poor slave, you will be worse than a negro—And then horrid poverty (without one's wife was better than an angel and had money)—Never mind my boy—Cheer up—One cannot live this solitary life, with groggy old age, friendless and cold and childless staring one in one's face, already beginning to wrinkle. Never mind, trust to chance—keep a sharp look out.—There is many a happy slave—

1958

---

4. The following are pencil notes in Darwin's handwriting, presumably dating from 1837 or 1838. Darwin married his cousin Emma Wedgwood on 29 January 1839.

5. Abbreviation used by scientists and logicians to mark the completion of a proof.

⇒+ PERSPECTIVES +⇐

Religion and Science

"If only the Geologists would let me alone, I could do very well, but those dreadful Hammers! I hear the clink of them at the end of every cadence of the Bible verses." John Ruskin's anxious words reflect the widespread fear that science was chipping away at the foundations of faith. The fossil record showed that the earth was vastly older than anyone had thought, thus casting doubt on the biblical account of Creation, conventionally dated around four thousand years before the birth of Christ. Suddenly a scale of millions and even billions of years was being employed. "The riddle of the rocks" having been deciphered, the physicist John Tyndall said in 1874, "the leaves of that stone book . . . carry the mind back into abysses of past time."

Yet, far from being opposed to science, many early Victorian clergymen were amateur geologists and naturalists. The word "scientist" did not even exist until 1840, and science was scarcely imagined as an independent profession: for all his love of natural history, Charles Darwin studied to be a clergyman. In his day, it was common to take a university degree with no scientific education at all. Until the mid-nineteenth century, science and religion had often been seen as being in harmony. In *Natural Theology* (1802) the philosopher and Anglican priest William Paley had proposed a famous analogy: when we see a complex mechanism such as a watch, we infer that the watch must have had a maker; similarly, when we see the order and beauty of the universe, we must infer the existence of a Creator. Paley's "Argument from Design" was enormously influential. As the geologist Hugh Miller put it, "I am confident that there is not half the ingenuity, or half the mathematical knowledge, displayed in the dome of St Paul's at London, that we find exhibited in the construction of this simple shell."

Increasingly, though, scientists began to question the evidence of God's artistry. In *Principles of Geology* (1830–1833), Charles Lyell argued that geological phenomena resulted from the gradual actions of nature over immense stretches of time. And in 1859, Darwin's *The Origin of Species* extended this perspective to the formation of living creatures, including human beings. Years of scientific observations had convinced him that the animate world is not the product of divine creation but of natural selection: "We can no longer argue that, for instance, the beautiful hinge of a bivalve shell must have been made by an intelligent being. . . . There seems to be no more design in the variability of organic beings and in the action of natural selection, than in the course which the wind blows."

Scientific methods, moreover, were being applied to the study of the Bible itself. Even as scientists undermined "natural" theology, a new wave of biblical criticism from Germany undermined the "revealed" theology given in the Bible. These scholars treated Scripture like any other text, probing into questions of dates and sources, authorship and authenticity. They concluded that Moses could not have written the Pentateuch, and that many episodes in the Bible could not be regarded as historically accurate; some even denied that Jesus was the son of God.

The claims of both science and the "Higher Criticism" provoked storms of controversy. They shattered certainties about the nature of truth, the meaning of life, and man's place in the universe. The historian J. A. Froude recalled the 1840s as a period when "All round us, the intellectual lightships had broken from their moorings. . . . The present generation . . . will never know what it was to find the lights all drifting, the compasses all awry, and nothing left to steer by except the stars." This was not only a personal problem; many assumed that a collapse of Christian faith would lead to the disintegration of society as a whole. The critic Walter Houghton points out the connection to the fear of revolution: in the reviews of *The Descent of Man* (1871) Darwin was severely censured for "revealing his zoological conclusions to the general public at a moment when the sky of Paris was red with the incendiary flames of the Commune."

Some—particularly the literal-minded Evangelicals—reacted to these upheavals by denying any validity to the new scientific theories; others struggled to repress their concerns.

The educator Thomas Arnold suggested that doubts "should be kept, I think, to ourselves, and not talked of even to our nearest friends." If we put a searching question to our neighbor, wrote Ruskin, we risk discovering "that he doubts of many things which we ourselves do not believe strongly enough to hear doubted without danger." To some Victorians, on the other hand, the new theories offered an opportunity for a fresh assessment of long-unquestioned beliefs. George Eliot wrote with exhilaration that her soul had been "liberated from the wretched giant's bed of dogmas on which it has been racked and stretched." The philosopher Leslie Stephen welcomed agnosticism: "I did not feel that the solid ground was giving way beneath my feet, but rather that I was being relieved of a cumbrous burden."

Stopping short of agnosticism, the liberal "Broad Church" centrists of the Church of England sought a clarified, "demythologized" faith, finding moral rather than historical truths in the old stories of creation. At times they treated even Jesus' miracles as more on a par with his parables than as crucial historical events. Bishop William Colenso's careful weighing of historical probabilities, excerpted below, struck many of his first readers as scandalous, but over time mainstream Church of England thought came to accept a comparable coexistence of myth and history in the biblical stories. The book of nature and the book of the acts of God alike now required active and engaged readers, in a world less of facts and certainties than of hypotheses and interpretations.

Thomas Babington Macaulay
1800–1859

Always a staunch believer in material progress, Macaulay extolled scientific achievements as entirely beneficial for society. In 1837 his lavish and unqualified praise of applied science did not jar any sensibilities, for religion and science had not yet clashed as violently as they were to do later in the century. Railroads and steamships, feats of engineering and astronomy, military and industrial technology—it was still possible to admire them all unreservedly. Macaulay's enthusiasm for science was untempered by any sense of the possible dangers of science, or of the threat science would soon pose to the very foundations of religious belief.

An additional work by Macaulay is included in Perspectives: The Industrial Landscape, page 1137.

from **Lord Bacon**
[SCIENCE AS PROGRESS]

It has lengthened life; it has mitigated pain; it has extinguished diseases; it has increased the fertility of the soil; it has given new securities to the mariner; it has furnished new arms to the warrior; it has spanned great rivers and estuaries with bridges of form unknown to our fathers; it has guided the thunderbolt innocuously from heaven to earth; it has lighted up the night with the splendour of the day; it has extended the range of the human vision; it has multiplied the power of the human muscles; it has accelerated motion; it has annihilated distance; it has facilitated intercourse, correspondence, all friendly offices, all despatch of business; it has enabled man to descend to the depths of the sea, to soar into the air, to penetrate securely into the noxious recesses of the earth, to traverse the land in cars which whirl along without horses, and the ocean in ships which run ten knots an hour against the wind. These are but a part of its fruits, and of its first fruits. For it is a philosophy which never rests, which has never attained, which is never perfect. Its law is progress. A point which yesterday was invisible is its goal today, and will be its starting-post to-morrow.

1837

✦ ✦ ✦

Charles Dickens
1812–1870

Victorian morality permeated British life in the mid-nineteenth century—but there was sharp disagreement as to how that morality should be fostered and expressed. In this selection, Dickens argues passionately for a relaxed standard of Sunday observance, against the strict rules that the Evangelicals were attempting to legislate. A broadly based group that included Methodists, Congregationalists, Baptists, and "Low Church" Anglicans, Evangelicals were concerned not only with individual salvation (through rigorous conduct, prayer, and Bible reading) but also with the moral reform of society. In the mid–1830s, Sir Andrew Agnew repeatedly proposed a Sunday Observance Bill in Parliament. As Dickens points out in his scathing attack, the effects of the Bill would have been felt disproportionately by the lower classes, for whom Sunday was the only day of relaxation; he argues that the cause of religion itself, as well as working people's well-being, would be harmed by overly strict observance.

For more about Dickens, see his principal listing on page 1462.

from Sunday Under Three Heads

The provisions of the bill introduced into the House of Commons by Sir Andrew Agnew, and thrown out by that House on the motion for the second reading, on the 18th of May in the present year, by a majority of 32, may very fairly be taken as a test of the length to which the fanatics, of which the honourable Baronet is the distinguished leader, are prepared to go. * * *

The proposed enactments of the bill are briefly these:—All work is prohibited on the Lord's day, under heavy penalties, increasing with every repetition of the offence. There are penalties for keeping shops open—penalties for drunkenness—penalties for keeping open houses of entertainment—penalties for being present at any public meeting or assembly—penalties for letting carriages, and penalties for hiring them—penalties for travelling in steam-boats, and penalties for taking passengers—penalties on vessels commencing their voyage on Sundays—penalties on the owners of cattle who suffer them to be driven on the Lord's day—penalties on constables who refuse to act, and penalties for resisting them when they do. In addition to these trifles, the constables are invested with arbitrary, vexatious, and most extensive powers; and all this in a bill which sets out with the hypocritical and canting declaration that "nothing is more acceptable to God than the *true and sincere* worship of Him according to His holy will, and that it is the bounden duty of Parliament to promote the observance of the Lord's day, by protecting every class of society against being required to sacrifice their comfort, health, religious privileges, and conscience, for the convenience, enjoyment, or supposed advantage of any other class on the Lord's day"! The idea of making a man truly moral through the ministry of constables, and sincerely religious under the influence of penalties, is worthy of the mind which could form such a mass of monstrous absurdity as this bill is composed of.
* * *

In the first place, it is by no means the worst characteristic of this bill, that it is a bill of blunders: it is, from beginning to end, a piece of deliberate cruelty, and crafty injustice. If the rich composed the whole population of this country, not a single comfort of one single man would be affected by it. It is directed exclusively, and without the exception of a solitary instance, against the amusements and recreations of the poor. * * *

Take the very first clause, the provision that no man shall be allowed to work on Sunday—"That no person, upon the Lord's day, shall do, or hire, or employ any person to do any manner of labour, or any work of his or her ordinary calling." What class of persons does this affect? The rich man? No. Menial servants, both male and female, are specially exempted from the operation of the bill. "Menial servants" are among the poor people. The bill has no regard for them. The Baronet's dinner must be cooked on Sunday, the Bishop's horses must be groomed, and the Peer's carriage must be driven. So the menial servants are put utterly beyond the pale of grace;— unless indeed, they are to go to heaven through the sanctity of their masters, and possibly they might think even that, rather an uncertain passport. * * *

With one exception, there are perhaps no clauses in the whole bill, so strongly illustrative of its partial operation, and the intention of its framer, as those which relate to travelling on Sunday. Penalties of ten, twenty, and thirty pounds, are mercilessly imposed upon coach proprietors who shall run their coaches on the Sabbath; one, two, and ten pounds upon those who hire, or let to hire, horses and carriages upon the Lord's day, but not one syllable about those who have no necessity to hire, because they have carriages and horses of their own; not one word of a penalty on liveried coachmen and footmen. The whole of the saintly venom is directed against the hired cabriolet, the humble fly, or the rumbling hackney coach, which enables a man of the poorer class to escape for a few hours from the smoke and dirt, in the midst of which he has been confined throughout the week: while the escutcheoned[1] carriage and the dashing cab, may whirl their wealthy owners to Sunday feasts and private oratorios, setting constables, informers, and penalties, at defiance. Again, in the description of the places of public resort which it is rendered criminal to attend on Sunday, there are no words comprising a very fashionable promenade. Public discussions, public debates, public lectures and speeches, are cautiously guarded against; for it is by their means that the people become enlightened enough, to deride the last efforts of bigotry and superstition. There is a stringent provision for punishing the poor man who spends an hour in a news-room, but there is nothing to prevent the rich one, from lounging away the day in the Zoological Gardens.

There is, in four words, a mock proviso, which affects to forbid travelling "with any animal" on the Lord's day. This, however, is revoked, as relates to the rich man, by a subsequent provision. We have then a penalty of not less than fifty, nor more than one hundred pounds, upon any person participating in the controul, or having the command of any vessel which shall commence her voyage on the Lord's day, should the wind prove favourable. The next time this bill is brought forward (which will no doubt be at an early period of the next session of Parliament) perhaps it will be better to amend this clause by declaring, that from and after the passing of the act, it shall be deemed unlawful for the wind to blow at all upon the Sabbath. It would remove a great deal of temptation from the owners and captains of vessels. * * *

---

1. Bearing a coat of arms.

Let us suppose such a bill as this, to have actually passed both branches of the legislature; to have received the royal assent; and to have come into operation. Imagine its effect in a great city like London.

Sunday comes, and brings with it a day of general gloom and austerity. The man who has been toiling hard all the week, has been looking towards the Sabbath, not as to a day of rest from labour, and healthy recreation, but as one of grievous tyranny and grinding oppression. The day which his Maker intended as a blessing, man has converted into a curse. Instead of being hailed by him as his period of relaxation, he finds it remarkable only as depriving him of every comfort and enjoyment. He has many children about him, all sent into the world at an early age, to struggle for a livelihood; one is kept in a warehouse all day, with an interval of rest too short to enable him to reach home, another walks four or five miles to his employment at the docks, a third earns a few shillings weekly, as an errand boy, or office messenger; and the employment of the man himself, detains him at some distance from his home from morning till night. Sunday is the only day on which they could all meet together, and enjoy a homely meal in social comfort; and now they sit down to a cold and cheerless dinner: the pious guardians of the man's salvation, having, in their regard for the welfare of his precious soul, shut up the bakers' shops.[2] The fire blazes high in the kitchen chimney of these well-fed hypocrites, and the rich steams of the savoury dinner scent the air. What care they to be told that this class of men have neither a place to cook in—nor means to bear the expense, if they had?

Look into your churches—diminished congregations, and scanty attendance. People have grown sullen and obstinate, and are becoming disgusted with the faith which condemns them to such a day as this, once in every seven. And as you cannot make people religious by Act of Parliament, or force them to church by constables, they display their feeling by staying away.

Turn into the streets, and mark the rigid gloom that reigns over everything around. The roads are empty, the fields are deserted, the houses of entertainment are closed. Groups of filthy and discontented-looking men, are idling about at the street corners, or sleeping in the sun; but there are no decently-dressed people of the poorer class, passing to and fro. Where should they walk to? It would take them an hour, at least, to get into the fields, and when they reached them, they could procure neither bit nor sup, without the informer and the penalty. Now and then, a carriage rolls smoothly on, or a well-mounted horseman followed by a liveried attendant, canters by; but with these exceptions, all is as melancholy and quiet, as if a pestilence had fallen on the city.

Bend your steps through the narrow and thickly-inhabited streets, and observe the sallow faces of the men and women, who are lounging at the doors, or lolling from the windows. Regard well, the closeness of these crowded rooms, and the noisome exhalations that rise from the drains and kennels; and then laud the triumph of religion and morality, which condemns people to drag their lives out in such stews[3] as these, and makes it criminal for them to eat or drink in the fresh air, or under the clear sky. * * *

It may be asked, what motives can actuate a man who has so little regard for the comfort of his fellow-beings, so little respect for their wants and necessities, and so

---

2. Lacking ovens at home, working people brought their dinners to cook at bakers' shops on Sundays. Dickens returned to the subject in A Christmas Carol, where the re-formed Scrooge is indignant about Sunday closings, particularly of bakeries; see page 1490–91.

3. Overheated, congested areas.

distorted a notion of the beneficence of his Creator. I reply, an envious, heartless, ill-conditioned dislike, to seeing those whom fortune has placed below him, cheerful and happy—an intolerant confidence in his own high worthiness before God, and a lofty impression of the demerits of others—pride, selfish pride, as inconsistent with the spirit of Christianity itself, as opposed to the example of its Founder upon earth.

1836

✦❉✦

David Friedrich Strauss
1808–1874

Evolution and geology were not the only threats to traditional Christian faith: German scholars who applied methods of historical and literary analysis to the Bible demonstrated that it was, as the historian J. A. Froude put it, "a human composition—parts of it of doubtful authenticity." Such scholarship, known as the "higher criticism," undermined the Bible's stature as divine revelation. Biblical criticism made Charles Kingsley, the Anglican clergyman associated with "Muscular Christianity," feel as though he were standing "on a cliff which is crumbling beneath one, and falling piecemeal into the dark sea." But it liberated George Eliot from her evangelical beliefs. In 1846 she helped bring German scholarship to the attention of the British public with her translation, excerpted here, of *Das Leben Jesu*, David Friedrich Strauss's controversial treatment of Jesus as a historical figure, not the son of God.

from The Life of Jesus Critically Examined
Translated by George Eliot

Having shown the possible existence of the mythical and the legendary in the gospels, both on extrinsic and intrinsic grounds, and defined their distinctive characteristics, it remains in conclusion to inquire how their actual presence may be recognized in individual cases?

The mythus[1] presents two phases; in the first place it is not history; in the second it is fiction, the product of the particular mental tendency of a certain community. These two phases afford the one a negative, the other a positive criterion, by which the mythus is to be recognized.

I. *Negative.* That an account is not historical—that the matter related could not have taken place in the manner described is evident.

First. When the narration is irreconcileable with the known and universal laws which govern the course of events. * * *

Secondly. An account which shall be regarded as historically valid must neither be inconsistent with itself, nor in contradiction with other accounts. * * *

It may here be asked: is it to be regarded as a contradiction if one account is wholly silent respecting a circumstance mentioned by another? In itself, apart from all other considerations, the argumentum ex silentio is of no weight; but it is certainly to be accounted of moment when, at the same time, it may be shown that had the author known the circumstance he could not have failed to mention it, and also that he must have known it had it actually occurred.

---

1. Myth; this was a contentious word to use in connection with Scripture.

II. *Positive.* The positive characters of legend and fiction are to be recognized sometimes in the form, sometimes in the substance of a narrative.

If the form be poetical, if the actors converse in hymns, and in a more diffuse and elevated strain than might be expected from their training and situations, such discourses, at all events, are not to be regarded as historical. The absence of these marks of the unhistorical do not however prove the historical validity of the narration, since the mythus often wears the most simple and apparently historical form: in which case the proof lies in the substance.

If the contents of a narrative strikingly accords with certain ideas existing and prevailing within the circle from which the narrative proceeded, which ideas themselves seem to be the product of preconceived opinions rather than of practical experience, it is more or less probable, according to circumstances, that such a narrative is of mythical origin. The knowledge of the fact, that the Jews were fond of representing their great men as the children of parents who had long been childless, cannot but make us doubtful of the historical truth of the statement that this was the case with John the Baptist;[2] knowing also that the Jews saw predictions every where in the writings of their prophets and poets, and discovered types[3] of the Messiah in all the lives of holy men recorded in their Scriptures; when we find details in the life of Jesus evidently sketched after the pattern of these prophecies and prototypes, we cannot but suspect that they are rather mythical than historical. * * *

Yet each of these tests, on the one hand, and each narrative on the other, considered apart, will rarely prove more than the possible or probable unhistorical character of the record. The concurrence of several such indications, is necessary to bring about a more definite result. The accounts of the visit of the Magi, and of the murder of the innocents at Bethlehem, harmonize remarkably with the Jewish Messianic notion, built upon the prophecy of Balaam, respecting the star which should come out of Jacob; and with the history of the sanguinary command of Pharaoh.[4] Still this would not alone suffice to stamp the narratives as mythical. But we have also the corroborative facts that the described appearance of the star is contrary to the physical, the alleged conduct of Herod to the psychological laws; that Josephus,[5] who gives in other respects so circumstantial an account of Herod, agrees with all other historical authorities in being silent concerning the Bethlehem massacre; and that the visit of the Magi together with the flight into Egypt related in the one Gospel, and the presentation in the temple related in another Gospel, mutually exclude one another.[6] Wherever, as in this instance, the several criteria of the mythical character concur, the result is certain, and certain in proportion to the accumulation of such grounds of evidence. * * *

In these last remarks we are, to a certain extent, anticipating the question which is, in conclusion, to be considered: viz., whether the mythical character is restricted to those features of the narrative, upon which such character is actually stamped; and whether a contradiction between two accounts invalidates one

2. Elizabeth, the mother of John the Baptist, was well past childbearing years when he was born. See Luke 1.5–25.
3. Antecedents who foreshadowed the coming of the Messiah.
4. The Magi were the three kings or wise men who visited the infant Jesus (Matthew 2.1); the "murder of the innocents" refers to King Herod's slaughter of all the male infants in Bethlehem (Matthew 2.16); Balaam's words in Numbers 24.17 have been interpreted as a prophecy concerning Jesus; the Pharaoh of Egypt, fearing the people of Israel, plotted to kill all the male infants born to them (Exodus 1.8, 22).
5. Flavius Josephus (37–c.100), Jewish historian.
6. Joseph and Mary fled into Egypt with their child, Jesus, after a dream warning of the wrath of Herod (Matthew 2.13–15); when Jesus was 12, his parents took him to the Temple in Jerusalem, where he amazed the rabbis with his wisdom (Luke 2.41–52).

account only, or both? That is to say, what is the precise boundary line between the historical and the unhistorical?—the most difficult question in the whole province of criticism.

In the first place, when two narratives mutually exclude one another, one only is thereby proved to be unhistorical. If one be true the other must be false, but though the one be false the other may be true. Thus, in reference to the original residence of the parents of Jesus, we are justified in adopting the account of Luke which places it at Nazareth, to the exclusion of that of Matthew, which plainly supposes it to have been at Bethlehem; and, generally speaking, when we have to choose between two irreconcileable accounts, in selecting as historical that which is the least opposed to the laws of nature, and has the least correspondence with certain national or party opinions. But upon a more particular consideration it will appear that, since one account is false, it is possible that the other may be so likewise: the existence of a mythus respecting some certain point, shows that the imagination has been active in reference to that particular subject; (we need only refer to the genealogies); and the historical accuracy of either of two such accounts cannot be relied upon, unless substantiated by its agreement with some other well-authenticated testimony.

Concerning the different parts of one and the same narrative: it might be thought for example, that though the appearance of an angel, and his announcement to Mary that she should be the Mother of the Messiah,[7] must certainly be regarded as unhistorical, still, that Mary should have indulged this hope before the birth of the child, is not in itself incredible. But what should have excited this hope in Mary's mind? It is at once apparent that that which is credible in itself is nevertheless unhistorical when it is so intimately connected with what is incredible that, if you discard the latter, you at the same time remove the basis on which the former rests. * * *

The following examples will serve to illustrate the mode of deciding in such cases. According to the narrative, as Mary entered the house and saluted her cousin Elizabeth, who was then pregnant, the babe leaped in her womb, she was filled with the Holy Ghost, and she immediately addressed Mary as the mother of the Messiah. This account bears indubitable marks of an unhistorical character. Yet, it is not, in itself, impossible that Mary should have paid a visit to her cousin, during which every thing went on quite naturally. The fact is, however, that there are psychological difficulties connected with this journey of the betrothed; and that the visit, and even the relationship of the two women, seem to have originated entirely in the wish to exhibit a connexion between the mother of John the Baptist, and the mother of the Messiah. Or when in the history of the transfiguration[8] it is stated, that the men who appeared with Jesus on the Mount were Moses and Elias; and that the brilliancy which illuminated Jesus was supernatural; it might seem here also that, after deducting the marvellous, the presence of two men and a bright morning beam might be retained as the historical facts. But the legend was predisposed, by virtue of the current idea concerning the relation of the Messiah to these two prophets, not merely to make any two men (whose persons, object, and conduct, if they were not what the narrative represents them, remain in the highest degree mysterious) into Moses and Elias, but to create the whole occurrence; and in like manner not merely to conceive of some certain illumination as a supernatural effulgence (which, if a natural one, is much exaggerated and misrepresented), but to create it at once after the pattern of the brightness which illuminated the face of Moses on Mount Sinai.

---

7. See Luke 1.26.
8. Jesus took several disciples up a mountain, "And was transfigured before them: and his face did shine as the sun, and his raiment was white as the light. And, behold, there appeared unto them Moses and Elias talking with him" (Matthew 17.1–3).

Hence is derived the following rule. Where not merely the particular nature and manner of an occurrence is critically suspicious, its external circumstances represented as miraculous and the like; but where likewise the essential substance and groundwork is either inconceivable in itself, or is in striking harmony with some Messianic idea of the Jews of that age, then not the particular alleged course and mode of the transaction only, but the entire occurrence must be regarded as unhistorical. Where on the contrary, the form only, and not the general contents of the narration, exhibits the characteristics of the unhistorical, it is at least possible to suppose a kernel of historical fact; although we can never confidently decide whether this kernel of fact actually exists, or in what it consists; unless, indeed, it be discoverable from other sources. In legendary narratives, or narratives embellished by the writer, it is less difficult,—by divesting them of all that betrays itself as fictitious imagery, exaggeration, &c.—by endeavouring to abstract from them every extraneous adjunct and to fill up every hiatus—to succeed, proximately at least, in separating the historical groundwork.

The boundary line, however, between the historical and the unhistorical, in records, in which as in our Gospels this latter element is incorporated, will ever remain fluctuating and unsusceptible of precise attainment. Least of all can it be expected that the first comprehensive attempt to treat these records from a critical point of view should be successful in drawing a sharply defined line of demarcation. In the obscurity which criticism has produced, by the extinction of all lights hitherto held historical, the eye must accustom itself by degrees to discriminate objects with precision; and at all events the author of this work, wishes especially to guard himself, in those places where he declares he knows not what happened, from the imputation of asserting that he knows that nothing happened.

1835; 1846

Charlotte Brontë
1816–1855

Charlotte Brontë's savage portrait in her novel *Jane Eyre* of an evangelical clergyman as a sadistic and hypocritical bully is based on a real-life figure, the founder of the school where her two elder sisters died. The Reverend Mr. Brocklehurst, who hectors a small child about death and hell-fire, represents the worst excesses of the Evangelical movement. Convinced of mankind's essentially sinful nature, Evangelicals stressed Bible reading, prayer, and regular examinations of conscience as the means to salvation. Brontë satirizes the self-serving piety which urges humility and self-denial on others—particularly dependents—while complacently exempting itself.

from Jane Eyre

I feared to return to the nursery, and feared to go forward to the parlour; ten minutes I stood in agitated hesitation; the vehement ringing of the breakfast-room bell decided me; I *must* enter.

"Who could want me?" I asked inwardly, as with both hands I turned the stiff door-handle which, for a second or two, resisted my efforts. "What should I see besides Aunt Reed in the apartment?—a man or a woman?" The handle turned, the door unclosed, and passing through and curtseying low, I looked up at—a black pillar!—such, at least, appeared to me, at first sight, the straight, narrow, sable-clad shape standing erect on the rug; the grim face at the top was like a carved mask, placed above the shaft by way of capital.

Mrs Reed occupied her usual seat by the fireside; she made a signal to me to approach; I did so, and she introduced me to the stony stranger with the words—

"This is the little girl respecting whom I applied to you."

He—for it was a man—turned his head slowly towards where I stood, and having examined me with the two inquisitive looking gray eyes which twinkled under a pair of bushy brows, said solemnly, and in a bass voice—

"Her size is small; what is her age?"

"Ten years."

"So much?" was the doubtful answer; and he prolonged his scrutiny for some minutes. Presently he addressed me—

"Your name, little girl?"

"Jane Eyre, sir."

In uttering these words I looked up: he seemed to me a tall gentleman, but then I was very little; his features were large, and they and all the lines of his frame were equally harsh and prim.

"Well, Jane Eyre, and are you a good child?"

Impossible to reply to this in the affirmative: my little world held a contrary opinion: I was silent. Mrs Reed answered for me by an expressive shake of the head, adding soon, "Perhaps the less said on that subject the better, Mr Brocklehurst."

"Sorry indeed to hear it! She and I must have some talk"; and bending from the perpendicular, he installed his person in the arm-chair, opposite Mrs Reed's. "Come here," he said.

I stepped across the rug: he placed me square and straight before him. What a face he had, now that it was almost on a level with mine! what a great nose! and what a mouth! and what large, prominent teeth!

"No sight so sad as that of a naughty child," he began, "especially a naughty little girl. Do you know where the wicked go after death?"

"They go to hell," was my ready and orthodox answer.

"And what is hell? Can you tell me that?"

"A pit full of fire."

"And should you like to fall into that pit, and to be burning there for ever?"

"No, sir."

"What must you do to avoid it?"

I deliberated a moment: my answer, when it did come, was objectionable: "I must keep in good health, and not die."

"How can you keep in good health? Children younger than you die daily. I buried a little child of five years old only a day or two since—a good little child, whose soul is now in heaven. It is to be feared the same could not be said of you, were you to be called thence."

Not being in a condition to remove his doubt, I only cast my eyes down on the two large feet planted on the rug, and sighed, wishing myself far enough away.

"I hope that sigh is from the heart, and that you repent of ever having been the occasion of discomfort to your excellent benefactress."

"Benefactress! benefactress!" said I inwardly: "they all call Mrs Reed my benefactress; if so, a benefactress is a disagreeable thing."

"Do you say your prayers night and morning?" continued my interrogator.

"Yes, sir."

"Do you read your Bible?"

"Sometimes."

"With pleasure? Are you fond of it?"

"I like Revelations, and the Book of Daniel, and Genesis, and Samuel, and a little bit of Exodus, and some parts of Kings and Chronicles, and Job and Jonah."

"And the Psalms? I hope you like them?"

"No, sir."

"No? Oh, shocking! I have a little boy, younger than you, who knows six Psalms by heart: and when you ask him which he would rather have, a ginger-bread-nut to eat, or a verse of a Psalm to learn, he says: 'Oh! the verse of a Psalm! angels sing Psalms,' says he; 'I wish to be a little angel here below.' He then gets two nuts in recompense for his infant piety."

"Psalms are not interesting," I remarked.

"That proves you to have a wicked heart; and you must pray to God to change it: to give you a new and clean one: to take away your heart of stone and give you a heart of flesh."

I was about to propound a question, touching the manner in which that operation of changing my heart was to be performed, when Mrs Reed interposed, telling me to sit down; she then proceeded to carry on the conversation herself.

1847

━━ ⛩ ━━

Arthur Hugh Clough
1819–1861

Clever, witty, and ironic, Arthur Hugh Clough satirized religious hypocrisy and bankrupt values. But his humor only thinly veiled his genuine concern at the erosion of Christianity's spiritual authority. Clough took religion seriously enough to resign his Oxford fellowship rather than subscribe to the Thirty-Nine Articles of Anglican doctrine. He used his poetry to probe the ways Victorians had adjusted their religion to suit an increasingly secular age. The title *Epi-strauss-ium* refers to David Friedrich Strauss, whose *Life of Jesus* denied the divinity of Christ: the poem concludes that the Sun/Son of God can still illuminate, despite skepticism about the authenticity of the gospels. *The Latest Decalogue* casts a cynical eye on a materialist version of the Ten Commandments. *"There is no God," the Wicked Saith*, a lyric interlude from his long poem *Dipsychus*, contrasts the self-absorption of doubters to those whose love, innocence, or suffering make them believers.

Epi-strauss-ium[1]

Matthew and Mark and Luke and holy John
Evanished all and gone!
Yea, he° that erst, his dusky curtains quitting,   *the sun*
Through Eastern pictured panes his level beams transmitting,
5   With gorgeous portraits blent,

---

1. "On-Strauss-ism."

On them his glories intercepted spent,
Southwestering now, through windows plainly glassed,
On the inside face his radiance keen hath cast,
And in the lustre lost, invisible and gone,
10 Are, say you, Matthew, Mark and Luke and holy John?
Lost, is it? lost, to be recovered never?
However,
The place of worship the meantime with light
Is, if less richly, more sincerely bright,
15 And in blue skies the Orb is manifest to sight.
1847   1869

The Latest Decalogue[1]

Thou shalt have one God only; who
Would be at the expense of two?
No graven images may be
Worshipped, except the currency:
5   Swear not at all; for for thy curse
Thine enemy is none the worse:
At church on Sunday to attend
Will serve to keep the world thy friend:
Honour thy parents; that is, all
10 From whom advancement may befall:

Thou shalt not kill; but needst not strive
Officiously to keep alive:
Do not adultery commit;
Advantage rarely comes of it:
15 Thou shalt not steal; an empty feat,
When it's so lucrative to cheat:
Bear not false witness; let the lie
Have time on its own wings to fly:
Thou shalt not covet; but tradition
20 Approves all forms of competition.

The sum of all is, thou shalt love,
If any body, God above:
At any rate shall never labour
More than thyself to love thy neighbour.

1862; 1951

from Dipsychus[1]
"There Is No God," the Wicked Saith

"There is no God," the wicked saith,
    "And truly it's a blessing,

---

1. The Ten Commandments. The last four lines were not published until 1951; they were added from Clough's manuscript.

1. Dipsychus ("two-souled" or "of two minds") is the hero of a long poem by Clough, published in 1865; this excerpt from scene 5 was published separately in 1862.

For what he might have done with us
    It's better only guessing."

5   "There is no God," a youngster thinks,
    "Or really, if there may be,
He surely didn't mean a man
    Always to be a baby."

"There is no God, or if there is,"
10   The tradesman thinks, "'twere funny
If he should take it ill in me
    To make a little money."

"Whether there be," the rich man says,
    "It matters very little,
15   For I and mine, thank somebody,
    Are not in want of victual."

Some others, also, to themselves
    Who scarce so much as doubt it,
Think there is none, when they are well,
20   And do not think about it.

But country folks who live beneath
    The shadow of the steeple;
The parson and the parson's wife,
    And mostly married people;

25   Youths green and happy in first love,
    So thankful for illusion;
And men caught out in what the world
    Calls guilt, in first confusion;

And almost every one when age,
30   Disease, or sorrows strike him,
Inclines to think there is a God,
    Or something very like Him.

1850   1862

✦ ✦ ✦

John William Colenso
1814–1883

Shortly after *The Origin of Species* appeared in 1859, an even greater furor erupted, this time with the publication of a work of biblical criticism written by an Anglican bishop. A mathematician who had become the Bishop of Natal in South Africa, Colenso was translating the Scriptures into Zulu when he began to have doubts about their historical veracity. His knowledge of geology made him realize that the Flood "could not possibly have taken place." Further research convinced him that Moses had not written the first five books of the Bible. Colenso was angrily attacked for challenging the divine authenticity of the Bible—he was even accused of insanity. He was deposed as bishop and excommunicated, though later reinstated. Colenso argued, however, that a vital religious belief could not ultimately conflict with the findings of historical scholarship, and that modern Christianity would be strengthened by being freed from outdated mythological beliefs.

from The Pentateuch and Book of Joshua Critically Examined

You will, of course, expect that, since I have had the charge of this Diocese, I have been closely occupied in the study of the Zulu tongue, and in translating the Scriptures into it. Through the blessing of God, I have now translated the New Testament completely, and several parts of the Old, among the rest the books of Genesis and Exodus. In this work I have been aided by intelligent natives; and, having also published a Zulu Grammar and Dictionary, I have acquired sufficient knowledge of the language, to be able to have intimate communion with the native mind. * * *

Here, however, as I have said, amidst my work in this land, I have been brought face to face with the very questions which I then put by. While translating the story of the Flood, I have had a simple-minded, but intelligent, native,—one with the docility of a child, but the reasoning powers of mature age,—look up, and ask, "Is all that true? Do you really believe that all this happened thus,—that all the beasts, and birds, and creeping things, upon the earth, large and small, from hot countries and cold, came thus by pairs, and entered into the ark with Noah? And did Noah gather food for them *all,* for the beasts and birds of prey, as well as the rest?" My heart answered in the words of the Prophet, "Shall a man speak lies in the Name of the Lord?" Zech.xiii.3. I dared not do so. My own knowledge of some branches of science, of Geology in particular, had been much increased since I left England; and I now knew for certain, on geological grounds, a fact, of which I had only had misgivings before, viz. that a *Universal* Deluge, such as the Bible manifestly speaks of, could not possibly have taken place in the way described in the Book of Genesis, not to mention other difficulties which the story contains. * * * Of course, I am well aware that some have attempted to show that Noah's Deluge was only a *partial* one. But such attempts have ever seemed to me to be made in the very teeth of the Scripture statements, which are as plain and explicit as words can possibly be. Nor is anything really gained by supposing the Deluge to have been partial. For, as waters must find their own level on the Earth's surface, without a special miracle, of which the Bible says nothing, a Flood, which should begin by covering the top of Ararat,[1] (if that were conceivable), or a much lower mountain, must necessarily become universal, and in due time sweep over the hills of Auvergne.[2] Knowing this, I felt that I dared not, as a servant of the God of Truth, urge my brother man to believe that, which I did not myself believe, which I knew to be untrue, as a matter-of-fact, historical, narrative. I gave him, however, such a reply as satisfied him for the time, without throwing any discredit upon the general veracity of the Bible history.

But I was thus driven,—against my will at first, I may truly say,—to search more deeply into these questions; and I have since done so, to the best of my power, with the means at my disposal in this colony. And now I tremble at the result of my enquiries, rather, I should do so, were it not that I believe firmly in a God of Righteousness and Truth and Love, who both "IS, and is a rewarder of them that diligently seek him." * * *

---

1. A mountain in Turkey on which Noah's ark was supposed to have landed at the end of the Flood (Genesis 8.4).   2. Part of the Massif Central in France.

The first five books of the Bible,—commonly called the Pentateuch (ηπεντατευχος βιβλος, Pentateuchus, sc. liber), or Book of Five Volumes,—are supposed by most English readers of the Bible to have been written by Moses, except the last chapter of Deuteronomy, which records the death of Moses, and which, of course, it is generally allowed, must have been added by another hand, perhaps that of Joshua. It is believed that Moses wrote under such special guidance and teaching of the Holy Spirit, that he was preserved from making any error in recording those matters, which came within his own cognisance, and was instructed also in respect of events, which took place before he was born,—before, indeed, there was a human being on the earth to take note of what was passing. He was in this way, it is supposed, enabled to write a true account of the Creation. And, though the accounts of the Fall and of the Flood, as well as of later events, which happened in the time of Abraham, Isaac, and Jacob, may have been handed down by tradition from one generation to another, and even, some of them, perhaps, written down in words, or represented in hieroglyphics, and Moses may, probably, have derived assistance from these sources also in the composition of his narrative, yet in all his statements, it is believed, he was under such constant control and superintendence of the Spirit of God, that he was kept from making any serious error, and certainly from writing anything altogether untrue. We may rely with undoubting confidence—such is the statement usually made—on the historical veracity, and infallible accuracy, of the Mosaic narrative in all its main particulars. * * *

But, among the many results of that remarkable activity in scientific enquiry of every kind, which, by God's own gift, distinguishes the present age, this also must be reckoned, that attention and labour are now being bestowed, more closely and earnestly than ever before, to search into the real foundations for such a belief as this. * * * The time is come, as I believe, in the Providence of God, when this question can no longer be put by,—when it must be resolutely faced, and the whole matter fully and freely examined, if we would be faithful servants of the God of Truth. * * *

The result of my enquiry is this, that I have arrived at the conviction,—as painful to myself at first, as it may be to my reader, though painful now no longer under the clear shining of the Light of Truth,—that the Pentateuch, as a whole, cannot possibly have been written by Moses, or by any one acquainted personally with the facts which it professes to describe, and, further, that the (so-called) Mosaic narrative, by whomsoever written, and though imparting to us, as I fully believe it does, revelations of the Divine Will and Character, cannot be regarded as *historically true.*

1862

———— ✠ ————

John Henry Cardinal Newman
1801–1890

Newman's conversion to Catholicism in 1845 sent shock waves throughout England. Newman, an Anglican clergyman and a leading figure in the Oxford Movement, was well known for his efforts to construct a *via media,* or middle way, between Protestantism and Catholicism. But his struggle to locate the authority of the Anglican church in early church history gradually convinced him that Rome was right. Anti-Catholic feeling was strong, and Newman's "going over" was regarded as a terrible betrayal of his friends and colleagues. But when Charles Kingsley incautiously accused him of lying, Newman finally got a chance to explain his conversion to the public; the *Apologia Pro Vita Sua* became a classic of spiritual autobiography. Unlike some of his contemporaries, whose religious beliefs were shaken by scientific discoveries and biblical criticism, Newman's faith never wavered: "Ten thousand difficulties do not make one doubt."

For more about Newman, see Perspectives: Victorian Ladies and Gentlemen, page 1626.

from Apologia Pro Vita Sua

from Chapter 1. History of My Religious Opinions to the Year 1833

I was brought up from a child to take great delight in reading the Bible; but I had no formed religious convictions till I was fifteen. Of course I had a perfect knowledge of my Catechism.[1]

After I was grown up, I put on paper my recollections of the thoughts and feelings on religious subjects, which I had at the time that I was a child and a boy,—such as had remained on my mind with sufficient prominence to make me then consider them worth recording. Out of these, written in the Long Vacation of 1820, and transcribed with additions in 1823, I select two, which are at once the most definite among them, and also have a bearing on my later convictions.

1. "I used to wish the Arabian Tales were true: my imagination ran on unknown influences, on magical powers, and talismans. . . . I thought life might be a dream, or I an Angel, and all this world a deception, my fellow-angels by a playful device concealing themselves from me, and deceiving me with the semblance of a material world."

Again: "Reading in the Spring of 1816 a sentence from [Dr. Watts's] 'Remnants of Time,'[2] entitled 'the Saints unknown to the world,' to the effect, that 'there is nothing in their figure or countenance to distinguish them,' &c, &c, I supposed he spoke of Angels who lived in the world, as it were disguised."

2. The other remark is this: "I was very superstitious, and for some time previous to my conversion [when I was fifteen] used constantly to cross myself on going into the dark."

Of course I must have got this practice from some external source or other; but I can make no sort of conjecture whence; and certainly no one had ever spoken to me on the subject of the Catholic religion, which I only knew by name. The French master was an *émigré* Priest, but he was simply made a butt, as French masters too commonly were in that day, and spoke English very imperfectly. There was a Catholic family in the village, old maiden ladies we used to think; but I knew nothing about them. I have of late years heard that there were one or two Catholic boys in the school; but either we were carefully kept from knowing this, or the knowledge of it made simply no impression on our minds. My brother[3] will bear witness how free the school was from Catholic ideas. * * *

---

1. A summary of religious doctrine (in Newman's case, the Church of England's) set forth in a series of questions and answers.
2. Isaac Watts (1674–1748), Nonconformist cleric; the full title is *The Improvement of the Mind, with a discourse* *on Education, and the Remnants of Time, employed in prose and verse.*
3. Francis William Newman (1805–1897), professor of Latin at University College, London, and a prominent freethinker.

When I was fifteen, (in the autumn of 1816), a great change of thought took place in me. I fell under the influences of a definite Creed, and received into my intellect impressions of dogma, which, through God's mercy, have never been effaced or obscured. * * * [I] believed that the inward conversion of which I was conscious, (and of which I still am more certain than that I have hands and feet,) would last into the next life, and that I was elected to eternal glory. I have no consciousness that this belief had any tendency whatever to lead me to be careless about pleasing God. I retained it till the age of twenty-one, when it gradually faded away; but I believe that it had some influence on my opinions, in the direction of those childish imaginations which I have already mentioned, viz. in isolating me from the objects which surrounded me, in confirming me in my mistrust of the reality of material phenomena, and making me rest in the thought of two and two only absolute and luminously self-evident beings, myself and my Creator;—for while I considered myself predestined to salvation, my mind did not dwell upon others, as fancying them simply passed over, not predestined to eternal death. I only thought of the mercy to myself. * * *

Calvinists[4] make a sharp separation between the elect and the world; there is much in this that is cognate or parallel to the Catholic doctrine; but they go on to say, as I understand them, very differently from Catholicism,—that the converted and the unconverted can be discriminated by man, that the justified are conscious of their state of justification, and that the regenerate cannot fall away. Catholics on the other hand shade and soften the awful antagonism between good and evil, which is one of their dogmas, by holding that there are different degrees of justification, that there is a great difference in point of gravity between sin and sin, that there is the possibility and the danger of falling away, and that there is no certain knowledge given to any one that he is simply in a state of grace, and much less that he is to persevere to the end:—of the Calvinistic tenets the only one which took root in my mind was the fact of heaven and hell, divine favour and divine wrath, of the justified and the unjustified. The notion that the regenerate and the justified were one and the same, and that the regenerate, as such, had the gift of perseverance, remained with me not many years, as I have said already. * * *

I am obliged to mention, though I do it with great reluctance, another deep imagination, which at this time, the autumn of 1816, took possession of me,—there can be no mistake about the fact; viz. that it would be the will of God that I should lead a single life. This anticipation, which has held its ground almost continuously ever since,—with the break of a month now and a month then, up to 1829, and, after that date, without any break at all,—was more or less connected in my mind with the notion, that my calling in life would require such a sacrifice as celibacy involved; as, for instance, missionary work among the heathen, to which I had a great drawing for some years. It also strengthened my feeling of separation from the visible world, of which I have spoken above.

from *Chapter 5. The Position of My Mind Since 1845*

From the time that I became a Catholic, of course I have no further history of my religious opinions to narrate. In saying this, I do not mean to say that my mind has

---

4. Followers of John Calvin (1509–1564), French theologian whose doctrines included predestination, the natural depravity of human beings, and salvation through God's grace.

been idle, or that I have given up thinking on theological subjects; but that I have had no variations to record, and have had no anxiety of heart whatever. I have been in perfect peace and contentment; I never have had one doubt. I was not conscious to myself, on my conversion, of any change, intellectual or moral, wrought in my mind. I was not conscious of firmer faith in the fundamental truths of Revelation, or of more self-command; I had not more fervour; but it was like coming into port after a rough sea; and my happiness on that score remains to this day without interruption.

Nor had I any trouble about receiving those additional articles, which are not found in the Anglican Creed. Some of them I believed already, but not any one of them was a trial to me. I made a profession of them upon my reception with the greatest ease, and I have the same ease in believing them now. I am far of course from denying that every article of the Christian Creed, whether as held by Catholics or by Protestants, is beset with intellectual difficulties; and it is simple fact, that, for myself, I cannot answer those difficulties. Many persons are very sensitive of the difficulties of Religion; I am as sensitive of them as any one; but I have never been able to see a connexion between apprehending those difficulties, however keenly, and multiplying them to any extent, and on the other hand doubting the doctrines to which they are attached. Ten thousand difficulties do not make one doubt, as I understand the subject; difficulty and doubt are incommensurate. There of course may be difficulties in the evidence; but I am speaking of difficulties intrinsic to the doctrines themselves, or to their relations with each other. A man may be annoyed that he cannot work out a mathematical problem, of which the answer is or is not given to him, without doubting that it admits of an answer, or that a certain particular answer is the true one. Of all points of faith, the being of a God is, to my own apprehension, encompassed with most difficulty, and yet borne in upon our minds with most power.

People say that the doctrine of Transubstantiation[1] is difficult to believe; I did not believe the doctrine till I was a Catholic. I had no difficulty in believing it, as soon as I believed that the Catholic Roman Church was the oracle of God, and that she had declared this doctrine to be part of the original revelation. It is difficult, impossible, to imagine, I grant;—but how is it difficult to believe? Yet Macaulay thought it so difficult to believe, that he had need of a believer in it of talents as eminent as Sir Thomas More,[2] before he could bring himself to conceive that the Catholics of an enlightened age could resist "the overwhelming force of the argument against it." "Sir Thomas More," he says, "is one of the choice specimens of wisdom and virtue; and the doctrine of transubstantiation is a kind of proof charge. A faith which stands that test, will stand any test." But for myself, I cannot indeed prove it, I cannot tell *how* it is; but I say, "Why should it not be? What's to hinder it? What do I know of substance or matter? just as much as the greatest philosophers, and that is nothing at all;"—so much is this the case, that there is a rising school of philosophy now, which considers phenomena to constitute the whole of our knowledge in physics. The Catholic doctrine leaves phenomena alone. It does not say that the phenomena go; on the contrary, it says that they remain; nor does it say that the same phenomena are in several places at once. It deals with what no one on earth knows any thing about, the material substances themselves. And, in like manner, of

1. Doctrine that the elements of bread and wine in the rite of Holy Communion are actually converted into the Body and Blood of Christ in all but external appearance.
2. Sir Thomas More (1478–1535) was an English states-man beheaded for his opposition to the church policy of Henry VIII. Macaulay invokes More in his 1840 review of Ranke's *History of the Popes*.

that majestic Article of the Anglican as well as of the Catholic Creed,—the doctrine of the Trinity in Unity.[3] What do I know of the Essence of the Divine Being? I know that my abstract idea of three is simply incompatible with my idea of one; but when I come to the question of concrete fact, I have no means of proving that there is not a sense in which one and three can equally be predicated of the Incommunicable God.

But I am going to take upon myself the responsibility of more than the mere Creed of the Church; as the parties accusing me are determined I shall do. They say, that now, in that I am a Catholic, though I may not have offences of my own against honesty to answer for, yet, at least, I am answerable for the offences of others, of my co-religionists, of my brother priests, of the Church herself. I am quite willing to accept the responsibility; and, as I have been able, as I trust, by means of a few words, to dissipate, in the minds of all those who do not begin with disbelieving me, the suspicion with which so many Protestants start, in forming their judgment of Catholics, viz. that our Creed is actually set up in inevitable superstition and hypocrisy, as the original sin of Catholicism; so now I will proceed, as before, identifying myself with the Church and vindicating it,—not of course denying the enormous mass of sin and error which exists of necessity in that world-wide multiform Communion,—but going to the proof of this one point, that its system is in no sense dishonest, and that therefore the upholders and teachers of that system, as such, have a claim to be acquitted in their own persons of that odious imputation.

Starting then with the being of a God, (which, as I have said, is as certain to me as the certainty of my own existence, though when I try to put the grounds of that certainty into logical shape I find a difficulty in doing so in mood and figure to my satisfaction,) I look out of myself into the world of men, and there I see a sight which fills me with unspeakable distress. The world seems simply to give the lie to that great truth, of which my whole being is so full; and the effect upon me is, in consequence, as a matter of necessity, as confusing as if it denied that I am in existence myself. If I looked into a mirror, and did not see my face, I should have the sort of feeling which actually comes upon me, when I look into this living busy world, and see no reflexion of its Creator. This is, to me, one of those great difficulties of this absolute primary truth, to which I referred just now. Were it not for this voice, speaking so clearly in my conscience and my heart, I should be an atheist, or a pantheist, or a polytheist when I looked into the world. I am speaking for myself only; and I am far from denying the real force of the arguments in proof of a God, drawn from the general facts of human society and the course of history, but these do not warm me or enlighten me; they do not take away the winter of my desolation, or make the buds unfold and the leaves grow within me, and my moral being rejoice. The sight of the world is nothing else than the prophet's scroll, full of "lamentations, and mourning, and woe."[4]

To consider the world in its length and breadth, its various history, the many races of man, their starts, their fortunes, their mutual alienation, their conflicts; and then their ways, habits, governments, forms of worship; their enterprises, their aimless courses, their random achievements and acquirements, the impotent conclusion of long-standing facts, the tokens so faint and broken of a superintending design, the blind evolution of what turn out to be great powers or truths, the progress of things, as if from unreasoning elements, not towards final causes, the greatness and littleness

---

3. The belief that God is three (Father, Son, and Holy   4. Ezekiel 2.9–10.
Spirit) and yet only one.

of man, his far-reaching aims, his short duration, the curtain hung over his futurity, the disappointments of life, the defeat of good, the success of evil, physical pain, mental anguish, the prevalence and intensity of sin, the pervading idolatries, the corruptions, the dreary hopeless irreligion, that condition of the whole race, so fearfully yet exactly described in the Apostle's words, "having no hope and without God in the world,"[5]—all this is a vision to dizzy and appal; and inflicts upon the mind the sense of a profound mystery, which is absolutely beyond human solution.

What shall be said to this heart-piercing, reason-bewildering fact? I can only answer, that either there is no Creator, or this living society of men is in a true sense discarded from His presence. Did I see a boy of good make and mind, with the tokens on him of a refined nature, cast upon the world without provision, unable to say whence he came, his birth-place or his family connexions, I should conclude that there was some mystery connected with his history, and that he was one, of whom, from one cause or other, his parents were ashamed. Thus only should I be able to account for the contrast between the promise and the condition of his being. And so I argue about the world;—*if* there be a God, *since* there is a God, the human race is implicated in some terrible aboriginal calamity. It is out of joint with the purposes of its Creator. This is a fact, a fact as true as the fact of its existence; and thus the doctrine of what is theologically called original sin becomes to me almost as certain as that the world exists, and as the existence of God.

And now, supposing it were the blessed and loving will of the Creator to interfere in this anarchical condition of things, what are we to suppose would be the methods which might be necessarily or naturally involved in His purpose of mercy? Since the world is in so abnormal a state, surely it would be no surprise to me, if the interposition were of necessity equally extraordinary—or what is called miraculous. But that subject does not directly come into the scope of my present remarks. Miracles as evidence, involve a process of reason, or an argument; and of course I am thinking of some mode of interference which does not immediately run into argument. I am rather asking what must be the face-to-face antagonist, by which to withstand and baffle the fierce energy of passion and the all-corroding, all-dissolving scepticism of the intellect in religious inquiries? I have no intention at all of denying, that truth is the real object of our reason, and that, if it does not attain to truth, either the premiss or the process is in fault; but I am not speaking here of right reason, but of reason as it acts in fact and concretely in fallen man. I know that even the unaided reason, when correctly exercised, leads to a belief in God, in the immortality of the soul, and in a future retribution; but I am considering the faculty of reason actually and historically; and in this point of view, I do not think I am wrong in saying that its tendency is towards a simple unbelief in matters of religion. No truth, however sacred, can stand against it, in the long run; and hence it is that in the pagan world, when our Lord came, the last traces of the religious knowledge of former times were all but disappearing from those portions of the world in which the intellect had been active and had had a career.

And in these latter days, in like manner, outside the Catholic Church things are tending,—with far greater rapidity than in that old time from the circumstance of the age,—to atheism in one shape or other. What a scene, what a prospect, does the

---

5. Ephesians 2.12.

whole of Europe present at this day! and not only Europe, but every government and every civilization through the world, which is under the influence of the European mind! Especially, for it most concerns us, how sorrowful, in the view of religion, even taken in its most elementary, most attenuated form, is the spectacle presented to us by the educated intellect of England, France, and Germany! Lovers of their country and of their race, religious men, external to the Catholic Church, have attempted various expedients to arrest fierce wilful human nature in its onward course, and to bring it into subjection. The necessity of some form of religion for the interests of humanity, has been generally acknowledged: but where was the concrete representative of things invisible, which would have the force and the toughness necessary to be a breakwater against the deluge? Three centuries ago the establishment of religion, material, legal, and social, was generally adopted as the best expedient for the purpose, in those countries which separated from the Catholic Church; and for a long time it was successful; but now the crevices of those establishments are admitting the enemy. Thirty years ago, education was relied upon: ten years ago there was a hope that wars would cease for ever, under the influence of commercial enterprise and the reign of the useful and fine arts; but will any one venture to say that there is any thing any where on this earth, which will afford a fulcrum for us, whereby to keep the earth from moving onwards? * * *

Supposing then it to be the Will of the Creator to interfere in human affairs, and to make provisions for retaining in the world a knowledge of Himself, so definite and distinct as to be proof against the energy of human scepticism, in such a case,—I am far from saying that there was no other way,—but there is nothing to surprise the mind, if He should think fit to introduce a power into the world, invested with the prerogative of infallibility in religious matters. Such a provision would be a direct, immediate, active, and prompt means of withstanding the difficulty; it would be an instrument suited to the need; and, when I find that this is the very claim of the Catholic Church, not only do I feel no difficulty in admitting the idea, but there is a fitness in it, which recommends it to my mind. And thus I am brought to speak of the Church's infallibility, as a provision, adapted by the mercy of the Creator, to preserve religion in the world, and to restrain that freedom of thought, which of course in itself is one of the greatest of our natural gifts, and to rescue it from its own suicidal excesses. And let it be observed that, neither here nor in what follows, shall I have occasion to speak directly of Revelation in its subject-matter, but in reference to the sanction which it gives to truths which may be known independently of it,—as it bears upon the defence of natural religion. I say, that a power, possessed of infallibility in religious teaching, is happily adapted to be a working instrument, in the course of human affairs, for smiting hard and throwing back the immense energy of the aggressive, capricious, untrustworthy intellect:—and in saying this, as in the other things that I have to say, it must still be recollected that I am all along bearing in mind my main purpose, which is a defence of myself.

I am defending myself here from a plausible charge brought against Catholics, as will be seen better as I proceed. The charge is this:—that I, as a Catholic, not only make profession to hold doctrines which I cannot possibly believe in my heart, but that I also believe in the existence of a power on earth, which at its own will imposes upon men any new set of *credenda* [beliefs], when it pleases, by a claim to infallibility; in consequence, that my own thoughts are not my own property; that I cannot tell that to-morrow I may not have to give up what I hold to-day, and that the necessary effect of such a condition of mind must be a degrading bondage, or a bitter inward rebellion relieving itself in secret infidelity, or the necessity of ignoring the whole subject of religion in a sort of disgust, and of mechanically saying every thing that the Church says, and leaving to others the defence of it. As then I have above spoken of the relation of my mind towards the Catholic Creed, so now I shall speak of the attitude which it takes up in the view of the Church's infallibility.

And first, the initial doctrine of the infallible teacher must be an emphatic protest against the existing state of mankind. Man had rebelled against his Maker. It was this that caused the divine interposition: and to proclaim it must be the first act of the divinely-accredited messenger. The Church must denounce rebellion as of all possible evils the greatest. She must have no terms with it; if she would be true to her Master, she must ban and anathematize it. This is the meaning of a statement of mine which has furnished matter for one of those special accusations to which I am at present replying: I have, however, no fault at all to confess in regard to it; I have nothing to withdraw, and in consequence I here deliberately repeat it. I said, "The Catholic Church holds it better for the sun and moon to drop from heaven, for the earth to fail, and for all the many millions on it to die of starvation in extremest agony, as far as temporal affliction goes, than that one soul, I will not say, should be lost, but should commit one single venial sin, should tell one wilful untruth, or should steal one poor farthing without excuse." I think the principle here enunciated to be the mere preamble in the formal credentials of the Catholic Church, as an Act of Parliament might begin with a "Whereas." It is because of the intensity of the evil which has possession of mankind, that a suitable antagonist has been provided against it; and the initial act of that divinely-commissioned power is of course to deliver her challenge and to defy the enemy. Such a preamble then gives a meaning to her position in the world, and an interpretation to her whole course of teaching and action. * * *

* * * We live in a wonderful age; the enlargement of the circle of secular knowledge just now is simply a bewilderment, and the more so, because it has the promise of continuing, and that with greater rapidity, and more signal results. Now these discoveries, certain or probable, have in matter of fact an indirect bearing upon religious opinions, and the question arises how are the respective claims of revelation and of natural science to be adjusted. Few minds in earnest can remain at ease without some sort of rational grounds for their religious belief; to reconcile theory and fact is almost an instinct of the mind. When then a flood of facts, ascertained or suspected, comes pouring in upon us, with a multitude of others in prospect, all believers in Revelation, be they Catholic or not, are roused to consider their bearing upon themselves, both for the honour of God, and from tenderness for those many souls who, in consequence of the confident tone of the schools of secular knowledge, are in danger of being led away into a bottomless liberalism of thought.

I am not going to criticize here that vast body of men, in the mass, who at this time would profess to be liberals in religion; and who look towards the discoveries of the age, certain or in progress, as their informants, direct or indirect, as to what they shall think about the unseen and the future. The Liberalism which gives a colour to society now, is very different from that character of thought which bore the name thirty or forty years ago. Now it is scarcely a party; it is the educated lay world.

1864

Thomas Henry Huxley
1825–1895

Huxley was known as "Darwin's bulldog" for the vigorous way he defended Darwin in the controversies over *The Origin of Species*. In 1860 he took on Bishop Wilberforce in a famous debate at Oxford: when the bishop asked sarcastically whether "it was through his grandfather or his grandmother that he claimed his descent from a monkey?" Huxley carried the day by replying that "he was not ashamed to have a monkey for his ancestor; but he would be ashamed to be connected with a man who used great gifts to obscure the truth." In *Evolution and Ethics* he built on Darwinian ideas, arguing that although humankind is the natural product of evolutionary forces, we are inescapably at war with nature. Huxley rejected any direct "social Darwinist" view of society as a struggle for the survival of the fittest, and sought instead to envision a humanist ethics free from natural and from supernatural control alike.

from Evolution and Ethics
from Prolegomena
[MAN'S WAR WITH NATURE]

It may be safely assumed that, two thousand years ago, before Caesar set foot in southern Britain,[1] the whole country-side visible from the windows of the room in which I write, was in what is called "the state of nature." Except, it may be, by raising a few sepulchral mounds, such as those which still, here and there, break the flowing contours of the downs, man's hands had made no mark upon it; and the thin veil of vegetation which overspread the broad-backed heights and the shelving sides of the coombs[2] was unaffected by his industry. The native grasses and weeds, the scattered patches of gorse, contended with one another for the possession of the scanty surface soil; they fought against the droughts of summer, the frosts of winter, and the furious gales which swept, with unbroken force, now from the Atlantic, and now from the North Sea, at all times of the year; they filled up, as they best might, the gaps made in their ranks by all sorts of underground and overground animal ravagers. One year with another, an average population, the floating balance of the unceasing struggle for existence among the indigenous plants, maintained itself. It is as little to be doubted, that an essentially similar state of nature prevailed, in this region, for many thousand years before the coming of Caesar; and there is no assignable reason for denying that it might continue to exist through an equally prolonged futurity, except for the intervention of man.

Reckoned by our customary standards of duration, the native vegetation, like the "everlasting hills" which it clothes, seems a type of permanence. The little Amarella Gentians, which abound in some places to-day, are the descendants of those that were trodden underfoot by the prehistoric savages who have left their flint tools about, here and there; and they followed ancestors which, in the climate of the glacial epoch, probably flourished better than they do now. Compared with the long past of this humble plant, all the history of civilized men is but an episode.

---

1. Julius Caesar conquered Britain for the Roman Empire   2. Deep valleys.
in the last century B.C.

Yet nothing is more certain than that, measured by the liberal scale of time-keeping of the universe, this present state of nature, however it may seem to have gone and to go on for ever, is but a fleeting phase of her infinite variety; merely the last of the series of changes which the earth's surface has undergone in the course of the millions of years of its existence. Turn back a square foot of the thin turf, and the solid foundation of the land, exposed in cliffs of chalk five hundred feet high on the adjacent shore, yields full assurance of a time when the sea covered the site of the "everlasting hills"; and when the vegetation of what land lay nearest, was as different from the present Flora of the Sussex downs, as that of Central Africa now is. No less certain is it that between the time during which the chalk was formed and that at which the original turf came into existence, thousands of centuries elapsed, in the course of which, the state of nature of the ages during which the chalk was deposited, passed into that which now is, by changes so slow that, in the coming and going of the generations of men, had such witnessed them, the contemporary conditions would have seemed to be unchanging and unchangeable.

But it is also certain that, before the deposition of the chalk, a vastly longer period had elapsed, throughout which it is easy to follow the traces of the same process of ceaseless modification and of the internecine struggle for existence of living things; and that even when we can get no further back, it is not because there is any reason to think we have reached the beginning, but because the trail of the most ancient life remains hidden, or has become obliterated.

Thus that state of nature of the world of plants, which we began by considering, is far from possessing the attribute of permanence. Rather its very essence is impermanence. It may have lasted twenty or thirty thousand years, it may last for twenty or thirty thousand years more, without obvious change; but, as surely as it has followed upon a very different state, so it will be followed by an equally different condition. That which endures is not one or another association of living forms, but the process of which the cosmos is the product, and of which these are among the transitory expressions. And in the living world, one of the most characteristic features of this cosmic process is the struggle for existence, the competition of each with all, the result of which is the selection, that is to say, the survival of those forms which, on the whole, are best adapted to the conditions which at any period obtain; and which are, therefore, in that respect, and only in that respect, the fittest. The acme reached by the cosmic process in the vegetation of the downs is seen in the turf, with its weeds and gorse. Under the conditions, they have come out of the struggle victorious; and, by surviving, have proved that they are the fittest to survive. * * *

As a natural process, of the same character as the development of a tree from its seed, or of a fowl from its egg, evolution excludes creation and all other kinds of supernatural intervention. As the expression of a fixed order, every stage of which is the effect of causes operating according to definite rules, the conception of evolution no less excludes that of chance. It is very desirable to remember that evolution is not an explanation of the cosmic process, but merely a generalized statement of the method and results of that process. And, further, that, if there is proof that the cosmic process was set going by any agent, then that agent will be the creator of it and of all its products, although supernatural intervention may remain strictly excluded from its further course.

So far as that limited revelation of the nature of things, which we call scientific knowledge, has yet gone, it tends, with constantly increasing emphasis, to the belief that, not merely the world of plants, but that of animals; not merely living things, but the whole fabric of the earth; not merely our planet, but the whole solar system; not merely our star and its satellites, but the millions of similar bodies which bear witness to the order which pervades boundless space, and has endured through boundless time; are all working out their predestined courses of evolution.

* * * Three or four years have elapsed since the state of nature, to which I have referred, was brought to an end, so far as a small patch of the soil is concerned, by the intervention of man. The patch was cut off from the rest by a wall; within the area thus protected, the native vegetation was, as far as possible, extirpated; while a colony of strange plants was imported and set down in its place. In short, it was made into a garden. At the present time, this artificially treated area presents an aspect extraordinarily different from that of so much of the land as remains in the state of nature, outside the wall. Trees, shrubs, and herbs, many of them appertaining to the state of nature of remote parts of the globe, abound and flourish. Moreover, considerable quantities of vegetables, fruits, and flowers are produced, of kinds which neither now exist, nor have ever existed, except under conditions such as obtain in the garden; and which, therefore, are as much works of the art of man as the frames and glass-houses in which some of them are raised. That the "state of Art," thus created in the state of nature by man, is sustained by and dependent on him, would at once become apparent, if the watchful supervision of the gardener were withdrawn, and the antagonistic influences of the general cosmic process were no longer sedulously warded off, or counteracted. The walls and gates would decay; quadrupedal and bipedal intruders would devour and tread down the useful and beautiful plants; birds, insects, blight, and mildew would work their will; the seeds of the native plants, carried by winds or other agencies, would immigrate, and in virtue of their long-earned special adaptation to the local conditions, these despised native weeds would soon choke their choice exotic rivals. A century or two hence, little beyond the foundations of the wall and of the houses and frames would be left, in evidence of the victory of the cosmic powers at work in the state of nature, over the temporary obstacles to their supremacy, set up by the art of the horticulturist.

It will be admitted that the garden is as much a work of art,[3] or artifice, as anything that can be mentioned. The energy localised in certain human bodies, directed by similarly localised intellects, has produced a collocation[4] of other material bodies which could not be brought about in the state of nature. The same proposition is true of all the works of man's hands, from a flint implement to a cathedral or a chronometer; and it is because it is true, that we call these things artificial, term them works of art, or artifice, by way of distinguishing them from the products of the cosmic process, working outside man, which we call natural, or works of nature. The distinction thus drawn between the works of nature and those of man, is universally recognised; and it is, as I conceive, both useful and justifiable. * * *

The process of colonization presents analogies to the formation of a garden which are highly instructive. Suppose a shipload of English colonists sent to form a settlement, in such a country as Tasmania was in the middle of the last century. On landing, they find themselves in the midst of a state of nature, widely different from that left behind them in everything but the most general physical conditions. The common plants, the common birds and quadrupeds, are as totally distinct as the men

3. The sense of the term "Art" is becoming narrowed; "work of Art" to most people means a picture, a statue, or a piece of *bijouterie*; by way of compensation "artist" has included in its wide embrace cooks and ballet girls, no less than painters and sculptors [Huxley's note].
4. Bringing together.

from anything to be seen on the side of the globe from which they come. The colonists proceed to put an end to this state of things over as large an area as they desire to occupy. They clear away the native vegetation, extirpate or drive out the animal population, so far as may be necessary, and take measures to defend themselves from the re-immigration of either. In their place, they introduce English grain and fruit trees; English dogs, sheep, cattle, horses; and English men; in fact, they set up a new Flora and Fauna and a new variety of mankind, within the old state of nature. Their farms and pastures represent a garden on a great scale, and themselves the gardeners who have to keep it up, in watchful antagonism to the old *régime*. Considered as a whole, the colony is a composite unit introduced into the old state of nature; and, thenceforward, a competitor in the struggle for existence, to conquer or be vanquished.

Under the conditions supposed, there is no doubt of the result, if the work of the colonists be carried out energetically and with intelligent combination of all their forces. On the other hand, if they are slothful, stupid, and careless; or if they waste their energies in contests with one another, the chances are that the old state of nature will have the best of it. The native savage will destroy the immigrant civilized man; of the English animals and plants some will be extirpated by their indigenous rivals, others will pass into the feral state and themselves become components of the state of nature. In a few decades, all other traces of the settlement will have vanished. * * *

Moralists of all ages and of all faiths, attending only to the relations of men towards one another in an ideal society, have agreed upon the "golden rule," "Do as you would be done by." In other words, let sympathy be your guide; put yourself in the place of the man towards whom your action is directed; and do to him what you would like to have done to yourself under the circumstances. However much one may admire the generosity of such a rule of conduct; however confident one may be that average men may be thoroughly depended upon not to carry it out to its full logical consequences; it is nevertheless desirable to recognise the fact that these consequences are incompatible with the existence of a civil state, under any circumstances of this world which have obtained, or, so far as one can see, are, likely to come to pass.

For I imagine there can be no doubt that the great desire of every wrongdoer is to escape from the painful consequences of his actions. If I put myself in the place of the man who has robbed me, I find that I am possessed by an exceeding desire not to be fined or imprisoned; if in that of the man who has smitten me on one cheek, I contemplate with satisfaction the absence of any worse result than the turning of the other cheek for like treatment. Strictly observed, the "golden rule" involves the negation of law by the refusal to put it in motion against law-breakers; and, as regards the external relations of a polity,[5] it is the refusal to continue the struggle for existence. It can be obeyed, even partially, only under the protection of a society which repudiates it. Without such shelter, the followers of the "golden rule" may indulge in hopes of heaven, but they must reckon with the certainty that other people will be masters of the earth.

What would become of the garden if the gardener treated all the weeds and slugs and birds and trespassers as he would like to be treated, if he were in their place? * * *

That progressive modification of civilization which passes by the name of the "evolution of society," is, in fact, a process of an essentially different character, both

---

5. Government.

from that which brings about the evolution of species, in the state of nature, and from that which gives rise to the evolution of varieties, in the state of art.

There can be no doubt that vast changes have taken place in English civilization since the reign of the Tudors.[6] But I am not aware of a particle of evidence in favour of the conclusion that this evolutionary process has been accompanied by any modification of the physical, or the mental, characters of the men who have been the subjects of it. I have not met with any grounds for suspecting that the average Englishmen of to-day are sensibly different from those that Shakspere knew and drew. We look into his magic mirror of the Elizabethan age, and behold, nowise darkly, the presentment of ourselves.

During these three centuries, from the reign of Elizabeth to that of Victoria, the struggle for existence between man and man has been so largely restrained among the great mass of the population (except for one or two short intervals of civil war), that it can have had little, or no, selective operation. As to anything comparable to direct selection, it has been practised on so small a scale that it may also be neglected. The criminal law, in so far as by putting to death, or by subjecting to long periods of imprisonment, those who infringe its provisions, it prevents the propagation of hereditary criminal tendencies; and the poor-law, in so far as it separates married couples, whose destitution arises from hereditary defects of character, are doubtless selective agents operating in favour of the non-criminal and the more effective members of society. But the proportion of the population which they influence is very small; and, generally, the hereditary criminal and the hereditary pauper have propagated their kind before the law affects them. In a large proportion of cases, crime and pauperism have nothing to do with heredity; but are the consequence, partly, of circumstances and, partly, of the possession of qualities, which, under different conditions of life, might have excited esteem and even admiration. It was a shrewd man of the world who, in discussing sewage problems, remarked that dirt is riches in the wrong place; and that sound aphorism has moral applications. The benevolence and open-handed generosity which adorn a rich man, may make a pauper of a poor one; the energy and courage to which the successful soldier owes his rise, the cool and daring subtlety to which the great financier owes his fortune, may very easily, under unfavourable conditions, lead their possessors to the gallows, or to the hulks. Moreover, it is fairly probable that the children of a "failure" will receive from their other parent just that little modification of character which makes all the difference. I sometimes wonder whether people, who talk so freely about extirpating the unfit, ever dispassionately consider their own history. Surely, one must be very "fit," indeed, not to know of an occasion, or perhaps two, in one's life, when it would have been only too easy to qualify for a place among the "unfit."

In my belief the innate qualities, physical, intellectual, and moral, of our nation have remained substantially the same for the last four or five centuries. If the struggle for existence has affected us to any serious extent (and I doubt it) it has been, indirectly, through our military and industrial wars with other nations. * * *

To return, once more, to the parallel of horticulture. In the modern world, the gardening of men by themselves is practically restricted to the performance, not of selection, but of that other function of the gardener, the creation of conditions more favourable than those of the state of nature; to the end of facilitating the free expan-

6. Reigned 1485–1603.

sion of the innate faculties of the citizen, so far as it is consistent with the general good. And the business of the moral and political philosopher appears to me to be the ascertainment, by the same method of observation, experiment, and ratiocination, as is practised in other kinds of scientific work, of the course of conduct which will best conduce to that end.

But, supposing this course of conduct to be scientifically determined and carefully followed out, it cannot put an end to the struggle for existence in the state of nature; and it will not so much as tend, in any way, to the adaptation of man to that state. Even should the whole human race be absorbed in one vast polity, within which "absolute political justice" reigns, the struggle for existence with the state of nature outside it, and the tendency to the return of the struggle within, in consequence of over-multiplication, will remain; and, unless men's inheritance from the ancestors who fought a good fight in the state of nature, their dose of original sin, is rooted out by some method at present unrevealed, at any rate to disbelievers in supernaturalism, every child born into the world will still bring with him the instinct of unlimited self-assertion. He will have to learn the lesson of self-restraint and renunciation. But the practice of self-restraint and renunciation is not happiness, though it may be something much better.

That man, as a "political animal," is susceptible of a vast amount of improvement, by education, by instruction, and by the application of his intelligence to the adaptation of the conditions of life to his higher needs, I entertain not the slightest doubt. But, so long as he remains liable to error, intellectual or moral; so long as he is compelled to be perpetually on guard against the cosmic forces, whose ends are not his ends, without and within himself; so long as he is haunted by inexpugnable memories and hopeless aspirations; so long as the recognition of his intellectual limitations forces him to acknowledge his incapacity to penetrate the mystery of existence; the prospect of attaining untroubled happiness, or of a state which can, even remotely, deserve the title of perfection, appears to me to be as misleading an illusion as ever was dangled before the eyes of poor humanity. And there have been many of them.

That which lies before the human race is a constant struggle to maintain and improve, in opposition to the State of Nature, the State of Art of an organized polity; in which, and by which, man may develop a worthy civilization, capable of maintaining and constantly improving itself, until the evolution of our globe shall have entered so far upon its downward course that the cosmic process resumes its sway; and, once more, the State of Nature prevails over the surface of our planet.

1893

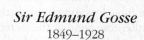

Sir Edmund Gosse
1849–1928

Gosse's autobiography relates his effort to forge an identity in opposition to loving but fanatical parents. His father, Philip Henry Gosse, was a prominent zoologist, and a zealous member of the Plymouth Brethren, a fundamentalist Evangelical sect. They disapproved of art and the imagination: the father was proud of not knowing a word of Shakespeare; the son devoted his life to literature. The turning point of Philip Gosse's career was his publication of *Omphalos* (1857), an absurd attempt to counter Darwin's impending *The Origin of Species* by arguing that the natural world presents a false picture of its own history: "God hid the fossils in the rocks." His argument was ridiculed by scientists and rejected even by churchmen, but it illustrates the desperate lengths to which some were willing to go to refute Darwin's theories.

from **Father and Son**

[NO FICTION OF ANY KIND]

I found my greatest pleasure in the pages of books. The range of these was limited, for story-books of every description were sternly excluded. No fiction of any kind, religious or secular, was admitted into the house. In this it was to my Mother, not to my Father, that the prohibition was due. She had a remarkable, I confess to me still somewhat un-accountable impression that "to tell a story," that is, to compose fictitious narrative of any kind, was a sin. She carried this conviction to extreme lengths. * * *

My own state, however, was, I should think, almost unique among the children of cultivated parents. In consequence of the stern ordinance which I have described, not a single fiction was read or told to me during my infancy. The rapture of the child who delays the process of going to bed by cajoling "a story" out of his mother or his nurse, as he sits upon her knee, well tucked up, at the corner of the nursery fire,—this was unknown to me. Never, in all my early childhood, did anyone address to me the affecting preamble, "Once upon a time!" I was told about missionaries, but never about pirates, I was familiar with humming-birds, but I had never heard of fairies. Jack the Giant-Killer, Rumpelstiltskin and Robin Hood were not of my acquaintance, and though I understood about wolves, Little Red Ridinghood was a stranger even by name. So far as my "dedication"[1] was concerned, I can but think that my parents were in error thus to exclude the imaginary from my outlook upon facts. They desired to make me truthful; the tendency was to make me positive and sceptical. Had they wrapped me in the soft folds of supernatural fancy, my mind might have been longer content to follow their traditions in an unquestioning spirit.

[A MOTH INTERRUPTS FAMILY PRAYERS]

Another instance of the remarkable way in which the interests of daily life were mingled, in our strange household, with the practice of religion, made an impression upon my memory. We had all three been much excited by a report that a certain dark geometer-moth, generated in underground stables, had been met with in Islington. Its name, I think, is *boletobia fuliginaria*, and I believe that it is excessively rare in England. We were sitting at family prayers, on a summer morning, I think in 1855, when through the open window a brown moth came sailing. My Mother immediately interrupted the reading of the Bible by saying to my Father, "O! Henry, do you think that can be *boletobia?*" My Father rose up from the sacred book, examined the insect, which had now perched, and replied: "No! it is only the common Vapourer, *orgygia antiqua*," resuming his seat, and the exposition of the Word, without any apology or embarrassment.

---

1. Earlier, Gosse described how when he was two months old, his mother had written a "solemn dedication of me to the Lord, which was repeated in public in my Mother's arms" at church. Similarly, in *Praeterita* Ruskin described how his mother "solemnly 'devoted me to God' before I was born; in imitation of Hannah."

[A Scientific Experiment in Idolatry]

My theological misdeeds culminated, however, in an act so puerile and preposterous that I should not venture to record it if it did not throw some glimmering of light on the subject which I have proposed to myself in writing these pages. My mind continued to dwell on the mysterious question of prayer. It puzzled me greatly to know why, if we were God's children, and if he was watching over us by night and day, we might not supplicate for toys and sweets and smart clothes as well as for the conversion of the heathen. * * *

All these matters drew my thoughts to the subject of idolatry, which was severely censured at the missionary meeting. I cross-examined my Father very closely as to the nature of this sin, and pinned him down to the categorical statement that idolatry consisted in praying to any one or anything but God himself. Wood and stone, in the words of the hymn, were peculiarly liable to be bowed down to by the heathen in their blindness. I pressed my Father further on this subject, and he assured me that God would be very angry, and would signify His anger, if any one, in a Christian country, bowed down to wood and stone. I cannot recall why I was so pertinacious on this subject, but I remember that my Father became a little restive under my cross-examination. I determined, however, to test the matter for myself, and one morning, when both my parents were safely out of the house, I prepared for the great act of heresy. I was in the morning-room on the ground-floor, where, with much labour, I hoisted a small chair on to the table close to the window. My heart was now beating as if it would leap out of my side, but I pursued my experiment. I knelt down on the carpet in front of the table, and looking up I said my daily prayer in a loud voice, only substituting the address "O Chair!" for the habitual one.

Having carried this act of idolatry safely through, I waited to see what would happen. It was a fine day, and I gazed up at the slip of white sky above the houses opposite, and expected something to appear in it. God would certainly exhibit his anger in some terrible form, and would chastise my impious and wilful action. I was very much alarmed, but still more excited; I breathed the high, sharp air of defiance. But nothing happened; there was not a cloud in the sky, not an unusual sound in the street. Presently I was quite sure that nothing would happen. I had committed idolatry, flagrantly and deliberately, and God did not care. The result of this ridiculous act was not to make me question the existence and power of God; those were forces which I did not dream of ignoring. But what it did was to lessen still further my confidence in my Father's knowledge of the Divine mind. My Father had said, positively, that if I worshipped a thing made of wood, God would manifest his anger. I had then worshipped a chair, made (or partly made) of wood, and God had made no sign whatever. My Father, therefore, was not really acquainted with the Divine practice in cases of idolatry. And with that, dismissing the subject, I dived again into the unplumbed depths of the "Penny Cyclopædia."

[Did God Hide the Fossils in the Rocks?]

So, through my Father's brain, in that year of scientific crisis, 1857, there rushed two kinds of thought, each absorbing, each convincing yet totally irreconcilable. There is a peculiar agony in the paradox that truth has two forms, each of them indisputable, yet each antagonistic to the other. It was this discovery, that there were two theories of physical life, each of which was true, but the truth of each incompatible with the truth of the other, which shook the spirit of my Father with perturbation. It was not, really, a paradox, it was a fallacy, if he could only have known it, but he allowed the turbid volume of superstition to drown the delicate stream of reason. He took one step in the service of truth, and then he drew back in an agony, and accepted the servitude of error.

This was the great moment in the history of thought when the theory of the mutability of species was preparing to throw a flood of light upon all departments of human speculation and action. It was becoming necessary to stand emphatically in one army or the other. Lyell[2] was surrounding himself with disciples, who were making strides in the direction of discovery. Darwin had long been collecting facts with regard to the variation of animals and plants. Hooker and Wallace, Asa Gray and even Agassiz,[3] each in his own sphere, were coming closer and closer to a perception of that secret which was first to reveal itself clearly to the patient and humble genius of Darwin. In the year before, in 1856, Darwin, under pressure from Lyell, had begun that modest statement of the new revelation, that "abstract of an essay," which developed so mightily into "The Origin of Species." Wollaston's "Variation of Species" had just appeared,[4] and had been a nine days' wonder in the wilderness.

On the other side, the reactionaries, although never dreaming of the fate which hung over them, had not been idle. In 1857 the astounding question had for the first time been propounded with contumely, "What, then, did we come from an orangoutang?" The famous "Vestiges of Creation"[5] had been supplying a sugar-and-water panacea for those who could not escape from the trend of evidence, and who yet clung to revelation. Owen[6] was encouraging reaction by resisting, with all the strength of his prestige, the theory of the mutability of species.

In this period of intellectual ferment, as when a great political revolution is being planned, many possible adherents were confidentially tested with hints and encouraged to reveal their bias in a whisper. It was the notion of Lyell, himself a great mover of men, that before the doctrine of natural selection was given to a world which would be sure to lift up at it a howl of execration, a certain body-guard of sound and experienced naturalists, expert in the description of species, should be privately made aware of its tenour. Among those who were thus initiated, or approached with a view towards possible illumination, was my Father. He was spoken to by Hooker, and later on by Darwin, after meetings of the Royal Society in the summer of 1857.

My Father's attitude towards the theory of natural selection was critical in his career, and, oddly enough, it exercised an immense influence on my own experience as a child. Let it be admitted at once, mournful as the admission is, that every instinct in his intelligence went out at first to greet the new light. It had hardly done so, when a recollection of the opening chapter of Genesis checked it at the outset. He consulted with Carpenter, a great investigator, but one who was fully as incapable

2. Sir Charles Lyell (1797–1875), Victorian Britain's most influential geologist, author of *Principles of Geology* (1830–1833), which argued that geological change had occurred gradually over vast periods of time, not through sudden and violent natural catastrophes. His theory was inconsistent with the Christian reckoning that the earth was only six thousand years old.
3. Sir Joseph Dalton Hooker (1817–1911), English botanist; Alfred Russel Wallace (1823–1913), co-originator, with Darwin, of the theory of evolution; Asa Gray (1810–1888), American botanist and taxonomist; Louis Agassiz (1807–1873), Swiss-American zoologist and ge-

ologist who studied the natural history of North America.
4. *On the Variation of Species* (1856) by Thomas Vernon Wollaston (1822–1878), entomologist and conchologist, and a friend of Darwin's.
5. The controversial *Vestiges of the Natural History of Creation* (1844), by the Scottish scientist Robert Chambers, introduced the British public to the idea of evolution, although in the context of a divine Creator.
6. Sir Richard Owen (1804–1892), naturalist and anatomist who attacked Darwin's theory of natural selection.

as himself of remodelling his ideas with regard to the old, accepted hypotheses. They both determined, on various grounds, to have nothing to do with the terrible theory, but to hold steadily to the law of the fixity of species. It was exactly at this juncture that we left London, and the slight and occasional, but always extremely salutary personal intercourse with men of scientific leading which my Father had enjoyed at the British Museum and at the Royal Society came to an end. His next act was to burn his ships, down to the last beam and log out of which a raft could have been made. By a strange act of wilfulness, he closed the doors upon himself for ever.

My Father had never admired Sir Charles Lyell. I think that the famous "Lord Chancellor manner" of the geologist intimidated him, and we undervalue the intelligence of those whose conversation puts us at a disadvantage. For Darwin and Hooker, on the other hand, he had a profound esteem, and I know not whether this had anything to do with the fact that he chose, for his impetuous experiment in reaction, the field of geology, rather than that of zoölogy or botany. Lyell had been threatening to publish a book on the geological history of Man, which was to be a bomb-shell flung into the camp of the catastrophists. My Father, after long reflection, prepared a theory of his own, which, as he fondly hoped, would take the wind out of Lyell's sails, and justify geology to godly readers of "Genesis." It was, very briefly, that there had been no gradual modification of the surface of the earth, or slow development of organic forms, but that when the catastrophic act of creation took place, the world presented, instantly, the structural appearance of a planet on which life had long existed.

The theory, coarsely enough, and to my Father's great indignation, was defined by a hasty press as being this—that God hid the fossils in the rocks in order to tempt geologists into infidelity. In truth, it was the logical and inevitable conclusion of accepting, literally, the doctrine of a sudden act of creation; it emphasised the fact that any breach in the circular course of nature could be conceived only on the supposition that the object created bore false witness to past processes, which had never taken place. For instance, Adam would certainly possess hair and teeth and bones in a condition which it must have taken many years to accomplish, yet he was created full-grown yesterday. He would certainly—though Sir Thomas Browne[7] denied it—display an *omphalos* [navel], yet no umbilical cord had ever attached him to a mother.

Never was a book cast upon the waters with greater anticipations of success than was this curious, this obstinate, this fanatical volume. My Father lived in a fever of suspense, waiting for the tremendous issue. This "Omphalos" of his, he thought, was to bring all the turmoil of scientific speculation to a close, fling geology into the arms of Scripture, and make the lion eat grass with the lamb. It was not surprising, he admitted, that there had been experienced an ever-increasing discord between the facts which geology brings to light and the direct statements of the early chapters of "Genesis." Nobody was to blame for that. My Father, and my Father alone, possessed the secret of the enigma; he alone held the key which could smoothly open the lock of geological mystery. He offered it, with a glowing gesture, to atheists and Christians alike. This was to be the universal panacea; this the system of intellectual therapeutics which could not but heal all the maladies of the age. But, alas! atheists and Christians alike looked at it and laughed, and threw it away.

---

7. Sir Thomas Browne (1605–1682), author and physician; his *Religio Medici* attempted to reconcile science and religion.

In the course of that dismal winter, as the post began to bring in private letters, few and chilly, and public reviews, many and scornful, my Father looked in vain for the approval of the churches, and in vain for the acquiescence of the scientific societies, and in vain for the gratitude of those "thousands of thinking persons," which he had rashly assured himself of receiving. As his reconciliation of Scripture statements and geological deductions was welcomed nowhere; as Darwin continued silent, and the youthful Huxley was scornful, and even Charles Kingsley,[8] from whom my Father had expected the most instant appreciation, wrote that he could not "give up the painful and slow conclusion of five and twenty years' study of geology, and believe that God has written on the rocks one enormous and superfluous lie,"—as all this happened or failed to happen, a gloom, cold and dismal, descended upon our morning teacups. It was what the poets mean by an "inspissated" gloom; it thickened day by day, as hope and self-confidence evaporated in thin clouds of disappointment. My Father was not prepared for such a fate. He had been the spoiled darling of the public, the constant favourite of the press, and now, like the dark angels of old,

> so huge a rout
> Encumbered him with ruin.

He could not recover from amazement at having offended everybody by an enterprise which had been undertaken in the cause of universal reconciliation.

1907

↦ END OF PERSPECTIVES: RELIGION AND SCIENCE ↤

Robert Browning
1812–1889

Julia Margaret Cameron, *Robert Browning*, 1866.

Throughout his life Robert Browning was something of an enigma, a Byronic dandy sporting lemon-yellow gloves and gorgeous waistcoats, who loved dining out and yet kept both his private life and poetic practice out of the conversation. He longed for public recognition but would not make his work more accessible by stepping from behind his elaborate artistic masks. Unable to reconcile the hearty dinner guest with the experimental poet, Henry James concluded that Browning lived equally on both sides of an inner wall which "contained an invisible door through which, working the lock at will, he could swiftly pass." Although Browning sometimes suggested that he was a mere ventriloquist or puppeteer, the genius with which he impersonated other voices extended the range and complexity of English poetry in bold new directions. More than any other nineteenth-century figure, Browning shaped the poetry of the twentieth, influencing British and American poets from Hardy and Yeats to Eliot, Pound, Frost, Lowell, and Stevens.

---

8. Huxley had been an early defender of Darwin's; Charles Kingsley (1819–1875) was a prominent clergyman.

Browning's early years were quiet, even sheltered. He was born in Camberwell, a rural suburb south of London, and with the exception of a year spent at London University, he lived at home with his parents and sister until the age of thirty-four. His father was an official in the Bank of England, and his mother a pious Nonconformist, both of whom encouraged their son in his passion for poetry, painting, and music. The chief source of his education was extensive, haphazard reading in his father's vast private library. Brought up to be a gentleman, Browning received lessons in dancing, fencing, boxing, drawing, and music, as well as Greek and Latin. His doting parents denied him nothing: when, at fourteen, he expressed an interest in the poetry of Shelley—whose works were unavailable because of his atheism—Browning's devout mother took him to London to find an out-of-print copy.

Uncertain what his genuine calling was, Browning considered and rejected careers in art, music, law, and business. A turning point came in October 1832, when he saw the aging Edmund Kean play Richard III. Stunned by the power of a performance in which the brilliant but weary actor alternately electrified and embarrassed the audience as he struggled to dominate his role, Browning found dramatic confirmation of his evolving theory that all personality was staged and variable. Taking Shakespeare as a model, he envisioned himself as performer, playwright, and stage manager of his own artistic world. That night he conceived a grand plan to "assume I know not how many different characters" in order to write poems, operas, novels, and speeches under different names so that "the world was never to guess" that Robert Browning had been the author.

It is a fascinating literary mystery why Browning should have wanted simultaneously to conceal his own identity and yet dazzle the world by impersonating other people—especially since the authors he most admired (Byron, Keats, and particularly Shelley) seemed to him to speak so personally. In 1833, Browning began his career anonymously with a long romantic poem, *Pauline*, in which he took an indirect approach, speaking through a narrator who confided: "I will tell / My state, as though 'twere none of mine." *Pauline* failed to sell a single copy, but the book found its way to John Stuart Mill, who commented that the poet possessed "a more intense and morbid self-consciousness than I ever knew in any sane being."

In the next decade Browning produced a string of introspective plays and experimental dramatic poems, including *Paracelsus* (1835), *Strafford* (1837), *Sordello* (1840), and *Pippa Passes* (1841). The notorious difficulty of these unpopular works gave Browning a reputation for obscurity that he labored for the rest of his life to overcome. But by the early 1840s he had discovered where his talent lay: applying to lyric poetry his theatrical instincts and his aversion to self-revelation, he found he could produce startling new effects. Henceforth he would present his audience with a cast of aberrant personalities, each starring in his or her own miniplay. In language adapted to their insecurities and obsessions, Browning's characters unwittingly reveal their own, often shocking secrets—but only if readers make the effort to follow the uncanny logic of their contorted confessions.

In the advertisement for his breakthrough book, *Dramatic Lyrics* (1842), Browning offered the disclaimer that, though the poems are "lyric in expression," they are the "utterances of so many imaginary persons, not mine." These imaginary persons range from the Greek goddess Artemis to lovers in a Venetian gondola, from a medieval damsel in distress to a Spanish monk so consumed by hatred that his soliloquy begins with a growl: "Gr-r-r." The sheer physicality of Browning's words, the thick-textured lines, the aggressive consonant clusters that seem to mock Tennyson's liquid vowels, the staccato lines and convoluted syntax that convey the twistings of tongue and mind struggling to express themselves—all are trademarks of Browning's style. As Gerard Manley Hopkins said, Browning talks like "a man bouncing up from table with his mouth full of bread and cheese and saying that he meant to stand no blasted nonsense."

Browning did not invent the poetic form known as the dramatic monologue—it is used in such classics as Marvell's *To His Coy Mistress* and Tennyson's *Ulysses*—but he brought the form to new levels of complexity. He usually situates his speakers in specific historical places and periods. Sometimes they are well-known figures from the past, such as the Italian painters

Andrea del Sarto and Fra Lippo Lippi, or literary characters, such as Caliban and Childe Roland. Browning catches them at a moment of great emotional intensity as they attempt to explain why they think and act as they do. In these passionate outbursts, they reveal their characters as much by idiomatic language, patterns of imagery, speech rhythms, and unintended ironies as by what they actually say.

Browning induces his readers to sympathize—even identify—with speakers of dubious morality and intentions. His gallery of rogues includes a duke who may have murdered his wife, a painter who savors his own cuckoldry, and a dying bishop who recalls with gusto the fleshly delights he has enjoyed. As the critic Robert Langbaum has pointed out, "the utter outrageousness" of such behavior "makes condemnation the least interesting response." Just as Satan becomes the most intriguing figure in *Paradise Lost*, so Browning's narrators elicit a reluctant fascination. Alternating between admiration and revulsion, and compelled by the intricacies of human motivation to suspend judgment, the reader struggles to come to terms with these disclosures.

This theatrical world of passionate utterance spilled over into reality in 1845, when Browning became the coauthor and hero of his own romantic drama. On January 10, he wrote a fan letter to the famous poet Elizabeth Barrett, whom he had never seen. He was thirty-three, she nearly forty, and her poetry was far better known than his. "I love your verses with all my heart," he wrote boldly, "—and I love you too." Her reply was encouraging, and thus began the century's most celebrated literary correspondence. She was an invalid suffering from tuberculosis, and they did not meet until May. But when Browning entered her darkened room, he fell instantly in love with the frail, fiery woman lying on her couch swathed in shawls and blankets. For more than a year and half they kept the nature of their relationship secret, to circumvent the wrath of her tyrannical father, who had permitted none of his children to marry. Finally, Browning decided they must break free: they were married secretly during a morning walk, in September 1846, and eloped to Italy, where they eventually settled in Florence.

Though their marriage was rhapsodic, Browning was frustrated with his art. Preoccupied with his wife, her work, their son "Pen" (born in 1849), and the charms of Florence, the usually prolific Browning wrote only one poem in the first three years of marriage and published just two books in the fifteen years they lived together. Though she acknowledged his genius, Elizabeth joined with her husband's friends in urging him to write "in the most directest and most impressive way, the mask thrown off." Unable or unwilling to do so, Browning gloomily found that he had acquired a further mask that he had not sought: that of "Mrs. Browning's husband."

Hoping finally to make his name with a wider public, Browning channeled his energies into a new project, fifty monologues published in 1855 as *Men and Women*. These animated self-portraits by artists, lovers, questors, skeptics, and impostors form a dazzling picture gallery containing many of Browning's greatest poems, including *Love Among the Ruins*, *Fra Lippo Lippi*, and *Childe Roland*. The plural title of *Men and Women* insists on the variability of human experience and the centrality of sexual difference to every individual's self-definition. But the book was poorly received at the time, except by the Pre-Raphaelites, and was soon overshadowed by the tumultuous acclaim bestowed on Elizabeth Barrett Browning's *Aurora Leigh* in 1856. Dejected by his readers' failure to make the effort to comprehend his art, Browning complained to his friend John Ruskin: "I cannot begin writing poetry till my imaginary reader has conceded licenses to me. . . . You would have me paint it all plain out, which can't be; but by various artifices I try to make shift with touches and bits of outlines which *succeed* if they bear the conception from me to you. You ought, I think, to keep pace with the thought."

Elizabeth Barrett Browning died suddenly in 1861 in Florence. "My life is fixed and sure now," the devastated widower wrote to his sister, "I shall live out the remainder in her direct influence." Browning returned to England with his son and settled down to a steady rhythm of writing and dining out. But with renewed vigor he resumed his demanding experiments with dramatic lyrics, more determined than ever to pursue the indirect forms of expression that the reading public had resisted.

The result was his second masterpiece, *The Ring and the Book*, a novel in verse published in four monthly installments, between 1868 and 1869. The poem reimagines a sensational seventeenth-century Roman murder trial. In extended monologues the various participants tell their versions of the story. We hear the pleas of the dying young bride Pompilia, her cruel husband Guido, her priest and would-be rescuer Caponsacchi, and then the rationale of the Pope, who decides the case. In this sordid tale of marital abuse and dubious justice, Browning explores the relativity of human understanding, the rights of women, and the role of religious belief in determining earthly action.

"Art remains the one way possible," the poet says, "Of speaking truth. . . . " But then, typically, he hedges his assertion: "—to mouths like mine, at least." In a world of becoming, no single perspective is ever sufficient, but Browning shows how, seen from the inside, each self, no matter how bizarre, finds words to justify its actions. Browning's truth is always contingent, evolving, and dependent on the flawed language we have to express it: "For how else know we save by worth of word?"

The success of *The Ring and the Book*, together with the increasing popularity of his earlier work, meant that in the 1870s and 1880s Browning was finally recognized as sharing with Tennyson the title of the era's leading poet. He was especially amused and gratified by the adulation of the Browning Societies that sprang up in England and around the world during his later years. When asked if he objected to the amateurish enthusiasm of the clubs that met to discuss his philosophy of life, he replied: "Object to it? No, I like it! . . . I have waited forty years for it, and now—I like it!" In the United States, where Browning mania hit hardest, brown clothing, curtains, and tableware became the rage, and his works were excerpted on railroad timetables. Mark Twain even gave a series of readings of which he boasted: "I can read Browning so Browning himself can understand it."

Browning's last book, *Asolando*, was published to wide acclaim the day he died at his son's home in Venice. Shortly before his death, Browning read aloud from the book's *Epilogue* the stanza that described his dogged determination to keep on striving in a world of limitation and imperfection: "One who never turned his back but marched breast forward, / Never doubted clouds would break." Ultimately, this confidence underlies the bold relativity and deep skepticism that animate Browning's work. Like Hopkins, Browning insists that all of nature, even human nature, bespeaks some part of an unknowable absolute. Thus everything becomes material for poetry, the dirty, deformed, and despicable no less than the beautiful, pure, and radiantly good. As Browning says in *Fra Lippo Lippi*, "This world's no blot for us, / Nor blank; it means intensely, and means good: / To find its meaning is my meat and drink."

Porphyria's Lover[1]

The rain set early in to-night,
    The sullen wind was soon awake,
It tore the elm-tops down for spite,
    And did its worst to vex the lake:
5   I listened with heart fit to break.
When glided in Porphyria; straight
    She shut the cold out and the storm,
And kneeled and made the cheerless grate
    Blaze up, and all the cottage warm;
10   Which done, she rose, and from her form

1. The poem was originally published with another of Browning's dramatic monologues, *Johannes Agricola in Meditation*, under the general title of *Madhouse Cells*.

Withdrew the dripping cloak and shawl,
　　And laid her soiled gloves by, untied
Her hat and let the damp hair fall,
　　And, last, she sat down by my side
15　　And called me. When no voice replied,
She put my arm about her waist,
　　And made her smooth white shoulder bare,
And all her yellow hair displaced,
　　And, stooping, made my cheek lie there,
20　　And spread, o'er all, her yellow hair,
Murmuring how she loved me—she
　　Too weak, for all her heart's endeavour,
To set its struggling passion free
　　From pride, and vainer ties dissever,
25　　And give herself to me for ever.
But passion sometimes would prevail,
　　Nor could to-night's gay feast restrain
A sudden thought of one so pale
　　For love of her, and all in vain:
30　　So, she was come through wind and rain.
Be sure I looked up at her eyes
　　Happy and proud; at last I knew
Porphyria worshipped me; surprise
　　Made my heart swell, and still it grew
35　　While I debated what to do.
That moment she was mine, mine, fair,
　　Perfectly pure and good: I found
A thing to do, and all her hair
　　In one long yellow string I wound
40　　Three times her little throat around,
And strangled her. No pain felt she;
　　I am quite sure she felt no pain.
As a shut bud that holds a bee,
　　I warily oped her lids: again
45　　Laughed the blue eyes without a stain.
And I untightened next the tress
　　About her neck; her cheek once more
Blushed bright beneath my burning kiss:
　　I propped her head up as before,
50　　Only, this time my shoulder bore
Her head, which droops upon it still:
　　The smiling rosy little head,
So glad it has its utmost will,
　　That all it scorned at once is fled,
55　　And I, its love, am gained instead!
Porphyria's love: she guessed not how
　　Her darling one wish would be heard.
And thus we sit together now,

60   And all night long we have not stirred,
        And yet God has not said a word!

c. 1835   1836, 1842

Soliloquy of the Spanish Cloister

1

Gr-r-r—there go, my heart's abhorrence!
    Water your damned flower-pots, do!
If hate killed men, Brother Lawrence,
    God's blood, would not mine kill you!
5 What? your myrtle-bush wants trimming?
    Oh, that rose has prior claims—
Needs its leaden vase filled brimming?
    Hell dry you up with its flames!

2

At the meal we sit together:
10   *Salve tibi!*° I must hear   *hail to thee*
Wise talk of the kind of weather,
    Sort of season, time of year:
Not a plenteous cork-crop: scarcely
    Dare we hope oak-galls,[1] *I doubt:*
15 *What's the Latin name for "parsley"?*
    What's the Greek name for Swine's Snout?°   *dandelion*

3

Whew! We'll have our platter burnished,
    Laid with care on our own shelf!
With a fire-new spoon we're furnished,
20   And a goblet for ourself,
Rinsed like something sacrificial
    Ere 'tis fit to touch our chaps°—   *chops, jaws*
Marked with L. for our initial!
    (He-he! There his lily snaps!)

4

25 *Saint*, forsooth! While brown Dolores
    Squats outside the Convent bank
With Sanchicha, telling stories,
    Steeping tresses in the tank,
Blue-black, lustrous, thick like horsehairs,
30   —Can't I see his dead eye glow,
Bright as't were a Barbary corsair's?[2]
    (That is, if he'd let it show!)

---

1. Growths on oaks which produce tannin.   2. A pirate from the Barbary Coast of Africa.

5

When he finishes refection,
    Knife and fork he never lays
35 Cross-wise, to my recollection,
    As do I, in Jesu's praise.
I the Trinity illustrate,
    Drinking watered orange-pulp—
In three sips the Arian[3] frustrate;
40   While he drains his at one gulp.

6

Oh, those melons? If he's able
    We're to have a feast! so nice!
One goes to the Abbot's table,
    All of us get each a slice.
45 How go on your flowers? None double?
    Not one fruit-sort can you spy?
Strange!—And I, too, at such trouble,
    Keep them close-nipped on the sly!

7

There's a great text in Galatians,
50   Once you trip on it, entails
Twenty-nine distinct damnations,
    One sure, if another fails:
If I trip him just a-dying,[4]
    Sure of heaven as sure can be,
55 Spin him round and send him flying
    Off to hell, a Manichee?°   *heretic*

8

Or, my scrofulous° French novel   *degenerate*
    On grey paper with blunt type!
Simply glance at it, you grovel
60   Hand and foot in Belial's gripe:[5]
If I double down its pages
    At the woeful sixteenth print,
When he gathers his greengages,°   *plums*
    Ope a sieve and slip it in't?

9

65 Or, there's Satan!—one might venture
    Pledge one's soul to him, yet leave
Such a flaw in the indenture
    As he'd miss till, past retrieve,
Blasted lay that rose-acacia

---

3. The Arian heresy denied the doctrine of the Trinity.
4. The speaker would like to ensure Brother Lawrence's damnation by tripping him up with St. Paul's difficult Epistle to the Galatians. Focusing on Galations 5.19–21, which lists 17 mortal sins, the speaker overlooks Gala- tians 5.14–15: "Thou shalt love thy neighbour as thyself. But if ye hate and devour one another, take heed that ye be not consumed one of another."
5. In the grip of the Devil.

70   We're so proud of! *Hy, Zy, Hine* . . . [6]
’St, there’s Vespers! *Plena gratiâ*
Ave, Virgo![7] Gr-r-r—you swine!

1839   1842

My Last Duchess[1]
Ferrara

That’s my last Duchess painted on the wall,
Looking as if she were alive. I call
That piece a wonder, now: Frà Pandolf’s[2] hands
Worked busily a day, and there she stands.
5 Will’t please you sit and look at her? I said
“Frà Pandolf” by design, for never read
Strangers like you that pictured countenance,
The depth and passion of its earnest glance,
But to myself they turned (since none puts by
10 The curtain I have drawn for you, but I)
And seemed as they would ask me, if they durst,
How such a glance came there; so, not the first
Are you to turn and ask thus. Sir, ’twas not
Her husband’s presence only, called that spot
15 Of joy into the Duchess’ cheek: perhaps
Frà Pandolf chanced to say “Her mantle laps
Over my lady’s wrist too much,” or “Paint
Must never hope to reproduce the faint
Half-flush that dies along her throat:” such stuff
20 Was courtesy, she thought, and cause enough
For calling up that spot of joy. She had
A heart—how shall I say?—too soon made glad,
Too easily impressed; she liked whate’er
She looked on, and her looks went everywhere.
25 Sir, ’twas all one! My favour at her breast,
The dropping of the daylight in the West,
The bough of cherries some officious fool
Broke in the orchard for her, the white mule
She rode with round the terrace—all and each
30 Would draw from her alike the approving speech,
Or blush, at least. She thanked men,—good! but thanked
Somehow—I know not how—as if she ranked
My gift of a nine-hundred-years-old name
With anybody’s gift. Who’d stoop to blame

6. The speaker considers selling his own soul to Satan in return for blasting Lawrence, but he would leave a clever loophole in the bargain and thus escape damnation himself. “*Hy, Zy, Hine*” may be the beginning of a curse against Lawrence.
7. “Full of Grace, hail, Virgin!”—a garbled form of the Ave Maria, or prayer to Mary. Vespers are evening prayers.

1. The speaker is modeled on Alfonso II, Duke of Ferrara, who married the 14-year-old Lucrezia de Medici in 1558. When she died three years later, poisoning was suspected. In 1565 the Duke married the daughter of Ferdinand I, Count of Tyrol.
2. Brother Pandolf, the imaginary painter of the duchess’s portrait.

35   This sort of trifling? Even had you skill
       In speech—(which I have not)—to make your will
       Quite clear to such an one, and say, "Just this
       Or that in you disgusts me; here you miss,
       Or there exceed the mark"—and if she let
40   Herself be lessoned so, nor plainly set
       Her wits to yours, forsooth, and made excuse,
       —E'en then would be some stooping; and I choose
       Never to stoop. Oh sir, she smiled, no doubt,
       Whene'er I passed her, but who passed without
45   Much the same smile? This grew; I gave commands;
       Then all smiles stopped together. There she stands
       As if alive. Will't please you rise? We'll meet
       The company below, then. I repeat,
       The Count your master's known munificence
50   Is ample warrant that no just pretence
       Of mine for dowry will be disallowed;
       Though his fair daughter's self, as I avowed
       At starting, is my object.[3] Nay, we'll go
       Together down, sir. Notice Neptune, though,
55   Taming a sea-horse, thought a rarity,
       Which Claus of Innsbruck cast in bronze for me!

1842   1842

How They Brought the Good News from Ghent to Aix[1]
(16——)

1

I sprang to the stirrup, and Joris, and he;
I galloped, Dirck galloped, we galloped all three;
"Good speed!" cried the watch, as the gate-bolts undrew;
"Speed!" echoed the wall to us galloping through;
5   Behind shut the postern,° the lights sank to rest,   *city gate*
    And into the midnight we galloped abreast.

2

Not a word to each other; we kept the great pace
Neck by neck, stride by stride, never changing our place;
I turned in my saddle and made its girths tight,
10 Then shortened each stirrup, and set the pique right,
    Rebuckled the cheek-strap, chained slacker the bit,
    Nor galloped less steadily Roland a whit.

3

'Twas moonset at starting; but while we drew near
Lokeren, the cocks crew and twilight dawned clear;

---

3. Only now does the reader learn that the duke is conducting negotiations for his second marriage and has been addressing the envoy of his bride-to-be's father.
1. Ghent, in Flanders, is about 100 miles from Aix-la-

Chapelle (present-day Aachen, in Germany). The route Browning describes—which he planned without a map—is more like 120 miles. Browning said he had no particular historical event in mind.

15   At Boom, a great yellow star came out to see;
        At Düffeld, 'twas morning as plain as could be;
        And from Mecheln church-steeple we heard the half-chime,
        So, Joris broke silence with, "Yet there is time!"

                                4

        At Aershot, up leaped of a sudden the sun,
20   And against him the cattle stood black every one,
        To stare thro' the mist at us galloping past,
        And I saw my stout galloper Roland at last,
        With resolute shoulders, each butting away
        The haze, as some bluff river headland its spray:

                                5

25   And his low head and crest, just one sharp ear bent back
        For my voice, and the other pricked out on his track;
        And one eye's black intelligence,—ever that glance
        O'er its white edge at me, his own master, askance!
        And the thick heavy spume-flakes which aye and anon
30   His fierce lips shook upwards in galloping on.

                                6

        By Hasselt, Dirck groaned; and cried Joris, "Stay spur!
        Your Roos galloped bravely, the fault's not in her,
        We'll remember at Aix"—for one heard the quick wheeze
        Of her chest, saw the stretched neck and staggering knees,
35   And sunk tail, and horrible heave of the flank,
        As down on her haunches she shuddered and sank.

                                7

        So, we were left galloping, Joris and I,
        Past Looz and past Tongres, no cloud in the sky;
        The broad sun above laughed a pitiless laugh,
40   'Neath our feet broke the brittle bright stubble like chaff;
        Till over by Dalhem a dome-spire sprang white,
        And "Gallop," gasped Joris, "for Aix is in sight!"

                                8

        "How they'll greet us!"—and all in a moment his roan
        Rolled neck and croup° over, lay dead as a stone;   rump
45   And there was my Roland to bear the whole weight
        Of the news which alone could save Aix from her fate,
        With his nostrils like pits full of blood to the brim,
        And with circles of red for his eye-sockets' rim.

                                9

        Then I cast loose my buffcoat, each holster let fall,
50   Shook off both my jack-boots, let go belt and all,
        Stood up in the stirrup, leaned, patted his ear,
        Called my Roland his pet-name, my horse without peer;
        Clapped my hands, laughed and sang, any noise, bad or good,
        Till at length into Aix Roland galloped and stood.

10

55   And all I remember is—friends flocking round
     As I sat with his head 'twixt my knees on the ground;
     And no voice but was praising this Roland of mine,
     As I poured down his throat our last measure of wine,
     Which (the burgesses voted by common consent)
60   Was no more than his due who brought good news from Ghent.
c. 1844   1845

Home-Thoughts, from Abroad

1

     Oh, to be in England
     Now that April's there,
     And whoever wakes in England
     Sees, some morning, unaware,
5   That the lowest boughs and the brushwood sheaf
     Round the elm-tree bole are in tiny leaf,
     While the chaffinch sings on the orchard bough
     In England—now!

2

     And after April, when May follows,
10   And the whitethroat° builds, and all the swallows!   sparrow
     Hark, where my blossomed pear-tree in the hedge
     Leans to the field and scatters on the clover
     Blossoms and dewdrops—at the bent spray's edge—
     That's the wise thrush; he sings each song twice over,
15   Lest you should think he never could recapture
     The first fine careless rapture!
     And though the fields look rough with hoary dew
     All will be gay when noontide wakes anew
     The buttercups, the little children's dower
20   —Far brighter than this gaudy melon-flower!
c. 1845   1845

Home-Thoughts, from the Sea

     Nobly, nobly Cape Saint Vincent[1] to the North-west died away;
     Sunset ran, one glorious blood-red, reeking into Cadiz Bay;
     Bluish 'mid the burning water, full in face Trafalgar[2] lay;
     In the dimmest North-east distance dawned Gibraltar grand and gray;
5   "Here and here did England help me: how can I help England?"—say,
     Whoso turns as I, this evening, turn to God to praise and pray,
     While Jove's planet° rises yonder, silent over Africa.   Jupiter
c. 1844   1845

1. Scene of Admiral Nelson's naval victory in 1797 off   2. In 1805 Nelson defeated Napoleon's fleets and was fa-
the coast of Portugal.   tally wounded himself off Cape Trafalgar in Spain.

The Bishop Orders His Tomb at Saint Praxed's Church[1]
Rome, 15—

     Vanity, saith the preacher, vanity![2]
     Draw round my bed: is Anselm keeping back?
     Nephews—sons mine[3] . . . ah God, I know not! Well—
     She, men would have to be your mother once,
5   Old Gandolf envied me, so fair she was!
     What's done is done, and she is dead beside,
     Dead long ago, and I am Bishop since,
     And as she died so must we die ourselves,
     And thence ye may perceive the world's a dream.
10   Life, how and what is it? As here I lie
     In this state-chamber, dying by degrees,
     Hours and long hours in the dead night, I ask
     "Do I live, am I dead?" Peace, peace seems all.
     Saint Praxed's ever was the church for peace;
15   And so, about this tomb of mine. I fought
     With tooth and nail to save my niche, ye know:
     —Old Gandolf me cozened,° despite my care;   *cheated*
     Shrewd was that snatch from out the corner South
     He graced his carrion with, God curse the same!
20   Yet still my niche is not so cramped but thence
     One sees the pulpit o' the epistle-side,[4]
     And somewhat of the choir, those silent seats,
     And up into the aery dome where live
     The angels, and a sunbeam's sure to lurk:
25   And I shall fill my slab of basalt there,
     And 'neath my tabernacle[5] take my rest,
     With those nine columns round me, two and two,
     The odd one at my feet where Anselm stands:
     Peach-blossom marble all, the rare, the ripe
30   As fresh-poured red wine of a mighty pulse.[6]
     —Old Gandolf with his paltry onion-stone,°   *cheap marble*
     Put me where I may look at him! True peach,
     Rosy and flawless: how I earned the prize!
     Draw close: that conflagration of my church
35   —What then? So much was saved if aught were missed!
     My sons, ye would not be my death? Go dig
     The white-grape vineyard where the oil-press stood,

1. John Ruskin admired Browning's portrait of a dying bishop's obsession with ordering a sumptuous tomb: "I know of no other piece of modern English, prose or poetry, in which there is so much told, as in these lines, of the Renaissance spirit—its worldliness, inconsistency, pride, hypocrisy, ignorance of itself, love of art, of luxury, and of good Latin. It is nearly all that I have said of the central Renaissance in thirty pages of the *Stones of Venice*, put into as many lines, Browning's also being the antecedent work" (*Modern Painters*, vol. 4, ch. 20, sec. 34).

2. "Vanity of vanities, saith the Preacher, vanity of vanities; all is vanity" (Ecclesiastes 1.2).
3. The supposedly celibate clergy could not marry but sometimes took mistresses; the Bishop euphemistically calls his illegitimate sons "nephews."
4. The right side, as one faces the altar, from which the Epistles of the New Testament are read.
5. Stone canopy beneath which the sculpted effigy of the bishop will repose on his tomb.
6. The pulpy mash of grapes from which strong wine could be made.

Drop water gently till the surface sink,
And if ye find . . . Ah God, I know not, I! . . .
40   Bedded in store of rotten fig-leaves soft,
And corded up in a tight olive-frail,°   basket
Some lump, ah God, of *lapis lazuli*,[7]
Big as a Jew's head cut off at the nape,
Blue as a vein o'er the Madonna's breast . . .
45   Sons, all have I bequeathed you, villas, all,
That brave Frascati[8] villa with its bath,
So, let the blue lump poise between my knees,
Like God the Father's globe on both his hands
Ye worship in the Jesu Church so gay,
50   For Gandolf shall not choose but see and burst!
Swift as a weaver's shuttle fleet our years:[9]
Man goeth to the grave, and where is he?
Did I say basalt for my slab, sons? Black—
'Twas ever antique-black I meant! How else
55   Shall ye contrast my frieze° to come beneath?   sculpted band
The bas-relief in bronze ye promised me,
Those Pans and Nymphs ye wot of, and perchance
Some tripod, thyrsus, with a vase or so,
The Saviour at his sermon on the mount,
60   Saint Praxed in a glory, and one Pan
Ready to twitch the Nymph's last garment off,
And Moses with the tables[1] . . . but I know
Ye mark me not! What do they whisper thee,
Child of my bowels, Anselm? Ah, ye hope
65   To revel down my villas while I gasp
Bricked o'er with beggar's mouldy travertine°   limestone
Which Gandolf from his tomb-top chuckles at!
Nay, boys, ye love me—all of jasper, then!
'Tis jasper ye stand pledged to, lest I grieve.
70   My bath must needs be left behind, alas!
One block, pure green as a pistachio-nut,
There's plenty jasper somewhere in the world—
And have I not Saint Praxed's ear to pray
Horses for ye, and brown Greek manuscripts,
75   And mistresses with great smooth marbly limbs?
—That's if ye carve my epitaph aright,
Choice Latin, picked phrase, Tully's every word,
No gaudy ware like Gandolf's second line—
Tully, my masters? Ulpian serves his need![2]

7. A semiprecious bright blue stone.
8. A resort near Rome.
9. Job 7.6: "My days are swifter than a weaver's shuttle
and are spent without hope." The next line alludes to Job
7.9 and 14.10.
1. The bronze bas-relief sculptures will mingle pagan and
Christian scenes, the goatlike lecherous Pan next to

Moses receiving the Ten Commandments. In *Contrasts*
(1841) A. W. Pugin criticized such juxtapositions, which
were typical of the Renaissance.
2. Domitius Ulpianus (A.D. 170–228) was considered inferior to Marcus Tullius Cicero (106–43 B.C.), regarded
during the Renaissance as the greatest Latin prose stylist.

80   And then how I shall lie through centuries,
     And hear the blessed mutter of the mass,
     And see God made and eaten all day long,[3]
     And feel the steady candle-flame, and taste
     Good strong thick stupefying incense-smoke!
85   For as I lie here, hours of the dead night,
     Dying in state and by such slow degrees,
     I fold my arms as if they clasped a crook,
     And stretch my feet forth straight as stone can point,
     And let the bedclothes, for a mortcloth, drop
90   Into great laps and folds of sculptor's-work:[4]
     And as yon tapers dwindle, and strange thoughts
     Grow, with a certain humming in my ears,
     About the life before I lived this life,
     And this life too, popes, cardinals and priests,
95   Saint Praxed at his sermon on the mount,[5]
     Your tall pale mother with her talking eyes,
     And new-found agate urns as fresh as day,
     And marble's language, Latin pure, discreet,
     —Aha, ELUCESCEBAT[6] quoth our friend?
100   No Tully, said I, Ulpian at the best!
     Evil and brief hath been my pilgrimage.[7]
     All *lapis*, all, sons! Else I give the Pope
     My villas! Will ye ever eat my heart?
     Ever your eyes were as a lizard's quick,
105   They glitter like your mother's for my soul,
     Or ye would heighten my impoverished frieze,
     Piece out its starved design, and fill my vase
     With grapes, and add a vizor and a Term,[8]
     And to the tripod ye would tie a lynx
110   That in his struggle throws the thyrsus down,
     To comfort me on my entablature°   *platform*
     Whereon I am to lie till I must ask
     "Do I live, am I dead?" There, leave me, there!
     For ye have stabbed me with ingratitude
115   To death—ye wish it—God, ye wish it! Stone—
     Gritstone, a-crumble![9] Clammy squares which sweat
     As if the corpse they keep were oozing through—
     And no more *lapis* to delight the world!
     Well go! I bless ye. Fewer tapers there,

3. According to the doctrine of transubstantiation, the bread and wine of Holy Communion become the body and blood of Christ.

4. As he lies in bed, the bishop positions himself like a carved effigy lying on a tomb, holding his ceremonial staff and draping his bedsheets like a "mortcloth" over a corpse.

5. Jesus gave the sermon on the mount, not St. Praxed (who was a woman); the bishop's mind is getting confused.

6. Gandolf's epitaph: "He was illustrious." The bishop disapproves of the verb form; Cicero would have written *elucebat*.

7. Cf. Genesis 47.9, where Jacob says: "The days of the years of my pilgrimage are an hundred and thirty years: few and evil have the days of the years of my life been."

8. The vizor of a helmet is sometimes represented in sculpture; the bishop suggests that his sons might also add a statue of Terminus, the Roman god of boundaries.

9. He fears they might use crumbly sandstone after all.

120   But in a row: and, going, turn your backs
        —Ay, like departing altar-ministrants,
        And leave me in my church, the church for peace,
        That I may watch at leisure if he leers—
        Old Gandolf, at me, from his onion-stone,
125   As still he envied me, so fair she was!

1844   1845

Meeting at Night

1

        The grey sea and the long black land;
        And the yellow half-moon large and low;
        And the startled little waves that leap
        In fiery ringlets from their sleep,
5   As I gain the cove with pushing prow,
        And quench its speed i' the slushy sand.

2

        Then a mile of warm sea-scented beach;
        Three fields to cross till a farm appears;
        A tap at the pane, the quick sharp scratch
10   And blue spurt of a lighted match
        And a voice less loud, thro' its joys and fears,
        Than the two hearts beating each to each!

                                                            1845

Parting at Morning

        Round the cape of a sudden came the sea,
        And the sun looked over the mountain's rim:
        And straight was a path of gold for him,°   *the sun*
        And the need of a world of men for me.

                                                            1845

A Toccata of Galuppi's[1]

1

        Oh, Galuppi, Baldassaro, this is very sad to find!
        I can hardly misconceive you; it would prove me deaf and blind;
        But although I take your meaning, 'tis with such a heavy mind!

2

        Here you come with your old music, and here's all the good it brings.
5   What, they lived once thus at Venice where the merchants were the kings,
        Where Saint Mark's is, where the Doges used to wed the sea with rings?[2]

1. Baldassare Galuppi (1706–1785) was a Venetian composer for harpsichord. (Baldassaro is Browning's spelling of the composer's name.) A toccata is a fast-moving keyboard composition that displays the performer's virtuosity. The speaker is an imaginary Englishman of the 19th century for whom the music of Galuppi evokes scenes of Venice—and thoughts of death.

2. The Doges of Venice performed an annual ceremony of throwing a gold ring into the water near St. Mark's church, celebrating Venice's maritime power through a symbolic marriage to the sea.

3

Ay, because the sea's the street there; and 'tis arched by . . . what you call
. . . Shylock's bridge with houses on it, where they kept the carnival:[3]
I was never out of England—it's as if I saw it all.

4

10   Did young people take their pleasure when the sea was warm in May?
Balls and masks begun at midnight, burning ever to midday,
When they made up fresh adventures for the morrow, do you say?

5

Was a lady such a lady, cheeks so round and lips so red,—
On her neck the small face buoyant, like a bell-flower on its bed,
15   O'er the breast's superb abundance where a man might base his head?

6

Well, and it was graceful of them—they'd break talk off and afford
—She, to bite her mask's black velvet—he, to finger on his sword,
While you sat and played Toccatas, stately at the clavichord?

7

What? Those lesser thirds[4] so plaintive, sixths diminished, sigh on sigh,
20   Told them something? Those suspensions, those solutions—"Must we die?"
Those commiserating sevenths—"Life might last! we can but try!"

8

"Were you happy?"—"Yes."—"And are you still as happy?"—"Yes. And you?"
—"Then, more kisses!"—"Did I stop them, when a million seemed so few?"
Hark, the dominant's persistence till it must be answered to!

9

25   So, an octave struck the answer. Oh, they praised you, I dare say!
"Brave Galuppi! that was music! good alike at grave and gay!
I can always leave off talking when I hear a master play!"

10

Then they left you for their pleasure: till in due time, one by one,
Some with lives that came to nothing, some with deeds as well undone,
30   Death stepped tacitly and took them where they never see the sun.

11

But when I sit down to reason, think to take my stand nor swerve,
While I triumph o'er a secret wrung from nature's close reserve,
In you come with your cold music till I creep thro' every nerve.

12

Yes, you, like a ghostly cricket, creaking where a house was burned:[5]
35   "Dust and ashes, dead and done with, Venice spent what Venice earned.
The soul, doubtless, is immortal—where a soul can be discerned.

3. The Rialto, a bridge over the Grand Canal, was the Venetian Merchants' Exchange where Shylock does business in *The Merchant of Venice*. Venice is famous for its celebrations of Carnival during the weeks preceding Lent.
4. Musical intervals, as are the sixths, sevenths, and octaves in later lines. Browning uses these and harmonic terms such as "suspension" and "dominant" evocatively—to convey the emotional effect of the toccata on the speaker—rather than in strict accordance with musical theory; there is no such interval as a "lesser third," for example.
5. Listening to Galuppi's music, the speaker imagines the lines that follow being spoken to him by the dead composer.

13

"Yours for instance: you know physics, something of geology,
Mathematics are your pastime; souls shall rise in their degree;
Butterflies may dread extinction,—you'll not die, it cannot be!

14

40   "As for Venice and her people, merely born to bloom and drop,
Here on earth they bore their fruitage, mirth and folly were the crop:
What of soul was left, I wonder, when the kissing had to stop?

15

"Dust and ashes!" So you creak it, and I want° the heart to scold.   lack
Dear dead women, with such hair, too—what's become of all the gold
45   Used to hang and brush their bosoms? I feel chilly and grown old.

1855

Memorabilia[1]

1

Ah, did you once see Shelley plain,
    And did he stop and speak to you
And did you speak to him again?
    How strange it seems and new!

2

5   But you were living before that,
    And also you are living after;
And the memory I started at—
    My starting moves your laughter.

3

I crossed a moor, with a name of its own
10   And a certain use in the world no doubt,
Yet a hand's-breadth of it shines alone
    'Mid the blank miles round about:

4

For there I picked up on the heather
    And there I put inside my breast
15   A moulted feather, an eagle-feather!
    Well, I forget the rest.

1851   1855

---

1. Things worthy of remembrance. Browning recalled meeting a man who had known Shelley, the poet he admired beyond all others: "I was one day in the shop of Hodgson, the well-known London bookseller, when a stranger came in, who, in the course of conversation with the bookseller, spoke of something that Shelley had once said to him. Suddenly the stranger paused, and burst into laughter as he observed me staring at him with blanched face; and . . . I still vividly remember how strangely the presence of a man who had seen and spoken with Shelley affected me."

Love Among the Ruins[1]

1

Where the quiet-coloured end of evening smiles,
    Miles and miles
On the solitary pastures where our sheep
    Half-asleep
5 Tinkle homeward thro' the twilight, stray or stop
    As they crop—
Was the site once of a city great and gay,
    (So they say)
Of our country's very capital, its prince
10 Ages since
Held his court in, gathered councils, wielding far
    Peace or war.

2

Now,—the country does not even boast a tree
    As you see,
15 To distinguish slopes of verdure, certain rills
    From the hills
Intersect and give a name to, (else they run
    Into one)
Where the domed and daring palace shot its spires
20 Up like fires
O'er the hundred-gated circuit of a wall
    Bounding all,
Made of marble, men might march on nor be pressed
    Twelve abreast.

3

25 And such plenty and perfection, see, of grass
    Never was!
Such a carpet as, this summer-time, o'erspreads
    And embeds
Every vestige of the city, guessed alone,
30 Stock or stone—
Where a multitude of men breathed joy and woe
    Long ago;
Lust of glory pricked their hearts up, dread of shame
    Struck them tame;
35 And that glory and that shame alike, the gold
    Bought and sold.

4

Now,—the single little turret that remains
    On the plains,

---

1. The poem's scenery suggests the Roman Campagna but may also allude to archaeological excavations at Babylon, Nineveh, and Egyptian Thebes. Browning invented this stanza form. See Edward Burne-Jones's painting of the same name (Color Plate 20).

By the caper° overrooted, by the gourd   *shrub*
40   Overscored,
While the patching houseleek's head of blossom winks
          Through the chinks—
Marks the basement whence a tower in ancient time
          Sprang sublime,
45 And a burning ring, all round, the chariots traced
          As they raced,
And the monarch and his minions and his dames
          Viewed the games.

                              5
And I know, while thus the quiet-coloured eve
50   Smiles to leave
To their folding, all our many-tinkling fleece
          In such peace,
And the slopes and rills in undistinguished grey
          Melt away—
55 That a girl with eager eyes and yellow hair
          Waits me there
In the turret whence the charioteers caught soul
          For the goal,
When the king looked, where she looks now, breathless, dumb
60   Till I come.

                              6
But he looked upon the city, every side,
          Far and wide,
All the mountains topped with temples, all the glades'
          Colonnades,
65 All the causeys,° bridges, aqueducts,—and then,   *causeways*
          All the men!
When I do come, she will speak not, she will stand,
          Either hand
On my shoulder, give her eyes the first embrace
70   Of my face,
Ere we rush, ere we extinguish sight and speech
          Each on each.

                              7
In one year they sent a million fighters forth
          South and North,
75 And they built their gods a brazen pillar high
          As the sky,
Yet reserved a thousand chariots in full force—
          Gold, of course.
Oh heart! oh blood that freezes, blood that burns!
80   Earth's returns
For whole centuries of folly, noise and sin!
          Shut them in,

With their triumphs and their glories and the rest!
    Love is best.

c. 1852   1855

"Childe Roland to the Dark Tower Came"[1]
(See Edgar's Song in "Lear")[2]

1

My first thought was, he lied in every word,
    That hoary cripple, with malicious eye
    Askance to watch the working of his lie
On mine, and mouth scarce able to afford
5   Suppression of the glee, that pursed and scored
    Its edge, at one more victim gained thereby.

2

What else should he be set for, with his staff?
    What, save to waylay with his lies, ensnare
    All travellers who might find him posted there,
10   And ask the road? I guessed what skull-like laugh
    Would break, what crutch 'gin write my epitaph
    For pastime in the dusty thoroughfare,

3

If at his counsel I should turn aside
    Into that ominous tract which, all agree,
15   Hides the Dark Tower. Yet acquiescingly
I did turn as he pointed: neither pride
Nor hope rekindling at the end descried,
    So much as gladness that some end might be.

4

For, what with my whole world-wide wandering,
20   What with my search drawn out thro' years, my hope
    Dwindled into a ghost not fit to cope
With that obstreperous joy success would bring,—
I hardly tried now to rebuke the spring
    My heart made, finding failure in its scope.

5

25   As when a sick man very near to death
    Seems dead indeed, and feels begin and end
    The tears and takes the farewell of each friend,

---

1. Roland was a hero of Charlemagne legends, and a "childe" was a young candidate for knighthood. Although critics have proposed many different interpretations of Roland's strange, nightmarish quest, Browning himself said only that the poem "came upon me as a kind of dream. I had to write it, then and there, and I finished it the same day, I believe. But it was simply that I had to do it. I did not know then what I meant beyond that, and I'm sure I don't know now. But I am very fond of it."

2. In Shakespeare's *King Lear*, Edgar, disguised as the mad beggar Poor Tom, sings: "Child Rowland to the dark tower came; / His word was still, 'Fie, foh and fum, / I smell the blood of a British man'" (3.4.181–83).

And hears one bid the other go, draw breath
Freelier outside, ("since all is o'er," he saith,
30   "And the blow fallen no grieving can amend;")

6

While some discuss if near the other graves
    Be room enough for this, and when a day
    Suits best for carrying the corpse away,
With care about the banners, scarves and staves:
35   And still the man hears all, and only craves
    He may not shame such tender love and stay.

7

Thus, I had so long suffered in this quest,
    Heard failure prophesied so oft, been writ
    So many times among "The Band"—to wit,
40   The knights who to the Dark Tower's search addressed
Their steps—that just to fail as they, seemed best,
    And all the doubt was now—should I be fit?

8

So, quiet as despair, I turned from him,
    That hateful cripple, out of his highway
45   Into the path he pointed. All the day
Had been a dreary one at best, and dim
Was settling to its close, yet shot one grim
    Red leer to see the plain catch its estray.°   *stray animal*

9

For mark! no sooner was I fairly found
50   Pledged to the plain, after a pace or two,
    Than, pausing to throw backward a last view
O'er the safe road, 'twas gone; grey plain all round:
Nothing but plain to the horizon's bound.
    I might go on; nought else remained to do.

10

55   So, on I went. I think I never saw
    Such starved ignoble nature; nothing throve:
    For flowers—as well expect a cedar grove!
But cockle, spurge,° according to their law   *weeds*
Might propagate their kind, with none to awe,
60   You'd think; a burr had been a treasure-trove.

11

No! penury, inertness and grimace,
    In some strange sort, were the land's portion. "See
    Or shut your eyes," said Nature peevishly,
"It nothing skills: I cannot help my case:
65   'Tis the Last Judgment's fire must cure this place,
    Calcine° its clods and set my prisoners free."   *burn to ashes*

12

If there pushed any ragged thistle-stalk
   Above its mates, the head was chopped; the bents°   *coarse grasses*
   Were jealous else. What made those holes and rents
70   In the dock's° harsh swarth leaves, bruised as to baulk   *weed*
All hope of greenness? 'tis a brute must walk
   Pashing° their life out, with a brute's intents.   *crushing*

13

As for the grass, it grew as scant as hair
   In leprosy; thin dry blades pricked the mud
75   Which underneath looked kneaded up with blood.
One stiff blind horse, his every bone a-stare,
Stood stupefied, however he came there:
   Thrust out past service from the devil's stud!

14

Alive? he might be dead for aught I know,
80   With that red gaunt and colloped neck a-strain,
   And shut eyes underneath the rusty mane;
Seldom went such grotesqueness with such woe;
I never saw a brute I hated so;
   He must be wicked to deserve such pain.

15

85   I shut my eyes and turned them on my heart.
   As a man calls for wine before he fights,
   I asked one draught of earlier, happier sights,
Ere fitly I could hope to play my part.
Think first, fight afterwards—the soldier's art:
90   One taste of the old time sets all to rights.

16

Not it! I fancied Cuthbert's reddening face
   Beneath its garniture of curly gold,
   Dear fellow, till I almost felt him fold
An arm in mine to fix me to the place,
95   That way he used. Alas, one night's disgrace!
   Out went my heart's new fire and left it cold.

17

Giles then, the soul of honour—there he stands
   Frank as ten years ago when knighted first.
   What honest man should dare (he said) he durst.
100   Good—but the scene shifts—faugh! what hangman-hands
Pin to his breast a parchment? His own bands
   Read it. Poor traitor, spit upon and curst!

18

Better this present than a past like that;
   Back therefore to my darkening path again!

105   No sound, no sight as far as eye could strain.
            Will the night send a howlet° or a bat?   *owl*
            I asked: when something on the dismal flat
                Came to arrest my thoughts and change their train.

                                    19
        A sudden little river crossed my path
110   As unexpected as a serpent comes.
                No sluggish tide congenial to the glooms;
        This, as it frothed by, might have been a bath
        For the fiend's glowing hoof—to see the wrath
                Of its black eddy bespate with flakes and spumes.

                                    20
115   So petty yet so spiteful! All along,
                Low scrubby alders kneeled down over it;
                Drenched willows flung them headlong in a fit
        Of mute despair, a suicidal throng:
        The river which had done them all the wrong,
120   Whate'er that was, rolled by, deterred no whit.

                                    21
        Which, while I forded,—good saints, how I feared
                To set my foot upon a dead man's cheek,
                Each step, or feel the spear I thrust to seek
        For hollows, tangled in his hair or beard!
125   —It may have been a water-rat I speared,
                But, ugh! it sounded like a baby's shriek.

                                    22
        Glad was I when I reached the other bank.
                Now for a better country. Vain presage!
                Who were the strugglers, what war did they wage,
130   Whose savage trample thus could pad° the dank   *tread*
        Soil to a plash? Toads in a poisoned tank,
                Or wild cats in a red-hot iron cage—

                                    23
        The fight must so have seemed in that fell cirque.°   *terrible arena*
                What penned them there, with all the plain to choose?
135   No foot-print leading to that horrid mews,
        None out of it. Mad brewage set to work
        Their brains, no doubt, like galley-slaves the Turk
                Pits for his pastime, Christians against Jews.

                                    24
        And more than that—a furlong on—why, there!
140   What bad use was that engine for, that wheel,
                Or brake, not wheel—that harrow fit to reel
        Men's bodies out like silk? with all the air
        Of Tophet's° tool, on earth left unaware,   *hell's*
                Or brought to sharpen its rusty teeth of steel.

25

145   Then came a bit of stubbed ground, once a wood,
        Next a marsh, it would seem, and now mere earth
        Desperate and done with; (so a fool finds mirth,
    Makes a thing and then mars it, till his mood
    Changes and off he goes!) within a rood°—   *quarter of an acre*
150   Bog, clay and rubble, sand and stark black dearth.

26

    Now blotches rankling, coloured gay and grim,
        Now patches where some leanness of the soil's
        Broke into moss or substances like boils;
    Then came some palsied oak, a cleft in him
155   Like a distorted mouth that splits its rim
        Gaping at death, and dies while it recoils.

27

    And just as far as ever from the end!
        Nought in the distance but the evening, nought
        To point my footstep further! At the thought,
160   A great black bird, Apollyon's[3] bosom-friend,
    Sailed past, nor beat his wide wing dragon-penned°   *pinioned*
        That brushed my cap—perchance the guide I sought.

28

    For, looking up, aware I somehow grew,
        'Spite of the dusk, the plain had given place
165   All round to mountains—with such name to grace
    Mere ugly heights and heaps now stolen in view.
    How thus they had surprised me,—solve it, you!
        How to get from them was no clearer case.

29

    Yet half I seemed to recognize some trick
170   Of mischief happened to me, God knows when—
        In a bad dream perhaps. Here ended, then,
    Progress this way. When, in the very nick
    Of giving up, one time more, came a click
        As when a trap shuts—you're inside the den!

30

175   Burningly it came on me all at once,
        This was the place! those two hills on the right,
        Crouched like two bulls locked horn in horn in fight;
    While to the left, a tall scalped mountain . . . Dunce,
    Dotard, a-dozing at the very nonce,°   *moment*
180   After a life spent training for the sight!

3. Devil mentioned in Revelation 9.11 and in Bunyan's *Pilgrim's Progress.*

31

What in the midst lay but the Tower itself?
    The round squat turret, blind as the fool's heart,[4]
    Built of brown stone, without a counterpart
In the whole world. The tempest's mocking elf
185   Points to the shipman thus the unseen shelf
    He strikes on, only when the timbers start.

32

Not see? because of night perhaps?—why, day
    Came back again for that! before it left,
    The dying sunset kindled through a cleft:
190   The hills, like giants at a hunting, lay,
Chin upon hand, to see the game at bay,—
    "Now stab and end the creature—to the heft!"°   *hilt*

33

Not hear? when noise was everywhere! it tolled
    Increasing like a bell. Names in my ears
195   Of all the lost adventurers my peers,—
How such a one was strong, and such was bold,
And such was fortunate, yet each of old
    Lost, lost! one moment knelled the woe of years.

34

There they stood, ranged along the hill-sides, met
200   To view the last of me, a living frame
    For one more picture! in a sheet of flame
I saw them and I knew them all. And yet
Dauntless the slug-horn[5] to my lips I set,
    And blew. "*Childe Roland to the Dark Tower came.*"

c. 1852   1855

<hr />

RESPONSE

Stevie Smith: Childe Rolandine[1]

Dark was the day for Childe Rolandine the artist
When she went to work as a secretary-typist
And as she worked she sang this song
Against oppression and the rule of wrong:

4. "The fool hath said in his heart, There is no God" (Psalm 14.1).
5. Scottish word for slogan, or battle cry, though Browning seems to mean "trumpet."
1. The British poet Stevie Smith (1902–1971), known for her playful, ironic, often prosaically straightforward verses, spent almost all her life in London. She began to write poetry while working as a secretary at a publishing house, and it was likely there that she conceived of Childe Rolandine, a modern female version of Browning's chivalric hero. While the exploitative drudgery of the office carries some of the symbolic weight of Browning's wasteland, Smith's heroine appears more able to transform the suffering of her quest into something lasting; she is an artist. Smith loved to read Romantic and Victorian poetry (*Thoughts about the Person from Porlock*, about the caller who interrupted Coleridge while he was writing *Kubla Khan*, is one of her best poems); and the reader may find an echo of Dante Gabriel Rossetti's *The Blessed Damozel* here in the final lines.

5   It is the privilege of the rich
       To waste the time of the poor
       To water with tears in secret
       A tree that grows in secret
       That bears fruit in secret
10   That ripened falls to the ground in secret
       And manures the parent tree
       Oh the wicked tree of hatred and the secret
       The sap rising and the tears falling.

       Likely also, sang the Childe, my soul will fry in hell
15   Because of this hatred, while in heaven my employer does well
       And why should he not, exacerbating though he be but generous
       Is it his fault I must work at a work that is tedious?
       Oh heaven sweet heaven keep my thoughts in their night den
       Do not let them by day be spoken.

20   But then she sang, Ah why not? tell all, speak, speak,
       Silence is vanity, speak for the whole truth's sake.

       And rising she took the bugle and put it to her lips, crying:
       There is a Spirit feeds on our tears, I give him mine,
       Mighty human feelings are his food
25   Passion and grief and joy his flesh and blood
       That he may live and grow fat we daily die
       This cropping One is our immortality.

       Childe Rolandine bowed her head and in the evening
       Drew the picture of the spirit from heaven.

                                                          1957

                          ❧

Fra Lippo Lippi[1]

       I am poor brother Lippo, by your leave!
       You need not clap your torches to my face.
       Zooks, what's to blame? you think you see a monk!
       What, 'tis past midnight, and you go the rounds,
5   And here you catch me at an alley's end
       Where sportive ladies leave their doors ajar?
       The Carmine's my cloister:[2] hunt it up,
       Do,—harry out, if you must show your zeal,
       Whatever rat, there, haps on his wrong hole,
10   And nip each softling of a wee white mouse,
       Weke, weke, that's crept to keep him company!
       Aha, you know your betters! Then, you'll take
       Your hand away that's fiddling on my throat,
       And please to know me likewise. Who am I?
15   Why, one, sir, who is lodging with a friend

---

1. Filippo Lippi (1406–1469) was an early Renaissance painter and monk whose life is described in Giorgio Vasari's *The Lives of the Painters* (1550, 1568); "Fra" means brother.

2. Santa Maria del Carmine, a Carmelite monastery in Florence.

Three streets off—he's a certain . . . how d'ye call?
Master—a . . . Cosimo of the Medici,[3]
I' the house that caps the corner. Boh! you were best!
Remember and tell me, the day you're hanged,
20   How you affected such a gullet's-gripe![4]
But you, sir,[5] it concerns you that your knaves
Pick up a manner nor discredit you:
Zooks, are we pilchards,° that they sweep the streets   sardines
And count fair prize what comes into their net?
25   He's Judas to a tittle, that man is![6]
Just such a face! Why, sir, you make amends:
Lord, I'm not angry! Bid your hangdogs go
Drink out this quarter-florin to the health
Of the munificent House that harbours me
30   (And many more beside, lads! more beside!)
And all's come square again. I'd like his face—
His, elbowing on his comrade in the door
With the pike and lantern,—for the slave that holds
John Baptist's head a-dangle by the hair
35   With one hand ("Look you, now," as who should say)
And his weapon in the other, yet unwiped!
It's not your chance to have a bit of chalk,
A wood-coal or the like? or you should see!
Yes, I'm the painter, since you style me so.
40   What, brother Lippo's doings, up and down,
You know them and they take you? like enough!
I saw the proper twinkle in your eye—
'Tell you, I liked your looks at very first.
Let's sit and set things straight now, hip to haunch.
45   Here's spring come, and the nights one makes up bands
To roam the town and sing out carnival,[7]
And I've been three weeks shut within my mew,
A-painting for the great man, saints and saints
And saints again. I could not paint all night—
50   Ouf! I leaned out of window for fresh air.
There came a hurry of feet and little feet,
A sweep of lute-strings, laughs, and whiffs of song,—
Flower o' the broom,
Take away love, and our earth is a tomb!
55   *Flower o' the quince,*
I let Lisa go, and what good in life since?
Flower o' the thyme[8]—and so on. Round they went.
Scarce had they turned the corner when a titter
Like the skipping of rabbits by moonlight,—three slim shapes,

---

3. Cosimo de' Medici (1389–1464), a banker and ruler of
Florence, was Lippi's patron.
4. How you choked me by the throat.
5. Lippi now addresses the leader of the watchmen.

6. One of the watchmen is the spitting image of Judas.
7. A season of festivities before Lent.
8. The "flower songs" Lippi sings are called *stornelli*,
three-line Tuscan folk songs.

60 And a face that looked up . . . zooks, sir, flesh and blood,
    That's all I'm made of! Into shreds it went,
    Curtain and counterpane and coverlet,
    All the bed-furniture—a dozen knots,
    There was a ladder! Down I let myself,
65 Hands and feet, scrambling somehow, and so dropped,
    And after them. I came up with the fun
    Hard by Saint Laurence,[9] hail fellow, well met,—
      Flower o' the rose,
      If I've been merry, what matter who knows?
70 And so as I was stealing back again
    To get to bed and have a bit of sleep
    Ere I rise up to-morrow and go work
    On Jerome[1] knocking at his poor old breast
    With his great round stone to subdue the flesh,
75 You snap me of the sudden. Ah, I see!
    Though your eye twinkles still, you shake your head—
    Mine's shaved[2]—a monk, you say—the sting's in that!
    If Master Cosimo announced himself,
    Mum's the word naturally; but a monk!
80 Come, what am I a beast for? tell us, now!
    I was a baby when my mother died
    And father died and left me in the street.
    I starved there, God knows how, a year or two
    On fig-skins, melon-parings, rinds and shucks,
85 Refuse and rubbish. One fine frosty day,
    My stomach being empty as your hat,
    The wind doubled me up and down I went.
    Old Aunt Lapaccia trussed me with one hand,
    (Its fellow was a stinger as I knew)
90 And so along the wall, over the bridge,
    By the straight cut to the convent. Six words there,
    While I stood munching my first bread that month:
    "So, boy, you're minded," quoth the good fat father
    Wiping his own mouth, 'twas refection-time,°—   *mealtime*
95 "To quit this very miserable world?
    Will you renounce" . . . "the mouthful of bread?" thought I;
    By no means! Brief, they made a monk of me;
    I did renounce the world, its pride and greed,
    Palace, farm, villa, shop and banking-house,
100 Trash, such as these poor devils of Medici
    Have given their hearts to—all at eight years old.
    Well, sir, I found in time, you may be sure,
    'Twas not for nothing—the good bellyful,
    The warm serge and the rope that goes all round,

9. The Church of San Lorenzo.
1. The pleasure-loving Lippi is painting the chaste and ascetic St. Jerome.

2. The tonsure, or partially shaved head, was the emblem of the monk.

105 And day-long blessed idleness beside!
"Let's see what the urchin's fit for"—that came next.
Not overmuch their way, I must confess.
Such a to-do! They tried me with their books:
Lord, they'd have taught me Latin in pure waste!

110 *Flower o' the clove,*
All the Latin I construe is, "amo," I love!
But, mind you, when a boy starves in the streets
Eight years together, as my fortune was,
Watching folk's faces to know who will fling

115 The bit of half-stripped grape-bunch he desires,
And who will curse or kick him for his pains,—
Which gentleman processional and fine,
Holding a candle to the Sacrament,
Will wink and let him lift a plate and catch

120 The droppings of the wax to sell again,
Or holla for the Eight[3] and have him whipped,—
How say I?—nay, which dog bites, which lets drop
His bone from the heap of offal in the street,—
Why, soul and sense of him grow sharp alike,

125 He learns the look of things, and none the less
For admonition from the hunger-pinch.
I had a store of such remarks, be sure,
Which, after I found leisure, turned to use.
I drew men's faces on my copy-books,

130 Scrawled them within the antiphonary's marge,[4]
Joined legs and arms to the long music-notes,
Found eyes and nose and chin for A's and B's,
And made a string of pictures of the world
Betwixt the ins and outs of verb and noun,

135 On the wall, the bench, the door. The monks looked black.
"Nay," quoth the Prior, "turn him out, d' ye say?
In no wise. Lose a crow and catch a lark.
What if at last we get our man of parts,
We Carmelites, like those Camaldolese

140 And Preaching Friars, to do our church up fine
And put the front on it that ought to be!"[5]
And hereupon he bade me daub away.
Thank you! my head being crammed, the walls a blank,
Never was such prompt disemburdening.

145 First, every sort of monk, the black and white,
I drew them, fat and lean: then, folk at church,
From good old gossips waiting to confess
Their cribs° of barrel-droppings, candle-ends,—   *small thefts*
To the breathless fellow at the altar-foot,

---

3. Send for the magistrates of Florence.
4. The margin of his hymnbook.
5. The Prior, or head of the monastery, wants to outdo

rival orders of monks by having Lippi paint the church
splendidly.

150   Fresh from his murder,⁶ safe and sitting there
With the little children round him in a row
Of admiration, half for his beard and half
For that white anger of his victim's son
Shaking a fist at him with one fierce arm,
155   Signing himself⁷ with the other because of Christ
(Whose sad face on the cross sees only this
After the passion° of a thousand years)   *suffering*
Till some poor girl, her apron o'er her head,
(Which the intense eyes looked through) came at eve
160   On tiptoe, said a word, dropped in a loaf,
Her pair of earrings and a bunch of flowers
(The brute took growling), prayed, and so was gone.
I painted all, then cried "'Tis ask and have;
Choose, for more's ready!"—laid the ladder flat,
165   And showed my covered bit of cloister-wall
The monks closed in a circle and praised loud
Till checked, taught what to see and not to see,
Being simple bodies,—"That's the very man!
Look at the boy who stoops to pat the dog!
170   That woman's like the Prior's niece⁸ who comes
To care about his asthma: it's the life!"
But there my triumph's straw-fire flared and funked;°   *smoked*
Their betters took their turn to see and say:
The Prior and the learned pulled a face
175   And stopped all that in no time. "How? what's here?
Quite from the mark of painting, bless us all!
Faces, arms, legs and bodies like the true
As much as pea and pea! it's devil's-game!
Your business is not to catch men with show,
180   With homage to the perishable clay,
But lift them over it, ignore it all,
Make them forget there's such a thing as flesh.
Your business is to paint the souls of men—
Man's soul, and it's a fire, smoke . . . no, it's not . . .
185   It's vapour done up like a new-born babe—
(In that shape when you die it leaves your mouth)
It's . . . well, what matters talking, it's the soul!
Give us no more of body than shows soul!
Here's Giotto,⁹ with his Saint a-praising God,
190   That sets us praising,—why not stop with him?
Why put all thoughts of praise out of our head
With wonder at lines, colours, and what not?
Paint the soul, never mind the legs and arms!
Rub all out, try at it a second time.

---

6. Criminals could take refuge in the church because it
was a sanctuary where civil law had no power.
7. Making the sign of the cross.

8. Probably a euphemism for the Prior's mistress.
9. Giotto di Bondone (c. 1266–1337), late-medieval Florentine artist and architect.

195   Oh, that white smallish female with the breasts,
       She's just my niece . . . Herodias, I would say,—
       Who went and danced and got men's heads cut off![1]
       Have it all out!" Now, is this sense, I ask?
       A fine way to paint soul, by painting body
200   So ill, the eye can't stop there, must go further
       And can't fare worse! Thus, yellow does for white
       When what you put for yellow's simply black,
       And any sort of meaning looks intense
       When all beside itself means and looks nought.
205   Why can't a painter lift each foot in turn,
       Left foot and right foot, go a double step,
       Make his flesh liker and his soul more like,
       Both in their order? Take the prettiest face,
       The Prior's niece . . . patron-saint—is it so pretty
210   You can't discover if it means hope, fear,
       Sorrow or joy? won't beauty go with these?
       Suppose I've made her eyes all right and blue,
       Can't I take breath and try to add life's flash,
       And then add soul and heighten them threefold?
215   Or say there's beauty with no soul at all—
       (I never saw it—put the case the same—)
       If you get simple beauty and nought else,
       You get about the best thing God invents:
       That's somewhat: and you'll find the soul you have missed,
220   Within yourself, when you return him thanks.
       "Rub all out!" Well, well, there's my life, in short,
       And so the thing has gone on ever since.
       I'm grown a man no doubt, I've broken bounds:
       You should not take a fellow eight years old
225   And make him swear to never kiss the girls.
       I'm my own master, paint now as I please—
       Having a friend, you see, in the Corner-house!°   *Medici palace*
       Lord, it's fast holding by the rings in front—
       Those great rings serve more purposes than just
230   To plant a flag in, or tie up a horse!
       And yet the old schooling sticks, the old grave eyes
       Are peeping o'er my shoulder as I work,
       The heads shake still—"It's art's decline, my son!
       You're not of the true painters, great and old;
235   Brother Angelico's the man, you'll find;
       Brother Lorenzo stands his single peer:[2]
       Fag° on at flesh, you'll never make the third!"   *struggle*
       Flower o' the pine,

---

1. The gospel of Matthew tells how Herod's niece Salomé danced before him and requested as a reward the head of John the Baptist (14.6–8). According to Vasari, however, it was Salomé's mother, Herodias, who danced.

2. Fra Angelico (1387–1455) and Lorenzo Monaco (1370–1425) were important painters in the traditional formalist style.

You keep your mistr . . . manners, and I'll stick to mine!
240 I'm not the third, then: bless us, they must know!
Don't you think they're the likeliest to know,
They with their Latin? So, I swallow my rage,
Clench my teeth, suck my lips in tight, and paint
To please them—sometimes do and sometimes don't;
245 For, doing most, there's pretty sure to come
A turn, some warm eve finds me at my saints—
A laugh, a cry, the business of the world—
(*Flower o' the peach,*
Death for us all, and his own life for each!)
250 And my whole soul revolves, the cup runs over,
The world and life's too big to pass for a dream,
And I do these wild things in sheer despite,
And play the fooleries you catch me at,
In pure rage! The old mill-horse, out at grass
255 After hard years, throws up his stiff heels so,
Although the miller does not preach to him
The only good of grass is to make chaff.°   straw
What would men have? Do they like grass or no—
May they or mayn't they? all I want's the thing
260 Settled for ever one way. As it is,
You tell too many lies and hurt yourself:
You don't like what you only like too much,
You do like what, if given you at your word,
You find abundantly detestable.
265 For me, I think I speak as I was taught;
I always see the garden and God there
A-making man's wife: and, my lesson learned,
The value and significance of flesh,
I can't unlearn ten minutes afterwards.

270   You understand me: I'm a beast, I know.
But see, now—why, I see as certainly
As that the morning-star's about to shine,
What will hap some day. We've a youngster here
Comes to our convent, studies what I do,
275 Slouches and stares and lets no atom drop:
His name is Guidi—he'll not mind the monks—
They call him Hulking Tom,[3] he lets them talk—
He picks my practice up—he'll paint apace,
I hope so—though I never live so long,
280 I know what's sure to follow. You be judge!
You speak no Latin more than I, belike,
However, you're my man, you've seen the world

---

3. Tommaso Guidi (1401–1428), called Masaccio ("Sloppy Tom"), was probably Lippi's teacher, but Browning casts him as his pupil. Both painters revolted against the highly stylized conventions of medieval art in favor of increased realism.

—The beauty and the wonder and the power,
The shapes of things, their colours, lights and shades,
285 Changes, surprises,—and God made it all!
—For what? Do you feel thankful, ay or no,
For this fair town's face, yonder river's line,
The mountain round it and the sky above,
Much more the figures of man, woman, child,
290 These are the frame to? What's it all about?
To be passed over, despised? or dwelt upon,
Wondered at? oh, this last of course!—you say.
But why not do as well as say,—paint these
Just as they are, careless what comes of it?
295 God's works—paint anyone, and count it crime
To let a truth slip. Don't object, "His works
Are here already; nature is complete:
Suppose you reproduce her—(which you can't)
There's no advantage! you must beat her, then."
300 For, don't you mark? we're made so that we love
First when we see them painted, things we have passed
Perhaps a hundred times nor cared to see;
And so they are better, painted—better to us,
Which is the same thing. Art was given for that;
305 God uses us to help each other so,
Lending our minds out. Have you noticed, now,
Your cullion's hanging face?[4] A bit of chalk,
And trust me but you should, though! How much more,
If I drew higher things with the same truth!
310 That were to take the Prior's pulpit-place,
Interpret God to all of you! Oh, oh,
It makes me mad to see what men shall do
And we in our graves! This world's no blot for us,
Nor blank; it means intensely, and means good:
315 To find its meaning is my meat and drink.
"Ay, but you don't so instigate to prayer!"
Strikes in the Prior: "when your meaning's plain
It does not say to folk—remember matins,°   *morning prayers*
Or, mind you fast next Friday!" Why, for this
320 What need of art at all? A skull and bones,
Two bits of stick nailed crosswise, or, what's best,
A bell to chime the hour with, does as well.
I painted a Saint Laurence six months since
At Prato, splashed the fresco in fine style:
325 "How looks my painting, now the scaffold's down?"
I ask a brother: "Hugely," he returns—
Already not one phiz° of your three slaves   *face*

4. That rascal's drooping face (or perhaps "born to be hanged"—cf. line 19).

Who turn the Deacon off his toasted side,[5]
But's scratched and prodded to our heart's content,
330 The pious people have so eased their own
With coming to say prayers there in a rage:
We get on fast to see the bricks beneath.
Expect another job this time next year,
For pity and religion grow i' the crowd—
335 Your painting serves its purpose!" Hang the fools!

    —That is—you'll not mistake an idle word
Spoke in a huff by a poor monk, God wot,
Tasting the air this spicy night which turns
The unaccustomed head like Chianti wine!
340 Oh, the church knows! don't misreport me, now!
It's natural a poor monk out of bounds
Should have his apt word to excuse himself:
And hearken how I plot to make amends.
I have bethought me: I shall paint a piece
345 . . . There's for you! Give me six months, then go, see
Something in Sant' Ambrogio's![6] Bless the nuns!
They want a cast o' my office. I shall paint
God in the midst, Madonna and her babe,
Ringed by a bowery flowery angel-brood,
350 Lilies and vestments and white faces, sweet
As puff on puff of grated orris-root
When ladies crowd to Church at midsummer.
And then i' the front, of course a saint or two—
Saint John, because he saves the Florentines,
355 Saint Ambrose, who puts down in black and white
The convent's friends and gives them a long day,
And Job, I must have him there past mistake,
The man of Uz (and Us without the z,
Painters who need his patience). Well, all these
360 Secured at their devotion, up shall come
Out of a corner when you least expect,
As one by a dark stair into a great light,
Music and talking, who but Lippo! I!—
Mazed, motionless and moonstruck—I'm the man!
365 Back I shrink—what is this I see and hear?
I, caught up with my monk's-things by mistake,
My old serge gown and rope that goes all round,
I, in this presence, this pure company!
Where's a hole, where's a corner for escape?
370 Then steps a sweet angelic slip of a thing
Forward, puts out a soft palm—"Not so fast!"
    —Addresses the celestial presence, "nay—

5. St. Laurence, a deacon who was martyred by being roasted, is reputed to have asked to be turned over, as he was done on one side.

6. Lippi's *Coronation of the Virgin* was painted for the church of Sant' Ambrogio's convent in Florence.

He made you and devised you, after all,
Though he's none of you! Could Saint John there draw—
375 His camel-hair[7] make up a painting-brush?
We come to brother Lippo for all that,
Iste perfecit opus!"[8] So, all smile—
I shuffle sideways with my blushing face
Under the cover of a hundred wings
380 Thrown like a spread of kirtles° when you're gay   skirts
And play hot cockles,[9] all the doors being shut,
Till, wholly unexpected, in there pops
The hothead husband! Thus I scuttle off
To some safe bench behind, not letting go
385 The palm of her, the little lily thing
That spoke the good word for me in the nick,
Like the Prior's niece . . . Saint Lucy, I would say.[1]
And so all's saved for me, and for the church
A pretty picture gained. Go, six months hence!
390 Your hand, sir, and good-bye: no lights, no lights!
The street's hushed, and I know my own way back,
Don't fear me! There's the grey beginning. Zooks!

1853   1855

The Last Ride Together

1

I said—Then, dearest, since 'tis so,
Since now at length my fate I know,
Since nothing all my love avails,
Since all, my life seemed meant for, fails,
5   Since this was written and needs must be—
My whole heart rises up to bless
Your name in pride and thankfulness!
Take back the hope you gave,—I claim
Only a memory of the same,
10   —And this beside, if you will not blame,
     Your leave for one more last ride with me.

2

My mistress bent that brow of hers;
Those deep dark eyes where pride demurs
When pity would be softening through,
15   Fixed me a breathing-while or two
     With life or death in the balance: right!

---

7. "And John was clothed with camel's hair, and with a girdle of a skin about his loins; and he did eat locusts and wild honey" (Mark 1.6). John the Baptist is the patron saint of Florence.
8. "This man made the work." These words appear beside a figure in the painting, which was assumed to be a self-portrait of Lippi. (It actually depicts the patron who ordered the painting.)
9. A blindfolded game, here a euphemism for sex.
1. Lippi will paint the Prior's "niece" as the virgin martyr Lucy, whom he has imagined interceding on his behalf with "the celestial presence" (lines 370–77).

The blood replenished me again;
My last thought was at least not vain:
I and my mistress, side by side
20 Shall be together, breathe and ride,
So, one day more am I deified.
    Who knows but the world may end to-night?

3

Hush! if you saw some western cloud
All billowy-bosomed, over-bowed
25 By many benedictions—sun's
And moon's and evening-star's at once—
    And so, you, looking and loving best,
Conscious grew, your passion drew
Cloud, sunset, moonrise, star-shine too,
30 Down on you, near and yet more near,
Till flesh must fade for heaven was here!—
Thus leant she and lingered—joy and fear!
    Thus lay she a moment on my breast.

4

Then we began to ride. My soul
35 Smoothed itself out, a long-cramped scroll
Freshening and fluttering in the wind.
Past hopes already lay behind.
    What need to strive with a life awry?
Had I said that, had I done this,
40 So might I gain, so might I miss.
Might she have loved me? just as well
She might have hated, who can tell!
Where had I been now if the worst befell?
    And here we are riding, she and I.

5

45 Fail I alone, in words and deeds?
Why, all men strive and who succeeds?
We rode; it seemed my spirit flew,
Saw other regions, cities new,
    As the world rushed by on either side.
50 I thought,—All labour, yet no less
Bear up beneath their unsuccess.
Look at the end of work, contrast
The petty done, the undone vast,
This present of theirs with the hopeful past!
55   I hoped she would love me; here we ride.

6

What hand and brain went ever paired?
What heart alike conceived and dared?
What act proved all its thought had been?
What will but felt the fleshy screen?

60   We ride and I see her bosom heave.
    There's many a crown for who can reach.
    Ten lines, a statesman's life in each!
    The flag stuck on a heap of bones,
    A soldier's doing! what atones?
65   They scratch his name on the Abbey-stones.[1]
       My riding is better, by their leave.

7

    What does it all mean, poet? Well,
    Your brains beat into rhythm, you tell
    What we felt only; you expressed
70   You hold things beautiful the best,
       And pace them in rhyme so, side by side.
    'Tis something, nay 'tis much: but then,
    Have you yourself what's best for men?
    Are you—poor, sick, old ere your time—
75   Nearer one whit your own sublime
    Than we who never have turned a rhyme?
       Sing, riding's a joy! For me, I ride.

8

    And you, great sculptor—so, you gave
    A score of years to Art, her slave,
80   And that's your Venus, whence we turn
    To yonder girl that fords the burn!°   *crosses the stream*
       You acquiesce, and shall I repine?
    What, man of music, you grown grey
    With notes and nothing else to say,
85   Is this your sole praise from a friend,
    "Greatly his opera's strains intend,
    But in music we know how fashions end!"
       I gave my youth; but we ride, in fine.

9

    Who knows what's fit for us? Had fate
90   Proposed bliss here should sublimate°   *make sublime, exalt*
    My being—had I signed the bond—
    Still one must lead some life beyond,
       Have a bliss to die with, dim-descried.[2]
    This foot once planted on the goal,
95   This glory-garland round my soul,
    Could I descry such? Try and test!
    I sink back shuddering from the quest.
    Earth being so good, would heaven seem best?
       Now, heaven and she are beyond this ride.

---

1. Glorious human achievement ends in a ten-line bio-graphical summary, a memorial flag, or a tomb in West-minster Abbey.

2. At death one looks forward to heavenly bliss (whereas, had his earthly love been successful, he might have had nothing better to hope for in heaven).

10

100   And yet—she has not spoke so long
    What if heaven be that, fair and strong
    At life's best, with our eyes upturned
    Whither life's flower is first discerned,
        We, fixed so, ever should so abide?
105   What if we still ride on, we two
    With life for ever old yet new,
    Changed not in kind but in degree,
    The instant made eternity,—
    And heaven just prove that I and she
110   Ride, ride together, for ever ride?

1855

Andrea del Sarto[1]
(called "The Faultless Painter")

But do not let us quarrel any more,
No, my Lucrezia; bear with me for once:
Sit down and all shall happen as you wish.
You turn your face, but does it bring your heart?
5   I'll work then for your friend's friend, never fear,
Treat his own subject after his own way,
Fix his own time, accept too his own price,
And shut the money into this small hand
When next it takes mine. Will it? tenderly?
10   Oh, I'll content him,—but to-morrow, Love!
I often am much wearier than you think,
This evening more than usual, and it seems
As if—forgive now—should you let me sit
Here by the window with your hand in mine
15   And look a half-hour forth on Fiesole,[2]
Both of one mind, as married people use,
Quietly, quietly the evening through,
I might get up to-morrow to my work
Cheerful and fresh as ever. Let us try.
20   To-morrow, how you shall be glad for this!
Your soft hand is a woman of itself,
And mine the man's bared breast she curls inside.
Don't count the time lost, neither; you must serve
For each of the five pictures we require:
25   It saves a model. So! keep looking so—
My serpentining beauty, rounds on rounds!

---

1. Browning's depiction of Andrea del Sarto (1486–1531), a technically gifted Florentine Renaissance painter who never quite lived up to his early promise, is based in part on Giorgio Vasari's *The Lives of the Painters* (1550, 1568). Vasari, who had been Andrea's pupil, considered that "had his spirit been as bold as his judgment was profound, he would doubtless have been unequaled. But a timidity of spirit and a yielding simple nature prevented him from exhibiting a burning ardour and dash that, joined to his other qualities, would have made him divine."
2. A suburb of Florence.

—How could you ever prick those perfect ears,
Even to put the pearl there! oh, so sweet—
My face, my moon, my everybody's moon,
30   Which everybody looks on and calls his,
And, I suppose, is looked on by in turn,
While she looks—no one's: very dear, no less.
You smile? why, there's my picture ready made,
There's what we painters call our harmony!
35   A common greyness silvers everything,³—
All in a twilight, you and I alike
—You, at the point of your first pride in me
(That's gone you know),—but I, at every point;
My youth, my hope, my art, being all toned down
40   To yonder sober pleasant Fiesole.
There's the bell clinking from the chapel-top;
That length of convent-wall across the way
Holds the trees safer, huddled more inside;
The last monk leaves the garden; days decrease,
45   And autumn grows, autumn in everything.
Eh? the whole seems to fall into a shape
As if I saw alike my work and self
And all that I was born to be and do,
A twilight-piece. Love, we are in God's hand.
50   How strange now, looks the life he makes us lead;
So free we seem, so fettered fast we are!
I feel he laid the fetter: let it lie!
This chamber for example—turn your head—
All that's behind us! You don't understand
55   Nor care to understand about my art,
But you can hear at least when people speak:
And that cartoon,° the second from the door   *drawing*
—It is the thing, Love! so such things should be—
Behold Madonna!—I am bold to say.
60   I can do with my pencil what I know,
What I see, what at bottom of my heart
I wish for, if I ever wish so deep—
Do easily, too—what I say, perfectly,
I do not boast, perhaps: yourself are judge,
65   Who listened to the Legate's⁴ talk last week,
And just as much they used to say in France.
At any rate 'tis easy, all of it!
No sketches first, no studies, that's long past:
I do what many dream of, all their lives,
70   —Dream? strive to do, and agonize to do,
And fail in doing. I could count twenty such

3. The grey tones of Andrea del Sarto's paintings were re-garded in Browning's day as characteristic of his art (rather than the effect of fading and aging); the unusually muted rhythms of this poem attempt to convey the same qualities of restraint and understatement.
4. A representative of the Pope.

On twice your fingers, and not leave this town,
Who strive—you don't know how the others strive
To paint a little thing like that you smeared
75   Carelessly passing with your robes afloat,—
Yet do much less, so much less, Someone[5] says,
(I know his name, no matter)—so much less!
Well, less is more, Lucrezia: I am judged.
There burns a truer light of God in them,
80   In their vexed beating stuffed and stopped-up brain,
Heart, or whate'er else, than goes on to prompt
This low-pulsed forthright craftsman's hand of mine.
Their works drop groundward, but themselves, I know,
Reach many a time a heaven that's shut to me,
85   Enter and take their place there sure enough,
Though they come back and cannot tell the world.
My works are nearer heaven, but I sit here.
The sudden blood of these men! at a word—
Praise them, it boils, or blame them, it boils too.
90   I, painting from myself and to myself,
Know what I do, am unmoved by men's blame
Or their praise either. Somebody remarks
Morello's[6] outline there is wrongly traced,
His hue mistaken; what of that? or else,
95   Rightly traced and well ordered; what of that?
Speak as they please, what does the mountain care?
Ah, but a man's reach should exceed his grasp,
Or what's a heaven for? All is silver-grey
Placid and perfect with my art: the worse!
100   I know both what I want and what might gain,
And yet how profitless to know, to sigh
"Had I been two, another and myself,
Our head would have o'erlooked the world!" No doubt.
Yonder's a work now, of that famous youth
105   The Urbinate who died five years ago.[7]
('Tis copied, George Vasari sent it me.)
Well, I can fancy how he did it all,
Pouring his soul, with kings and popes to see,
Reaching, that heaven might so replenish him,
110   Above and through his art—for it gives way;
That arm is wrongly put—and there again—
A fault to pardon in the drawing's lines,
Its body, so to speak: its soul is right,
He means right—that, a child may understand.
115   Still, what an arm! and I could alter it:
But all the play, the insight and the stretch—

5. Probably Michelangelo.
6. A mountain near Florence.
7. Raphael (1483–1520) was born in Urbino. Thus the poem is set in 1525 (when, far from being in autumnal decline, Andrea was at the height of his powers).

Out of me, out of me! And wherefore out?
Had you enjoined them on me, given me soul,
We might have risen to Rafael, I and you!
120   Nay, Love, you did give all I asked, I think—
More than I merit, yes, by many times.
But had you—oh, with the same perfect brow,
And perfect eyes, and more than perfect mouth,
And the low voice my soul hears, as a bird
125   The fowler's pipe, and follows to the snare—
Had you, with these the same, but brought a mind!
Some women do so. Had the mouth there urged
"God and the glory! never care for gain.
The present by the future, what is that?
130   Live for fame, side by side with Agnolo![8]
Rafael is waiting: up to God, all three!"
I might have done it for you. So it seems:
Perhaps not. All is as God over-rules.
Beside, incentives come from the soul's self;
135   The rest avail not. Why do I need you?
What wife had Rafael, or has Agnolo?
In this world, who can do a thing, will not;
And who would do it, cannot, I perceive:
Yet the will's somewhat—somewhat, too, the power—
140   And thus we half-men struggle. At the end,
God, I conclude, compensates, punishes.
'Tis safer for me, if the award be strict,
That I am something underrated here,
Poor this long while, despised, to speak the truth.
145   I dared not, do you know, leave home all day,
For fear of chancing on the Paris lords.[9]
The best is when they pass and look aside;
But they speak sometimes; I must bear it all.
Well may they speak! That Francis, that first time,
150   And that long festal year at Fontainebleau!
I surely then could sometimes leave the ground,
Put on the glory, Rafael's daily wear,
In that humane great monarch's golden look,—
One finger in his beard or twisted curl
155   Over his mouth's good mark that made the smile,
One arm about my shoulder, round my neck,
The jingle of his gold chain in my ear,
I painting proudly with his breath on me,
All his court round him, seeing with his eyes,
160   Such frank French eyes, and such a fire of souls

8. Michelangelo (Michel Agnolo Buonarroti), Italian painter (1475–1564).
9. In 1518 Andrea was invited to Fontainebleau by the French king, Francis I, who became his patron. Rumor had it that when he left the court to return to Italy, the king entrusted him with funds, which he spent on a house for Lucrezia. Now he is ashamed to face the scorn of visiting French nobles.

Profuse, my hand kept plying by those hearts,—
And, best of all, this, this, this face beyond,
This in the background, waiting on my work,
To crown the issue with a last reward!

165 A good time, was it not, my kingly days?
And had you not grown restless . . . but I know—
'Tis done and past; 'twas right, my instinct said;
Too live the life grew, golden and not grey,
And I'm the weak-eyed bat no sun should tempt

170 Out of the grange whose four walls make his world.
How could it end in any other way?
You called me, and I came home to your heart.
The triumph was—to reach and stay there; since
I reached it ere the triumph, what is lost?

175 Let my hands frame your face in your hair's gold,
You beautiful Lucrezia that are mine!
"Rafael did this, Andrea painted that;
The Roman's[1] is the better when you pray,
But still the other's Virgin was his wife—"

180 Men will excuse me. I am glad to judge
Both pictures in your presence; clearer grows
My better fortune, I resolve to think.
For, do you know, Lucrezia, as God lives,
Said one day Agnolo, his very self,

185 To Rafael . . . I have known it all these years . . .
(When the young man was flaming out his thoughts
Upon a palace-wall for Rome to see,
Too lifted up in heart because of it)
"Friend, there's a certain sorry little scrub[2]

190 Goes up and down our Florence, none cares how,
Who, were he set to plan and execute
As you are, pricked on by your popes and kings,
Would bring the sweat into that brow of yours!"
To Rafael's!—And indeed the arm is wrong.

195 I hardly dare . . . yet, only you to see,
Give the chalk here—quick, thus the line should go!
Ay, but the soul! he's Rafael! rub it out!
Still, all I care for, if he spoke the truth,
(What he? why, who but Michel Agnolo?

200 Do you forget already words like those?)[3]
If really there was such a chance, so lost,—
Is, whether you're—not grateful—but more pleased.
Well, let me think so. And you smile indeed!
This hour has been an hour! Another smile?

205 If you would sit thus by me every night
I should work better, do you comprehend?

---

1. Raphael worked in Rome after 1509.
2. I.e., Andrea, who is boasting to Lucrezia that

Michelangelo once praised his abilities to Raphael.
3. Lucrezia, bored, has lost the thread of Andrea's story.

I mean that I should earn more, give you more.
See, it is settled dusk now; there's a star;
Morello's gone, the watch-lights show the wall,
210   The cue-owls[4] speak the name we call them by.
Come from the window, love,—come in, at last,
Inside the melancholy little house
We built to be so gay with. God is just.
King Francis may forgive me: oft at nights
215   When I look up from painting, eyes tired out,
The walls become illumined, brick from brick
Distinct, instead of mortar, fierce bright gold,
That gold of his I did cement them with!
Let us but love each other. Must you go?
220   That Cousin here again?[5] he waits outside?
Must see you—you, and not with me? Those loans?
More gaming debts to pay? you smiled for that?
Well, let smiles buy me! have you more to spend?
While hand and eye and something of a heart
225   Are left me, work's my ware, and what's it worth?
I'll pay my fancy. Only let me sit
The grey remainder of the evening out,
Idle, you call it, and muse perfectly
How I could paint, were I but back in France,
230   One picture, just one more—the Virgin's face,
Not yours this time! I want you at my side
To hear them—that is, Michel Agnolo—
Judge all I do and tell you of its worth.
Will you? To-morrow, satisfy your friend.
235   I take the subjects for his corridor,
Finish the portrait out of hand—there, there,
And throw him in another thing or two
If he demurs; the whole should prove enough
To pay for this same Cousin's freak. Beside,
240   What's better and what's all I care about,
Get you the thirteen scudi° for the ruff!   *coins*
Love, does that please you? Ah, but what does he,
The Cousin! what does he to please you more?

I am grown peaceful as old age to-night.
245   I regret little, I would change still less.
Since there my past life lies, why alter it?
The very wrong to Francis!—it is true
I took his coin, was tempted and complied,
And built this house and sinned, and all is said.
250   My father and my mother died of want.[6]
Well, had I riches of my own? you see

4. Owls whose cry sounds like the Italian word *ciù*.
5. Lucrezia's lover, whose gambling debts Andrea has already agreed to pay (lines 5–10).

6. Vasari claimed that Andrea abandoned his aged parents and spent his money on Lucrezia and her family.

How one gets rich! Let each one bear his lot.
They were born poor, lived poor, and poor they died:
And I have laboured somewhat in my time
255 And not been paid profusely. Some good son
Paint my two hundred pictures—let him try!
No doubt, there's something strikes a balance. Yes,
You loved me quite enough, it seems to-night.
This must suffice me here. What would one have?
260 In heaven, perhaps, new chances, one more chance—
Four great walls in the New Jerusalem,[7]
Meted° on each side by the angel's reed,   *measured*
For Leonard,[8] Rafael, Agnolo and me
To cover—the three first without a wife,
265 While I have mine! So—still they overcome
Because there's still Lucrezia,—as I choose.

Again the Cousin's whistle! Go, my Love.
c. 1853   1855

Two in the Campagna[1]

1

I wonder do you feel to-day
    As I have felt since, hand in hand,
We sat down on the grass, to stray
    In spirit better through the land,
5 This morn of Rome and May?

2

For me, I touched a thought, I know,
    Has tantalized me many times,
(Like turns of thread the spiders throw
    Mocking across our path) for rhymes
10 To catch at and let go.

3

Help me to hold it! First it left
    The yellowing fennel, run to seed
There, branching from the brickwork's cleft,
    Some old tomb's ruin: yonder weed
15 Took up the floating weft,°   *weaving threads*

4

Where one small orange cup amassed
    Five beetles,—blind and green they grope
Among the honey-meal: and last,
    Everywhere on the grassy slope
20 I traced it. Hold it fast!

7. Cf. Revelation 21.10–21.
8. Leonardo da Vinci (1452–1519), third in the trio of great Italian Renaissance artists whom del Sarto has failed to equal.
1. The countryside around Rome, a plain dotted with ancient ruins.

5

The champaign° with its endless fleece   *countryside*
    Of feathery grasses everywhere!
Silence and passion, joy and peace,
    An everlasting wash of air—
25   Rome's ghost since her decease.

6

Such life here, through such lengths of hours,
    Such miracles performed in play,
Such primal naked forms of flowers,
    Such letting nature have her way
30   While heaven looks from its towers!

7

How say you? Let us, O my dove,
    Let us be unashamed of soul,
As earth lies bare to heaven above!
    How is it under our control
35   To love or not to love?

8

I would that you were all to me,
    You that are just so much, no more.
Nor yours nor mine, nor slave nor free!
    Where does the fault lie? What the core
40   O' the wound, since wound must be?

9

I would I could adopt your will,
    See with your eyes, and set my heart
Beating by yours, and drink my fill
    At your soul's springs,—your part my part
45   In life, for good and ill.

10

No. I yearn upward, touch you close,
    Then stand away. I kiss your cheek,
Catch your soul's warmth,—I pluck the rose
    And love it more than tongue can speak—
50   Then the good minute goes.

11

Already how am I so far
    Out of that minute? Must I go
Still like the thistle-ball, no bar,
    Onward, whenever light winds blow
55   Fixed by no friendly star?

12

Just when I seemed about to learn!
    Where is the thread now? Off again!

The old trick! Only I discern—
    Infinite passion, and the pain
60   Of finite hearts that yearn.

1854   1855

A Woman's Last Word[1]

1

Let's contend no more, Love,
    Strive nor weep:
All be as before, Love,
    —Only sleep!

2

5   What so wild as words are?
    I and thou
In debate, as birds are,
    Hawk on bough![2]

3

See the creature stalking
10   While we speak!
Hush and hide the talking,
    Cheek on cheek!

4

What so false as truth is,
    False to thee?
15   Where the serpent's tooth is
    Shun the tree—

5

Where the apple reddens
    Never pry—
Lest we lose our Edens,
20   Eve and I.

6

Be a god and hold me
    With a charm!
Be a man and fold me
    With thine arm!

7

25   Teach me, only teach, Love!
    As I ought
I will speak thy speech, Love,
    Think thy thought—

1. The title refers to the notion that a woman always has the last word in a quarrel.

2. As birds are threatened with destruction by a hawk, so their love is threatened by the violence of their words.

8

Meet, if thou require it,
30   Both demands,
Laying flesh and spirit
          In thy hands.

9

That shall be to-morrow
          Not to-night:
35   I must bury sorrow
          Out of sight:

10

—Must a little weep, Love,
          (Foolish me!)
And so fall asleep, Love,
40   Loved by thee.

1855

Caliban Upon Setebos[1]
Or Natural Theology[2] in the Island

"Thou thoughtest that I was altogether such a one as thyself."[3]

['Will sprawl, now that the heat of day is best,
Flat on his belly in the pit's much mire,
With elbows wide, fists clenched to prop his chin.
And, while he kicks both feet in the cool slush,
5   And feels about his spine small eft-things° course,   lizards
Run in and out each arm, and make him laugh:
And while above his head a pompion-plant,°   pumpkin plant
Coating the cave-top as a brow its eye,
Creeps down to touch and tickle hair and beard,
10   And now a flower drops with a bee inside,
And now a fruit to snap at, catch and crunch,—
He looks out o'er yon sea which sunbeams cross
And recross till they weave a spider-web
(Meshes of fire, some great fish breaks at times)
15   And talks to his own self, howe'er he please,

---

1. Caliban is the "monster" in Shakespeare's *Tempest*. A native of the island on which Prospero and his daughter Miranda have been shipwrecked, he is compelled by Prospero's magic powers and authority to do his drudgework. Setebos is his deity, and the poem is his meditation "upon" his god, whom he imagines in terms strictly limited to his own small world and his own primitive emotional state. He assumes Setebos must be like himself: petty, jealous, willful, at times cruel in his random exercise of power. Fearful of being overheard and punished, Caliban hopes to fool Setebos by referring to himself in the third person, "he" (a capitalized "He" refers to Sete-

bos). The poem evokes both ongoing theological debates about the nature of God and the meaning of suffering, and more specifically Victorian concerns about evolution: the nature of the human species, our origins, and our relationship to other animals. The first 23 lines are in brackets, suggesting that Caliban is musing to himself, rather than speaking aloud.
2. Knowledge of God based on natural evidence rather than the evidence of divine revelation.
3. In Psalm 50.21 God addresses these words to the wicked.

Touching that other, whom his dam[4] called God.
Because to talk about Him, vexes—ha,
Could He but know! and time to vex is now,
When talk is safer than in winter-time.
20 Moreover Prosper and Miranda sleep
In confidence he drudges at their task,
And it is good to cheat the pair, and gibe,
Letting the rank tongue blossom into speech.]

Setebos, Setebos, and Setebos!
25 'Thinketh, He dwelleth i' the cold o' the moon.

'Thinketh He made it, with the sun to match,
But not the stars; the stars came otherwise;
Only made clouds, winds, meteors, such as that:
Also this isle, what lives and grows thereon,
30 And snaky sea which rounds and ends the same.

'Thinketh, it came of being ill at ease:
He hated that He cannot change His cold,
Nor cure its ache. 'Hath spied an icy fish
That longed to 'scape the rock-stream where she lived,
35 And thaw herself within the lukewarm brine
O' the lazy sea her stream thrusts far amid,
A crystal spike 'twixt two warm walls of wave;
Only, she ever sickened, found repulse
At the other kind of water, not her life,
40 (Green-dense and dim-delicious, bred o' the sun)
Flounced back from bliss she was not born to breathe,
And in her old bounds buried her despair,
Hating and loving warmth alike: so He.

'Thinketh, He made thereat the sun, this isle,
45 Trees and the fowls here, beast and creeping thing.
Yon otter, sleek-wet, black, lithe as a leech;
Yon auk,° one fire-eye in a ball of foam,   *sea bird*
That floats and feeds; a certain badger brown
He hath watched hunt with that slant white-wedge eye
50 By moonlight; and the pie° with the long tongue   *magpie*
That pricks deep into oakwarts for a worm,
And says a plain word when she finds her prize,
But will not eat the ants; the ants themselves
That build a wall of seeds and settled stalks
55 About their hole—He made all these and more,
Made all we see, and us, in spite: how else?
He could not, Himself, make a second self
To be His mate; as well have made Himself:
He would not make what he mislikes or slights,

---

4. His mother, the witch Sycorax, who worships Setebos.

60 An eyesore to Him, or not worth His pains:
    But did, in envy, listlessness or sport,
    Make what Himself would fain, in a manner, be—
    Weaker in most points, stronger in a few,
    Worthy, and yet mere playthings all the while,
65 Things He admires and mocks too,—that is it.
    Because, so brave, so better though they be,
    It nothing skills if He begin to plague.[5]
    Look now, I melt a gourd-fruit into mash,
    Add honeycomb and pods, I have perceived,
70 Which bite like finches when they bill and kiss,—
    Then, when froth rises bladdery,° drink up all,   bubbly
    Quick, quick, till maggots scamper through my brain;
    Last, throw me on my back i' the seeded thyme,
    And wanton, wishing I were born a bird.
75 Put case, unable to be what I wish,
    I yet could make a live bird out of clay:
    Would not I take clay, pinch my Caliban
    Able to fly?—for, there, see, he hath wings,
    And great comb like the hoopoe's[6] to admire,
80 And there, a sting to do his foes offence,
    There, and I will that he begin to live,
    Fly to yon rock-top, nip me off the horns
    Of grigs° high up that make the merry din,   crickets
    Saucy through their veined wings, and mind me not.
85 In which feat, if his leg snapped, brittle clay,
    And he lay stupid-like,—why, I should laugh;
    And if he, spying me, should fall to weep,
    Beseech me to be good, repair his wrong,
    Bid his poor leg smart less or grow again,—
90 Well, as the chance were, this might take or else
    Not take my fancy: I might hear his cry,
    And give the mankin three sound legs for one,
    Or pluck the other off, leave him like an egg,
    And lessoned he was mine and merely clay.
95 Were this no pleasure, lying in the thyme,
    Drinking the mash, with brain become alive,
    Making and marring clay at will? So He.

    'Thinketh, such shows nor right nor wrong in Him,
    Nor kind, nor cruel: He is strong and Lord.
100 'Am strong myself compared to yonder crabs
    That march now from the mountain to the sea,
    'Let twenty pass, and stone the twenty-first,
    Loving not, hating not, just choosing so.
    'Say, the first straggler that boasts purple spots

---

5. Strength and bravery are useless if God decides to   6. A brightly plumed tropical bird.
plague His creatures.

105   Shall join the file, one pincer twisted off;
        'Say, this bruised fellow shall receive a worm,
        And two worms he whose nippers end in red;
        As it likes me each time, I do: so He.[7]

        Well then, 'supposeth He is good i' the main,
110   Placable if His mind and ways were guessed,
        But rougher than His handiwork, be sure!
        Oh, He hath made things worthier than Himself,
        And envieth that, so helped, such things do more
        Than He who made them! What consoles but this?
115   That they, unless through Him, do nought at all,
        And must submit: what other use in things?
        'Hath cut a pipe of pithless elder joint
        That, blown through, gives exact the scream o' the jay
        When from her wing you twitch the feathers blue:
120   Sound this, and little birds that hate the jay
        Flock within stone's throw, glad their foe is hurt:
        Put case such pipe could prattle and boast forsooth
        "I catch the birds, I am the crafty thing,
        I make the cry my maker cannot make
125   With his great round mouth; he must blow through mine!"
        Would not I smash it with my foot? So He.

        But wherefore rough, why cold and ill at ease?
        Aha, that is a question! Ask, for that,
        What knows,—the something over Setebos
130   That made Him, or He, may be, found and fought,
        Worsted, drove off and did to nothing,° perchance.   *destroyed*
        There may be something quiet o'er His head,
        Out of His reach, that feels nor joy nor grief,
        Since both derive from weakness in some way.
135   I joy because the quails come; would not joy
        Could I bring quails here when I have a mind:
        This Quiet, all it hath a mind to, doth.
        'Esteemeth stars the outposts of its couch,
        But never spends much thought nor care that way.
140   It may look up, work up,—the worse for those
        It works on! 'Careth but for Setebos[8]
        The many-handed as a cuttle-fish,
        Who, making Himself feared through what He does,
        Looks up, first, and perceives he cannot soar
145   To what is quiet and hath happy life;
        Next looks down here, and out of very spite
        Makes this a bauble-world to ape yon real,

---

7. Caliban's notion of God's arbitrary rewards and punishments resembles Calvinist doctrines of predestination, the belief that God has preordained certain souls for salvation.

8. Caliban will worship only Setebos, and not "the Quiet" that he imagines may have created Setebos.

These good things to match those as hips[9] do grapes.
'Tis solace making baubles, ay, and sport.

150   Himself peeped late, eyed Prosper at his books
Careless and lofty, lord now of the isle:
Vexed, 'stitched a book of broad leaves, arrow-shaped,
Wrote thereon, he knows what, prodigious words;
Has peeled a wand and called it by a name;

155   Weareth at whiles for an enchanter's robe
The eyed skin of a supple oncelot;°   *ocelot*
And hath an ounce° sleeker than youngling mole,   *leopard*
A four-legged serpent he makes cower and couch,
Now snarl, now hold its breath and mind his eye.

160   And saith she is Miranda and my wife:
'Keeps for his Ariel[1] a tall pouch-bill crane
He bids go wade for fish and straight disgorge;
Also a sea-beast, lumpish, which he snared,
Blinded the eyes of, and brought somewhat tame,

165   And split its toe-webs, and now pens the drudge
In a hole o' the rock and calls him Caliban;
A bitter heart that bides its time and bites.
'Plays thus at being Prosper in a way,
Taketh his mirth with make-believes: so He.

170   His dam held that the Quiet made all things
Which Setebos vexed only: 'holds not so.
Who made them weak, meant weakness He might vex.
Had He meant other, while His hand was in,
Why not make horny eyes no thorn could prick,

175   Or plate my scalp with bone against the snow,
Or overscale my flesh 'neath joint and joint,
Like an orc's[2] armour? Ay,—so spoil His sport!
He is the One now: only He doth all.
'Saith, He may like, perchance, what profits Him.

180   Ay, himself loves what does him good; but why?
'Gets good no otherwise. This blinded beast
Loves whoso places flesh-meat on his nose,
But, had he eyes, would want no help, but hate
Or love, just as it liked him: He hath eyes.

185   Also it pleaseth Setebos to work,
Use all His hands, and exercise much craft,
By no means for the love of what is worked.
'Tasteth, himself, no finer good i' the world
When all goes right, in this safe summer-time,

190   And he wants little, hungers, aches not much,
Than trying what to do with wit and strength.
'Falls to make something: 'piled yon pile of turfs,

---

9. Rosehips are the hard, inedible fruit of wild roses.   2. Orca, killer whale.
1. Ariel is a clever island spirit who serves Prospero.

And squared and stuck there squares of soft white chalk,
And, with a fish-tooth, scratched a moon on each,
195   And set up endwise certain spikes of tree,
And crowned the whole with a sloth's skull a-top,
Found dead i' the woods, too hard for one to kill.
No use at all i' the work, for work's sole sake;
'Shall some day knock it down again: so He.

200   'Saith He is terrible: watch His feats in proof!
One hurricane will spoil six good months' hope.
He hath a spite against me, that I know,
Just as He favours Prosper, who knows why?
So it is, all the same, as well I find.
205   'Wove wattles³ half the winter, fenced them firm
With stone and stake to stop she-tortoises
Crawling to lay their eggs here: well, one wave,
Feeling the foot of Him upon its neck,
Gaped as a snake does, lolled out its large tongue,
210   And licked the whole labour flat: so much for spite.
'Saw a ball flame down late⁴ (yonder it lies)
Where, half an hour before, I slept i' the shade:
Often they scatter sparkles: there is force!
'Dug up a newt He may have envied once
215   And turned to stone, shut up inside a stone.
Please Him and hinder this?—What Prosper does?⁵
Aha, if He would tell me how! Not He!
There is the sport: discover how or die!
All need not die, for of the things o' the isle
220   Some flee afar, some dive, some run up trees;
Those at His mercy,—why, they please Him most
When . . . when . . . well, never try the same way twice!
Repeat what act has pleased, He may grow wroth.
You must not know His ways, and play Him off,
225   Sure of the issue. 'Doth the like himself:
'Spareth a squirrel that it nothing fears
But steals the nut from underneath my thumb,
And when I threat, bites stoutly in defence:
'Spareth an urchin° that contrariwise,   hedgehog
230   Curls up into a ball, pretending death
For fright at my approach: the two ways please.
But what would move my choler° more than this,   rage
That either creature counted on its life
To-morrow and next day and all days to come,
235   Saying, forsooth, in the inmost of its heart,
"Because he did so yesterday with me,
And otherwise with such another brute,

---

3. Twigs woven to construct a barrier or shelter.   5. I.e., shall I try to imitate Prospero in pleasing Serebos,
4. I saw a meteorite fall recently.   and thus avoid the newt's fate?

So must he do henceforth and always."—Ay?
Would teach the reasoning couple what "must" means!
240   'Doth as he likes, or wherefore Lord? So He.

'Conceiveth all things will continue thus,
And we shall have to live in fear of Him
So long as He lives, keeps His strength: no change,
If He have done His best, make no new world
245   To please Him more, so leave off watching this,—
If He surprise not even the Quiet's self
Some strange day,—or, suppose, grow into it
As grubs grow butterflies: else, here are we,
And there is He, and nowhere help at all.

250   'Believeth with the life, the pain shall stop.
His dam held different, that after death
He both plagued enemies and feasted friends:[6]
Idly! He doth His worst in this our life,
Giving just respite lest we die through pain,
255   Saving last pain for worst,—with which, an end.
Meanwhile, the best way to escape His ire
Is, not to seem too happy. 'Sees, himself,
Yonder two flies, with purple films and pink,
Bask on the pompion-bell above: kills both.
260   'Sees two black painful beetles roll their ball
On head and tail as if to save their lives:
Moves them the stick away they strive to clear.

Even so, 'would have Him misconceive, suppose
This Caliban strives hard and ails no less,
265   And always, above all else, envies Him;
Wherefore he mainly dances on dark nights,
Moans in the sun, gets under holes to laugh,
And never speaks his mind save housed as now:
Outside, 'groans, curses. If He caught me here,
270   O'erheard this speech, and asked "What chucklest at?"
'Would, to appease Him, cut a finger off,
Or of my three kid yearlings burn the best,
Or let the toothsome apples rot on tree,
Or push my tame beast for the orc to taste:
275   While myself lit a fire, and made a song
And sung it, "What I hate, be consecrate
To celebrate Thee and Thy state, no mate
For Thee; what see for envy in poor me?"
Hoping the while, since evils sometimes mend,
280   Warts rub away and sores are cured with slime,

6. Caliban believes there is no life after death, but Sycorax thought there would be punishment for some, reward for others.

That some strange day, will either the Quiet catch
And conquer Setebos, or likelier He
Decrepit may doze, doze, as good as die.

285 [What, what? A curtain o'er the world at once!
Crickets stop hissing; not a bird—or, yes,
There scuds His raven that has told Him all!
It was fool's play, this prattling! Ha! The wind
Shoulders the pillared dust, death's house o' the move,
And fast invading fires begin![7] White blaze—
290 A tree's head snaps—and there, there, there, there, there
His thunder follows! Fool to gibe at Him!
Lo! 'Lieth flat and loveth Setebos!
'Maketh his teeth meet through his upper lip,
Will let those quails fly, will not eat this month
295 One little mess of whelks,° so he may 'scape!]   *shellfish*
1859–1860   1864

Epilogue to *Asolando*[1]

At the midnight in the silence of the sleep-time,
    When you set your fancies free,
Will they pass to where—by death, fools think, imprisoned—
Low he lies who once so loved you, whom you loved so,
5   —Pity me?

Oh to love so, be so loved, yet so mistaken!
    What had I on earth to do
With the slothful, with the mawkish, the unmanly?
Like the aimless, helpless, hopeless, did I drivel
10   —Being—who?

One who never turned his back but marched breast forward,
    Never doubted clouds would break,
Never dreamed, though right were worsted, wrong would triumph,
Held we fall to rise, are baffled to fight better,
15   Sleep to wake.

No, at noonday in the bustle of man's work-time
    Greet the unseen[2] with a cheer!
Bid him forward, breast and back as either should be,
"Strive and thrive!" cry "Speed,°—fight on, fare ever   *Godspeed*
20   There as here!"
c. 1889   1889

---

7. Caliban thinks Setebos has heard his blasphemy and is
sending the approaching thunderstorm to punish him.
1. *Asolando* was Browning's last book, published in London on the same day he died at his son's house in Venice.
Asolo is a village near Venice that Browning had loved

for 50 years; it is the setting of his early poem, *Pippa
Passes* (1841). The poem is addressed to a loved one who
survives the speaker.
2. The speaker, once he is dead.

━━ ≒◆≒ ━━

Charles Dickens

1812–1870

Charles Dickens was the most popular novelist of his century. Anthony Trollope observed that Dickens's works could be found "in every house in which books are kept." He published his novels in monthly or weekly parts, and whole families would gather in suspense to hear a newly published episode read aloud. He was equally renowned in America: a ship arriving in New York from England was mobbed by crowds frantic to learn whether one of his characters, Little Nell, had died.

Dickens's own story was like a rags-to-riches fairy tale. His parents were lower-middle class, precariously clinging to gentility as they drifted downward into poverty. As a boy he was sent to school and taken to the theater; he read voraciously and amused himself by impersonating his favorite characters: "I have been Tom Jones . . . for a week together. I have sustained my own idea of Roderick Random for a month at a stretch."

But before Dickens was twelve, family fortunes took a turn for the worse. He was taken out of school and later sent to work for six months beside common laboring boys in a warehouse. For the rest of his life he would wonder bitterly "how I could have been so easily cast away at such an age." Many years later he wrote: "No words can express the secret agony of my soul as I sunk into this companionship; compared these every day associates with those of my happier childhood; and felt my early hopes of growing up to be a learned and distinguished man, crushed in my breast."

As if this were not dreadful enough, his father was arrested for debt and thrown into the Marshalsea debtors' prison, where his wife and younger children soon joined him. The twelve-year-old Charles was left to fend for himself. Even after his father was released, Charles's mother opposed his decision to take the boy away from the factory: "I never afterwards forgot, I never shall forget, I never can forget, that my mother was warm for my being sent back."

Dickens went on to become England's most celebrated novelist, but no achievements could erase the terrible memory of shame: "My whole nature was so penetrated with the grief and humiliation . . . that even now, famous and caressed and happy, I often forget in my dreams that I have a dear wife and children; even that I am a man; and wander desolately back to that time of my life." The traumatic recollections of his family's disgrace and his own abandonment motivated both his intense ambition for success and also his lifelong sympathy with suffering children.

As a young man, Dickens became a parliamentary reporter, then began writing. First *Sketches by Boz* (1836–1837) appeared, then *Pickwick Papers* (1836–1837), using the method of serial publication that he would continue with all his novels. Pickwick-mania suddenly swept the nation as readers of all classes were captivated by Dickens's humor.

In the next five years Dickens—still only in his twenties—produced four more long novels: *Oliver Twist* (1837–1839), *Nicholas Nickleby* (1838–1839), *The Old Curiosity Shop* (1840–1841), and *Barnaby Rudge* (1841). These early novels satirize the cruelties of workhouses and orphanages, bad schools, inhuman factories, and hideous slums. They reflect Dickens's growing compassion for orphans, outcasts, and the afflicted, and his outrage at the hypocrisies of a society that exploited them. Some readers missed the merry fun of Pickwick, but most welcomed his new earnestness. *The Old Curiosity Shop* in particular was a triumph, a runaway bestseller of over a hundred thousand copies.

In 1842 Dickens embarked on a trip to America, where he was given a hero's welcome. Bursting with enthusiasm for the young democracy, he was soon disillusioned, for when he complained about the pirating of his books (foreign authors did not have copyright protection in the United States until 1891), American newspapers attacked him as greedy. They were even more offended by *American Notes* (1842): far from lauding American landscapes and public institutions, Dickens's account of his travels focused obsessively on prisons and lunatic asylums. His moral crusading on behalf of the poor, the insane, and the imprisoned struck readers as a boorish affront to national honor. His next novel, *Martin Chuzzlewit* (1843–1844), set partially in America, did not mend matters; in fact, it was his first experience of failure.

Dickens was alarmed to realize that the public's love affair with his novels was at a low ebb, but he wooed them afresh with *A Christmas Carol* (1843). This parable of redemption and metamorphosis is one of Dickens's most representative works. The story of Scrooge, the cantankerous old miser who repents, dramatizes the fundamental Dickensian theme of rebirth. Scrooge's selfishness and coldness anticipate a host of later characters with frozen hearts. Scrooge's recollections of his unloved boyhood evoke Dickens's own past and illustrate his preoccupation with the insidious effects of a warped childhood.

These concerns pervaded Dickens's subsequent novels: in *Dombey and Son* (1846–1848) Mr. Dombey stonily spurns his daughter's love. The hero of *David Copperfield* (1849–1850) is maltreated by a repressive stepfather, then shipped off to a harsh boarding school. *Bleak House* (1852–1853) is full of unwanted orphans, including the illegitimate Esther and the illiterate Jo. In *Hard Times* (1854) the children are oppressed by a grinding system of education, and in *Little Dorrit* (1855–1857) the protagonist's childhood has been stunted by a narrow system of religion.

Dickens's extraordinary productivity was matched by his prodigious energy. In addition to writing one massive novel after another, he was actively involved in public affairs and charitable projects, including a home for "fallen women." In 1850 he founded *Household Words*, a weekly magazine later incorporated into *All the Year Round*, which he edited until his death. He serialized three of his novels in these periodicals, and contributed frequent essays. His exuberant vitality also found outlet in the theater; he loved performing in amateur theatricals and, later on, giving readings of his own works. An actor at heart, Dickens revelled in the applause and admiration of an audience.

Even amid these successes, Dickens kept returning to the theme of imprisonment: in *Little Dorrit* the Marshalsea debtors' prison in London had been the dominant setting; in *A Tale of Two Cities* (1859) it is the French Bastille. In *Great Expectations* (1860–1861) an escaped convict turns out to be the hidden agent behind the hero's transformation into a gentleman. In Dickens's last completed novel, *Our Mutual Friend* (1864–1865), the Thames becomes a river of the dead where outcasts scrounge a living by pickpocketing drowned bodies: "I can't get away from it," says the daughter of one of these river rats.

As these grim images suggest, there was a darker side to Dickens's art. Despite his flourishing career and convivial nature, Dickens felt a lifelong sense of restlessness and loss, of some "happiness I have missed in life." His unsatisfying marriage gradually came to seem claustrophobic, and Dickens's decision in 1858 to separate from his wife, after ten children and more than two decades together, did considerable harm to his reputation. Flamboyant and charming, Dickens was also emotionally insecure. In his later years he wore himself out with an arduous round of public readings, courting audiences nightly by bringing his famous characters to life on stage. Exhausted from his unceasing activities, Dickens collapsed and died while still at work on his last novel, *The Mystery of Edwin Drood* (1870). He was only fifty-eight. From America Longfellow wrote: "I never knew an author's death to cause such general mourning. It is no exaggeration to say that this whole country is stricken with grief."

Contemporary readers, associating Dickens with jollity, were sometimes alienated by his indignation about the human costs of industrialism and materialism. His attack on the complacent brutality of laissez-faire capitalism in *Hard Times* irritated conservatives, as did his portrayal of Sir Leicester Dedlock, a doddering aristocrat, in *Bleak House*. Meanwhile, the liberal John Stuart Mill—author of *The Subjection of Women*—was annoyed by Mrs. Jellyby, Dickens's satirical portrait of a woman who neglects her home and family to devote herself to philanthropic causes.

But Dickens's comic genius always enabled him to combine serious themes with laughter. His novels are populated with an extraordinary gallery of peculiar characters, whose names—

Scrooge, Gradgrind, Uriah Heep, Mr Micawber, Oliver Twist, Fagin—have become part of the language. Dickens delighted in the absurd, but he was also an astute observer of human nature, and he insisted that his memorable eccentrics were true to life: "Mrs Nickleby herself, sitting bodily before me in a solid chair, once asked me whether I believed there ever was such a woman." Keenly aware of how figures of speech pervade everyday language, Dickens gloried in flights of linguistic fancy: literalizing metaphors, personifying inanimate objects, turning people into their possessions, and using verbal ticks to limn a character or construct a scene. This attention to how language creates and reveals personality not only made Dickens a brilliant comic novelist; it also, especially in his later novels, helped him probe the darker sides of human nature with the psychological acuity of one of his fans, Sigmund Freud.

Later generations of readers have sometimes found Dickens's sentimentality hard to take: Oscar Wilde said that "one must have a heart of stone to read the death of Little Nell without laughing." But they have also been fascinated by Dickens's deftly elaborated symbolism. Almost all his works are permeated by a dominant symbol-system (railways in *Dombey and Son*, prisons in *Little Dorrit*, dustheaps in *Our Mutual Friend*) that helped him establish thematic unity among the monthly installments. With an inventiveness of character and density of imagery equaled only by Shakespeare, Dickens worked out in astonishing detail the complex connections binding members of a society to their environment, to their institutions, and to each other. He is the quintessential urban novelist: his mythic vision of Victorian London is so intense, surprising, and phantasmagoric that the fractured, paranoid modernist landscapes of Conrad, T. S. Eliot, Joyce, and Woolf all seem to have originated with Dickens.

Additional works by Dickens are included in Perspectives: The Industrial Landscape, page 1137, and Perspectives: Religion and Science, page 1376.

For additional resources on Dickens, go to *The Longman Anthology of British Literature* Web site at www.ablongman.com/damroschbritlit3e.

A CHRISTMAS CAROL   An instant success when it was first published in December 1843, *A Christmas Carol* is still the best-known work of Victorian short fiction. Thackeray called it "a national benefit" and noted that it provoked such an outpouring of Yuletide conviviality that "had the book appeared a fortnight earlier all the prize cattle would have been gobbled up in pure love and friendship, Epping denuded of sausages, and not a turkey left in Norfolk." Even before Dickens gave his tour-de-force readings of the story, pirated productions filled the stages and bookstalls. Its overwhelming popularity has turned this fable of moral metamorphosis into a cultural icon.

But *A Christmas Carol* is not all holiday cheer. Near its beginning Ebenezer Scrooge brusquely refuses to contribute to charity: "Are there no prisons?" he asks. Dickens is satirizing his society's harsh treatment of the indigent; as the Poor Law of 1834 had established, paupers were little better than criminals, to be incarcerated in workhouses for the crime of poverty. Echoing Thomas Malthus, the grim analyst of overpopulation, Scrooge says that if the poor would rather die than subsist in workhouses, "they had better do it, and decrease the surplus population."

Like Carlyle's *Past and Present*, published earlier in 1843, *A Christmas Carol* is in part a response to the Hungry Forties, a period of high unemployment and suffering among factory workers. Both Dickens and Carlyle expose the brutality of laissez-faire capitalism, where profit is the only goal, and employers and employees are united by nothing except the "cash nexus." Scrooge's gradual awakening to a more generous sense of responsibility toward his dependents and fellow beings illustrates the redemptive power of imaginative sympathy.

A Christmas Carol is a story of catharsis and renewal, of a crabbed old miser who miraculously gets a second chance at life. His change of heart is brought about by ghostly visitors who lead him on a tour of his past: Scrooge pities his own solitary boyhood, delights in recalling Ali Baba and Robinson Crusoe, and grieves for his dead sister and lost love. These dream visions offer insight into the psychological sources of Scrooge's monstrous egotism, and the similarities to Dickens's own childhood suggest an autobiographical identification with his character. By recovering his past, Scrooge recovers his humanity.

A Christmas Carol is thus both an allegory of social responsibility and a fable of individual transformation through symbolic rebirth. Beside himself with joy, Scrooge splutters "I'm quite a baby. Never mind. I don't care. I'd rather be a baby." Like Wordsworth and Blake, Dickens explores the nature of memory and childhood, innocence and experience, exalting the power of the imagination to transcend a fallen world. But he situates these archetypal themes in a classically Dickensian fairy-tale universe, where inanimate objects, from bedposts to buildings, come to life and the supernatural permeates the prosaic.

A Christmas Carol
Stave One
MARLEY'S GHOST

Marley was dead: to begin with. There is no doubt whatever about that. The register of his burial was signed by the clergyman, the clerk, the undertaker, and the chief mourner. Scrooge signed it: and Scrooge's name was good upon 'Change, for anything he chose to put his hand to. Old Marley was as dead as a door-nail.

Mind! I don't mean to say that I know, of my own knowledge, what there is particularly dead about a door-nail. I might have been inclined, myself, to regard a coffin-nail as the deadest piece of ironmongery in the trade. But the wisdom of our ancestors is in the simile; and my unhallowed hands shall not disturb it, or the Country's done for. You will therefore permit me to repeat, emphatically, that Marley was as dead as a door-nail.

Scrooge knew he was dead? Of course he did. How could it be otherwise? Scrooge and he were partners for I don't know how many years. Scrooge was his sole executor, his sole administrator, his sole assign, his sole residuary legatee,[1] his sole friend and sole mourner. And even Scrooge was not so dreadfully cut up by the sad event, but that he was an excellent man of business on the very day of the funeral, and solemnised it with an undoubted bargain.

The mention of Marley's funeral brings me back to the point I started from. There is no doubt that Marley was dead. This must be distinctly understood, or nothing wonderful can come of the story I am going to relate. If we were not perfectly convinced that Hamlet's Father died before the play began,[2] there would be nothing more remarkable in his taking a stroll at night, in an easterly wind, upon his own ramparts, than there would be in any other middle-aged gentleman rashly turning out after dark in a breezy spot—say Saint Paul's Churchyard for instance—literally to astonish his son's weak mind.

Scrooge never painted out Old Marley's name. There it stood, years afterwards, above the warehouse door: Scrooge and Marley. The firm was known as Scrooge and Marley. Sometimes people new to the business called Scrooge Scrooge, and sometimes Marley, but he answered to both names: it was all the same to him.

---

1. Legal terms meaning that Scrooge was Marley's only heir.

2. In Shakespeare's *Hamlet*, the appearance of the ghost of Hamlet's murdered father sets the plot in motion.

Oh! but he was a tight-fisted hand at the grindstone, Scrooge! a squeezing, wrenching, grasping, scraping, clutching, covetous old sinner! Hard and sharp as flint, from which no steel had ever struck out generous fire; secret, and self-contained, and solitary as an oyster. The cold within him froze his old features, nipped his pointed nose, shrivelled his cheek, stiffened his gait; made his eyes red, his thin lips blue; and spoke out shrewdly in his grating voice. A frosty rime was on his head, and on his eyebrows, and his wiry chin. He carried his own low temperature always about with him; he iced his office in the dog-days;[3] and didn't thaw it one degree at Christmas.

External heat and cold had little influence on Scrooge. No warmth could warm, nor wintry weather chill him. No wind that blew was bitterer than he, no falling snow was more intent upon its purpose, no pelting rain less open to entreaty. Foul weather didn't know where to have him. The heaviest rain, and snow, and hail, and sleet, could boast of the advantage over him in only one respect. They often "came down"[4] handsomely, and Scrooge never did.

Nobody ever stopped him in the street to say, with gladsome looks, "My dear Scrooge, how are you? when will you come to see me?" No beggars implored him to bestow a trifle, no children asked him what it was o'clock, no man or woman ever once in all his life inquired the way to such and such a place, of Scrooge. Even the blindmen's dogs appeared to know him; and when they saw him coming on, would tug their owners into doorways and up courts; and then would wag their tails as though they said, "no eye at all is better than an evil eye, dark master!"

But what did Scrooge care? It was the very thing he liked. To edge his way along the crowded paths of life, warning all human sympathy to keep its distance, was what the knowing ones call "nuts" to Scrooge.[5]

Once upon a time—of all the good days in the year, on Christmas Eve—old Scrooge sat busy in his counting-house. It was cold, bleak, biting weather: foggy withal: and he could hear the people in the court outside, go wheezing up and down, beating their hands upon their breasts, and stamping their feet upon the pavement-stones to warm them. The city clocks had only just gone three, but it was quite dark already: it had not been light all day: and candles were flaring in the windows of the neighbouring offices, like ruddy smears upon the palpable brown air. The fog came pouring in at every chink and keyhole, and was so dense without, that although the court was of the narrowest, the houses opposite were mere phantoms. To see the dingy cloud come drooping down, obscuring everything, one might have thought that Nature lived hard by, and was brewing on a large scale.

The door of Scrooge's counting-house was open that he might keep his eye upon his clerk, who in a dismal little cell beyond, a sort of tank, was copying letters. Scrooge had a very small fire, but the clerk's fire was so very much smaller that it looked like one coal. But he couldn't replenish it, for Scrooge kept the coal-box in his own room; and so surely as the clerk came in with the shovel, the master predicted that it would be necessary for them to part. Wherefore the clerk put on his white comforter,[6] and tried to warm himself at the candle; in which effort, not being a man of a strong imagination, he failed.

"A merry Christmas, uncle! God save you!" cried a cheerful voice. It was the voice of Scrooge's nephew, who came upon him so quickly that this was the first intimation he had of his approach.

3. The hot weather of late summer.
4. A pun, playing on the slang meaning, to give money.
5. A source of pleasure to him (slang).
6. A long scarf.

"Bah!" said Scrooge, "Humbug!"

He had so heated himself with rapid walking in the fog and frost, this nephew of Scrooge's, that he was all in a glow; his face was ruddy and handsome; his eyes sparkled, and his breath smoked again.

"Christmas a humbug, uncle!" said Scrooge's nephew. "You don't mean that, I am sure?"

"I do," said Scrooge. "Merry Christmas! What right have you to be merry? what reason have you to be merry? You're poor enough."

"Come, then," returned the nephew gaily. "What right have you to be dismal? what reason have you to be morose? You're rich enough."

Scrooge having no better answer ready on the spur of the moment, said, "Bah!" again; and followed it up with "Humbug."

"Don't be cross, uncle," said the nephew.

"What else can I be," returned the uncle, "when I live in such a world of fools as this? Merry Christmas! Out upon merry Christmas! What's Christmas time to you but a time for paying bills without money; a time for finding yourself a year older, and not an hour richer; a time for balancing your books and having every item in 'em through a round dozen of months presented dead against you? If I could work my will," said Scrooge, indignantly, "every idiot who goes about with 'Merry Christmas,' on his lips, should be boiled with his own pudding, and buried with a stake of holly through his heart. He should!"

"Uncle!" pleaded the nephew.

"Nephew!" returned the uncle, sternly, "keep Christmas in your own way, and let me keep it in mine."

"Keep it!" repeated Scrooge's nephew. "But you don't keep it."

"Let me leave it alone, then," said Scrooge. "Much good may it do you! Much good it has ever done you!"

"There are many things from which I might have derived good, by which I have not profited, I dare say," returned the nephew: "Christmas among the rest. But I am sure I have always thought of Christmas time, when it has come round—apart from the veneration due to its sacred name and origin, if anything belonging to it can be apart from that—as a good time: a kind, forgiving, charitable, pleasant time: the only time I know of, in the long calendar of the year, when men and women seem by one consent to open their shut-up hearts freely, and to think of people below them as if they really were fellow-passengers to the grave, and not another race of creatures bound on other journeys. And therefore, uncle, though it has never put a scrap of gold or silver in my pocket, I believe that it *has* done me good, and *will* do me good; and I say, God bless it!"

The clerk in the tank involuntarily applauded: becoming immediately sensible of the impropriety, he poked the fire, and extinguished the last frail spark for ever.

"Let me hear another sound from *you*," said Scrooge, "and you'll keep your Christmas by losing your situation. You're quite a powerful speaker, sir," he added, turning to his nephew. "I wonder you don't go into Parliament."

"Don't be angry, uncle. Come! Dine with us to-morrow."

Scrooge said that he would see him—yes, indeed he did. He went the whole length of the expression, and said that he would see him in that extremity first.[7]

---

7. I.e., that he would see his nephew in hell first.

"But why?" cried Scrooge's nephew. "Why?"

"Why did you get married?" said Scrooge.

"Because I fell in love."

"Because you fell in love!" growled Scrooge, as if that were the only one thing in the world more ridiculous than a merry Christmas. "Good afternoon!"

"Nay, uncle, but you never came to see me before that happened. Why give it as a reason for not coming now?"

"Good afternoon," said Scrooge.

"I want nothing from you; I ask nothing of you; why cannot we be friends?"

"Good afternoon," said Scrooge.

"I am sorry, with all my heart, to find you so resolute. We have never had any quarrel, to which I have been a party. But I have made the trial in homage to Christmas, and I'll keep my Christmas humour to the last. So A Merry Christmas, uncle!"

"Good afternoon!" said Scrooge.

"And A Happy New Year!"

"Good afternoon!" said Scrooge.

His nephew left the room without an angry word, notwithstanding. He stopped at the outer door to bestow the greetings of the season on the clerk, who, cold as he was, was warmer than Scrooge; for he returned them cordially.

"There's another fellow," muttered Scrooge; who overheard him: "my clerk, with fifteen shillings a-week, and a wife and family, talking about a merry Christmas. I'll retire to Bedlam."[8]

This lunatic, in letting Scrooge's nephew out, had let two other people in. They were portly gentlemen, pleasant to behold, and now stood, with their hats off, in Scrooge's office. They had books and papers in their hands, and bowed to him.

"Scrooge and Marley's, I believe," said one of the gentlemen, referring to his list. "Have I the pleasure of addressing Mr Scrooge, or Mr Marley?"

"Mr Marley has been dead these seven years," Scrooge replied. "He died seven years ago, this very night."

"We have no doubt his liberality is well represented by his surviving partner," said the gentleman, presenting his credentials.

It certainly was; for they had been two kindred spirits. At the ominous word "liberality," Scrooge frowned, and shook his head, and handed the credentials back.

"At this festive season of the year, Mr Scrooge," said the gentleman, taking up a pen, "it is more than usually desirable that we should make some slight provision for the poor and destitute, who suffer greatly at the present time. Many thousands are in want of common necessaries; hundreds of thousands are in want of common comforts, sir."

"Are there no prisons?" asked Scrooge.

"Plenty of prisons," said the gentleman, laying down the pen again.

"And the Union workhouses?"[9] demanded Scrooge. "Are they still in operation?"

"They are. Still," returned the gentleman, "I wish I could say they were not."

"The Treadmill[1] and the Poor Law are in full vigour, then?" said Scrooge.

"Both very busy, sir."

8. An insane asylum.
9. Established under the Poor Law Amendment Act of 1834, the workhouses provided a place of refuge for the poor but offered degrading subsistence conditions, justified by the theory that the inhabitants of workhouses ought to be worse off than the poorest of the gainfully employed.
1. Prisoners were required to perform meaningless hard labor, such as walking on treadmills.

"Oh! I was afraid, from what you said at first, that something had occurred to stop them in their useful course," said Scrooge. "I'm very glad to hear it."

"Under the impression that they scarcely furnish Christian cheer of mind or body to the multitude," returned the gentleman, "a few of us are endeavouring to raise a fund to buy the Poor some meat and drink, and means of warmth. We choose this time because it is a time, of all others, when Want is keenly felt, and Abundance rejoices. What shall I put you down for?"

"Nothing!" Scrooge replied.

"You wish to be anonymous?"

"I wish to be left alone," said Scrooge. "Since you ask me what I wish, gentlemen, that is my answer. I don't make merry myself at Christmas, and I can't afford to make idle people merry. I help to support the establishments I have mentioned: they cost enough: and those who are badly off must go there."

"Many can't go there; and many would rather die."

"If they would rather die," said Scrooge, "they had better do it, and decrease the surplus population.[2] Besides—excuse me—I don't know that."

"But you might know it," observed the gentleman.

"It's not my business," Scrooge returned. "It's enough for a man to understand his own business, and not to interfere with other people's. Mine occupies me constantly. Good afternoon, gentlemen!"

Seeing clearly that it would be useless to pursue their point, the gentlemen withdrew. Scrooge resumed his labours with an improved opinion of himself, and in a more facetious temper than was usual with him.

Meanwhile the fog and darkness thickened so, that people ran about with flaring links,[3] proffering their services to go before horses in carriages, and conduct them on their way. The ancient tower of a church, whose gruff old bell was always peeping slily down at Scrooge out of a gothic window in the wall, became invisible, and struck the hours and quarters in the clouds, with tremulous vibrations afterwards, as if its teeth were chattering in its frozen head up there. The cold became intense. In the main street, at the corner of the court, some labourers were repairing the gas-pipes, and had lighted a great fire in a brazier, round which a party of ragged men and boys were gathered: warming their hands and winking their eyes before the blaze in rapture. The water-plug being left in solitude, its overflowings sullenly congealed, and turned to misanthropic ice. The brightness of the shops where holly sprigs and berries crackled in the lamp-heat of the windows, made pale faces ruddy as they passed. Poulterers' and grocers' trades became a splendid joke: a glorious pageant, with which it was next to impossible to believe that such dull principles as bargain and sale had anything to do. The Lord Mayor, in the stronghold of the mighty Mansion House, gave orders to his fifty cooks and butlers to keep Christmas as a Lord Mayor's household should; and even the little tailor, whom he had fined five shillings on the previous Monday for being drunk and blood-thirsty in the streets, stirred up to-morrow's pudding in his garret, while his lean wife and the baby sallied out to buy the beef.

Foggier yet, and colder! Piercing, searching, biting cold. If the good Saint Dunstan[4] had but nipped the Evil Spirit's nose with a touch of such weather as that, instead of using his familiar weapons, then indeed he would have roared to lusty purpose. The

2. In 1803, Thomas Malthus published his *Essay on the Principle of Population*, warning that unchecked population growth would lead to starvation.

3. Torches.

4. St. Dunstan was a smith who once seized the devil by the nose with a pair of red-hot pincers.

owner of one scant young nose, gnawed and mumbled by the hungry cold as bones are gnawed by dogs, stooped down at Scrooge's keyhole to regale him with a Christmas carol: but at the first sound of—

> "God bless you merry gentleman!
> May nothing you dismay!"

Scrooge seized the ruler with such energy of action, that the singer fled in terror, leaving the keyhole to the fog and even more congenial frost.

At length the hour of shutting up the counting-house arrived. With an ill-will Scrooge dismounted from his stool, and tacitly admitted the fact to the expectant clerk in the Tank, who instantly snuffed his candle out, and put on his hat.

"You'll want all day to-morrow, I suppose?" said Scrooge.

"If quite convenient, sir."

"It's not convenient," said Scrooge, "and it's not fair. If I was to stop half-a-crown for it, you'd think yourself ill used, I'll be bound?"

The clerk smiled faintly.

"And yet," said Scrooge, "you don't think *me* ill used, when I pay a day's wages for no work."

The clerk observed that it was only once a year.

"A poor excuse for picking a man's pocket every twenty-fifth of December!" said Scrooge, buttoning his great-coat to the chin. "But I suppose you must have the whole day. Be here all the earlier next morning!"

The clerk promised that he would; and Scrooge walked out with a growl. The office was closed in a twinkling, and the clerk, with the long ends of his white comforter dangling below his waist (for he boasted no great-coat), went down a slide on Cornhill, at the end of a lane of boys, twenty times, in honour of its being Christmas-eve, and then ran home to Camden Town[5] as hard as he could pelt, to play at blind-man's-buff.

Scrooge took his melancholy dinner in his usual melancholy tavern; and having read all the newspapers, and beguiled the rest of the evening with his banker's-book, went home to bed. He lived in chambers which had once belonged to his deceased partner. They were a gloomy suite of rooms, in a lowering pile of building up a yard, where it had so little business to be, that one could scarcely help fancying it must have run there when it was a young house, playing at hide-and-seek with other houses, and have forgotten the way out again. It was old enough now, and dreary enough, for nobody lived in it but Scrooge, the other rooms being all let out as offices. The yard was so dark that even Scrooge, who knew its every stone, was fain to grope with his hands. The fog and frost so hung about the black old gateway of the house, that it seemed as if the Genius of the Weather sat in mournful meditation on the threshold.

Now, it is a fact, that there was nothing at all particular about the knocker on the door, except that it was very large. It is also a fact, that Scrooge had seen it night and morning during his whole residence in that place; also that Scrooge had as little of what is called fancy about him as any man in the City of London, even including—which is a bold word—the corporation, aldermen, and livery. Let it also be borne in mind that Scrooge had not bestowed one thought on Marley, since his

---

5. A northern suburb of London; in Dickens's era the home of the working poor.

last mention of his seven-years' dead partner that afternoon. And then let any man explain to me, if he can, how it happened that Scrooge, having his key in the lock of the door, saw in the knocker, without its undergoing any intermediate process of change: not a knocker, but Marley's face.

Marley's face. It was not in impenetrable shadow as the other objects in the yard were, but had a dismal light about it, like a bad lobster in a dark cellar. It was not angry or ferocious, but looked at Scrooge as Marley used to look: with ghostly spectacles turned up upon its ghostly forehead. The hair was curiously stirred, as if by breath or hot-air; and though the eyes were wide open, they were perfectly motionless. That, and its livid colour, made it horrible; but its horror seemed to be, in spite of the face and beyond its control, rather than a part of its own expression.

As Scrooge looked fixedly at this phenomenon, it was a knocker again.

To say that he was not startled, or that his blood was not conscious of a terrible sensation to which it had been a stranger from infancy, would be untrue. But he put his hand upon the key he had relinquished, turned it sturdily, walked in, and lighted his candle.

He *did* pause, with a moment's irresolution, before he shut the door; and he *did* look cautiously behind it first, as if he half-expected to be terrified with the sight of Marley's pigtail sticking out into the hall. But there was nothing on the back of the door, except the screws and nuts that held the knocker on; so he said "Pooh, pooh!" and closed it with a bang.

The sound resounded through the house like thunder. Every room above, and every cask in the wine-merchant's cellars below, appeared to have a separate peal of echoes of its own. Scrooge was not a man to be frightened by echoes. He fastened the door, and walked across the hall, and up the stairs: slowly too: trimming his candle as he went.

You may talk vaguely about driving a coach-and-six up a good old flight of stairs, or through a bad young Act of Parliament; but I mean to say you might have got a hearse up that staircase, and taken it broadwise, with the splinter-bar towards the wall, and the door towards the balustrades: and done it easy. There was plenty of width for that, and room to spare; which is perhaps the reason why Scrooge thought he saw a locomotive hearse going on before him in the gloom. Half a dozen gas-lamps out of the street wouldn't have lighted the entry too well, so you may suppose that it was pretty dark with Scrooge's dip.[6]

Up Scrooge went, not caring a button for that: darkness is cheap, and Scrooge liked it. But before he shut his heavy door, he walked through his rooms to see that all was right. He had just enough recollection of the face to desire to do that.

Sitting room, bed-room, lumber-room. All as they should be. Nobody under the table, nobody under the sofa; a small fire in the grate; spoon and basin ready; and the little saucepan of gruel[7] (Scrooge had a cold in his head) upon the hob.[8] Nobody under the bed; nobody in the closet; nobody in his dressing-gown, which was hanging up in a suspicious attitude against the wall. Lumber-room as usual. Old fire-guard, old shoes, two fish-baskets, washing-stand on three legs, and a poker.

Quite satisfied, he closed his door, and locked himself in; double-locked himself in, which was not his custom. Thus secured against surprise, he took off his cravat;

6. Candle.
7. Thin porridge.

8. A shelf in the fireplace where something may be kept warm.

put on his dressing-gown and slippers, and his night-cap; and sat down before the fire to take his gruel.

It was a very low fire indeed; nothing on such a bitter night. He was obliged to sit close to it, and brood over it, before he could extract the least sensation of warmth from such a handful of fuel. The fireplace was an old one, built by some Dutch merchant long ago, and paved all round with quaint Dutch tiles, designed to illustrate the Scriptures. There were Cains and Abels; Pharaoh's daughters, Queens of Sheba, Angelic messengers descending through the air on clouds like feather-beds, Abrahams, Belshazzars, Apostles putting off to sea in butter-boats, hundreds of figures to attract his thoughts; and yet that face of Marley, seven years dead, came like the ancient Prophet's rod,[9] and swallowed up the whole. If each smooth tile had been a blank at first, with power to shape some picture on its surface from the disjointed fragments of his thoughts, there would have been a copy of old Marley's head on every one.

"Humbug!" said Scrooge; and walked across the room.

After several turns, he sat down again. As he threw his head back in the chair, his glance happened to rest upon a bell, a disused bell, that hung in the room, and communicated for some purpose now forgotten with a chamber in the highest story of the building. It was with great astonishment, and with a strange, inexplicable dread, that as he looked, he saw this bell begin to swing. It swung so softly in the outset that it scarcely made a sound; but soon it rang out loudly, and so did every bell in the house.

This might have lasted half a minute, or a minute, but it seemed an hour. The bells ceased as they had begun, together. They were succeeded by a clanking noise, deep down below; as if some person were dragging a heavy chain over the casks in the wine-merchant's cellar. Scrooge then remembered to have heard that ghosts in haunted houses were described as dragging chains.

The cellar-door flew open with a booming sound, and then he heard the noise much louder, on the floors below; then coming up the stairs; then coming straight towards his door.

"It's humbug still!" said Scrooge. "I won't believe it."

His colour changed though, when, without a pause, it came on through the heavy door, and passed into the room before his eyes. Upon its coming in, the dying flame leaped up, as though it cried "I know him! Marley's Ghost!" and fell again.

The same face: the very same. Marley in his pig-tail, usual waistcoat, tights, and boots; the tassels on the latter bristling, like his pigtail, and his coat-skirts, and the hair upon his head. The chain he drew was clasped about his middle. It was long, and wound about him like a tail; and it was made (for Scrooge observed it closely) of cash-boxes, keys, padlocks, ledgers, deeds, and heavy purses wrought in steel. His body was transparent: so that Scrooge, observing him, and looking through his waistcoat, could see the two buttons on his coat behind.

Scrooge had often heard it said that Marley had no bowels, but he had never believed it until now.

No, nor did he believe it even now. Though he looked the phantom through and through, and saw it standing before him; though he felt the chilling influence of its death-cold eyes; and marked the very texture of the folded kerchief bound about

---

9. Aaron, the brother of Moses, transformed his rod into a serpent, which swallowed up those of the magicians of Egypt (Exodus 7.12).

its head and chin, which wrapper he had not observed before: he was still incredulous, and fought against his senses.

"How now!" said Scrooge, caustic and cold as ever. "What do you want with me?"

"Much!"—Marley's voice, no doubt about it.

"Who are you?"

"Ask me who I *was*."

"Who *were* you then?" said Scrooge, raising his voice. "You're particular—for a shade." He was going to say "*to* a shade," but substituted this, as more appropriate.

"In life I was your partner, Jacob Marley."

"Can you—can you sit down?" asked Scrooge, looking doubtfully at him.

"I can."

"Do it then."

Scrooge asked the question, because he didn't know whether a ghost so transparent might find himself in a condition to take a chair; and felt that in the event of its being impossible, it might involve the necessity of an embarrassing explanation. But the ghost sat down on the opposite side of the fireplace, as if he were quite used to it.

"You don't believe in me," observed the Ghost.

"I don't," said Scrooge.

"What evidence would you have of my reality, beyond that of your senses?"

"I don't know," said Scrooge.

"Why do you doubt your senses?"

"Because," said Scrooge, "a little thing affects them. A slight disorder of the stomach makes them cheats. You may be an undigested bit of beef, a blot of mustard, a crumb of cheese, a fragment of an underdone potato. There's more of gravy than of grave about you, whatever you are!"

Scrooge was not much in the habit of cracking jokes, nor did he feel, in his heart, by any means waggish then. The truth is, that he tried to be smart, as a means of distracting his own attention, and keeping down his terror; for the spectre's voice disturbed the very marrow in his bones.

To sit, staring at those fixed, glazed eyes, in silence for a moment, would play, Scrooge felt, the very deuce with him. There was something very awful, too, in the spectre's being provided with an infernal atmosphere of its own. Scrooge could not feel it himself, but this was clearly the case; for though the Ghost sat perfectly motionless, its hair, and skirts, and tassels, were still agitated as by the hot vapour from an oven.

"You see this toothpick?" said Scrooge, returning quickly to the charge, for the reason just assigned; and wishing, though it were only for a second, to divert the vision's stony gaze from himself.

"I do," replied the Ghost.

"You are not looking at it," said Scrooge.

"But I see it," said the Ghost, "notwithstanding."

"Well!" returned Scrooge. "I have but to swallow this, and be for the rest of my days persecuted by a legion of goblins, all of my own creation. Humbug, I tell you—humbug!"

At this, the spirit raised a frightful cry, and shook its chain with such a dismal and appalling noise, that Scrooge held on tight to his chair, to save himself from falling in a swoon. But how much greater was his horror, when the phantom taking off the bandage round its head, as if it were too warm to wear in-doors, its lower jaw dropped down upon its breast!

Scrooge fell upon his knees, and clasped his hands before his face.

"Mercy!" he said. "Dreadful apparition, why do you trouble me?"

"Man of the worldly mind!" replied the Ghost, "do you believe in me or not?"

"I do," said Scrooge. "I must. But why do spirits walk the earth, and why do they come to me?"

"It is required of every man," the Ghost returned, "that the spirit within him should walk abroad among his fellowmen, and travel far and wide; and if that spirit goes not forth in life, it is condemned to do so after death. It is doomed to wander through the world—oh, woe is me!—and witness what it cannot share, but might have shared on earth, and turned to happiness!"

Again the spectre raised a cry, and shook its chain and wrung its shadowy hands.

"You are fettered," said Scrooge, trembling. "Tell me why?"

"I wear the chain I forged in life," replied the Ghost. "I made it link by link, and yard by yard; I girded it on of my own free will, and of my own free will I wore it. Is its pattern strange to you?"

Scrooge trembled more and more.

"Or would you know," pursued the Ghost, "the weight and length of the strong coil you bear yourself? It was full as heavy and as long as this, seven Christmas Eves ago. You have laboured on it, since. It is a ponderous chain!"

Scrooge glanced about him on the floor, in the expectation of finding himself surrounded by some fifty or sixty fathoms of iron cable: but he could see nothing.

"Jacob," he said, imploringly. "Old Jacob Marley, tell me more. Speak comfort to me, Jacob."

"I have none to give," the Ghost replied. "It comes from other regions, Ebenezer Scrooge, and is conveyed by other ministers, to other kinds of men. Nor can I tell you what I would. A very little more is all permitted to me. I cannot rest, I cannot stay, I cannot linger anywhere. My spirit never walked beyond our counting-house—mark me!—in life my spirit never roved beyond the narrow limits of our money-changing hole; and weary journeys lie before me!"

It was a habit with Scrooge, whenever he became thoughtful, to put his hands in his breeches pockets. Pondering on what the Ghost had said, he did so now, but without lifting up his eyes, or getting off his knees.

"You must have been very slow about it, Jacob," Scrooge observed, in a business-like manner, though with humility and deference.

"Slow!" the Ghost repeated.

"Seven years dead," mused Scrooge. "And travelling all the time?"

"The whole time," said the Ghost. "No rest, no peace. Incessant torture of remorse."

"You travel fast?" said Scrooge.

"On the wings of the wind," replied the Ghost.

"You might have got over a great quantity of ground in seven years," said Scrooge.

The Ghost, on hearing this, set up another cry, and clanked its chain so hideously in the dead silence of the night, that the Ward[1] would have been justified in indicting it for a nuisance.

"Oh! captive, bound, and double-ironed," cried the phantom, "not to know, that ages of incessant labour by immortal creatures, for this earth must pass into eternity before the good of which it is susceptible is all developed. Not to know that any Christian spirit working kindly in its little sphere, whatever it may be, will find its mortal life too short for its vast means of usefulness. Not to know that no space of regret can make amends for one life's opportunity misused! Yet such was I! Oh! such was I!"

---

1. A constable who patrolled the streets of London at night.

"But you were always a good man of business, Jacob," faultered Scrooge, who now began to apply this to himself.

"Business!" cried the Ghost, wringing its hands again. "Mankind was my business. The common welfare was my business; charity, mercy, forbearance, and benevolence, were, all, my business. The dealings of my trade were but a drop of water in the comprehensive ocean of my business!"

It held up its chain at arm's length, as if that were the cause of all its unavailing grief, and flung it heavily upon the ground again.

"At this time of the rolling year," the spectre said, "I suffer most. Why did I walk through crowds of fellow-beings with my eyes turned down, and never raise them to that blessed Star which led the Wise Men to a poor abode? Were there no poor homes to which its light would have conducted *me!*"

Scrooge was very much dismayed to hear the spectre going on at this rate, and began to quake exceedingly.

"Hear me!" cried the Ghost. "My time is nearly gone."

"I will," said Scrooge. "But don't be hard upon me! Don't be flowery, Jacob! Pray!"

"How it is that I appear before you in a shape that you can see, I may not tell. I have sat invisible beside you many and many a day."

It was not an agreeable idea. Scrooge shivered, and wiped the perspiration from his brow.

"That is no light part of my penance," pursued the Ghost. "I am here to-night to warn you, that you have yet a chance and hope of escaping my fate. A chance and hope of my procuring, Ebenezer."

"You were always a good friend to me," said Scrooge. "Thank'ee!"

"You will be haunted," resumed the Ghost, "by Three Spirits."

Scrooge's countenance fell almost as low as the Ghost's had done.

"Is that the chance and hope you mentioned, Jacob?" he demanded, in a faultering voice.

"It is."

"I—I think I'd rather not," said Scrooge.

"Without their visits," said the Ghost, "you cannot hope to shun the path I tread. Expect the first to-morrow, when the bell tolls one."

"Couldn't I take 'em all at once, and have it over, Jacob?" hinted Scrooge.

"Expect the second on the next night at the same hour. The third upon the next night when the last stroke of twelve has ceased to vibrate. Look to see me no more; and look that, for your own sake, you remember what has passed between us!"

When it had said these words, the spectre took its wrapper from the table, and bound it round its head, as before. Scrooge knew this, by the smart sound its teeth made, when the jaws were brought together by the bandage. He ventured to raise his eyes again, and found his supernatural visitor confronting him in an erect attitude, with its chain wound over and about its arm.

The apparition walked backward from him; and at every step it took, the window raised itself a little, so that when the spectre reached it, it was wide open. It beckoned Scrooge to approach, which he did. When they were within two paces of each other, Marley's Ghost held up its hand, warning him to come no nearer. Scrooge stopped.

Not so much in obedience, as in surprise and fear: for on the raising of the hand, he became sensible of confused noises in the air; incoherent sounds of lamentation and regret; wailings inexpressibly sorrowful and self-accusatory. The spectre, after listening for a moment, joined in the mournful dirge; and floated out upon the bleak, dark night.

Scrooge followed to the window: desperate in his curiosity. He looked out.

The air filled with phantoms, wandering hither and thither in restless haste, and moaning as they went. Every one of them wore chains like Marley's Ghost; some few (they might be guilty governments) were linked together; none were free. Many had been personally known to Scrooge in their lives. He had been quite familiar with one old ghost, in a white waistcoat, with a monstrous iron safe attached to its ankle, who cried piteously at being unable to assist a wretched woman with an infant, whom it saw below, upon a door-step. The misery with them all was, clearly, that they sought to interfere, for good, in human matters, and had lost the power for ever.

Whether these creatures faded into mist, or mist enshrouded them, he could not tell. But they and their spirit voices faded together; and the night became as it had been when he walked home.

Scrooge closed the window, and examined the door by which the Ghost had entered. It was double-locked, as he had locked it with his own hands, and the bolts were undisturbed. He tried to say "Humbug!" but stopped at the first syllable. And being, from the emotion he had undergone, or the fatigues of the day, or his glimpse of the Invisible World, or the dull conversation of the Ghost, or the lateness of the hour, much in need of repose; went straight to bed, without undressing, and fell asleep upon the instant.

Stave Two
THE FIRST OF THE THREE SPIRITS

When Scrooge awoke, it was so dark, that looking out of bed, he could scarcely distinguish the transparent window from the opaque walls of his chamber. He was endeavouring to pierce the darkness with his ferret eyes, when the chimes of a neighbouring church struck the four quarters. So he listened for the hour.

To his great astonishment the heavy bell went on from six to seven, and from seven to eight, and regularly up to twelve; then stopped. Twelve! It was past two when he went to bed. The clock was wrong. An icicle must have got into the works. Twelve!

He touched the spring of his repeater, to correct this most preposterous clock. Its rapid little pulse beat twelve; and stopped.

"Why, it isn't possible," said Scrooge, "that I can have slept through a whole day and far into another night. It isn't possible that anything has happened to the sun, and this is twelve at noon!"

The idea being an alarming one, he scrambled out of bed, and groped his way to the window. He was obliged to rub the frost off with the sleeve of his dressing-gown before he could see anything; and could see very little then. All he could make out was, that it was still very foggy and extremely cold, and that there was no noise of people running to and fro, and making a great stir, as there unquestionably would have been if night had beaten off bright day, and taken possession of the world. This was a great relief, because "three days after sight of this First of Exchange pay to Mr Ebenezer Scrooge or his order," and so forth, would have become a mere United States' security[2] if there were no days to count by.

Scrooge went to bed again, and thought, and thought, and thought it over and over and over, and could make nothing of it. The more he thought, the more perplexed he was; and the more he endeavoured not to think, the more he thought.

2. Individual American states borrowed heavily from foreign capitalists in the 1830s; in 1837 a financial crisis caused many to default.

Marley's Ghost bothered him exceedingly. Every time he resolved within himself, after mature inquiry, that it was all a dream, his mind flew back again, like a strong spring released, to its first position, and presented the same problem to be worked all through, "Was it a dream or not?"

Scrooge lay in this state until the chimes had gone three quarters more, when he remembered, on a sudden, that the Ghost had warned him of a visitation when the bell tolled one. He resolved to lie awake until the hour was passed; and, considering that he could no more go to sleep than go to Heaven, this was perhaps the wisest resolution in his power.

The quarter was so long, that he was more than once convinced he must have sunk into a doze unconsciously, and missed the clock. At length it broke upon his listening ear.

"Ding, dong!"

"A quarter past," said Scrooge, counting.

"Ding, dong!"

"Half past!" said Scrooge.

"Ding, dong!"

"A quarter to it," said Scrooge.

"Ding, dong!"

"The hour itself," said Scrooge, triumphantly, "and nothing else!"

He spoke before the hour bell sounded, which it now did with a deep, dull, hollow, melancholy ONE. Light flashed up in the room upon the instant, and the curtains of his bed were drawn.

The curtains of his bed were drawn aside, I tell you, by a hand. Not the curtains at his feet, nor the curtains at his back, but those to which his face was addressed. The curtains of his bed were drawn aside; and Scrooge, starting up into a half-recumbent attitude, found himself face to face with the unearthly visitor who drew them: as close to it as I am now to you, and I am standing in the spirit at your elbow.

It was a strange figure—like a child: yet not so like a child as like an old man, viewed through some supernatural medium, which gave him the appearance of having receded from the view, and being diminished to a child's proportions. Its hair, which hung about its neck and down its back, was white as if with age; and yet the face had not a wrinkle in it, and the tenderest bloom was on the skin. The arms were very long and muscular; the hands the same, as if its hold were of uncommon strength. Its legs and feet, most delicately formed, were, like those upper members, bare. It wore a tunic of the purest white; and round its waist was bound a lustrous belt, the sheen of which was beautiful. It held a branch of fresh green holly in its hand; and, in singular contradiction of that wintry emblem, had its dress trimmed with summer flowers. But the strangest thing about it was, that from the crown of its head there sprung a bright clear jet of light, by which all this was visible; and which was doubtless the occasion of its using, in its duller moments, a great extinguisher for a cap,[3] which it now held under its arm.

Even this, though, when Scrooge looked at it with increasing steadiness, was *not* its strangest quality. For as its belt sparkled and glittered now in one part and now in another, and what was light one instant, at another time was dark, so the figure itself fluctuated in its distinctness: being now a thing with one arm, now with one leg, now with twenty legs, now a pair of legs without a head, now a head without a body: of

3. A candle snuffer.

which dissolving parts, no outline would be visible in the dense gloom wherein they melted away. And in the very wonder of this, it would be itself again; distinct and clear as ever.

"Are you the Spirit, sir, whose coming was foretold to me?" asked Scrooge.

"I am!"

The voice was soft and gentle. Singularly low, as if instead of being so close beside him, it were at a distance.

"Who, and what are you?" Scrooge demanded.

"I am the Ghost of Christmas Past."

"Long Past?" inquired Scrooge: observant of its dwarfish stature.

"No. Your past."

Perhaps, Scrooge could not have told anybody why, if anybody could have asked him; but he had a special desire to see the Spirit in his cap; and begged him to be covered.

"What!" exclaimed the Ghost, "would you so soon put out, with worldly hands, the light I give? Is it not enough that you are one of those whose passions made this cap, and force me through whole trains of years to wear it low upon my brow!"

Scrooge reverently disclaimed all intention to offend, or any knowledge of having wilfully "bonneted" the Spirit at any period of his life. He then made bold to inquire what business brought him there.

"Your welfare!" said the Ghost.

Scrooge expressed himself much obliged, but could not help thinking that a night of unbroken rest would have been more conducive to that end. The Spirit must have heard him thinking for it said immediately:

"Your reclamation, then. Take heed!"

It put out its strong hand as it spoke, and clasped him gently by the arm.

"Rise! and walk with me!"

It would have been in vain for Scrooge to plead that the weather and the hour were not adapted to pedestrian purposes; that bed was warm, and the thermometer a long way below freezing; that he was clad but lightly in his slippers, dressing-gown, and nightcap; and that he had a cold upon him at that time. The grasp, though gentle as a woman's hand, was not to be resisted. He rose: but finding that the Spirit made towards the window, clasped its robe in supplication.

"I am a mortal," Scrooge remonstrated, "and liable to fall."

"Bear but a touch of my hand *there*," said the Spirit, laying it upon his heart, "and you shall be upheld in more than this!"

As the words were spoken, they passed through the wall, and stood upon an open country road, with fields on either hand. The city had entirely vanished. Not a vestige of it was to be seen. The darkness and the mist had vanished with it, for it was a clear, cold, winter day, with snow upon the ground.

"Good Heaven!" said Scrooge, clasping his hands together, as he looked about him. "I was bred in this place. I was a boy here!"

The Spirit gazed upon him mildly. Its gentle touch, though it had been light and instantaneous, appeared still present to the old man's sense of feeling. He was conscious of a thousand odours floating in the air, each one connected with a thousand thoughts, and hopes, and joys, and cares long, long, forgotten!

"Your lip is trembling," said the Ghost. "And what is that upon your cheek?"

Scrooge muttered, with an unusual catching in his voice, that it was a pimple; and begged the Ghost to lead him where he would.

"You recollect the way?" inquired the Spirit.

"Remember it!" cried Scrooge with fervour—"I could walk it blindfold."

"Strange to have forgotten it for so many years!" observed the Ghost. "Let us go on."

They walked along the road; Scrooge recognising every gate, and post, and tree; until a little market-town appeared in the distance, with its bridge, its church, and winding river. Some shaggy ponies now were seen trotting towards them with boys upon their backs, who called to other boys in country gigs and carts, driven by farmers. All these boys were in great spirits, and shouted to each other, until the broad fields were so full of merry music, that the crisp air laughed to hear it.

"These are but shadows of the things that have been," said the Ghost. "They have no consciousness of us."

The jocund travellers came on; and as they came, Scrooge knew and named them every one. Why was he rejoiced beyond all bounds to see them! Why did his cold eye glisten, and his heart leap up as they went past! Why was he filled with gladness when he heard them give each other Merry Christmas, as they parted at crossroads and bye-ways, for their several homes! What was merry Christmas to Scrooge? Out upon merry Christmas! What good had it ever done to him?

"The school is not quite deserted," said the Ghost. "A solitary child, neglected by his friends, is left there still."

Scrooge said he knew it. And he sobbed.

They left the high-road, by a well remembered lane, and soon approached a mansion of dull red brick, with a little weathercock-surmounted cupola on the roof, and a bell hanging in it. It was a large house, but one of broken fortunes; for the spacious offices were little used, their walls were damp and mossy, their windows broken, and their gates decayed. Fowls clucked and strutted in the stables; and the coach-houses and sheds were over-run with grass. Nor was it more retentive of its ancient state, within; for entering the dreary hall, and glancing through the open doors of many rooms, they found them poorly furnished, cold, and vast. There was an earthy savour in the air, a chilly bareness in the place, which associated itself somehow with too much getting up by candle-light, and not too much to eat.

They went, the Ghost and Scrooge, across the hall, to a door at the back of the house. It opened before them, and disclosed a long, bare, melancholy room, made barer still by lines of plain deal forms and desks. At one of these a lonely boy was reading near a feeble fire; and Scrooge sat down upon a form, and wept to see his poor forgotten self as he had used to be.

Not a latent echo in the house, not a squeak and scuffle from the mice behind the panelling, not a drip from the half-thawed water-spout in the dull yard behind, not a sigh among the leafless boughs of one despondent poplar, not the idle swinging of an empty store-house door, no, not a clicking in the fire, but fell upon the heart of Scrooge with a softening influence, and gave a freer passage to his tears.

The Spirit touched him on the arm, and pointed to his younger self, intent upon his reading. Suddenly a man, in foreign garments: wonderfully real and distinct to look at: stood outside the window, with an axe stuck in his belt, and leading an ass laden with wood by the bridle.

"Why, it's Ali Baba!"[4] Scrooge exclaimed in ecstasy. "It's dear old honest Ali Baba! Yes, yes, I know! One Christmas time, when yonder solitary child was left here all alone, he *did* come, for the first time, just like that. Poor boy! And Valentine," said Scrooge,

4. From *The Arabian Nights*.

"and his wild brother, Orson;[5] there they go! And what's his name, who was put down in his drawers, asleep, at the Gate of Damascus; don't you see him! And the Sultan's Groom turned upside-down by the Genii; there he is upon his head! Serve him right. I'm glad of it. What business had *he* to be married to the Princess!"

To hear Scrooge expending all the earnestness of his nature on such subjects, in a most extraordinary voice between laughing and crying; and to see his heightened and excited face; would have been a surprise to his business friends in the city, indeed.

"There's the Parrot!" cried Scrooge. "Green body and yellow tail, with a thing like a lettuce growing out of the top of his head; there he is! Poor Robin Crusoe, he called him, when he came home again after sailing round the island. 'Poor Robin Crusoe, where have you been, Robin Crusoe?' The man thought he was dreaming, but he wasn't. It was the Parrot, you know. There goes Friday, running for his life to the little creek! Halloa! Hoop! Halloo!"[6]

Then, with a rapidity of transition very foreign to his usual character, he said, in pity for his former self, "Poor boy!" and cried again.

"I wish," Scrooge muttered, putting his hand in his pocket, and looking about him, after drying his eyes with his cuff: "but it's too late now."

"What is the matter?" asked the Spirit.

"Nothing," said Scrooge. "Nothing. There was a boy singing a Christmas Carol at my door last night. I should like to have given him something: that's all."

The Ghost smiled thoughtfully, and waved its hand: saying as it did so, "Let us see another Christmas!"

Scrooge's former self grew larger at the words, and the room became a little darker and more dirty. The panels shrunk, the windows cracked; fragments of plaster fell out of the ceiling, and the naked laths were shown instead; but how all this was brought about, Scrooge knew no more than you do. He only knew that it was quite correct; that everything had happened so; that there he was, alone again, when all the other boys had gone home for the jolly holidays.

He was not reading now, but walking up and down despairingly. Scrooge looked at the Ghost, and with a mournful shaking of his head, glanced anxiously towards the door.

It opened; and a little girl, much younger than the boy, came darting in, and putting her arms about his neck, and often kissing him, addressed him as her "Dear, dear brother."

"I have come to bring you home, dear brother!" said the child, clapping her tiny hands, and bending down to laugh. "To bring you home, home, home!"

"Home, little Fan?" returned the boy.

"Yes!" said the child, brimful of glee. "Home, for good and all. Home, for ever and ever. Father is so much kinder than he used to be, that home's like Heaven! He spoke so gently to me one dear night when I was going to bed, that I was not afraid to ask him once more if you might come home; and he said Yes, you should; and sent me in a coach to bring you. And you're to be a man!" said the child, opening her eyes, "and are never to come back here; but first, we're to be together all the Christmas long, and have the merriest time in all the world."

"You are quite a woman, little Fan!" exclaimed the boy.

---

5. The medieval story of the knight Valentine, and his brother Orson who had been reared as a wild man in the woods, had become a popular folktale by Dickens's time.

6. The incidents in this paragraph allude to Daniel Defoe's *Robinson Crusoe* (1719).

She clapped her hands and laughed, and tried to touch his head; but being too little, laughed again, and stood on tiptoe to embrace him. Then she began to drag him, in her childish eagerness, towards the door; and he, nothing loth to go, accompanied her.

A terrible voice in the hall cried, "Bring down Master Scrooge's box, there!" and in the hall appeared the schoolmaster himself, who glared on Master Scrooge with a ferocious condescension, and threw him into a dreadful state of mind by shaking hands with him. He then conveyed him and his sister into the veriest old well of a shivering best-parlour that ever was seen, where the maps upon the wall, and the celestial and terrestrial globes in the windows were waxy with cold. Here he produced a decanter of curiously light wine, and a block of curiously heavy cake, and administered instalments of those dainties to the young people: at the same time, sending out a meagre servant to offer a glass of "something" to the postboy, who answered that he thanked the gentleman, but if it was the same tap as he had tasted before, he had rather not. Master Scrooge's trunk being by this time tied on to the top of the chaise, the children bade the schoolmaster good-bye right willingly; and getting into it, drove gaily down the garden-sweep: the quick wheels dashing the hoar-frost and snow from off the dark leaves of the evergreens like spray.

"Always a delicate creature, whom a breath might have withered," said the Ghost. "But she had a large heart!"

"So she had," cried Scrooge. "You're right. I'll not gainsay it, Spirit. God forbid!"

"She died a woman," said the Ghost, "and had, as I think, children."

"One child," Scrooge returned.

"True," said the Ghost. "Your nephew!"

Scrooge seemed uneasy in his mind; and answered briefly, "Yes."

Although they had but that moment left the school behind them, they were now in the busy thoroughfares of a city, where shadowy passengers passed and repassed; where shadowy carts and coaches battled for the way, and all the strife and tumult of a real city were. It was made plain enough, by the dressing of the shops, that here too it was Christmas time again; but it was evening, and the streets were lighted up.

The Ghost stopped at a certain warehouse door, and asked Scrooge if he knew it.

"Know it!" said Scrooge. "Was I apprenticed here?"

They went in. At sight of an old gentleman in a Welch wig,[7] sitting behind such a high desk, that if he had been two inches taller he must have knocked his head against the ceiling, Scrooge cried in great excitement:

"Why, it's old Fezziwig! Bless his heart; it's Fezziwig alive again!"

Old Fezziwig laid down his pen, and looked up at the clock, which pointed to the hour of seven. He rubbed his hands; adjusted his capacious waistcoat; laughed all over himself, from his shoes to his organ of benevolence;[8] and called out in a comfortable, oily, rich, fat, jovial voice:

"Yo ho, there! Ebenezer! Dick!"

Scrooge's former self, now grown a young man, came briskly in, accompanied by his fellow-'prentice.

"Dick Wilkins, to be sure!" said Scrooge to the Ghost. "Bless me, yes. There he is. He was very much attached to me, was Dick. Poor Dick! Dear, dear!"

7. A knit cap.
8. The top of the forehead. Phrenology, a system for ana- lyzing character based on the shape of the head, was widely credited in Victorian times.

"Yo ho, my boys!" said Fezziwig. "No more work tonight. Christmas Eve, Dick. Christmas, Ebenezer! Let's have the shutters up," cried old Fezziwig, with a sharp clap of his hands, "before a man can say, Jack Robinson!"

You wouldn't believe how those two fellows went at it! They charged into the street with the shutters—one, two, three—had 'em up in their places—four, five, six—barred 'em and pinned 'em—seven, eight, nine—and came back before you could have got to twelve, panting like race-horses.

"Hilli-ho!" cried old Fezziwig, skipping down from the high desk, with wonderful agility. "Clear away, my lads, and let's have lots of room here! Hilli-ho, Dick! Chirrup, Ebenezer!"

Clear away! There was nothing they wouldn't have cleared away, or couldn't have cleared away, with old Fezziwig looking on. It was done in a minute. Every movable was packed off, as if it were dismissed from public life for evermore; the floor was swept and watered, the lamps were trimmed, fuel was heaped upon the fire; and the warehouse was as snug, and warm, and dry, and bright a ball-room, as you would desire to see upon a winter's night.

In came a fiddler with a music-book, and went up to the lofty desk, and made an orchestra of it, and tuned like fifty stomach-aches. In came Mrs Fezziwig, one vast substantial smile. In came the three Miss Fezziwigs, beaming and lovable. In came the six young followers whose hearts they broke. In came all the young men and women employed in the business. In came the housemaid, with her cousin, the baker. In came the cook, with her brother's particular friend, the milkman. In came the boy from over the way, who was suspected of not having board enough from his master; trying to hide himself behind the girl from next door but one, who was proved to have had her ears pulled by her Mistress. In they all came, one after another; some shyly, some boldly, some gracefully, some awkwardly, some pushing, some pulling; in they all came, anyhow and everyhow. Away they all went, twenty couple at once, hands half round and back again the other way; down the middle and up again; round and round in various stages of affectionate grouping; old top couple always turning up in the wrong place; new top couple starting off again, as soon as they got there; all top couples at last, and not a bottom one to help them. When this result was brought about, old Fezziwig, clapping his hands to stop the dance, cried out, "Well done!" and the fiddler plunged his hot face into a pot of porter, especially provided for that purpose. But scorning rest upon his reappearance, he instantly began again, though there were no dancers yet, as if the other fiddler had been carried home, exhausted, on a shutter; and he were a bran-new man resolved to beat him out of sight, or perish.

There were more dances, and there were forfeits, and more dances, and there was cake, and there was negus, and there was a great piece of Cold Roast, and there was a great piece of Cold Boiled, and there were mince-pies, and plenty of beer. But the great effect of the evening came after the Roast and Boiled, when the fiddler (an artful dog, mind! The sort of man who knew his business better than you or I could have told it him!) struck up "Sir Roger de Coverley." Then old Fezziwig stood out to dance with Mrs Fezziwig. Top couple, too; with a good stiff piece of work cut out for them; three or four and twenty pair of partners; people who were not to be trifled with; people who *would* dance, and had no notion of walking.

But if they had been twice as many: ah, four times: old Fezziwig would have been a match for them, and so would Mrs Fezziwig. As to *her*, she was worthy to be his partner in every sense of the term. If that's not high praise, tell me higher, and I'll use it. A positive light appeared to issue from Fezziwig's calves. They shone in every part of the dance like moons. You couldn't have predicted, at any given time, what would become of 'em next. And when old Fezziwig and Mrs Fezziwig had gone all through the dance; advance and retire, hold hands with your partner; bow and curtsey; corkscrew; thread-the-needle, and back again to your place; Fezziwig "cut"[9]—cut so deftly, that he appeared to wink with his legs, and came upon his feet again without a stagger.

When the clock struck eleven, this domestic ball broke up. Mr and Mrs Fezziwig took their stations, one on either side the door, and shaking hands with every person individually as he or she went out, wished him or her a Merry Christmas. When everybody had retired but the two 'prentices, they did the same to them; and thus the cheerful voices died away, and the lads were left to their beds; which were under a counter in the back-shop.

During the whole of this time, Scrooge had acted like a man out of his wits. His heart and soul were in the scene, and with his former self. He corroborated everything, remembered everything, enjoyed everything, and underwent the strangest agitation. It was not until now, when the bright faces of his former self and Dick were turned from them, that he remembered the Ghost, and became conscious that it was looking full upon him, while the light upon its head burnt very clear.

"A small matter," said the Ghost, "to make these silly folks so full of gratitude."

"Small!" echoed Scrooge.

The Spirit signed to him to listen to the two apprentices, who were pouring out their hearts in praise of Fezziwig: and when he had done so, said,

"Why! Is it not? He has spent but a few pounds of your mortal money: three or four, perhaps. Is that so much that he deserves this praise?"

"It isn't that," said Scrooge, heated by the remark, and speaking unconsciously like his former, not his latter, self. "It isn't that, Spirit. He has the power to render us happy or unhappy; to make our service light or burdensome; a pleasure or a toil. Say that his power lies in words and looks; in things so slight and insignificant that it is impossible to add and count 'em up: what then? The happiness he gives, is quite as great as if it cost a fortune."

He felt the Spirit's glance, and stopped.

"What is the matter?" asked the Ghost.

"Nothing particular," said Scrooge.

"Something, I think?" the Ghost insisted.

"No," said Scrooge, "No. I should like to be able to say a word or two to my clerk just now! That's all."

His former self turned down the lamps as he gave utterance to the wish; and Scrooge and the Ghost again stood side by side in the open air.

"My time grows short," observed the Spirit. "Quick!"

This was not addressed to Scrooge, or to any one whom he could see, but it produced an immediate effect. For again Scrooge saw himself. He was older now; a man in the prime of life. His face had not the harsh and rigid lines of later years; but it had begun to wear the signs of care and avarice. There was an eager, greedy, restless motion in the eye, which showed the passion that had taken root, and where the shadow of the growing tree would fall.

---

9. A "cut" in dancing meant to leap in the air and wiggle the legs back and forth quickly.

He was not alone, but sat by the side of a fair young girl in a mourning-dress: in whose eyes there were tears, which sparkled in the light that shone out of the Ghost of Christmas Past.

"It matters little," she said, softly. "To you, very little. Another idol has displaced me; and if it can cheer and comfort you in time to come, as I would have tried to do, I have no just cause to grieve."

"What Idol has displaced you?" he rejoined.

"A golden one."

"This is the even-handed dealing of the world!" he said. "There is nothing on which it is so hard as poverty; and there is nothing it professes to condemn with such severity as the pursuit of wealth!"

"You fear the world too much," she answered, gently. "All your other hopes have merged into the hope of being beyond the chance of its sordid reproach. I have seen your nobler aspirations fall off one by one, until the master-passion, Gain, engrosses you. Have I not?"

"What then?" he retorted. "Even if I have grown so much wiser, what then? I am not changed towards you."

She shook her head.

"Am I?"

"Our contract is an old one. It was made when we were both poor and content to be so, until, in good season, we could improve our worldly fortune by our patient industry. You *are* changed. When it was made, you were another man."

"I was a boy," he said impatiently.

"Your own feeling tells you that you were not what you are," she returned. "I am. That which promised happiness when we were one in heart, is fraught with misery now that we are two. How often and how keenly I have thought of this, I will not say. It is enough that I *have* thought of it, and can release you."

"Have I ever sought release?"

"In words. No. Never."

"In what, then?"

"In a changed nature; in an altered spirit; in another atmosphere of life; another Hope as its great end. In everything that made my love of any worth or value in your sight. If this had never been between us," said the girl, looking mildly, but with steadiness, upon him; "tell me, would you seek me out and try to win me now? Ah, no!"

He seemed to yield to the justice of this supposition, in spite of himself. But he said, with a struggle, "You think not."

"I would gladly think otherwise if I could," she answered, "Heaven knows! When I have learned a Truth like this, I know how strong and irresistible it must be. But if you were free to-day, to-morrow, yesterday, can even I believe that you would choose a dowerless girl—you who, in your very confidence with her, weigh everything by Gain: or, choosing her, if for a moment you were false enough to your one guiding principle to do so, do I not know that your repentance and regret would surely follow? I do; and I release you. With a full heart, for the love of him you once were."

He was about to speak; but with her head turned from him, she resumed.

"You may—the memory of what is past half makes me hope you will—have pain in this. A very, very brief time, and you will dismiss the recollection of it, gladly, as an unprofitable dream, from which it happened well that you awoke. May you be happy in the life you have chosen!"

She left him; and they parted.

"Spirit!" said Scrooge, "show me no more! Conduct me home. Why do you delight to torture me?"

"One shadow more!" exclaimed the Ghost.

"No more!" cried Scrooge. "No more. I don't wish to see it. Show me no more!"

But the relentless Ghost pinioned him in both his arms, and forced him to observe what happened next.

They were in another scene and place: a room, not very large or handsome, but full of comfort. Near to the winter fire sat a beautiful young girl, so like the last that Scrooge believed it was the same, until he saw *her*, now a comely matron, sitting opposite her daughter. The noise in this room was perfectly tumultuous, for there were more children there, than Scrooge in his agitated state of mind could count; and, unlike the celebrated herd in the poem,[1] they were not forty children conducting themselves like one, but every child was conducting itself like forty. The consequences were uproarious beyond belief; but no one seemed to care; on the contrary, the mother and daughter laughed heartily, and enjoyed it very much; and the latter, soon beginning to mingle in the sports, got pillaged by the young brigands most ruthlessly. What would I not have given to be one of them! Though I never could have been so rude, no, no! I wouldn't for the wealth of all the world have crushed that braided hair, and torn it down; and for the precious little shoe, I wouldn't have plucked it off, God bless my soul! to save my life. As to measuring her waist in sport, as they did, bold young brood, I couldn't have done it; I should have expected my arm to have grown round it for a punishment, and never come straight again. And yet I should have dearly liked, I own, to have touched her lips; to have questioned her, that she might have opened them; to have looked upon the lashes of her downcast eyes, and never raised a blush; to have let loose waves of hair, an inch of which would be a keepsake beyond price: in short, I should have liked, I do confess, to have had the lightest licence of a child, and yet been man enough to know its value.

But now a knocking at the door was heard, and such a rush immediately ensued that she with laughing face and plundered dress was borne towards it the centre of a flushed and boisterous group, just in time to greet the father, who came home attended by a man laden with Christmas toys and presents. Then the shouting and the struggling, and the onslaught that was made on the defenceless porter! The scaling him with chairs for ladders, to dive into his pockets, despoil him of brown-paper parcels, hold on tight by his cravat, hug him round the neck, pommel his back, and kick his legs in irrepressible affection! The shouts of wonder and delight with which the development of every package was received! The terrible announcement that the baby had been taken in the act of putting a doll's frying-pan into his mouth, and was more than suspected of having swallowed a fictitious turkey, glued on a wooden platter! The immense relief of finding this a false alarm! The joy, and gratitude, and ecstasy! They are all indescribable alike. It is enough that by degrees the children and their emotions got out of the parlour and by one stair at a time, up to the top of the house; where they went to bed, and so subsided.

And now Scrooge looked on more attentively than ever, when the master of the house, having his daughter leaning fondly on him, sat down with her and her mother at his own fireside; and when he thought that such another creature, quite as graceful

---

1. A reference to Wordsworth's *Written in March*: "The cattle are grazing, / Their heads never raising; / There are forty feeding like one!"

and as full of promise, might have called him father, and been a spring-time in the haggard winter of his life, his sight grew very dim indeed.

"Belle," said the husband, turning to his wife with a smile, "I saw an old friend of yours this afternoon."

"Who was it?"

"Guess!"

"How can I? Tut, don't I know," she added in the same breath, laughing as he laughed. "Mr Scrooge."

"Mr Scrooge it was. I passed his office window; and as it was not shut up, and he had a candle inside, I could scarcely help seeing him. His partner lies upon the point of death, I hear; and there he sat alone. Quite alone in the world, I do believe."

"Spirit!" said Scrooge in a broken voice, "remove me from this place."

"I told you these were shadows of the things that have been," said the Ghost. "That they are what they are, do not blame me!"

"Remove me!" Scrooge exclaimed. "I cannot bear it!"

He turned upon the Ghost, and seeing that it looked upon him with a face, in which in some strange way there were fragments of all the faces it had shown him, wrestled with it.

"Leave me! Take me back. Haunt me no longer!"

In the struggle, if that can be called a struggle in which the Ghost with no visible resistance on its own part was undisturbed by any effort of its adversary, Scrooge observed that its light was burning high and bright; and dimly connecting that with its influence over him, he seized the extinguisher-cap, and by a sudden action pressed it down upon its head.

The Spirit dropped beneath it, so that the extinguisher covered its whole form; but though Scrooge pressed it down with all his force, he could not hide the light: which streamed from under it, in an unbroken flood upon the ground.

He was conscious of being exhausted, and overcome by an irresistible drowsiness; and, further, of being in his own bedroom. He gave the cap a parting squeeze, in which his hand relaxed; and had barely time to reel to bed, before he sank into a heavy sleep.

Stave Three
THE SECOND OF THE THREE SPIRITS

Awaking in the middle of a prodigiously tough snore, and sitting up in bed to get his thoughts together, Scrooge had no occasion to be told that the bell was again upon the stroke of One. He felt that he was restored to consciousness in the right nick of time, for the especial purpose of holding a conference with the second messenger despatched to him through Jacob Marley's intervention. But, finding that he turned uncomfortably cold when he began to wonder which of his curtains this new spectre would draw back, he put them every one aside with his own hands; and lying down again, established a sharp look-out all round the bed. For he wished to challenge the Spirit on the moment of its appearance, and did not wish to be taken by surprise and made nervous.

Gentlemen of the free-and-easy sort, who plume themselves on being acquainted with a move or two, and being usually equal to the time-of-day, express the wide range of their capacity for adventure by observing that they are good for anything from pitch-and-toss to manslaughter; between which opposite extremes, no

Hablot K. Browne ("Phiz"), *Mr. Scrooge Extinguishing the Spirit*. Mr. Scrooge uses a giant extinguisher cap (for snuffing candles or oil lamps) to escape the reproachful haunting of the Ghost of Christmas Past. The illustrator Hablot K. Browne (1815–1882), who called himself "Phiz" to complement Dickens's nickname "Boz," closely collaborated with the author on ten of his novels, thereby indelibly imprinting the faces and forms of Dickens's characters on the Victorian consciousness. Here Browne produces a stark yet comic image of Scrooge's ineffectual struggle to repress his selfish past and his awakening conscience: "but though Scrooge pressed it down with all his force, he could not hide the light: which streamed from under it."

doubt, there lies a tolerably wide and comprehensive range of subjects. Without venturing for Scrooge quite as hardily as this, I don't mind calling on you to believe that he was ready for a good broad field of strange appearances, and that nothing between a baby and a rhinoceros would have astonished him very much.

Now, being prepared for almost anything, he was not by any means prepared for nothing; and, consequently, when the Bell struck One, and no shape appeared, he was taken with a violent fit of trembling. Five minutes, ten minutes, a quarter of an hour went by, yet nothing came. All this time, he lay upon his bed, the very core and centre of a blaze of ruddy light, which streamed upon it when the clock proclaimed the hour; and which being only light, was more alarming than a dozen ghosts, as he was powerless to make out what it meant, or would be at; and was sometimes apprehensive that he might be at that very moment an interesting case of spontaneous combustion,[2] without having the consolation of knowing it. At last, however, he began to think—as you or I would have thought at first; for it is always the person not in the predicament who knows what ought to have been done in it, and would unquestionably have done it too—at last, I say, he began to think that the source and secret of this ghostly light might be in the adjoining room: from whence, on further tracing it, it seemed to shine. This idea taking full possession of his mind, he got up softly and shuffled in his slippers to the door.

The moment Scrooge's hand was on the lock, a strange voice called him by his name, and bade him enter. He obeyed.

It was his own room. There was no doubt about that. But it had undergone a surprising transformation. The walls and ceiling were so hung with living green, that it looked a perfect grove, from every part of which, bright gleaming berries glistened. The crisp leaves of holly, mistletoe, and ivy reflected back the light, as if so many little mirrors had been scattered there; and such a mighty blaze went roaring up the chimney, as that dull petrification of a hearth had never known in Scrooge's time, or Marley's, or for many and many a winter season gone. Heaped up on the floor, to form a kind of throne, were turkeys, geese, game, poultry, brawn, great joints of meat, sucking-pigs, long wreaths of sausages, mince-pies, plum-puddings, barrels of oysters, red-hot chestnuts, cherry-cheeked apples, juicy oranges, luscious pears, immense twelfth-cakes,[3] and seething bowls of punch, that made the chamber dim with their delicious steam. In easy state upon this couch, there sat a jolly Giant, glorious to see; who bore a glowing torch, in shape not unlike Plenty's horn, and held it up, high up, to shed its light on Scrooge, as he came peeping round the door.

"Come in!" exclaimed the Ghost. "Come in! and know me better, man!"

Scrooge entered timidly, and hung his head before this Spirit. He was not the dogged Scrooge he had been; and though the Spirit's eyes were clear and kind, he did not like to meet them.

"I am the Ghost of Christmas Present," said the Spirit. "Look upon me!"

Scrooge reverently did so. It was clothed in one simple deep green robe, or mantle, bordered with white fur. This garment hung so loosely on the figure, that its capacious breast was bare, as if disdaining to be warded or concealed by any artifice. Its feet, observable beneath the ample folds of the garment, were also bare; and on its head it wore no other covering than a holly wreath, set here and there with shining icicles. Its dark brown curls were long and free: free as its genial face, its sparkling eye, its open hand, its cheery voice, its unconstrained demeanour, and its joyful air. Girded round its middle was an antique scabbard; but no sword was in it, and the ancient sheath was eaten up with rust.

"You have never seen the like of me before!" exclaimed the Spirit.

"Never," Scrooge made answer to it.

"Have never walked forth with the younger members of my family; meaning (for I am very young) my elder brothers born in these later years?" pursued the Phantom.

"I don't think I have," said Scrooge. "I am afraid I have not. Have you had many brothers, Spirit?"

"More than eighteen hundred," said the Ghost.

---

2. Dickens was fascinated by the theory that under certain conditions a human body could go up in flames spontaneously; in his novel *Bleak House* the rag-and-bone dealer, Krook, perishes this way.

3. Decorated cakes eaten on Twelfth Night (January 5), the eve of Epiphany; traditionally, the end of Christmas festivities.

"A tremendous family to provide for!" muttered Scrooge.

The Ghost of Christmas Present rose.

"Spirit," said Scrooge submissively, "conduct me where you will. I went forth last night on compulsion, and I learnt a lesson which is working now. To-night, if you have aught to teach me, let me profit by it."

"Touch my robe!"

Scrooge did as he was told, and held it fast.

Holly, mistletoe, red berries, ivy, turkeys, geese, game, poultry, brawn, meat, pigs, sausages, oysters, pies, puddings, fruit, and punch, all vanished instantly. So did the room, the fire, the ruddy glow, the hour of night, and they stood in the city streets on Christmas morning, where (for the weather was severe) the people made a rough, but brisk and not unpleasant kind of music, in scraping the snow from the pavement in front of their dwellings, and from the tops of their houses: whence it was mad delight to the boys to see it come plumping down into the road below, and splitting into artificial little snow-storms.

The house fronts looked black enough, and the windows blacker, contrasting with the smooth white sheet of snow upon the roofs, and with the dirtier snow upon the ground; which last deposit had been ploughed up in deep furrows by the heavy wheels of carts and waggons; furrows that crossed and re-crossed each other hundreds of times where the great streets branched off, and made intricate channels, hard to trace, in the thick yellow mud and icy water. The sky was gloomy, and the shortest streets were choked up with a dingy mist, half thawed, half frozen, whose heavier particles descended in a shower of sooty atoms, as if all the chimneys in Great Britain had, by one consent, caught fire, and were blazing away to their dear hearts' content. There was nothing very cheerful in the climate or the town, and yet was there an air of cheerfulness abroad that the clearest summer air and brightest summer sun might have endeavoured to diffuse in vain.

For the people who were shovelling away on the housetops were jovial and full of glee; calling out to one another from the parapets, and now and then exchanging a facetious snow-ball—better-natured missile far than many a wordy jest—laughing heartily if it went right, and not less heartily if it went wrong. The poulterers' shops were still half open, and the fruiterers' were radiant in their glory. There were great round, pot-bellied baskets of chestnuts, shaped like the waistcoats of jolly old gentlemen, lolling at the doors, and tumbling out into the street in their apoplectic opulence. There were ruddy, brown-faced, broad-girthed Spanish Onions, shining in the fatness of their growth like Spanish Friars; and winking from their shelves in wanton slyness at the girls as they went by, and glanced demurely at the hung-up mistletoe. There were pears and apples, clustered high in blooming pyramids; there were bunches of grapes, made in the shopkeepers' benevolence to dangle from conspicuous hooks, that people's mouths might water gratis as they passed; there were piles of filberts, mossy and brown, recalling, in their fragrance, ancient walks among the woods, and pleasant shufflings ankle deep through withered leaves; there were Norfolk Biffins,[4] squab and swarthy, setting off the yellow of the oranges and lemons, and, in the great compactness of their juicy persons, urgently entreating and beseeching to be carried home in paper bags and eaten after dinner. The very gold and silver fish, set forth among these choice fruits in a bowl, though members of a dull

4. Cooking apples.

and stagnant-blooded race, appeared to know that there was something going on; and, to a fish, went gasping round and round their little world in slow and passionless excitement.

The Grocers'! oh the Grocers'! nearly closed, with perhaps two shutters down, or one; but through those gaps such glimpses! It was not alone that the scales descending on the counter made a merry sound, or that the twine and roller parted company so briskly, or that the canisters were rattled up and down like juggling tricks, or even that the blended scents of tea and coffee were so grateful to the nose, or even that the raisins were so plentiful and rare, the almonds so extremely white, the sticks of cinnamon so long and straight, the other spices so delicious, the candied fruits so caked and spotted with molten sugar as to make the coldest lookers-on feel faint and subsequently bilious. Nor was it that the figs were moist and pulpy, or that the French plums blushed in modest tartness from their highly-decorated boxes, or that everything was good to eat and in its Christmas dress: but the customers were all so hurried and so eager in the hopeful promise of the day, that they tumbled up against each other at the door, clashing their wicker baskets wildly, and left their purchases upon the counter, and came running back to fetch them, and committed hundreds of the like mistakes in the best humour possible; while the Grocer and his people were so frank and fresh that the polished hearts with which they fastened their aprons behind might have been their own, worn outside for general inspection, and for Christmas daws to peck at if they chose.[5]

But soon the steeples called good people all, to church and chapel, and away they came, flocking through the streets in their best clothes, and with their gayest faces. And at the same time there emerged from scores of bye streets, lanes, and nameless turnings, innumerable people, carrying their dinners to the bakers' shops.[6] The sight of these poor revellers appeared to interest the Spirit very much, for he stood with Scrooge beside him in a baker's doorway, and taking off the covers as their bearers passed, sprinkled incense on their dinners from his torch. And it was a very uncommon kind of torch, for once or twice when there were angry words between some dinner-carriers who had jostled each other, he shed a few drops of water on them from it, and their good humour was restored directly. For they said, it was a shame to quarrel upon Christmas Day. And so it was! God love it, so it was!

In time the bells ceased, and the bakers' were shut up; and yet there was a genial shadowing forth of all these dinners and the progress of their cooking, in the thawed blotch of wet above each baker's oven; where the pavement smoked as if its stones were cooking too.

"Is there a peculiar flavour in what you sprinkle from your torch?" asked Scrooge.

"There is. My own."

"Would it apply to any kind of dinner on this day?" asked Scrooge.

"To any kindly given. To a poor one most."

"Why to a poor one most?" asked Scrooge.

"Because it needs it most."

"Spirit," said Scrooge, after a moment's thought, "I wonder you, of all the beings in the many worlds about us, should desire to cramp these people's opportunities of innocent enjoyment."

5. Cf. *Othello*, 1.1.65–66: "But I will wear my heart upon my sleeve / For daws to peck at."
6. Bakers were forbidden to bake bread on Sundays and holidays, so working-class families brought their meals to cook in the ovens.

"I!" cried the Spirit.

"You would deprive them of their means of dining every seventh day, often the only day on which they can be said to dine at all," said Scrooge. "Wouldn't you?"

"I!" cried the Spirit.

"You seek to close these places on the Seventh Day?"[7] said Scrooge. "And it comes to the same thing."

"I seek!" exclaimed the Spirit.

"Forgive me if I am wrong. It has been done in your name, or at least in that of your family," said Scrooge.

"There are some upon this earth of yours," returned the Spirit, "who lay claim to know us, and who do their deeds of passion, pride, ill-will, hatred, envy, bigotry, and selfishness in our name, who are as strange to us and all our kith and kin, as if they had never lived. Remember that, and charge their doings on themselves, not us."

Scrooge promised that he would; and they went on, invisible, as they had been before, into the suburbs of the town. It was a remarkable quality of the Ghost (which Scrooge had observed at the baker's) that notwithstanding his gigantic size, he could accommodate himself to any place with ease; and that he stood beneath a low roof quite as gracefully and like a supernatural creature, as it was possible he could have done in any lofty hall.

And perhaps it was the pleasure the good Spirit had in showing off this power of his, or else it was his own kind, generous, hearty nature, and his sympathy with all poor men, that led him straight to Scrooge's clerk's; for there he went, and took Scrooge with him, holding to his robe; and on the threshold of the door the Spirit smiled, and stopped to bless Bob Cratchit's dwelling with the sprinkling of his torch. Think of that! Bob had but fifteen "Bob" a-week himself; he pocketed on Saturdays but fifteen copies of his Christian name; and yet the Ghost of Christmas Present blessed his four-roomed house!

Then up rose Mrs Cratchit, Cratchit's wife, dressed out but poorly in a twice-turned gown,[8] but brave in ribbons, which are cheap and make a goodly show for sixpence; and she laid the cloth, assisted by Belinda Cratchit, second of her daughters, also brave in ribbons; while Master Peter Cratchit plunged a fork into the saucepan of potatoes, and getting the corners of his monstrous shirt-collar (Bob's private property, conferred upon his son and heir in honour of the day) into his mouth, rejoiced to find himself so gallantly attired, and yearned to show his linen in the fashionable Parks. And now two smaller Cratchits, boy and girl, came tearing in, screaming that outside the baker's they had smelt the goose, and known it for their own; and basking in luxurious thoughts of sage and onion, these young Cratchits danced about the table, and exalted Master Peter Cratchit to the skies, while he (not proud, although his collars nearly choked him) blew the fire, until the slow potatoes bubbling up, knocked loudly at the saucepan-lid to be let out and peeled.

"What has ever got your precious father then," said Mrs Cratchit. "And your brother, Tiny Tim; and Martha warn't as late last Christmas Day by half-an-hour!"

"Here's Martha, mother!" said a girl, appearing as she spoke.

"Here's Martha, mother!" cried the two young Cratchits. "Hurrah! There's *such* a goose, Martha!"

---

7. Dickens strongly opposed efforts in the 1830s to pass a Sunday Observance Bill limiting the recreations of working people on their only day off. (See *Sunday Under Three Heads* in Perspectives: Religion and Science, page 1378.)
8. A worn out and remade dress.

"Why, bless your heart alive, my dear, how late you are!" said Mrs Cratchit, kissing her a dozen times, and taking off her shawl and bonnet for her, with officious zeal.

"We'd a deal of work to finish up last night," replied the girl, "and had to clear away this morning, mother!"

"Well! Never mind so long as you are come," said Mrs Cratchit. "Sit ye down before the fire, my dear, and have a warm, Lord bless ye!"

"No no! There's father coming," cried the two young Cratchits, who were everywhere at once. "Hide Martha, hide!"

So Martha hid herself, and in came little Bob, the father, with at least three feet of comforter exclusive of the fringe, hanging down before him; and his thread-bare clothes darned up and brushed, to look seasonable; and Tiny Tim upon his shoulder. Alas for Tiny Tim, he bore a little crutch, and had his limbs supported by an iron frame!

"Why, where's our Martha?" cried Bob Cratchit looking round.

"Not coming," said Mrs Cratchit.

"Not coming!" said Bob, with a sudden declension in his high spirits; for he had been Tim's blood horse[9] all the way from church, and had come home rampant. "Not coming upon Christmas Day!"

Martha didn't like to see him disappointed, if it were only in joke; so she came out prematurely from behind the closet door, and ran into his arms, while the two young Cratchits hustled Tiny Tim, and bore him off into the wash-house, that he might hear the pudding singing in the copper.

"And how did little Tim behave?" asked Mrs Cratchit, when she had rallied Bob on his credulity and Bob had hugged his daughter to his heart's content.

"As good as gold," said Bob, "and better. Somehow he gets thoughtful sitting by himself so much, and thinks the strangest things you ever heard. He told me, coming home, that he hoped the people saw him in the church, because he was a cripple, and it might be pleasant to them to remember upon Christmas Day, who made lame beggars walk and blind men see."

Bob's voice was tremulous when he told them this, and trembled more when he said that Tiny Tim was growing strong and hearty.

His active little crutch was heard upon the floor, and back came Tiny Tim before another word was spoken, escorted by his brother and sister to his stool before the fire; and while Bob, turning up his cuffs—as if, poor fellow, they were capable of being made more shabby—compounded some hot mixture in a jug with gin and lemons, and stirred it round and round and put it on the hob to simmer; Master Peter, and the two ubiquitous young Cratchits went to fetch the goose, with which they soon returned in high procession.

Such a bustle ensued that you might have thought a goose the rarest of all birds; a feathered phenomenon, to which a black swan was a matter of course; and in truth it was something very like it in that house. Mrs Cratchit made the gravy (ready beforehand in a little saucepan) hissing hot; Master Peter mashed the potatoes with incredible vigour; Miss Belinda sweetened up the apple-sauce; Martha dusted the hot plates; Bob took Tiny Tim beside him in a tiny corner at the table; the two young Cratchits set chairs for everybody, not forgetting themselves, and mounting guard upon their posts, crammed spoons into their mouths, lest they should shriek for goose before their turn came to be helped. At last the dishes were set on, and grace was said. It was succeeded by a breathless pause, as Mrs Cratchit, looking slowly all along

---

9. I.e., Bob was carrying Tim on his shoulders.

the carving-knife, prepared to plunge it in the breast; but when she did, and when the long expected gush of stuffing issued forth, one murmur of delight arose all round the board, and even Tiny Tim, excited by the two young Cratchits, beat on the table with the handle of his knife, and feebly cried Hurrah!

There never was such a goose. Bob said he didn't believe there ever was such a goose cooked. Its tenderness and flavour, size and cheapness, were the themes of universal admiration. Eked out by the apple-sauce and mashed potatoes, it was a sufficient dinner for the whole family; indeed, as Mrs Cratchit said with great delight (surveying one small atom of a bone upon the dish), they hadn't ate it all at last! Yet every one had had enough, and the youngest Cratchits in particular, were steeped in sage and onion to the eyebrows! But now, the plates being changed by Miss Belinda, Mrs Cratchit left the room alone—too nervous to bear witnesses—to take the pudding up, and bring it in.

Suppose it should not be done enough! Suppose it should break in turning out! Suppose somebody should have got over the wall of the back-yard, and stolen it, while they were merry with the goose: a supposition at which the two young Cratchits became livid! All sorts of horrors were supposed.

Hallo! A great deal of steam! The pudding was out of the copper. A smell like a washing-day! That was the cloth. A smell like an eating-house, and a pastry cook's next door to each other, with a laundress's next door to that! That was the pudding. In half a minute Mrs Cratchit entered: flushed, but smiling proudly: with the pudding, like a speckled cannon-ball, so hard and firm, blazing in half of half-a-quartern of ignited brandy, and bedight with Christmas holly stuck into the top.

Oh, a wonderful pudding! Bob Cratchit said, and calmly too, that he regarded it as the greatest success achieved by Mrs Cratchit since their marriage. Mrs Cratchit said that now the weight was off her mind, she would confess she had had her doubts about the quantity of flour. Everybody had something to say about it, but nobody said or thought it was at all a small pudding for a large family. It would have been flat heresy to do so. Any Cratchit would have blushed to hint at such a thing.

At last the dinner was all done, the cloth was cleared, the hearth swept, and the fire made up. The compound in the jug being tasted, and considered perfect, apples and oranges were put upon the table, and a shovel-full of chestnuts on the fire. Then all the Cratchit family drew round the hearth, in what Bob Cratchit called a circle, meaning half a one; and at Bob Cratchit's elbow stood the family display of glass; two tumblers, and a custard-cup without a handle.

These held the hot stuff from the jug, however, as well as golden goblets would have done; and Bob served it out with beaming looks, while the chestnuts on the fire sputtered and crackled noisily. Then Bob proposed:

"A Merry Christmas to us all, my dears. God bless us!"

Which all the family re-echoed.

"God bless us every one!" said Tiny Tim, the last of all.

He sat very close to his father's side, upon his little stool. Bob held his withered little hand in his, as if he loved the child, and wished to keep him by his side, and dreaded that he might be taken from him.

"Spirit," said Scrooge, with an interest he had never felt before, "tell me if Tiny Tim will live."

"I see a vacant seat," replied the Ghost, "in the poor chimney corner, and a crutch without an owner, carefully preserved. If these shadows remain unaltered by the Future, the child will die."

"No, no," said Scrooge. "Oh no, kind Spirit! say he will be spared."

"If these shadows remain unaltered by the Future, none other of my race," returned the Ghost, "will find him here. What then? If he be like to die, he had better do it, and decrease the surplus population."

Scrooge hung his head to hear his own words quoted by the Spirit, and was overcome with penitence and grief.

"Man," said the Ghost, "if man you be in heart, not adamant, forbear that wicked cant until you have discovered What the surplus is, and Where it is. Will you decide what men shall live, what men shall die? It may be, that in the sight of Heaven, you are more worthless and less fit to live than millions like this poor man's child. Oh God! to hear the Insect on the leaf pronouncing on the too much life among his hungry brothers in the dust!"

Scrooge bent before the Ghost's rebuke, and trembling cast his eyes upon the ground. But he raised them speedily, on hearing his own name.

"Mr Scrooge!" said Bob; "I'll give you Mr Scrooge, the Founder of the Feast!"

"The Founder of the Feast indeed!" cried Mrs Cratchit, reddening. "I wish I had him here. I'd give him a piece of my mind to feast upon, and I hope he'd have a good appetite for it."

"My dear," said Bob, "the children; Christmas Day."

"It should be Christmas Day, I am sure," said she, "on which one drinks the health of such an odious, stingy, hard, unfeeling man as Mr Scrooge. You know he is, Robert! Nobody knows it better than you do, poor fellow!"

"My dear," was Bob's mild answer, "Christmas Day."

"I'll drink his health for your sake and the Day's," said Mrs Cratchit, "not for his. Long life to him! A merry Christmas and a happy new year!—he'll be very merry and very happy, I have no doubt!"

The children drank the toast after her. It was the first of their proceedings which had no heartiness in it. Tiny Tim drank it last of all, but he didn't care twopence for it. Scrooge was the Ogre of the family. The mention of his name cast a dark shadow on the party, which was not dispelled for full five minutes.

After it had passed away, they were ten times merrier than before, from the mere relief of Scrooge the Baleful being done with. Bob Cratchit told them how he had a situation in his eye for Master Peter, which would bring in, if obtained, full five-and-sixpence weekly. The two young Cratchits laughed tremendously at the idea of Peter's being a man of business; and Peter himself looked thoughtfully at the fire from between his collars, as if he were deliberating what particular investments he should favour when he came into the receipt of that bewildering income. Martha, who was a poor apprentice at a milliner's, then told them what kind of work she had to do, and how many hours she worked at a stretch, and how she meant to lie a-bed tomorrow morning for a good long rest; to-morrow being a holiday she passed at home. Also how she had seen a countess and a lord some days before, and how the lord "was much about as tall as Peter"; at which Peter pulled up his collars so high that you couldn't have seen his head if you had been there. All this time the chestnuts and the jug went round and round; and bye and bye they had a song, about a lost child travelling in the snow, from Tiny Tim; who had a plaintive little voice, and sang it very well indeed.

There was nothing of high mark in this. They were not a handsome family; they were not well dressed; their shoes were far from being water-proof; their clothes were scanty; and Peter might have known, and very likely did, the inside of a pawnbroker's. But they were happy, grateful, pleased with one another, and contented with the time; and when they faded, and looked happier yet in the bright sprinklings of the Spirit's torch at parting, Scrooge had his eye upon them, and especially on Tiny Tim, until the last.

By this time it was getting dark, and snowing pretty heavily; and as Scrooge and the Spirit went along the streets, the brightness of the roaring fires in kitchens, parlours, and all sorts of rooms, was wonderful. Here, the flickering of the blaze showed preparations for a cosy dinner, with hot plates baking through and through before the fire, and deep red curtains, ready to be drawn, to shut out cold and darkness. There, all the children of the house were running out into the snow to meet their married sisters, brothers, cousins, uncles, aunts, and be the first to greet them. Here, again, were shadows on the window-blind of guests assembling; and there a group of handsome girls, all hooded and fur-booted, and all chattering at once, tripped lightly off to some near neighbour's house; where, woe upon the single man who saw them enter—artful witches: well they knew it—in a glow!

But if you had judged from the numbers of people on their way to friendly gatherings, you might have thought that no one was at home to give them welcome when they got there, instead of every house expecting company, and piling up its fires half-chimney high. Blessings on it, how the Ghost exulted! How it bared its breadth of breast, and opened its capacious palm, and floated on, outpouring, with a generous hand, its bright and harmless mirth on everything within its reach! The very lamplighter, who ran on before dotting the dusky street with specks of light, and who was dressed to spend the evening somewhere, laughed out loudly as the Spirit passed: though little kenned the lamplighter that he had any company but Christmas!

And now, without a word of warning from the Ghost, they stood upon a bleak and desert moor, where monstrous masses of rude stone were cast about, as though it were the burial-place of giants; and water spread itself wheresoever it listed—or would have done so, but for the frost that held it prisoner; and nothing grew but moss and furze, and coarse, rank grass. Down in the west the setting sun had left a streak of fiery red, which glared upon the desolation for an instant, like a sullen eye, and frowning lower, lower, lower yet, was lost in the thick gloom of darkest night.

"What place is this?" asked Scrooge.

"A place where Miners live, who labour in the bowels of the earth," returned the Spirit. "But they know me. See!"

A light shone from the window of a hut, and swiftly they advanced towards it. Passing through the wall of mud and stone, they found a cheerful company assembled round a glowing fire. An old, old man and woman, with their children and their children's children, and another generation beyond that, all decked out gaily in their holiday attire. The old man, in a voice that seldom rose above the howling of the wind upon the barren waste, was singing them a Christmas song; it had been a very old song when he was a boy; and from time to time they all joined in the chorus. So surely as they raised their voices, the old man got quite blithe and loud; and so surely as they stopped, his vigour sang again.

The Spirit did not tarry here, but bade Scrooge hold his robe, and passing on above the moor, sped whither? Not to sea? To sea. To Scrooge's horror, looking back, he saw the last of the land, a frightful range of rocks, behind them; and his ears were deafened by the thundering of water, as it rolled, and roared, and raged among the dreadful caverns it had worn, and fiercely tried to undermine the earth.

Built upon a dismal reef of sunken rocks, some league or so from shore, on which the waters chafed and dashed, the wild year through, there stood a solitary lighthouse. Great heaps of sea-weed clung to its base, and storm-birds—born of the wind one might suppose, as sea-weed of the water—rose and fell about it, like the waves they skimmed.

But even here, two men who watched the light had made a fire, that through the loophole in the thick stone wall shed out a ray of brightness on the awful sea. Joining their horny hands over the rough table at which they sat, they wished each other Merry Christmas in their can of grog; and one of them: the elder, too, with his face all damaged and scarred with hard weather, as the figure-head of an old ship might be: struck up a sturdy song that was like a Gale in itself.

Again the Ghost sped on, above the black and heaving sea—on, on—until, being far away, as he told Scrooge, from any shore, they lighted on a ship. They stood beside the helmsman at the wheel, the look-out in the bow, the officers who had the watch; dark, ghostly figures in their several stations; but every man among them hummed a Christmas tune, or had a Christmas thought, or spoke below his breath to his companion of some bygone Christmas Day, with homeward hopes belonging to it. And every man on board, waking or sleeping, good or bad, had had a kinder word for another on that day than on any day in the year; and had shared to some extent in its festivities; and had remembered those he cared for at a distance, and had known that they delighted to remember him.

It was a great surprise to Scrooge, while listening to the moaning of the wind, and thinking what a solemn thing it was to move on through the lonely darkness over an unknown abyss, whose depths were secrets as profound as Death: it was a great surprise to Scrooge, while thus engaged, to hear a hearty laugh. It was a much greater surprise to Scrooge to recognise it as his own nephew's, and to find himself in a bright, dry, gleaming room, with the Spirit standing smiling by his side, and looking at that same nephew with approving affability!

"Ha, ha!" laughed Scrooge's nephew. "Ha, ha, ha!"

If you should happen, by any unlikely chance, to know a man more blest in a laugh than Scrooge's nephew, all I can say is, I should like to know him too. Introduce him to me, and I'll cultivate his acquaintance.

It is a fair, even-handed, noble adjustment of things, that while there is infection in disease and sorrow, there is nothing in the world so irresistibly contagious as laughter and good-humour. When Scrooge's nephew laughed in this way: holding his sides, rolling his head, and twisting his face into the most extravagant contortions: Scrooge's niece, by marriage, laughed as heartily as he. And their assembled friends being not a bit behindhand, roared out, lustily.

"Ha, ha! Ha, ha, ha, ha!"

"He said that Christmas was a humbug, as I live!" cried Scrooge's nephew. "He believed it too!"

"More shame for him, Fred!" said Scrooge's niece, indignantly. Bless those women; they never do anything by halves. They are always in earnest.

She was very pretty: exceedingly pretty. With a dimpled, surprised-looking, capital face; a ripe little mouth, that seemed made to be kissed—as no doubt it was; all kinds of good little dots about her chin, that melted into one another when she laughed; and the sunniest pair of eyes you ever saw in any little creature's head. Altogether she was what you would have called provoking, you know; but satisfactory too. Oh, perfectly satisfactory!

"He's a comical old fellow," said Scrooge's nephew, "that's the truth: and not so pleasant as he might be. However, his offences carry their own punishment, and I have nothing to say against him."

"I'm sure he is very rich, Fred," hinted Scrooge's niece. "At least you always tell me so."

"What of that, my dear!" said Scrooge's nephew. "His wealth is of no use to him. He don't do any good with it. He don't make himself comfortable with it. He hasn't the satisfaction of thinking—ha, ha, ha!—that he is ever going to benefit Us with it."

"I have no patience with him," observed Scrooge's niece. Scrooge's niece's sisters, and all the other ladies, expressed the same opinion.

"Oh, I have!" said Scrooge's nephew. "I am sorry for him; I couldn't be angry with him if I tried. Who suffers by his ill whims! Himself, always. Here, he takes it into his head to dislike us, and he won't come and dine with us. What's the consequence? He don't lose much of a dinner."

"Indeed, I think he loses a very good dinner," interrupted Scrooge's niece. Everybody else said the same, and they must be allowed to have been competent judges, because they had just had dinner; and, with the dessert upon the table, were clustered round the fire, by lamplight.

"Well! I'm very glad to hear it," said Scrooge's nephew, "because I haven't great faith in these young housekeepers. What do *you* say, Topper?"

Topper had clearly got his eye upon one of Scrooge's niece's sisters, for he answered that a bachelor was a wretched outcast, who had no right to express an opinion on the subject. Whereat Scrooge's niece's sister—the plump one with the lace tucker: not the one with the roses—blushed.

"Do go on, Fred," said Scrooge's niece, clapping her hands. "He never finishes what he begins to say! He is such a ridiculous fellow!"

Scrooge's nephew revelled in another laugh, and as it was impossible to keep the infection off; though the plump sister tried hard to do it with aromatic vinegar; his example was unanimously followed.

"I was going to say," said Scrooge's nephew, "that the consequence of his taking a dislike to us, and not making merry with us, is, as I think, that he loses some pleasant moments, which could do him no harm. I am sure he loses pleasanter companions than he can find in his own thoughts, either in his mouldy old office, or his dusty chambers. I mean to give him the same chance every year, whether he likes it or not, for I pity him. He may rail at Christmas till he dies, but he can't help thinking better of it—I defy him—if he finds me going there, in good temper, year after year, and saying Uncle Scrooge, how are you? If it only puts him in the vein to leave his poor clerk fifty pounds, *that's* something; and I think I shook him, yesterday."

It was their turn to laugh now, at the notion of his shaking Scrooge. But being thoroughly good-natured, and not much caring what they laughed at, so that they laughed at any rate, he encouraged them in their merriment, and passed the bottle, joyously.

After tea, they had some music. For they were a musical family, and knew what they were about, when they sung a Glee or Catch,[1] I can assure you: especially Topper, who could growl away in the bass like a good one, and never swell the large veins in his forehead, or get red in the face over it. Scrooge's niece played well upon the harp; and played among other tunes a simple little air (a mere nothing: you might learn to whistle it in two minutes), which had been familiar to the child who fetched Scrooge from the boarding-school, as he had been reminded by the Ghost of Christmas Past. When this strain of music sounded, all the things that Ghost had shown him, came upon his mind; he softened more and more; and thought that if he could

---

1. A glee is an unaccompanied song for three or more voices; a catch is a round.

have listened to it often, years ago, he might have cultivated the kindnesses of life for his own happiness with his own hands, without resorting to the sexton's spade that buried Jacob Marley.

But they didn't devote the whole evening to music. After a while they played at forfeits;[2] for it is good to be children sometimes, and never better than at Christmas, when its mighty Founder was a child himself. Stop! There was first a game at blind-man's buff. Of course there was. And I no more believe Topper was really blind than I believe he had eyes in his boots. My opinion is, that it was a done thing between him and Scrooge's nephew; and that the Ghost of Christmas Present knew it. The way he went after that plump sister in the lace tucker, was an outrage on the credulity of human nature. Knocking down the fire-irons, tumbling over the chairs, bumping against the piano, smothering himself among the curtains, wherever she went, there went he. He always knew where the plump sister was. He wouldn't catch anybody else. If you had fallen up against him, as some of them did, and stood there; he would have made a feint of endeavouring to seize you, which would have been an affront to your understanding; and would instantly have sidled off in the direction of the plump sister. She often cried out that it wasn't fair; and it really was not. But when at last, he caught her; when, in spite of all her silken rustlings, and her rapid flutterings past him, he got her into a corner whence there was no escape; then his conduct was the most execrable. For his pretending not to know her; his pretending that it was necessary to touch her head-dress, and further to assure himself of her identity by pressing a certain ring upon her finger, and a certain chain about her neck; was vile, monstrous! No doubt she told him her opinion of it, when, another blind-man being in office, they were so very confidential together, behind the curtains.

Scrooge's niece was not one of the blind-man's buff party, but was made comfortable with a large chair and a footstool, in a snug corner, where the Ghost and Scrooge were close behind her. But she joined in the forfeits, and loved her love to admiration with all the letters of the alphabet. Likewise at the game of How, When, and Where, she was very great, and to the secret joy of Scrooge's nephew, beat her sisters hollow: though they were sharp girls too, as Topper could have told you. There might have been twenty people there, young and old, but they all played, and so did Scrooge; for wholly forgetting in the interest he had in what was going on, that his voice made no sound in their ears, he sometimes came out with his guess quite loud, and very often guessed quite right, too; for the sharpest needle, best Whitechapel,[3] warranted not to cut in the eye, was not sharper than Scrooge: blunt as he took it in his head to be.

The Ghost was greatly pleased to find him in this mood, and looked upon him with such favour that he begged like a boy to be allowed to stay until the guests departed. But this the Spirit said could not be done.

"Here's a new game," said Scrooge. "One half hour, Spirit, only one!"

It was a Game called Yes and No, where Scrooge's nephew had to think of something, and the rest must find out what; he only answering to their questions yes or no as the case was. The brisk fire of questioning to which he was exposed, elicited from him that he was thinking of an animal, a live animal, rather a disagreeable animal, a savage animal, an animal that growled and grunted sometimes, and talked sometimes, and lived in London, and walked about the streets, and wasn't made a show of,

2. A game in which penalties are exacted when the player makes a mistake.

3. Whitechapel, a district in East London, was known for its manufacturing.

and wasn't led by anybody, and didn't live in a menagerie, and was never killed in a market, and was not a horse, or an ass, or a cow, or a bull, or a tiger, or a dog, or a pig, or a cat, or a bear. At every fresh question that was put to him, this nephew burst into a fresh roar of laughter; and was so inexpressibly tickled, that he was obliged to get up off the sofa and stamp. At last the plump sister, falling into a similar state, cried out:

"I have found it out! I know what it is, Fred! I know what it is!"

"What is it?" cried Fred.

"It's your Uncle Scro-o-o-o-oge!"

Which it certainly was. Admiration was the universal sentiment, though some objected that the reply to "Is it a bear?" ought to have been "Yes;" inasmuch as an an-swer in the negative was sufficient to have diverted their thoughts from Mr Scrooge, supposing they had ever had any tendency that way.

"He has given us plenty of merriment, I am sure," said Fred, "and it would be un-grateful not to drink his health. Here is a glass of mulled wine ready to our hand at the moment; and I say 'Uncle Scrooge!'"

"Well! Uncle Scrooge!" they cried.

"A Merry Christmas and a Happy New Year to the old man, whatever he is!" said Scrooge's nephew. "He wouldn't take it from me, but may he have it, neverthe-less. Uncle Scrooge!"

Uncle Scrooge had imperceptibly become so gay and light of heart, that he would have pledged the unconscious company in return, and thanked them in an in-audible speech, if the Ghost had given him time. But the whole scene passed off in the breath of the last word spoken by his nephew; and he and the Spirit were again upon their travels.

Much they saw, and far they went, and many homes they visited, but always with a happy end. The Spirit stood beside sick beds, and they were cheerful; on foreign lands, and they were close at home; by struggling men, and they were patient in their greater hope; by poverty, and it was rich. In almshouse, hospital, and jail, in misery's every refuge, where vain man in his little brief authority[4] had not made fast the door, and barred the Spirit out, he left his blessing, and taught Scrooge his precepts.

It was a long night, if it were only a night; but Scrooge had his doubts of this, be-cause the Christmas Holidays appeared to be condensed into the space of time they passed together. It was strange, too, that while Scrooge remained unaltered in his outward form, the Ghost grew older, clearly older. Scrooge had observed this change, but never spoke of it, until they left a children's Twelfth Night party, when, looking at the Spirit as they stood together in an open place, he noticed that its hair was gray.

"Are spirits' lives so short?" asked Scrooge.

"My life upon this globe, is very brief," replied the Ghost. "It ends to-night."

"To-night!" cried Scrooge.

"To-night at midnight. Hark! The time is drawing near."

The chimes were ringing the three quarters past eleven at that moment.

"Forgive me if I am not justified in what I ask," said Scrooge, looking intently at the Spirit's robe, "but I see something strange, and not belonging to yourself, protrud-ing from your skirts. Is it a foot or a claw!"

"It might be a claw, for the flesh there is upon it," was the Spirit's sorrowful re-ply. "Look here."

4. *Measure for Measure*, 2.2.121–22: "but man, proud man, / Dress'd in a little brief authority."

From the foldings of its robe, it brought two children; wretched, abject, frightful, hideous, miserable. They knelt down at its feet, and clung upon the outside of its garment.

"Oh, Man! look here. Look, look, down here!" exclaimed the Ghost.

They were a boy and girl. Yellow, meagre, ragged, scowling, wolfish; but prostrate, too, in their humility. Where graceful youth should have filled their features out, and touched them with its freshest tints, a stale and shrivelled hand, like that of age, had pinched, and twisted them, and pulled them into shreds. Where angels might have sat enthroned, devils lurked; and glared out menacing. No change, no degradation, no perversion of humanity, in any grade, through all the mysteries of wonderful creation, has monsters half so horrible and dread.

Scrooge started back, appalled. Having them shown to him in this way, he tried to say they were fine children, but the words choked themselves, rather than be parties to a lie of such enormous magnitude.

"Spirit! are they yours?" Scrooge could say no more.

"They are Man's," said the Spirit, looking down upon them. "And they cling to me, appealing from their fathers. This boy is Ignorance. This girl is Want. Beware them both, and all of their degree, but most of all beware this boy, for on his brow I see that written which is Doom, unless the writing be erased. Deny it!" cried the Spirit, stretching out its hand towards the city. "Slander those who tell it ye! Admit it for your factious purposes, and make it worse. And bide the end!"

"Have they no refuge or resource?" cried Scrooge.

"Are there no prisons?" said the Spirit, turning on him for the last time with his own words. "Are there no workhouses?"

The bell struck twelve.

Scrooge looked about him for the Ghost, and saw it not. As the last stroke ceased to vibrate, he remembered the prediction of old Jacob Marley, and lifting up his eyes, beheld a solemn Phantom, draped and hooded, coming, like a mist along the ground, towards him.

Stave Four
THE LAST OF THE SPIRITS

The Phantom slowly, gravely, silently, approached. When it came near him, Scrooge bent down upon his knee; for in the very air through which this Spirit moved it seemed to scatter gloom and mystery.

It was shrouded in a deep black garment, which concealed its head, its face, its form, and left nothing of it visible save one outstretched hand. But for this it would have been difficult to detach its figure from the night, and separate it from the darkness by which it was surrounded.

He felt that it was tall and stately when it came beside him, and that its mysterious presence filled him with a solemn dread. He knew no more, for the Spirit neither spoke nor moved.

"I am in the presence of the Ghost of Christmas Yet To Come?" said Scrooge.

The Spirit answered not, but pointed onward with its hand.

"You are about to show me shadows of the things that have not happened, but will happen in the time before us," Scrooge pursued. "Is that so, Spirit?"

The upper portion of the garment was contracted for an instant in its folds, as if the Spirit had inclined its head. That was the only answer he received.

Although well used to ghostly company by this time, Scrooge feared the silent shape so much that his legs trembled beneath him, and he found that he could hardly stand when he prepared to follow it. The Spirit paused a moment, as observing his condition, and giving him time to recover.

But Scrooge was all the worse for this. It thrilled him with a vague uncertain horror, to know that behind the dusky shroud, there were ghostly eyes intently fixed upon him, while he, though he stretched his own to the utmost, could see nothing but a spectral hand and one great heap of black.

"Ghost of the Future!" he exclaimed, "I fear you more than any Spectre I have seen. But as I know your purpose is to do me good, and as I hope to live to be another man from what I was, I am prepared to bear you company, and do it with a thankful heart. Will you not speak to me?"

It gave him no reply. The hand was pointed straight before them.

"Lead on!" said Scrooge. "Lead on! The night is waning fast, and it is precious time to me, I know. Lead on, Spirit!"

The Phantom moved away as it had come towards him. Scrooge followed in the shadow of its dress, which bore him up, he thought, and carried him along.

They scarcely seemed to enter the city; for the city rather seemed to spring up about them, and encompass them of its own act. But there they were, in the heart of it; on 'Change, amongst the merchants; who hurried up and down, and chinked the money in their pockets, and conversed in groups, and looked at their watches, and trifled thoughtfully with their great gold seals; and so forth, as Scrooge had seen them often.

The Spirit stopped beside one little knot of business men. Observing that the hand was pointed to them, Scrooge advanced to listen to their talk.

"No," said a great fat man with a monstrous chin, "I don't know much about it, either way. I only know he's dead."

"When did he die?" inquired another.

"Last night, I believe."

"Why, what was the matter with him?" asked a third, taking a vast quantity of snuff out of a very large snuff-box. "I thought he'd never die."

"God knows," said the first, with a yawn.

"What has he done with his money?" asked a red-faced gentleman with a pendulous excrescence on the end of his nose, that shook like the gills of a turkey-cock.

"I haven't heard," said the man with the large chin, yawning again. "Left it to his Company, perhaps. He hasn't left it to me. That's all I know."

This pleasantry was received with a general laugh.

"It's likely to be a very cheap funeral," said the same speaker; "for upon my life I don't know of anybody to go to it. Suppose we make up a party and volunteer?"

"I don't mind going if a lunch is provided," observed the gentleman with the excrescence on his nose. "But I must be fed, if I make one."

Another laugh.

"Well, I am the most disinterested among you, after all," said the first speaker, "for I never wear black gloves, and I never eat lunch. But I'll offer to go, if anybody else will. When I come to think of it, I'm not at all sure that I wasn't his most particular friend; for we used to stop and speak whenever we met. Bye, bye!"

Speakers and listeners strolled away, and mixed with other groups. Scrooge knew the men, and looked towards the Spirit for an explanation.

The Phantom glided on into a street. Its finger pointed to two persons meeting. Scrooge listened again, thinking that the explanation might lie here.

He knew these men, also, perfectly. They were men of business: very wealthy, and of great importance. He had made a point always of standing well in their esteem: in a business point of view, that is; strictly in a business point of view.

"How are you?" said one.

"How are you?" returned the other.

"Well!" said the first. "Old Scratch[5] has got his own at last, hey?"

"So I am told," returned the second. "Cold, isn't it?"

"Seasonable for Christmas time. You're not a skaiter, I suppose?"

"No. No. Something else to think of. Good morning!"

Not another word. That was their meeting, their conversation, and their parting.

Scrooge was at first inclined to be surprised that the Spirit should attach importance to conversations apparently so trivial; but feeling assured that they must have some hidden purpose, he set himself to consider what it was likely to be. They could scarcely be supposed to have any bearing on the death of Jacob, his old partner, for that was Past, and this Ghost's province was the Future. Nor could he think of any one immediately connected with himself, to whom he could apply them. But nothing doubting that to whomsoever they applied they had some latent moral for his own improvement, he resolved to treasure up every word he heard, and everything he saw; and especially to observe the shadow of himself when it appeared. For he had an expectation that the conduct of his future self would give him the clue he missed, and would render the solution of these riddles easy.

He looked about in that very place for his own image; but another man stood in his accustomed corner, and though the clock pointed to his usual time of day for being there, he saw no likeness of himself among the multitudes that poured in through the Porch. It gave him little surprise, however; for he had been revolving in his mind a change of life, and thought and hoped he saw his new-born resolutions carried out in this.

Quiet and dark, beside him stood the Phantom, with its outstretched hand. When he roused himself from his thoughtful quest, he fancied from the turn of the hand, and its situation in reference to himself, that the Unseen Eyes were looking at him keenly. It made him shudder, and feel very cold.

They left the busy scene, and went into an obscure part of the town, where Scrooge had never penetrated before although he recognised its situation, and its bad repute. The ways were foul and narrow; the shops and houses wretched; the people half-naked, drunken, slipshod, ugly. Alleys and archways, like so many cesspools, disgorged their offences of smell, and dirt, and life, upon the straggling streets; and the whole quarter reeked with crime, with filth, and misery.

Far in this den of infamous resort, there was a low-browed, beetling shop, below a pent-house roof,[6] where iron, old rags, bottles, bones, and greasy offal, were bought. Upon the floor within, were piled up heaps of rusty keys, nails, chains, hinges, files, scales, weights, and refuse iron of all kinds. Secrets that few would like to scrutinise were bred and hidden in mountains of unseemly rags, masses of corrupted fat, and sepulchres of bones. Sitting in among the wares he dealt in, by a charcoal-stove, made of old bricks, was a gray-haired rascal, nearly seventy years of age; who had screened himself from the cold air without, by a frousy curtaining of miscellaneous tatters, hung upon a line; and smoked his pipe in all the luxury of calm retirement.

5. The devil.   6. A roof sloping out from a building.

Scrooge and the Phantom came into the presence of this man, just as a woman with a heavy bundle slunk into the shop. But she had scarcely entered, when another woman, similarly laden, came in too; and she was closely followed by a man in faded black, who was no less startled by the sight of them, than they had been upon the recognition of each other. After a short period of blank astonishment, in which the old man with the pipe had joined them, they all three burst into a laugh.

"Let the charwoman alone to be the first!" cried she who had entered first. "Let the laundress alone to be the second; and let the undertaker's man alone to be the third. Look here, old Joe, here's a chance! If we haven't all three met here without meaning it."

"You couldn't have met in a better place," said old Joe, removing his pipe from his mouth. "Come into the parlour. You were made free of it long ago, you know; and the other two an't strangers. Stop till I shut the door of the shop. Ah! How it skreeks! There an't such a rusty bit of metal in the place as its own hinges, I believe; and I'm sure there's no such old bones here, as mine. Ha, ha! We're all suitable to our calling, we're well matched. Come into the parlour. Come into the parlour."

The parlour was the space behind the screen of rags. The old man raked the fire together with an old stair-rod, and having trimmed his smoky lamp (for it was night), with the stem of his pipe, put it in his mouth again.

While he did this, the woman who had already spoken threw her bundle on the floor and sat down in a flaunting manner on a stool; crossing her elbows on her knees, and looking with a bold defiance at the other two.

"What odds then! What odds, Mrs Dilber?" said the woman. "Every person has a right to take care of themselves. *He* always did!"

"That's true, indeed!" said the laundress. "No man more so."

"Why then, don't stand staring as if you was afraid, woman; who's the wiser? We're not going to pick holes in each other's coats, I suppose?"

"No, indeed!" said Mrs Dilber and the man together. "We should hope not."

"Very well, then!" cried the woman. "That's enough. Who's the worse for the loss of a few things like these? Not a dead man, I suppose."

"No, indeed," said Mrs Dilber, laughing.

"If he wanted to keep 'em after he was dead, a wicked old screw," pursued the woman, "why wasn't he natural in his lifetime? If he had been, he'd have had somebody to look after him when he was struck with Death, instead of lying gasping out his last there, alone by himself."

"It's the truest word that ever was spoke," said Mrs Dilber. "It's a judgment on him."

"I wish it was a little heavier one," replied the woman; "and it should have been, you may depend upon it, if I could have laid my hands on anything else. Open that bundle, old Joe, and let me know the value of it. Speak out plain. I'm not afraid to be the first, nor afraid for them to see it. We knew pretty well that we were helping ourselves, before we met here, I believe. It's no sin. Open the bundle, Joe."

But the gallantry of her friends would not allow of this; and the man in faded black, mounting the breach first, produced *his* plunder. It was not extensive. A seal or two, a pencil-case, a pair of sleeve-buttons, and a brooch of no great value, were all. They were severally examined and appraised by old Joe, who chalked the sums he was disposed to give for each, upon the wall, and added them up into a total when he found there was nothing more to come.

"That's your account," said Joe, "and I wouldn't give another sixpence, if I was to be boiled for not doing it. Who's next?"

Mrs Dilber was next. Sheets and towels, a little wearing apparel, two old-fashioned silver teaspoons, a pair of sugar-tongs, and a few boots. Her account was stated on the wall in the same manner.

"I always give too much to ladies. It's a weakness of mine, and that's the way I ruin myself," said old Joe. "That's your account. If you asked me for another penny, and made it an open question, I'd repent of being so liberal and knock off half-a-crown."

"And now undo my bundle, Joe," said the first woman.

Joe went down on his knees for the greater convenience of opening it, and having unfastened a great many knots, dragged out a large and heavy roll of some dark stuff.

"What do you call this?" said Joe. "Bed-curtains!"

"Ah!" returned the woman, laughing and leaning forward on her crossed arms. "Bed-curtains!"

"You don't mean to say you took 'em down, rings and all, with him lying there?" said Joe.

"Yes I do," replied the woman. "Why not?"

"You were born to make your fortune," said Joe, "and you'll certainly do it."

"I certainly shan't hold my hand, when I get anything in it by reaching it out, for the sake of such a man as He was, I promise you, Joe," returned the woman coolly. "Don't drop that oil upon the blankets, now."

"His blankets?" asked Joe.

"Whose else's do you think?" replied the woman. "He isn't likely to take cold without 'em, I dare say."

"I hope he didn't die of anything catching? Eh?" said old Joe, stopping in his work, and looking up.

"Don't you be afraid of that," returned the woman. "I an't so fond of his company that I'd loiter about him for such things, if he did. Ah! you may look through that shirt till your eyes ache; but you won't find a hole in it, nor a threadbare place. It's the best he had, and a fine one too. They'd have wasted it, if it hadn't been for me."

"What do you call wasting of it?" asked old Joe.

"Putting it on him to be buried in, to be sure," replied the woman with a laugh. "Somebody was fool enough to do it, but I took it off again. If calico an't good enough for such a purpose, it isn't good enough for anything. It's quite as becoming to the body. He can't look uglier than he did in that one."

Scrooge listened to this dialogue in horror. As they sat grouped about their spoil, in the scanty light afforded by the old man's lamp, he viewed them with a detestation and disgust, which could hardly have been greater, though they had been obscene demons, marketing the corpse itself.

"He, ha!" laughed the same woman, when old Joe, producing a flannel bag with money in it, told out their several gains upon the ground. "This is the end of it, you see! He frightened every one away from him when he was alive, to profit us when he was dead! Ha, ha, ha!"

"Spirit!" said Scrooge, shuddering from head to foot. "I see, I see. The case of this unhappy man might be my own. My life tends that way, now. Merciful Heaven, what is this!"

He recoiled in terror, for the scene had changed, and now he almost touched a bed: a bare, uncurtained bed: on which, beneath a ragged sheet, there lay a something covered up, which, though it was dumb, announced itself in awful language.

The room was very dark, too dark to be observed with any accuracy, though Scrooge glanced round it in obedience to a secret impulse, anxious to know what kind of room it was. A pale light, rising in the outer air, fell straight upon the bed; and on it, plundered and bereft, unwatched, unwept, uncared for, was the body of this man.

Scrooge glanced towards the Phantom. Its steady hand was pointed to the head. The cover was so carelessly adjusted that the slightest raising of it, the motion of a finger upon Scrooge's part, would have disclosed the face. He thought of it, felt how easy it would be to do, and longed to do it; but had no more power to withdraw the veil than to dismiss the spectre at his side.

Oh cold, cold, rigid, dreadful Death, set up thine altar here, and dress it with such terrors as thou hast at thy command: for this is thy dominion! But of the loved, revered, and honoured head, thou canst not turn one hair to thy dread purposes, or make one feature odious. It is not that the hand is heavy and will fall down when released; it is not that the heart and pulse are still; but that the hand WAS open, generous, and true; the heart brave, warm, and tender; and the pulse a man's. Strike, Shadow, strike! And see his good deeds springing from the wound, to sow the world with life immortal!

No voice pronounced these words in Scrooge's ears, and yet he heard them when he looked upon the bed. He thought, if this man could be raised up now, what would be his foremost thoughts? Avarice, hard dealing, griping cares? They have brought him to a rich end, truly!

He lay, in the dark empty house, with not a man, a woman, or a child, to say that he was kind to me in this or that, and for the memory of one kind word I will be kind to him. A cat was tearing at the door, and there was a sound of gnawing rats beneath the hearth-stone. What *they* wanted in the room of death, and why they were so restless and disturbed, Scrooge did not dare to think.

"Spirit!" he said, "this is a fearful place. In leaving it, I shall not leave its lesson, trust me. Let us go!"

Still the Ghost pointed with an unmoved finger to the head.

"I understand you," Scrooge returned, "and I would do it, if I could. But I have not the power, Spirit. I have not the power."

Again it seemed to look upon him.

"If there is any person in the town, who feels emotion caused by this man's death," said Scrooge quite agonised, "show that person to me, Spirit, I beseech you!"

The Phantom spread its dark robe before him for a moment, like a wing; and withdrawing it, revealed a room by daylight, where a mother and her children were.

She was expecting some one, and with anxious eagerness; for she walked up and down the room; started at every sound; looked out from the window; glanced at the clock; tried, but in vain, to work with her needle; and could hardly bear the voices of the children in their play.

At length the long-expected knock was heard. She hurried to the door, and met her husband; a man whose face was care-worn and depressed, though he was young. There was a remarkable expression in it now; a kind of serious delight of which he felt ashamed, and which he struggled to repress.

He sat down to the dinner that had been hoarding for him by the fire; and when she asked him faintly what news (which was not until after a long silence), he appeared embarrassed how to answer.

"Is it good," she said, "or bad?"—to help him.

"Bad," he answered.

"We are quite ruined?"

"No. There is hope yet, Caroline."

"If *he* relents," she said, amazed, "there is! Nothing is past hope, if such a miracle has happened."

"He is past relenting," said her husband. "He is dead."

She was a mild and patient creature if her face spoke truth; but she was thankful in her soul to hear it, and she said so, with clasped hands. She prayed forgiveness the next moment, and was sorry; but the first was the emotion of her heart.

"What the half-drunken woman whom I told you of last night, said to me, when I tried to see him and obtain a week's delay; and what I thought was a mere excuse to avoid me; turns out to have been quite true. He was not only very ill, but dying, then."

"To whom will our debt be transferred?"

"I don't know. But before that time we shall be ready with the money; and even though we were not, it would be bad fortune indeed to find so merciless a creditor in his successor. We may sleep to-night with light hearts, Caroline!"

Yes. Soften it as they would, their hearts were lighter. The children's faces, hushed and clustered round to hear what they so little understood, were brighter; and it was a happier house for this man's death! The only emotion that the Ghost could show him, caused by the event, was one of pleasure.

"Let me see some tenderness connected with a death," said Scrooge; "or that dark chamber, Spirit, which we left just now, will be for ever present to me."

The Ghost conducted him through several streets familiar to his feet; and as they went along, Scrooge looked here and there to find himself, but nowhere was he to be seen. They entered poor Bob Cratchit's house; the dwelling he had visited before; and found the mother and the children seated round the fire.

Quiet. Very quiet. The noisy little Cratchits were as still as statues in one corner, and sat looking up at Peter, who had a book before him. The mother and her daughters were engaged in sewing. But surely they were very quiet!

"'And He took a child, and set him in the midst of them.'"[7]

Where had Scrooge heard those words? He had not dreamed them. The boy must have read them out, as he and the Spirit crossed the threshold. Why did he not go on?

The mother laid her work upon the table, and put her hand up to her face.

"The colour hurts my eyes," she said.

The colour? Ah, poor Tiny Tim!

"They're better now again," said Cratchit's wife. "It makes them weak by candle-light; and I wouldn't show weak eyes to your father when he comes home, for the world. It must be near his time."

"Past it rather," Peter answered, shutting up his book. "But I think he's walked a little slower than he used, these few last evenings, mother."

They were very quiet again. At last she said, and in a steady, cheerful voice, that only faultered once:

"I have known him walk with—I have known him walk with Tiny Tim upon his shoulder, very fast indeed."

"And so have I," cried Peter. "Often."

"And so have I!" exclaimed another. So had all.

"But he was very light to carry," she resumed, intent upon her work, "and his father loved him so, that it was no trouble—no trouble. And there is your father at the door!"

7. Matthew 18.2.

She hurried out to meet him; and little Bob in his comforter—he had need of it, poor fellow—came in. His tea was ready for him on the hob, and they all tried who should help him to it most. Then the two young Cratchits got upon his knees and laid, each child a little cheek, against his face, as if they said, "Don't mind it, father. Don't be grieved!"

Bob was very cheerful with them, and spoke pleasantly to all the family. He looked at the work upon the table, and praised the industry and speed of Mrs Cratchit and the girls. They would be done long before Sunday, he said.

"Sunday! You went to-day then, Robert?" said his wife.

"Yes, my dear," returned Bob. "I wish you could have gone. It would have done you good to see how green a place it is. But you'll see it often. I promised him that I would walk there on a Sunday. My little, little child!" cried Bob. "My little child!"

He broke down all at once. He couldn't help it. If he could have helped it, he and his child would have been farther apart perhaps than they were.

He left the room, and went up stairs into the room above, which was lighted cheerfully, and hung with Christmas. There was a chair set close beside the child, and there were signs of some one having been there, lately. Poor Bob sat down in it, and when he had thought a little and composed himself, he kissed the little face. He was reconciled to what had happened, and went down again quite happy.

They drew about the fire, and talked; the girls and mother working still. Bob told them of the extraordinary kindness of Mr Scrooge's nephew, whom he had scarcely seen but once, and who, meeting him in the street that day, and seeing that he looked a little—"just a little down you know" said Bob, inquired what had happened to distress him. "On which," said Bob, "for he is the pleasantest-spoken gentleman you ever heard, I told him. 'I am heartily sorry for it, Mr Cratchit,' he said, 'and heartily sorry for your good wife.' By the bye, how he ever knew *that*, I don't know."

"Knew what, my dear."

"Why, that you were a good wife," replied Bob.

"Everybody knows that!" said Peter.

"Very well observed, my boy!" cried Bob. "I hope they do. 'Heartily sorry,' he said, 'for your good wife. If I can be of any service to you in any way,' he said, giving me his card, 'that's where I live. Pray come to me.' Now, it wasn't," cried Bob, "for the sake of anything he might be able to do for us, so much as for his kind way, that this was quite delightful. It really seemed as if he had known our Tiny Tim, and felt with us."

"I'm sure he's a good soul!" said Mrs Cratchit.

"You would be surer of it, my dear," returned Bob, "if you saw and spoke to him. I shouldn't be at all surprised, mark what I say, if he got Peter a better situation."

"Only hear that, Peter," said Mrs Cratchit.

"And then," cried one of the girls, "Peter will be keeping company with some one, and setting up for himself."

"Get along with you!" retorted Peter, grinning.

"It's just as likely as not," said Bob, "one of these days; though there's plenty of time for that, my dear. But however and whenever we part from one another, I am sure we shall none of us forget poor Tiny Tim—shall we—or this first parting that there was among us?"

"Never, father!" cried they all.

"And I know," said Bob, "I know, my dears, that when we recollect how patient and how mild he was; although he was a little, little child; we shall not quarrel easily among ourselves, and forget poor Tiny Tim in doing it."

"No, never, father!" they all cried again.

"I am very happy," said little Bob, "I am very happy!"

Mrs Cratchit kissed him, his daughters kissed him, the two young Cratchits kissed him, and Peter and himself shook hands. Spirit of Tiny Tim, thy childish essence was from God!

"Spectre," said Scrooge, "something informs me that our parting moment is at hand. I know it, but I know not how. Tell me what man that was whom we saw lying dead?"

The Ghost of Christmas Yet To Come conveyed him, as before—though at a different time, he thought: indeed, there seemed no order in these latter visions, save that they were in the Future—into the resorts of business men, but showed him not himself. Indeed, the Spirit did not stay for anything, but went straight on, as to the end just now desired, until besought by Scrooge to tarry for a moment.

"This court," said Scrooge, "through which we hurry now, is where my place of occupation is, and has been for a length of time. I see the house. Let me behold what I shall be, in days to come."

The Spirit stopped; the hand was pointed elsewhere.

"The house is yonder," Scrooge exclaimed. "Why do you point away?"

The inexorable finger underwent no change.

Scrooge hastened to the window of his office, and looked in. It was an office still, but not his. The furniture was not the same, and the figure in the chair was not himself. The Phantom pointed as before.

He joined it once again, and wondering why and whither he had gone, accompanied it until they reached an iron gate. He paused to look round before entering.

A churchyard. Here, then, the wretched man whose name he had now to learn, lay underneath the ground. It was a worthy place. Walled in by houses; overrun by grass and weeds, the growth of vegetation's death, not life; choked up with too much burying; fat with repleted appetite. A worthy place!

The Spirit stood among the graves, and pointed down to One. He advanced towards it trembling. The Phantom was exactly as it had been, but he dreaded that he saw new meaning in its solemn shape.

"Before I draw nearer to that stone to which you point," said Scrooge, "answer me one question. Are these the shadows of the things that Will be, or are they shadows of things that May be, only?"

Still the Ghost pointed downward to the grave by which it stood.

"Men's courses will foreshadow certain ends, to which, if persevered in, they must lead," said Scrooge. "But if the courses be departed from, the ends will change. Say it is thus with what you show me!"

The Spirit was immovable as ever.

Scrooge crept towards it, trembling as he went; and following the finger, read upon the stone of the neglected grave his own name, EBENEZER SCROOGE.

"Am I that man who lay upon the bed?" he cried, upon his knees.

The finger pointed from the grave to him, and back again.

"No, Spirit! Oh, no, no!"

The finger still was there.

"Spirit!" he cried, tight clutching at its robe, "hear me! I am not the man I was. I will not be the man I must have been but for this intercourse. Why show me this, if I am past all hope?"

For the first time the hand appeared to shake.

"Good Spirit," he pursued, as down upon the ground he fell before it: "Your nature intercedes for me, and pities me. Assure me that I yet may change these shadows you have shown me, by an altered life!"

The kind hand trembled.

"I will honour Christmas in my heart, and try to keep it all the year. I will live in the Past, Present, and the Future. The Spirits of all Three shall strive within me. I will not shut out the lessons that they teach. Oh, tell me I may sponge away the writing on this stone!"

In his agony, he caught the spectral hand. It sought to free itself, but he was strong in his entreaty, and detained it. The Spirit, stronger yet, repulsed him.

Holding up his hands in a last prayer to have his fate reversed, he saw an alteration in the Phantom's hood and dress. It shrunk, collapsed, and dwindled down into a bedpost.

Stave Five
THE END OF IT

Yes! and the bedpost was his own. The bed was his own, the room was his own. Best and happiest of all, the Time before him was his own, to make amends in!

"I will live in the Past, the Present, and the Future!" Scrooge repeated, as he scrambled out of bed. "The Spirits of all Three shall strive within me. Oh Jacob Marley! Heaven, and the Christmas Time be praised for this! I say it on my knees, old Jacob; on my knees!"

He was so fluttered and so glowing with his good intentions, that his broken voice would scarcely answer to his call. He had been sobbing violently in his conflict with the Spirit, and his face was wet with tears.

"They are not torn down," cried Scrooge, folding one of his bed-curtains in his arms, "they are not torn down, rings and all. They are here: I am here: the shadows of the things that would have been, may be dispelled. They will be. I know they will!"

His hands were busy with his garments all this time: turning them inside out, putting them on upside down, tearing them, mislaying them, making them parties to every kind of extravagance.

"I don't know what to do!" cried Scrooge, laughing and crying in the same breath; and making a perfect Laocoön of himself with his stockings.[8] I am as light as a feather, I am as happy as an angel, I am as merry as a school-boy. I am as giddy as a drunken man. A merry Christmas to everybody! A happy New Year to all the world! Hallo here! Whoop! Hallo!"

He had frisked into the sitting-room, and was now standing there: perfectly winded.

"There's the saucepan that the gruel was in!" cried Scrooge, starting off again, and frisking round the fire-place. "There's the door, by which the Ghost of Jacob Marley entered! There's the corner where the Ghost of Christmas Present, sat! There's the window where I saw the wandering Spirits! It's all right, it's all true, it all happened. Ha ha ha!"

Really, for a man who had been out of practice for so many years, it was a splendid laugh, a most illustrious laugh. The father of a long, long line of brilliant laughs!

8. Scrooge struggles with his stockings as Laocoön struggles with two sea serpents (see Virgil's *Aeneid*, Book 2).

"I don't know what day of the month it is!" said Scrooge. "I don't know how long I've been among the Spirits. I don't know anything. I'm quite a baby. Never mind. I don't care. I'd rather be a baby. Hallo! Whoop! Hallo here!"

He was checked in his transports by the churches ringing out the lustiest peals he had ever heard. Clash, clang, hammer, ding, dong, bell. Bell, dong, ding, hammer, clang, clash! Oh, glorious, glorious!

Running to the window, he opened it, and put out his head. No fog, no mist; clear, bright, jovial, stirring, cold; cold, piping for the blood to dance to; Golden sunlight; Heavenly sky; sweet fresh air; merry bells. Oh, glorious. Glorious!

"What's to-day?" cried Scrooge, calling downward to a boy in Sunday clothes, who perhaps had loitered in to look about him.

"EH?" returned the boy, with all his might of wonder.

"What's to-day, my fine fellow?" said Scrooge.

"To-day!" replied the boy. "Why, CHRISTMAS DAY."

"It's Christmas Day!" said Scrooge to himself. "I haven't missed it. The Spirits have done it all in one night. They can do anything they like. Of course they can. Of course they can. Hallo, my fine fellow!"

"Hallo!" returned the boy.

"Do you know the Poulterer's, in the next street but one, at the corner?" Scrooge inquired.

"I should hope I did," replied the lad.

"An intelligent boy!" said Scrooge. "A remarkable boy! Do you know whether they've sold the prize Turkey that was hanging up there? Not the little prize Turkey: the big one?"

"What, the one as big as me?" returned the boy.

"What a delightful boy!" said Scrooge. "It's a pleasure to talk to him. Yes, my buck!"

"It's hanging there now," replied the boy.

"Is it?" said Scrooge. "Go and buy it."

"Walk-ER!"[9] exclaimed the boy.

"No, no," said Scrooge, "I am in earnest. Go and buy it, and tell 'em to bring it here, that I may give them the direction where to take it. Come back with the man, and I'll give you a shilling. Come back with him in less than five minutes, and I'll give you half-a-crown!"

The boy was off like a shot. He must have had a steady hand at a trigger who could have got a shot off half so fast.

"I'll send it to Bob Cratchit's!" whispered Scrooge, rubbing his hands, and splitting with a laugh. "He shan't know who sends it. It's twice the size of Tiny Tim. Joe Miller[1] never made such a joke as sending it to Bob's will be!"

The hand in which he wrote the address was not a steady one, but write it he did, somehow, and went down stairs to open the street door, ready for the coming of the poulterer's man. As he stood there, waiting his arrival, the knocker caught his eye.

"I shall love it, as long as I live!" cried Scrooge, patting it with his hand. "I scarcely ever looked at it before. What an honest expression it has in its face! It's a wonderful knocker!—Here's the Turkey. Hallo! Whoop! How are you! Merry Christmas!"

It *was* a Turkey! He never could have stood upon his legs, that bird. He would have snapped 'em short off in a minute, like sticks of sealing-wax.

---

9. Cockney exclamation of incredulity.   1. Eighteenth-century actor and comedian. *Joe Miller's Jests* (1739) was a popular jokebook.

"Why, it's impossible to carry that to Camden Town," said Scrooge. "You must have a cab."

The chuckle with which he said this, and the chuckle with which he paid for the Turkey, and the chuckle with which he paid for the cab, and the chuckle with which he recompensed the boy, were only to be exceeded by the chuckle with which he sat down breathless in his chair again, and chuckled till he cried.

Shaving was not an easy task, for his hand continued to shake very much; and shaving requires attention, even when you don't dance while you are at it. But if he had cut the end of his nose off, he would have put a piece of sticking-plaister over it, and been quite satisfied.

He dressed himself "all in his best," and at last got out into the streets. The people were by this time pouring forth, as he had seen them with the Ghost of Christmas Present; and walking with his hands behind him, Scrooge regarded every one with a delighted smile. He looked so irresistibly pleasant, in a word, that three or four good-humoured fellows said, "Good morning, sir! A merry Christmas to you!" And Scrooge said often afterwards, that of all the blithe sounds he had ever heard, those were the blithest in his ears.

He had not gone far, when coming on towards him he beheld the portly gentleman, who had walked into his counting-house the day before and said, "Scrooge and Marley's, I believe?" It sent a pang across his heart to think how this old gentleman would look upon him when they met; but he knew what path lay straight before him, and he took it.

"My dear sir," said Scrooge, quickening his pace, and taking the old gentleman by both his hands. "How do you do? I hope you succeeded yesterday. It was very kind of you. A merry Christmas to you, sir!"

"Mr Scrooge?"

"Yes," said Scrooge. "That is my name, and I fear it may not be pleasant to you. Allow me to ask your pardon. And will you have the goodness"—here Scrooge whispered in his ear.

"Lord bless me!" cried the gentleman, as if his breath were gone. "My dear Mr Scrooge, are you serious?"

"If you please," said Scrooge. "Not a farthing less. A great many back-payments are included in it, I assure you. Will you do me that favour?"

"My dear sir," said the other, shaking hands with him. "I don't know what to say to such munifi—"

"Don't say anything, please," retorted Scrooge. "Come and see me. Will you come and see me?"

"I will!" cried the old gentleman. And it was clear he meant to do it.

"Thank'ee," said Scrooge. "I am much obliged to you. I thank you fifty times. Bless you!"

He went to church, and walked about the streets, and watched the people hurrying to and fro, and patted children on the head, and questioned beggars, and looked down into the kitchens of houses, and up to the windows; and found that everything could yield him pleasure. He had never dreamed that any walk—that anything—could give him so much happiness. In the afternoon, he turned his steps towards his nephew's house.

He passed the door a dozen times, before he had the courage to go up and knock. But he made a dash, and did it:

"Is your master at home, my dear?" said Scrooge to the girl. Nice girl! Very.

"Yes, sir."

"Where is he, my love?" said Scrooge.

"He's in the dining-room, sir, along with mistress. I'll show you up stairs, if you please."

"Thank'ee. He knows me," said Scrooge, with his hand already on the dining-room lock. "I'll go in here, my dear."

He turned it gently, and sidled his face in, round the door. They were looking at the table (which was spread out in great array); for these young housekeepers are always nervous on such points, and like to see that everything is right.

"Fred!" said Scrooge.

Dear heart alive, how his niece by marriage started! Scrooge had forgotten, for the moment, about her sitting in the corner with the footstool, or he wouldn't have done it, on any account.[2]

"Why bless my soul!" cried Fred, "who's that?"

"It's I. Your uncle Scrooge. I have come to dinner. Will you let me in, Fred?"

Let him in! It is a mercy he didn't shake his arm off. He was at home in five minutes. Nothing could be heartier. His niece looked just the same. So did Topper when *he* came. So did the plump sister, when *she* came. So did every one when *they* came. Wonderful party, wonderful games, wonderful unanimity, won-der-ful happiness!

But he was early at the office next morning. Oh, he was early there. If he could only be there first, and catch Bob Cratchit coming late! That was the thing he had set his heart upon.

And he did it; yes, he did! The clock struck nine. No Bob. A quarter past. No Bob. He was full eighteen minutes and a half behind his time. Scrooge sat with his door wide open, that he might see him come into the Tank.

His hat was off, before he opened the door; his comforter too. He was on his stool in a jiffy; driving away with his pen, as if he were trying to overtake nine o'clock.

"Hallo!" growled Scrooge, in his accustomed voice as near as he could feign it. "What do you mean by coming here at this time of day?"

"I am very sorry, sir," said Bob. "I *am* behind my time."

"You are?" repeated Scrooge. "Yes. I think you are. Step this way, if you please."

"It's only once a year, sir," pleaded Bob, appearing from the Tank. "It shall not be repeated. I was making rather merry yesterday, sir."

"Now, I'll tell you what, my friend," said Scrooge, "I am not going to stand this sort of thing any longer. And therefore," he continued, leaping from his stool, and giving Bob such a dig in the waistcoat that he staggered back into the Tank again: "and therefore I am about to raise your salary!"

Bob trembled, and got a little nearer to the ruler. He had a momentary idea of knocking Scrooge down with it; holding him; and calling to the people in the court for help and a strait-waistcoat.

"A merry Christmas, Bob!" said Scrooge, with an earnestness that could not be mistaken, as he clapped him on the back. "A merrier Christmas, Bob, my good fellow, than I have given you, for many a year! I'll raise your salary, and endeavour to assist your struggling family, and we will discuss your affairs this very afternoon, over a Christmas bowl of smoking bishop,[3] Bob! Make up the fires, and buy another coal-scuttle before you dot another i, Bob Cratchit!"

---

2. Scrooge alludes to the fact that Fred's wife is pregnant.   3. A hot punch made of red wine, oranges, sugar, and spices.

Scrooge was better than his word. He did it all, and infinitely more; and to Tiny Tim, who did NOT die, he was a second father. He became as good a friend, as good a master, and as good a man, as the good old city knew, or any other good old city, town, or borough, in the good old world. Some people laughed to see the alteration in him, but he let them laugh, and little heeded them; for he was wise enough to know that nothing ever happened on this globe, for good, at which some people did not have their fill of laughter in the outset; and knowing that such as these would be blind anyway, he thought it quite as well that they should wrinkle up their eyes in grins, as have the malady in less attractive forms. His own heart laughed: and that was quite enough for him.

He had no further intercourse with Spirits, but lived upon the Total Abstinence Principle, ever afterwards; and it was always said of him, that he knew how to keep Christmas well, if any man alive possessed the knowledge. May that be truly said of us, and all of us! And so, as Tiny Tim observed, God bless Us, Every One!

The End

1843

from A Walk in a Workhouse

A few Sundays ago, I formed one of the congregation assembled in the chapel of a large metropolitan Workhouse.[1] With the exception of the clergyman and clerk, and a very few officials, there were none but paupers present. The children sat in the galleries; the women in the body of the chapel, and in one of the side aisles; the men in the remaining aisle. The service was decorously performed, though the sermon might have been much better adapted to the comprehension and to the circumstances of the hearers. The usual supplications were offered, with more than the usual significancy in such a place, for the fatherless children and widows, for all sick persons and young children, for all that were desolate and oppressed, for the comforting and helping of the weak-hearted, for the raising-up of them that had fallen; for all that were in danger, necessity, and tribulation. The prayers of the congregation were desired "for several persons in the various wards, dangerously ill"; and others who were recovering returned their thanks to Heaven.

Among this congregation, were some evil-looking young women, and beetle-browed young men; but not many—perhaps that kind of characters kept away. Generally, the faces (those of the children excepted) were depressed and subdued, and wanted colour. Aged people were there, in every variety. Mumbling, blear-eyed, spectacled, stupid, deaf, lame; vacantly winking in the gleams of sun that now and then crept in through the open doors, from the paved yard; shading their listening ears, or blinking eyes, with their withered hands; poring over their books, leering at nothing, going to sleep, crouching and drooping in corners. There were weird old women, all skeleton within, all bonnet and cloak without, continually wiping their eyes with dirty dusters of pocket-handkerchiefs; and there were ugly old crones, both male and female, with a ghastly kind of contentment upon them which was not at all comforting to see. Upon the whole, it was the dragon, Pauperism, in a very weak and impotent condition; toothless, fangless, drawing his breath heavily enough, and hardly worth chaining up.

---

1. Dickens visited a London workhouse on 5 May 1850. He published this account in his magazine *Household Words* on May 25.

When the service was over, I walked with the humane and conscientious gentleman whose duty it was to take that walk, that Sunday morning, through the little world of poverty enclosed within the workhouse walls. It was inhabited by a population of some fifteen hundred or two thousand paupers, ranging from the infant newly born or not yet come into the pauper world, to the old man dying on his bed.

In a room opening from a squalid yard, where a number of listless women were lounging to and fro, trying to get warm in the ineffectual sunshine of the tardy May morning—in the "Itch Ward,"[2] not to compromise the truth—a woman such as Hogarth[3] has often drawn was hurriedly getting on her gown, before a dusty fire. She was the nurse, or wardswoman, of that insalubrious department—herself a pauper—flabby, raw-boned, untidy—unpromising and coarse of aspect as need be. But, on being spoken to about the patients whom she had in charge, she turned round, with her shabby gown half on, half off, and fell a crying with all her might. Not for show, not querulously, not in any mawkish sentiment, but in the deep grief and affliction of her heart; turning away her dishevelled head: sobbing most bitterly, wringing her hands, and letting fall abundance of great tears, that choked her utterance. What was the matter with the nurse of the itch-ward? Oh, "the dropped child" was dead! Oh, the child that was found in the street, and she had brought up ever since, had died an hour ago, and see where the little creature lay, beneath this cloth! The dear, the pretty dear!

The dropped child seemed too small and poor a thing for Death to be in earnest with, but Death had taken it; and already its diminutive form was neatly washed, composed, and stretched as if in sleep upon a box. I thought I heard a voice from Heaven saying, It shall be well for thee, O nurse of the itch-ward, when some less gentle pauper does those offices to thy cold form, that such as the dropped child are the angels who behold my Father's face!

In another room, were several ugly old women crouching, witch-like, round a hearth, and chattering and nodding, after the manner of the monkeys. "All well here? And enough to eat?" A general chattering and chuckling; at last an answer from a volunteer. "Oh yes gentleman! Bless you gentleman! Lord bless the parish of St. So-and-So! It feed the hungry, Sir, and give drink to the thirsty, and it warm them which is cold, so it do, and good luck to the parish of St. So-and-So, and thankee gentleman!" Elsewhere, a party of pauper nurses were at dinner. "How do you get on?" "Oh pretty well Sir! We works hard, and we lives hard—like the sodgers!"[4]

In another room, a kind of purgatory or place of transition, six or eight noisy madwomen were gathered together, under the superintendence of one sane attendant. Among them was a girl of two or three and twenty, very prettily dressed, of most respectable appearance, and good manners, who had been brought in from the house where she had lived as domestic servant (having, I suppose, no friends), on account of being subject to epileptic fits, and requiring to be removed under the influence of a very bad one. She was by no means of the same stuff, or the same breeding, or the same experience, or in the same state of mind, as those by whom she was surrounded; and she pathetically complained, that the daily association and the nightly noise made her worse, and was driving her mad—which was perfectly evident. The case was noted for enquiry and redress, but she said she had already been there for some weeks.

2. Scabies or mange.
3. William Hogarth (1697–1764) was an English en-
graver of moral and satirical subjects.
4. Soldiers.

If this girl had stolen her mistress's watch, I do not hesitate to say she would, in all probability, have been infinitely better off. * * * We have come to this absurd, this dangerous, this monstrous pass, that the dishonest felon is, in respect of cleanliness, order, diet, and accommodation, better provided for, and taken care of, than the honest pauper.

And this conveys no special imputation on the workhouse of the parish of St So-and-So, where, on the contrary, I saw many things to commend. It was very agreeable, recollecting that most infamous and atrocious enormity committed at Tooting[5]—an enormity which, a hundred years hence, will still be vividly remembered in the bye-ways of English life, and which has done more to engender a gloomy discontent and suspicion among many thousands of the people than all the Chartist[6] leaders could have done in all their lives—to find the pauper children in this workhouse looking robust and well, and apparently the objects of very great care. In the Infant School—a large, light, airy room at the top of the building—the little creatures, being at dinner, and eating their potatoes heartily, were not cowed by the presence of strange visitors, but stretched out their small hands to be shaken, with a very pleasant confidence. And it was comfortable to see two mangy pauper rocking-horses rampant in a corner. In the girls' school, where the dinner was also in progress, everything bore a cheerful and healthy aspect. The meal was over, in the boys' school, by the time of our arrival there, and the room was not yet quite re-arranged; but the boys were roaming unrestrained about a large and airy yard, as any other school-boys might have done. Some of them had been drawing large ships upon the schoolroom wall; and if they had a mast with shrouds and stays set up for practice (as they have in the Middlesex House of Correction), it would be so much the better. At present, if a boy should feel a strong impulse upon him to learn the art of going aloft, he could only gratify it, I presume, as the men and women paupers gratify their aspirations after better board and lodging, by smashing as many workhouse windows as possible, and being promoted to prison.

In one place, the Newgate[7] of the workhouse, a company of boys and youths were locked up in a yard alone; their day-room being a kind of kennel where the casual poor used formerly to be littered down at night. Divers of them had been there some long time. "Are they never going away?" was the natural enquiry. "Most of them are crippled, in some form or other," said the Wardsman, "and not fit for anything." They slunk about, like dispirited wolves or hyaenas; and made a pounce at their food when it was served out, much as those animals do. The big-headed idiot shuffling his feet along the pavement, in the sunlight outside, was a more agreeable object everyway.

Groves of babies in arms; groves of mothers and other sick women in bed; groves of lunatics; jungles of men in stone-paved downstairs day-rooms, waiting for their dinners; longer and longer groves of old people, in upstairs Infirmary wards, wearing out life, God knows how—this was the scenery through which the walk lay, for two hours. In some of these latter chambers, there were pictures stuck against the wall, and a neat display of crockery and pewter on a kind of sideboard; now and then it was a treat to see a plant or two; in almost every ward, there was a cat.

5. A reference to the baby-farm run by Bartholomew Drouet at Tooting, which was responsible for the deaths of many children due to disease and neglect.
6. The Chartist movement of 1838–1848 sought to address social and economic injustices through political reform; it was regarded with suspicion by the upper and middle classes.
7. A famous prison.

In all of these Long Walks of aged and infirm, some old people were bed-ridden, and had been for a long time; some were sitting on their beds half-naked; some dying in their beds; some out of bed, and sitting at a table near the fire. A sullen or lethargic indifference to what was asked, a blunted sensibility to everything but warmth and food, a moody absence of complaint as being of no use, a dogged silence and resentful desire to be left alone again, I thought were generally apparent. On our walking into the midst of one of these dreary perspectives of old men, nearly the following little dialogue took place, the nurse not being immediately at hand:

"All well here?"

No answer. An old man in a Scotch cap sitting among others on a form at the table, eating out of a tin porringer, pushes back his cap a little to look at us, claps it down on his forehead again with the palm of his hand, and goes on eating.

"All well here?" (repeated.)

No answer. Another old man sitting on his bed, paralytically peeling a boiled potato, lifts his head, and stares.

"Enough to eat?"

No answer. Another old man, in bed, turns himself and coughs.

"How are *you* to day?" To the last old man.

That old man says nothing; but another old man, a tall old man of a very good address, speaking with perfect correctness, comes forward from somewhere, and volunteers an answer. The reply almost always proceeds from a volunteer, and not from the person looked at or spoken to.

"We are very old, Sir," in a mild, distinct voice. "We can't expect to be well, most of us."

"Are you comfortable?"

"I have no complaint to make, Sir." With a half shake of his head, a half shrug of his shoulders, and a kind of apologetic smile.

"Enough to eat?"

"Why, Sir, I have but a poor appetite," with the same air as before; "and yet I get through my allowance very easily."

"But," showing a porringer with a Sunday dinner in it; "here is a portion of mutton, and three potatoes. You can't starve on that?"

"Oh dear no, Sir," with the same apologetic air. "Not starve."

"What do you want?"

"We have very little bread, Sir. It's an exceedingly small quantity of bread."

The nurse, who is now rubbing her hands at the questioner's elbow, interferes with, "It ain't much raly, Sir. You see they've only six ounces a day, and when they've took their breakfast, there *can* only be a little left for night, Sir."

Another old man, hitherto invisible, rises out of his bedclothes, as out of a grave, and looks on.

"You have tea at night?" The questioner is still addressing the well-spoken old man.

"Yes, Sir, we have tea at night."

"And you save what bread you can from the morning, to eat with it?"

"Yes, Sir—if we can save any."

"And you want more to eat with it?"

"Yes, Sir." With a very anxious face.

The questioner, in the kindness of his heart, appears a little discomposed, and changes the subject.

"What has become of the old man who used to lie in that bed in the corner?"

The nurse don't remember what old man is referred to. There has been such a many old men. The well-spoken old man is doubtful. The spectral old man who has come to life in bed says, "Billy Stevens." Another old man who has previously had his head in the fireplace pipes out, "Charley Walters."

Something like a feeble interest is awakened. I suppose Charley Walters had conversation in him.

"He's dead!" says the piping old man.

Another old man, with one eye screwed up, hastily displaces the piping old man, and says:

"Yes! Charley Walters died in that bed, and—and—"

"Billy Stevens," persists the spectral old man.

"No, no! and Johnny Rogers died in that bed, and—and—they're both on 'em dead—and Sam'l Bowyer," this seems very extraordinary to him, "he went out!"

With this he subsides, and all the old men (having had quite enough of it) subside, and the spectral old man goes into his grave again, and takes the shade of Billy Stevens with him.

As we turn to go out at the door, another previously invisible old man, a hoarse old man in a flannel gown, is standing there, as if he had just come up through the floor.

"I beg your pardon, Sir, could I take the liberty of saying a word?"

"Yes; what is it?"

"I am greatly better in my health, Sir; but what I want, to get me quite round," with his hand on his throat, "is a little fresh air, Sir. It has always done my complaint so much good, Sir. The regular leave for going out, comes round so seldom, that if the gentlemen, next Friday, would give me leave to go out walking, now and then—for only an hour or so, Sir!—"

Who could wonder, looking through those weary vistas of bed and infirmity, that it should do him good to meet with some other scenes, and assure himself that there was something else on earth? Who could help wondering why the old men lived on as they did; what grasp they had on life; what crumbs of interest or occupation they could pick up from its bare board; whether Charley Walters had ever described to them the days when he kept company with some old pauper woman in the bud, or Billy Stevens ever told them of the time when he was a dweller in the far-off foreign land called Home!

The morsel of burnt child, lying in another room, so patiently, in bed, wrapped in lint, and looking steadfastly at us with his bright quiet eyes when we spoke to him kindly, looked as if the knowledge of these things, and of all the tender things there are to think about, might have been in his mind—as if he thought, with us, that there was a fellow-feeling in the pauper nurses which appeared to make them more kind to their charges than the race of common nurses in the hospitals—as if he mused upon the Future of some older children lying around him in the same place, and thought it best, perhaps, all things considered, that he should die—as if he knew, without fear, of those many coffins, made and unmade, piled up in the store below—and of his unknown friend, "the dropped child," calm upon the box-lid covered with a cloth. But there was something wistful and appealing, too, in his tiny face, as if, in the midst of all the hard necessities and incongruities he pondered on, he pleaded, in behalf of the helpless and the aged poor, for a little more liberty—and a little more bread.

1850

cᴕᴥᴗ

COMPANION READINGS
Dickens at Work: Recollections by His Children and Friends[1]
[DICKENS'S ELDEST SON, CHARLEY, RECALLS HIS FATHER'S HABITS]

As to his system of work, it was the same wherever he was. No city clerk was ever more methodical or orderly than he; no humdrum, monotonous, conventional task could ever have been discharged with more punctuality or with more businesslike regularity, than he gave to the work of his imagination and fancy. At something before ten he would sit down—every day with very, very rare exceptions—to his desk which, as to its papers, its writing materials, and the quaint little bronze figures which he delighted in having before him, was as neat and as orderly as everything else in and about the house, and would there remain until lunch time—sometimes, if he were much engrossed with any particular point or had something in hand which he was very anxious to finish there and then, until later. Whether he could get on satisfactorily with the work in hand mattered nothing. He had no faith in the waiting-for-inspiration theory, nor did he fall into the opposite error of forcing himself willy-nilly to turn out so much manuscript every day, as was Mr Anthony Trollope's plan, for instance.[2] It was his business to sit at his desk during just those particular hours in the day, my father used to say, and, whether the day turned out well or ill, there he sat accordingly. * * *

When he was writing one of his long stories and had become deeply interested in the working-out of his plot and the evolution of his characters, he lived, I am sure, two lives, one with us and one with his fictitious people, and I am equally certain that the children of his brain were much more real to him at times than we were. I have, often and often, heard him complain that he could *not* get the people of his imagination to do what he wanted, and that they would insist on working out their histories in *their* way and not *his*. I can very well remember his describing their flocking round his table in the quiet hours of a summer morning when he was—an unusual circumstance with him—at work very early, each one of them claiming and demanding instant personal attention. And at such times he would often fall to consider the matter in hand even during his walks. There was no mistaking the silence into which he fell on such occasions. It was not the silence only of a pause in conversation, but the silence of engrossing thought, not, one felt, to be broken or interrupted lightly. Many a mile have I walked with him thus—he striding along with his regular four-miles-an-hour swing; his eyes looking straight before him, his lips slightly working, as they generally did when he sat thinking and writing; almost unconscious of companionship, and keeping half a pace or so ahead. When he had worked out what had come into his mind he would drop back again into line—again, I am sure, almost unconsciously—and the conversation would be resumed, as if there had been no appreciable break or interval at all.

1934

---

1. The following selections are drawn from *Dickens: Interviews and Recollections*, 2 vols., ed. Philip Collins, 1981.
2. In his *Autobiography* (1883) Anthony Trollope revealed that his method of producing novels was "to write with my watch before me, and to require from myself 250 words every quarter of an hour."

[DICKENS'S DAUGHTER MAMIE DESCRIBES SEEING HER FATHER AT WORK]

He was usually alone when at work, though there were, of course, some occasional exceptions, and I myself constituted such an exception. * * * I had a long and serious illness, with an almost equally long convalescence.[3] During the latter, my father suggested that I should be carried every day into his study to remain with him, and, although I was fearful of disturbing him, he assured me that he desired to have me with him. On one of these mornings, I was lying on the sofa endeavouring to keep perfectly quiet, while my father wrote busily and rapidly at his desk, when he suddenly jumped from his chair and rushed to a mirror which hung near, and in which I could see the reflection of some extraordinary facial contortions which he was making. He returned rapidly to his desk, wrote furiously for a few moments, and then went again to the mirror. The facial pantomime was resumed, and then turning toward, but evidently not seeing, me, he began talking rapidly in a low voice. Ceasing this soon, however, he returned once more to his desk, where he remained silently writing until luncheon time. It was a most curious experience for me, and one of which I did not, until later years, fully appreciate the purport. Then I knew that with his natural intensity he had thrown himself completely into the character that he was creating, and that for the time being he had not only lost sight of his surroundings, but had actually become in action, as in imagination, the creature of his pen.

1897

[AN AMERICAN FRIEND, JAMES FIELDS, RECALLS WALKING WITH DICKENS]

His favorite mode of exercise was walking; and when in America, scarcely a day passed, no matter what the weather, that he did not accomplish his eight or ten miles. It was on these expeditions that he liked to recount to the companion of his rambles stories and incidents of his early life; and when he was in the mood, his fun and humor knew no bounds. He would then frequently discuss the numerous characters in his delightful books, and would act out, on the road, dramatic situations, where Nickleby or Copperfield or Swiveller[4] would play distinguished parts. I remember he said, on one of these occasions, that during the composition of his first stories he could never entirely dismiss the characters about whom he happened to be writing; that while the Old Curiosity Shop was in process of composition Little Nell followed him about everywhere; that while he was writing Oliver Twist Fagin the Jew would never let him rest, even in his most retired moments; that at midnight and in the morning, on the sea and on the land, Tiny Tim and Little Bob Cratchit were ever tugging at his coat-sleeve, as if impatient for him to get back to his desk and continue the story of their lives. * * * He said, also, that when the children of his brain had once been launched, free and clear of him, into the world, they would sometimes turn up in the most unexpected manner to look their father in the face.

Sometimes he would pull my arm while we were walking together and whisper, "Let us avoid Mr Pumblechook, who is crossing the street to meet us"; or, "Mr Micawber is coming; let us turn down this alley to get out of his way." He always seemed to enjoy the fun of his comic people, and had unceasing mirth over Mr Pickwick's misadventures. * * * The growing up of characters in his mind never lost for him a sense of

3. She was ill in 1854, when Dickens was writing Hard Times.

4. The names mentioned throughout this passage are all characters from Dickens's novels.

the marvellous. "What an unfathomable mystery there is in it all!" he said one day. Taking up a wineglass, he continued: "Suppose I choose to call this a *character*, fancy it a man, endue it with certain qualities; and soon the fine filmy webs of thought, almost impalpable, coming from every direction, we know not whence, spin and weave about it, until it assumes form and beauty, and becomes instinct with life."

1872

Kate Field
Dickens Giving a Reading of A Christmas Carol[1]

He comes! A lithe, energetic man, of medium stature, crosses the platform at the brisk gait of five miles an hour, and takes his position behind the table. This is Charles Dickens, whose name has been a household word in England and America for thirty years; whose books have been the joy and solace of many a weary heart and head. * * *

Ah, that Christmas dinner! I feel as if I were eating every morsel of it. Peter mashes the potatoes with incredible energy; Belinda sweetens the apple-sauce, and smacks her lips so loudly in the tasting as to prove that it could not be better; "the two young Cratchits," "cram spoons into their mouths, lest they should shriek for goose before their turn"; and Tiny Tim "beats on the table with the handle of his knife, as he feebly cries, 'Hoorray! Hoorray! Hoorray!'" in such a still, small voice. Moreover, there is that goose! I see it with my naked eye. And O, the pudding! * * * Dickens's sniffing and smelling of that pudding would make a starving family believe that they had swallowed it, holly and all. It is infectious.

What Dickens *does* is frequently infinitely better than anything he says, or the way he says it; yet the doing is as delicate and intangible as the odor of violets, and can be no better indicated. Nothing of its kind can be more touchingly beautiful than the manner in which Bob Cratchit—previous to proposing "a merry Christmas to us all, my dears, God bless us"—stoops down, with tears in his eyes, and places Tiny Tim's withered little hand in his, "as if he loved the child, and wished to keep him by his side, and dreaded that he might be taken from him." It is pantomime worthy of the finest actor.

Equally clever is Bob's attempt to pacify Mrs Cratchit, when, upon being desired to toast "Mr Scrooge, the Founder of the Feast," this amiable lady displays an amount of temper of which we never believed her capable. "My dear!" says Bob, in an expostulatory tone, "my dear! the children! Christmas day!" pointing mysteriously to each one with inimitable *naïveté*. Bob's picture ought to be taken at this moment. Indeed, now I think of it, I am astonished that artists who illustrate such of Dickens's books as are read by him do not make him their model. They can never approach his conception, they can never equal his execution, and to the virtue of truth would be added the charm of resembling the author.

Admirable is Mrs Cratchit's ungracious drinking to Scrooge's health, and Martha's telling how she had seen a lord, and how he "was much about as tall as Peter!" It is a charming cabinet picture, and so likewise is the glimpse of Christmas at Scrooge's nephew's. The plump sister is "satisfactory, O, perfectly satisfactory," and

1. Kate Field (1839–1896) was an American journalist and actress who attended more than two dozen of Dickens's readings from his works in Boston and New York.

Topper is a magnificent fraud on the understanding, a side-splitting fraud. I see Fred get off the sofa and *stamp* at his own fun, and I hear the plump sister's voice when she guesses the wonderful riddle, "It's your uncle Scro-o-o-o-oge!" Altogether, Dickens is better than any comedy. * * *

I do not see how *A Christmas Carol* can be read and acted better. The only improvement possible is in "The Ghosts," who are perhaps too monotonous,—a way ghosts have when they return to earth. It is generally believed that ghosts, being "damp, moist, uncomfortable bodies," lose their voices beyond redemption and are obliged to pipe through eternity on one key. I am at a loss to see the wisdom of this hypothesis. Solemnity and monotony are not synonymous terms, yet every theatrical ghost insists that they are, and Dickens is no exception to the rule. If monotony be excusable in any one, however, it is in him; for when one actor is obliged to represent *twenty-three different characters,* giving to every one an individual tone, he may be pardoned if his ghosts are not colloquial.

1871

POPULAR SHORT FICTION

During the 1880s and 1890s, short stories enjoyed a golden age in Britain. H. G. Wells said that "People talked about them tremendously, compared them, and ranked them. That was the thing that mattered." Yet short stories had been popular in America and Europe for decades before they caught on in Britain. Previously, the public's appetite for fiction had been sated by novels, which often appeared serially in the leading periodicals. Although many novelists, including Charles Dickens, George Eliot, Anthony Trollope, and Wilkie Collins, occasionally tried their hand at short fiction, three-decker novels were far more profitable—and far more prestigious. Where the novel might be regarded as "serious," stories smacked of the sensational. Henry James observed that "the little story is but scantily relished in England, where readers take their fiction rather by the volume than by the page." Not until late in the century did writers such as Stevenson, Kipling, and Doyle build their careers on short stories, and only then did the genre gain the status of a distinct artistic form.

The growing visibility of short stories was fueled by innovations in the printing process that allowed low-cost mass-circulation periodicals to flourish; Somerset Maugham later argued that "the rich abundance of short stories during the nineteenth century was directly occasioned by the opportunity which the periodicals afforded." Thanks in part to the rage for Sherlock Holmes, *The Strand* sold half-a-million copies a month during the 1890s. Literary magazines were often shaped by the taste and vision of the founding editor; *Household Words,* for example—where Elizabeth Gaskell first published *Cranford*—bore the characteristic stamp of its creator, Charles Dickens.

The market for cheap reading matter was strengthened by the excitement of new-found and nearly universal literacy. The demands of an expanding readership spurred the development of the short story as an emerging literary form, one that ran the gamut from mystery stories, detective stories, and ghost stories to fairy tales, fables, and fantasies. The best story writers have always made every detail count; they achieve powerful effects through poetic compression of meaning into a narrow space. But they must do more than convey a unified mood or atmosphere; Hardy believed that their subject matter should be exceptional, too: "We tale-tellers are all Ancient Mariners, and none of us is warranted in stopping Wedding Guests (in other words, the hurrying public) unless he has something more unusual to relate than the ordinary experience of every average man and woman."

The four examples that follow suggest the range of technique and experience the short story form could accommodate. Other Victorian fiction in this anthology includes Charles Dickens's *Christmas Carol,* Rudyard Kipling's *Without Benefit of Clergy,* Ada Leverson's *Suggestion,* and Max Beerbohm's *Enoch Soames.*

Elizabeth Gaskell
1810–1865

The narrator of *Cranford* speaks of having "vibrated all my life" between the rural setting of Cranford and a nearby commercial city. The same was true of Elizabeth Gaskell, who grew up in the small town of Knutsford, but went to live in the industrial city of Manchester after her marriage to a Unitarian minister in 1832. She grappled with the changes wrought by industrialism in novels of social protest, including *Mary Barton* (1848), *Ruth* (1853), and *North and South* (1855). Even in the idyllic village of Cranford, the "obnoxious" new railroad impinges dramatically. The middle-aged spinsters with their out-of-date clothes and manners are only dimly aware of the bustling modern world; they linger on as representatives of a bygone era. The story is set in the 1830s, when Dickens's lively comic novel *Pickwick Papers* was hot off the presses, the epitome of modern literature; the Cranford ladies' preference for the stately prose of the eighteenth-century Dr. Johnson humorously dramatizes a society in transition. The young narrator records their eccentricities fondly, but with a subtle sense of the absurd. Yet despite their faintly ridiculous obsession with gentility and "elegant economy," the women of Cranford retain the humanity, compassion, and moral integrity conspicuously lacking in the industrial world.

Our Society at Cranford[1]

In the first place, Cranford is in possession of the Amazons;[2] all the holders of houses above a certain rent are women. If a married couple come to settle in the town, somehow the gentleman disappears; he is either fairly frightened to death by being the only man in the Cranford evening parties, or he is accounted for by being with his regiment, his ship, or closely engaged in business all the week in the great neighbouring commercial town of Drumble,[3] distant only twenty miles on a railroad. In short, whatever does become of the gentlemen, they are not at Cranford. What could they do if they were there? The surgeon has his round of thirty miles, and sleeps at Cranford; but every man cannot be a surgeon. For keeping the trim gardens full of choice flowers without a weed to speck them; for frightening away little boys who look wistfully at the said flowers through the railings; for rushing out at the geese that occasionally venture into the gardens if the gates are left open; for deciding all questions of literature and politics without troubling themselves with unnecessary reasons or arguments; for obtaining clear and correct knowledge of everybody's affairs in the

1. First published as a self-contained story in December 1851 in *Household Words,* a periodical edited by Charles Dickens. Although Gaskell later said that "I never meant to write more," Dickens persuaded her to continue the story in subsequent issues. In 1853 the collected sketches appeared in book form as *Cranford.*
2. In Greek legend, the Amazons were fierce warriors who formed an all-female state.
3. Manchester.

parish; for keeping their neat maid-servants in admirable order; for kindness (somewhat dictatorial) to the poor, and real tender good offices to each other whenever they are in distress, the ladies of Cranford are quite sufficient. "A man," as one of them observed to me once, "is *so* in the way in the house!" Although the ladies of Cranford know all each other's proceedings, they are exceedingly indifferent to each other's opinions. Indeed, as each has her own individuality, not to say eccentricity, pretty strongly developed, nothing is so easy as verbal retaliation; but, somehow, good-will reigns among them to a considerable degree.

The Cranford ladies have only an occasional little quarrel, spirited out in a few peppery words and angry jerks of the head; just enough to prevent the even tenor of their lives from becoming too flat. Their dress is very independent of fashion; as they observe, "What does it signify how we dress here at Cranford, where everybody knows us?" And if they go from home, their reason is equally cogent, "What does it signify how we dress here, where nobody knows us?" The materials of their clothes are, in general, good and plain, and most of them are nearly as scrupulous as Miss Tyler, of cleanly memory;[4] but I will answer for it, the last gigot, the last tight and scanty petticoat in wear in England, was seen in Cranford—and seen without a smile.[5]

I can testify to a magnificent family red silk umbrella, under which a gentle little spinster, left alone of many brothers and sisters, used to patter to church on rainy days. Have you any red silk umbrellas in London? We had a tradition of the first that had ever been seen in Cranford; and the little boys mobbed it, and called it "a stick in petticoats." It might have been the very red silk one I have described, held by a strong father over a troop of little ones; the poor little lady—the survivor of all—could scarcely carry it.

Then there were rules and regulations for visiting and calls; and they were announced to any young people who might be staying in the town, with all the solemnity with which the old Manx laws were read once a year on the Tinwald Mount.[6]

"Our friends have sent to inquire how you are after your journey to-night, my dear" (fifteen miles in a gentleman's carriage); "they will give you some rest tomorrow, but the next day, I have no doubt, they will call; so be at liberty after twelve—from twelve to three are our calling hours."

Then, after they had called—

"It is the third day; I dare say your mamma has told you, my dear, never to let more than three days elapse between receiving a call and returning it; and also, that you are never to stay longer than a quarter of an hour."

"But am I to look at my watch? How am I to find out when a quarter of an hour has passed?"

"You must keep thinking about the time, my dear, and not allow yourself to forget it in conversation."

As everybody had this rule in their minds, whether they received or paid a call, of course no absorbing subject was ever spoken about. We kept ourselves to short sentences of small talk, and were punctual to our time.

I imagine that a few of the gentlefolks of Cranford were poor, and had some difficulty in making both ends meet; but they were like the Spartans,[7] and concealed

---

4. The aunt of Robert Southey (1774–1843)—Poet Laureate at the time when *Cranford* takes place—was famous for her passion for cleanliness.
5. By the mid-1830s, the old-fashioned leg-of-mutton sleeve and straight skirt had given way to the hooped skirt.

6. The population of the Isle of Man customarily assembled once a year on Tynwald Hill to hear the new laws read aloud.
7. The Spartans of ancient Greece were known for their courage and self-control in the face of hardship.

their smart under a smiling face. We none of us spoke of money, because that subject savoured of commerce and trade, and though some might be poor, we were all aristocratic. The Cranfordians had that kindly *esprit de corps* which made them overlook all deficiencies in success when some among them tried to conceal their poverty. When Mrs Forrester, for instance, gave a party in her baby-house of a dwelling, and the little maiden disturbed the ladies on the sofa by a request that she might get the tea-tray out from underneath, every one took this novel proceeding as the most natural thing in the world, and talked on about household forms and ceremonies as if we all believed that our hostess had a regular servants' hall, second table, with housekeeper and steward, instead of the one little charity-school maiden,[8] whose short ruddy arms could never have been strong enough to carry the tray upstairs, if she had not been assisted in private by her mistress, who now sat in state, pretending not to know what cakes were sent up, though she knew, and we knew, and she knew that we knew, and we knew that she knew that we knew, she had been busy all the morning making tea-bread and sponge-cakes.

There were one or two consequences arising from this general but unacknowledged poverty, and this very much acknowledged gentility, which were not amiss, and which might be introduced into many circles of society to their great improvement. For instance, the inhabitants of Cranford kept early hours, and clattered home in their pattens,[9] under the guidance of a lantern-bearer, about nine o'clock at night; and the whole town was abed and asleep by half-past ten. Moreover, it was considered "vulgar" (a tremendous word in Cranford) to give anything expensive, in the way of eatable or drinkable, at the evening entertainments. Wafer bread-and-butter and sponge-biscuits were all that the Honourable Mrs Jamieson gave; and she was sister-in-law to the late Earl of Glenmire, although she did practise such "elegant economy."

"Elegant economy!" How naturally one falls back into the phraseology of Cranford! There, economy was always "elegant," and money-spending always "vulgar and ostentatious;" a sort of sour-grapeism which made us very peaceful and satisfied. I never shall forget the dismay felt when a certain Captain Brown came to live at Cranford, and openly spoke about his being poor—not in a whisper to an intimate friend, the doors and windows being previously closed, but in the public street! in a loud military voice! alleging his poverty as a reason for not taking a particular house. The ladies of Cranford were already rather moaning over the invasion of their territories by a man and a gentleman. He was a half-pay captain,[1] and had obtained some situation on a neighbouring railroad, which had been vehemently petitioned against by the little town;[2] and if, in addition to his masculine gender, and his connection with the obnoxious railroad, he was so brazen as to talk of being poor—why, then, indeed, he must be sent to Coventry.[3] Death was as true and as common as poverty; yet people never spoke about that, loud out in the streets. It was a word not to be mentioned to ears polite. We had tacitly agreed to ignore that any with whom we associated on terms of visiting equality could ever be prevented by poverty from doing anything that they wished. If we walked to or from a party, it was because the night was *so* fine, or the air *so* refreshing, not because sedan-chairs were expensive.[4] If we wore

---

8. Charity schools trained poor children for domestic work; that one such pupil formed Mrs. Forrester's entire domestic staff indicates her meager standard of living.
9. Wooden platform shoes to protect one's shoes from mud.
1. A retired officer who stayed on reserve at half pay.

2. The railroads were new, and still looked on with suspicion by many country-dwellers.
3. Ostracized.
4. Enclosed chairs carried by servants; more common in the 18th century.

prints, instead of summer silks, it was because we preferred a washing material; and so on, till we blinded ourselves to the vulgar fact that we were, all of us, people of very moderate means. Of course, then, we did not know what to make of a man who could speak of poverty as if it was not a disgrace. Yet, somehow, Captain Brown made himself respected in Cranford, and was called upon, in spite of all resolutions to the contrary. I was surprised to hear his opinions quoted as authority at a visit which I paid to Cranford about a year after he had settled in the town. My own friends had been among the bitterest opponents of any proposal to visit the Captain and his daughters, only twelve months before; and now he was even admitted in the tabooed hours before twelve. True, it was to discover the cause of a smoking chimney, before the fire was lighted; but still Captain Brown walked upstairs, nothing daunted, spoke in a voice too large for the room, and joked quite in the way of a tame man about the house. He had been blind to all the small slights, and omissions of trivial ceremonies, with which he had been received. He had been friendly, though the Cranford ladies had been cool; he had answered small sarcastic compliments in good faith; and with his manly frankness had overpowered all the shrinking which met him as a man who was not ashamed to be poor. And, at last, his excellent masculine common sense, and his facility in devising expedients to overcome domestic dilemmas, had gained him an extraordinary place as authority among the Cranford ladies. He himself went on in his course, as unaware of his popularity as he had been of the reverse; and I am sure he was startled one day when he found his advice so highly esteemed as to make some counsel which he had given in jest to be taken in sober, serious earnest.

It was on this subject: An old lady had an Alderney cow, which she looked upon as a daughter. You could not pay the short quarter of an hour call without being told of the wonderful milk or wonderful intelligence of this animal. The whole town knew and kindly regarded Miss Betsy Barker's Alderney; therefore great was the sympathy and regret when, in an unguarded moment, the poor cow tumbled into a lime-pit.[5] She moaned so loudly that she was soon heard and rescued; but meanwhile the poor beast had lost most of her hair, and came out looking naked, cold, and miserable, in a bare skin. Everybody pitied the animal, though a few could not restrain their smiles at her droll appearance. Miss Betsy Barker absolutely cried with sorrow and dismay; and it was said she thought of trying a bath of oil. This remedy, perhaps, was recommended by some one of the number whose advice she asked; but the proposal, if ever it was made, was knocked on the head by Captain Brown's decided "Get her a flannel waistcoat and flannel drawers, ma'am, if you wish to keep her alive. But my advice is, kill the poor creature at once."

Miss Betsy Barker dried her eyes, and thanked the Captain heartily; she set to work, and by-and-by all the town turned out to see the Alderney meekly going to her pasture, clad in dark grey flannel. I have watched her myself many a time. Do you ever see cows dressed in grey flannel in London?

Captain Brown had taken a small house on the outskirts of the town, where he lived with his two daughters. He must have been upwards of sixty at the time of the first visit I paid to Cranford after I had left it as a residence. But he had a wiry, well-trained, elastic figure, a stiff military throw-back of his head, and a springing step, which made him appear much younger than he was. His eldest daughter looked almost as old as himself, and betrayed the fact that his real was more than his apparent age. Miss Brown must have been forty; she had a sickly, pained, careworn expression

5. A pit in which tanners dress skins with lime to remove the hair.

on her face, and looked as if the gaiety of youth had long faded out of sight. Even when young she must have been plain and hard featured. Miss Jessie Brown was ten years younger than her sister, and twenty shades prettier. Her face was round and dimpled. Miss Jenkyns once said, in a passion against Captain Brown (the cause of which I will tell you presently), "that she thought it was time for Miss Jessie to leave off her dimples, and not always to be trying to look like a child." It was true there was something childlike in her face; and there will be, I think, till she dies, though she should live to a hundred. Her eyes were large blue wondering eyes, looking straight at you; her nose was unformed and snub, and her lips were red and dewy; she wore her hair, too, in little rows of curls, which heightened this appearance. I do not know whether she was pretty or not; but I liked her face, and so did everybody, and I do not think she could help her dimples. She had something of her father's jauntiness of gait and manner; and any female observer might detect a slight difference in the attire of the two sisters—that of Miss Jessie being about two pounds per annum more expensive than Miss Brown's. Two pounds was a large sum in Captain Brown's annual disbursements.

Such was the impression made upon me by the Brown family when I first saw them all together in Cranford Church. The Captain I had met before—on the occasion of the smoky chimney, which he had cured by some simple alteration in the flue. In church, he held his double eye-glass to his eyes during the Morning Hymn, and then lifted up his head erect and sang out loud and joyfully. He made the responses louder than the clerk—an old man with a piping feeble voice, who, I think, felt aggrieved at the Captain's sonorous bass, and quavered higher and higher in consequence.

On coming out of church, the brisk Captain paid the most gallant attention to his two daughters. He nodded and smiled to his acquaintances; but he shook hands with none until he had helped Miss Brown to unfurl her umbrella, had relieved her of her prayer-book, and had waited patiently till she, with trembling nervous hands, had taken up her gown to walk through the wet roads.

I wondered what the Cranford ladies did with Captain Brown at their parties. We had often rejoiced, in former days, that there was no gentleman to be attended to, and to find conversation for, at the card-parties. We had congratulated ourselves upon the snugness of the evenings; and, in our love for gentility, and distaste of mankind, we had almost persuaded ourselves that to be a man was to be "vulgar"; so that when I found my friend and hostess, Miss Jenkyns, was going to have a party in my honour, and that Captain and the Miss Browns were invited, I wondered much what would be the course of the evening. Card-tables, with green baize tops, were set out by daylight, just as usual; it was the third week in November, so the evenings closed in about four. Candles, and clean packs of cards were arranged on each table. The fire was made up; the neat maid-servant had received her last directions; and there we stood, dressed in our best, each with a candle-lighter in our hands, ready to dart at the candles as soon as the first knock came. Parties in Cranford were solemn festivities, making the ladies feel gravely elated as they sat together in their best dresses. As soon as three had arrived, we sat down to "Preference," I being the unlucky fourth.[6] The next four comers were put down immediately to another table; and presently the tea-trays, which I had seen set out in the store-room as I passed in

---

6. "Unlucky" because only three people can play this card game at once; the dealer has to sit out.

the morning, were placed each on the middle of a card-table. The china was delicate egg-shell; the old-fashioned silver glittered with polishing; but the eatables were of the slightest description. While the trays were yet on the tables, Captain and the Miss Browns came in; and I could see that, somehow or other, the Captain was a favourite with all the ladies present. Ruffled brows were smoothed, sharp voices lowered at his approach. Miss Brown looked ill, and depressed almost to gloom. Miss Jessie smiled as usual, and seemed nearly as popular as her father. He immediately and quietly assumed the man's place in the room; attended to every one's wants, lessened the pretty maid-servant's labour by waiting on empty cups and bread-and-butterless ladies; and yet did it all in so easy and dignified a manner, and so much as if it were a matter of course for the strong to attend to the weak, that he was a true man throughout. He played for threepenny points with as grave an interest as if they had been pounds; and yet, in all his attention to strangers, he had an eye on his suffering daughter—for suffering I was sure she was, though to many eyes she might only appear to be irritable. Miss Jessie could not play cards: but she talked to the sitters-out, who, before her coming, had been rather inclined to be cross. She sang, too, to an old cracked piano, which I think had been a spinet[7] in its youth. Miss Jessie sang "Jock of Hazeldean"[8] a little out of tune; but we were none of us musical, though Miss Jenkyns beat time, out of time, by way of appearing to be so.

It was very good of Miss Jenkyns to do this; for I had seen that, a little before, she had been a good deal annoyed by Miss Jessie Brown's unguarded admission (à propos of Shetland wool) that she had an uncle, her mother's brother, who was a shopkeeper in Edinburgh. Miss Jenkyns tried to drown this confession by a terrible cough—for the Honourable Mrs Jamieson was sitting at the card-table nearest Miss Jessie, and what would she say or think if she found out she was in the same room with a shopkeeper's niece! But Miss Jessie Brown (who had no tact, as we all agreed the next morning) *would* repeat the information, and assure Miss Pole she could easily get her the identical Shetland wool required, "through my uncle, who has the best assortment of Shetland goods of any one in Edinbro'." It was to take the taste of this out of our mouths, and the sound of this out of our ears, that Miss Jenkyns proposed music; so I say again, it was very good of her to beat time to the song.

When the trays re-appeared with biscuits and wine, punctually at a quarter to nine, there was conversation, comparing of cards, and talking over tricks; but by-and-by Captain Brown sported a bit of literature.

"Have you seen any numbers of 'The Pickwick Papers'?" said he. (They were then publishing in parts.)[9] "Capital thing!"

Now Miss Jenkyns was daughter of a deceased rector of Cranford; and, on the strength of a number of manuscript sermons, and a pretty good library of divinity, considered herself literary, and looked upon any conversation about books as a challenge to her. So she answered and said, "Yes, she had seen them; indeed, she might say she had read them."

"And what do you think of them?" exclaimed Captain Brown. "Aren't they famously good?"

---

7. An earlier keyboard instrument, popular before the invention of the piano.
8. A ballad written in 1816 by Sir Walter Scott.
9. Dickens published The Pickwick Papers serially in 1836 and 1837 under the pseudonym "Boz." Although this form of publication was considered "vulgar," the humorous escapades of Mr. Pickwick were phenomenally successful. When *Cranford* first appeared in Dickens's *Household Words*, he substituted Thomas Hood for himself, to Gaskell's annoyance.

So urged, Miss Jenkyns could not but speak.

"I must say, I don't think they are by any means equal to Dr Johnson.[1] Still, perhaps, the author is young. Let him persevere, and who knows what he may become if he will take the great Doctor for his model?" This was evidently too much for Captain Brown to take placidly; and I saw the words on the tip of his tongue before Miss Jenkyns had finished her sentence.

"It is quite a different sort of thing, my dear madam," he began.

"I am quite aware of that," returned she. "And I make allowances, Captain Brown."

"Just allow me to read you a scene out of this month's number," pleaded he. "I had it only this morning, and I don't think the company can have read it yet."

"As you please," said she, settling herself with an air of resignation. He read the account of the "swarry" which Sam Weller gave at Bath.[2] Some of us laughed heartily. I did not dare, because I was staying in the house. Miss Jenkyns sat in patient gravity. When it was ended, she turned to me, and said with mild dignity—

"Fetch me 'Rasselas,'[3] my dear, out of the bookroom."

When I brought it to her, she turned to Captain Brown—

"Now allow me to read you a scene, and then the present company can judge between your favourite, Mr Boz, and Dr Johnson."

She read one of the conversations between Rasselas and Imlac, in a high-pitched majestic voice: and when she had ended, she said, "I imagine I am now justified in my preference of Dr Johnson as a writer of fiction." The Captain screwed his lips up, and drummed on the table, but he did not speak. She thought she would give a finishing blow or two.

"I consider it vulgar, and below the dignity of literature, to publish in numbers."

"How was the Rambler[4] published, ma'am?" asked Captain Brown in a low voice, which I think Miss Jenkyns could not have heard.

"Dr Johnson's style is a model for young beginners. My father recommended it to me when I began to write letters—I have formed my own style upon it; I recommend it to your favourite."

"I should be very sorry for him to exchange his style for any such pompous writing," said Captain Brown.

Miss Jenkyns felt this as a personal affront, in a way of which the Captain had not dreamed. Epistolary writing she and her friends considered as her forte. Many a copy of many a letter have I seen written and corrected on the slate, before she "seized the half-hour just previous to post-time to assure" her friends of this or of that; and Dr Johnson was, as she said, her model in these compositions. She drew herself up with dignity, and only replied to Captain Brown's last remark by saying, with marked emphasis on every syllable, "I prefer Dr Johnson to Mr Boz."

It is said—I won't vouch for the fact—that Captain Brown was heard to say, sotto voce, "D—n Dr Johnson!" If he did, he was penitent afterwards, as he showed by going to stand near Miss Jenkyns's arm-chair, and endeavouring to beguile her into

1. Samuel Johnson (1708–1784) born more than a hundred years before Dickens, was noted for his stately, balanced prose.
2. A reference to an episode in Pickwick Papers where Mr. Pickwick's servant Sam Weller attends a "soirée" for the footmen at Bath. The quick-witted Sam mocks the pompous servants, but they don't realize it.
3. Rasselas is a series of dialogues on moral themes between the prince of Abyssinia and his spiritual mentor, Imlac. Unlike the lively Pickwick, it is a serious and slow-paced philosophical work.
4. A periodical started in 1750 by Dr. Johnson and written almost entirely by himself.

conversation on some more pleasing subject. But she was inexorable. The next day she made the remark I have mentioned about Miss Jessie's dimples.

2

It was impossible to live a month at Cranford and not know the daily habits of each resident; and long before my visit was ended I knew much concerning the whole Brown trio. There was nothing new to be discovered respecting their poverty; for they had spoken simply and openly about that from the very first. They made no mystery of the necessity for their being economical. All that remained to be discovered was the Captain's infinite kindness of heart, and the various modes in which, unconsciously to himself, he manifested it. Some little anecdotes were talked about for some time after they occurred. As we did not read much, and as all the ladies were pretty well suited with servants, there was a dearth of subjects for conversation. We therefore discussed the circumstance of the Captain taking a poor old woman's dinner out of her hands one very slippery Sunday. He had met her returning from the bakehouse as he came from church, and noticed her precarious footing; and, with the grave dignity with which he did everything, he relieved her of her burden, and steered along the street by her side, carrying her baked mutton and potatoes safely home.[5] This was thought very eccentric; and it was rather expected that he would pay a round of calls, on the Monday morning, to explain and apologise to the Cranford sense of propriety: but he did no such thing: and then it was decided that he was ashamed, and was keeping out of sight. In a kindly pity for him, we began to say, "After all, the Sunday morning's occurrence showed great goodness of heart," and it was resolved that he should be comforted on his next appearance amongst us; but, lo! he came down upon us, untouched by any sense of shame, speaking loud and bass as ever, his head thrown back, his wig as jaunty and well-curled as usual, and we were obliged to conclude he had forgotten all about Sunday.

Miss Pole and Miss Jessie Brown had set up a kind of intimacy on the strength of the Shetland wool and the new knitting stitches; so it happened that when I went to visit Miss Pole I saw more of the Browns than I had done while staying with Miss Jenkyns, who had never got over what she called Captain Brown's disparaging remarks upon Dr Johnson as a writer of light and agreeable fiction. I found that Miss Brown was seriously ill of some lingering, incurable complaint, the pain occasioned by which gave the uneasy expression to her face that I had taken for unmitigated crossness. Cross, too, she was at times, when the nervous irritability occasioned by her disease became past endurance. Miss Jessie bore with her at these times, even more patiently than she did with the bitter self-upbraidings by which they were invariably succeeded. Miss Brown used to accuse herself, not merely of hasty and irritable temper, but also of being the cause why her father and sister were obliged to pinch, in order to allow her the small luxuries which were necessaries in her condition. She would so fain have made sacrifices for them, and have lightened their cares, that the original generosity of her disposition added acerbity to her temper. All this was borne by Miss Jessie and her father with more than placidity—with absolute tenderness. I forgave Miss Jessie her singing out of tune, and her juvenility of dress, when I saw her at home. I came to perceive that Captain Brown's dark Brutus wig and

5. Poor people often brought their meals to cook in the ovens of bake shops on Sundays and holidays.

padded coat[6] (alas! too often threadbare) were remnants of the military smartness of his youth, which he now wore unconsciously. He was a man of infinite resources, gained in his barrack experience. As he confessed, no one could black his boots to please him except himself; but, indeed, he was not above saving the little maid-servant's labours in every way—knowing, most likely, that his daughter's illness made the place a hard one.

He endeavoured to make peace with Miss Jenkyns soon after the memorable dispute I have named, by a present of a wooden fire-shovel (his own making), having heard her say how much the grating of an iron one annoyed her. She received the present with cool gratitude, and thanked him formally. When he was gone, she bade me put it away in the lumber-room; feeling, probably, that no present from a man who preferred Mr Boz to Dr Johnson could be less jarring than an iron fire-shovel.

Such was the state of things when I left Cranford and went to Drumble. I had, however, several correspondents, who kept me *au fait* as to the proceedings of the dear little town. There was Miss Pole, who was becoming as much absorbed in crochet as she had been once in knitting, and the burden of whose letter was something like, "But don't you forget the white worsted at Flint's" of the old song; for at the end of every sentence of news came a fresh direction as to some crochet commission which I was to execute for her. Miss Matilda Jenkyns (who did not mind being called Miss Matty, when Miss Jenkyns was not by) wrote nice, kind, rambling letters, now and then venturing into an opinion of her own; but suddenly pulling herself up, and either begging me not to name what she had said, as Deborah thought differently, and *she* knew, or else putting in a postscript to the effect that, since writing the above, she had been talking over the subject with Deborah, and was quite convinced that, &c.—(here probably followed a recantation of every opinion she had given in the letter). Then came Miss Jenkyns—Debōrah, as she liked Miss Matty to call her, her father having once said that the Hebrew name ought to be so pronounced. I secretly think she took the Hebrew prophetess for a model in character; and, indeed, she was not unlike the stern prophetess[7] in some ways, making allowance, of course, for modern customs and difference in dress. Miss Jenkyns wore a cravat, and a little bonnet like a jockey-cap, and altogether had the appearance of a strong-minded woman; although she would have despised the modern idea of women being equal to men. Equal, indeed! she knew they were superior. But to return to her letters. Everything in them was stately and grand like herself. I have been looking them over (dear Miss Jenkyns, how I honoured her!), and I will give an extract, more especially because it relates to our friend Captain Brown:—

"The Honourable Mrs Jamieson has only just quitted me; and, in the course of conversation, she communicated to me the intelligence that she had yesterday received a call from her revered husband's quondam[8] friend, Lord Mauleverer. You will not easily conjecture what brought his lordship within the precincts of our little town. It was to see Captain Brown, with whom, it appears, his lordship was acquainted in the 'plumed wars,' and who had the privilege of averting destruction from his lordship's head when some great peril was impending over it, off the misnomered Cape of Good Hope. You know our friend the Honourable Mrs Jamieson's deficiency in the spirit of innocent curiosity; and you will therefore not be so much

6. A short, curly hairstyle popular during the French Revolution; padded coats were fashionable in the early 19th century.

7. Deborah was one of the leaders of Israel (Judges 4–5).
8. Former.

surprised when I tell you she was quite unable to disclose to me the exact nature of the peril in question. I was anxious, I confess, to ascertain in what manner Captain Brown, with his limited establishment, could receive so distinguished a guest; and I discovered that his lordship retired to rest, and, let us hope, to refreshing slumbers, at the Angel Hotel; but shared the Brunonian[9] meals during the two days that he honoured Cranford with his august presence. Mrs Johnson, our civil butcher's wife, informs me that Miss Jessie purchased a leg of lamb; but, besides this, I can hear of no preparation whatever to give a suitable reception to so distinguished a visitor. Perhaps they entertained him with 'the feast of reason and the flow of soul;'[1] and to us, who are acquainted with Captain Brown's sad want of relish for 'the pure wells of English undefiled,'[2] it may be matter for congratulation that he has had the opportunity of improving his taste by holding converse with an elegant and refined member of the British aristocracy. But from some mundane failings who is altogether free?"

Miss Pole and Miss Matty wrote to me by the same post. Such a piece of news as Lord Mauleverer's visit was not to be lost on the Cranford letter-writers: they made the most of it. Miss Matty humbly apologised for writing at the same time as her sister, who was so much more capable than she to describe the honour done to Cranford; but in spite of a little bad spelling, Miss Matty's account gave me the best idea of the commotion occasioned by his lordship's visit, after it had occurred; for, except the people at the Angel, the Browns, Mrs Jamieson, and a little lad his lordship had sworn at for driving a dirty hoop against the aristocratic legs, I could not hear of any one with whom his lordship had held conversation.

My next visit to Cranford was in the summer. There had been neither births, deaths, nor marriages since I was there last. Everybody lived in the same house, and wore pretty nearly the same well-preserved, old-fashioned clothes. The greatest event was, that Miss Jenkynses had purchased a new carpet for the drawing-room. Oh, the busy work Miss Matty and I had in chasing the sunbeams, as they fell in an afternoon right down on this carpet through the blindless window! We spread newspapers over the places, and sat down to our book or our work; and, lo! in a quarter of an hour the sun had moved, and was blazing away on a fresh spot; and down again we went on our knees to alter the position of the newspapers. We were very busy, too, one whole morning, before Miss Jenkyns gave her party, in following her directions, and in cutting out and stitching together pieces of newspaper so as to form little paths to every chair set for the expected visitors, lest their shoes might dirty or defile the purity of the carpet. Do you make paper paths for every guest to walk upon in London?

Captain Brown and Miss Jenkyns were not very cordial to each other. The literary dispute, of which I had seen the beginning, was a "raw," the slightest touch on which made them wince. It was the only difference of opinion they had ever had; but that difference was enough. Miss Jenkyns could not refrain from talking *at* Captain Brown; and, though he did not reply, he drummed with his fingers, which action she felt and resented as very disparaging to Dr Johnson. He was rather ostentatious in his preference of the writings of Mr Boz; would walk through the streets so absorbed in them that he all but ran against Miss Jenkyns; and though his apologies were earnest and sincere, and though he did not, in fact, do more than startle her and himself, she

9. A pretentious, Latinized version of Brown, part of Miss Jenkyns's unintentionally comic imitation of the style of Dr. Johnson.
1. Alexander Pope, *Imitations of Horace*, Satire 1, Book 2.128

(1733).
2. Edmund Spenser, *The Faerie Queene* 4.2.32 (1596); the reference is to Chaucer.

owned to me she had rather he had knocked her down, if he had only been reading a higher style of literature. The poor, brave Captain! he looked older, and more worn, and his clothes were very threadbare. But he seemed as bright and cheerful as ever, unless he was asked about his daughter's health.

"She suffers a great deal, and she must suffer more: we do what we can to alleviate her pain;—God's will be done!" He took off his hat at these last words. I found, from Miss Matty, that everything had been done, in fact. A medical man, of high repute in that country neighbourhood, had been sent for, and every injunction he had given was attended to, regardless of expense. Miss Matty was sure they denied themselves many things in order to make the invalid comfortable; but they never spoke about it; and as for Miss Jessie!—"I really think she's an angel," said poor Miss Matty, quite overcome. "To see her way of bearing with Miss Brown's crossness, and the bright face she puts on after she's been sitting up a whole night and scolded above half of it, is quite beautiful. Yet she looks as neat and as ready to welcome the Captain at breakfast-time as if she had been asleep in the Queen's bed all night. My dear! you could never laugh at her prim little curls or her pink bows again if you saw her as I have done." I could only feel very penitent, and greet Miss Jessie with double respect when I met her next. She looked faded and pinched; and her lips began to quiver, as if she was very weak, when she spoke of her sister. But she brightened, and sent back the tears that were glittering in her pretty eyes, as she said—

"But, to be sure, what a town Cranford is for kindness! I don't suppose any one has a better dinner than usual cooked but the best part of all comes in a little covered basin for my sister. The poor people will leave their earliest vegetables at our door for her. They speak short and gruff, as if they were ashamed of it; but I am sure it often goes to my heart to see their thoughtfulness." The tears now came back and overflowed; but after a minute or two she began to scold herself, and ended by going away the same cheerful Miss Jessie as ever.

"But why does not this Lord Mauleverer do something for the man who saved his life?" said I.

"Why, you see, unless Captain Brown has some reason for it, he never speaks about being poor; and he walked along by his lordship looking as happy and cheerful as a prince; and as they never called attention to their dinner by apologies, and as Miss Brown was better that day, and all seemed bright, I dare say his lordship never knew how much care there was in the background. He did send game in the winter pretty often, but now he is gone abroad."

I had often occasion to notice the use that was made of fragments and small opportunities in Cranford; the rose-leaves that were gathered ere they fell to make into a potpourri for some one who had no garden; the little bundles of lavender flowers sent to strew the drawers of some town-dweller, or to burn in the chamber of some invalid. Things that many would despise, and actions which it seemed scarcely worth while to perform, were all attended to in Cranford. Miss Jenkyns stuck an apple full of cloves, to be heated and smell pleasantly in Miss Brown's room; and as she put in each clove she uttered a Johnsonian sentence. Indeed, she never could think of the Browns without talking Johnson; and, as they were seldom absent from her thoughts just then, I heard many a rolling, three-piled sentence.

Captain Brown called one day to thank Miss Jenkyns for many little kindnesses, which I did not know until then that she had rendered. He had suddenly become like an old man; his deep bass voice had a quavering in it, his eyes looked dim, and the lines on his face were deep. He did not—could not—speak cheerfully of his daughter's state, but he talked with manly, pious resignation, and not much. Twice over he said, "What Jessie has been to us, God only knows!" and after the second time, he got up hastily, shook hands all round without speaking, and left the room.

That afternoon we perceived little groups in the street, all listening with faces aghast to some tale or other. Miss Jenkyns wondered what could be the matter for some time before she took the undignified step of sending Jenny out to inquire.

Jenny came back with a white face of terror. "Oh, ma'am! oh, Miss Jenkyns, ma'am! Captain Brown is killed by them nasty cruel railroads!" and she burst into tears. She, along with many others, had experienced the poor Captain's kindness.

"How?—where—where? Good God! Jenny, don't waste time in crying, but tell us something." Miss Matty rushed out into the street at once, and collared the man who was telling the tale.

"Come in—come to my sister at once, Miss Jenkyns, the rector's daughter. Oh, man, man! say it is not true," she cried, as she brought the affrighted carter, sleeking down his hair, into the drawing-room, where he stood with his wet boots on the new carpet, and no one regarded it.

"Please, mum, it is true. I seed it myself," and he shuddered at the recollection. "The Captain was a-reading some new book as he was deep in, a-waiting for the down train; and there was a little lass as wanted to come to its mammy, and gave its sister the slip, and came toddling across the line. And he looked up sudden, at the sound of the train coming, and seed the child, and he darted on the line and cotched it up, and his foot slipped, and the train came over him in no time. O Lord, Lord! Mum, it's quite true—and they've come over to tell his daughters. The child's safe, though, with only a bang on its shoulder as he threw it to its mammy. Poor Captain would be glad of that, mum, wouldn't he? God bless him!" The great rough carter puckered up his manly face, and turned away to hide his tears. I turned to Miss Jenkyns. She looked very ill, as if she were going to faint, and signed to me to open the window.

"Matilda, bring me my bonnet. I must go to those girls. God pardon me, if ever I have spoken contemptuously to the Captain!"

Miss Jenkyns arrayed herself to go out, telling Miss Matilda to give the man a glass of wine. While she was away, Miss Matty and I huddled over the fire, talking in a low and awestruck voice. I know we cried quietly all the time.

Miss Jenkyns came home in a silent mood, and we durst not ask her many questions. She told us that Miss Jessie had fainted, and that she and Miss Pole had had some difficulty in bringing her round; but that, as soon as she recovered, she begged one of them to go and sit with her sister.

"Mr Hoggins says she cannot live many days, and she shall be spared this shock," said Miss Jessie, shivering with feelings to which she dared not give way.

"But how can you manage, my dear?" asked Miss Jenkyns; "you cannot bear up, she must see your tears."

"God will help me—I will not give way—she was asleep when the news came; she may be asleep yet. She would be so utterly miserable, not merely at my father's death, but to think of what would become of me; she is so good to me." She looked up earnestly in their faces with her soft true eyes, and Miss Pole told Miss Jenkyns afterwards she could hardly bear it, knowing, as she did, how Miss Brown treated her sister.

However, it was settled according to Miss Jessie's wish. Miss Brown was to be told her father had been summoned to take a short journey on railway business. They had managed it in some way—Miss Jenkyns could not exactly say how. Miss Pole was to stop with Miss Jessie. Mrs Jamieson had sent to inquire. And this was all we heard that night; and a sorrowful night it was. The next day a full account of the fatal accident was in the county paper which Miss Jenkyns took in. Her eyes were very weak, she said, and she asked me to read it. When I came to the "gallant gentleman was deeply engaged in the perusal of a number of 'Pickwick,' which he had just received," Miss Jenkyns shook her head long and solemnly, and then sighed out, "Poor, dear, infatuated man!"

The corpse was to be taken from the station to the parish church, there to be interred. Miss Jessie had set her heart on following it to the grave; and no dissuasives could alter her resolve. Her restraint upon herself made her almost obstinate; she resisted all Miss Pole's entreaties and Miss Jenkyns's advice. At last Miss Jenkyns gave up the point; and after a silence, which I feared portended some deep displeasure against Miss Jessie, Miss Jenkyns said she should accompany the latter to the funeral.

"It is not fit for you to go alone. It would be against both propriety and humanity were I to allow it."

Miss Jessie seemed as if she did not half like this arrangement; but her obstinacy, if she had any, had been exhausted in her determination to go to the interment. She longed, poor thing, I have no doubt, to cry alone over the grave of the dear father to whom she had been all in all, and to give way, for one little half-hour, uninterrupted by sympathy and unobserved by friendship. But it was not to be. That afternoon Miss Jenkyns sent out for a yard of black crape, and employed herself busily in trimming the little black silk bonnet I have spoken about. When it was finished she put it on, and looked at us for approbation—admiration she despised. I was full of sorrow, but, by one of those whimsical thoughts which come unbidden into our heads, in times of deepest grief, I no sooner saw the bonnet than I was reminded of a helmet; and in that hybrid bonnet, half helmet, half jockey-cap, did Miss Jenkyns attend Captain Brown's funeral, and, I believe, supported Miss Jessie with a tender, indulgent firmness which was invaluable, allowing her to weep her passionate fill before they left.

Miss Pole, Miss Matty, and I, meanwhile attended to Miss Brown: and hard work we found it to relieve her querulous and never-ending complaints. But if we were so weary and dispirited, what must Miss Jessie have been! Yet she came back almost calm, as if she had gained a new strength. She put off her mourning dress, and came in, looking pale and gentle, thanking us each with a soft long pressure of the hand. She could even smile—a faint, sweet, wintry smile—as if to reassure us of her power to endure; but her look made our eyes fill suddenly with tears, more than if she had cried outright.

It was settled that Miss Pole was to remain with her all the watching livelong night; and that Miss Matty and I were to return in the morning to relieve them, and give Miss Jessie the opportunity for a few hours of sleep. But when the morning came, Miss Jenkyns appeared at the breakfast-table, equipped in her helmet-bonnet, and ordered Miss Matty to stay at home, as she meant to go and help to nurse. She was evidently in a state of great friendly excitement, which she showed by eating her breakfast standing, and scolding the household all round.

No nursing—no energetic strong-minded woman could help Miss Brown now. There was that in the room as we entered which was stronger than us all, and made us shrink into solemn awestruck helplessness. Miss Brown was dying. We hardly knew her voice, it was so devoid of the complaining tone we had always associated with it. Miss Jessie told me afterwards that it, and her face too, were just what they had been formerly, when her mother's death left her the young anxious head of the family, of whom only Miss Jessie survived.

She was conscious of her sister's presence, though not, I think, of ours. We stood a little behind the curtain: Miss Jessie knelt with her face near her sister's, in order to catch the last soft awful whispers.

"Oh, Jessie! Jessie! How selfish I have been! God forgive me for letting you sacrifice yourself for me as you did! I have so loved you—and yet I have thought only of myself. God forgive me!"

"Hush, love! hush!" said Miss Jessie, sobbing.

"And my father! my dear, dear father! I will not complain now, if God will give me strength to be patient. But, oh, Jessie! tell my father how I longed and yearned to see him at last, and to ask his forgiveness. He can never know now how I loved him—oh! if I might but tell him, before I die! What a life of sorrow his has been, and I have done so little to cheer him!"

A light came into Miss Jessie's face. "Would it comfort you, dearest, to think that he does know?—would it comfort you, love, to know that his cares, his sorrows"—Her voice quivered, but she steadied it into calmness—"Mary! he has gone before you to the place where the weary are at rest.[3] He knows now how you loved him."

A strange look, which was not distress, came over Miss Brown's face. She did not speak for some time, but then we saw her lips form the words, rather than heard the sound—"Father, mother, Harry, Archy;"—then, as if it were a new idea throwing a filmy shadow over her darkened mind—"But you will be alone, Jessie!"

Miss Jessie had been feeling this all during the silence, I think; for the tears rolled down her cheeks like rain, at these words, and she could not answer at first. Then she put her hands together tight, and lifted them up, and said—but not to us—

"Though He slay me, yet will I trust in Him."[4]

In a few moments more Miss Brown lay calm and still—never to sorrow or murmur more.

After this second funeral, Miss Jenkyns insisted that Miss Jessie should come to stay with her rather than go back to the desolate house, which, in fact, we learned from Miss Jessie, must now be given up, as she had not wherewithal to maintain it. She had something above twenty pounds a year, besides the interest of the money for which the furniture would sell; but she could not live upon that: and so we talked over her qualifications for earning money.

"I can sew neatly," said she, "and I like nursing. I think, too, I could manage a house, if any one would try me as housekeeper; or I would go into a shop, as saleswoman, if they would have patience with me at first."

Miss Jenkyns declared, in an angry voice, that she should do no such thing; and talked to herself about "some people having no idea of their rank as a captain's daughter," nearly an hour afterwards, when she brought Miss Jessie up a basin of delicately-made arrowroot, and stood over her like a dragoon until the last spoonful was finished; then she disappeared. Miss Jessie began to tell me some more of the plans which had suggested themselves to her, and insensibly fell into talking of the days that were past and gone, and interested me so much I neither knew nor heeded how time passed. We were both startled when Miss Jenkyns reappeared, and caught us crying. I was afraid lest she would be displeased, as she often said that crying hindered digestion, and I knew she wanted Miss Jessie to get strong; but, instead, she looked queer and excited, and fidgeted round us without saying anything. At last she spoke.

"I have been so much startled—no, I've not been at all startled—don't mind me, my dear Miss Jessie—I've been very much surprised—in fact, I've had a caller, whom you knew once, my dear Miss Jessie"—

Miss Jessie went very white, then flushed scarlet, and looked eagerly at Miss Jenkyns.

"A gentleman, my dear, who wants to know if you would see him."

"Is it?—it is not"—stammered out Miss Jessie—and got no farther.

"This is his card," said Miss Jenkyns, giving it to Miss Jessie; and while her head was bent over it, Miss Jenkyns went through a series of winks and odd faces to me, and formed her lips into a long sentence, of which, of course, I could not understand a word.

"May he come up?" asked Miss Jenkyns, at last.

"Oh, yes! certainly!" said Miss Jessie, as much as to say, this is your house, you may show any visitor where you like. She took up some knitting of Miss Matty's and began to be very busy, though I could see how she trembled all over.

Miss Jenkyns rang the bell, and told the servant who answered it to show Major Gordon upstairs; and, presently, in walked a tall, fine, frank-looking man of forty or upwards. He shook hands with Miss Jessie; but he could not see her eyes, she kept them so fixed on the ground. Miss Jenkyns asked me if I would come and help her to tie up the preserves in the store-room; and, though Miss Jessie plucked at my gown, and even looked up at me with begging eye, I durst not refuse to go where Miss Jenkyns asked. Instead of tying up preserves in the store-room, however, we went to talk in the dining-room; and there Miss Jenkyns told me what Major Gordon had told her; how he had served in the same regiment with Captain Brown, and had become acquainted with Miss Jessie, then a sweet-looking, blooming girl of eighteen; how the acquaintance had grown into love on his part, though it had been some years before he had spoken; how, on becoming possessed, through the will of an uncle, of a good estate in Scotland, he had offered and been refused, though with so much agitation and evident distress that he was sure she was not indifferent to him; and how he had discovered that the obstacle was the fell disease which was, even then, too surely threatening her sister. She had mentioned that the surgeons foretold intense suffering; and there was no one but herself to nurse her poor Mary, or cheer and comfort her father during the time of illness. They had had long discussions; and on her refusal to pledge herself to him as his wife when all should be over, he had grown angry, and broken off entirely, and gone abroad, believing that she was a cold-hearted person whom he would do well to forget. He had been travelling in the East, and was on his return home when, at Rome, he saw the account of Captain Brown's death in *Galignani*.[5]

Just then Miss Matty, who had been out all the morning, and had only lately returned to the house, burst in with a face of dismay and outraged propriety.

"Oh, goodness me!" she said. "Deborah, there's a gentleman sitting in the drawing-room with his arm round Miss Jessie's waist!" Miss Matty's eyes looked large with terror.

5. An English newspaper published in Paris and read by tourists and expatriates.

Miss Jenkyns snubbed her down in an instant.

"The most proper place in the world for his arm to be in. Go away, Matilda, and mind your own business." This from her sister, who had hitherto been a model of feminine decorum, was a blow for poor Miss Matty, and with a double shock she left the room.

The last time I ever saw poor Miss Jenkyns was many years after this. Mrs Gordon had kept up a warm and affectionate intercourse with all at Cranford. Miss Jenkyns, Miss Matty, and Miss Pole had all been to visit her, and returned with wonderful accounts of her house, her husband, her dress, and her looks. For, with happiness, something of her early bloom returned; she had been a year or two younger than we had taken her for. Her eyes were always lovely, and, as Mrs Gordon, her dimples were not out of place. At the time to which I have referred, when I last saw Miss Jenkyns, that lady was old and feeble, and had lost something of her strong mind. Little Flora Gordon was staying with the Misses Jenkyns, and when I came in she was reading aloud to Miss Jenkyns, who lay feeble and changed on the sofa. Flora put down the *Rambler* when I came in.

"Ah!" said Miss Jenkyns, "you find me changed, my dear. I can't see as I used to do. If Flora were not here to read to me, I hardly know how I should get through the day. Did you ever read the *Rambler?* It's a wonderful book—wonderful! and the most improving reading for Flora" (which I dare say it would have been, if she could have read half the words without spelling, and could have understood the meaning of a third), "better than that strange old book, with the queer name, poor Captain Brown was killed for reading—that book by Mr Boz, you know—'Old Poz'; when I was a girl—but that's a long time ago—I acted Lucy in 'Old Poz.'"[6] She babbled on long enough for Flora to get a good long spell at the "Christmas Carol,"[7] which Miss Matty had left on the table.

1851, 1853

⊹ ⊰⧓⊱ ⊹

Thomas Hardy
1840–1928

Son of a mason and a maidservant, Thomas Hardy spent most of his life in Dorset, one of the most remote and unpopulated counties in England. In his fiction Dorset became a mythic place called "Wessex," a primitive and powerful imaginative realm central to his art. In the lives of farmers, shepherds, and milkmaids, Hardy found the tragic passion of King Lear, whom he liked to think had once roamed Egdon Heath: "I consider . . . that the domestic emotions have throbbed in Wessex nooks with as much intensity as in the palaces of Europe." Hardy's fiction explores the ironies of fate, the intense suffering of failed love, and the powerlessness of human beings in the face of an indifferent universe. He wrote with sympathy and understanding about the lives of women, and the psychological insight with which he approached sexuality and the unconscious prefigures D. H. Lawrence. His best-known novels include *Far from the Madding Crowd* (1874), *The Return of the Native* (1878), *The Mayor of Casterbridge* (1886), and

---

6. A children's play by Maria Edgeworth (1795); Lucy is the young heroine.

7. Published by Dickens in 1843. The topicality of Dickens's works helps date the events of *Cranford*.

Tess of the d'Urbervilles (1891), but after the hostile reception of *Jude the Obscure* (1896) he renounced novel writing in favor of poetry.

He also produced enough short stories to fill four volumes, beginning with *Wessex Tales* (1888). These stories, which include *The Withered Arm,* were written during a time of agricultural crisis in England—the worst harvest of the century was in 1879—but were set a half century earlier, also a time of crop failures, rick burnings, and rural misery. Hardy was anxious to record a disappearing way of life: "Village tradition—a vast mass of unwritten folk-lore, local chronicle, local topography, and nomenclature—is absolutely sinking, has nearly sunk, into eternal oblivion." His stories are rooted in the local details of Dorset life, but he was less concerned with sociological realism than with the fragility of things, a sense of ancient mystery and the strange workings of destiny. The oral quality of Hardy's narrative voice preserves the mood of a rural community handing down folk belief in supernatural omens, weird dreams, and conjurer's remedies. Hardy himself was grounded in local history; concerning *The Withered Arm,* he said that "its cardinal incidents are true, both the women who figure in the story having been known to me." His father had seen an eighteen-year-old boy hung merely for watching a rick burn: "Nothing my father ever said to me drove the tragedy of Life so deeply into my mind."

For more about Hardy, see his principal listing on page 2295.

The Withered Arm[1]
1. A Lorn Milkmaid

It was an eight-cow dairy, and the troop of milkers, regular and supernumerary,[2] were all at work; for, though the time of year was as yet but early April, the feed lay entirely in water-meadows and the cows were "in full pail."[3] The hour was about six in the evening, and three-fourths of the large, red, rectangular animals having been finished off, there was opportunity for a little conversation.

"He brings home his bride tomorrow, I hear. They've come as far as Anglebury to-day."

The voice seemed to proceed from the carcass of the cow called Cherry, but the speaker was a milking-woman, whose face was buried in the flank of that motionless beast.

"Has anybody seen her?" said another.

There was a negative response from the first. "Though they say she's a rosy-cheeked, tisty-tosty[4] little body enough," she added; and as the milkmaid spoke she turned her face so that she could glance past her cow's tail to the other side of the barton, where a thin faded woman of thirty milked somewhat apart from the rest.

"Years younger than he, they say," continued the second, with also a glance of reflectiveness in the same direction.

"How old do you call him, then?"

"Thirty or so."

"More like forty," broke in an old milkman near, in a long white pinafore or "wropper," and with the brim of his hat tied down, so that he looked like a woman. "'A was born before our Great Weir was builded, and I hadn't man's wages when I laved water there."

---

1. First published in *Blackwood's Edinburgh Magazine* in January 1888.
2. Extra workers.

3. Giving a great deal of milk.
4. Appealingly plump.

The discussion waxed so warm that the purr of the milk-streams became jerky, till a voice from another cow's belly cried with authority, "Now, then, what the Turk do it matter to us about Farmer Lodge's age, or Farmer Lodge's new mis'ess! I shall have to pay him nine pound a-year for the rent of every one of these milchers, whatever his age or hers. Get on with your work, or 'twill be dark before we have done. The evening is pinking in a'ready." This speaker was the dairyman himself, by whom the milkmaids and men were employed.

Nothing more was said publicly about Farmer Lodge's wedding, but the first woman murmured under her cow to her next neighbour, "'Tis hard for she," signifying the thin worn milkmaid aforesaid.

"Oh no," said the second. "He hasn't spoken to Rhoda Brook for years."

When the milking was done they washed their pails and hung them on a many-forked stand made of the peeled limb of an oak-tree, set upright in the earth, and resembling a colossal antlered horn. The majority then dispersed in various directions homeward. The thin woman who had not spoken was joined by a boy of twelve or thereabout, and the twain went away up the field also.

Their course lay apart from that of the others, to a lonely spot high above the water-meads, and not far from the border of Egdon Heath,[5] whose dark countenance was visible in the distance as they drew nigh to their home.

"They've just been saying down in barton that your father brings his young wife home from Anglebury to-morrow," the woman observed. "I shall want to send you for a few things to market, and you'll be pretty sure to meet 'em."

"Yes, mother," said the boy. "Is father married, then?"

"Yes. . . . You can give her a look, and tell me what she's like, if you do see her."

"Yes, mother."

"If she's dark or fair, and if she's tall—as tall as I. And if she seems like a woman who has ever worked for a living, or one that has been always well off, and has never done anything, and shows marks of the lady on her, as I expect she do."

"Yes."

They crept up the hill in the twilight, and entered the cottage. It was thatched, and built of mud-walls, the surface of which had been washed by many rains into channels and depressions that left none of the original flat face visible; while here and there a rafter showed like a bone protruding through the skin.

She was kneeling down in the chimney-corner, before two pieces of turf[6] laid together with the heather inwards, blowing at the red-hot ashes with her breath till the turves flamed. The radiance lit her pale cheek, and made her dark eyes, that had once been handsome, seem handsome anew. "Yes," she resumed, "see if she is dark or fair, and if you can, notice if her hands are white; if not, see if they look as though she had ever done housework, or are milker's hands like mine."

The boy again promised, inattentively this time, his mother not observing that he was cutting a notch with his pocket-knife in the beech-backed chair.

2. The Young Wife

The road from Anglebury to Stickleford is in general level; but there is one place where a sharp ascent breaks its monotony. Farmers homeward-bound from the former market-town, who trot all the rest of the way, walk their horses up this short incline.

---

5. In Hardy's Wessex writings, Egdon Heath is an ancient and mysterious landscape, often associated with primitive and supernatural powers.
6. Peat, burned for fuel.

The next evening, while the sun was yet bright, a handsome new gig, with a lemon-coloured body and red wheels, was spinning westward along the level highway at the heels of a powerful mare. The driver was a yeoman[7] in the prime of life, cleanly shaven like an actor, his face being toned to that bluish vermilion hue which so often graces a thriving farmer's features when returning home after successful dealings in the town. Beside him sat a woman, many years his junior—almost, indeed, a girl. Her face too was fresh in colour, but it was of a totally different quality—soft and evanescent, like the light under a heap of rose-petals.

Few people travelled this way, for it was not a turnpike road; and the long white riband of gravel that stretched before them was empty, save of one small scarce-moving speck, which presently resolved itself into the figure of a boy, who was creeping on at a snail's pace, and continually looking behind him—the heavy bundle he carried being some excuse for, if not the reason of, his dilatoriness. When the bouncing gig-party slowed at the bottom of the incline above mentioned, the pedestrian was only a few yards in front. Supporting the large bundle by putting one hand on his hip, he turned and looked straight at the farmer's wife as though he would read her through and through, pacing along abreast of the horse.

The low sun was full in her face, rendering every feature, shade, and contour distinct, from the curve of her little nostril to the colour of her eyes. The farmer, though he seemed annoyed at the boy's persistent presence, did not order him to get out of the way; and thus the lad preceded them, his hard gaze never leaving her, till they reached the top of the ascent, when the farmer trotted on with relief in his lineaments—having taken no outward notice of the boy whatever.

"How that poor lad stared at me!" said the young wife.

"Yes, dear; I saw that he did."

"He is one of the village, I suppose?"

"One of the neighbourhood. I think he lives with his mother a mile or two off."

"He knows who we are, no doubt?"

"Oh yes. You must expect to be stared at just at first, my pretty Gertrude."

"I do,—though I think the poor boy may have looked at us in the hope we might relieve him of his heavy load, rather than from curiosity."

"Oh no," said her husband, off-handedly. "These country lads will carry a hundredweight once they get it on their backs; besides, his pack had more size than weight in it. Now, then, another mile and I shall be able to show you our house in the distance—if it is not too dark before we get there." The wheels spun round, and particles flew from their periphery as before, till a white house of ample dimensions revealed itself, with farm-buildings and ricks at the back.

Meanwhile the boy had quickened his pace, and turning up a by-lane some mile and half short of the white farmstead, ascended towards the leaner pastures, and so on to the cottage of his mother.

She had reached home after her day's milking at the outlying dairy, and was washing cabbage at the doorway in the declining light. "Hold up the net a moment," she said, without preface, as the boy came up.

He flung down his bundle, held the edge of the cabbage-net, and as she filled its meshes with the dripping leaves she went on, "Well, did you see her?"

"Yes; quite plain."

---

7. A small farmer who works his own land.

"Is she ladylike?"

"Yes; and more. A lady complete."

"Is she young?"

"Well, she's growed up, and her ways are quite a woman's."

"Of course. What colour is her hair and face?"

"Her hair is lightish, and her face like a real live doll's."

"Her eyes, then, are not dark like mine?"

"No—of a bluish turn, and her mouth is very nice and red; and when she smiles, her teeth show white."

"Is she tall?" said the woman sharply.

"I couldn't see. She was sitting down."

"Then do you go to Stickleford church to-morrow morning: she's sure to be there. Go early and notice her walking in, and come home and tell me if she's taller than I."

"Very well, mother. But why don't you go and see for yourself?"

"*I* go to see her! I wouldn't look up at her if she were to pass my window this instant. She was with Mr Lodge, of course. What did he say or do?"

"Just the same as usual."

"Took no notice of you?"

"None."

Next day the mother put a clean shirt on the boy, and started him off for Stickleford church. He reached the ancient little pile when the door was just being opened, and he was the first to enter. Taking his seat by the font, he watched all the parishioners file in. The well-to-do Farmer Lodge came nearly last; and his young wife, who accompanied him, walked up the aisle with the shyness natural to a modest woman who had appeared thus for the first time. As all other eyes were fixed upon her, the youth's stare was not noticed now.

When he reached home his mother said "Well?" before he had entered the room.

"She is not tall. She is rather short," he replied.

"Ah!" said his mother, with satisfaction.

"But she's very pretty—very. In fact, she's lovely." The youthful freshness of the yeoman's wife had evidently made an impression even on the somewhat hard nature of the boy.

"That's all I want to hear," said his mother quickly. "Now, spread the table-cloth. The hare you caught is very tender; but mind that nobody catches you.[8]— You've never told me what sort of hands she had."

"I have never seen 'em. She never took off her gloves."

"What did she wear this morning?"

"A white bonnet and a silver-coloured gownd. It whewed and whistled so loud when it rubbed against the pews that the lady coloured up more than ever for very shame at the noise, and pulled it in to keep it from touching; but when she pushed into her seat, it whewed more than ever. Mr Lodge, he seemed pleased, and his waistcoat stuck out, and his great golden seals hung like a lord's; but she seemed to wish her noisy gownd anywhere but on her."

"Not she! However, that will do now."

---

8. The boy has been poaching, an offense punishable by prison.

These descriptions of the newly married couple were continued from time to time by the boy at his mother's request, after any chance encounter he had had with them. But Rhoda Brook, though she might easily have seen young Mrs Lodge for herself by walking a couple of miles, would never attempt an excursion towards the quarter where the farmhouse lay. Neither did she, at the daily milking in the dairyman's yard on Lodge's outlying second farm, ever speak on the subject of the recent marriage. The dairyman, who rented the cows of Lodge, and knew perfectly the tall milkmaid's history, with manly kindliness always kept the gossip in the cow-barton from annoying Rhoda. But the atmosphere thereabout was full of the subject during the first days of Mrs Lodge's arrival; and from her boy's description and the casual words of the other milkers, Rhoda Brook could raise a mental image of the unconscious Mrs Lodge that was realistic as a photograph.

3. A Vision

One night, two or three weeks after the bridal return, when the boy was gone to bed, Rhoda sat a long time over the turf ashes that she had raked out in front of her to extinguish them. She contemplated so intently the new wife, as presented to her in her mind's eye over the embers, that she forgot the lapse of time. At last, wearied with her day's work, she too retired.

But the figure which had occupied her so much during this and the previous days was not to be banished at night. For the first time Gertrude Lodge visited the supplanted woman in her dreams. Rhoda Brook dreamed—if her assertion that she really saw, before falling asleep, was not to be believed—that the young wife, in the pale silk dress and white bonnet, but with features shockingly distorted, and wrinkled as by age, was sitting upon her chest as she lay. The pressure of Mrs Lodge's person grew heavier; the blue eyes peered cruelly into her face; and then the figure thrust forward its left hand mockingly, so as to make the wedding-ring it wore glitter in Rhoda's eyes. Maddened mentally, and nearly suffocated by pressure, the sleeper struggled; the incubus,[9] still regarding her, withdrew to the foot of the bed, only, however, to come forward by degrees, resume her seat, and flash her left hand as before.

Gasping for breath, Rhoda, in a last desperate effort, swung out her right hand, seized the confronting spectre by its obtrusive left arm, and whirled it backward to the floor, starting up herself as she did so with a low cry.

"Oh, merciful heaven!" she cried, sitting on the edge of the bed in a cold sweat, "that was not a dream—she was here!"

She could feel her antagonist's arm within her grasp even now—the very flesh and bone of it, as it seemed. She looked on the floor whither she had whirled the spectre, but there was nothing to be seen.

Rhoda Brook slept no more that night, and when she went milking at the next dawn they noticed how pale and haggard she looked. The milk that she drew quivered into the pail; her hand had not calmed even yet, and still retained the feel of the arm. She came home to breakfast as wearily as if it had been supper-time.

"What was that noise in your chimmer,[1] mother, last night?" said her son. "You fell off the bed, surely?"

"Did you hear anything fall? At what time?"

---

9. An evil spirit that oppresses sleepers.   1. Chamber.

"Just when the clock struck two."

She would not explain, and when the meal was done went silently about her household work, the boy assisting her, for he hated going afield on the farms, and she indulged his reluctance. Between eleven and twelve the garden-gate clicked, and she lifted her eyes to the window. At the bottom of the garden, within the gate, stood the woman of her vision. Rhoda seemed transfixed.

"Ah, she said she would come!" exclaimed the boy, also observing her.

"Said so—when? How does she know us?"

"I have seen and spoken to her. I talked to her yesterday."

"I told you," said the mother, flushing indignantly, "never to speak to anybody in that house, or go near the place."

"I did not speak to her till she spoke to me. And I did not go near the place. I met her in the road."

"What did you tell her?"

"Nothing. She said, 'Are you the poor boy who had to bring the heavy load from market?' And she looked at my boots, and said they would not keep my feet dry if it came on wet, because they were so broken. I told her I lived with my mother, and we had enough to do to keep ourselves, and that's how it was; and she said then, 'I'll come and bring you some better boots, and see your mother.' She gives away things to other folks in the meads[2] besides us."

Mrs Lodge was by this time close to the door—not in her silk, as Rhoda had seen her in the bed-chamber, but in a morning hat, and gown of common light material, which became her better than silk. On her arm she carried a basket.

The impression remaining from the night's experience was still strong. Brook had almost expected to see the wrinkles, the scorn, and the cruelty on her visitor's face. She would have escaped an interview, had escape been possible. There was, however, no back-door to the cottage, and in an instant the boy had lifted the latch to Mrs Lodge's gentle knock.

"I see I have come to the right house," said she, glancing at the lad, and smiling. "But I was not sure till you opened the door."

The figure and action were those of the phantom; but her voice was so indescribably sweet, her glance so winning, her smile so tender, so unlike that of Rhoda's midnight visitant, that the latter could hardly believe the evidence of her senses. She was truly glad that she had not hidden away in sheer aversion, as she had been inclined to do. In her basket Mrs Lodge brought the pair of boots that she had promised to the boy, and other useful articles.

At these proofs of a kindly feeling towards her and hers, Rhoda's heart reproached her bitterly. This innocent young thing should have her blessing and not her curse. When she left them a light seemed gone from the dwelling. Two days later she came again to know if the boots fitted; and less than a fortnight after that paid Rhoda another call. On this occasion the boy was absent.

"I walk a good deal," said Mrs Lodge, "and your house is the nearest outside our own parish. I hope you are well. You don't look quite well."

Rhoda said she was well enough; and indeed, though the paler of the two, there was more of the strength that endures in her well-defined features and large frame, than in the soft-cheeked young woman before her. The conversation became quite

2. Meadows.

confidential as regarded their powers and weaknesses; and when Mrs Lodge was leaving, Rhoda said, "I hope you will find this air agree with you, ma'am, and not suffer from the damp of the meads."

The younger one replied that there was not much doubt of it, her general health being usually good. "Though, now you remind me," she added, "I have one little ailment which puzzles me. It is nothing serious, but I cannot make it out."

She uncovered her left hand and arm; and their outline confronted Rhoda's gaze as the exact original of the limb she had beheld and seized in her dream. Upon the pink round surface of the arm were faint marks of an unhealthy colour, as if produced by a rough grasp. Rhoda's eyes became riveted on the discolorations; she fancied that she discerned in them the shape of her own four fingers.

"How did it happen?" she said mechanically.

"I cannot tell," replied Mrs Lodge, shaking her head. "One night when I was sound asleep, dreaming I was away in some strange place, a pain suddenly shot into my arm there, and was so keen as to awaken me. I must have struck it in the daytime, I suppose, though I don't remember doing so." She added, laughing, "I tell my dear husband that it looks just as if he had flown into a rage and struck me there. Oh, I daresay it will soon disappear."

"Ha, ha! Yes. . . . On what night did it come?"

Mrs Lodge considered, and said it would be a fortnight ago on the morrow. "When I awoke, I could not remember where I was," she added, "till the clock striking two reminded me."

She had named the night and the hour of Rhoda's spectral encounter, and Brook felt like a guilty thing. The artless disclosure startled her; she could not understand the coincidence; and all the scenery of that ghastly night returned with double vividness to her mind.

"Oh, can it be," she said to herself, when her visitor had departed, "that I exercise a malignant power over people against my own will?" She knew that she had been slyly called a witch since her fall; but never having understood why that particular stigma had been attached to her, it had passed disregarded. Could this be the explanation, and had such things as this ever happened before?

4. A Suggestion

The summer drew on, and Rhoda Brook almost dreaded to meet Mrs Lodge again, notwithstanding that her feeling for the young wife amounted wellnigh to affection. Something in her own individuality seemed to convict Rhoda of crime. Yet a fatality sometimes would direct the steps of the latter to the outskirts of Stickleford whenever she left her house for any other purpose than her daily work; and hence it happened that their next encounter was out of doors. Rhoda could not avoid the subject which had so mystified her, and after the first few words she stammered, "I hope your—arm is well again, ma'am?" She had perceived with consternation that Gertrude Lodge carried her left arm stiffly.

"No; it is not quite well. Indeed it is no better at all; it is rather worse. It pains me dreadfully sometimes."

"Perhaps you had better go to a doctor, ma'am."

She replied that she had already seen a doctor. Her husband had insisted upon her going to one. But the surgeon had not seemed to understand the afflicted limb at all; he had told her to bathe it in hot water, and she had bathed it, but the treatment had done no good.

"Will you let me see it?" said the milkwoman.

Mrs Lodge pushed up her sleeve and disclosed the place, which was a few inches above the wrist. As soon as Rhoda Brook saw it, she could hardly preserve her composure. There was nothing of the nature of a wound, but the arm at that point had a shrivelled look, and the outline of the four fingers appeared more distinct than at the former time. Moreover, they were imprinted in precisely the relative position of her clutch upon the arm in the trance; the first finger towards Gertrude's wrist, and the fourth towards her elbow.

What the impress resembled seemed to have struck Gertrude herself since their last meeting. "It looks almost like finger-marks," she said; adding with a faint laugh, "my husband says it is as if some witch, or the devil himself, had taken hold of me there, and blasted the flesh."

Rhoda shivered. "That's fancy," she said hurriedly. "I wouldn't mind it, if I were you."

"I shouldn't so much mind it," said the younger, with hesitation, "if—if I hadn't a notion that it makes my husband—dislike me—no, love me less. Men think so much of personal appearance."

"Some do—he for one."

"Yes; and he was very proud of mine, at first."

"Keep your arm covered from his sight."

"Ah—he knows the disfigurement is there!" She tried to hide the tears that filled her eyes.

"Well, ma'am, I earnestly hope it will go away soon."

And so the milkwoman's mind was chained anew to the subject by a horrid sort of spell as she returned home. The sense of having been guilty of an act of malignity increased, affect as she might to ridicule her superstition. In her secret heart Rhoda did not altogether object to a slight diminution of her successor's beauty, by whatever means it had come about; but she did not wish to inflict upon her physical pain. For though this pretty young woman had rendered impossible any reparation which Lodge might have made her for his past conduct, everything like resentment at her unconscious usurpation had quite passed away from the elder's mind.

If the sweet and kindly Gertrude Lodge only knew of the scene in the bed-chamber, what would she think? Not to inform her of it seemed treachery in the presence of her friendliness; but tell she could not of her own accord—neither could she devise a remedy.

She mused upon the matter the greater part of the night; and the next day, after the morning milking, set out to obtain another glimpse of Gertrude Lodge if she could, being held to her by a gruesome fascination. By watching the house from a distance the milkmaid was presently able to discern the farmer's wife in a ride she was taking alone—probably to join her husband in some distant field. Mrs Lodge perceived her, and cantered in her direction.

"Good morning, Rhoda!" she said, when she had come up. "I was going to call."

Rhoda noticed that Mrs Lodge held the reins with some difficulty.

"I hope—the bad arm," said Rhoda.

"They tell me there is possibly one way by which I might be able to find out the cause, and so perhaps the cure, of it," replied the other anxiously. "It is by going to some clever man over in Egdon Heath. They did not know if he was still alive—and I cannot remember his name at this moment; but they said that you knew more of his movements than anybody else hereabout, and could tell me if he were still to be consulted. Dear me—what was his name? But you know."

"Not Conjuror Trendle?" said her thin companion, turning pale.

"Trendle—yes. Is he alive?"

"I believe so," said Rhoda, more reluctantly.

"Why do you call him conjuror?"

"Well—they say—they used to say he was a—he had powers other folks have not."

"Oh, how could my people be so superstitious as to recommend a man of that sort! I thought they meant some medical man. I shall think no more of him."

Rhoda looked relieved, and Mrs Lodge rode on. The milkwoman had inwardly seen, from the moment she heard of her having been mentioned as a reference for this man, that there must exist a sarcastic feeling among the work-folk that a sorceress would know the whereabouts of the exorcist. They suspected her, then. A short time ago this would have given no concern to a woman of her common-sense. But she had good reason to be superstitious now; and she had been seized with sudden dread that this Conjuror Trendle might name her as the malignant influence which was blasting the fair person of Gertrude, and so lead her friend to hate her for ever, and to treat her as some fiend in human shape.

But all was not over. Two days after, a shadow intruded into the window-pattern thrown on Rhoda Brook's floor by the afternoon sun. The woman opened the door at once, almost breathlessly.

"Are you alone?" said Gertrude. She seemed to be no less harassed and anxious than Brook herself.

"Yes," said Rhoda.

"The place on my arm seems worse, and troubles me!" the young farmer's wife went on. "It is so mysterious! I do hope it will not be a permanent blemish. I have again been thinking of what they said about Conjuror Trendle. I don't really believe in such men, but I should not mind just visiting him, from curiosity—though on no account must my husband know. Is it far to where he lives?"

"Yes—five miles," said Rhoda, backwardly. "In the heart of Egdon."

"Well, I should have to walk. Could not you go with me to show me the way—say to-morrow afternoon?"

"Oh, not I—that is," the milkwoman murmured, with a start of dismay. Again the dread seized her that something to do with her fierce act in the dream might be revealed, and her character in the eyes of the most useful friend she had ever had be ruined irretrievably.

Mrs Lodge urged, and Rhoda finally assented, though with much misgiving. Sad as the journey would be to her, she could not conscientiously stand in the way of a possible remedy for her patron's strange affliction. It was agreed that, to escape suspicion of their mystic intent, they should meet at the edge of the heath, at the corner of a plantation which was visible from the spot where they now stood.

5. Conjuror Trendle

By the next afternoon, Rhoda would have done anything to escape this inquiry. But she had promised to go. Moreover, there was a horrid fascination at times in becoming instrumental in throwing such possible light on her own character as would reveal her to be something greater in the occult world than she had ever herself suspected.

She started just before the time of day mentioned between them, and half an hour's brisk walking brought her to the south-eastern extension of the Egdon tract of country, where the fir plantation was. A slight figure, cloaked and veiled, was already there. Rhoda recognised, almost with a shudder, that Mrs Lodge bore her left arm in a sling.

They hardly spoke to each other, and immediately set out on their climb into the interior of this solemn country, which stood high above the rich alluvial soil they had left half an hour before. It was a long walk; thick clouds made the atmosphere dark, though it was as yet only early afternoon; and the wind howled dismally over the hills of the heath—not improbably the same heath which had witnessed the agony of the Wessex King Ina, presented to after-ages as Lear. Gertrude Lodge talked most, Rhoda replying with monosyllabic preoccupation. She had a strange dislike to walking on the side of her companion where hung the afflicted arm, moving round to the other when inadvertently near it. Much heather had been brushed by their feet when they descended upon a cart-track, beside which stood the house of the man they sought.

He did not profess his remedial practices openly, or care anything about their continuance, his direct interests being those of a dealer in furze,[3] turf, "sharp sand," and other local products. Indeed, he affected not to believe largely in his own powers, and when warts that had been shown him for cure miraculously disappeared—which it must be owned they infallibly did—he would say lightly, "Oh, I only drink a glass of grog upon 'em—perhaps it's all chance," and immediately turn the subject.

He was at home when they arrived, having in fact seen them descending into his valley. He was a grey-bearded man, with a reddish face, and he looked singularly at Rhoda the first moment he beheld her. Mrs Lodge told him her errand; and then with words of self-disparagement he examined her arm.

"Medicine can't cure it," he said, promptly. "'Tis the work of an enemy."

Rhoda shrank into herself, and drew back.

"An enemy? What enemy?" asked Mrs Lodge.

He shook his head. "That's best known to yourself," he said. "If you like I can show the person to you, though I shall not myself know who it is. I can do no more; and don't wish to do that."

She pressed him; on which he told Rhoda to wait outside where she stood, and took Mrs Lodge into the room. It opened immediately from the door; and, as the latter remained ajar, Rhoda Brook could see the proceedings without taking part in them. He brought a tumbler from the dresser, nearly filled it with water, and fetching an egg, prepared it in some private way; after which he broke it on the edge of the glass, so that the white went in and the yolk remained. As it was getting gloomy, he took the glass and its contents to the window, and told Gertrude to watch them closely. They leant over the table together, and the milkwoman could see the opaline hue of the egg fluid changing form as it sank in the water, but she was not near enough to define the shape that it assumed.

"Do you catch the likeness of any face or figure as you look?" demanded the conjuror of the young woman.

She murmured a reply, in tones so low as to be inaudible to Rhoda, and continued to gaze intently into the glass. Rhoda turned, and walked a few steps away.

When Mrs Lodge came out, and her face was met by the light, it appeared exceedingly pale—as pale as Rhoda's—against the sad dun shades of the upland's garniture. Trendle shut the door behind her, and they at once started homeward together. But Rhoda perceived that her companion had quite changed.

"Did he charge much?" she asked, tentatively.

"Oh no—nothing. He would not take a farthing," said Gertrude.

"And what did you see?" inquired Rhoda.

---

3. Shrub found on the heath and burned as fuel.

"Nothing I—care to speak of." The constraint in her manner was remarkable; her face was so rigid as to wear an oldened aspect, faintly suggestive of the face in Rhoda's bed-chamber.

"Was it you who first proposed coming here?" Mrs Lodge suddenly inquired, after a long pause. "How very odd, if you did."

"No. But I am not sorry we have come, all things considered," she replied. For the first time a sense of triumph possessed her, and she did not altogether deplore that the young thing at her side should learn that their lives had been antagonised by other influences than their own.

The subject was no more alluded to during the long and dreary walk home. But in some way or other a story was whispered about the many-dairied Swenn valley that winter that Mrs Lodge's gradual loss of the use of her left arm was owing to her being "overlooked"[4] by Rhoda Brook. The latter kept her own counsel about the incubus, but her face grew sadder and thinner; and in the spring she and her boy disappeared from the neighbourhood of Stickleford.

6. A Second Attempt

Half-a-dozen years passed away, and Mr and Mrs Lodge's married experience sank into prosiness, and worse. The farmer was usually gloomy and silent: the woman whom he had wooed for her grace and beauty was contorted and disfigured in the left limb; moreover, she had brought him no child, which rendered it likely that he would be the last of a family who had occupied that valley for some two hundred years. He thought of Rhoda Brook and her son; and feared this might be a judgment from heaven upon him.

The once blithe-hearted and enlightened Gertrude was changing into an irritable, superstitious woman, whose whole time was given to experimenting upon her ailment with every quack remedy she came across. She was honestly attached to her husband, and was ever secretly hoping against hope to win back his heart again by regaining some at least of her personal beauty. Hence it arose that her closet was lined with bottles, packets, and ointment-pots of every description—nay, bunches of mystic herbs, charms, and books of necromancy,[5] which in her schoolgirl time she would have ridiculed as folly.

"Damned if you won't poison yourself with these apothecary messes and witch mixtures some time or other," said her husband, when his eye chanced to fall upon the multitudinous array.

She did not reply, but turned her sad soft glance upon him in such heart-swollen reproach that he looked sorry for his words. "I only meant it for your good, you know, Gertrude," he added.

"I'll clear out the whole lot, and destroy them," said she, huskily, "and attempt such remedies no more!"

"You want somebody to cheer you," he observed. "I once thought of adopting a boy; but he is too old now. And he is gone away I don't know where."

She guessed to whom he alluded; for Rhoda Brook's story had in the course of years become known to her; though not a word had ever passed between her hus-

4. Given the evil eye.   5. Sorcery.

band and herself on the subject. Neither had she ever spoken to him of her visit to Conjuror Trendle, and of what was revealed to her, or she thought was revealed to her, by that solitary heath-man.

She was now five-and-twenty; but she seemed older. "Six years of marriage, and only a few months of love," she sometimes whispered to herself. And then she thought of the apparent cause, and said, with a tragic glance at her withering limb, "If I could only again be as I was when he first saw me!"

She obediently destroyed her nostrums and charms; but there remained a hankering wish to try something else—some other sort of cure altogether. She had never revisited Trendle since she had been conducted to the house of the solitary by Rhoda against her will; but it now suddenly occurred to Gertrude that she would, in a last desperate effort at deliverance from this seeming curse, again seek out the man, if he yet lived. He was entitled to a certain credence, for the indistinct form he had raised in the glass had undoubtedly resembled the only woman in the world who—as she now knew, though not then—could have a reason for bearing her ill-will. The visit should be paid.

This time she went alone, though she nearly got lost on the heath, and roamed a considerable distance out of her way. Trendle's house was reached at last, however: he was not indoors, and instead of waiting at the cottage she went to where his bent figure was pointed out to her at work a long way off. Trendle remembered her, and laying down the handful of furze-roots which he was gathering and throwing into a heap, he offered to accompany her in her homeward direction, as the distance was considerable and the days were short. So they walked together, his head bowed nearly to the earth, and his form of a colour with it.

"You can send away warts and other excrescences, I know," she said; "why can't you send away this?" And the arm was uncovered.

"You think too much of my powers!" said Trendle; "and I am old and weak now, too. No, no; it is too much for me to attempt in my own person. What have ye tried?"

She named to him some of the hundred medicaments and counter-spells which she had adopted from time to time. He shook his head.

"Some were good enough," he said, approvingly; "but not many of them for such as this. This is of the nature of a blight, not of the nature of a wound; and if you ever do throw it off, it will be all at once."

"If I only could!"

"There is only one chance of doing it known to me. It has never failed in kindred afflictions,—that I can declare. But it is hard to carry out, and especially for a woman."

"Tell me!" said she.

"You must touch with the limb the neck of a man who's been hanged."

She started a little at the image he had raised.

"Before he's cold—just after he's cut down," continued the conjuror, impassively.

"How can that do good?"

"It will turn the blood and change the constitution. But, as I say, to do it is hard. You must get into jail, and wait for him when he's brought off the gallows. Lots have done it, though perhaps not such pretty women as you. I used to send dozens for skin complaints. But that was in former times. The last I sent was in '13—near twenty years ago."

He had no more to tell her; and, when he had put her into a straight track homeward, turned and left her, refusing all money as at first.

7. A Ride

The communication sank deep into Gertrude's mind. Her nature was rather a timid one; and probably of all remedies that the white wizard could have suggested there was not one which would have filled her with so much aversion as this, not to speak of the immense obstacles in the way of its adoption.

Casterbridge, the county-town, was a dozen or fifteen miles off; and though in those days, when men were executed for horse-stealing, arson, and burglary, an assize[6] seldom passed without a hanging, it was not likely that she could get access to the body of the criminal unaided. And the fear of her husband's anger made her reluctant to breathe a word of Trendle's suggestion to him or to anybody about him.

She did nothing for months, and patiently bore her disfigurement as before. But her woman's nature, craving for renewed love, through the medium of renewed beauty (she was but twenty-five), was ever stimulating her to try what, at any rate, could hardly do her any harm. "What came by a spell will go by a spell surely," she would say. Whenever her imagination pictured the act she shrank in terror from the possibility of it: then the words of the conjuror, "It will turn your blood," were seen to be capable of a scientific no less than a ghastly interpretation; the mastering desire returned, and urged her on again.

There was at this time but one county paper, and that her husband only occasionally borrowed. But old-fashioned days had old-fashioned means, and news was extensively conveyed by word of mouth from market to market or from fair to fair; so that, whenever such an event as an execution was about to take place, few within a radius of twenty miles were ignorant of the coming sight; and, so far as Stickleford was concerned, some enthusiasts had been known to walk all the way to Casterbridge and back in one day, solely to witness the spectacle. The next assizes were in March; and when Gertrude Lodge heard that they had been held, she inquired stealthily at the inn as to the result, as soon as she could find opportunity.

She was, however, too late. The time at which the sentences were to be carried out had arrived, and to make the journey and obtain admission at such short notice required at least her husband's assistance. She dared not tell him, for she had found by delicate experiment that these smouldering village beliefs made him furious if mentioned, partly because he half entertained them himself. It was therefore necessary to wait for another opportunity.

Her determination received a fillip from learning that two epileptic children had attended from this very village of Stickleford many years before with beneficial results, though the experiment had been strongly condemned by the neighbouring clergy. April, May, June passed; and it is no overstatement to say that by the end of the last-named month Gertrude wellnigh longed for the death of a fellow-creature. This time she made earlier inquiries, and was altogether more systematic in her proceedings. Moreover, the season was summer, between the haymaking and the harvest, and in the leisure thus afforded her husband had been holiday-taking away from home.

The assizes were in July, and she went to the inn as before. There was to be one execution—only one, for arson.

Her greatest problem was not how to get to Casterbridge, but what means she should adopt for obtaining admission to the jail. Though access for such purposes had

---

6. Assize courts met twice a year and were presided over by circuit judges.

formerly never been denied, the custom had fallen into desuetude; and in contemplating her possible difficulties, she was again almost driven to fall back upon her husband. But, on sounding him about the assizes, he was so uncommunicative, so more than usually cold, that she did not proceed, and decided that whatever she did she would do alone.

Fortune, obdurate hitherto, showed her unexpected favour. On the Thursday before the Saturday fixed for the execution, Lodge remarked to her that he was going away from home for another day or two on business at a fair, and that he was sorry he could not take her with him.

She exhibited on this occasion so much readiness to stay at home that he looked at her in surprise. Time had been when she would have shown deep disappointment at the loss of such a jaunt. However, he lapsed into his usual taciturnity, and on the day named left Stickleford.

It was now her turn. She at first had thought of driving, but on reflection held that driving would not do, since it would necessitate her keeping to the turnpike-road, and so increase by tenfold the risk of her ghastly errand being found out. She decided to ride, and avoid the beaten track, notwithstanding that in her husband's stables there was no animal just at present which by any stretch of imagination could be considered a lady's mount, in spite of his promise before marriage to always keep a mare for her. He had, however, many horses, fine ones of their kind; and among the rest was a serviceable creature, an equine Amazon, with a back as broad as a sofa, on which Gertrude had occasionally taken an airing when unwell. This horse she chose.

On Friday afternoon one of the men brought it round. She was dressed, and before going down looked at her shrivelled arm. "Ah!" she said to it, "if it had not been for you this terrible ordeal would have been saved me!"

When strapping up the bundle in which she carried a few articles of clothing, she took occasion to say to the servant, "I take these in case I should not get back tonight from the person I am going to visit. Don't be alarmed if I am not in by ten, and close up the house as usual. I shall be at home to-morrow for certain." She meant then to privately tell her husband: the deed accomplished was not like the deed projected. He would almost certainly forgive her.

And then the pretty palpitating Gertrude Lodge went from her husband's homestead in a course directly the opposite of that towards Casterbridge. As soon as she was out of sight she took the first turning to the left, which led into Egdon, and on entering the heath wheeled round, and set out in a course due westerly. A more private way down the county could not be imagined; and as to direction, she had merely to keep her horse's head to a point a little to the right of the sun. She knew that she would light upon a furze-cutter or cottager of some sort from time to time, from whom she might correct her course.

Though the date was comparatively recent, Egdon was much less fragmentary in character than now. The attempts—successful and otherwise—at cultivation on the lower slopes, which intrude and break up the original heath into small detached heaths, had not been carried far: Enclosure Acts[7] had not taken effect, and the banks and fences which now exclude the cattle of those villagers who formerly enjoyed

7. Traditionally villagers could graze their animals on common lands, but the Enclosure Acts fenced off these lands, causing hardship in rural areas.

rights of commonage thereon, and the carts of those who had turbary privileges[8] which kept them in firing all the year round, were not erected. Gertrude therefore rode along with no other obstacles than the prickly furze-bushes, the mats of heather, the white water-courses, and the natural steeps and declivities of the ground.

Her horse was sure, if heavy-footed and slow, and though a draught animal, was easy-paced; had it been otherwise, she was not a woman who could have ventured to ride over such a bit of country with a half-dead arm. It was therefore nearly eight o'clock when she drew rein to breathe the mare on the last outlying high point of heath-land towards Casterbridge, previous to leaving Egdon for the cultivated valleys.

She halted before a pond, flanked by the ends of two hedges; a railing ran through the centre of the pond, dividing it in half. Over the railing she saw the low green country; over the green trees the roofs of the town; over the roofs a white flat façade, denoting the entrance to the county jail. On the roof of this front specks were moving about; they seemed to be workmen erecting something. Her flesh crept. She descended slowly, and was soon amid corn-fields and pastures. In another half-hour, when it was almost dusk, Gertrude reached the White Hart, the first inn of the town on that side.

Little surprise was excited by her arrival: farmers' wives rode on horseback then more than they do now; though for that matter, Mrs Lodge was not imagined to be a wife at all; the innkeeper supposed her some harum-scarum young woman who had come to attend "hang-fair"[9] next day. Neither her husband nor herself ever dealt in Casterbridge market, so that she was unknown. While dismounting she beheld a crowd of boys standing at the door of a harness-maker's shop just above the inn, looking inside it with deep interest.

"What is going on there?" she asked of the ostler.

"Making the rope for to-morrow."

She throbbed responsively, and contracted her arm.

"'Tis sold by the inch afterwards," the man continued. "I could get ye a bit, miss, for nothing, if you'd like?"

She hastily repudiated any such wish, all the more from a curious creeping feeling that the condemned wretch's destiny was becoming interwoven with her own; and having engaged a room for the night, sat down to think.

Up to this time she had formed but the vaguest notions about her means of obtaining access to the prison. The words of the cunning-man returned to her mind. He had implied that she should use her beauty, impaired though it was, as a pass-key. In her inexperience she knew little about jail functionaries; she had heard of a high sheriff and an under-sheriff, but dimly only. She knew, however, that there must be a hangman, and to the hangman she determined to apply.

8. A Water-Side Hermit

At this date, and for several years after, there was a hangman to almost every jail. Gertrude found, on inquiry, that the Casterbridge official dwelt in a lonely cottage by a deep slow river flowing under the cliff on which the prison buildings were situate—

---

8. The right to cut turf for fuel on common land.   9. Crowds often came from far away to watch public hangings.

the stream being the self-same one, though she did not know it, which watered the Stickleford meads lower down in its course.

Having changed her dress, and before she had eaten or drunk—for she could not take her ease till she had ascertained some particulars—Gertrude pursued her way by a path along the water-side to the cottage indicated. Passing thus the outskirts of the jail, she discerned on the level roof over the gateway three rectangular lines against the sky, where the specks had been moving in her distant view; she recognised what the erection was, and passed quickly on. Another hundred yards brought her to the executioner's house, which a boy pointed out. It stood close to the same stream, and was hard by a weir, the waters of which emitted a steady roar.

While she stood hesitating the door opened, and an old man came forth shading a candle with one hand. Locking the door on the outside, he turned to a flight of wooden steps fixed against the end of the cottage, and began to ascend them, this being evidently the staircase to his bedroom. Gertrude hastened forward, but by the time she reached the foot of the ladder he was at the top. She called to him loudly enough to be heard above the roar of the weir; he looked down and said, "What d'ye want here?"

"To speak to you a minute."

The candle-light, such as it was, fell upon her imploring, pale, upturned face, and Davies (as the hangman was called) backed down the ladder. "I was just going to bed," he said; "'Early to bed and early to rise,' but I don't mind stopping a minute for such a one as you. Come into house." He reopened the door, and preceded her to the room within.

The implements of his daily work, which was that of a jobbing gardener, stood in a corner, and seeing probably that she looked rural, he said, "If you want me to undertake country work I can't come, for I never leave Casterbridge for gentle nor simple—not I. Though sometimes I make others leave," he added slyly.

"Yes, yes! That's it! Tomorrow!"

"Ah! I thought so. Well, what's the matter about that? 'Tis no use to come here about the knot—folks do come continually, but I tell 'em one knot is as merciful as another if ye keep it under the ear. Is the unfortunate man a relation; or, I should say, perhaps" (looking at her dress) "a person who's been in your employ?"

"No. What time is the execution?"

"The same as usual—twelve o'clock, or as soon after as the London mail-coach gets in. We always wait for that, in case of a reprieve."

"Oh—a reprieve—I hope not!" she said involuntarily.

"Well,—he, he!—as a matter of business, so do I! But still, if ever a young fellow deserved to be let off, this one does; only just turned eighteen, and only present by chance when the rick[1] was fired. Howsomever, there's not much risk of it, as they are obliged to make an example of him, there having been so much destruction of property that way lately."

"I mean," she explained, "that I want to touch him for a charm, a cure of an affliction, by the advice of a man who has proved the virtue of the remedy."

"Oh yes, miss! Now I understand. I've had such people come in past years. But it didn't strike me that you looked of a sort to require blood-turning. What's the complaint? The wrong kind for this, I'll be bound."

---

1. Thatched stack of hay; rick burning was a form of agricultural protest.

"My arm." She reluctantly showed the withered skin.

"Ah!—'tis all a-scram!" said the hangman, examining it.

"Yes," said she.

"Well," he continued with interest, "that *is* the class o' subject, I'm bound to admit. I like the look of the place; it is truly as suitable for the cure as any I ever saw. 'Twas a knowing man that sent 'ee, whoever he was."

"You can contrive for me all that's necessary?" she said, breathlessly.

"You should really have gone to the governor of the jail, and your doctor with 'ee, and given your name and address—that's how it used to be done, if I recollect. Still, perhaps, I can manage it for a trifling fee."

"Oh, thank you! I would rather do it this way, as I should like it kept private."

"Lover not to know, eh?"

"No—husband."

"Aha! Very well. I'll get 'ee a touch of the corpse."

"Where is it now?" she said, shuddering.

"It?—*he*, you mean; he's living yet. Just inside that little small winder up there in the glum." He signified the jail on the cliff above.

She thought of her husband and her friends. "Yes, of course," she said; "and how am I to proceed?"

He took her to the door. "Now, do you be waiting at the little wicket in the wall, that you'll find up there in the lane, not later than one o'clock. I will open it from the inside, as I shan't come home to dinner till he's took down. Good night. Be punctual; and if you don't want anybody to know 'ee, wear a veil. Ah—once I had such a daughter as you!"

She went away, and climbed the path above, to assure herself that she would be able to find the wicket next day. Its outline was soon visible to her—a narrow opening in the outer wall of the prison-yard. The steep was so great that, having reached the wicket, she stopped a moment to breathe; and looking back upon the water-side cot, saw the hangman again ascending his outdoor staircase. He entered the loft or chamber to which it led, and in a few minutes extinguished his light.

The town clock struck ten, and she returned to the White Hart as she had come.

9. A Rencounter

It was one o'clock on Saturday. Gertrude Lodge, having been admitted to the jail as above described, was sitting in a waiting-room within the second gate, which stood under a classic archway of ashlar,[2] then comparatively modern, and bearing the inscription, "COVNTY GAOL: 1793." This had been the façade she saw from the heath the day before. Near at hand was a passage to the roof on which the gallows stood.

The town was thronged, and the market suspended; but Gertrude had seen scarcely a soul. Having kept her room till the hour of the appointment, she had proceeded to the spot by a way which avoided the open space below the cliff where the spectators had gathered; but she could, even now, hear the multitudinous babble of their voices, out of which rose at intervals the hoarse croak of a single voice, uttering the words, "Last dying speech and confession!" There had been no reprieve, and the execution was over; but the crowd still waited to see the body taken down.

---

2. Square-hewn stone.

Soon the persistent girl heard a trampling overhead, then a hand beckoned to her, and, following directions, she went out and crossed the inner paved court beyond the gatehouse, her knees trembling so that she could scarcely walk. One of her arms was out of its sleeve, and only covered by her shawl.

On the spot to which she had now arrived were two trestles, and before she could think of their purpose she heard heavy feet descending stairs somewhere at her back. Turn her head she would not, or could not, and, rigid in this position, she was conscious of a rough coffin passing her shoulder, borne by four men. It was open, and in it lay the body of a young man, wearing the smockfrock of a rustic, and fustian breeches. It had been thrown into the coffin so hastily that the skirt of the smock-frock was hanging over. The burden was temporarily deposited on the trestles.

By this time the young woman's state was such that a grey mist seemed to float before her eyes, on account of which, and the veil she wore, she could scarcely discern anything: it was as though she had half-fainted and could not finish.

"Now," said a voice close at hand, and she was just conscious that it had been addressed to her.

By a last strenuous effort she advanced, at the same time hearing persons approaching behind her. She bared her poor curst arm; and Davies, taking her hand, held it so that the arm lay across the dead man's neck, upon a line the colour of an unripe blackberry, which surrounded it.

Gertrude shrieked: "the turn o' the blood," predicted by the conjuror, had taken place. But at that moment a second shriek rent the air of the enclosure: it was not Gertrude's, and its effect upon her was to make her start round.

Immediately behind her stood Rhoda Brook, her face drawn, and her eyes red with weeping. Behind Rhoda stood her own husband; his countenance lined, his eyes dim, but without a tear.

"D—n you! what are you doing here?" he said, hoarsely.

"Hussy—to come between us and our child now!" cried Rhoda. "This is the meaning of what Satan showed me in the vision! You are like her at last!" And clutching the bare arm of the younger woman, she pulled her unresistingly back against the wall. Immediately Brook had loosened her hold the fragile young Gertrude slid down against the feet of her husband. When he lifted her up she was unconscious.

The mere sight of the twain had been enough to suggest to her that the dead young man was Rhoda's son. At that time the relatives of an executed convict had the privilege of claiming the body for burial, if they chose to do so; and it was for this purpose that Lodge was awaiting the inquest with Rhoda. He had been summoned by her as soon as the young man was taken in the crime, and at different times since; and he had attended in court during the trial. This was the "holiday" he had been indulging in of late. The two wretched parents had wished to avoid exposure; and hence had come themselves for the body, a waggon and sheet for its conveyance and covering being in waiting outside.

Gertrude's case was so serious that it was deemed advisable to call to her the surgeon who was at hand. She was taken out of the jail into the town; but she never reached home alive. Her delicate vitality, sapped perhaps by the paralysed arm, collapsed under the double shock that followed the severe strain, physical and mental, to which she had subjected herself during the previous twenty-four hours. Her blood had been "turned" indeed—too far. Her death took place in the town three days after.

Her husband was never seen in Casterbridge again; once only in the old market-place at Anglebury, which he had so much frequented, and very seldom in public anywhere. Burdened at first with moodiness and remorse, he eventually changed for the better, and appeared as a chastened and serious-minded man. Soon after attending the funeral of his poor young wife, he took steps towards giving up the farms in Stickleford and the adjoining parish, and, having sold every head of his stock, he went away to Port-Bredy, at the other end of the county, living there in solitary lodgings till his death two years later of a painless decline. It was then found that he had bequeathed the whole of his not inconsiderable property to a reformatory for boys, subject to the payment of a small annuity to Rhoda Brook, if she could be found to claim it.

For some time she could not be found; but eventually she reappeared in her old parish,—absolutely refusing, however, to have anything to do with the provision made for her. Her monotonous milking at the dairy was resumed, and followed for many long years, till her form became bent, and her once abundant dark hair white and worn away at the forehead—perhaps by long pressure against the cows. Here, sometimes, those who knew her experiences would stand and observe her, and wonder what sombre thoughts were beating inside that impassive, wrinkled brow, to the rhythm of the alternating milk-streams.

1888

━━┥ ☰◈☰ ┝━━

Sir Arthur Conan Doyle
1859–1930

Sherlock Holmes may not have been the first detective in English fiction, but he quickly became *the* detective, a near-mythic character whose cloak and deerstalker cap, pipe and magnifying glass have defined our image of the "private eye" for over a century. Edgar Allan Poe, Charles Dickens, and Wilkie Collins had preceded Doyle in creating detectives of their own, but Doyle's genius was to construct a rational aesthete: Holmes's languid manner and bohemian tastes suggest *fin de siècle* decadence, but his suave imperturbability stems from his extraordinary powers of reasoning and observation. A quintessentially urban figure, Sherlock Holmes penetrates the foggy chaos of London with his mastery of disguise and his uncanny ability to guess occupations through telltale signs. In an urban world of anonymous strangers, Holmes can "place" people instantly, deciphering the clues to identity that elude and perplex the ordinary observer. Like his plodding sidekick Watson, readers trail along in the wake of Holmes's deft ratiocinations, awed and reassured by his effortless omniscience. His successful detections keep at bay threats to middle-class values and social harmony; he offers a comforting promise of legibility, order, and justice.

Holmes's adventures appeared monthly in *The Strand Magazine*, and they were the making of Arthur Conan Doyle, a doctor-turned-writer who capitalized on the Victorian fascination with crime. So wildly popular was his brilliant investigator that when Doyle grew bored and decided to slay his hero, the public wore mourning-bands, and Doyle was forced to revive him. Indeed, Sherlock Holmes has always seemed oddly more real than his creator: T. S. Eliot wrote that when we talk of Holmes, "we invariably fall into the fancy of his existence." To this day, thousands of letters are addressed to him at 221B Baker Street.

A Scandal in Bohemia[1]

To Sherlock Holmes she is always *the* woman. I have seldom heard him mention her under any other name. In his eyes she eclipses and predominates the whole of her sex. It was not that he felt any emotion akin to love for Irene Adler. All emotions, and that one particularly, were abhorrent to his cold, precise, but admirably balanced mind. He was, I take it, the most perfect reasoning and observing machine that the world has seen; but, as a lover, he would have placed himself in a false position. He never spoke of the softer passions, save with a gibe and a sneer. They were admirable things for the observer—excellent for drawing the veil from men's motives and actions. But for the trained reasoner to admit such intrusions into his own delicate and finely adjusted temperament was to introduce a distracting factor which might throw a doubt upon all his mental results. Grit in a sensitive instrument, or a crack in one of his own high-power lenses, would not be more disturbing than a strong emotion in a nature such as his. And yet there was but one woman to him, and that woman was the late Irene Adler, of dubious and questionable memory.

I had seen little of Holmes lately. My marriage had drifted us away from each other. My own complete happiness, and the home-centred interests which rise up around the man who first finds himself master of his own establishment, were sufficient to absorb all my attention; while Holmes, who loathed every form of society with his whole Bohemian soul,[2] remained in our lodgings in Baker-street, buried among his old books, and alternating from week to week between cocaine and ambition, the drowsiness of the drug, and the fierce energy of his own keen nature. He was still, as ever, deeply attracted by the study of crime, and occupied his immense faculties and extraordinary powers of observation in following out those clues, and clearing up those mysteries, which had been abandoned as hopeless by the official police. From time to time I heard some vague account of his doings: of his summons to Odessa in the case of the Trepoff murder, of his clearing up of the singular tragedy of the Atkinson brothers at Trincomalee, and finally of the mission which he had accomplished so delicately and successfully for the reigning family of Holland. Beyond these signs of his activity, however, which I merely shared with all the readers of the daily press, I knew little of my former friend and companion.

One night—it was on the 20th of March, 1888—I was returning from a journey to a patient (for I had now returned to civil practice),[3] when my way led me through Baker-street. As I passed the well-remembered door, which must always be associated in my mind with my wooing, and with the dark incidents of the Study in Scarlet,[4] I was seized with a keen desire to see Holmes again, and to know how he was employing his extraordinary powers. His rooms were brilliantly lit, and, even as I looked up, I saw his tall spare figure pass twice in a dark silhouette against the blind. He was pacing the room swiftly, eagerly, with his head sunk upon his chest, and his hands clasped behind him. To me, who knew his every mood and habit, his attitude and manner told their own story. He was at work again. He had arisen out of his drug-created dreams, and was hot upon the scent of some new problem. I rang the bell, and was shown up to the chamber which had formerly been in part my own.

1. First published in *The Strand Magazine* in July 1891.
2. Like the artists in Henri Murger's *Scènes de la vie de Bohème* (1848), Holmes's tastes are aesthetic and eccentric. His bohemianism contrasts with the conventional soul of the King of Bohemia later in the story.

3. Watson, who had been invalided out of the Army medical corps, had resumed private practice upon his marriage.
4. Doyle's first Sherlock Holmes novel (1887).

His manner was not effusive. It seldom was; but he was glad, I think, to see me. With hardly a word spoken, but with a kindly eye, he waved me to an armchair, threw across his case of cigars, and indicated a spirit case and a gasogene in the corner.[5] Then he stood before the fire, and looked me over in his singular introspective fashion.

"Wedlock suits you," he remarked. "I think, Watson, that you have put on seven and a half pounds since I saw you."

"Seven," I answered.

"Indeed, I should have thought a little more. Just a trifle more, I fancy, Watson. And in practice again, I observe. You did not tell me that you intended to go into harness."

"Then, how do you know?"

"I see it, I deduce it. How do I know that you have been getting yourself very wet lately, and that you have a most clumsy and careless servant girl?"

"My dear Holmes," said I, "this is too much. You would certainly have been burned, had you lived a few centuries ago.[6] It is true that I had a country walk on Thursday and came home in a dreadful mess; but, as I have changed my clothes, I can't imagine how you deduce it. As to Mary Jane, she is incorrigible, and my wife has given her notice; but there again I fail to see how you work it out."

He chuckled to himself and rubbed his long nervous hands together.

"It is simplicity itself," said he; "my eyes tell me that on the inside of your left shoe, just where the fire-light strikes it, the leather is scored by six almost parallel cuts. Obviously they have been caused by someone who has very carelessly scraped round the edges of the sole in order to remove crusted mud from it. Hence, you see, my double deduction that you had been out in vile weather, and that you had a particularly malignant boot-slitting specimen of the London slavey.[7] As to your practice, if a gentleman walks into my rooms smelling of iodoform, with a black mark of nitrate of silver upon his right fore-finger, and a bulge on the side of his top-hat to show where he has secreted his stethoscope, I must be dull indeed, if I do not pronounce him to be an active member of the medical profession."

I could not help laughing at the ease with which he explained his process of deduction. "When I hear you give your reasons," I remarked, "the thing always appears to me to be so ridiculously simple that I could easily do it myself, though at each successive instance of your reasoning I am baffled, until you explain your process. And yet I believe that my eyes are as good as yours."

"Quite so," he answered, lighting a cigarette, and throwing himself down into an armchair. "You see, but you do not observe. The distinction is clear. For example, you have frequently seen the steps which lead up from the hall to this room."

"Frequently."

"How often?"

"Well, some hundreds of times."

"Then how many are there?"

"How many! I don't know."

"Quite so! You have not observed. And yet you have seen. That is just my point. Now, I know that there are seventeen steps, because I have both seen and observed.

5. I.e., he invited Watson to make himself a drink (a gasogene makes carbonated water).
6. I.e., his uncanny powers would have led to his being burned at the stake as a warlock.
7. Maidservant.

By the way, since you are interested in these little problems, and since you are good enough to chronicle one or two of my trifling experiences, you may be interested in this." He threw over a sheet of thick pink-tinted notepaper which had been lying open upon the table. "It came by the last post," said he. "Read it aloud."

The note was undated, and without either signature or address.

"There will call upon you to-night, at a quarter to eight o'clock," it said, "a gentleman who desires to consult you upon a matter of the very deepest moment. Your recent services to one of the Royal Houses of Europe have shown that you are one who may safely be trusted with matters which are of an importance which can hardly be exaggerated. This account of you we have from all quarters received. Be in your chamber then at that hour, and do not take it amiss if your visitor wear a mask."

"This is indeed a mystery," I remarked. "What do you imagine that it means?"

"I have no data yet. It is a capital mistake to theorise before one has data. Insensibly one begins to twist facts to suit theories, instead of theories to suit facts. But the note itself. What do you deduce from it?"

I carefully examined the writing, and the paper upon which it was written.

"The man who wrote it was presumably well to do," I remarked, endeavouring to imitate my companion's processes. "Such paper could not be bought under half a crown a packet. It is peculiarly strong and stiff."

"Peculiar—that is the very word," said Holmes. "It is not an English paper at all. Hold it up to the light."

I did so, and saw a large E with a small g, a P, and a large G with a small t woven into the texture of the paper.

"What do you make of that?" asked Holmes.

"The name of the maker, no doubt; or his monogram, rather."

"Not at all. The G with the small t stands for 'Gesellschaft,' which is the German for 'Company.' It is a customary contraction like our 'Co.' P, of course, stands for 'Papier.' Now for the Eg. Let us glance at our Continental Gazetteer." He took down a heavy brown volume from his shelves. "Eglow, Eglonitz—here we are, Egria. It is in a German-speaking country—in Bohemia,[8] not far from Carlsbad. 'Remarkable as being the scene of the death of Wallenstein, and for its numerous glass factories and paper mills.' Ha, ha, my boy, what do you make of that?" His eyes sparkled, and he sent up a great blue triumphant cloud from his cigarette.

"The paper was made in Bohemia," I said.

"Precisely. And the man who wrote the note is a German. Do you note the peculiar construction of the sentence—'This account of you we have from all quarters received.' A Frenchman or Russian could not have written that. It is the German who is so uncourteous to his verbs. It only remains, therefore, to discover what is wanted by this German who writes upon Bohemian paper, and prefers wearing a mask to showing his face. And here he comes, if I am not mistaken, to resolve all our doubts."

As he spoke there was the sharp sound of horses' hoofs and grating wheels against the curb, followed by a sharp pull at the bell. Holmes whistled.

"A pair, by the sound," said he. "Yes," he continued, glancing out of the window. "A nice little brougham and a pair of beauties.[9] A hundred and fifty guineas apiece. There's money in this case, Watson, if there is nothing else."

8. Country in Eastern Central Europe, then part of the Austrian Empire, now part of the Czech Republic. Prague was the capital.

9. A closed four-wheeled carriage drawn by two horses.

"I think that I had better go, Holmes."

"Not a bit, Doctor. Stay where you are. I am lost without my Boswell.[1] And this promises to be interesting. It would be a pity to miss it."

"But your client—"

"Never mind him. I may want your help, and so may he. Here he comes. Sit down in that armchair, Doctor, and give us your best attention."

A slow and heavy step, which had been heard upon the stairs and in the passage, paused immediately outside the door. Then there was a loud and authoritative tap.

"Come in!" said Holmes.

A man entered who could hardly have been less than six feet six inches in height, with the chest and limbs of a Hercules. His dress was rich with a richness which would, in England, be looked upon as akin to bad taste. Heavy bands of Astrakhan[2] were slashed across the sleeves and fronts of his double-breasted coat, while the deep blue cloak which was thrown over his shoulders was lined with flame-coloured silk, and secured at the neck with a brooch which consisted of a single flaming beryl. Boots which extended half way up his calves, and which were trimmed at the tops with rich brown fur, completed the impression of barbaric opulence which was suggested by his whole appearance. He carried a broad-brimmed hat in his hand, while he wore across the upper part of his face, extending down past the cheek-bones, a black vizard mask,[3] which he had apparently adjusted that very moment, for his hand was still raised to it as he entered. From the lower part of the face he appeared to be a man of strong character, with a thick, hanging lip, and a long straight chin, suggestive of resolution pushed to the length of obstinacy.

"You had my note?" he asked, with a deep harsh voice and a strongly marked German accent. "I told you that I would call." He looked from one to the other of us, as if uncertain which to address.

"Pray take a seat," said Holmes. "This is my friend and colleague, Dr Watson, who is occasionally good enough to help me in my cases. Whom have I the honour to address?"

"You may address me as the Count Von Kramm, a Bohemian nobleman. I understand that this gentleman, your friend, is a man of honour and discretion, whom I may trust with a matter of the most extreme importance. If not, I should much prefer to communicate with you alone."

I rose to go, but Holmes caught me by the wrist and pushed me back into my chair. "It is both, or none," said he. "You may say before this gentleman anything which you may say to me."

The Count shrugged his broad shoulders. "Then I must begin," said he, "by binding you both to absolute secrecy for two years, at the end of that time the matter will be of no importance. At present it is not too much to say that it is of such weight that it may have an influence upon European history."

"I promise," said Holmes.

"And I."

"You will excuse this mask," continued our strange visitor. "The august person who employs me wishes his agent to be unknown to you, and I may confess at once that the title by which I have just called myself is not exactly my own."

---

1. James Boswell (1740–1795), biographer of Samuel Johnson.
2. A luxurious wool, made from lambs that are killed in their mother's womb.
3. A mask that conceals the eyes.

"I was aware of it," said Holmes dryly.

"The circumstances are of great delicacy, and every precaution has to be taken to quench what might grow to be an immense scandal and seriously compromise one of the reigning families of Europe. To speak plainly, the matter implicates the great House of Ormstein, hereditary kings of Bohemia."

"I was also aware of that," murmured Holmes, settling himself down in his armchair, and closing his eyes.

Our visitor glanced with some apparent surprise at the languid, lounging figure of the man who had been no doubt depicted to him as the most incisive reasoner, and most energetic agent in Europe. Holmes slowly reopened his eyes, and looked impatiently at his gigantic client.

"If your Majesty would condescend to state your case," he remarked, "I should be better able to advise you."

The man sprang from his chair, and paced up and down the room in uncontrollable agitation. Then, with a gesture of desperation, he tore the mask from his face and hurled it upon the ground. "You are right," he cried, "I am the King. Why should I attempt to conceal it?"

"Why, indeed?" murmured Holmes. "Your Majesty had not spoken before I was aware that I was addressing Wilhelm Gottsreich Sigismond von Ormstein, Grand Duke of Cassel-Felstein, and hereditary King of Bohemia."

"But you can understand," said our strange visitor, sitting down once more and passing his hand over his high, white forehead, "you can understand that I am not accustomed to doing such business in my own person. Yet the matter was so delicate that I could not confide it to an agent without putting myself in his power. I have come *incognito* from Prague for the purpose of consulting you."

"Then, pray consult," said Holmes, shutting his eyes once more.

"The facts are briefly these: Some five years ago, during a lengthy visit to Warsaw, I made the acquaintance of the well-known adventuress Irene Adler. The name is no doubt familiar to you."

"Kindly look her up in my index, Doctor," murmured Holmes, without opening his eyes. For many years he had adopted a system of docketing all paragraphs concerning men and things, so that it was difficult to name a subject or a person on which he could not at once furnish information. In this case I found her biography sandwiched in between that of a Hebrew Rabbi and that of a staff-commander who had written a monograph upon the deep sea fishes.

"Let me see," said Holmes. "Hum! Born in New Jersey in the year 1858. Contralto—hum! La Scala,[4] hum! Prima donna Imperial Opera of Warsaw—Yes! Retired from operatic stage—ha! Living in London—quite so! Your Majesty, as I understand, became entangled with this young person, wrote her some compromising letters, and is now desirous of getting those letters back."

"Precisely so. But how—"

"Was there a secret marriage?"

"None."

"No legal papers or certificates?"

"None."

"Then I fail to follow your Majesty. If this young person should produce her letters for blackmailing or other purposes, how is she to prove their authenticity?"

4. A famous opera house in Milan.

"There is the writing."

"Pooh, pooh! Forgery."

"My private notepaper."

"Stolen."

"My own seal."

"Imitated."

"My photograph."

"Bought."

"We were both in the photograph."

"Oh dear! That is very bad! Your Majesty has indeed committed an indiscretion."

"I was mad—insane."

"You have compromised yourself seriously."

"I was only Crown Prince then. I was young. I am but thirty now."

"It must be recovered."

"We have tried and failed."

"Your Majesty must pay. It must be bought."

"She will not sell."

"Stolen, then."

"Five attempts have been made. Twice burglars in my pay ransacked her house. Once we diverted her luggage when she travelled. Twice she has been waylaid. There has been no result."

"No sign of it?"

"Absolutely none."

Holmes laughed. "It is quite a pretty little problem," said he.

"But a very serious one to me," returned the King, reproachfully.

"Very, indeed. And what does she propose to do with the photograph?"

"To ruin me."

"But how?"

"I am about to be married."

"So I have heard."

"To Clotilde Lothman von Saxe-Meningen, second daughter of the King of Scandinavia. You may know the strict principles of her family. She is herself the very soul of delicacy. A shadow of a doubt as to my conduct would bring the matter to an end."

"And Irene Adler?"

"Threatens to send them the photograph. And she will do it. I know that she will do it. You do not know her, but she has a soul of steel. She has the face of the most beautiful of women, and the mind of the most resolute of men. Rather than I should marry another woman, there are no lengths to which she would not go—none."

"You are sure that she has not sent it yet?"

"I am sure."

"And why?"

"Because she has said that she would send it on the day when the betrothal was publicly proclaimed. That will be next Monday."

"Oh, then, we have three days yet," said Holmes, with a yawn. "That is very fortunate, as I have one or two matters of importance to look into just at present. Your Majesty will, of course, stay in London for the present?"

"Certainly. You will find me at the Langham, under the name of the Count Von Kramm."

"Then I shall drop you a line to let you know how we progress."

"Pray do so. I shall be all anxiety."

"Then, as to money?"

"You have *carte blanche*."[5]

"Absolutely?"

"I tell you that I would give one of the provinces of my kingdom to have that photograph."

"And for present expenses?"

The king took a heavy chamois leather bag from under his cloak, and laid it on the table.

"There are three hundred pounds in gold, and seven hundred in notes," he said.

Holmes scribbled a receipt upon a sheet of his note-book, and handed it to him.

"And mademoiselle's address?" he asked.

"Is Briony Lodge, Serpentine-avenue, St. John's Wood."[6]

Holmes took a note of it. "One other question," said he. "Was the photograph a cabinet?"[7]

"It was."

"Then, good night, your Majesty, and I trust that we shall soon have some good news for you. And good night, Watson," he added, as the wheels of the Royal brougham rolled down the street. "If you will be good enough to call tomorrow afternoon, at three o'clock, I should like to chat this little matter over with you."

2

At three o'clock precisely I was at Baker-street, but Holmes had not yet returned. The landlady informed me that he had left the house shortly after eight o'clock in the morning. I sat down beside the fire, however, with the intention of awaiting him, however long he might be. I was already deeply interested in his inquiry, for, though it was surrounded by none of the grim and strange features which were associated with the two crimes which I have already recorded,[8] still, the nature of the case and the exalted station of his client gave it a character of its own. Indeed, apart from the nature of the investigation which my friend had on hand, there was something in his masterly grasp of a situation, and his keen, incisive reasoning, which made it a pleasure to me to study his system of work, and to follow the quick, subtle methods by which he disentangled the most inextricable mysteries. So accustomed was I to his invariable success that the very possibility of his failing had ceased to enter into my head.

It was close upon four before the door opened, and a drunken-looking groom, ill-kempt and side-whiskered, with an inflamed face and disreputable clothes, walked into the room. Accustomed as I was to my friend's amazing powers in the use of disguises, I had to look three times before I was certain that it was indeed he. With a nod he vanished into the bedroom, whence he emerged in five minutes tweed-suited and respectable, as of old. Putting his hands into his pockets, he stretched out his legs in front of the fire, and laughed heartily for some minutes.

"Well, really!" he cried, and then he choked; and laughed again until he was obliged to lie back, limp and helpless, in the chair.

"What is it?"

"It's quite too funny. I am sure you could never guess how I employed my morning, or what I ended by doing."

5. I.e., complete freedom of action and unlimited funds.
6. A London area favored by authors, artists, and well-known courtesans.
7. A cabinet photo was 5$\frac{1}{2}$ by 4 inches.
8. In *A Study in Scarlet* (1887) and *The Sign of the Four* (1890).

"I can't imagine. I suppose that you have been watching the habits, and perhaps the house, of Miss Irene Adler."

"Quite so, but the sequel was rather unusual. I will tell you, however. I left the house a little after eight o'clock this morning, in the character of a groom out of work. There is a wonderful sympathy and freemasonry among horsey men. Be one of them, and you will know all that there is to know. I soon found Briony Lodge. It is a *bijou* villa,[9] with a garden at the back, but built out in front right up to the road, two stories. Chubb lock to the door. Large sitting-room on the right side, well furnished, with long windows almost to the floor, and those preposterous English window fasteners which a child could open. Behind there was nothing remarkable, save that the passage window could be reached from the top of the coach-house. I walked round it and examined it closely from every point of view, but without noting anything else of interest.

"I then lounged down the street, and found, as I expected, that there was a mews[1] in a lane which runs down by one wall of the garden. I lent the ostlers a hand in rubbing down their horses, and I received in exchange twopence, a glass of half-and-half, two fills of shag tobacco, and as much information as I could desire about Miss Adler, to say nothing of half a dozen other people in the neighbourhood in whom I was not in the least interested, but whose biographies I was compelled to listen to."

"And what of Irene Adler?" I asked.

"Oh, she has turned all the men's heads down in that part. She is the daintiest thing under a bonnet on this planet. So say the Serpentine-mews, to a man. She lives quietly, sings at concerts, drives out at five every day, and returns at seven sharp for dinner. Seldom goes out at other times, except when she sings. Has only one male visitor, but a good deal of him. He is dark, handsome, and dashing; never calls less than once a day, and often twice. He is a Mr Godfrey Norton, of the Inner Temple.[2] See the advantages of a cabman as a confidant. They had driven him home a dozen times from Serpentine-mews, and knew all about him. When I had listened to all that they had to tell, I began to walk up and down near Briony Lodge once more, and to think over my plan of campaign.

"This Godfrey Norton was evidently an important factor in the matter. He was a lawyer. That sounded ominous. What was the relation between them, and what the object of his repeated visits? Was she his client, his friend, or his mistress? If the former, she had probably transferred the photograph to his keeping. If the latter, it was less likely. On the issue of this question depended whether I should continue my work at Briony Lodge, or turn my attention to the gentleman's chambers in the Temple. It was a delicate point, and it widened the field of my inquiry. I fear that I bore you with these details, but I have to let you see my little difficulties, if you are to understand the situation."

"I am following you closely," I answered.

"I was still balancing the matter in my mind, when a hansom cab drove up to Briony Lodge, and a gentleman sprang out. He was a remarkably handsome man, dark, aquiline, and moustached—evidently the man of whom I had heard. He appeared to be in a great hurry, shouted to the cabman to wait, and brushed past the maid who opened the door with the air of a man who was thoroughly at home.

"He was in the house about half an hour, and I could catch glimpses of him, in the windows of the sitting-room, pacing up and down, talking excitedly and waving

9. A small, charming house.
1. A back lane, used for stables and deliveries.

2. One of the four Inns of Court, where the offices and residences of barristers are located.

his arms. Of her I could see nothing. Presently he emerged, looking even more flurried than before. As he stepped up to the cab, he pulled a gold watch from his pocket and looked at it earnestly. 'Drive like the devil,' he shouted, 'first to Gross & Hankey's in Regent-street, and then to the church of St. Monica in the Edgware-road. Half a guinea if you do it in twenty minutes!'

"Away they went, and I was just wondering whether I should not do well to follow them, when up the lane came a neat little landau, the coachman with his coat only half buttoned, and his tie under his ear, while all the tags of his harness were sticking out of the buckles. It hadn't pulled up before she shot out of the hall door and into it. I only caught a glimpse of her at the moment, but she was a lovely woman, with a face that a man might die for.

"'The Church of St. Monica, John,' she cried, 'and half a sovereign if you reach it in twenty minutes.'

"This was quite too good to lose, Watson. I was just balancing whether I should run for it, or whether I should perch behind her landau, when a cab came through the street. The driver looked twice at such a shabby fare; but I jumped in before he could object. 'The Church of St. Monica,' said I, 'and half a sovereign if you reach it in twenty minutes.' It was twenty-five minutes to twelve, and of course it was clear enough what was in the wind.[3]

"My cabby drove fast. I don't think I ever drove faster, but the others were there before us. The cab and the landau with their steaming horses were in front of the door when I arrived. I paid the man, and hurried into the church. There was not a soul there save the two whom I had followed and a surpliced clergyman, who seemed to be expostulating with them. They were all three standing in a knot in front of the altar. I lounged up the side aisle like any other idler who has dropped into a church. Suddenly, to my surprise, the three at the altar faced round to me, and Godfrey Norton came running as hard as he could towards me.

"'Thank God!' he cried. 'You'll do. Come! Come!'

"'What then?' I asked.

"'Come man, come, only three minutes, or it won't be legal.'

"I was half dragged up to the altar, and, before I knew where I was, I found myself mumbling responses which were whispered in my ear, and vouching for things of which I knew nothing, and generally assisting in the secure tying up of Irene Adler, spinster, to Godfrey Norton, bachelor. It was all done in an instant, and there was the gentleman thanking me on the one side and the lady on the other, while the clergyman beamed on me in front. It was the most preposterous position in which I ever found myself in my life, and it was the thought of it that started me laughing just now. It seems that there had been some informality about their licence, that the clergyman absolutely refused to marry them without a witness of some sort, and that my lucky appearance saved the bridegroom from having to sally out into the streets in search of a best man. The bride gave me a sovereign, and I mean to wear it on my watch chain in memory of the occasion."

"This is a very unexpected turn of affairs," said I; "and what then?"

"Well, I found my plans very seriously menaced. It looked as if the pair might take an immediate departure, and so necessitate very prompt and energetic measures on my part. At the church door, however, they separated, he driving back to the Temple, and she to her own house. 'I shall drive out in the Park at five as usual,' she

3. Until 1886, marriages could only be legally performed before noon.

said as she left him. I heard no more. They drove away in different directions, and I went off to make my own arrangements."

"Which are?"

"Some cold beef and a glass of beer," he answered, ringing the bell. "I have been too busy to think of food, and I am likely to be busier still this evening. By the way, Doctor, I shall want your co-operation."

"I shall be delighted."

"You don't mind breaking the law?"

"Not in the least."

"Nor running a chance of arrest?"

"Not in a good cause."

"Oh, the cause is excellent!"

"Then I am your man."

"I was sure that I might rely on you."

"But what is it you wish?"

"When Mrs Turner has brought in the tray I will make it clear to you. Now," he said, as he turned hungrily on the simple fare that our landlady had provided, "I must discuss it while I eat, for I have not much time. It is nearly five now. In two hours we must be on the scene of action. Miss Irene, or Madame, rather, returns from her drive at seven. We must be at Briony Lodge to meet her."

"And what then?"

"You must leave that to me. I have already arranged what is to occur. There is only one point on which I must insist. You must not interfere, come what may. You understand?"

"I am to be neutral?"

"To do nothing whatever. There will probably be some small unpleasantness. Do not join in it. It will end in my being conveyed into the house. Four or five minutes afterwards the sitting-room window will open. You are to station yourself close to that open window."

"Yes."

"You are to watch me, for I will be visible to you."

"Yes."

"And when I raise my hand—so—you will throw into the room what I give you to throw, and will, at the same time, raise the cry of fire. You quite follow me?"

"Entirely."

"It is nothing very formidable," he said, taking a long cigar-shaped roll from his pocket. "It is an ordinary plumber's smoke rocket,[4] fitted with a cap at either end to make it self-lighting. Your task is confined to that. When you raise your cry of fire, it will be taken up by quite a number of people. You may then walk to the end of the street, and I will rejoin you in ten minutes. I hope that I have made myself clear?"

"I am to remain neutral, to get near the window, to watch you, and, at the signal, to throw in this object, then to raise the cry of fire, and to await you at the corner of the street."

"Precisely."

"Then you may entirely rely on me."

"That is excellent. I think perhaps it is almost time that I prepared for the new *rôle* I have to play."

---

4. A device to test pipes for leaks.

He disappeared into his bedroom, and returned in a few minutes in the character of an amiable and simple-minded Nonconformist clergyman. His broad black hat, his baggy trousers, his white tie, his sympathetic smile, and general look of peering and benevolent curiosity were such as Mr John Hare[5] alone could have equalled. It was not merely that Holmes changed his costume. His expression, his manner, his very soul seemed to vary with every fresh part that he assumed. The stage lost a fine actor, even as science lost an acute reasoner, when he became a specialist in crime.

It was a quarter past six when we left Baker-street, and it still wanted ten minutes to the hour when we found ourselves in Serpentine-avenue. It was already dusk, and the lamps were just being lighted as we paced up and down in front of Briony Lodge, waiting for the coming of its occupant. The house was just such as I had pictured it from Sherlock Holmes's succinct description, but the locality appeared to be less private than I expected. On the contrary, for a small street in a quiet neighbourhood, it was remarkably animated. There was a group of shabbily-dressed men smoking and laughing in a corner, a scissors grinder with his wheel,[6] two guardsmen who were flirting with a nurse-girl, and several well-dressed young men who were lounging up and down with cigars in their mouths.

"You see," remarked Holmes, as we paced to and fro in front of the house, "this marriage rather simplifies matters. The photograph becomes a double-edged weapon now. The chances are that she would be as averse to its being seen by Mr Godfrey Norton, as our client is to its coming to the eyes of his Princess. Now the question is—Where are we to find the photograph?"

"Where, indeed?"

"It is most unlikely that she carries it about with her. It is cabinet size. Too large for easy concealment about a woman's dress. She knows that the King is capable of having her waylaid and searched. Two attempts of the sort have already been made. We may take it then that she does not carry it about with her."

"Where, then?"

"Her banker or her lawyer. There is that double possibility. But I am inclined to think neither. Women are naturally secretive, and they like to do their own secreting. Why should she hand it over to anyone else? She could trust her own guardianship, but she could not tell what indirect or political influence might be brought to bear upon a business man. Besides, remember that she had resolved to use it within a few days. It must be where she can lay her hands upon it. It must be in her own house."

"But it has twice been burgled."

"Pshaw! They did not know how to look."

"But how will you look?"

"I will not look."

"What then?"

"I will get her to show me."

"But she will refuse."

"She will not be able to. But I hear the rumble of wheels. It is her carriage. Now carry out my orders to the letter."

As he spoke the gleam of the sidelights of a carriage came round the curve of the avenue. It was a smart little landau which rattled up to the door of Briony Lodge. As it pulled up one of the loafing men at the corner dashed forward to open the door in the hope of earning a copper, but was elbowed away by another loafer who had rushed up with the same intention. A fierce quarrel broke out, which was increased by the two

5. A popular character actor of the era.   6. A door-to-door knife sharpener.

guardsmen, who took sides with one of the loungers, and by the scissors grinder, who was equally hot upon the other side. A blow was struck, and in an instant the lady, who had stepped from her carriage, was the centre of a little knot of flushed and struggling men who struck savagely at each other with their fists and sticks. Holmes dashed into the crowd to protect the lady; but, just as he reached her, he gave a cry and dropped to the ground, with the blood running freely down his face. At his fall the guardsmen took to their heels in one direction and the loungers in the other, while a number of better dressed people who had watched the scuffle without taking part in it, crowded in to help the lady and to attend to the injured man. Irene Adler, as I will still call her, had hurried up the steps; but she stood at the top with her superb figure outlined against the lights of the hall, looking back into the street.

"Is the poor gentleman much hurt?" she asked.

"He is dead," cried several voices.

"No, no, there's life in him," shouted another. "But he'll be gone before you can get him to hospital."

"He's a brave fellow," said a woman. "They would have had the lady's purse and watch if it hadn't been for him. They were a gang, and a rough one too. Ah, he's breathing now."

"He can't lie in the street. May we bring him in, marm?"

"Surely. Bring him into the sitting-room. There is a comfortable sofa. This way, please!"

Slowly and solemnly he was borne into Briony Lodge, and laid out in the principal room, while I still observed the proceedings from my post by the window. The lamps had been lit, but the blinds had not been drawn, so that I could see Holmes as he lay upon the couch. I do not know whether he was seized with compunction at that moment for the part he was playing, but I know that I never felt more heartily ashamed of myself in my life than when I saw the beautiful creature against whom I was conspiring, or the grace and kindliness with which she waited upon the injured man. And yet it would be the blackest treachery to Holmes to draw back now from the part which he had entrusted to me. I hardened my heart, and took the smoke-rocket from under my ulster.[7] After all, I thought, we are not injuring her. We are but preventing her from injuring another.

Holmes had sat up upon the couch, and I saw him motion like a man who is in need of air. A maid rushed across and threw open the window. At the same instant I saw him raise his hand, and at the signal I tossed my rocket into the room with a cry of "Fire." The word was no sooner out of my mouth than the whole crowd of spectators, well dressed and ill—gentlemen, ostlers, and servant maids—joined in a general shriek of "Fire." Thick clouds of smoke curled through the room, and out at the open window. I caught a glimpse of rushing figures, and a moment later the voice of Holmes from within, assuring them that it was a false alarm. Slipping through the shouting crowd I made my way to the corner of the street, and in ten minutes was rejoiced to find my friend's arm in mine, and to get away from the scene of uproar. He walked swiftly and in silence for some few minutes, until we had turned down one of the quiet streets which lead towards the Edgware-road.

"You did it very nicely, Doctor," he remarked. "Nothing could have been better. It is all right."

---

7. A long, loose overcoat.

"You have the photograph!"

"I know where it is."

"And how did you find out?"

"She showed me, as I told you that she would."

"I am still in the dark."

"I do not wish to make a mystery," said he laughing. "The matter was perfectly simple. You, of course, saw that everyone in the street was an accomplice. They were all engaged for the evening."

"I guessed as much."

"Then, when the row broke out, I had a little moist red paint in the palm of my hand. I rushed forward, fell down, clapped my hand to my face, and became a piteous spectacle. It is an old trick."

"That also I could fathom."

"Then they carried me in. She was bound to have me in. What else could she do? And into her sitting-room, which was the very room which I suspected. It lay between that and her bedroom, and I was determined to see which. They laid me on a couch, I motioned for air, they were compelled to open the window, and you had your chance."

"How did that help you?"

"It was all-important. When a woman thinks that her house is on fire, her instinct is at once to rush to the thing which she values most. It is a perfectly overpowering impulse, and I have more than once taken advantage of it. In the case of the Darlington Substitution Scandal it was of use to me, and also in the Arnsworth Castle business. A married woman grabs at her baby—an unmarried one reaches for her jewel box. Now it was clear to me that our lady of to-day had nothing in the house more precious to her than what we are in quest of. She would rush to secure it. The alarm of fire was admirably done. The smoke and shouting were enough to shake nerves of steel. She responded beautifully. The photograph is in a recess behind a sliding panel just above the right bell pull. She was there in an instant, and I caught a glimpse of it as she half drew it out. When I cried out that it was a false alarm, she replaced it, glanced at the rocket, rushed from the room, and I have not seen her since. I rose, and, making my excuses, escaped from the house. I hesitated whether to attempt to secure the photograph at once; but the coachman had come in, and, as he was watching me narrowly, it seemed safer to wait. A little over-precipitance may ruin all."

"And now?" I asked.

"Our quest is practically finished. I shall call with the King to-morrow, and with you, if you care to come with us. We will be shown into the sitting-room to wait for the lady, but it is probable that when she comes she may find neither us nor the photograph. It might be a satisfaction to His Majesty to regain it with his own hands."

"And when will you call?"

"At eight in the morning. She will not be up, so that we shall have a clear field. Besides, we must be prompt, for this marriage may mean a complete change in her life and habits. I must wire to the King without delay."

We had reached Baker-street, and had stopped at the door. He was searching his pockets for the key, when someone passing said:—

"Good-night, Mister Sherlock Holmes."

There were several people on the pavement at the time, but the greeting appeared to come from a slim youth in an ulster who had hurried by.

"I've heard that voice before," said Holmes, staring down the dimly lit street. "Now, I wonder who the deuce that could have been."

Sidney Paget, *Good-night, Mr. Sherlock Holmes*. At the doorway of 221B Baker Street, Watson and Holmes (disguised as a clergyman) are hailed by a mysterious stranger. The artist Sidney Paget (1850–1908), who illustrated the Sherlock Holmes stories as they appeared in *The Strand Magazine* in the early 1890s, was responsible for creating the instantly recognizable image of Holmes as the tall, lean, hook-nosed sleuth who smokes a curved meerschaum pipe and wears a deerstalker cap and cloak when out on the trail of a criminal. But Doyle made his detective as adept at disguise as at deduction. In almost every story, Holmes becomes someone else in order to pass unnoticed at all levels of society. Here Paget explores one of Doyle's main themes, that skill in disguise must be matched by skill in penetrating the disguises of others.

3

I slept at Baker-street that night, and we were engaged upon our toast and coffee in the morning when the King of Bohemia rushed into the room.

"You have really got it!" he cried, grasping Sherlock Holmes by either shoulder, and looking eagerly into his face.

"Not yet."

"But you have hopes?"

"I have hopes."

"Then, come. I am all impatience to be gone."

"We must have a cab."

"No, my brougham is waiting."

"Then that will simplify matters." We descended, and started off once more for Briony Lodge.

"Irene Adler is married," remarked Holmes.

"Married! When?"

"Yesterday."

"But to whom?"

"To an English lawyer named Norton."

"But she could not love him?"

"I am in hopes that she does."

"And why in hopes?"

"Because it would spare your Majesty all fear of future annoyance. If the lady loves her husband, she does not love your Majesty. If she does not love your Majesty, there is no reason why she should interfere with your Majesty's plan."

"It is true. And yet—! Well! I wish she had been of my own station! What a queen she would have made!" He relapsed into a moody silence which was not broken, until we drew up in Serpentine-avenue.

The door of Briony Lodge was open, and an elderly woman stood upon the steps. She watched us with a sardonic eye as we stepped from the brougham.

"Mr Sherlock Holmes, I believe?" said she.

"I am Mr Holmes," answered my companion, looking at her with a questioning and rather startled gaze.

"Indeed! My mistress told me that you were likely to call. She left this morning with her husband, by the 5.15 train from Charing-cross, for the Continent."

"What!" Sherlock Holmes staggered back, white with chagrin and surprise. "Do you mean that she has left England?"

"Never to return."

"And the papers?" asked the King, hoarsely. "All is lost."

"We shall see." He pushed past the servant, and rushed into the drawing-room, followed by the King and myself. The furniture was scattered about in every direction, with dismantled shelves, and open drawers, as if the lady had hurriedly ransacked them before her flight. Holmes rushed at the bell-pull, tore back a small sliding shutter, and, plunging in his hand, pulled out a photograph and a letter. The photograph was of Irene Adler herself in evening dress, the letter was superscribed to "Sherlock Holmes, Esq. To be left till called for." My friend tore it open, and we all three read it together. It was dated at midnight of the preceding night, and ran in this way:—

"MY DEAR MR SHERLOCK HOLMES,—You really did it very well. You took me in completely. Until after the alarm of fire, I had not a suspicion. But then, when I found how I had betrayed myself, I began to think. I had been warned against you months ago. I had been told that, if the King employed an agent, it would certainly be you. And your address had been given me. Yet, with all this, you made me reveal what you wanted to know. Even after I became suspicious, I found it hard to think evil of such a dear, kind old clergyman. But, you know, I have been trained as an actress myself. Male costume is nothing new to me. I often take advantage of the freedom which it gives. I sent John, the coachman, to watch you, ran upstairs, got into my walking clothes, as I call them, and came down just as you departed.

"Well, I followed you to your door, and so made sure that I was really an object of interest to the celebrated Mr Sherlock Holmes. Then I, rather imprudently, wished you good night, and started for the Temple to see my husband.

"We both thought the best resource was flight, when pursued by so formidable an antagonist; so you will find the nest empty when you call to-morrow. As to the photograph, your client may rest in peace. I love and am loved by a better man than he. The King may do what he will without hindrance from one whom he has cruelly wronged. I keep it only to safeguard myself, and to preserve a weapon which will always secure me from any steps which he might take in the future. I leave a photograph which he might care to possess; and I remain, dear Mr Sherlock Holmes, very truly yours,

"IRENE NORTON, *née* ADLER."

"What a woman—oh, what a woman!" cried the King of Bohemia, when we had all three read this epistle. "Did I not tell you how quick and resolute she was? Would she not have made an admirable queen? Is it not a pity that she was not on my level?"

"From what I have seen of the lady, she seems, indeed, to be on a very different level to your Majesty," said Holmes, coldly. "I am sorry that I have not been able to bring your Majesty's business to a more successful conclusion."

"On the contrary, my dear sir," cried the King. "Nothing could be more successful. I know that her word is inviolate. The photograph is now as safe as if it were in the fire."

"I am glad to hear your Majesty say so."

"I am immensely indebted to you. Pray tell me in what way I can reward you. This ring—." He slipped an emerald snake ring from his finger, and held it out upon the palm of his hand.

"Your Majesty has something which I should value even more highly," said Holmes.

"You have but to name it."

"This photograph!"

The King stared at him in amazement.

"Irene's photograph!" he cried. "Certainly, if you wish it."

"I thank your Majesty. Then there is no more to be done in the matter. I have the honour to wish you a very good morning." He bowed, and, turning away without observing the hand which the King had stretched out to him, he set off in my company for his chambers.

And that was how a great scandal threatened to affect the kingdom of Bohemia, and how the best plans of Mr Sherlock Holmes were beaten by a woman's wit. He used to make merry over the cleverness of women, but I have not heard him do it of late. And when he speaks of Irene Adler, or when he refers to her photograph, it is always under the honourable title of *the* woman.

1891

RESPONSE
Jamyang Norbu: from The Mandala of Sherlock Holmes[1]
[A PUKKA VILLAIN]

Runnymeade Cottage was just outside Chota Simla.[2] Behind the cottage was a mule track which, seven miles beyond Chota Simla, led to the Hindustan–Thibet (or H–T) road. Sometimes our lessons would be disturbed by the sound of bells, as

1. Sherlock Holmes and Holmes-like figures have proven irresistible to writers since Arthur Conan Doyle's day. Holmes has appeared in more books and films than any other literary character in modern times. A particularly striking reincarnation of Holmes is found in *Sherlock Holmes: The Missing Years* (1999) by the Tibetan novelist Jamyang Norbu, who lives in exile in India and wrote this novel in English. This postmodern mystery story imagines what Holmes might have been up to during the two years he "disappeared" after Doyle tried to kill him off. When Holmes's fans insisted he return, Doyle had Holmes reappear, claiming he had been off wandering in Tibet. Norbu takes the opportunity to tell this tale, in a

comic rewriting of Doyle in the style of Kipling's novel *Kim*. Norbu gives a postcolonial slant to the classic detective, in an homage to Victorian fiction that is also an indirect portrayal of Tibet's struggle for independence from China. In the chapter included here, the novel's narrator, an Indian civil servant (and old Kipling character) named Hurree Chunder Mookerjee is studying Holmes while they stay in northern India on the way to Tibet. This chapter gives a lively portrait of Holmes as seen in contemporary perspective and in more than one role.

2. The eastern part of Simla, in the foothills of the Himalayas, a summer resort and hill station of the British occupying India.

Thibetan traders plodded along the track with their panniered mules. Occasionally lamas in weathered wine-red robes would go past, twirling their prayer wheels, and half naked sanyasis[3] with begging bowls of polished coco-de-mer and blackbuck skins would make their way to some distant cave-shrine, where they would spend the summer fed by the nearest village. Pahari[4] herdsmen in warm putoo (home-spun wool) coats would pass through with their flocks of goats and sheep, sometimes playing strange tunes on bamboo flutes.

I would explain to Mr Holmes the background of these various people—their origins, religious customs and so on and so forth. He took a great deal of interest in them. Sometimes he would stop a Thibetan muleteer or a Ladakhi trader[5] and try out his Thibetan on them. They would smoke his tobacco and laugh with amazement when the strange sahib spoke to them, haltingly maybe, but unmistakably in their own language. Months passed in this manner: in study, long walks and conversation, without even a hint of Colonel Moran or his society's activities ever disturbing the peace at Runnymeade Cottage.

It was this tranquillity that permitted me the leisure to examine Mr Holmes's personality and uncover traits in it that were not at all tranquil. He was not a happy man. It seemed that the great powers he possessed were sometimes more of a curse than a blessing to him. His cruel clarity of vision seemed often to deny him the comfort of those illusions that permit most of humankind to go through their short lives absorbed in their small problems and humble pleasures, oblivious of the misery surrounding them and their own inevitably wretched ends. When his powers thus overwhelmed him, Sherlock Holmes would, unfortunately, take certain injurious drugs such as morphine and cocaine in daily injections for many weeks.

Aside from this unhappy habit, there was much in Mr Holmes that was lofty and spiritual. He was celibate, and did not seem to have any desire for such human foibles as wealth, power, fame or comeliness. He could have been an ascetic in a mountain cave, for the simplicity of his life.

Strickland came up for Christmas. Simla was deep in snow, but up at the cottage, sitting before a roaring log fire, we warmed ourselves with potent beverages, and listened to Strickland's report. The case had made no progress. In spite of the strenuous efforts by the Bombay police, no link could be established between the dead Portuguese clerk and Colonel Moran. Also, no witnesses had been found who had seen anything remotely suspicious at the time the clerk had been shot in front of the police station. Strickland had attempted to rattle the Colonel's self-assurance by sending in "beaters" to flush him out of his lair. He had posted policemen in civilian attire around the Colonel's house and club, and had even had half-a-dozen following him wherever he went. But Colonel Moran was not a man easily shaken by such tactics, and stuck to his daily routine as if the "beaters" did not exist at all. Once, on leaving his club, he had even made one of the policeman hold his horse, and subsequently tipped him a rupee. A cool rogue, the Colonel sahib.

Strickland also had instructions for me from another Colonel, our department head, Colonel Creighton. I was to remain with Mr Sherlock Holmes for the time being and make myself useful to him in whatever way he wanted. I was also to take

3. Ascetic Hindu holy men, devotees of Shiva, here carrying bowls made from the coconut-like shell of the coco-de-mer tree, and wearing skins of the blackbuck, a common Indian antelope.

4. A Hindu people of Nepal.
5. Ladakh or "Little Tibet" is a mountainous district in the Indian state of Jammu and Kashmir.

every precaution against any further attempt on Mr Holmes's life—and I was to look sharp about it! The last comment—quite uncalled for—was probably Colonel Creighton's way of expressing his disapproval of the way I had been caught with my dhoti[6] down; when Colonel Moran's thugs had made their abortive attempt to murder Sherlock Holmes on the Frontier Mall. Being a scrupulously honest sort of chap I had not hesitated to include the incident in my report to the Colonel, even though it had not really shown me up in the best of lights. Even if I hadn't, the Colonel would have learnt about it one way or the other—he was that sort of person.

Well, we babus[7] have our pride. I was determined never to have such an embarrassing situation repeated again. So I doubled my precautions, instructed my informers and agents to increase their vigilance, and even employed, full-time, a couple of little chokras,[8] to keep an eye around the vicinity of Runnymeade Cottage for anyone who might take undue interest in the cottage or its occupant. In my line of work it is axiomatic that time and energy spent on precaution are never wasted. Sure enough, within a week the truth of this was demonstrated, Q.E.D.

One day one of the ragged little urchins, the one with the particularly runny nose, came running to my house at the lower bazaar. "Babuji.[9] A strange man appeared at the back of the sahib's house a short while ago," the boy said, sniffing in a disgusting manner.

"And what of it?" I asked impatiently. "All manner of men pass by the track behind the house."

"Nay, Babuji. I his man did more. He entered the house."

"Kya? What manner of man was he?"

"He looked like a real budmaash,[1] Babuji. He had long matted hair and was dressed belike as a Bhotia, in brown woollen bukoo and sheepskin cap. He also had a burra talwar, stuck in his belt."

"And what of the sahib?" I enquired anxiously.

"We know not, Babuji. We saw him not."

I imagined Mr Holmes peacefully sitting at his desk going over his Thibetan declensions, or happily performing one of his malodorous experiments, while an assassin silently approached him from behind, a glittering sword raised in his hands. I felt slightly sick.

Reaching under my bed, I quickly dragged out my tin trunk. Rummaging in it I finally found the small nickel-plated revolver that I had, some years ago, purchased at the Multani bazaar in Cabul. However, I must confess that I am a hopeless shot. In fact I could never quite get over the inconvenient but purely involuntary habit of closing my eyes dam' tight when pulling the trigger. But being ever averse to the crudities of violence I had always considered the bally thing as an object to be used more in terrorem than in mortiferus[2]—so the standards of my marksmanship did not really matter too much.

I puffed up to the cottage behind the boy. The other chokra was waiting by the bend in the road, just before Runnymeade Cottage.

"Ohe, Sunnoo," the boy with me called to his friend, "what has happened?"

6. A cloth worn by Indian men, wrapped about the legs and waist.
7. Native Indian clerks, government officials.
8. Street boy.
9. "Sir"—respectful address derived from "babu."

1. A desperado, here a Bhotia, or person from the kingdom of Bhutan, near Tibet, wearing a bukoo or gown, and carrying a burra talwar or Tibetan broadsword.
2. More to scare than to kill.

"Kuch nahin," the other replied, "the man is still in the house."

"And the sahib?" I enquired anxiously, fingering the pistol under my coat.

"I have not seen him at all, Babuji."

"What of the servant?"

"He went to the bazaar an hour ago—before the Bhotia man entered the house."

"Both of you stay here quietly. I'm going to take a look," said I, as confidently as I could. I was not very happy about it, but it had to be done. I approached the cottage from the east side where there were the least number of windows, walking as lightly as my hundred and twenty seers[3] of corporeal flesh permitted. I managed to scramble over the picket fence without any difficulty—just a few scratches and a slightly torn dhoti—and sidled up to the stone wall of the cottage. Then I crept up to the front door and prepared for action. Girding up my loins—in this case quite literally as I had to tie the loose ends of my dhoti around my loins for the sake of comfort and convenience—and closing my hand on the butt of my revolver, I slowly pushed the door open.

The small parlour was empty, but I noticed that the door of the study-cum-living room was ajar. With nerves tingling I tip-toed over and peeked in.

A pukka[4] villain of a hill-man stood by the side table near the fire-place, rifling through Mr Holmes's papers. He looked decidedly sinister. His small slanting eyes peered furtively at the papers that he clutched with thin dirty fingers. A scraggly moustache dropped around the sides of his greasy lips. His long hair matted with dirt complemented the filthy sheep-skin cap that partly covered it. He wore a bukoo, or woollen gown of Thibetan cut, and felt boots of Tartar design. His Thibetan broadsword, I was relieved to note, was firmly in its scabbard, stuck into the belt of his robe. He looked quite the budmaash, or desperado, and was probably one of those bad characters from the upper reaches of Gharwal[5] who specialised in robbing pilgrims proceeding to Mount Kailash.

But what was he doing? If he was a robber, he should be packing away whatever articles of value he could lay his hands on, and not poring through other people's correspondence—which he certainly could not read in any case. There was a mystery here, and I would not solve it by dithering in the parlour.

Cocking the hammer of the revolver, I entered the room. "Khabardar!"[6] I said in a brave voice. He turned towards me slowly. The blighter looked even more villainous than I had previously supposed. His greasy lips curled into a sneer and he placed his hands akimbo on his hips. "Take heed, budmaash," I expostulated firmly. "Thou hast only to touch the hilt of thy sword and I will most surely blow thee to Jehannum[7] on a lead ball."

He must have been impressed by my stern demeanour for he suddenly fell on his knees and babbled apologies and excuses in a queer mixture of bad Hindustani and Thibetan. "Forgive thy slave, Lord and Master. I only came to take back what is rightfully mine. What was stolen from me by the tall English sahib. My sacred ghau, my charm-box. Even now it hangs there on the wall of this unbeliever's house."

Mr Holmes stealing his charm-box? What tommy-rot did this smooth-tongued villain expect me to believe. I moved my head to look at the wall where he was

---

3. Seer, a variable unit of Indian measure, about a kilogram, or 2.2 pounds.
4. Genuine.
5. A desolate Himalayan region. Mount Kailish is a Himalayan peak.
6. "Take warning."
7. Hell.

pointing but there was no charm-box there. When I turned back to the rascal to give him a piece of my mind, Sherlock Holmes stood smiling at me by the fireplace.

"I do wish you wouldn't grip the revolver so tightly, Huree," said he in his dry, unemotional way. "After all, the thing may have a hair trigger, you know."

"Good Heavens, Mr. Holmes!" I cried in amazement. "This takes the bally biscuit.[8] How the deuce an' all . . . "

"Confess that you were absolutely taken in," said he, chuckling to himself and throwing his cap, wig, and false moustache on the armchair.

"Why, certainly, Sir. It was a most extraordinary thespian performance. But you should not pull my leg like that, Mr Holmes. I was very worried about your safety."

"I owe you an apology for that. I certainly did not intend this disguise to be some kind of practical joke on you. This is my passport to Thibet."

"But surely it is too dan. . . "

"You were fooled by it, were you not? You thought I was a Bhotia trader."

"A Bhotia bandit, Sir. Not a trader."

"But a Bhotia, nonetheless."

"Well, I cannot deny that, Mr Holmes . . . By Jove, you were, if I may say so, a Bhotia to the boot heels; a Bhotia *ad vivium*,[9] if you will pardon the expression. But I must still beg you not to be rash, Sir. After all I am responsible for your welfare—and a trip to Thibet demands much more than an adequate disguise. You will require pack animals, provisions, medicines, tents, tin-openers, etcetera, etcetera—and at least the services of an experienced and faithful guide."

"Someone like yourself, perhaps?"

"Me, Sir? Ah . . . ahem. Well. I was really not implying that at all. But for the sake of argument—why not?"

"Why not, indeed. So why don't you come with me?"

"Mr Holmes, it is a deuced attractive proposition. After all I am a scientific man, and what is a little danger and discomfort to the insignificant self, when weighed against the opportunities to extend the frontiers of human knowledge—which we will, no doubt, be doing on this proposed venture."

"No doubt."

"But alas, Sir. I unfortunately happen to be in official harness, and can only proceed on such voyages on receipt of authorised instructions, *ex cathedra*."

"Which would be Colonel Creighton's?"

"Most unfortunately, yes, Mr Holmes."

"Well, I shall have to speak to the Colonel about it, won't I?"

"But the Colonel will surely object. He may even blame me . . . "

"Spare me your anxieties, I beg you," he said, raising his hand in an imperious manner. "Leave it to me." He took off his Thibetan robe. "Now I would be much obliged if, on your way home you would kindly return this costume to Lurgan,[1] and that horrible wig and moustache to the manager of the Gaiety Theatre."

8. British slang response to an astounding event; "that takes the cake" would be an American equivalent.
9. True to life.

1. A shopkeeper and police agent who supplied Holmes with the robe.

John Ruskin
1819–1900

John Ruskin began his career as the most perceptive English art critic of the nineteenth century. But for Ruskin, art was inextricably linked to the moral temper of the age in which it was produced. Thus he was drawn inevitably from art criticism to social criticism, denouncing ugliness and injustice as aspects of the same spiritual decline. His prodigious output of books on painting, literature, architecture, politics, and society culminated with a beautiful and moving autobiography, *Praeterita*, which means "of things past."

For all the magnificence of his prose and the brilliance of his vision, John Ruskin was a rather peculiar man. He was the only child of middle-class parents who lived in the suburbs near London and whose dearest wish, he wrote, was "to make an evangelical clergyman of me." Forbidden toys, he passed his time studying the patterns in the nursery carpet and garden leaves, delighting already in the visual pleasures that would engross him all his life. His upbringing was strict, secluded, and overprotected: he was educated at home until his mother accompanied him to Oxford, where she remained for the duration of his studies.

Perhaps because he was so sheltered, Ruskin's love life was a series of disastrous ordeals. As a teenager he suffered a hopeless passion for Adèle Domecq, who was rich, French, and Catholic—unsuitable on every count. Later, a miserable six-year marriage to his cousin Effie Gray was annulled on the grounds of nonconsummation (she then married the Pre-Raphaelite painter John Everett Millais, with whom she had many children). The annulment created a scandal, and the whole episode was so painful that Ruskin omitted any reference to his marriage in *Praeterita*. Finally, he became morbidly obsessed with Rose La Touche, thirty years his junior, and only nine years old when he met her. His tragic relationship with her became a secret thread running through his later work.

Ruskin's intensity of vision was already evident in his first book, *Modern Painters*, in which he declared that "to see clearly is poetry, prophecy, and religion—all in one." Ruskin insisted that the impressionistic canvasses of J. M. W. Turner were actually more faithful to nature than the carefully rendered detail of Dutch realists. Reading *Modern Painters*, Charlotte Brontë wrote: "I feel . . . as if I had been walking blindfold—this book seems to give me eyes." Published over seventeen years (1843–1860), the five volumes of *Modern Painters* reflect their author's changing preoccupations: from art and nature in the early volumes to humanism and society in the last one, following an experience of religious "unconversion" in 1858.

From boyhood Ruskin loved to travel on the Continent, and his autobiography relates with deep pleasure the many journeys he took, usually with his parents. Venice aroused him to write what the critic John Rosenberg has called "the most elaborate and eloquent monument to a city in our literature," *The Stones of Venice* (1851–1853). Ruskin's Venice is "a ghost upon the sands of the sea, so weak—so quiet,—so bereft of all but her loveliness." The decline and fall of the Venetian empire serves as a warning to the British, which, "if it forget their example, may be led through prouder eminence to less pitied destruction."

The book's central chapter, *The Nature of Gothic*, became the touchstone for Ruskin's subsequent radical social critique of England. He argues that Gothic workmanship, though rude and imperfect, reflected a culture that respected the individual soul of the workman. Societies which demand machinelike perfection dehumanize the craftsman, turning him into a soulless operative. Ruskin thus mingled his hymn to the beauty of Venice with a scathing indictment of the Industrial Revolution.

In *Modern Manufacture and Design* (1859) and *Unto This Last* (1862), Ruskin turned from architecture to economics, raging like a biblical prophet against the savagery of laissez-faire capitalism and exhorting employers to take responsibility for the well-being of their workers. Contemporary response was hostile, but Ruskin's reforms have had a lasting influence on radical political thinkers from the founders of the British Labour Party to Gandhi, who felt himself transformed by reading *Unto This Last:* "All Ruskin's words captivated me . . . I lay awake all night and there and then I decided to change my whole life."

Ruskin's later writings became increasingly fragmented as he suffered a long, slow decline into madness. "The doctors said I went mad . . . from overwork," he wrote, but "I went mad because nothing came of my work." Yet from 1871 to 1884 he was able to lecture about art at Oxford and to produce an impassioned series of open letters to English workmen, entitled *Fors Clavigera*. Many of the letters describe the Guild of St. George, a utopian society Ruskin had founded. Tormented by the brutality and folly he saw everywhere around him, Ruskin chose in his final work to record only "what it gives me joy to remember." In the serene and radiant *Praeterita* (1885–1889), which was to inspire Proust's *Remembrance of Things Past*, Ruskin transcended his apocalyptic fury to produce one of the most enchanting yet poignant autobiographies ever written in English.

from Modern Painters
from Definition of Greatness in Art[1]

Painting, or art generally, as such, with all its technicalities, difficulties, and particular ends, is nothing but a noble and expressive language, invaluable as the vehicle of thought, but by itself nothing. He who has learned what is commonly considered the whole art of painting, that is, the art of representing any natural object faithfully, has as yet only learned the language by which his thoughts are to be expressed. He has done just as much towards being that which we ought to respect as a great painter, as a man who has learnt how to express himself grammatically and melodiously has towards being a great poet. The language is, indeed, more difficult of acquirement in the one case than in the other, and possesses more power of delighting the sense, while it speaks to the intellect; but it is, nevertheless, nothing more than language, and all those excellences which are peculiar to the painter as such, are merely what rhythm, melody, precision, and force are in the words of the orator and the poet, necessary to their greatness, but not the tests of their greatness. It is not by the mode of representing and saying, but by what is represented and said, that the respective greatness either of the painter or the writer is to be finally determined. * * *

If I say that the greatest picture is that which conveys to the mind of the spectator the greatest number of the greatest ideas, I have a definition which will include as subjects of comparison every pleasure which art is capable of conveying. If I were to say, on the contrary, that the best picture was that which most closely imitated nature, I should assume that art could only please by imitating nature; and I should cast out of the pale of criticism those parts of works of art which are not imitative, that is to say, intrinsic beauties of colour and form, and those works of art wholly, which, like the Arabesques of Raffaelle in the Loggias,[2] are not imitative at all. Now, I want a definition of art wide enough to include all its varieties of aim. I do not say, therefore, that the art is greatest which gives most pleasure, because perhaps there is some art whose end is to teach, and not to please. I do not say that the art is greatest which teaches us most, because perhaps there is some art whose end is to please, and not to

1. From vol. 1, part 1, sec. 1, ch. 2.
2. The Italian Renaissance painter Raphael (1483–1520) decorated the Loggia of the Vatican with arabesques, wall paintings of interwoven foliage, animals, and human figures.

teach. I do not say that the art is greatest which imitates best, because perhaps there is some art whose end is to create and not to imitate. But I say that the art is greatest which conveys to the mind of the spectator, by any means whatsoever, the greatest number of the greatest ideas; and I call an idea great in proportion as it is received by a higher faculty of the mind, and as it more fully occupies, and in occupying, exercises and exalts, the faculty by which it is received.

If this, then, be the definition of great art, that of a great artist naturally follows. He is the greatest artist who has embodied, in the sum of his works, the greatest number of the greatest ideas.

1843

from *Of Water, As Painted by Turner*
["THE SLAVE SHIP"][1]

But, I think, the noblest sea that Turner[2] has ever painted, and, if so, the noblest certainly ever painted by man, is that of the Slave Ship, the chief Academy picture of the Exhibition of 1840.[3] It is a sunset on the Atlantic, after prolonged storm; but the storm is partially lulled, and the torn and streaming rain-clouds are moving in scarlet lines to lose themselves in the hollow of the night. The whole surface of sea included in the picture is divided into two ridges of enormous swell, not high, nor local, but a low broad heaving of the whole ocean, like the lifting of its bosom by deep-drawn breath after the torture of the storm. Between these two ridges the fire of the sunset falls along the trough of the sea, dyeing it with an awful but glorious light, the intense and lurid splendour which burns like gold, and bathes like blood. Along this fiery path and valley, the tossing waves by which the swell of the sea is restlessly divided, lift themselves in dark, indefinite, fantastic forms, each casting a faint and ghastly shadow behind it along the illumined foam. They do not rise everywhere, but three or four together in wild groups, fitfully and furiously, as the under strength of the swell compels or permits them; leaving between them treacherous spaces of level and whirling water, now lighted with green and lamp-like fire, now flashing back the gold of the declining sun, now fearfully dyed from above with the undistinguishable images of the burning clouds, which fall upon them in flakes of crimson and scarlet, and give to the reckless waves the added motion of their own fiery flying. Purple and blue, the lurid shadows of the hollow breakers are cast upon the mist of night, which gathers cold and low, advancing like the shadow of death upon the guilty ship[4] as it labours amidst the lightning of the sea, its thin masts written upon the sky in lines of blood, girded with condemnation in that fearful hue which signs the sky with horror, and mixes its flaming flood with the sunlight, and, cast far along the desolate heave of the sepulchral waves, incarnadines the multitudinous sea.[5]

I believe, if I were reduced to rest Turner's immortality upon any single work, I should choose this. Its daring conception, ideal in the highest sense of the word, is

1. From vol. 1, part 2, sec. 5, ch. 3.
2. J. M. W. Turner (1775–1851), English Romantic landscape painter. See Color Plate 5.
3. In 1844 Ruskin's father gave him this dramatic painting; it now hangs in the Museum of Fine Arts in Boston. The annual exhibition of the Royal Academy of Arts was the primary showcase for new paintings.
4. She is a slaver, throwing her slaves overboard. The near sea is encumbered with corpses [Ruskin's note].
5. "No, this my hand will rather / The multitudinous seas incarnadine, / Making the green one red" (*Macbeth* 2.2.59–61).

based on the purest truth, and wrought out with the concentrated knowledge of a life; its colour is absolutely perfect, not one false or morbid hue in any part or line, and so modulated that every square inch of canvas is a perfect composition; its drawing as accurate as fearless; the ship buoyant, bending, and full of motion; its tones as true as they are wonderful; and the whole picture dedicated to the most sublime of subjects and impressions (completing thus the perfect system of all truth, which we have shown to be formed by Turner's works)—the power, majesty, and deathfulness of the open, deep, illimitable sea.

1843

from The Stones of Venice
from *The Nature of Gothic*[1]

I shall endeavour therefore to give the reader in this chapter an idea, at once broad and definite, of the true nature of *Gothic* architecture, properly so called; not of that of Venice only, but of universal Gothic: for it will be one of the most interesting parts of our subsequent inquiry to find out how far Venetian architecture reached the universal or perfect type of Gothic, and how far it either fell short of it, or assumed foreign and independent forms.

The principal difficulty in doing this arises from the fact that every building of the Gothic period differs in some important respect from every other; and many include features which, if they occurred in other buildings, would not be considered Gothic at all; so that all we have to reason upon is merely, if I may be allowed so to express it, a greater or less degree of *Gothicness* in each building we examine. And it is this Gothicness,—the character which, according as it is found more or less in a building, makes it more or less Gothic,—of which I want to define the nature. * * * That is to say, pointed arches do not constitute Gothic, nor vaulted roofs, nor flying buttresses, nor grotesque sculptures; but all or some of these things, and many other things with them, when they come together so as to have life. * * *

* * * We shall find that Gothic architecture has external forms and internal elements. Its elements are certain mental tendencies of the builders, legibly expressed in it; as fancifulness, love of variety, love of richness, and such others. Its external forms are pointed arches, vaulted roofs, etc. And unless both the elements and the forms are there, we have no right to call the style Gothic. It is not enough that it has the Form, if it have not also the power and life. It is not enough that it has the Power, if it have not the form. * * *

I believe, then, that the characteristic or moral elements of Gothic are the following, placed in the order of their importance:

1. Savageness.
2. Changefulness.
3. Naturalism.
4. Grotesqueness.
5. Rigidity.
6. Redundance.

These characters are here expressed as belonging to the building; as belonging to the builder, they would be expressed thus:—1. Savageness or Rudeness. 2. Love of

1. From vol. 2, ch. 6.

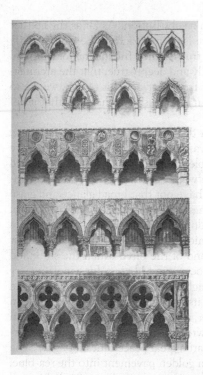

John Ruskin, *Windows of the Early Gothic Palaces*. Ruskin was a skilled draftsman, and in *The Stones of Venice* he provided many of his own illustrations to show readers just what was valuable—by which he meant expressive of the honest and devout spirit of the builders, sculptors, and painters—in Venetian art. Here, he says, "I have arranged some of the more delicate and finished examples of Gothic work" of the thirteenth century. The three windows at the top left, for example, "are entirely wrought in brick, with exquisite mouldings, not cast, but *moulded in the clay by the hand,* so that there is not one piece of the arch like another." Ruskin also wanted his readers to appreciate the interplay of round and pointed elements, as the Roman and Gothic styles engage in a struggle for supremacy, as well as the careful detailing, enabling each ornament to differ from the next. The feeling that produced these arches, Ruskin contends, is "the root of all that is greatest in Christian art . . . the life-blood of all manly work thenceforward in Europe." The style reaches its height in the intricate bottom arcade, from the Ducal Palace. If British workmen and builders could learn from the solidity and beauty of Gothic architecture, Ruskin concludes, "we may have a school of domestic architecture in the nineteenth century, which will make our children grateful to us, and proud of us, till the thirtieth."

Change. 3. Love of Nature. 4. Disturbed Imagination. 5. Obstinacy. 6. Generosity. And I repeat, that the withdrawal of any one, or any two, will not at once destroy the Gothic character of a building, but the removal of a majority of them will. I shall proceed to examine them in their order.

(1.) SAVAGENESS. I am not sure when the word "Gothic" was first generically applied to the architecture of the North; but I presume that, whatever the date of its original usage, it was intended to imply reproach, and express the barbaric character of the nations among whom that architecture arose. It never implied that they were literally of Gothic lineage, far less that their architecture had been originally invented by the Goths themselves;[2] but it did imply that they and their buildings together exhibited a degree of sternness and rudeness, which, in contradistinction to the character of Southern and Eastern nations, appeared like a perpetual reflection of the contrast between the Goth and the Roman in their first encounter. And when that fallen Roman, in the utmost impotence of his luxury, and insolence of his guilt, became the model for the imitation of civilized Europe,[3] at the close of the so-called Dark ages, the word Gothic became a term of unmitigated contempt, not unmixed with aversion. From that contempt, by the exertion of the antiquaries and architects of this century, Gothic architecture has been sufficiently vindicated; and perhaps some among us, in our admiration of the magnificent science of its structure, and sacredness of its expression, might desire that the term of ancient reproach should be withdrawn, and some other, of more apparent honourableness, adopted in its place.

2. The Goths, a Germanic people who overran the Roman Empire, were regarded as barbarians.
3. A reference to the Renaissance rediscovery of the classical world. Ruskin despised Renaissance architecture, which he found excessively ornate and morally suspect.

There is no chance, as there is no need, of such a substitution. As far as the epithet was used scornfully, it was used falsely; but there is no reproach in the word, rightly understood; on the contrary, there is a profound truth, which the instinct of mankind almost unconsciously recognizes. It is true, greatly and deeply true, that the architecture of the North is rude and wild; but it is not true, that, for this reason, we are to condemn it, or despise. Far otherwise: I believe it is in this very character that it deserves our profoundest reverence.

The charts of the world which have been drawn up by modern science have thrown into a narrow space the expression of a vast amount of knowledge, but I have never yet seen any one pictorial enough to enable the spectator to imagine the kind of contrast in physical character which exists between Northern and Southern countries. We know the differences in detail, but we have not that broad glance and grasp which would enable us to feel them in their fulness. We know that gentians grow on the Alps, and olives on the Apennines; but we do not enough conceive for ourselves that variegated mosaic of the world's surface which a bird sees in its migration, that difference between the district of the gentian and of the olive which the stork and the swallow see far off, as they lean upon the sirocco wind.[4] Let us, for a moment, try to raise ourselves even above the level of their flight, and imagine the Mediterranean lying beneath us like an irregular lake, and all its ancient promontories sleeping in the sun: here and there an angry spot of thunder, a grey stain of storm, moving upon the burning field; and here and there a fixed wreath of white volcano smoke, surrounded by its circle of ashes; but for the most part a great peacefulness of light, Syria and Greece, Italy and Spain, laid like pieces of a golden pavement into the sea-blue, chased, as we stoop nearer to them, with bossy beaten work of mountain chains, and glowing softly with terraced gardens, and flowers heavy with frankincense, mixed among masses of laurel, and orange, and plumy palm, that abate with their grey-green shadows the burning of the marble rocks, and of the ledges of porphyry[5] sloping under lucent sand. Then let us pass farther towards the north, until we see the orient colours change gradually into a vast belt of rainy green, where the pastures of Switzerland, and poplar valleys of France, and dark forests of the Danube and Carpathians stretch from the mouths of the Loire to those of the Volga, seen through clefts in grey swirls of rain-cloud and flaky veils of the mist of the brooks, spreading low along the pasture lands: and then, farther north still, to see the earth heave into mighty masses of leaden rock and heathy moor, bordering with a broad waste of gloomy purple that belt of field and wood, and splintering into irregular and grisly islands amidst the northern seas, beaten by storm, and chilled by ice-drift, and tormented by furious pulses of contending tide, until the roots of the last forests fail from among the hill ravines, and the hunger of the north wind bites their peaks into barrenness; and, at last, the wall of ice, durable like iron, sets, deathlike, its white teeth against us out of the polar twilight. And, having once traversed in thought this gradation of the zoned iris of the earth in all its material vastness, let us go down nearer to it, and watch the parallel change in the belt of animal life; the multitudes of swift and brilliant creatures that glance in the air and sea, or tread the sands of the southern zone; striped zebras and spotted leopards, glistening serpents, and birds arrayed in purple and scarlet. Let us contrast their delicacy and brilliancy of colour, and swiftness of motion, with the frost-cramped strength, and shaggy covering, and dusky

4. Hot Mediterranean wind.   5. Dark red or purple rock.

plumage of the northern tribes; contrast the Arabian horse with the Shetland, the tiger and leopard with the wolf and bear, the antelope with the elk, the bird of paradise with the osprey; and then, submissively acknowledging the great laws by which the earth and all that it bears are ruled throughout their being, let us not condemn, but rejoice in the expression by man of his own rest in the statutes of the lands that gave him birth. Let us watch him with reverence as he sets side by side the burning gems, and smooths with soft sculpture the jasper pillars, that are to reflect a ceaseless sunshine, and rise into a cloudless sky: but not with less reverence let us stand by him, when, with rough strength and hurried stroke, he smites an uncouth animation out of the rocks which he has torn from among the moss of the moorland, and heaves into the darkened air the pile of iron buttress and rugged wall, instinct with work of an imagination as wild and wayward as the northern sea; creatures of ungainly shape and rigid limb, but full of wolfish life; fierce as the winds that beat, and changeful as the clouds that shade them.

There is, I repeat, no degradation, no reproach in this, but all dignity and honourableness: and we should err grievously in refusing either to recognize as an essential character of the existing architecture of the North, or to admit as a desirable character in that which it yet may be, this wildness of thought, and roughness of work; this look of mountain brotherhood between the cathedral and the Alp; this magnificence of sturdy power, put forth only the more energetically because the fine finger-touch was chilled away by the frosty wind, and the eye dimmed by the moor-mist, or blinded by the hail; this out-speaking of the strong spirit of men who may not gather redundant fruitage from the earth, nor bask in dreamy benignity of sunshine, but must break the rock for bread, and cleave the forest for fire, and show, even in what they did for their delight, some of the hard habits of the arm and heart that grew on them as they swung the axe or pressed the plough.

If, however, the savageness of Gothic architecture, merely as an expression of its origin among Northern nations, may be considered, in some sort, a noble character, it possesses a higher nobility still, when considered as an index, not of climate, but of religious principle.

In the 13th and 14th paragraphs of Chapter XXI of the first volume of this work, it was noticed that the systems of architectural ornament, properly so called, might be divided into three:—1. Servile ornament, in which the execution or power of the inferior workman is entirely subjected to the intellect of the higher;—2. Constitutional ornament, in which the executive inferior power is, to a certain point, emancipated and independent, having a will of its own, yet confessing its inferiority and rendering obedience to higher powers;—and 3. Revolutionary ornament, in which no executive inferiority is admitted at all. I must here explain the nature of these divisions at somewhat greater length.

Of Servile ornament, the principal schools are the Greek, Ninevite,[6] and Egyptian; but their servility is of different kinds. The Greek master-workman was far advanced in knowledge and power above the Assyrian or Egyptian. Neither he nor those for whom he worked could endure the appearance of imperfection in anything; and, therefore, what ornament he appointed to be done by those beneath him was composed of mere geometrical forms,—balls, ridges, and perfectly symmetrical foliage,—which could be executed with absolute precision by line and rule, and were as

6. Nineveh was an ancient Assyrian city.

perfect in their way, when completed, as his own figure sculpture. The Assyrian and Egyptian, on the contrary, less cognisant of accurate form in anything, were content to allow their figure sculpture to be executed by inferior workmen, but lowered the method of its treatment to a standard which every workman could reach, and then trained him by discipline so rigid, that there was no chance of his falling beneath the standard appointed. The Greek gave to the lower workman no subject which he could not perfectly execute. The Assyrian gave him subjects which he could only execute imperfectly, but fixed a legal standard for his imperfection. The workman was, in both systems, a slave.

But in the mediaeval, or especially Christian, system of ornament, this slavery is done away with altogether; Christianity having recognized, in small things as well as great, the individual value of every soul. But it not only recognizes its value; it confesses its imperfection, in only bestowing dignity upon the acknowledgment of unworthiness. That admission of lost power and fallen nature, which the Greek or Ninevite felt to be intensely painful, and, as far as might be, altogether refused, the Christian makes daily and hourly, contemplating the fact of it without fear, as tending, in the end, to God's greater glory. Therefore, to every spirit which Christianity summons to her service, her exhortation is: Do what you can, and confess frankly what you are unable to do; neither let your effort be shortened for fear of failure, nor your confession silenced for fear of shame. And it is, perhaps, the principal admirableness of the Gothic schools of architecture, that they thus receive the results of the labour of inferior minds; and out of fragments full of imperfection, and betraying that imperfection in every touch, indulgently raise up a stately and unaccusable whole.

But the modern English mind has this much in common with that of the Greek, that it intensely desires, in all things, the utmost completion or perfection compatible with their nature. This is a noble character in the abstract, but becomes ignoble when it causes us to forget the relative dignities of that nature itself, and to prefer the perfectness of the lower nature to the imperfection of the higher; not considering that as, judged by such a rule, all the brute animals would be preferable to man, because more perfect in their functions and kind. * * * And therefore, while in all things that we see or do, we are to desire perfection, and strive for it, we are nevertheless not to set the meaner thing, in its narrow accomplishment, above the nobler thing, in its mighty progress; not to esteem smooth minuteness above shattered majesty; not to prefer mean victory to honourable defeat; not to lower the level of our aim, that we may the more surely enjoy the complacency of success. But, above all, in our dealings with the souls of other men, we are to take care how we check, by severe requirement or narrow caution, efforts which might otherwise lead to a noble issue; and, still more, how we withhold our admiration from great excellencies, because they are mingled with rough faults. Now, in the make and nature of every man, however rude or simple, whom we employ in manual labour, there are some powers for better things; some tardy imagination, torpid capacity of emotion, tottering steps of thought, there are, even at the worst; and in most cases it is all our own fault that they *are* tardy or torpid. But they cannot be strengthened, unless we are content to take them in their feebleness, and unless we prize and honour them in their imperfection above the best and most perfect manual skill. And this is what we have to do with all our labourers; to look for the *thoughtful* part of them, and get that out of them, whatever we lose for it, whatever faults and errors we are obliged to take with it. For the best that is in them cannot manifest itself, but in company with much error. Understand this clearly: You can teach a man to draw a straight line, and to cut one; to strike a curved line, and to carve it; and to copy and carve any number of given lines or forms, with admirable speed and perfect precision; and you find his work perfect of its kind: but if you ask him to think about any of those forms, to consider if he cannot find any better in his own head, he stops; his execution becomes hesitating; he thinks, and ten to one he thinks wrong; ten to one he makes a mistake in the first touch he gives to his work as a thinking being. But you have made a man of him for all that. He was only a machine before, an animated tool.

And observe, you are put to stern choice in this matter. You must either make a tool of the creature, or a man of him. You cannot make both. Men were not intended to work with the accuracy of tools, to be precise and perfect in all their actions. If you will have that precision out of them, and make their fingers measure degrees like cogwheels, and their arms strike curves like compasses, you must unhumanize them. All the energy of their spirits must be given to make cogs and compasses of themselves. All their attention and strength must go to the accomplishment of the mean act. The eye of the soul must be bent upon the finger-point, and the soul's force must fill all the invisible nerves that guide it, ten hours a day, that it may not err from its steely precision, and so soul and sight be worn away, and the whole human being be lost at last—a heap of sawdust, so far as its intellectual work in this world is concerned: saved only by its Heart, which cannot go into the form of cogs and compasses, but expands, after the ten hours are over, into fireside humanity. On the other hand, if you will make a man of the working creature, you cannot make a tool. Let him but begin to imagine, to think, to try to do anything worth doing; and the engine-turned precision is lost at once. Out come all his roughness, all his dulness, all his incapability; shame upon shame, failure upon failure, pause after pause: but out comes the whole majesty of him also; and we know the height of it only when we see the clouds settling upon him. And, whether the clouds be bright or dark, there will be transfiguration behind and within them.

And now, reader, look round this English room of yours, about which you have been proud so often, because the work of it was so good and strong, and the ornaments of it so finished. Examine again all those accurate mouldings, and perfect polishings, and unerring adjustments of the seasoned wood and tempered steel. Many a time you have exulted over them, and thought how great England was, because her slightest work was done so thoroughly. Alas! if read rightly, these perfectnesses are signs of a slavery in our England a thousand times more bitter and more degrading than that of the scourged African, or helot[7] Greek. Men may be beaten, chained, tormented, yoked like cattle, slaughtered like summer flies, and yet remain in one sense, and the best sense, free. But to smother their souls within them, to blight and hew into rotting pollards[8] the suckling branches of their human intelligence, to make the flesh and skin which, after the worm's work on it, is to see God,[9] into leathern thongs to yoke machinery with,—this is to be slave-masters indeed; and there might be more freedom in England, though her feudal lords' lightest words were worth men's lives, and though the blood of the vexed husbandman dropped in the furrows of her fields, than there is while the animation of her multitudes is sent like fuel to feed the factory smoke, and the strength of them is given daily to be wasted into the fineness of a web, or racked into the exactness of a line.

7. Serf or slave.
8. Trees that are artificially shaped by pruning.

9. "And though after my skin worms destroy this body, yet in my flesh shall I see God" (Job 19.26).

And, on the other hand, go forth again to gaze upon the old cathedral front, where you have smiled so often at the fantastic ignorance of the old sculptors: examine once more those ugly goblins, and formless monsters, and stern statues, anatomiless and rigid; but do not mock at them, for they are signs of the life and liberty of every workman who struck the stone; a freedom of thought, and rank in scale of being, such as no laws, no charters, no charities can secure; but which it must be the first aim of all Europe at this day to regain for her children.

Let me not be thought to speak wildly or extravagantly. It is verily this degradation of the operative into a machine, which, more than any other evil of the times, is leading the mass of the nations everywhere into vain, incoherent, destructive struggling for a freedom of which they cannot explain the nature to themselves. Their universal outcry against wealth, and against nobility, is not forced from them either by the pressure of famine, or the sting of mortified pride. These do much, and have done much in all ages; but the foundations of society were never yet shaken as they are at this day. It is not that men are ill fed, but that they have no pleasure in the work by which they make their bread, and therefore look to wealth as the only means of pleasure. It is not that men are pained by the scorn of the upper classes, but they cannot endure their own; for they feel that the kind of labour to which they are condemned is verily a degrading one, and makes them less than men. Never had the upper classes so much sympathy with the lower, or charity for them, as they have at this day, and yet never were they so much hated by them: for, of old, the separation between the noble and the poor was merely a wall built by law; now it is a veritable difference in level of standing, a precipice between upper and lower grounds in the field of humanity, and there is pestilential air at the bottom of it. ＊ ＊ ＊

We have much studied and much perfected, of late, the great civilized invention of the division of labour; only we give it a false name. It is not, truly speaking, the labour that is divided; but the men:—Divided into mere segments of men—broken into small fragments and crumbs of life; so that all the little piece of intelligence that is left in a man is not enough to make a pin, or a nail, but exhausts itself in making the point of a pin or the head of a nail. Now it is a good and desirable thing, truly, to make many pins in a day; but if we could only see with what crystal sand their points were polished,—sand of human soul, much to be magnified before it can be discerned for what it is—we should think there might be some loss in it also. And the great cry that rises from all our manufacturing cities, louder than their furnace blast, is all in very deed for this,—that we manufacture everything there except men; we blanch cotton, and strengthen steel, and refine sugar, and shape pottery; but to brighten, to strengthen, to refine, or to form a single living spirit, never enters into our estimate of advantages. And all the evil to which that cry is urging our myriads can be met only in one way: not by teaching nor preaching, for to teach them is but to show them their misery, and to preach to them, if we do nothing more than preach, is to mock at it. It can be met only by a right understanding, on the part of all classes, of what kinds of labour are good for men, raising them, and making them happy; by a determined sacrifice of such convenience, or beauty, or cheapness as is to be got only by the degradation of the workman; and by equally determined demand for the products and results of healthy and ennobling labour.

And how, it will be asked, are these products to be recognized, and this demand to be regulated? Easily: by the observance of three broad and simple rules:

1. Never encourage the manufacture of any article not absolutely necessary, in the production of which *Invention* has no share.

2. Never demand an exact finish for its own sake, but only for some practical or noble end.

3. Never encourage imitation or copying of any kind, except for the sake of preserving records of great works.

The second of these principles is the only one which directly rises out of the consideration of our immediate subject; but I shall briefly explain the meaning and extent of the first also, reserving the enforcement of the third for another place.

1. Never encourage the manufacture of anything not necessary, in the production of which invention has no share.

For instance. Glass beads are utterly unnecessary, and there is no design or thought employed in their manufacture. They are formed by first drawing out the glass into rods; these rods are chopped up into fragments of the size of beads by the human hand, and the fragments are then rounded in the furnace. The men who chop up the rods sit at their work all day, their hands vibrating with a perpetual and exquisitely timed palsy, and the beads dropping beneath their vibration like hail. Neither they, nor the men who draw out the rods or fuse the fragments, have the smallest occasion for the use of any single human faculty; and every young lady, therefore, who buys glass beads is engaged in the slave-trade, and in a much more cruel one than that which we have so long been endeavouring to put down.

But glass cups and vessels may become the subjects of exquisite invention; and if in buying these we pay for the invention, that is to say, for the beautiful form, or colour, or engraving, and not for mere finish of execution, we are doing good to humanity.

So, again, the cutting of precious stones, in all ordinary cases, requires little exertion of any mental faculty; some tact and judgment in avoiding flaws, and so on, but nothing to bring out the whole mind. Every person who wears cut jewels merely for the sake of their value is, therefore, a slave-driver.

But the working of the goldsmith, and the various designing of grouped jewellery and enamel-work, may become the subject of the most noble human intelligence. Therefore, money spent in the purchase of well-designed plate, of precious engraved vases, cameos, or enamels, does good to humanity; and, in work of this kind, jewels may be employed to heighten its splendour; and their cutting is then a price paid for the attainment of a noble end, and thus perfectly allowable.

I shall perhaps press this law farther elsewhere, but our immediate concern is chiefly with the second, namely, never to demand an exact finish, when it does not lead to a noble end. For observe, I have only dwelt upon the rudeness of Gothic, or any other kind of imperfectness, as admirable, where it was impossible to get design or thought without it. If you are to have the thought of a rough and untaught man, you must have it in a rough and untaught way; but from an educated man, who can without effort express his thoughts in an educated way, take the graceful expression, and be thankful. Only *get* the thought, and do not silence the peasant because he cannot speak good grammar, or until you have taught him his grammar. Grammar and refinement are good things, both, only be sure of the better thing first. And thus in art, delicate finish is desirable from the greatest masters, and is always given by them. In some places Michael Angelo, Leonardo, Phidias, Perugino, Turner,[1] all finished with the most exquisite care; and the finish they give always leads to the fuller

---

1. Michelangelo Buonarroti (1475–1564), Italian painter, sculptor, architect, and poet; Leonardo da Vinci (1452–1519), Italian painter, sculptor, architect, and engineer; Phidias (5th century B.C.), ancient Greek sculptor; Pietro Vannucci Perugino (1446–1523), Italian painter; J. M. W. Turner (1775–1851), English painter.

accomplishment of their noble purposes. But lower men than these cannot finish, for it requires consummate knowledge to finish consummately, and then we must take their thoughts as they are able to give them. So the rule is simple: Always look for invention first, and after that, for such execution as will help the invention, and as the inventor is capable of without painful effort, and *no more*. Above all, demand no refinement of execution where there is no thought, for that is slaves' work, unredeemed. Rather choose rough work than smooth work, so only that the practical purpose be answered, and never imagine there is reason to be proud of anything that may be accomplished by patience and sand-paper.

I shall only give one example, which however will show the reader what I mean, from the manufacture already alluded to, that of glass. Our modern glass is exquisitely clear in its substance, true in its form, accurate in its cutting. We are proud of this. We ought to be ashamed of it. The old Venice glass was muddy, inaccurate in all its forms, and clumsily cut, if at all. And the old Venetian was justly proud of it. For there is this difference between the English and Venetian workman, that the former thinks only of accurately matching his patterns, and getting his curves perfectly true and his edges perfectly sharp, and becomes a mere machine for rounding curves and sharpening edges; while the old Venetian cared not a whit whether his edges were sharp or not, but he invented a new design for every glass that he made, and never moulded a handle or a lip without a new fancy in it. And therefore, though some Venetian glass is ugly and clumsy enough when made by clumsy and uninventive workmen, other Venetian glass is so lovely in its forms that no price is too great for it; and we never see the same form in it twice. Now you cannot have the finish and the varied form too. If the workman is thinking about his edges, he cannot be thinking of his design; if of his design, he cannot think of his edges. Choose whether you will pay for the lovely form or the perfect finish, and choose at the same moment whether you will make the worker a man or a grindstone.

Nay, but the reader interrupts me,—"If the workman can design beautifully, I would not have him kept at the furnace. Let him be taken away and made a gentleman, and have a studio, and design his glass there, and I will have it blown and cut for him by common workmen, and so I will have my design and my finish too."

All ideas of this kind are founded upon two mistaken suppositions: the first, that one man's thoughts can be, or ought to be, executed by another man's hands; the second, that manual labour is a degradation, when it is governed by intellect.

On a large scale, and in work determinable by line and rule, it is indeed both possible and necessary that the thoughts of one man should be carried out by the labour of others; in this sense I have already defined the best architecture to be the expression of the mind of manhood by the hands of childhood. But on a smaller scale, and in a design which cannot be mathematically defined, one man's thoughts can never be expressed by another: and the difference between the spirit of touch of the man who is inventing, and of the man who is obeying directions, is often all the difference between a great and a common work of art. How wide the separation is between original and second-hand execution, I shall endeavour to show elsewhere; it is not so much to our purpose here as to mark the other and more fatal error of despising manual labour when governed by intellect; for it is no less fatal an error to despise it when thus regulated by intellect, than to value it for its own sake. We are always in these days endeavouring to separate the two; we want one man to be always thinking, and another to be always working, and we call one a gentleman, and the other an operative; whereas the workman ought often to be thinking, and the thinker often to be working, and both should be gentlemen, in the best sense. As it is, we make both un-gentle, the one envying, the other despising, his brother; and the mass of society is made up of morbid thinkers, and miserable workers. Now it is only by labour that thought can be made healthy, and only by thought that labour can be made happy, and the two cannot be separated with impunity. * * *

I should be led far from the matter in hand, if I were to pursue this interesting subject. Enough, I trust, has been said to show the reader that the rudeness or imper-fection which at first rendered the term "Gothic" one of reproach is indeed, when rightly understood, one of the most noble characters of Christian architecture, and not only a noble but an *essential* one. It seems a fantastic paradox, but it is neverthe-less a most important truth, that no architecture can be truly noble which is *not* im-perfect. And this is easily demonstrable. For since the architect, whom we will sup-pose capable of doing all in perfection, cannot execute the whole with his own hands, he must either make slaves of his workmen in the old Greek, and present Eng-lish fashion, and level his work to a slave's capacities, which is to degrade it; or else he must take his workmen as he finds them, and let them show their weaknesses to-gether with their strength, which will involve the Gothic imperfection, but render the whole work as noble as the intellect of the age can make it.

But the principle may be stated more broadly still. I have confined the illustra-tion of it to architecture, but I must not leave it as if true of architecture only. Hith-erto I have used the words imperfect and perfect merely to distinguish between work grossly unskilful, and work executed with average precision and science; and I have been pleading that any degree of unskilfulness should be admitted, so only that the labourer's mind had room for expression. But, accurately speaking, no good work whatever can be perfect, and *the demand for perfection is always a sign of a misunder-standing of the ends of art.*

This for two reasons, both based on everlasting laws. The first, that no great man ever stops working till he has reached his point of failure: that is to say, his mind is al-ways far in advance of his powers of execution, and the latter will now and then give way in trying to follow it; besides that he will always give to the inferior portions of his work only such inferior attention as they require; and according to his greatness he becomes so accustomed to the feeling of dissatisfaction with the best he can do, that in moments of lassitude or anger with himself he will not care though the be-holder be dissatisfied also. I believe there has only been one man who would not ac-knowledge this necessity, and strove always to reach perfection, Leonardo; the end of his vain effort being merely that he would take ten years to a picture and leave it un-finished. And therefore, if we are to have great men working at all, or less men doing their best, the work will be imperfect, however beautiful. Of human work none but what is bad can be perfect, in its own bad way.[2]

The second reason is, that imperfection is in some sort essential to all that we know of life. It is the sign of life in a mortal body, that is to say, of a state of progress and change. Nothing that lives is, or can be, rigidly perfect; part of it is decaying, part nascent. The foxglove blossom,—a third part bud, a third part past, a third part in

2. The Elgin marbles are supposed by many persons to be "perfect." In the most important portions they indeed approach perfection, but only there. The draperies are unfinished, the hair and wool of the animals are unfinished, and the entire bas-reliefs of the frieze are roughly cut [Ruskin's note]. The Elgin marbles are sculptures (including the Parthenon frieze) that were taken from Athens to England by Lord Elgin at the beginning of the 19th century.

full bloom,—is a type of the life of this world. And in all things that live there are certain irregularities and deficiencies which are not only signs of life, but sources of beauty. No human face is exactly the same in its lines on each side, no leaf perfect in its lobes, no branch in its symmetry. All admit irregularity as they imply change; and to banish imperfection is to destroy expression, to check exertion, to paralyze vitality. All things are literally better, lovelier, and more beloved for the imperfections which have been divinely appointed, that the law of human life may be Effort, and the law of human judgment, Mercy.

Accept this then for a universal law, that neither architecture nor any other noble work of man can be good unless it be imperfect; and let us be prepared for the otherwise strange fact, which we shall discern clearly as we approach the period of the Renaissance, that the first cause of the fall of the arts of Europe was a relentless requirement of perfection, incapable alike either of being silenced by veneration for greatness, or softened into forgiveness of simplicity.

Thus far then of the Rudeness or Savageness, which is the first mental element of Gothic architecture. It is an element in many other healthy architectures also, as the Byzantine and Romanesque; but true Gothic cannot exist without it.

1851–1853

from Modern Manufacture and Design[1]

The changes in the state of this country are now so rapid, that it would be wholly absurd to endeavour to lay down laws of art education for it under its present aspect and circumstances; and therefore I must necessarily ask, how much of it do you seriously intend within the next fifty years to be coal-pit, brick-field, or quarry? For the sake of distinctness of conclusion, I will suppose your success absolute: that from shore to shore the whole of the island is to be set as thick with chimneys as the masts stand in the docks of Liverpool: that there shall be no meadows in it; no trees; no gardens; only a little corn grown upon the housetops, reaped and threshed by steam: that you do not leave even room for roads, but travel either over the roofs of your mills, on viaducts; or under their floors, in tunnels: that, the smoke having rendered the light of the sun unserviceable, you work always by the light of your own gas: that no acre of English ground shall be without its shaft and its engine; and therefore, no spot of English ground left, on which it shall be possible to stand, without a definite and calculable chance of being blown off it, at any moment, into small pieces.

Under these circumstances, (if this is to be the future of England,) no designing or any other development of beautiful art will be possible. Do not vex your minds, nor waste your money with any thought or effort in the matter. Beautiful art can only be produced by people who have beautiful things about them, and leisure to look at them; and unless you provide some elements of beauty for your workmen to be surrounded by, you will find that no elements of beauty can be invented by them.

I was struck forcibly by the bearing of this great fact upon our modern efforts at ornamentation in an afternoon walk, last week, in the suburbs of one of our large manufacturing towns. I was thinking of the difference in the effect upon the designer's mind, between the scene which I then came upon, and the scene which would have presented itself to the eyes of any designer of the Middle Ages, when he left his workshop. Just outside the town I came upon an old English cottage, or mansion, I hardly know which to call it, set close under the hill, and beside the river, perhaps built somewhere in the Charleses' times,[2] with mullioned windows and a low arched porch; round which, in the little triangular garden, one can imagine the family as they used to sit in old summer times, the ripple of the river heard faintly through the sweetbriar hedge, and the sheep on the far-off wolds shining in the evening sunlight. There, uninhabited for many and many a year, it had been left in unregarded havoc of ruin; the garden-gate still swung loose to its latch; the garden, blighted utterly into a field of ashes, not even a weed taking root there; the roof torn into shapeless rents; the shutters hanging about the windows in rags of rotten wood; before its gate, the stream which had gladdened it now soaking slowly by, black as ebony and thick with curdling scum; the bank above it trodden into unctuous, sooty slime: far in front of it, between it and the old hills, the furnaces of the city foaming forth perpetual plague of sulphurous darkness; the volumes of their storm clouds coiling low over a waste of grassless fields, fenced from each other, not by hedges, but by slabs of square stone, like gravestones, riveted together with iron.

That was your scene for the designer's contemplation in his afternoon walk at Rochdale. Now fancy what was the scene which presented itself, in his afternoon walk, to a designer of the Gothic school of Pisa—Nino Pisano,[3] or any of his men.

On each side of a bright river he saw rise a line of brighter palaces, arched and pillared, and inlaid with deep red porphyry, and with serpentine; along the quays before their gates were riding troops of knights, noble in face and form, dazzling in crest and shield; horse and man one labyrinth of quaint colour and gleaming light—the purple, and silver, and scarlet fringes flowing over the strong limbs and clashing mail, like sea-waves over rocks at sunset. Opening on each side from the river were gardens, courts, and cloisters; long successions of white pillars among wreaths of vine; leaping of fountains through buds of pomegranate and orange: and still along the garden paths, and under and through the crimson of the pomegranate shadows, moving slowly, groups of the fairest women that Italy ever saw—fairest, because purest and thoughtfullest; trained in all high knowledge, as in all courteous art—in dance, in song, in sweet wit, in lofty learning, in loftier courage, in loftiest love—able alike to cheer, to enchant, or save, the souls of men. Above all this scenery of perfect human life, rose dome and bell-tower, burning with white alabaster and gold: beyond dome and bell-tower the slopes of mighty hills, hoary with olive; far in the north, above a purple sea of peaks of solemn Apennine, the clear, sharp-cloven Carrara mountains sent up their steadfast flames of marble summit into amber sky; the great sea itself, scorching with expanse of light, stretching from their feet to the Gorgonian isles; and over all these, ever present, near or far—seen through the leaves of vine, or imaged with all its march of clouds in the Arno's stream, or set with its depth of blue close against the golden hair and burning cheek of lady and knight,—that untroubled and sacred sky, which was to all men, in those days of innocent faith, indeed the unquestioned abode of spirits, as the earth was of men; and which opened straight through its gates of cloud and veils of dew into the awfulness of the eternal world;—a heaven in which every cloud that passed was literally the chariot of an angel, and every ray of its Evening and Morning streamed from the throne of God.

What think you of that for a school of design?

---

2. In the 17th century.

3. Either Nicola Pisano (1220–1284) or his son Giovanni, Italian sculptors.

I do not bring this contrast before you as a ground of hopelessness in our task; neither do I look for any possible renovation of the Republic of Pisa, at Bradford, in the nineteenth century; but I put it before you in order that you may be aware precisely of the kind of difficulty you have to meet, and may then consider with yourselves how far you can meet it. To men surrounded by the depressing and monotonous circumstances of English manufacturing life, depend upon it, design is simply impossible. This is the most distinct of all the experiences I have had in dealing with the modern workman. He is intelligent and ingenious in the highest degree—subtle in touch and keen in sight: but he is, generally speaking, wholly destitute of designing power. And if you want to give him the power, you must give him the materials, and put him in the circumstances for it. Design is not the offspring of idle fancy: it is the studied result of accumulative observation and delightful habit. Without observation and experience, no design—without peace and pleasurableness in occupation, no design—and all the lecturings, and teachings, and prizes, and principles of art, in the world, are of no use, so long as you don't surround your men with happy influences and beautiful things. It is impossible for them to have right ideas about colour, unless they see the lovely colours of nature unspoiled; impossible for them to supply beautiful incident and action in their ornament, unless they see beautiful incident and action in the world about them. Inform their minds, refine their habits, and you form and refine their designs; but keep them illiterate, uncomfortable, and in the midst of unbeautiful things, and whatever they do will still be spurious, vulgar, and valueless.

I repeat, that I do not ask you nor wish you to build a new Pisa for them. We don't want either the life or the decorations of the thirteenth century back again; and the circumstances with which you must surround your workmen are those simply of happy modern English life, because the designs you have now to ask for from your workmen are such as will make modern English life beautiful. All that gorgeousness of the Middle Ages, beautiful as it sounds in description, noble as in many respects it was in reality, had, nevertheless, for foundation and for end, nothing but the pride of life—the pride of the so-called superior classes; a pride which supported itself by violence and robbery, and led in the end to the destruction both of the arts themselves and the States in which they flourished.

The great lesson of history is, that all the fine arts hitherto—having been supported by the selfish power of the noblesse, and never having extended their range to the comfort or the relief of the mass of the people—the arts, I say, thus practised, and thus matured, have only accelerated the ruin of the States they adorned; and at the moment when, in any kingdom, you point to the triumphs of its greatest artists, you point also to the determined hour of the kingdom's decline. The names of great painters are like passing bells: in the name of Velasquez, you hear sounded the fall of Spain; in the name of Titian, that of Venice; in the name of Leonardo, that of Milan; in the name of Raphael, that of Rome. And there is profound justice in this; for in proportion to the nobleness of the power is the guilt of its use for purposes vain or vile; and hitherto the greater the art, the more surely has it been used, and used solely, for the decoration of pride, or the provoking of sensuality. Another course lies open to us. We may abandon the hope—or if you like the words better—we may disdain the temptation, of the pomp and grace of Italy in her youth. For us there can be no more the throne of marble—for us no more the vault of gold—but for us there is the loftier and lovelier privilege of bringing the power and charm of art within the reach of the humble and the poor; and as the magnificence of past ages failed by its narrowness and its pride, ours may prevail and continue, by its universality and its lowliness. * * *

* * * And you must remember always that your business, as manufacturers, is to form the market, as much as to supply it. If, in shortsighted and reckless eagerness for wealth, you catch at every humour of the populace as it shapes itself into momentary demand—if, in jealous rivalry with neighbouring States, or with other producers, you try to attract attention by singularities, novelties, and gaudinesses—to make every design an advertisement, and pilfer every idea of a successful neighbour's, that you may insidiously imitate it, or pompously eclipse—no good design will ever be possible to you, or perceived by you. You may, by accident, snatch the market; or, by energy, command it; you may obtain the confidence of the public, and cause the ruin of opponent houses; or you may, with equal justice of fortune, be ruined by them. But whatever happens to you, this, at least, is certain, that the whole of your life will have been spent in corrupting public taste and encouraging public extravagance. Every preference you have won by gaudiness must have been based on the purchaser's vanity; every demand you have created by novelty has fostered in the consumer a habit of discontent; and when you retire into inactive life, you may, as a subject of consolation for your declining years, reflect that precisely according to the extent of your past operations, your life has been successful in retarding the arts, tarnishing the virtues, and confusing the manners of your country.

1859

The Storm-Cloud of the Nineteenth Century
Lecture I[1]

Let me first assure my audience that I have no *arrière pensée*[2] in the title chosen for this lecture. I might, indeed, have meant, and it would have been only too like me to mean, any number of things by such a title;—but, to-night, I mean simply what I have said, and propose to bring to your notice a series of cloud phenomena, which, so far as I can weigh existing evidence, are peculiar to our own times; yet which have not hitherto received any special notice or description from meteorologists.

So far as the existing evidence, I say, of former literature can be interpreted, the storm-cloud—or more accurately plague-cloud, for it is not always stormy—which I am about to describe to you, never was seen but by now living, or *lately* living eyes. It is not yet twenty years that this—I may well call it, wonderful—cloud has been, in its essence, recognizable. There is no description of it, so far as I have read, by any ancient observer. Neither Homer nor Virgil, neither Aristophanes nor Horace, acknowledge any such clouds among those compelled by Jove. Chaucer has no word of

1. Given at the London Institution, 4 February 1884, followed by a second and final lecture a week later. The impassioned, almost hypersensitive lectures mix pioneering environmentalism, based on careful observation and record-keeping, with Ruskin's biblically inflected sense of dread; the Storm-Cloud contains a grim moral message for all beneath its shadow. Over the course of his lifetime Ruskin's immensely acute vision registered climactic changes as finely as any scientific instrument, but he could not and would not separate any observation from moral considerations—and human failings. In the second lecture, Ruskin remarked that "had the weather when I was young been such as it is now, no book such as *Modern Painters* ever would... have been written," since that work was founded on "the beauty and blessing of nature," whereas now "month by month the darkness gains upon the day, and the ashes of the Antipodes glare through the night." The glaring ashes that troubled Ruskin were those of Krakatau, whose eruption in Java in 1883 also produced the horrifying reddish sky recorded in Edvard Munch's painting *The Scream*.
2. Ulterior motive or hidden meaning.

them, nor Dante; Milton none, nor Thomson.[3] In modern times, Scott, Wordsworth, and Byron are alike unconscious of them; and the most-observant and descriptive of scientific men, De Saussure[4] is utterly silent concerning them. Taking up the traditions of air from the year before Scott's death, I am able, by my own constant and close observation, to certify you that in the forty following years (1831 to 1871 approximately—for the phenomena in question came on gradually)—no such clouds as these are, and are now often for months without intermission, were ever seen in the skies of England, France, or Italy.

In those old days, when weather was fine, it was luxuriously fine; when it was bad—it was often abominably bad, but it had its fit of temper and was done with it—it didn't sulk for three months without letting you see the sun,—nor send you one cyclone inside out, every Saturday afternoon, and another outside in, every Monday morning.

In fine weather the sky was either blue or clear in its light; the clouds, either white or golden, adding to, not abating, the lustre of the sky. In wet weather, there were two different species of clouds,—those of beneficent rain, which for distinction's sake I will call the non-electric rain-cloud, and those of storm, usually charged highly with electricity. The beneficent rain-cloud was indeed often extremely dull and grey for days together, but gracious nevertheless, felt to be doing good, and often to be delightful after drought; capable also of the most exquisite colouring, under certain conditions; and continually traversed in clearing by the rainbow:—and, secondly, the storm-cloud, always majestic, often dazzlingly beautiful, and felt also to be beneficent in its own way, affecting the mass of the air with vital agitation, and purging it from the impurity of all morbific elements.

In the entire system of the Firmament, thus seen and understood, there appeared to be, to all the thinkers of those ages, the incontrovertible and unmistakable evidence of a Divine Power in creation, which had fitted, as the air for human breath, so the clouds for human sight and nourishment;—the Father who was in heaven feeding day by day the souls of His children with marvels, and satisfying them with bread, and so filling their hearts with food and gladness. * * *

The first time I recognized the clouds brought by the plague-wind as distinct in character was in walking back from Oxford, after a hard day's work, to Abingdon,[5] in the early spring of 1871: it would take too long to give you any account this evening of the particulars which drew my attention to them; but during the following months I had too frequent opportunities of verifying my first thoughts of them, and on the first of July in that year wrote the description of them which begins the *Fors Clavigera*[6] of August, thus:—

"It is the first of July, and I sit down to write by the dismallest light that ever yet I wrote by; namely, the light of this midsummer morning, in mid-England (Matlock, Derbyshire),[7] in the year 1871.

"For the sky is covered with grey cloud;—not rain-cloud, but a dry black veil, which no ray of sunshine can pierce; partly diffused in mist, feeble mist, enough to make distant

---

3. James Thomson (1700–1748), whose poem *The Seasons* (1726–1730), contains many descriptions of British weather.
4. The geologist and naturalist Horace Bénédict de Saussure, author of *Voyages in the Alps* (1779–1796), the third man ever to scale Mont Blanc.
5. Market town about six miles south of Oxford.

6. Ruskin's series of open letters to British workingmen, published irregularly from 1871 until 1884. The Latin words mean "Fate, the club-bearer," and are taken from Horace's *Odes* 1. 35.
7. A scenic area in north-central England, much developed during the Industrial Revolution due to its abundant water power.

objects unintelligible, yet without any substance, or wreathing, or colour of its own. And everywhere the leaves of the trees are shaking fitfully, as they do before a thunderstorm; only not violently, but enough to show the passing to and fro of a strange, bitter, blighting wind. Dismal enough, had it been the first morning of its kind that summer had sent. But during all this spring, in London, and at Oxford, through meagre March, through changelessly sullen April, through despondent May, and darkened June, morning after morning has come grey-shrouded thus.

"And it is a new thing to me, and a very dreadful one. I am fifty years old, and more; and since I was five, have gleaned the best hours of my life in the sun of spring and summer mornings; and I never saw such as these, till now.

"And the scientific men are busy as ants, examining the sun and the moon, and the seven stars, and can tell me all about *them*, I believe, by this time; and how they move, and what they are made of.

"And I do not care, for my part, two copper spangles how they move, nor what they are made of. I can't move them any other way than they go, nor make them of anything else, better than they are made. But I would care much and give much, if I could be told where this bitter wind comes from, and what *it* is made of.

"For, perhaps, with forethought, and fine laboratory science, one might make it of something else.

"It looks partly as if it were made of poisonous smoke; very possibly it may be: there are at least two hundred furnace chimneys in a square of two miles on every side of me. But mere smoke would not blow to and fro in that wild way. It looks more to me as if it were made of dead men's souls—such of them as are not gone yet where they have to go, and may be flitting hither and thither, doubting, themselves, of the fittest place for them.

"You know, if there are such things as souls, and if ever any of them haunt places where they have been hurt, there must be many above us, just now, displeased enough!"

The last sentence refers of course to the battles of the Franco-German campaign[8] which was especially horrible to me, in its digging, as the Germans should have known, a moat flooded with waters of death between the two nations for a century to come.

Since that Midsummer day, my attention, however otherwise occupied, has never relaxed in its record of the phenomena characteristic of the plague-wind; and I now define for you, as briefly as possible, the essential signs of it.

(1.) It is a wind of darkness,—all the former conditions of tormenting winds, whether from the north or east, were more or less capable of co-existing with sunlight, and often with steady and bright sunlight; but whenever, and wherever the plague-wind blows, be it but for ten minutes, the sky is darkened instantly.

(2.) It is a malignant *quality* of wind, unconnected with any one quarter of the compass; it blows indifferently from all, attaching its own bitterness and malice to the worst characters of the proper winds of each quarter. It will blow either with drenching rain, or dry rage, from the south,—with ruinous blasts from the west,— with bitterest chills from the north,—and with venomous blight from the east.

Its own favourite quarter, however, is the south-west, so that it is distinguished in its malignity equally from the Bise of Provence, which is a north wind always, and from our own old friend, the east.

(3.) It always blows *tremulously,* making the leaves of the trees shudder as if they were all aspens, but with a peculiar fitfulness which gives them—and I watch them

8. The Franco-Prussian war of 1870–1871, in which nearly 200,000 persons died.

this moment as I write—an expression of anger as well as of fear and distress. You may see the kind of quivering, and hear the ominous whimpering, in the gusts that precede a great thunderstorm; but plague-wind is more panic-struck, and feverish; and its sound is a hiss instead of a wail.

When I was last at Avallon, in South France, I went to see *Faust* played at the little country theatre: it was done with scarcely any means of pictorial effect, except a few old curtains, and a blue light or two. But the night on the Brocken[9] was nevertheless extremely appalling to me,—a strange ghastliness being obtained in some of the witch scenes merely by fine management of gesture and drapery; and in the phantom scenes, by the half-palsied, half-furious, faltering or fluttering past of phantoms stumbling as into graves; as if of not only soulless, but senseless, Dead, moving with the very action, the rage, the decrepitude, and the trembling of the plague-wind.

(4.) Not only tremulous at every moment, it is also *intermittent* with a rapidity quite unexampled in former weather. There are, indeed, days—and weeks, on which it blows without cessation, and is as inevitable as the Gulf Stream; but also there are days when it is contending with healthy weather, and on such days it will remit for half an hour, and the sun will begin to show itself, and then the wind will come back and cover the whole sky with clouds in ten minutes; and so on, every half-hour, through the whole day; so that it is often impossible to go on with any kind of drawing in colour, the light being never for two seconds the same from morning till evening.

(5.) It degrades, while it intensifies, ordinary storm; but before I read you any description of its efforts in this kind, I must correct an impression which has got abroad through the papers, that I speak as if the plague-wind blew now always, and there were no more any natural weather. On the contrary, the winter of 1878–9 was one of the most healthy and lovely I ever saw ice in;–Coniston lake[1] shone under the calm clear frost in one marble field, as strong as the floor of Milan Cathedral, half a mile across and four miles down; and the first entries in my diary which I read you shall be from the 22nd to 26th June, 1876, of perfectly lovely and natural weather: * * *

"Monday, 26th June, 1876.

Yesterday an entirely perfect summer light on the Old Man; Lancaster Bay all clear; Ingleborough and the great Pennine fault as on a map.[2] Divine beauty of western colour on thyme and rose,—then twilight of clearest *warm* amber far into night, of *pale* amber all night long; hills dark-clear against it.

"And so it continued, only growing more intense in blue and sunlight, all day. After breakfast, I came in from the well under strawberry bed, to say I had never seen anything like it, so pure or intense, in Italy; and so it went glowing on, cloudless, with soft north wind, all day."

"16th July.

"The sunset almost too bright *through the blinds* for me to read Humboldt[3] at tea by, finally, new moon like a lime-light, reflected on breeze-struck water; traces, across dark calm, of reflected hills."

---

9. In Goethe's drama *Faust* (1808), witches meet at night on the high mountain of Brocken in central Germany.
1. Coniston, in the Lake District, is the site of Ruskin's home, Brantwood.
2. Sites in the Lake District.

3. Alexander von Humboldt (1769–1859), German geologist and naturalist described by Darwin as "the greatest scientific traveler who ever lived," a founder of modern meteorology.

These extracts are, I hope, enough to guard you against the absurdity of supposing that it only means that I am myself soured, or doting, in my old age, and always in an ill humour. Depend upon it, when old men are worth anything, they are better-humoured than young ones; and have learned to see what good there is, and pleasantness, in the world they are likely so soon to have orders to quit.

Now then—take the following sequences of accurate description of thunderstorm, *with* plague-wind. * * *

"*Brantwood, 13th August*, 1879.

"The most terrific and horrible thunderstorm, this morning, I ever remember. It waked me at six, or a little before—then rolling incessantly, like railway luggage trains, quite ghastly in its mockery of them—the air one loathsome mass of sultry and foul fog, like smoke; scarcely raining at all, but increasing to heavier rollings, with flashes quivering vaguely through all the air, and at last terrific double streams of reddish-violent fire, not forked or zigzag, but rippled rivulets—two at the same instant some twenty to thirty degrees apart, and lasting on the eye at least half a second, with grand artillery-peals following; not rattling crashes, or irregular cracklings, but delivered volleys. It lasted an hour, then passed off, clearing a little, without rain to speak of,—not a glimpse of blue,—and now, half-past seven, seems settling down again into Manchester devil's darkness.

"Quarter to eight, morning.—Thunder returned, all the air collapsed into one black fog, the hills invisible, and scarcely visible the opposite shore; heavy rain in short fits, and frequent though less formidable, flashes, and shorter thunder. While I have written this sentence the cloud has again dissolved itself, like a nasty solution in a bottle, with miraculous and unnatural rapidity, and the hills are in sight again; a double-forked flash—rippled, I mean, like the others—starts into its frightful ladder of light between me and Wetherlam, as I raise my eyes. All black above, a rugged spray cloud on the Eaglet. (The 'Eaglet' is my own name for the bold and elevated crag to the west of the little lake above Coniston mines. It had no name among the country people, and is one of the most conspicuous features of the mountain chain, as seen from Brantwood.)

"Half-past eight.—Three times light and three times dark since last I wrote, and the darkness seeming each time as it settles more loathsome, at last stopping my reading in mere blindness. One lurid gleam of white cumulus in upper lead-blue sky, seen for half a minute through the sulphurous chimney-pot vomit of blackguardly cloud beneath, where its rags were thinnest."

"*Thursday, 22nd Feb.* 1883.

"Yesterday a fearfully dark mist all afternoon, with steady, south plague-wind of the bitterest, nastiest, poisonous blight, and fretful flutter. I could scarcely stay in the wood for the horror of it. To-day, really rather bright blue, and bright semi-cumuli, with the frantic Old Man[4] blowing sheaves of lancets and chisels across the lake—not in strength enough, or whirl enough, to raise it in spray, but tracing every squall's outline in black on the silver grey waves, and whistling meanly, and as if on a flute made of a file."

---

4. An 800-meter tall crag overlooking Coniston Water.

"Sunday, 17th August, 1879.

"Raining in foul drizzle, slow and steady; sky pitchdark, and I just get a little light by sitting in the bow-window; diabolic clouds over everything: and looking over my kitchen garden yesterday, I found it one miserable mass of weeds gone to seed, the roses in the higher garden putrefied into brown sponges, feeling like dead snails; and the half-ripe strawberries all rotten at the stalks."

(6.) And now I come to the most important sign of the plague-wind and the plague-cloud: that in bringing on their peculiar darkness, they *blanch* the sun instead of reddening it. And here I must note briefly to you the uselessness of observation by instruments, or machines, instead of eyes. In the first year when I had begun to notice the specialty of the plague-wind, I went of course to the Oxford observatory to consult its registrars. They have their anemometer always on the twirl, and can tell you the force, or at least the pace, of a gale, by day or night. But the anemometer can only record for you how often it has been driven round, not at all whether it went round *steadily*, or went round *trembling*. And on that point depends the entire question whether it is a plague breeze or a healthy one: and what's the use of telling you whether the wind's strong or not, when it can't tell you whether it's a strong medicine, or a strong poison? * * *

Blanched Sun,—blighted grass—blinded man.—If, in conclusion, you ask me for any conceivable cause or meaning of these things—I can tell you none, according to your modern beliefs; but I can tell you what meaning it would have borne to the men of old time. Remember, for the last twenty years, England, and all foreign nations, either tempting her, or following her, have blasphemed the name of God deliberately and openly; and have done iniquity by proclamation, every man doing as much injustice to his brother as it is in his power to do. Of states in such moral gloom every seer of old predicted the physical gloom, saying, "The light shall be darkened in the heavens thereof, and the stars shall withdraw their shining."[5] All Greek, all Christian, all Jewish prophecy insists on the same truth through a thousand myths; but of all the chief, to former thought, was the fable of the Jewish warrior and prophet, for whom the sun hasted not to go down,[6] with which I leave you to compare at leisure the physical result of your own wars and prophecies, as declared by your own elect journal not fourteen days ago,—that the Empire of England, on which formerly the sun never set, has become one on which he never rises.[7]

What is best to be done, do you ask me? The answer is plain. Whether you can affect the signs of the sky or not, you *can* the signs of the times. Whether you can bring the *sun* back or not, you can assuredly bring back your own cheerfulness, and your own honesty. You may not be able to say to the winds, "Peace; be still," but you can cease from the insolence of your own lips, and the troubling of your own passions. And all *that* it would be extremely well to do, even though the day *were* coming when the sun should be as darkness, and the moon as blood. But, the paths of rectitude and piety once regained, who shall say that the promise of old time would not be found to hold for us also?—"Bring ye all the tithes into my storehouse, and prove me now herewith, saith the Lord God, if I will not open you the windows of heaven, and pour you out a blessing, that there shall not be room enough to receive it."[8]

1884

5. A biblical citation combining Isaiah 5.30 and Joel 3.15.
6. In the Bible the Lord kept the sun from setting so that Joshua could win a battle; see Joshua 10.12–14.

7. The year 1883 ended with a totally sunless week in London, according to the *Pall Mall Gazette* (2 January 1884).
8. See Malachi 3.10.

from **Praeterita**[1]
Preface

I have written these sketches of effort and incident in former years for my friends; and for those of the public who have been pleased by my books.

I have written them therefore, frankly, garrulously, and at ease; speaking, of what it gives me joy to remember, at any length I like—sometimes very carefully of what I think it may be useful for others to know; and passing in total silence things which I have no pleasure in reviewing, and which the reader would find no help in the account of. My described life has thus become more amusing than I expected to myself, as I summoned its long past scenes for present scrutiny:—its main methods of study, and principles of work, I feel justified in commending to other students; and very certainly any habitual readers of my books will understand them better, for having knowledge as complete as I can give them of the personal character which, without endeavour to conceal, I yet have never taken pains to display, and even, now and then, felt some freakish pleasure in exposing to the chance of misinterpretation.

I write these few prefatory words on my father's birthday, in what was once my nursery in his old house,—to which he brought my mother and me, sixty-two years since, I being then four years old. What would otherwise in the following pages have been little more than an old man's recreation in gathering visionary flowers in fields of youth, has taken, as I wrote, the nobler aspect of a dutiful offering at the grave of parents who trained my childhood to all the good it could attain, and whose memory makes declining life cheerful in the hope of being soon again with them.

HERNE HILL, 10*th May*, 1885.

from *The Springs of Wandel*[1]

I am, and my father was before me, a violent Tory of the old school;—Walter Scott's school, that is to say, and Homer's. I name these two out of the numberless great Tory writers, because they were my own two masters. I had Walter Scott's novels, and the *Iliad* (Pope's translation), for constant reading when I was a child, on week-days: on Sunday, their effect was tempered by *Robinson Crusoe* and the *Pilgrim's Progress*; my mother having it deeply in her heart to make an evangelical clergyman of me. Fortunately, I had an aunt more evangelical than my mother; and my aunt gave me cold mutton for Sunday's dinner, which—as I much preferred it hot—greatly diminished the influence of the *Pilgrim's Progress*; and the end of the matter was, that I got all the noble imaginative teaching of Defoe and Bunyan, and yet—am not an evangelical clergyman.

I had, however, still better teaching than theirs, and that compulsorily, and every day of the week.

Walter Scott and Pope's Homer were reading of my own election, and my mother forced me, by steady daily toil, to learn long chapters of the Bible by heart; as well as to read it every syllable through, aloud, hard names and all, from Genesis to the Apocalypse, about once a year: and to that discipline—patient, accurate, and resolute—I owe, not only a knowledge of the book, which I find occasionally serviceable, but much of my general power of taking pains, and the best part of my taste in literature. * * *

---

1. The title of Ruskin's autobiography means "Of things past." *Praeterita* was written when Ruskin was an old man enduring ever-more-frequent bouts of madness. Marcel Proust admired the book so much that he claimed to know it by heart.

1. Wandel was a river near Croydon that Ruskin loved.

The aunt who gave me cold mutton on Sundays was my father's sister: she lived at Bridge-end, in the town of Perth, and had a garden full of gooseberry-bushes, sloping down to the Tay, with a door opening to the water, which ran past it, clear-brown over the pebbles three or four feet deep; swift-eddying,—an infinite thing for a child to look down into.

My father began business as a wine-merchant, with no capital, and a considerable amount of debts bequeathed him by my grandfather. He accepted the bequest, and paid them all before he began to lay by anything for himself,—for which his best friends called him a fool, and I, without expressing any opinion as to his wisdom, which I knew in such matters to be at least equal to mine, have written on the granite slab over his grave that he was "an entirely honest merchant." As days went on he was able to take a house in Hunter Street, Brunswick Square, No. 54, (the windows of it, fortunately for me, commanded a view of a marvellous iron post, out of which the water-carts were filled through beautiful little trap-doors, by pipes like boa-constrictors; and I was never weary of contemplating that mystery, and the delicious dripping consequent); and as years went on, and I came to be four or five years old, he could command a postchaise and pair for two months in the summer, by help of which, with my mother and me, he went the round of his country customers. * * *

To my farther great benefit, as I grew older, I thus saw nearly all the noblemen's houses in England; in reverent and healthy delight of uncovetous admiration,—perceiving, as soon as I could perceive any political truth at all, that it was probably much happier to live in a small house, and have Warwick Castle to be astonished at, than to live in Warwick Castle and have nothing to be astonished at; but that, at all events, it would not make Brunswick Square in the least more pleasantly habitable, to pull Warwick Castle down. And at this day, though I have kind invitations enough to visit America, I could not, even for a couple of months, live in a country so miserable as to possess no castles. * * *

* * * My mother's general principles of first treatment were, to guard me with steady watchfulness from all avoidable pain or danger; and, for the rest, to let me amuse myself as I liked, provided I was neither fretful nor troublesome. But the law was, that I should find my own amusement. No toys of any kind were at first allowed;—and the pity of my Croydon aunt for my monastic poverty in this respect was boundless. On one of my birthdays, thinking to overcome my mother's resolution by splendour of temptation, she bought the most radiant Punch and Judy[2] she could find in all the Soho bazaar—as big as a real Punch and Judy, all dressed in scarlet and gold, and that would dance, tied to the leg of a chair. I must have been greatly impressed, for I remember well the look of the two figures, as my aunt herself exhibited their virtues. My mother was obliged to accept them; but afterwards quietly told me it was not right that I should have them; and I never saw them again.

Nor did I painfully wish, what I was never permitted for an instant to hope, or even imagine, the possession of such things as one saw in toy-shops. I had a bunch of keys to play with, as long as I was capable only of pleasure in what glittered and jingled; as I grew older, I had a cart, and a ball; and when I was five or six years old, two boxes of well-cut wooden bricks. With these modest, but, I still think, entirely sufficient possessions, and being always summarily whipped if I cried, did not do as I was bid, or tumbled on the stairs, I soon attained serene and secure methods of life and

---

2. Punch and Judy were puppets whose antics had delighted English audiences since the mid-17th century.

motion; and could pass my days contentedly in tracing the squares and comparing the colours of my carpet;—examining the knots in the wood of the floor, or counting the bricks in the opposite houses; with rapturous intervals of excitement during the filling of the water-cart, through its leathern pipe, from the dripping iron post at the pavement edge; or the still more admirable proceedings of the turncock, when he turned and turned till a fountain sprang up in the middle of the street. But the carpet, and what patterns I could find in bed-covers, dresses, or wall-papers to be examined, were my chief resources. * * *

My mother had, as she afterwards told me, solemnly "devoted me to God" before I was born; in imitation of Hannah.[3]

Very good women are remarkably apt to make away with their children prematurely, in this manner. * * *

"Devoting me to God," meant, as far as my mother knew herself what she meant, that she would try to send me to college, and make a clergyman of me: and I was accordingly bred for "the Church." My father, who—rest be to his soul—had the exceedingly bad habit of yielding to my mother in large things and taking his own way in little ones, allowed me, without saying a word, to be thus withdrawn from the sherry trade as an unclean thing; not without some pardonable participation in my mother's ultimate views for me. For, many and many a year afterwards, I remember, while he was speaking to one of our artist friends, who admired Raphael, and greatly regretted my endeavours to interfere with that popular taste,—while my father and he were condoling with each other on my having been impudent enough to think I could tell the public about Turner and Raphael,—instead of contenting myself, as I ought, with explaining the way of their souls' salvation to them—and what an amiable clergyman was lost in me,—"Yes," said my father, with tears in his eyes—(true and tender tears, as ever father shed,) "he would have been a Bishop."

Luckily for me, my mother, under these distinct impressions of her own duty, and with such latent hopes of my future eminence, took me very early to church;—where, in spite of my quiet habits, and my mother's golden vinaigrette, always indulged to me there, and there only, with its lid unclasped that I might see the wreathed open pattern above the sponge, I found the bottom of the pew so extremely dull a place to keep quiet in, (my best story-books being also taken away from me in the morning,) that, as I have somewhere said before, the horror of Sunday used even to cast its prescient gloom as far back in the week as Friday—and all the glory of Monday, with church seven days removed again, was no equivalent for it.

Notwithstanding, I arrived at some abstract in my own mind of the Rev. Mr. Howell's sermons; and occasionally, in imitation of him, preached a sermon at home over the red sofa cushions;—this performance being always called for by my mother's dearest friends, as the great accomplishment of my childhood. The sermon was, I believe, some eleven words long; very exemplary, it seems to me, in that respect—and I still think must have been the purest gospel, for I know it began with, "People, be good."

from *Herne-Hill Almond Blossoms*

And it is perhaps already time to mark what advantage and mischief, by the chances of life up to seven years old, had been irrevocably determined for me.

---

3. Hannah, the mother of the prophet Samuel, dedicates him to the Lord in his infancy (1 Samuel 1.22).

I will first count my blessings (as a not unwise friend once recommended me to do, continually; whereas I have a bad trick of always numbering the thorns in my fingers and not the bones in them).

And for best and truest beginning of all blessings, I had been taught the perfect meaning of Peace, in thought, act, and word.

I never had heard my father's or mother's voice once raised in any question with each other; nor seen an angry, or even slightly hurt or offended, glance in the eyes of either. I had never heard a servant scolded; nor even suddenly, passionately, or in any severe manner, blamed. I had never seen a moment's trouble or disorder in any household matter; nor anything whatever either done in a hurry, or undone in due time. I had no conception of such a feeling as anxiety; my father's occasional vexation in the afternoons, when he had only got an order for twelve butts after expecting one for fifteen, as I have just stated, was never manifested to *me*; and itself related only to the question whether his name would be a step higher or lower in the year's list of sherry exporters; for he never spent more than half his income, and therefore found himself little incommoded by occasional variations in the total of it. I had never done any wrong that I knew of—beyond occasionally delaying the commitment to heart of some improving sentence, that I might watch a wasp on the window pane, or a bird in the cherry tree; and I had never seen any grief.

Next to this quite priceless gift of Peace, I had received the perfect understanding of the natures of Obedience and Faith. I obeyed word, or lifted finger, of father or mother, simply as a ship her helm; not only without idea of resistance, but receiving the direction as a part of my own life and force, and helpful law, as necessary to me in every moral action as the law of gravity in leaping. And my practice in Faith was soon complete: nothing was ever promised me that was not given; nothing ever threatened me that was not inflicted, and nothing ever told me that was not true.

Peace, obedience, faith; these three for chief good; next to these, the habit of fixed attention with both eyes and mind—on which I will not further enlarge at this moment, this being the main practical faculty of my life, causing Mazzini[1] to say of me, in conversation authentically reported, a year or two before his death, that I had "the most analytic mind in Europe." An opinion in which, so far as I am acquainted with Europe, I am myself entirely disposed to concur.

Lastly, an extreme perfection in palate and all other bodily senses, given by the utter prohibition of cake, wine, comfits, or, except in carefullest restriction, fruit; and by fine preparation of what food was given me. Such I esteem the main blessings of my childhood;—next, let me count the equally dominant calamities.

First, that I had nothing to love.

My parents were—in a sort—visible powers of nature to me, no more loved than the sun and the moon: only I should have been annoyed and puzzled if either of them had gone out; (how much, now, when both are darkened!)—still less did I love God; not that I had any quarrel with Him, or fear of Him; but simply found what people told me was His service, disagreeable; and what people told me was His book, not entertaining. I had no companions to quarrel with, neither; nobody to assist, and nobody to thank. Not a servant was ever allowed to do anything for me, but what it was their duty to do; and why should I have been grateful to the cook for cooking, or the gardener for gardening,—when the one dared not give me a baked potato without

1. Guiseppe Mazzini (1805–1872), Italian revolutionary leader.

asking leave, and the other would not let my ants' nests alone, because they made the walks untidy? The evil consequence of all this was not, however, what might perhaps have been expected, that I grew up selfish or unaffectionate; but that, when affection did come, it came with violence utterly rampant and unmanageable, at least by me, who never before had anything to manage.

For (second of chief calamities) I had nothing to endure. Danger or pain of any kind I knew not: my strength was never exercised, my patience never tried, and my courage never fortified. Not that I was ever afraid of anything,—either ghosts, thunder, or beasts; and one of the nearest approaches to insubordination which I was ever tempted into as a child, was in passionate effort to get leave to play with the lion's cubs in Wombwell's menagerie.

Thirdly. I was taught no precision nor etiquette of manners; it was enough if, in the little society we saw, I remained unobtrusive, and replied to a question without shyness: but the shyness came later, and increased as I grew conscious of the rudeness arising from the want of social discipline, and found it impossible to acquire, in advanced life, dexterity in any bodily exercise, skill in any pleasing accomplishment, or ease and tact in ordinary behaviour.

Lastly, and chief of evils. My judgment of right and wrong, and powers of independent action, were left entirely undeveloped; because the bridle and blinkers were never taken off me. Children should have their times of being off duty, like soldiers; and when once the obedience, if required, is certain, the little creature should be very early put for periods of practice in complete command of itself; set on the bare-backed horse of its own will, and left to break it by its own strength. But the ceaseless authority exercised over my youth left me, when cast out at last into the world, unable for some time to do more than drift with its vortices.

My present verdict, therefore, on the general tenor of my education at that time, must be, that it was at once too formal and too luxurious; leaving my character, at the most important moment for its construction, cramped indeed, but not disciplined; and only by protection innocent, instead of by practice virtuous. My mother saw this herself, and but too clearly, in later years; and whenever I did anything wrong, stupid, or hard-hearted,—(and I have done many things that were all three,)—always said, "It is because you were too much indulged."

from *Schaffhausen and Milan*[1]

The poor modern slaves and simpletons who let themselves be dragged like cattle, or felled timber, through the countries they imagine themselves visiting, can have no conception whatever of the complex joys, and ingenious hopes, connected with the choice and arrangement of the travelling carriage in old times. The mechanical questions first, of strength—easy rolling—steady and safe poise of persons and luggage; the general stateliness of effect to be obtained for the abashing of plebeian beholders; the cunning design and distribution of store-cellars under the seats, secret drawers under front windows, invisible pockets under padded lining, safe from dust, and accessible only by insidious slits, or necromantic valves like Aladdin's trap-door * * *

---

1. In this chapter Ruskin recalls the carriage trips through Europe that he took with his parents beginning in 1833. It was in Schaffhausen, Switzerland, that he had his first sight of the Alps, which were to be such an important feature of his lifework.

all this was an imaginary journey in itself, with every pleasure, and none of the discomfort, of practical travelling. * * *

* * * We never travelled on Sunday; my father and I nearly always went—as philosophers—to mass, in the morning, and my mother, in pure good-nature to us, (I scarcely ever saw in her a trace of feminine curiosity,) would join with us in some such profanity as a drive on the Corso, or the like, in the afternoon. But we all, even my father, liked a walk in the fields better, round an Alpine châlet village. * * *

The Black Forest! The fall of Schaffhausen! The chain of the Alps! within one's grasp for Sunday! What a Sunday, instead of customary Walworth and the Dulwich fields! My impassioned petition at last carried it, and the earliest morning saw us trotting over the bridge of boats to Kehl, and in the eastern light I well remember watching the line of the Black Forest hills enlarge and rise, as we crossed the plain of the Rhine. "Gates of the hills"; opening for me to a new life—to cease no more, except at the Gates of the Hills whence one returns not. * * *

The road got into more barren heights by the mid-day, the hills arduous; once or twice we had to wait for horses, and we were still twenty miles from Schaffhausen at sunset; it was past midnight when we reached her closed gates. The disturbed porter had the grace to open them—not quite wide enough; we carried away one of our lamps in collision with the slanting bar as we drove through the arch. How much happier the privilege of dreamily entering a mediaeval city, though with the loss of a lamp, than the free ingress of being jammed between a dray and a tramcar at a railroad station! * * *

We must have still spent some time in town-seeing, for it was drawing towards sunset, when we got up to some sort of garden promenade—west of the town, I believe; and high above the Rhine, so as to command the open country across it to the south and west. At which open country of low undulation, far into blue,—gazing as at one of our own distances from Malvern of Worcestershire, or Dorking of Kent,—suddenly—behold—beyond!

There was no thought in any of us for a moment of their being clouds. They were clear as crystal, sharp on the pure horizon sky, and already tinged with rose by the sinking sun. Infinitely beyond all that we had ever thought or dreamed,—the seen walls of lost Eden could not have been more beautiful to us; not more awful, round heaven, the walls of sacred Death.

It is not possible to imagine, in any time of the world, a more blessed entrance into life, for a child of such a temperament as mine. True, the temperament belonged to the age: a very few years,—within the hundred,—before that, no child could have been born to care for mountains, or for the men that lived among them, in that way. Till Rousseau's time, there had been no "sentimental" love of nature;[2] and till Scott's, no such apprehensive love of "all sorts and conditions of men," not in the soul merely, but in the flesh. St. Bernard of La Fontaine,[3] looking out to Mont Blanc with his child's eyes, sees above Mont Blanc the Madonna; St. Bernard of Talloires,[4] not the Lake of Annecy, but the dead between Martigny and Aosta. But for me, the Alps and their people were alike beautiful in their snow, and their humanity; and I wanted, neither for them nor myself, sight of any thrones in heaven but the rocks, or of any spirits in heaven but the clouds.

2. Jean-Jacques Rousseau (1712–1778), Swiss-born French writer and philosopher, often wrote of his yearning for a greater closeness to nature.
3. Bernard of Clairvaux (c. 1090–1153), Cistercian monk and abbot.
4. Bernard of Aosta (d. 1081), priest known for the care he took of Alpine travelers; the patron saint of mountain climbers.

* * * I went down that evening from the garden-terrace of Schaffhausen with my destiny fixed in all of it that was to be sacred and useful. To that terrace, and the shore of the Lake of Geneva, my heart and faith return to this day, in every impulse that is yet nobly alive in them, and every thought that has in it help or peace.

from *The Grande Chartreuse*[1]

This breaking down of my Puritan faith, being the matter probably most important to many readers of my later books, shall be traced in this chapter to the sorrowful end. * * *

* * * I had never cared for ornamental design until in 1850 or '51 I chanced, at a bookseller's in a back alley, on a little fourteenth-century Hours of the Virgin, not of refined work, but extremely rich, grotesque, and full of pure colour.

The new worlds which every leaf of this book opened to me, and the joy I had, counting their letters and unravelling their arabesques as if they had all been of beaten gold,—as many of them indeed were,—cannot be told. * * *

* * * For truly a well-illuminated missal is a fairy cathedral full of painted windows, bound together to carry in one's pocket, with the music and the blessing of all its prayers besides.

And then followed, of course, the discovery that all beautiful prayers were Catholic,—all wise interpretations of the Bible Catholic;—and every manner of Protestant written services whatsoever either insolently altered corruptions, or washed-out and ground-down rags and débris of the great Catholic collects, litanies, and songs of praise.

"But why did not you become a Catholic at once, then?"

It might as well be asked, Why did not I become a fire-worshipper? I *could* become nothing but what I was, or was growing into. I no more believed in the living Pope than I did in the living Khan of Tartary. * * *

The most stern practical precept of that doctrine still holding me,—it is curiously inbound with all the rest,—was the Sabbath keeping; the idea that one was not to seek one's own pleasure on Sunday, nor to do anything useful. Gradually, in honest Bible reading, I saw that Christ's first article of teaching was to unbind the yoke of the Sabbath. * * *

Nevertheless, the great passages in the Old Testament regarding its observance held their power over me, nor have ceased to do so; but the inveterate habit of being unhappy all Sunday did not in any way fulfil the order to call the Sabbath a delight.

I have registered the year 1858 as the next, after 1845, in which I had complete guidance of myself. Couttet[2] met me at Basle, and I went on to Rheinfelden with great joy, and stayed to draw town and bridges completely (two of the studies are engraved in *Modern Painters*).

I think it was the second Sunday there, and no English church. I had read the service with George,[3] and gone out afterwards alone for a walk up a lovely dingle on the Black Forest side of the Rhine, where every pretty cottage was inscribed, in fair old German characters, with the date of its building, the names of the married pair who had built it, and a prayer. * * *

---

1. Carthusian monastery in the French Alps that Ruskin and his father visited together. In this section Ruskin traces the steps leading to his "unconversion" in 1858 from the Evangelicalism of his parents.

2. An Alpine guide in the Chamonix valley below Mont Blanc; Ruskin passed many holidays with him.
3. Ruskin's valet.

Very happy in my Sunday walk, I gathered what wild flowers were in their first springing, and came home with a many-coloured cluster, in which the dark-purple orchis was chief. I had never examined its structure before, and by this afternoon sunlight did so with care; also it seemed to me wholly right to describe it as I examined; and to draw the outlines as I described, though with a dimly alarmed consciousness of its being a new fact in existence for me, that I should draw on Sunday. * * *

* * * In this state of mind, a fit took me of hunger for city life again, military bands, nicely-dressed people, and shops with something inside. And I emphasized Couttet's disapproval of the whole tour, by announcing to him suddenly that I was going, of all places in the world, to Turin! * * *

There, one Sunday morning, I made my way in the south suburb to a little chapel which, by a dusty roadside, gathered to its unobserved door the few sheep of the old Waldensian faith[4] who had wandered from their own pastures under Monte Viso into the worldly capital of Piedmont.

The assembled congregation numbered in all some three or four and twenty, of whom fifteen or sixteen were grey-haired women. Their solitary and clerkless preacher, a somewhat stunted figure in a plain black coat, with a cracked voice, after leading them through the languid forms of prayer which are all that in truth are possible to people whose present life is dull and its terrestrial future unchangeable, put his utmost zeal into a consolatory discourse on the wickedness of the wide world, more especially of the plain of Piedmont and city of Turin, and on the exclusive favour with God, enjoyed by the between nineteen and twenty-four elect members of his congregation, in the streets of Admah and Zeboim.[5]

Myself neither cheered nor greatly alarmed by this doctrine, I walked back into the condemned city, and up into the gallery where Paul Veronese's Solomon and the Queen of Sheba[6] glowed in full afternoon light. The gallery windows being open, there came in with the warm air, floating swells and falls of military music, from the courtyard before the palace, which seemed to me more devotional, in their perfect art, tune, and discipline, than anything I remembered of evangelical hymns. And as the perfect colour and sound gradually asserted their power on me, they seemed finally to fasten me in the old article of Jewish faith, that things done delightfully and rightly were always done by the help and in the Spirit of God.

Of course that hour's meditation in the gallery of Turin only concluded the courses of thought which had been leading me to such end through many years. There was no sudden conversion possible to me, either by preacher, picture, or dulcimer. But, that day, my evangelical beliefs were put away, to be debated of no more.

from *Joanna's Care*[1]

I draw back to my own home, twenty years ago, permitted to thank Heaven once more for the peace, and hope, and loveliness of it, and the Elysian walks with Joanie, and Paradisiacal with Rosie,[2] under the peach-blossom branches by the little glitter-

---

4. Italian Calvinist sect, based in Piedmont, a mountainous region near Turin.
5. Deuteronomy 29.23 refers to the Lord overthrowing "Sodom, and Gomorrah, Admah, and Zeboim."
6. This painting by Paolo Veronese (1528–1588), an Italian painter of lushly colored feasts and festivities, symbolized for Ruskin all that was missing in the narrow Evangelical outlook on art and life.
1. Ruskin's health was failing, and his mind growing con-

fused as he dictated this final chapter of *Praeterita* to his Scottish cousin Joan (or Joanna), who looked after him in his later years. She was married to Arthur Severn, son of the painter Joseph Severn.
2. Rose La Touche (1849–1875) was an Irish girl with whom Ruskin had fallen desperately in love when she was nine and he forty; he felt despair after her early death.

ing stream which I had paved with crystal for them. I had built behind the highest cluster of laurels a reservoir, from which, on sunny afternoons, I could let a quite rippling film of water run for a couple of hours down behind the hayfield, where the grass in spring still grew fresh and deep. There used to be always a corncrake or two in it. Twilight after twilight I have hunted that bird, and never once got glimpse of it: the voice was always at the other side of the field, or in the inscrutable air or earth. And the little stream had its falls, and pools, and imaginary lakes. Here and there it laid for itself lines of graceful sand; there and here it lost itself under beads of chalcedony. It wasn't the Liffey, nor the Nith, nor the Wandel; but the two girls were surely a little cruel to call it "The Gutter"! Happiest times, for all of us, that ever were to be; not but that Joanie and her Arthur are giddy enough, both of them yet, with their five little ones, but they have been sorely anxious about me, and I have been sorrowful enough for myself, since ever I lost sight of that peach-blossom avenue. "Eden-land" Rosie calls it sometimes in her letters. Whether its tiny river were of the waters of Abana, or Euphrates, or Thamesis, I know not, but they were sweeter to my thirst than the fountains of Trevi or Branda.[3]

How things bind and blend themselves together! The last time I saw the Fountain of Trevi, it was from Arthur's father's room—Joseph Severn's, where we both took Joanie to see him in 1872, and the old man made a sweet drawing of his pretty daughter-in-law, now in her schoolroom; he himself then eager in finishing his last picture of the Marriage in Cana,[4] which he had caused to take place under a vine trellis, and delighted himself by painting the crystal and ruby glittering of the changing rivulet of water out of the Greek vase, glowing into wine. Fonte Branda I last saw with Charles Norton,[5] under the same arches where Dante saw it. We drank of it together, and walked together that evening on the hills above, where the fireflies among the scented thickets shone fitfully in the still undarkened air. *How* they shone! moving like fine-broken starlight through the purple leaves. How they shone! through the sunset that faded into thunderous night as I entered Siena three days before, the white edges of the mountainous clouds still lighted from the west, and the openly golden sky calm behind the Gate of Siena's heart, with its still golden words, "Cor magis tibi Sena pandit,"[6] and the fireflies everywhere in sky and cloud rising and falling, mixed with the lightning, and more intense than the stars.

BRANTWOOD,
June 19th, 1889.

⊷ ⊠◈⊠ ⊶

Florence Nightingale
1820–1910

Revered as "the Lady of the Lamp," Florence Nightingale was in fact a high-powered administrator who reformed the British Army medical service and helped to found the profession of modern nursing. In 1854 she led a group of nurses to attend wounded soldiers in the Crimean

---

3. Fountains in Rome and Siena.
4. Scene of Christ's first miracle, in which he transforms water into wine. See John 1.1–11.
5. Charles Eliot Norton (1827–1908), American man of letters, and the first professor of art history at Harvard.

He and Ruskin met in 1855 and conducted an epistolary friendship for many years.
6. The inscription over the city gate reads: "More than her gates, Siena opens her heart to you."

War, where unsanitary conditions and colossal mismanagement had created a disaster. Her administrative genius saved countless lives, and she was acclaimed as a national heroine. For the rest of her life she was a legend, and thanks to her mythic reputation she was able to initiate widespread health reforms. Although her sister Parthe complained that Florence actually "was a shocking nurse," the sentimentalized image of the angel of mercy made her accomplishments more palatable to the Victorians.

She was reared in a wealthy family horrified by her desire to enter nursing and bitterly opposed to her plans to pursue such a disreputable and unladylike occupation. "It was as if I had wanted to be a kitchen-maid," she said. Indeed, they saw no need for her to seek any occupation at all. But from an early age, Nightingale rebelled against the social obligations and feminine pursuits—needlework, music, watercolors—with which a well-bred young lady was expected to fill her day. In her diary she wrote: "What am I that I am not in harmony with all this, that their life is not good enough for me? . . . A profession, a trade, a necessary occupation, something to fill & employ all my faculties, I have always felt essential to me. . . . Why, oh my God, cannot I be satisfied with the life that satisfies so many people?"

Nightingale was unusually well-educated for a woman, since her father taught his daughters classics, philosophy, science, and languages. Yet her parents initially refused her request to study mathematics with a tutor. Her mother lamented, "We are ducks who have hatched a wild swan." For many years her mother and sister used emotional blackmail to thwart her ambition for a useful vocation. At thirty-two she still had not broken free, and her frustrations found vent in an autobiographical essay, *Cassandra*, which vividly depicts her impatience with the conventional lives of women.

Although it was never published during her lifetime, *Cassandra* was privately circulated and immediately began to take its place in the literature of feminist protest. John Stuart Mill alluded to the essay in *The Subjection of Women*, and in her classic book about women writers, *A Room of One's Own* (1929), Virginia Woolf quoted Nightingale's anguished complaint, "women never have an half hour . . . that they can call their own." The critic Elaine Showalter calls *Cassandra* "a major text of English feminism, a link between Wollstonecraft and Woolf." Denouncing the enforced frivolity of women's lives, and insisting on privacy and time as the necessary conditions for creative work, Nightingale paved the way for later feminist thinkers.

Cassandra[1]

1

The voice of one crying in the *crowd*,
"Prepare ye the way of the Lord."[2]

One often comes to be thus wandering alone in the bitterness of life without. It might be that such an one might be tempted to seek an escape in hope of a more congenial sphere. Yet, perhaps, if prematurely we dismiss ourselves from this world, all may even have to be suffered through again—the premature birth may not contribute to the production of another being, which must be begun again from the beginning.

---

1. Cassandra was a Trojan princess to whom Apollo gave the gift of foretelling the future; when she refused his advances, he doomed her to have her prophecies ignored. Elaine Showalter notes: "The myth suggests that women who refuse sexuality and love are denied a voice, indeed can be driven mad by their society." Nightingale had refused an offer of marriage from Richard Monckton Milnes.

2. Cf. Isaiah 40.3: "The voice of him that crieth in the wilderness, Prepare ye the way of the Lord."

Such an one longs to replunge into the happy unconscious sleep of the rest of the race! they slumber in one another's arms—they are not yet awake. To them evil and suffering are not, for they are not conscious of evil. While one alone, awake and prematurely alive to it, must wander out in silence and solitude—such an one has awakened too early, has risen up too soon, has rejected the companionship of the race, unlinked to any human being. Such an one sees the evil they do not see, and yet has no power to discover the remedy for it.

Why have women passion, intellect, moral activity—these three—and a place in society where no one of the three can be exercised? Men say that God punishes for complaining. No, but men are angry with misery. They are irritated with women for not being happy. They take it as a personal offence. To God alone may women complain, without insulting Him!

And women, who are afraid, while in words they acknowledge that God's work is good, to say, Thy will be *not* done (declaring another order of society from that which He has made), go about maudling to each other and teaching to their daughters that "women have no passions." In the conventional society, which men have made for women, and women have accepted, they *must* have none, they *must* act the farce of hypocrisy, the lie that they are without passion—and therefore what else can they say to their daughters, without giving the lie to themselves?

"Suffering, sad" female "humanity!" What are these feelings which they are taught to consider as disgraceful, to deny to themselves? What form do the Chinese feet assume when denied their proper development? If the young girls of the "higher classes," who never commit a false step, whose justly earned reputations were never sullied even by the stain which the fruit of mere "knowledge of good and evil" leaves behind, were to speak, and say what are their thoughts employed upon, their *thoughts*, which alone are free, what would they say?

That, with the phantom companion of their fancy, they talk (not love, they are too innocent, too pure, too full of genius and imagination for that, but) they talk, in fancy, of that which interests them most; they seek a companion for their every thought; the companion they find not in reality they seek in fancy, or, if not that, if not absorbed in endless conversations, they see themselves engaged with him in stirring events, circumstances which call out the interest wanting to them. Yes, fathers, mothers, you who see your daughter proudly rejecting all semblance of flirtation, primly engaged in the duties of the breakfast table, you little think how her fancy compensates itself by endless interviews and sympathies (sympathies either for ideas or events) with the fancy's companion of the hour! And you say, "She is not susceptible. Women have no passion." Mothers, who cradle yourselves in visions about the domestic hearth, how many of your sons and daughters are *there*, do you think, while sitting round under your complacent maternal eye? Were you there yourself during your own (now forgotten) girlhood?

What are the thoughts of these young girls while one is singing Schubert, another is reading the Review, and a third is busy embroidering? Is not one fancying herself the nurse of some new friend in sickness; another engaging in romantic dangers with him, such as call out the character and afford more food for sympathy than the monotonous events of domestic society; another undergoing unheard-of trials under the observation of some one whom she has chosen as the companion of her dream? another having a loving and loved companion in the life she is living, which many do not want to change?

And is not all this most natural, inevitable? Are they, who are too much ashamed of it to confess it even to themselves, to be blamed for that which cannot be otherwise, the causes of which stare one in the face, *if one's eyes were not closed?* Many struggle against this as a "snare." No Trappist ascetic watches or fasts more in the body than these do in the soul! They understand the discipline of the Thebaïd[3]—the life-long agonies to which those strong moral Mohicans subjected themselves. How cordially they could do the same, in order to escape the worse torture of wandering "vain imaginations." But the laws of God for moral well-being are not thus to be obeyed. We fast mentally, scourge ourselves morally, use the intellectual hairshirt, in order to subdue that perpetual day-dreaming, which is so dangerous! We resolve "this day month I will be free from it"; twice a day with prayer and written record of the times when we have indulged in it, we endeavor to combat it. Never, with the slightest success. By mortifying vanity we do ourselves no good. It is the want of interest in our life which produces it; by filling up that want of interest in our life we can alone remedy it. And, did we even see this, how can we make the difference? How obtain the interest which Society declares *she* does not want, and *we* cannot want?

What are novels? What is the secret of the charm of every romance that ever was written? The first thing in a good novel is to place the persons together in circumstances which naturally call out the high feelings and thoughts of the character which afford food for sympathy between them on these points—romantic events they are called. The second is that the heroine has *generally* no family ties (almost *invariably* no mother), or, if she has, these do not interfere with her entire independence.

These two things constitute the main charm of reading novels. Now, in as far as these are good and not spurious interests, let us see what we have to correspond with them in real life. Can high sympathies be fed upon the opera, the exhibitions, the gossip of the House of Commons, and the political caricature? If, together, man and woman approach any of the high questions of social, political, or religious life, they are said (and justly—under our present disqualifications) to be going "too far." That such things can be!

"Is it Thou, Lord?" And He said, "It is I." Let our hearts be still.

2

Yet I would spare no pang,
    Would wish no torture less,
The more that anguish racks,
    The earlier it will bless.[4]

Give us back our suffering, we cry to Heaven in our hearts—suffering rather than indifferentism; for out of nothing comes nothing.[5] But out of suffering may come the cure. Better have pain than paralysis! A hundred struggle and drown in the breakers. One discovers the new world. But rather, ten times rather, die in the surf, heralding the way to that new world, than stand idly on the shore!

Passion, intellect, moral activity—these three have never been satisfied in woman. In this cold and oppressive conventional atmosphere, they cannot be satisfied. To say more on this subject would be to enter into the whole history of society, of the present state of civilization.

---

3. Latin epic poem written c. A.D. 92 by Statius about a protracted military campaign against Thebes.
4. Cf. Emily Brontë: "Yet I would lose no sting, would wish no torture less; / The more that anguish racks the earlier it will bless" (*The Prisoner: A Fragment*, 1846).
5. Cf. *King Lear* 1.1.90: "Nothing will come of nothing."

Look at that lizard—"It is not hot," he says, "I like it. The atmosphere which enervates you is life to me." The state of society which some complain of makes others happy. Why should these complain to those? *They* do not suffer. *They* would not understand it, any more than that lizard would comprehend the sufferings of a Shetland sheep.

The progressive world is necessarily divided into two classes—those who take the best of what there is and enjoy it—those who wish for something better and try to create it. Without these two classes, the world would be badly off. They are the very conditions of progress, both the one and the other. Were there none who were discontented with what they have, the world would never reach anything better. And, through the other class, which is constantly taking the best of what the first is creating for them, a balance is secured, and that which is conquered is held fast. But with neither class must we quarrel for not possessing the privileges of the other. The laws of the nature of each make it impossible.

Is discontent a privilege?

Yes, it is a privilege to suffer for your race—a privilege not reserved to the Redeemer and the martyrs alone, but one enjoyed by numbers in every age.

The common-place life of thousands; and in that is its only interest—its only merit as a history: viz., that it *is* the type of common sufferings—the story of one who has not the courage to resist nor to submit to the civilization of her time—is this.

Poetry and imagination begin life. A child will fall on its knees on the gravel walk at the sight of a pink hawthorn in full flower, when it is by itself, to praise God for it.

Then comes intellect. It wishes to satisfy the wants which intellect creates for it. But there is a physical, not moral, impossibility of supplying the wants of the intellect in the state of civilization at which we have arrived. The stimulus, the training, the time, are all three wanting to us; or, in other words, the means and inducements are not there.

Look at the poor lives which we lead. It is a wonder that we are so good as we are, not that we are so bad. In looking round we are struck with the power of the organizations we see, not with their want of power. Now and then, it is true, we are conscious that *there* is an inferior organization, but, in general, just the contrary. Mrs A. has the imagination, the poetry of a Murillo,[6] and has sufficient power of execution to show that she might have had a great deal more. Why is she not a Murillo? From a material difficulty, not a mental one. If she has a knife and fork in her hands during three hours of the day, she cannot have a pencil or brush. Dinner is the great sacred ceremony of this day, the great sacrament. To be absent from dinner is equivalent to being ill. Nothing else will excuse us from it. Bodily incapacity is the only apology valid. If she has a pen and ink in her hands during other three hours, writing answers for the penny post; again, she cannot have her pencil, and so *ad infinitum* through life. People have no type[7] before them in their lives, neither fathers and mothers, nor the children themselves. They look at things in detail. They say, "It is very desirable that A., my daughter, should go to such a party, should know such a lady, should sit by such a person." It is true. But what standard have they before them? of the nature and destination of man? The very words are rejected as pedantic. But might they not, at least, have a type in their minds that such an one might be a

6. Bartoleme Murillo (1618–1682), Spanish painter.   7. Model.

discoverer through her intellect, such another through her art, a third through her moral power?

Women often try one branch of intellect after another in their youth, *e.g.*, mathematics. But that, least of all, is compatible with the life of "society." It is impossible to follow up anything systematically. Women often long to enter some man's profession where they would find direction, competition (or rather opportunity of measuring the intellect with others), and, above all, time.

In those wise institutions, mixed as they are with many follies, which will last as long as the human race lasts, because they are adapted to the wants of the human race; those institutions which we call monasteries, and which, embracing much that is contrary to the laws of nature, are yet better adapted to the union of the life of action and that of thought than any other mode of life with which we are acquainted; in many such, four and a half hours, at least, are daily set aside for thought, rules are given for thought, training and opportunity afforded. Among us, there is no time appointed for this purpose, and the difficulty is that, in our social life, we must be always doubtful whether we ought not to be with somebody else or be doing something else.

Are men better off than women in this?

If one calls upon a friend in London and sees her son in the drawing-room, it strikes one as odd to find a young man sitting idling in his mother's drawing-room in the morning. For men, who are seen much in those haunts, there is no end of the epithets we have; "knights of the carpet," "drawing-room heroes," "ladies' men." But suppose we were to see a number of men in the morning sitting round a table in the drawing-room, looking at prints, doing worsted work, and reading little books, how we should laugh! A member of the House of Commons was once known to do worsted work. Of another man was said, "His only fault is that he is too good; he drives out with his mother every day in the carriage, and if he is asked anywhere he answers that he must dine with his mother, but, if she can spare him, he will come in to tea, and he does not come."

Now, why is it more ridiculous for a man than for a woman to do worsted work and drive out every day in the carriage? Why should we laugh if we were to see a parcel of men sitting round a drawing-room table in the morning, and think it all right if they were women?

Is man's time more valuable than woman's? or is the difference between man and woman this, that woman has confessedly nothing to do?

Women are never supposed to have any occupation of sufficient importance *not* to be interrupted, except "suckling their fools";[8] and women themselves have accepted this, have written books to support it, and have trained themselves so as to consider whatever they do as *not* of such value to the world or to others, but that they can throw it up at the first "claim of social life." They have accustomed themselves to consider intellectual occupation as a merely selfish amusement, which it is their "duty" to give up for every trifler more selfish than themselves.

A young man (who was afterwards useful and known in his day and generation) when busy reading and sent for by his proud mother to shine in some morning visit, came; but, after it was over, he said, "Now, remember, this is not to happen again. I

---

8. In *Othello* the villain Iago says that a woman's role is merely "To suckle fools and chronicle small beer"—i.e., to nurse babies and keep track of trifling matters (2.1.159).

came that you might not think me sulky, but I shall not come again." But for a young woman to send such a message to her mother and sisters, how impertinent it would be! A woman of great administrative powers said that she never undertook anything which she "could not throw by at once, if necessary."

How do we explain then the many cases of women who have distinguished themselves in classics, mathematics, even in politics?

Widowhood, ill-health, or want of bread, these three explanations or excuses are supposed to justify a woman in taking up an occupation. In some cases, no doubt, an indomitable force of character will suffice without any of these three, but such are rare.

But see how society fritters away the intellects of those committed to her charge! It is said that society is necessary to sharpen the intellect. But what do we seek society for? It does sharpen the intellect, because it is a kind of *tour-de-force* to say something at a pinch,—unprepared and uninterested with any subject, to improvise something under difficulties. But what "go we out for to seek?" To take the chance of some one having something to say which we want to hear or of our finding something to say which *they* want to hear? You have a little to say, but not much. You often make a stipulation with some one else, "Come in ten minutes, for I shall not be able to find enough to spin out longer than that." You are not to talk of anything very interesting, for the essence of society is to prevent any long conversations and all *tête-à-têtes*.[9] "Glissez, n'appuyez pas"[1] is its very motto. The praise of a good *"maîtresse de maison"* consists in this, that she allows no one person to be too much absorbed in, or too long about, a conversation. She always recalls them to their "duty." People do not go into the company of their fellow-creatures for what would seem a very sufficient reason, namely, that they have something to say to them, or something that they want to hear from them; but in the vague hope that they may find something to say.

Then as to solitary opportunities. Women never have half an hour in all their lives (excepting before or after anybody is up in the house) that they can call their own, without fear of offending or of hurting some one. Why do people sit up so late, or, more rarely, get up so early? Not because the day is not long enough, but because they have "no time in the day to themselves."

If we do attempt to do anything in company, what is the system of literary exercise which we pursue? Everybody reads aloud out of their own book or newspaper—or, every five minutes, something is said. And what is it to be "read aloud to"? The most miserable exercise of the human intellect. Or rather, is it any exercise at all? It is like lying on one's back, with one's hands tied and having liquid poured down one's throat. Worse than that, because suffocation would immediately ensue and put a stop to this operation. But no suffocation would stop the other.

So much for the satisfaction of the intellect. Yet for a married woman in society, it is even worse. A married woman was heard to wish that she could break a limb that she might have a little time to herself. Many take advantage of the fear of "infection" to do the same.

It is a thing *so* accepted among women that they have nothing to do, that one woman has not the least scruple in saying to another, "I will come and spend the morning with you." And you would be thought quite surly and absurd, if you were to

---

9. Private conversations (French).
1. Slide along, don't push (French); i.e., remain light and superficial rather than engage ideas seriously. *Maîtresse de maison* means housewife.

refuse it on the plea of occupation. Nay, it is thought a mark of amiability and affection, if you are "on such terms" that you can "come in" "any morning you please."

In a country house, if there is a large party of young people, "You will spend the morning with us," they say to the neighbours, "we will drive together in the afternoon," "to-morrow we will make an expedition, and we will spend the evening together." And this is thought friendly, and spending time in a pleasant manner. So women play through life. Yet time is the most valuable of all things. If they had come every morning and afternoon and robbed us of half-a-crown we should have had redress from the police. But it is laid down, that our time is of no value. If you offer a morning visit to a professional man, and say, "I will just stay an hour with you, if you will allow me, till so and so comes back to fetch me;" it costs him the earnings of an hour, and therefore he has a right to complain. But women have no right, because it is "*only* their time."

Women have no means given them, whereby they *can* resist the "claims of social life." They are taught from their infancy upwards that it is wrong, ill-tempered, and a misunderstanding of "woman's mission"[2] (with a great M.) if they do not allow themselves *willingly* to be interrupted at all hours. If a woman has once put in a claim to be treated as a man by some work of science or art or literature, which she can *show* as the "fruit of her leisure," then she will be considered justified in *having* leisure (hardly, perhaps, even then). But if not, not. If she has nothing to show, she must resign herself to her fate.

3

"I like riding about this beautiful place, why don't you? I like walking about the garden, why don't you?" is the common expostulation—as if we were children, whose spirits rise during a fortnight's holidays, who think that they will last for ever—and look neither backwards nor forwards.

Society triumphs over many. They wish to regenerate the world with their institutions, with their moral philosophy, with their love. Then they sink to living from breakfast till dinner, from dinner till tea, with a little worsted work, and to looking forward to nothing but bed.

When shall we see a life full of steady enthusiasm, walking straight to its aim, flying home, as that bird is now, against the wind—with the calmness and the confidence of one who knows the laws of God and can apply them?

What *do* we see? We see great and fine organizations deteriorating. We see girls and boys of seventeen, before whose noble ambitions, heroic dreams, and rich endowments we bow our heads, as before *God incarnate in the flesh*. But, ere they are thirty, they are withered, paralysed, extinguished. "We have forgotten our visions," they say themselves.

The "dreams of youth" have become a proverb. That organizations, early rich, fall far short of their promise has been repeated to satiety. But is it extraordinary that it should be so? For do we ever *utilize* this heroism? Look how it lives upon itself and perishes for lack of food. We do not know what to do with it. We had rather that it should not be there. Often we laugh at it. Always we find it troublesome. Look at the poverty of our life! Can we expect anything else but poor creatures to come out of it? Did Michael Angelo's genius fail, did Pascal's die in its bud,

2. A popular book of this title was published in 1839 by Sarah Lewis.

did Sir Isaac Newton become a common-place sort of man?[3] In two of these cases the knife wore out the sheath. But the knife itself did not become rusty, till the body was dead or infirm.

Why cannot we *make use* of the noble rising heroisms of our own day, instead of leaving them to rust?

They have nothing to do.

Are they to be employed in sitting in the drawing-room, saying words which may as well not be said, which could be said as well if *they* were not there?

Women often strive to live by intellect. The clear, brilliant, sharp radiance of intellect's moonlight rising upon such an expanse of snow is dreary, it is true, but some love its solemn desolation, its silence, its solitude—if they are but *allowed* to live in it; if they are not perpetually baulked and disappointed. But a woman cannot live in the light of intellect. Society forbids it. Those conventional frivolities, which are called her "duties," forbid it. Her "domestic duties," high-sounding words, which, for the most part, are but bad habits (which she has not the courage to enfranchise herself from, the strength to break through) forbid it. What are these duties (or bad habits)?—Answering a multitude of letters which lead to nothing, from her so-called friends—keeping herself up to the level of the world that she may furnish her quota of amusement at the breakfast-table; driving out her company in the carriage. And all these things are exacted from her by her family which if she is good and affectionate, will have more influence with her than the world.

What wonder if, wearied out, sick at heart with hope deferred, the springs of will broken, not seeing clearly *where* her duty lies, she abandons intellect as a vocation and takes it only, as we use the moon, by glimpses through her tight-closed window-shutters?

The family? It is too narrow a field for the development of an immortal spirit, be that spirit male or female. The chances are a thousand to one that, in that small sphere, the task for which that immortal spirit is destined by the qualities and the gifts which its Creator has placed within it, will not be found.

The family uses people, *not* for what they are, nor for what they are intended to be, but for what it wants them for—for its own uses. It thinks of them not as what God has made them, but as the something which *it* has arranged that they shall be. If it wants some one to sit in the drawing-room, *that* some one is to be supplied by the family, though that member may be destined for science, or for education, or for active superintendence by God, *i.e.*, by the gifts within.

This system dooms some minds to incurable infancy, others to silent misery.

And family boasts that it has performed its mission well, in as far as it has enabled the individual to say, "I have *no* peculiar work, nothing but what the moment brings me, nothing that I cannot throw up at once at anybody's claim;" in as far, that is, as it has *destroyed* the individual life. And the individual thinks that a great victory has been accomplished, when, at last, she is able to say that she has "no personal desires or plans." What is this but throwing the gifts of God aside as worthless, and substituting for them those of the world?

Marriage is the only chance (and it is but a chance) offered to women for escape from this death; and how eagerly and how ignorantly it is embraced!

---

3. Michelangelo Buonarroti (1475–1564), Italian Renaissance artist; Blaise Pascal (1623–1662), French philosopher and mathematician; Sir Isaac Newton (1642–1727), mathematician and scientist.

At present we live to impede each other's satisfactions; competition, domestic life, society, what is it all but this? We go somewhere where we are not wanted and where we don't want to go. What else is conventional life? *Passivity* when we want to be active. So many hours spent every day in passively doing what conventional life tells us, when we would so gladly be at work.

And is it a wonder that all individual life is extinguished?

Women dream of a great sphere of steady, not sketchy benevolence, of moral activity, for which they would fain be trained and fitted, instead of working in the dark, neither knowing nor registering whither their steps lead, whether farther from or nearer to the aim.

For how do people exercise their moral activity now? We visit, we teach, we talk, among "the poor"; we are told, "don't look for the fruits, cast thy bread upon the waters: for thou shalt find it after many days." Certainly "don't look," for you won't see. You will *not* "find it," and then you would "strike work."

How different would be the heart for the work, and how different would be the success, if we learnt our work as a serious study, and followed it out steadily as a profession!

Were the physician to set to work at *his* trade, as the philanthropist does at his, how many bodies would he not spoil before he cured one!

We set the treatment of bodies so high above the treatment of souls, that the physician occupies a higher place in society than the school-master. The governess is to have every one of God's gifts; she is to do that which the mother herself is incapable of doing; but our son must not degrade himself by marrying the governess, nor our daughter the tutor, though she might marry the medical man.

But my medical man does do something for me, it is said, my tutor has done nothing.

This is true, this is the real reason. And what a condemnation of the state of mental science it is! Low as is physical science, that of the mind is still lower.

Women long for an education to teach them *to teach*, to teach them the laws of the human mind and how to apply them—and knowing how imperfect, in the present state of the world, such an education must be, they long for experience, not patch-work experience, but experience followed up and systematized, to enable them to know what they are about and *where* they are "casting their bread" and whether it is "*bread*" or a stone.

How should we learn a language if we were to give to it an hour a week? A fortnight's steady application would make more way in it than a year of such patch-work. A "lady" can hardly go to "her school" two days running. She cannot leave the breakfast-table—or she must be fulfilling some little frivolous "duty," which others ought not to exact, or which might just as well be done some other time.

Dreaming always—never accomplishing; thus women live—too much ashamed of their dreams, which they think "romantic," to tell them where they will be laughed at, even if not considered wrong.

With greater strength of purpose they might accomplish something. But if they were strong, all of them, they would not need to have their story told, for all the world would read it in the mission they have fulfilled. It is for common place, every-day characters that we tell our tale—because it is the sample of hundreds of lives (or rather deaths) of persons who cannot fight with society, or who, unsupported by the sympathies about them, give up their own destiny as not worth the fierce and continued struggle necessary to accomplish it. One struggle they *could* make and be free (and, in the Church of Rome, many, many, unallured by any other motive, make this one struggle to enter a convent); but the perpetual series of petty spars, with discouragements between, and doubts as to whether they are right—these wear out the very life necessary to make them.

If a man were to follow up his profession or occupation at odd times, how would he do it? Would he become skilful in that profession? It is acknowledged by women themselves that they are inferior in every occupation to men. Is it wonderful? *They* do *everything* at "odd times."

And if a woman's music and drawing are only used by her as an amusement (a *pass-time*, as it is called), is it wonderful that she tires of them, that she becomes disgusted with them?

In every dream of the life of intelligence or that of activity, women are accompanied by a phantom—the phantom of sympathy, guiding, lighting the way—even if they do not marry. Some few sacrifice marriage, because they must sacrifice all other life if they accept that. That man and woman have an equality of duties and rights is accepted by woman even less than by man. Behind *his* destiny woman must annihilate herself, must be only his complement. A woman dedicates herself to the vocation of her husband; she fills up and performs the subordinate parts in it. But if she has any destiny, any vocation of her own, she must renounce it, in nine cases out of ten. Some few, like Mrs Somerville, Mrs Chisholm, Mrs Fry,[4] have not done so; but these are exceptions. The fact is that woman has so seldom any vocation of her own, that it does not much signify; she has none to renounce. A man gains everything by marriage: he gains a "help-mate," but a woman does not.

But if ever women come into contact with sickness, and crime, and poverty in masses, how the practical reality of life revives them! They are exhausted, like those who live on opium or on novels, all their lives—exhausted with feelings which lead to no action. If they see and enter into a continuous line of action, with a full and interesting life, with training constantly kept up to the occupation, occupation constantly testing the training—it is the *beau-idéal* of practical, not theoretical, education—they are re-tempered, their life is filled, they have found their work, and the means to do it.

Women, when they are young, sometimes think that an actress's life is a happy one—not for the sake of the admiration, not for the sake of the fame; but because in the morning she studies, in the evening she embodies those studies: she has the means of testing and correcting them by practice, and of resuming her studies in the morning, to improve the weak parts, remedy the failures, and in the evening try the corrections again. It is, indeed, true that, even after middle age, with such exercise of faculty, there is no end to the progress which may be made.

Some are only deterred from suicide because it is in the most distinct manner to say to God: "I will not, I will not do as Thou wouldst have me," and because it is "no use."

To have no food for our heads, no food for our hearts, no food for our activity, is that nothing? If we have no food for the body, how we do cry out, how all the world hears of it, how all the newspapers talk of it, with a paragraph headed in great capital letters, DEATH FROM STARVATION! But suppose one were to put a paragraph in the "Times," *Death of Thought from Starvation,* or *Death of Moral Activity from Starvation,*

---

4. Mary Somerville (1780–1872), scientist; Caroline Chisholm (1808–1877), philanthropist who helped emigrants to settle in Australia; Elizabeth Fry (1780–1845), philanthropist and prison reformer.

how people would stare, how they would laugh and wonder! One would think we had no heads nor hearts, by the total indifference of the public towards them. Our bodies are the only things of any consequence.

We have nothing to do which raises us, no food which agrees with us. We can never pursue any object for a single two hours, for we can never command any regular leisure or solitude; and in social or domestic life one is bound, under pain of being thought sulky, to make a remark every two minutes.

Men are on the side of society; they blow hot and cold; they say, "Why can't you employ yourself in society?" and then, "Why don't you talk in society?" I can pursue a connected conversation, or I can be silent; but to drop a remark, as it is called, every two minutes, how wearisome it is! It is impossible to pursue the current of one's own thoughts, because one must keep oneself ever on the alert "to say something;" and it is impossible to say what one is thinking, because the essence of a remark is not to be a thought, but an impression. With what labour women have toiled to break down all individual and independent life, in order to fit themselves for this social and domestic existence, thinking it right! And when they have killed themselves to do it, they have awakened (too late) to think it wrong.

For, later in life, women could not make use of leisure and solitude if they had it! Like the Chinese woman, who could not make use of her feet, if she were brought into European life.

Some have an attention like a battering-ram, which, slowly brought to bear, can work upon a subject for any length of time. They can work ten hours just as well as two upon the same thing. But this age would have men like the musket, which you can load so fast that nothing but its heating in the process puts any limit to the number and frequency of times of firing, and at as many different objects as you please.

So, later in life, people cannot use their battering-ram. Their attention, like society's, goes off in a thousand different directions. They are an hour before they can fix it; and by the time it is fixed, the leisure is gone. They become incapable of consecutive or strenuous work.

What these suffer—even physically—from the want of such work no one can tell. The accumulation of nervous energy, which has had nothing to do during the day, makes them feel every night, when they go to bed, as if they were going mad; and they are obliged to lie long in bed in the morning to let it evaporate and keep it down.

At last they suffer at once from disgust of the one and incapacity for the other— from loathing of conventional idleness and powerlessness to do work when they have it. "Now go, you have several hours," say people, "you have all the afternoon to yourself." When they are all frittered away, they are to begin to work. When they are broken up into little bits, they are to hew away.

4

Moral activity? There is scarcely such a thing possible! Everything is sketchy. The world does nothing but sketch. One Lady Bountiful sketches a school, but it never comes to a finished study; she can hardly work at it two weeks consecutively. Here and there a solitary individual, it is true, makes a really careful study,—as Mrs Chisholm of emigration—as Miss Carpenter of reformatory discipline.[5] But, in gen-

5. Mary Carpenter (1807–1892), philanthropist who promoted reformatory schools.

eral, a "lady" has too many sketches on hand. She has a sketch of society, a sketch of her children's education, sketches of her "charities," sketches of her reading. She is like a painter who should have five pictures in his studio at once, and giving now a stroke to one, and now a stroke to another, till he had made the whole round, should continue this routine to the end.

All life is sketchy,—the poet's verse (compare Tennyson, Milnes, and Mrs Browning[6] with Milton or even Byron: it is not the difference of genius which strikes one so much as the unfinished state of these modern sketches compared with the studies of the old masters),—the artist's picture, the author's composition—all are rough, imperfect, incomplete, even as works of art.

And how can it be otherwise? A "leader" out of a newspaper, an article out of a review, five books read aloud in the course of an evening, such is our literature. What mind can stand three leading articles every morning as its food?

When shall we see a woman making a *study* of what she does? Married women cannot; for a man would think, if his wife undertook any great work with the intention of carrying it out,—of making anything but a sham of it—that she would "suckle his fools and chronicle his small beer" less well for it,—that he would not have so good a dinner—that she would destroy, as it is called, his domestic life.

The intercourse of man and woman—how frivolous, how unworthy it is! Can we call *that* the true vocation of woman—her high career? Look round at the marriages which you know. The true marriage—that noble union, by which a man and woman become together the one perfect being—probably does not exist at present upon earth.

It is not surprising that husbands and wives seem so little part of one another. It is surprising that there is so much love as there is. For there is no food for it. What does it live upon—what nourishes it? Husbands and wives never seem to have anything to say to one another. What do they talk about? Not about any great religious, social, political questions or feelings. They talk about who shall come to dinner, who is to live in this lodge and who in that, about the improvement of the place, or when they shall go to London. If there are children, they form a common subject of some nourishment. But, even then, the case is oftenest thus,—the husband is to think of how they are to get on in life; the wife of bringing them up at home.

But any real communion between husband and wife—any descending into the depths of their being, and drawing out thence what they find and comparing it—do we ever dream of such a thing? Yes, we may dream of it during the season of "passion"; but we shall not find it afterwards. We even *expect* it to go off, and lay our account that it will. If the husband has, by chance, gone into the depths of *his* being, and found anything there unorthodox, he, oftenest, conceals it carefully from his wife,—he is afraid of "unsettling her opinions."

What is the mystery of passion, spiritually speaking? For there *is* a passion of the Spirit. *Blind* passion, as it has most truly been called, seems to come on in man without his exactly knowing why, without his *at all* knowing why for *this* person rather than for *that,* and (whether it has been satisfied or unsatisfied) to go off again after a while, as it came, also without his knowing why.

The woman's passion is generally more lasting.

---

6. Three contemporary poets; Richard Monckton Milnes (1809–1885) had proposed to Nightingale and been turned down.

It is possible that this difference may be, because there is really more in man than in woman. There is nothing in her for him to have this intimate communion *with*. He cannot impart to her his religious beliefs, if he have any, because she would be "shocked." Religious men are and must be heretics now—for we must not pray, except in a "form" of words, made beforehand—or think of God but with a pre-arranged idea.

With the man's political ideas, if they extend beyond the merest party politics, she has no sympathy.

His social ideas, if they are "advanced," she will probably denounce without knowing why, as savouring of "socialism" (a convenient word, which covers a multitude of new ideas and offences). For woman is "by birth a Tory,"—has been often said—by education a "Tory," we mean.

Woman has nothing but her affections,—and this makes her at once more loving and less loved.

But is it surprising that there should be so little real marriage, when we think what the process is which leads to marriage?

Under the eyes of an always present mother and sisters (of whom even the most refined and intellectual cannot abstain from a jest upon the subject, who think it their *duty* to be anxious, to watch every germ and bud of it) the acquaintance begins. It is fed—upon what?—the gossip of art, musical and pictorial, the party politics of the day, the chit-chat of society, and people marry or sometimes they don't marry, discouraged by the impossibility of knowing any more of one another than this will furnish.

They prefer to marry in *thought,* to hold imaginary conversations with one another in idea, rather than, on such a flimsy pretext of communion, to take the chance (*certainty* it cannot be) of having more to say to one another in marriage.

Men and women meet now *to be idle*. Is it extraordinary that they do not know each other, and that, in their mutual ignorance, they form no surer friendships? Did they meet to *do* something together, then indeed they might form some real tie.

But, as it is, *they* are not there, it is only a mask which is there—a mouth-piece of ready-made sentences about the "topics of the day;" and then people rail against men for choosing a woman "for her face"—why, what else do they see?

It is very well to say "be prudent, be careful, try to know each other." But how are you to know each other?

Unless a woman has lost all pride, how is it possible for her, under the eyes of all her family, to indulge in long exclusive conversations with a man? "Such a thing" must not take place till after her "engagement." And how is she to make an engagement, if "such a thing" has not taken place?

Besides, young women at home have so little to occupy and to interest them—they have so little reason for *not* quitting their home, that a young and independent man cannot look at a girl without giving rise to "expectations," if not on her own part, on that of her family. Happy he, if he is not said to have been "trifling with her feelings," or "disappointing her hopes!" Under these circumstances, how can a man, who has any pride or any principle, become acquainted with a woman in such a manner as to *justify* them in marrying?

There are four ways in which people marry. First, accident or relationship has thrown them together in their childhood, and acquaintance has grown up naturally and unconsciously. Accordingly, in novels, it is generally cousins who marry; and *now* it seems the only natural thing—the only possible way of making an intimacy. And yet, we know that intermarriage between relations is in direct contravention of the laws of nature for the well-being of the race; witness the Quakers, the Spanish grandees, the royal races, the secluded valleys of mountainous countries, where madness, degeneration of race, defective organization and cretinism flourish and multiply.

The second way, and by far the most general, in which people marry, is this. A woman, thoroughly uninterested at home, and having formed a slight acquaintance with some accidental person, accepts him, if he "falls in love" with her, as it is technically called, and takes the chance. Hence the vulgar expression of marriage being a lottery, which it most truly is, for that the *right* two should come together has as many chances against it as there are blanks in any lottery.

The third way is, that some person is found sufficiently independent, sufficiently careless of the opinions of others, or sufficiently without modesty to speculate thus:— "It is worth while that I should become acquainted with so and so. I do not care what his or her opinion of me is, if, *after* having become acquainted, to do which can bear no other construction in people's eyes than a desire of marriage, I retreat." But there is this to be said, that it is doubtful whether, under this unnatural tension, which, to all susceptible characters, such a disregard of the opinions which they care for must be, a healthy or a natural feeling can grow up.

And now they are married—that is to say, two people have received the licence of a man in a white surplice. But they are no more man and wife for that than Louis XIV and the Infanta of Spain, married by proxy, were man and wife. The woman who has sold herself for an establishment, in what is she superior to those we may not name?

Lastly, in a few rare, very rare, cases, such as circumstances, always provided in novels, but seldom to be met with in real life, present—whether the accident of parents' neglect, or of parents' unusual skill and wisdom, or of having no parents at all, which is generally the case in novels—or marrying out of the person's rank of life, by which the usual restraints are removed, and there is room and play left for attraction—or extraordinary events, isolation, misfortunes, which many wish for, even though their imaginations be not tainted by romance-reading; such alternatives as these give food and space for the development of character and mutual sympathies.

But a girl, if she has any pride, is so ashamed of having any thing she wishes to say out of the hearing of her own family, she thinks it must be something so very wrong, that it is ten to one, if she have the opportunity of saying it, that she will not.

And yet she is spending her life, perhaps, in dreaming of accidental means of unrestrained communion.

And then it is thought pretty to say that "Women have no passion." If passion is excitement in the daily social intercourse with men, women think about marriage much more than men do; it is the only event of their lives. It ought to be a sacred event, but surely not the only event of a woman's life, as it is now. Many women spend their lives in asking men to marry them, in a refined way. Yet it is true that women are seldom in love. How can they be?

How cruel are the revulsions which high-minded women suffer! There was one who loved, in connexion with great deeds, noble thoughts, devoted feelings. They met after an interval. It was at one of those crowded parties of Civilization which we call Society. His only careless passing remark was, "The buzz to-night is like a manufactory."[7] Yet he loved her.

---

7. Apparently Milnes said something like this to Nightingale when they met at a party after she had refused his proposal.

5

"L'enthousiasme est la faiblesse d'un temps où l'intelligence monte très haut, en-
traînée par l'imagination, et tombe très bas, écrasée par une réalité, sans poésie et
sans grandeur."[8]

Women dream till they have no longer the strength to dream; those dreams
against which they so struggle, so honestly, vigorously, and conscientiously, and so in
vain, yet which are their life, without which they could not have lived; those dreams
go at last. All their plans and visions seem vanished, and they know not where; gone,
and they cannot recall them. They do not even remember them. And they are left
without the food either of reality or of hope.

Later in life, they neither desire nor dream, neither of activity, nor of love, nor of
intellect. The last often survives the longest. They wish, if their experiences would
benefit anybody, to give them to some one. But they never find an hour free in which
to collect their thoughts, and so discouragement becomes ever deeper and deeper,
and they less and less capable of undertaking anything.

It seems as if the female spirit of the world were mourning everlastingly over
blessings, *not* lost, but which she has never had, and which, in her discouragement,
she feels that she never will have, they are so far off.

The more complete a woman's organization, the more she will feel it, till at last
there shall arise a woman, who will resume, in her own soul, all the sufferings of her
race, and that woman will be the Saviour of her race.

Jesus Christ raised women above the condition of mere slaves, mere ministers to
the passions of the man, raised them by his sympathy, to be ministers of God. He
gave them moral activity. But the Age, the World, Humanity, must give them the
means to exercise this moral activity, must give them intellectual cultivation, spheres
of action.

There is perhaps no century where the woman shows so meanly as in this.[9] Because her education seems entirely to have parted company with her vocation; there
is no longer unity between the woman as inwardly developed, and as outwardly manifested.

In the last century it was not so. In the succeeding one let us hope that it will no
longer be so.

But now she is like the Archangel Michael as he stands upon Saint Angelo at
Rome. She has an immense provision of wings, which seem as if they would bear her
over earth and heaven; but when she tries to use them, she is petrified into stone, her
feet are grown into the earth, chained to the bronze pedestal.

Nothing can well be imagined more painful than the present position of woman,
unless, on the one hand, she renounces all outward activity and keeps herself within
the magic sphere, the bubble of her dreams; or, on the other, surrendering all aspiration, she gives herself to her real life, soul and body. For those to whom it is possible,

---

8. Enthusiasm is the weakness of an age during which intelligence soars, swept along by the imagination, and
then plummets, crushed by a reality without poetry and
without grandeur (French).
9. At almost every period of social life, we find, as it were,
two under currents running different ways. There is the
noble woman who dreams [of] following out her useful
vocation; but there is also the selfish dreamer now, who is
ever turning to something new, regardless of the expectations she has voluntarily excited, who is ever talking
about "making a life for herself," heedless that she is
spoiling another life, undertaken, perhaps, at her own
bidding. This is the ugly reverse of the medal [Nightin-
gale's note].

the latter is best; for out of activity may come thought, out of mere aspiration can come nothing.

But now—when the young imagination is so high and so developed, and reality is so narrow and conventional—there is no more parallelism between life in the thought and life in the actual than between the corpse, which lies motionless in its narrow bed, and the spirit, which, in our imagination, is at large among the stars.

The ideal life is passed in noble schemes of good consecutively followed up, of devotion to a great object, of sympathy given and received for high ideas and generous feelings. The actual life is passed in sympathy given and received for a dinner, a party, a piece of furniture, a house built or a garden laid out well, in devotion to your guests—(a too real devotion, for it implies that of all your time)—in schemes of schooling for the poor, which you follow up perhaps in an odd quarter of an hour, between luncheon and driving out in the carriage—broth and dripping are included in the plan—and the rest of your time goes in ordering the dinner, hunting for a governess for your children, and sending pheasants and apples to your poorer relations. Is there anything in *this* life which can be called an Incarnation of the ideal life within? Is it a wonder that the unhappy woman should prefer to keep them entirely separate? not to take the bloom off her Ideal by mixing it up with her Actual; not to make her Actual still more unpalatable by trying to *inform* it with her Ideal? And then she is blamed, and her own sex unites against her, for not being content with the "day of small things." She is told that "trifles make the sum of human things;" they do indeed. She is contemptuously asked, "Would she abolish domestic life?" Men are afraid that their houses will not be so comfortable, that their wives will make themselves "remarkable"—women, that they will make themselves distasteful to men; they write books (and very wisely) to teach themselves to dramatize "little things," to persuade themselves that "domestic life is their sphere" and to idealize the "sacred hearth."[1] Sacred it is indeed. Sacred from the touch of their sons almost as soon as they are out of childhood—from its dulness and its tyrannous trifling *these* recoil. Sacred from the grasp of their daughters' affections, upon which it has so light a hold that they seize the first opportunity of marriage, *their* only chance of emancipation. The "sacred hearth;" sacred to their husband's sleep, their sons' absence in the body and their daughters' in mind.

Oh! mothers, who talk about this hearth, how much do you know of your sons' real life, how much of your daughters' imaginary one? Awake, ye women, all ye that sleep, awake! If this domestic life were so very good, would your young men wander away from it, your maidens think of something else?

The time is come when women must do something more than the "domestic hearth," which means nursing the infants, keeping a pretty house, having a good dinner and an entertaining party.

You say, "It is true, our young men see visions, and our maidens dream dreams, but what of? Does not the woman intend to marry, and have over again what she has at home? and the man ultimately too?" Yes, but not the same; she *will* have the same, that is, if circumstances are not altered to prevent it; but her *idéal* is very different, though that *idéal* and the reality will never come together to mould each other. And it is not only the unmarried woman who dreams. The married woman also holds long imaginary conversations but too often.

---

1. A reference to female conduct books, such as those by Sarah Stickney Ellis; see page 1632.

6

We live in the world, it is said, and must walk in its ways.

Was Christ called a complainer against the world? Yet all these great teachers and preachers, must have had a most deep and ingrained sense, a continual gnawing feeling of the miseries and wrongs of the world. Otherwise they would not have been impelled to devote life and death to redress them. Christ, Socrates, Howard,[2] they must have had no ear for the joys, compared to that which they had for the sorrows of the world.

They acted, however, and we complain. The great reformers of the world turn into the great misanthropists, if circumstances or organisation do not permit them to act. Christ, if He had been a woman, might have been nothing but a great complainer. Peace be with the misanthropists! They have made a step in progress; the next will make them great philanthropists; they are divided but by a line.

The next Christ will perhaps be a female Christ. But do we see one woman who looks like a female Christ? or even like "the messenger before" her "face," to go before her and prepare the hearts and minds for her?

To this will be answered that half the inmates of Bedlam[3] begin in this way, by fancying that they are "the Christ."[4]

People talk about imitating Christ, and imitate Him in the little trifling formal things, such as washing the feet, saying his prayer, and so on; but if any one attempts the real imitation of Him, there are no bounds to the outcry with which the presumption of that person is condemned.

For instance, Christ was saying something to the people one day, which interested Him very much, and interested them very much; and Mary and his brothers came in the middle of it, and wanted to interrupt Him, and take Him home to dinner, very likely—(how natural that story is! does it not speak more home than any historic evidences of the Gospel's reality?), and He, instead of being angry with their interruption of Him in such an important work for some trifling thing, answers, "Who is my mother and who are my brethren? Whosoever shall do the will of my Father which is in heaven, the same is my brother and sister and mother."[5] But if *we* were to say that, we should be accused of "destroying the family tie," of "diminishing the obligation of the home duties."

He might well say, "Heaven and earth shall pass away, but my words shall not pass away."[6] His words will never pass away. If He had said, "Tell them that I am engaged at this moment in something very important; that the instruction of the multitude ought to go before any personal ties; that I will remember to come when I have done," no one would have been impressed by His words; but how striking is that, "Behold my mother and my brethren!"

2. John Howard (1726–1790), philanthropist and prison reformer.
3. London lunatic asylum.
4. It is quite true that insanity, sensuality, and monstrous fraud have constantly assumed to be "the Christ," *vide* the *Agapemone*, and the Mormons. "Believing" a man of the name of Prince "to be the tabernacle of God on earth," poor deluded women transfer to him all their stock in the Three per Cents. We hear of the Mormons, &c., being the "recipients and mouth-pieces of God's spirit." They profess to be "incarnations of the Deity," "witnesses of the Almighty, solely knowing God's will, and being the medium of communicating it to man," and so forth. It does not appear to us that this blasphemy is very dangerous to the cause of true religion in general, any more than forgery is very dangerous to commerce in general. It is the universal dishonesty in religion, as in trade, which is really dangerous [Nightingale's note]. The Church of the Agapemone was founded in an English village in 1849 by H. J. Prince, who claimed to be the personification of the Holy Ghost, but the sect was discovered to be engaging in promiscuous and immoral behavior.
5. Matthew 12.46–50.
6. Matthew 24.35.

7

The dying woman to her mourners:[7]—"Oh! if you knew how gladly I leave this life, how much more courage I feel to take the chance of another, than of anything I see before me in this, you would put on your wedding-clothes instead of mourning for me!"

"But," they say, "so much talent! so many gifts! such good which you might have done!"

"The world will be put back some little time by my death," she says; "you see I estimate my powers at least as highly as you can; but it is by the death which has taken place some years ago in me, not by the death which is about to take place now." And so is the world put back by the death of every one who has to sacrifice the development of his or her peculiar gifts (which were meant, not for selfish gratification, but for the improvement of that world) to conventionality.

"My people were like children playing on the shore of the eighteenth century. I was their hobby-horse, their plaything; and they drove me to and fro, dear souls! never weary of the play themselves, till I, who had grown to woman's estate and to the ideas of the nineteenth century, lay down exhausted, my mind closed to hope, my heart to strength.

"Free—free—oh! divine freedom, art thou come at last? Welcome, beautiful death!"

Let neither name nor date be placed on her grave, still less the expression of regret or of admiration; but simply the words, "I believe in God."

1852; 1859   1928

---

7. Cassandra, who can neither find happiness in life, nor alter it, dies [Nightingale's note].

⊯ PERSPECTIVES ⊯

Victorian Ladies and Gentlemen

As Victorian society prospered, social divisions became more fluid, but at the same time class consciousness became more intense. The terms "lady" and "gentleman" had enormous significance, particularly for those aspiring to these ranks, or for those in danger of slipping out of them. Some social distinctions were obvious: regardless of conduct, people born into the aristocracy and landed gentry were indisputably ladies and gentlemen; people who worked with their hands in home, field, or factory were not. The upper and lower boundaries of the middle class were blurred, however, and everyone was alert to fine gradations. Manners, money, birth, occupation, and leisure time were crucial indicators of social standing, determining not only one's place in society but one's freedom to act, speak, learn, and earn.

Ladies and gentlemen endeavored to conform to the ideology of separate spheres that dominated Victorian thinking about gender. Middle-class women were to preside over the domestic sphere, the home and family, while men entered the fray of the world. Woman's "mission" was to provide a sanctified haven from the rough-and-tumble world of business and politics. Her virtuous passivity, selflessness, and spiritual purity gave her moral authority in the social and domestic realm. The first mass-circulation women's periodical, launched in 1852, was called, significantly, *Englishwoman's Domestic Magazine*.

Meanwhile, the world of action and aggression belonged to men: as Ruskin put it in *Sesame and Lilies* (1865): "The man, in his rough work in the open world, must encounter all peril and trial . . . often he must be wounded, or subdued, often misled; and *always* hardened. But he guards the woman from all this; within his house, as ruled by her . . . need enter no danger, no temptation, no cause of error or offense." Tennyson's *The Princess* (1847) gave the polarization of gender roles the aura of timeless law:

> Man for the field and woman for the hearth:
> Man for the sword and for the needle she:
> Man with the head and woman with the heart:
> Man to command and woman to obey:
> All else confusion.

Among middle-class men, the clearest social division was between those who had attended a public school (an elite boarding school) and those who had not. The ideal of gentlemanliness inculcated by these schools became a way for society to remake the upstart middle classes in the image of the aristocracy. Emphasizing character over intellect, the public schools taught boys how to assimilate the manners and customs of those above them socially, and gave them a familiarity with Greek, Latin, and school games such as cricket and rugby—hallmarks of an upper-class education. Instilling the values of duty, loyalty, and public service, these schools helped to create a new administrative elite, based more on merit and training than birth, who ran both the Civil Service and the Empire. Sustained by the "old boy" network, in which former schoolmates assisted each other's careers, graduates of places such as Eton, Harrow, Winchester, and Rugby could look forward to positions of influence and affluence.

Although the daughters of some well-to-do families might attend a fashionable boarding school, education was not primarily what determined a woman's claim to be considered a lady. Her position derived from her parents or her husband, and her unproductive leisure was a visible signal of rank. Since aspirations to "refinement" effectively precluded middle-class women from employment, ladies had, as the novelist Dinah Maria Mulock put it in 1858, "literally nothing whatever to do." She complained that "their whole energies are devoted to the massacre of old Time. They prick him to death with crochet and embroidery needles;

The Parliamentary Female, from *Punch* magazine, 1853. A caption offered this dialogue:

FATHER OF THE FAMILY: Come, dear; we so seldom go out together now—Can't you take us all to the Play to-night?

MISTRESS OF THE HOUSE, AND M.P.: How you talk, Charles! Don't you see that I am too Busy. I have a Committee to-morrow morning, and I have my Speech on the Great Crochet Question to prepare for the evening.

strum him deaf with piano and harp playing—*not* music; cut him up with morning visitors, or leave his carcass in ten-minute parcels at every 'friend's' house they can think of." In her autobiography Harriet Martineau described the expectations in her day: "It was not thought proper for young ladies to study very conspicuously. . . . If ever I shut myself into my own room for an hour of solitude, I knew it was at the risk of being sent for to join the sewing-circle, or to read aloud."

It was a way of life that at once exalted women and paralyzed them. They could not work outside the home; they could not vote; they had no legal rights, even over their own children; they could not attend university or enter the professions. Legally, they were classed with criminals, idiots, and minors. Rejecting women's education, the painter Edward Burne-Jones argued, "The great point is, not that they should understand us, but that they should worship and obey us." Ironically, only economic necessity or illness could liberate a lady from the burden of enforced idleness. When Harriet Martineau's family went bankrupt, she was enabled to pursue her dream of authorship, for "we had lost our gentility." Similarly, the death of both parents freed Mary Kingsley to travel, and her own recurrent ill health allowed Isabella Bird to go off in search of a "cure." (See Perspectives: Travel and Empire, page 1888.) Florence Nightingale made time for a career by taking to her bed, where only her persistent indisposition released her from the demands of family and social life. Definitions of masculinity and femininity were earnestly contested throughout the period—with increasingly sharp assaults on traditional roles coming from aesthetes and decadents at the end of the century. The following selections illustrate the kinds of arguments and experiences that figured prominently in debates on gender roles in the early and mid-Victorian periods.

Frances Power Cobbe
1822–1904

The education of girls from well-to-do families lacked intellectual challenge, partly because of the belief that the female mind was incapable of serious effort, and partly because the goal was to produce "Ornaments of Society" who would catch husbands. The elaborate and expensive clothes worn by Frances Power Cobbe and her fellow pupils further reinforced their essentially decorative function. Although Cobbe recalls her teachers' horror at the idea that a woman's education might ever be put to any practical use, she herself became an active philanthropist, reformer, and feminist, who pressed for female suffrage and for women's access to university education and the professions.

from Life of Frances Power Cobbe As Told by Herself
[A FASHIONABLE ENGLISH BOARDING SCHOOL]

When it came to my turn to receive education, it was not in London but in Brighton that the ladies' schools most in estimation were to be found. There were even then (about 1836) not less than a hundred such establishments in the town, but that at No. 32, Brunswick Terrace, of which Miss Runciman and Miss Roberts were mistresses, and which had been founded some time before by a celebrated Miss Poggi, was supposed to be *nec pluribus impar* [equal to the best]. It was, at all events, the most outrageously expensive, the nominal tariff of £120 or £130 per annum representing scarcely a fourth of the charges for "extras" which actually appeared in the bills of many of the pupils. My own, I know, amounted to 1,000 for two years' schooling.[1]

I shall write of this school quite frankly, since the two poor ladies, well-meaning but very unwise, to whom it belonged have been dead for nearly thirty years, and it can hurt nobody to record my conviction that a better system than theirs could scarcely have been devised had it been designed to attain the maximum of cost and labour and the minimum of solid results. It was the typical Higher Education of the period, carried out to the extreme of expenditure and high pressure.

Profane persons were apt to describe our school as a Convent, and to refer to the back door of our garden, whence we issued on our dismal diurnal[2] walks, as the "postern." If we in any degree resembled nuns, however, it was assuredly not those of either a Contemplative or Silent Order. The din of our large double schoolrooms was something frightful. Sitting in either of them, four pianos might be heard going at once in rooms above and around us, while at numerous tables scattered about the rooms there were girls reading aloud to the governesses and reciting lessons in English, French, German, and Italian. This hideous clatter continued the entire day till we went to bed at night, there being no time whatever allowed for recreation, unless the dreary hour of walking with our teachers (when we recited our verbs), could so be described by a fantastic imagination. In the midst of the uproar we were obliged to write our exercises, to compose our themes, and to commit to memory whole pages of prose. On Saturday afternoons, instead of play, there was a terrible ordeal generally known as the "Judgment Day." The two school-mistresses sat side by side, solemn and

---

1. Compare this figure to the 20 pounds per year that Charlotte Brontë was earning in 1841 as a private governess.　　2. Daily.

stern, at the head of the long table. Behind them sat all the governesses as Assessors. On the table were the books wherein our evil deeds of the week were recorded; and round the room against the wall, seated on stools of penitential discomfort, we sat, five-and-twenty "damosels," anything but "Blessed,"[3] expecting our sentences according to our ill-deserts. It must be explained that the fiendish ingenuity of some teacher had invented for our torment a system of imaginary "cards," which we were supposed to "lose" (though we never gained any) whenever we had not finished all our various lessons and practisings every night before bed-time, or whenever we had been given the mark for "stooping," or had been impertinent, or had been "turned" in our lessons, or had been marked "P" by the music master, or had been convicted of "disorder" (e.g., having our long shoe-strings untied), or, lastly, had told lies! Any one crime in this heterogeneous list entailed the same penalty, namely, the sentence, "You have lost your card, Miss So-and-so, for such and such a thing;" and when Saturday came round, if three cards had been lost in the week, the law wreaked its justice on the unhappy sinner's head! Her confession having been wrung from her at the awful judgment-seat above described, and the books having been consulted, she was solemnly scolded and told to sit in the corner for the rest of the evening! Anything more ridiculous than the scene which followed can hardly be conceived. I have seen (after a week in which a sort of feminine barring-out had taken place) no less than nine young ladies obliged to sit for hours in the angles of the three rooms, like naughty babies, with their faces to the wall; half of them being quite of marriageable age, and all dressed, as was de rigueur [the rule] with us every day, in full evening attire of silk or muslin, with gloves and kid slippers. Naturally, Saturday evenings, instead of affording some relief to the incessant overstrain of the week, were looked upon with terror as the worst time of all. Those who escaped the fell destiny of the corner were allowed, if they chose, to write to their parents, but our letters were perforce committed at night to the schoolmistress to seal, and were not as may be imagined, exactly the natural outpouring of our sentiments as regarded those ladies and their school.

Our household was a large one. It consisted of the two schoolmistresses and joint proprietors, of the sister of one of them and another English governess; of a French, an Italian, and a German lady teacher; of a considerable staff of respectable servants; and finally of twenty-five or twenty-six pupils, varying in age from nine to nineteen. All the pupils were daughters of men of some standing, mostly country gentlemen, members of Parliament, and offshoots of the peerage. There were several heiresses amongst us, and one girl whom we all liked and recognised as the beauty of the school, the daughter of Horace Smith, author of Rejected Addresses. On the whole, looking back after the long interval, it seems to me that the young creatures there assembled were full of capabilities for widely extended usefulness and influence. Many were decidedly clever and nearly all were well disposed. There was very little malice or any other vicious ideas or feelings, and no worldliness at all amongst us. * * *

But all this fine human material was deplorably wasted. Nobody dreamed that any one of us could in later life be more or less than an "Ornament of Society." That a pupil in that school should ever become an artist, or authoress, would have been looked upon by both Miss Runciman and Miss Roberts as a deplorable dereliction. Not that which was good in itself or useful to the community, or even that which

3. An allusion to Dante Gabriel Rossetti's poem, The Blessed Damozel (see page 1713).

would be delightful to ourselves, but that which would make us admired in society, was the *raison d'être* [reason for being] of each acquirement. Everything was taught us in the inverse ratio of its true importance. At the bottom of the scale were Morals and Religion, and at the top were Music and Dancing; miserably poor music, too, of the Italian school then in vogue, and generally performed in a showy and tasteless manner on harp or piano. I can recall an amusing instance in which the order of precedence above described was naïvely betrayed by one of our schoolmistresses when she was admonishing one of the girls who had been detected in a lie. "Don't you know, you naughty girl," said Miss R. impressively, before the whole school: "don't you know we had *almost* rather find you have a P—" (the mark of Pretty Well) "in your music, than tell such falsehoods?"

It mattered nothing whether we had any "music in our souls" or any voices in our throats, equally we were driven through the dreary course of practising daily for a couple of hours under a German teacher, and then receiving lessons twice or three times a week from a music master (Griesbach by name) and a singing master. Many of us, myself in particular, in addition to these had a harp master, a Frenchman named Labarre, who gave us lessons at a guinea apiece, while we could only play with one hand at a time. Lastly there were a few young ladies who took instructions in the new instruments, the concertina and the accordion!

The waste of money involved in all this, the piles of useless music, and songs never to be sung, for which our parents had to pay, and the loss of priceless time for ourselves, were truly deplorable; and the result of course in many cases (as in my own) complete failure. One day I said to the good little German teacher, who nourished a hopeless attachment for Schiller's Marquis Posa,[4] and was altogether a sympathetic person, "My dear Fraulein, I mean to practise this piece of Beethoven's till I conquer it." "My dear," responded the honest Fraulein, "you do practice that piece for seex hours a day, and you do live till you are seexty, at the end you will *not* play it!" Yet so hopeless a pupil was compelled to learn for years, not only the piano, but the harp and singing!

Next to music in importance in our curriculum came dancing. The famous old Madame Michaud and her husband both attended us constantly, and we danced to their direction in our large play-room (*lucus a non lucendo*[5]), till we had learned not only all the dances in use in England in that ante-polka epoch, but almost every national dance in Europe, the Minuet, the Gavotte, the Cachucha, the Bolero, the Mazurka, and the Tarantella. To see the stout old lady in her heavy green velvet dress, with furbelow[6] a foot deep of sable, going through the latter cheerful performance for our ensample, was a sight not to be forgotten. Beside the dancing we had "calisthenic" lessons every week from a "Capitaine." Somebody, who put us through manifold exercises with poles and dumbbells. How much better a few good country scrambles would have been than all these calisthenics it is needless to say, but our dismal walks were confined to parading the esplanade[7] and neighbouring terraces. Our parties never exceeded six, a governess being one of the number, and we looked down from an immeasurable height of superiority on the processions of twenty and thirty girls belonging to other schools. The governess who accompanied us had

---

4. In Friedrich von Schiller's play *Don Carlos* (1787), Posa is a self-sacrificing advocate of religious tolerance and democratic rule.
5. An ironic Latin phrase for naming something after

what it lacks; Cobbe means that there was no play to be found in that playroom.
6. Showy fringe.
7. A public promenade.

enough to do with her small party, for it was her duty to utilise these brief hours of bodily exercise by hearing us repeat our French, Italian or German verbs, according to her own nationality.

Next to Music and Dancing and Deportment, came Drawing, but that was not a sufficiently *voyant* [remarkable] accomplishment, and no great attention was paid to it; the instruction also being of a second-rate kind, except that it included lessons in perspective which have been useful to me ever since. Then followed Modern Languages. No Greek or Latin were heard of at the school, but French, Italian and German were chattered all day long, our tongues being only set at liberty at six o'clock to speak English. *Such* French, such Italian, and such German as we actually spoke may be more easily imagined than described. We had bad "Marks" for speaking wrong languages, *e.g.*, French when we were bound to speak Italian or German, and a dreadful mark for bad French, which was transferred from one to another all day long, and was a fertile source of tears and quarrels, involving as it did a heavy lesson out of Noel et Chapsal's Grammar on the last holder at night. We also read in each language every day to the French, Italian and German ladies, recited lessons to them, and wrote exercises for the respective masters who attended every week. * * *

Naturally after (a very long way after) foreign languages came the study of English. We had a writing and arithmetic master (whom we unanimously abhorred and despised, though one and all of us grievously needed his instructions) and an "English master," who taught us to write "themes," and to whom I, for one, feel that I owe, perhaps, more than to any other teacher in that school, few as were the hours which we were permitted to waste on so insignificant an art as composition in our native tongue! * * *

Lastly, as I have said, in point of importance, came our religious instruction. Our well-meaning schoolmistresses thought it was obligatory on them to teach us something of the kind, but, being very obviously altogether worldly women themselves, they were puzzled how to carry out their intentions. They marched us to church every Sunday when it did not rain, and they made us on Sunday mornings repeat the Collect and Catechism; but beyond these exercises of body and mind, it was hard for them to see what to do for our spiritual welfare. One Ash Wednesday, I remember, they provided us with a dish of salt-fish, and when this was removed to make room for the roast mutton, they addressed us in a short discourse, setting forth the merits of fasting, and ending by the remark that they left us free to take meat or not as we pleased, but that they hoped we should fast; "it would be good for our souls AND OUR FIGURES!"

Each morning we were bound publicly to repeat a text out of certain little books, called *Daily Bread,* left in our bedrooms, and always scanned in frantic haste while "doing-up" our hair at the glass, or gabbled aloud by one damsel so occupied while her room-fellow (there were never more than two in each bed-chamber) was splashing about behind the screen in her bath. Down, when the prayer-bell rang, both were obliged to hurry and breathlessly to await the chance of being called on first to repeat the text of the day, the penalty for oblivion being the loss of a "card." Then came a chapter of the Bible, read verse by verse amongst us, and then our books were shut and a solemn question was asked. On one occasion I remember it was: "What have you just been reading, Miss S——?" Miss S——(now a lady of high rank and fashion, whose small wits had been wool-gathering) peeped surreptitiously into her Bible again, and then responded with just confidence, "The First Epistle, Ma'am, of *General Peter.*"[8]

8. Instead of *The First Epistle General of Peter.*

It is almost needless to add, in concluding these reminiscences, that the hetero-geneous studies pursued in this helter-skelter fashion were of the smallest possible utility in later life; each acquirement being of the shallowest and most imperfect kind, and all real education worthy of the name having to be begun on our return home, after we had been pronounced "finished."

1894

Sarah Stickney Ellis
1799–1872

Author of numerous popular guides to female conduct, including *The Women of England* (1839), *The Daughters of England* (1842), *The Wives of England* (1843), and *The Mothers of England* (1845), Sarah Stickney Ellis advised women to accept their inferiority to men and devote themselves to the happiness and moral elevation of their brothers, husbands, and sons. Idealizing the family home as the center of middle-class English life, Ellis fostered the notion of women's separate domestic sphere. Although she ran a school for girls, Ellis dis-couraged intellectual ambitions, demanding precisely the sort of self-sacrificing domesticity that Florence Nightingale, and many other talented and capable women, found so intolerably confining.

from The Women of England:
Their Social Duties and Domestic Habits
[THE INFLUENCE OF WOMEN]

It is not to be presumed that women *possess* more power than men; but happily for them, such are their early impressions, associations, and general position in the world, that their moral feelings are less liable to be impaired by the pecuniary objects which too often constitute the chief end of man, and which, even under the limita-tions of better principle, necessarily engage a large portion of his thoughts. There are many humble-minded women, not remarkable for any particular intellectual endow-ments, who yet possess so clear a sense of the right and wrong of individual actions, as to be of essential service in aiding the judgments of their husbands, brothers, or sons, in those intricate affairs in which it is sometimes difficult to dissever worldly wisdom from religious duty.

* * * And surely they now need more than ever all the assistance which Provi-dence has kindly provided, to win them away from this warfare, to remind them that they are hastening on towards a world into which none of the treasures they are amassing can be admitted; and, next to those holier influences which operate through the medium of revelation, or through the mysterious instrumentality of Di-vine love, I have little hesitation in saying, that the society of woman in her highest moral capacity, is best calculated to effect this purpose.

How often has man returned to his home with a mind confused by the many voices, which in the mart, the exchange, or the public assembly, have addressed themselves to his inborn selfishness, or his worldly pride; and while his integrity was shaken, and his resolution gave way beneath the pressure of apparent necessity, or the insidious pretences of expediency, he has stood corrected before the clear eye of woman, as it looked directly to the naked truth, and detected the lurking evil of the specious act he was about to commit. Nay, so potent may have become this secret influence, that he may have borne it about with him like a kind of second conscience, for mental reference, and spiritual counsel, in moments of trial; and when the snares of the world were around him, and temptations from within and without have bribed over the witness in his own bosom, he has thought of the humble monitress who sat alone, guarding the fireside comforts of his distant home; and the remembrance of her character, clothed in moral beauty, has scattered the clouds before his mental vision, and sent him back to that beloved home, a wiser and a better man.

The women of England, possessing the grand privilege of being better instructed than those of any other country, in the minutiae of domestic comfort, have obtained a degree of importance in society far beyond what their unobtrusive virtues would appear to claim. The long-established customs of their country have placed in their hands the high and holy duty of cherishing and protecting the minor morals of life, from whence springs all that is elevated in purpose, and glorious in action. The sphere of their direct personal influence is central, and consequently small; but its extreme operations are as widely extended as the range of human feeling. They may be less striking in society than some of the women of other countries, and may feel themselves, on brilliant and stirring occasions, as simple, rude, and unsophisticated in the popular science of excitement; but as far as the noble daring of Britain has sent forth her adventurous sons, and that is to every point of danger on the habitable globe, they have borne along with them a generosity, a disinterestedness, and a moral courage, derived in no small measure from the female influence of their native country.

It is a fact well worthy of our most serious attention, and one which bears immediately upon the subject under consideration, that the present state of our national affairs is such as to indicate that the influence of woman in counteracting the growing evils of society is about to be more needed than ever. * * *

Will an increase of intellectual attainments, or a higher style of accomplishments, effect this purpose? Will the common-place frivolities of morning calls, or an interminable range of superficial reading, enable them to assist their brothers, their husbands, or their sons in becoming happier and better men?—No: let the aspect of society be what it may, man is a social being, and beneath the hard surface he puts on, to fit him for the wear and tear of every day, he has a heart as true to the kindly affections of our nature, as that of woman—as true, though not as suddenly awakened to every pressing call. He has therefore need of all her sisterly services—and under the pressure of the present times, he needs them more than ever—to foster in his nature, and establish in his character that higher tone of feeling, without which he can enjoy nothing beyond a kind of animal existence. * * *

In order to ascertain what kind of education is most effective in making woman what she ought to be, the best method is to inquire into the character, station, and peculiar duties of woman throughout the largest portion of her earthly career; and then ask, for what she is most valued, admired, and beloved?

In answer to this, I have little hesitation in saying,—For her disinterested kindness. Look at all the heroines, whether of romance or reality—at all the female characters that are held up to universal admiration—at all who have gone down to honoured graves, amongst the tears and the lamentations of their survivors. Have these been the learned, the accomplished women; the women who could speak many languages, who could solve problems, and elucidate systems of philosophy? No: or if they have, they have also been women who were dignified with the majesty of moral greatness—women who regarded not themselves, their own feebleness, or their own susceptibility of pain, but who, endued with an almost super-human energy, could trample under foot every impediment that intervened between them and the accomplishment of some great object upon which their hopes were fixed, while that object was wholly unconnected with their own personal exaltation or enjoyment, and related only to some beloved object, whose suffering was their sorrow, whose good their gain. * * *

Never yet, however, was woman great, because she had great acquirements; nor can she ever be great in herself—personally, and without instrumentality—as an object, not an agent. * * *

Let us single out from any particular seminary a child who has been there from the years of ten to fifteen, and reckon, if it can be reckoned, the pains that have been spent in making that child a proficient in Latin. Have the same pains been spent in making her disinterestedly kind? And yet what man is there in existence who would not rather his wife should be free from selfishness, than be able to read Virgil without the use of a dictionary. * * *

Taking into consideration the various excellencies and peculiarities of woman, I am inclined to think that the sphere which of all others admits of the highest development of her character, is the chamber of sickness; and how frequently and mournfully familiar are the scenes in which she is thus called to act and feel, let the private history of every family declare.

There is but a very small proportion of the daughters of farmers, manufacturers, and tradespeople, in England, who are ever called upon for their Latin, their Italian, or even for their French; but all women in this sphere of life are liable to be called upon to visit and care for the sick; and if in the hour of weakness and of suffering, they prove to be unacquainted with any probable means of alleviation, and wholly ignorant of the most judicious and suitable mode of offering relief and consolation, they are indeed deficient in one of the highest attainments in the way of usefulness, to which a woman can aspire. * * *

Women have the choice of many means of bringing their principles into exercise, and of obtaining influence, both in their own domestic sphere, and in society at large. Amongst the most important of these is *conversation*, an engine so powerful upon the minds and characters of mankind in general, that beauty fades before it, and wealth in comparison is but as leaden coin. If match-making were indeed the great object of human life, I should scarcely dare to make this assertion, since few men choose women for their conversation, where wealth or beauty are to be had. * * *

* * * But if she has no intellectual hold upon her husband's heart, she must inevitably become that most helpless and pitiable of earthly objects—a slighted wife.

Conversation, understood in its proper character, as distinct from mere talk, might rescue her from this. Not conversation upon books, if her husband happens to be a fox-hunter; nor upon fox-hunting, if he is a book-worm; but exactly that kind of conversation which is best adapted to his tastes and habits, yet at the same time capable of leading him a little out of both into a wider field of observation, and subjects he may never have derived amusement from before, simply from the fact of their never having been presented to his notice.—How pleasantly the evening hours may be made to pass, when a woman who really can converse, will thus beguile the time. But, on the other hand, how wretched is the portion of that man who dreads the dulness of his own fireside! who sees the clog of his existence ever seated there—the same, in the deadening influence she has upon his spirits to-day, as yesterday, to-morrow, and the next day, and the next!

1839

Charlotte Brontë
1816–1855

To be a governess or schoolteacher was one of the very few professions open to a middle-class woman, but it was not an enviable life. Rarely was the governess treated as an equal by her employers, even though she was expected to be a "lady." Poorly paid and often rudely treated, she could be fired at a moment's notice, for there was an abundance of needy single women eager to take her place. Charlotte Brontë's novel *Jane Eyre* (1847) portrayed the social isolation of a governess, who is ridiculed to her face by visiting ladies. Brontë's own experiences were unhappy, as this letter to her sister reveals. In another letter, Brontë wrote that it was better to be "a housemaid or kitchen girl, rather than a baited, trampled, desolate, distracted governess."

from Letter to Emily Brontë[1]
[The Horrors of Governessing]

STONEGAPPE, June 8th, 1839

* * * I have striven hard to be pleased with my new situation. The country, the house, and the grounds are, as I have said, divine. But, alack-a-day! there is such a thing as seeing all beautiful around you—pleasant woods, winding white paths, green lawns, and blue sunshiny sky—and not having a free moment or a free thought left to enjoy them in. The children are constantly with me, and more riotous, perverse, unmanageable cubs never grew. As for correcting them, I soon quickly found that was entirely out of the question: they are to do as they like. A complaint to Mrs Sidgwick brings only black looks upon oneself, and unjust, partial excuses to screen the children. I have tried that plan once. It succeeded so notably that I shall try it no more. I said in my last letter that Mrs Sidgwick did not know me. I now begin to find that she does not intend to know me, that she cares nothing in the world about me except to contrive how the greatest possible quantity of labour may be squeezed out of me, and to that end she overwhelms me with oceans of needlework, yards of cambric to hem, muslin nightcaps to make, and, above all things, dolls to dress. I do not think she likes me at all, because I can't help being shy in such an entirely novel scene, surrounded as I have hitherto been by strange and constantly changing faces. I used to think I should like to be in the stir of grand folks' society but I have had enough of it—it is dreary work to look on and listen. I see now more clearly than I have ever done before that a private governess has no existence, is not considered as a living and rational being except as connected with the wearisome duties she has to fulfil. While she is teaching the children, working for them, amusing them, it is all right. If she steals a moment for herself she is a nuisance. Nevertheless, Mrs Sidgwick is universally considered an amiable woman. Her manners are fussily affable. She talks a

---

1. Text taken from *The Brontës: Their Lives, Friendships and Correspondence*, vol. 1 (1933, rpt. 1980).

Richard Redgrave, *The Poor Teacher*, 1844. Narrative painting was enormously popular with the Victorians, who delighted in "reading" the story in symbolic visual details and drawing a moral from it. Here Redgrave, whose sisters were governesses, draws attention to his subject's social and emotional isolation. Dressed in mourning, the solitary governess sits indoors while her gaily-clad pupils skip rope in the sunlight, apparently indifferent to the bad news contained in her black-bordered letter. She has been playing "Home Sweet Home" on the piano. With copy books still to correct, she is about to consume her supper, a meager slice of bread and a tiny cup of tea. Contemporary observers speculated that she was an orphan, whose pallor revealed that she was already wasting away from illness and overwork.

great deal, but as it seems to me not much to the purpose. Perhaps I may like her better after a while. At present I have no call to her. Mr Sidgwick is in my opinion a hundred times better—less profession, less bustling condescension, but a far kinder heart. It is very seldom that he speaks to me, but when he does I always feel happier and more settled for some minutes after. He never asks me to wipe the children's smutty noses or tie their shoes or fetch their pinafores or set them a chair. * * *

Anne Brontë
1820–1849

Like her older sisters, Charlotte and Emily, Anne Brontë tried to earn her living as a governess. All of them were made miserable by the constant drudgery and humiliations, and by being cut off, as governesses usually were, from family and friends. Her autobiographical novel

Agnes Grey (1847) dramatizes Anne Brontë's own experience of working as a governess. Initially, she had looked forward to the job: "How delightful it would be to be a governess!" says Agnes: "To go out into the world; to enter into a new life; to act for myself; to exercise my unused faculties." But Agnes had not yet realized the drawbacks of a governess's anomalous social status: caught between disrespectful children and contemptuous parents, she was made grimly conscious of her dependent position.

from Agnes Grey
[THE GOVERNESS TORMENTED BY HER CHARGES]

I returned, however, with unabated vigour to my work—a more arduous task than any one can imagine, who has not felt something like the misery of being charged with the care and direction of a set of mischievous turbulent rebels, whom his utmost exertions cannot bind to their duty; while, at the same time, he is responsible for their conduct to a higher power, who exacts from him what cannot be achieved without the aid of the superior's more potent authority: which, either from indolence, or the fear of becoming unpopular with the said rebellious gang, the latter refuses to give. I can conceive few situations more harassing than that wherein, however you may long for success, however you may labour to fulfil your duty, your efforts are baffled and set at nought by those beneath you, and unjustly censured and misjudged by those above. * * *

I particularly remember one wild, snowy afternoon, soon after my return in January; the children had all come up from dinner, loudly declaring that they meant "to be naughty"; and they had well kept their resolution, though I had talked myself hoarse, and wearied every muscle in my throat, in the vain attempt to reason them out of it. I had got Tom pinned up in a corner, whence, I told him, he should not escape till he had done his appointed task. Meantime, Fanny had possessed herself of my work-bag, and was rifling its contents—and spitting into it besides. I told her to let it alone, but to no purpose, of course.

"Burn it, Fanny!" cried Tom; and *this* command she hastened to obey. I sprang to snatch it from the fire, and Tom darted to the door.

"Mary Ann, throw her desk[1] out of the window!" cried he: and my precious desk, containing my letters and papers, my small amount of cash, and all my valuables, was about to be precipitated from the three-story window. I flew to rescue it. Meanwhile Tom had left the room, and was rushing down the stairs, followed by Fanny. Having secured my desk, I ran to catch them, and Mary Ann came scampering after. All three escaped me, and ran out of the house into the garden, where they plunged about in the snow, shouting and screaming in exultant glee.

What must I do? If I followed them, I should probably be unable to capture one, and only drive them farther away; if I did not, how was I to get them in? and what would their parents think of me, if they saw or heard the children rioting, hatless, bonnetless, gloveless, and bootless, in the deep, soft snow?

While I stood in this perplexity, just without the door, trying by grim looks and angry words, to awe them into subjection, I heard a voice behind me, in harshly piercing tones, exclaiming,—

"Miss Grey! Is it possible? What, in the devil's name, can you be thinking about?"

"I can't get them in, sir," said I, turning round, and beholding Mr Bloomfield, with his hair on end, and his pale blue eyes bolting from their sockets.

---

1. Portable box for writing materials and letters, sometimes with a sloping surface for writing on.

"But I INSIST upon their being got in!" cried he, approaching nearer, and looking perfectly ferocious.

"Then, sir, you must call them yourself, if you please, for they won't listen to me," I replied, stepping back.

"Come in with you, you filthy brats! or I'll horsewhip you, every one!" roared he; and the children instantly obeyed. "There, you see! they come at the first word!"

"Yes, when *you* speak."

"And it's very strange, that when you've the care of 'em, you've no better control over 'em than that!—Now, there they are, gone upstairs with their nasty snowy feet! Do go after 'em and see them made decent, for Heaven's sake!"

That gentleman's mother was then staying in the house; and, as I ascended the stairs and passed the drawing-room door, I had the satisfaction of hearing the old lady declaiming aloud to her daughter-in-law to this effect (for I could only distinguish the most emphatic words)—

"Gracious Heavens!—never in all my life!—!—get their death as sure as—! Do you think, my dear, she's a *proper person?* Take my word for it—"

I heard no more, but that sufficed.

1847

John Henry Cardinal Newman
1801–1890

The ideal of gentlemanliness was central to the Victorians' notion of themselves, yet for a society in flux it was a concept increasingly difficult to pin down. What exactly *was* a gentleman? In most people's minds, property, birth, courage, and athleticism were essential ingredients. And, of course, a gentleman was assumed to be a Christian. But John Henry Cardinal Newman distinguishes between the two: in a series of lectures about the purposes of a liberal education he said that while the gentleman has "a cultivated intellect, a delicate taste, a candid, equitable, dispassionate mind, a noble and courteous bearing in the conduct of life . . . they are no guarantee for sanctity or even for conscientiousness; they may attach to the man of the world, to the profligate, to the heartless." Thus for Newman, who was both, a gentleman is not necessarily a Christian: one may have character and education but not faith. He subtly suggests the vanity behind the gentleman's courtesy; gentility and virtue are not necessarily the same thing.

For more about Newman, see Perspectives: Religion and Science, page 1376.

from The Idea of a University
[A DEFINITION OF A GENTLEMAN]

Hence it is that it is almost a definition of a gentleman to say he is one who never inflicts pain. This description is both refined and, as far as it goes, accurate. He is mainly occupied in merely removing the obstacles which hinder the free and unembarrassed action of those about him; and he concurs with their movements rather than takes the initiative himself. His benefits may be considered as parallel to what are called comforts or conveniences in arrangements of a personal nature: like an easy chair or a good fire, which do their part in dispelling cold and fatigue, though nature provides both means of rest and animal heat without them. The true gentleman in like manner carefully avoids whatever may cause a jar or a jolt in the minds of those with whom he is cast;—all clashing of opinion, or collision of feeling, all restraint, or suspicion, or gloom, or resentment; his great concern being to make every one at their ease and at home. He has his eyes on all his company; he is tender towards the bashful, gentle towards the distant, and merciful towards the absurd; he can recollect to whom he is speaking; he guards against unseasonable allusions, or topics which may irritate; he is seldom prominent in conversation, and never wearisome. He makes light of favours while he does them, and seems to be receiving when he is conferring. He never speaks of himself except when compelled, never defends himself by a mere retort, he has no ears for slander or gossip, is scrupulous in imputing motives to those who interfere with him, and interprets every thing for the best. He is never mean or little in his disputes, never takes unfair advantage, never mistakes personalities or sharp sayings for arguments, or insinuates evil which he dare not say out. From a longsighted prudence, he observes the maxim of the ancient sage, that we should ever conduct ourselves towards our enemy as if he were one day to be our friend. He has too much good sense to be affronted at insults, he is too well employed to remember injuries, and too indolent to bear malice. He is patient, forbearing, and resigned, on philosophical principles; he submits to pain, because it is inevitable, to bereavement, because it is irreparable, and to death, because it is his destiny. If he engages in controversy of any kind, his disciplined intellect preserves him from the blundering discourtesy of better, perhaps, but less educated minds; who, like blunt weapons, tear and hack instead of cutting clean, who mistake the point in argument, waste their strength on trifles, misconceive their adversary, and leave the question more involved than they find it. He may be right or wrong in his opinion, but he is too clear-headed to be unjust; he is as simple as he is forcible, and as brief as he is decisive. Nowhere shall we find greater candour, consideration, indulgence: he throws himself into the minds of his opponents, he accounts for their mistakes. He knows the weakness of human reason as well as its strength, its province and its limits. If he be an unbeliever, he will be too profound and large-minded to ridicule religion or to act against it; he is too wise to be a dogmatist or fanatic in his infidelity. He respects piety and devotion; he even supports institutions as venerable, beautiful, or useful, to which he does not assent; he honours the ministers of religion, and it contents him to decline its mysteries without assailing or denouncing them. He is a friend of religious toleration, and that, not only because his philosophy has taught him to look on all forms of faith with an impartial eye, but also from the gentleness and effeminacy of feeling, which is the attendant on civilization.

1852

Caroline Norton
1808–1877

In the nineteenth century, a woman's person and property were at her husband's disposal, not merely by custom but by law. The thinking was that "husband and wife are one person, and the husband is that person." The celebrated case of Caroline Norton, trapped in a disastrous marriage to a brutal man, helped bring this injustice into the public eye. Her husband denied her access to their three sons (a father had sole custody of his children) and tried to seize her earnings as a writer. Norton's passionate and articulate agitation aided passage of the Infant Custody Act (1839) and the Divorce and Matrimonial Causes Act (1857). But not until after her death, with the Married Women's Property Act of 1882, did married women finally gain the right to hold property.

from A Letter to the Queen

A married woman in England has *no legal existence:* her being is absorbed in that of her husband. Years of separation or desertion can not alter this position. Unless divorced by special enactment in the House of Lords, the legal fiction holds her to be "*one*" with her husband, even though she may never see or hear of him.

She has no possessions, unless by special settlement; her property is *his* property. Lord Ellenborough mentions a case in which a sailor bequeathed "all he was worth" to a woman he cohabited with; and afterwards married, in the West Indies, a woman of considerable fortune. At this man's death it was held,—notwithstanding the hardship of the case,—that the will swept away from his widow, in favour of his mistress, every shilling of the property. It is now provided that a will shall be revoked by marriage: but the claim of *the husband* to all that is his wife's exists in full force. An English wife has no legal right even to her clothes or ornaments; her husband may take them and sell them if he pleases, even though they be the gifts of relatives or friends, or bought before marriage.

An English wife cannot make a will. She may have children or kindred whom she may earnestly desire to benefit;—she may be separated from her husband, who may be living with a mistress; no matter: the law gives what she has to him, and no will she could make would be valid.

An English wife cannot legally claim her own earnings. Whether wages for manual labour, or payment for intellectual exertion, whether she weed potatoes, or keep a school, her salary is *the husband's;* and he could compel a second payment, and treat the first as void, if paid to the wife without his sanction.

An English wife may not leave her husband's house. Not only can he sue her for "restitution of conjugal rights," but he has a right to enter the house of any friend or relation with whom she may take refuge, and who may "harbour her,"—as it is termed,—and carry her away by force, with or without the aid of the police.

If the wife sue for separation for cruelty, it must be "cruelty that endangers life or limb," and if she has once forgiven, or, in legal phrase, "*condoned*" his offences, she cannot plead them; though her past forgiveness only proves that she endured as long as endurance was possible.

If her husband take proceedings for a divorce, she is not, in the first instance, allowed to defend herself. She has no means of proving the falsehood of his allegation. She is not represented by attorney, nor permitted to be considered a party to the suit between him and her supposed lover, for "damages." Lord Brougham affirmed in the House of Lords: "*in the action the character of the woman was at immediate issue, although she was not prosecuted. The consequence not unfrequently was, that the character of a woman was sworn away; instances were known in which, by collusion between the husband and a pretended paramour, the character of the wife has been destroyed. All this could take place, and yet the wife had no defence; she was excluded from Westminster-hall, and behind her back, by the principles of our jurisprudence, her character was tried between her husband and the man called her paramour.*"

If an English wife be guilty of infidelity, her husband can divorce *her* so as to marry again; but she cannot divorce the husband *a vinculo,*[1] however profligate he

1. A nullification of the marriage, granted only for reasons of mental incompetence, sexual impotence, or fraud.

may be. No law court can divorce in England. A special Act of Parliament annulling the marriage, is passed for each case. The House of Lords grants this almost as a matter of course to the husband, but not to the wife. In only four instances (two of which were cases of incest), has the wife obtained a divorce to marry again.

She cannot prosecute for a libel. Her husband must prosecute; and in cases of enmity and separation, of course she is without a remedy.

She cannot sign a lease, or transact responsible business.

She cannot claim support, as a matter of personal right, from her husband. The general belief and nominal rule is, that her husband is "bound to maintain her." That is not the law. He is not bound to *her*. He is bound to his country; bound to see that she does not cumber the parish in which she resides. If it be proved that means sufficient are at her disposal, from relatives or friends, her husband is quit of his obligation, and need not contribute a farthing:[2] even if he have deserted her; or be in receipt of money which is hers by inheritance. * * *

Separation from her husband by consent, or for his ill usage, does not alter their mutual relation. He retains the right to divorce her *after* separation,—as before,—though he himself be unfaithful.

Her being, on the other hand, of spotless character, and without reproach, gives her no advantage in law. She may have withdrawn from his roof knowing that he lives with "his faithful housekeeper": having suffered personal violence at his hands; having "condoned" much, and being able to prove it by unimpeachable testimony: or he may have shut the doors of her house against her: all this is quite immaterial: the law takes no cognisance of which is to blame. As *her husband*, he has a right to all that is hers: as *his wife*, she has no right to anything that is his. As her husband, he may divorce her (if truth or false swearing can do it): as his wife, the utmost "divorce" she could obtain, is permission to reside alone,—married to his name. The marriage ceremony is a civil bond for him,—and an indissoluble sacrament for her; and the rights of mutual property which that ceremony is ignorantly supposed to confer, are made absolute for him, and null for her.

Of course, an opposite picture may be drawn. There are bad, wanton, irreclaimable women, as there are vicious, profligate, tyrannical men: but the difference is *this*: that to punish and restrain bad wives, there are laws, and very severe laws (to say nothing of social condemnation); while to punish or restrain bad husbands, there is, in England, no adequate law whatever. Indeed, the English law holds out a sort of premium on infidelity; for there is no doubt that the woman, who is divorced for a lover and marries him, suffers less (except in conscience) than the woman who *does not deserve to suffer at all*—the wife of a bad husband, who can inflict what he pleases, whether she remain in her home, or attempt to leave it.

Such, however, is "the law": and if anything could add to the ridicule, confusion, and injustice of its provision, it would be the fact, that though it is law for the rich, it is not law for the poor; and though it is the law in England, it is not the law in Scotland!

It is not law for the poor.

Since the days of Henry VIII, for whose passions it was contrived, our method of divorce has remained an indulgence sacred to the aristocracy of England. The poorer classes have no form of divorce amongst them. The rich man makes a new marriage, having divorced his wife in the House of Lords: his new marriage is legal; his children

2. A quarter of a penny.

are legitimate; his bride occupies, in all respects, the same social position as if he had never previously been wedded. The poor man makes a new marriage, *not* having divorced his wife in the House of Lords; his new marriage is null; his children are bastards; and he himself is liable to be put on his trial for bigamy: the allotted punishment for which crime, at one time was hanging, and is now imprisonment. Not always offending knowingly,—for nothing can exceed the ignorance of the poor on this subject; they believe a Magistrate can divorce them, that an absence of seven years constitutes a nullity of the marriage tie, or that they can give each other reciprocal permission to divorce: and among some of our rural populations, the grosser belief prevails, that a man may legally *sell* his wife, and so break the bond of union! They believe anything,—rather than what is the fact,—viz., that *they* cannot do legally, that which they know is done legally in the classes above them; that the comfort of the rich man's home, or the indulgence of the rich man's passions, receives a consideration in England which the poor need not expect to obtain.

It is not the law of Scotland. In your Majesty's kingdom, nothing but "The rapid running of the silver Tweed" divides that portion of the realm where women are protected by law,—from that portion where they are *unprotected*, though living under the same Sovereign and the same government!

1855

George Eliot
1819–1880

George Eliot was the pen name of Mary Ann Evans, who scandalized Victorian society by her decision in 1854 to live openly with a married man. Her family refused to have anything more to do with the "fallen woman," but the socially outcast Eliot went on to become one of the most revered novelists of the age. Writing under a male pseudonym, she discovered her creative genius in midlife and published a series of highly successful novels, including *Adam Bede* (1859), *The Mill on the Floss* (1860), *Silas Marner* (1861), *Romola* (1863), *Felix Holt* (1866), *Middlemarch* (1871–1872), and *Daniel Deronda* (1876). Although her formal education had ended at sixteen, George Eliot read widely on her own, teaching herself foreign languages and studying philosophy and theology; in her thirties, she became an editor of the influential *Westminster Review*. In this essay, she argues eloquently against the popular notion that an ignorant woman makes the best wife: "Men pay a heavy price for their reluctance to encourage self-help and independent resources in women."

 For additional resources on Eliot, go to *The Longman Anthology of British Literature* Web site at www.ablongman.com/damroschbritlit3e.

Margaret Fuller and Mary Wollstonecraft[1]

The dearth of new books just now gives us time to recur to less recent ones which we have hitherto noticed but slightly; and among these we choose the late edition of Margaret Fuller's *Woman in the Nineteenth Century*, because we think it has been

---

1. This essay, originally published in *The Leader* (1855), reviews two influential feminist works. Margaret Fuller (1810–1850), an American associated with the New England transcendentalist movement, was the author of *Woman in the Nineteenth Century* (1843; 1855). Mary Wollstonecraft (1759–1797), the wife of William Godwin and mother of Mary Shelley, was best known for writing *A Vindication of the Rights of Woman* (1792), page 281. See also Perspectives: The Wollstonecraft Controversy and the Rights of Women, page 319.

unduly thrust into the background by less comprehensive and candid productions on the same subject. Notwithstanding certain defects of taste and a sort of vague spiritualism and grandiloquence which belong to all but the very best American writers, the book is a valuable one: it has the enthusiasm of a noble and sympathetic nature, with the moderation and breadth and large allowance of a vigorous and cultivated understanding. There is no exaggeration of woman's moral excellence or intellectual capabilities; no injudicious insistence on her fitness for this or that function hitherto engrossed by men; but a calm plea for the removal of unjust laws and artificial restrictions, so that the possibilities of her nature may have room for full development, a wisely stated demand to disencumber her of the

> parasitic forms
> That seem to keep her up, but drag her down—
> And leave her field to burgeon and to bloom
> From all within her, make herself her own
> To give or keep, to live and learn and be
> All that not harms distinctive womanhood.[2]

It is interesting to compare this essay of Margaret Fuller's, published in its earliest form in 1843, with a work on the position of woman, written between sixty and seventy years ago—we mean Mary Wollstonecraft's *Rights of Woman*. The latter work was not continued beyond the first volume; but so far as this carries the subject, the comparison, at least in relation to strong sense and loftiness of moral tone, is not at all disadvantageous to the woman of the last century. There is in some quarters a vague prejudice against the *Rights of Woman* as in some way or other a reprehensible book, but readers who go to it with this impression will be surprised to find it eminently serious, severely moral, and withal rather heavy—the true reason, perhaps, that no edition has been published since 1796, and that it is now rather scarce. There are several points of resemblance, as well as of striking difference, between the two books. A strong understanding is present in both; but Margaret Fuller's mind was like some regions of her own American continent, where you are constantly stepping from the sunny "clearings" into the mysterious twilight of the tangled forest—she often passes in one breath from forcible reasoning to dreamy vagueness; moreover, her unusually varied culture gives her great command of illustration. Mary Wollstonecraft, on the other hand, is nothing if not rational; she has no erudition, and her grave pages are lit up by no ray of fancy. In both writers we discern, under the brave bearing of a strong and truthful nature, the beating of a loving woman's heart, which teaches them not to undervalue the smallest offices of domestic care or kindliness. But Margaret Fuller, with all her passionate sensibility, is more of the literary woman, who would not have been satisfied without intellectual production; Mary Wollstonecraft, we imagine, wrote not at all for writing's sake, but from the pressure of other motives. So far as the difference of date allows, there is a striking coincidence in their trains of thought; indeed, every important idea in the *Rights of Woman*, except the combination of home education with a common day-school for boys and girls, reappears in Margaret Fuller's essay.

One point on which they both write forcibly is the fact that, while men have a horror of such faculty or culture in the other sex as tends to place it on a level with

2. Tennyson, *The Princess* 7.253–58; see page 1259.

their own, they are really in a state of subjection to ignorant and feeble-minded women. Margaret Fuller says:—

> Wherever man is sufficiently raised above extreme poverty or brutal stupidity, to care for the comforts of the fireside, or the bloom and ornament of life, woman has always power enough, if she choose to exert it, and is usually disposed to do so, in proportion to her ignorance and childish vanity. Unacquainted with the importance of life and its purposes, trained to a selfish coquetry and love of petty power, she does not look beyond the pleasure of making herself felt at the moment, and governments are shaken and commerce broken up to gratify the pique of a female favourite. The English shopkeeper's wife does not vote, but it is for her interest that the politician canvasses by the coarsest flattery.

Again:—

> All wives, bad or good, loved or unloved, inevitably influence their husbands from the power their position not merely gives, but necessitates of colouring evidence and infusing feelings in hours when the—patient, shall I call him?—is off his guard.

Hear now what Mary Wollstonecraft says on the same subject:—

> Women have been allowed to remain in ignorance and slavish dependence many, very many years, and still we hear of nothing but their fondness of pleasure and sway, their preference of rakes and soldiers, their childish attachment to toys, and the vanity that makes them value accomplishments more than virtues. History brings forward a fearful catalogue of the crimes which their cunning has produced, when the weak slaves have had sufficient address to overreach their masters. . . . When, therefore, I call women slaves, I mean in a political and civil sense; for indirectly they obtain too much power, and are debased by their exertions to obtain illicit sway. . . . The libertinism,[3] and even the virtues of superior men, will always give women of some description great power over them; and these weak women, under the influence of childish passions and selfish vanity, *will throw a false light over the objects which the very men view with their eyes who ought to enlighten their judgment.* Men of fancy, and those sanguine[4] characters who mostly hold the helm of human affairs in general, relax in the society of women; and surely I need not cite to the most superficial reader of history the numerous examples of vice and oppression which the private intrigues of female favourites have produced; not to dwell on the mischief that naturally arises from the blundering interposition of well-meaning folly. *For in the transactions of business it is much better to have to deal with a knave than a fool, because a knave adheres to some plan, and any plan of reason may be seen through sooner than a sudden flight of folly.* The power which vile and foolish women have had over wise men who possessed sensibility is notorious.

There is a notion commonly entertained among men that an instructed woman, capable of having opinions, is likely to prove an impracticable yoke-fellow, always pulling one way when her husband wants to go the other, oracular in tone, and prone to give curtain lectures[5] on metaphysics. But surely, so far as obstinacy is concerned, your unreasoning animal is the most unmanageable of creatures, where you are not allowed to settle the question by a cudgel, a whip and bridle, or even a string to the leg. For our own parts, we see no consistent or commodious medium between the old plan of corporal discipline and that thorough education of women which will make them rational beings in the highest sense of the word. Wherever weakness is not

---

3. Licentiousness.
4. Confident.

5. I.e., she would lecture him privately, behind the bed curtains.

harshly controlled it must *govern*, as you may see when a strong man holds a little child by the hand, how he is pulled hither and thither, and wearied in his walk by his submission to the whims and feeble movements of his companion. A really cultured woman, like a really cultured man, will be ready to yield in trifles. So far as we see, there is no indissoluble connexion between infirmity of logic and infirmity of will, and a woman quite innocent of an opinion in philosophy, is as likely as not to have an indomitable opinion about the kitchen. As to airs of superiority, no woman ever had them in consequence of true culture, but only because her culture was shallow or unreal, only as a result of what Mrs Malaprop[6] well calls "the ineffectual qualities in a woman"—mere acquisitions carried about, and not knowledge thoroughly assimilated so as to enter into the growth of the character.

To return to Margaret Fuller, some of the best things she says are on the folly of absolute definitions of woman's nature and absolute demarcations of woman's mission. "Nature," she says, "seems to delight in varying the arrangements, as if to show that she will be fettered by no rule; and we must admit the same varieties that she admits." Again: "If nature is never bound down, nor the voice of inspiration stifled, that is enough. We are pleased that women should write and speak, if they feel need of it, from having something to tell; but silence for ages would be no misfortune, if that silence be from divine command, and not from man's tradition." And here is a passage, the beginning of which has been often quoted:—

> If you ask me what offices they (women) may fill, I reply—any. I do not care what case you put; let them be sea-captains if you will. I do not doubt there are women well fitted for such an office, and, if so, I should be as glad as to welcome the Maid of Saragossa, or the Maid of Missolonghi, or the Suliote heroine, or Emily Plater.[7] I think women need, especially at this juncture, a much greater range of occupation than they have, to rouse their latent powers. . . . In families that I know, some little girls like to saw wood, others to use carpenter's tools. Where these tastes are indulged, cheerfulness and good-humour are promoted. Where they are forbidden, because "such things are not proper for girls," they grow sullen and mischievous. Fouriet[8] had observed these wants of women, as no one can fail to do who watches the desires of little girls, or knows the *ennui* that haunts grown women, except where they make to themselves a serene little world by art of some kind. He, therefore, in proposing a great variety of employments, in manufactures or the care of plants and animals, allows for one third of women as likely to have a taste for masculine pursuits, one third of men for feminine. . . . I have no doubt, however, that a large proportion of women would give themselves to the same employments as now, because there are circumstances that must lead them. Mothers will delight to make the nest soft and warm. Nature would take care of that; no need to clip the wings of any bird that wants to soar and sing, or finds in itself the strength of pinion[9] for a migratory flight unusual to its kind. The difference would be that *all* need not be constrained to employments for which *some* are unfit.

A propos of the same subject, we find Mary Wollstonecraft offering a suggestion which the women of the United States have already begun to carry out. She says:—

> Women, in particular, all want to be ladies. Which is simply to have nothing to do, but listlessly to go they scarcely care where, for they cannot tell what. But what have women

---

6. In Richard Sheridan's play *The Rivals* (1775), Mrs. Malaprop misuses words in hilarious ways: when complimented on her "intellectual accomplishments," she replies: "Ah! few gentlemen, nowadays, know how to value the ineffectual qualities in a woman!"

7. Women who fought heroically for their countries.
8. Charles Fourier, French social reformer and author of *The New Industrial World* (1829–1830).
9. Wing.

to do in society? I may be asked, but to loiter with easy grace; surely you would not condemn them all to suckle fools and chronicle small beer.[1] No. *Women might certainly study the art of healing, and be physicians as well as nurses. . . .* Business of various kinds they might likewise pursue, if they were educated in a more orderly manner. . . . Women would not then marry for a support, as men accept of places under government, and neglect the implied duties.

Men pay a heavy price for their reluctance to encourage self-help and independent resources in women. The precious meridian years of many a man of genius have to be spent in the toil of routine, that an "establishment" may be kept up for a woman who can understand none of his secret yearnings, who is fit for nothing but to sit in her drawing-room like a doll-Madonna in her shrine. No matter. Anything is more endurable than to change our established formulae about women, or to run the risk of looking up to our wives instead of looking down on them. *Sit divus, dummodo non sit vivus* (let him be a god, provided he be not living), said the Roman magnates of Romulus;[2] and so men say of women, let them be idols, useless absorbents of precious things, provided we are not obliged to admit them to be strictly fellow-beings, to be treated, one and all, with justice and sober reverence.

On one side we hear that woman's position can never be improved until women themselves are better; and, on the other, that women can never become better until their position is improved—until the laws are made more just, and a wider field opened to feminine activity. But we constantly hear the same difficulty stated about the human race in general. There is a perpetual action and reaction between individuals and institutions; we must try and mend both by little and little—the only way in which human things can be mended. Unfortunately, many over-zealous champions of women assert their actual equality with men—nay, even their moral superiority to men—as a ground for their release from oppressive laws and restrictions. They lose strength immensely by this false position. If it were true, then there would be a case in which slavery and ignorance nourished virtue, and so far we should have an argument for the continuance of bondage. But we want freedom and culture for woman, because subjection and ignorance have debased her, and with her, Man; for—

> If she be small, slight-natured, miserable,
> How shall men grow?[3]

Both Margaret Fuller and Mary Wollstonecraft have too much sagacity to fall into this sentimental exaggeration. Their ardent hopes of what women may become do not prevent them from seeing and painting women as they are. On the relative moral excellence of men and women Mary Wollstonecraft speaks with the most decision:—

> Women are supposed to possess more sensibility,[4] and even humanity, than men, and their strong attachments and instantaneous emotions of compassion are given as proofs; but the clinging affection of ignorance has seldom anything noble in it, and may mostly be resolved into selfishness, as well as the affection of children and brutes. I have known many weak women whose sensibility was entirely engrossed by their husbands; and as for their humanity, it was very faint indeed, or rather it was only a transient emotion of com-

1. Iago's view of women in *Othello* 2.1.159.
2. Romulus and Remus were the legendary founders of Rome. After Romulus vanished in a thunderstorm, he was worshipped as the god Quirinus; in *Lives* Plutarch says the patricians were suspected of murdering Romulus and starting the rumor of his translation to godhood to keep people from inquiring too closely into his disappearance.
3. Tennyson, *The Princess* 7.249–50; see page 1259.
4. Awareness of and responsiveness to emotions.

passion. Humanity does not consist "in a squeamish ear," says an eminent orator. "It belongs to the mind as well as to the nerves." But this kind of exclusive affection, though it degrades the individual, should not be brought forward as a proof of the inferiority of the sex, because it is the natural consequence of confined views; for even women of superior sense, having their attention turned to little employments and private plans, rarely rise to heroism, unless when spurred on by love! and love, as an heroic passion, like genius, appears but once in an age. I therefore agree with the moralist who asserts "that women have seldom so much generosity as men"; and that their narrow affections, to which justice and humanity are often sacrificed, render the sex apparently inferior, especially as they are commonly inspired by men; but I contend that the heart would expand as the understanding gained strength, if women were not depressed[5] from their cradles.

We had marked several other passages of Margaret Fuller's for extract, but as we do not aim at an exhaustive treatment of our subject, and are only touching a few of its points, we have, perhaps, already claimed as much of the reader's attention as he will be willing to give to such desultory material.

1855

Thomas Hughes
1822–1896

Thomas Hughes's famous portrait of Victorian public school life was based on his own experiences at Rugby under the headmastership of Thomas Arnold, the renowned educator and father of Matthew Arnold. Appointed in 1828, Arnold brought an evangelical fervor to the task of reforming the English public schools so as to instill moral character and Christian virtue in the future leaders of society. He made team sports a big part of school life; the playing fields would foster physical prowess, courage, and manliness. The curriculum was dominated by Latin and Greek—the hallmarks of a gentleman's education—but scholarship wasn't really the point: musing about his reasons for sending his son to Rugby, Tom Brown's father declares, "I don't care a straw for Greek particles. . . . If he'll only turn out a brave, helpful, truth-telling Englishman, and a gentleman, and a Christian, that's all I want."

from Tom Brown's School Days
[THE HEAD BOY ADDRESSES THE SCHOOL]

Then Warner, the head of the house,[1] gets up and wants to speak, but he can't, for every boy knows what's coming; and the big boys who sit at the tables pound them and cheer; and the small boys who stand behind pound one another, and cheer, and rush about the hall cheering. Then silence being made, Warner reminds them of the old School-house custom of drinking the healths, on the first night of singing, of those who are going to leave at the end of the half. "He sees that they know what he is going to say already—(loud cheers)—and so won't keep them, but only ask them to treat the toast as it deserves. It is the head of the eleven, the head of big-side football, their leader on this glorious day—Pater[2] Brooke!"

---

5. Repressed, kept down.
1. A public school such as Rugby would be divided into houses; Tom Brown belongs to the School-house, which

has just beaten the whole of the School in a rugby match.
2. Father (Latin). Brooke is "head of the eleven," i.e., captain of the School-house rugby team.

And away goes the pounding and cheering again, becoming deafening when old Brooke gets on his legs: till, a table having broken down, and a gallon or so of beer been upset, and all throats getting dry, silence ensues, and the hero speaks, leaning his hands on the table, and bending a little forwards. No action, no tricks or oratory; plain, strong, and straight, like his play.

"Gentlemen of the School-house! I am very proud of the way in which you have received my name, and I wish I could say all I should like in return. But I know I shan't. However, I'll do the best I can to say what seems to me ought to be said by a fellow who's just going to leave, and who has spent a good slice of his life here. Eight years it is, and eight such years as I can never hope to have again. So now I hope you'll all listen to me—(loud cheers of 'that we will')—for I'm going to talk seriously. You're bound to listen to me, for what's the use of calling me 'pater,' and all that, if you don't mind what I say? And I'm going to talk seriously, because I feel so. It's a jolly time, too, getting to the end of the half, and a goal kicked by us first day— (tremendous applause)—after one of the hardest and fiercest day's play I can remember in eight years—(frantic shoutings). The School played splendidly, too, I will say, and kept it up to the last. That last charge of theirs would have carried away a house. I never thought to see anything again of old Crab there, except little pieces, when I saw him tumbled over by it—(laughter and shouting, and great slapping on the back of Jones by the boys nearest him). Well, but we beat 'em—(cheers). Ay, but why did we beat 'em? answer me that—(shouts of 'your play'). Nonsense! 'Twasn't the wind and kick-off either—that wouldn't do it. 'Twasn't because we've half-a-dozen of the best players in the school, as we have. I wouldn't change Warner, and Hedge, and Crab, and the young un, for any six on their side—(violent cheers). But half-a-dozen fellows can't keep it up for two hours against two hundred. Why is it, then? I'll tell you what I think. It's because we've more reliance on one another, more of a house feeling, more fellowship than the School can have. Each of us knows and can depend on his next hand man better—that's why we beat 'em to-day. We've union, they've division—there's the secret—(cheers). But how's this to be kept up? How's it to be improved? That's the question. For I take it, we're all in earnest about beating the School, whatever else we care about. I know I'd sooner win two School-house matches running than get the Balliol scholarship[3] any day—(frantic cheers).

"Now, I'm as proud of the house as any one. I believe it's the best house in the school, out-and-out—(cheers). But it's a long way from what I want to see it. First, there's a deal of bullying going on. I know it well. I don't pry about and interfere; that only makes it more underhand, and encourages the small boys to come to us with their fingers in their eyes telling tales, and so we should be worse off than ever. It's very little kindness for the sixth[4] to meddle generally—you youngsters, mind that. You'll be all the better football players for learning to stand it, and to take your own parts, and fight it through. But depend on it, there's nothing breaks up a house like bullying. Bullies are cowards, and one coward makes many; so good-bye to the School-house match if bullying gets ahead here. (Loud applause from the small boys, who look meaningly at Flashman and other boys at the tables.) Then there's fuddling about in the public-house, and drinking bad spirits, and punch, and such rot-gut stuff. That won't make good drop-kicks or charges of you, take my word for it. You get plenty of good beer here, and that's enough for you; and drinking isn't fine or manly, whatever some of you may think of it. * * *

---

3. Prize scholarship to attend Balliol College at Oxford.   4. The sixth form—i.e., the oldest boys, who were in charge of the younger ones.

* * * But before I sit down I must give you a toast to be drunk with three-times-three and all the honours. It's a toast which I hope every one of us, wherever he may go hereafter, will never fail to drink when he thinks of the brave bright days of his boyhood. It's a toast which should bind us all together, and to those who've gone before, and who'll come after us here. It is the dear old School-house—the best house of the best school in England!"

1857

Isabella Beeton
1836–1865

The home was a near-sacred institution in Victorian England, and when Isabella Beeton published her book of advice on household management it became a best-seller second only to the Bible. In over a thousand pages of small print, she instructed women on matters ranging from the supervision of servants to the care of the sick, from meal planning to proper conduct during a social call. Mrs. Beeton's portrait of the mistress of the house reflects a complex, somewhat contradictory sense of a woman's role: she is at once "the commander of an army"—with the housekeeper as her "second in command"—and a lady of leisure, enjoying "the pleasures of literature" and "the innocent delights of the garden." Yet, like a child, she needs to be scolded to rise early and be punctual. Although Mrs. Beeton was just twenty-four, she was respected as an oracle in the domestic sphere; her cookbook is still used today. She died in childbirth at twenty-eight.

from The Book of Household Management

I must frankly own, that if I had known, beforehand, that this book would have cost me the labour which it has, I should never have been courageous enough to commence it. What moved me, in the first instance, to attempt a work like this, was the discomfort and suffering which I had seen brought upon men and women by household mismanagement. I have always thought that there is no more fruitful source of family discontent than a housewife's badly-cooked dinners and untidy ways. Men are now so well served out of doors,—at their clubs, well-ordered taverns, and dining-houses, that in order to compete with the attractions of these places, a mistress must be thoroughly acquainted with the theory and practice of cookery, as well as be perfectly conversant with all the other arts of making and keeping a comfortable home. * * *

As with the Commander of an Army, or the leader of any enterprise, so is it with the mistress of a house. Her spirit will be seen through the whole establishment; and just in proportion as she performs her duties intelligently and thoroughly, so will her domestics follow in her path. Of all those acquirements, which more particularly belong to the feminine character, there are none which take a higher rank, in our estimation, than such as enter into a knowledge of household duties; for on these are perpetually dependent the happiness, comfort, and well-being of a family. * * *

Early Rising is one of the most Essential Qualities which enter into good Household Management, as it is not only the parent of health, but of innumerable other advantages. Indeed, when a mistress is an early riser, it is almost certain that her house will be orderly and well-managed. On the contrary, if she remain in bed till a late hour, then the domestics, who, as we have before observed, invariably partake somewhat of their mistress's character, will surely become sluggards. * * *

Friendships should not be hastily formed, nor the heart given, at once, to every new-comer. There are ladies who uniformly smile at, and approve everything and everybody, and who possess neither the courage to reprehend vice, nor the generous warmth to defend virtue. The friendship of such persons is without attachment, and their love without affection or even preference. * * *

Hospitality is a most Excellent Virtue; but care must be taken that the love of company, for its own sake, does not become a prevailing passion; for then the habit is no longer hospitality, but dissipation. * * * With respect to the continuance of friendships * * * it may be found necessary, in some cases, for a mistress to relinquish, on assuming the responsibility of a house-hold, many of those commenced in the earlier part of her life. * * *

In Conversation, Trifling Occurrences, such as small disappointments, petty annoyances, and other every-day incidents, should never be mentioned to your friends. The extreme injudiciousness of repeating these will be at once apparent, when we reflect on the unsatisfactory discussions which they too frequently occasion, and on the load of advice which they are the cause of being tendered, and which is, too often, of a kind neither to be useful nor agreeable. * * * If the mistress be a wife, never let an account of her husband's failings pass her lips. * * *

After Breakfast is over, it will be well for the mistress to make a round of the kitchen and other offices, to see that all are in order, and that the morning's work has been properly performed by the various domestics. The orders for the day should then be given, and any questions which the domestics desire to ask, respecting their several departments, should be answered, and any special articles they may require, handed to them from the store-closet. * * *

After this General Superintendence of her servants, the mistress, if a mother of a young family, may devote herself to the instruction of some of its younger members, or to the examination of the state of their wardrobe, leaving the later portion of the morning for reading, or for some amusing recreation. * * *

Unless the means of the mistress be very circumscribed, and she be obliged to devote a great deal of her time to the making of her children's clothes, and other economical pursuits, it is right that she should give some time to the pleasures of literature, the innocent delights of the garden, and to the improvement of any special abilities for music, painting, and other elegant arts, which she may, happily, possess. * * *

After Luncheon, Morning Calls and Visits may be made and received. These may be divided under three heads: those of ceremony, friendship, and congratulation or condolence. Visits of ceremony, or courtesy, which occasionally merge into those of friendship, are to be paid under various circumstances. Thus, they are uniformly required after dining at a friend's house, or after a ball, picnic, or any other party. These visits should be short, a stay of from fifteen to twenty minutes being quite sufficient. A lady paying a visit may remove her boa or neckerchief; but neither her shawl nor bonnet.

When other visitors are announced, it is well to retire as soon as possible, taking care to let it appear that their arrival is not the cause. When they are quietly seated, and the bustle of their entrance is over, rise from your chair, taking a kind leave of the hostess, and bowing politely to the guests. Should you call at an inconvenient time, not having ascertained the luncheon hour, or from any other inadvertence, retire as soon as possible, without, however, showing that you feel yourself an intruder. It is not difficult for any well-bred or even good-tempered person, to know what to say on such an occasion, and, on politely withdrawing, a promise can be made to call again, if the lady you have called on, appear really disappointed.

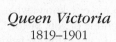

In Paying Visits of Friendship, it will not be so necessary to be guided by etiquette as in paying visits of ceremony; and if a lady be pressed by her friend to remove her shawl and bonnet, it can be done if it will not interfere with her subsequent arrangements. * * * During these visits, the manners should be easy and cheerful, and the subjects of conversation such as may be readily terminated. Serious discussions or arguments are to be altogether avoided.

1861

Queen Victoria
1819–1901

Queen Victoria, who ruled from 1837 to 1901, was the most prominent woman of the age, and during her reign the monarchy came to symbolize the far-flung power of the British Empire. Although she was a capable woman who wielded genuine political influence, she felt uncomfortably thrust into greatness and often deplored the contradictions of her position. A firm believer in the notion that men and women should occupy separate spheres, the queen regarded campaigns for women's rights as "dangerous and unchristian and unnatural." The mother of nine children, Victoria was revered as the embodiment of domestic propriety, but her views on maternity were decidedly unsentimental. Her letters to her eldest daughter lament the sufferings of pregnancy, and in the 1850s Queen Victoria pioneered the use of chloroform in childbirth, thus making anesthesia acceptable for other women.

Letters and Journal Entries on the Position of Women
Journal[1]

20 June 1837

I was awoke at 6 o'clock by Mamma,[2] who told me that the Archbishop of Canterbury and Lord Conyngham were here, and wished to see me. I got out of bed and went into my sitting-room (only in my dressing-gown), and alone, and saw them. Lord Conyngham then acquainted me that my poor Uncle, the King, was no more, and had expired at 12 minutes p. 2 this morning, and consequently that I am Queen. Lord Conyngham knelt down and kissed my hand, at the same time delivering to me the official announcement of the poor King's demise. The Archbishop then told me that the Queen[3] was desirous that he should come and tell me the details of the last moments of my poor, good Uncle; he said that he had directed his mind to religion and had died in a perfectly happy, quiet state of mind, and was quite prepared for his death. He added that the King's sufferings at the last were not very great but that there was a good deal of uneasiness. Lord Conyngham, who I charged to express my feelings of condolence and sorrow to the poor Queen, returned directly to Windsor. I then went to my room and dressed.

Since it has pleased Providence to place me in this station, I shall do my utmost to fulfil my duty towards my country; I am very young and perhaps in many, though

1. From *Queen Victoria in Her Letters and Journals*, ed. Christopher Hibbert (1985).
2. Victoria's mother was the widow of Edward, Duke of Kent, the fourth son of George III. Since Edward died when Victoria was an infant, she was brought up by her mother. She had just turned 18 when she became queen on the death of her uncle, King William IV.
3. Adelaide, the widow of William IV.

not in all things, inexperienced, but I am sure, that very few have more real good will and more real desire to do what is fit and right than I have. * * *

To Princess Frederick William[4]

24 March 1858

That you should feel shy sometimes I can easily understand. I do so very often to this hour. But being married gives one one's position which nothing else can. Think however what it was for me, a girl of 18 all alone, not brought up at court as you were—but very humbly at Kensington Palace—with trials and difficulties, to receive and be everywhere the first! No, no one knows what a life of difficulties mine was—and is! How thankful I am that none of you, please God! ever will have that anomalous and trying position. Now do enter into this in your letters, you so seldom do that, except to answer a question.

Now to reply to your observation that you find a married woman has much more liberty than an unmarried one; in one sense of the word she has,—but what I meant was—in a physical point of view—and if you have hereafter (as I had constantly for the first 2 years of my marriage)—aches—and sufferings and miseries and plagues—which you must struggle against—and enjoyments etc. to give up—constant precautions to take, you will feel the yoke of a married woman! Without that—certainly it is unbounded happiness—if one has a husband one worships! It is a foretaste of heaven. And you have a husband who adores you, and is, I perceive, ready to meet every wish and desire of your's. I had 9 times for 8 months[5] to bear with those above-named enemies and real misery (besides many duties) and I own it tried me sorely; one feels so pinned down—one's wings clipped—in fact, at the best (and few were or are better than I was) only half oneself—particularly the first and second time. This I call the "shadow side" as much as being torn away from one's loved home, parents and brothers and sisters. And therefore—I think our sex a most unenviable one.

26 May 1858

The horrid news contained in Fritz's letter to Papa [that the Princess was pregnant] upset us dreadfully. The more so as I feel certain almost it will all end in nothing.

15 June 1858

What you say of the pride of giving life to an immortal soul is very fine, dear, but I own I cannot enter into that; I think much more of our being like a cow or a dog at such moments; when our poor nature becomes so very animal and unecstatic—but for you, dear, if you are sensible and reasonable not in ecstasy nor spending your day with nurses and wet nurses, which is the ruin of many a refined and intellectual young lady, without adding to her real maternal duties, a child will be a great resource. Above all, dear, do remember never to lose the modesty of a young girl towards others (without being prude); though you are married don't become a matron

---

4. This and the following letters on marriage and childbirth are from *Dearest Child: Letters between Queen Victoria and the Princess Royal, 1858–1861*, ed. Roger Fulford (1964). On 25 January 1858, at the age of 17, Victoria's eldest daughter had married Prince Frederick ("Fritz"), later Crown Prince of Prussia. Her mother wrote her frequent letters full of maternal advice.
5. Victoria alludes to her nine pregnancies.

Edwin Landseer, *Windsor Castle in Modern Times*, 1841–1845, showing Queen Victoria and Prince Albert at home with their eldest child Princess Victoria.

at once to whom everything can be said, and who minds saying nothing herself—I remained particular to a degree (indeed feel so now) and often feel shocked at the confidences of other married ladies. I fear abroad they are very indelicate about these things.

29 January 1859

God be praised for all his mercies, and for bringing you safely through this awful time![6] Our joy, our gratitude knows no bounds.

My precious darling, you suffered much more that I ever did—and how I wish I could have lightened them for you! Poor dear Fritz—how he will have suffered for you! I think and feel much for him; the dear little boy if I could but see him for one minute, give you one kiss. It is hard, very hard. But we are so happy, so grateful! And people here are all in ecstasies—such pleasure, such delight—as if it was their own prince and so it is too! All the children so delighted! You will and must feel so thankful all is over! But don't be alarmed for the future, it never can be so bad again!

---

6. After a difficult and dangerous labor, Victoria's daughter had given birth on 27 January 1859; her son was the future Kaiser Wilhelm II, who led Germany against England in World War I.

20 April 1859

I really think I shall never let your sisters marry—certainly not to be so constantly away and see so little of their parents—as till now, you have done, contrary to all that I was originally promised and told. I am so glad to see that you so entirely enter into all my feelings as a mother. Yes, dearest, it is an awful moment to have to give one's innocent child up to a man, be he ever so kind and good—and to think of all that she must go through! I can't say what I suffered, what I felt—what struggles I had to go through—(indeed I have not quite got over it yet) and that last night when we took you to your room, and you cried so much, I said to Papa as we came back "after all, it is like taking a poor lamb to be sacrificed." You now know—what I meant, dear. I know that God has willed it so and that these are the trials which we poor women must go through; no father, no man can feel this! Papa never would enter into it all! As in fact he seldom can in my very violent feelings. It really makes me shudder when I look around at all your sweet, happy, unconscious sisters—and think that I must give them up too—one by one!! Our dear Alice,[7] has seen and heard more (of course not what no one ever can know before they marry and before they have had children) than you did, from your marriage—and quite enough to give her a horror rather of marrying.

4 May 1859

Abstractedly, I have no *tendre* for them [babies] till they have become a little human; an ugly baby is a very nasty object—and the prettiest is frightful when undressed—till about four months; in short as long as they have their big body and little limbs and that terrible frog-like action. But from four months, they become prettier and prettier. And I repeat it—your child would delight me at any age.

15 June 1859

Now I must scold you a wee bit for an observation which really seems at variance with your own expressions. You say "how glad" Ada[8] "must be" at being again in that most charming situation, which you yourself very frequently told me last year was so wretched. How can anyone, who has not been married above two years and three quarters, (like Ada) rejoice at being a third time in that condition? I positively think those ladies who are always *enceinte* quite disgusting; it is more like a rabbit or guinea-pig than anything else and really it is not very nice.

16 May 1860

All marriage is such a lottery—the happiness is always an exchange—though it may be a very happy one—still the poor woman is bodily and morally the husband's slave. That always sticks in my throat. When I think of a merry, happy, free young girl—and look at the ailing, aching state a young wife generally is doomed to—which you can't deny is the penalty of marriage.

17 November 1860

My beloved child, these lines are to wish you heartily and warmly joy of your 20th birthday—an important age—though married nearly three years and with two children it seems but of little consequence. Still to bid adieu to one's "teens" is a serious thing!

7. Princess Alice, Victoria's second daughter, was 15.   Schleswig-Holstein.
8. The Queen's niece, married to Prince Frederick of

18 December 1861

What is to become of us all?[9] Of the unhappy country, of Europe, of all? For you all, the loss of such a father is totally irreparable! I will do all I can to follow out all his wishes—to live for you all and for my duties. But how I, who leant on him for all and everything—without whom I did nothing, moved not a finger, arranged not a print or photograph, didn't put on a gown or bonnet if he didn't approve it shall be able to go on, to live, to move, to help myself in difficult moments? How I shall long to ask his advice! Oh! it is too, too weary! The day—the night (above all the night) is too sad and weary. The days never pass! I try to feel and think that I am living on with him, and that his pure and perfect spirit is guiding and leading me and inspiring me!

Sweet little Beatrice comes to lie in my bed every morning which is a comfort. I long so to cling to and clasp a loving being. Oh! how I admired Papa! How in love I was with him! How everything about him was beautiful and precious in my eyes! Oh! how, how I miss all, all! Oh! Oh! the bitterness of this—of this woe!

To William Gladstone[1]

6 May 1870

The circumstances respecting the Bill to give women the same position as men with respect to Parliamentary franchise gives her an opportunity to observe that she had for some time past wished to call Mr Gladstone's attention to the mad & utterly demoralizing movement of the present day to place women in the same position as to professions—as *men;*—& amongst others, in the *Medical Line.*

* * * And she is *most* anxious that it should be known how she not only disapproves but *abhors* the attempts to destroy all propriety & womanly feeling which will inevitably be the result of what has been proposed. The Queen is a woman herself—& knows what an anomaly her *own* position is:—but that can be reconciled with reason & propriety tho' it is a terribly difficult & trying one. But to tear away all the barriers which surround a woman, & to propose that they should study with *men*—things which could not be named before them—certainly not *in a mixed* audience—would be to introduce a total disregard of what must be considered as belonging to the rules & principles of morality.

The Queen feels so strongly upon this dangerous & unchristian & unnatural cry & movement of "woman's rights,"—in which she knows Mr Gladstone *agrees,* (as he sent her that excellent Pamphlet by Lady) that she is most anxious that Mr Gladstone & others should take some steps to check this alarming danger & to make whatever use they can of her name. * * *

Let woman be what God intended; a helpmate for a man—but with totally different duties & vocations.

---

9. Victoria was grief stricken at the death of her husband, Prince Albert, on 14 December 1861; after his death she mourned him obsessively, going into virtual seclusion for many years. Beatrice was her ninth child, born in 1857. This letter is from *Queen Victoria in Her Letters and Journals,* ed. Christopher Hibbert (1985).
1. Gladstone (1809–1898) was the prime minister in four Liberal governments (1868–1874, 1880–1885, 1886, 1892–1894). This letter is from *The Queen and Mr. Gladstone* (1933) edited by Philip Guedalla. The Queen refers to the recurrence of the proposal to give women the vote, first presented to the House of Commons in 1866 by J. S. Mill.

To Sir Theodore Martin[2]

29 May 1870

The Queen is most anxious to enlist every one who can speak or write to join in checking this mad, wicked folly of "Woman's Rights," with all its attendant horrors, on which her poor feeble sex is bent, forgetting every sense of womanly feeling and propriety. Lady—ought to get a *good whipping*.

It is a subject which makes the Queen so furious that she cannot contain herself. God created men and women different—then let them remain each in their own position. Tennyson has some beautiful lines on the difference of men and women in *The Princess*.[3] Woman would become the most hateful, heartless, and disgusting of human beings were she allowed to unsex herself; and where would be the protection which man was intended to give the weaker sex? The Queen is sure that Mrs Martin agrees with her.

⊢ ⊨⟡⊨ ⊣

Sir Henry Newbolt
1862–1938

Sir Henry Newbolt's rousing patriotic poems make explicit the link between public school games and the romantic ideology of empire. Schoolboy sports were not merely about keeping fit; with their emphasis on manliness, mettle, and pluck, they were preparing the upper classes to regard imperialism as a grand adventure. School loyalty merged with national patriotism. Games fostered the notion that wars were won by team spirit, holding up the side, and never quitting. Young English officers carried this schoolboy code into combat: they saw war itself as a "great game," and battlefields as playing fields. Their letters from the front during World War I described the action in the language of sports. One officer actually dribbled a soccer ball as he led his men to their deaths in the battle of the Somme.

Vitaï Lampada[1]

There's a breathless hush in the Close[2] to-night—
    Ten to make and the match to win—
A bumping pitch and a blinding light,
    An hour to play and the last man in.
5 And it's not for the sake of a ribboned coat,
    Or the selfish hope of a season's fame,
But his Captain's hand on his shoulder smote—
    "Play up! play up! and play the game!"

---

2. This letter is from *Queen Victoria As I Knew Her* (1908) by Sir Theodore Martin, a lawyer and man of letters.

3. See *The Princess* (page 1259): "For woman is not undevelopt man, / But diverse: could we make her as the man, / Sweet Love were slain: his dearest bond is this, / Not like to like, but like in difference."

1. The Torch of Life; a reference to a relay race, described in Lucretius's *De Rerum Natura*, where runners hand off a flaming torch.

2. The playing fields at a public school.

The sand of the desert is sodden red,—

10   Red with the wreck of a square that broke;—
    The Gatling's[3] jammed and the Colonel dead,
    And the regiment blind with dust and smoke.
The river of death has brimmed his banks,
    And England's far, and Honour a name,
15   But the voice of a schoolboy rallies the ranks:
    "Play up! play up! and play the game!"

This is the word that year by year,
    While in her place the School is set,
Every one of her sons must hear,
20   And none that hears it dare forget.
This they all with a joyful mind
    Bear through life like a torch in flame,
And falling fling to the host behind—
25   "Play up! play up! and play the game!"

        1897

➤✦ END OF PERSPECTIVES: VICTORIAN LADIES AND GENTLEMEN ✦←

Matthew Arnold
1822–1888

Matthew Arnold and his wife Frances Wightman Arnold, 1860s,
carte de visite photographs by Elliot and Fry, London.

"I am glad you like the Gipsy Scholar," Matthew Arnold wrote to a friend in 1853, "—but what does it *do* for you?" No Victorian gave more attention than Arnold to the momentous question of how art should affect an audience, and no writer was ever more tortured by it. For much as he delighted in creating the "pleasing melancholy" of *The Scholar-Gipsy*, one of his greatest poems, Arnold felt that literature must directly address the moral needs of readers, "to *animate* and *ennoble* them." This concern with the practical emotional effects of art, Arnold said simply, is "the basis of my nature—and of my poetics."

But in trying to realize his goal, Arnold became a deeply divided man. Author of the era's most distinctive poems of alienation and doubt, he gave up poetry to work for the public good,

3. An early form of machine gun.

passionately defending classic literature as a means of remaking the materialist society he abhorred. As a social critic, he aspired to embody his ideal of a balanced mind, to be a man "who saw life steadily and saw it whole." But as a private individual he viewed himself as a forlorn romantic quester, disenchanted with modernity. Unable to believe in the religion of the past and unwilling to accept the secular values of the present, he described himself as "wandering between two worlds, one dead, / The other powerless to be born." Arnold is unique among the eminent Victorian writers, admired equally for his heartfelt poetry of disillusionment and for his sophisticated prose aimed at pragmatic social reform.

Matthew Arnold was the oldest son of Dr. Thomas Arnold, headmaster of Rugby School, who had become famous for reshaping the curriculum to instill a healthy respect for Christian values, classical languages, and competitive games. Matthew's mother, Mary Penrose Arnold, encouraged her son to be creative, self-conscious, and alert to the comic or dramatic side of daily events. Nicknamed "Crabby" by his father when he wore leg braces for two years, Arnold adopted a sidelong, crab-like approach to his goal of becoming a poet. A lazy, dilettantish, facetious student, Arnold managed through last-minute heroics to win the top prizes: a scholarship in 1840 to Balliol College, Oxford; the renowned Newdigate Prize for poetry in 1843; and in 1845 a Fellowship at Oriel College.

Throughout his life, Arnold seemed most comfortable outdoors and free of the classroom, whether blasting away at game on the English moors (he was a terrible shot) or hiking in the Alps. He spent his early childhood at Laleham, a village on the Thames, perhaps the source of his frequent river imagery. When he should have been studying at Oxford, he roamed the idyllic countryside surrounding it, hunting, fishing, and composing verses. He once pranced naked on a riverbank after swimming, prompting a rebuke from a passing clergyman. Waving his towel, Arnold replied: "Is it possible that you see anything indelicate in the human form divine?"

In 1847 Arnold became private secretary to the liberal politician Lord Lansdowne, spending most of his time in London, working on his poetry, and arguing about poetry and religion with his best friend, the poet Arthur Hugh Clough. They both agreed on the spiritual bankruptcy of modern life: "These are damned times," Arnold wrote to Clough in 1849; "everything is against one . . . the absence of great *natures*, the unavoidable contact with millions of small ones . . . our own selves, and the sickening consciousness of our difficulties."

Arnold dealt with these difficulties by casting them in poetic form. His first book of poems, *The Strayed Reveller, and Other Poems*, by "A," appeared in 1849, followed by *Empedocles on Etna, and Other Poems* (1852) and *Poems* (1853). Many other important poems, including *Dover Beach,* also date from this fertile period, though not published until later, in *Poems, Second Series* (1855) and *New Poems* (1867).

Arnold's finest poetry is imbued with a love of the countryside. He spent family vacations in the Lake District, whose beauty and poetic associations made a deep impression on him. His parents were friendly with Wordsworth, who was to become the chief influence on Arnold's poetry; when Wordsworth died he mourned, "who will teach us how to feel?" Like Wordsworth, Arnold evokes memorable landscapes in many of his key works in order to ponder the relation between hidden emotions and external objects, and to explore the themes of lost childhood, nostalgia for the past, and the quest for identity. But Arnold rarely found in nature a means of contact with other people or with a deeper self: "The disease of the present age," he wrote in his journal, "is divorce from oneself."

Arnold felt a growing dissatisfaction with his society and with his own poetry. In a controversial preface to his *Poems* of 1853, he justified not reprinting his major earlier work, *Empedocles on Etna,* because he felt that it failed to "inspirit and rejoice" readers and teach them how to live. He went on to condemn poetry that merely presents "a continuous state of mental distress . . . unrelieved by incident, hope, or resistance; in which there is everything to be endured, nothing to be done." In these words he accurately summed up—and dismissed—what was most powerful and moving in his own work.

Provoking a heated debate about the poet's relation to contemporary life, Arnold urged that modern poets should turn from their own troubles to build upon timeless, universal "great actions," such as those found in Sophocles and Aeschylus. The Victorian age, he concluded, was an unlikely source of poetic material, because it was "an age wanting in moral grandeur . . . an age of spiritual discomfort."

Too much a man of his time to be able to follow his own advice, Arnold largely abandoned poetry after the mid-1850s. In 1851, two important events occurred that contributed to this abdication: his marriage to Frances Lucy Wightman and his taking a job as a school inspector to support his family. This turned out to be a grueling position assessing the quality of instruction in government-funded schools for the poor. Initially surmising that the job would do well enough "for the next three or four years," Arnold doggedly kept at it for thirty-five years, traveling constantly throughout Britain and later in Europe. He soon realized the importance of expanding and reforming public education, arguing for the schools' crucial role "in civilizing the next generation of the lower classes, who, as things are going, will have most of the political power of the country in their hands."

Thus the anguished poet transformed himself into an energetic public servant, strenuously trying to remedy with his progressive criticism a society that he privately despaired of as hopelessly materialist. In 1857 Arnold was elected Professor of Poetry at Oxford University. He was the first to lecture in English rather than Latin, and for the next ten years he used the occasion of his public lectures to reach the broadest possible audience, promoting his belief that a careful reading of classic literature produces civilizing and morally sustaining effects. He reworked many of his lectures into books and essays, including On Translating Homer (1861) and On the Modern Element in Literature (1869). The work begun at Oxford eventually helped establish literature as a cornerstone of university programs in the liberal arts.

In 1865 Arnold published Essays in Criticism, which began with his famous essay, The Function of Criticism at the Present Time. There he argued that criticism is "a free creative activity," one that may well be the most useful and satisfying activity available to an inquiring mind in a modern, unpoetical era. With examples ranging from high art to tabloid journalism, Arnold revealed how British thought is entangled in class relations and political exigencies; his essay anticipates the scope and methods of modern culture studies. In his most important work of social criticism, Culture and Anarchy (1869), Arnold called for "disinterested" analysis free of partisan politics. He deplored English pride in "doing as one likes" and found in the self-serving behavior of all classes an anarchic lack of concern for the public good. Only education, he contended, could unite the antagonistic factions of British society, by teaching respect for beauty and intellect—what Arnold termed the virtues of "sweetness and light."

The mocking irony, Olympian assurance, and lucid, cascading style of these works make them exhilarating—or exasperating—reading. Arnold's high-minded attitudes enraged many of his opponents, and his loftiness of tone led even his friends and family to nickname him "the Emperor." For Arnold, education was a lifelong task, and few measured up to the cosmopolitan, European standards he set. He was particularly savage with anyone he considered guilty of self-interest or fuzzy thinking, and he attacked politicians and bishops by name. Leslie Stephen, Virginia Woolf's father, remarked satirically that "I often wished . . . that I too had a little sweetness and light that I might be able to say such nasty things of my enemies."

In the 1870s, Arnold scandalized many people with his attacks on orthodox religion in St. Paul and Protestantism (1870), Literature and Dogma (1873), and God and the Bible (1875). In The Study of Poetry (1880), he went so far as to argue that "most of what now passes for religion and philosophy will be replaced by poetry."

In 1883, weary, in debt, and desperate to retire, Arnold tried to raise money by selecting, with his daughter Nelly, 365 mottoes to create a Matthew Arnold Birthday Book. In the same year he went on a money-making lecture tour of the United States, meeting with mixed success. The chief intellectual product of his travel was Discourses in America (1885), which contained his essay Literature and Science. There, Arnold defended the idea of a liberal arts education founded on ancient and modern literatures against Thomas Huxley's contention in *Science and Culture* (1881) that an education based on the natural sciences would do just as well. Arnold felt that the debate had particular relevance for Americans, whose respect for "the average man" was fraught with "danger to the ideal of a high and rare excellence," best conveyed by a humanistic education. Arnold died suddenly of a heart attack in 1888.

Arnold was not a prophetic critic like Carlyle, nor a visionary poet of social reform like Elizabeth Barrett Browning, nor a moral crusader like Dickens. Instead, Arnold offered thoughtful prescriptions for guiding a changing and increasingly democratic society to a fuller understanding of its problems, and a more effective realization of its goals. As a school inspector he developed a deeper understanding of ineffective institutions and the ignorance of the British public than any other important Victorian author. While few have agreed fully with his pronouncements on literature and society, he has influenced almost every significant English-speaking critic since his time, including T. S. Eliot, F. R. Leavis, Lionel Trilling, and Raymond Williams.

Arnold has remained a literary force to be reckoned with as well. In its honest, introspective, sometimes awkward way, Arnold's poetry speaks unforgettably of the anxieties of his era. Though he saw himself as having "less poetical sentiment than Tennyson, and less intellectual vigor and abundance than Browning," he felt that his more balanced "fusion" of these qualities would continue to assure him an audience. His open approach to his innermost feelings is echoed almost everywhere in modern poetry.

Isolation. To Marguerite[1]

We were apart; yet, day by day,
I bade my heart more constant be.
I bade it keep the world away,
And grow a home for only thee;
5   Nor feared but thy love likewise grew,
Like mine, each day, more tried, more true.

The fault was grave! I might have known,
What far too soon, alas! I learned—
The heart can bind itself alone,
10   And faith may oft be unreturned.
Self-swayed our feelings ebb and swell—
Thou lov'st no more;—Farewell! Farewell!

Farewell!—and thou, thou lonely heart,
Which never yet without remorse
15   Even for a moment didst depart
From thy remote and spheréd course
To haunt the place where passions reign—
Back to thy solitude again!

Back! with the conscious thrill of shame
20   Which Luna felt, that summer-night,
Flash through her pure immortal frame,
When she forsook the starry height
To hang over Endymion's sleep
Upon the pine-grown Latmian steep.

1. The identity of Marguerite has long been a puzzle. She has been variously identified as an unknown woman whom Arnold met in Switzerland in the 1840s, or as Mary Claude, an Englishwoman whom he knew at about the same time.

25 Yet she, chaste queen, had never proved
 How vain a thing is mortal love,
 Wandering in Heaven, far removed.
 But thou hast long had place to prove
30 This truth—to prove, and make thine own:
 "Thou hast been, shalt be, art, alone."

 Or, if not quite alone, yet they
 Which touch thee are unmating things—
 Ocean and clouds and night and day;
 Lorn autumns and triumphant springs;
35 And life, and others' joy and pain,
 And love, if love, of happier men.

 Of happier men—for they, at least,
 Have *dreamed* two human hearts might blend
 In one, and were through faith released
40 From isolation without end
 Prolonged; nor knew, although not less
 Alone than thou, their loneliness.

1849   1857

To Marguerite—Continued

 Yes! in the sea of life enisled,
 With echoing straits between us thrown,
 Dotting the shoreless watery wild,
 We mortal millions live *alone*.
5 The islands feel the enclasping flow,
 And then their endless bounds they know.

 But when the moon their hollows lights,
 And they are swept by balms of spring,
 And in their glens, on starry nights,
10 The nightingales divinely sing;
 And lovely notes, from shore to shore,
 Across the sounds and channels pour—

 Oh! then a longing like despair
 Is to their farthest caverns sent;
15 For surely once, they feel, we were
 Parts of a single continent!
 Now round us spreads the watery plain—
 Oh might our marges meet again!

 Who ordered, that their longing's fire
20 Should be, as soon as kindled, cooled?
 Who renders vain their deep desire?—
 A God, a God their severance ruled!
 And bade betwixt their shores to be
 The unplumbed, salt, estranging sea.

1849   1852

Dover Beach

The sea is calm to-night.
The tide is full, the moon lies fair
Upon the straits; on the French coast the light
Gleams and is gone; the cliffs of England stand,
5   Glimmering and vast, out in the tranquil bay.
Come to the window, sweet is the night-air!
Only, from the long line of spray
Where the sea meets the moon-blanched land,
Listen! you hear the grating roar
10   Of pebbles which the waves draw back, and fling,
At their return, up the high strand,
Begin, and cease, and then again begin,
With tremulous cadence slow, and bring
The eternal note of sadness in.

15   Sophocles long ago
Heard it on the Aegean,[1] and it brought
Into his mind the turbid ebb and flow
Of human misery; we
Find also in the sound a thought,
20   Hearing it by this distant northern sea.

The Sea of Faith
Was once, too, at the full, and round earth's shore
Lay like the folds of a bright girdle° furled.   *sash*
But now I only hear
25   Its melancholy, long, withdrawing roar,
Retreating, to the breath
Of the night-wind, down the vast edges drear
And naked shingles° of the world.   *pebble beaches*

Ah, love, let us be true
30   To one another! for the world, which seems
To lie before us like a land of dreams,
So various, so beautiful, so new,
Hath really neither joy, nor love, nor light,
Nor certitude, nor peace, nor help for pain;
35   And we are here as on a darkling plain
Swept with confused alarms of struggle and flight,
Where ignorant armies clash by night.

c. 1851   1867

---

1. Sophocles was a 5th century B.C. Greek dramatist; the Aegean Sea lies between Greece and Turkey.

RESPONSE
Anthony Hecht: The Dover Bitch
A Criticism of Life[1]

for Andrews Wanning

So there stood Matthew Arnold and this girl
With the cliffs of England crumbling away behind them,
And he said to her, "Try to be true to me,
And I'll do the same for you, for things are bad
5   All over, etc., etc."
Well now, I knew this girl. It's true she had read
Sophocles in a fairly good translation
And caught that bitter allusion to the sea,
But all the time he was talking she had in mind
10   The notion of what his whiskers would feel like
On the back of her neck. She told me later on
That after a while she got to looking out
At the lights across the channel, and really felt sad,
Thinking of all the wine and enormous beds
15   And blandishments in French and the perfumes.
And then she got really angry. To have been brought
All the way down from London, and then be addressed
As a sort of mournful cosmic last resort
Is really tough on a girl, and she was pretty.
20   Anyway, she watched him pace the room
And finger his watch-chain and seem to sweat a bit,
And then she said one or two unprintable things.
But you mustn't judge her by that. What I mean to say is,
She's really all right. I still see her once in a while
25   And she always treats me right. We have a drink
And I give her a good time, and perhaps it's a year
Before I see her again, but there she is,
Running to fat, but dependable as they come.
And sometimes I bring her a bottle of *Nuit d'Amour*.[2]

1967

1. The Pulitzer Prize–winning American poet Anthony Hecht (1923–2004) was known for a polished, musical verse whose beauty was built on dark undertones. But he had a lighter side, and here he uses his fascination with literary history to imagine how the self-involved "cosmic" concerns of a poet like Arnold (or Hecht) might strike a woman more interested in sex than in Sophocles. With its memorable setting and uneasy mixture of desire and doubt, *Dover Beach* is perhaps the single most popular poem of the Victorian era; it has played host to endless interpretations. Many scholars believe that Arnold wrote the poem to his wife on his honeymoon, so Hecht's outrageous but intriguing suggestion that the poem's auditor is a woman of easy virtue shows just how open the text is to a reader's imagination. But is Hecht's worldly speaker any more open-minded than Arnold's? And in Arnold's poem, can we even be sure a man is speaking? Hecht's subtitle wryly alludes to Arnold's famous definition in *The Study of Poetry* (1880) that poetry is "a criticism of life."
2. Night of Love (French); presumably a perfume.

Lines Written in Kensington Gardens[1]

In this lone, open glade I lie,
Screened by deep boughs on either hand;
And at its end, to stay the eye,
Those black-crowned, red-boled pine-trees stand!

5   Birds here make song, each bird has his,
Across the girdling city's hum.
How green under the boughs it is!
How thick the tremulous sheep-cries come!

Sometimes a child will cross the glade
10   To take his nurse his broken toy;
Sometimes a thrush flit overhead
Deep in her unknown day's employ.

Here at my feet what wonders pass,
What endless, active life is here!
15   What blowing daisies, fragrant grass!
An air-stirred forest, fresh and clear.

Scarce fresher is the mountain-sod
Where the tired angler lies, stretched out,
And, eased of basket and of rod,
20   Counts his day's spoil, the spotted trout.

In the huge world, which roars hard by,
Be others happy if they can!
But in my helpless cradle I
Was breathed on by the rural Pan.

25   I, on men's impious uproar hurled,
Think often, as I hear them rave,
That peace has left the upper world
And now keeps only in the grave.

Yet here is peace for ever new!
30   When I who watch them am away,
Still all things in this glade go through
The changes of their quiet day.

Then to their happy rest they pass!
The flowers upclose, the birds are fed,
35   The night comes down upon the grass,
The child sleeps warmly in his bed.

Calm soul of all things! make it mine
To feel, amid the city's jar,
That there abides a peace of thine,
40   Man did not make, and cannot mar.

1. A park in London.

The will to neither strive nor cry,
The power to feel with others give!
Calm, calm me more! nor let me die
Before I have begun to live.

c. 1852   1852

The Buried Life

Light flows our war of mocking words, and yet,
Behold, with tears mine eyes are wet!
I feel a nameless sadness o'er me roll.
Yes, yes, we know that we can jest,
5 We know, we know that we can smile!
But there's a something in this breast,
To which thy light words bring no rest,
And thy gay smiles no anodyne.
Give me thy hand, and hush awhile,
10 And turn those limpid eyes on mine,
And let me read there, love! thy inmost soul.

Alas! is even love too weak
To unlock the heart, and let it speak?
Are even lovers powerless to reveal
15 To one another what indeed they feel?
I knew the mass of men concealed
Their thoughts, for fear that if revealed
They would by other men be met
With blank indifference, or with blame reproved;
20 I knew they lived and moved
Tricked in disguises, alien to the rest
Of men, and alien to themselves—and yet
The same heart beats in every human breast!

But we, my love!—doth a like spell benumb
25 Our hearts, our voices? must we too be dumb?

Ah! well for us, if even we,
Even for a moment, can get free
Our heart, and have our lips unchained;
For that which seals them hath been deep-ordained!

30 Fate, which foresaw
How frivolous a baby man would be—
By what distractions he would be possessed,
How he would pour himself in every strife,
And well-nigh change his own identity—
35 That it might keep from his capricious play
His genuine self, and force him to obey
Even in his own despite his being's law,
Bade through the deep recesses of our breast
The unregarded river of our life

40   Pursue with indiscernible flow its way;
    And that we should not see
    The buried stream, and seem to be
    Eddying at large in blind uncertainty,
    Though driving on with it eternally.

45   But often, in the world's most crowded streets,
    But often, in the din of strife,
    There rises an unspeakable desire
    After the knowledge of our buried life;
    A thirst to spend our fire and restless force
50   In tracking out our true, original course;
    A longing to inquire
    Into the mystery of this heart which beats
    So wild, so deep in us—to know
    Whence our lives come and where they go.
55   And many a man in his own breast then delves,
    But deep enough, alas! none ever mines.
    And we have been on many thousand lines,
    And we have shown, on each, spirit and power;
    But hardly have we, for one little hour,
60   Been on our own line, have we been ourselves—
    Hardly had skill to utter one of all
    The nameless feelings that course through our breast,
    But they course on for ever unexpressed.
    And long we try in vain to speak and act
65   Our hidden self, and what we say and do
    Is eloquent, is well—but 'tis not true!
    And then we will no more be racked
    With inward striving, and demand
    Of all the thousand nothings of the hour
70   Their stupefying power;
    Ah yes, and they benumb us at our call!
    Yet still, from time to time, vague and forlorn,
    From the soul's subterranean depth upborne
    As from an infinitely distant land,
75   Come airs, and floating echoes, and convey
    A melancholy into all our day.

    Only—but this is rare—
    When a belovéd hand is laid in ours,
    When, jaded with the rush and glare
80   Of the interminable hours,
    Our eyes can in another's eyes read clear,
    When our world-deafened ear
    Is by the tones of a loved voice caressed—
    A bolt is shot back somewhere in our breast,
85   And a lost pulse of feeling stirs again.
    The eye sinks inward, and the heart lies plain,
    And what we mean, we say, and what we would, we know.

A man becomes aware of his life's flow,
And hears its winding murmur; and he sees
90   The meadows where it glides, the sun, the breeze.

And there arrives a lull in the hot race
Wherein he doth for ever chase
That flying and elusive shadow, rest.
An air of coolness plays upon his face,
95   And an unwonted calm pervades his breast.
And then he thinks he knows
The hills where his life rose,
And the sea where it goes.

                                        1852

Stanzas from the Grande Chartreuse[1]

Through Alpine meadows soft-suffused
With rain, where thick the crocus blows,
Past the dark forges long disused,
The mule-track from Saint Laurent goes.
5   The bridge is crossed, and slow we ride,
Through forest, up the mountain-side.

The autumnal evening darkens round,
The wind is up, and drives the rain;
While, hark! far down, with strangled sound
10   Doth the Dead Guier's stream[2] complain,
Where that wet smoke, among the woods,
Over his boiling cauldron broods.

Swift rush the spectral vapours white
Past limestone scars with ragged pines,
15   Showing—then blotting from our sight!
Halt—through the cloud-drift something shines!
High in the valley, wet and drear,
The huts of Courrerie appear.

Strike leftward! cries our guide; and higher
20   Mounts up the stony forest-way.
At last the encircling trees retire;
Look! through the showery twilight grey
What pointed roofs are these advance?
A palace of the Kings of France?

25   Approach, for what we seek is here!
Alight, and sparely sup, and wait
For rest in this outbuilding near;
Then cross the sward and reach that gate.

---

1. Monastery in the French Alps founded by the Carthusians, an ascetic and contemplative order; Arnold visited it on his honeymoon in September 1851.

2. The Guiers Mort River flows down past the monastery and joins the Guiers Vif (or Living Guiers) in the valley.

Knock; pass the wicket! Thou art come
30   To the Carthusians' world-famed home.

The silent courts, where night and day
Into their stone-carved basins cold
The splashing icy fountains play—
The humid corridors behold!
35   Where, ghostlike in the deepening night,
Cowled forms brush by in gleaming white.

The chapel, where no organ's peal
Invests the stern and naked prayer—
With penitential cries they kneel
40   And wrestle; rising then, with bare
And white uplifted faces stand,
Passing the Host from hand to hand;[3]

Each takes, and then his visage wan
Is buried in his cowl once more.
45   The cells!—the suffering Son of Man
Upon the wall—the knee-worn floor—
And where they sleep, that wooden bed,
Which shall their coffin be, when dead![4]

The library, where tract and tome
50   Not to feed priestly pride are there,
To hymn the conquering march of Rome,
Nor yet to amuse, as ours are!
They paint of souls the inner strife,
Their drops of blood, their death in life.

55   The garden, overgrown—yet mild,
See, fragrant herbs are flowering there![5]
Strong children of the Alpine wild
Whose culture is the brethren's care;
Of human tasks their only one,
60   And cheerful works beneath the sun.

Those halls, too, destined to contain
Each its own pilgrim-host of old,
From England, Germany, or Spain—
All are before me! I behold
65   The House, the Brotherhood austere!
—And what am I, that I am here?

For rigorous teachers seized my youth,
And purged its faith, and trimmed its fire,

3. Arnold's mistake. When taking Holy Communion, the Carthusians receive the wafer ("the Host") directly on their tongues, rather than in their hands, as Anglicans do.
4. Carthusians are buried in their habits, on bare wooden planks; they do not sleep in coffins, as is sometimes believed.
5. A reference to Chartreuse, the liqueur that the monks make from aromatic herbs and brandy and sell as a source of income.

Showed me the high, white star of Truth,
70   There bade me gaze, and there aspire.
Even now their whispers pierce the gloom:
What dost thou in this living tomb?

Forgive me, masters of the mind![6]
At whose behest I long ago
75   So much unlearnt, so much resigned—
I come not here to be your foe!
I seek these anchorites, not in ruth,[7]
To curse and to deny your truth;

Not as their friend, or child, I speak!
80   But as, on some far northern strand,
Thinking of his own Gods, a Greek
In pity and mournful awe might stand
Before some fallen Runic stone—
For both were faiths, and both are gone.

85   Wandering between two worlds, one dead,
The other powerless to be born,
With nowhere yet to rest my head,
Like these, on earth I wait forlorn.
Their faith, my tears, the world deride—
90   I come to shed them at their side.

Oh, hide me in your gloom profound,
Ye solemn seats of holy pain!
Take me, cowled forms, and fence me round,
Till I possess my soul again;
95   Till free my thoughts before me roll,
Not chafed by hourly false control!

For the world cries your faith is now
But a dead time's exploded dream;
My melancholy, sciolists[8] say,
100   Is a past mode, an outworn theme—
As if the world had ever had
A faith, or sciolists been sad!

Ah, if it *be* passed, take away,
At least, the restlessness, the pain;
105   Be man henceforth no more a prey
To these out-dated stings again!
The nobleness of grief is gone—
Ah, leave us not the fret alone!

But—if you cannot give us ease—
110   Last of the race of them who grieve,

6. I.e., those writers who had influenced Arnold to conclude that Christianity is no longer tenable.
7. Remorse for his rationalism.
8. Superficial pretenders to learning.

Here leave us to die out with these
Last of the people who believe!
Silent, while years engrave the brow;
Silent—the best are silent now.

115 Achilles ponders in his tent,[9]
The kings of modern thought are dumb;
Silent they are, though not content,
And wait to see the future come.
They have the grief men had of yore,
120 But they contend and cry no more.

Our fathers[1] watered with their tears
This sea of time whereon we sail,
Their voices were in all men's ears
Who passed within their puissant hail.
125 Still the same ocean round us raves,
But we stand mute, and watch the waves.

For what availed it, all the noise
And outcry of the former men?
Say, have their sons achieved more joys,
130 Say, is life lighter now than then?
The sufferers died, they left their pain—
The pangs which tortured them remain.

What helps it now, that Byron bore,
With haughty scorn which mocked the smart,
135 Through Europe to the Aetolian shore[2]
The pageant of his bleeding heart?
That thousands counted every groan,
And Europe made his woe her own?

What boots it, Shelley! that the breeze
140 Carried thy lovely wail away,
Musical through Italian trees
Which fringe thy soft blue Spezzian bay?[3]
Inheritors of thy distress
Have restless hearts one throb the less?

145 Or are we easier, to have read,
O Obermann![4] the sad, stern page,
Which tells us how thou hidd'st thy head
From the fierce tempest of thine age
In the lone brakes of Fontainebleau,
150 Or chalets near the Alpine snow?

---

9. At the start of Homer's *Iliad*, Achilles sulked in his
tent and refused to fight the Trojans.
1. The previous generation of writers, the Romantics.
2. The part of Greece where Byron died in 1824, fighting
for Greek independence.
3. The Gulf of Spezzia in Italy, where Shelley drowned in

1822.
4. In *Obermann* (1804), a novel by Etienne Pivert de
Senancour, the melancholy hero flees to a remote alpine
valley, from which he writes letters describing his solitude
and his devotion to nature. Arnold wrote several poems
and a critical essay on *Obermann*.

Ye slumber in your silent grave!
The world, which for an idle day
Grace to your mood of sadness gave,
Long since hath flung her weeds° away.   *mourning clothes*
155   The eternal trifler breaks your spell;
But we—we learnt your lore too well!

Years hence, perhaps, may dawn an age,
More fortunate, alas! than we,
Which without hardness will be sage,
160   And gay without frivolity.
Sons of the world, oh, speed those years;
But, while we wait, allow our tears!

Allow them! We admire with awe
The exulting thunder of your race;
165   You give the universe your law,
You triumph over time and space!
Your pride of life, your tireless powers,
We laud them, but they are not ours.

We are like children reared in shade
170   Beneath some old-world abbey wall,
Forgotten in a forest-glade,
And secret from the eyes of all.
Deep, deep the greenwood round them waves,
Their abbey, and its close° of graves!   *enclosed yard*

175   But, where the road runs near the stream,
Oft through the trees they catch a glance
Of passing troops in the sun's beam—
Pennon, and plume, and flashing lance!
Forth to the world those soldiers fare,
180   To life, to cities, and to war!

And through the wood, another way,
Faint bugle-notes from far are borne,
Where hunters gather, staghounds bay,
Round some fair forest-lodge at morn.
185   Gay dames are there, in sylvan green;
Laughter and cries—those notes between!

The banners flashing through the trees
Make their blood dance and chain their eyes;
That bugle-music on the breeze
190   Arrests them with a charmed surprise.
Banner by turns and bugle woo:
Ye shy recluses, follow too!

O children, what do ye reply?—
"Action and pleasure, will ye roam
195   Through these secluded dells to cry
And call us?—but too late ye come!

Too late for us your call ye blow,
Whose bent was taken long ago.

200   "Long since we pace this shadowed nave;
We watch those yellow tapers shine,
Emblems of hope over the grave,
In the high altar's depth divine;
The organ carries to our ear
Its accents of another sphere.

205   "Fenced early in this cloistral round
Of reverie, of shade, of prayer,
How should we grow in other ground?
How can we flower in foreign air?
—Pass, banners, pass, and bugles, cease;
210   And leave our desert to its peace!"

c. 1852   1855

THE SCHOLAR-GIPSY   While at Oxford in the mid-1840s, Arnold read the seventeenth-century tale of a young man who left his studies at the university to join a band of gypsies, intending to master their lore. Fascinated by the story, Arnold imagined the scholar still wandering the hills around Oxford, magically untouched by time and change. The poem Arnold eventually wrote, circa 1853, celebrated his own youth at Oxford, "the *freest* and most delightful part, perhaps, of my life," he told his brother Tom, "when with you and Clough . . . I shook off all the bonds and formalities of the place, and enjoyed the spring of life and that unforgotten Oxfordshire and Berkshire country." Arnold accompanied the poem with a note based on his source, Joseph Glanvill's *Vanity of Dogmatizing* (1661):

> There was very lately a lad in the University of Oxford, who was by his poverty forced to leave his studies there; and at last to join himself to a company of vagabond gipsies. Among these extravagant people, by the insinuating subtilty of his carriage, he quickly got so much of their love and esteem as that they discovered to him their mystery. After he had been a pretty while well exercised in the trade, there chanced to ride by a couple of scholars, who had formerly been of his acquaintance. They quickly spied out their old friend among the gipsies; and he gave them an account of the necessity which drove him to that kind of life, and told them that the people he went with were not such impostors as they were taken for, but that they had a traditional kind of learning among them, and could do wonders by the power of imagination, their fancy binding that of others: that himself had learned much of their art, and when he had compassed the whole secret, he intended, he said, to leave their company, and give the world an account of what he had learned.

The Scholar-Gipsy

Go, for they call you, shepherd, from the hill;
    Go, shepherd, and untie the wattled cotes![1]
        No longer leave thy wistful flock unfed,
        Nor let thy bawling fellows rack their throats,
5   Nor the cropped herbage shoot another head.
            But when the fields are still,
        And the tired men and dogs all gone to rest,

---

1. Fences made of woven sticks, used to pen sheep.

And only the white sheep are sometimes seen
Cross and recross the strips of moon-blanched green,
10   Come, shepherd, and again begin the quest!

Here, where the reaper was at work of late—
In this high field's dark corner, where he leaves
His coat, his basket, and his earthen cruse,°   *jug*
And in the sun all morning binds the sheaves,
15   Then here, at noon, comes back his stores to use—
Here will I sit and wait,
While to my ear from uplands far away
The bleating of the folded° flocks is borne,   *penned up*
With distant cries of reapers in the corn—
20   All the live murmur of a summer's day.

Screened is this nook o'er the high, half-reaped field,
And here till sun-down, shepherd! will I be.
Through the thick corn the scarlet poppies peep,
And round green roots and yellowing stalks I see
25   Pale pink convolvulus° in tendrils creep;   *morning glory*
And air-swept lindens yield
Their scent, and rustle down their perfumed showers
Of bloom on the bent grass where I am laid,
And bower me from the August sun with shade;
30   And the eye travels down to Oxford's towers.

And near me on the grass lies Glanvil's book—
Come, let me read the oft-read tale again!
The story of the Oxford scholar poor,
Of pregnant parts° and quick inventive brain,   *bursting with ideas*
35   Who, tired of knocking at preferment's door,
One summer-morn forsook
His friends, and went to learn the gipsy-lore,
And roamed the world with that wild brotherhood,
And came, as most men deemed, to little good,
40   But came to Oxford and his friends no more.

But once, years after, in the country-lanes,
Two scholars, whom at college erst he knew,
Met him, and of his way of life enquired;
Whereat he answered, that the gipsy-crew,
45   His mates, had arts to rule as they desired
The workings of men's brains,
And they can bind them to what thoughts they will.
"And I," he said, "the secret of their art,
When fully learned, will to the world impart;
50   But it needs heaven-sent moments for this skill."

This said, he left them, and returned no more.
But rumours hung about the country-side,
That the lost Scholar long was seen to stray,
Seen by rare glimpses, pensive and tongue-tied,

55   In hat of antique shape, and cloak of grey,
            The same the gipsies wore.
        Shepherds had met him on the Hurst[2] in spring;
            At some lone alehouse in the Berkshire moors,
            On the warm ingle-bench, the smock-frocked boors[3]
60   Had found him seated at their entering,

        But, 'mid their drink and clatter, he would fly.
        And I myself seem half to know thy looks,
            And put the shepherds, wanderer! on thy trace;
            And boys who in lone wheatfields scare the rooks
65   I ask if thou hast passed their quiet place;
                Or in my boat I lie
        Moored to the cool bank in the summer-heats,
            'Mid wide grass meadows which the sunshine fills,
            And watch the warm, green-muffled Cumner hills,
70   And wonder if thou haunt'st their shy retreats.

        For most, I know, thou lov'st retiréd ground!
        Thee at the ferry Oxford riders blithe,
            Returning home on summer-nights, have met
        Crossing the stripling Thames at Bab-lock-hithe,
75   Trailing in the cool stream thy fingers wet,
                As the punt's° rope chops round;   *small boat*
        And leaning backward in a pensive dream,
            And fostering in thy lap a heap of flowers
            Plucked in shy fields and distant Wychwood bowers,
80   And thine eyes resting on the moonlit stream.

        And then they land, and thou art seen no more!
        Maidens, who from the distant hamlets come
            To dance around the Fyfield elm in May,
        Oft through the darkening fields have seen thee roam,
85   Or cross a stile into the public way.
                Oft thou hast given them store
        Of flowers—the frail-leafed, white anemone,
            Dark bluebells drenched with dews of summer eves,
            And purple orchises with spotted leaves—
90   But none hath words she can report of thee.

        And, above Godstow Bridge, when hay-time's here
        In June, and many a scythe in sunshine flames,
            Men who through those wide fields of breezy grass
        Where black-winged swallows haunt the glittering Thames,
95   To bathe in the abandoned lasher pass,[4]
                Have often passed thee near
        Sitting upon the river bank o'ergrown;

2. Hill near Oxford; most of the places mentioned are in the countryside around Oxford.

3. Rustic peasants; an ingle-bench is beside the fireplace.

4. Pool where water spilling over a dam collects.

Marked thine outlandish garb, thy figure spare,
　　Thy dark vague eyes, and soft abstracted air—
100　　But, when they came from bathing, thou wast gone!

At some lone homestead in the Cumner hills,
　　Where at her open door the housewife darns,
　　Thou hast been seen, or hanging on a gate
　　To watch the threshers in the mossy barns.
105　　　　Children, who early range these slopes and late
　　　　　For cresses from the rills,
　　Have known thee eying, all an April-day,
　　　　The springing pastures and the feeding kine;
　　And marked thee, when the stars come out and shine,
110　　Through the long dewy grass move slow away.

In autumn, on the skirts of Bagley Wood—
　　Where most the gipsies by the turf-edged way
　　　　Pitch their smoked tents, and every bush you see
　　With scarlet patches tagged and shreds of grey,[5]
115　　　　Above the forest-ground called Thessaly—
　　　　　The blackbird, picking food,
　　Sees thee, nor stops his meal, nor fears at all;
　　　　So often has he known thee past him stray,
　　　　Rapt, twirling in thy hand a withered spray,
120　　And waiting for the spark from heaven to fall.

And once, in winter, on the causeway chill
　　Where home through flooded fields foot-travellers go,
　　　　Have I not passed thee on the wooden bridge,
　　Wrapped in thy cloak and battling with the snow,
125　　　　Thy face tow'rd Hinksey and its wintry ridge?
　　　　　And thou hast climbed the hill,
　　And gained the white brow of the Cumner range;
　　　　Turned once to watch, while thick the snowflakes fall,
　　　　The line of festal light in Christ-Church hall[6]—
130　　Then sought thy straw in some sequestered grange.

But what—I dream! Two hundred years are flown
　　Since first thy story ran through Oxford halls,
　　　　And the grave Glanvil did the tale inscribe
　　That thou wert wandered from the studious walls
135　　　　To learn strange arts, and join a gipsy-tribe;
　　　　　And thou from earth art gone
　　Long since, and in some quiet churchyard laid—
　　　　Some country-nook, where o'er thy unknown grave
　　　　Tall grasses and white flowering nettles wave,
140　　Under a dark, red-fruited yew-tree's shade.

---

5. Gypsies spread their clothes on bushes to dry.　　6. The dining hall of Christ Church, an Oxford college.

—No, no, thou hast not felt the lapse of hours!
  For what wears out the life of mortal men?
    'Tis that from change to change their being rolls;
  'Tis that repeated shocks, again, again,
145   Exhaust the energy of strongest souls
      And numb the elastic powers.
  Till having used our nerves with bliss and teen,°   *grief*
    And tired upon a thousand schemes our wit,
    To the just-pausing Genius[7] we remit
150 Our worn-out life, and are—what we have been.

  Thou hast not lived, why should'st thou perish, so?
    Thou hadst *one* aim, *one* business, *one* desire;
      Else wert thou long since numbered with the dead!
    Else hadst thou spent, like other men, thy fire!
155   The generations of thy peers are fled,
        And we ourselves shall go;
  But thou possessest an immortal lot,
      And we imagine thee exempt from age
      And living as thou liv'st on Glanvil's page,
160 Because thou hadst—what we, alas! have not.

  For early didst thou leave the world, with powers
    Fresh, undiverted to the world without,
      Firm to their mark, not spent on other things;
    Free from the sick fatigue, the languid doubt,
165   Which much to have tried, in much been baffled, brings.
        O life unlike to ours!
  Who fluctuate idly without term or scope,
      Of whom each strives, nor knows for what he strives,
      And each half-lives a hundred different lives;
170 Who wait like thee, but not, like thee, in hope.

  Thou waitest for the spark from heaven! and we,
    Light half-believers of our casual creeds,
      Who never deeply felt, nor clearly willed,
    Whose insight never has borne fruit in deeds,
175   Whose vague resolves never have been fulfilled;
      For whom each year we see
  Breeds new beginnings, disappointments new;
    Who hesitate and falter life away,
    And lose to-morrow the ground won to-day—
180 Ah! do not we, wanderer! await it too?

  Yes, we await it!—but it still delays,
    And then we suffer! and amongst us one,[8]
      Who most has suffered, takes dejectedly

---

7. The guardian spirit that the ancients believed accompanied a person through life; here it pauses for only a moment to receive back the life it has shepherded.

8. Either Goethe, whom Arnold admired, or Tennyson, whose *In Memoriam* had recently been published.

His seat upon the intellectual throne;
185   And all his store of sad experience he
       Lays bare of wretched days;
Tells us his misery's birth and growth and signs,
     And how the dying spark of hope was fed,
     And how the breast was soothed, and how the head,
190   And all his hourly varied anodynes.

This for our wisest! and we others pine,
     And wish the long unhappy dream would end,
       And waive all claim to bliss, and try to bear;
With close-lipped patience for our only friend,
195   Sad patience, too near neighbour to despair—
       But none has hope like thine!
Thou through the fields and through the woods dost stray,
     Roaming the country-side, a truant boy,
     Nursing thy project in unclouded joy,
200   And every doubt long blown by time away.

O born in days when wits were fresh and clear,
     And life ran gaily as the sparkling Thames;
       Before this strange disease of modern life,
     With its sick hurry, its divided aims,
205   Its heads o'ertaxed, its palsied hearts, was rife—
       Fly hence, our contact fear!
Still fly, plunge deeper in the bowering wood!
     Averse, as Dido did with gesture stern
     From her false friend's approach in Hades turn,[9]
210   Wave us away, and keep thy solitude!

Still nursing the unconquerable hope,
     Still clutching the inviolable shade,
       With a free, onward impulse brushing through,
     By night, the silvered branches of the glade—
215   Far on the forest-skirts, where none pursue,
       On some mild pastoral slope
Emerge, and resting on the moonlit pales
     Freshen thy flowers as in former years
     With dew, or listen with enchanted ears,
220   From the dark dingles,° to the nightingales!   *small wooded valleys*

But fly our paths, our feverish contact fly!
     For strong the infection of our mental strife,
       Which, though it gives no bliss, yet spoils for rest;
     And we should win thee from thy own fair life,
225   Like us distracted, and like us unblest.
       Soon, soon thy cheer would die,

9. In Virgil's *Aeneid*, Dido, queen of Carthage, kills herself after her lover, Aeneas, deserts her. When they meet in Hades, she turns away sternly.

Thy hopes grow timorous, and unfixed thy powers,
   And thy clear aims be cross and shifting made;
   And then thy glad perennial youth would fade,
230   Fade, and grow old at last, and die like ours.

Then fly our greetings, fly our speech and smiles!
   —As some grave Tyrian trader,[1] from the sea,
   Descried at sunrise an emerging prow
   Lifting the cool-haired creepers stealthily,
235   The fringes of a southward-facing brow
         Among the Aegean isles;
   And saw the merry Grecian coaster come,
      Freighted with amber grapes, and Chian wine,
      Green, bursting figs, and tunnies steeped in brine—
240   And knew the intruders on his ancient home,

The young light-hearted masters of the waves—
   And snatched his rudder, and shook out more sail;
   And day and night held on indignantly
   O'er the blue Midland waters with the gale,
245   Betwixt the Syrtes[2] and soft Sicily,
         To where the Atlantic raves
   Outside the western straits; and unbent sails
      There, where down cloudy cliffs, through sheets of foam,
      Shy traffickers, the dark Iberians come;
250   And on the beach undid his corded bales.[3]

c. 1853   1853

East London[1]

'Twas August, and the fierce sun overhead
Smote on the squalid streets of Bethnal Green,
And the pale weaver, through his windows seen
In Spitalfields, looked thrice dispirited.

5   I met a preacher there I knew, and said:
"Ill and o'erworked, how fare you in this scene?"
"Bravely!" said he; "for I of late have been
Much cheered with thoughts of Christ, *the living bread*."

O human soul! as long as thou canst so
10   Set up a mark of everlasting light,
Above the howling senses' ebb and flow,

---

1. From Tyre, capital of ancient Phoenicia, in Northern Africa. The poet urges the solitary scholar to shun modern contacts just as he imagines the Tyrian trader once fled from intrusive Greeks.
2. Shoals off North Africa.
3. The last stanza continues the comparison between the scholar and the Tyrian. According to Herodotus's *History* 4.196, the Carthaginians—who came originally from Tyre—would sail out of the Mediterranean to West Africa, place their bales on the beach, and withdraw to their ships. The timid inhabitants would then set gold by the goods and withdraw in turn; thus the two sides could do business and never meet. Arnold's "shy traffickers" are not Africans but "dark Iberians" (Spanish or Portuguese). He implies that in them—people reminiscent of the dark-skinned reclusive gypsies who "trade" in the Oxford countryside—the sensitive Tyrian has found others as wary as he is.
1. The East End was the home of the poor and the working classes; Bethnal Green (line 2) and Spitalfields (line 4) are districts in the East End.

To cheer thee, and to right thee if thou roam—
Not with lost toil thou labourest through the night!
Thou mak'st the heaven thou hop'st indeed thy home.

c. 1863   1867

West London[1]

Crouched on the pavement, close by Belgrave Square,
A tramp I saw, ill, moody, and tongue-tied.
A babe was in her arms, and at her side
A girl; their clothes were rags, their feet were bare.

5   Some labouring men, whose work lay somewhere there,
Passed opposite; she touched her girl, who hied
Across, and begged, and came back satisfied.
The rich she had let pass with frozen stare.

Thought I: "Above her state this spirit towers;
10   She will not ask of aliens, but of friends,
Of sharers in a common human fate.

She turns from that cold succour, which attends
The unknown little from the unknowing great,
And points us to a better time than ours."

c. 1863   1867

Thyrsis[1]
*A Monody, to commemorate the author's friend,
Arthur Hugh Clough, who died at Florence, 1861*

How changed is here each spot man makes or fills!
    In the two Hinkseys[2] nothing keeps the same;
        The village street its haunted mansion lacks,
        And from the sign is gone Sibylla's name,[3]
5   And from the roofs the twisted chimney-stacks—
            Are ye too changed, ye hills?
    See, 'tis no foot of unfamiliar men
        To-night from Oxford up your pathway strays!
        Here came I often, often, in old days—
10   Thyrsis and I; we still had Thyrsis then.

---

1. The West End was the neighborhood of the wealthy. Belgrave Square is a particularly fashionable area.

1. By the 1860s, Arnold had nearly given up writing poetry. But he made an exception to produce this tribute to his lifelong friend, Arthur Hugh Clough. After Clough died unexpectedly in 1861, Arnold revisited the scenes of their student wanderings in the Oxford countryside, meditating on the fate of youthful ideals. Following in the tradition of pastoral elegies such as Milton's *Lycidas* and Shelley's *Adonais*, Arnold gives Clough the classical name of a shepherd-poet: "Thyrsis" appears in Virgil's seventh eclogue, as does his friend and rival "Corydon," the name Arnold takes for himself. *Thyrsis* has the same stanza form as *The Scholar-Gipsy*, both influenced by Keats's *Ode to a Nightingale*. For Clough's own poetry, see Perspectives: Religion and Science, page 1386.

2. North and South Hinksey, villages near Oxford. The places named in the poem—Childsworth Farm, Ilsley Downs, etc.—are in the Thames Valley and the Cumner Hills in Oxfordshire.

3. Sibylla Kerr kept a tavern in South Hinksey.

Runs it not here, the track by Childsworth Farm,
   Past the high wood, to where the elm-tree crowns
      The hill behind whose ridge the sunset flames?
The signal-elm, that looks on Ilsley Downs,
15   The Vale, the three lone weirs, the youthful Thames?
         This winter-eve is warm,
Humid the air! leafless, yet soft as spring,
      The tender purple spray on copse and briers!
      And that sweet city with her dreaming spires,
20 She needs not June for beauty's heightening,

Lovely all times she lies, lovely to-night!—
   Only, methinks, some loss of habit's power
      Befalls me wandering through this upland dim.
   Once passed I blindfold here, at any hour;
25   Now seldom come I, since I came with him.
         That single elm-tree bright
Against the west—I miss it! is it gone?
      We prized it dearly; while it stood, we said,
      Our friend, the Gipsy-Scholar, was not dead;
30 While the tree lived, he in these fields lived on.

Too rare, too rare, grow now my visits here,
   But once I knew each field, each flower, each stick;
      And with the country-folk acquaintance made
By barn in threshing time, by new-built rick.
35   Here, too, our shepherd-pipes we first assayed.
         Ah me! this many a year
My pipe is lost, my shepherd's holiday!
      Needs must I lose them, needs with heavy heart
      Into the world and wave of men depart;
40 But Thyrsis of his own will went away.[4]

It irked him to be here, he could not rest.
   He loved each simple joy the country yields,
      He loved his mates; but yet he could not keep,
For that a shadow loured on the fields,
45   Here with the shepherds and the silly° sheep.   *innocent*
         Some life of men unblest
He knew, which made him droop, and filled his head.
      He went; his piping took a troubled sound
      Of storms that rage outside our happy ground;
50 He could not wait their passing, he is dead.

So, some tempestuous morn in early June,
   When the year's primal burst of bloom is o'er,
      Before the roses and the longest day—

4. In 1848 Clough had resigned his fellowship at Oriel College, Oxford, rather than subscribe to the Thirty-Nine Articles of Anglican doctrine.

When garden-walks and all the grassy floor
55   With blossoms red and white of fallen May
        And chestnut-flowers are strewn—
So have I heard the cuckoo's parting cry,
        From the wet field, through the vexed garden-trees,
        Come with the volleying rain and tossing breeze:
60   *The bloom is gone, and with the bloom go I!*

Too quick despairer, wherefore wilt thou go?
        Soon will the high Midsummer pomps come on,
        Soon will the musk carnations break and swell,
        Soon shall we have gold-dusted snapdragon,
65   Sweet-William with his homely cottage-smell,
        And stocks in fragrant blow;
Roses that down the alleys shine afar,
        And open, jasmine-muffled lattices,
        And groups under the dreaming garden-trees,
70   And the full moon, and the white evening-star.

He hearkens not! light comer, he is flown!
        What matters it? next year he will return,
        And we shall have him in the sweet spring-days,
        With whitening hedges, and uncrumpling fern,
75   And blue-bells trembling by the forest-ways,
        And scent of hay new-mown.
But Thyrsis never more we swains° shall see;   *youths, shepherds*
        See him come back, and cut a smoother reed,
        And blow a strain the world at last shall heed—
80   For Time, not Corydon, hath conquered thee!

Alack, for Corydon no rival now!
        But when Sicilian shepherds lost a mate,
        Some good survivor with his flute would go,
        Piping a ditty sad for Bion's fate;[5]
85   And cross the unpermitted ferry's flow,[6]
        And relax Pluto's brow,
And make leap up with joy the beauteous head
        Of Proserpine, among whose crownéd hair
        Are flowers first opened on Sicilian air,
90   And flute his friend, like Orpheus, from the dead.[7]

O easy access to the hearer's grace
        When Dorian shepherds[8] sang to Proserpine!
        For she herself had trod Sicilian fields,
        She knew the Dorian water's gush divine,

---

5. A poet who died in Sicily; a pastoral elegy was composed for him by Moschus, a Greek poet.
6. I.e., cross the River Styx to the underworld, ruled by Pluto. When Pluto's bride Proserpine returned aboveground in Sicily each spring, she made the flowers blossom.

7. The musician Orpheus was allowed to enter Hades in search of his dead wife, Eurydice.
8. Dorian Greeks colonized Sicily; the "Dorian strain" (line 97) is the simple, direct style of pastoral poetry in which Moschus, Bion, and Theocritus wrote.

95   She knew each lily white which Enna[9] yields,
            Each rose with blushing face;
        She loved the Dorian pipe, the Dorian strain.
            But ah, of our poor Thames she never heard!
            Her foot the Cumner cowslips never stirred;
100   And we should tease her with our plaint in vain!

        Well! wind-dispersed and vain the words will be,
            Yet, Thyrsis, let me give my grief its hour
                In the old haunt, and find our tree-topped hill!
            Who, if not I, for questing here hath power?
105   I know the wood which hides the daffodil,
                I know the Fyfield tree,
            I know what white, what purple fritillaries°   *meadow flowers*
                The grassy harvest of the river-fields,
                Above by Ensham, down by Sandford, yields,
110   And what sedged brooks are Thames's tributaries;

        I know these slopes; who knows them if not I?
            But many a dingle° on the loved hill-side,   *small wooded valley*
                With thorns once studded, old, white-blossomed trees,
            Where thick the cowslips grew, and far descried
115   High towered the spikes of purple orchises,
                    Hath since our day put by
            The coronals° of that forgotten time;   *circlets worn on head*
                Down each green bank hath gone the ploughboy's team,
                And only in the hidden brookside gleam
120   Primroses, orphans of the flowery prime.

        Where is the girl, who by the boatman's door,
            Above the locks, above the boating throng,
                Unmoored our skiff when through the Wytham flats,
            Red loosestrife and blond meadow-sweet among
125   And darting swallows and light water-gnats,
                    We tracked the shy Thames shore?
            Where are the mowers, who, as the tiny swell
                Of our boat passing heaved the river-grass,
                Stood with suspended scythe to see us pass?
130   They all are gone, and thou art gone as well!

        Yes, thou art gone! and round me too the night
            In ever-nearing circle weaves her shade.
                I see her veil draw soft across the day,
            I feel her slowly chilling breath invade
135   The cheek grown thin, the brown hair sprent° with grey;   *sprinkled*
                    I feel her finger light
            Laid pausefully upon life's headlong train;
                The foot less prompt to meet the morning dew,

---

9. A Sicilian town near which Pluto had abducted Proserpine.

The heart less bounding at emotion new,
140   And hope, once crushed, less quick to spring again.

And long the way appears, which seemed so short
    To the less practised eye of sanguine youth;
      And high the mountain-tops, in cloudy air,
    The mountain-tops where is the throne of Truth,
145   Tops in life's morning-sun so bright and bare!
          Unbreachable the fort
    Of the long-battered world uplifts its wall;
      And strange and vain the earthly turmoil grows,
      And near and real the charm of thy repose,
150   And night as welcome as a friend would fall.

But hush! the upland hath a sudden loss
    Of quiet!—Look, adown the dusk hill-side,
      A troop of Oxford hunters going home,
    As in old days, jovial and talking, ride!
155   From hunting with the Berkshire hounds they come.
          Quick! let me fly, and cross
    Into yon farther field!—'Tis done; and see,
      Backed by the sunset, which doth glorify
      The orange and pale violet evening-sky,
160   Bare on its lonely ridge, the Tree! the Tree!

I take the omen! Eve° lets down her veil,   *evening*
    The white fog creeps from bush to bush about,
      The west unflushes, the high stars grow bright,
    And in the scattered farms the lights come out.
165   I cannot reach the signal-tree to-night,
          Yet, happy omen, hail!
    Hear it from thy broad lucent Arno-vale[1]
      (For there thine earth-forgetting eyelids keep
      The morningless and unawakening sleep
170   Under the flowery oleanders pale),

Hear it, O Thyrsis, still our tree is there!
    Ah, vain! These English fields, this upland dim,
      These brambles pale with mist engarlanded,
    That lone, sky-pointing tree, are not for him;
175   To a boon° southern country he is fled,   *bounteous*
          And now in happier air,
    Wandering with the great Mother's[2] train divine
      (And purer or more subtle soul than thee,
      I trow,° the mighty Mother doth not see)   *believe*
180   Within a folding of the Apennine,[3]

---

1. Clough was buried in Florence, in the valley of the Arno River.
2. Demeter, the mother of Proserpine and goddess of agri-culture.
3. A mountain chain on the Italian peninsula.

Thou hearest the immortal chants of old!
   Putting his sickle to the perilous grain
     In the hot cornfield of the Phrygian king,[4]
  For thee the Lityerses-song again
185   Young Daphnis with his silver voice doth sing;
       Sings his Sicilian fold,
  His sheep, his hapless love, his blinded eyes—
    And how a call celestial round him rang,
    And heavenward from the fountain-brink he sprang,
190 And all the marvel of the golden skies.

There thou art gone, and me thou leavest here
   Sole in these fields! yet will I not despair.
    Despair I will not, while I yet descry
  'Neath the mild canopy of English air
195   That lonely tree against the western sky.
       Still, still these slopes, 'tis clear,
  Our Gipsy-Scholar haunts, outliving thee!
    Fields where soft sheep from cages pull the hay,
    Woods with anemones in flower till May,
200 Know him a wanderer still; then why not me?

A fugitive and gracious light he seeks,
   Shy to illumine; and I seek it too.
    This does not come with houses or with gold,
  With place, with honour, and a flattering crew;
205   'Tis not in the world's market bought and sold—
       But the smooth-slipping weeks
  Drop by, and leave its seeker still untired;
    Out of the heed of mortals he is gone,
    He wends unfollowed, he must house alone;
210 Yet on he fares, by his own heart inspired.

Thou too, O Thyrsis, on like quest wast bound;
   Thou wanderedst with me for a little hour!
    Men gave thee nothing; but this happy quest,
  If men esteemed thee feeble, gave thee power,
215   If men procured thee trouble, gave thee rest.
       And this rude Cumner ground,
  Its fir-topped Hurst, its farms, its quiet fields,
    Here cam'st thou in thy jocund youthful time,

4. Daphnis, the ideal Sicilian shepherd of Greek pastoral poetry, was said to have followed into Phrygia his mistress Piplea, who had been carried off by robbers, and to have found her in the power of the king of Phrygia, Lityerses. Lityerses used to make strangers try a contest with him in reaping corn and to put them to death if he overcame them. Hercules arrived in time to save Daphnis, took upon himself the reaping-contest with Lityerses, overcame him, and slew him. The Lityerses-song connected with this tradition was, like the Linus-song, one of the early plaintive strains of Greek popular poetry, and used to be sung by corn-reapers. Other traditions represented Daphnis as beloved by a nymph who exacted from him an oath to love no one else. He fell in love with a princess, and was struck blind by the jealous nymph. Mercury, who was his father, raised him to Heaven, and made a fountain spring up in the place from which he ascended. At this fountain the Sicilians offered yearly sacrifices [Arnold's note, from Servius's commentary on Virgil's *Eclogues*].

Here was thine height of strength, thy golden prime!
220   And still the haunt beloved a virtue yields.

What though the music of thy rustic flute
    Kept not for long its happy, country tone;
        Lost it too soon, and learnt a stormy note
    Of men contention-tossed, of men who groan,
225   Which tasked thy pipe too sore, and tired thy throat—[5]
            It failed, and thou wast mute!
Yet hadst thou alway visions of our light,
    And long with men of care thou couldst not stay,
    And soon thy foot resumed its wandering way,
230   Left human haunt, and on alone till night.

Too rare, too rare, grow now my visits here!
    'Mid city-noise, not, as with thee of yore,
        Thyrsis! in reach of sheep-bells is my home.
    —Then through the great town's harsh, heart-wearying roar,
235   Let in thy voice a whisper often come,
        To chase fatigue and fear:
Why faintest thou? I wandered till I died.
Roam on! The light we sought is shining still.
Dost thou ask proof? Our tree yet crowns the hill,
240   *Our Scholar travels yet the loved hill-side.*

1866

from The Function of Criticism at the Present Time[1]

Many objections have been made to a proposition which, in some remarks of mine on translating Homer, I ventured to put forth; a proposition about criticism, and its importance at the present day. I said: "Of the literature of France and Germany, as of the intellect of Europe in general, the main effort, for now many years, has been a critical effort; the endeavour, in all branches of knowledge, theology, philosophy, history, art, science, to see the object as in itself it really is."[2] I added, that owing to the operation in English literature of certain causes, "almost the last thing for which one would come to English literature is just that very thing which now Europe most desires,—criticism;" and that the power and value of English literature was thereby impaired. More than one rejoinder declared that the importance I here assigned to criticism was excessive, and asserted the inherent superiority of the creative effort of the human spirit over its critical effort. And the other day, having been led by Mr. Shairp's excellent notice of Wordsworth[3] to turn again to his biography, I found, in the words of this great man, whom I, for one, must always listen to with the profoundest respect, a sentence passed on the critic's business, which seems to justify every possible disparagement of it. Wordsworth says in one of his letters:—

5. Despite the ironic tone of many of his poems, Clough took to heart—even more than Arnold—the social and religious disarray of Victorian England. His poetic production fell off toward the end of his life.
1. This essay, which introduced Arnold's *Essays in Criticism* (1865), was his critical manifesto. In it he argues that criticism, in the best sense, can have positive intel-

lectual and spiritual effects, not only on creative writers but on society as a whole, teaching people to think critically about the political, religious, and aesthetic problems confronting them.
2. From *On Translating Homer* (1861).
3. J. C. Shairp, *Wordsworth: The Man and the Poet* (1864).

"The writers in these publications" (the Reviews), "while they prosecute their inglorious employment, can not be supposed to be in a state of mind very favourable for being affected by the finer influences of a thing so pure as genuine poetry."

And a trustworthy reporter of his conversation quotes a more elaborate judgment to the same effect:—

"Wordsworth holds the critical power very low, infinitely lower than the inventive; and he said to-day that if the quantity of time consumed in writing critiques on the works of others were given to original composition, of whatever kind it might be, it would be much better employed; it would make a man find out sooner his own level, and it would do infinitely less mischief. A false or malicious criticism may do much injury to the minds of others; a stupid invention, either in prose or verse, is quite harmless."[4]

It is almost too much to expect of poor human nature, that a man capable of producing some effect in one line of literature, should, for the greater good of society, voluntarily doom himself to impotence and obscurity in another. Still less is this to be expected from men addicted to the composition of the "false or malicious criticism" of which Wordsworth speaks. However, everybody would admit that a false or malicious criticism had better never have been written. Everybody, too, would be willing to admit, as a general proposition, that the critical faculty is lower than the inventive. But is it true that criticism is really, in itself, a baneful and injurious employment; is it true that all time given to writing critiques on the works of others would be much better employed if it were given to original composition, of whatever kind this may be? Is it true that Johnson had better have gone on producing more *Irenes* instead of writing his *Lives of the Poets*;[5] nay, is it certain that Wordsworth himself was better employed in making his Ecclesiastical Sonnets than when he made his celebrated Preface, so full of criticism, and criticism of the works of others?[6] Wordsworth was himself a great critic, and it is to be sincerely regretted that he has not left us more criticism; Goethe[7] was one of the greatest of critics, and we may sincerely congratulate ourselves that he has left us so much criticism. Without wasting time over the exaggeration which Wordsworth's judgment on criticism clearly contains, or over an attempt to trace the causes,—not difficult, I think, to be traced,—which may have led Wordsworth to this exaggeration, a critic may with advantage seize an occasion for trying his own conscience, and for asking himself of what real service at any given moment the practice of criticism either is or may be made to his own mind and spirit, and to the minds and spirits of others.

The critical power is of lower rank than the creative. True; but in assenting to this proposition, one or two things are to be kept in mind. It is undeniable that the exercise of a creative power, that a free creative activity, is the highest function of man; it is proved to be so by man's finding in it his true happiness. But it is undeniable, also, that men may have the sense of exercising this free creative activity in other ways than in producing great works of literature or art; if it were not so, all but a very few men would be shut out from the true happiness of all men. They may have it in well-doing, they may have it in learning, they may have it even in criticising.

4. See Christopher Wordsworth, *Memoirs of William Wordsworth* (1851) 2.53 and 2.439.
5. Samuel Johnson's *Irene* (1736) was a lifeless verse tragedy; *Lives of the English Poets* (1779–1781) was his crowning critical achievement.
6. Wordsworth's Preface to *Lyrical Ballads* (1800; rev. 1802) defined English Romanticism; his *Ecclesiastical Sonnets* (1822) are far less memorable.
7. Johann Wolfgang von Goethe (1749–1832), German novelist, poet, and dramatist.

This is one thing to be kept in mind. Another is, that the exercise of the creative power in the production of great works of literature or art, however high this exercise of it may rank, is not at all epochs and under all conditions possible; and that therefore labour may be vainly spent in attempting it, which might with more fruit be used in preparing for it, in rendering it possible. This creative power works with elements, with materials; what if it has not those materials, those elements, ready for its use? In that case it must surely wait till they are ready. Now, in literature,—I will limit myself to literature, for it is about literature that the question arises,—the elements with which the creative power works are ideas; the best ideas, on every matter which literature touches, current at the time. At any rate we may lay it down as certain that in modern literature no manifestation of the creative power not working with these can be very important or fruitful. And I say *current* at the time, not merely accessible at the time; for creative literary genius does not principally show itself in discovering new ideas, that is rather the business of the philosopher. The grand work of literary genius is a work of synthesis and exposition, not of analysis and discovery; its gift lies in the faculty of being happily inspired by a certain intellectual and spiritual atmosphere, by a certain order of ideas, when it finds itself in them; of dealing divinely with these ideas, presenting them in the most effective and attractive combinations,—making beautiful works with them, in short. But it must have the atmosphere, it must find itself amidst the order of ideas, in order to work freely; and these it is not so easy to command. This is why great creative epochs in literature are so rare, this is why there is so much that is unsatisfactory in the productions of many men of real genius; because for the creation of a master-work of literature two powers must concur, the power of the man and the power of the moment, and the man is not enough without the moment; the creative power has, for its happy exercise, appointed elements, and those elements are not in its own control.

Nay, they are more within the control of the critical power. It is the business of the critical power, as I said in the words already quoted, "in all branches of knowledge, theology, philosophy, history, art, science, to see the object as in itself it really is." Thus it tends, at last, to make an intellectual situation of which the creative power can profitably avail itself. It tends to establish an order of ideas, if not absolutely true, yet true by comparison with that which it displaces; to make the best ideas prevail. Presently these new ideas reach society, the touch of truth is the touch of life, and there is a stir and growth everywhere; out of this stir and growth come the creative epochs of literature.

Or, to narrow our range, and quit these considerations of the general march of genius and of society,—considerations which are apt to become too abstract and impalpable,—every one can see that a poet, for instance, ought to know life and the world before dealing with them in poetry; and life and the world being in modern times very complex things, the creation of a modern poet, to be worth much, implies a great critical effort behind it; else it must be a comparatively poor, barren, and short-lived affair. This is why Byron's poetry had so little endurance in it, and Goethe's so much; both Byron and Goethe had a great productive power, but Goethe's was nourished by a great critical effort providing the true materials for it, and Byron's was not; Goethe knew life and the world, the poet's necessary subjects, much more comprehensively and thoroughly than Byron. He knew a great deal more of them, and he knew them much more as they really are.

It has long seemed to me that the burst of creative activity in our literature, through the first quarter of this century, had about it in fact something premature;

and that from this cause its productions are doomed, most of them, in spite of the sanguine hopes which accompanied and do still accompany them, to prove hardly more lasting than the productions of far less splendid epochs. And this prematureness comes from its having proceeded without having its proper data, without sufficient materials to work with. In other words, the English poetry of the first quarter of this century, with plenty of energy, plenty of creative force, did not know enough. This makes Byron so empty of matter, Shelley so incoherent, Wordsworth even, profound as he is, yet so wanting in completeness and variety. Wordsworth cared little for books, and disparaged Goethe. I admire Wordsworth, as he is, so much that I cannot wish him different; and it is vain, no doubt, to imagine such a man different from what he is, to suppose that he *could* have been different. But surely the one thing wanting to make Wordsworth an even greater poet than he is,—his thought richer, and his influence of wider application,—was that he should have read more books, among them, no doubt, those of that Goethe whom he disparaged without reading him.

But to speak of books and reading may easily lead to a misunderstanding here. It was not really books and reading that lacked to our poetry at this epoch; Shelley had plenty of reading, Coleridge had immense reading. Pindar and Sophocles—as we all say so glibly, and often with so little discernment of the real import of what we are saying—had not many books; Shakespeare was no deep reader. True; but in the Greece of Pindar and Sophocles, in the England of Shakespeare, the poet lived in a current of ideas in the highest degree animating and nourishing to the creative power; society was, in the fullest measure, permeated by fresh thought, intelligent and alive. And this state of things is the true basis for the creative power's exercise, in this it finds its data, its materials, truly ready for its hand; all the books and reading in the world are only valuable as they are helps to this. Even when this does not actually exist, books and reading may enable a man to construct a kind of semblance of it in his own mind, a world of knowledge and intelligence in which he may live and work. This is by no means an equivalent to the artist for the nationally diffused life and thought of the epochs of Sophocles or Shakespeare; but, besides that it may be a means of preparation for such epochs, it does really constitute, if many share in it, a quickening and sustaining atmosphere of great value. Such an atmosphere the many-sided learning and the long and widely-combined critical effort of Germany formed for Goethe, when he lived and worked. There was no national glow of life and thought there as in the Athens of Pericles or the England of Elizabeth.[8] That was the poet's weakness. But there was a sort of equivalent for it in the complete culture and unfettered thinking of a large body of Germans. That was his strength. In the England of the first quarter of this century there was neither a national glow of life and thought, such as we had in the age of Elizabeth, nor yet a culture and a force of learning and criticism such as were to be found in Germany. Therefore the creative power of poetry wanted, for success in the highest sense, materials and a basis; a thorough interpretation of the world was necessarily denied to it.

* * *

But epochs of concentration cannot well endure for ever; epochs of expansion, in the due course of things, follow them. Such an epoch of expansion seems to be opening in this country. In the first place all danger of a hostile forcible pressure of foreign ideas upon our practice has long disappeared; like the traveller in the fable,

8. Athens was at its peak during the time of the statesman and orator Pericles (d. 429 B.C.).

therefore, we begin to wear our cloak a little more loosely.[9] Then, with a long peace, the ideas of Europe steal gradually and amicably in, and mingle, though in infinitesimally small quantities at a time, with our own notions. Then, too, in spite of all that is said about the absorbing and brutalising influence of our passionate material progress, it seems to me indisputable that this progress is likely, though not certain, to lead in the end to an apparition of intellectual life; and that man, after he has made himself perfectly comfortable and has now to determine what to do with himself next, may begin to remember that he has a mind, and that the mind may be made the source of great pleasure. I grant it is mainly the privilege of faith, at present, to discern this end to our railways, our business, and our fortune-making; but we shall see if, here as elsewhere, faith is not in the end the true prophet. Our ease, our travelling, and our unbounded liberty to hold just as hard and securely as we please to the practice to which our notions have given birth, all tend to beget an inclination to deal a little more freely with these notions themselves, to canvass them a little, to penetrate a little into their real nature. Flutterings of curiosity, in the foreign sense of the word, appear amongst us, and it is in these that criticism must look to find its account. Criticism first; a time of true creative activity, perhaps,—which, as I have said, must inevitably be preceded amongst us by a time of criticism,—hereafter, when criticism has done its work.

It is of the last importance that English criticism should clearly discern what rule for its course, in order to avail itself of the field now opening to it, and to produce fruit for the future, it ought to take. The rule may be summed up in one word,—*disinterestedness*.[1] And how is criticism to show disinterestedness? By keeping aloof from what is called "the practical view of things;" by resolutely following the law of its own nature, which is to be a free play of the mind on all subjects which it touches. By steadily refusing to lend itself to any of those ulterior, political, practical considerations about ideas, which plenty of people will be sure to attach to them, which perhaps ought often to be attached to them, which in this country at any rate are certain to be attached to them quite sufficiently, but which criticism has really nothing to do with. Its business is, as I have said, simply to know the best that is known and thought in the world, and by in its turn making this known, to create a current of true and fresh ideas. Its business is to do this with inflexible honesty, with due ability; but its business is to do no more, and to leave alone all questions of practical consequences and applications, questions which will never fail to have due prominence given to them. Else criticism, besides being really false to its own nature, merely continues in the old rut which it has hitherto followed in this country, and will certainly miss the chance now given to it. For what is at present the bane of criticism in this country? It is that practical considerations cling to it and stifle it. It subserves interests not its own. Our organs of criticism are organs of men and parties having practical ends to serve, and with them those practical ends are the first thing and the play of mind the second; so much play of mind as is compatible with the prosecution of those practical ends is all that is wanted. An organ like the *Revue des Deux Mondes*,[2] having for its main function to understand and utter the best that is known and

9. In Aesop's fable the wind and the sun had a contest to see which could make a traveler take off his cloak; when the wind blew, the traveler clutched his cloak tighter, but when the sun shone, he removed it, showing that persuasion is more effective than force.

1. Not lack of interest but impartiality and critical objectivity. Arnold derived this central concept from the French critic Charles Augustin Sainte-Beuve (1804–1869).
2. Intellectual Parisian magazine founded in 1829.

thought in the world, existing, it may be said, as just an organ for a free play of the mind, we have not. But we have the *Edinburgh Review*, existing as an organ of the old Whigs, and for as much play of the mind as may suit its being that; we have the *Quarterly Review*, existing as an organ of the Tories, and for as much play of mind as may suit its being that; we have the *British Quarterly Review*, existing as an organ of the political Dissenters, and for as much play of mind as may suit its being that; we have the *Times*, existing as an organ of the common, satisfied, well-to-do Englishman, and for as much play of mind as may suit its being that. And so on through all the various fractions, political and religious, of our society; every fraction has, as such, its organ of criticism, but the notion of combining all fractions in the common pleasure of a free disinterested play of mind meets with no favour. Directly this play of mind wants to have more scope, and to forget the pressure of practical considerations a little, it is checked, it is made to feel the chain. We saw this the other day in the extinction, so much to be regretted, of the *Home and Foreign Review*. Perhaps in no organ of criticism in this country was there so much knowledge, so much play of mind; but these could not save it. The *Dublin Review* subordinates play of mind to the practical business of English and Irish Catholicism, and lives. It must needs be that men should act in sects and parties, that each of these sects and parties should have its organ, and should make this organ subserve the interests of its action; but it would be well, too, that there should be a criticism, not the minister of these interests, not their enemy, but absolutely and entirely independent of them. No other criticism will ever attain any real authority or make any real way towards its end,—the creating a current of true and fresh ideas.

It is because criticism has so little kept in the pure intellectual sphere, has so little detached itself from practice, has been so directly polemical and controversial, that it has so ill accomplished, in this country, its best spiritual work; which is to keep man from a self-satisfaction which is retarding and vulgarising, to lead him towards perfection, by making his mind dwell upon what is excellent in itself, and the absolute beauty and fitness of things. A polemical practical criticism makes men blind even to the ideal imperfection of their practice, makes them willingly assert its ideal perfection, in order the better to secure it against attack; and clearly this is narrowing and baneful for them. If they were reassured on the practical side, speculative considerations of ideal perfection they might be brought to entertain, and their spiritual horizon would thus gradually widen. Sir Charles Adderley[3] says to the Warwickshire farmers:—

"Talk of the improvement of breed! Why, the race we ourselves represent, the men and women, the old Anglo-Saxon race, are the best breed in the whole world. . . . The absence of a too enervating climate, too unclouded skies, and a too luxurious nature, has produced so vigorous a race of people, and has rendered us so superior to all the world."

Mr Roebuck[4] says to the Sheffield cutlers:—

"I look around me and ask what is the state of England? Is not property safe? Is not every man able to say what he likes? Can you not walk from one end of England to the other in perfect security? I ask you whether, the world over or in past history, there is anything like it? Nothing. I pray that our unrivalled happiness may last."

3. Conservative member of Parliament and landowner (1814–1905).
4. John Arthur Roebuck (1801–1879), a radical but na-tionalistic member of Parliament for the industrial city of Sheffield.

Now obviously there is a peril for poor human nature in words and thoughts of such exuberant self-satisfaction, until we find ourselves safe in the streets of the Celestial City.

> Das wenige verschwindet leicht dem Blicke
> Der vorwärts sieht, wie viel noch übrig bleibt—[5]

says Goethe; "the little that is done seems nothing when we look forward and see how much we have yet to do." Clearly this is a better line of reflection for weak humanity, so long as it remains on this earthly field of labour and trial.

But neither Sir Charles Adderley nor Mr Roebuck is by nature inaccessible to considerations of this sort. They only lose sight of them owing to the controversial life we all lead, and the practical form which all speculation takes with us. They have in view opponents whose aim is not ideal, but practical; and in their zeal to uphold their own practice against these innovators, they go so far as even to attribute to this practice an ideal perfection. Somebody has been wanting to introduce a six-pound franchise,[6] or to abolish church-rates, or to collect agricultural statistics by force, or to diminish local self-government. How natural, in reply to such proposals, very likely improper or ill-timed, to go a little beyond the mark, and to say stoutly, "Such a race of people as we stand, so superior to all the world! The old Anglo-Saxon race, the best breed in the whole world! I pray that our unrivalled happiness may last! I ask you whether, the world over or in past history, there is anything like it?" And so long as criticism answers this dithyramb[7] by insisting that the old Anglo-Saxon race would be still more superior to all others if it had no church-rates, or that our unrivalled happiness would last yet longer with a six-pound franchise, so long will the strain, "The best breed in the whole world!" swell louder and louder, everything ideal and refining will be lost out of sight, and both the assailed and their critics will remain in a sphere, to say the truth, perfectly unvital, a sphere in which spiritual progression is impossible. But let criticism leave church-rates and the franchise alone, and in the most candid spirit, without a single lurking thought of practical innovation, confront with our dithyramb this paragraph on which I stumbled in a newspaper immediately after reading Mr Roebuck:—

"A shocking child murder has just been committed at Nottingham. A girl named Wragg left the workhouse there on Saturday morning with her young illegitimate child. The child was soon afterwards found dead on Mapperly Hills, having been strangled. Wragg is in custody."

Nothing but that; but, in juxtaposition with the absolute eulogies of Sir Charles Adderley and Mr Roebuck, how eloquent, how suggestive are those few lines! "Our old Anglo-Saxon breed, the best in the whole world!"—how much that is harsh and ill-favoured there is in this best! *Wragg!* If we are to talk of ideal perfection, of "the best in the whole world," has any one reflected what a touch of grossness in our race, what an original shortcoming in the more delicate spiritual perceptions, is shown by the natural growth amongst us of such hideous names,—Higginbottom, Stiggins, Bugg! In Ionia and Attica they were luckier in this respect than "the best race in the world;" by the Ilissus there was no Wragg, poor thing! And "our unrivalled happiness;"—what an element of grimness, bareness, and hideousness mixes with it and

5. Goethe, *Iphigenie auf Tauris* 1.2.91–92.
6. A proposal to extend voting rights to anyone who owned property worth six pounds annual rent. Church
rates were taxes to support the Church of England.
7. A Greek choric song of wild or inflated style; Arnold uses it to mean an exaggerated, excited statement.

blurs it; the workhouse, the dismal Mapperly Hills,[8]—how dismal those who have seen them will remember;—the gloom, the smoke, the cold, the strangled illegitimate child! "I ask you whether, the world over or in past history, there is anything like it?" Perhaps not, one is inclined to answer; but at any rate, in that case, the world is [not] very much to be pitied. And the final touch,—short, bleak, and inhuman: *Wragg is in custody.* The sex lost in the confusion of our unrivalled happiness; or (shall I say?) the superfluous Christian name lopped off by the straightforward vigour of our old Anglo-Saxon breed! There is profit for the spirit in such contrasts as this; criticism serves the cause of perfection by establishing them. By eluding sterile conflict, by refusing to remain in the sphere where alone narrow and relative conceptions have any worth and validity, criticism may diminish its momentary importance, but only in this way has it a chance of gaining admittance for those wider and more perfect conceptions to which all its duty is really owed. Mr Roebuck will have a poor opinion of an adversary who replies to his defiant songs of triumph only by murmuring under his breath, *Wragg is in custody;* but in no other way will these songs of triumph be induced gradually to moderate themselves, to get rid of what in them is excessive and offensive, and to fall into a softer and truer key.

It will be said that it is a very subtle and indirect action which I am thus prescribing for criticism, and that, by embracing in this manner the Indian virtue of detachment and abandoning the sphere of practical life, it condemns itself to a slow and obscure work. Slow and obscure it may be, but it is the only proper work of criticism. The mass of mankind will never have any ardent zeal for seeing things as they are; very inadequate ideas will always satisfy them. On these inadequate ideas reposes, and must repose, the general practice of the world. That is as much as saying that whoever sets himself to see things as they are will find himself one of a very small circle; but it is only by this small circle resolutely doing its own work that adequate ideas will ever get current at all. The rush and roar of practical life will always have a dizzying and attracting effect upon the most collected spectator, and tend to draw him into its vortex; most of all will this be the case where that life is so powerful as it is in England. But it is only by remaining collected, and refusing to lend himself to the point of view of the practical man, that the critic can do the practical man any service; and it is only by the greatest sincerity in pursuing his own course, and by at last convincing even the practical man of his sincerity, that he can escape misunderstandings which perpetually threaten him.

For the practical man is not apt for fine distinctions, and yet in these distinctions truth and the highest culture greatly find their account. But it is not easy to lead a practical man,—unless you reassure him as to your practical intentions, you have no chance of leading him,—to see that a thing which he has always been used to look at from one side only, which he greatly values, and which, looked at from that side, quite deserves, perhaps, all the prizing and admiring which he bestows upon it,—that this thing, looked at from another side, may appear much less beneficent and beautiful, and yet retain all its claims to our practical allegiance. Where shall we find language innocent enough, how shall we make the spotless purity of our intentions evident enough, to enable us to say to the political Englishman that the British Constitution itself, which, seen from the practical side, looks such a magnificent organ of progress and virtue, seen from the speculative side,—with its compromises, its love of facts, its horror of theory, its studied avoidance of clear thoughts,—that, seen

8. Arnold contrasts these hills near the industrial coal-mining area of Nottingham with the Ilissus, a river in ancient pastoral Greece.

from this side, our august Constitution sometimes looks,—forgive me, shade of Lord Somers![9]—a colossal machine for the manufacture of Philistines?[1] How is Cobbett[2] to say this and not be misunderstood, blackened as he is with the smoke of a lifelong conflict in the field of political practice? how is Mr Carlyle to say it and not be misunderstood, after his furious raid into this field with his *Latter-day Pamphlets*?[3] how is Mr Ruskin, after his pugnacious political economy?[4] I say, the critic must keep out of the region of immediate practice in the political, social, humanitarian sphere, if he wants to make a beginning for that more free speculative treatment of things, which may perhaps one day make its benefits felt even in this sphere, but in a natural and thence irresistible manner.

Do what he will, however, the critic will still remain exposed to frequent misunderstandings, and nowhere so much as in this country. For here people are particularly indisposed even to comprehend that without this free disinterested treatment of things, truth and the highest culture are out of the question. So immersed are they in practical life, so accustomed to take all their notions from this life and its processes, that they are apt to think that truth and culture themselves can be reached by the processes of this life, and that it is an impertinent singularity to think of reaching them in any other. "We are all *terrae filii*" [sons of the earth], cries their eloquent advocate; "all Philistines together. Away with the notion of proceeding by any other course than the course dear to the Philistines; let us have a social movement, let us organise and combine a party to pursue truth and new thought, let us call it *the liberal party*, and let us all stick to each other, and back each other up. Let us have no nonsense about independent criticism, and intellectual delicacy, and the few and the many. Don't let us trouble ourselves about foreign thought; we shall invent the whole thing for ourselves as we go along. If one of us speaks well, applaud him; if one of us speaks ill, applaud him too; we are all in the same movement, we are all liberals, we are all in pursuit of truth." In this way the pursuit of truth becomes really a social, practical, pleasurable affair, almost requiring a chairman, a secretary, and advertisements; with the excitement of an occasional scandal, with a little resistance to give the happy sense of difficulty overcome; but, in general, plenty of bustle and very little thought. To act is so easy, as Goethe says; to think is so hard! It is true that the critic has many temptations to go with the stream, to make one of the party of movement, one of these *terrae filii*; it seems ungracious to refuse to be a *terrae filius*, when so many excellent people are; but the critic's duty is to refuse, or, if resistance is vain, at least to cry with Obermann: *Périssons en résistant*.[5]

* * *

If I have insisted so much on the course which criticism must take where politics and religion are concerned, it is because, where these burning matters are in question, it is most likely to go astray. I have wished, above all, to insist on the attitude which criticism should adopt towards things in general; on its right tone and temper of mind. But then comes another question as to the subject-matter which literary criticism should most seek. Here, in general, its course is determined for it by the idea

9. John, Lord Somers (1651–1716), statesman who presided over the formulation of the Declaration of Rights after the abdication of James II.
1. Arnold likened the middle classes, with their stubborn resistance to ideas, to the Philistines who fought against the Israelites.
2. William Cobbett (1762–1835), radical journalist and reformer who served for several years in Parliament.

3. In *Latter-day Pamphlets* (1850) Carlyle expressed his antidemocratic views in a tone seen by many as hysterical.
4. In *Unto This Last* (1862) Ruskin turned from art criticism to social reform, attacking laissez-faire economics.
5. "Let us die fighting," from Etienne Pivert de Senancour's romantic novel *Obermann* (1804).

which is the law of its being; the idea of a disinterested endeavour to learn and propagate the best that is known and thought in the world, and thus to establish a current of fresh and true ideas. By the very nature of things, as England is not all the world, much of the best that is known and thought in the world cannot be of English growth, must be foreign; by the nature of things, again, it is just this that we are least likely to know, while English thought is streaming in upon us from all sides, and takes excellent care that we shall not be ignorant of its existence. The English critic of literature, therefore, must dwell much on foreign thought, and with particular heed on any part of it, which, while significant and fruitful in itself, is for any reason specially likely to escape him. Again, judging is often spoken of as the critic's one business, and so in some sense it is; but the judgment which almost insensibly forms itself in a fair and clear mind, along with fresh knowledge, is the valuable one; and thus knowledge, and ever fresh knowledge, must be the critic's great concern for himself. And it is by communicating fresh knowledge, and letting his own judgment pass along with it,—but insensibly, and in the second place, not the first, as a sort of companion and clue, not as an abstract lawgiver,—that the critic will generally do most good to his readers. Sometimes, no doubt, for the sake of establishing an author's place in literature, and his relation to a central standard (and if this is not done, how are we to get at our *best in the world?*) criticism may have to deal with a subject-matter so familiar that fresh knowledge is out of the question, and then it must be all judgment; an enunciation and detailed application of principles. Here the great safeguard is never to let oneself become abstract, always to retain an intimate and lively consciousness of the truth of what one is saying, and, the moment this fails us, to be sure that something is wrong. Still, under all circumstances, this mere judgment and application of principles is, in itself, not the most satisfactory work to the critic; like mathematics, it is tautological, and cannot well give us, like fresh learning, the sense of creative activity.

But stop, some one will say; all this talk is of no practical use to us whatever; this criticism of yours is not what we have in our minds when we speak of criticism; when we speak of critics and criticism, we mean critics and criticism of the current English literature of the day; when you offer to tell criticism its function, it is to this criticism that we expect you to address yourself. I am sorry for it, for I am afraid I must disappoint these expectations. I am bound by my own definition of criticism: *a disinterested endeavour to learn and propagate the best that is known and thought in the world.* How much of current English literature comes into this "best that is known and thought in the world?" Not very much, I fear; certainly less, at this moment, than of the current literature of France or Germany. Well, then, am I to alter my definition of criticism, in order to meet the requirements of a number of practising English critics, who, after all, are free in their choice of a business? That would be making criticism lend itself just to one of those alien practical considerations, which, I have said, are so fatal to it. One may say, indeed, to those who have to deal with the mass—so much better disregarded—of current English literature, that they may at all events endeavour, in dealing with this, to try it, so far as they can, by the standard of the best that is known and thought in the world; one may say, that to get anywhere near this standard, every critic should try and possess one great literature, at least, besides his own; and the more unlike his own, the better. But, after all, the criticism I am really concerned with,—the criticism which alone can much help us for the future, the criticism which, throughout Europe, is at the present day meant, when so much stress is laid on the importance of criticism and the critical spirit,—is a criticism which regards Europe as being, for intellectual and spiritual purposes, one great confederation, bound to a joint action and working to a common result; and whose members have, for their proper outfit, a knowledge of Greek, Roman, and Eastern antiquity, and of one another. Special, local, and temporary advantages being put out of account, that modern nation will in the intellectual and spiritual sphere make most progress, which most thoroughly carries out this programme. And what is that but saying that we too, all of us, as individuals, the more thoroughly we carry it out, shall make the more progress?

There is so much inviting us!—what are we to take? what will nourish us in growth towards perfection? That is the question which, with the immense field of life and of literature lying before him, the critic has to answer; for himself first, and afterwards for others. In this idea of the critic's business the essays brought together in the following pages have had their origin; in this idea, widely different as are their subjects, they have, perhaps, their unity.

I conclude with what I said at the beginning: to have the sense of creative activity is the great happiness and the great proof of being alive, and it is not denied to criticism to have it; but then criticism must be sincere, simple, flexible, ardent, ever widening its knowledge. Then it may have, in no contemptible measure, a joyful sense of creative activity; a sense which a man of insight and conscience will prefer to what he might derive from a poor, starved, fragmentary, inadequate creation. And at some epochs no other creation is possible.

Still, in full measure, the sense of creative activity belongs only to genuine creation; in literature we must never forget that. But what true man of letters ever can forget it? It is no such common matter for a gifted nature to come into possession of a current of true and living ideas, and to produce amidst the inspiration of them, that we are likely to underrate it. The epochs of Aeschylus and Shakespeare make us feel their preeminence. In an epoch like those is, no doubt, the true life of literature; there is the promised land, towards which criticism can only beckon. That promised land it will not be ours to enter, and we shall die in the wilderness: but to have desired to enter it, to have saluted it from afar, is already, perhaps, the best distinction among contemporaries; it will certainly be the best title to esteem with posterity.

1864, 1865

from **Culture and Anarchy**[1]
from Sweetness and Light

The disparagers of culture make its motive curiosity; sometimes, indeed, they make its motive mere exclusiveness and vanity. The culture which is supposed to plume itself on a smattering of Greek and Latin is a culture which is begotten by nothing so intellectual as curiosity; it is valued either out of sheer vanity and ignorance or else as

1. Arnold's most important work of social criticism, *Culture and Anarchy* (1869) grew out of his final Oxford lecture in 1867. Deploring English pride in "doing as one likes," Arnold connected the self-serving behavior of all classes to the worst effects of laissez-faire capitalism. He felt that Britain was heading toward anarchy; no one seemed to have any concern for the public good. The best of Western culture, Arnold contended, depends on a balance between the Judeo-Christian emphasis on moral conduct (Hebraism) and the Greek ideal of intellectual and artistic cultivation (Hellenism). But in his view a Puritan "strictness of conscience" was now impeding a classical "spontaneity of consciousness." There was only one way to bridge the gap between privileged "Barbarians" (the aristocracy), intolerant "Philistines" (the middle classes), and the uneducated "Populace" (the working classes): by spreading to all parts of society a Hellenistic respect for beauty and intellect—what Arnold termed "sweetness and light."

an engine of social and class distinction, separating its holder, like a badge or title, from other people who have not got it. No serious man would call this *culture*, or attach any value to it, as culture, at all. To find the real ground for the very different estimate which serious people will set upon culture, we must find some motive for culture in the terms of which may lie a real ambiguity; and such a motive the word *curiosity* gives us.

I have before now pointed out that we English do not, like the foreigners, use this word in a good sense as well as in a bad sense. With us the word is always used in a somewhat disapproving sense. A liberal and intelligent eagerness about the things of the mind may be meant by a foreigner when he speaks of curiosity, but with us the word always conveys a certain notion of frivolous and unedifying activity. In the *Quarterly Review*, some little time ago, was an estimate of the celebrated French critic, M. Sainte-Beuve,[2] and a very inadequate estimate it in my judgment was. And its inadequacy consisted chiefly in this: that in our English way it left out of sight the double sense really involved in the word *curiosity*, thinking enough was said to stamp M. Sainte-Beuve with blame if it was said that he was impelled in his operations as a critic by curiosity, and omitting either to perceive that M. Sainte-Beuve himself, and many other people with him, would consider that this was praiseworthy and not blameworthy, or to point out why it ought really to be accounted worthy of blame and not of praise. For as there is a curiosity about intellectual matters which is futile, and merely a disease, so there is certainly a curiosity,—a desire after the things of the mind simply for their own sakes and for the pleasure of seeing them as they are,—which is, in an intelligent being, natural and laudable. Nay, and the very desire to see things as they are implies a balance and regulation of mind which is not often attained without fruitful effort, and which is the very opposite of the blind and diseased impulse of mind which is what we mean to blame when we blame curiosity. Montesquieu[3] says: "The first motive which ought to impel us to study is the desire to augment the excellence of our nature, and to render an intelligent being yet more intelligent." This is the true ground to assign for the genuine scientific passion, however manifested, and for culture, viewed simply as a fruit of this passion; and it is a worthy ground, even though we let the term *curiosity* stand to describe it.

But there is of culture another view, in which not solely the scientific passion, the sheer desire to see things as they are, natural and proper in an intelligent being, appears as the ground of it. There is a view in which all the love of our neighbour, the impulses towards action, help, and beneficence, the desire for removing human error, clearing human confusion, and diminishing human misery, the noble aspiration to leave the world better and happier than we found it,—motives eminently such as are called social,—come in as part of the grounds of culture, and the main and pre-eminent part. Culture is then properly described not as having its origin in curiosity, but as having its origin in the love of perfection; it is *a study of perfection*. It moves by the force, not merely or primarily of the scientific passion for pure knowledge, but also of the moral and social passion for doing good. As, in the first view of it, we took for its worthy motto Montesquieu's words: "To render an intelligent being yet more intelligent!" so, in the second view of it, there is no better motto which it

---

2. Charles Augustine Sainte-Beuve (1804–1869), French critic whom Arnold admired.

3. Baron de la Brède et de Montesquieu (1689–1755), French political and legal philosopher.

can have than these words of Bishop Wilson: "To make reason and the will of God prevail!"[4] * * *

The pursuit of perfection, then, is the pursuit of sweetness and light.[5] He who works for sweetness and light, works to make reason and the will of God prevail. He who works for machinery, he who works for hatred, works only for confusion. Culture looks beyond machinery, culture hates hatred; culture has one great passion, the passion for sweetness and light. It has one even yet greater!—the passion for making them *prevail*. It is not satisfied till we *all* come to a perfect man; it knows that the sweetness and light of the few must be imperfect until the raw and unkindled masses of humanity are touched with sweetness and light. If I have not shrunk from saying that we must work for sweetness and light, so neither have I shrunk from saying that we must have a broad basis, must have sweetness and light for as many as possible. Again and again I have insisted how those are the happy moments of humanity, how those are the marking epochs of a people's life, how those are the flowering times for literature and art and all the creative power of genius, when there is a *national* glow of life and thought, when the whole of society is in the fullest measure permeated by thought, sensible to beauty, intelligent and alive. Only it must be *real* thought and *real* beauty; *real* sweetness and *real* light. Plenty of people will try to give the masses, as they call them, an intellectual food prepared and adapted in the way they think proper for the actual condition of the masses. The ordinary popular literature is an example of this way of working on the masses. Plenty of people will try to indoctrinate the masses with the set of ideas and judgments constituting the creed of their own profession or party. Our religious and political organisations give an example of this way of working on the masses. I condemn neither way; but culture works differently. It does not try to teach down to the level of inferior classes; it does not try to win them for this or that sect of its own, with ready-made judgments and watchwords. It seeks to do away with classes; to make the best that has been thought and known in the world current everywhere; to make all men live in an atmosphere of sweetness and light, where they may use ideas, as it uses them itself, freely,—nourished, and not bound by them.

* * *

from *Doing as One Likes*

It is said that a man with my theories of sweetness and light is full of antipathy against the rougher or coarser movements going on around him, that he will not lend a hand to the humble operation of uprooting evil by their means, and that therefore the believers in action grow impatient with him. But what if rough and coarse action, ill-calculated action, action with insufficient light, is, and has for a long time been, our bane? What if our urgent want now is, not to act at any price, but rather to lay in a stock of light for our difficulties? In that case, to refuse to lend a hand to the rougher and coarser movements going on round us, to make the primary need, both for oneself and others, to consist in enlightening ourselves and qualifying ourselves to

4. Thomas Wilson (1663–1755), Bishop of Sodor and Man. His *Maxims*, though little known, were a favorite of Arnold's.
5. The phrase comes from a fable in Swift's *The Battle of the Books* (1704): the Bee (representing ancient culture) ventures forth to fill its hive with honey and wax for light-giving candles, but the home-bound Spider (representing modern culture) produces from itself only cobwebs and poison. The Bee thus provides "the two noblest of things, which are sweetness and light."

act less at random, is surely the best and in real truth the most practical line our endeavours can take. So that if I can show what my opponents call rough or coarse action, but what I would rather call random and ill-regulated action,—action with insufficient light, action pursued because we like to be doing something and doing it as we please, and do not like the trouble of thinking and the severe constraint of any kind of rule,—if I can show this to be, at the present moment, a practical mischief and dangerous to us, then I have found a practical use for light in correcting this state of things, and have only to exemplify how, in cases which fall under everybody's observation, it may deal with it.

When I began to speak of culture, I insisted on our bondage to machinery, on our proneness to value machinery as an end in itself, without looking beyond it to the end for which alone, in truth, it is valuable. Freedom, I said, was one of those things which we thus worshipped in itself, without enough regarding the ends for which freedom is to be desired. In our common notions and talk about freedom, we eminently show our idolatry of machinery. Our prevalent notion is,—and I quoted a number of instances to prove it,—that it is a most happy and important thing for a man merely to be able to do as he likes. On what he is to do when he is thus free to do as he likes, we do not lay so much stress. Our familiar praise of the British Constitution under which we live, is that it is a system of checks,—a system which stops and paralyses any power in interfering with the free action of individuals. To this effect Mr Bright,[6] who loves to walk in the old ways of the Constitution, said forcibly in one of his great speeches, what many other people are every day saying less forcibly, that the central idea of English life and politics is *the assertion of personal liberty*. Evidently this is so; but evidently, also, as feudalism, which with its ideas and habits of subordination was for many centuries silently behind the British Constitution, dies out, and we are left with nothing but our system of checks, and our notion of its being the great right and happiness of an Englishman to do as far as possible what he likes, we are in danger of drifting towards anarchy. We have not the notion, so familiar on the Continent and to antiquity, of *the State*,—the nation in its collective and corporate character, entrusted with stringent powers for the general advantage, and controlling individual wills in the name of an interest wider than that of individuals. We say, what is very true, that this notion is often made instrumental to tyranny; we say that a State is in reality made up of the individuals who compose it, and that every individual is the best judge of his own interests. Our leading class is an aristocracy, and no aristocracy likes the notion of a State-authority greater than itself, with a stringent administrative machinery superseding the decorative inutilities of lord-lieutenancy, deputy-lieutenancy, and the *posse comitatus*,[7] which are all in its own hands. Our middle class, the great representative of trade and Dissent, with its maxims of every man for himself in business, every man for himself in religion, dreads a powerful administration which might somehow interfere with it; and besides, it has its own decorative inutilities of vestrymanship and guardianship, which are to this class what lord-lieutenancy and the county magistracy are to the aristocratic class, and a stringent administration might either take these functions out of its hands, or prevent its exercising them in its own comfortable, independent manner, as at present.

6. John Bright (1811–1889), Quaker radical who led the left wing of the Liberal Party under Gladstone.
7. Power of the county (Latin); a "posse" was an outdated method of preserving public order by local authority rather than by the government.

Then as to our working class. This class, pressed constantly by the hard daily compulsion of material wants, is naturally the very centre and stronghold of our national idea, that it is man's ideal right and felicity to do as he likes. I think I have somewhere related how M. Michelet said to me of the people of France, that it was "a nation of barbarians civilised by the conscription."[8] He meant that through their military service the idea of public duty and of discipline was brought to the mind of these masses, in other respects so raw and uncultivated. Our masses are quite as raw and uncultivated as the French; and so far from their having the idea of public duty and of discipline, superior to the individual's self-will, brought to their mind by a universal obligation of military service, such as that of the conscription,—so far from their having this, the very idea of a conscription is so at variance with our English notion of the prime right and blessedness of doing as one likes, that I remember the manager of the Clay Cross works in Derbyshire told me during the Crimean war, when our want of soldiers was much felt and some people were talking of a conscription, that sooner than submit to a conscription the population of that district would flee to the mines, and lead a sort of Robin Hood life under ground.

For a long time, as I have said, the strong feudal habits of subordination and deference continued to tell upon the working class. The modern spirit has now almost entirely dissolved those habits, and the anarchical tendency of our worship of freedom in and for itself, of our superstitious faith, as I say, in machinery, is becoming very manifest. More and more, because of this our blind faith in machinery, because of our want of light to enable us to look beyond machinery to the end for which machinery is valuable, this and that man, and this and that body of men, all over the country, are beginning to assert and put in practice an Englishman's right to do what he likes; his right to march where he likes, meet where he likes, enter where he likes, hoot as he likes, threaten as he likes, smash as he likes. All this, I say, tends to anarchy; and though a number of excellent people, and particularly my friends of the Liberal or progressive party, as they call themselves, are kind enough to reassure us by saying that these are trifles, that a few transient outbreaks of rowdyism signify nothing, that our system of liberty is one which itself cures all the evils which it works, that the educated and intelligent classes stand in overwhelming strength and majestic repose, ready, like our military force in riots, to act at a moment's notice,—yet one finds that one's Liberal friends generally say this because they have such faith in themselves and their nostrums,[9] when they shall return, as the public welfare requires, to place and power. But this faith of theirs one cannot exactly share, when one has so long had them and their nostrums at work, and sees that they have not prevented our coming to our present embarrassed condition. And one finds, also, that the outbreaks of rowdyism tend to become less and less of trifles, to become more frequent rather than less frequent; and that meanwhile our educated and intelligent classes remain in their majestic repose, and somehow or other, whatever happens, their overwhelming strength, like our military force in riots, never does act.

How, indeed, *should* their overwhelming strength act, when the man who gives an inflammatory lecture, or breaks down the park railings,[1] or invades a Secretary of State's office, is only following an Englishman's impulse to do as he likes; and our own conscience tells us that we ourselves have always regarded this impulse as something primary and sacred? Mr Murphy lectures at Birmingham,[2] and showers on the Catholic population of that town "words," says the Home Secretary, "only fit to be addressed to thieves or murderers." What then? Mr Murphy has his own reasons of several kinds. He suspects the Roman Catholic Church of designs upon Mrs Murphy; and he says if mayors and magistrates do not care for their wives and daughters, he does. But, above all, he is doing as he likes; or, in worthier language, asserting his personal liberty. "I will carry out my lectures if they walk over my body as a dead corpse; and I say to the Mayor of Birmingham that he is my servant while I am in Birmingham, and as my servant he must do his duty and protect me." Touching and beautiful words, which find a sympathetic chord in every British bosom! The moment it is plainly put before us that a man is asserting his personal liberty, we are half disarmed; because we are believers in freedom, and not in some dream of a right reason to which the assertion of our freedom is to be subordinated. Accordingly, the Secretary of State had to say that although the lecturer's language was "only fit to be addressed to thieves or murderers," yet, "I do not think he is to be deprived, I do not think that anything I have said could justify the inference that he is to be deprived, of the right of protection in a place built by him for the purpose of these lectures; because the language was not language which afforded grounds for a criminal prosecution." No, nor to be silenced by Mayor, or Home Secretary, or any administrative authority on earth, simply on their notion of what is discreet and reasonable! This is in perfect consonance with our public opinion, and with our national love for the assertion of personal liberty. * * *

Now, if culture, which simply means trying to perfect oneself, and one's mind as part of oneself, brings us light, and if light shows us that there is nothing so very blessed in merely doing as one likes, that the worship of the mere freedom to do as one likes is worship of machinery, that the really blessed thing is to like what right reason ordains, and to follow her authority, then we have got a practical benefit out of culture. We have got a much wanted principle, a principle of authority, to counteract the tendency to anarchy which seems to be threatening us. * * *

Well, then, what if we tried to rise above the idea of class to the idea of the whole community, *the State,* and to find our centre of light and authority there? Every one of us has the idea of country, as a sentiment; hardly any one of us has the idea of *the State,* as a working power. And why? Because we habitually live in our ordinary selves, which do not carry us beyond the ideas and wishes of the class to which we happen to belong. And we are all afraid of giving to the State too much power, because we only conceive of the State as something equivalent to the class in occupation of the executive government, and are afraid of that class abusing power to its own purposes. If we strengthen the State with the aristocratic class in occupation of the executive government, we imagine we are delivering ourselves up captive to the ideas and wishes of our fierce aristocratical baronet; if with the middle class in occupation of the executive government, to those of our truculent middle-class Dissenting minister;[3] if with the working class, to those of its notorious tribune, Mr Bradlaugh.[4] And with much justice; owing to the exaggerated notion which we English, as I have said, entertain of the right and blessedness of the mere doing as one likes, of

---

2. In 1867 William Murphy, an anti-Catholic agitator, delivered a series of lectures in Birmingham that led to riots.
3. Rev. William Cattle, chairman at William Murphy's anti-Catholic lectures (see n. 2).

4. Charles Bradlaugh, radical agitator, eventually the first atheist Member of Parliament.

the affirming oneself, and oneself just as it is. People of the aristocratic class want to affirm their ordinary selves, their likings and dislikings; people of the middle class the same, people of the working class the same. By our everyday selves, however, we are separate, personal, at war; we are only safe from one another's tyranny when no one has any power; and this safety, in its turn, cannot save us from anarchy. And when, therefore, anarchy presents itself as a danger to us, we know not where to turn.

But by our *best self* we are united, impersonal, at harmony. We are in no peril from giving authority to this, because it is the truest friend we all of us can have; and when anarchy is a danger to us, to this authority we may turn with sure trust. Well, and this is the very self which culture, or the study of perfection, seeks to develop in us; at the expense of our old untransformed self, taking pleasure only in doing what it likes or is used to do, and exposing us to the risk of clashing with every one else who is doing the same! So that our poor culture, which is flouted as so unpractical, leads us to the very ideas capable of meeting the great want of our present embarrassed times! We want an authority, and we find nothing but jealous classes, checks, and a dead-lock; culture suggests the idea of *the State*. We find no basis for a firm State-power in our ordinary selves; culture suggests one to us in our *best self*.[5] * * *

from *Hebraism and Hellenism*

This fundamental ground is our preference of doing to thinking. Now this preference is a main element in our nature, and as we study it we find ourselves opening up a number of large questions on every side.

Let me go back for a moment to Bishop Wilson, who says: "First, never go against the best light you have; secondly, take care that your light be not darkness."[6] We show, as a nation, laudable energy and persistence in walking according to the best light we have, but are not quite careful enough, perhaps, to see that our light be not darkness. This is only another version of the old story that energy is our strong point and favourable characteristic, rather than intelligence. But we may give to this idea a more general form still, in which it will have a yet larger range of application. We may regard this energy driving at practice, this paramount sense of the obligation of duty, self-control, and work, this earnestness in going manfully with the best light we have, as one force. And we may regard the intelligence driving at those ideas which are, after all, the basis of right practice, the ardent sense for all the new and changing combinations of them which man's development brings with it, the indomitable impulse to know and adjust them perfectly, as another force. And these two forces we may regard as in some sense rivals,—rivals not by the necessity of their own nature, but as exhibited in man and his history,—and rivals dividing the empire of the world between them. And to give these forces names from the two races of men who have supplied the most signal and splendid manifestations of them, we may call them respectively the forces of Hebraism and Hellenism.[7] Hebraism and Hellenism,—between these two points of influence moves our world. At one time it feels

5. Chapter 3, omitted here, explores the class-bound "ordinary selves" that Arnold wishes to transcend: the "Barbarian" aristocracy who value individualism, courage, and athleticism over intellect and sensitivity; the middle-class Philistines who stubbornly resist new ideas; and the dangerously "raw and half-developed" working class he calls simply "the Populace."
6. Quoting Thomas Wilson, *Maxims* (see page 1697, n. 4).

7. In Arnold's view Hebraism (the Judeo-Christian tradition) emphasizes duty, industriousness, and a sense of sin. In contrast, Hellenism (the Greek tradition) values rationality, "clearness of mind," and the quest for perfection. While Arnold emphasizes the importance of both traditions, it is Hellenism that he associates with sweetness and light.

more powerfully the attraction of one of them, at another time of the other; and it ought to be, though it never is, evenly and happily balanced between them.

The final aim of both Hellenism and Hebraism, as of all great spiritual disciplines, is no doubt the same: man's perfection or salvation. The very language which they both of them use in schooling us to reach this aim is often identical. * * *

Still, they pursue this aim by very different courses. The uppermost idea with Hellenism is to see things as they really are; the uppermost idea with Hebraism is conduct and obedience. Nothing can do away with this ineffaceable difference. The Greek quarrel with the body and its desires is, that they hinder right thinking; the Hebrew quarrel with them is, that they hinder right acting. * * *

* * * Eighteen hundred years ago it was altogether the hour of Hebraism. Primitive Christianity was legitimately and truly the ascendant force in the world at that time, and the way of mankind's progress lay through its full development. Another hour in man's development began in the fifteenth century, and the main road of his progress then lay for a time through Hellenism. Puritanism was no longer the central current of the world's progress, it was a side stream crossing the central current and checking it. The cross and the check may have been necessary and salutary, but that does not do away with the essential difference between the main stream of man's advance and a cross or side stream. For more than two hundred years the main stream of man's advance has moved towards knowing himself and the world, seeing things as they are, spontaneity of consciousness; the main impulse of a great part, and that the strongest part, of our nation has been towards strictness of conscience. They have made the secondary the principal at the wrong moment, and the principal they have at the wrong moment treated as secondary. This contravention of the natural order has produced, as such contravention always must produce, a certain confusion and false movement, of which we are now beginning to feel, in almost every direction, the inconvenience. In all directions our habitual courses of action seem to be losing efficaciousness, credit, and control, both with others and even with ourselves. Everywhere we see the beginnings of confusion, and we want a clue to some sound order and authority. This we can only get by going back upon the actual instincts and forces which rule our life, seeing them as they really are, connecting them with other instincts and forces, and enlarging our whole view and rule of life.

from *Porro Unum Est Necessarium*[8]

* * * Sweetness and light evidently have to do with the bent or side in humanity which we call Hellenic. Greek intelligence has obviously for its essence the instinct for what Plato calls the true, firm, intelligible law of things; the law of light, of seeing things as they are. Even in the natural sciences, where the Greeks had not time and means adequately to apply this instinct, and where we have gone a great deal further than they did, it is this instinct which is the root of the whole matter and the ground of all our success; and this instinct the world has mainly learnt of the Greeks, inasmuch as they are humanity's most signal manifestation of it. Greek art, again, Greek beauty, have their root in the same impulse to see things as they really are, inasmuch as Greek art and beauty rest on fidelity to nature,—the *best* nature,—and on a delicate discrimination of what this best nature is. To say we work for sweetness and

---

8. In Luke 10.42 Jesus tells Mary that only "one thing is needful"; he appears to mean faith. According to Arnold, the Puritan middle classes think "the one thing needful" is their own narrow "Hebraic" sense of moral conduct.

light, then, is only another way of saying that we work for Hellenism. But, oh! cry many people, sweetness and light are not enough; you must put strength or energy along with them, and make a kind of trinity of strength, sweetness and light, and then, perhaps, you may do some good. That is to say, we are to join Hebraism, strictness of the moral conscience, and manful walking by the best light we have, together with Hellenism, inculcate both, and rehearse the praises of both.

Or, rather, we may praise both in conjunction, but we must be careful to praise Hebraism most. "Culture," says an acute, though somewhat rigid critic, Mr Sidgwick,[9] "diffuses sweetness and light. I do not undervalue these blessings, but religion gives fire and strength, and the world wants fire and strength even more than sweetness and light." By religion, let me explain, Mr Sidgwick here means particularly that Puritanism on the insufficiency of which I have been commenting and to which he says I am unfair. Now, no doubt, it is possible to be a fanatical partisan of light and the instincts which push us to it, a fanatical enemy of strictness of moral conscience and the instincts which push us to it. A fanaticism of this sort deforms and vulgarises the well-known work, in some respects so remarkable, of the late Mr Buckle.[1] Such a fanaticism carries its own mark with it, in lacking sweetness; and its own penalty, in that, lacking sweetness, it comes in the end to lack light too. And the Greeks,—the great exponents of humanity's bent for sweetness and light united, of its perception that the truth of things must be at the same time beauty,—singularly escaped the fanaticism which we moderns, whether we Hellenise or whether we Hebraise, are so apt to show. They arrived,— though failing, as has been said, to give adequate practical satisfaction to the claims of man's moral side,—at the idea of a comprehensive adjustment of the claims of both the sides in man, the moral as well as the intellectual, of a full estimate of both, and of a reconciliation of both; an idea which is philosophically of the greatest value, and the best of lessons for us moderns. So we ought to have no difficulty in conceding to Mr Sidgwick that manful walking by the best light one has,—fire and strength as he calls it,—has its high value as well as culture, the endeavour to see things in their truth and beauty, the pursuit of sweetness and light. But whether at this or that time, and to this or that set of persons, one ought to insist most on the praises of fire and strength, or on the praises of sweetness and light, must depend, one would think, on the circumstances and needs of that particular time and those particular persons. And all that we have been saying, and indeed any glance at the world around us shows that with us, with the most respectable and strongest part of us, the ruling force is now, and long has been, a Puritan force,—the care for fire and strength, strictness of conscience, Hebraism, rather than the care for sweetness and light, spontaneity of consciousness, Hellenism.

Well, then, what is the good of our now rehearsing the praises of fire and strength to ourselves, who dwell too exclusively on them already? When Mr Sidgwick says so broadly, that the world wants fire and strength even more than sweetness and light, is he not carried away by a turn for broad generalisation? does he not forget that the world is not all of one piece, and every piece with the same needs at the same time? It may be true that the Roman world at the beginning of our era, or Leo the Tenth's Court at the time of the Reformation, or French society in the eighteenth century,[2] needed fire and strength even more than sweetness and light. But

9. Henry Sidgwick, Cambridge philosopher who in 1867 had published a response to *Culture and Its Enemies*, the lecture that became the first chapter of *Culture and Anarchy*.
1. Henry Thomas Buckle, whose *History of Civilisation in England* (1857–1861) attributed historical events to geography.

2. The courts of the Roman emperor Nero (A.D. 54–68), of Pope Leo X (1513–1521), and of Louis XV (1715–1774) were renowned for worldly luxury and excess.

can it be said that the Barbarians who overran the empire needed fire and strength even more than sweetness and light; or that the Puritans needed them more; or that Mr Murphy, the Birmingham lecturer, and his friends, need them more?

The Puritan's great danger is that he imagines himself in possession of a rule telling him the *unum necessarium*, or one thing needful, and that he then remains satisfied with a very crude conception of what this rule really is and what it tells him, thinks he has now knowledge and henceforth needs only to act, and, in this danger-ous state of assurance and self-satisfaction, proceeds to give full swing to a number of the instincts of his ordinary self. Some of the instincts of his ordinary self he has, by the help of his rule of life, conquered; but others which he has not conquered by this help he is so far from perceiving to need subjugation, and to be instincts of an inferior self, that he even fancies it to be his right and duty, in virtue of having conquered a limited part of himself, to give unchecked swing to the remainder. He is, I say, a vic-tim of Hebraism, of the tendency to cultivate strictness of conscience rather than spontaneity of consciousness. And what he wants is a larger conception of human nature, showing him the number of other points at which his nature must come to its best, besides the points which he himself knows and thinks of. There is no *unum nec-essarium*, or one thing needful, which can free human nature from the obligation of trying to come to its best at all these points. The real *unum necessarium* for us is to come to our best at all points. Instead of our "one thing needful," justifying in us vul-garity, hideousness, ignorance, violence,—our vulgarity, hideousness, ignorance, vio-lence, are really so many touchstones which try our one thing needful, and which prove that in the state, at any rate, in which we ourselves have it, it is not all we want. And as the force which encourages us to stand staunch and fast by the rule and ground we have is Hebraism, so the force which encourages us to go back upon this rule, and to try the very ground on which we appear to stand, is Hellenism,—a turn for giving our consciousness free play and enlarging its range. And what I say is, not that Hellenism is always for everybody more wanted than Hebraism, but that for Mr Murphy at this particular moment, and for the great majority of us his fellow-countrymen, it is more wanted. * * *

from *Conclusion*

And so we bring to an end what we had to say in praise of culture, and in evidence of its special utility for the circumstances in which we find ourselves, and the confusion which environs us. Through culture seems to lie our way, not only to perfection, but even to safety. Resolutely refusing to lend a hand to the imperfect operations of our Liberal friends, disregarding their impatience, taunts, and reproaches, firmly bent on trying to find in the intelligible laws of things a firmer and sounder basis for future practice than any which we have at present, and believ-ing this search and discovery to be, for our generation and circumstances, of yet more vital and pressing importance than practice itself, we nevertheless may do more, perhaps, we poor disparaged followers of culture, to make the actual present, and the frame of society in which we live, solid and seaworthy, than all which our bustling politicians can do.

For we have seen how much of our disorders and perplexities is due to the disbe-lief, among the classes and combinations of men, Barbarian or Philistine, which have hitherto governed our society, in right reason, in a paramount best self; to the in-evitable decay and break-up of the organisations by which, asserting and expressing in these organisations their ordinary self only, they have so long ruled us; and to their irresolution, when the society, which their conscience tells them they have made and still manage not with right reason but with their ordinary self, is rudely shaken, in offering resistance to its subverters. But for us,—who believe in right reason, in the duty and possibility of extricating and elevating our best self, in the progress of humanity towards perfection,—for us the framework of society, that theatre on which this august drama has to unroll itself, is sacred; and whoever administers it, and however we may seek to remove them from their tenure of administration, yet, while they administer, we steadily and with undivided heart support them in repressing anarchy and disorder; because without order there can be no society, and without society there can be no human perfection.

And this opinion of the intolerableness of anarchy we can never forsake, however our Liberal friends may think a little rioting, and what they call popular demonstrations, useful sometimes to their own interests and to the interests of the valuable practical operations they have in hand, and however they may preach the right of an Englishman to be left to do as far as possible what he likes, and the duty of his government to indulge him and connive as much as possible and abstain from all harshness of repression. And even when they artfully show us operations which are undoubtedly precious, such as the abolition of the slave-trade, and ask us if, for their sake, foolish and obstinate governments may not wholesomely be frightened by a little disturbance, the good design in view and the difficulty of overcoming opposition to it being considered,—still we say no, and that monster-processions in the streets and forcible irruptions into the parks, even in professed support of this good design, ought to be unflinchingly forbidden and repressed; and that far more is lost than is gained by permitting them. Because a State in which law is authoritative and sovereign, a firm and settled course of public order, is requisite if man is to bring to maturity anything precious and lasting now, or to found anything precious and lasting for the future. * * *

1867–1868; 1869

from The Study of Poetry[1]

"The future of poetry is immense, because in poetry, where it is worthy of its high destinies, our race, as time goes on, will find an ever surer and surer stay. There is not a creed which is not shaken, not an accredited dogma which is not shown to be questionable, not a received tradition which does not threaten to dissolve. Our religion has materialised itself in the fact, in the supposed fact; it has attached its emotion to the fact, and now the fact is failing it. But for poetry the idea is everything; the rest is a world of illusion, of divine illusion. Poetry attaches its emotion to the idea; the idea *is* the fact. The strongest part of our religion to-day is its unconscious poetry."[2]

Let me be permitted to quote these words of my own, as uttering the thought which should, in my opinion, go with us and govern us in all our study of poetry. In

---

1. This influential essay, first published in 1880, is notable not only for its theory of absolute poetic excellence, independent of historical or personal taste, but also for the broad classical and modern European context in which it evaluates English literature.
2. From Arnold's introduction to *The Hundred Greatest Men* (1879).

the present work[3] it is the course of one great contributory stream to the world-river of poetry that we are invited to follow. We are here invited to trace the stream of English poetry. But whether we set ourselves, as here, to follow only one of the several streams that make the mighty river of poetry, or whether we seek to know them all, our governing thought should be the same. We should conceive of poetry worthily, and more highly than it has been the custom to conceive of it. We should conceive of it as capable of higher uses, and called to higher destinies, than those which in general men have assigned to it hitherto. More and more mankind will discover that we have to turn to poetry to interpret life for us, to console us, to sustain us. Without poetry, our science will appear incomplete; and most of what now passes with us for religion and philosophy will be replaced by poetry. Science, I say, will appear incomplete without it. For finely and truly does Wordsworth call poetry "the impassioned expression which is in the countenance of all science"[4]; and what is a countenance without its expression? Again, Wordsworth finely and truly calls poetry "the breath and finer spirit of all knowledge:" our religion, parading evidences such as those on which the popular mind relies now; our philosophy, pluming itself on its reasonings about causation and finite and infinite being; what are they but the shadows and dreams and false shows of knowledge? The day will come when we shall wonder at ourselves for having trusted to them, for having taken them seriously; and the more we perceive their hollowness, the more we shall prize "the breath and finer spirit of knowledge" offered to us by poetry.

But if we conceive thus highly of the destinies of poetry, we must also set our standard for poetry high, since poetry, to be capable of fulfilling such high destinies, must be poetry of a high order of excellence. We must accustom ourselves to a high standard and to a strict judgment. * * * For in poetry the distinction between excellent and inferior, sound and unsound or only half-sound, true and untrue or only half-true, is of paramount importance. It is of paramount importance because of the high destinies of poetry. In poetry, as a criticism of life under the conditions fixed for such a criticism by the laws of poetic truth and poetic beauty, the spirit of our race will find, we have said, as time goes on and as other helps fail, its consolation and stay. But the consolation and stay will be of power in proportion to the power of the criticism of life. And the criticism of life will be of power in proportion as the poetry conveying it is excellent rather than inferior, sound rather than unsound or half-sound, true rather than untrue or half-true.

The best poetry is what we want; the best poetry will be found to have a power of forming, sustaining, and delighting us, as nothing else can. * * *

Yes; constantly, in reading poetry, a sense for the best, the really excellent, and of the strength and joy to be drawn from it, should be present in our minds and should govern our estimate of what we read. But this real estimate, the only true one, is liable to be superseded, if we are not watchful, by two other kinds of estimate, the historic estimate and the personal estimate, both of which are fallacious. A poet or a poem may count to us historically, they may count to us on grounds personal to ourselves, and they may count to us really. They may count to us historically. The course of development of a nation's language, thought, and poetry, is profoundly interesting; and by regarding a poet's work as a stage in this course of development we may easily

3. *The English Poets* (1880), ed. T. H. Ward, an anthology of English poetry that this essay originally introduced.   4. Preface to *Lyrical Ballads* (1802).

bring ourselves to make it of more importance as poetry than in itself it really is, we may come to use a language of quite exaggerated praise in criticising it; in short, to over-rate it. So arises in our poetic judgments the fallacy caused by the estimate which we may call historic. Then, again, a poet or a poem may count to us on grounds personal to ourselves. Our personal affinities, likings, and circumstances, have great power to sway our estimate of this or that poet's work, and to make us attach more importance to it as poetry than in itself it really possesses, because to us it is, or has been, of high importance. Here also we over-rate the object of our interest, and apply to it a language of praise which is quite exaggerated. And thus we get the source of a second fallacy in our poetic judgments—the fallacy caused by an estimate which we may call personal. * * *

Indeed there can be no more useful help for discovering what poetry belongs to the class of the truly excellent, and can therefore do us most good, than to have always in one's mind lines and expressions of the great masters, and to apply them as a touchstone to other poetry. Of course we are not to require this other poetry to resemble them; it may be very dissimilar. But if we have any tact we shall find them, when we have lodged them well in our minds, an infallible touchstone for detecting the presence or absence of high poetic quality, and also the degree of this quality, in all other poetry which we may place beside them. Short passages, even single lines, will serve our turn quite sufficiently. Take the two lines which I have just quoted from Homer,[5] the poet's comment on Helen's mention of her brothers;—or take his

> Ἀ δειλώ, τί σφῶϊ δόμεν Πηληΐ ἄνακτι
> θνητω; ὑμεις δ' ἐστὸν ἀγήρω τ' ἀθανάτω τε.
> ἦ ἵνα 'δυστήνοισι μετ' ανδράσιν ἄλγε' ἔχητον;[6]

the address of Zeus to the horses of Peleus;—or take finally his

> Καὶ σέ, γέρον, τὸ πρὶν μὲν ἀκούομεν ὄλβιον εἶναι[7]

the words of Achilles to Priam, a suppliant before him. Take that incomparable line and a half of Dante, Ugolino's tremendous words—

> Io non piangeva; sì dentro impietrai.
> Piangevan elli . . .[8]

take the lovely words of Beatrice to Virgil—

> Io son fatta da Dio, sua mercè, tale,
> Che la vostra miseria non mi tange,
> Nè fiamma d'esto incendio non m'assale . . .[9]

5. "So said she; they long since in Earth's soft arms were reposing, / There, in their own dear land, their father-land, Lacedaemon." *Iliad* 3.243–44 (translated by Dr. Hawtrey) [Arnold's note].
6. "Ah, unhappy pair, why gave we you to King Peleus, to a mortal? but ye are without old age, and immortal. Was it that with men born to misery ye might have sorrow?" *Iliad* 17.443–45 [Arnold's note].
7. "Nay, and thou too, old man, in former days wast, as we hear, happy." *Iliad* 24.543 [Arnold's note].
8. "I wailed not, so of stone grew I within;—*they* wailed." *Inferno* 33.49–50 [Arnold's note].
9. "Of such sort hath God, thanked be His mercy, made me, that your misery toucheth me not, neither doth the flame of this fire strike me." *Inferno* 2.91–93 [Arnold's note].

take the simple, but perfect, single line—

> In la sua volontade è nostra pace.[1]

Take of Shakespeare a line or two of Henry the Fourth's expostulation with sleep—

> Wilt thou upon the high and giddy mast
> Seal up the ship-boy's eyes, and rock his brains
> In cradle of the rude imperious surge . . .[2]

and take, as well, Hamlet's dying request to Horatio—

> If thou didst ever hold me in thy heart,
> Absent thee from felicity awhile,
> And in this harsh world draw thy breath in pain
> To tell my story . . .[3]

Take of Milton that Miltonic passage—

> Darken'd so, yet shone
> Above them all the archangel; but his face
> Deep scars of thunder had intrench'd, and care
> Sat on his faded cheek . . .[4]

add two such lines as—

> And courage never to submit or yield
> And what is else not to be overcome . . .[5]

and finish with the exquisite close to the loss of Proserpine, the loss

> . . . which cost Ceres all that pain
> To seek her through the world.[6]

These few lines, if we have tact and can use them, are enough even of themselves to keep clear and sound our judgments about poetry, to save us from fallacious estimates of it, to conduct us to a real estimate.

The specimens I have quoted differ widely from one another, but they have in common this: the possession of the very highest poetical quality. If we are thoroughly penetrated by their power, we shall find that we have acquired a sense enabling us, whatever poetry may be laid before us, to feel the degree in which a high poetical quality is present or wanting there. Critics give themselves great labour to draw out what in the abstract constitutes the characters of a high quality of poetry. It is much better simply to have recourse to concrete examples;—to take specimens of poetry of the high, the very highest quality, and to say: The characters of a high quality of poetry are what is expressed *there*. They are far better recognised by being felt in the verse of the master, than by being perused in the prose of the critic. Nevertheless if we are urgently pressed to give some critical account of them, we may safely, perhaps, venture on laying down, not indeed how and why the characters arise, but where and in what they arise. They are in the matter and substance of the poetry, and they are in its manner and style. Both of these, the substance and matter on the one hand, the style and manner on the other, have a mark, an accent, of high beauty, worth, and

1. "In His will is our peace." *Paradiso* 3.85 [Arnold's note].
2. *2 Henry IV* 3.1.18–20.
3. *Hamlet* 5.2.348–51.

4. *Paradise Lost* 1.599–602.
5. *Paradise Lost* 1.108–109.
6. *Paradise Lost* 4.271–72.

power. But if we are asked to define this mark and accent in the abstract, our answer must be: No, for we should thereby be darkening the question, not clearing it. The mark and accent are as given by the substance and matter of that poetry, by the style and manner of that poetry, and of all other poetry which is akin to it in quality.

Only one thing we may add as to the substance and matter of poetry, guiding ourselves by Aristotle's profound observation that the superiority of poetry over history consists in its possessing a higher truth and a higher seriousness (φιλοσοφώτερον καὶ σπουδαιότερον).[7] Let us add, therefore, to what we have said, this: that the substance and matter of the best poetry acquire their special character from possessing, in an eminent degree, truth and seriousness. We may add yet further, what is in itself evident, that to the style and manner of the best poetry their special character, their accent, is given by their diction, and, even yet more, by their movement. And though we distinguish between the two characters, the two accents, of superiority, yet they are nevertheless vitally connected one with the other. The superior character of truth and seriousness, in the matter and substance of the best poetry, is inseparable from the superiority of diction and movement marking its style and manner. The two superiorities are closely related, and are in steadfast proportion one to the other. So far as high poetic truth and seriousness are wanting to a poet's matter and substance, so far also, we may be sure, will a high poetic stamp of diction and movement be wanting to his style and manner. In proportion as this high stamp of diction and movement, again, is absent from a poet's style and manner, we shall find, also, that high poetic truth and seriousness are absent from his substance and matter.

So stated, these are but dry generalities; their whole force lies in their application. And I could wish every student of poetry to make the application of them for himself. Made by himself, the application would impress itself upon his mind far more deeply than made by me. Neither will my limits allow me to make any full application of the generalities above propounded; but in the hope of bringing out, at any rate, some significance in them, and of establishing an important principle more firmly by their means, I will, in the space which remains to me, follow rapidly from the commencement the course of our English poetry with them in my view. * * *

* * * Chaucer's power of fascination * * * is enduring; his poetical importance does not need the assistance of the historic estimate; it is real. He is a genuine source of joy and strength, which is flowing still for us and will flow always. He will be read, as time goes on, far more generally than he is read now. His language is a cause of difficulty for us; but so also, and I think in quite as great a degree, is the language of Burns. In Chaucer's case, as in that of Burns, it is a difficulty to be unhesitatingly accepted and overcome.

* * * We have only to call to mind the Prologue to *The Canterbury Tales*. The right comment upon it is Dryden's: "It is sufficient to say, according to the proverb, that *here is God's plenty*." And again: "He is a perpetual fountain of good sense."[8] It is by a large, free, sound representation of things, that poetry, this high criticism of life, has truth of substance; and Chaucer's poetry has truth of substance.

Of his style and manner, if we think first of the romance-poetry and then of Chaucer's divine liquidness of diction, his divine fluidity of movement, it is difficult to speak temperately. * * * Chaucer is the father of our splendid English poetry; he is our "well of English undefiled,"[9] because by the lovely charm of his diction, the

---

7. *Poetics* 9.3.
8. From Dryden's preface to *Fables Ancient and Modern* (1700).

9. Spenser said this of Chaucer in *The Faerie Queene* 4.2.32.

lovely charm of his movement, he makes an epoch and founds a tradition. In Spenser, Shakespeare, Milton, Keats, we can follow the tradition of the liquid diction, the fluid movement, of Chaucer; at one time it is his liquid diction of which in these poets we feel the virtue, and at another time it is his fluid movement. And the virtue is irresistible. * * *

And yet Chaucer is not one of the great classics. His poetry transcends and effaces, easily and without effort, all the romance-poetry of Catholic Christendom; it transcends and effaces all the English poetry contemporary with it, it transcends and effaces all the English poetry subsequent to it down to the age of Elizabeth. Of such avail is poetic truth of substance, in its natural and necessary union with poetic truth of style. And yet, I say, Chaucer is not one of the great classics. He has not their accent. What is wanting to him is suggested by the mere mention of the name of the first great classic of Christendom, the immortal poet who died eighty years before Chaucer,—Dante. The accent of such verse as

> In la sua volontade è nostra pace . . .

is altogether beyond Chaucer's reach; we praise him, but we feel that this accent is out of the question for him. It may be said that it was necessarily out of the reach of any poet in the England of that stage of growth. Possibly; but we are to adopt a real, not a historic, estimate of poetry. However we may account for its absence, something is wanting, then, to the poetry of Chaucer, which poetry must have before it can be placed in the glorious class of the best. And there is no doubt what that something is. It is the σπουδαιότης, the high and excellent seriousness, which Aristotle assigns as one of the grand virtues of poetry. The substance of Chaucer's poetry, his view of things and his criticism of life, has largeness, freedom, shrewdness, benignity; but it has not this high seriousness. Homer's criticism of life has it, Dante's has it, Shakespeare's has it. It is this chiefly which gives to our spirits what they can rest upon; and with the increasing demands of our modern ages upon poetry, this virtue of giving us what we can rest upon will be more and more highly esteemed. * * *

For my present purpose I need not dwell on our Elizabethan poetry, or on the continuation and close of this poetry in Milton. We all of us profess to be agreed in the estimate of this poetry; we all of us recognise it as great poetry, our greatest, and Shakespeare and Milton as our poetical classics. The real estimate, here, has universal currency. With the next age of our poetry divergency and difficulty begin. An historic estimate of that poetry has established itself; and the question is, whether it will be found to coincide with the real estimate. * * *

Are Dryden and Pope poetical classics? Is the historic estimate, which represents them as such, and which has been so long established that it cannot easily give way, the real estimate? Wordsworth and Coleridge, as is well known, denied it; but the authority of Wordsworth and Coleridge does not weigh much with the young generation, and there are many signs to show that the eighteenth century and its judgments are coming into favour again. Are the favourite poets of the eighteenth century classics? * * *

We are to regard Dryden as the puissant and glorious founder, Pope as the splendid high priest, of our age of prose and reason, of our excellent and indispensable eighteenth century. For the purposes of their mission and destiny their poetry, like their prose, is admirable. Do you ask me whether Dryden's verse, take it almost where you will, is not good?

> A milk-white Hind, immortal and unchanged,
> Fed on the lawns and in the forest ranged.[1]

I answer: Admirable for the purposes of the inaugurator of an age of prose and reason. Do you ask me whether Pope's verse, take it almost where you will, is not good?

> To Hounslow Heath I point, and Banstead Down;
> Thence comes your mutton, and these chicks my own.[2]

I answer: Admirable for the purposes of the high priest of an age of prose and reason. But do you ask me whether such verse proceeds from men with an adequate poetic criticism of life, from men whose criticism of life has a high seriousness, or even, without that high seriousness, has poetic largeness, freedom, insight, benignity? Do you ask me whether the application of ideas to life in the verse of these men, often a powerful application, no doubt, is a powerful *poetic* application? Do you ask me whether the poetry of these men has either the matter or the inseparable manner of such an adequate poetic criticism; whether it has the accent of

> Absent thee from felicity awhile . . .

or of

> And what is else not to be overcome . . .

or of

> O martyr souded to virginitee![3]

I answer: It has not and cannot have them; it is the poetry of the builders of an age of prose and reason. Though they may write in verse, though they may in a certain sense be masters of the art of versification, Dryden and Pope are not classics of our poetry, they are classics of our prose.

Gray is our poetical classic of that literature and age; the position of Gray is singular, and demands a word of notice here. He has not the volume or the power of poets who, coming in times more favourable, have attained to an independent criticism of life. But he lived with the great poets, he lived, above all, with the Greeks, through perpetually studying and enjoying them; and he caught their poetic point of view for regarding life, caught their poetic manner. The point of view and the manner are not self-sprung in him, he caught them of others; and he had not the free and abundant use of them. But whereas Addison and Pope never had the use of them, Gray had the use of them at times. He is the scantiest and frailest of classics in our poetry, but he is a classic. * * *

At any rate the end to which the method and the estimate are designed to lead, and from leading to which, if they do lead to it, they get their whole value,—the benefit of being able clearly to feel and deeply to enjoy the best, the truly classic, in poetry,—is an end, let me say it once more at parting, of supreme importance. We are often told that an era is opening in which we are to see multitudes of a common sort of readers, and masses of a common sort of literature; that such readers do not want

---

1. *The Hind and the Panther* (1867) 1.1–2.
2. *Imitations of Horace* (1737), Satire 2.2.143–44.
3. *The Prioress's Tale* (line 127) in Chaucer's *Canterbury*

Tales. Arnold noted that "souded" derives from "the French *soudé*: soldered, fixed fast."

and could not relish anything better than such literature, and that to provide it is becoming a vast and profitable industry. Even if good literature entirely lost currency with the world, it would still be abundantly worth while to continue to enjoy it by oneself. But it never will lose currency with the world, in spite of momentary appearances; it never will lose supremacy. Currency and supremacy are insured to it, not indeed by the world's deliberate and conscious choice, but by something far deeper,—by the instinct of self-preservation in humanity.

1880

⊷ ⊨✢⊨ ⊷

Dante Gabriel Rossetti
1828–1882

"If any man has any poetry in him he should paint it," Dante Gabriel Rossetti once said. Like Blake, whose work he rediscovered for a Victorian audience, Rossetti was gifted as both a poet and painter. So many of Rossetti's poems became subjects of his own paintings—and vice versa—that his friend James McNeill Whistler once suggested combining the two: "Why not frame the sonnet?"

Christened Gabriele Charles Dante, Rossetti rearranged his name to signal his determination to devote himself to what was most spiritual in love, poetry, and art. He grew up in London in a poor but exceptionally cultivated milieu: his father was an ardent Italian poet, patriot, and Dante scholar in exile; his mother was a devout, half-Italian but very English governess. His sister Christina composed poetry before she was old enough to write it down. Dante himself showed such early signs of genius that he was spared work and sent to art school despite his family's poverty. In 1848 Dante joined with two other young students at the Royal Academy, William Holman Hunt and John Everett Millais, to found the Pre-Raphaelite Brotherhood.

Rossetti published his early poems, including *The Blessed Damozel,* in the Pre-Raphaelite journal, *The Germ,* in 1850. His paintings of the time exhibit many traits of the short-lived group: a flattened picture plane, luminous detail, careful observation of nature, purity of line and color, and an earnest treatment of religious subjects that sought to capture the intensity of feeling of art before Raphael—i.e., before the High Renaissance.

Members of the group soon went their separate ways, and Rossetti's own art and writing became increasingly preoccupied with two subjects that often overlapped: a "medievalism" that lost itself in densely designed interpretations of scenes from Dante and Malory, and a luscious, almost claustrophobic exploration of love in its most spiritual and sensuous manifestations. Rossetti's distinctive style included elements that shaped the meaning of "Pre-Raphaelitism" as a literary and artistic term: vivid color, formal harmony, and symbolic detail used to create distant (and decidedly un-Victorian) settings for the expression of amorous passion.

Bohemian, gregarious, brilliant, and worldly, Rossetti moved in a circle of artists and writers that included Ruskin, William Morris, Swinburne, Edward Burne-Jones, Whistler, George Meredith, and Ford Madox Brown. The wittiness of *The Burden of Nineveh,* about the eventual decline of the British Empire, and the jaded sophistication of *Jenny,* about a poet's night with a prostitute, convey a different side of Rossetti: the urbane and self-assured Londoner who was the center of attention at any gathering, who taught art at the Working Men's College, and who for a while shared his house with a menagerie that included kangaroos, peacocks, and a wombat.

But Rossetti's personal life was erratic, eccentric, and often miserable. As one critic put it: "He married a woman he did not love, loved a woman he could not marry, and lived with a woman he neither loved nor married." The woman he married, in 1860, was the poet, artist, and model Elizabeth Siddall. She committed suicide in 1862, a devastating event that Rossetti commemorated by portraying her as a transfigured Beatrice (Dante's love lost early to death) in his painting *Beata Beatrix* (c. 1863). In a fit of remorse Rossetti thrust the manuscript of his poems into her coffin at the funeral—only to exhume them years later in order to publish his first collection, *Poems* (1870). By then he had fallen hopelessly in love with William Morris's wife, Jane, who posed for many of his later portrait-fantasies, among them *Astarte Syrica* (1877) and *Proserpine* (1873–1877). The woman he finally lived with was Fanny Cornforth, who also modeled for Rossetti's languid, steamy fantasies of long-necked, thick-haired beauties.

In 1871 the poet Robert Buchanan published a scathing attack on Rossetti, *The Fleshly School of Poetry*. Rossetti counterattacked in 1872 with *The Stealthy School of Criticism*, but the experience wounded him deeply, contributing to declining health and mental depression, aggravated by large doses of narcotics and whiskey. Spiritual and sensuous at the same time, Rossetti could not seem to find happiness in a world scandalized by his efforts to unite these qualities in art and life. He had approached his ideal most fully, perhaps, in *The Blessed Damozel*, where he transformed the Dantesque vision of a heavenly beloved by giving her a very Rossettian physical body: he could not separate the purity of his passion from the warmth of her bosom. It was this combination of eroticism and idealism, together with his commingling of the visual and the poetic, that made Rossetti's work a decisive force in the shaping of English aestheticism, the Arts and Crafts movement, and art nouveau. And it was Rossetti's powerful influence on the symbolist poets of the *fin de siècle* that made Yeats declare of his own youthful aspirations that he was "in all things Pre-Raphaelite."

The Blessed Damozel[1]

The blessed damozel leaned out
   From the gold bar of Heaven;
Her eyes were deeper than the depth
   Of waters stilled at even;
5   She had three lilies in her hand,
   And the stars in her hair were seven.

Her robe, ungirt from clasp to hem,
   No wrought flowers did adorn,
But a white rose of Mary's gift,
10   For service meetly worn;
Her hair that lay along her back
   Was yellow like ripe corn.

Herseemed° she scarce had been a day   *it seemed to her*
   One of God's choristers;
15   The wonder was not yet quite gone
   From that still look of hers;
Albeit, to them she left, her day
   Had counted as ten years.

1. Damsel, young woman. Rossetti explained the connection between this poem and Edgar Allan Poe's *The Raven* (1844): "I saw that Poe had done the utmost it was possible to do with the grief of the lover on earth, and so I determined to reverse the conditions, and give utterance to the yearning of the loved one in heaven" (quoted in T. Hall Caine's *Recollections of Dante Gabriel Rossetti*, 1882). See Rossetti's painting *The Blessed Damozel*, Color Plate 17.

     (To one, it is ten years of years.

20   . . . Yet now, and in this place,

     Surely she leaned o'er me—her hair

         Fell all about my face . . .

     Nothing: the autumn-fall of leaves.

         The whole year sets apace.)

25   It was the rampart of God's house

         That she was standing on;

     By God built over the sheer depth

         The which is Space begun;

     So high, that looking downward thence

30   She scarce could see the sun.

     It lies in Heaven, across the flood

         Of ether, as a bridge.

     Beneath, the tides of day and night

         With flame and darkness ridge

35   The void, as low as where this earth

         Spins like a fretful midge.

     Around her, lovers, newly met

         'Mid deathless love's acclaims,

     Spoke evermore among themselves

40   Their heart-remembered names;

     And the souls mounting up to God

         Went by her like thin flames.

     And still she bowed herself and stooped

         Out of the circling charm;

45   Until her bosom must have made

         The bar she leaned on warm,

     And the lilies lay as if asleep

         Along her bended arm.

     From the fixed place of Heaven she saw

50   Time like a pulse shake fierce

     Through all the worlds. Her gaze still strove

         Within the gulf to pierce

     Its path; and now she spoke as when

         The stars sang in their spheres.

55   The sun was gone now; the curled moon

         Was like a little feather

     Fluttering far down the gulf; and now

         She spoke through the still weather.

     Her voice was like the voice the stars

60   Had when they sang together.

     (Ah sweet! Even now, in that bird's song,

         Strove not her accents there,

     Fain to be hearkened? When those bells

         Possessed the mid-day air,

65 Strove not her steps to reach my side
  Down all the echoing stair?)

"I wish that he were come to me,
  For he will come," she said.
"Have I not prayed in Heaven?—on earth,
70 Lord, Lord, has he not pray'd?
Are not two prayers a perfect strength?
  And shall I feel afraid?

"When round his head the aureole° clings,   *halo*
  And he is clothed in white,
75 I'll take his hand and go with him
  To the deep wells of light;
As unto a stream we will step down,
  And bathe there in God's sight.

"We two will stand beside that shrine,
80 Occult,° withheld, untrod,   *hidden*
Whose lamps are stirred continually
  With prayer sent up to God;
And see our old prayers, granted, melt
  Each like a little cloud.

85 "We two will lie i' the shadow of
  That living mystic tree[2]
Within whose secret growth the Dove
  Is sometimes felt to be,
While every leaf that His plumes touch
90 Saith His Name audibly.

"And I myself will teach to him,
  I myself, lying so,
The songs I sing here; which his voice
  Shall pause in, hushed and slow,
95 And find some knowledge at each pause,
  Or some new thing to know."

(Alas! we two, we two, thou say'st!
  Yea, one wast thou with me
That once of old. But shall God lift
100 To endless unity
The soul whose likeness with thy soul
  Was but its love for thee?)

"We two," she said, "will seek the groves
  Where the lady Mary is,
105 With her five handmaidens, whose names
  Are five sweet symphonies,
Cecily, Gertrude, Magdalen,
  Margaret and Rosalys.

2. The tree of life; cf. Revelation 22.2.

     "Circlewise sit they, with bound locks
110   And foreheads garlanded;
     Into the fine cloth white like flame
         Weaving the golden thread,
     To fashion the birth-robes for them
         Who are just born, being dead.

115   "He shall fear, haply, and be dumb:
         Then will I lay my cheek
     To his, and tell about our love,
         Not once abashed or weak:
     And the dear Mother will approve
120   My pride, and let me speak.

     "Herself shall bring us, hand in hand,
         To Him round whom all souls
     Kneel, the clear-ranged unnumbered heads
         Bowed with their aureoles:
125   And angels meeting us shall sing
         To their citherns and citoles.[3]

     "There will I ask of Christ the Lord
         Thus much for him and me:—
     Only to live as once on earth
130   With Love,—only to be,
     As then awhile, for ever now
         Together, I and he."

     She gazed and listened and then said,
         Less sad of speech than mild,—
135   "All this is when he comes." She ceased.
         The light thrilled towards her, fill'd
     With angels in strong level flight.
         Her eyes prayed, and she smil'd.

     (I saw her smile.) But soon their path
140   Was vague in distant spheres:
     And then she cast her arms along
         The golden barriers,
     And laid her face between her hands,
         And wept. (I heard her tears.)

1847   1850

The Woodspurge[1]

The wind flapped loose, the wind was still,
Shaken out dead from tree and hill:
I had walked on at the wind's will,—
I sat now, for the wind was still.

---

3. Stringed instruments from the Middle Ages and Renaissance.

1. A flowering weed that exudes a milky fluid.

5   Between my knees my forehead was,—
       My lips, drawn in, said not Alas!
       My hair was over in the grass,
       My naked ears heard the day pass.

       My eyes, wide open, had the run
10   Of some ten weeds to fix upon;
       Among those few, out of the sun,
       The woodspurge flowered, three cups in one.

       From perfect grief there need not be
       Wisdom or even memory:
15   One thing then learnt remains to me,—
       The woodspurge has a cup of three.

1856   1870

from **The House of Life**
The Sonnet

       A Sonnet is a moment's monument,—
          Memorial from the Soul's eternity
          To one dead deathless hour. Look that it be,
       Whether for lustral° rite or dire portent,   purification
5   Of its own arduous fulness reverent:
          Carve it in ivory or in ebony,
          As Day or Night may rule; and let Time see
       Its flowering crest impearled and orient.

       A Sonnet is a coin: its face reveals
10   The soul,—its converse, to what Power 'tis due:—[1]
       Whether for tribute to the august appeals
          Of Life, or dower in Love's high retinue,
       It serve; or, 'mid the dark wharf's cavernous breath,
       In Charon's[2] palm it pay the toll to Death.

1880   1881

4. Lovesight

       When do I see thee most, belovèd one?
          When in the light the spirits of mine eyes
          Before thy face, their altar, solemnize
       The worship of that Love through thee made known?
5   Or when in the dusk hours, (we two alone,)
          Close-kissed and eloquent of still replies
          Thy twilight-hidden glimmering visage lies,
       And my soul only sees thy soul its own?

1. Cf. Luke 20.21–26.   2. The ferryman whom the dead would pay to row them
                                         across the River Styx of Hades.

O love, my love! if I no more should see
10   Thyself, nor on the earth the shadow of thee,
        Nor image of thine eyes in any spring,—
    How then should sound upon Life's darkening slope
    The ground-whirl of the perished leaves of Hope,
        The wind of Death's imperishable wing?

1869   1870

6. The Kiss

What smouldering senses in death's sick delay
    Or seizure of malign vicissitude
    Can rob this body of honour, or denude
This soul of wedding-raiment worn to-day?
5   For lo! even now my lady's lips did play
        With these my lips such consonant interlude
        As laurelled Orpheus[1] longed for when he wooed
The half-drawn hungering face with that last lay.

I was a child beneath her touch,—a man
10   When breast to breast we clung, even I and she,—
    A spirit when her spirit looked through me,—
A god when all our life-breath met to fan
Our life-blood, till love's emulous ardours ran,
    Fire within fire, desire in deity.

1869   1870

Nuptial Sleep[1]

At length their long kiss severed, with sweet smart:
    And as the last slow sudden drops are shed
    From sparkling eaves when all the storm has fled,
So singly flagged the pulses of each heart.
5   Their bosoms sundered, with the opening start
        Of married flowers to either side outspread
        From the knit stem; yet still their mouths, burnt red,
Fawned on each other where they lay apart.

Sleep sank them lower than the tide of dreams,
10   And their dreams watched them sink, and slid away.
Slowly their souls swam up again, through gleams
    Of watered light and dull drowned waifs of day;
Till from some wonder of new woods and streams
    He woke, and wondered more: for there she lay.

1869   1870

1. Orpheus tried to rescue his wife Eurydice from the underworld by the power of his music. She was permitted to leave provided he did not look back at her, but he disobeyed and she had to return to Hades. In his grief he wandered the earth for years.
1. In a review titled The Fleshly School of Poetry (1871), the poet and critic Robert Buchanan viciously attacked Rossetti for having "so sickening a desire to reproduce the sensual mood." Buchanan singled out Nuptial Sleep: "we merely shudder at the shameless nakedness." Rossetti omitted this poem from the 1881 edition of his work.

The Burden of Nineveh[1]

In our Museum galleries
To-day I lingered o'er the prize
Dead Greece vouchsafes to living eyes,—
Her Art for ever in fresh wise
5   From hour to hour rejoicing me.
Sighing I turned at last to win
Once more the London dirt and din;
And as I made the swing-door spin
And issued, they were hoisting in
10   A wingèd beast[2] from Nineveh.

A human face the creature wore,
And hoofs behind and hoofs before,
And flanks with dark runes° fretted o'er.   *archaic letters*
'Twas bull, 'twas mitred Minotaur,[3]
15   A dead disbowelled mystery:
The mummy of a buried faith
Stark from the charnel[4] without scathe,
Its wings stood for the light to bathe,—
Such fossil cerements° as might swathe   *shrouds*
20   The very corpse of Nineveh.

The print of its first rush-wrapping,
Wound ere it dried, still ribbed the thing.
What song did the brown maidens sing,
From purple mouths alternating,
25   When that was woven languidly?
What vows, what rites, what prayers preferr'd,
What songs has the strange image heard?
In what blind vigil stood interr'd
For ages, till an English word
30   Broke silence first at Nineveh?

Oh when upon each sculptured court,
Where even the wind might not resort,—
O'er which Time passed, of like import
With the wild Arab boys at sport,—
35   A living face looked in to see:—
Oh seemed it not—the spell once broke—
As though the carven warriors woke,
As though the shaft the string forsook,
The cymbals clashed, the chariots shook,
40   And there was life in Nineveh?

1. The title comes from the beginning of the biblical Book of Nahum, a prophetic oracle concerning the fall of Nineveh. The capital of the powerful Assyrian Empire, Nineveh was destroyed in 600 B.C. and buried under drifting sand. Many of the details of the poem derive from Sir Austen Henry Layard's accounts of his excavations at Nineveh in 1845–1851.
2. A massive Assyrian statue of a winged bull with the head of a man is being brought into the British Museum.
3. A mythical monster, half bull and half man, kept at the center of a labyrinth by King Minos of Crete.
4. A building holding dead bodies.

On London stones our sun anew
The beast's recovered shadow threw.
(No shade that plague of darkness knew,
No light, no shade, while older grew
45   By ages the old earth and sea.)
Lo thou! could all thy priests have shown
Such proof to make thy godhead known?
From their dead Past thou liv'st alone;
And still thy shadow is thine own,
50   Even as of yore in Nineveh.

That day whereof we keep record,
When near thy city-gates the Lord
Sheltered His Jonah with a gourd,[5]
This sun, (I said) here present, pour'd
55   Even thus this shadow that I see.
This shadow has been shed the same
From sun and moon,—from lamps which came
For prayer,—from fifteen days of flame,
The last, while smouldered to a name
60   Sardanapalus'[6] Nineveh.

Within thy shadow, haply, once
Sennacherib[7] has knelt, whose sons
Smote him between the altar-stones:
Or pale Semiramis[8] her zones
65   Of gold, her incense brought to thee,
In love for grace, in war for aid: . . .
Ay, and who else? . . . till 'neath thy shade
Within his trenches newly made
Last year the Christian knelt and pray'd—
70   Not to thy strength—in Nineveh.[9]

Now, thou poor god, within this hall
Where the blank windows blind the wall
From pedestal to pedestal,
The kind of light shall on thee fall
75   Which London takes the day to be:
While school-foundations in the act
Of holiday, three files compact,
Shall learn to view thee as a fact
Connected with that zealous tract:
80   "ROME,—Babylon and Nineveh."[1]

5. The Hebrew prophet Jonah was sent by God to chastise the wicked Ninevites. Angry because God spared the
repentant city, Jonah sat outside it: "And the Lord God
prepared a gourd, and made it to come up over Jonah,
that it might be a shadow over his head, to deliver him
from his grief. So Jonah was exceedingly glad of the
gourd" (Jonah 4.5–6).
6. King of Assyria in the 9th century B.C. who burned his
treasure and himself to avoid capture.

7. King of Assyria, 705–681 B.C., who was murdered, possibly by his sons.
8. A legendary Assyrian queen, renowned for her wisdom
and beauty, Semiramis was supposed to have been the
founder of Babylon. Hoping to achieve success in love
and war, she offered gold and incense to idols.
9. During the excavation, the Tiyari workmen held their
services in the shadow of the great bulls [Rossetti's note].
1. Capitals of ancient empires, all fallen.

Deemed they of this, those worshippers,
When, in some mythic chain of verse
Which man shall not again rehearse,
The faces of thy ministers
85   Yearned pale with bitter ecstasy?
Greece, Egypt, Rome,—did any god
Before whose feet men knelt unshod
Deem that in this unblest abode
Another scarce more unknown god
90   Should house with him, from Nineveh?

Ah! in what quarries lay the stone
From which this pillared pile has grown,
Unto man's need how long unknown,
Since those thy temples, court and cone,
95   Rose far in desert history?
Ah! what is here that does not lie
All strange to thine awakened eye?
Ah! what is here can testify
(Save that dumb presence of the sky)
100   Unto thy day and Nineveh?

Why, of those mummies in the room
Above, there might indeed have come
One out of Egypt to thy home,
An alien. Nay, but were not some
105   Of these thine own "antiquity"?
And now,—they and their gods and thou
All relics here together,—now
Whose profit? whether bull or cow,[2]
Isis or Ibis,[3] who or how,
110   Whether of Thebes[4] or Nineveh?

The consecrated metals found,
And ivory tablets, underground,
Winged teraphim° and creatures crown'd.   *idols*
When air and daylight filled the mound,
115   Fell into dust immediately.
And even as these, the images
Of awe and worship,—even as these,—
So, smitten with the sun's increase,
Her glory mouldered and did cease
120   From immemorial Nineveh.

The day her builders made their halt,
Those cities of the lake of salt[5]

2. Deities of the ancient Near East often took the forms of these animals.
3. Isis was an Egyptian goddess, Ibis an Egyptian moon-god; Rossetti may have been thinking of Iblis, chief of the evil spirits in pre-Islamic Arabian lore.
4. City in ancient Egypt, sacked by the Assyrians in 661 B.C.; its ruined temples and tombs still survive.
5. Sodom and Gomorrah, near the salty Dead Sea, were destroyed for their wickedness (Genesis 19).

Stood firmly 'stablished without fault,
Made proud with pillars of basalt,
125   With sardonyx and porphyry.
The day that Jonah bore abroad
To Nineveh the voice of God,
A brackish lake lay in his road,
Where erst Pride fixed her sure abode,
130   As then in royal Nineveh.

The day when he, Pride's lord and Man's,
Showed all the kingdoms at a glance
To Him before whose countenance
The years recede, the years advance,
135   And said, Fall down and worship me:—
'Mid all the pomp beneath that look,
Then stirred there, haply, some rebuke,
Where to the wind the Salt Pools[6] shook,
And in those tracts, of life forsook,
140   That knew thee not, O Nineveh!

Delicate harlot! On thy throne
Thou with a world beneath thee prone
In state for ages sat'st alone;
And needs were years and lustres flown
145   Ere strength of man could vanquish thee:
Whom even thy victor foes must bring,
Still royal, among maids that sing
As with doves' voices, taboring°   drumming
Upon their breasts, unto the King,—
150   A kingly conquest, Nineveh!

. . . Here woke my thought. The wind's slow sway
Had waxed°; and like the human play   increased
Of scorn that smiling spreads away,
The sunshine shivered off the day:
155   The callous wind, it seemed to me,
Swept up the shadow from the ground:
And pale as whom the Fates astound,
The god forlorn stood winged and crown'd:
Within I knew the cry lay bound
160   Of the dumb soul of Nineveh.

And as I turned, my sense half shut
Still saw the crowds of kerb and rut[7]
Go past as marshalled to the strut
Of ranks in gypsum[8] quaintly cut.
165   It seemed in one same pageantry
They followed forms which had been erst;
To pass, till on my sight should burst

6. Areas of low salty ground in ancient Nineveh.   8. Plaster of paris, used to make casts of ancient sculpture.
7. Common people of the curbstone and gutter.

That future of the best or worst
When some may question which was first,
170   Of London or of Nineveh.

For as that Bull-god once did stand
And watched the burial-clouds of sand,
Till these at last without a hand
Rose o'er his eyes, another land,
175   And blinded him with destiny:—
So may he stand again; till now,
In ships of unknown sail and prow,
Some tribe of the Australian plough
Bear him afar,—a relic now
180   Of London, not of Nineveh!

Or it may chance indeed that when
Man's age is hoary among men,—
His centuries threescore and ten,[9]—
His furthest childhood shall seem then
185   More clear than later times may be:
Who, finding in this desert place
This form, shall hold us for some race
That walked not in Christ's lowly ways,
But bowed its pride and vowed its praise
190   Unto the God of Nineveh.

The smile rose first,—anon drew nigh
The thought: . . . Those heavy wings spread high,
So sure of flight, which do not fly;
That set gaze never on the sky;
195   Those scriptured flanks it cannot see;
Its crown, a brow-contracting load;
Its planted feet which trust the sod: . . .
(So grew the image as I trod:)
O Nineveh, was this thy God,—
200   Thine also, mighty Nineveh?

1850   1856

—◄═◆═►—

Christina Rossetti
1830–1894

"Here is a great discovery," Christina Rossetti wrote to her brother Dante Gabriel in 1870, as he tried to advise her about her poetic career: "'Women are not Men,' and you must not expect me to possess a tithe of your capacities, though I humbly—or proudly—lay claim to family-likeness." The remark hints at many sides of Rossetti's complex nature: her modest yet firm manner; the

9. The Bible gives the human life span as "threescore years and ten" (or seventy years); thus, Rossetti is referring to when the human race has lived out its time.

touch of irony in her deference; and the "family-likeness" not only of poetic genius but personal temperament—their parents called them the "two storms" in childhood because they were both difficult, irritable, volatile, and creative. Her declaration signals Rossetti's recognition that as a woman and artist she had had to take a very different path from her more famous brother. She renounced from an early age any pleasures or relationships that did not conform to her strict Anglo-Catholic principles—even to the point of giving up chess because it made her too eager to win. Instead she found poetic fulfillment in haunting lyrics about goblin men and love beyond the grave.

Rossetti was born in London in 1830, the youngest of four precocious children of Gabriele Rossetti, an Italian poet-in-exile, and his English-Italian wife, Frances Polidori, whose brother John was Byron's physician and traveling companion. Amid a stream of foreign visitors the bilingual Rossetti children listened to animated discussions of art, music, and revolutionary politics. This atmosphere "made us . . . not a little different from British children," her brother William recalled, "and, when Dante and Christina Rossetti proved, as poetic writers, somewhat devious from the British tradition and the insular mind, we may say, if not 'so much the better,' at any rate, 'no wonder.'"

Like many Victorian women of letters, Christina Rossetti suffered from mysterious maladies that served to protect her time and talent. "I am rejoiced to feel that my health does really unfit me for miscellaneous governessing en permanence," she confided to William in 1855. Freed from "the necessity of teaching the small daughters of the neighbouring hairdresser or the neighbouring pork-butcher their p's and q's," she was "anxious to secure any literary pickings which might offer."

Shy, devout, and self-sacrificing, Rossetti nevertheless found time for a literary and social life that included as acquaintances Browning, Ruskin, Swinburne, Lewis Carroll, Edmund Gosse, and the Pre-Raphaelites. She modeled as the Virgin Mary in two of Dante Gabriel's finest paintings, The Girlhood of Mary Virgin (1848–1849) and Ecce Ancilla Domini (1849–1850). Because of her sex, Christina was denied membership in the Pre-Raphaelite Brotherhood, but she did publish her first poems in their journal, The Germ, in 1850. With the appearance of Goblin Market and Other Poems in 1862, she acquired a growing critical and popular following. Hailed by Gosse as the "High Priestess of Pre-Raphaelitism" because of her superb technique and keenness of observation, she won even wider fame as an author of religious poetry, inspiring, among others, Gerard Manley Hopkins.

Admirers of Rossetti's passionate, frustrated love poetry have long puzzled over the scanty details of her romantic life. She rejected two suitors because she found their faith wanting. Early biographers assumed that these broken relationships blighted Rossetti's life, but recently critics have regarded her choice of a single life as an act of artistic self-preservation. For Christina not only witnessed Dante's tormented affairs but also had the opportunity to view passion's consequences in a clinical light during the decade she worked as a volunteer at the Highgate House of Charity for "fallen women."

Though brightened by many touches of humor, Rossetti's writing focuses mostly on religious topics or some combination of themes arising from troubled love, grave illness, and anticipations of death—themes she must have pondered during the extended periods she spent taking care of dying family members at home, beginning with her father and continuing with her sister, her brother Dante, her mother (who was always her closest companion), and two maiden aunts. Despite severe illness in later life, she maintained a strict professionalism toward her career, publishing new work during the 1870s and 1880s, then issuing revised editions until her death in 1894.

A spontaneous writer whose lucidity of phrasing has sometimes caused readers to overlook her emotional and symbolic depths, Rossetti mastered a variety of forms, ranging from hymns and a sonnet-sequence to nursery rhymes and a well-known Christmas carol, In the Bleak Mid-Winter. Like Emily Dickinson, whose poems she admired when the first selection was published in 1890, Rossetti displays a quirky independence of vision, mingling the morbid, the whimsical, the cooly ironic. What is today her most famous poem, *Goblin Market,* features the enticements of sensual knowledge. Regarded chiefly as a children's tale in the nineteenth century, the poem has subsequently attracted much critical attention, including analyses of it as a struggle between self and soul, a comment on sex as a capitalist commodity, a parable of feminist solidarity, a lesson about poetry's subversive power, and a lesbian love story. This fable about the danger of desire provides insight into the dualistic world of Victorian fantasy. Magical events permitted writers and readers to enter forbidden realms of violence, temptation, and transformation, yet moralized endings sought to tame even the wildest tales for social and ethical instruction. Something similar may be said of Christina Rossetti's life and art: a stormy nature finds release in the tight formal control of the polished artist.

Song

She sat and sang alway
 By the green margin of a stream,
Watching the fishes leap and play
 Beneath the glad sunbeam.

5 I sat and wept away
  Beneath the moon's most shadowy beam,
Watching the blossoms of the May
  Weep leaves into the stream.

I wept for memory;
10 She sang for hope that is so fair:
My tears were swallowed by the sea;
  Her songs died on the air.

1848   1862

Song

When I am dead, my dearest,
 Sing no sad songs for me;
Plant thou no roses at my head,
 Nor shady cypress tree:
5 Be the green grass above me
  With showers and dewdrops wet;
And if thou wilt, remember,
  And if thou wilt, forget.

I shall not see the shadows,
10 I shall not feel the rain;
I shall not hear the nightingale
  Sing on, as if in pain:
And dreaming through the twilight
  That doth not rise nor set,
15 Haply° I may remember,   *perhaps*
  And haply may forget.

1848   1862

Remember

Remember me when I am gone away,
   Gone far away into the silent land;
   When you can no more hold me by the hand,
Nor I half turn to go yet turning stay.
5   Remember me when no more day by day
   You tell me of our future that you planned:
   Only remember me; you understand
It will be late to counsel then or pray.
Yet if you should forget me for a while
10   And afterwards remember, do not grieve:
     For if the darkness and corruption leave
     A vestige of the thoughts that once I had,
Better by far you should forget and smile
     Than that you should remember and be sad.

1849   1862

After Death

The curtains were half drawn, the floor was swept
   And strewn with rushes, rosemary and may[1]
   Lay thick upon the bed on which I lay,
Where thro' the lattice ivy-shadows crept.
5   He leaned above me, thinking that I slept
   And could not hear him; but I heard him say:
   "Poor child, poor child:" and as he turned away
Came a deep silence, and I knew he wept.
He did not touch the shroud, or raise the fold
10   That hid my face, or take my hand in his,
     Or ruffle the smooth pillows for my head:
     He did not love me living; but once dead
He pitied me; and very sweet it is
     To know he still is warm tho' I am cold.

1849   1862

A Pause

They made the chamber sweet with flowers and leaves,
   And the bed sweet with flowers on which I lay;
   While my soul, love-bound, loitered on its way.
I did not hear the birds about the eaves,
5   Nor hear the reapers talk among the sheaves:
   Only my soul kept watch from day to day,
   My thirsty soul kept watch for one away:—
Perhaps he loves, I thought, remembers, grieves.
At length there came the step upon the stair,

---

1. Flowers traditionally associated with death.

10   Upon the lock the old familiar hand:
      Then first my spirit seemed to scent the air
          Of Paradise; then first the tardy sand
      Of time ran golden; and I felt my hair
          Put on a glory, and my soul expand.

1853   1896

Echo

      Come to me in the silence of the night;
          Come in the speaking silence of a dream;
      Come with soft rounded cheeks and eyes as bright
          As sunlight on a stream;
5   Come back in tears,
      O memory, hope, love of finished years.

      Oh dream how sweet, too sweet, too bitter sweet,
          Whose wakening should have been in Paradise,
      Where souls brimfull of love abide and meet;
10   Where thirsting longing eyes
              Watch the slow door
      That opening, letting in, lets out no more.

      Yet come to me in dreams, that I may live
          My very life again tho' cold in death:
15   Come back to me in dreams, that I may give
          Pulse for pulse, breath for breath:
              Speak low, lean low,
      As long ago, my love, how long ago.

1854   1862

Dead Before Death

      Ah! changed and cold, how changed and very cold!
          With stiffened smiling lips and cold calm eyes:
          Changed, yet the same; much knowing, little wise;
      This was the promise of the days of old!
5   Grown hard and stubborn in the ancient mould,
          Grown rigid in the sham of lifelong lies:
      We hoped for better things as years would rise,
      But it is over as a tale once told.
      All fallen the blossom that no fruitage bore,
10   All lost the present and the future time,
      All lost, all lost, the lapse that went before:
      So lost till death shut-to the opened door,
          So lost from chime to everlasting chime,
      So cold and lost for ever evermore.

1854   1862

Cobwebs

It is a land with neither night nor day,
   Nor heat nor cold, nor any wind, nor rain,
   Nor hills nor valleys; but one even plain
Stretches thro' long unbroken miles away:
5 While thro' the sluggish air a twilight grey
   Broodeth; no moons or seasons wax and wane,
   No ebb and flow are there along the main,
No bud-time no leaf-falling there for aye,
No ripple on the sea, no shifting sand,
10   No beat of wings to stir the stagnant space,
No pulse of life thro' all the loveless land:
And loveless sea; no trace of days before,
No guarded home, no toil-won restingplace
No future hope no fear for evermore.

1855   1896

A Triad

Three sang of love together: one with lips
   Crimson, with cheeks and bosom in a glow,
Flushed to the yellow hair and finger tips;
   And one there sang who soft and smooth as snow
5   Bloomed like a tinted hyacinth at a show;
And one was blue with famine after love,
   Who like a harpstring snapped rang harsh and low
The burden of what those were singing of.
One shamed herself in love; one temperately
10   Grew gross in soulless love, a sluggish wife;
One famished died for love. Thus two of three
   Took death for love and won him after strife;
One droned in sweetness like a fattened bee:
   All on the threshold, yet all short of life.

1856   1862

In an Artist's Studio

One face looks out from all his canvasses,[1]
   One selfsame figure sits or walks or leans;
   We found her hidden just behind those screens,
That mirror gave back all her loveliness.
5   A queen in opal or in ruby dress,
   A nameless girl in freshest summer greens,
A saint, an angel;—every canvass means
The same one meaning, neither more nor less.
He feeds upon her face by day and night,

---

1. Christina's brother, William Michael Rossetti, wrote: "The reference is apparently to our brother's studio, and to his constantly repeated heads of the lady whom he afterwards married, Miss Siddal."

10   And she with true kind eyes looks back on him
     Fair as the moon and joyful as the light:
       Not wan with waiting, not with sorrow dim;
     Not as she is, but was when hope shone bright;
       Not as she is, but as she fills his dream.

1856   1896

A Birthday

My heart is like a singing bird
  Whose nest is in a watered shoot;
My heart is like an apple tree
  Whose boughs are bent with thickset fruit;
5 My heart is like a rainbow shell
   That paddles in a halcyon° sea;   *serene*
My heart is gladder than all these
  Because my love is come to me.

Raise me a dais[1] of silk and down;
10   Hang it with vair[2] and purple dyes;
Carve it in doves and pomegranates,
   And peacocks with a hundred eyes;
Work it in gold and silver grapes,
   In leaves and silver fleurs-de-lys;
15 Because the birthday of my life
   Is come, my love is come to me.

1857   1861

An Apple-Gathering

I plucked pink blossoms from mine apple tree
  And wore them all that evening in my hair:
Then in due season when I went to see
  I found no apples there.

5 With dangling basket all along the grass
   As I had come I went the selfsame track:
My neighbours mocked me while they saw me pass
   So empty-handed back.

Lilian and Lilias smiled in trudging by,
10   Their heaped-up basket teazed me like a jeer;
Sweet-voiced they sang beneath the sunset sky,
   Their mother's home was near.

Plump Gertrude passed me with her basket full,
   A stronger hand than hers helped it along;
15 A voice talked with her thro' the shadows cool
   More sweet to me than song.

---

1. A platform for a throne or seat of honor.   2. A gray and white squirrel whose fur was highly prized.

Ah Willie, Willie, was my love less worth
    Than apples with their green leaves piled above?
I counted rosiest apples on the earth
20   Of far less worth than love.

So once it was with me you stooped to talk
    Laughing and listening in this very lane:
To think that by this way we used to walk
    We shall not walk again!

25 I let my neighbours pass me, ones and twos
    And groups; the latest said the night grew chill,
And hastened: but I loitered, while the dews
    Fell fast I loitered still.

1857   1862

Winter: My Secret

I tell my secret? No indeed, not I:
Perhaps some day, who knows?
But not today; it froze, and blows, and snows,
And you're too curious: fie!
5 You want to hear it? well:
Only, my secret's mine, and I won't tell.

Or, after all, perhaps there's none:
Suppose there is no secret after all,
But only just my fun.
10 Today's a nipping day, a biting day;
In which one wants a shawl,
A veil, a cloak, and other wraps:
I cannot ope to every one who taps,
And let the draughts come whistling thro' my hall;
15 Come bounding and surrounding me,
Come buffeting, astounding me,
Nipping and clipping thro' my wraps and all.
I wear my mask for warmth: who ever shows
His nose to Russian snows
20 To be pecked at by every wind that blows?
You would not peck? I thank you for good will,
Believe, but leave that truth untested still.

Spring's an expansive time: yet I don't trust
March with its peck of dust,
25 Nor April with its rainbow-crowned brief showers,
Nor even May, whose flowers
One frost may wither thro' the sunless hours.

Perhaps some languid summer day,
When drowsy birds sing less and less,
30 And golden fruit is ripening to excess,

If there's not too much sun nor too much cloud,
And the warm wind is neither still nor loud,
Perhaps my secret I may say,
Or you may guess.

1857   1862

Up-Hill

Does the road wind up-hill all the way?
    Yes, to the very end.
Will the day's journey take the whole long day?
    From morn to night, my friend.

5   But is there for the night a resting-place?
    A roof for when the slow dark hours begin.
May not the darkness hide it from my face?
    You cannot miss that inn.

Shall I meet other wayfarers at night?
10   Those who have gone before.
Then must I knock, or call when just in sight?
    They will not keep you standing at that door.

Shall I find comfort, travel-sore and weak?
    Of labour you shall find the sum.
15   Will there be beds for me and all who seek?
    Yea, beds for all who come.

1858   1862

Goblin Market

Morning and evening
Maids heard the goblins cry:
"Come buy our orchard fruits,
Come buy, come buy:
5   Apples and quinces,
Lemons and oranges,
Plump unpecked cherries,
Melons and raspberries,
Bloom-down-cheeked peaches,
10   Swart°-headed mulberries,   *dark*
Wild free-born cranberries,
Crab-apples, dewberries,
Pine-apples, blackberries,
Apricots, strawberries;—
15   All ripe together
In summer weather,—
Morns that pass by,
Fair eves that fly;
Come buy, come buy:
20   Our grapes fresh from the vine,

"Buy from us with @ golden curl"

Dante Gabriel Rossetti, frontispiece to the first edition of Christina Rossetti's *Goblin Market*, 1862.

Pomegranates full and fine,
Dates and sharp bullaces,
Rare pears and greengages,
Damsons[1] and bilberries,
25   Taste them and try:
Currants and gooseberries,
Bright-fire-like barberries,
Figs to fill your mouth,
Citrons from the South,
30   Sweet to tongue and sound to eye;
Come buy, come buy."

Evening by evening
Among the brookside rushes,
Laura bowed her head to hear,
35   Lizzie veiled her blushes:
Crouching close together
In the cooling weather,
With clasping arms and cautioning lips,

1. Bullaces, greengages, and damsons are types of plums.

With tingling cheeks and finger tips.
40   "Lie close," Laura said,
Pricking up her golden head:
"We must not look at goblin men,
We must not buy their fruits:
Who knows upon what soil they fed
45   Their hungry thirsty roots?"
"Come buy," call the goblins
Hobbling down the glen.
"Oh," cried Lizzie, "Laura, Laura,
You should not peep at goblin men."
50   Lizzie covered up her eyes,
Covered close lest they should look;
Laura reared her glossy head,
And whispered like the restless brook:
"Look, Lizzie, look, Lizzie,
55   Down the glen tramp little men.
One hauls a basket,
One bears a plate,
One lugs a golden dish
Of many pounds weight.
60   How fair the vine must grow
Whose grapes are so luscious;
How warm the wind must blow
Thro' those fruit bushes."
"No," said Lizzie: "No, no, no;
65   Their offers should not charm us,
Their evil gifts would harm us."
She thrust a dimpled finger
In each ear, shut eyes and ran:
Curious Laura chose to linger
70   Wondering at each merchant man.
One had a cat's face,
One whisked a tail,
One tramped at a rat's pace,
One crawled like a snail,
75   One like a wombat prowled obtuse and furry,
One like a ratel[2] tumbled hurry skurry.
She heard a voice like voice of doves
Cooing all together:
They sounded kind and full of loves
80   In the pleasant weather.

Laura stretched her gleaming neck
Like a rush-imbedded swan,
Like a lily from the beck,°   *brook*
Like a moonlit poplar branch,

2. A tropical badgerlike nocturnal animal (pronounced "ray-tell").

85   Like a vessel at the launch
        When its last restraint is gone.

        Backwards up the mossy glen
        Turned and trooped the goblin men,
        With their shrill repeated cry,
90   "Come buy, come buy."
        When they reached where Laura was
        They stood stock still upon the moss,
        Leering at each other,
        Brother with queer brother;
95   Signalling each other,
        Brother with sly brother.
        One set his basket down,
        One reared his plate;
        One began to weave a crown
100   Of tendrils, leaves and rough nuts brown
        (Men sell not such in any town);
        One heaved the golden weight
        Of dish and fruit to offer her:
        "Come buy, come buy," was still their cry.
105   Laura stared but did not stir,
        Longed but had no money:
        The whisk-tailed merchant bade her taste
        In tones as smooth as honey,
        The cat-faced purr'd,
110   The rat-paced spoke a word
        Of welcome, and the snail-paced even was heard;
        One parrot-voiced and jolly
        Cried "Pretty Goblin" still for "Pretty Polly;"—
        One whistled like a bird.

115   But sweet-tooth Laura spoke in haste:
        "Good folk, I have no coin;
        To take were to purloin:
        I have no copper in my purse,
        I have no silver either,
120   And all my gold is on the furze³
        That shakes in windy weather
        Above the rusty heather."
        "You have much gold upon your head,"
        They answered all together:
125   "Buy from us with a golden curl."
        She clipped a precious golden lock,
        She dropped a tear more rare than pearl,
        Then sucked their fruit globes fair or red:
        Sweeter than honey from the rock.

3. An evergreen shrub that grows on the heath.

130 Stronger than man-rejoicing wine,
 Clearer than water flowed that juice;
 She never tasted such before,
 How should it cloy with length of use?
 She sucked and sucked and sucked the more
135 Fruits which that unknown orchard bore;
 She sucked until her lips were sore;
 Then flung the emptied rinds away
 But gathered up one kernel-stone,
 And knew not was it night or day
140 As she turned home alone.

 Lizzie met her at the gate
 Full of wise upbraidings:
 "Dear, you should not stay so late,
 Twilight is not good for maidens;
145 Should not loiter in the glen
 In the haunts of goblin men.
 Do you not remember Jeanie,
 How she met them in the moonlight,
 Took their gifts both choice and many,
150 Ate their fruits and wore their flowers
 Plucked from bowers
 Where summer ripens at all hours?
 But ever in the noonlight
 She pined and pined away;
155 Sought them by night and day,
 Found them no more but dwindled and grew grey;
 Then fell with the first snow,
 While to this day no grass will grow
 Where she lies low:
160 I planted daisies there a year ago
 That never blow.
 You should not loiter so."
 "Nay, hush," said Laura:
 "Nay, hush, my sister:
165 I ate and ate my fill,
 Yet my mouth waters still;
 Tomorrow night I will
 Buy more:" and kissed her:
 "Have done with sorrow;
170 I'll bring you plums tomorrow
 Fresh on their mother twigs,
 Cherries worth getting;
 You cannot think what figs
 My teeth have met in,
175 What melons icy-cold
 Piled on a dish of gold
 Too huge for me to hold,
 What peaches with a velvet nap,

Pellucid° grapes without one seed: *translucent*
180   Odorous indeed must be the mead
      Whereon they grow, and pure the wave they drink
      With lilies at the brink,
      And sugar-sweet their sap."

      Golden head by golden head,
185   Like two pigeons in one nest
      Folded in each other's wings,
      They lay down in their curtained bed:
      Like two blossoms on one stem,
      Like two flakes of new-fall'n snow,
190   Like two wands of ivory
      Tipped with gold for awful° kings.   *awe-inspiring*
      Moon and stars gazed in at them,
      Wind sang to them lullaby,
      Lumbering owls forbore to fly,
195   Not a bat flapped to and fro
      Round their rest:
      Cheek to cheek and breast to breast
      Locked together in one nest.

      Early in the morning
200   When the first cock crowed his warning,
      Neat like bees, as sweet and busy,
      Laura rose with Lizzie:
      Fetched in honey, milked the cows,
      Aired and set to rights the house,
205   Kneaded cakes of whitest wheat,
      Cakes for dainty mouths to eat,
      Next churned butter, whipped up cream,
      Fed their poultry, sat and sewed;
      Talked as modest maidens should:
210   Lizzie with an open heart,
      Laura in an absent dream,
      One content, one sick in part;
      One warbling for the mere bright day's delight,
      One longing for the night.

215   At length slow evening came:
      They went with pitchers to the reedy brook;
      Lizzie most placid in her look,
      Laura most like a leaping flame.
      They drew the gurgling water from its deep;
220   Lizzie plucked purple and rich golden flags,
      Then turning homewards said: "The sunset flushes
      Those furthest loftiest crags;
      Come, Laura, not another maiden lags,
      No wilful squirrel wags,
225   The beasts and birds are fast asleep."

But Laura loitered still among the rushes
And said the bank was steep.

And said the hour was early still,
The dew not fall'n, the wind not chill:
230   Listening ever, but not catching
The customary cry,
"Come buy, come buy,"
With its iterated jingle
Of sugar-baited words:
235   Not for all her watching
Once discerning even one goblin
Racing, whisking, tumbling, hobbling;
Let alone the herds
That used to tramp along the glen,
240   In groups or single,
Of brisk fruit-merchant men.
Till Lizzie urged, "O Laura, come;
I hear the fruit-call but I dare not look:
You should not loiter longer at this brook:
245   Come with me home.
The stars rise, the moon bends her arc,
Each glowworm winks her spark,
Let us get home before the night grows dark:
For clouds may gather
250   Tho' this is summer weather,
Put out the lights and drench us thro';
Then if we lost our way what should we do?"

Laura turned cold as stone
To find her sister heard that cry alone,
255   That goblin cry,
"Come buy our fruits, come buy."
Must she then buy no more such dainty fruit?
Must she no more such succous° pasture find,   *juicy*
Gone deaf and blind?
260   Her tree of life drooped from the root:
She said not one word in her heart's sore ache;
But peering thro' the dimness, nought discerning,
Trudged home, her pitcher dripping all the way;
So crept to bed, and lay
265   Silent till Lizzie slept;
Then sat up in a passionate yearning,
And gnashed her teeth for baulked desire, and wept
As if her heart would break.

Day after day, night after night,
270   Laura kept watch in vain
In sullen silence of exceeding pain.
She never caught again the goblin cry:

"Come buy, come buy;"—
She never spied the goblin men
275   Hawking their fruits along the glen:
But when the noon waxed bright
Her hair grew thin and gray;
She dwindled, as the fair full moon doth turn
To swift decay and burn
280   Her fire away.

One day remembering her kernel-stone
She set it by a wall that faced the south;
Dewed it with tears, hoped for a root,
Watched for a waxing shoot,
285   But there came none;
It never saw the sun,
It never felt the trickling moisture run:
While with sunk eyes and faded mouth
She dreamed of melons, as a traveller sees
290   False waves in desert drouth
With shade of leaf-crowned trees,
And burns the thirstier in the sandful breeze.

She no more swept the house,
Tended the fowls or cows,
295   Fetched honey, kneaded cakes of wheat,
Brought water from the brook:
But sat down listless in the chimney-nook
And would not eat.

Tender Lizzie could not bear
300   To watch her sister's cankerous° care   *festering*
Yet not to share.
She night and morning
Caught the goblins' cry:
"Come buy our orchard fruits,
305   Come buy, come buy:"—
Beside the brook, along the glen,
She heard the tramp of goblin men,
The voice and stir
Poor Laura could not hear;
310   Longed to buy fruit to comfort her,
But feared to pay too dear.
She thought of Jeanie in her grave,
Who should have been a bride;
But who for joys brides hope to have
315   Fell sick and died
In her gay prime,
In earliest Winter time,
With the first glazing rime,
With the first snow-fall of crisp Winter time.

320   Till Laura dwindling
        Seemed knocking at Death's door:
        Then Lizzie weighed no more
        Better and worse;
        But put a silver penny in her purse,
325   Kissed Laura, crossed the heath with clumps of furze
        At twilight, halted by the brook:
        And for the first time in her life
        Began to listen and look.

        Laughed every goblin
330   When they spied her peeping:
        Came towards her hobbling,
        Flying, running, leaping,
        Puffing and blowing,
        Chuckling, clapping, crowing,
335   Clucking and gobbling,
        Mopping and mowing,
        Full of airs and graces,
        Pulling wry faces,
        Demure grimaces,
340   Cat-like and rat-like,
        Ratel- and wombat-like,
        Snail-paced in a hurry,
        Parrot-voiced and whistler,
        Helter skelter, hurry skurry,
345   Chattering like magpies,
        Fluttering like pigeons,
        Gliding like fishes,—
        Hugged her and kissed her,
        Squeezed and caressed her:
350   Stretched up their dishes,
        Panniers, and plates:
        "Look at our apples
        Russet and dun,
        Bob at our cherries,
355   Bite at our peaches,
        Citrons and dates,
        Grapes for the asking,
        Pears red with basking
        Out in the sun,
360   Plums on their twigs;
        Pluck them and suck them,
        Pomegranates, figs."—

        "Good folk," said Lizzie,
        Mindful of Jeanie:
365   "Give me much and many:"—
        Held out her apron,

Tossed them her penny.
"Nay, take a seat with us,
Honour and eat with us,"
370   They answered grinning:
"Our feast is but beginning.
Night yet is early,
Warm and dew-pearly,
Wakeful and starry:
375   Such fruits as these
No man can carry;
Half their bloom would fly,
Half their dew would dry,
Half their flavour would pass by.
380   Sit down and feast with us,
Be welcome guest with us,
Cheer you and rest with us."—
"Thank you," said Lizzie: "But one waits
At home alone for me:
385   So without further parleying,
If you will not sell me any
Of your fruits tho' much and many,
Give me back my silver penny
I tossed you for a fee."—
390   They began to scratch their pates,
No longer wagging, purring,
But visibly demurring,
Grunting and snarling.
One called her proud,
395   Cross-grained, uncivil;
Their tones waxed loud,
Their looks were evil.
Lashing their tails
They trod and hustled her,
400   Elbowed and jostled her,
Clawed with their nails,
Barking, mewing, hissing, mocking,
Tore her gown and soiled her stocking,
Twitched her hair out by the roots,
405   Stamped upon her tender feet,
Held her hands and squeezed their fruits
Against her mouth to make her eat.
White and golden Lizzie stood,
Like a lily in a flood,—
410   Like a rock of blue-veined stone
Lashed by tides obstreperously,—
Like a beacon left alone
In a hoary roaring sea,
Sending up a golden fire,—
415   Like a fruit-crowned orange-tree

White with blossoms honey-sweet
Sore beset by wasp and bee,—
Like a royal virgin town
Topped with gilded dome and spire
420   Close beleaguered by a fleet
Mad to tug her standard down.

One may lead a horse to water,
Twenty cannot make him drink.
Tho' the goblins cuffed and caught her,
425   Coaxed and fought her,
Bullied and besought her,
Scratched her, pinched her black as ink,
Kicked and knocked her,
Mauled and mocked her,
430   Lizzie uttered not a word;
Would not open lip from lip
Lest they should cram a mouthful in:
But laughed in heart to feel the drip
Of juice that syrupped all her face,
435   And lodged in dimples of her chin,
And streaked her neck which quaked like curd.
At last the evil people
Worn out by her resistance
Flung back her penny, kicked their fruit
440   Along whichever road they took,
Not leaving root or stone or shoot;
Some writhed into the ground,
Some dived into the brook
With ring and ripple,
445   Some scudded on the gale without a sound,
Some vanished in the distance.
In a smart, ache, tingle,
Lizzie went her way;
Knew not was it night or day;
450   Sprang up the bank, tore thro' the furze,
Threaded copse and dingle,
And heard her penny jingle
Bouncing in her purse,
Its bounce was music to her ear.
455   She ran and ran
As if she feared some goblin man
Dogged her with gibe or curse
Or something worse:
But not one goblin skurried after,
460   Nor was she pricked by fear;
The kind heart made her windy-paced
That urged her home quite out of breath with haste
And inward laughter.

She cried "Laura," up the garden,
465 "Did you miss me?
Come and kiss me.
Never mind my bruises,
Hug me, kiss me, suck my juices
Squeezed from goblin fruits for you,
470 Goblin pulp and goblin dew.
Eat me, drink me, love me;
Laura, make much of me:
For your sake I have braved the glen
And had to do with goblin merchant men."

475 Laura started from her chair,
Flung her arms up in the air,
Clutched her hair:
"Lizzie, Lizzie, have you tasted
For my sake the fruit forbidden?
480 Must your light like mine be hidden,
Your young life like mine be wasted,
Undone in mine undoing
And ruined in my ruin,
Thirsty, cankered, goblin-ridden?"—
485 She clung about her sister,
Kissed and kissed and kissed her:
Tears once again
Refreshed her shrunken eyes,
Dropping like rain
490 After long sultry drouth;
Shaking with aguish fear, and pain,
She kissed and kissed her with a hungry mouth.

Her lips began to scorch,
That juice was wormwood to her tongue,
495 She loathed the feast:
Writhing as one possessed she leaped and sung,
Rent all her robe, and wrung
Her hands in lamentable haste,
And beat her breast.
500 Her locks streamed like the torch
Borne by a racer at full speed,
Or like the mane of horses in their flight,
Or like an eagle when she stems° the light   *makes headway against*
Straight toward the sun,
505 Or like a caged thing freed,
Or like a flying flag when armies run.

Swift fire spread thro' her veins, knocked at her heart,
Met the fire smouldering there
And overbore its lesser flame;
510 She gorged on bitterness without a name:

Ah! fool, to choose such part
Of soul-consuming care!
Sense failed in the mortal strife:
Like the watch-tower of a town

515   Which an earthquake shatters down,
Like a lightning-stricken mast,
Like a wind-uprooted tree
Spun about,
Like a foam-topped waterspout

520   Cast down headlong in the sea,
She fell at last;
Pleasure past and anguish past,
Is it death or is it life?

Life out of death.

525   That night long Lizzie watched by her,
Counted her pulse's flagging stir,
Felt for her breath,
Held water to her lips, and cooled her face
With tears and fanning leaves:

530   But when the first birds chirped about their eaves,
And early reapers plodded to the place
Of golden sheaves,
And dew-wet grass
Bowed in the morning winds so brisk to pass,

535   And new buds with new day
Opened of cup-like lilies on the stream,
Laura awoke as from a dream,
Laughed in the innocent old way,
Hugged Lizzie but not twice or thrice;

540   Her gleaming locks showed not one thread of grey,
Her breath was sweet as May
And light danced in her eyes.

Days, weeks, months, years
Afterwards, when both were wives

545   With children of their own;
Their mother-hearts beset with fears,
Their lives bound up in tender lives;
Laura would call the little ones
And tell them of her early prime,

550   Those pleasant days long gone
Of not-returning time:
Would talk about the haunted glen,
The wicked, quaint fruit-merchant men,
Their fruits like honey to the throat

555   But poison in the blood;
(Men sell not such in any town:)
Would tell them how her sister stood
In deadly peril to do her good,

And win the fiery antidote:
560   Then joining hands to little hands
Would bid them cling together,
"For there is no friend like a sister
In calm or stormy weather;
To cheer one on the tedious way,
565   To fetch one if one goes astray,
To lift one if one totters down,
To strengthen whilst one stands."

1859   1862

"No, Thank You, John"

I never said I loved you, John:
    Why will you teaze me day by day,
And wax a weariness to think upon
    With always "do" and "pray"?

5   You know I never loved you, John;
    No fault of mine made me your toast:
Why will you haunt me with a face as wan
    As shows an hour-old ghost?

I dare say Meg or Moll would take
10   Pity upon you, if you'd ask:
And pray don't remain single for my sake
    Who can't perform that task.

I have no heart?—Perhaps I have not;
    But then you're mad to take offence
15   That I don't give you what I have not got:
    Use your own common sense.

Let bygones be bygones:
    Don't call me false, who owed not to be true:
I'd rather answer "No" to fifty Johns
20   Than answer "Yes" to you.

Let's mar our pleasant days no more,
    Song-birds of passage, days of youth:
Catch at today, forget the days before:
    I'll wink at your untruth.

25   Let us strike hands as hearty friends;
    No more, no less; and friendship's good:
Only don't keep in view ulterior ends,
    And points not understood

In open treaty. Rise above
30   Quibbles and shuffling off and on:

Here's friendship for you if you like; but love,—
    No, thank you, John.

1860   1862

Promises Like Pie-Crust[1]

Promise me no promises,
    So will I not promise you;
Keep we both our liberties,
    Never false and never true:
5   Let us hold the die uncast,
    Free to come as free to go;
For I cannot know your past,
    And of mine what can you know?

You, so warm, may once have been
10   Warmer towards another one;
I, so cold, may once have seen
    Sunlight, once have felt the sun:
Who shall show us if it was
    Thus indeed in time of old?
15   Fades the image from the glass
    And the fortune is not told.

If you promised, you might grieve
    For lost liberty again;
If I promised, I believe
20   I should fret to break the chain:
Let us be the friends we were,
    Nothing more but nothing less;
Many thrive on frugal fare
    Who would perish of excess.

1861   1896

In Progress

Ten years ago it seemed impossible
    That she should ever grow so calm as this,
    With self-remembrance in her warmest kiss
And dim dried eyes like an exhausted well.
5   Slow-speaking when she has some fact to tell,
    Silent with long-unbroken silences,
    Centred in self yet not unpleased to please,
Gravely monotonous like a passing bell.

Mindful of drudging daily common things,
10   Patient at pastime, patient at her work,
Wearied perhaps but strenuous certainly.

1. English proverb: "Promises are like pie-crust, made to be broken."

Sometimes I fancy we may one day see
    Her head shoot forth seven stars from where they lurk
And her eyes lightnings and her shoulders wings.

1862   1896

What Would I Give?

What would I give for a heart of flesh to warm me thro',
Instead of this heart of stone ice-cold whatever I do;
Hard and cold and small, of all hearts the worst of all.

What would I give for words, if only words would come;
5   But now in its misery my spirit has fallen dumb:
O merry friends, go your way, I have never a word to say.

What would I give for tears, not smiles but scalding tears,
To wash the black mark clean, and to thaw the frost of years,
To wash the stain ingrain and to make me clean again.

1864   1866

A Life's Parallels

Never on this side of the grave again,
    On this side of the river,
On this side of the garner of the grain,
    Never,—

5   Ever while time flows on and on and on,
    That narrow noiseless river,
Ever while corn bows heavy-headed, wan,
    Ever,—

Never despairing, often fainting, rueing,°   *regretting*
10   But looking back, ah never!
Faint yet pursuing, faint yet still pursuing
    Ever.

                                                                                    1881

from Later Life
17

Something this foggy day, a something which
    Is neither of this fog nor of today,
    Has set me dreaming of the winds that play
Past certain cliffs, along one certain beach,
5   And turn the topmost edge of waves to spray:
    Ah pleasant pebbly strand so far away,
So out of reach while quite within my reach,
    As out of reach as India or Cathay!°   *China*
I am sick of where I am and where I am not,
10   I am sick of foresight and of memory,
    I am sick of all I have and all I see,

I am sick of self, and there is nothing new;
Oh weary impatient patience of my lot!—
Thus with myself: how fares it, Friends, with you?

1881

Sleeping at Last

Sleeping at last, the trouble & tumult over,
Sleeping at last, the struggle & horror past,
Cold & white out of sight of friend & of lover
Sleeping at last.

5   No more a tired heart downcast or overcast,
No more pangs that wring or shifting fears that hover,
Sleeping at last in a dreamless sleep locked fast.

Fast asleep. Singing birds in their leafy cover
Cannot wake her, nor shake her the gusty blast.
10   Under the purple thyme & the purple clover
Sleeping at last.

c. 1893   1896

William Morris
1834–1896

William Morris personified the Victorian fascination with medievalism. As a child he rode his pony dressed in a little suit of armor, and devoured Sir Walter Scott's novels about knights and chivalry. Later he came under the spell of Pugin's *Contrasts*, Carlyle's *Past and Present,* and Ruskin's essay *The Nature of Gothic*. Morris succeeded in a multitude of roles—poet and prose writer, artist, designer, craftsman, printer, political reformer—and his many endeavors were united by his strong distaste for the nineteenth century and his romantic yearning to recapture the lost beauty, harmony, and sense of community of the Middle Ages.

Morris's first book of poems, *The Defence of Guenevere and Other Poems* (1858), was a disaster in the eyes of the critics, yet it contains some of his best and most vivid poetry. His portrait of King Arthur's queen is powerful and sympathetic: while tied to the stake awaiting execution for adultery, Guenevere delivers a proud and passionate protest to her accusers. Her erotic energy is striking, especially in an era that idealized languid sexless women.

Morris's later verse continued to be set in the past, whether the classical world, as in *The Life and Death of Jason* (1867), or the medieval world, in *The Earthly Paradise* (1868). These books established his reputation as a poet—he was nearly chosen as Poet Laureate following Tennyson's death in 1892—while offering a seductive invitation to escape the evils of contemporary life: "Forget six counties overhung with smoke, / Forget the snorting steam and piston stroke, / Forget the spreading of the hideous town. . . . "

Morris was strongly influenced by the painting and poetry of the Pre-Raphaelite Brotherhood, particularly that of Dante Gabriel Rossetti. In 1859 the upper-class, Oxford-educated Morris married one of Rossetti's models, Jane Burden, a stableman's daughter legendary for her stunning beauty. As he struggled to paint his portrait of her as Queen Guenevere (see Color

Plate 16), he scrawled on the canvas, "I cannot paint you, but I love you." The restless, voluble husband and famously silent wife were opposites in many ways, and they had a troubled marriage, exacerbated by her long love affair with Rossetti.

In 1861 Morris helped found "The Firm" of Morris & Co. and began designing furniture, stained glass, tapestries, wallpapers, and textiles. Appalled by the hideously ornate taste of the period, Morris became the central figure of the British "Arts and Crafts" movement, which revolutionized the decorative arts. His pioneering designs, inspired by medieval motifs, were linked to his larger social and political vision, for he shared Ruskin's aim of copying nature faithfully and respecting the artistic freedom of the individual workman. In *The Beauty of Life*, a lecture delivered in 1880, Morris issued his memorable dictum: "Have nothing in your houses which you do not know to be useful or believe to be beautiful." His designs are still popular today, and the magnificent stained glass windows he created along with Rossetti, Ford Madox Brown, and Edward Burne-Jones can still be seen in numerous English churches.

Morris left his mark on the era in a remarkable number of ways. Enthusiastic about Iceland and its sagas, he learned the language, visited the country twice, and became the leading English translator of Icelandic literature. Dedicated to preserving Britain's architectural heritage from overzealous "restoration," he established the Society for the Protection of Ancient Buildings. And in 1890 he founded the Kelmscott Press, reviving the art of book decoration and printing sumptuous editions of *The Canterbury Tales* and other English classics.

Ultimately Morris's opposition to the age in which he lived led him to turn his prodigious energies to politics, and in the 1880s he became a leader of the British socialist movement. He was well aware of the irony that his politics were a rebellion against his own class, yet his private wealth had given him the freedom to pursue his numerous interests. Fervently dedicated to the cause, he lectured, organized, and wrote socialist essays, songs, and poems. In 1890 he published *News from Nowhere*, a futuristic fantasy in which London becomes an ideal pastoral community, and mechanization gives way to medieval-style handicrafts.

Morris's ideas were a mixture of socialism and medievalism, romanticism and utopianism. His diverse achievements were united by a concern for how best to live: how to design simple and beautiful objects for daily use, how to organize society for the good of the whole community, how to write literature that proposes an alternative vision to the ugliness and greed of nineteenth-century capitalist Britain.

The Defence of Guenevere[1]

> But, knowing now that they would have her speak,
> She threw her wet hair backward from her brow,
> Her hand close to her mouth touching her cheek,
>
> As though she had had there a shameful blow,
> 5   And feeling it shameful to feel aught but shame
> All through her heart, yet felt her cheek burned so,
>
> She must a little touch it; like one lame
> She walked away from Gauwaine,[2] with her head
> Still lifted up; and on her cheek of flame

1. The poem is based on Thomas Malory's *Morte D'Arthur* (1470), which describes the conflict that arises in the legendary kingdom of Arthur when Queen Guenevere and Sir Launcelot are suspected of adultery. Malory does not depict Guenevere on trial for her life; this is Morris's own invention. Chained to the stake, she speaks in passionate self-defense, revealing strengths and weaknesses of character in a manner that recalls Browning's dramatic monologues. Guenevere also takes the offensive, seeking to sway her judges with an array of rhetorical tactics, including analogy, autobiography, counter-accusation, appeals for sympathy and empathy, sophistry, and physical gestures.

2. Arthur's nephew, and a knight of the Round Table, Gauwaine was one of the chief accusers of Guenevere and Launcelot.

10   The tears dried quick; she stopped at last and said:
      "O knights and lords, it seems but little skill°   use
      To talk of well-known things past now and dead.

      "God wot° I ought to say, I have done ill,   knows
      And pray you all forgiveness heartily!
15   Because you must be right, such great lords—still

      "Listen, suppose your time were come to die,
      And you were quite alone and very weak;
      Yea, laid a dying while very mightily

      "The wind was ruffling up the narrow streak
20   Of river through your broad lands running well:
      Suppose a hush should come, then some one speak:

      " 'One of these cloths is heaven, and one is hell,
      Now choose one cloth for ever; which they be,
      I will not tell you, you must somehow tell

25   " 'Of your own strength and mightiness; here, see!'
      Yea, yea, my lord, and you to ope your eyes,
      At foot of your familiar bed to see

      "A great God's angel standing, with such dyes,°   colors
      Not known on earth, on his great wings, and hands
30   Held out two ways, light from the inner skies

      "Showing him well, and making his commands
      Seem to be God's commands, moreover, too,
      Holding within his hands the cloths on wands;

      "And one of these strange choosing cloths was blue,
35   Wavy and long, and one cut short and red;
      No man could tell the better of the two.

      "After a shivering half-hour you said:
      'God help! heaven's colour, the blue;' and he said: 'hell.'
      Perhaps you then would roll upon your bed,

40   "And cry to all good men that loved you well,
      'Ah Christ! if only I had known, known, known;'
      Launcelot went away, then I could tell,

      "Like wisest man how all things would be, moan,
      And roll and hurt myself, and long to die,
45   And yet fear much to die for what was sown.

      "Nevertheless you, O Sir Gauwaine, lie,
      Whatever may have happened through these years,
      God knows I speak truth, saying that you lie."

      Her voice was low at first, being full of tears,
50   But as it cleared, it grew full loud and shrill,
      Growing a windy shriek in all men's ears,

A ringing in their startled brains, until
She said that Gauwaine lied, then her voice sunk,
And her great eyes began again to fill,

55   Though still she stood right up, and never shrunk,
But spoke on bravely, glorious lady fair!
Whatever tears her full lips may have drunk,

She stood, and seemed to think, and wrung her hair,
Spoke out at last with no more trace of shame,
60   With passionate twisting of her body there:

"It chanced upon a day that Launcelot came
To dwell at Arthur's court: at Christmas-time
This happened; when the heralds sung his name,

"'Son of King Ban of Benwick,'³ seemed to chime
65   Along with all the bells that rang that day,
O'er the white roofs, with little change of rhyme.

"Christmas and whitened winter passed away,
And over me the April sunshine came,
Made very awful with black hail-clouds, yea

70   "And in the Summer I grew white with flame,
And bowed my head down—Autumn, and the sick
Sure knowledge things would never be the same,

"However often Spring might be most thick
Of blossoms and buds, smote on me, and I grew
75   Careless of most things, let the clock tick, tick,

"To my unhappy pulse, that beat right through
My eager body; while I laughed out loud,
And let my lips curl up at false or true,

"Seemed cold and shallow without any cloud.
80   Behold my judges, then the cloths were brought;
While I was dizzied thus, old thoughts would crowd,

"Belonging to the time ere I was bought
By Arthur's great name and his little love;
Must I give up for ever then, I thought,

85   "That which I deemed would ever round me move
Glorifying all things; for a little word,⁴
Scarce ever meant at all, must I now prove

"Stone-cold for ever? Pray you, does the Lord
Will that all folks should be quite happy and good?
90   I love God now a little, if this cord⁵

---

3. Launcelot is the son of King Ban of Brittany.   5. Her bond with Launcelot.
4. Her vow of marriage to Arthur.

"Were broken, once for all what striving could
Make me love anything in earth or heaven?
So day by day it grew, as if one should

"Slip slowly down some path worn smooth and even,
95   Down to a cool sea on a summer day;
Yet still in slipping there was some small leaven

"Of stretched hands catching small stones by the way,
Until one surely reached the sea at last,
And felt strange new joy as the worn head lay

100   "Back, with the hair like sea-weed; yea all past
Sweat of the forehead, dryness of the lips,
Washed utterly out by the dear waves o'ercast,

"In the lone sea, far off from any ships!
Do I not know now of a day in Spring?
105   No minute of that wild day ever slips

"From out my memory; I hear thrushes sing,
And wheresoever I may be, straightway
Thoughts of it all come up with most fresh sting:

"I was half mad with beauty on that day,
110   And went without my ladies all alone,
In a quiet garden walled round every way;

"I was right joyful of that wall of stone,
That shut the flowers and trees up with the sky,
And trebled all the beauty: to the bone,

115   "Yea right through to my heart, grown very shy
With weary thoughts, it pierced, and made me glad;
Exceedingly glad, and I knew verily,

"A little thing just then had made me mad;
I dared not think, as I was wont to do,
120   Sometimes, upon my beauty; if I had

"Held out my long hand up against the blue,
And, looking on the tenderly darken'd fingers,
Thought that by rights one ought to see quite through,

"There, see you, where the soft still light yet lingers,
125   Round by the edges; what should I have done,
If this had joined with yellow spotted singers,°   *birds*

"And startling green drawn upward by the sun?
But shouting, loosed out, see now! all my hair,
And trancedly stood watching the west wind run

130   "With faintest half-heard breathing sound—why there
I lose my head e'en now in doing this;
But shortly listen—In that garden fair

"Came Launcelot walking; this is true, the kiss
Wherewith we kissed in meeting that spring day,
135   I scarce dare talk of the remember'd bliss,

"When both our mouths went wandering in one way,
And aching sorely, met among the leaves;
Our hands being left behind strained far away.

"Never within a yard of my bright sleeves
140   Had Launcelot come before—and now, so nigh!
After that day why is it Guenevere grieves?

"Nevertheless you, O Sir Gauwaine, lie,
Whatever happened on through all those years,
God knows I speak truth, saying that you lie.

145   "Being such a lady could I weep these tears
If this were true? A great queen such as I
Having sinn'd this way, straight her conscience sears;

"And afterwards she liveth hatefully,
Slaying and poisoning, certes° never weeps,—   certainly
150   Gauwaine, be friends now, speak me lovingly.

"Do I not see how God's dear pity creeps
All through your frame, and trembles in your mouth?
Remember in what grave your mother sleeps,

"Buried in some place far down in the south,
155   Men are forgetting as I speak to you;
By her head sever'd in that awful drouth

"Of pity that drew Agravaine's fell blow,[6]
I pray your pity! let me not scream out
For ever after, when the shrill winds blow

160   "Through half your castle-locks! let me not shout
For ever after in the winter night
When you ride out alone! in battle-rout

"Let not my rusting tears make your sword light!°   weak
Ah! God of mercy, how he turns away!
165   So, ever must I dress me to the fight;

"So—let God's justice work! Gauwaine, I say,
See me hew down your proofs: yea, all men know
Even as you said how Mellyagraunce[7] one day,

"One bitter day in la Fausse Garde,[8] for so
170   All good knights held it after, saw—
Yea, sirs, by cursed unknightly outrage; though

---

6. Gawaine's mother had been accused of adultery, and his brother Agravaine had beheaded her.
7. Mellyagraunce, a knight who had accused Guenevere of adultery, had been challenged and killed by Launcelot.
8. "The False Castle." Guenevere disdainfully contrasts Mellyagraunce's castle with Launcelot's, the "Joyous Garde."

"You, Gauwaine, held his word without a flaw,
This Mellyagraunce saw blood upon my bed[9]—
Whose blood then pray you? is there any law

175 "To make a queen say why some spots of red
Lie on her coverlet? or will you say:
'Your hands are white, lady, as when you wed,

" 'Where did you bleed?' and must I stammer out: 'Nay,
I blush indeed, fair lord, only to rend
180 My sleeve up to my shoulder, where there lay

" 'A knife-point last night:' so must I defend
The honour of the lady Guenevere?
Not so, fair lords, even if the world should end

"This very day, and you were judges here
185 Instead of God. Did you see Mellyagraunce
When Launcelot stood by him? what white fear

"Curdled his blood, and how his teeth did dance,
His side sink in? as my knight cried and said:
'Slayer of unarm'd men, here is a chance!

190 " 'Setter of traps,[1] I pray you guard your head,
By God I am so glad to fight with you,
Stripper of ladies, that my hand feels lead

" 'For driving weight; hurrah now! draw and do,
For all my wounds are moving in my breast,
195 And I am getting mad with waiting so.'

"He struck his hands together o'er the beast,
Who fell down flat and grovell'd at his feet,
And groan'd at being slain so young—'at least.'

"My knight said: 'Rise you, sir, who are so fleet
200 At catching ladies, half-arm'd will I fight,
My left side all uncovered!' then I weet,°   know

"Up sprang Sir Mellyagraunce with great delight
Upon his knave's face; not until just then
Did I quite hate him, as I saw my knight

205 "Along the lists look to my stake and pen
With such a joyous smile, it made me sigh
From agony beneath my waist-chain,[2] when

"The fight began, and to me they drew nigh;
Ever Sir Launcelot kept him on the right,
210 And traversed warily, and ever high

9. In Malory, Guenevere and some of her knights are confined in Mellyagraunce's castle after a battle. Finding blood on her sheets, Mellyagraunce believes she has slept with one of her wounded knights and accuses her of adultery. Her partner was actually Launcelot, who cut himself climbing into her room.
1. Mellyagraunce had tried to prevent Launcelot from championing the Queen's honor by trapping him in a dungeon.
2. Guenevere is chained to a stake at which she is to be burnt unless Launcelot defeats her accuser.

"And fast leapt caitiff's° sword, until my knight   *coward's*
Sudden threw up his sword to his left hand,
Caught it, and swung it; that was all the fight,

"Except a spout of blood on the hot land;
215   For it was hottest summer; and I know
I wonder'd how the fire, while I should stand,

"And burn, against the heat, would quiver so,
Yards above my head; thus these matters went;
Which things were only warnings of the woe

220   "That fell on me. Yet Mellyagraunce was shent,°   *destroyed*
For Mellyagraunce had fought against the Lord;
Therefore, my lords, take heed lest you be blent°   *blinded*

"With all this wickedness; say no rash word
Against me, being so beautiful; my eyes,
225   Wept all away to grey, may bring some sword

"To drown you in your blood; see my breast rise,
Like waves of purple sea, as here I stand;
And how my arms are moved in wonderful wise,

"Yea also at my full heart's strong command,
230   See through my long throat how the words go up
In ripples to my mouth; how in my hand

"The shadow lies like wine within a cup
Of marvellously colour'd gold; yea now
This little wind is rising, look you up,

235   "And wonder how the light is falling so
Within my moving tresses: will you dare,
When you have looked a little on my brow,

"To say this thing is vile? or will you care
For any plausible lies of cunning woof,°   *weaving*
240   When you can see my face with no lie there

"For ever? am I not a gracious proof—
'But in your chamber Launcelot was found'—
Is there a good knight then would stand aloof,

"When a queen says with gentle queenly sound:
245   'O true as steel, come now and talk with me,
I love to see your step upon the ground

" 'Unwavering, also well I love to see
That gracious smile light up your face, and hear
Your wonderful words, that all mean verily

250 " 'The thing they seem to mean: good friend, so dear
To me in everything, come here to-night,
Or else the hours will pass most dull and drear;

" 'If you come not, I fear this time I might
Get thinking over much of times gone by,
255 When I was young, and green hope was in sight:

" 'For no man cares now to know why I sigh;
And no man comes to sing me pleasant songs,
Nor any brings me the sweet flowers that lie

" 'So thick in the gardens; therefore one so longs
260 To see you, Launcelot; that we may be
Like children once again, free from all wrongs

" 'Just for one night.' Did he not come to me?
What thing could keep true Launcelot away
If I said, 'Come?' There was one less than three

265 "In my quiet room that night, and we were gay;
Till sudden I rose up, weak, pale, and sick,
Because a bawling broke our dream up, yea

"I looked at Launcelot's face and could not speak,
For he looked helpless too, for a little while;
270 Then I remember how I tried to shriek,

"And could not, but fell down; from tile to tile
The stones they threw up rattled o'er my head
And made me dizzier; till within a while

"My maids were all about me, and my head
275 On Launcelot's breast was being soothed away
From its white chattering, until Launcelot said—

"By God! I will not tell you more to-day,
Judge any way you will—what matters it?
You know quite well the story of that fray,

280 "How Launcelot still'd their bawling, the mad fit
That caught up Gauwaine—all, all, verily,
But just that which would save me; these things flit.

"Nevertheless you, O Sir Gauwaine, lie,
Whatever may have happen'd these long years,
285 God knows I speak truth, saying that you lie!

"All I have said is truth, by Christ's dear tears."
She would not speak another word, but stood
Turn'd sideways; listening, like a man who hears

His brother's trumpet sounding through the wood
290 Of his foes' lances. She lean'd eagerly,
And gave a slight spring sometimes, as she could

At last hear something really; joyfully
Her cheek grew crimson, as the headlong speed
Of the roan charger drew all men to see,
295 The knight who came was Launcelot at good need.

1858

The Haystack in the Floods[1]

Had she come all the way for this,
To part at last without a kiss?
Yea, had she borne the dirt and rain
That her own eyes might see him slain
5   Beside the haystack in the floods?

Along the dripping leafless woods,
The stirrup touching either shoe,
She rode astride as troopers do;
With kirtle kilted° to her knee,   *skirt hitched up*
10   To which the mud splash'd wretchedly;
And the wet dripp'd from every tree
Upon her head and heavy hair,
And on her eyelids broad and fair;
The tears and rain ran down her face.
15   By fits and starts they rode apace,
And very often was his place
Far off from her; he had to ride
Ahead, to see what might betide
When the roads cross'd; and sometimes, when
20   There rose a murmuring from his men,
Had to turn back with promises;
Ah me! she had but little ease;
And often for pure doubt and dread
She sobb'd, made giddy in the head
25   By the swift riding; while, for cold,
Her slender fingers scarce could hold
The wet reins; yea, and scarcely, too,
She felt the foot within her shoe
Against the stirrup: all for this,
30   To part at last without a kiss
Beside the haystack in the floods.

For when they near'd that old soak'd hay,
They saw across the only way

1. The poem takes place after the French defeat by the English at Poitiers in 1356. Sir Robert de Marny, an English knight, and his French mistress, Jehane, are trying to reach safety in Gascony, which is held by the English.

That Judas, Godmar,[2] and the three
35   Red running lions dismally
Grinn'd from his pennon,° under which   *flag*
In one straight line along the ditch,
They counted thirty heads.

                    So then,
While Robert turn'd round to his men,
40   She saw at once the wretched end,
And, stooping down, tried hard to rend
Her coif the wrong way from her head,
And hid her eyes; while Robert said:
"Nay, love, 'tis scarcely two to one,
45   At Poitiers where we made them run
So fast—why, sweet my love, good cheer,
The Gascon frontier is so near,
Nought after this."

                    But, "O!" she said,
"My God! my God! I have to tread
50   The long way back without you; then
The court at Paris; those six men;
The gratings of the Chatelet;
The swift Seine on some rainy day
Like this, and people standing by
55   And laughing, while my weak hands try
To recollect how strong men swim.[3]
All this, or else a life with him,
For which I should be damned at last.
Would God that this next hour were past!"

60   He answer'd not, but cried his cry,
"St. George for Marny!" cheerily;
And laid his hand upon her rein.
Alas! no man of all his train
Gave back that cheery cry again;
65   And, while for rage his thumb beat fast
Upon his sword-hilts, some one cast
About his neck a kerchief long,
And bound him.

                    Then they went along
To Godmar; who said: "Now, Jehane,
70   Your lover's life is on the wane
So fast, that, if this very hour
You yield not as my paramour,

2. Godmar is betraying them into French hands (like Judas, the disciple who betrayed Jesus to the Romans).
3. Jehane is saying that, without Robert to protect her, she will be imprisoned in the Chatelet in Paris, tried by six judges, and subjected to an ordeal by water to determine her guilt or innocence. Line 108 suggests that if she did not drown, she would be burned at the stake.

He will not see the rain leave off—
Nay, keep your tongue from gibe and scoff,
75   Sir Robert, or I slay you now."

She laid her hand upon her brow,
Then gazed upon the palm, as though
She thought her forehead bled, and—"No!"
She said, and turn'd her head away,
80   As there were nothing else to say,
And everything were settled: red
Grew Godmar's face from chin to head:
"Jehane, on yonder hill there stands
My castle, guarding well my lands:
85   What hinders me from taking you,
And doing that I list to do
To your fair wilful body, while
Your knight lies dead?"

                              A wicked smile
Wrinkled her face, her lips grew thin,
90   A long way out she thrust her chin:
"You know that I should strangle you
While you were sleeping; or bite through
Your throat, by God's help—ah!" she said,
"Lord Jesus, pity your poor maid!
95   For in such wise they hem me in,
I cannot choose but sin and sin,

Whatever happens: yet I think
They could not make me eat or drink,
And so should I just reach my rest."
100   "Nay, if you do not my behest,
O Jehane! though I love you well,"
Said Godmar, "would I fail to tell
All that I know?" "Foul lies," she said.
"Eh? lies, my Jehane? by God's head,
105   At Paris folks would deem them true!
Do you know, Jehane, they cry for you:
'Jehane the brown! Jehane the brown!
Give us Jehane to burn or drown!'—
Eh—gag me Robert!—sweet my friend,
110   This were indeed a piteous end
For those long fingers, and long feet,
And long neck, and smooth shoulders sweet;
An end that few men would forget
That saw it—So, an hour yet:
115   Consider, Jehane, which to take
Of life or death!"

                              So, scarce awake,
Dismounting, did she leave that place,

And totter some yards: with her face
Turn'd upward to the sky she lay,
120   Her head on a wet heap of hay,
And fell asleep: and while she slept,
And did not dream, the minutes crept
Round to the twelve again; but she,
Being waked at last, sigh'd quietly,
125   And strangely childlike came, and said:
"I will not." Straightway Godmar's head,
As though it hung on strong wires, turn'd
Most sharply round, and his face burn'd.

For Robert—both his eyes were dry,
130   He could not weep, but gloomily
He seem'd to watch the rain; yea, too,
His lips were firm; he tried once more
To touch her lips; she reach'd out, sore
And vain desire so tortured them,
135   The poor grey lips, and now the hem
Of his sleeve brush'd them.
                                           With a start
Up Godmar rose, thrust them apart;
From Robert's throat he loosed the bands
Of silk and mail; with empty hands
140   Held out, she stood and gazed, and saw
The long bright blade without a flaw
Glide out from Godmar's sheath, his hand
In Robert's hair; she saw him bend
Back Robert's head; she saw him send
145   The thin steel down; the blow told well,
Right backward the knight Robert fell,
And moaned as dogs do, being half dead,
Unwitting, as I deem: so then
Godmar turn'd grinning to his men,
150   Who ran, some five or six, and beat
His head to pieces at their feet.

Then Godmar turn'd again and said:
"So, Jehane, the first fitte[4] is read!
Take note, my lady, that your way
155   Lies backward to the Chatelet!"
She shook her head and gazed awhile
At her cold hands with a rueful smile,
As though this thing had made her mad.

This was the parting that they had
160   Beside the haystack in the floods.

1858

4. Canto or section of a poem.

from **The Beauty of Life**[1]

As I look round on this assemblage, and think of all that it represents, I cannot choose but be moved to the soul by the troubles of the life of civilized man, and the hope that thrusts itself through them; I cannot refrain from giving you once again the message with which, as it seems, some chance-hap has charged me: that message is, in short, to call on you to face the latest danger which civilization is threatened with, a danger of her own breeding: that men in struggling towards the complete attainment of all the luxuries of life for the strongest portion of their race should deprive their whole race of all the beauty of life: a danger that the strongest and wisest of mankind, in striving to attain to a complete mastery over Nature, should destroy her simplest and widest-spread gifts, and thereby enslave simple people to them, and themselves to themselves, and so at last drag the world into a second barbarism more ignoble, and a thousandfold more hopeless, than the first. ✳ ✳ ✳

That the beauty of life is a thing of no moment, I suppose few people would venture to assert, and yet most civilized people act as if it were of none, and in so doing are wronging both themselves and those that are to come after them; for that beauty, which is what is meant by *art*, using the word in its widest sense, is, I contend, no mere accident to human life, which people can take or leave as they choose, but a positive necessity of life, if we are to live as nature meant us to; that is, unless we are content to be less than men. ✳ ✳ ✳

You, of this great and famous town, for instance, which has had so much to do with the Century of Commerce,[2] your gains are obvious to all men, but the price you have paid for them is obvious to many—surely to yourselves most of all: I do not say that they are not worth the price; I know that England and the world could very ill afford to exchange the Birmingham of to-day for the Birmingham of the year 1700: but surely if what you have gained be more than a mockery, you cannot stop at those gains, or even go on always piling up similar ones. Nothing can make me believe that the present condition of your Black Country[3] yonder is an unchangeable necessity of your life and position: such miseries as this were begun and carried on in pure thoughtlessness, and a hundredth part of the energy that was spent in creating them would get rid of them. ✳ ✳ ✳

For again I say that therein rich people have defrauded themselves as well as the poor: you will see a refined and highly educated man nowadays, who has been to Italy and Egypt and where not, who can talk learnedly enough (and fantastically enough sometimes) about art, and who has at his fingers' ends abundant lore concerning the art and literature of past days, sitting down without signs of discomfort in a house, that with all its surroundings is just brutally vulgar and hideous: all his education has not done more for him than that.

The truth is, that in art, and in other things besides, the laboured education of a few will not raise even those few above the reach of the evils that beset the ignorance of the great mass of the population: the brutality of which such a huge stock has been accumulated lower down will often show without much peeling through the selfish refinement of those who have let it accumulate. The lack of art, or rather the murder of art, that

---

1. A lecture delivered before the Birmingham Society of Arts and School of Design, 19 February 1880.
2. Birmingham was a major manufacturing center in the 19th century.

3. The region around Birmingham was called the "Black Country" because of the proliferation of coal mines and factory smoke.

curses our streets from the sordidness of the surroundings of the lower classes, has its exact counterpart in the dulness and vulgarity of those of the middle classes, and the double-distilled dulness, and scarcely less vulgarity of those of the upper classes. * * *

So once more I say, if in any matters civilization has gone astray, the remedy lies not in standing still, but in more complete civilization.

Now whatever discussion there may be about that often used and often misused word, I believe all who hear me will agree with me in believing from their hearts, and not merely in saying in conventional phrase, that the civilization which does not carry the whole people with it is doomed to fall, and give place to one which at least aims at doing so.

We talk of the civilization of the ancient peoples, of the classical times: well, civilized they were no doubt, some of their folk at least: an Athenian citizen for instance led a simple, dignified, almost perfect life; but there were drawbacks to happiness perhaps in the lives of his slaves: and the civilization of the ancients was founded on slavery. * * *

What, therefore, can we do, to guard traditions of time past that we may not one day have to begin anew from the beginning with none to teach us? What are we to do, that we may take heed to, and spread the decencies of life, so that at the least we may have a field where it will be possible for art to grow when men begin to long for it: what finally can we do, each of us, to cherish some germ of art, so that it may meet with others, and spread and grow little by little into the thing that we need? * * *

In the first place, many and many a beautiful and ancient building is being destroyed all over civilized Europe as well as in England, because it is supposed to interfere with the convenience of the citizens, while a little forethought might save it without trenching on that convenience; but even apart from that, I say that if we are not prepared to put up with a little inconvenience in our lifetimes for the sake of preserving a monument of art which will elevate and educate, not only ourselves, but our sons, and our sons' sons, it is vain and idle of us to talk about art—or education either. Brutality must be bred of such brutality. * * *

Surely if it be worth while troubling ourselves about the works of art of to-day, of which any amount almost can be done, since we are yet alive, it is worth while spending a little care, forethought, and money in preserving the art of bygone ages, of which (woe worth the while!) so little is left, and of which we can never have any more, whatever good hap the world may attain to.

No man who consents to the destruction or the mutilation of an ancient building has any right to pretend that he cares about art; or has any excuse to plead in defence of his crime against civilization and progress, save sheer brutal ignorance.

But before I leave this subject I must say a word or two about the curious invention of our own days called Restoration, a method of dealing with works of bygone days which, though not so degrading in its spirit as downright destruction, is nevertheless little better in its results on the condition of those works of art; it is obvious that I have no time to argue the question out to-night, so I will only make these assertions:

That ancient buildings, being both works of art and monuments of history, must obviously be treated with great care and delicacy: that the imitative art of to-day is not, and cannot be the same thing as ancient art, and cannot replace it; and that therefore if we superimpose this work on the old, we destroy it both as art and as a record of history: lastly, that the natural weathering of the surface of a building is beautiful, and its loss disastrous.

Now the restorers hold the exact contrary of all this: they think that any clever architect to-day can deal off-hand successfully with the ancient work; that while all things else have changed about us since (say) the thirteenth century, art has not changed, and that our workmen can turn out work identical with that of the thirteenth century; and, lastly, that the weather-beaten surface of an ancient building is worthless, and to be got rid of wherever possible. * * *

It will give us trouble no doubt, all this care of our possessions: but there is more trouble to come; for I must now speak of something else, of possessions which should be common to all of us, of the green grass, and the leaves, and the waters, of the very light and air of heaven, which the Century of Commerce has been too busy to pay any heed to. And first let me remind you that I am supposing every one here present professes to care about art.

Well, there are some rich men among us whom we oddly enough call manufacturers, by which we mean capitalists who pay other men to organize manufacturers; these gentlemen, many of whom buy pictures and profess to care about art, burn a deal of coal: there is an Act in existence which was passed to prevent them sometimes and in some places from pouring a dense cloud of smoke over the world, and, to my thinking, a very lame and partial Act it is:[4] but nothing hinders these lovers of art from being a law to themselves, and making it a point of honour with them to minimize the smoke nuisance as far as their own works are concerned; and if they don't do so, when mere money, and even a very little of that, is what it will cost them, I say that their love of art is a mere pretence: how can you care about the image of a landscape when you show by your deeds that you don't care for the landscape itself? or what right have you to shut yourself up with beautiful form and colour when you make it impossible for other people to have any share in these things? * * *

Again, I must ask what do you do with the trees on a site that is going to be built over? do you try to save them, to adapt your houses at all to them? do you understand what treasures they are in a town or a suburb? or what a relief they will be to the hideous dog-holes which (forgive me!) you are probably going to build in their places? I ask this anxiously, and with grief in my soul, for in London and its suburbs we always begin by clearing a site till it is as bare as the pavement: I really think that almost anybody would have been shocked, if I could have shown him some of the trees that have been wantonly murdered in the suburb in which I live (Hammersmith to wit), amongst them some of those magnificent cedars, for which we along the river used to be famous once.

But here again see how helpless those are who care about art or nature amidst the hurry of the Century of Commerce.

Pray do not forget, that any one who cuts down a tree wantonly or carelessly, especially in a great town or its suburbs, need make no pretence of caring about art.

What else can we do to help to educate ourselves and others in the path of art, to be on the road to attaining an *Art made by the people and for the people as a joy to the maker and the user?*

Why, having got to understand something of what art was, having got to look upon its ancient monuments as friends that can tell us something of times bygone, and whose faces we do not wish to alter, even though they be worn by time and grief: having got to spend money and trouble upon matters of decency, great and little;

4. Probably the Sanitary Act of 1866. Throughout the 19th century both local and national laws were passed to control the noxious environmental effects of the Industrial Revolution. But the acts were not well enforced, and manufacturers promoted the view that smoke was a visible symbol of Britain's economic progress.

having made it clear that we really do care about nature even in the suburbs of a big town—having got so far, we shall begin to think of the houses in which we live.

For I must tell you that unless you are resolved to have good and rational architecture, it is, once again, useless your thinking about art at all.

I have spoken of the popular arts, but they might all be summed up in that one word Architecture; they are all parts of that great whole, and the art of house-building begins it all: if we did not know how to dye or to weave; if we had neither gold, nor silver, nor silk; and no pigments to paint with, but half-a-dozen ochres and umbers, we might yet frame a worthy art that would lead to everything, if we had but timber, stone, and lime, and a few cutting tools to make these common things not only shelter us from wind and weather, but also express the thoughts and aspirations that stir in us. * * *

Now I do not think the greatest of optimists would deny that, taking us one and all, we are at present housed in a perfectly shameful way, and since the greatest part of us have to live in houses already built for us, it must be admitted that it is rather hard to know what to do, beyond waiting till they tumble about our ears. * * *

However, I must try to answer the question I have supposed put, how are we to pay for decent houses?

It seems to me that, by a great piece of good luck, the way to pay for them is by doing that which alone can produce popular art among us: living a simple life, I mean. Once more I say that the greatest foe to art is luxury, art cannot live in its atmosphere.

When you hear of the luxuries of the ancients, you must remember that they were not like our luxuries, they were rather indulgence in pieces of extravagant folly than what we to-day call luxury; which perhaps you would rather call comfort: well, I accept the word, and say that a Greek or Roman of the luxurious time would stare astonished could he be brought back again and shown the comforts of a well-to-do middle-class house.

But some, I know, think that the attainment of these very comforts is what makes the difference between civilization and uncivilization, that they are the essence of civilization. Is it so indeed? Farewell my hope then!—I had thought that civilization meant the attainment of peace and order and freedom, of goodwill between man and man, of the love of truth and the hatred of injustice, and by consequence the attainment of the good life which these things breed, a life free from craven fear, but full of incident: that was what I thought it meant, not more stuffed chairs and more cushions, and more carpets and gas, and more dainty meat and drink—and therewithal more and sharper differences between class and class.

If that be what it is, I for my part wish I were well out of it, and living in a tent in the Persian desert, or a turf hut on the Iceland hill-side. But however it be, and I think my view is the true view, I tell you that art abhors that side of civilization, she cannot breathe in the houses that lie under its stuffy slavery.

Believe me, if we want art to begin at home, as it must, we must clear our houses of troublesome superfluities that are for ever in our way: conventional comforts that are no real comforts, and do but make work for servants and doctors: if you want a golden rule that will fit everybody, this is it:

Have nothing in your houses that you do not know to be useful, or believe to be beautiful.

And if we apply that rule strictly, we shall in the first place show the builders and such-like servants of the public what we really want, we shall create a demand for real art, as the phrase goes; and in the second place, we shall surely have more money to pay for decent houses.

Perhaps it will not try your patience too much if I lay before you my idea of the fittings necessary to the sitting-room of a healthy person: a room, I mean, which he would not have to cook in much, or sleep in generally, or in which he would not have to do any very litter-making manual work.

First a book-case with a great many books in it: next a table that will keep steady when you write or work at it: then several chairs that you can move, and a bench that you can sit or lie upon: next a cupboard with drawers: next, unless either the book-case or the cupboard be very beautiful with painting or carving, you will want pictures or engravings, such as you can afford, only not stopgaps, but real works of art on the wall; or else the wall itself must be ornamented with some beautiful and restful pattern: we shall also want a vase or two to put flowers in, which latter you must have sometimes, especially if you live in a town. Then there will be the fireplace of course, which in our climate is bound to be the chief object in the room.

That is all we shall want, especially if the floor be good; if it be not, as, by the way, in a modern house it is pretty certain not to be, I admit that a small carpet which can be bundled out of the room in two minutes will be useful, and we must also take care that it is beautiful, or it will annoy us terribly.

Now unless we are musical, and need a piano (in which case, as far as beauty is concerned, we are in a bad way), that is quite all we want: and we can add very little to these necessaries without troubling ourselves and hindering our work, our thought, and our rest.

If these things were done at the least cost for which they could be done well and solidly, they ought not to cost much; and they are so few, that those that could afford to have them at all, could afford to spend some trouble to get them fitting and beautiful: and all those who care about art ought to take great trouble to do so, and to take care that there be no sham art amongst them, nothing that it has degraded a man to make or sell. And I feel sure, that if all who care about art were to take this pains, it would make a great impression upon the public.

This simplicity you may make as costly as you please or can, on the other hand: you may hang your walls with tapestry instead of whitewash or paper; or you may cover them with mosaic, or have them frescoed by a great painter: all this is not luxury, if it be done for beauty's sake, and not for show: it does not break our golden rule: *Have nothing in your houses which you do not know to be useful or believe to be beautiful.*

All art starts from this simplicity; and the higher the art rises, the greater the simplicity. I have been speaking of the fittings of a dwelling-house—a place in which we eat and drink, and pass familiar hours; but when you come to places which people want to make more specially beautiful because of the solemnity or dignity of their uses, they will be simpler still, and have little in them save the bare walls made as beautiful as may be. St. Mark's at Venice has very little furniture in it, much less than most Roman Catholic churches: its lovely and stately mother St. Sophia of Constantinople had less still, even when it was a Christian church:[5] but we need not go either to Venice or Stamboul to take note of that: go into one of our own mighty Gothic naves (do any of you remember the first time you did so?) and note how the huge free space satisfies and elevates you, even now when win-

5. The Basilica di San Marco is the heart of Venice. It was partly inspired by Hagia Sophia, a perfect example of Byzantine architecture, built by the Emperor Justinian between 532 and 537; when the Turks conquered Constantinople (present-day Istanbul—"Stamboul") in 1453, the church became a mosque; today it is a museum.

dow and wall are stripped of ornament: then think of the meaning of simplicity and absence of encumbering gewgaws.

Now after all, for us who are learning art, it is not far to seek what is the surest way to further it; that which most breeds art is art; every piece of work that we do which is well done, is so much help to the cause; every piece of pretence and half-heartedness is so much hurt to it. Most of you who take to the practice of art can find out in no very long time whether you have any gifts for it or not: if you have not, throw the thing up, or you will have a wretched time of it yourselves, and will be damaging the cause by laborious pretence: but if you have gifts of any kind, you are happy indeed beyond most men; for your pleasure is always with you, nor can you be intemperate in the enjoyment of it, and as you use it, it does not lessen, but grows: if you are by chance weary of it at night, you get up in the morning eager for it; or if perhaps in the morning it seems folly to you for a while, yet presently, when your hand has been moving a little in its wonted way, fresh hope has sprung up beneath it and you are happy again. While others are getting through the day like plants thrust into the earth, which cannot turn this way or that but as the wind blows them, you know what you want, and your will is on the alert to find it, and you, whatever happens, whether it be joy or grief, are at least alive. * * *

* * * What I want to do to-night is to put definitely before you a cause for which to strive.

That cause is the Democracy of Art, the ennobling of daily and common work, which will one day put hope and pleasure in the place of fear and pain, as the forces which move men to labour and keep the world a-going. * * *

I know indeed that men, wearied by the pettiness of the details of the strife, their patience tried by hope deferred, will at whiles, excusably enough, turn back in their hearts to other days, when if the issues were not clearer, the means of trying them were simpler; when, so stirring were the times, one might even have atoned for many a blunder and backsliding by visibly dying for the cause. To have breasted the Spanish pikes at Leyden, to have drawn sword with Oliver:[6] that may well seem to us at times amidst the tangles of to-day a happy fate: for a man to be able to say, I have lived like a fool, but now I will cast away fooling for an hour, and die like a man—there is something in that certainly: and yet 'tis clear that few men can be so lucky as to die for a cause, without having first of all lived for it. And as this is the most that can be asked from the greatest man that follows a cause, so it is the least that can be taken from the smallest.

So to us who have a Cause at heart, our highest ambition and our simplest duty are one and the same thing: for the most part we shall be too busy doing the work that lies ready to our hands, to let impatience for visibly great progress vex us much; but surely since we are servants of a Cause, hope must be ever with us, and sometimes perhaps it will so quicken our vision that it will outrun the slow lapse of time, and show us the victorious days when millions of those who now sit in darkness will be enlightened by an *Art made by the people and for the people, a joy to the maker and the user.*

1880

---

6. The Dutch inhabitants of Leyden defended it against Spanish attack in 1574; Oliver died alongside Roland defending the pass at Roncevalles against the Moors.

Algernon Charles Swinburne
1837–1909

Algernon Charles Swinburne is the most notorious bad boy in English poetry. His verse contains everything calculated to affront a "respectable" audience—incest, sadomasochism, necrophilia, atheism, cannibalism, aestheticism, revolutionary politics—all conveyed in virtuoso rhythms that intensify his lurid, seductive appeal. Drunk or sober, sliding naked down banisters or rhapsodizing over the Marquis de Sade, Swinburne managed to offend people wherever he went. Yet despite the uproar, his extraordinary talent won him many admirers. Ruskin regarded him as a force of nature: "I should as soon think of finding fault with you as with a thundercloud or a nightshade blossom." Tennyson declared: "Swinburne is a reed through which all things blow into music."

Raised on the Isle of Wight, the son of an admiral and an earl's daughter, Swinburne was obsessed with the sea. His family nicknamed him "Seagull," and his earliest memory was "being held up naked in my father's arms . . . then shot like a stone from a sling through the air, shouting and laughing with delight, head foremost into the coming wave." The surging rhythms of his lines give proof of what he called "my endless passionate returns to the sea in all my verse."

Educated at Eton and Oxford, he became friends with Dante Gabriel Rossetti and William Morris in the late 1850s and embarked on a wild, bohemian life in London, where he dazzled people with impromptu recitations of his own erotic verse. But he was devastated when his beloved cousin Mary Gordon married in 1865. Her "loss" was the major event in his adult emotional life, inspiring many poems that dwell on the curiously pleasurable pain of unrequited love. Swinburne spent another fourteen self-destructive yet amazingly productive years in London, punctuated by visits to flagellation brothels, drunken sprees, seizures, breakdowns, and recuperations. In 1879 he was taken into "protective custody" by his friend Theodore Watts-Dunton, and spent his last three decades living quietly in the rural suburb of Putney.

Swinburne burst upon public notice with two key works: *Atalanta in Calydon* (1865), an effort to recreate in English the measures and feeling of Greek tragedy, and *Poems and Ballads* (1866), sixty-two lyrics of metric genius and scandalous subject matter. These revealed his particular flair for decadent dramatic monologues and poems. His speakers include a necrophiliac lover in *The Leper*, a connoisseur of erotic cruelty in *Dolores*, an incestuous mother in *Phaedra*, and a wary admirer of a nymphomaniac Roman empress in *Faustine*. Public outrage was nearly unanimous: even a friend who conceded Swinburne's "audacious courage" and musical "swing of words" accused the author of "grovelling down among the nameless shameless abominations which inspire him with such frenzied delight." *Punch* suggested simply that the poet should change his name to "Swineborn."

When he wasn't writing flagellation pornography for the amusement of his friends, Swinburne wrote more poems, two novels, and influential critical essays. His lush prose and fervent worship of beauty for its own sake made him an important influence on the Aesthetes, especially Walter Pater. Swinburne's outrageous acts and radical sympathies made him *the* symbol of social, political, and religious revolt in Victorian Britain. His friend and biographer Edmund Gosse recalled: "He was not merely a poet, but a flag, and not merely a flag but the Red Flag incarnate."

Swinburne is most admired for his startling style. Like his hero Shelley, he tried "to render the effect of the thing rather than the thing itself." Desiring to convey sensations acutely, Swinburne glorified all the senses except sight. This approach is so rare in English poetry that he is often accused of caring more for sound effects than ideas or images. Poets like Browning or Hopkins challenge the reader because of their intense particularity; Swinburne challenges because he is so diffuse—his deluge of words threatens to overwhelm the reader with hypnotic cadences and intricate, echoing patterns of association.

Yet, as T. S. Eliot declared, "his diffuseness is one of his glories." Like J. M. W. Turner, the English painter who said "indistinctness is my forte," Swinburne thrives on elemental forces of nature clashing and combining. He constructs his stanzas by piling up parallels and contrasts. Passionate about love's impossibility, he weaves his rich textures mostly from monosyllables, discovering in the process what the critic John D. Rosenberg calls "the bleak beauty of little words." As Ezra Pound remarked, summing up the effect of his verse, "no one else has made such music in English . . . the passion, not merely for political, but also for personal, liberty is the bedrock of Swinburne's writing."

The Leper[1]

Nothing is better, I well think,
　　Than love; the hidden well-water
Is not so delicate to drink:
　　This was well seen of me and her.

5　　I served her in a royal house;
　　I served her wine and curious meat.
For will to kiss between her brows,
　　I had no heart to sleep or eat.

Mere scorn God knows she had of me,
10　　A poor scribe, nowise great or fair,
Who plucked his clerk's hood back to see
　　Her curled-up lips and amorous hair.

I vex my head with thinking this.
　　Yea, though God always hated me,
15 And hates me now that I can kiss
　　Her eyes, plait up her hair to see

How she then wore it on the brows,
　　Yet am I glad to have her dead
Here in this wretched wattled° house　　　　　*built of sticks*
20　　Where I can kiss her eyes and head.

---

1. Suffering from an infectious disease that eats away parts of the body, lepers were often shunned or forced into isolated colonies; their disease was regarded as a sign of moral contagion, and they were required to shout "unclean" as they approached other people. A necrophilic love-fantasy recounted by a medieval scribe, this dramatic monologue ranks with Browning's *Porphyria's Lover* as one of the most deliberately disturbing works of the Victorian era. Swinburne, who perpetrated other literary hoaxes, created a fictitious 16th-century French source, which he appended as a note. Translated, it reads in part: "Now it happened that a noble damsel named Yolande de Sallières, being afflicted and utterly wasted by this terrible disease . . . none of the lovers who so often had embraced and kissed her very tenderly was willing to shelter any longer so ugly a woman and so detestable a sinner. Only a clerk who had been at first her servant and go-between in matters of love took her in. . . . They say that this wicked man and accursed clerk, recalling the great but now ravaged beauty of this woman, often delighted in kissing her foul and leprous mouth and in caressing her gently with his loving hands. And he also died of this same abominable disease."

Nothing is better, I well know,
    Than love; no amber in cold sea
Or gathered berries under snow:
    That is well seen of her and me.

25   Three thoughts I make my pleasure of:
    First I take heart and think of this:
That knight's gold hair she chose to love,
    His mouth she had such will to kiss.

Then I remember that sundawn
30   I brought him by a privy way
Out at her lattice,[2] and thereon
    What gracious words she found to say.

(Cold rushes for such little feet—
    Both feet could lie into my hand.
35   A marvel was it of my sweet
    Her upright body could so stand.)

"Sweet friend, God give you thank and grace;
    Now am I clean and whole of shame,
Nor shall men burn me in the face
40   For my sweet fault that scandals them."

I tell you over word by word.
    She, sitting edgewise on her bed,
Holding her feet, said thus. The third,
    A sweeter thing than these, I said.

45   God, that makes time and ruins it
    And alters not, abiding God,
Changed with disease her body sweet,
    The body of love wherein she abode.

Love is more sweet and comelier
50   Than a dove's throat strained out to sing.
All they spat out and cursed at her
    And cast her forth for a base thing.

They cursed her, seeing how God had wrought
    This curse to plague her, a curse of his.
55   Fools were they surely, seeing not
    How sweeter than all sweet she is.

He that had held her by the hair,
    With kissing lips blinding her eyes,

2. He secretly leads the knight to her latticed window or door.

Felt her bright bosom, strained and bare,
    Sigh under him, with short mad cries

Out of her throat and sobbing mouth
    And body broken up with love,
With sweet hot tears his lips were loth
    Her own should taste the savour of,

Yea, he inside whose grasp all night
    Her fervent body leapt or lay,
Stained with sharp kisses red and white,
    Found her a plague to spurn away.

I hid her in this wattled house,
    I served her water and poor bread.
For joy to kiss between her brows
    Time upon time I was nigh dead.

Bread failed; we got but well-water
    And gathered grass with dropping seed.
I had such joy of kissing her,
    I had small care to sleep or feed.

Sometimes when service made me glad
    The sharp tears leapt between my lids,
Falling on her, such joy I had
    To do the service God forbids.

"I pray you let me be at peace,
    Get hence, make room for me to die."
She said that: her poor lip would cease,
    Put up to mine, and turn to cry.

I said, "Bethink yourself how love
    Fared in us twain, what either did;
Shall I unclothe my soul thereof?
    That I should do this, God forbid."

Yea, though God hateth us, he knows
    That hardly in a little thing
Love faileth of the work it does
    Till it grow ripe for gathering.

Six months, and now my sweet is dead
    A trouble takes me; I know not
If all were done well, all well said,
    No word or tender deed forgot.

Too sweet, for the least part in her,
    To have shed life out by fragments; yet,
Could the close mouth catch breath and stir,
    I might see something I forget.

Six months, and I sit still and hold
    In two cold palms her cold two feet.
Her hair, half grey half ruined gold,
    Thrills me and burns me in kissing it.

105   Love bites and stings me through, to see
        Her keen face made of sunken bones.
    Her worn-off eyelids madden me,
        That were shot through with purple once.

She said, "Be good with me; I grow
110   So tired for shame's sake, I shall die
If you say nothing:" even so.
    And she is dead now, and shame put by.

Yea, and the scorn she had of me
    In the old time, doubtless vexed her then.
115   I never should have kissed her. See
       What fools God's anger makes of men!

She might have loved me a little too,
    Had I been humbler for her sake.
But that new shame could make love new
120   She saw not—yet her shame did make.

I took too much upon my love,
    Having for such mean service done
Her beauty and all the ways thereof,
    Her face and all the sweet thereon.

125   Yea, all this while I tended her,
       I know the old love held fast his part:
I know the old scorn waxed heavier,
    Mixed with sad wonder, in her heart.

It may be all my love went wrong—
130   A scribe's work writ awry and blurred,
Scrawled after the blind evensong°—   *evening prayer*
    Spoilt music with no perfect word.

But surely I would fain have done
    All things the best I could. Perchance
135   Because I failed, came short of one,
       She kept at heart that other man's.

I am grown blind with all these things:
    It may be now she hath in sight
Some better knowledge; still there clings
140   The old question. Will not God do right?

1866

from The Triumph of Time[1]
I Will Go Back to the Great Sweet Mother

I will go back to the great sweet mother,
    Mother and lover of men, the sea.
I will go down to her, I and none other,
260   Close with her, kiss her and mix her with me;
Cling to her, strive with her, hold her fast:
O fair white mother, in days long past
Born without sister, born without brother,
    Set free my soul as thy soul is free.

265   O fair green-girdled mother of mine,
    Sea, that art clothed with the sun and the rain,
Thy sweet hard kisses are strong like wine,
    Thy large embraces are keen like pain.
Save me and hide me with all thy waves,
270   Find me one grave of thy thousand graves,
Those pure cold populous graves of thine
    Wrought without hand in a world without stain.

I shall sleep, and move with the moving ships,
    Change as the winds change, veer in the tide;
275   My lips will feast on the foam of thy lips,
    I shall rise with thy rising, with thee subside;
Sleep, and not know if she[2] be, if she were,
Filled full with life to the eyes and hair,
As a rose is fulfilled to the roseleaf tips
280   With splendid summer and perfume and pride.

This woven raiment of nights and days,
    Were it once cast off and unwound from me,
Naked and glad would I walk in thy ways,
    Alive and aware of thy ways and thee;
285   Clear of the whole world, hidden at home,
Clothed with the green and crowned with the foam,
A pulse of the life of thy straits and bays,
    A vein in the heart of the streams of the sea.

Fair mother, fed with the lives of men,
290   Thou art subtle and cruel of heart, men say.
Thou hast taken, and shalt not render again;

---

1. *The Triumph of Time* is a long monologue in which the speaker laments that his love has forsaken him; he wishes that they had died together. In this excerpt the speaker envisions finding comfort by drowning his sorrows—or himself—in the sea.
2. The woman he has lost.

Thou art full of thy dead, and cold as they.
But death is the worst that comes of thee;
Thou art fed with our dead, O mother, O sea,
295   But when hast thou fed on our hearts? or when,
    Having given us love, hast thou taken away?

O tender-hearted, O perfect lover,
    Thy lips are bitter, and sweet thine heart.
The hopes that hurt and the dreams that hover,
300   Shall they not vanish away and apart?
But thou, thou art sure, thou art older than earth;
Thou art strong for death and fruitful of birth;
Thy depths conceal and thy gulfs discover;
    From the first thou wert; in the end thou art.

1866

Hymn to Proserpine[1]
(After the Proclamation in Rome of the Christian Faith)
VICISTI, GALILAEE[2]

I have lived long enough, having seen one thing, that love hath an end;
Goddess and maiden and queen, be near me now and befriend.
Thou art more than the day or the morrow, the seasons that laugh or that weep;
For these give joy and sorrow; but thou, Proserpina, sleep.
5   Sweet is the treading of wine, and sweet the feet of the dove;
But a goodlier gift is thine than foam of the grapes or love.
Yea, is not even Apollo, with hair and harpstring of gold,
A bitter God to follow, a beautiful God to behold?
I am sick of singing: the bays[3] burn deep and chafe: I am fain
10   To rest a little from praise and grievous pleasure and pain.
For the Gods we know not of, who give us our daily breath,
We know they are cruel as love or life, and lovely as death.
O Gods dethroned and deceased, cast forth, wiped out in a day!
From your wrath is the world released, redeemed from your chains, men say.
15   New Gods are crowned in the city; their flowers have broken your rods;
They are merciful, clothed with pity, the young compassionate Gods.
But for me their new device is barren, the days are bare;
Things long past over suffice, and men forgotten that were.
Time and the Gods are at strife; ye dwell in the midst thereof,
20   Draining a little life from the barren breasts of love.

1. Proserpine (Persephone) was the queen of the under-world. The daughter of Demeter (Ceres), the goddess of planting and harvest, she was abducted by Hades and forced to live as his consort in the underworld for six months of each year.
2. "Thou hast conquered, O Galilean." Legend has it that these words were spoken by the Roman Emperor Julian the Apostate (331–363) on his deathbed. The Galilean is Jesus, and the proclamation in the subtitle is Constantine's Edict of Milan in 313, which extended religious tolerance to Christians. Julian had tried to discourage the spread of Christianity and promote a return to paganism. The speaker of the poem, a Roman poet, shares Julian's admiration for the traditional gods.
3. Leaves from the poet's laurel wreath.

I say to you, cease, take rest; yea, I say to you all, be at peace,
Till the bitter milk of her breast and the barren bosom shall cease.
Wilt thou yet take all, Galilean? but these thou shalt not take,
The laurel, the palms and the paean, the breasts of the nymphs in the brake;
25   Breasts more soft than a dove's, that tremble with tenderer breath;
And all the wings of the Loves, and all the joy before death;
All the feet of the hours that sound as a single lyre,
Dropped and deep in the flowers, with strings that flicker like fire.
More than these wilt thou give, things fairer than all these things?
30   Nay, for a little we live, and life hath mutable wings.
A little while and we die; shall life not thrive as it may?
For no man under the sky lives twice, outliving his day.
And grief is a grievous thing, and a man hath enough of his tears:
Why should he labour, and bring fresh grief to blacken his years?
35   Thou hast conquered, O pale Galilean; the world has grown grey from thy breath;
We have drunken of things Lethean,[4] and fed on the fullness of death.
Laurel is green for a season, and love is sweet for a day;
But love grows bitter with treason, and laurel outlives not May.
Sleep, shall we sleep after all? for the world is not sweet in the end;
40   For the old faiths loosen and fall, the new years ruin and rend.
Fate is a sea without shore, and the soul is a rock that abides;
But her ears are vexed with the roar and her face with the foam of the tides.
O lips that the live blood faints in, the leavings of racks and rods!
O ghastly glories of saints, dead limbs of gibbeted Gods![5]
45   Though all men abase them before you in spirit, and all knees bend,
I kneel not neither adore you, but standing, look to the end.
All delicate days and pleasant, all spirits and sorrows are cast
Far out with the foam of the present that sweeps to the surf of the past:
Where beyond the extreme sea-wall, and between the remote sea-gates,
50   Waste water washes, and tall ships founder, and deep death waits:
Where, mighty with deepening sides, clad about with the seas as with wings,
And impelled of invisible tides, and fulfilled of unspeakable things,
White-eyed and poisonous-finned, shark-toothed and serpentine-curled,
Rolls, under the whitening wind of the future, the wave of the world.
55   The depths stand naked in sunder behind it, the storms flee away;
In the hollow before it the thunder is taken and snared as a prey;
In its sides is the north-wind bound; and its salt is of all men's tears;
With light of ruin, and sound of changes, and pulse of years;
With travail of day after day, and with trouble of hour upon hour;
60   And bitter as blood is the spray; and the crests are as fangs that devour:
And its vapour and storm of its steam as the sighing of spirits to be;
And its noise as the noise in a dream; and its depth as the roots of the sea:
And the height of its heads as the height of the utmost stars of the air:
And the ends of the earth at the might thereof tremble, and time is made bare.

---

4. The River Lethe in the underworld; the dead who drank of its waters forgot their past.

5. A reference to the Crucifixion.

65   Will ye bridle the deep sea with reins, will ye chasten the high sea with rods?
     Will ye take her to chain her with chains, who is older than all ye Gods?
     All ye as a wind shall go by, as a fire shall ye pass and be past;
     Ye are Gods, and behold, ye shall die, and the waves be upon you at last.
     In the darkness of time, in the deeps of the years, in the changes of things,
70   Ye shall sleep as a slain man sleeps, and the world shall forget you for kings.
     Though the feet of thine high priests tread where thy lords and our forefathers trod,
     Though these that were Gods are dead, and thou being dead art a God,
     Though before thee the throned Cytherean[6] be fallen, and hidden her head,
     Yet thy kingdom shall pass, Galilean, thy dead shall go down to thee dead.
75   Of the maiden thy mother men sing as a goddess with grace clad around;
     Thou art throned where another was king; where another was queen she is crowned.
     Yea, once we had sight of another: but now she is queen, say these.
     Not as thine, not as thine was our mother, a blossom of flowering seas,
     Clothed round with the world's desire as with raiment, and fair as the foam,
80   And fleeter than kindled fire, and a goddess, and mother of Rome.[7]
     For thine came pale and a maiden, and sister to sorrow; but ours,
     Her deep hair heavily laden with odour and colour of flowers,
     White rose of the rose-white water, a silver splendour, a flame,
     Bent down unto us that besought her, and earth grew sweet with her name.
85   For thine came weeping, a slave among slaves, and rejected; but she
     Came flushed from the full-flushed wave, and imperial, her foot on the sea.
     And the wonderful waters knew her, the winds and the viewless ways,
     And the roses grew rosier, and bluer the sea-blue stream of the bays.
     Ye are fallen, our lords, by what token? we wist that ye should not fall.
90   Ye were all so fair that are broken; and one more fair than ye all.
     But I turn to her[8] still, having seen she shall surely abide in the end;
     Goddess and maiden and queen, be near me now and befriend.
     O daughter of earth, of my mother, her crown and blossom of birth,
     I am also, I also, thy brother; I go as I came unto earth.
95   In the night where thine eyes are as moons are in heaven, the night where thou art,
     Where the silence is more than all tunes, where sleep overflows from the heart,
     Where the poppies are sweet as the rose in our world, and the red rose is white,
     And the wind falls faint as it blows with the fume of the flowers of the night,
     And the murmur of spirits that sleep in the shadow of Gods from afar
100 Grows dim in thine ears and deep as the deep dim soul of a star,
     In the sweet low light of thy face, under heavens untrod by the sun,
     Let my soul with their souls find place, and forget what is done and undone.
     Thou art more than the Gods who number the days of our temporal breath;
     For these give labour and slumber; but thou, Proserpina, death.
105 Therefore now at thy feet I abide for a season in silence. I know
     I shall die as my fathers died, and sleep as they sleep; even so.
     For the glass of the years is brittle wherein we gaze for a span;

6. Aphrodite (Venus) was born near the island of Cythera.   8. Proserpine.
7. Aphrodite was the mother of Aeneas, the founder of
Rome.

A little soul for a little bears up this corpse which is man.
So long I endure, no longer; and laugh not again, neither weep.
110   For there is no God found stronger than death; and death is a sleep.

1866

A Forsaken Garden[1]

In a coign[2] of the cliff between lowland and highland,
   At the sea-down's edge between windward and lee,
Walled round with rocks as an inland island,
   The ghost of a garden fronts the sea.
5   A girdle of brushwood and thorn encloses
   The steep square slope of the blossomless bed
Where the weeds that grew green from the graves of its roses
    Now lie dead.

The fields fall southward, abrupt and broken,
10   To the low last edge of the long lone land.
If a step should sound or a word be spoken,
   Would a ghost not rise at the strange guest's hand?
So long have the grey bare walks lain guestless,
   Through branches and briars if a man make way,
15 He shall find no life but the sea-wind's, restless
    Night and day.

The dense hard passage is blind and stifled
   That crawls by a track none turn to climb
To the strait waste place that the years have rifled
20   Of all but the thorns that are touched not of time.
The thorns he spares when the rose is taken;
   The rocks are left when he wastes the plain.
The wind that wanders, the weeds wind-shaken,
    These remain.

25 Not a flower to be pressed of the foot that falls not;
   As the heart of a dead man the seed-plots are dry;
From the thicket of thorns whence the nightingale calls not,
   Could she call, there were never a rose to reply.
Over the meadows that blossom and wither
30   Rings but the note of a sea-bird's song;
Only the sun and the rain come hither
    All year long.

The sun burns sere and the rain dishevels
One gaunt bleak blossom of scentless breath.
35 Only the wind here hovers and revels

---

1. The poem is set at East Dene on the Isle of Wight,
where Swinburne grew up.   2. Corner.

In a round where life seems barren as death.
Here there was laughing of old, there was weeping,
    Haply, of lovers none ever will know,
Whose eyes went seaward a hundred sleeping
40   Years ago.

Heart handfast in heart as they stood, "Look thither,"
    Did he whisper? "look forth from the flowers to the sea;
For the foam-flowers endure when the rose-blossoms wither,
    And men that love lightly may die—but we?"
45 And the same wind sang and the same waves whitened,
    And or ever the garden's last petals were shed,
In the lips that had whispered, the eyes that had lightened,
    Love was dead.

Or they loved their life through, and then went whither?
50   And were one to the end—but what end who knows?
Love deep as the sea as a rose must wither,
    As the rose-red seaweed that mocks the rose.
Shall the dead take thought for the dead to love them?
    What love was ever as deep as a grave?
55 They are loveless now as the grass above them
    Or the wave.

All are at one now, roses and lovers,
    Not known of the cliffs and the fields and the sea.
Not a breath of the time that has been hovers
60   In the air now soft with a summer to be.
Not a breath shall there sweeten the seasons hereafter
    Of the flowers or the lovers that laugh now or weep,
When as they that are free now of weeping and laughter
    We shall sleep.

65 Here death may deal not again for ever;
    Here change may come not till all change end.
From the graves they have made they shall rise up never,
    Who have left nought living to ravage and rend.
Earth, stones, and thorns of the wild ground growing,
70   While the sun and the rain live, these shall be;
Till a last wind's breath upon all these blowing
    Roll the sea.

Till the slow sea rise and the sheer cliff crumble,
    Till terrace and meadow the deep gulfs drink,
75 Till the strength of the waves of the high tides humble
    The fields that lessen, the rocks that shrink,
Here now in his triumph where all things falter,
    Stretched out on the spoils that his own hand spread,
As a god self-slain on his own strange altar,
80   Death lies dead.

1876

Walter Pater
1839–1894

"It doesn't matter what is said as long as it is said beautifully." The young Walter Pater's casual, deliberately shocking remark forecast a career that would undermine Victorian confidence in the morality of art and spark a transition to the Aesthetic creed of "art for art's sake." But if Pater was, as Oscar Wilde said, "the most perfect master of English prose now creating amongst us," *what* he said also mattered immensely. He was an elegant pioneer of subjective, impressionistic criticism, intent on subverting moral and religious absolutes.

Pater's first publication, on Coleridge (1866), announced his main theme: "To the modern spirit nothing is or can be rightly known except relatively." Pater dismissed the notion of critical objectivity, preferring to explore art's effect on himself. In preface to *The Renaissance*, he startled his readers by asking: "What is this song or picture, this engaging personality presented in life or in a book, to *me?*"

As a boy, Pater loved to play at being a priest; his schoolmates called him "Parson Pater." Even though he lost his faith at Oxford, scandalizing friends with his irreverent talk, he was so attracted to the beauty of church ritual that he considered ordination anyway. Instead, in 1864 he became a Fellow of Brasenose College, Oxford. Regarded by friends as a "queer, strange creature," Pater developed a reputation for wittily trivializing serious topics. After his first tutorial with Pater, Gerard Manley Hopkins noted in his diary: "Pater talking two hours against Xtianity." From 1869 onward, Pater lived with his two sisters, first at Oxford, then in London. Their house was an Aesthetic oasis, decorated with Morris wallpaper, blue china pots, delicate embroidery, engravings from Botticelli, and a few artfully arranged flowers. The teas they gave for students subtly challenged decorum, as Pater's favored guests were young athletes who approached a Greek ideal of male beauty.

The publication of *Studies in the History of the Renaissance* (1873) brought Pater both recognition and notoriety. His appointment as university proctor appears to have been blocked because the amoral tone of his writing drew attention to his private behavior—a romantic friendship with an undergraduate. His reputation also suffered from his well-known influence on Oscar Wilde. Pater's efforts to defend himself were characteristically prim: "I wish they would not call me a hedonist. It gives such a wrong impression to those who do not know Greek."

Yet *The Renaissance* became the key book of the Aesthetic movement. It marked the end of High Victorianism by displacing reverence for the organicism and spirituality of medieval society—as imagined by Carlyle, Ruskin, and Morris—in favor of the sensuous, pagan self-consciousness and materiality of Renaissance artists like Botticelli and Leonardo. Pater denied that morality had anything to do with art, or that organized religion had any claim on the individual. Arguing that life was sheer flux—"that strange perpetual weaving and unweaving of ourselves"—Pater insisted that the intense appreciation of passionate, beautiful, transitory moments mattered more than anything else. Life's aim, he concluded, is "not the fruit of experience, but experience itself." Wilde called *The Renaissance* "the holy writ of beauty."

In 1878 Pater transformed his earliest memories into *The Child in the House*, a haunting exploration of how identity is born. Later, he obliquely elaborated his own moral sensibility in the dreamy novel *Marius the Epicurean* (1885), in which his pagan protagonist dies alongside a Christian martyr who befriends him. The works of Pater's last decade include the quasi-autobiographical musings in *Imaginary Portraits* (1887); his finest book of literary criticism, *Appreciations, with an Essay on Style* (1889); *Plato and Platonism* (1893), and a posthumous unfinished novel, *Gaston de Latour* (1896).

Elevating criticism to an expressive art, Pater opened new possibilities both for critics and for English prose. Though Arnold had claimed that criticism should "see the object as in itself it really is," Pater asserted that first one had to "know one's own impression as it really is" and make that elusive feeling, as Wilde put it, the "starting point for a new creation." As Wilde saw, Pater's famous description of the Mona Lisa achieves independent stature as a work of art. Yeats admired the passage so much he pronounced it the first modern poem, and reprinted it—in free verse form—at the start of his *Oxford Book of Modern Verse* (1936). Pater's emphasis on flux, sensation, perception, and the mysteries of identity—all that betokened the "quickened, multiplied consciousness" of modern life—carried his influence far beyond Aestheticism. Joyce imitated him in *A Portrait of the Artist* and *Ulysses,* and Wilde, Hopkins, Symons, Yeats, Eliot, Pound, and Woolf all acknowledged their debt to him. As he announced in his famous essay on style: "imaginative prose" is "the special art of the modern world."

from The Renaissance
Preface

Many attempts have been made by writers on art and poetry to define beauty in the abstract, to express it in the most general terms, to find some universal formula for it. The value of these attempts has most often been in the suggestive and penetrating things said by the way. Such discussions help us very little to enjoy what has been well done in art or poetry, to discriminate between what is more and what is less excellent in them, or to use words like beauty, excellence, art, poetry, with a more precise meaning than they would otherwise have. Beauty, like all other qualities presented to human experience, is relative; and the definition of it becomes unmeaning and useless in proportion to its abstractness. To define beauty, not in the most abstract but in the most concrete terms possible, to find not its universal formula, but the formula which expresses most adequately this or that special manifestation of it, is the aim of the true student of aesthetics.

"To see the object as in itself it really is,"[1] has been justly said to be the aim of all true criticism whatever; and in aesthetic criticism the first step towards seeing one's object as it really is, is to know one's own impression as it really is, to discriminate it, to realise it distinctly. The objects with which aesthetic criticism deals—music, poetry, artistic and accomplished forms of human life—are indeed receptacles of so many powers or forces: they possess, like the products of nature, so many virtues or qualities. What is this song or picture, this engaging personality presented in life or in a book, to *me?* What effect does it really produce on me? Does it give me pleasure? and if so, what sort or degree of pleasure? How is my nature modified by its presence, and under its influence? The answers to these questions are the original facts with which the aesthetic critic has to do; and, as in the study of light, of morals, of number, one must realise such primary data for one's self, or not at all. And he who experiences these impressions strongly, and drives directly at the discrimination and analysis of them, has no need to trouble himself with the abstract question what beauty is in itself, or what its exact relation to truth or experience—metaphysical questions, as unprofitable as metaphysical questions elsewhere. He may pass them all by as being, answerable or not, of no interest to him.

The aesthetic critic, then, regards all the objects with which he has to do, all works of art, and the fairer forms of nature and human life, as powers or forces producing pleasurable sensations, each of a more or less peculiar or unique kind. This influence he feels, and wishes to explain, by analysing and reducing it to its elements.

---

1. Quoting Matthew Arnold, *The Function of Criticism at the Present Time* (page 1685).

To him, the picture, the landscape, the engaging personality in life or in a book, *La Gioconda*, the hills of Carrara, Pico of Mirandola,[2] are valuable for their virtues, as we say, in speaking of a herb, a wine, a gem; for the property each has of affecting one with a special, a unique, impression of pleasure. Our education becomes complete in proportion as our susceptibility to these impressions increases in depth and variety. And the function of the aesthetic critic is to distinguish, to analyse, and separate from its adjuncts, the virtue by which a picture, a landscape, a fair personality in life or in a book, produces this special impression of beauty or pleasure, to indicate what the source of that impression is, and under what conditions it is experienced. His end is reached when he has disengaged that virtue, and noted it, as a chemist notes some natural element, for himself and others; and the rule for those who would reach this end is stated with great exactness in the words of a recent critic of Sainte-Beuve:—
De se borner à connaître de près les belles choses, et à s'en nourrir en exquis amateurs, en humanistes accomplis.[3]

What is important, then, is not that the critic should possess a correct abstract definition of beauty for the intellect, but a certain kind of temperament, the power of being deeply moved by the presence of beautiful objects. He will remember always that beauty exists in many forms. To him all periods, types, schools of taste, are in themselves equal. In all ages there have been some excellent workmen, and some excellent work done. The question he asks is always:—In whom did the stir, the genius, the sentiment of the period find itself? where was the receptacle of its refinement, its elevation, its taste? "The ages are all equal," says William Blake, "but genius is always above its age."[4]

Often it will require great nicety to disengage this virtue from the commoner elements with which it may be found in combination. Few artists, not Goethe or Byron even, work quite cleanly, casting off all *débris*, and leaving us only what the heat of their imagination has wholly fused and transformed. Take, for instance, the writings of Wordsworth. The heat of his genius, entering into the substance of his work, has crystallised a part, but only a part, of it; and in that great mass of verse there is much which might well be forgotten. But scattered up and down it, sometimes fusing and transforming entire compositions, like the Stanzas on *Resolution and Independence*, or the *Ode on the Recollections of Childhood*,[5] sometimes, as if at random, depositing a fine crystal here or there, in a matter it does not wholly search through and transmute, we trace the action of his unique, incommunicable faculty, that strange, mystical sense of a life in natural things, and of man's life as a part of nature, drawing strength and colour and character from local influences, from the hills and streams, and from natural sights and sounds. Well! that is the *virtue*, the active principle in Wordsworth's poetry; and then the function of the critic of Wordsworth is to follow up that active principle, to disengage it, to mark the degree in which it penetrates his verse.

The subjects of the following studies are taken from the history of the *Renaissance*, and touch what I think the chief points in that complex, many-sided movement. I have explained in the first of them what I understand by the word,

---

2. *La Gioconda* is another title for the *Mona Lisa* by Leonardo da Vinci (1452–1519); the hills of Carrara contain marble quarries; Pico della Mirandola (1463–1494) was an Italian philosopher and classical scholar about whom Pater wrote an essay in *The Renaissance*.
3. To limit oneself to knowing beautiful things well, and to be nourished by them, as might an exquisite amateur or an accomplished humanist (French). In fact, this was written by Charles Sainte-Beuve (1804–1869).
4. From Blake's annotations to *The Works of Sir Joshua Reynolds*.
5. The actual title of Wordsworth's poem is *Ode: Intimations of Immortality from Recollections of Early Childhood*.

giving it a much wider scope than was intended by those who originally used it to denote that revival of classical antiquity in the fifteenth century which was only one of many results of a general excitement and enlightening of the human mind, but of which the great aim and achievements of what, as Christian art, is often falsely opposed to the Renaissance, were another result. This outbreak of the human spirit may be traced far into the middle age itself, with its motives already clearly pronounced, the care for physical beauty, the worship of the body, the breaking down of those limits which the religious system of the middle age imposed on the heart and the imagination. I have taken as an example of this movement, this earlier Renaissance within the middle age itself, and as an expression of its qualities, two little compositions in early French; not because they constitute the best possible expression of them, but because they help the unity of my series, inasmuch as the Renaissance ends also in France, in French poetry, in a phase of which the writings of Joachim du Bellay[6] are in many ways the most perfect illustration. The Renaissance, in truth, put forth in France an aftermath, a wonderful later growth, the products of which have to the full that subtle and delicate sweetness which belongs to a refined and comely decadence, just as its earliest phases have the freshness which belongs to all periods of growth in art, the charm of *ascêsis* [self-denial], of the austere and serious girding of the loins in youth.

But it is in Italy, in the fifteenth century, that the interest of the Renaissance mainly lies,—in that solemn fifteenth century which can hardly be studied too much, not merely for its positive results in the things of the intellect and the imagination, its concrete works of art, its special and prominent personalities, with their profound aesthetic charm, but for its general spirit and character, for the ethical qualities of which it is a consummate type.

The various forms of intellectual activity which together make up the culture of an age, move for the most part from different starting-points, and by unconnected roads. As products of the same generation they partake indeed of a common character, and unconsciously illustrate each other; but of the producers themselves, each group is solitary, gaining what advantage or disadvantage there may be in intellectual isolation. Art and poetry, philosophy and the religious life, and that other life of refined pleasure and action in the conspicuous places of the world, are each of them confined to its own circle of ideas, and those who prosecute either of them are generally little curious of the thoughts of others. There come, however, from time to time, eras of more favourable conditions, in which the thoughts of men draw nearer together than is their wont, and the many interests of the intellectual world combine in one complete type of general culture. The fifteenth century in Italy is one of these happier eras, and what is sometimes said of the age of Pericles is true of that of Lorenzo:[7]—it is an age productive in personalities, many-sided, centralised, complete. Here, artists and philosophers and those whom the action of the world has elevated and made keen, do not live in isolation, but breathe a common air, and catch light and heat from each other's thoughts. There is a spirit of general elevation and enlightenment in which all alike communicate. The unity of this spirit gives unity to all the various products of the Renaissance; and it is to this intimate alliance with mind, this participation in the best thoughts which that age produced, that the art of Italy in the fifteenth century owes much of its grave dignity and influence.

6. French poet and critic, (1524–1560), about whom Pater wrote an essay in *The Renaissance*.
7. Pericles, Athenian statesman during the 5th century B.C.; Lorenzo de Medici (1449–1492), Florentine ruler and patron of the arts.

I have added an essay on Winckelmann,[8] as not incongruous with the studies which precede it, because Winckelmann, coming in the eighteenth century, really belongs in spirit to an earlier age. By his enthusiasm for the things of the intellect and the imagination for their own sake, by his Hellenism, his life-long struggle to attain to the Greek spirit, he is in sympathy with the humanists of a previous century. He is the last fruit of the Renaissance, and explains in a striking way its motive and tendencies.

1873

from *Leonardo da Vinci*
[LA GIOCONDA][1]

La Gioconda is, in the truest sense, Leonardo's masterpiece, the revealing instance of his mode of thought and work. In suggestiveness, only the *Melancholia* of Dürer[2] is comparable to it; and no crude symbolism disturbs the effect of its subdued and graceful mystery. We all know the face and hands of the figure, set in its marble chair, in that circle of fantastic rocks, as in some faint light under sea. Perhaps of all ancient pictures time has chilled it least. As often happens with works in which invention seems to reach its limit, there is an element in it given to, not invented by, the master. In that inestimable folio of drawings, once in the possession of Vasari, were certain designs by Verrocchio,[3] faces of such impressive beauty that Leonardo in his boyhood copied them many times. It is hard not to connect with these designs of the elder, by-past master, as with its germinal principle, the unfathomable smile, always with a touch of something sinister in it, which plays over all Leonardo's work. Besides, the picture is a portrait. From childhood we see this image defining itself on the fabric of his dreams; and but for express historical testimony, we might fancy that this was but his ideal lady, embodied and beheld at last. What was the relationship of a living Florentine to this creature of his thought? By what strange affinities had the dream and the person grown up thus apart, and yet so closely together? Present from the first incorporeally in Leonardo's brain, dimly traced in the designs of Verrocchio, she is found present at last in *Il Giocondo's* house. That there is much of mere portraiture in the picture is attested by the legend that by artificial means, the presence of mimes and flute-players, that subtle expression was protracted on the face. Again, was it in four years and by renewed labour never really completed, or in four months and as by stroke of magic, that the image was projected?

The presence that rose thus so strangely beside the waters, is expressive of what in the ways of a thousand years men had come to desire. Hers is the head upon which all "the ends of the world are come,"[4] and the eyelids are a little weary. It is a beauty wrought out from within upon the flesh, the deposit, little cell by cell, of strange thoughts and fantastic reveries and exquisite passions. Set it for a moment beside one of those white Greek goddesses or beautiful women of antiquity, and how would they

8. Johann Joachim Winckelmann (1717–1768), German classicist and art historian.
1. Better known as the *Mona Lisa,* this painting by Italian Renaissance artist and inventor Leonardo da Vinci (1452–1519) hangs in the Louvre Museum in Paris. The model was probably the wife of Francesco del Giocondo; hence, "La Gioconda."
2. Engraving of the spirit of Melancholy, represented as a seated female figure, by the German artist Albrecht

Dürer (1471–1528).
3. Andrea del Verrocchio (1435–1488), Florentine painter and sculptor; Giorgio Vasari (1511–1574), was the author of *Lives of the Most Excellent Italian Painters.*
4. "Now all these things happened unto them for examples: and they are written for our admonition, upon whom the ends of the world are come" (1 Corinthians 10.11).

be troubled by this beauty, into which the soul with all its maladies has passed! All the thoughts and experience of the world have etched and moulded there, in that which they have of power to refine and make expressive the outward form, the animalism of Greece, the lust of Rome, the mysticism of the middle age with its spiritual ambition and imaginative loves, the return of the Pagan world, the sins of the Borgias.[5] She is older than the rocks among which she sits; like the vampire, she has been dead many times, and learned the secrets of the grave; and has been a diver in deep seas, and keeps their fallen day about her; and trafficked for strange webs with Eastern merchants and, as Leda, was the mother of Helen of Troy, and, as Saint Anne, the mother of Mary;[6] and all this has been to her but as the sound of lyres and flutes, and lives only in the delicacy with which it has moulded the changing lineaments, and tinged the eyelids and the hands. The fancy of a perpetual life, sweeping together ten thousand experiences, is an old one; and modern philosophy has conceived the idea of humanity as wrought upon by, and summing up in itself, all modes of thought and life. Certainly Lady Lisa might stand as the embodiment of the old fancy, the symbol of the modern idea.

1871

Conclusion[1]

Λέγει που Ἡράκλειτος ὅτι πάντα χωρεῖ καὶ οὐδὲν μένι[2]

To regard all things and principles of things as inconstant modes or fashions has more and more become the tendency of modern thought. Let us begin with that which is without—our physical life. Fix upon it in one of its more exquisite intervals, the moment, for instance, of delicious recoil from the flood of water in summer heat. What is the whole physical life in that moment but a combination of natural elements to which science gives their names? But those elements, phosphorus and lime and delicate fibres, are present not in the human body alone: we detect them in places most remote from it. Our physical life is a perpetual motion of them—the passage of the blood, the waste and repairing of the lenses of the eye, the modification of the tissues of the brain under every ray of light and sound—processes which science reduces to simpler and more elementary forces. Like the elements of which we are composed, the action of these forces extends beyond us: it rusts iron and ripens corn. Far out on every side of us those elements are broadcast, driven in many currents; and birth and gesture and death and the springing of violets from the grave[3] are but a few out of ten thousand resultant combinations. That clear, perpetual outline of face and limb is but an image of ours, under which we group them—a design in a web, the actual threads of which pass out beyond it. This at least of flamelike our life has, that it is but the concurrence, renewed from moment to moment, of forces parting sooner or later on their ways.

---

5. An Italian Renaissance family notorious for their ruthlessness in the pursuit of power.

6. A bold juxtaposition of St. Anne, mother of the Virgin Mary, with the mythic Leda, who gave birth to Helen of Troy after being raped by Zeus.

1. This brief "Conclusion" was omitted in the second edition of this book, as I conceived it might possibly mislead some of those young men into whose hands it might fall. On the whole, I have thought it best to reprint it here, with some slight changes which bring it closer to my original meaning. I have dealt more fully in *Marius the Epicurean* with the thoughts suggested by it [Pater's note to the third edition, 1888].

2. Heraclitus says, All things give way; nothing remaineth [Pater's translation, from Plato's *Cratylus*].

3. When Ophelia is being buried, her brother says: "Lay her i' th' earth; / And from her fair and unpolluted flesh / May violets spring!" (*Hamlet* 5.1.238–40).

Or if we begin with the inward world of thought and feeling, the whirlpool is still more rapid, the flame more eager and devouring. There it is no longer the gradual darkening of the eye, the gradual fading of colour from the wall—movements of the shore-side, where the water flows down indeed, though in apparent rest—but the race of the mid-stream, a drift of momentary acts of sight and passion and thought. At first sight experience seems to bury us under a flood of external objects, pressing upon us with a sharp and importunate reality, calling us out of ourselves in a thousand forms of action. But when reflexion begins to play upon those objects they are dissipated under its influence; the cohesive force seems suspended like some trick of magic; each object is loosed into a group of impressions—colour, odour, texture—in the mind of the observer. And if we continue to dwell in thought on this world, not of objects in the solidity with which language invests them, but of impressions, unstable, flickering, inconsistent, which burn and are extinguished with our consciousness of them, it contracts still further: the whole scope of observation is dwarfed into the narrow chamber of the individual mind. Experience, already reduced to a group of impressions, is ringed round for each one of us by that thick wall of personality through which no real voice has ever pierced on its way to us, or from us to that which we can only conjecture to be without. Every one of those impressions is the impression of the individual in his isolation, each mind keeping as a solitary prisoner its own dream of a world. Analysis goes a step farther still, and assures us that those impressions of the individual mind to which, for each one of us, experience dwindles down, are in perpetual flight; that each of them is limited by time, and that as time is infinitely divisible, each of them is infinitely divisible also; all that is actual in it being a single moment, gone while we try to apprehend it, of which it may ever be more truly said that it has ceased to be than that it is. To such a tremulous wisp constantly re-forming itself on the stream, to a single sharp impression, with a sense in it, a relic more or less fleeting, of such moments gone by, what is real in our life fines itself down. It is with this movement, with the passage and dissolution of impressions, images, sensations, that analysis leaves off—that continual vanishing away, that strange, perpetual weaving and unweaving of ourselves.

Philosophiren, says Novalis, *ist dephlegmatisiren vivificiren.*[4] The service of philosophy, of speculative culture, towards the human spirit, is to rouse, to startle it to a life of constant and eager observation. Every moment some form grows perfect in hand or face; some tone on the hills or the sea is choicer than the rest; some mood of passion or insight or intellectual excitement is irresistibly real and attractive to us,—for that moment only. Not the fruit of experience, but experience itself, is the end. A counted number of pulses only is given to us of a variegated, dramatic life. How may we see in them all that is to be seen in them by the finest senses? How shall we pass most swiftly from point to point, and be present always at the focus where the greatest number of vital forces unite in their purest energy?

To burn always with this hard, gemlike flame, to maintain this ecstasy, is success in life. In a sense it might even be said that our failure is to form habits: for, after all, habit is relative to a stereotyped world, and meantime it is only the roughness of the eye that makes any two persons, things, situations, seem alike. While all melts under

---

4. "To philosophize is to become unsluggish, to come alive." Novalis is the pseudonym of Friedrich von Hardenberg (1772–1801), a German Romantic writer.

our feet, we may well grasp at any exquisite passion, or any contribution to knowledge that seems by a lifted horizon to set the spirit free for a moment, or any stirring of the senses, strange dyes, strange colours, and curious odours, or work of the artist's hands, or the face of one's friend. Not to discriminate every moment some passionate attitude in those about us, and in the very brilliancy of their gifts some tragic dividing of forces on their ways, is, on this short day of frost and sun, to sleep before evening. With this sense of the splendour of our experience and of its awful brevity, gathering all we are into one desperate effort to see and touch, we shall hardly have time to make theories about the things we see and touch. What we have to do is to be for ever curiously testing new opinions and courting new impressions, never acquiescing in a facile orthodoxy of Comte, or of Hegel,[5] or of our own. Philosophical theories or ideas, as points of view, instruments of criticism, may help us to gather up what might otherwise pass unregarded by us. "Philosophy is the microscope of thought."[6] The theory or idea or system which requires of us the sacrifice of any part of this experience, in consideration of some interest into which we cannot enter, or some abstract theory we have not identified with ourselves, or of what is only conventional, has no real claim upon us.

One of the most beautiful passages of Rousseau is that in the sixth book of the *Confessions*,[7] where he describes the awakening in him of the literary sense. An undefinable taint of death had clung always about him, and now in early manhood he believed himself smitten by mortal disease. He asked himself how he might make as much as possible of the interval that remained; and he was not biassed by anything in his previous life when he decided that it must be by intellectual excitement, which he found just then in the clear, fresh writings of Voltaire.[8] Well! we are all *condamnés*, as Victor Hugo[9] says: we are all under sentence of death but with a sort of indefinite reprieve—*les hommes sont tous condamnés à mort avec des sursis indéfinis*: we have an interval, and then our place knows us no more. Some spend this interval in listlessness, some in high passions, the wisest, at least among "the children of this world,"[1] in art and song. For our one chance lies in expanding that interval, in getting as many pulsations as possible into the given time. Great passions may give us this quickened sense of life, ecstasy and sorrow of love, the various forms of enthusiastic activity, disinterested or otherwise, which come naturally to many of us. Only be sure it is passion—that it does yield you this fruit of a quickened, multiplied consciousness. Of such wisdom, the poetic passion, the desire of beauty, the love of art for its own sake, has most. For art comes to you proposing frankly to give nothing but the highest quality to your moments as they pass, and simply for those moments' sake.

1868   1868, 1873

5. Auguste Comte (1798–1857), French philosopher, was the founder of positivism; George W. F. Hegel (1770–1831), was a major German philosopher of history and of art.
6. Victor Hugo, *Les Misérables* (1862) pt. 5, bk. 2, ch. 2.
7. The *Confessions* is an autobiographical work by Jean-Jacques Rousseau (1712–1778), French writer and philosopher.
8. The critic Donald Hill notes that Rousseau never mentions reading Voltaire (1694–1778), French writer and skeptic.
9. Condemned. Victor Hugo, French novelist; the passage Pater quotes is from *Le dernier jour d'un condamné* (1832).
1. "And the Lord commended the unjust steward, because he had done wisely; for the children of this world are in their generation wiser than the children of light" (Luke 16.8).

from The Child in the House[1]

As Florian Deleal walked, one hot afternoon, he overtook by the wayside a poor aged man, and, as he seemed weary with the road, helped him on with the burden which he carried, a certain distance. And as the man told his story, it chanced that he named the place, a little place in the neighbourhood of a great city, where Florian had passed his earliest years, but which he had never since seen, and, the story told, went forward on his journey comforted. And that night, like a reward for his pity, a dream of that place came to Florian, a dream which did for him the office of the finer sort of memory, bringing its object to mind with a great clearness, yet, as sometimes happens in dreams, raised a little above itself, and above ordinary retrospect. The true aspect of the place, especially of the house there in which he had lived as a child,[2] the fashion of its doors, its hearths, its windows, the very scent upon the air of it, was with him in sleep for a season; only, with tints more musically blent on wall and floor, and some finer light and shadow running in and out along its curves and angles, and with all its little carvings daintier. He awoke with a sigh at the thought of almost thirty years which lay between him and that place, yet with a flutter of pleasure still within him at the fair light, as if it were a smile, upon it. And it happened that this accident of his dream was just the thing needed for the beginning of a certain design he then had in view, the noting, namely, of some things in the story of his spirit—in that process of brain-building by which we are, each one of us, what we are. With the image of the place so clear and favourable upon him, he fell to thinking of himself therein, and how his thoughts had grown up to him. In that half-spiritualised house he could watch the better, over again, the gradual expansion of the soul which had come to be there—of which indeed, through the law which makes the material objects about them so large an element in children's lives, it had actually become a part; inward and outward being woven through and through each other into one inextricable texture—half, tint and trace and accident of homely colour and form, from the wood and the bricks; half, mere soul-stuff, floated thither from who knows how far. In the house and garden of his dream he saw a child moving, and could divide the main streams at least of the winds that had played on him, and study so the first stage in that mental journey.

The *old house,* as when Florian talked of it afterwards he always called it, (as all children do, who can recollect a change of home, soon enough but not too soon to mark a period in their lives) really was an old house; and an element of French descent in its inmates—descent from Watteau, the old court-painter, one of whose gallant pieces still hung in one of the rooms[3]—might explain, together with some other things, a noticeable trimness and comely whiteness about everything there—the curtains, the couches, the paint on the walls with which the light and shadow played so delicately; might explain also the tolerance of the great poplar in the garden, a tree most often despised by English people, but which French people love, having observed a certain fresh way its leaves have of dealing with the wind, making it sound, in never so slight a stirring of the air, like running water.

---

1. First published in *Macmillan's Magazine* in August 1878, *The Child in the House* is a fictionalized autobiographical sketch, written when Pater was 41. Florian Deleal may represent Pater himself, but many details of his childhood have been altered.
2. Florian's house appears to be a composite of Pater's childhood home in Enfield (a village north of London)

and his aunt's larger house in Kent. When Pater was 14, the family moved to Canterbury so that he could attend the King's School there.
3. Jean Antoine Watteau (1684–1721), French painter about whom Pater wrote an essay in *Imaginary Portraits* (1887).

The old-fashioned, low wainscoting went round the rooms, and up the staircase with carved balusters and shadowy angles, landing half-way up at a broad window, with a swallow's nest below the sill, and the blossom of an old pear-tree showing across it in late April, against the blue, below which the perfumed juice of the find of fallen fruit in autumn was so fresh. At the next turning came the closet which held on its deep shelves the best china. Little angel faces and reedy flutings stood out round the fireplace of the children's room. And on the top of the house, above the large attic, where the white mice ran in the twilight—an infinite, unexplored wonderland of childish treasures, glass beads, empty scent-bottles still sweet, thrum[4] of coloured silks, among its lumber—a flat space of roof, railed round, gave a view of the neighbouring steeples; for the house, as I said, stood near a great city, which sent up heavenwards, over the twisting weather-vanes, not seldom, its beds of rolling cloud and smoke, touched with storm or sunshine. But the child of whom I am writing did not hate the fog because of the crimson lights which fell from it sometimes upon the chimneys, and the whites which gleamed through its openings, on summer mornings, on turret or pavement. For it is false to suppose that a child's sense of beauty is dependent on any choiceness or special fineness, in the objects which present themselves to it, though this indeed comes to be the rule with most of us in later life; earlier, in some degree, we see inwardly; and the child finds for itself, and with unstinted delight, a difference for the sense, in those whites and reds through the smoke on very homely buildings, and in the gold of the dandelions at the road-side, just beyond the houses, where not a handful of earth is virgin and untouched, in the lack of better ministries to its desire of beauty.

This house then stood not far beyond the gloom and rumours of the town, among high garden-wall, bright all summer-time with Golden-rod, and brown-and-golden Wall-flower—*Flos Parietis*, as the children's Latin-reading father taught them to call it, while he was with them. Tracing back the threads of his complex spiritual habit, as he was used in after years to do, Florian found that he owed to the place many tones of sentiment afterwards customary with him, certain inward lights under which things most naturally presented themselves to him. The coming and going of travellers to the town along the way, the shadow of the streets, the sudden breath of the neighbouring gardens, the singular brightness of bright weather there, its singular darknesses which linked themselves in his mind to certain engraved illustrations in the old big Bible at home, the coolness of the dark, cavernous shops round the great church, with its giddy winding stair up to the pigeons and the bells—a citadel of peace in the heart of the trouble—all this acted on his childish fancy, so that ever afterwards the like aspects and incidents never failed to throw him into a well-recognised imaginative mood, seeming actually to have become a part of the texture of his mind. Also, Florian could trace home to this point a pervading preference in himself for a kind of comeliness and dignity, an *urbanity* literally, in modes of life, which he connected with the pale people of towns, and which made him susceptible to a kind of exquisite satisfaction in the trimness and well-considered grace of certain things and persons he afterwards met with, here and there, in his way through the world.

So the child of whom I am writing lived on there quietly; things without thus ministering to him, as he sat daily at the window with the birdcage hanging below it, and his mother taught him to read, wondering at the ease with which he learned, and

4. Scraps.

at the quickness of his memory. The perfume of the little flowers of the lime-tree fell through the air upon them like rain; while time seemed to move ever more slowly to the murmur of the bees in it, till it almost stood still on June afternoons. How insignificant, at the moment, seem the influences of the sensible things[5] which are tossed and fall and lie about us, so, or so, in the environment of early childhood. How indelibly, as we afterwards discover, they affect us; with what capricious attractions and associations they figure themselves on the white paper, the smooth wax,[6] of our ingenuous souls, as "with lead in the rock for ever,"[7] giving form and feature, and as it were assigned house-room in our memory, to early experiences of feeling and thought, which abide with us ever afterwards, thus, and not otherwise. The realities and passions, the rumours of the greater world without, steal in upon us, each by its own special little passage-way, through the wall of custom about us; and never afterwards quite detach themselves from this or that accident, or trick, in the mode of their first entrance to us. Our susceptibilities, the discovery of our powers, manifold experiences—our various experiences of the coming and going of bodily pain, for instance—belong to this or the other well-remembered place in the material habitation—that little white room with the window across which the heavy blossoms could beat so peevishly in the wind, with just that particular catch or throb, such a sense of teasing in it, on gusty mornings; and the early habitation thus gradually becomes a sort of material shrine or sanctuary of sentiment; a system of visible symbolism interweaves itself through all our thoughts and passions; and irresistibly, little shapes, voices, accidents—the angle at which the sun in the morning fell on the pillow—become parts of the great chain wherewith we are bound.

Thus far, for Florian, what all this had determined was a peculiarly strong sense of home—so forcible a motive with all of us—prompting to us our customary love of the earth, and the larger part of our fear of death, that revulsion we have from it, as from something strange, untried, unfriendly; though life-long imprisonment, they tell you, and final banishment from home is a thing bitterer still; the looking forward to but a short space, a mere childish *goûter* [snack] and dessert of it, before the end, being so great a resource of effort to pilgrims and wayfarers, and the soldier in distant quarters, and lending, in lack of that, some power of solace to the thought of sleep in the home churchyard, at least—dead cheek by dead cheek, and with the rain soaking in upon one from above.

So powerful is this instinct, and yet accidents like those I have been speaking of so mechanically determine it; its essence being indeed the early familiar, as constituting our ideal, or typical conception, of rest and security. Out of so many possible conditions, just this for you and that for me, brings ever the unmistakeable realisation of the delightful *chez soi*;[8] this for the Englishman, for me and you, with the closely-drawn white curtain and the shaded lamp; that, quite other, for the wandering Arab, who folds his tent every morning, and makes his sleeping-place among haunted ruins, or in old tombs.

With Florian then the sense of home became singularly intense, his good fortune being that the special character of his home was in itself so essentially home-like. As after many wanderings I have come to fancy that some parts of Surrey and Kent are,

---

5. Things perceptible to the senses.
6. A reference to the *tabula rasa*, or blank page, which represents the unformed human mind in John Locke's *Essay Concerning Human Understanding* (1690).

7. "Oh that my words were now written! oh that they were printed in a book! That they were graven with an iron pen and lead in the rock for ever!" (Job 19.23–24).
8. Feeling of being at home (French).

for Englishmen, the true landscape, true home-counties, by right, partly, of a certain earthy warmth in the yellow of the sand below their gorse-bushes, and of a certain grey-blue mist after rain, in the hollows of the hills there, welcome to fatigued eyes, and never seen farther south; so I think that the sort of house I have described, with precisely those proportions of red-brick and green, and with a just perceptible monotony in the subdued order of it, for its distinguishing note, is for Englishmen at least typically home-life. And so for Florian that general human instinct was reinforced by this special home-likeness in the place his wandering soul had happened to light on, as, in the second degree, its body and earthly tabernacle; the sense of harmony between his soul and its physical environment became, for a time at least, like perfectly played music, and the life led there singularly tranquil and filled with a curious sense of self-possession. * * *

I have remarked how, in the process of our brain-building, as the house of thought in which we live gets itself together, like some airy bird's-nest of floating thistle-down and chance straws, compact at last, little accidents have their consequence; and thus it happened that, as he walked one evening, a garden gate, usually closed, stood open; and lo! within, a great red hawthorn in full flower, embossing heavily the bleached and twisted trunk and branches, so aged that there were but few green leaves thereon—a plumage of tender, crimson fire out of the heart of the dry wood. The perfume of the tree had now and again reached him, in the currents of the wind, over the wall, and he had wondered what might be behind it, and was now allowed to fill his arms with the flowers—flowers enough for all the old blue-china pots along the chimney-piece, making *fête* [festivity] in the children's room. Was it some periodic moment in the expansion of soul within him, or mere trick of heat in the heavily-laden summer air? But the beauty of the thing struck home to him feverishly; and in dreams all night he loitered along a magic roadway of crimson flowers, which seemed to open ruddily in thick, fresh masses about his feet, and fill softly all the little hollows in the banks on either side. Always afterwards, summer by summer, as the flowers came on, the blossom of the red hawthorn still seemed to him absolutely the reddest of all things; and the goodly crimson, still alive in the works of old Venetian masters or old Flemish tapestries, called out always from afar the recollection of the flame in those perishing little petals, as it pulsed gradually out of them, kept long in the drawers of an old cabinet. Also then, for the first time, he seemed to experience a passionateness in his relation to fair outward objects, an inexplicable excitement in their presence, which disturbed him, and from which he half longed to be free. A touch of regret or desire mingled all night with the remembered presence of the red flowers, and their perfume in the darkness about him; and the longing for some undivined, entire possession of them was the beginning of a revelation to him, growing ever clearer, with the coming of the gracious summer guise of fields and trees and persons in each succeeding year, of a certain, at times seemingly exclusive, predominance in his interests, of beautiful physical things, a kind of tyranny of the senses over him. * * *

So he yielded himself to these things, to be played upon by them like a musical instrument, and began to note with deepening watchfulness, but always with some puzzled, unutterable longing in his enjoyment, the phases of the seasons and of the growing or waning day, down even to the shadowy changes wrought on bare wall or ceiling—the light cast up from the snow, bringing out their darkest angles; the brown light in the cloud, which meant rain; that almost too austere clearness, in the protracted light of the lengthening day, before warm weather began, as if it lingered but to make a severer workday, with the school-books opened earlier and later; that beam of June sunshine, at last, as he lay awake before the time, a way of gold-dust across the darkness; all the humming, the freshness, the perfume of the garden seemed to lie upon it—and coming in one afternoon in September, along the red gravel walk, to look for a basket of yellow crab-apples left in the cool, old parlour, he remembered it the more, and how the colours struck upon him, because a wasp on one bitten apple stung him, and he felt the passion of sudden, severe pain. * * *

Also, as he felt this pressure upon him of the sensible world, then, as often afterwards, there would come another sort of curious questioning how the last impressions of eye and ear might happen to him, how they would find him—the scent of the last flower, the soft yellowness of the last morning, the last recognition of some object of affection, hand or voice; it could not be but that the latest look of the eyes, before their final closing, would be strangely vivid; one would go with the hot tears, the cry, the touch of the wistful bystander, impressed how deeply on one! or would it be, perhaps, a mere frail retiring of all things, great or little, away from one, into a level distance?

For with this desire of physical beauty mingled itself early the fear of death—the fear of death intensified by the desire of beauty. Hitherto he had never gazed upon dead faces, as sometimes, afterwards, at the *Morgue* in Paris, or in that fair cemetery at Munich, where all the dead must go and lie in state before burial, behind glass windows, among the flowers and incense and holy candles—the aged clergy with their sacred ornaments, the young men in their dancing-shoes and spotless white linen— after which visits, those waxen, resistless faces would always live with him for many days, making the broadest sunshine sickly. The child had heard indeed of the death of his father, and how, in the Indian station, a fever had taken him, so that though not in action he had yet died as a soldier;[9] and hearing of the "resurrection of the just,"[1] he could think of him as still abroad in the world, somehow, for his protection—a grand, though perhaps rather terrible figure, in beautiful soldier's things, like the figure in the picture of Joshua's Vision in the Bible[2]—and of that, round which the mourners moved so softly, and afterwards with such solemn singing, as but a worn-out garment left at a deserted lodging. So it was, until on a summer day he walked with his mother through a fair churchyard. In a bright dress he rambled among the graves, in the gay weather, and so came, in one corner, upon an open grave for a child—a dark space on the brilliant grass—the black mould lying heaped up round it, weighing down the little jewelled branches of the dwarf rose-bushes in flower. And therewith came, full-grown, never wholly to leave him, with the certainty that even children do sometimes die, the physical horror of death, with its wholly selfish recoil from the association of lower forms of life, and the suffocating weight above. No benign, grave figure in beautiful soldier's things any longer abroad in the world for his protection! only a few poor, piteous bones; and above them, possibly, a certain sort of figure he hoped not to see. For sitting one day in the garden below an open window, he heard people talking, and could not but listen, how, in a sleepless hour, a sick woman had seen one of the dead sitting beside her, come to call her hence; and from the broken talk evolved with much clearness the notion that not all those dead people had really departed to the churchyard, nor were quite so

---

9. Pater's own father, a doctor who treated the poor of Enfield, died when Pater was a small child.
1. "And thou shalt be blessed; for they cannot recompense thee: for thou shalt be recompensed at the resurrection of the just" (Luke 14.14).
2. "Behold, there stood a man over against him with his

sword drawn in his hand: and Joshua went unto him, and said unto him, Art thou for us, or for our adversaries? And he said, Nay; but as captain of the host of the LORD am I now come. And Joshua fell on his face to the earth, and did worship" (Joshua 5.13–15).

motionless as they looked, but led a secret, half-fugitive life in their old homes, quite free by night, though sometimes visible in the day, dodging from room to room, with no great goodwill towards those who shared the place with them. * * *

To most children the sombre questionings to which impressions like these attach themselves, if they come at all, are actually suggested by religious books, which therefore they often regard with much secret distaste, and dismiss, as far as possible, from their habitual thoughts as a too depressing element in life. To Florian such impressions, these misgivings as to the ultimate tendency of the years, of the relationship between life and death, had been suggested spontaneously in the natural course of his mental growth by a strong innate sense for the soberer tones in things, further strengthened by actual circumstances; and religious sentiment, that system of biblical ideas in which he had been brought up, presented itself to him as a thing that might soften and dignify, and light up as with a "lively hope,"[3] a melancholy already deeply settled in him. So he yielded himself easily to religious impressions, and with a kind of mystical appetite for sacred things; the more as they came to him through a saintly person who loved him tenderly,[4] and believed that this early pre-occupation with them already marked the child out for a saint. He began to love, for their own sakes, church lights, holy days, all that belonged to the comely order of the sanctuary, the secrets of its white linen, and holy vessels, and fonts of pure water; and its hieratic purity and simplicity became the type of something he desired always to have about him in actual life. * * *

Sensibility—the desire of physical beauty—a strange biblical awe, which made any reference to the unseen act on him like solemn music—these qualities the child took away with him, when, at about the age of twelve years, he left the old house, and was taken to live in another place. He had never left home before, and, anticipating much from this change, had long dreamed over it, jealously counting the days till the time fixed for departure should come; had been a little careless about others even, in his strong desire for it—when Lewis fell sick, for instance, and they must wait still two days longer. At last the morning came, very fine; and all things—the very pavement with its dust, at the roadside—seemed to have a white, pearl-like lustre in them. They were to travel by a favourite road on which he had often walked a certain distance, and on one of those two prisoner days, when Lewis was sick, had walked farther than ever before, in his great desire to reach the new place. They had started and gone a little way when a pet bird was found to have been left behind, and must even now—so it presented itself to him—have already all the appealing fierceness and wild self-pity at heart of one left by others to perish of hunger in a closed house; and he returned to fetch it, himself in hardly less stormy distress. But as he passed in search of it from room to room, lying so pale, with a look of meekness in their denudation, and at last through that little, stripped white room, the aspect of the place touched him like the face of one dead; and a clinging back towards it came over him, so intense that he knew it would last long, and spoiling all his pleasure in the realisation of a thing so eagerly anticipated. And so, with the bird found, but himself in an agony of home-sickness, thus capriciously sprung up within him, he was driven quickly away, far into the rural distance, so fondly speculated on, of that favourite country-road.

1878

---

3. "Blessed be the God and Father of our Lord Jesus Christ, which according to his abundant mercy hath begotten us again unto a lively hope by the resurrection of Jesus Christ from the dead" (1 Peter 1.3).
4. Perhaps John Keble, a leader of the Oxford Movement whom Pater met in 1854.

Gerard Manley Hopkins
1844–1889

Gerard Manley Hopkins is the most modern of Victorian poets, and the most Victorian of modern poets. His stunningly original poems were, with a few exceptions, not published until 1918, placing him at first glance in the company of Eliot and Pound. But his struggle to maintain religious faith, his respect for conventional verse forms, and his quest to find proof of God's work in nature all mark him as quintessentially Victorian. Hopkins combines a microscopic keenness of vision with a Joycean genius for compound words, new coinages, unexpected rhymes, and startling distortions of syntax. The result is a poetry of modernist intensity and compression, fraught with bold ellipses and daring line breaks, but nonetheless dedicated to describing a world "charged with the grandeur of God." Orthodox and self-denying in matters of religion, Hopkins was also the era's most radical literary rebel.

Hopkins was born into a prosperous, pious Anglican family. After attending school in London, he went in 1863 to study classics at Balliol College, Oxford, where the agnostic aesthete Walter Pater was one of his tutors. At the same time, Hopkins came under the influence of the "Oxford Movement." He read John Henry Newman's account of his gravitation toward Roman Catholicism in *Apologia Pro Vita Sua*; subsequent talks with Newman led to Hopkins's own agonizing conversion to Catholicism in 1866. In 1868 he entered the novitiate of the Society of Jesus and burned almost all his early, Keatsian poems. He called his action the "slaughter of the innocents," and resolved "to write no more, as not belonging to my profession, unless it were by the wish of my superiors."

Seven years of poetic silence ensued, as Hopkins studied for the priesthood. But he was also meditating on his idiosyncratic theories of poetic composition. When five nuns were drowned in a shipwreck in 1875, he was suddenly moved to compose the first poem in his new style, *The Wreck of the Deutschland*. But there was no audience prepared to fathom his highly wrought style. Hopkins offered the work to a Jesuit magazine but, he said, "they dared not print it." He never again tried to publish.

Hopkins was ordained a Jesuit priest in 1877. Joyous, he produced a series of radiant sonnets celebrating the presence of God in nature. But his remaining years tested his faith sorely. Often in ill-health, he labored as a parish priest and teacher throughout Britain, including missionary work in the slums of Liverpool. He suffered physically and spiritually from the "vice and horrors" he found in his dreary urban duties: "It made even life a burden to me," he confessed. Then in 1884 he was appointed Professor of Greek and Latin at the Catholic, newly formed University College in Dublin. Already estranged from his family and the English church, he felt separated from his country, too. "I am in Ireland now," he wrote in a sonnet, "now I am at a third / Remove." Yet even as he despaired of accomplishing work of lasting value, he produced many of his best poems, including the famed "terrible sonnets" that describe his sense of spiritual and poetic sterility. Exhausted by his strenuous duties, Hopkins died in Dublin of typhoid at the age of forty-five.

Although Hopkins read the important nineteenth-century poets with care, he deliberately carved his own way. "The effect of studying masterpieces," he said, "is to make me admire and do otherwise." In his journals Hopkins often sounds like an English Thoreau, finely attuned to every nuance of the natural world. His entries are always searching to grasp the essential particularity of a thing, its inner landscape—what he called "inscape." Elaborating his theory in a letter to Robert Bridges, an Oxford friend who later became Poet Laureate, Hopkins admitted that "no doubt my poetry errs on the side of oddness. . . . it is the vice of distinctiveness to become queer." But he asserted the absolute importance of such "distinctiveness"—this "design, pattern or what I am in the habit of calling *inscape* is what I above all aim at in poetry." Hopkins needed another term to express the dynamic energy that not only makes the inscape cohere but also projects it outward toward the observer. This force that both unifies an object and arouses the senses of its beholder Hopkins called "instress." Taken together, the terms "inscape" and "instress" convey the organic beauty that for Hopkins speaks of God's presence in nature.

To apply these concepts poetically, Hopkins developed a new verse line based on "sprung rhythm." As in Old English poetry or nursery rhymes, each line in sprung rhythm has a fixed number of stresses, but the number and placement of unstressed syllables can vary widely. Many poets had employed individual lines of this type, but Hopkins took the idea of flexible metrics to new heights. He loaded his lines with internal rhyme, alliteration, assonance, and strong Anglo-Saxon words, and drove them forward with crashing consonants and wrenching enjambments. Responding to Bridges's confusion, he explained: "Why do I employ sprung rhythm at all? Because it is the nearest to the rhythm of prose, that is the native and natural rhythm of speech, the least forced, the most rhetorical and emphatic of all possible rhythms." Since Hopkins connected the sight and sound of individual words to the religious intensity with which he viewed objects in nature, the effect is akin to impassioned prayer. "My verse is less to be read than heard," he concluded; "it is oratorical."

In his later poetry a tangle of religious and sexual imagery expresses his sense of thwarted love and meager poetic production. He portrays himself as a sapless tree, or as barren sand: "I am soft sift / In an hourglass." In 1885 he wrote to Bridges in frustration, "if I could but produce work I should not mind its being buried, silenced, and going no further; but it kills me to be time's eunuch and never to beget." Such passages, with their images of sexual impotency, poetic infertility, and self-abnegation, suggest what Bridges called "the naked encounter of sensualism and asceticism" in Hopkins's work.

Despite his disclaimers, Hopkins was preoccupied with his lack of an audience. He once informed Bridges: "You are my public and I hope to convert you." Missionary-like, Hopkins's poetry seeks to "convert" the reader with its ecstatic particularity, its intensity of perception. But he speaks of his efforts as a one-way correspondence to God and his public; his poems are "cries like dead letters sent / To dearest him that lives alas! away." Hopkins could not have known that Bridges, despite his difficulty grasping these "dead letters," would finally publish the poems to great acclaim at the close of World War I. Then, like the works of Emily Dickinson and Vincent Van Gogh, they would suddenly seize a central artistic place in a past that had been unaware of their existence. And yet, Hopkins did recognize that his mingling of sensuality and spirituality allied him with another great proto-modernist. "I always knew in my heart Walt Whitman's mind to be more like my own than any other man's living," he told Bridges. "As he is a great scoundrel this is not a pleasant confession."

God's Grandeur

The world is charged with the grandeur of God.
  It will flame out, like shining from shook foil;[1]
  It gathers to a greatness, like the ooze of oil
Crushed.[2] Why do men then now not reck° his rod?   *heed*
5 Generations have trod, have trod, have trod;
    And all is seared with trade; bleared, smeared with toil;
    And wears man's smudge and shares man's smell: the soil
  Is bare now, nor can foot feel, being shod.

1. I mean foil in its sense of leaf or tinsel .... Shaken goldfoil gives off broad glares like sheet lightning and also, and this is true of nothing else, owing to its zigzag dints and creasings and network of small many cornered facets, a sort of fork lightning too [Hopkins's note].
2. Oil made by crushing seeds or olives.

And for° all this, nature is never spent;   *despite*
10   There lives the dearest freshness deep down things;
And though the last lights off the black West went
          Oh, morning, at the brown brink eastward, springs—
Because the Holy Ghost over the bent
          World broods with warm breast and with ah! bright wings.
1877   1895

The Starlight Night

Look at the stars! look, look up at the skies!
          O look at all the fire-folk sitting in the air!
          The bright boroughs, the circle-citadels there!
Down in dim woods the diamond delves!° the elves'-eyes!   *quarries*
5   The grey lawns cold where gold, where quickgold[1] lies!
          Wind-beat whitebeam![2] airy abeles° set on a flare!   *poplars*
          Flake-doves sent floating forth at a farmyard scare!—
Ah well! it is all a purchase, all is a prize.

Buy then! bid then!—What?—Prayer, patience, alms, vows.
10   Look, look: a May-mess,[3] like on orchard boughs!
          Look! March-bloom, like on mealed-with-yellow sallows![4]
These are indeed the barn; withindoors house
The shocks.[5] This piece-bright paling° shuts the spouse   *picket fence*
          Christ home, Christ and his mother and all his hallows.°   *saints*
1877   1918

Spring

Nothing is so beautiful as spring—
          When weeds, in wheels, shoot long and lovely and lush;
          Thrush's eggs look little low heavens, and thrush
Through the echoing timber does so rinse and wring
5   The ear, it strikes like lightnings to hear him sing;
          The glassy peartree leaves and blooms, they brush
          The descending blue; that blue is all in a rush
With richness; the racing lambs too have fair their fling.

What is all this juice and all this joy?
10   A strain of the earth's sweet being in the beginning
In Eden garden.—Have, get, before it cloy,
          Before it cloud, Christ, lord, and sour with sinning,

---

1. To describe the dew glittering on the lawns, Hopkins
has coined a word analogous to "quicksilver."
2. A tree whose leaves have white silky hair on the un-
derside.
3. An abundance of blossoming spring growth.
4. Willow trees stained with yellow spots.

5. Sheaves. Cf. Matthew 13.30: "Let both grow together
until the harvest: and in the time of harvest I will say to
the reapers, Gather ye together first the tares, and bind
them in bundles to burn them: but gather the wheat into
my barn."

Innocent mind and Mayday in girl and boy,
  Most, O maid's child,[1] thy choice and worthy the winning.

1877   1893

The Windhover:[1]
To Christ Our Lord

I caught this morning morning's minion,[2] king-
  dom of daylight's dauphin,[3] dapple-dawn-drawn Falcon, in his riding
  Of the rolling level underneath him steady air, and striding
High there, how he rung upon the rein[4] of a wimpling wing
5   In his ecstasy! then off, off forth on swing,
  As a skate's heel sweeps smooth on a bow-bend: the hurl and gliding
  Rebuffed the big wind. My heart in hiding
Stirred for a bird,—the achieve of, the mastery of the thing!

Brute beauty and valour and act, oh, air, pride, plume, here
10   Buckle! AND the fire that breaks from thee then, a billion
Times told lovelier, more dangerous, O my chevalier!

  No wonder of it: shéer plód makes plough down sillion[5]
Shine, and blue-bleak embers, ah my dear,
  Fall, gall[6] themselves, and gash gold-vermilion.

1877   1918

Pied[1] Beauty

Glory be to God for dappled things—
  For skies of couple-colour as a brinded[2] cow;
    For rose-moles all in stipple[3] upon trout that swim;
Fresh-firecoal chestnut-falls;[4] finches' wings;
5   Landscape plotted and pieced—fold, fallow, and plough;[5]
    And áll trádes, their gear and tackle and trim.°   *equipment*

All things counter,[6] original, spare, strange;
  Whatever is fickle, freckled (who knows how?)
    With swift, slow; sweet, sour; adazzle, dim;
10 He fathers-forth whose beauty is past change:
    Praise him.

1877   1918

---

1. Jesus, son of the Virgin Mary.
1. Kestrel falcon—a small hawk—that appears to hover in the air.
2. Darling, from the French *mignon*.
3. The dauphin was the heir to the French throne.
4. In falconry, a bird rings when it rises in spirals (like a horse circling at the end of a tether or rein). Wimpling means rippling.
5. The furrows of a plowed field.

6. Break their surfaces.
1. Blotched with different colors.
2. Brindled, having dark patches on a tawny ground.
3. Stippled, painted or drawn with dots instead of lines.
4. Chestnuts as bright as coals [Hopkins's journal].
5. Landscape of differently colored fields, some used as pasture ("fold"), some lying fallow, some plowed.
6. Contrary; "spare" means rare.

Hurrahing in Harvest[1]

Summer ends now; now, barbarous in beauty, the stooks° arise   *sheaves*
   Around; up above, what wind-walks! what lovely behaviour
   Of silk-sack clouds! has wilder, wilful-wavier
Meal-drift moulded ever and melted across skies?

5   I walk, I lift up, I lift up heart, eyes,
   Down all that glory in the heavens to glean our Saviour;
   And, éyes, heárt, what looks, what lips yet gave you a
Rapturous love's greeting of realer, of rounder replies?

And the azurous hung hills are his world-wielding shoulder
10   Majestic—as a stallion stalwart, very-violet-sweet!—
These things, these things were here and but the beholder
   Wanting; which two when they once meet,
The heart rears wings bold and bolder
   And hurls for him, O half hurls earth for him off under his feet.

1877   1918

Binsey Poplars
felled 1879

My aspens dear, whose airy cages quelled,
Quelled or quenched in leaves the leaping sun,
All felled, felled, are all felled;
   Of a fresh and following folded rank
5   Not spared, not one
       That dandled a sandalled
     Shadow that swam or sank
On meadow and river and wind-wandering weed-winding bank.

O if we but knew what we do
10   When we delve or hew—
   Hack and rack the growing green!
    Since country is so tender
   To touch, her being só slender,
   That, like this sleek and seeing ball°   *eye*
15   But a prick will make no eye at all,
   Where we, even where we mean
     To mend her we end her,
   When we hew or delve:
After-comers cannot guess the beauty been.
20   Ten or twelve, only ten or twelve
    Strokes of havoc únselve
    The sweet especial scene,

---

1. The Hurrahing sonnet was the outcome of half an hour of extreme enthusiasm as I walked home alone one day from fishing in the Elwy [letter to Bridges, 1877].

Rural scene, a rural scene,
Sweet especial rural scene.

1879   1918

Duns Scotus's Oxford[1]

Towery city and branchy between towers;
Cuckoo-echoing, bell-swarmèd, lark-charmèd, rook-racked, river-rounded;
The dapple-eared lily below thee; that country and town did
Once encounter in, here coped[2] and poisèd powers;

5   Thou hast a base and brickish skirt there,[3] sours
That neighbour-nature thy grey beauty is grounded
Best in; graceless growth, thou hast confounded
Rural rural keeping[4]—folk, flocks, and flowers.

Yet ah! this air I gather and I release
10   He lived on; these weeds and waters, these walls are what
He haunted who of all men most sways my spirits to peace;

Of realty° the rarest-veinèd unraveller; a not   reality
Rivalled insight, be rival Italy or Greece;
Who fired France for Mary without spot.[5]

1879   1918

Felix Randal

Felix Randal the farrier,[1] O he is dead then? my duty all ended,
Who have watched his mould of man, big-boned and hardy-handsome
Pining, pining, till time when reason rambled in it and some
Fatal four disorders, fleshed there, all contended?

5   Sickness broke him. Impatient he cursed at first, but mended
Being anointed[2] and all; though a heavenlier heart began some
Months earlier, since I had our sweet reprieve and ransom[3]
Tendered to him. Ah well, God rest him all road ever he offended!

This seeing the sick endears them to us, us too it endears.
10   My tongue had taught thee comfort, touch had quenched thy tears,
Thy tears that touched my heart, child, Felix, poor Felix Randal;

1. Johannes Duns Scotus (1266?–1308) was a theologian who lectured at Oxford. In 1872 Hopkins read Scotus with great excitement, finding in Scotus's principle of individuation a corroboration of his own evolving theory of inscape and instress. Each thing, said Scotus, has its own special quality or "Thisness" that the intellect and senses immediately fasten upon; this concrete being becomes a starting point for abstracting universal principles. Scotus thus provided Hopkins with a theological rationale that liberated him to pursue his own individuality, as a poet celebrating the specificity of all God's creations. See journal entry for 19 July 1872, page 1801.
2. Met and matched, as balanced equals or opponents.

3. The red brick outskirts of Oxford, built in the 19th century, contrast unfavorably with the grey stone medieval center.
4. The new suburbs have upset the old balance between Oxford and its rural surroundings.
5. In Paris, Duns Scotus promoted the doctrine of the Immaculate Conception, that Mary was born without original sin.
1. Blacksmith.
2. Having received Extreme Unction, the sacrament for the dying.
3. Confession, absolution, and Holy Communion.

How far from then forethought of, all thy more boisterous years,
When thou at the random⁴ grim forge, powerful amidst peers,
Didst fettle° for the great grey drayhorse his bright and battering sandal!   *prepare*

1880   1918

Spring and Fall:
to a young child

Márgarét, are you gríeving
Over Goldengrove unleaving?
Leáves, líke the things of man, you
With your fresh thoughts care for, can you?
5   Áh! ás the heart grows older
It will come to such sights colder
By and by, nor spare a sigh
Though worlds of wanwood leafmeal lie;¹
And yet you wíll weep and know why.
10   Now no matter, child, the name:
Sórrow's spríngs áre the same.
Nor mouth had, no nor mind, expressed
What heart heard of, ghost° guessed: *spirit*
It ís the blight man was born for,
15   It is Margaret you mourn for.

1880   1918

As Kingfishers Catch Fire

As kingfishers catch fire, dragonflies dráw fláme;
As tumbled over rim in roundy wells
Stones ring; like each tucked° string tells, each hung bell's   *plucked*
Bow swung finds tongue to fling out broad its name;
5   Each mortal thing does one thing and the same:
Deals out that being indoors each one dwells;
Selves—goes itself; *myself* it speaks and spells;
Crying *Whát I dó is me: for that I came.*

Í say móre: the just man justices;
10   Kéeps gráce; thát keeps all his goings graces;
Acts in God's eye what in God's eye he is—
Chríst—for Christ plays in ten thousand places,
Lovely in limbs, and lovely in eyes not his
To the Father through the features of men's faces.

1881–1882?   1918

---

4. Built of rough irregular stones.

1. The leaves of pale trees lie scattered; "leafmeal" is derived from "piecemeal."

[Carrion Comfort][1]

Not, I'll not, carrion comfort, Despair, not feast on thee;
Not untwist—slack they may be—these last strands of man
In me ór, most weary, cry *I can no more*. I can;
Can something, hope, wish day come, not choose not to be.
5   But ah, but O thou terrible, why wouldst thou rude on me
Thy wring-world right foot rock? lay a lionlimb against me? scan
With darksome devouring eyes my bruisèd bones? and fan,
O in turns of tempest, me heaped there; me frantic to avoid thee and flee?

Why? That my chaff might fly; my grain lie, sheer and clear.
10   Nay in all that toil, that coil,[2] since (seems) I kissed the rod,
Hand rather,[3] my heart lo! lapped strength, stole joy, would laugh, chéer.
Cheer whom though? the hero whose heaven-handling flung me, fóot tród
Me? or me that fought him? O which one? is it each one? That night, that year
Of now done darkness I wretch lay wrestling with (my God!) my God.

1885   1918

No Worst, There Is None

No worst, there is none. Pitched past pitch of grief,
More pangs will, schooled at forepangs, wilder wring.
Comforter, where, where is your comforting?
Mary, mother of us, where is your relief?
5   My cries heave, herds-long;[1] huddle in a main, a chief
Woe, world-sorrow; on an age-old anvil wince and sing—
Then lull, then leave off. Fury had shrieked "No ling-
ering! Let me be fell°: force° I must be brief."   *fierce/perforce*

O the mind, mind has mountains; cliffs of fall
10   Frightful, sheer, no-man-fathomed. Hold them cheap
May who ne'er hung there. Nor does long our small
Durance° deal with that steep or deep. Here! creep,   *endurance*
Wretch, under a comfort serves in a whirlwind: all
Life death does end and each day dies with sleep.

1885   1918

I Wake and Feel the Fell of Dark, Not Day

I wake and feel the fell[1] of dark, not day.
What hours, O what black hoürs we have spent
This night! what sights you, heart, saw; ways you went!
And more must, in yet longer light's delay.
5   With witness I speak this. But where I say
Hours I mean years, mean life. And my lament

---

1. The title was added by Robert Bridges. This poem is one of the "terrible sonnets" of 1885, as are the next two.
2. Turmoil.
3. I.e., the hand that holds the rod the speaker has kissed.

1. Like a cry of sheep or cattle repeated successively the length of the herd.
1. Gall, bitterness; but also a hide or covering; a wasteland; as an adjective, "fell" means fierce or cruel.

Is cries countless, cries like dead letters sent
To dearest him that lives alas! away.

    I am gall, I am heartburn. God's most deep decree
10   Bitter would have me taste: my taste was me;
Bones built in me, flesh filled, blood brimmed the curse.
    Selfyeast of spirit a dull dough sours. I see
The lost° are like this, and their scourge to be   *souls in Hell*
As I am mine, their sweating selves; but worse.

1885   1918

That Nature Is a Heraclitean Fire[1]
and of the Comfort of the Resurrection

Cloud-puffball, torn tufts, tossed pillows | flaunt forth, then
    chevy° on an air-   *race*
built thoroughfare: heaven-roysterers, in gay-gangs | they throng; they
    glitter in marches.
Down roughcast, down dazzling whitewash, | wherever an elm arches,
Shivelights[2] and shadowtackle in long | lashes lace, lance, and pair.
5   Delightfully the bright wind boisterous | ropes, wrestles, beats earth bare
Of yestertempest's creases; | in pool and rut peel parches
Squandering ooze to squeezed | dough, crust, dust; stanches,[3] starches
Squadroned masks and manmarks | treadmire toil there
Footfretted in it. Million-fuelèd, | nature's bonfire burns on.
10   But quench her bonniest, dearest | to her, her clearest-selvèd spark
Man, how fast his firedint, | his mark on mind, is gone!
Both are in an unfathomable, all is in an enormous dark
Drowned. O pity and indig | nation! Manshape, that shone
Sheer off, disseveral,[4] a star, | death blots black out; nor mark
15   Is any of him at all so stark
But vastness blurs and time | beats level. Enough! the Resurrection,
A heart's-clarion! Away grief's gasping, | joyless days, dejection.
                Across my foundering deck shone
A beacon, an eternal beam. | Flesh fade, and mortal trash
20   Fall to the residuary worm; | world's wildfire, leave but ash:
                In a flash, at a trumpet crash,
I am all at once what Christ is, | since he was what I am, and
This Jack, joke, poor potsherd,[5] | patch,[6] matchwood, immortal diamond,
                Is immortal diamond.

1888   1918

1. The Greek philosopher Heraclitus (c. 535 B.C.–475 B.C.) taught that the basic element of the universe was fire, and that all things were constantly in flux as mere transient manifestations of that fire. Hopkins sets this idea against his belief in the resurrection of an immortal, unchanging Christ.

2. Slivers of light.
3. Makes staunch or firm.
4. Neologism combining "dissever" and "several."
5. A broken piece of pottery.
6. Fool.

Thou Art Indeed Just, Lord

Justus quidem tu es, Domine, si disputem tecum: verumtamen
justa loquar ad te: Quare via impiorum prosperatur? & c.[1]

Thou art indeed just, Lord, if I contend
With thee; but, sir, so what I plead is just.
Why do sinners' ways prosper? and why must
Disappointment all I endeavour end?
5   Wert thou my enemy, O thou my friend,
How wouldst thou worse, I wonder, than thou dost
Defeat, thwart me? Oh, the sots and thralls of lust
Do in spare hours more thrive than I that spend,
Sir, life upon thy cause. See, banks and brakes°   *thickets*
10 Now, leavèd how thick! lacèd they are again
With fretty chervil,° look, and fresh wind shakes   *cow-parsley*
Them; birds build—but not I build; no, but strain,
Time's eunuch, and not breed one work that wakes.
Mine, O thou lord of life, send my roots rain.

1889   1893

from Journal
[ON "INSCAPE" AND "INSTRESS"]

End of March and beginning of April [1871]—This is the time to study inscape in the spraying[1] of trees, for the swelling buds carry them to a pitch which the eye could not else gather—for out of much much more, out of little not much, out of nothing nothing: in these sprays at all events there is a new world of inscape. The male ashes are very boldly jotted with the heads of the bloom which tuft the outer ends of the branches. The staff of each of these branches is closely knotted with the places where buds are or have been, so that it is something like a finger which has been tied up with string and keeps the marks. They are in knops[2] of a pair, one on each side, and the knops are set alternately, at crosses with the knops above and the knops below, the bud of course is a short smoke-black pointed nail-head or beak pieced of four lids or nippers. Below it, like the hollow below the eye or the piece between the knuckle and the root of the nail, is a half-moon-shaped sill as if once chipped from the wood and this gives the twig its quaining[3] in the outline. When the bud breaks at first it shews a heap of fruity purplish anthers[4] looking something like unripe elder-berries but these push open into richly-branched tree-pieces coloured buff and brown, shaking out loads of pollen, and drawing the tuft as a whole into peaked quains—mainly four, I think, two bigger and two smaller * * *

April 22—But such a lovely damasking in the sky as today I never felt before. The blue was charged with simple instress, the higher, zenith sky earnest and frowning, lower more light and sweet. High up again, breathing through woolly coats of cloud or on the quains and branches of the flying pieces it was the true exchange of

---

1. The first lines of the poem translate these words from Jeremiah 12.1.
1. Sprouting, flowering.
2. Buds.

3. Wedge shape.
4. The part of the flower's stamen that contains the pollen.

crimson, nearer the earth / against the sun / it was turquoise, and in the opposite south-western bay below the sun it was like clear oil but just as full of colour, shaken over with slanted flashing "travellers," all in flight, stepping one behind the other, their edges tossed with bright ravelling, as if white napkins were thrown up in the sun but not quite at the same moment so that they were all in a scale down the air falling one after the other to the ground * * *

May 9— * * * This day and May 11 the bluebells in the little wood between the College[5] and the highroad and in one of the Hurst Green cloughs.[6] In the little wood / opposite the light / they stood in blackish spreads or sheddings like the spots on a snake. The heads are then like thongs and solemn in grain and grape-colour. But in the clough / through the light / they came in falls of sky-colour washing the brows and slacks of the ground with vein-blue, thickening at the double, vertical themselves and the young grass and brake fern combed vertical, but the brake struck the upright of all this with light winged transomes. It was a lovely sight.—The bluebells in your hand baffle you with their inscape, made to every sense: if you draw your fingers through them they are lodged and struggle / with a shock of wet heads; the long stalks rub and click and flatten to a fan on one another like your fingers themselves would when you passed the palms hard across one another, making a brittle rub and jostle like the noise of a hurdle strained by leaning against; then there is the faint honey smell and in the mouth the sweet gum when you bite them. But this is easy, it is the eye they baffle. They give one a fancy of panpipes and of some wind instrument with stops—a trombone perhaps. The overhung necks—for growing they are little more than a staff with a simple crook but in water, where they stiffen, they take stronger turns, in the head like sheephooks or, when more waved throughout, like the waves riding through a whip that is being smacked—what with these overhung necks and what with the crisped ruffled bells dropping mostly on one side and the gloss these have at their footstalks they have an air of the knights at chess. Then the knot or "knoop" of buds some shut, some just gaping, which makes the pencil of the whole spike, should be noticed: the inscape of the flower most finely carried out in the siding of the axes, each striking a greater and greater slant, is finished in these clustered buds, which for the most part are not straightened but rise to the end like a tongue and this and their tapering and a little flattening they have make them look like the heads of snakes * * *

July 19 [1872]— * * * Stepped into a barn of ours, a great shadowy barn, where the hay had been stacked on either side, and looking at the great rudely arched timberframes—principals(?) and tie-beams, which make them look like bold big As with the cross-bar high up—I thought how sadly beauty of inscape was unknown and buried away from simple people and yet how near at hand it was if they had eyes to see it and it could be called out everywhere again * * *

After the examinations we went for our holiday out to Douglas in the Isle of Man Aug. 3. At this time I had first begun to get hold of the copy of Scotus on the Sentences[7] in the Baddely library and was flush with a new stroke of enthusiasm. It may come to nothing or it may be a mercy from God. But just then when I took in any inscape of the sky or sea I thought of Scotus

5. Stonyhurst, the Jesuit seminary where Hopkins was studying for the priesthood.
6. Ravines.

7. The major work of the medieval theologian Duns Scotus, *Opus Oxoniense*, is a commentary on the Bible, Aristotle, and the *Sentences* of the theologian Peter Lombard.

Dec. 12—A Blandyke.[8] Hard frost, bright sun, a sky of blue "water". On the fells with Mr. Lucas.[9] Parlick Pike and that ridge ruddy with fern and evening light. Ground sheeted with taut tattered streaks of crisp gritty snow. Green-white tufts of long bleached grass like heads of hair or the crowns of heads of hair, each a whorl of slender curves, one tuft taking up another—however these I might have noticed any day. I saw the inscape though freshly, as if my eye were still growing, though with a companion the eye and the ear are for the most part shut and instress cannot come.

* * *

Feb. 24 [1873]—In the snow flat-topped hillocks and shoulders outlined with wavy edges, ridge below ridge, very like the grain of wood in line and in projection like relief maps. These the wind makes I think and of course drifts, which are in fact snow waves. The sharp nape of a drift is sometimes broken by slant flutes or channels. I think this must be when the wind after shaping the drift first has changed and cast waves in the body of the wave itself. All the world is full of inscape and chance left free to act falls into an order as well as purpose: looking out of my window I caught it in the random clods and broken heaps of snow made by the cast of a broom. * * *

April 8—The ashtree growing in the corner of the garden was felled. It was lopped first: I heard the sound and looking out and seeing it maimed there came at that moment a great pang and I wished to die and not to see the inscapes of the world destroyed any more

from Letter to R. W. Dixon[1]
[On Sprung Rhythm]

5 October 1878

Very Reverend and Dear Sir,

* * * You ask, do I write verse myself. What I had written I burnt before I became a Jesuit and resolved to write no more, as not belonging to my profession, unless it were by the wish of my superiors; so for seven years I wrote nothing but two or three little presentation pieces which occasion called for. But when in the winter of '75 the Deutschland was wrecked in the mouth of the Thames and five Franciscan nuns, exiles from Germany by the Falck Laws, aboard of her were drowned I was affected by the account and happening to say so to my rector he said that he wished someone would write a poem on the subject. On this hint I set to work and, though my hand was out at first, produced one. I had long had haunting my ear the echo of a new rhythm which now I realised on paper. To speak shortly, it consists in scanning by accents or stresses alone, without any account of the number of syllables, so that a foot may be one strong syllable or it may be many light and one strong. I do not say the idea is altogether new; there are hints of it in music, in nursery rhymes and popular jingles, in the poets themselves, and, since then, I have seen it talked about as a thing possible in critics. Here are instances—"*Díng, dóng, béll; Pússy's ín the wéll; Whó pút her ín? Líttle Jóhnny Thín. Whó púlled her óut? Líttle Jóhnny Stóut.*" For if each line has three stresses or three feet it follows that some of the feet are of one syllable only. So too "*Óne, twó, Búckle my shóe*" *passim.* In Campbell you have "Ánd

8. At Stonyhurst, Blandyke was the name for a monthly holiday.
9. Herbert Lucas (1852–1933), Jesuit writer and lecturer.
1. Richard Watson Dixon (1833–1900), Anglican clergy-
man, poet, and associate of the Pre-Raphaelites. As Hopkins's former schoolmaster, he was the first to recognize his pupil's poetic gifts.

their fléet alóng the *déep próudly* shóne"—"Ít was tén of Ápril *mórn bý* the chíme" etc; in Shakspere "Whý shd. *thís* désert bé?" corrected wrongly by the editors; in Moore a little melody I cannot quote; etc. But no one has professedly used it and made it the principle throughout, that I know of. Nevertheless to me it appears, I own, to be a better and more natural principle than the ordinary system, much more flexible, and capable of much greater effects. However I had to mark the stresses in blue chalk, and this and my rhymes carried on from one line into another and certain chimes suggested by the Welsh poetry I had been reading (what they call *cynghanedd*) and a great many more oddnesses could not but dismay an editor's eye, so that when I offered it to our magazine the *Month*, though at first they accepted it, after a time they withdrew and dared not print it. After writing this I held myself free to compose, but cannot find it in my conscience to spend time upon it; so I have done little and shall do less. But I wrote a shorter piece on the Eurydice, also in "sprung rhythm", as I call it, but simpler, shorter, and without marks, and offered the *Month* that too, but they did not like it either. Also I have written some sonnets and a few other little things; some in sprung rhythm, with various other experiments—as "outriding feet," that is parts of which do not count in the scanning (such as you find in Shakspere's later plays, but as a licence, whereas mine are rather calculated effects); others in the ordinary scanning *counterpointed* (this is counterpoint: "*Hóme to* his móther's hóuse *prívate* retúrned" and "*Bút to vánquish* by wísdom héllish wíles" etc[2]); others, one or two, in common uncounterpointed rhythm. But even the impulse to write is wanting, for I have no thought of publishing. * * *

Believe me, dear Sir, very sincerely yours

Gerard Hopkins

Lewis Carroll
1832–1898

With their disconcerting mix of fantasy and parody, wordplay and violent, outrageous nonsense, *Alice in Wonderland* (1865) and its sequel, *Through the Looking Glass* (1871), enchanted the Victorian public. The Alice stories make fun of manners, school lessons, politics, royalty, and the values of the middle class. Lewis Carroll's rare ability to enter the imaginative world of childhood, coupled with his surrealistic, tumultuous vision of what would entertain a ten-year-old, transformed children's literature. His extravagant, eccentric characters—the White Rabbit, the Mad Hatter, the Cheshire Cat, Tweedledee and Tweedledum—badger Alice with absurd advice, but ultimately the books themselves offer no moral whatsoever.

The creator of Wonderland was a shy but playful professor of mathematics named Charles Lutwidge Dodgson. He had settled early on the chief activities of his life: puzzling over logical problems and entertaining children. The oldest son of an Anglican clergyman, Dodgson delighted his seven sisters and three brothers with his puppet shows, invented games, and comic writing. A prize-winning student at Rugby School, he went on to Oxford, where he became a fellow of Christ Church in 1855. Some readers find it peculiar that the greatest nonsense writer in English should also be the author of *Curiosa Mathematica: A New Theory of Parallels* (1888) and *Symbolic Logic* (1896), but others have enjoyed the mathematical and logical

2. From Milton's *Paradise Regained* (1671), 4.639 and 1.175.

brainteasers embedded in his stories. His sense of fun emerged in his serious work, too, as in a passage in a textbook he wrote where Euclid's ghost tries to prevent a professor from altering his classical geometry manual.

Dodgson was the epitome of the Oxford don—set in his ways, devoted to his work and his spinster sisters, a confirmed bachelor who kept the same cluttered rooms in college for thirty years. To separate the retiring scholar from the irreverent author of fiction and poetry, Dodgson invented a pseudonym: he reversed his first two names, translated them into Latin, and then back again, with schoolboy mistakes, into English. "Lewis Carroll" became in some sense an uninhibited alter ego. Like all instructors at Oxford, Dodgson was an ordained clergyman. The insecure Reverend Dodgson could not bear to hear a religious joke, yet Lewis Carroll gleefully parodied hymns and moralizing poems. While the identity of the Reverend Dodgson and Mr. Carroll was an open secret, Dodgson refused to acknowledge publicly the authorship of the Alice books. When Queen Victoria, who was a fan of *Alice*, asked him to send her a copy of his next book, he duly obliged with an inscribed copy of *An Elementary Treatise on Determinants* (1867), by C. L. Dodgson. And when a dinner guest unwittingly raised the forbidden topic, Dodgson fled the house. Like Alice, he seems to have been "very fond of pretending to be two people."

The story of how *Alice in Wonderland* came to be written is famous. On 4 July 1862 Dodgson and another don, Robinson Duckworth, invited Alice Liddell, daughter of the Dean of Christ Church, and her sisters on a boating trip. The children clamored for a story, and Dodgson obliged, inventing tales about a fictional child also named Alice. "In a desperate attempt to strike out some new line of fairy lore," Dodgson recalled, he precipitated his heroine "straight down a rabbit hole . . . without the least idea what was to happen afterwards." Later on, at Alice Liddell's request, he began drafting a fuller version which he illustrated himself. Revised, the book was published with superb illustrations by John Tenniel. When it was finally presented to Alice on the third anniversary of the boat trip in 1865, the actual Alice was already thirteen, though her fictional counterpart was only seven.

Even in a pre-Freudian era, Dodgson's friends were struck by his unusual interest in little girls. He invited them to tea and escorted them on outings. He struck up conversations with girls on trains and at the seaside, and afterward wrote them letters. He also took their pictures. Dodgson took up photography in 1856, the same year he created "Lewis Carroll." Though he produced fine portraits of Tennyson, Thackeray, Ruskin, and the Rossettis, his passion was photographing children. He preferred his sitters to be solitary and, if possible, nude. He wrote to one mother, "what I like best of all is to have *two* hours of leisure time before me, *one* child to photograph, and *no* restrictions as to costume! (It is a descending Arithmetical Series—2, 1, 0)." While the *Dictionary of Literary Biography* concludes that his attentions were "pronounced though proper," it is hard nowadays not to find his behavior rather odd. In any case, it is clear that the story of Alice would never have been told without Dodgson's extraordinary desire to please one particular little girl.

The fractured narrative structure of *Alice's Adventures* combines the abrupt, topsy-turvy transitions of nursery rhymes with some of the classic motifs of Western literature. It is part quest-romance toward a miniature Edenic garden, part Dantean descent into a fearful underworld. Mocking didactic literature and rejecting the sentimental view of childhood, Dodgson sends a bold but nervous Alice into a menacing, anarchic landscape replete with birth trauma (the fall down the hole), identity crisis ("Who in the world am I?"), and exaggerated growth pangs ("sending presents to one's own feet!"). In Wonderland, sudden change is the keynote—Alice's body, the rules of society, and even animal species suffer unexpected transformations—as Dodgson invokes Victorian anxiety about the instability of a world racked by speed, industry, and evolutionary theory.

One of Dodgson's innovations was the seamless way his narrative incorporates the poetic "lessons" that Alice hears or recites. Shredding conventional pieties, the poems crazily spoof the dignity of old age ("You are old, Father William"), the instructive events of animal fables ("The Lobster Quadrille," "The Walrus and the Carpenter"), and the purported wisdom of rural folk ("The White Knight's Song"). Even Dodgson's dedicatory verse, "Child of the Pure Unclouded Brow," refuses to honor its genre: instead of celebrating innocence, its ominous view of "bedtime" reveals an underlying fear of growth, sex, and death that lurks at the heart of the Alice stories. Dodgson's scenes frequently take on a nightmarish quality based on estrangement from the body, whether by physical constriction, painful alteration, or some form of extinction, such as "shutting up like a telescope."

Cumulatively, the "lessons" given to Alice and her readers bespeak a universe of randomness and chance, where rules are ridiculous, animals loquacious, everybody illogical, and words arbitrary and out of control. "Lewis Carroll" reveled in what Charles Dodgson repressed, and this subversive, exhilarating flirting with excesses of language and behavior has led not only to the popularity of the Alice stories but to innumerable interpretations. Are they allegories about the Church of England, studies in pyschological and social regression, devastating attacks on English education? For some critics, Lewis Carroll expresses Dodgson's deepest religious doubts—in a world of nonsense, there is no divine guidance shaping human life or guaranteeing the meaning of sacred texts. Others see his irrepressible wordplay as a joyful liberation from the Victorian prison house of stuffy etiquette and stifling morality. The variety of responses even in his own day did not surprise Dodgson/Carroll. As he explained to perplexed readers, "words mean more than we mean to express whenever we use them, so a whole book ought to mean a great deal more than the writer meant."

from **Alice's Adventures in Wonderland**
Chapter 1. Down the Rabbit-Hole

Alice was beginning to get very tired of sitting by her sister on the bank and of having nothing to do: once or twice she had peeped into the book her sister was reading, but it had no pictures or conversations in it, "and what is the use of a book," thought Alice, "without pictures or conversations?"

So she was considering, in her own mind (as well as she could, for the hot day made her feel very sleepy and stupid), whether the pleasure of making a daisy-chain would be worth the trouble of getting up and picking the daisies, when suddenly a White Rabbit with pink eyes ran close by her.

There was nothing so *very* remarkable in that; nor did Alice think it so *very* much out of the way to hear the Rabbit say to itself "Oh dear! Oh dear! I shall be too late!" (when she thought it over afterwards it occurred to her that she ought to have wondered at this, but at the time it all seemed quite natural); but, when the Rabbit actually *took a watch out of its waistcoat-pocket,* and looked at it, and then hurried on, Alice started to her feet, for it flashed across her mind that she had never before seen a rabbit with either a waistcoat-pocket, or a watch to take out of it, and burning with curiosity, she ran across the field after it, and was just in time to see it pop down a large rabbit-hole under the hedge.

In another moment down went Alice after it, never once considering how in the world she was to get out again.

The rabbit-hole went straight on like a tunnel for some way, and then dipped suddenly down, so suddenly that Alice had not a moment to think about stopping herself before she found herself falling down what seemed to be a very deep well.

Either the well was very deep, or she fell very slowly, for she had plenty of time as she went down to look about her, and to wonder what was going to happen next. First, she tried to look down and make out what she was coming to, but it was too dark to see anything: then she looked at the sides of the well, and noticed that they were filled with cupboards and book-shelves: here and there she saw maps and pictures hung upon pegs. She took down a jar from one of the shelves as she passed: it was labeled "ORANGE MARMALADE," but to her great disappointment it was empty: she did not like to drop the jar, for fear of killing somebody underneath, so managed to put it into one of the cupboards as she fell past it.

"Well!" thought Alice to herself. "After such a fall as this, I shall think nothing of tumbling down-stairs! How brave they'll all think me at home! Why, I wouldn't say anything about it, even if I fell off the top of the house!" (Which was very likely true.)

Down, down, down. Would the fall *never* come to an end? "I wonder how many miles I've fallen by this time?" she said aloud. "I must be getting somewhere near the centre of the earth. Let me see: that would be four thousand miles down, I think—" (for, you see, Alice had learnt several things of this sort in her lessons in the school-room, and though this was not a *very* good opportunity for showing off her knowledge, as there was no one to listen to her, still it was good practice to say it over) "—yes, that's about the right distance, but then I wonder what Latitude or Longitude I've got to?" (Alice had not the slightest idea what Latitude was, or Longitude either, but she thought they were nice grand words to say.)

Presently she began again. "I wonder if I shall fall right *through* the earth! How funny it'll seem to come out among the people that walk with their heads downwards! The antipathies,[1] I think—" (she was rather glad there *was* no one listening, this time, as it didn't sound at all the right word) "—but I shall have to ask them what the name of the country is, you know. Please, Ma'am, is this New Zealand? Or Australia?" (and she tried to curtsey as she spoke—fancy, *curtseying* as you're falling through the air! Do you think you could manage it?) "And what an ignorant little girl she'll think me for asking! No, it'll never do to ask: perhaps I shall see it written up somewhere."

Down, down, down. There was nothing else to do, so Alice soon began talking again. "Dinah'll miss me very much to-night, I should think!" (Dinah was the cat.) "I hope they'll remember her saucer of milk at tea-time. Dinah, my dear! I wish you were down here with me! There are no mice in the air, I'm afraid, but you might catch a bat, and that's very like a mouse, you know. But do cats eat bats, I wonder?" And here Alice began to get rather sleepy, and went on saying to herself, in a dreamy sort of way, "Do cats eat bats? Do cats eat bats?" and sometimes "Do bats eat cats?" for, you see, as she couldn't answer either question, it didn't much matter which way she put it. She felt that she was dozing off, and had just begun to dream that she was walking hand in hand with Dinah, and was saying to her, very earnestly, "Now, Dinah, tell me the truth: did you ever eat a bat?" when suddenly, thump! thump! down she came upon a heap of sticks and dry leaves, and the fall was over.

Alice was not a bit hurt, and she jumped up on to her feet in a moment: she looked up, but it was all dark overhead: before her was another long passage, and the White Rabbit was still in sight, hurrying down it. There was not a moment to be lost: away went Alice like the wind, and was just in time to hear it say, as it turned a corner, "Oh my ears and whiskers, how late it's getting!" She was close behind it when she turned the corner, but the Rabbit was no longer to be seen: she found herself in a long, low hall, which was lit up by a row of lamps hanging from the roof.

There were doors all round the hall, but they were all locked; and when Alice had been all the way down one side and up the other, trying every door, she walked sadly down the middle, wondering how she was ever to get out again.

Suddenly she came upon a little three-legged table, all made of solid glass: there was nothing on it but a tiny golden key, and Alice's first idea was that this might be-

1. Alice means "Antipodes," or places on opposite sides of the globe; for England, that would be Australia.

long to one of the doors of the hall; but, alas! either the locks were too large, or the key was too small, but at any rate it would not open any of them. However, on the second time round, she came upon a low curtain she had not noticed before, and behind it was a little door about fifteen inches high: she tried the little golden key in the lock, and to her great delight it fitted!

Alice opened the door and found that it led into a small passage, not much larger than a rat-hole: she knelt down and looked along the passage into the loveliest garden you ever saw. How she longed to get out of that dark hall, and wander about among those beds of bright flowers and those cool fountains, but she could not even get her head through the doorway: "and even if my head *would* go through," thought poor Alice, "it would be of very little use without my shoulders. Oh, how I wish I could shut up like a telescope! I think I could, if I only knew how to begin." For, you see, so many out-of-the-way things had happened lately, that Alice had begun to think that very few things indeed were really impossible.

There seemed to be no use in waiting by the little door, so she went back to the table, half hoping she might find another key on it, or at any rate a book of rules for shutting people up like telescopes: this time she found a little bottle on it ("which certainly was not here before," said Alice), and tied around the neck of the bottle was a paper label, with the words "DRINK ME" beautifully printed on it in large letters.

It was all very well to say "Drink me," but the wise little Alice was not going to do *that* in a hurry. "No, I'll look first," she said, "and see whether it's marked '*poison*' or not"; for she had read several nice little stories about children who had got burnt, and eaten up by wild beasts, and other unpleasant things, all because they *would* not remember the simple rules their friends had taught them: such as, that a red-hot poker will burn you if you hold it too long; and that, if you cut your finger *very* deeply with a knife, it usually bleeds; and she had never forgotten that, if you drink much from a bottle marked "poison," it is almost certain to disagree with you, sooner or later.

However, this bottle was *not* marked "poison," so Alice ventured to taste it, and, finding it very nice (it had, in fact, a sort of mixed flavour of cherry-tart, custard, pine-apple, roast turkey, toffy, and hot buttered toast), she very soon finished it off.

*　　　*　　　*　　　*

*　　　*　　　*

*　　　*　　　*　　　*

"What a curious feeling!" said Alice. "I must be shutting up like a telescope!"

And so it was indeed: she was now only ten inches high, and her face brightened up at the thought that she was now the right size for going through the little door into that lovely garden. First, however, she waited for a few minutes to see if she was going to shrink any further: she felt a little nervous about this; "for it might end, you know," said Alice to herself, "in my going out altogether, like a candle. I wonder what I should be like then?" And she tried to fancy what the flame of a candle looks like after the candle is blown out, for she could not remember ever having seen such a thing.

After a while, finding that nothing more happened, she decided on going into the garden at once; but, alas for poor Alice! when she got to the door, she found she had forgotten the little golden key, and when she went back to the table for it, she found she could not possibly reach it: she could see it quite plainly through the glass, and she tried her best to climb up one of the legs of the table, but it was too slippery; and when she had tired herself out with trying, the poor little thing sat down and cried.

"Come, there's no use in crying like that!" said Alice to herself rather sharply. "I advise you to leave off this minute!" She generally gave herself very good advice (though she very seldom followed it), and sometimes she scolded herself so severely as to bring tears into her eyes; and once she remembered trying to box her own ears for having cheated herself in a game of croquet she was playing against herself, for this curious child was very fond of pretending to be two people. "But it's no use now," thought poor Alice, "to pretend to be two people! Why, there's hardly enough of me left to make *one* respectable person!"

Soon her eye fell on a little glass box that was lying under the table: she opened it, and found in it a very small cake, on which the words "EAT ME" were beautifully marked in currants. "Well, I'll eat it," said Alice, "and if it makes me grow larger, I can reach the key; and if it makes me grow smaller, I can creep under the door: so either way I'll get into the garden, and I don't care which happens!"

She ate a little bit, and said anxiously to herself "Which way? Which way?", holding her hand on the top of her head to feel which way it was growing; and she was quite surprised to find that she remained the same size. To be sure, this is what generally happens when one eats cake; but Alice had got so much into the way of expecting nothing but out-of-the-way things to happen, that it seemed quite dull and stupid for life to go on in the common way.

So she set to work, and very soon finished off the cake.

* * *

from *Chapter 2. The Pool of Tears*

"Curiouser and curiouser!" cried Alice (she was so much surprised, that for the moment she quite forgot how to speak good English). "Now I'm opening out like the largest telescope that ever was! Good-bye, feet!" (for when she looked down at her feet, they seemed to be almost out of sight, they were getting so far off). "Oh, my poor little feet, I wonder who will put on your shoes and stockings for you now, dears? I'm sure *I* sha'n't be able! I shall be a great deal too far off to trouble myself about you: you must manage the best way you can—but I must be kind to them," thought Alice, "or perhaps they wo'n't walk the way I want to go! Let me see. I'll give them a new pair of boots every Christmas."

And she went on planning to herself how she would manage it. "They must go by the carrier," she thought; "and how funny it'll seem, sending presents to one's own feet! And how odd the directions will look!

> *Alice's Right Foot, Esq.*
> *Hearthrug,*
> *near the Fender,*[2]
> *(with Alice's love).*

Oh dear, what nonsense I'm talking!"

Just at this moment her head struck against the roof of the hall: in fact she was now rather more than nine feet high, and she at once took up the little golden key and hurried off to the garden door.

Poor Alice! It was as much as she could do, lying down on one side, to look through into the garden with one eye; but to get through was more hopeless than ever: she sat down and began to cry again.

"You ought to be ashamed of yourself," said Alice, "a great girl like you," (she might well say this), "to go on crying in this way! Stop this moment, I tell you!" But she went on all the same, shedding gallons of tears, until there was a large pool around her, about four inches deep, and reaching half down the hall.

2. A low fence in front of a fireplace to keep coals from falling out.

John Tenniel, illustration to *Alice in Wonderland*, 1865.

After a time she heard a little pattering of feet in the distance, and she hastily dried her eyes to see what was coming. It was the White Rabbit returning, splendidly dressed, with a pair of white kid-gloves in one hand and a large fan in the other: he came trotting along in a great hurry, muttering to himself, as he came, "Oh! The Duchess, the Duchess! Oh! *Wo'n't* she be savage if I've kept her waiting!" Alice felt so desperate that she was ready to ask help of any one: so, when the Rabbit came near her, she began, in a low, timid voice, "If you please, Sir—" The Rabbit started violently, dropped the white kid-gloves and the fan, and scurried away into the darkness as hard as he could go.

Alice took up the fan and gloves, and, as the hall was very hot, she kept fanning herself all the time she went on talking. "Dear, dear! How queer everything is to-day! And yesterday things went on just as usual. I wonder if I've changed in the night? Let me think: was I the same when I got up this morning? I almost think I can remember feeling a little different. But if I'm not the same, the next question is 'Who in the world am I?' Ah, *that's* the great puzzle!" And she began thinking over all the children she knew that were of the same age as herself, to see if she could have been changed for any of them.

"I'm sure I'm not Ada," she said, "for her hair goes in such long ringlets, and mine doesn't go in ringlets at all; and I'm sure I ca'n't be Mabel, for I know all sorts of things, and she, oh, she knows such a very little! Besides, *she's* she, and *I'm* I, and— oh dear, how puzzling it all is! I'll try if I know all the things I used to know. Let me see: four times five is twelve, and four times six is thirteen, and four times seven is— oh dear! I shall never get to twenty at that rate! However, the Multiplication-Table doesn't signify: let's try Geography. London is the capital of Paris, and Paris is the capital of Rome, and Rome—no, *that's* all wrong, I'm certain! I must have been changed for Mabel! I'll try and say 'How doth the little—'," and she crossed her hands on her lap as if she were saying lessons, and began to repeat it, but her voice sounded hoarse and strange, and the words did not come the same as they used to do:—

> *"How doth the little crocodile*
> *Improve his shining tail,*
> *And pour the waters of the Nile*
> *On every golden scale!*

> *"How cheerfully he seems to grin,*
> *How neatly spreads his claws,*
> *And welcomes little fishes in,*
> *With gently smiling jaws!*[3]

"I'm sure those are not the right words," said poor Alice, and her eyes filled with tears again as she went on, "I must be Mabel after all, and I shall have to go and live in that poky little house, and have next to no toys to play with, and oh, ever so many lessons to learn! No, I've made up my mind about it: if I'm Mabel, I'll stay down here. It'll be no use their putting their heads down and saying 'Come up again, dear!' I shall only look up and say 'Who am I, then? Tell me that first, and then, if I like being that person, I'll come up: if not, I'll stay down here till I'm somebody else'—but, oh dear!" cried Alice, with a sudden burst of tears, "I do wish they *would* put their heads down! I am so *very* tired of being all alone here!"

You are old, Father William[1]

"You are old, Father William," the young man said,
　"And your hair has become very white;
And yet you incessantly stand on your head—
　Do you think, at your age, it is right?"

5　　"In my youth," Father William replied to his son,
　"I feared it might injure the brain;
But, now that I'm perfectly sure I have none,
　Why, I do it again and again."

"You are old," said the youth, "as I mentioned before,
10　　And have grown most uncommonly fat;
Yet you turned a back-somersault in at the door—
　Pray, what is the reason of that?"

"In my youth," said the sage, as he shook his grey locks,
　"I kept all my limbs very supple
15　By the use of this ointment—one shilling the box—
　Allow me to sell you a couple?"

"You are old," said the youth, "and your jaws are too weak
　For anything tougher than suet;

---

3. The poem Alice is trying to recite is Isaac Watts's *Against Idleness and Mischief* (1715): "How doth the little busy bee / Improve each shining hour, / And gather honey all the day / from every opening flower! / How skillfully she builds her cell! / How neatly she spreads the wax! / And labours hard to store it well / With the sweet food she makes."

1. From *Alice's Adventures in Wonderland* (ch. 5). The Caterpillar orders Alice to recite a pious poem, Robert Southey's *The Old Man's Comforts, and How He Gained Them* (1799); to her own dismay, what comes out of her mouth is this parody.

Yet you finished the goose, with the bones and the beak—
20   Pray, how did you manage to do it?"

"In my youth," said his father, "I took to the law,
    And argued each case with my wife;
And the muscular strength, which it gave to my jaw
    Has lasted the rest of my life."

25   "You are old," said the youth, "one would hardly suppose
    That your eye was as steady as ever;
Yet you balanced an eel on the end of your nose—
    What made you so awfully clever?"

"I have answered three questions, and that is enough,"
30   Said his father. "Don't give yourself airs!
Do you think I can listen all day to such stuff?
    Be off, or I'll kick you down-stairs!"

The Lobster-Quadrille[1]

"Will you walk a little faster?" said a whiting to a snail,
"There's a porpoise close behind us, and he's treading on my tail.
See how eagerly the lobsters and the turtles all advance!
They are waiting on the shingle[2]—will you come and join the dance?
5   Will you, wo'n't you, will you, wo'n't you, will you join the dance?
    Will you, wo'n't you, will you, wo'n't you, wo'n't you join the dance?

"You can really have no notion how delightful it will be
When they take us up and throw us, with the lobsters, out to sea!"
But the snail replied "Too far, too far!", and gave a look askance—
10   Said he thanked the whiting kindly, but he would not join the dance.
    Would not, could not, would not, could not, could not join the dance.
    Would not, could not, would not, could not, could not join the dance.

"What matters it how far we go?" his scaly friend replied.
"There is another shore, you know, upon the other side.
15   The further off from England the nearer is to France—
Then turn not pale, beloved snail, but come and join the dance.
    Will you, wo'n't you, will you, wo'n't you, will you join the dance?
    Will you, wo'n't you, will you, wo'n't you, wo'n't you join the dance?"

from Through the Looking Glass
Child of the pure unclouded brow[1]

Child of the pure unclouded brow
    And dreaming eyes of wonder!
Though time be fleet, and I and thou
    Are half a life asunder,

---

1. From *Alice's Adventures in Wonderland* (ch. 10); the Mock-Turtle sings this, "very slowly and sadly." It is a parody of Mary Howitt's moralistic poem, *The Spider and the Fly* (1834), which begins, "'Will you walk into my parlor?' said the Spider to the Fly, / 'Tis the prettiest lit-

tle parlor that ever you did spy.'"
2. Pebble beach.
1. Introductory poem to *Through the Looking Glass* (1871), the sequel to *Alice*.

5   Thy loving smile will surely hail
       The love-gift of a fairy-tale.

       I have not seen thy sunny face,
           Nor heard thy silver laughter:
       No thought of me shall find a place
10   In thy young life's hereafter—
       Enough that now thou wilt not fail
       To listen to my fairy-tale.

       A tale begun in other days,
           When summer suns were glowing—
15   A simple chime, that served to time
           The rhythm of our rowing—
       Whose echoes live in memory yet,
       Though envious years would say "forget."

       Come, hearken then, ere voice of dread,
20   With bitter tidings laden,
       Shall summon to unwelcome bed
           A melancholy maiden!
       We are but older children, dear,
       Who fret to find our bedtime near.

25   Without, the frost, the blinding snow,
           The storm-wind's moody madness—
       Within, the firelight's ruddy glow,
           And childhood's nest of gladness.
       The magic words shall hold thee fast:
30   Thou shalt not heed the raving blast.

       And, though the shadow of a sigh
           May tremble through the story,
       For "happy summer days" gone by,
           And vanish'd summer glory—
35   It shall not touch, with breath of bale,
       The pleasance[2] of our fairy-tale.

Jabberwocky[1]

       'Twas brillig, and the slithy toves
           Did gyre and gimble in the wabe:
       All mimsy were the borogoves,
           And the mome raths outgrabe.

5   "Beware the Jabberwock, my son!
           The jaws that bite, the claws that catch!

---

2. Pleasance was Alice Liddell's middle name. By 1871, when *Through the Looking-Glass* was published, Alice Liddel was 16; in the book she is seven.
1. From *Through the Looking-Glass* (ch. 1). Alice finds a book in which all the words are printed backwards; when

she realizes it's a Looking-glass book, she holds it up to the mirror and reads this poem. Afterwards she remarks that "it's *rather* hard to understand!" Later in *Through the Looking Glass* Humpty Dumpty explicates the poem (see below).

Beware the Jubjub bird, and shun
　　The frumious Bandersnatch!"

He took his vorpal sword in hand:
10　　Long time the manxome foe he sought—
So rested he by the Tumtum tree,
　　And stood awhile in thought.

And, as in uffish thought he stood,
　　The Jabberwock, with eyes of flame,
15　Came whiffling through the tulgey wood,
　　And burbled as it came!

One, two! One, two! And through and through
　　The vorpal blade went snicker-snack!
He left it dead, and with its head
20　　He went galumphing back.

"And, hast thou slain the Jabberwock?
　　Come to my arms, my beamish boy!
O frabjous day! Callooh! Callay!"
　　He chortled in his joy.

25　'Twas brillig, and the slithy toves
　　Did gyre and gimble in the wabe:
All mimsy were the borogoves,
　　And the mome raths outgrabe.

[HUMPTY DUMPTY ON JABBERWOCKY][1]

"You seem very clever at explaining words, Sir," said Alice. "Would you kindly tell me the meaning of the poem called 'Jabberwocky'?"

"Let's hear it," said Humpty Dumpty. "I can explain all the poems that ever were invented—and a good many that haven't been invented just yet."

This sounded very hopeful, so Alice repeated the first verse:—

> "'Twas brillig, and the slithy toves
> Did gyre and gimble in the wabe:
> All mimsy were the borogoves,
> And the mome raths outgrabe."

"That's enough to begin with," Humpty Dumpty interrupted: "there are plenty of hard words there. 'Brillig' means four o'clock in the afternoon—the time when you begin broiling things for dinner."

"That'll do very well," said Alice: "and 'slithy'?"

"Well, 'slithy' means 'lithe and slimy.' 'Lithe' is the same as 'active.' You see it's like a portmanteau[2]—there are two meanings packed up into one word."

---

1. From *Through the Looking-Glass* (ch. 6).
2. A word formed by combining two other words (e.g., *brunch, motel*). In the preface to *The Hunting of the Snark* (1876), Carroll wrote about the "hard words" in *Jabberwocky*: "Humpty Dumpty's theory, of two meanings packed into one word like a portmanteau, seems to me the right explanation for all. For instance, take the two words

'fuming' and 'furious.' Make up your mind that you will say both words, but leave it unsettled which you will say first. Now open your mouth and speak. If your thoughts incline ever so little towards 'fuming,' you will say 'fuming-furious,' if they turn, by even a hair's breadth, towards 'furious,' you will say 'furious-fuming,' but if you have the rarest of gifts, a perfectly balanced mind, you will say 'frumious.'"

"I see it now," Alice remarked thoughtfully: "and what are 'toves'?"

"Well 'toves' are something like badgers—they're something like lizards—and they're something like corkscrews."

"They must be very curious-looking creatures."

"They are that," said Humpty Dumpty; "also they make their nests under sun-dials—also they live on cheese."

"And what's to 'gyre' and to 'gimble'?"

"To 'gyre' is to go round and round like a gyroscope. To 'gimble' is to make holes like a gimlet."

"And 'the wabe' is the grass-plot round a sun-dial, I suppose?" said Alice, surprised at her own ingenuity.

"Of course it is. It's called 'wabe' you know, because it goes a long way before it, and a long way behind it—"

"And a long way beyond it on each side," Alice added.

"Exactly so. Well then, 'mimsy' is 'flimsy and miserable' (there's another portmanteau for you). And a 'borogove' is a thin shabby-looking bird with its feathers sticking out all round—something like a live mop."

"And then 'mome raths'?" said Alice. "I'm afraid I'm giving you a great deal of trouble."

"Well, a 'rath' is a sort of green pig: but 'mome' I'm not certain about. I think it's short for 'from home'—meaning that they'd lost their way, you know."

"And what does 'outgrabe' mean?"

"Well, 'outgribing' is something between bellowing and whistling, with a kind of sneeze in the middle: however, you'll hear it done, maybe—down in the wood yonder—and, when you've once heard it, you'll be *quite* content. Who's been repeating all that hard stuff to you?"

"I read it in a book," said Alice.

The Walrus and the Carpenter[1]

The sun was shining on the sea,
    Shining with all his might:
He did his very best to make
    The billows smooth and bright—
5 And this was odd, because it was
    The middle of the night.

The moon was shining sulkily,
    Because she thought the sun
Had got no business to be there
10   After the day was done—
"It's very rude of him," she said,
    "To come and spoil the fun!"

The sea was wet as wet could be,
    The sands were dry as dry.
15 You could not see a cloud, because

---

1. From *Through the Looking Glass* (ch. 4); Tweedledee recites this poem to Alice, choosing it because it "is the longest."

No cloud was in the sky:
No birds were flying overhead—
   There were no birds to fly.

The Walrus and the Carpenter
20   Were walking close at hand:
They wept like anything to see
   Such quantities of sand:
"If this were only cleared away,"
   They said, "it would be grand!"

25 "If seven maids with seven mops
   Swept it for half a year,
Do you suppose," the Walrus said,
   "That they could get it clear?"
"I doubt it," said the Carpenter,
30   And shed a bitter tear.

"O Oysters, come and walk with us!"
   The Walrus did beseech.
"A pleasant walk, a pleasant talk,
   Along the briny beach:
35 We cannot do with more than four,
   To give a hand to each."

The eldest Oyster looked at him,
   But never a word he said:
The eldest Oyster winked his eye,
40   And shook his heavy head—
Meaning to say he did not choose
   To leave the oyster-bed.

But four young Oysters hurried up,
   All eager for the treat:
45 Their coats were brushed, their faces washed,
   Their shoes were clean and neat—
And this was odd, because, you know,
   They hadn't any feet.

Four other Oysters followed them,
50   And yet another four;
And thick and fast they came at last,
   And more, and more, and more—
All hopping through the frothy waves,
   And scrambling to the shore.

55 The Walrus and the Carpenter
   Walked on a mile or so,
And then they rested on a rock
   Conveniently low:
And all the little Oysters stood
60   And waited in a row.

"The time has come," the Walrus said,
    "To talk of many things:
Of shoes—and ships—and sealing wax—
    Of cabbages—and kings—
65 And why the sea is boiling hot—
    And whether pigs have wings."

"But wait a bit," the Oysters cried,
    "Before we have our chat;
For some of us are out of breath,
70   And all of us are fat!"
"No hurry!" said the Carpenter.
    They thanked him much for that.

"A loaf of bread," the Walrus said,
    "Is what we chiefly need:
75 Pepper and vinegar besides
    Are very good indeed—
Now, if you're ready, Oysters dear,
    We can begin to feed."

"But not on us!" the Oysters cried,
80   Turning a little blue.
"After such kindness, that would be
    A dismal thing to do!"
"The night is fine," the Walrus said.
    "Do you admire the view?"

85 "It was so kind of you to come!
    And you are very nice!"
The Carpenter said nothing but
    "Cut us another slice.
I wish you were not quite so deaf—
90   I've had to ask you twice!"

"It seems a shame," the Walrus said,
    "To play them such a trick.
After we've brought them out so far,
    And made them trot so quick!"
95 The Carpenter said nothing but
    "The butter's spread too thick!"

"I weep for you," the Walrus said:
    "I deeply sympathize."
With sobs and tears he sorted out
100   Those of the largest size,
Holding his pocket-handkerchief
    Before his streaming eyes.

"O Oysters," said the Carpenter,
    "You've had a pleasant run!
105 Shall we be trotting home again?"

But answer came there none—
And this was scarcely odd, because
    They'd eaten every one.

The White Knight's Song[1]

I'll tell thee everything I can:
    There's little to relate.
I saw an aged aged man,
    A-sitting on a gate.
"Who are you, aged man?" I said.
    "And how is it you live?"
And his answer trickled through my head,
    Like water through a sieve.

He said "I look for butterflies
    That sleep among the wheat:
I make them into mutton-pies,
    And sell them in the street.
I sell them unto men," he said,
    "Who sail on stormy seas;
And that's the way I get my bread—
    A trifle, if you please."

But I was thinking of a plan
    To dye one's whiskers green,
And always use so large a fan
    That they could not be seen.
So, having no reply to give
    To what the old man said,
I cried "Come, tell me how you live!"
    And thumped him on the head.

His accents mild took up the tale:
    He said "I go my ways,
And when I find a mountain-rill,
    I set it in a blaze;
And thence they make a stuff they call
    Rowland's Macassar-Oil—
Yet twopence-halfpenny is all
    They give me for my toil."

But I was thinking of a way
    To feed oneself on batter,
And so go on from day to day
    Getting a little fatter.
I shook him well from side to side,
    Until his face was blue:

---

1. From *Through the Looking Glass* (ch. 8); the White Knight sings it to Alice. It is a parody of Wordsworth's *Resolution and Independence* (see page 520).

"Come, tell me how you live," I cried,
40   "And what it is you do!"

He said "I hunt for haddocks' eyes
    Among the heather bright,
And work them into waistcoat-buttons
    In the silent night.
45 And these I do not sell for gold
    Or coin of silvery shine,
But for a copper halfpenny,
    And that will purchase nine.

"I sometimes dig for buttered rolls,
50   Or set limed twigs for crabs:
I sometimes search for grassy knolls
    For wheels of Hansom-cabs.
And that's the way" (he gave a wink)
    "By which I get my wealth—
55 And very gladly will I drink
    Your Honour's noble health."

I heard him then, for I had just
    Completed my design
To keep the Menai bridge from rust
60   By boiling it in wine.
I thanked him much for telling me
    The way he got his wealth,
But chiefly for his wish that he
    Might drink my noble health.

65 And now, if e'er by chance I put
    My fingers into glue,
Or madly squeeze a right-hand foot
    Into a left-hand shoe,
Or if I drop upon my toe
70   A very heavy weight,
I weep, for it reminds me so
    Of that old man I used to know—

Whose look was mild, whose speech was slow,
Whose hair was whiter than the snow,
75 Whose face was very like a crow,
With eyes, like cinders, all aglow,
Who seemed distracted with his woe,
Who rocked his body to and fro,
And muttered mumblingly and low,
80 As if his mouth were full of dough,
Who snorted like a buffalo—
That summer evening long ago,
    A-sitting on a gate.

⇒ PERSPECTIVES ⇐

Imagining Childhood

The nineteenth century has been called the Golden Age of children's literature, for the period saw a remarkable flourishing of writing for and about children. Much of this writing aimed not merely to instruct or admonish children but to delight them. Lewis Carroll's *Alice* books may be the best-known examples, but they are hardly alone: Edward Lear produced several enormously popular volumes of nonsense, writers from John Ruskin to Oscar Wilde tried their hand at the modern fairy tale, Christina Rossetti and Robert Louis Stevenson produced deceptively simple nursery rhymes, and fantasy writing by Charles Kingsley, George MacDonald, and Edith Nesbit paved the way for early-twentieth-century classics such as *Peter Pan*, *The Wind in the Willows*, and *Winnie-the-Pooh*. In addition, the era saw an explosion of adventure stories by novelists such as Rudyard Kipling and Robert Louis Stevenson; of detective fiction, most famously by Sir Arthur Conan Doyle (see *A Scandal in Bohemia*, page 1557); and of tales of ghosts and the supernatural (see Charles Dickens's *A Christmas Carol*, page 1464 and Thomas Hardy's *The Withered Arm*, page 1538). Thomas Hughes's *Tom Brown's School Days* (see page 1647) gave rise to another popular genre known as the "school story."

Although the distinction between writing for adults and writing for children was less marked than it is today, much of this literature was produced with a juvenile audience in mind. But it wasn't just the audience who was young: child protagonists featured in countless Victorian novels. The first child hero, Dickens's Oliver Twist (1837), was soon followed by Charlotte Brontë's Jane Eyre, Emily Brontë's Cathy Earnshaw and Heathcliff, William Makepeace Thackeray's Amelia Sedley and Becky Sharp, George Eliot's Tom and Maggie Tulliver—and, of course, a host of subsequent child protagonists in Dickens's own novels, from David Copperfield to Pip. The youthful characters who filled the pages of nineteenth-century fiction served, in part, as vehicles for the authors to come to terms with their own early years. Many of the best-known writers for children, including Dickens, Carroll, and Lear, had memories of difficult childhoods; hence, they frequently idealized and sentimentalized childhood or fantasized about escape to secret gardens and wonderlands. Simultaneously, the century saw a flood of autobiographical writing, excerpts from which can be found throughout this anthology: Mill, Darwin, Ruskin, Nightingale, Cobbe, Gosse, as well as Pater's autobiographical fiction, *The Child in the House*.

Although childhood was often part of the plot in eighteenth-century novels, it was Blake and Wordsworth who made children into central characters. The Victorians built on the Romantic vision of the child as source of both innocence and imagination, a vision expressed by Wordsworth in his ode *Intimations of Immortality*: "And not in utter nakedness, / But trailing clouds of glory do we come / From God, who is our home." Such ideas about the natural goodness of children owed much to the French philosopher Jean-Jacques Rousseau (1712–1778), who saw children's instinctive innocence as a spiritual touchstone for adults.

The Victorians were engaged in an ongoing debate about the meaning and nature of childhood. What was special about that period of life? Were children born in original sin and thus in need of perpetual training and vigilance in order to ensure the salvation of their souls? Or were they born in a state of innocence, only gradually to be sullied through initiation into adult cares? Did children possess heightened perceptions that would gradually fade with time? Did they have a clearer vision or a purer moral nature? Were their minds really blank slates— John Locke's *tabula rasa*—upon which teaching and experience would later be imprinted? Or did they have inborn instincts, innate predispositions? (Darwin, for example, observed in his baby that ideas arose "independently of any instruction.")

The answers to such questions determined, among other things, how children were brought up. Evangelical households subordinated every other aim and pleasure to the goal of saving the souls of their offspring: strict Sabbath observance meant putting away all the toys except Noah's

Advertisement for Pears' soap. Children in earlier eras were often depicted as miniature adults, standing stiffly beside their parents in dignified family portraits. Victorian painters, aided by photographs, tried to convey their liveliness and playfulness. The painting here was created in 1886 by Sir John Everett Millais, one of the original Pre-Raphaelites, and depicts his grandson wearing a Little Lord Fauntleroy suit and blowing bubbles—symbol of the ephemeral beauty of childhood. Millais called it *A Child's World*. But this sort of idealization of childhood readily leant itself to commercialization, and without Millais's knowledge, the owner of his picture sold it to the Pears Soap Company, along with the rights to reproduction. Retitled *Bubbles* and shown with a bar of soap added at the lower right and the word "Pears" in the upper left, the art-advertisement went on to become one of the most widely diffused images in the British Empire.

ark and reading only sermons or perhaps *Pilgrim's Progress*. The results of such an upbringing are vividly described in autobiographies by John Ruskin and Edmund Gosse (see pages 1599 and 1403). Darwin, ever the scientist, regarded his children as part and parcel of the natural world and thus as objects of study every bit as fascinating as finches or coral reefs; he preferred, therefore, to work on his children's "good feelings" rather than exert authoritarian control.

The Victorians were the first generation of parents to be bombarded with books on child rearing; the 1830s alone saw the publication of *Advice to Young Men . . . on How to Be a Father* (1829), *The Mother at Home, or the Principles of Maternal Duty* (1830), *Nursery Government* (1836), *Thoughts of a Parent on Education* (1837), *Hints to Mothers* (1837), *Physical Education, or the Nurture and Management of Children* (1838), and *Advice to Mothers* (1839). Such books were full of information about bathing, dressing, feeding, and disciplining children; some even offered suggestions for decorating the nursery. All of this sometimes conflicting advice could confuse well-meaning and well-read parents: as Elizabeth Gaskell exclaimed anxiously in the diary she kept from 1835 to 1838 to record her feelings as a first-time mother, "Books do so differ." Gaskell herself was most influenced by *L'Education progressive* (1828–1832), written by a French mother who took issue with Rousseau on the question of parental authority: "Perhaps Rousseau has made you uneasy as to the lawfulness of your authority. But if your child be exposed to a real danger . . . your theories are all forgotten." Such books put a great deal of pressure on conscientious women to live up to the high responsibilities of maternity; child rearing was no longer considered merely a matter of affection and common sense.

The novelist Anthony Trollope—whose own, notoriously miserable childhood he later recorded in his autobiography—disapproved of permissive American methods of upbringing:

> I must protest that American babies are an unhappy race. They eat and drink just as they please; they are never punished; they are never banished, snubbed, and kept in the back ground as children are kept with us; and yet they are wretched and uncomfortable. My heart has bled for them as I have heard them squalling by the hour together in agonies of discontent and dyspepsia. Can it be, I wonder, that the children are happier when they are made to obey orders and are sent to bed at six o'clock, than when allowed to regulate their own conduct; that bread and milk is more favourable to laughter and soft childish ways than beefsteak and pickles three times a day; that an occasional whipping, even, will conduce to rosy cheeks? It is an idea which I should never dare to broach to an American mother; but I must confess that after my travels on the western continent my opinions have a tendency in that direction. Beefsteak and pickles certainly produce smart[1] little men and women. Let that be taken for granted. But rosy laughter and winning childish ways are, I fancy, the produce of bread and milk.

Trollope's observations give a glimpse of contemporary British nursery life, with its strict discipline, bland diet, and early bedtimes. Middle- and upper-class children spent most of their day under the care of nurses and governesses, seeing their parents only at scheduled times. Trollope subscribes to a prevalent ideal of childhood—rosy cheeks and soft childish ways—that he feels should be protected; the American system of a rich diet and early independence encourages children to grow up too soon, to become "smart little men and women."

For some, there were nurseries and nannies; for others, factories and mines—American children weren't the only ones growing up too soon. The comfortable childhoods depicted in *Alice's Adventures in Wonderland* or *A Child's Garden of Verses*—full of toys and storybooks, nice clothes and good manners—existed alongside appalling child labor and poverty. Children

---

1. Trollope probably means "shrewd." Other English travelers to America, including Trollope's mother, Frances Trollope, and Isabella Bird, also deplored the "smartness" of American children and their passion for making money.

as young as five or six put in twelve-hour days as chimney sweeps or mill workers. Large numbers of children were employed in domestic service or agricultural labor. Others worked in coal mines or as street hawkers or prostitutes. Thus, while popular ideology regarded children as innocents to be cherished, admired, and safeguarded, they were very often allowed to endure unspeakable wretchedness.

Of course, these were not the *same* children; as the following remarks on pregnancy illustrate, class distinctions were taken for granted: "We know that it is utterly impossible for the wife of the labouring man to give up work, and, what is called 'take care of herself,' as others can. Nor is it necessary. 'The back is made for its burthen.' It would be just as injurious for the labourer's wife to give up her daily work, as for the lady to take to sweeping her own carpets or cooking the dinner" (from *Cassell's Household Guide*). As with the mother-to-be, so with the child: the privileges of one class and the sufferings of the other were divinely appointed, or at least inevitable. As a Nottingham master sweep explained, many customers *insisted* on having their chimneys swept by children rather than machines, even "ladies who professed to pity the boys." For further reading about the lives of working children, see Blake's "The Chimney Sweeper" (page 174), as well as the testimony of child workers excerpted from the Parliamentary Papers (page 1143) and Henry Mayhew's accounts of his interviews with street children (page 1158).

The nineteenth century saw gradual improvement in the lot of such children, beginning with the Factory Act of 1833, which limited those under thirteen to an eight-hour work day. It was the first time that childhood had been legally defined by age. The findings of the Children's Employment Commission of 1842–1843 shocked the public conscience, but not until 1901 was a Factory Act passed to prohibit children under twelve from employment in any factory or workshop. In other areas, too, humanitarian efforts slowly brought about protective legislation: the Education Act of 1870 made the first move toward compulsory education, and the 1889 Prevention of Cruelty to Children Act enabled authorities to remove abused children from the custody of their parents. The imprisonment of children under sixteen was not abolished until 1908.

Any discussion of Victorian childhood must also consider the reality of infant mortality. Throughout much of the century, the death rate in England remained fairly constant at over 15 percent of live births (the lowest in Europe). But in industrialized cities, the figure was far higher. Even at midcentury, as many as half of all children did not survive to see their fifth birthday. In addition to malnutrition and poor hygiene, the lack of antibiotics made many deaths from childhood diseases unavoidable. Yet it is a mistake to think that people in earlier times were resigned to losing their children. Darwin wrote a heartbreaking account of the death of his ten-year-old daughter Annie; when her infant son succumbed to scarlet fever, Elizabeth Gaskell wrote, "I don't believe Heaven itself can obliterate the memory of that agony." Then, as now, the loss of a child was one of life's worst blows. It is hardly surprising, then, that pathetic deathbed scenes figure largely in Victorian literature: the most notorious is the death of Little Nell in Dickens's *The Old Curiosity Shop* (1841), which made grown men sob. In contrast, Christina Rossetti's nursery lyrics "*Why did baby die*" and "*Baby lies so fast asleep*" treat the topic with a poignant matter-of-factness.

Child mortality was only one of many complex factors that led the Victorians to make a cult of childhood. They fetishized eternal youth, from Little Nell to Dorian Gray, and on to Peter Pan. Some men, including Ruskin and Carroll and Lear, sought out young children for intense friendships. The notion that the spiritual purity of a young child could bring about the moral redemption of an adult became a frequent theme, from *A Christmas Carol* to Frances Hodgson Burnett's *Little Lord Fauntleroy* (1886). In the same year that Burnett's novel sparked a craze for dressing boys in velvet suits, lace collars, and long curls, John Everett Millais painted his grandson blowing bubbles in just such an outfit. The portrait of this golden-headed child became one of the most popular images of the century. It evokes a vision of childhood as a golden, fragile realm of innocence, a paradisiacal time that many idealized and longed to recapture. The great children's writers, themselves often in revolt against the strictures of adult society, created imaginary worlds for the amusement of their younger readers and the solace of their older ones. Fairy tales and fantasies, anarchic nonsense verse and thrilling tales of adventure, all were part of the period's ongoing discovery and recovery of childhood. As Charles Dickens wrote, in an essay called *Frauds on Fairies* (1853), "everyone who has considered the subject knows full well that a nation without fancy, without some romance, never did, never can, never will, hold a great place under the sun."

For additional writing for children, see Rudyard Kipling's *Just So Stories*, page 1874.

Charles Darwin
1809–1882

"My first child was born on December 27th, 1839, and I at once commenced to make notes on the first dawn of the various expressions which he exhibited, for I felt convinced, even at this early period, that the most complex and fine shades of expression must all have had a gradual and natural origin." Darwin thus explains in his *Autobiography* how he carefully observed the behavior of his baby, recording his findings with the same objectivity and detachment he brought to any other subject of scientific inquiry. His speculations are free of any sentimentality about children or any religious concerns about their innate guilt or innocence; rather, his approach is typically and sometimes amusingly "Darwinian." He wonders whether throwing things in anger is an inherited male trait and whether a child's fear of large animals derives from a primal memory of "ancient savage times." He matter-of-factly notes similarities between the human infant and various animals: his baby's instinctive anger reminds him of the snapping jaws of a young crocodile, and he contrasts his son's pleasure in looking at himself in the mirror to the puzzlement of apes (and his younger sister). In a final surprise, Darwin hints at a permissive system of child rearing more associated with contemporary America than Victorian England. Although written in 1839–1841, this path-breaking study in child development was not published until 1877.

For more about Charles Darwin, see his principal listing on page 1345.

from A Biographical Sketch of an Infant

During the first seven days various reflex actions, namely sneezing, hickuping, yawning, stretching, and of course sucking and screaming, were well performed by my infant. On the seventh day, I touched the naked sole of his foot with a bit of paper, and he jerked it away, curling at the same time his toes, like a much older child when tickled. The perfection of these reflex movements shows that the extreme imperfection of the voluntary ones is not due to the state of the muscles or of the coordinating centres, but to that of the seat of the will. * * *

* * *

Anger.—It was difficult to decide at how early an age anger was felt; on his eighth day he frowned and wrinkled the skin round his eyes before a crying fit, but this may have been due to pain or distress, and not to anger. When about ten weeks old, he was given some rather cold milk and he kept a slight frown on his forehead all the time that he was sucking, so that he looked like a grown-up person made cross from being compelled to do something which he did not like. When nearly four months old, and perhaps much earlier, there could be no doubt, from the manner in which the blood gushed into his whole face and scalp, that he easily got into a violent passion. A small cause sufficed; thus, when a little over seven months old, he screamed with rage because a lemon slipped away and he could not seize it with his hands.

When eleven months old, if a wrong plaything was given him, he would push it away and beat it; I presume that the beating was an instinctive sign of anger, like the snapping of the jaws by a young crocodile just out of the egg, and not that he imagined he could hurt the plaything. When two years and three months old, he became a great adept at throwing books or sticks, &c., at anyone who offended him; and so it was with some of my other sons. On the other hand, I could never see a trace of such aptitude in my infant daughters; and this makes me think that a tendency to throw objects is inherited by boys.

Fear.—This feeling probably is one of the earliest which is experienced by infants, as shown by their starting at any sudden sound when only a few weeks old, followed by crying. Before the present one was 4$\frac{1}{2}$ months old I had been accustomed to make close to him many strange and loud noises, which were all taken as excellent jokes, but at this period I one day made a loud snoring noise which I had never done before; he instantly looked grave and then burst out crying. Two or three days afterwards, I made through forgetfulness the same noise with the same result. About the same time (*viz.* on the 137th day) I approached with my back towards him and then stood motionless: he looked very grave and much surprised, and would soon have cried, had I not turned round; then his face instantly relaxed into a smile. It is well known how intensely older children suffer from vague and undefined fears, as from the dark, or in passing an obscure corner in a large hall, &c. I may give as an instance that I took the child in question, when 2$\frac{1}{2}$ years old, to the Zoological Gardens, and he enjoyed looking at all the animals which were like those that he knew, such as deer, antelopes &c., and all the birds, even the ostriches, but was much alarmed at the various larger animals in cages. He often said afterwards that he wished to go again, but not to see "beasts in houses"; and we could in no manner account for his fear. May we not suspect that the vague but very real fears of children, which are quite independent of experience, are the inherited effects of real dangers and abject superstitions during ancient savage times? It is quite conformable with what we know of the transmission of formerly well-developed characters, that they should appear at an early period of life, and afterwards disappear.

* * *

Affection.—This probably arose very early in life, if we may judge by his smiling at those who had charge of him when under two months old; though I had no distinct evidence of his distinguishing and recognizing anyone, until he was nearly four months old. When nearly five months old, he plainly showed his wish to go to his nurse. But he did not spontaneously exhibit affection by overt acts until a little above a year old, namely, by kissing several times his nurse who had been absent for a short time. With respect to the allied feeling of sympathy, this was clearly shown at 6 months and 11 days by his melancholy face, with the corners of his mouth well depressed, when his nurse pretended to cry. Jealousy was plainly exhibited when I fondled a large doll, and when I weighed his infant sister, he being 15$\frac{1}{2}$ months old. Seeing how strong a feeling jealousy is in dogs, it would probably be exhibited by infants at an earlier age than that just specified, if they were tried in a fitting manner.

Association of Ideas, Reason, &c.—The first action which exhibited, as far as I observed, a kind of practical reasoning, has already been noticed, namely, the slipping his hand down my finger so as to get the end of it into his mouth; and this happened on the 114th day. When four and a half months old, he repeatedly smiled at my image and his own in a mirror, and no doubt mistook them for real objects; but he showed sense in being evidently surprised at my voice coming from behind him. Like all infants he much enjoyed thus looking at himself, and in less than two months perfectly understood that it was an image; for if I made quite silently any odd grimace, he would suddenly turn round to look at me. He was, however, puzzled at the age of seven months, when being out of doors he saw me on the inside of a large plate-glass window, and seemed in doubt whether or not it was an image. Another of my infants, a little girl, when exactly a year old, was not nearly so acute, and seemed quite perplexed at the image of a person in a mirror approaching her from behind. The higher apes which I tried with a small looking-glass behaved differently; they placed their hands behind the glass, and in doing so showed their sense, but far from taking pleasure in looking at themselves they got angry and would look no more.

When five months old, associated ideas arising independently of any instruction became fixed in his mind; thus as soon as his hat and cloak were put on, he was very cross if he was not immediately taken out of doors. When exactly seven months old, he made the great step of associating his nurse with her name, so that if I called it out he would look round for her. Another infant used to amuse himself by shaking his head laterally: we praised and imitated him, saying "Shake your head"; and when he was seven months old, he would sometimes do so on being told without any other guide. * * * The facility with which associated ideas due to instruction and others spontaneously arising were acquired, seemed to me by far the most strongly marked of all the distinctions between the mind of an infant and that of the cleverest full-grown dog that I have ever known. What a contrast does the mind of an infant present to that of the pike, described by Professor Möbius,[1] who during three whole months dashed and stunned himself against a glass partition which separated him from some minnows; and when, after at least learning that he could not attack them with impunity, he was placed in the aquarium with these same minnows, then in a persistent and senseless manner he would not attack them!

* * *

Moral Sense.—The first sign of moral sense was noticed at the age of nearly 13 months. I said "Doddy (his nickname) won't give poor papa a kiss,—naughty Doddy". These words, without doubt, made him feel slightly uncomfortable; and at last when I had returned to my chair, he protruded his lips as a sign that he was ready to kiss me; and he then shook his hand in an angry manner until I came and received his kiss. Nearly the same little scene recurred in a few days, and the reconciliation seemed to give him so much satisfaction, that several times afterwards he pretended to be angry and slapped me, and then insisted on giving me a kiss. So that here we have a touch of the dramatic art, which is so strongly pronounced in most young children. About this time it became easy to work on his feelings and make him do whatever was wanted. When 2 years and 3 months old, he gave his last bit of gingerbread to his little sister, and then cried out with high self-approbation "Oh kind Doddy, kind Doddy." Two months later, he became extremely sensitive to ridicule, and was so suspicious that he often thought people who were laughing and talking together were laughing at him. A little later (2 years and 7½ months old) I met him coming out of the dining room with his eyes unnaturally bright, and an odd unnatural or affected manner, so that I went into the room to see who was there, and found that he had been taking pounded sugar, which he had been told not to do. As he had never been in any way punished, his odd manner certainly was not due to fear, and I suppose it was pleasurable excitement struggling with conscience. A fortnight afterwards, I met him coming out of the same room, and he was eyeing his pinafore which he had carefully rolled up; and again his manner was so

---

1. Karl August Möbius (1825–1908), German zoologist and marine biologist.

odd that I determined to see what was within his pinafore, notwithstanding that he said that there was nothing and repeatedly commanded me to "go away," and I found it stained with pickle-juice; so that here was carefully planned deceit. As this child was educated solely by working on his good feelings, he soon became as truthful, open, and tender, as anyone could desire.

1839–1841   1877

━━◆◆◆◆━━

Moral Verses

Much of what was written for children in the nineteenth century had a strong flavor of the didactic and morally improving, as illustrated by the anonymous *Table Rules for Little Folks*. The lessons could be hard-hitting: the popular but unsentimental Eliza Cook's little mouse actually *dies* as a punishment for not sharing his cake with his brothers! Translated into English in 1848, Heinrich Hoffmann's *Struwwelpeter* was the first sustained parody of the "awful warnings" of earlier moral verse; he inspired many imitators, most notably Hilaire Belloc's *Cautionary Tales for Children* (1907). Yet it's never quite clear whether Hoffmann is truly mocking the awful warnings or comically reinventing them—for the "sin" of defying his parents by refusing his soup, Augustus ends up dead. In a different vein Thomas Miller, a popular working-class poet, sought to arouse the moral sympathies of his young readers with the plight of the freezing and half-starved watercress seller; the implied contrast with their own comfort would presumably teach them to be grateful for their blessings. In contrast, the Scots poem *Willie Winkie*—the title character is the personification of Sleep—takes a cheerful view of mischievous "weans" who won't go to bed.

Table Rules for Little Folks

<blockquote>

In silence I must take my seat,
And give God thanks before I eat;
Must for my food in patience wait,
Till I am asked to hand my plate;
5   I must not scold, nor whine, nor pout,
Nor move my chair nor plate about;
With knife, or fork, or napkin ring,
I must not play, nor must I sing.
I must not speak a useless word,
10   For children should be seen, not heard;
I must not talk about my food,
Nor fret if I don't think it good;
I must not say, "The bread is old,"
"The tea is hot," "The coffee's cold";
15   My mouth with food I must not crowd,
Nor while I'm eating speak aloud;
Must turn my head to cough or sneeze,
And when I ask, say "If you please";
The tablecloth I must not spoil,
20   Nor with my food my fingers soil;
Must keep my seat when I have done,
Nor round the table sport or run;

</blockquote>

When told to rise, then I must put
My chair away with noiseless foot;
25 And lift my heart to God above,
In praise for all his wondrous love.

c. 1858

Eliza Cook: The Mouse and the Cake

A mouse found a beautiful piece of plum cake,
The richest and sweetest that mortal could make;
'Twas heavy with citron and fragrant with spice,
And covered with sugar all sparkling as ice.

5 "My stars!" cried the mouse, while his eye beamed with glee,
"Here's a treasure I've found: what a feast it will be;
But, hark! there's a noise, 'tis my brothers at play;
So I'll hide with the cake, lest they wander this way.

"Not a bit shall they have, for I know I can eat
10 Every morsel myself, and I'll have such a treat."
So off went the mouse as he held the cake fast;
While his hungry young brothers went scampering past.

He nibbled, and nibbled, and panted, but still
He kept gulping it down till he made himself ill;
15 Yet he swallowed it all, and 'tis easy to guess,
He was soon so unwell that he groaned with distress.

His family heard him, and as he grew worse,
They sent for the doctor, who made him rehearse
How he'd eaten the cake to the very last crumb,
20 Without giving his playmates and relatives some.

"Ah me!" cried the doctor, "advice is too late;
You must die before long, so prepare for your fate.
If you had but divided the cake with your brothers,
'Twould have done you no harm, and been good for the others.

25 "Had you shared it, the treat had been wholesome enough;
But eaten by *one*, it was dangerous stuff;
So prepare for the worst—" and the word had scarce fled,
When the doctor turned round, and the patient was dead.

Now all little people the lesson may take,
30 And *some* large ones may learn from the mouse and the cake;
Not to be over-selfish with what we may gain,
Or the best of our pleasures may turn into pain.

1849

Heinrich Hoffmann: The Story of Augustus who would Not have any Soup

Augustus was a chubby lad;
Fat ruddy cheeks Augustus had:

And everybody saw with joy
The plump and hearty, healthy boy.
5   He ate and drank as he was told,
And never let his soup get cold.
But one day, one cold winter's day,
He screamed out "Take the soup away!
O take the nasty soup away!
10   I won't have any soup today."

Next day, now look, the picture shows
How lank and lean Augustus grows!
Yet, though he feels so weak and ill,
The naughty fellow cries out still
15   "Not any soup for me, I say:
O take the nasty soup away!
I *won't* have any soup today."

The third day comes: Oh what a sin!
To make himself so pale and thin.
20   Yet, when the soup is put on table,
He screams, as loud as he is able,
"Not any soup for me, I say:
O take the nasty soup away!
I WON'T have any soup today."

25   Look at him, now the fourth day's come!
He scarcely weighs a sugar-plum;
He's like a little bit of thread,
And, on the fifth day, he was—dead!

1844   1848

Thomas Miller: The Watercress Seller[1]

Now all aloud the wind and rain
Beat sharp upon the window pane,
And though 'tis hardly light,
I hear that little girl go by,
5   Who does "Fine watercresses" cry,
Morning, and noon, and night.

I saw her pass by yesterday,
The snow upon the pavement lay,
Her hair was white with sleet;
10   She shook with cold, as she did cry,
"Fine watercresses, come and buy,"
And naked were her feet.

And with one hand, so red and cold,
She did her tattered bonnet hold,
15   The other held her shawl,

1. See also Henry Mayhew, the *Watercress Girl*, page 1158.

Which was too thin to keep her warm,
But naked left each little arm,
    It was so very small.

Her watercresses froze together,
20 Yet she, through the cold, bitter weather,
    Went on from street to street:
And thus she goes out every day,
For she can earn no other way
    The bread which she doth eat.

1850

William Miller: Willie Winkie

Wee Willie Winkie rins through the town,	
Up stairs and doon stairs in his nicht-gown,	
Tirling° at the window, crying at the lock,	*rapping*
"Are the weans° in their bed, for it's now ten o'clock?"	*children*
5 "Hey, Willie Winkie, are ye coming ben?°	*in*
The cat's singing grey thrums° to the sleeping hen,	*purring*
The dog's spelder'd° on the floor, and disna gie a cheep,	*sprawled*
But here's a waukrife° laddie, that winna fa' asleep."	*wakeful*
Onything but sleep, you rogue! glow'ring like the moon,	
10 Rattling in an airn° jug wi' an airn spoon,	*iron*
Rumbling, tumbling round about, crawing like a cock,	
Skirling like a kenna-what,° wauk'ning sleeping fock.	*shrieking like anything*
"Hey, Willie Winkie—the wean's in a creel,°	*in a state*
Wambling° aff a bodie's knee like a very eel,	*squirming*
15 Rugging° at the cat's lug,° and ravelling a'her thrums—	*tugging / ear*
Hey, Willie Winkie—see, there he comes!"	
Wearied is the mither° that has a stoorie° wean,	*mother / restless*
A wee stumpie stoussie,° that canna rin his lane,°	*little munchkin / cannot run alone*
That has a battle aye wi' sleep before he'll close an e'e—	
20 But a kiss frae aff his rosy lips gies strength anew to me.	

1841

Edward Lear
1812–1888

"I see life as basically tragic and futile and the only thing that matters is making little jokes," wrote the landscape painter Edward Lear in his diary. The twentieth child of a bankrupt stockbroker, he suffered from depression and poor health. Yet this unhappy, enigmatic figure produced some of the most amusing writing of the era, accompanied by his own surreal sketches. Like Lewis Carroll, whose *Alice* (1865) appeared nearly twenty years after Lear's *A Book of Nonsense* (1846), Lear created an absurdist nonsense world in reaction to the stuffy conventions of Victorian social life. His sense of himself as a misfit is reflected not only in the autobiographical *How Pleasant to Know Mr. Lear*, but also in the gallery of eccentrics who people his limericks. Many of his peculiar Old Men and whimsical Young Ladies come to a violent end at the hands of a mocking and intolerant "they"; others do away with themselves for no apparent reason, suggesting nihilism at the heart of nonsense. In later verses, such as *The Owl and the Pussy-Cat*, alienation is transformed as preposterously mismatched couples enact a fantasy of joyful romantic escape. The bouncing energy of Lear's verses and the chaotic anarchy of his nonsense vision culminate in the Jumblies' fantastical and nutty adventures at sea.

[SELECTED LIMERICKS]

There was an Old Man with a beard,
Who said, "It is just as I feared!—
Two Owls and a Hen, four Larks and a Wren,
Have all built their nests in my beard!"

There was an Old Man with a nose,
Who said, "If you choose to suppose,
That my nose is too long, you are certainly wrong!"
That remarkable Man with a nose.

There was a Young Lady of Norway,
Who casually sat in a doorway;
When the door squeezed her flat, she exclaimed "What of that?"
This courageous Young Lady of Norway.

There was an Old Man of the Dee,
Who was sadly annoyed by a flea;
When he said, "I will scratch it"—they gave him a hatchet,
Which grieved that Old Man of the Dee.

There was an Old Man of Whitehaven,
Who danced a quadrille with a Raven;
But they said—"It's absurd, to encourage this bird!"
So they smashed that Old Man of Whitehaven.

There was a young lady, whose nose,
Continually prospers and grows;
When it grew out of sight, she exclaimed in a fright,
"Oh! Farewell to the end of my nose!"

The Owl and the Pussy-Cat

1

The Owl and the Pussy-cat went to sea
   In a beautiful pea-green boat,
They took some honey, and plenty of money,
   Wrapped up in a five-pound note.
The Owl looked up to the stars above,
   And sang to a small guitar,
"O lovely Pussy! O Pussy, my love,
   What a beautiful Pussy you are,
     You are,

10   You are!
       What a beautiful Pussy you are!"

                           2

       Pussy said to the Owl, "You elegant fowl!
           How charmingly sweet you sing!
       O let us be married! too long we have tarried:
15   But what shall we do for a ring?"
       They sailed away, for a year and a day,
           To the land where the Bong-tree grows
       And there in a wood a Piggy-wig stood
           With a ring at the end of his nose,
20   His nose,
               His nose,
           With a ring at the end of his nose.

                           3

       "Dear Pig, are you willing to sell for one shilling
           Your ring?" Said the Piggy, "I will."
25   So they took it away, and were married next day
           By the Turkey who lives on the hill.
       They dined on mince, and slices of quince,
           Which they ate with a runcible spoon;
       And hand in hand, on the edge of the sand,
30   They danced by the light of the moon,
               The moon,
               The moon,
           They danced by the light of the moon.

                                                    1871

The Jumblies

                           1

       They went to sea in a Sieve, they did,
           In a Sieve they went to sea:
       In spite of all their friends could say,
       On a winter's morn, on a stormy day,
5   In a Sieve they went to sea!
       And when the Sieve turned round and round,
       And every one cried, "You'll all be drowned!"
       They called aloud, "Our Sieve ain't big,
       But we don't care a button! we don't care a fig!
10   In a Sieve we'll go to sea!"
               Far and few, far and few,
                   Are the lands where the Jumblies live;
               Their heads are green, and their hands are blue,
                   And they went to sea in a Sieve.

2

15   They sailed away in a Sieve, they did,
          In a Sieve they sailed so fast,
      With only a beautiful pea-green veil
      Tied with a riband by way of a sail,
          To a small tobacco-pipe mast;
20   And every one said, who saw them go,
      "O won't they be soon upset, you know!
      For the sky is dark, and the voyage is long,
      And happen what may, it's extremely wrong
          In a Sieve to sail so fast!"
25   Far and few, far and few,
                  Are the lands where the Jumblies live;
              Their heads are green, and their hands are blue,
                  And they went to sea in a Sieve.

3

      The water it soon came in, it did,
30   The water it soon came in;
      So to keep them dry, they wrapped their feet
      In a pinky paper all folded neat,
          And they fastened it down with a pin.
      And they passed the night in a crockery-jar,
35   And each of them said, "How wise we are!
      Though the sky be dark, and the voyage be long,
      Yet we never can think we were rash or wrong,
          While round in our Sieve we spin!"
              Far and few, far and few,
40   Are the lands where the Jumblies live;
              Their heads are green, and their hands are blue,
                  And they went to sea in a Sieve.

4

      And all night long they sailed away;
          And when the sun went down,
45   They whistled and warbled a moony song
      To the echoing sound of a coppery gong,
          In the shade of the mountains brown.
      "O Timballo! How happy we are,
      When we live in a sieve and a crockery-jar,
50   And all night long in the moonlight pale,
      We sail away with a pea-green sail,
          In the shade of the mountains brown!"
              Far and few, far and few,
                  Are the lands where the Jumblies live;
55   Their heads are green, and their hands are blue,
                  And they went to sea in a Sieve.

5

They sailed to the Western Sea, they did,
    To a land all covered with trees,
And they bought an Owl, and a useful Cart,
60   And a pound of Rice, and a Cranberry Tart,
        And a hive of silvery Bees.
And they bought a Pig, and some green Jack-daws,
And a lovely Monkey with lollipop paws,
And forty bottles of Ring-Bo-Ree,
65   And no end of Stilton Cheese.
            Far and few, far and few,
                Are the lands where the Jumblies live;
            Their heads are green, and their hands are blue,
                And they went to sea in a Sieve.

6

70   And in twenty years they all came back,
        In twenty years or more,
And every one said, "How tall they've grown!
For they've been to the Lakes, and the Torrible Zone,
        And the hills of the Chankly Bore;
75   And they drank their health, and gave them a feast
Of dumplings made of beautiful yeast;
And every one said, "If we only live,
We too will go to sea in a Sieve,—
        To the hills of the Chankly Bore!"
80   Far and few, far and few,
                Are the lands where the Jumblies live;
            Their heads are green, and their hands are blue,
                And they went to sea in a Sieve.

1871

How pleasant to know Mr. Lear!

How pleasant to know Mr. Lear!
    Who has written such volumes of stuff!
Some think him ill-tempered and queer,
    But a few think him pleasant enough.

5   His mind is concrete and fastidious,
        His nose is remarkably big;
His visage is more or less hideous,
        His beard it resembles a wig.

He has ears, and two eyes, and ten fingers,
10   Leastways if you reckon two thumbs:
Long ago he was one of the singers,
        But now he is one of the dumbs.

He sits in a beautiful parlour,
    With hundreds of books on the wall;
15   He drinks a great deal of Marsala,
    But never gets tipsy at all.

He has many friends, laymen and clerical;
    Old Foss is the name of his cat;
His body is perfectly spherical,
20   He weareth a runcible hat.

When he walks in a waterproof white,
    The children run after him so!
Calling out, "He's come out in his night-
    Gown, that crazy old Englishman, oh!"

25   He weeps by the side of the ocean,
    He weeps on the top of the hill;
He purchases pancakes and lotion,
    And chocolate shrimps from the mill.

He reads but he cannot speak Spanish,
30   He cannot abide ginger-beer;
Ere the days of his pilgrimage vanish,
    How pleasant to know Mr. Lear!

1879   1912

Christina Rossetti
1830–1894

Christina Rossetti's brother Dante called the poems of *Sing-Song* "admirable things, alternating between merest babyism and a sort of Blakish wisdom and tenderness." A carefully constructed sequence of 121 lyrics—illustrated in the original edition by Pre-Raphaelite artist Arthur Hughes—*Sing-Song* chronicles with nursery-rhyme simplicity a child's life from cradle to grave. In catchy tempos that often mimic the activity portrayed, Rossetti describes the child's development and learning: from factual lessons and moral instruction ("What does the bee do?") to thoughtful nonsense ("When fishes set umbrellas up") and musings on time and change ("I caught a little ladybird").

With their subtle, ironic, movingly casual reflections on gender, mortality, and the larger rhythms of life, Rossetti's poems address adults as well as children. The series is full of images of motionless babies—dead or slumbering? The final poem, a lullaby that ends with characteristic ambiguity ("Never wake:— / Baby, sleep"), seems to hint chillingly at the widespread practice of infanticide. Like *Goblin Market* (1862), *Sing-Song* is animated by the tension between Rossetti's conflicting desires: to unleash and yet tame her imaginative life. Playfulness wars with old-fashioned didacticism: "If a pig wore a wig" is preceded by "A pocket handkerchief to hem." Unlike the open-ended pranks that annoy Lewis Carroll's Alice and cast her schooling in doubt, Rossetti's nonsense riddles quickly rein in the wacky possibilities they open up: "A pin has a head but no hair." As Rossetti herself said, "Puns and such like are a frivolous crew likely to misbehave unless kept within strict bounds."

For more about Christina Rossetti, see her principal listing on page 1723.

Arthur Hughes, illustration to *If I were a Queen*, 1872.

from **Sing-Song: A Nursery Rhyme Book**
Rhymes Dedicated
without Permission
to the Baby
Who Suggested Them

Angels at the foot,
   And Angels at the head,
And like a curly little lamb
   My pretty babe in bed.

     * * *

Why did baby die,
Making Father sigh,
Mother cry?

Flowers, that bloom to die,
5   Make no reply
Of "why?"
But bow and die.

     * * *

"If I were a Queen,
   What would I do?
I'd make you King,
   And I'd wait on you."

5   "If I were a King,
   What would I do?

I'd make you Queen,
    For I'd marry you."

———————

What are heavy? sea-sand and sorrow:
What are brief? to-day and to-morrow:
What are frail? Spring blossoms and youth:
What are deep? the ocean and truth.

———————

Stroke a flint, and there is nothing to admire:
Strike a flint, and forthwith flash out sparks of fire.

* * *

"Twist me a crown of wind-flowers;
    That I may fly away
To hear the singers at their song.
    And players at their play."

5   "Put on your crown of wind-flowers:
    But whither would you go?"
"Beyond the surging of the sea
    And the storms that blow."

"Alas! your crown of wind-flowers
10   Can never make you fly:
I twist them in a crown to-day,
    And to-night they die."

* * *

A pocket handkerchief to hem—
    Oh dear, oh dear, oh dear!
How many stitches it will take
    Before it's done, I fear.

5   Yet set a stitch and then a stitch,
    And stitch and stitch away,
Till stitch by stitch the hem is done—
    And after work is play!

———————

If a pig wore a wig,
    What could we say?
Treat him as a gentleman,
    And say "Good-day."

5   If his tail chanced to fail,
    What could we do?—
Send him to the tailoress
    To get one new.

* * *

What is pink? a rose is pink
By the fountain's brink.
What is red? a poppy's red
In its barley bed.
5 What is blue? the sky is blue
Where the clouds float thro'.

What is white? a swan is white
Sailing in the light.
What is yellow? pears are yellow,
10   Rich and ripe and mellow.
What is green? the grass is green,
With small flowers between.
What is violet? clouds are violet
In the summer twilight.
15   What is orange? why, an orange,
Just an orange!

* * *

A pin has a head, but has no hair;
A clock has a face, but no mouth there;
Needles have eyes, but they cannot see;
A fly has a trunk without lock or key;
5   A timepiece may lose; but cannot win;
A corn-field dimples without a chin;
A hill has no leg, but has a foot;
A wine-glass a stem, but not a root;
A watch has hands, but no thumb or finger;
10   A boot has a tongue, but is no singer;
Rivers run, though they have no feet;
A saw has teeth, but it does not eat;
Ash-trees have keys, yet never a lock;
And baby crows, without being a cock.

* * *

When fishes set umbrellas up
    If the rain-drops run,
Lizards will want their parasols
    To shade them from the sun.

* * *

There is one that has a head without an eye,
    And there's one that has an eye without a head:
You may find the answer if you try;
    And when all is said,
Half the answer hangs upon a thread.

* * *

Who has seen the wind?
    Neither I nor you:
But when the leaves hang trembling
    The wind is passing thro'.

5   Who has seen the wind?
    Neither you nor I:
But when the trees bow down their heads
    The wind is passing by.

* * *

An emerald is as green as grass;
    A ruby red as blood;
A sapphire shines as blue as heaven;
    A flint lies in the mud.

5 A diamond is a brilliant stone,
  To catch the world's desire;
 An opal holds a fiery spark;
  But a flint holds fire.

    * * *

 I caught a little ladybird°   *ladybug*
  That flies far away;
 I caught a little lady wife
  That is both staid and gay.

5 Come back, my scarlet ladybird,
  Back from far away;
 I weary of my dolly wife,
  My wife that cannot play.

 She's such a senseless wooden thing
10 She stares the livelong day;
 Her wig of gold is stiff and cold
  And cannot change to grey.

    * * *

 What does the bee do?
  Bring home honey.
 And what does Father do?
  Bring home money.
5 And what does Mother do?
  Lay out the money.
 And what does baby do?
  Eat up the honey.

    * * *

 Baby lies so fast asleep
  That we cannot wake her:
 Will the Angels clad in white
  Fly from heaven to take her?

5 Baby lies so fast asleep
  That no pain can grieve her;
 Put a snowdrop in her hand,
  Kiss her once and leave her.

              1872, 1893

⊷ ⊷⬥⊷ ⊶

Robert Louis Stevenson
1850–1894

The Scottish author of adventure novels such as *Treasure Island* (1883) and *Kidnapped* (1886), Robert Louis Stevenson also produced the century's most important collection of poems for children, the immensely popular *A Child's Garden of Verses* (1885). The poems are written from a child's perspective yet tinged with adult nostalgia for lost innocence and simplicity. Like Stevenson himself, who suffered from poor health, the protagonist is a sickly child with a vivid imaginative life. The poems recreate the child's world: his delight in make-believe, his wonder at the moon and stars and wind, his curiosity about dreams and shadows. They also evoke the more everyday experiences of having to worry about good manners and to go to bed while it's still light out. Yet along with the pleasures of teatime and toys, cozy counterpanes and dreamy reverie, runs a thread of anxiety, as though middle-class comforts are bulwarks against nighttime fears. The precariousness of this world is suggested, too, in the child's awareness of how poor children and foreign children do not have the security of regular meals and a rich papa. The wider world entices the child, who longs to visit foreign lands or venture out at night like the lamplighter, yet his desire to explore mingles with a fearful sense of the dangers that lurk abroad.

For more about Robert Louis Stevenson, see his principal listing on page 1937.

from **A Child's Garden of Verses**
Bed in Summer

In winter I get up at night
And dress by yellow candle-light.
In summer, quite the other way,
I have to go to bed by day.

5   I have to go to bed and see
The birds still hopping on the tree,
Or hear the grown-up people's feet
Still going past me in the street.

And does it not seem hard to you,
10   When all the sky is clear and blue,
And I should like so much to play,
To have to go to bed by day?

Whole Duty of Children

A child should always say what's true
And speak when he is spoken to,
And behave mannerly at table;
At least as far as he is able.

Looking Forward

When I am grown to man's estate
I shall be very proud and great,
And tell the other girls and boys
Not to meddle with my toys.

The Land of Counterpane°   bedspread

When I was sick and lay a-bed,
I had two pillows at my head,
And all my toys beside me lay
To keep me happy all the day.

5   And sometimes for an hour or so
I watched my leaden soldiers go,

With different uniforms and drills,
Among the bed-clothes, through the hills;

And sometimes sent my ships in fleets
10   All up and down among the sheets;
Or brought my trees and houses out,
And planted cities all about.

I was the giant great and still
That sits upon the pillow-hill,
15   And sees before him, dale and plain,
The pleasant land of counterpane.

The Land of Nod

From breakfast on through all the day
At home among my friends I stay,
But every night I go abroad
Afar into the land of Nod.

5   All by myself I have to go,
With none to tell me what to do—
All alone beside the streams
And up the mountain-sides of dreams.

The strangest things are there for me,
10   Both things to eat and things to see,
And many frightening sights abroad
Till morning in the land of Nod.

Try as I like to find the way,
I never can get back by day,
15   Nor can remember plain and clear
The curious music that I hear.

System

Every night my prayers I say,
And get my dinner every day;
And every day that I've been good,
I get an orange after food.

5   The child that is not clean and neat,
With lots of toys and things to eat,
He is a naughty child, I'm sure—
Or else his dear papa is poor.

Escape at Bedtime

The lights from the parlour and kitchen shone out
    Through the blinds and the windows and bars;
And high overhead and all moving about,

There were thousands of millions of stars.
5   There ne'er were such thousands of leaves on a tree,
          Nor of people in church or the Park,
      As the crowds of the stars that looked down upon me,
          And that glittered and winked in the dark.

      The Dog, and the Plough, and the Hunter, and all,
10   And the star of the sailor, and Mars,
      These shone in the sky, and the pail by the wall
          Would be half full of water and stars.
      They saw me at last, and they chased me with cries,
          And they soon had me packed into bed;
15   But the glory kept shining and bright in my eyes,
          And the stars going round in my head.

Happy Thought

The world is so full of a number of things,
I'm sure we should all be as happy as kings.

Good and Bad Children

      Children, you are very little,
      And your bones are very brittle;
      If you would grow great and stately,
      You must try to walk sedately.

5   You must still be bright and quiet,
      And content with simple diet;
      And remain, through all bewild'ring,
      Innocent and honest children.

      Happy hearts and happy faces,
10   Happy play in grassy places—
      That was how, in ancient ages,
      Children grew to kings and sages.

      But the unkind and the unruly,
      And the sort who eat unduly,
15   They must never hope for glory—
      Theirs is quite a different story!

      Cruel children, crying babies,
      All grow up as geese and gabies,
      Hated, as their age increases,
20   By their nephews and their nieces.

Foreign Children

Little Indian, Sioux or Crow,
Little frosty Eskimo,

Little Turk or Japanee,
O! don't you wish that you were me?

5   You have seen the scarlet trees
And the lions over seas;
You have eaten ostrich eggs,
And turned the turtles off their legs.

Such a life is very fine,
10   But it's not so nice as mine:
You must often, as you trod,
Have wearied *not* to be abroad.

You have curious things to eat,
I am fed on proper meat;
15   You must dwell beyond the foam,
But I am safe and live at home.
    Little Indian, Sioux or Crow,
    Little frosty Eskimo,
    Little Turk or Japanee,
20   O! don't you wish that you were me?

The Lamplighter

My tea is nearly ready and the sun has left the sky;
It's time to take the window to see Leerie going by;
For every night at teatime and before you take your seat,
With lantern and with ladder he comes posting up the street.

5   Now Tom would be a driver and Maria go to sea,
And my papa's a banker and as rich as he can be;
But I, when I am stronger and can choose what I'm to do,
O Leerie, I'll go round at night and light the lamps with you!

For we are very lucky, with a lamp before the door,
10   And Leerie stops to light it as he lights so many more;
And O! before you hurry by with ladder and with light,
O Leerie, see a little child and nod to him to-night!

Shadow March

All round the house is the jet-black night;
    It stares through the window-pane;
It crawls in the corners, hiding from the light,
    And it moves with the moving flame.

5   Now my little heart goes a-beating like a drum,
    With the breath of the Bogie in my hair;
And all round the candle the crooked shadows come,
    And go marching along up the stair.

The shadow of the balusters, the shadow of the lamp,
10   The shadow of the child that goes to bed—
All the wicked shadows coming tramp, tramp, tramp,
        With the black night overhead.

                                                    1885

＊＋ ᵌ◈ᵌ ＋＊

Hilaire Belloc
1870–1953

Born in France, Hilaire Belloc grew up in England, where he became a novelist, biographer, journalist, essayist, critic, and travel writer. His book of whimsical verse, *The Bad Child's Book of
Beasts* (1896), was a runaway best-seller, soon followed by *More Beasts for Worse Children* (1897).
These lively comic verses parody the heavy-handed moral lessons for children so prevalent earlier in the century. Their wry sophistication and subversive energy make them as entertaining for
adults as for children—though it is the adults who usually appear pompous and slightly absurd.
The illustrations by Belloc's friend Basil Blackwood interact cleverly with the texts, as in *The
Tiger*, where the image of the tiger's bulging stomach elucidates why the overworked mother
might find such a creature a handy pet. The jovial ruthlessness of *Cautionary Tales for Children*
(1907) seems directly inspired by Heinrich Hoffmann's *Struwwelpeter* (1848).

from **The Bad Child's Book of Beasts**
Introduction

I call you bad, my little child,
    Upon the title page,
Because a manner rude and wild
    Is common at your age.

5   The Moral of this priceless work
        (If rightly understood)
    Will make you—from a little Turk—
        Unnaturally good.

    Do not as evil children do,
10   Who on the slightest grounds
    Will imitate the Kangaroo,
        With wild unmeaning bounds.

    Do not as children badly bred,
        Who eat like little Hogs,
15 And when they have to go to bed
        Will whine like Puppy Dogs:

    Who take their manners from the Ape,
        Their habits from the Bear,
    Indulge the loud unseemly jape,°   joke
20   And never brush their hair.

But so control your actions that
    Your friends may all repeat,
"This child is dainty as the cat
    And as the Owl discreet."

1896

The Yak

As a friend to the children commend me the Yak.
    You will find it exactly the thing:
It will carry and fetch, you can ride on its back,
    Or lead it about with a string.

5   The Tartar who dwells on the plains of Thibet
        (A desolate region of snow)
Has for centuries made it a nursery pet,
        And surely the Tartar should know!

Then tell your papa where the Yak can be got,
10   And if he is awfully rich
He will buy you the creature—or else he will *not*.
        (I cannot be positive which.)

1896

The Tiger

The Tiger, on the other hand,

is kittenish and mild,
He makes a pretty playfellow for any little child;
And mothers of large families (who claim to common sense)

Will find a Tiger well repay the trouble and expense.

1896

from Cautionary Tales for Children
Jim
Who ran away from his Nurse, and was eaten by a Lion

There was a boy whose name was Jim;
His friends were very good to him.
They gave him tea, and cakes, and jam,
And slices of delicious ham,
5   And chocolate with pink inside,
And little tricycles to ride,
And read him stories through and through,
And even took him to the Zoo—
But there it was the dreadful fate
10   Befell him, which I now relate.

You know—at least you *ought* to know,
For I have often told you so—
That children never are allowed
To leave their nurses in a crowd;
15   Now this was Jim's especial foible,
He ran away when he was able,
And on this inauspicious day
He slipped his hand and ran away!
He hadn't gone a yard when—Bang!
20   With open jaws, a lion sprang,
And hungrily began to eat
The boy: beginning at his feet.

Now, just imagine how it feels
When first your toes and then your heels,
25   And then by gradual degrees,
Your shins and ankles, calves and knees,
Are slowly eaten, bit by bit,
No wonder Jim detested it!

No wonder that he shouted "Hi!"
30   The honest keeper heard his cry,
     Though very fat he almost ran
     To help the little gentleman.
     "Ponto!" he ordered as he came
     (For Ponto was the lion's name),
35   "Ponto!" he cried, with angry frown.
     "Let go, Sir! Down, Sir! Put it down!"

     The lion made a sudden stop,
     He let the dainty morsel drop,
     And slunk reluctant to his cage,
40   Snarling with disappointed rage.
     But when he bent him over Jim,
     The honest keeper's eyes were dim.
     The lion having reached his head,
     The miserable boy was dead!

45   When Nurse informed his parents, they
     Were more concerned than I can say:—
     His Mother, as she dried her eyes,
     Said, "Well—it gives me no surprise,
     He would not do as he was told!"
50   His Father, who was self-controlled,
     Bade all the children round attend
     To James's miserable end,
     And always keep a-hold of Nurse
     For fear of finding something worse.

                                              1907

Beatrix Potter
1866–1943

Anticipating Kenneth Grahame's *The Wind in the Willows* (1908) and A. A. Milne's *Winnie-the-Pooh* (1926), Beatrix Potter's books take place in a magical pastoral landscape inhabited by talking animals who lead remarkably domestic middle-class English lives. *The Tale of Peter Rabbit* began as a letter to comfort a sick child; but its popularity encouraged Potter to write many more little books for children, twenty-three in all, populated by a gallery of rabbits and squirrels and mice, illustrated with her own exquisite watercolors and told with an elegant economy of style. Although it may initially seem to be a moral fable—the naughty Peter disobeys his mother and goes to bed without supper—there is more than a hint of subversiveness in this tale. To the mischievous hero, "Don't go into Mr McGregor's garden" sounds like an implicit invitation rather than a warning. Peter ventures into a forbidden paradise, braves an assortment of dangers, and returns safely home to domestic warmth and maternal comfort. This archetypal story of transgression and redemption is told with humorous understatement; a comic providence watches over Peter, who pays for his temporary escape with scarcely a moment's repentance.

The Tale of Peter Rabbit

Once upon a time there were four little Rabbits, and their names were—Flopsy, Mopsy, Cotton-tail, and Peter.

They lived with their Mother in a sand-bank, underneath the root of a very big fir-tree.

"Now, my dears," said old Mrs Rabbit one morning, "you may go into the fields or down the lane, but don't go into Mr McGregor's garden: your Father had an accident there; he was put in a pie by Mrs McGregor."

"Now run along, and don't get into mischief. I am going out."

Then old Mrs Rabbit took a basket and her umbrella, and went through the wood to the baker's. She bought a loaf of brown bread and five currant buns.

Flopsy, Mopsy, and Cotton-tail, who were good little bunnies, went down the lane to gather blackberries: but Peter, who was very naughty, ran straight away to Mr McGregor's garden, and squeezed under the gate!

First he ate some lettuces and some French beans; and then he ate some radishes; and then, feeling rather sick, he went to look for some parsley.

But round the end of a cucumber frame, whom should he meet but Mr McGregor!

Mr McGregor was on his hands and knees planting out young cabbages, but he jumped up and ran after Peter, waving a rake and calling out, "Stop thief!"

Peter was most dreadfully frightened; he rushed all over the garden, for he had forgotten the way back to the gate.

He lost one of his shoes among the cabbages, and the other shoe amongst the potatoes.

After losing them, he ran on four legs and went faster, so that I think he might have got away altogether if he had not unfortunately run into a gooseberry net, and got caught by the large buttons on his jacket. It was a blue jacket with brass buttons, quite new.

Peter gave himself up for lost, and shed big tears; but his sobs were overheard by some friendly sparrows, who flew to him in great excitement, and implored him to exert himself.

Mr McGregor came up with a sieve, which he intended to pop upon the top of Peter; but Peter wriggled out just in time, leaving his jacket behind him. And rushed into the toolshed, and jumped into a can. It would have been a beautiful thing to hide in, if it had not had so much water in it.

Mr McGregor was quite sure that Peter was somewhere in the tool-shed, perhaps hidden underneath a flower-pot. He began to turn them over carefully, looking under each.

Presently Peter sneezed—"Kertyschoo!" Mr McGregor was after him in no time.

And tried to put his foot upon Peter, who jumped out of a window, upsetting three plants. The window was too small for Mr McGregor, and he was tired of running after Peter. He went back to his work.

Peter sat down to rest; he was out of breath and trembling with fright, and he had not the least idea which way to go. Also he was very damp with sitting in that can.

After a time he began to wander about, going lippity—lippity—not very fast, and looking all round.

He found a door in a wall; but it was locked, and there was no room for a fat little rabbit to squeeze underneath.

An old mouse was running in and out over the stone doorstep, carrying peas and beans to her family in the wood. Peter asked her the way to the gate, but she had such a large pea in her mouth that she could not answer. She only shook her head at him. Peter began to cry.

Then he tried to find his way straight across the garden, but he became more and more puzzled. Presently, he came to a pond where Mr McGregor filled his water-cans. A white cat was staring at some gold-fish, she sat very, very still, but now and then the tip of her tail twitched as if it were alive. Peter thought it best to go away without speaking to her; he had heard about cats from his cousin, little Benjamin Bunny.

He went back towards the tool-shed, but suddenly, quite close to him, he heard the noise of a hoe—scr-r-ritch, scratch, scratch, scritch. Peter scuttered underneath the bushes. But presently, as nothing happened, he came out, and climbed upon a wheelbarrow and peeped over. The first thing he saw was Mr McGregor hoeing onions. His back was turned towards Peter, and beyond him was the gate!

Peter got down very quietly off the wheelbarrow, and started running as fast as he could go, along a straight walk behind some black-currant bushes.

Mr McGregor caught sight of him at the corner, but Peter did not care. He slipped underneath the gate, and was safe at last in the wood outside the garden.

Mr McGregor hung up the little jacket and the shoes for a scare-crow to frighten the blackbirds.

Peter never stopped running or looked behind him till he got home to the big fir-tree.

He was so tired that he flopped down upon the nice soft sand on the floor of the rabbit-hole and shut his eyes. His mother was busy cooking; she wondered what he had done with his clothes. It was the second little jacket and pair of shoes that Peter had lost in a fortnight!

I am sorry to say that Peter was not very well during the evening.

His mother put him to bed, and made some camomile tea; and she gave a dose of it to Peter!

"One table-spoonful to be taken at bed-time."

But Flopsy, Mopsy, and Cotton-tail had bread and milk and blackberries for supper.

THE END

1893   1902

—•—⊨◈⊨—•—

Daisy Ashford
1881–1972

The Young Visiters has been called "the greatest novel ever written by a nine-year-old." Margaret Mary ("Daisy") Ashford wrote the book in 1890, but it was not published for nearly thirty years, when the manuscript was rediscovered. Thanks in part to a preface by J. M. Barrie (the author of *Peter Pan*), it became an instant best-seller in 1919. By then in her late thirties, Ashford was able to marry on the proceeds; she lived a modest uneventful life until her death at ninety. She had written nothing since the age of thirteen, when she renounced her earlier ambition to become "an authoress." No one could quite believe that *The Young Visiters* had been produced by a child of nine: Winston Churchill, for one, was convinced that Barrie had written it himself, and a journalist is said to have chased the publisher down a London street shouting, "Did he or did she?" The novel is a comic masterpiece, an unintentionally hilarious portrait of late Victorian high life as seen from the nursery. The peregrinations of Mr. Salteena and Ethel are recounted with a mixture of exuberance, innocence, and misspelling. Ashford's readings of adult social codes are remarkably astute; she intuitively grasps the relationships between class and money, sex and social ambition.

from The Young Visiters; or, Mr Salteena's Plan
Quite a Young Girl

Mr Salteena was an elderly man of 42 and was fond of asking peaple to stay with him. He had quite a young girl staying with him of 17 named Ethel Monticue. Mr Salteena had dark short hair and mustache and wiskers which were very black and twisty. He was middle sized and he had very pale blue eyes. He had a pale brown suit but on Sundays he had a black one and he had a topper[1] every day as he thorght it more becoming. Ethel Monticue had fair hair done on the top and blue eyes. She had a blue velvit frock which had grown rarther short in the sleeves. She had a black straw hat and kid gloves.

One morning Mr Salteena came down to brekfast and found Ethel had come down first which was strange. Is the tea made Ethel he said rubbing his hands. Yes said Ethel and such a quear shaped parcel has come for you Yes indeed it was a quear shape parcel it was a hat box tied down very tight and a letter stuffed between the string. Well well said Mr Salteena parcels do turn quear I will read the letter first and so saying he tore open the letter and this is what it said

MY DEAR ALFRED.

I want you to come for a stop with me so I have sent you a top hat wraped up in tishu paper inside the box. Will you wear it staying with me because it is very uncommon. Please bring one of your young ladies whichever is the prettiest in the face.

I remain Yours truely
BERNARD CLARK

Well said Mr Salteena I shall take you to stay Ethel and fancy him sending me a top hat. Then Mr S. opened the box and there lay the most splendid top hat of a lovly rich tone rarther like grapes with a ribbon round compleat.

Well said Mr Salteena peevishly I dont know if I shall like it the bow of the ribbon is too flighty for my age. Then he sat down and eat the egg which Ethel had so kindly laid for him. After he had finished his meal he got down and began to write to Bernard Clark he ran up stairs on his fat legs and took out his blotter with a loud sniff and this is what he wrote

MY DEAR BERNARD

Certinly I shall come and stay with you next Monday I will bring Ethel Monticue commonly called Miss M. She is very active and pretty. I do hope I shall enjoy myself with you. I am fond of digging in the garden and I am parshial to ladies if they are nice I suppose it is my nature. I am not quite a gentleman but you would hardly notice it but cant be helped anyhow. We will come by the 3–15.

Your old and valud friend
ALFRED SALTEENA

1. Top hat.

Perhaps my readers will be wondering why Bernard Clark had asked Mr Salteena to stay with him. He was a lonely man in a remote spot and he liked peaple and partys but he did not know many. What rot muttered Bernard Clark as he read Mr Salteenas letter. He was rarther a presumshious man.

from *Starting Gaily*

When the great morning came Mr Salteena did not have an egg for his brekfast in case he should be sick on the jorney.

What top hat will you wear asked Ethel.

I shall wear my best black and my white alpacka coat to keep off the dust and flies replied Mr Salteena.

I shall put some red ruge on my face said Ethel because I am very pale owing to the drains in this house.

You will look very silly said Mr Salteena with a dry laugh.

Well so will you said Ethel in a snappy tone and she ran out of the room with a very superier run throwing out her legs behind and her arms swinging in rithum.

Well said the owner of the house she has a most idiotick run.

Presently Ethel came back in her best hat and a lovly velvit coat of royal blue. Do I look nice in my get up she asked.

Mr Salteena survayed her. You look rarther rash my dear your colors dont quite match your face but never mind I am just going up to say goodbye to Rosalind the housemaid.

Well dont be long said Ethel. Mr S. skipped upstairs to Rosalinds room. Goodbye Rosalind he said I shall be back soon and I hope I shall enjoy myself.

I make no doubt of that sir said Rosalind with a blush as Mr Salteena silently put 2/6 on the dirty toilet cover.

Take care of your bronkitis said Mr S. rarther bashfully and he hastilly left the room waving his hand carelessly to the housemaid.

Come along cried Ethel powdering her nose in the hall let us get into the cab. Mr Salteena did not care for powder but he was an unselfish man so he dashed into the cab. Sit down said Ethel as the cabman waved his whip you are standing on my luggage. Well I am paying for the cab said Mr S. so I might be allowed to put my feet were I like.

They traveled 2nd class in the train and Ethel was longing to go first but thought perhaps least said soonest mended. Mr Salteena got very excited in the train about his visit. Ethel was calm but she felt excited inside. Bernard has a big house said Mr S. gazing at Ethel he is inclined to be rich.

Oh indeed said Ethel looking at some cows flashing past the window. Mr S. felt rarther disheartened so he read the paper till the train stopped and the porters shouted Rickamere station. We had better collect our traps said Mr Salteena and just then a very exalted footman in a cocked hat and olive green uniform put his head in at the window. Are you for Rickamere Hall he said in impressive tones.

Well yes I am said Mr Salteena and so is this lady.

Very good sir said the noble footman if you will alight I will see to your luggage there is a convayance awaiting you.

Oh thankyou thankyou said Mr S. and he and Ethel stepped along the platform. Outside they found a lovely cariage lined with olive green cushons to match the footman and the horses had green bridles and bows on their manes and tails. They got gingerly in. Will he bring our luggage asked Ethel nervously.

I expect so said Mr Salteena lighting a very long cigar.

Do we tip him asked Ethel quietly.

Well no I dont think so not yet we had better just thank him perlitely.

Just then the footman staggered out with the bagage. Ethel bowed gracefully over the door of the cariage and Mr S. waved his hand as each bit of luggage was hoisted up to make sure it was all there. Then he said thankyou my good fellow very politely. Not at all sir said the footman and touching his cocked hat he jumped actively to the box.

I was right not to tip him whispered Mr Salteena the thing to do is to leave 2/6 on your dressing table when your stay is over.

Does he find it asked Ethel who did not really know at all how to go on at a visit. I beleeve so replied Mr Salteena anyhow it is quite the custom and we cant help it if he does not. Now my dear what do you think of the sceenery

Very nice said Ethel gazing at the rich fur rug on her knees. Just then the cariage rolled into a beautifull drive with tall trees and big red flowers growing amid shiny dark leaves. Presently the haughty coachman pulled up with a great clatter at a huge front door with tall pillers each side a big iron bell and two very clean scrapers. The doors flung open as if by majic causing Ethel to jump and a portly butler appeared on the scene with a very shiny shirt front and a huge pale face. Welcome sir he exclaimed good naturedly as Mr Salteena alighted rarther quickly from the viacle and please to step inside.

Mr Salteena stepped in as bid followed by Ethel. The footman again struggled with the luggage and the butler Francis Minnit by name kindly lent a hand. The hall was very big and hung round with guns and mats and ancesters giving it a gloomy but a grand air. The butler then showed them down a winding corridoor till he came to a door which he flung open shouting Mr Salteena and a lady sir.

A tall man of 29 rose from the sofa. He was rarther bent in the middle with very nice long legs fairish hair and blue eyes. Hullo Alf old boy he cried so you have got here all safe and no limbs broken.

None thankyou Bernard replied Mr Salteena shaking hands and let me introduce Miss Monticue she is very pleased to come for this visit. Oh yes gasped Ethel blushing through her red ruge. Bernard looked at her keenly and turned a dark red. I am glad to see you he said I hope you will enjoy it but I have not arranged any partys yet as I dont know anybody.

Dont worry murmered Ethel I dont mix much in Societly and she gave him a dainty smile.

* * *

I have given the best spare room to Miss Monticue said Bernard with a gallant bow and yours turning to Mr Salteena opens out of it so you will be nice and friendly both the rooms have big windows and a handsome view.

How charming said Ethel. Yes well let us go up replied Bernard and he led the way up many a winding stairway till they came to an oak door with some lovly swans and bull rushes painted on it. Here we are he cried gaily. Ethels room was indeed a handsome compartment with purple silk curtains and a 4 post bed draped with the same shade. The toilit set was white and mouve and there were some violets in a costly varse. Oh I say cried Ethel in supprise. I am glad you like it said Bernard and here we have yours Alf. He opened the dividing doors and portrayed a smaller but dainty room all in pale yellow and wild primroses. My own room is next the bath room said Bernard it is decerated dark red as I have somber tastes. The bath room has got a tip up bason and a hose thing for washing your head.

A good notion said Mr Salteena who was secretly getting jellus.

Here we will leave our friends to unpack and end this Chapter.

from *Mr Salteenas Plan*

Mr Salteena woke up rarther early next day and was supprised and delighted to find Horace the footman entering with a cup of tea.

Oh thankyou my man said Mr Salteena rolling over in the costly bed. Mr Clark is nearly out of the bath sir anounced Horace I will have great plesure in turning it on for you if such is your desire. Well yes you might said Mr Salteena seeing it was the idear and Horace gave a profound bow.

Ethel are you getting up shouted Mr Salteena.

Very nearly replied Ethel faintly from the next room.

I say said Mr Salteena excitedly I have had some tea in bed.

So have I replied Ethel.

Then Mr Salteena got into a mouve dressing goun with yellow tassles and siezing his soap he wandered off to the bath room which was most sumpshous. It had a lovly white shiny bath and sparkling taps and several towels arrayed in readiness by thourghtful Horace. It also had a step for climbing up the bath and other good dodges of a rich nature. Mr Salteena washed himself well and felt very much better. After brekfast Mr Salteena asked Bernard if he could have some privite conversation with him. Well yes replied Bernard if you will come into my study we can have a few words.

Cant I come too muttered Ethel sulkily.

No my dear said Mr Salteena this is privite.

Perhaps later I might have a privite chat with you Miss Monticue said Bernard kindly.

Oh do lets said Ethel.

Then Bernard and Mr S. strolled to the study and sat upon two arm chairs. Fire away said Bernard lighting his pipe. Well I cant exactly do that said Mr Salteena in slow tones it is a searious matter and you can advise me as you are a thorugh gentleman I am sure.

Well yes said Bernard what can I do for you eh Alf?

You can help me perhaps to be more like a gentleman said Mr Salteena getting rarther hot I am quite alright as they say but I would like to be the real thing can it be done he added slapping his knees.

I dont quite know said Bernard it might take a good time.

Might it said Mr S. but I would slave for years if need be. Bernard scratched his head. Why dont you try the Crystal Pallace he asked several peaple Earls and even dukes have privite compartments there.[2]

But I am not an Earl said Mr Salteena in a purplexed tone.

True replied Bernard but I understand there are sort of students there who want to get into the War Office and notable banks.

Would that be a help asked Mr Salteena egerly.

Well it might said Bernard I can give you a letter to my old pal the Earl of Clincham who lives there he might rub you up and by mixing with him you would probably grow more seemly.

Oh ten thousand thanks said Mr Salteena I will go there as soon as it can be arranged if you would be so kind as to keep an eye on Ethel while I am away.

Oh yes said Bernard I may be running up to town for a few days and she could come too.

2. The Crystal Palace was a huge glass and iron structure in London designed to house the Great Exhibition of 1851 (see photo, page 1108); it was not a palace where aristocrats had apartments.

You are too kind said Mr Salteena and I dont think you will find her any trouble.

No I dont think I shall said Bernard she is a pretty girl cheerful and active. And he blushed rarther red.

[MR SALTEENA GOES TO THE CRYSTAL PALACE IN LONDON TO MEET THE EARL OF CLINCHAM]

The Earl gave a slight cough and gazed at Mr Salteena thourghtfully.

Have you much money he asked and are you prepared to spend a good deal.

Oh yes quite gasped Mr Salteena I have plenty in the bank and £10 in ready gold in my purse.

You see these compartments are the haunts of the Aristockracy said the earl and they are kept going by peaple who have got something funny in their family and who want to be less mere if you can comprehend.

Indeed I can said Mr Salteena.

Personally I am a bit parshial to mere people said his Lordship but the point is that we charge a goodly sum for our training here but however if you cant pay you need not join.

I can and will proclaimed Mr Salteena and he placed a £10 note on the desk. His Lordship slipped it in his trouser pocket. It will be £42 before I have done with you he said but you can pay me here and there as convenient.

Oh thankyou cried Mr Salteena.

Not at all said the Earl and now to bissness. While here you will live in compartments in the basement known as Lower Range. You will get many hints from the Groom of the Chambers as to clothes and ettiquett to menials. You will mix with me for grammer and I might take you out hunting or shooting sometimes to give you a few tips. Also I have lots of ladies partys which you will attend occasionally.

Mr Salteenas eyes flashed with excitement. I shall enjoy that he cried.

from *A Gay Call*
[ETHEL GOES TO LONDON WITH BERNARD CLARK, THEN CALLS ON THE EARL]

What pleasant compartments you have cried Ethel in rarther a socierty tone.

Fairly so so responded the Earl do you live in London he added in a loud tone as someone was playing a very difficult peice on the piano.

Well no I dont said Ethel my home is really in Northumberland but I am at present stopping with Mr Clark at the Gaierty Hotel she continued in a somewhat showing off tone.

Oh I see said the earl well shall I introduce you to a few of my friends.

Oh please do said Ethel with a dainty blow at her nose.

The earl disserppeard into the madding crowd and presently came back with a middle aged gentleman. This is Lord Hyssops he said my friend Miss Monticue he added genially.

Ethel turned a dull yellaw. Lord Hyssops she said in a faint voice why it is Mr Salteena I know him well.

Hush cried the Earl it is a title bestowd recently by my friend the Prince of Wales. Yes indeed murmered Mr Salteena deeply flabber-gasted by the ready wit of the earl.

Oh indeed said Ethel in a peevish tone well how do you come to be here.

I am stopping with his Lordship said Mr Salteena and have a set of compartments in the basement so there.

I dont care said huffy Ethel I am in handsome rooms at the Gaierty.

Nothing could be nicer I am sure struck in the earl what do you say Hyssops eh.

Doubtless it is charming said Mr Salteena who was wanting peace tell me Ethel how did you leave Bernard.

I have not left him said Ethel in an annoying voice I am stopping with him at the gaierty and we have been to lots of theaters and dances.

Well I am glad you are enjoying yourself said Mr Salteena kindly you had been looking pale of late.

No wonder in your stuffy domain cried Ethel well have you got any more friends she added turning to the earl.

Well I will see said the obliging earl and he once more disapeared.

I dont know why you should turn against me Ethel said Mr Salteena in a low tone.

Ethel patted her hair and looked very sneery. Well I call it very mystearious you going off and getting a title said Ethel and I think our friendship had better stop as no doubt you will soon be marrying a duchess or something.

Not at all said Mr Salteena you must know Ethel he said blushing a deep red I always wished to marry you some fine day.

This is news to me cried Ethel still peevish.

But not to me murmered Mr Salteena and his voice trembled in his chest. I may add that I have always loved you and now I seem to do so madly he added passionately.

But I dont love you responded Ethel.

But if you married me you might get to said Mr Salteena.

I think not replied Ethel and all the same it is very kind of you to ask me and she smiled more nicely at him.

This is agony cried Mr Salteena clutching hold of a table my life will be sour grapes and ashes without you.

Be a man said Ethel in a gentle whisper and I shall always think of you in a warm manner.

from *A Proposale*

Let us now bask under the spreading trees said Bernard in a passiunate tone.

Oh yes lets said Ethel and she opened her dainty parasole and sank down upon the long green grass. She closed her eyes but she was far from asleep. Bernard sat beside her in profound silence gazing at her pink face and long wavy eye lashes. He puffed at his pipe for some moments while the larks gaily caroled in the blue sky. Then he edged a trifle closer to Ethels form.

Ethel he murmured in a trembly voice.

Oh what is it said Ethel hastily sitting up.

Words fail me ejaculated Bernard horsly my passion for you is intense he added fervently. It has grown day and night since I first beheld you.

Oh said Ethel in susprise I am not prepared for this and she lent back against the trunk of the tree.

Bernard placed one arm tightly round her. When will you marry me Ethel he uttered you must be my wife it has come to that I love you so intensely that if you say no I shall perforce dash my body to the brink of yon muddy river he panted wildly.

Oh dont do that implored Ethel breathing rarther hard.

Then say you love me he cried.

Oh Bernard she sighed fervently I certinly love you madly you are to me like a Heathen god she cried looking at his manly form and handsome flashing face I will indeed marry you.

How soon gasped Bernard gazing at her intensly.

As soon as possible said Ethel gently closing her eyes.

My Darling whispered Bernard and he seiezed her in his arms we will be marrid next week.

Oh Bernard muttered Ethel this is so sudden.

No no cried Bernard and taking the bull by both horns he kissed her violently on her dainty face. My bride to be he murmered several times.

Ethel trembled with joy as she heard the mistick words.

Oh Bernard she said little did I ever dream of such as this and she suddenly fainted into his out stretched arms.

Oh I say gasped Bernard and laying the dainty burden on the grass he dashed to the waters edge and got a cup full of the fragrant river to pour on his true loves pallid brow.

She soon came to and looked up with a sickly smile Take me back to the Gaierty hotel she whispered faintly.

With plesure my darling said Bernard I will just pack up our viands ere I unloose the boat.

Ethel felt better after a few drops of champagne and began to tidy her hair while Bernard packed the remains of the food. Then arm in arm they tottered to the boat.

I trust you have not got an illness my darling murmured Bernard as he helped her in.

Oh no I am very strong said Ethel I fainted from joy she added to explain matters.

Oh I see said Bernard handing her a cushon well some people do he added kindly and so saying they rowed down the dark stream now flowing silently beneath a golden moon. All was silent as the lovers glided home with joy in their hearts and radiance on their faces only the sound of the mystearious water lapping against the frail vessel broke the monotony of the night.

So I will end my chapter.

How It Ended

Mr Salteena by the aid of the earl and the kindness of the Prince of Wales managed to get the job his soul craved and any day might be seen in Hyde park or Pickadilly galloping madly after the Royal Carrage in a smart suit of green velvit with knicker-bockers compleat. At first he was rarther terrified as he was not used to riding and he found his horse bumped him a good deal and he had to cling on desperatly to its flowing main. At other times the horse would stop dead and Mr Salteena would use his spurs and bad languige with no avail. But he soon got more used to his fresh and sultry steed and His Royal Highness seemed satisfide.

The Earl continued his merry life at the Compartments till finally he fell in love with one of the noble ladies who haunted them. She was not so pretty as Ethel as she had rarther a bulgy figure and brown eyes but she had lovely raven tresses a pointed nose and a rose like complexion of a dainty hue. She had very nice feet and plenty of money. Her name was called Lady Helena Herring and her age was 25 and she mated well with the earl.

Mr Salteena grew very lonely after the earl was marrid and he could not bear a single life any more so failing Ethel he marrid one of the maids in waiting at Buckingham palace by name Bessie Topp a plesant girl of 18 with a round red face and rarther stary eyes.

So now that all our friends are marrid I will add a few words about their familys. Ethel and Bernard returned from their Honymoon with a son and hair a nice fat baby called Ignatius Bernard. They soon had six more children four boys and three girls and some of them were twins which was very exciting.

The Earl only got two rarther sickly girls called Helen and Marie because the last one looked slightly french.

Mr Salteena had a large family of 10 five of each but he grew very morose as the years rolled by and his little cottage was very noisy and his wife was a bit annoying at times especially when he took to dreaming of Ethel and wishing he could have marrid her. Still he was a pius man in his way and found relief in prayer.

Bernard Clark was the happiest of our friends as he loved Ethel to the bitter end and so did she him and they had a nice house too.

The Earl soon got tired of his sickly daughters and his wife had a savage temper so he thourght he would divorce her and try again but he gave up the idear after several attempts and decided to offer it up as a Mortification.[3]

So now my readers we will say farewell to the characters in this book.

1890   1919

⇢⊷ END OF PERSPECTIVES: IMAGINING CHILDHOOD ⊷⇠

⊶⊱⊷

Rudyard Kipling
1865–1936

"The infant monster," Henry James called him. In his early twenties the "shockingly precocious" Rudyard Kipling was already a literary celebrity, acclaimed for his vivid stories of life in India. Like Dickens, to whom he was inevitably compared, Kipling was both popular and prolific. In addition to hundreds of short stories, he wrote poetry, essays, and children's books, including the *Jungle Books* (1894, 1895) and *Just So Stories* (1902). He also wrote several novels, of which the best-known are *The Light That Failed* (1890), *Captains Courageous* (1896–1897), and *Kim* (1901). In 1907 he became the first English writer to win the Nobel Prize for literature.

Rudyard Kipling was born in Bombay, and his idyllic early years gave him a lifelong attachment to India. He and his younger sister were cared for by indulgent servants with whom they spoke Hindustani; English was almost a second language, "haltingly translated out of the vernacular idiom that one thought and dreamed in." But when he was five years old Kipling's parents sent the children "home" to England, where they were badly treated by the English family who were paid to look after them. They did not see their parents for five years. After this period of bitter unhappiness, boarding school came as a relief; Kipling later recorded his experiences of schoolboy life in the stories of *Stalky & Co.* (1899).

---

3. As a penance (for one's sins).

In 1882, not yet seventeen, Kipling returned to India to work as a journalist. Once again the people and landscape got under his skin: "I would wander till dawn in all manner of odd places—liquor-shops, gambling- and opium-dens . . . wayside entertainments such as puppet-shows, native dances; or in and about the narrow gullies under the Mosque of Wazir Khan for the sheer sake of looking." After seven years in India, he returned to England with a growing literary reputation, for his first collection of stories, *Plain Tales from the Hills* (1888), had caught the public's imagination. His exotic settings and vigorous prose struck readers as fresh and original—particularly in contrast to the writing of his jaded *fin-de-siècle* contemporaries. Somerset Maugham described the magic of Kipling's Indian stories: "They give you the tang of the East, the smell of the bazaars, the torpor of the rains, the heat of the sun-scorched earth, the rough life of the barracks."

Kipling married an American and lived in Vermont for several years, but eventually the couple settled in Sussex. Kipling wrote: "I am slowly discovering England which is the most wonderful foreign land I have ever been in." Although he was always something of an outsider in England, his love for the English countryside is reflected in much of his later writing, including the haunting story, *They*, and the children's book *Puck of Pook's Hill* (1906).

Many critics consider Kipling the greatest short story writer in English. Describing his own economy of style, Kipling wrote that tightening up his stories had taught him "that a tale from which pieces have been raked out is like a fire that has been poked." His intense and enigmatic stories reveal a meticulous attention to detail. In addition, Kipling captured the cadences of everyday speech in many dialects and accents—Indian, Cockney, Yorkshire, Irish, Sussex—and he was adept with an astonishing range of narrative voices. He particularly excelled at reproducing the slang and shoptalk of the rough-and-ready men doing the work of empire: soldiers, sailors, engineers. Kipling's genius for capturing the "language of common men,"—to use Wordsworth's phrase from his preface to *Lyrical Ballads* (1800)—is even more pronounced in his poetry than in his prose. *Barrack-Room Ballads* (1892), for instance, pursues the Wordsworthian fascination with the imaginative side of ordinary life, but life as it is lived at the ends of a far-flung Empire, to the tempo of a military band. His first book of poems, *Departmental Ditties* (1886), revealed that he had learned his swinging rhythms and ballad meters from Swinburne and Scott, while he also admired the American dialect styles of Bret Harte, Mark Twain, and Joel Chandler Harris's Uncle Remus stories.

Fusing these varied influences with subject matter that was completely new to English verse, he deliberately rejected the introspective poetry of private life that the Aesthetes were making fashionable. Instead Kipling produced a public-oriented poetry that dealt with the wider world of Empire, using poetry as a vehicle to express the social and political views of his down-to-earth narrators. Though his exceptional skill with rhyme and meter has been widely praised, people often quote Kipling without realizing it, when they use such phrases as "a good cigar is a Smoke," "the female of the species," "but that is another story," or "the White Man's burden."

At times Kipling has been better known for his political views than for his literary works. But attention to the more reactionary moments of his later life (his opposition to Home Rule in India, for instance) has obscured the complexity of his attitudes. His opinions of imperialism, the colonies, and people of other cultures can be extremely hard to pin down. Like Robert Browning or Joseph Conrad, he adopts a range of narrative devices and speaking voices, presenting himself in a variety of roles, from the common British soldier to the Islamic sage. Though he is often accused of supporting British imperialism, Kipling persistently probes the human toll that empire building takes on those who bear the brunt of it: British soldiers and administrators on the one hand and native soldiers and servants on the other.

A reading of Kipling's work on its own terms reveals a complicated art in which human qualities such as love, fidelity, and devotion to duty can bridge national and racial boundaries. What comes through strongly in Kipling's writing is his respect for hard work and his admiration for courage in the face of death. He satirizes and condemns vanity and bullying among all peoples. Above all else, perhaps, he is fascinated with both subtle and crude manifestations of English power: its uses, abuses, and—especially—its painful responsibilities. Kipling's sympathy for both colonized and colonizer, as well as his evident pleasure in the myriad inflections and accents of speech, makes his work, as the critic Craig Raine has said, "the expression of a profoundly democratic artistry."

See also Perspectives: Travel and Empire on page 1888.

Without Benefit of Clergy[1]

"But if it be a girl?"

"Lord of my life, it cannot be. I have prayed for so many nights, and sent gifts to Sheikh Badl's shrine so often, that I know God will give us a son—a man-child that shall grow into a man. Think of this and be glad. My mother shall be his mother till I can take him again, and the mullah[2] of the Pattan mosque shall cast his nativity—God send he be born in an auspicious hour!—and then, and then thou wilt never weary of me, thy slave."

"Since when hast thou been a slave, my queen?"

"Since the beginning—till this mercy[3] came to me. How could I be sure of thy love when I knew that I had been bought with silver?"

"Nay, that was the dowry. I paid it to thy mother."

"And she has buried it, and sits upon it all day long like a hen. What talk is yours of dower! I was bought as though I had been a Lucknow dancing-girl[4] instead of a child."

"Art thou sorry for the sale?"

"I have sorrowed; but to-day I am glad. Thou wilt never cease to love me now?—answer, my king."

"Never—never. No."

"Not even though the mem-log—the white women of thy own blood—love thee? And remember, I have watched them driving in the evening; they are very fair."

"I have seen fire-balloons[5] by the hundred. I have seen the moon, and—then I saw no more fire-balloons."

Ameera clapped her hands and laughed. "Very good talk," she said. Then with an assumption of great stateliness: "It is enough. Thou hast my permission to depart,—if thou wilt."

The man did not move. He was sitting on a low red-lacquered couch in a room furnished only with a blue and white floor-cloth, some rugs, and a very complete collection of native cushions. At his feet sat a woman of sixteen, and she was all but all the world in his eyes. By every rule and law she should have been otherwise, for he was an Englishman, and she a Mussulman's daughter bought two years before from her mother, who, being left without money, would have sold Ameera shrieking to the Prince of Darkness if the price had been sufficient.

It was a contract entered into with a light heart; but even before the girl had reached her bloom she came to fill the greater portion of John Holden's life. For her,

---

1. First published in *Macmillan's Magazine* (1890). "Benefit of clergy" means the traditional right of clergymen to be tried by a church court; Kipling, however, means that the union of the two protagonists has not been blessed by the clergy—i.e., they are unmarried.

2. Muslim religious leader.
3. I.e., her pregnancy.
4. Dancing girls were considered prostitutes; Ameera's mother has sold her as if she were a prostitute.
5. Hot-air balloons.

and the withered hag her mother, he had taken a little house overlooking the great red-walled city, and found,—when the marigolds had sprung up by the well in the courtyard, and Ameera had established herself according to her own ideas of comfort, and her mother had ceased grumbling at the inadequacy of the cooking-places, the distance from the daily market, and at matters of house-keeping in general,— that the house was to him his home. Any one could enter his bachelor's bungalow by day or night, and the life that he led there was an unlovely one. In the house in the city his feet only could pass beyond the outer courtyard to the women's rooms; and when the big wooden gate was bolted behind him he was king in his own territory, with Ameera for queen. And there was going to be added to this kingdom a third person whose arrival Holden felt inclined to resent. It interfered with his perfect happiness. It disarranged the orderly peace of the house that was his own. But Ameera was wild with delight at the thought of it, and her mother not less so. The love of a man, and particularly a white man, was at the best an inconstant affair, but it might, both women argued, be held fast by a baby's hands. "And then," Ameera would always say, "then he will never care for the white *mem-log*. I hate them all—I hate them all."

"He will go back to his own people in time," said the mother; "but by the blessing of God that time is yet afar off."

Holden sat silent on the couch thinking of the future, and his thoughts were not pleasant. The drawbacks of a double life are manifold. The Government, with singular care, had ordered him out of the station for a fortnight on special duty in the place of a man who was watching by the bedside of a sick wife. The verbal notification of the transfer had been edged by a cheerful remark that Holden ought to think himself lucky in being a bachelor and a free man. He came to break the news to Ameera.

"It is not good," she said slowly, "but it is not all bad. There is my mother here, and no harm will come to me—unless indeed I die of pure joy. Go thou to thy work and think no troublesome thoughts. When the days are done I believe . . . nay, I am sure. And—and then I shall lay *him* in thy arms, and thou wilt love me for ever. The train goes tonight, at midnight is it not? Go now, and do not let thy heart be heavy by cause of me. But thou wilt not delay in returning? Thou wilt not stay on the road to talk to the bold white *mem-log*. Come back to me swiftly, my life."

As he left the courtyard to reach his horse that was tethered to the gatepost, Holden spoke to the white-haired old watchman who guarded the house, and bade him under certain contingencies despatch the filled-up telegraph-form that Holden gave him. It was all that could be done, and with the sensations of a man who has attended his own funeral Holden went away by the night-mail to his exile. Every hour of the day he dreaded the arrival of the telegram, and every hour of the night he pictured to himself the death of Ameera. In consequence his work for the State was not of first-rate quality, nor was his temper towards his colleagues of the most amiable. The fortnight ended without a sign from his home, and, torn to pieces by his anxieties, Holden returned to be swallowed up for two precious hours by a dinner at the club, wherein he heard, as a man hears in a swoon, voices telling him how execrably he had performed the other man's duties, and how he had endeared himself to all his associates. Then he fled on horseback through the night with his heart in his mouth. There was no answer at first to his blows on the gate, and he had just wheeled his horse round to kick it in when Pir Khan appeared with a lantern and held his stirrup.

"Has aught occurred?" said Holden.

"The news does not come from my mouth, Protector of the Poor, but—" He held out his shaking hand as befitted the bearer of good news who is entitled to a reward.

Holden hurried through the courtyard. A light burned in the upper room. His horse neighed in the gateway and he heard a shrill little wail that sent all the blood into the apple of his throat. It was a new voice, but it did not prove that Ameera was alive.

"Who is there?" he called up the narrow brick staircase.

There was a cry of delight from Ameera, and then the voice of the mother, tremulous with old age and pride—"We be two women and—the—man—thy—son."

On the threshold of the room Holden stepped on a naked dagger, that was laid there to avert ill-luck, and it broke at the hilt under his impatient heel.

"God is great!" cooed Ameera in the half-light. "Thou hast taken his misfortunes on thy head."

"Ay, but how is it with thee, life of my life? Old woman, how is it with her?"

"She has forgotten her sufferings for joy that the child is born. There is no harm; but speak softly," said the mother.

"It only needed thy presence to make me all well," said Ameera. "My king, thou hast been very long away. What gifts hast thou for me? Ah, ah! It is I that bring gifts this time. Look, my life, look. Was there ever such a babe? Nay, I am too weak even to clear my arm from him."

"Rest then, and do not talk. I am here, *bachari* (little woman)."

"Well said, for there is a bond and a heel-rope (*peecharee*) between us now that nothing can break. Look—canst thou see in this light? He is without spot or blemish. Never was such a man-child. *Ya illah!* [My God] he shall be a pundit[6]—no, a trooper of the Queen. And, my life, dost thou love me as well as ever, though I am faint and sick and worn? Answer truly."

"Yea. I love as I have loved, with all my soul. Lie still, pearl, and rest."

"Then do not go. Sit by my side here—so. Mother, the lord of this house needs a cushion. Bring it." There was an almost imperceptible movement on the part of the new life that lay in the hollow of Ameera's arm. "Aho!" she said, her voice breaking with love. "The babe is a champion from his birth. He is kicking me in the side with mighty kicks. Was there ever such a babe! And he is ours to us—thine and mine. Put thy hand on his head, but carefully, for he is very young, and men are unskilled in such matters."

Very cautiously Holden touched with the tips of his fingers the downy head.

"He is of the Faith," said Ameera; "for lying here in the night-watches I whispered the call to prayer and the profession of faith into his ears. And it is most marvellous that he was born upon a Friday,[7] as I was born. Be careful of him, my life; but he can almost grip with his hands."

Holden found one helpless little hand that closed feebly on his finger. And the clutch ran through his limbs till it settled about his heart. Till then his sole thought had been for Ameera. He began to realize that there was some one else in the world, but he could not feel that it was a veritable son with a soul. He sat down to think, and Ameera dozed lightly.

"Get hence, *sahib*,"[8] said her mother under her breath. "It is not good that she should find you here on waking. She must be still."

6. Teacher.
7. The Islamic holy day.

8. A deferential term meaning lord or master.

"I go," said Holden submissively. "Here be rupees. See that my *baba* gets fat and finds all that he needs."

The chink of the silver roused Ameera. "I am his mother, and no hireling," she said weakly. "Shall I look to him more or less for the sake of money? Mother, give it back. I have born my lord a son."

The deep sleep of weakness came upon her almost before the sentence was completed. Holden went down to the courtyard very softly with his heart at ease. Pir Khan, the old watchman, was chuckling with delight. "This house is now complete," he said, and without further comment thrust into Holden's hands the hilt of a sabre worn many years ago when he, Pir Khan, served the Queen in the police. The bleat of a tethered goat came from the well-kerb.

"There be two," said Pir Khan, "two goats of the best. I bought them, and they cost much money; and since there is no birth-party assembled their flesh will be all mine. Strike craftily, *sahib!* 'Tis an ill-balanced sabre at the best. Wait till they raise their heads from cropping the marigolds."

"And why?" said Holden, bewildered.

"For the birth-sacrifice. What else? Otnerwise the child being unguarded from fate may die. The Protector of the Poor knows the fitting words to be said."

Holden had learned them once with little thought that he would ever speak them in earnest. The touch of the cold sabre-hilt in his palm turned suddenly to the clinging grip of the child up stairs—the child that was his own son—and a dread of loss filled him.

"Strike!" said Pir Khan. "Never life came into the world but life was paid for it. See, the goats have raised their heads. Now! With a drawing cut!"

Hardly knowing what he did Holden cut twice as he muttered the Mohammedan prayer that runs:—"Almighty! In place of this my son I offer life for life, blood for blood, head for head, bone for bone, hair for hair, skin for skin." The waiting horse snorted and bounded in his pickets at the smell of the raw blood that spirted over Holden's riding-boots.

"Well smitten!" said Pir Khan wiping the sabre. "A swordsman was lost in thee. Go with a light heart, Heaven-born. I am thy servant, and the servant of thy son. May the Presence live a thousand years and. . . . the flesh of the goats is all mine?" Pir Khan drew back richer by a month's pay. Holden swung himself into the saddle and rode off through the low-hanging wood-smoke of the evening. He was full of riotous exultation, alternating with a vast vague tenderness directed towards no particular object, that made him choke as he bent over the neck of his uneasy horse. "I never felt like this in my life," he thought. "I'll go to the club and pull myself together."

A game of pool was beginning, and the room was full of men. Holden entered, eager to get to the light and the company of his fellows, singing at the top of his voice:

> In Baltimore a-walking, a lady I did meet!

"Did you?" said the club-secretary from his corner. "Did she happen to tell you that your boots were wringing wet? Great goodness, man, it's blood!"

"Bosh!" said Holden, picking his cue from the rack. "May I cut in? It's dew. I've been riding through high crops. My faith! my boots are in a mess though!

> And if it be a girl she shall wear a wedding ring,
> And if it be a boy he shall fight for his king,
> With his dirk, and his cap, and his little jacket blue,
> He shall walk the quarter-deck—"

"Yellow on blue—green next player," said the marker monotonously.

"He *shall walk the quarter-deck*,—am I green, marker? He *shall walk the quarter-deck*,—eh! that's a bad shot,—*as his daddy used to do!*"

"I don't see that you have anything to crow about," said a zealous junior civilian acidly. "The Government is not exactly pleased with your work when you relieved Sanders."

"Does that mean a wigging[9] from head-quarters?" said Holden with an abstracted smile. "I think I can stand it."

The talk beat up round the ever-fresh subject of each man's work, and steadied Holden till it was time to go to his dark empty bungalow, where his butler received him as one who knew all his affairs. Holden remained awake for the greater part of the night, and his dreams were pleasant ones.

2

"How old is he now?"

"*Ya illah!* What a man's question! He is all but six weeks old; and on this night I go up to the house-top with thee, my life, to count the stars. For that is auspicious. And he was born on a Friday under the sign of the sun, and it has been told to me that he will outlive us both and get wealth. Can we wish for aught better, beloved?"

"There is nothing better. Let us go up to the roof, and thou shalt count the stars—but a few only, for the sky is heavy with cloud."

"The winter rains are late, and maybe they come out of season. Come, before all the stars are hid. I have put on my richest jewels."

"Thou hast forgotten the best of all."

"Ai! Ours. He comes also. He has never yet seen the skies."

Ameera climbed the narrow staircase that led to the flat roof. The child, placid and unwinking, lay in the hollow of her right arm, gorgeous in silver-fringed muslin with a small skull-cap on his head. Ameera wore all that she valued most. The diamond nose-stud that takes the place of the Western patch[1] in drawing attention to the curve of the nostril, the gold ornament in the centre of the forehead studded with tallow-drop emeralds and flawed rubies, the heavy circlet of beaten gold that was fastened round her neck by the softness of the pure metal, and the chinking curb-patterned silver anklets hanging low over the rosy ankle-bone. She was dressed in jade-green muslin as befitted a daughter of the Faith, and from shoulder to elbow and elbow to wrist ran bracelets of silver tied with floss silk, frail glass bangles slipped over the wrist in proof of the slenderness of the hand, and certain heavy gold bracelets that had no part in her country's ornaments but, since they were Holden's gift and fastened with a cunning European snap, delighted her immensely.

They sat down by the low white parapet of the roof, overlooking the city and its lights.

"They are happy down there," said Ameera. "But I do not think that they are as happy as we. Nor do I think the white *mem-log* are as happy. And thou?"

"I know they are not."

"How dost thou know?"

"They give their children over to the nurses."

"I have never seen that," said Ameera with a sigh, "nor do I wish to see. *Ahi!*"— she dropped her head on Holden's shoulder,—"I have counted forty stars, and I am tired. Look at the child, love of my life, he is counting too."

The baby was staring with round eyes at the dark of the heavens. Ameera placed him in Holden's arms, and he lay there without a cry.

"What shall we call him among ourselves?" she said. "Look! Art thou ever tired of looking? He carries thy very eyes. But the mouth—"

"Is thine, most dear. Who should know better than I?"

"'Tis such a feeble mouth. Oh, so small! And yet it holds my heart between its lips. Give him to me now. He has been too long away."

"Nay, let him lie; he has not yet begun to cry."

"When he cries thou wilt give him back—eh! What a man of mankind thou art! If he cried he were only the dearer to me. But, my life, what little name shall we give him?"

The small body lay close to Holden's heart. It was utterly helpless and very soft. He scarcely dared to breathe for fear of crushing it. The caged green parrot that is regarded as a sort of guardian spirit in most native households moved on its perch and fluttered a drowsy wing.

"There is the answer," said Holden. "Mian Mittu has spoken. He shall be the parrot. When he is ready he will talk mightily and run about. Mian Mittu is the parrot in thy—in the Mussulman tongue, is it not?"

"Why put me so far off?" said Ameera fretfully. "Let it be like unto some English name—but not wholly. For he is mine."

"Then call him Tota, for that is likest English."

"Ay, Tota, and that is still the parrot. Forgive me, my lord, for a minute ago, but in truth he is too little to wear all the weight of Mian Mittu for name. He shall be Tota—our Tota to us. Hearest thou, oh, small one? Littlest, thou art Tota." She touched the child's cheek, and he waking wailed, and it was necessary to return him to his mother, who soothed him with the wonderful rhyme of *Aré koko, Ja ré koko!* which says:

> Oh, crow! Go crow! Baby's sleeping sound,
> And the wild plums grow in the jungle, only a penny a pound.
> Only a penny a pound, *baba*, only a penny a pound.

Reassured many times as to the price of those plums, Tota cuddled himself down to sleep. The two sleek, white well-bullocks in the courtyard were steadily chewing the cud of their evening meal; old Pir Khan squatted at the head of Holden's horse, his police sabre across his knees, pulling drowsily at a big water-pipe that croaked like a bull-frog in a pond. Ameera's mother sat spinning in the lower verandah, and the wooden gate was shut and barred. The music of a marriage procession came to the roof above the gentle hum of the city, and a string of flying-foxes crossed the face of the low moon.

"I have prayed," said Ameera after a long pause, "I have prayed for two things. First, that I may die in thy stead if thy death is demanded, and in the second that I may die in the place of the child. I have prayed to the Prophet and to Beebee Miriam [the Virgin Mary]. Thinkest thou either will hear?"

"From thy lips who would not hear the lightest word?"

"I asked for straight talk, and thou hast given me sweet talk. Will my prayers be heard?"

"How can I say? God is very good."

"Of that I am not sure. Listen now. When I die, or the child dies, what is thy fate? Living, thou wilt return to the bold white *mem-log*, for kind calls to kind."

"Not always."

"With a woman, no; with a man it is otherwise. Thou wilt in this life, later on, go back to thine own folk. That I could almost endure, for I should be dead. But in thy very death thou wilt be taken away to a strange place and a paradise that I do not know."

"Will it be paradise?"

"Surely, for who would harm thee? But we two—I and the child—shall be elsewhere, and we cannot come to thee, nor canst thou come to us. In the old days, before the child was born, I did not think of these things; but now I think of them always. It is very hard talk."

"It will fall as it will fall. Tomorrow we do not know, but to-day and love we know well. Surely we are happy now."

"So happy that it were well to make our happiness assured. And thy Beebee Miriam should listen to me; for she is also a woman. But then she would envy me! It is not seemly for men to worship a woman."

Holden laughed aloud at Ameera's little spasm of jealousy.

"Is it not seemly? Why didst thou not turn me from worship of thee, then?"

"Thou a worshipper! And of me! My king, for all thy sweet words, well I know that I am thy servant and thy slave, and the dust under thy feet. And I would not have it otherwise. See!"

Before Holden could prevent her she stooped forward and touched his feet; recovering herself with a little laugh she hugged Tota closer to her bosom. Then, almost savagely—

"Is it true that the bold white *mem-log* live for three times the length of my life? Is it true that they make their marriages not before they are old women?"

"They marry as do others—when they are women."

"That I know, but they wed when they are twenty-five. Is that true?"

"That is true."

"*Ya illah!* At twenty-five! Who would of his own will take a wife even of eighteen? She is a woman—ageing every hour. Twenty-five! I shall be an old woman at that age, and—Those *mem-log* remain young for ever. How I hate them!"

"What have they to do with us?"

"I cannot tell. I know only that there may now be alive on this earth a woman ten years older than I who may come to thee and take thy love ten years after I am an old woman, grey headed, and the nurse of Tota's son. That is unjust and evil. They should die too."

"Now, for all thy years thou art a child, and shalt be picked up and carried down the staircase."

"Tota! Have a care for Tota, my lord! Thou at least art as foolish as any babe!" Ameera tucked Tota out of harm's way in the hollow of her neck, and was carried down stairs laughing in Holden's arms, while Tota opened his eyes and smiled after the manner of the lesser angels.

He was a silent infant, and, almost before Holden could realize that he was in the world, developed into a small gold-coloured little god and unquestioned despot of the house overlooking the city. Those were months of absolute happiness to Holden and Ameera—happiness withdrawn from the world, shut in behind the wooden gate that Pir Khan guarded. By day Holden did his work with an immense pity for such as were not so fortunate as himself, and a sympathy for small children that amazed and amused many mothers at the little station-gatherings. At nightfall he returned to Ameera,—Ameera full of the wondrous doings of Tota, how he had been seen to clap his hands together and move his fingers with intention and purpose—which was manifestly a miracle—how later, he had of his own initiative crawled out of his low bedstead on to the floor and swayed on both feet for the space of three breaths.

"And they were long breaths, for my heart stood still with delight," said Ameera.

Then he took the beasts into his councils—the well-bullocks, the little grey squirrels, the mongoose that lived in a hole near the well, and especially Mian Mittu, the parrot, whose tail he grievously pulled, and Mian Mittu screamed till Ameera and Holden arrived.

"Oh, villain! Child of strength! This to thy brother on the house-top! *Tobah, tobah!* Fie! Fie! But I know a charm to make him wise as Suleiman and Aflatoun [Solomon and Plato]. Now look," said Ameera. She drew from an embroidered bag a handful of almonds. "See! we count seven. In the name of God!"

She placed Mian Mittu, very angry and rumpled, on the top of his cage, and seating herself between the babe and the bird she cracked and peeled an almond less white than her teeth. "This is a true charm, my life, and do not laugh. See! I give the parrot one half and Tota the other." Mian Mittu with careful beak took his share from between Ameera's lips, and she kissed the other half into the mouth of the child, who ate it slowly with wondering eyes. "This I will do each day of seven, and without doubt he who is ours will be a bold speaker and wise. Eh, Tota, what wilt thou be when thou art a man and I am grey-headed?" Tota tucked his fat legs into adorable creases. He could crawl, but he was not going to waste the spring of his youth in idle speech. He wanted Mian Mittu's tail to tweak.

When he was advanced to the dignity of a silver belt—which, with a magic-square engraved on silver and hung round his neck, made up the greater part of his clothing—he staggered on a perilous journey down the garden to Pir Khan and proffered him all his jewels in exchange for one little ride on Holden's horse, having seen his mother's mother chaffering with pedlars in the verandah. Pir Khan wept and set the untried feet on his own grey head in sign of fealty, and brought the bold adventurer to his mother's arms, vowing that Tota would be a leader of men ere his beard was grown.

One hot evening while he sat on the roof between his father and mother watching the never-ending warfare of the kites, that the city boys flew, he demanded a kite of his own with Pir Khan to fly it, because he had a fear of dealing with anything larger than himself, and when Holden called him a "spark," he rose to his feet and answered slowly in defence of his newfound individuality: "*Hum 'park nahin hai. Hom admi hai.* (I am no spark, but a man.)"

The protest made Holden choke and devote himself very seriously to a consideration of Tota's future. He need hardly have taken the trouble. The delight of that life was too perfect to endure. Therefore it was taken away as many things are taken away in India—suddenly and without warning. The little lord of the house, as Pir Khan called him, grew sorrowful and complained of pains who had never known the meaning of pain. Ameera, wild with terror, watched him through the night, and in the dawning of the second day the life was shaken out of him by fever—the seasonal autumn fever. It seemed altogether impossible that he could die, and neither Ameera nor Holden at first believed the evidence of the little body on the bedstead. Then Ameera beat her head against the wall and would have flung herself down the well in the garden had Holden not restrained her by main force.

One mercy only was granted to Holden. He rode to his office in broad daylight and found waiting him an unusually heavy mail that demanded concentrated attention and hard work. He was not, however, alive to this kindness of the gods.

3

The first shock of a bullet is no more than a brisk pinch. The wrecked body does not send in its protest to the soul till ten or fifteen seconds later. Holden realized his pain slowly, exactly as he had realized his happiness, and with the same imperious necessity for hiding all trace of it. In the beginning he only felt that there had been a loss, and that Ameera needed comforting, where she sat with her head on her knees shivering as Mian Mittu from the house-top called, *Tota! Tota! Tota!* Later all his world and the daily life of it rose up to hurt him. It was an outrage that any one of the children at the band-stand in the evening should be alive and clamorous, when his own child lay dead. It was more than mere pain when one of them touched him, and stories told by over-fond fathers of their children's latest performances cut him to the quick. He could not declare his pain. He had neither help, comfort, nor sympathy; and Ameera at the end of each weary day would lead him through the hell of self-questioning reproach which is reserved for those who have lost a child, and believe that with a little—just a little more care—it might have been saved.

"Perhaps," Ameera would say, "I did not take sufficient heed. Did I, or did I not? The sun on the roof that day when he played so long alone and I was—*ahi!* braiding my hair—it may be that the sun then bred the fever. If I had warned him from the sun he might have lived. But, oh my life, say that I am guiltless! Thou knowest that I loved him as I love thee. Say that there is no blame on me, or I shall die—I shall die!"

"There is no blame,—before God, none. It was written and how could we do aught to save? What has been, has been. Let it go, beloved."

"He was all my heart to me. How can I let the thought go when my arm tells me every night that he is not here? *Ahi! Ahi!* Oh Tota come back to me—come back again, and let us be all together as it was before!"

"Peace, peace! For thine own sake, and for mine also, if thou lovest me—rest."

"By this I know thou dost not care; and how shouldst thou? The white men have hearts of stone and souls of iron. Oh that I had married a man of mine own people—though he beat me, and had never eaten the bread of an alien!"

"Am I an alien—mother of my son?"

"What else—*sahib?* . . . Oh forgive me—forgive! The death has driven me mad. Thou art the life of my heart, and the light of my eyes, and the breath of my life, and—and I have put thee from me though it was but for a moment. If thou goest away to whom shall I look for help? Do not be angry. Indeed, it was the pain that spoke and not thy slave."

"I know, I know. We be two who were three. The greater need therefore that we should be one."

They were sitting on the roof as of custom. The night was a warm one in early spring, and sheet-lightning was dancing on the horizon to a broken tune played by far-off thunder. Ameera settled herself in Holden's arms.

"The dry earth is lowing like a cow for the rain, and I—I am afraid. It was not like this when we counted the stars. But thou lovest me as much as before, though a bond is taken away? Answer!"

"I love more because a new bond has come out of the sorrow that we have eaten together, and that thou knowest."

"Yea, I knew," said Ameera in a very small whisper. "But it is good to hear thee say so, my life, who art so strong to help. I will be a child no more, but a woman and an aid to thee. Listen! Give me my sitar[2] and I will sing bravely."

She took the light silver-studded sitar and began a song of the great hero Rajah Rasalu. The hand failed on the strings, the tune halted, checked, and at a low note turned off to the poor little nursery-rhyme about the wicked crow:

> And the wild plums grow in the jungle, only a penny a pound.
> Only a penny a pound, baba—only . . .

Then came the tears, and the piteous rebellion against fate till she slept, moaning a little in her sleep, with the right arm thrown clear of the body as though it protected something that was not there. It was after this night that life became a little easier for Holden. The ever-present pain of loss drove him into his work, and the work repaid him by filling up his mind for eight or nine hours a day. Ameera sat alone in the house and brooded, but grew happier when she understood that Holden was more at ease, according to the custom of women. They touched happiness again, but this time with caution.

"It was because we loved Tota that he died. The jealousy of God was upon us," said Ameera. "I have hung up a large black jar before our window to turn the evil eye from us, and we must make no protestations of delight but go softly underneath the stars, lest God find us out. Is that not good talk, worthless one?"

She had shifted the accent on the word that means "beloved," in proof of the sincerity of her purpose. But the kiss that followed the new christening was a thing that any deity might have envied. They went about henceforward saying, "It is naught, it is naught;" and hoping that all the Powers heard.

The Powers were busy on other things. They had allowed thirty million people four years of plenty wherein men fed well and the crops were certain and the birthrate rose year by year: the districts reported a purely agricultural population varying from nine hundred to two thousand to the square mile of the overburdened earth; and the Member for Lower Tooting,[3] wandering about India in top-hat and frockcoat talked largely of the benefits of British rule, and suggested as the one thing needful the establishment of a duly qualified electoral system and a general bestowal of the franchise. His long-suffering hosts smiled and made him welcome, and when he paused to admire, with pretty picked words, the blossom of the blood-red dhak tree that had flowered untimely for a sign of what was coming, they smiled more than ever.

It was the Deputy Commissioner of Kot-Kumharsen, staying at the club for a day, who lightly told a tale that made Holden's blood run cold as he overheard the end.

"He won't bother any one any more. Never saw a man so astonished in my life. By Jove, I thought he meant to ask a question in the House about it. Fellow-passenger in his ship—dined next him—bowled over by cholera and died in eighteen hours. You needn't laugh, you fellows. The Member for Lower Tooting is awfully angry about it; but he's more scared. I think he's going to take his enlightened self out of India."

2. Indian stringed instrument.
3. A Member of Parliament who has come to India to give advice on matters about which, Kipling suggests, he knows nothing.

"I'd give a good deal if he were knocked over. It might keep a few vestrymen[4] of his kidney to their own parish. But what's this about cholera? It's full early for anything of that kind," said a warden of an unprofitable salt-lick.

"Don't know," said the Deputy Commissioner reflectively. "We've got locusts with us. There's sporadic cholera all along the north—at least we're calling it sporadic for decency's sake. The spring crops are short in five districts, and nobody seems to know where the rains are. It's nearly March now. I don't want to scare anybody, but it seems to me that Nature's going to audit her accounts with a big red pencil this summer."

"Just when I wanted to take leave, too!" said a voice across the room.

"There won't be much leave this year, but there ought to be a great deal of promotion. I've come in to persuade the Government to put my pet canal on the list of famine relief-works. It's an ill-wind that blows no good. I shall get that canal finished at last."

"Is it the old programme then," said Holden; "famine, fever, and cholera?"

"Oh no. Only local scarcity and an unusual prevalence of seasonal sickness. You'll find it all in the reports if you live till next year. You're a lucky chap. You haven't got a wife to put out of harm's way. The hill-stations ought to be full of women this year."

"I think you're inclined to exaggerate the talk in the *bazars*," said a young civilian in the Secretariat. "Now I have observed——"

"I dare say you have," said the Deputy Commissioner, "but you've a great deal more to observe, my son. In the meantime, I wish to observe to you——" and he drew him aside to discuss the construction of the canal that was so dear to his heart. Holden went to his bungalow and began to understand that he was not alone in the world, and also that he was afraid for the sake of another,—which is the most soul-satisfying fear known to man.

Two months later, as the Deputy had foretold, Nature began to audit her accounts with a red pencil. On the heels of the spring-reapings came a cry for bread, and the Government, which had decreed that no man should die of want, sent wheat. Then came the cholera from all four quarters of the compass. It struck a pilgrim-gathering of half a million at a sacred shrine. Many died at the feet of their god; the others broke and ran over the face of the land carrying the pestilence with them. It smote a walled city and killed two hundred a day. The people crowded the trains, hanging on to the foot-boards and squatting on the roofs of the carriages, and the cholera followed them, for at each station they dragged out the dead and the dying. They died by the roadside, and the horses of the Englishmen shied at the corpses in the grass. The rains did not come, and the earth turned to iron lest man should escape death by hiding in her. The English sent their wives away to the hills and went about their work, coming forward as they were bidden to fill the gaps in the fighting-line. Holden, sick with fear of losing his chiefest treasure on earth, had done his best to persuade Ameera to go away with her mother to the Himalayas.

"Why should I go?" said she one evening on the roof.

"There is sickness, and people are dying, and all the white *mem-log* have gone."

"All of them?"

"All—unless perhaps there remain some old scald-head who vexes her husband's heart by running risk of death."

---

4. Members of a Church of England parish council; Kipling uses the term satirically to refer to Members of Parliament.

"Nay; who stays is my sister, and thou must not abuse her, for I will be a scald-head too. I am glad all the bold *mem-log* are gone."

"Do I speak to a woman or a babe? Go to the hills and I will see to it that thou goest like a queen's daughter. Think, child. In a red-lacquered bullock cart, veiled and curtained, with brass peacocks upon the pole and red cloth hangings. I will send two orderlies for guard and—"

"Peace! Thou art the babe in speaking thus. What use are those toys to me? He would have patted the bullocks and played with the housings. For his sake, per-haps,—thou hast made me very English—I might have gone. Now, I will not. Let the *mem-log* run."

"Their husbands are sending them, beloved."

"Very good talk. Since when hast thou been my husband to tell me what to do? I have but born thee a son. Thou art only all the desire of my soul to me. How shall I depart when I know that if evil befall thee by the breadth of so much as my littlest fingernail—is that not small?—I should be aware of it though I were in paradise. And here, this summer thou mayst die—*ai, janee,* die! and in dying they might call to tend thee a white woman, and she would rob me in the last of thy love!"

"But love is not born in a moment or on a death-bed!"

"What dost thou know of love, stone-heart? She would take thy thanks at least and, by God and the Prophet and Beebee Miriam the mother of thy Prophet, that I will never endure. My lord and my love, let there be no more foolish talk of going away. Where thou art, I am. It is enough." She put an arm round his neck and a hand on his mouth.

There are not many happinesses so complete as those that are snatched under the shadow of the sword. They sat together and laughed, calling each other openly by every pet name that could move the wrath of the gods. The city below them was locked up in its own torments. Sulphur fires blazed in the streets; the conches in the Hindu temples screamed and bellowed, for the gods were inattentive in those days. There was a service in the great Mahomedan shrine, and the call to prayer from the minarets was almost unceasing. They heard the wailing in the houses of the dead, and once the shriek of a mother who had lost a child and was calling for its return. In the grey dawn they saw the dead borne out through the city gates, each litter with its own little knot of mourners. Wherefore they kissed each other and shivered.

It was a red and heavy audit, for the land was very sick and needed a little breathing-space ere the torrent of cheap life should flood it anew. The children of immature fathers and undeveloped mothers made no resistance. They were cowed and sat still, waiting till the sword should be sheathed in November if it were so willed. There were gaps among the English, but the gaps were filled. The work of su-perintending famine-relief, cholera-sheds, medicine-distribution, and what little san-itation was possible, went forward because it was so ordered.

Holden had been told to keep himself in readiness to move to replace the next man who should fall. There were twelve hours in each day when he could not see Ameera, and she might die in three. He was considering what his pain would be if he could not see her for three months, or if she died out of his sight. He was absolutely certain that her death would be demanded—so certain that when he looked up from the telegram and saw Pir Khan breathless in the doorway, he laughed aloud, "And?" said he,——

"When there is a cry in the night and the spirit flutters into the throat, who has a charm that will restore? Come swiftly, Heaven-born! It is the black cholera."

Holden galloped to his home. The sky was heavy with clouds, for the long deferred rains were near and the heat was stifling. Ameera's mother met him in the courtyard, whimpering, "She is dying. She is nursing herself into death. She is all but dead. What shall I do, *sahib?*"

Ameera was lying in the room in which Tota had been born. She made no sign when Holden entered because the human soul is a very lonely thing and, when it is getting ready to go away, hides itself in a misty borderland where the living may not follow. The black cholera does its work quietly and without explanation. Ameera was being thrust out of life as though the Angel of Death had himself put his hand upon her. The quick breathing seemed to show that she was neither afraid nor in pain, but neither eyes nor mouth gave any answer to Holden's kisses. There was nothing to be said or done. Holden could only wait and suffer. The first drops of the rain began to fall on the roof and he could hear shouts of joy in the parched city.

The soul came back a little and the lips moved. Holden bent down to listen. "Keep nothing of mine," said Ameera. "Take no hair from my head. *She* would make thee burn it later on. That flame I should feel. Lower! Stoop lower! Remember only that I was thine and bore thee a son. Though thou wed a white woman to-morrow, the pleasure of receiving in thy arms thy first son is taken from thee for ever. Remember me when thy son is born—the one that shall carry thy name before all men. His misfortunes be on my head. I bear witness—I bear witness"—the lips were forming the words on his ear—"that there is no God but—thee, beloved!"

Then she died. Holden sat still, and all thought was taken from him,—till he heard Ameera's mother lift the curtain.

"Is she dead, *sahib?*"

"She is dead."

"Then I will mourn, and afterwards take an inventory of the furniture in this house. For that will be mine. The *sahib* does not mean to resume it? It is so little, so very little, *sahib*, and I am an old woman. I would like to lie softly."

"For the mercy of God be silent, a while. Go out and mourn where I cannot hear."

"*Sahib*, she will be buried in four hours."

"I know the custom. I shall go ere she is taken away. That matter is in thy hands. Look to it, that the bed on which—on which she lies—"

"Aha! That beautiful red-lacquered bed. I have long desired——"

"That the bed is left here untouched for my disposal. All else in the house is thine. Hire a cart, take everything, go hence, and before sunrise let there be nothing in this house but that which I have ordered thee to respect."

"I am an old woman. I would stay at least for the days of mourning, and the rains have just broken. Whither shall I go?"

"What is that to me? My order is that there is a going. The house-gear is worth a thousand rupees and my orderly shall bring thee a hundred rupees to-night."

"That is very little. Think of the cart-hire."

"It shall be nothing unless thou goest, and with speed. O woman, get hence and leave me to my dead!"

The mother shuffled down the staircase, and in her anxiety to take stock of the house-fittings forgot to mourn. Holden stayed by Ameera's side and the rain roared on the roof. He could not think connectedly by reason of the noise, though he made many attempts to do so. Then four sheeted ghosts glided dripping into the room and stared at him through their veils. They were the washers of the dead. Holden left the room and went out to his horse. He had come in a dead, stifling calm through ankle-deep dust. He found the court-yard a rain-lashed pond alive with frogs; a torrent of yellow water ran under the gate, and a roaring wind drove the bolts of the rain like buck-shot against the mud walls. Pir Khan was shivering in his little hut by the gate, and the horse was stamping uneasily in the water.

"I have been told the *sahib*'s order," said Pir Khan. "It is well. This house is now desolate. I go also, for my monkey-face would be a reminder of that which has been. Concerning the bed, I will bring that to thy house yonder in the morning; but remember, *sahib*, it will be to thee a knife turned in a green wound. I go upon a pilgrimage, and I will take no money. I have grown fat in the protection of the Presence whose sorrow is my sorrow. For the last time I hold his stirrup."

He touched Holden's foot with both hands and the horse sprang out into the road, where the creaking bamboos were whipping the sky and all the frogs were chuckling. Holden could not see for the rain in his face. He put his hands before his eyes and muttered,

"Oh you brute! You utter brute!"

The news of his trouble was already in his bungalow. He read the knowledge in his butler's eyes when Ahmed Khan brought in food, and for the first and last time in his life laid a hand upon his master's shoulder, saying: "Eat, *sahib*, eat. Meat is good against sorrow. I also have known. Moreover the shadows come and go, *sahib*; the shadows come and go. These be curried eggs."

Holden could neither eat nor sleep. The heavens sent down eight inches of rain in that night and washed the earth clean. The waters tore down walls, broke roads, and scoured open the shallow graves on the Mahomedan burying-ground. All next day it rained, and Holden sat still in his house considering his sorrow. On the morning of the third day he received a telegram which said only: "Rickells, Myndonie. Dying. Holden relieve. Immediate." Then he thought that before he departed he would look at the house wherein he had been master and lord. There was a break in the weather, and the rank earth steamed with vapour.

He found that the rains had torn down the mud pillars of the gateway, and the heavy wooden gate that had guarded his life hung lazily from one hinge. There was grass three inches high in the courtyard; Pir Khan's lodge was empty, and the sodden thatch sagged between the beams. A gray squirrel was in possession of the verandah, as if the house had been untenanted for thirty years instead of three days. Ameera's mother had removed everything except some mildewed matting. The *tick-tick* of the little scorpions as they hurried across the floor was the only sound in the house. Ameera's room and the other one where Tota had lived were heavy with mildew; and the narrow staircase leading to the roof was streaked and stained with rain-borne mud. Holden saw all these things, and came out again to meet in the road Durga Dass, his landlord,—portly, affable, clothed in white muslin, and driving a C-spring buggy. He was overlooking his property to see how the roofs stood the stress of the first rains.

"I have heard," said he, "you will not take this place any more, *sahib*?"

"What are you going to do with it?"

"Perhaps I shall let it again."

"Then I will keep it on while I am away."

Durga Dass was silent for some time. "You shall not take it on, *sahib*," he said. "When I was a young man I also——, but to-day I am a member of the Municipality. Ho! Ho! No. When the birds have gone what need to keep the nest? I will have it pulled down—the timber will sell for something always. It shall be pulled down, and the Municipality shall make a road across, as they desire, from the burning-*ghaut*[5] to the city wall, so that no man may say where this house stood."

1890

from JUST SO STORIES[1]

How the Whale Got His Throat

In the sea, once upon a time, O my Best Beloved, there was a Whale, and he ate fishes. He ate the starfish and the garfish, and the crab and the dab, and the plaice and the dace, and the skate and his mate, and the mackereel and the pickereel, and the really truly twirly-whirly eel. All the fishes he could find in all the sea he ate with his mouth—so! Till at last there was only one small fish left in all the sea, and he was a small 'Stute Fish,[2] and he swam a little behind the Whale's right ear, so as to be out of harm's way. Then the Whale stood up on his tail and said, "I'm hungry." And the small 'Stute Fish said in a small 'stute voice, "Noble and generous Cetacean, have you ever tasted Man?"

"No," said the Whale. "What is it like?"

"Nice," said the small 'Stute Fish. "Nice but nubbly."

"Then fetch me some," said the Whale, and he made the sea froth up with his tail.

"One at a time is enough," said the 'Stute Fish. "If you swim to latitude Fifty North, longitude Forty West (that is magic), you will find, sitting on a raft, in the middle of the sea, with nothing on but a pair of blue canvas breeches, a pair of suspenders (you must not forget the suspenders, Best Beloved), and a jack-knife, one shipwrecked Mariner, who, it is only fair to tell you, is a man of infinite-resource-and-sagacity."

So the Whale swam and swam to latitude Fifty North, longitude Forty West, as fast as he could swim, and on a raft, in the middle of the sea, with nothing to wear except a pair of blue canvas breeches, a pair of suspenders (you must particularly remember the suspenders, Best Beloved), and a jack-knife, he found one single, solitary shipwrecked Mariner, trailing his toes in the water. (He had his mummy's leave to paddle,[3] or else he would never have done it, because he was a man of infinite-resource-and-sagacity.)

Then the Whale opened his mouth back and back and back till it nearly touched his tail, and he swallowed the shipwrecked Mariner, and the raft he was sitting on, and his blue canvas breeches, and the suspenders (which you must not forget, and the jack-knife—He swallowed them all down into his warm, dark, inside cupboards, and then he smacked his lips—so, and turned round three times on his tail.

But as soon as the Mariner, who was a man of infinite-resource-and-sagacity, found himself truly inside the Whale's warm, dark, inside cupboards, he stumped and he jumped and he thumped and he bumped, and he pranced and he danced, and he banged and he clanged, and he hit and he bit, and he leaped and he creeped, and he prowled and he howled, and he hopped and he dropped, and he cried and he sighed,

---

5. Place where bodies are cremated.

1. *Just So Stories for Little Children* (1902) contains 12 stories and 12 poems, most of which were first published in various magazines between 1897 and 1902. They show the influence of the time Kipling spent in South Africa. G. K. Chesterton said of them: "The peculiar splendour . . . of these new Kipling stories is the fact that they do not read like fairy tales told to children by the modern fireside, so much as like fairy tales told to men in the morning of the world."

2. Astute or clever fish.

3. To dangle one's feet in the water idly; to wade.

and he crawled and he bawled, and he stepped and he lepped, and he danced horn-pipes where he shouldn't, and the Whale felt most unhappy indeed. (*Have* you forgotten the suspenders?)

So he said to the 'Stute Fish, "This man is very nubbly, and besides he is making me hiccough. What shall I do?"

"Tell him to come out," said the 'Stute Fish.

So the Whale called down his own throat to the shipwrecked Mariner, "Come out and behave yourself. I've got the hiccoughs."

"Nay, nay!" said the Mariner. "Not so, but far otherwise. Take me to my natal-shore and the white-cliffs-of-Albion,[4] and I'll think about it." And he began to dance more than ever.

"You had better take him home," said the 'Stute Fish to the Whale. "I ought to have warned you that he is a man of infinite-resource-and-sagacity."

So the Whale swam and swam and swam, with both flippers and his tail, as hard as he could for the hiccoughs; and at last he saw the Mariner's natal-shore and the white-cliffs-of-Albion, and he rushed half-way up the beach, and opened his mouth wide and wide and wide, and said, "Change here for Winchester, Ashuelot, Nashua, Keene, and stations on the *Fitch*burg Road;"[5] and just as he said "Fitch" the Mariner walked out of his mouth. But while the Whale had been swimming, the Mariner, who was indeed a person of infinite-resource-and-sagacity, had taken his jack-knife and cut up the raft into a little square grating all running criss-cross, and he had tied it firm with his suspenders (*now* you know why you were not to forget the suspenders!), and he dragged that grating good and tight into the Whale's throat, and there it stuck! Then he recited the following *Sloka* [stanza], which, as you have not heard it, I will now proceed to relate—

> By means of a grating
> I have stopped your ating.

For the Mariner he was also an Hi-ber-ni-an.[6] And he stepped out on the shingle, and went home to his mother, who had given him leave to trail his toes in the water; and he married and lived happily ever afterward. So did the Whale. But from that day on, the grating in his throat, which he could neither cough up nor swallow down, prevented him eating anything except very, very small fish; and that is the reason why whales nowadays never eat men or boys or little girls.

The small 'Stute Fish went and hid himself in the mud under the Door-sills of the Equator. He was afraid that the Whale might be angry with him.

The Sailor took the jack-knife home. He was wearing the blue canvas breeches when he walked out on the shingle. The suspenders were left behind, you see, to tie the grating with; and that is the end of *that* tale.

*

> When the cabin port-holes are dark and green
>   Because of the seas outside;
> When the ship goes *wop* (with a wiggle between)
> And the steward falls into the soup-tureen,
>   And the trunks begin to slide;
> When Nursey lies on the floor in a heap,

---

4. Chalk cliffs of Dover; Albion is another name for England.

5. The whale is impersonating a train conductor.

6. Irishman.

And Mummy tells you to let her sleep,
And you aren't waked or washed or dressed,
    Why, then you will know (if you haven't guessed)
    You're "Fifty North and Forty West!"

1897

How the Camel Got His Hump

Now this is the next tale, and it tells how the Camel got his big hump.

In the beginning of years, when the world was so new and all, and the Animals were just beginning to work for Man, there was a Camel, and he lived in the middle of a Howling Desert because he did not want to work; and besides, he was a Howler himself. So he ate sticks and thorns and tamarisks[1] and milkweed and prickles, most 'scruciating idle; and when anybody spoke to him he said "Humph!" Just "Humph!" and no more.

Presently the Horse came to him on Monday morning, with a saddle on his back and a bit in his mouth, and said, "Camel, O Camel, come out and trot like the rest of us."

"Humph!" said the Camel and the Horse went away and told the Man.

Presently the Dog came to him, with a stick in his mouth, and said, "Camel, O Camel, come and fetch and carry like the rest of us."

"Humph!" said the Camel; and the Dog went away and told the Man.

Presently the Ox came to him, with the yoke on his neck and said, "Camel, O Camel, come and plough like the rest of us."

"Humph!" said the Camel; and the Ox went away and told the Man.

At the end of the day the Man called the Horse and the Dog and the Ox together, and said, "Three, O Three, I'm very sorry for you (with the world so new-and-all); but that Humph-thing in the Desert can't work, or he would have been here by now, so I am going to leave him alone, and you must work double-time to make up for it."

That made the Three very angry (with the world so new-and-all), and they held a palaver, and an *indaba*, and a *punchayet*, and a pow-wow[2] on the edge of the Desert; and the Camel came chewing milkweed *most* 'scruciating idle, and laughed at them. Then he said "Humph!" and went away again.

Presently there came along the Djinn[3] in charge of All Deserts, rolling in a cloud of dust (Djinns always travel that way because it is Magic), and he stopped to palaver and pow-wow with the Three.

"Djinn of All Deserts," said the Horse, "*is* it right for any one to be idle, with the world so new-and-all?"

"Certainly not," said the Djinn.

"Well," said the Horse, "there's a thing in the middle of your Howling Desert (and he's a Howler himself) with a long neck and long legs, and he hasn't done a stroke of work since Monday morning. He won't trot."

"Whew!" said the Djinn, whistling, "that's my Camel, for all the gold in Arabia! What does he say about it?"

"He says 'Humph!'" said the Dog; "and he won't fetch and carry."

---

1. Desert shrubs.
2. The preceding terms are all synonyms for a conference or discussion.
3. Genie.

"Does he say anything else?"

"Only 'Humph!'; and he won't plough," said the Ox.

"Very good," said the Djinn. "I'll humph him if you will kindly wait a minute."

The Djinn rolled himself up in his dust-cloak, and took a bearing across the desert, and found the Camel most 'scruciatingly idle, looking at his own reflection in a pool of water.

"My long and bubbling friend," said the Djinn, "what's this I hear of your doing no work, with the world so new-and-all?"

"Humph!" said the Camel.

The Djinn sat down, with his chin in his hand, and began to think a Great Magic, while the Camel looked at his own reflection in the pool of water.

"You've given the Three extra work ever since Monday morning, all on account of your 'scruciating idleness," said the Djinn; and he went on thinking Magics, with his chin in his hand.

"Humph!" said the Camel.

"I shouldn't say that again if I were you," said the Djinn; "you might say it once too often. Bubbles, I want you to work."

And the Camel said "Humph!" again; but no sooner had he said it than he saw his back, that he was so proud of, puffing up and puffing up into a great big lolloping humph.

"Do you see that?" said the Djinn. "That's your very own humph that you've brought upon your very own self by not working. To-day is Thursday, and you've done no work since Monday, when the work began. Now you are going to work."

"How can I," said the Camel, "with this humph on my back?"

"That's made a-purpose," said the Djinn, "all because you missed those three days. You will be able to work now for three days without eating, because you can live on your humph; and don't you ever say I never did anything for you. Come out of the Desert and go to the Three, and behave. Humph yourself!"

And the Camel humphed himself, humph and all, and went away to join the Three. And from that day to this the Camel always wears a humph (we call it "hump" now, not to hurt his feelings); but he has never yet caught up with the three days that he missed at the beginning of the world, and he has never yet learned how to behave.

> The Camel's hump is an ugly lump
>   Which well you may see at the Zoo;
> But uglier yet is the hump we get
>   From having too little to do.
>
> 5   Kiddies and grown-ups too-oo-oo,
>   If we haven't enough to do-oo-oo,
>   We get the hump—
>   Cameelious hump—
>   The hump that is black and blue!
>
> 10 We climb out of bed with a frouzly head
>   And a snarly-yarly voice.
>   We shiver and scowl and we grunt and we growl
>   At our bath and our boots and our toys;
>
>   And there ought to be a corner for me
> 15   (And I know there is one for you)

> When we get the hump—
> Cameelious hump—
> The hump that is black and blue!

> The cure for this ill is not to sit still,
> 20   Or frowst with a book by the fire;
> But to take a large hoe and a shovel also,
>   And dig till you gently perspire.

> And then you will find that the sun and the wind
> And the Djinn of the Garden too,
> 25   Have lifted the hump—
>   The horrible hump—
> The hump that is black and blue!

> I get it as well as you-oo-oo—
> If I haven't enough to do-oo-oo—
> 30   We all get hump—
>   Cameelious hump—
> Kiddies and grown ups-too!

1897

How the Leopard Got His Spots

In the days when everybody started fair, Best Beloved, the Leopard lived in a place called the High Veldt.[1] 'Member it wasn't the Low Veldt, or the Bush Veldt, or the Sour Veldt, but the 'sclusively bare, hot, shiny High Veldt, where there was sand and sandy-coloured rock and 'sclusively tufts of sandy-yellowish grass. The Giraffe and the Zebra and the Eland and the Koodoo and the Hartebeest[2] lived there; and they were 'sclusively sandy-yellow-brownish all over; but the Leopard, he was the 'sclusivest sandiest-yellowish-brownest of them all—a greyish-yellowish catty-shaped kind of beast, and he matched the 'sclusively yellowish-greyish-brownish colour of the High Veldt to one hair. This was very bad for the Giraffe and the Zebra and the rest of them; for he would lie down by a 'sclusively yellowish-greyish-brownish stone or clump of grass, and when the Giraffe or the Zebra or the Eland or the Koodoo or the Bush-Buck or the Bonte-Buck came by he would surprise them out of their jumpsome lives. He would indeed! And, also, there was an Ethiopian with bows and arrows (a 'sclusively greyish-brownish-yellowish man he was then), who lived on the High Veldt with the Leopard; and the two used to hunt together—the Ethiopian with his bows and arrows, and the Leopard 'sclusively with his teeth and claws—till the Giraffe and the Eland and the Koodoo and the Quagga[3] and all the rest of them didn't know which way to jump, Best Beloved. They didn't indeed!

After a long time—things lived for ever so long in those days—they learned to avoid anything that looked like a Leopard or an Ethiopian; and bit by bit—the Giraffe began it, because his legs were the longest—they went away from the High Veldt. They scuttled for days and days and days till they came to a great forest, 'sclusively full of trees and bushes and stripy, speckly, patchy-blatchy shadows, and there

1. Open grassy plain.
2. Varieties of African antelope, as are Bush-Buck and   Bonte-Buck, mentioned below.
3. Zebra-like animal, extinct since the 19th century.

Kipling himself illustrated the *Just So Stories,* showing here how the man and the leopard (in the lower foreground) learned to blend in with their surroundings to hunt their prey, the giraffe (above the man near the crook of the tree) and the zebra (in the woods above the leopard). While today it is unusual for authors to be also skilled artists, learning to draw was part of the Victorian gentleman or lady's education. William Makepeace Thackeray illustrated his novels, John Ruskin's watercolors rivaled those of the artists he critiqued, Lewis Carroll did the first depictions of Alice's adventures, the poet Gerard Manley Hopkins sketched plants and self-portraits in his journals, and Beatrix Potter's pictures of Peter Rabbit and his fellow animals are still world famous.

they hid: and after another long time, what with standing half in the shade and half out of it, and what with the slippery-slidy shadows of the trees falling on them, the Giraffe grew blotchy, and the Zebra grew stripy, and the Eland and the Koodoo grew darker, with little wavy grey lines on their backs like bark on a tree trunk; and so, though you could hear them and smell them, you could very seldom see them, and then only when you knew precisely where to look. They had a beautiful time in the 'sclusively speckly-spickly shadows of the forest, while the Leopard and the Ethiopian ran about over the 'sclusively greyish-yellowish-reddish High Veldt outside, wondering where all their breakfasts and their dinners and their teas had gone. At last they were so hungry that they ate rats and beetles and rock-rabbits, the Leopard and the Ethiopian, and then they had the Big Tummy-ache, both together; and then they met Baviaan—the dog-headed, barking Baboon, who is Quite the Wisest Animal in All South Africa.

Said Leopard to Baviaan (and it was a very hot day), "Where has all the game gone?"

And Baviaan winked. *He* knew.

Said the Ethiopian to Baviaan, "Can you tell me the present habitat of the aboriginal Fauna?" (That meant just the same thing, but the Ethiopian always used long words. He was a grown-up.)

And Baviaan winked. *He* knew.

Then said Baviaan, "The game has gone into other spots; and my advice to you, Leopard, is to go into other spots as soon as you can."

And the Ethiopian said, "That is all very fine, but I wish to know whither the aboriginal Fauna has migrated."

Then said Baviaan, "The aboriginal Fauna has joined the aboriginal Flora because it was high time for a change; and my advice to you, Ethiopian, is to change as soon as you can."

That puzzled the Leopard and the Ethiopian, but they set off to look for the aboriginal Flora, and presently, after ever so many days, they saw a great, high, tall forest full of tree trunks all 'sclusively speckled and sprottled and spottled, dotted and splashed and slashed and hatched and cross-hatched with shadows. (Say that quickly aloud, and you will see how *very* shadowy the forest must have been.)

"What is this," said the Leopard, "that is so 'sclusively dark, and yet so full of little pieces of light?"

"I don't know," said the Ethiopian, "but it ought to be the aboriginal Flora. I can smell Giraffe, and I can hear Giraffe, but I can't see Giraffe."

"That's curious," said the Leopard. "I suppose it is because we have just come in out of the sunshine. I can smell Zebra, and I can hear Zebra, but I can't see Zebra."

"Wait a bit," said the Ethiopian. "It's a long time since we've hunted 'em. Perhaps we've forgotten what they were like."

"Fiddle!" said the Leopard. "I remember them perfectly on the High Veldt, especially their marrow-bones. Giraffe is about seventeen feet high, of a 'sclusively fulvous golden-yellow from head to heel; and Zebra is about four and a half feet high, of a 'sclusively grey-fawn colour from head to heel."

"Umm," said the Ethiopian, looking into the speckly-spickly shadows of the aboriginal Flora-forest. "Then they ought to show up in this dark place like ripe bananas in a smokehouse."

But they didn't. The Leopard and the Ethiopian hunted all day; and though they could smell them and hear them, they never saw one of them.

"For goodness' sake," said the Leopard at tea-time, "let us wait till it gets dark. This daylight hunting is a perfect scandal."

So they waited till dark, and then the Leopard heard something breathing sniffily in the starlight that fell all stripy through the branches, and he jumped at the noise, and it smelt like Zebra, and it felt like Zebra, and when he knocked it down it kicked like Zebra, but he couldn't see it. So he said, "Be quiet, O you person without any form. I am going to sit on your head till morning, because there is something about you that I don't understand."

Presently he heard a grunt and a crash and a scramble, and the Ethiopian called out, "I've caught a thing that I can't see. It smells like Giraffe, and it kicks like Giraffe, but it hasn't any form."

"Don't you trust it," said the Leopard. "Sit on its head till the morning—same as me. They haven't any form—any of 'em."

So they sat down on them hard till bright morning-time, and then Leopard said, "What have you at your end of the table, Brother?"

The Ethiopian scratched his head and said, "It ought to be 'sclusively a rich fulvous orange-tawny from head to heel, and it ought to be Giraffe; but it is covered all over with chestnut blotches. What have you at *your* end of the table, Brother?"

And the Leopard scratched his head and said, "It ought to be 'sclusively a delicate greyish-fawn, and it ought to be Zebra; but it is covered all over with black and purple stripes. What in the world have you been doing to yourself, Zebra? Don't you know that if you were on the High Veldt I could see you ten miles off? You haven't any form."

"Yes," said the Zebra, "but this isn't the High Veldt. Can't you see?"

"I can now," said the Leopard. "But I couldn't all yesterday. How is it done?"

"Let us up," said the Zebra, "and we will show you."

They let the Zebra and the Giraffe get up; and Zebra moved away to some little thornbushes where the sunlight fell all stripy, and Giraffe moved off to some tallish trees where the shadows fell all blotchy.

"Now watch," said the Zebra and the Giraffe. "This is the way it's done. One—two—three! And where's your breakfast?"

Leopard stared, and Ethiopian stared, but all they could see were stripy shadows and blotched shadows in the forest, but never a sign of Zebra and Giraffe. They had just walked off and hidden themselves in the shadowy forest.

"Hi! Hi!" said the Ethiopian. "That's a trick worth learning. Take a lesson by it, Leopard. You show up in this dark place like a bar of soap in a coal-scuttle."

"Ho! Ho!" said the Leopard. "Would it surprise you very much to know that you show up in this dark place like a mustard-plaster on a sack of coals?"

"Well, calling names won't catch dinner," said the Ethiopian. "The long and the little of it is that we don't match our backgrounds. I'm going to take Baviaan's advice. He told me I ought to change; and as I've nothing to change except my skin I'm going to change that."

"What to?" said the Leopard, tremendously excited.

"To a nice working blackish-brownish colour, with a little purple in it, and touches of slaty-blue. It will be the very thing for hiding in hollows and behind trees."

So he changed his skin then and there, and the Leopard was more excited than ever; he had never seen a man change his skin before.

"But what about me?" he said, when the Ethiopian had worked his last little finger into his fine new black skin.

"You take Baviaan's advice too. He told you to go into spots."

"So I did," said the Leopard. "I went into other spots as fast as I could. I went into this spot with you, and a lot of good it has done me."

"Oh," said the Ethiopian, "Baviaan didn't mean spots in South Africa. He meant spots on your skin."

"What's the use of that?" said the Leopard.

"Think of Giraffe," said the Ethiopian. "Or if you prefer stripes, think of Zebra. They find their spots and stripes give them per-fect satisfaction."

"Umm," said the Leopard. "I wouldn't look like Zebra—not for ever so."

"Well, make up your mind," said the Ethiopian, "because I'd hate to go hunting without you, but I must if you insist on looking like a sun-flower against a tarred fence."

"I'll take spots, then," said the Leopard; "but don't make 'em too vulgar-big. I wouldn't look like Giraffe—not for ever so."

"I'll make 'em with the tips of my fingers," said the Ethiopian. "There's plenty of black left on my skin still. Stand over!"

Then the Ethiopian put his five fingers close together (there was plenty of black left on his new skin still) and pressed them all over the Leopard, and wherever the five fingers touched they left five little black marks, all close together. You can see them on any Leopard's skin you like, Best Beloved. Sometimes the fingers slipped and the marks got a little blurred; but if you look closely at any Leopard now you will see that there are always five spots—off five fat black finger-tips.

"Now you *are* a beauty!" said the Ethiopian. "You can lie out on the bare ground and look like a heap of pebbles. You can lie out on the naked rocks and look like a piece of pudding-stone. You can lie out on a leafy branch and look like sunshine sifting through the leaves; and you can lie right across the centre of a path and look like nothing in particular. Think of that and purr!"

"But if I'm all this," said the Leopard, "why didn't you go spotty too?"

"Oh, plain black's best for a nigger," said the Ethiopian. "Now come along and we'll see if we can't get even with Mr. One-Two-Three-Where's-your-Breakfast!"

So they went away and lived happily ever afterward, Best Beloved. That is all.

Oh, now and then you will hear grown-ups say, "Can the Ethiopian change his skin or the Leopard his spots?" I don't think even grown-ups would keep on saying such a silly thing if the Leopard and the Ethiopian hadn't done it once—do you? But they will never do it again, Best Beloved. They are quite contented as they are.

> I AM the Most Wise Baviaan, saying in most wise tones,
> "Let us melt into the landscape—just us two by our lones."
> People have come—in a carriage—calling. But Mummy is there. . . .
> Yes, I can go if you take me—Nurse says she don't care.
> Let's go up to the pig-sties and sit on the farmyard rails!
> Let's say things to the bunnies, and watch 'em skitter their tails!
> Let's—oh, anything, daddy, so long as it's you and me,
> And going truly exploring, and not being in till tea!
> Here's your boots (I've brought 'em), and here's your cap and stick,
> And here's your pipe and tobacco. Oh, come along out of it—quick.

1902

Gunga Din

You may talk o' gin and beer
When you're quartered safe out 'ere,
An' you're sent to penny-fights an' Aldershot[1] it;
But when it comes to slaughter
5   You will do your work on water,
An' you'll lick the bloomin' boots of 'im that's got it.
Now in Injia's sunny clime,
Where I used to spend my time
A-servin' of 'Er Majesty the Queen,
10   Of all them blackfaced crew
The finest man I knew

---

1. The speaker is back from India, addressing recruits who will be training at Aldershot, a military camp in Hampshire.

Was our regimental bhisti,° Gunga Din.   *water carrier*
    He was "Din! Din! Din!
    "You limpin' lump o' brick-dust, Gunga Din!
15   "Hi! Slippy *hitherao!*°   *come here*
      "Water, get it! *Panee lao,*°   *bring water quickly*
    "You squidgy-nosed old idol, Gunga Din."

The uniform 'e wore
Was nothin' much before,
20 An' rather less than 'arf o' that be'ind,
For a piece o' twisty rag
An' a goatskin water-bag
Was all the field-equipment 'e could find.
When the sweatin' troop-train lay
25 In a sidin' through the day,
Where the 'eat would make your bloomin' eyebrows crawl,
We shouted "Harry By!"[2]
Till our throats were bricky-dry,
Then we wopped 'im 'cause 'e couldn't serve us all.
30   It was "Din! Din! Din!
    "You 'eathen, where the mischief 'ave you been?
      "You put some *juldee*° in it   *speed*
      "Or I'll *marrow*° you this minute   *hit*
    "If you don't fill up my helmet, Gunga Din!"

35 'E would dot an' carry one
Till the longest day was done;
An' 'e didn't seem to know the use o' fear.
If we charged or broke or cut,
You could bet your bloomin' nut,
40 'E'd be waitin' fifty paces right flank rear.
With 'is mussick° on 'is back,   *water-bag*
'E would skip with our attack,
An' watch us till the bugles made "Retire,"
An' for all 'is dirty 'ide
45 'E was white, clear white, inside
When 'e went to tend the wounded under fire!
    It was "Din! Din! Din!"
    With the bullets kickin' dust-spots on the green.
      When the cartridges ran out,
50   You could hear the front-ranks shout,
    "Hi! ammunition-mules an' Gunga Din!"

I shan't forgit the night
When I dropped be'ind the fight
With a bullet where my belt-plate should 'a' been.
55 I was chokin' mad with thirst,

2. *Hari bhai*, Hindustani for "Hey, brother!"

An' the man that spied me first
Was our good old grinnin', gruntin' Gunga Din.
'E lifted up my 'ead,
An' he plugged me where I bled,
60   An' 'e guv me 'arf-a-pint o' water green.
It was crawlin' and it stunk,
But of all the drinks I've drunk,
I'm gratefullest to one from Gunga Din.
          It was "Din! Din! Din!
65   "'Ere's a beggar with a bullet through 'is spleen;
          "'E's chawin' up the ground,
          "An' 'e's kickin' all around:
      "For Gawd's sake git the water, Gunga Din!"

      'E carried me away
70   To where a dooli° lay,   *stretcher*
      An' a bullet come an' drilled the beggar clean.
      'E put me safe inside,
      An' just before 'e died,
      "I 'ope you liked your drink," sez Gunga Din.
75   So I'll meet 'im later on
      At the place where 'e is gone—
      Where it's always double drill and no canteen.
      'E'll be squattin' on the coals
      Givin' drink to poor damned souls,
80   An' I'll get a swig in hell from Gunga Din!
          Yes, Din! Din! Din!
      You Lazarushian-leather³ Gunga Din!
          Though I've belted you and flayed you,
          By the livin' Gawd that made you,
85   You're a better man than I am, Gunga Din!

                                                    1890

The Widow at Windsor¹

'Ave you 'eard o' the Widow at Windsor
    With a hairy gold crown on 'er 'ead?
She 'as ships on the foam—she 'as millions at 'ome,
    An' she pays us poor beggars in red.²
5   (Ow, poor beggars in red!)
There's 'er nick on the cavalry 'orses,³
    There's 'er mark on the medical stores—
An' 'er troopers⁴ you'll find with a fair wind be'ind
    That takes us to various wars.
10   (Poor beggars!—barbarious wars!)

3. Kipling has coined a phrase, a cross between Russian leather (like Gunga Din's skin) and Lazarus, the beggar in Luke 16 who goes to heaven while the rich man who spurned him burns in hell begging for a drink of water.
1. Queen Victoria, who entered into lifelong mourning after the death of her husband, Prince Albert, in 1861.
2. British soldiers wore red coats.
3. Army horses had a nick on their hooves identifying them as property of the queen.
4. Troopships.

Then 'ere's to the Widow at Windsor,
   An' 'ere's to the stores an' the guns,
The men an' the 'orses what makes up the forces
   O' Missis Victorier's sons.
15   (Poor beggars! Victorier's sons!)

Walk wide o' the Widow at Windsor,
   For 'alf o' Creation she owns:
We 'ave bought 'er the same with the sword an' the flame,
   An' we've salted it down with our bones.
20   (Poor beggars!—it's blue with our bones!)
Hands off o' the sons o' the Widow,
   Hands off o' the goods in 'er shop,
For the Kings must come down an' the Emperors frown
   When the Widow at Windsor says "Stop!"
25   (Poor beggars!—we're sent to say "Stop!")
   Then 'ere's to the Lodge o' the Widow,
      From the Pole to the Tropics it runs[5]—
   To the Lodge that we tile with the rank an' the file,
      An' open in form with the guns.
30   (Poor beggars!—it's always they guns!)

We 'ave 'eard o' the Widow at Windsor,
   It's safest to leave 'er alone:
For 'er sentries we stand by the sea an' the land
   Wherever the bugles are blown.
35   (Poor beggars!—an' don't we get blown!)
Take 'old o' the Wings o' the Mornin',[6]
   An' flop round the earth till you're dead;
But you won't get away from the tune that they play[7]
   To the bloomin' old rag over'ead.
40   (Poor beggars!—it's 'ot over'ead!)
   Then 'ere's to the Sons o' the Widow,
      Wherever, 'owever they roam.
   'Ere's all they desire, an' if they require
      A speedy return to their 'ome.
45   (Poor beggars!—they'll never see 'ome!)

1890

Recessional[1]
1897

God of our fathers, known of old,
   Lord of our far-flung battle-line,
Beneath whose awful Hand we hold

---

5. The Lodge is being used as a synonym for the British Empire, with a probable allusion to Freemasonry, a secret society whose members group themselves into "lodges" or local chapters. Kipling was a Freemason.
6. "If I take the wings of the morning / And dwell in the uttermost parts of the sea" (Psalm 139.9).
7. *God Save the Queen*, the British national anthem.
1. Hymn sung at the end of a church service. Kipling wrote this cautionary hymn for Queen Victoria's Diamond Jubilee.

Dominion over palm and pine—
5 Lord God of Hosts, be with us yet,
  Lest we forget—lest we forget![2]

 The tumult and the shouting dies;
  The Captains and the Kings depart:
 Still stands Thine ancient sacrifice,
10 An humble and a contrite heart.[3]
 Lord God of Hosts, be with us yet,
  Lest we forget—lest we forget!

 Far-called, our navies melt away;
  On dune and headland sinks the fire:[4]
15 Lo, all our pomp of yesterday
  Is one with Nineveh and Tyre![5]
 Judge of the Nations, spare us yet,
  Lest we forget—lest we forget!

 If, drunk with sight of power, we loose
20 Wild tongues that have not Thee in awe,
 Such boastings as the Gentiles use,
  Or lesser breeds without the Law[6]—
 Lord God of Hosts, be with us yet,
  Lest we forget—lest we forget!

25 For heathen heart that puts her trust
  In reeking tube and iron shard,
 All valiant dust that builds on dust,
  And guarding, calls not Thee to guard,
 For frantic boast and foolish word—
30 Thy mercy on Thy People, Lord!

If—[1]

If you can keep your head when all about you
 Are losing theirs and blaming it on you,
If you can trust yourself when all men doubt you,
 But make allowance for their doubting too;
5 If you can wait and not be tired by waiting,
  Or being lied about, don't deal in lies,
 Or being hated, don't give way to hating,
  And yet don't look too good, nor talk too wise:

---

2. "Then beware lest thou forget the Lord, which brought thee forth out of the land of Egypt" (Deuteronomy 6.21).
3. Paraphrasing Psalm 51.17.
4. Celebratory bonfires were lit all over Britain in honor of the Jubilee.
5. The ruined capitals of once-great empires.
6. "For when the Gentiles, which have not the law, do by nature the things contained in the law, these having not the law, are a law unto themselves" (Romans 2.14).

Kipling associates the English with the Chosen People, and the rest of the world with the Gentiles.
1. First published in the *American Magazine* in October 1910, *If* soon became one of the best-known poems of the day. It was reprinted widely; Kipling included it in his children's book *Rewards and Fairies* (1910). Its theme and meter recall Browning's *Epilogue* to *Asolando*; see page 1461.

If you can dream—and not make dreams your master;
10   If you can think—and not make thoughts your aim;
If you can meet with Triumph and Disaster
    And treat those two impostors just the same;
If you can bear to hear the truth you've spoken
    Twisted by knaves to make a trap for fools,
15 Or watch the things you gave your life to, broken,
    And stoop and build 'em up with worn-out tools:

If you can make one heap of all your winnings
    And risk it on one turn of pitch-and-toss,[2]
And lose, and start again at your beginnings
20   And never breathe a word about your loss;
If you can force your heart and nerve and sinew
    To serve your turn long after they are gone,
And so hold on when there is nothing in you
    Except the Will which says to them: "Hold on!"

25 If you can talk with crowds and keep your virtue,
    Or walk with Kings—nor lose the common touch,
If neither foes nor loving friends can hurt you,
    If all men count with you, but none too much;
If you can fill the unforgiving minute
30   With sixty seconds' worth of distance run,
Yours is the Earth and everything that's in it,
    And—which is more—you'll be a Man, my son!

                              1910

2. Game in which players pitch coins.

⇒⧉ PERSPECTIVES ⧉⇐

Travel and Empire

Daylight at Last! The Advance Column of the Emin Pasha Relief Expedition Emerging from the Great Forest. From Henry Morton Stanley, *In Darkest Africa*, 1890. In his best-selling book, the journalist and explorer H. M. Stanley described his near-fatal expedition to rescue Edward Schnitzer, who held office as the Emin Pasha, governor of the British Equatorial Province of Egypt. The governor had been trapped by rebels at a frontier fort on the shore of Lake Albert in east central Africa. Stanley reached the lake after a grueling overland trek from the Congo. Here, walking stick in hand, Stanley surveys the scene with heroic sangfroid as his native troops rejoice at his success in guiding them through the hostile wilderness to their destination.

The Victorians were enthusiastic travelers. Although the explorers of previous centuries had mapped most of the globe, there still remained vast areas of "blank space" to be charted, and geographical mysteries, such as the source of the Nile, to be solved. Scientific and ethnographic research motivated travelers such as Charles Darwin, who spent five years sailing around the world as the naturalist on board the *Beagle*.

But new discovery was not the only enticement to travel. Some, such as the legendary David Livingstone, left home to undertake missionary work. Others, like Isabella Bird and Robert Louis Stevenson, traveled to regain their health. And then there were those who traveled for sheer pleasure on the new steamships and railways. The Grand Tour of the Continent, previously possible only for the rich, gradually became accessible to the middle classes. By midcentury the travel agent Thomas Cook had introduced the concept of organized group trips, and the phrase "a Cook's tour" entered the language.

The antiquities of Italy and Greece aroused romantic enthusiasm, as did the sublimity of the Alpine peaks. The budding sport of mountain climbing produced its own brand of travel literature, with Edward Whymper's *Scrambles Amongst the Alps* (1871) and Leslie Stephen's *The Playground of Europe* (1871) among the classics of this genre. Controversy surrounding the questions of democracy and slavery made America an intriguing destination—though Americans did not always appreciate the pointed criticism of their country by British travelers such as Frances Trollope and Charles Dickens.

Part of the appeal of travel literature lies in the way that it enables the stay-at-home reader to experience the world vicariously, to see through the eyes of others. The armchair traveler enters Mecca with Richard Burton, rides in a cattle roundup with Isabella Bird, floats down the Ogowé River with Mary Kingsley. Despite the lure of such colorful incidents, travel writing has often based its claim to be taken seriously on its status as a "nonfiction" genre. Travel writers may adopt a tone of factual reportage presenting Useful Information: as Kingsley asserts in her preface to *Travels in West Africa*, "if you go there you will find things as I have said." Yet works of travel are highly selective and self-conscious. They employ a variety of literary devices, including humor and irony, metaphor and imagery, that convey the outlook and prejudices of the author. They carefully construct their narrative voices: Trollope's sarcastic mockery, Kinglake's airy light-heartedness, Burton's bravado, Stanley's doggedness, Kingsley's jauntiness. Their protagonists become heroes or heroines engaged in epic struggles against blizzards and bandits, cannibals and crocodiles.

Thus, if travel represents exploration and adventure, it also offers an opportunity to shape one's own identity, first on the journey itself and later in the recounting of it. In Britain Henry Stanley was a nobody and Isabella Bird an invalid spinster, but they recreated themselves by battling hardships in foreign lands. Particularly for women, travel meant an escape from the constraints of domesticity, and a chance to try out new roles: cowboy, trader, pilgrim, scientist, writer. Yet this liberation of the individual from the boundaries of class or gender was not unproblematic: the Victorian search for self-discovery against a backdrop of exotic otherness was implicated in the politics of empire. Most obviously, Stanley's explorations helped open the way for Belgian exploitation of the Congo and the European "Scramble" to divide up Africa. Even Mary Kingsley, who opposed the more aggressive policies of imperialism and sought to convey the richness of African cultures, did not question Britain's right to plant its flag and conduct trade.

Travelers search for many things, among them lost innocence, an unspoiled paradise, and the supposed origins of civilization in more "primitive" cultures. Frances Trollope sought to find a democratic utopia in America; Isabella Bird believed she had found Eden in the Rocky Mountains. Inevitably, travelers project their own desires onto other landscapes and cultures. Yet Victorian travelers were not naive about the impossibility of achieving true objectivity, of writing from outside one's own culture. Alexander Kinglake's solution to the dilemma was to proclaim that subjectivity offers its own kind of truth: the traveler "tells you of objects, not as he knows them to be, but as they seemed to him."

+ ≡✧≡ +

Frances Trollope
1780–1863

Frances Trollope went to America in 1827 with three of her children to start a new life, leaving her bankrupt husband to look after their young son, Anthony, the future novelist. Her attempt to establish a business in Cincinnati failed, which may help explain her disillusion with America. She loathed Americans' vulgarity, their assumption of equality, and their provincial ignorance of culture. *Domestic Manners of the Americans* (1832) was hugely popular in England—where her satire of the young democracy fed the debate about extending the franchise in the Reform Bill of 1832—but she was reviled by thin-skinned American readers. Unlike his outraged countrymen, Mark Twain wrote: "She knew her subject well, and she set it forth fairly and squarely without any weak ifs and ands and buts. She deserved gratitude, but it is an error to suppose she got it."

from Domestic Manners of the Americans
[THE MISSISSIPPI]

On the 4th of November, 1827, I sailed from London, accompanied by my son and two daughters; and after a favourable, though somewhat tedious voyage, arrived on Christmas-day at the mouth of the Mississippi.

The first indication of our approach to land was the appearance of this mighty river pouring forth its muddy mass of waters, and mingling with the deep blue of the Mexican Gulf. The shores of this river are so utterly flat, that no object upon them is perceptible at sea; and we gazed with pleasure on the muddy ocean that met us; for it told us we were arrived, and seven weeks of sailing had wearied us; yet it was not without a feeling like regret that we passed from the bright blue waves, whose varying aspect had so long furnished our chief amusement, into the murky stream which now received us.

Large flights of pelicans were seen standing upon the long masses of mud which rose above the surface of the waters, and a pilot came to guide us over the bar, long before any other indication of land was visible.

I never beheld a scene so utterly desolate as this entrance of the Mississippi. Had Dante seen it, he might have drawn images of another Bolgia from its horrors.[1] One only object rears itself above the eddying waters: this is the mast of a vessel long since wrecked in attempting to cross the bar; and it still stands, a dismal witness of the destruction that has been, and a boding prophet of that which is to come.

By degrees bulrushes of enormous growth become visible, and a few more miles of mud brought us within sight of a cluster of huts called the Balize, by far the most miserable station that I ever saw made the dwelling of man, but I was told that many families of pilots and fishermen lived there.

For several miles above its mouth, the Mississippi presents no objects more interesting than mud banks, monstrous bulrushes, and now and then a huge crocodile luxuriating in the slime. Another circumstance that gives to this dreary scene an aspect of desolation, is the incessant appearance of vast quantities of drift wood, which is

---

1. Malebolgia, the eighth circle of hell in Dante's *Inferno*, contains ten "bolgias," or ditches, where the worst sinners are punished.

ever finding its way to the different mouths of the Mississippi. Trees of enormous length, often bearing their branches, and still oftener their uptorn roots entire, the victims of the frequent hurricane, come floating down the stream. Sometimes several of these, entangled together, collect among their boughs a quantity of floating rubbish, that gives the mass the appearance of a moving island, bearing a forest, with its roots mocking the heavens; while the dishonoured branches lash the tide in idle vengeance: this, as it approaches the vessel, and glides swiftly past, looks like the fragment of a world in ruins. * * *

The gentlemen in the cabin (we had no ladies) would certainly, neither from their language, manners, nor appearance, have received that designation in Europe; but we soon found their claim to it rested on more substantial ground; for we heard them nearly all addressed by the titles of general, colonel, and major. On mentioning these military dignities to an English friend some time afterwards, he told me that he too had made the voyage with the same description of company, but remarking that there was not a single captain among them, he made the observation to a fellow-passenger, and asked how he accounted for it. "Oh, sir, the captains are all on deck" was the reply.

Our honours, however, were not all military; for we had a judge among us. I know it is equally easy and invidious to ridicule the peculiarities of appearance and manner in people of a different nation from ourselves; we may, too, at the same moment be undergoing the same ordeal in their estimation; and, moreover, I am by no means disposed to consider whatever is new to me as therefore objectionable; but, nevertheless, it was impossible not to feel repugnance to many of the novelties that now surrounded me.

The total want of all the usual courtesies of the table, the voracious rapidity with which the viands were seized and devoured; the strange uncouth phrases and pronunciation; the loathsome spitting, from the contamination of which it was absolutely impossible to protect our dresses; the frightful manner of feeding with their knives, till the whole blade seemed to enter into the mouth; and the still more frightful manner of cleaning the teeth afterwards with a pocket-knife, soon forced us to feel that we were not surrounded by the generals, colonels, and majors of the old world; and that the dinner-hour was to be anything rather than an hour of enjoyment. * * *

Among other sights of desolation which mark this region, condemned of Nature, the lurid glare of a burning forest was almost constantly visible after sunset; and when the wind so willed, the smoke arising from it floated in heavy vapour over our heads. Not all the novelty of the scene, not all its vastness, could prevent its heavy horror wearying the spirits. Perhaps the dinners and suppers I have described may help to account for this; but certain it is, that when we had wondered for a week at the ceaseless continuity of forest; had first admired, and then wearied of the festooned drapery of Spanish moss; when we had learned to distinguish the different masses of timber that passed us, or that we passed, as a "snag," a "log," or a "sawyer"; when we had finally made up our minds that the gentlemen of the Kentucky and Ohio military establishments were not of the same genus as those of the Tuileries and St James's,[2] we began to wish that we could sleep more hours away. As we advanced to the northward, we were no longer cheered by the beautiful border of palmettoes: and even the amusement of occasionally spying out a sleeping crocodile was over. * * *

2. Fashionable parks in Paris and London.

[SERVANTS]

The greatest difficulty in organising a family establishment in Ohio, is getting servants, or, as it is there called, "getting help"; for it is more than petty treason to the republic to call a free citizen a *servant*. The whole class of young women, whose bread depends upon their labour, are taught to believe that the most abject poverty is preferable to domestic service. Hundreds of half-naked girls work in the paper-mills, or in any other manufactory, for less than half the wages they would receive in service; but they think their equality is compromised by the latter, and nothing but the wish to obtain some particular article of finery will ever induce them to submit to it. A kind friend, however, exerted herself so effectually for me, that a tall stately lass soon presented herself, saying "I be come to help you." The intelligence was very agreeable, and I welcomed her in the most gracious manner possible, and asked what I should give her by the year.

"O Gimini!" exclaimed the damsel, with a loud laugh, "you be a downright Englisher, sure enough. I should like to see a young lady engage by the year in America! I hope I shall get a husband before many months, or I expect I shall be an outright old maid, for I be most seventeen already: besides, mayhap I may want to go to school. You must just give me a dollar and a half a week, and mother's slave Phillis must come over once a week, I expect, from t'other side the water, to help me clean."

I agreed to the bargain, of course with all dutiful submission; and seeing she was preparing to set to work in a yellow dress, *parsemé* [strewn] with red roses, I gently hinted, that I thought it was a pity to spoil so fine a gown, and that she had better change it.

"'Tis just my best and my worst" she answered; "for I've got no other."

And in truth I found that this young lady had left the paternal mansion with no more clothes of any kind than what she had on. I immediately gave her money to purchase what was necessary for cleanliness and decency, and set to work with my daughters to make her a gown. She grinned applause when our labour was completed; but never uttered the slightest expression of gratitude for that, or for any thing else we could do for her. She was constantly asking us to lend her different articles of dress, and when we declined it, she said: "Well, I never seed such grumpy folks as you be; there is several young ladies of my acquaintance what goes to live out now and then with the old women about the town, and they and their gurls always lends them what they asks for; I guess you English thinks we should poison your things, just as bad as if we was negurs." Here I beg to assure the reader, that whenever I give conversations, they were not made *à loisir* [at leisure], but were written down immediately after they occurred, with all the verbal fidelity my memory permitted.

This young lady left me at the end of two months; because I refused to lend her money enough to buy a silk dress to go to a ball, saying: "Then 'tis not worth my while to stay any longer." * * *

[SOCIETY]

Such being the difficulties respecting domestic arrangements, it is obvious, that the ladies who are brought up amongst them cannot have leisure for any great development of mind; it is, in fact, out of the question: and, remembering this, it is more surprising that some among them should be very pleasing, than that none should be highly instructed.

Had I passed as many evenings in company in any other town that I ever visited as I did in Cincinnati, I should have been able to give some little account of the conversations I had listened to; but, upon reading over my notes, and then taxing my memory to the utmost to supply the deficiency, I can scarcely find a trace of any thing that deserves the name. Such as I have, shall be given in their place. But, whatever may be the talents of the persons who meet together in society, the very shape, form, and arrangement of the meeting is sufficient to paralyse conversation. The women invariably herd together at one part of the room, and the men at the other; but, in justice to Cincinnati, I must acknowledge that this arrangement is by no means peculiar to that city, or to the western side of the Alleghanies. Sometimes a small attempt at music produces a partial re-union; a few of the most daring youths, animated by the consciousness of curled hair and smart waistcoats, approach the pianoforte, and begin to mutter a little to the half-grown pretty things, who are comparing with one another "how many quarters' music they have had." Where the mansion is of sufficient dignity to have two drawing-rooms, the piano, the little ladies, and the slender gentlemen, are left to themselves, and on such occasions the sound of laughter is often heard to issue from among them. But the fate of the more dignified personages, who are left in the other room, is extremely dismal. The gentlemen spit, talk of elections and the price of produce, and spit again. The ladies look at each other's dresses till they know every pin by heart; talk of Parson Somebody's last sermon on the day of judgment, on Dr. T'otherbody's new pills for dyspepsia, till the "tea" is announced, when they all console themselves together for whatever they may have suffered in keeping awake, by taking more tea, coffee, hot cake and custard, hoe cake, johnny cake, waffle cake, and dodger cake, pickled peaches and preserved cucumbers, ham, turkey, hung beef, apple-sauce, and pickled oysters, than ever were prepared in any other country of the known world. After this massive meal is over, they return to the drawing-room, and it always appeared to me that they remained together as long as they could bear it, and then they rise *en masse*, cloak, bonnet, shawl, and exit. * * *

[AMUSEMENT]

I never saw any people who appeared to live so much without amusement as the Cincinnatians. Billiards are forbidden by law, so are cards. To sell a pack of cards in Ohio subjects the seller to a penalty of fifty dollars. They have no public balls, excepting, I think, six, during the Christmas holidays. They have no concerts. They have no dinner-parties.

They have a theatre, which is, in fact, the only public amusement of this triste little town; but they seem to care little about it, and either from economy or distaste, it is very poorly attended. Ladies are rarely seen there, and by far the larger proportion of females deem it an offence against religion to witness the representation of a play. It is in the churches and chapels of the town that the ladies are to be seen in full costume: and I am tempted to believe that a stranger from the continent of Europe would be inclined, on first reconnoitring the city, to suppose that the places of worship were the theatres and cafés of the place. No evening in the week but brings throngs of the young and beautiful to the chapels and meeting-houses, all dressed with care, and sometimes with great pretension; it is there that all display is made, and all fashionable distinction sought. The proportion of gentlemen attending these evening meetings is very small, but often, as might be expected, a sprinkling of smart young clerks makes this sedulous display of ribbons and ringlets intelligible and natural. Were it not for the churches, indeed, I think there might be a general bonfire of best bonnets, for I never could discover any other use for them.

The ladies are too actively employed in the interior of their houses to permit much parading in full dress for morning visits. There are no public gardens or lounging shops of fashionable resort, and were it not for public worship, and private tea-drinkings, all the ladies in Cincinnati would be in danger of becoming perfect recluses.

The influence which the ministers of all the innumerable religious sects throughout America have on the females of their respective congregations, approaches very nearly to what we read of in Spain, or in other strictly Roman Catholic countries. There are many causes for this peculiar influence. Where equality of rank is affectedly acknowledged by the rich, and clamorously claimed by the poor, distinction and preeminence are allowed to the clergy only. This gives them high importance in the eyes of the ladies. I think, also, that it is from the clergy only that the women of America receive that sort of attention which is so dearly valued by every female heart throughout the world. With the priests of America the women hold that degree of influential importance which, in the countries of Europe, is allowed them throughout all orders and ranks of society, except, perhaps, the very lowest; and in return for this they seem to give their hearts and souls into their keeping. I never saw, or read of, any country where religion had so strong a hold upon the women, or a slighter hold upon the men. * * *

[SCHOOLS]

Cincinnati contains many schools, but of their rank or merit I had very little opportunity of judging; the only one which I visited was kept by Dr Lock, a gentleman who appears to have liberal and enlarged opinions on the subject of female education. Should his system produce practical results proportionably excellent, the ladies of Cincinnati will probably, some years hence, be much improved in their powers of companionship. I attended the annual public exhibition at this school, and perceived, with some surprise, that the higher branches of science were among the studies of the pretty creatures I saw assembled there. One lovely girl of sixteen *took her degree* in mathematics, and another was examined in moral philosophy. They blushed so sweetly, and looked so beautifully puzzled and confounded, that it might have been difficult for an abler judge than I was, to decide how far they merited the diplomas they received.

This method of letting young ladies graduate, and granting them diplomas on quitting the establishment, was quite new to me; at least, I do not remember to have heard of anything similar elsewhere. I should fear that the time allowed to the fair graduates of Cincinnati for the acquirement of these various branches of education, would seldom be sufficient to permit their reaching the eminence in each which their enlightened instructor anticipates. "A quarter's" mathematics, or "two quarters'" political economy, moral philosophy, algebra and quadratic equations, would seldom, I should think, enable the teacher and the scholar, by their joint efforts, to lay in such a stock of these sciences as would stand the wear and tear of half a score of children, and one help. * * *

[HOGS]

It seems hardly fair to quarrel with a place because its staple commodity is not pretty, but I am sure I should have liked Cincinnati much better if the people had not dealt so very largely in hogs. The immense quantity of business done in this line would hardly be believed by those who had not witnessed it. I never saw a newspaper without remarking such advertisements as the following:

> "Wanted, immediately, 4,000 fat hogs."
> "For sale, 2,000 barrels of prime pork."

But the annoyance came nearer than this; if I determined upon a walk up Main Street, the chances were five hundred to one against my reaching the shady side without brushing by a snout fresh dripping from the kennel; when we had screwed our courage to the enterprise of mounting a certain noble-looking sugarloaf hill, that promised pure air and a fine view, we found the brook we had to cross, at its foot, red with the stream from a pig slaughter-house; while our noses, instead of meeting "the thyme that loves the green hill's breast," were greeted by odours that I will not describe, and which I heartily hope my readers cannot imagine; our feet, that on leaving the city had expected to press the flowery sod, literally got entangled in pigs' tails and jaw-bones; and thus the prettiest walk in the neighbourhood was interdicted for ever. * * *

[LITERATURE]

On one occasion, but not at the house of Mr Flint,[3] I passed an evening in company with a gentleman, said to be a scholar, and a man of reading; he was also what is called a *serious* gentleman, and he appeared to have pleasure in feeling that his claim to distinction was acknowledged in both capacities. There was a very amiable *serious* lady in the company, to whom he seemed to trust for the development of his celestial pretensions, and to me he did the honour of addressing most of his terrestrial superiority. The difference between us was, that when he spoke to her, he spoke as to a being who, if not his equal, was at least deserving high distinction; and he gave her smiles, such as Michael might have vouchsafed to Eve.[4] To me he spoke as Paul to the offending Jews;[5] he did not, indeed, shake his raiment at me, but he used his pocket-handkerchief so as to answer the purpose; and if every sentence did not end with "I am clean," pronounced by his lips, his tone, his look, his action, fully supplied the deficiency.

Our poor Lord Byron,[6] as may be supposed, was the bull's-eye against which every dart in his black little quiver was aimed. I had never heard any serious gentleman talk of Lord Byron at full length before, and I listened attentively. It was evident that the noble passages which are graven on the hearts of the genuine lovers of poetry had altogether escaped the serious gentleman's attention; and it was equally evident that he knew by rote all those that they wish the mighty master had never written. I told him so, and I shall not soon forget the look he gave me.

Of other authors his knowledge was very imperfect, but his criticisms very amusing. Of Pope, he said: "He is so entirely gone by, that in *our* country it is considered quite fustian[7] to speak of him."

But I persevered, and named *The Rape of the Lock*[8] as evincing some little talent, and being in a tone that might still hope for admittance in the drawing-room; but, on

---

3. An acquaintance in Cincinnati whom she called "one of the most talented men I ever met."
4. In Milton's *Paradise Lost*, Book 11, God sends the archangel Michael to cast Adam and Eve out of Paradise. Michael softens the blow for Eve, sending "gentle Dreams" to calm her.
5. The apostle Paul "testified to the Jews that Jesus was Christ. And when they opposed themselves, and blasphemed, he shook his raiment, and said unto them, Your blood be upon your own heads; I am clean: from henceforth I will go unto the Gentiles" (Acts 18.5–6).
6. Byron first gained fame with *Childe Harold's Pilgrimage* (1812–1818), which included rhapsodic passages about the great cities and natural wonders of Europe. His descriptive set pieces were often memorized. But the brooding passion and hints of unspeakable sins that characterized some of his protagonists distressed many readers.
7. Pretentious and banal.
8. Pope's mock-heroic epic poem (1714).

the mention of this poem, the serious gentleman became almost as strongly agitated as when he talked of *Don Juan;* and I was unfeignedly at a loss to comprehend the nature of his feelings, till he muttered, with an indignant shake of the handkerchief: "The very title!"

At the name of Dryden he smiled, and the smile spoke as plainly as a smile could speak "How the old woman twaddles!"

"We only know Dryden by quotations, madam, and these, indeed, are found only in books that have long since had their day."

"And Shakspeare, sir?"

"Shakspeare, madam, is obscene, and, thank God, we are sufficiently advanced to have found it out! If we must have the abomination of stage plays, let them at least be marked by the refinement of the age in which we live."[9]

This was certainly being *au courant du jour* [up-to-date].

Of Massinger he knew nothing. Of Ford he had never heard. Gray had had his day. Prior he had never read, but understood he was a very childish writer.[1] Chaucer and Spenser he tied in a couple, and dismissed by saying, that he thought it was neither more nor less than affectation to talk of authors who wrote in a tongue no longer intelligible.

This was the most literary conversation I was ever present at in Cincinnati.

1832

━✦═✦✦═✦━

Thomas Babington Macaulay
1800–1859

Historian, poet, and politician, Thomas Babington Macaulay devoted his immense oratorical and literary talents to demonstrating the superiority of English culture and institutions. His works, including a best-selling *History of England*, proved so popular that Lord Acton called them "a key to half the prejudices of our age." Yet the most influential of Macaulay's writings may have been the short position papers or "minutes" that he prepared as a member of the Supreme Council of India, a government body that was part of the transfer of colonial power from the privately run East India Company to the British crown. Macaulay spent four years in India, from 1834 to 1838, during which he studied the legal and educational systems. The reforms he backed included freedom of the press, the equality of Indians and Europeans under law, and the creation of a British-influenced method of national education.

The *Minute on Indian Education* was prompted by a fierce battle over how to interpret an 1813 act of Parliament that provided funds for "the revival and promotion of literature and the encouragement of the learned natives of India, and for the introduction and promotion of a knowledge of the sciences among the inhabitants of British territories." The "Orientalist" party wanted the government to maintain its current policy of aiding students to study Sanskrit and Arabic in institutions of higher learning. But Macaulay sided with the "Anglicists" (some of whom were Indians), claiming that "of all foreign tongues, the English tongue is that which would be the most useful to our native subjects." Persuaded by Macaulay, the governor-

9. Shakespeare's language was often regarded as too vulgar; in 1818 Thomas Bowdler published his *Family Shakespeare,* a popular expurgated version that removed language he considered coarse or improper. Trollope was frequently astonished by the prudery and puritanism of Americans. 1. Philip Massinger (1583–1640) and John Ford (1586–c. 1639), Jacobean playwrights; Thomas Gray (1716–1771) and Matthew Prior (1664–1721), English poets.

general, Lord William Bentinck, adopted policies in line with the Anglicist position. Today India has the third largest English-speaking population in the world, an estimated thirty million people, and similar debates about the value—or tyranny—of English as a "global language" continue across the planet.

For more about Macaulay, see Perspectives: The Industrial Landscape, page 1141, and Perspectives: Religion and Science, page 1377.

from Minute on Indian Education

* * * A sum is set apart "for the revival and promotion of literature and the encouragement of the learned natives of India, and for the introduction and promotion of a knowledge of the sciences among the inhabitants of the British territories." It is argued, or rather taken for granted, that by literature the Parliament can have only meant Arabic and Sanscrit literature, that they never would have given the honourable appellation of a "learned native" to a native who was familiar with the poetry of Milton, the metaphysics of Locke, and the physics of Newton; but that they meant to designate by that name only such persons as might have studied in the sacred books of the Hindoos all the usages of cusa-grass, and all the mysteries of absorption into the Deity. This does not appear to be a very satisfactory interpretation. To take a parallel case; suppose that the Pacha of Egypt, a country once superior in knowledge to the nations of Europe, but now sunk far below them, were to appropriate a sum for the purpose of "reviving and promoting literature, and encouraging learned natives of Egypt," would anybody infer that he meant the youth of his pachalic to give years to the study of hieroglyphics, to search into all the doctrines disguised under the fable of Osiris, and to ascertain with all possible accuracy the ritual with which cats and onions were anciently adored? Would he be justly charged with inconsistency, if, instead of employing his young subjects in deciphering obelisks, he were to order them to be instructed in the English and French languages, and in all the sciences to which those languages are the chief keys?

* * *

* * * We have a fund to be employed as Government shall direct for the intellectual improvement of the people of this country. The simple question is, what is the most useful way of employing it?

All parties seem to be agreed on one point, that the dialects commonly spoken among the natives of this part of India contain neither Literary nor scientific information, and are, moreover so poor and rude that, until they are enriched from some other quarter, it will not be easy to translate any valuable work into them. It seems to be admitted on all sides that the intellectual improvement of those classes of the people who have the means of pursuing higher studies can at present be effected only by means of some language not vernacular amongst them.

What, then, shall that language be? One half of the Committee maintain that it should be the English. The other half strongly recommend the Arabic and Sanscrit. The whole question seems to me to be, which language is the best worth knowing?

I have no knowledge of either Sanscrit or Arabic.—But I have done what I could to form a correct estimate of their value. I have read translations of the most celebrated Arabic and Sanscrit works. I have conversed both here and at home with men distinguished by their proficiency in the Eastern tongues. I am quite ready to take the Oriental learning at the valuation of the Orientalists themselves. I have never found one among them who could deny that a single shelf of a good European library was worth the whole native literature of India and Arabia. The intrinsic superiority of the Western literature is, indeed, fully admitted by those members of the Committee who support the Oriental plan of education.

It will hardly be disputed, I suppose, that the department of literature in which the Eastern writers stand highest is poetry. And I certainly never met with any Orientalist who ventured to maintain that the Arabic and Sanscrit poetry could be compared to that of the great European nations. But, when we pass from works of imagination to works in which facts are recorded and general principles investigated, the superiority of the Europeans becomes absolutely immeasurable. It is, I believe, no exaggeration to say, that all the historical information which has been collected from all the books written in the Sanscrit language is less valuable than what may be found in the most paltry abridgments used at preparatory schools in England. In every branch of physical or moral philosophy the relative position of the two nations is nearly the same.

How, then, stands the case? We have to educate a people who cannot at present be educated by means of their mother-tongue. We must teach them some foreign language. The claims of our own language it is hardly necessary to recapitulate. It stands preeminent even among the languages of the West. It abounds with works of imagination not inferior to the noblest which Greece has bequeathed to us; with models of every species of eloquence; with historical compositions, which, considered merely as narratives, have seldom been surpassed, and which, considered as vehicles of ethical and political instruction, have never been equalled; with just and lively representations of human life and human nature; with the most profound speculations on metaphysics, morals, government, jurisprudence, and trade; with full and correct information respecting every experimental science which tends to preserve the health, to increase the comfort, or to expand the intellect of man. Whoever knows that language, has ready access to all the vast intellectual wealth, which all the wisest nations of the earth have created and hoarded in the course of ninety generations. It may safely be said that the literature now extant in that language is of far greater value than all the literature which three hundred years ago was extant in all the languages of the world together. Nor is this all. In India, English is the language spoken by the ruling class. It is spoken by the higher class of natives at the seats of Government. It is likely to become the language of commerce throughout the seas of the East. It is the language of two great European communities which are rising, the one in the south of Africa, the other in Australasia; communities which are every year becoming more important, and more closely connected with our Indian empire. Whether we look at the intrinsic value of our literature, or at the particular situation of this country, we shall see the strongest reason to think that, of all foreign tongues, the English tongue is that which would be the most useful to our native subjects.

The question now before us is simply whether, when it is in our power to teach this language, we shall teach languages in which, by universal confession, there are no books on any subject which deserve to be compared to our own; whether, when we can teach European science, we shall teach systems which, by universal confession, whenever they differ from those of Europe, differ for the worse; and whether, when we can patronise sound Philosophy and true History, we shall countenance, at the public expense, medical doctrines which would disgrace an English Farrier[1]—Astronomy, which would move laughter in girls at an English boarding school—History, abounding with kings thirty feet high, and reigns thirty thousand years long—and Geography, made up of seas of treacle and seas of butter.

1. Blacksmith.

We are not without experience to guide us. History furnishes several analogous cases, and they all teach the same lesson. There are in modern times, to go no further, two memorable instances of a great impulse given to the mind of a whole society—of prejudices overthrown—of knowledge diffused—of taste purified—of arts and sciences planted in countries which had recently been ignorant and barbarous.

The first instance to which I refer is the great revival of letters among the Western nations at the close of the fifteenth and the beginning of the sixteenth century. At that time almost everything that was worth reading was contained in the writings of the ancient Greeks and Romans. Had our ancestors acted as the Committee of Public Instruction has hitherto acted; had they neglected the language of Cicero and Tacitus;[2] had they confined their attention to the old dialects of our own island; had they printed nothing and taught nothing at the universities but Chronicles in Anglo-Saxon and Romances in Norman-French, would England have been what she now is? What the Greek and Latin were to the contemporaries of More and Ascham,[3] our tongue is to the people of India. The literature of England is now more valuable than that of classical antiquity. I doubt whether the Sanscrit literature be as valuable as that of our Saxon and Norman progenitors. In some departments—in History, for example—I am certain that it is much less so.

Another instance may be said to be still before our eyes. Within the last hundred and twenty years, a nation which had previously been in a state as barbarous as that in which our ancestors were before the Crusades, has gradually emerged from the ignorance in which it was sunk, and has taken its place among civilised communities—I speak of Russia. There is now in that country a large educated class, abounding with persons fit to serve the state in the highest functions, and in nowise inferior to the most accomplished men who adorn the best circles of Paris and London. There is reason to hope that this vast empire, which in the time of our grandfathers was probably behind the Punjab,[4] may, in the time of our grandchildren, be pressing close on France and Britain in the career of improvement. And how was this change effected? Not by flattering national prejudices; not by feeding the mind of the young Muscovite[5] with the old woman's stories which his rude fathers had believed: not by filling his head with lying legends about St. Nicholas:[6] not by encouraging him to study the great question, whether the world was or was not created on the 13th of September: not by calling him "a learned native," when he has mastered all these points of knowledge: but by teaching him those foreign languages in which the greatest mass of information had been laid up, and thus putting all that information within his reach. The languages of Western Europe civilized Russia. I cannot doubt that they will do for the Hindoo what they have done for the Tartar.[7]

* * *

* * * It is said that the Sanscrit and Arabic are the languages in which the sacred books of a hundred millions of people are written, and that they are, on that account, entitled to peculiar encouragement. Assuredly it is the duty of the British Government in India to be not only tolerant, but neutral on all religious questions. But to encourage the study of a literature admitted to be of small intrinsic value only because that literature inculcates the most serious errors on the most important

---

2. Latin.
3. Sir Thomas More (1478–1535) and Roger Ascham (1515–1568), English humanist scholars.
4. Region in the northwest Indian subcontinent.
5. Native of Moscow.

6. The patron saint of Russia.
7. Purportedly savage Central Asian; the Tartars originally made up the army of Genghis Khan but were later incorporated into the Russian Empire.

subjects, is a course hardly reconcilable with reason, with morality, or even with that very neutrality which ought, as we all agree, to be sacredly preserved. It is confessed that a language is barren of useful knowledge. We are told to teach it because it is fruitful of monstrous superstitions. We are to teach false history, false astronomy, false medicine, because we find them in company with a false religion. We abstain, and I trust shall always abstain, from giving any public encouragement to those who are engaged in the work of converting natives to Christianity. And, while we act thus, can we reasonably and decently bribe men out of the revenues of the state to waste their youth in learning how they are to purify themselves after touching an ass, or what text of the Vedas[8] they are to repeat to expiate the crime of killing a goat?

It is taken for granted by the advocates of Oriental learning that no native of this country can possibly attain more than a mere smattering of English. They do not attempt to prove this; but they perpetually insinuate it. They designate the education which their opponents recommend as a mere spelling-book education. They assume it as undeniable, that the question is between a profound knowledge of Hindoo and Arabian literature and science on the one side, and a superficial knowledge of the rudiments of English on the other. This is not merely an assumption, but an assumption contrary to all reason and experience. We know that foreigners of all nations do learn our language sufficiently to have access to all the most abstruse knowledge which it contains, sufficiently to relish even the more delicate graces of our most idiomatic writers. There are in this very town natives who are quite competent to discuss political or scientific questions with fluency and precision in the English language. I have heard the very question on which I am now writing discussed by native gentlemen with a liberality and an intelligence which would do credit to any member of the Committee of Public Instruction. Indeed, it is unusual to find, even in the literary circles of the continent, any foreigner who can express himself in English with so much facility and correctness as we find in many Hindoos. Nobody, I suppose, will contend that English is so difficult to a Hindoo as Greek to an Englishman. Yet an intelligent English youth, in a much smaller number of years than our unfortunate pupils pass at the Sanscrit college, becomes able to read, to enjoy, and even to imitate, not unhappily, the composition of the best Greek authors. Less than half the time which enables an English youth to read Herodotus and Sophocles ought to enable a Hindoo to read Hume and Milton.

To sum up what I have said: I think it clear that we are not fettered by the Act of Parliament of 1813; that we are not fettered by any pledge expressed or implied; that we are free to employ our funds as we choose; that we ought to employ them in teaching what is best worth knowing; that English is better worth knowing than Sanscrit or Arabic; that the natives are desirous to be taught English, and are not desirous to be taught Sanscrit or Arabic; that neither as the languages of law, nor as the languages of religion, have the Sanscrit and Arabic any peculiar claim to our encouragement; that it is possible to make natives of this country thoroughly good English scholars, and that to this end our efforts ought to be directed.

In one point I fully agree with the gentlemen to whose general views I am opposed. I feel, with them, that it is impossible for us, with our limited means, to attempt to educate the body of the people. We must at present do our best to form a class who may be interpreters between us and the millions whom we govern; a class of persons, Indian in blood and colour, but English in taste, in opinions, in morals, and in intellect. To that class we may leave it to refine the vernacular dialects of the country, to enrich those dialects with terms of science borrowed from the Western

8. Collection of sacred Hindu texts written in Sanskrit.

nomenclature, and to render them by degrees fit vehicles for conveying knowledge to the great mass of the population.

1835

━━ ≠≡ ━━

Alexander William Kinglake
1809–1891

Eothen (1844) is the story of a lighthearted romp through the Near East, a pleasure trip in which the prosperous young Kinglake indulged himself after graduating from Cambridge, before settling down to a long and respectable law career. He addressed the book—written ten years after the journey—to his friend Eliot Warburton, who was planning a similar trip. Kinglake's intimate and breezy style made his book an instant success. The contemporary travel writer Jan Morris calls it "one of the most original, graceful, and creative of all travel books, which has cast a sort of spell over the *genre* from that day to this."

from Eothen[1]
[The Self-Conscious Traveller]

It is right to forewarn people * * * that the book is quite superficial in its character. I have endeavoured to discard from it all valuable matter derived from the works of others, and it appears to me that my efforts in this direction have been attended with great success; I believe I may truly acknowledge, that from all details of geographical discovery, or antiquarian research—from all display of "sound learning, and religious knowledge"—from all historical and scientific illustrations—from all useful statistics—from all political disquisitions—and from all good moral reflections, the volume is thoroughly free.

My excuse for the book is its truth: you and I know a man, fond of hazarding elaborate jokes, who, whenever a story of his happens not to go down as wit, will evade the awkwardness of the failure, by bravely maintaining that all he has said is pure fact. I can honestly take this decent though humble mode of escape. My narrative is not merely righteous in matters of fact (where fact is in question), but it is true in this larger sense—it conveys, not those impressions which *ought to have been* produced upon any "well constituted mind," but those which were really and truly received at the time of his rambles, by a headstrong and not very amiable traveller, whose prejudices in favour of other people's notions were then exceedingly slight. As I have felt so I have written; and the result is, that there will often be found in my narrative a jarring discord between the associations properly belonging to interesting sites, and the tone in which I speak of them. This seemingly perverse mode of treating the subject is forced upon me by my plan of adhering to sentimental truth, and really does not result from any impertinent wish to tease or trifle with readers. I ought, for instance, to have felt as strongly in Judaea, as in Galilee,[2] but it was not so in fact: the religious sentiment (born in solitude) which had heated my brain in the Sanctuary of Nazareth was rudely chilled at the foot of Zion,[3] by disenchanting

---

1. "*Eothen*" is, I hope, almost the only hard word to be found in the book; it ... signifies "from the early dawn",—"from the East" [Kinglake's footnote].
2. Judaea was the southern part of Israel; Galilee, in the north, is where Jesus grew up.

3. The Sanctuary is the church built in Nazareth in 356 on the spot where the Virgin Mary was supposed to have received the Annunciation; Zion is one of the hills in Jerusalem.

scenes, and this change is accordingly disclosed by the perfectly worldly tone in which I speak of Jerusalem and Bethlehem.

My notion of dwelling precisely upon those matters which happened to interest me, and upon none other, would of course be intolerable in a regular book of travels. If I had been passing through countries not previously explored, it would have been sadly perverse to withhold careful descriptions of admirable objects, merely because my own feelings of interest in them may have happened to flag; but where the countries which one visits have been thoroughly and ably described, and even artistically illustrated by others, one is fully at liberty to say as little (though not quite so much) as one chooses. Now a traveller is a creature not always looking at sights—he remembers (how often!) the happy land of his birth—he has, too, his moments of humble enthusiasm about fire, and food—about shade, and drink; and if he gives to these feelings anything like the prominence which really belonged to them at the time of his travelling, he will not seem a very good teacher; once having determined to write the sheer truth concerning the things which chiefly have interested him, he must, and he will, sing a sadly long strain about Self; he will talk for whole pages together about his bivouac fire, and ruin the Ruins of Baalbec[4] with eight or ten cold lines.

But it seems to me that this egotism of a traveller, however incessant—however shameless and obtrusive, must still convey some true ideas of the country through which he has passed. His very selfishness—his habit of referring the whole external world to his own sensations, compels him, as it were, in his writings, to observe the laws of perspective;—he tells you of objects, not as he knows them to be, but as they seemed to him. The people, and the things that most concern him personally, however mean and insignificant, take large proportions in his picture, because they stand so near to him. He shows you his Dragoman,[5] and the gaunt features of his Arabs—his tent—his kneeling camels—his baggage strewed upon the sand:—but the proper wonders of the land—the cities—the mighty ruins and monuments of bygone ages, he throws back faintly in the distance. It is thus that he felt, and thus he strives to repeat, the scenes of the Elder World. You may listen to him for ever without learning much in the way of Statistics; but, perhaps, if you bear with him long enough, you may find yourself slowly and faintly impressed with the realities of Eastern Travel.

* * *

[CEREMONIAL VISITS]

Yet, unless you can contrive to learn a little of the language, you will be rather bored by your visits of ceremony; the intervention of the Dragoman is fatal to the spirit of conversation. I think I should mislead you if I were to attempt to give the substance of any particular conversation with Orientals. A traveller may write and say that, "the Pasha[6] of So-and-So was particularly interested in the vast progress which has been made in the application of steam, and appeared to understand the structure of our machinery—that he remarked upon the gigantic results of our manufacturing industry—showed that he possessed considerable knowledge of our Indian affairs, and of the constitution of the Company, and expressed a lively admiration of the many sterling qualities for which the people of England are distinguished." But

4. Site of an ancient city in Lebanon, where the Phoenicians built a temple to the sun-god Baal.
5. Interpreter and guide.

6. High-ranking Turkish official, usually the governor of a province or a military commander.

the heap of commonplaces thus quietly attributed to the Pasha will have been founded perhaps on some such talking as this:—

PASHA. The Englishman is welcome; most blessed among hours is this, the hour of his coming.

DRAGOMAN (to the Traveller). The Pasha pays you his compliments.

TRAVELLER. Give him my best compliments in return, and say I'm delighted to have the honour of seeing him.

DRAGOMAN (to the Pasha). His Lordship, this Englishman, Lord of London, Scorner of Ireland, Suppressor of France, has quitted his governments, and left his enemies to breathe for a moment, and has crossed the broad waters in strict disguise, with a small but eternally faithful retinue of followers, in order that he might look upon the bright countenance of the Pasha among Pashas—the Pasha of the everlasting Pashalik of Karagholookoldour.

TRAVELLER (to his Dragoman). What on earth have you been saying about London? The Pasha will be taking me for a mere cockney. Have not I told you *always* to say, that I am from a branch of the family of Mudcombe Park, and that I am to be a magistrate for the county of Bedfordshire, only I've not qualified, and that I should have been a Deputy-Lieutenant, if it had not been for the extraordinary conduct of Lord Mountpromise, and that I was a candidate for Boughton-Soldborough at the last election, and that I should have won easy if my committee had not been bribed. I wish to heaven that if you *do* say any thing about me, you'd tell the simple truth.

DRAGOMAN —[is silent].

PASHA. What says the friendly Lord of London? is there aught that I can grant him within the Pashalik of Karagholookoldour?

DRAGOMAN (growing sulky and literal). This friendly Englishman—this branch of Mudcombe—this head purveyor of Boughton-Soldborough—this possible policeman of Bedfordshire is recounting his achievements and the number of his titles.

PASHA. The end of his honours is more distant than the ends of the earth, and the catalogue of his glorious deeds is brighter than the firmament of heaven!

DRAGOMAN (to the Traveller). The Pasha congratulates your Excellency.

TRAVELLER. About Boughton-Soldborough? The deuce he does!* * *

[CONSTANTINOPLE]

All the while that I stayed at Constantinople the plague was prevailing, but not with any violence; its presence, however, lent a mysterious and exciting, though not very pleasant, interest to my first knowledge of a great oriental city; it gave tone and colour to all I saw and all I felt—a tone and a colour sombre enough, but true, and well befitting the dreary monuments of past power and splendour. With all that is most truly oriental in its character the plague is associated: it dwells with the faithful in the holiest quarters of their city. The coats and the hats of Pera[7] are held to be nearly as innocent of infection as they are ugly in shape and fashion; but the rich furs and the costly shawls, the broidered slippers and the gold-laden saddle-cloths—the fragrance of burning aloes and the rich aroma of patchouli[8]—these are the signs that mark the familiar home of plague. You go out from your queenly London—the centre of the greatest and strongest amongst all earthly dominions—you go out thence, and

---

7. Pera was a suburb of Constantinople inhabited by Europeans; it was divided from the rest of the city by the Golden Horn, a narrow inlet of the Bosporous.
8. Heavy perfume.

travel on to the capital of an Eastern Prince—you find but a waning power, and a faded splendour, that inclines you to laugh and mock; but let the infernal Angel of Plague be at hand, and he, more mighty than armies, more terrible than Suleyman[9] in his glory, can restore such pomp and majesty to the weakness of the imperial city, that if, *when HE is there*, you must still go prying amongst the shades of this dead empire, at least you will tread the path with seemly reverence and awe.

It is the firm faith of almost all the Europeans living in the East, that plague is conveyed by the touch of infected substances, and that the deadly atoms especially lurk in all kinds of clothes and furs: it is held safer to breathe the same air with a man sick of the plague, and even to come into contact with his skin, than to be touched by the smallest particle of woollen or of thread which may have been within the reach of possible infection. If this be a right notion, the spread of the malady must be materially aided by the observance of a custom prevailing amongst the people of Stamboul.[1] It is this: when an Osmanlee[2] dies, one of his dresses is cut up, and a small piece of it is sent to each of his friends as a memorial of the departed—a fatal present, according to the opinion of the Franks,[3] for it too often forces the living not merely to remember the dead man, but to follow and bear him company.

The Europeans during the prevalence of the plague, if they are forced to venture into the streets, will carefully avoid the touch of every human being whom they pass: their conduct in this respect shows them strongly in contrast with the "true believers." The Moslem stalks on serenely, as though he were under the eye of his God, and were "equal to either fate." The Franks go crouching, and slinking from death, and some (those chiefly of French extraction) will fondly strive to fence out Destiny with shining capes of oilskin!

For some time you may manage by great care to thread your way through the streets of Stamboul without incurring contact; for the Turks, though scornful of the terrors felt by the Franks, are generally very courteous in yielding to that which they hold to be a useless and impious precaution, and will let you pass safe, if they can. It is impossible, however, that your immunity can last for any length of time, if you move about much through the narrow streets and lanes of a crowded city.

As for me, I soon got "compromised." After one day of rest the prayers of my hostess began to lose their power of keeping me from the pestilent side of the Golden Horn.[4] Faithfully promising to shun the touch of all imaginable substances, however enticing, I set off very cautiously, and held my way uncompromised till I reached the water's edge; but before my caïque[5] was quite ready, some rueful-looking fellows came rapidly shambling down the steps with a plague-stricken corpse, which they were going to bury amongst the faithful on the other side of the water. I contrived to be so much in the way of this brisk funeral, that I was not only touched by the men bearing the body, but also, I believe, by the foot of the dead man, as it hung lolling out of the bier. The accident gave me such a strong interest in denying the soundness of the contagion theory that I did in fact deny and repudiate it altogether: and from that time, acting upon my own convenient view of the matter, I went wherever I chose, without taking any serious pains to avoid a touch. It seems to me now very likely the Europeans are right, and that the plague may be really conveyed by contagion; but

9. Suleiman the Magnificent, head of the Ottoman Empire 1520–1566.
1. Istanbul, formerly Constantinople.
2. Turk.
3. Europeans.
4. I.e., could not persuade him to stay in Pera rather than venture across the water to see the rest of the city.
5. Light boat.

during the whole time of my remaining in the East my views on this subject more nearly approached to those of the fatalists; and so, when afterwards the plague of Egypt came dealing his blows around me, I was able to live amongst the dying without that alarm and anxiety which would inevitably have pressed upon my mind, if I had allowed myself to believe that every passing touch was really a probable death-stroke.

And perhaps as you make your difficult way through a steep and narrow alley, shut in between blank walls, and little frequented by passers, you meet one of those coffin-shaped bundles of white linen that implies an Ottoman lady. Painfully struggling against the obstacles to progression interposed by the many folds of her clumsy drapery, by her big mud boots, and especially by her two pairs of slippers, she works her way on full awkwardly enough, but yet there is something of womanly consciousness in the very labour and effort with which she tugs and lifts the burden of her charms: she is closely followed by her women slaves. Of her very self you see nothing, except the dark, luminous eyes that stare against your face, and the tips of the painted fingers depending like rosebuds from out of the blank bastions of the fortress. She turns, and turns again, and carefully glances around her on all sides, to see that she is safe from the eyes of Mussulmans, and then suddenly withdrawing the yashmak,[6] she shines upon your heart and soul with all the pomp and might of her beauty. And this, it is not the light, changeful grace that leaves you to doubt whether you have fallen in love with a body, or only a soul; it is the beauty that dwells secure in the perfectness of hard, downright outlines, and in the glow of generous colour. There is fire, though, too—high courage, and fire enough in the untamed mind, or spirit, or whatever it is which drives the breath of pride through those scarcely parted lips.

You smile at pretty women—you turn pale before the beauty that is great enough to have dominion over you. She sees, and exults in your giddiness; she sees and smiles; then, presently, with a sudden movement, she lays her blushing fingers upon your arm, and cries out "Yumourdjak!" (Plague! meaning, "there is a present of the plague for you!") This is her notion of a witticism: it is a very old piece of fun, no doubt—quite an oriental Joe Miller;[7] but the Turks are fondly attached not only to the institutions, but also to the jokes of their ancestors; so, the lady's silvery laugh rings joyously in your ears, and the mirth of her women is boisterous and fresh, as though the bright idea of giving the plague to a Christian had newly lit upon the earth. * * *

[TROY]

It was not the recollection of school nor college learning, but the rapturous and earnest reading of my childhood which made me bend forward so longingly to the plains of Troy.

Away from our people and our horses, Methley[8] and I went loitering along, by the willowy banks of a stream that crept in quietness through the low, even plain. There was no stir of weather over-head—no sound of rural labour—no sign of life in the land, but all the earth was dead and still, as though it had lain for thrice a thousand years under the leaden gloom of one unbroken sabbath.

6. Thick veil worn by Muslim women; it covers the entire face except for the eyes.
7. Old joke; *Joe Miller's Jests* was published in 1739.

8. John Savile, Lord Pollington (1809–1860)—called "Methley" after the name of his estate—Kinglake's companion during the early part of his travels.

Softly and sadly the poor, dumb, patient stream went winding, and winding along, through its shifting pathway; in some places its waters were parted, and then again, lower down, they would meet once more. I could see that the stream from year to year was finding itself new channels, and flowed no longer in its ancient track, but I knew that the springs which fed it were high on Ida—the springs of Simois and Scamander![9]

It was coldly, and thanklessly, and with vacant unsatisfied eyes that I watched the slow coming, and the gliding away, of the waters. I tell myself now, as a profane fact, that I did indeed stand by that river (Methley gathered some seeds from the bushes that grew there), but, since that I am away from his banks, "divine Scamander" has recovered the proper mystery belonging to him as an unseen deity; a kind of indistinctness, like that which belongs to far antiquity, has spread itself over my memory of the winding stream that I saw with these very eyes. One's mind regains in absence that dominion over earthly things which has been shaken by the rude contact; you force yourself hardily into the material presence of a mountain or a river, whose name belongs to poetry and ancient religion, rather than to the external world; your feelings, wound up and kept ready for some sort of half-expected rapture, are chilled and borne down for the time under all this load of real earth and water, but, let these once pass out of sight, and then again the old fanciful notions are restored, and the mere realities which you have just been looking at are thrown back so far into distance, that the very event of your intrusion upon such scenes begins to look dim and uncertain as though it belonged to mythology. * * *

[GALILEE]

I passed by Cana, and the house of the marriage feast prolonged by miraculous wine; I came to the field in which our Saviour had rebuked the Scotch Sabbath-keepers of that period, by suffering his disciples to pluck corn on the Lord's day; I rode over the ground where the fainting multitude had been fed, and they showed me some massive fragments—the relics (they said) of that wondrous banquet, now turned into stone.[1] The petrifaction was most complete.

I ascended the height where our Lord was standing when he wrought the miracle. The hill rose lofty enough to show me the fairness of the land on all sides; but I have an ancient love for the mere features of a lake, and so, forgetting all else when I reached the summit, I looked away eagerly to the eastward. There she lay, the Sea of Galilee. Less stern than Wastwater—less fair than gentle Windermere—she had still the winning ways of an English lake:[2] she caught from the smiling heavens unceasing light and changeful phases of beauty; and with all this brightness on her face, she yet clung fondly to the dull he-looking mountain at her side, as though she would

> Soothe him with her finer fancies,
> Touch him with her lighter thought.[3]

---

9. Zeus watched the Trojan War from the summit of Mount Ida. The Simois is a tributary of the River Scamander. When the Trojans fled the wrath of Achilles in Homer's *Iliad,* the river-god Scamander tried to protect them.
1. References to various Gospel stories: Jesus performed the miracle of changing water into wine for a wedding feast in Cana; he allowed his disciples to pluck grain on the Sabbath, even though work was forbidden; and he fed a crowd of five thousand with five loaves and two fishes.
2. Thoughts of the English Lake District distract Kinglake from contemplating the Sea of Galilee, where Jesus met his first two disciples, the fishermen Peter and Andrew (Matthew 4.18, Mark 1.16).
3. Adapted from Tennyson's *Locksley Hall* (line 54).

If one might judge of men's real thoughts by their writings, it would seem that there are people who can visit an interesting locality, and follow up continuously the exact train of thought that ought to be suggested by the historical associations of the place. A person of this sort can go to Athens, and think of nothing later than the age of Pericles—can live with the Scipios as long as he stays in Rome.[4] I am not thus docile: it is only by snatches, and for few moments together, that I can really associate a place with its proper history.

"There at Tiberias,[5] and along this western shore towards the North, and upon the bosom too of the lake, our Saviour and his disciples———" Away flew those recollections, and my mind strained eastward, because that that farthest shore was the end of the world that belongs to man the dweller—the beginning of the other and veiled world that is held by the strange race, whose life (like the pastime of Satan) is a "going to and fro upon the face of the earth."[6] From those grey hills right away to the gates of Bagdad stretched forth the mysterious "Desert"—not a pale, void, sandy tract, but a land abounding in rich pastures—a land without cities or towns, without any "respectable" people, or any "respectable" things, yet yielding its eighty thousand cavalry to the beck of a few old men. But once more—"Tiberias—the plain of Gennesareth—the very earth on which I stood—that the deep, low tones of the Saviour's voice should have gone forth into Eternity from out of the midst of these hills and these valleys!"—Ay, ay, but yet again the calm face of the lake was uplifted, and smiled upon my eyes with such familiar gaze that the "deep low tones" were hushed— the listening multitudes all passed away, and instead there came to me a loving thought from over the seas in England—a thought more sweet than Gospel to a wilful mortal like this. * * *

[ON THE BANKS OF JORDAN]

If a man, and an Englishman, be not born of his mother with a Chiffney-bit in his mouth,[7] there comes to him a time for loathing the wearisome ways of society—a time for not liking tamed people—a time for not sitting in pews—a time for impugning the foregone opinions of men, and haughtily dividing truth from falsehood—a time, in short, for questioning, scoffing, and railing—for speaking lightly of the very opera, and all our most cherished institutions. It is from nineteen to two or three and twenty, perhaps, that this war of the man against men is like to be waged most sullenly. You are yet in this smiling England, but you find yourself bending your way to the dark sides of her mountains,—climbing the dizzy crags,—exulting in the fellowship of mists and clouds, and watching the storms how they gather, or proving the mettle of your mare upon the broad and dreary downs, because that you feel congenially with the yet unparcelled earth. A little while you are free, and unlabelled, like the ground that you compass; but Civilization is watching to throw her lasso; you will be surely enclosed, and sooner or later brought down to a state of mere usefulness— your grey hills will be curiously sliced into acres, and roods, and perches, and you, for all you sit so wilful in your saddle, you will be caught—you will be taken up from travel, as a colt from grass, to be trained, and tried, and matched, and run. This in time; but first come continental tours, and the moody longing for eastern travel: the

4. Pericles (c. 495–429 B.C.), statesman during the peak of Athenian greatness; Scipio Africanus (237–183 B.C.), known as Scipio the Elder, and his son (known as Scipio the Younger), were Roman generals.
5. City on the western shore of the Sea of Galilee.
6. Job 2.2.
7. A bit for a horse's bridle—i.e., if a man is not born already tamed.

downs and the moors of England can hold you no longer; with larger stride you burst away from these slips and patches of free land—you thread your path through the crowds of Europe, and at last, on the banks of Jordan, you joyfully know that you are upon the very frontier of all accustomed respectabilities. There, on the other side of the river (you can swim it with one arm), there reigns the people that will be like to put you to death, for *not* being a vagrant, for *not* being a robber, for *not* being armed and houseless. There is comfort in that—health, comfort, and strength to one who is aching from very weariness of that poor, dear, middle-aged, deserving, accomplished, pedantic, and pains-taking governess, Europe.

1844

—+——≡♦≡——+—

Sir Richard Francis Burton
1821–1890

The archetypal Victorian explorer, Richard Burton was a gifted linguist fluent in two dozen languages, including Arabic and Persian. In 1853 he undertook a daring and controversial journey to visit the holy cities of Mecca and Medina, forbidden to non-Muslims. Burton disguised himself as an Afghani doctor, spent two months in Cairo perfecting the role, then set forth with a group of genuine pilgrims, none of whom penetrated his disguise. He was an unorthodox and restless adventurer, whose later exploits included searching for the source of the Nile, discovering Lake Tanganyika, and translating *The Arabian Nights* in a scandalously frank manner. After his death, his widow burned many of his papers in an effort to sanitize his reputation.

from A Personal Narrative of a Pilgrimage to El-Medinah and Meccah
[AMBUSHED ON THE ROAD TO MECCAH]

I have entitled this account of my summer's tour through Al-Hijaz,[1] a Personal Narrative, and I have laboured to make its nature correspond with its name, simply because "it is the personal that interests mankind." Many may not follow my example; but some perchance will be curious to see what measures I adopted, in order to appear suddenly as an Eastern upon the stage of Oriental life; and as the recital may be found useful by future adventurers, I make no apology for the egotistical semblance of the narrative. Those who have felt the want of some "silent friend" to aid them with advice, when it must not be asked, will appreciate what may appear to the uninterested critic mere outpourings of a mind full of self.

On the evening of April 3, 1853, I left London for Southampton. By the advice of a brother officer, Captain (now Colonel) Henry Grindlay, of the Bengal Cavalry,—little thought at that time the adviser or the advised how valuable was the suggestion!—my Eastern dress was called into requisition before leaving town, and all my "impedimenta" were taught to look exceedingly Oriental. Early the next day a "Persian Prince," accompanied by Captain Grindlay, embarked on board the Peninsular and Oriental Company's magnificent screw steamer "Bengal."

---

1. Hejaz, a region in western Saudi Arabia on the Red Sea; the capital is Mecca, the holy city of Islam.

A fortnight was profitably spent in getting into the train of Oriental manners. For what polite Chesterfield[2] says of the difference between a gentleman and his reverse,—namely, that both perform the same offices of life, but each in a several and widely different way—is notably as applicable to the manners of the Eastern as of the Western man. Look, for instance, at that Indian Moslem drinking a glass of water. With us the operation is simple enough, but his performance includes no fewer than five novelties. In the first place he clutches his tumbler as though it were the throat of a foe; secondly, he ejaculates, "In the name of Allah the Compassionate, the Merciful!" before wetting his lips; thirdly, he imbibes the contents, swallowing them, not sipping them as he ought to do, and ending with a satisfied grunt; fourthly, before setting down the cup, he sighs forth, "Praise be to Allah!"—of which you will understand the full meaning in the Desert; and, fifthly, he replies, "May Allah make it pleasant to thee!" in answer to his friend's polite "Pleasurably and health!" Also he is careful to avoid the irreligious action of drinking the pure element in a standing position, mindful, however, of the three recognised exceptions, the fluid of the Holy Well Zemzem, water distributed in charity, and that which remains after Wuzu, the lesser ablution. Moreover, in Europe, where both extremities are used indiscriminately, one forgets the exclusive use of the right hand, the manipulation of the rosary, the abuse of the chair,—your genuine Oriental gathers up his legs, looking almost as comfortable in it as a sailor upon the back of a high-trotting horse—the rolling gait with the toes straight to the front, the grave look and the habit of pious ejaculations. * * *

* * * After long deliberation about the choice of nations, I became a "Pathán."[3] Born in India of Afghan parents, who had settled in the country, educated at Rangoon, and sent out to wander, as men of that race frequently are, from early youth, I was well guarded against the danger of detection by a fellow-countryman. To support the character requires a knowledge of Persian, Hindustani and Arabic, all of which I knew sufficiently well to pass muster; any trifling inaccuracy was charged upon my long residence at Rangoon. * * *

Pilgrims, especially those from Turkey, carry, I have said, a "Hamail," to denote their holy errand. This is a pocket Koran, in a handsome gold-embroidered crimson velvet or red morocco case, slung by red silk cords over the left shoulder. It must hang down by the right side, and should never depend below the waist-belt. For this I substituted a most useful article. To all appearance a "Hamail," it had inside three compartments; one for my watch and compass, the second for ready money, and the third contained penknife, pencils, and slips of paper, which I could hold concealed in the hollow of my hand. These were for writing and drawing: opportunities of making a "fair copy" into the diary-book, are never wanting to the acute traveller. He must, however, beware of sketching before the Badawin,[4] who would certainly proceed to extreme measures, suspecting him to be a spy or a sorcerer. Nothing so effectually puzzles these people as the Frankish[5] habit of putting everything on paper; their imaginations are set at work, and then the worst may be expected from them. The only safe way of writing in presence of a Badawi would be when drawing out a horoscope or preparing a charm; he also objects not, if you can warm his heart upon the subject, to seeing you take notes in a book of genealogies. You might begin with,

2. Philip Stanhope, fourth Earl of Chesterfield (1694–1773), wrote letters of advice to his son; they became a kind of handbook on conduct.

3. The Indian name of an Afghan [Burton's note].
4. Bedouin, nomadic Arab tribes of the desert.
5. European.

"And you, men of Harb, on what origin do you pride yourselves?" And while the listeners became fluent upon the, to them, all-interesting theme, you could put down whatever you please upon the margin. The townspeople are more liberal, and years ago the Holy Shrines have been drawn, surveyed and even lithographed, by Eastern artists: still, if you wish to avoid all suspicion, you must rarely be seen with pen or with pencil in hand. * * *

[By July 1853, Burton had reached Al-Madinah, where he spent several weeks sight-seeing. He then joined a caravan of other pilgrims bound across the desert for Meccah.]

Having pitched the tent and eaten and slept, we prepared to perform the ceremony of *Al-Ihram* (assuming the pilgrim-garb), as Al-Zaribah is the Mikat, or the appointed place. Between the noonday and the afternoon prayers a barber attended to shave our heads, cut our nails, and trim our mustachios. Then, having bathed and perfumed ourselves,—the latter is a questionable point,—we donned the attire, which is nothing but two new cotton cloths, each six feet long by three and a half broad, white, with narrow red stripes and fringes: in fact, the costume called *Al-Eddeh*, in the baths at Cairo. One of these sheets, technically termed the *Rida*, is thrown over the back, and, exposing the arm and shoulder, is knotted at the right side in the style *Wishah*. The *Izar* is wrapped round the loins from waist to knee, and, knotted or tucked in at the middle, supports itself. Our heads were bare, and nothing was allowed upon the instep. It is said that some clans of Arabs still preserve this religious but most uncomfortable costume; it is doubtless of ancient date, and to this day, in the regions lying west of the Red Sea, it continues to be the common dress of the people.

After the toilette, we were placed with our faces in the direction of Meccah, and ordered to say aloud, "I vow this Ihram of Hajj (the pilgrimage) and the Umrah (the Little pilgrimage) to Allah Almighty!" Having thus performed a two-bow prayer, we repeated, without rising from the sitting position, these words, "O Allah! verily I purpose the Hajj and the Umrah, then enable me to accomplish the two, and accept them both of me, and make both blessed to me!" Followed the *Talbiyat*, or exclaiming—

> "Here I am! O Allah! here am I—
> No partner hast Thou, here am I;
> Verily the praise and the grace are Thine, and the empire—
> No partner hast Thou, here am I!"

And we were warned to repeat these words as often as possible, until the conclusion of the ceremonies. Then Shaykh Abdullah, who acted as director of our consciences, bade us be good pilgrims, avoiding quarrels, immorality, bad language, and light conversation. We must so reverence life that we should avoid killing game, causing an animal to fly, and even pointing it out for destruction; nor should we scratch ourselves, save with the open palm, lest vermin be destroyed, or a hair uprooted by the nail. We were to respect the sanctuary by sparing the trees, and not to pluck a single blade of grass. As regards personal considerations, we were to abstain from all oils, perfumes, and unguents; from washing the head with mallow or with lote leaves; from dyeing, shaving, cutting, or vellicating[6] a single pile or hair; and though we

6. Plucking.

might take advantage of shade, and even form it with upraised hands, we must by no means cover our sconces.[7] For each infraction of these ordinances we must sacrifice a sheep; and it is commonly said by Moslems that none but the Prophet could be perfect in the intricacies of pilgrimage. Old Ali[8] began with an irregularity: he declared that age prevented his assuming the garb, but that, arrived at Meccah, he would clear himself by an offering.

The wife and daughters of a Turkish pilgrim of our party assumed the Ihram at the same time as ourselves. They appeared dressed in white garments; and they had exchanged the Lisam, that coquettish fold of muslin which veils without concealing the lower part of the face, for a hideous mask, made of split, dried, and plaited palm-leaves, with two "bulls'-eyes" for light. I could not help laughing when these strange figures met my sight, and, to judge from the shaking of their shoulders, they were not less susceptible to the merriment which they had caused.

At three P.M. we left Al-Zaribah, travelling towards the South-West, and a wondrously picturesque scene met the eye. Crowds hurried along, habited in the pilgrim-garb, whose whiteness contrasted strangely with their black skins; their newly shaven heads glistening in the sun, and their long black hair streaming in the wind. The rocks rang with shouts of *Labbayk! Labbayk!* At a pass we fell in with the Wahhabis, accompanying the Baghdad Caravan, screaming "Here am I"; and, guided by a large loud kettle-drum, they followed in double file the camel of a standard-bearer, whose green flag bore in huge white letters the formula of the Moslem creed. They were wild-looking mountaineers, dark and fierce, with hair twisted into thin Dalik or plaits: each was armed with a long spear, a matchlock,[9] or a dagger. They were seated upon coarse wooden saddles, without cushions or stirrups, a fine saddle-cloth alone denoting a chief. The women emulated the men; they either guided their own dromedaries, or, sitting in pillion,[1] they clung to their husbands; veils they disdained, and their countenances certainly belonged not to a "soft sex." These Wahhabis were by no means pleasant companions. Most of them were followed by spare dromedaries, either unladen or carrying water-skins, fodder, fuel, and other necessaries for the march. The beasts delighted in dashing furiously through our file, which being lashed together, head and tail, was thrown each time into the greatest confusion. And whenever we were observed smoking, we were cursed aloud for Infidels and Idolaters.

Looking back at Al-Zaribah, soon after our departure, I saw a heavy nimbus settle upon the hill-tops, a sheet of rain being stretched between it and the plain. The low grumbling of thunder sounded joyfully in our ears. We hoped for a shower, but were disappointed by a dust-storm, which ended with a few heavy drops. There arose a report that the Badawin had attacked a party of Meccans with stones, and the news caused men to look exceeding grave.

At five P.M. we entered the wide bed of the Fiumara, down which we were to travel all night. Here the country falls rapidly towards the sea, as the increasing heat of the air, the direction of the watercourses, and signs of violence in the torrent-bed show. The Fiumara varies in breadth from a hundred and fifty feet to three-quarters of a mile; its course, I was told, is towards the South-West, and it enters the sea near Jeddah. The channel is a coarse sand, with here and there masses of sheet rock and patches of thin vegetation.

7. Heads.
8. Ali bin Ya Sin, a decrepit old man who guided parties of pilgrims to Mecca.
9. Musket.
1. On a cushion set behind the saddle.

At about half-past five P.M. we entered a suspicious-looking place. On the right was a stony buttress, along whose base the stream, when there is one, swings; and to this depression was our road limited by the rocks and thorn trees which filled the other half of the channel. The left side was a precipice, grim and barren, but not so abrupt as its brother. Opposite us the way seemed barred by piles of hills, crest rising above crest into the far blue distance. Day still smiled upon the upper peaks, but the lower slopes and the Fiumara bed were already curtained with grey sombre shade.

A damp seemed to fall upon our spirits as we approached this Valley Perilous. I remarked that the voices of the women and children sank into silence, and the loud Labbayk of the pilgrims were gradually stilled. Whilst still speculating upon the cause of this phenomenon, it became apparent. A small curl of the smoke, like a lady's ringlet, on the summit of the right-hand precipice, caught my eye; and simultaneous with the echoing crack of the matchlock, a high-trotting dromedary in front of me rolled over upon the sands,—a bullet had split its heart,—throwing the rider a goodly somersault of five or six yards.

Ensued terrible confusion; women screamed, children cried, and men vociferated, each one striving with might and main to urge his animal out of the place of death. But the road being narrow, they only managed to jam the vehicles in a solid immovable mass. At every matchlock shot, a shudder ran through the huge body, as when the surgeon's scalpel touches some more sensitive nerve. The Irregular horsemen, perfectly useless, galloped up and down over the stones, shouting to and ordering one another. The Pasha of the army had his carpet spread at the foot of the left-hand precipice, and debated over his pipe with the officers what ought to be done. No good genius whispered "Crown the heights."

Then it was that the conduct of the Wahhabis found favour in my eyes. They came up, galloping their camels,—

> Torrents less rapid, and less rash,—

with their elf-locks tossing in the wind, and their flaring matches casting a strange lurid light over their features. Taking up a position, one body began to fire upon the Utaybah robbers, whilst two or three hundred, dismounting, swarmed up the hill under the guidance of the Sharif Zayd. I had remarked this nobleman at Al-Madinah as a model specimen of the pure Arab. Like all Sharifs, he is celebrated for bravery, and has killed many with his own hand. When urged at Al-Zaribah to ride into Meccah, he swore that he would not leave the Caravan till in sight of the walls; and, fortunately for the pilgrims, he kept his word. Presently the firing was heard far in our rear, the robbers having fled. The head of the column advanced, and the dense body of pilgrims opened out. Our forced halt was now exchanged for a flight. It required much management to steer our Desert-craft clear of danger; but Shaykh Mas'ud was equal to the occasion. That many were not, was evident by the boxes and baggage that strewed the shingles. I had no means of ascertaining the number of men killed and wounded: reports were contradictory, and exaggeration unanimous. The robbers were said to be a hundred and fifty in number; their object was plunder, and they would eat the shot camels. But their principal ambition was the boast, "We, the Utaybah, on such and such a night, stopped the Sultan's Mahmil one whole hour in the Pass."

At the beginning of the skirmish I had primed my pistols, and sat with them ready for use. But soon seeing that there was nothing to be done, and wishing to make an impression,—nowhere does Bobadil[2] now "go down" so well as in the East,—I called aloud for my supper. Shaykh Nur, exanimate with fear, could not move. The boy Mohammed ejaculated only an "Oh, sir!" and the people around exclaimed in disgust, "By Allah, he eats!" Shaykh Abdullah, the Meccan, being a man of spirit, was amused by the spectacle. "Are these Afghan manners, Effendim?"[3] he enquired from the Shugduf[4] behind me. "Yes," I replied aloud, "in my country we always dine before an attack of robbers, because that gentry is in the habit of sending men to bed supperless." The Shaykh laughed aloud, but those around him looked offended. * * *

* * *

There at last it lay, the bourn of my long and weary Pilgrimage, realising the plans and hopes of many and many a year. The mirage medium of Fancy invested the huge catafalque[5] and its gloomy pall with peculiar charms. There were no giant fragments of hoar antiquity as in Egypt, no remains of graceful and harmonious beauty as in Greece and Italy, no barbarous gorgeousness as in the buildings of India; yet the view was strange, unique—and how few have looked upon the celebrated shrine! I may truly say that, of all the worshippers who clung weeping to the curtain, or who pressed their beating hearts to the stone, none felt for the moment a deeper emotion than did the Haji from the far-north. It was as if the poetical legends of the Arab spoke truth, and that the waving wings of angels, not the sweet breeze of morning, were agitating and swelling the black covering of the shrine. But, to confess humbling truth, theirs was the high feeling of religious enthusiasm, mine was the ecstasy of gratified pride.

1855, 1893

Isabella Bird
1831–1904

Isabella Bird was a semi-invalid who became one of the most energetic travelers of her day. In remote locations, she forgot her ailments, but whenever she returned home to Edinburgh she felt ill until she could go off boldly adventuring once more. In the American West she covered 800 miles alone on horseback and had a romantic interlude with a desperado named Mountain Jim, whom she described in a letter to her sister as "a man any woman might love, but no sane woman would marry." Her lively letters were published—in an edited version—as *A Lady's Life in the Rocky Mountains* (1878). She later married her physician, John Bishop, and settled down: she remarked that while she would like to visit New Guinea, it was hardly a place you could take a man to. After Bishop died five years later, Bird resumed traveling, exploring the wildest parts of Tibet, India, Persia, Korea, China, and Morocco. She published almost a dozen travel books and was the first woman elected to the Royal Geographical Society. She died at seventy-two, with her bags packed for China.

2. Bluster; from the name of a character in Ben Jonson's play *Every Man in His Humour* (1598).
3. Master; a man of property, education, or authority.

4. Litter borne on a camel's back.
5. Ceremonial coffin.

from A Lady's Life in the Rocky Mountains

[*In 1873 Bird spent several months in the Rocky Mountains on her way home to Britain after traveling in the Hawaiian islands (then called the Sandwich islands). Although she longed to visit Estes Park, a remote valley high in the mountains of Colorado, she was advised to stay lower down with the Chalmers, a family of settlers who she imagined were running a proper boardinghouse. She arrived after nine hours of traveling through rough country in a horse-drawn buggy, and was appalled to discover nothing but a miserable log cabin.*]

[WESTERN SETTLERS, OR "BEING AGREEABLE"]

Canyon, *September 12*

＊ ＊ ＊ I got down and found a single room of the rudest kind, with the wall at one end partially broken down, holes in the roof, holes for windows, and no furniture but two chairs and two unplaned wooden shelves, with some sacks of straw upon them for beds. There was an adjacent cabin room, with a stove, benches, and table, where they cooked and ate, but this was all. A hard, sad-looking woman looked at me measuringly. She said that they sold milk and butter to parties who camped in the canyon, that they had never had any boarders but two asthmatic old ladies, but they would take me for five dollars per week if I "would make myself agreeable." ＊ ＊ ＊

September 16

Five days here, and I am no nearer Estes Park. How the days pass I know not; I am weary of the limitations of this existence. This is "a life in which nothing ever happens." When the buggy disappeared, I felt as if I had cut the bridge behind me. I sat down and knitted for some time—my usual resource under discouraging circumstances. I really did not know how I should get on. There was no table, no bed, no basin, no towel, no glass, no window, no fastening on the door. The roof was in holes, the logs were unchinked, and one end of the cabin was partially removed! Life was reduced to its simplest elements. I went out; the family all had something to do, and took no notice of me. I went back, and then an awkward girl of sixteen, with uncombed hair, and a painful repulsiveness of face and air, sat on a log for half an hour and stared at me. I tried to draw her into talk, but she twirled her fingers and replied snappishly in monosyllables. Could I by any effort "make myself agreeable?" I wondered. ＊ ＊ ＊

Canyon, *September*

The absence of a date shows my predicament. *They* have no newspaper; *I* have no almanack; the father is away for the day, and none of the others can help me, and they look contemptuously upon my desire for information on the subject. ＊ ＊ ＊ My life has grown less dull from theirs having become more interesting to me, and as I have "made myself agreeable," we are on fairly friendly terms. My first move in the direction of fraternising was, however, snubbed. A few days ago, having finished my own work, I offered to wash up the plates, but Mrs. C., with a look which conveyed more than words, a curl of her nose, and a sneer in her twang, said, "Guess you'll make more work nor you'll do. Those hands of yours" (very brown and coarse they were) "ain't no good; never done nothing, I guess." Then to her awkward daughter: "This woman says she'll wash up! Ha! ha! look at her arms and hands!" This was the nearest approach to a laugh I have heard, and have never seen even a tendency towards a smile. Since then I have risen in their estimation by improvising a lamp—Hawaiian fashion—by putting a wisp of rag into a tin of fat. They have actually condescended to sit up till the stars come out since.

* * *

But oh! what a hard, narrow life it is with which I am now in contact! A narrow and unattractive religion, which I believe still to be genuine, and an intense but narrow patriotism, are the only higher influences. Chalmers came from Illinois nine years ago, pronounced by the doctors to be far gone in consumption, and in two years he was strong. They are a queer family; somewhere in the remote Highlands I have seen such another. Its head is tall, gaunt, lean, and ragged, and has lost one eye. On an English road one would think him a starving or a dangerous beggar. He is slightly intelligent, very opinionated, and wishes to be thought well-informed, which he is not. He belongs to the straitest sect of Reformed Presbyterians ("Psalm-singers"), but exaggerates anything of bigotry and intolerance which may characterise them, and rejoices in truly merciless fashion over the excision of the philanthropic Mr. Stuart, of Philadelphia, for worshipping with congregations which sing hymns. His great boast is that his ancestors were Scottish Covenanters.[1] He considers himself a profound theologian, and by the pine logs at night discourses to me on the mysteries of the eternal counsels and the divine decrees. Colorado, with its progress and its future, is also a constant theme. He hates England with a bitter, personal hatred, and regards any allusions which I make to the progress of Victoria as a personal insult. He trusts to live to see the downfall of the British monarchy and the disintegration of the empire. He is very fond of talking, and asks me a great deal about my travels, but if I speak favourably of the climate or resources of any other country, he regards it as a slur on Colorado.

They have one hundred and sixty acres of land, a "squatter's claim," and an invaluable water-power. He is a lumberer, and has a saw-mill of a very primitive kind. I notice that every day something goes wrong with it, and this is the case throughout. If he wants to haul timber down, one or other of the oxen cannot be found; or if the timber is actually under way, a wheel or a part of the harness gives way, and the whole affair is at a standstill for days. The cabin is hardly a shelter, but is allowed to remain in ruins because the foundation of a frame-house was once dug. A horse is always sure to be lame for want of a shoe-nail, or a saddle to be useless from a broken buckle, and the waggon and harness are a marvel of temporary shifts, patchings, and insecure linkings with strands of rope. Nothing is ever ready or whole when it is wanted. Yet Chalmers is a frugal, sober, hard-working man, and he, his eldest son, and a "hired man" "rise early," "going forth to their work and labour till the evening;" and if they do not "late take rest," they truly "eat the bread of carefulness." It is hardly surprising that nine years of persevering shiftlessness[2] should have resulted in nothing but the ability to procure the bare necessaries of life.

Of Mrs. C. I can say less. She looks like one of the English poor women of our childhood—lean, clean, toothless, and speaks, like some of them, in a piping, discontented voice, which seems to convey a personal reproach. All her waking hours are spent in a large sun-bonnet. She is never idle for one minute, is severe and hard, and despises everything but work. I think she suffers from her husband's shiftlessness. She

1. Protestants who repudiated both Catholicism and Anglicanism. They were, at times, fanatical supporters of the independence of the Scottish Church.
2. Inefficiency.

always speaks of me as "this" or "that woman." The family consists of a grown-up son, a shiftless, melancholy-looking youth, who possibly pines for a wider life; a girl of sixteen, a sour, repellent-looking creature, with as much manners as a pig; and three hard, unchildlike younger children. By the whole family all courtesy and gentleness of act or speech seem regarded as "works of the flesh," if not of "the devil." They knock over all one's things without apologising or picking them up, and when I thank them for anything they look grimly amazed. I feel that they think it sinful that I do not work as hard as they do. I wish I could show them "a more excellent way." This hard greed, and the exclusive pursuit of gain, with the indifference to all which does not aid in its acquisition, are eating up family love and life throughout the West. I write this reluctantly, and after a total experience of nearly two years in the United States.[3] They seem to have no "Sunday clothes," and few of any kind. The sewing-machine, like most other things, is out of order. One comb serves the whole family. Mrs. C. is cleanly in her person and dress, and the food, though poor, is clean. Work, work, work, is their day and their life. * * *

Sunday was a dreadful day. The family kept the Commandment literally, and did no work. Worship was conducted twice, and was rather longer than usual. Chalmers does not allow of any books in his house but theological works, and two or three volumes of dull travels, so the mother and children slept nearly all day. The man attempted to read a well-worn copy of *Boston's Fourfold State*,[4] but shortly fell asleep, and they only woke up for their meals. Friday and Saturday had been passably cool, with frosty nights, but on Saturday night it changed, and I have not felt anything like the heat of Sunday since I left New Zealand, though the mercury was not higher than 91°. It was sickening, scorching, melting, unbearable, from the mere power of the sun's rays. It was an awful day, and seemed as if it would never come to an end. The cabin, with its mud roof under the shade of the trees, gave a little shelter, but it was occupied by the family, and I longed for solitude. I took the *Imitation of Christ*,[5] and strolled up the canyon among the withered, crackling leaves, in much dread of snakes, and lay down on a rough table which some passing emigrant had left, and soon fell asleep. When I awoke it was only noon. The sun looked wicked as it blazed like a white magnesium light. A large tree-snake (quite harmless) hung from the pine under which I had taken shelter, and looked as if it were going to drop upon me. I was covered with black flies. The air was full of a busy, noisy din of insects, and snakes, locusts, wasps, flies, and grasshoppers were all rioting in the torrid heat. Would the sublime philosophy of Thomas à Kempis, I wondered, have given way under this? All day I seemed to hear in mockery the clear laugh of the Hilo streams, and the drip of Kona showers, and to see as in a mirage the perpetual green of windward Hawaii. I was driven back to the cabin in the late afternoon, and in the evening listened for two hours to abuse of my own country, and to sweeping condemnations of all religionists outside of the brotherhood of "Psalm-singers." * * *

* * * You will now have some idea of my surroundings. It is a moral, hard, unloving, unlovely, unrelieved, unbeautified, grinding life. These people live in a discomfort and lack of ease and refinement which seems only possible to people of British

3. This trip was Bird's fourth to the United States.
4. Thomas Boston (1676–1732), an Evangelical clergyman in the Church of Scotland, was the author of *The Fourfold State of Human Nature*. Boston's doctrines were harsh and unforgiving: "The godly husband shall say

Amen to the condemnation of her who lay in his bosom: the godly parents shall say *Hallelujah*, at the passing of the sentence against their ungodly child."
5. Mystical work by Thomas à Kempis (1380–1471), German monk.

stock. A "foreigner" fills his cabin with ingenuities and elegancies, and a Hawaiian or South Sea Islander makes his grass house both pretty and tasteful. Add to my surroundings a mighty canyon, impassable both above and below, and walls of mountains with an opening some miles off to the vast prairie sea.[6] * * *

[ESTES PARK AND THE ROUNDUP]

ESTES PARK!!! *September 28*

I wish I could let those three notes of admiration go to you instead of a letter. They mean everything that is rapturous and delightful—grandeur, cheerfulness, health, enjoyment, novelty, freedom, etc. etc. I have just dropped into the very place I have been seeking, but in everything it exceeds all my dreams. There is health in every breath of air; I am much better already, and get up to a seven o'clock breakfast without difficulty. It is quite comfortable—in the fashion that I like. I have a log cabin, raised on six posts, all to myself, with a skunk's lair underneath it, and a small lake close to it. There is a frost every night, and all day it is cool enough for a roaring fire. The ranchman [Griffith Evans], who is half hunter half stockman, and his wife are jovial, hearty Welsh people from Llanberis, who laugh with loud, cheery British laughs, sing in parts down to the youngest child, are free-hearted and hospitable, and pile the pitch-pine logs half-way up the great rude chimney. There has been fresh meat each day since I came, delicious bread baked daily, excellent potatoes, tea and coffee, and an abundant supply of milk like cream. I have a clean hay bed with six blankets, and there are neither bugs nor fleas. The scenery is the most glorious I have ever seen, and is above us, around us, at the very door. * * *

[*Bird had ridden for many hours to reach Estes Park; at the entrance to the valley she passed the log cabin where a notorious outlaw lived.*]

* * * His face was remarkable. He is a man about forty-five, and must have been strikingly handsome. He has large grey-blue eyes, deeply set, with well-marked eyebrows, a handsome aquiline nose, and a very handsome mouth. His face was smooth shaven except for a dense mustache and imperial.[7] Tawny hair, in thin uncared-for curls, fell from under his hunter's cap and over his collar. One eye was entirely gone, and the loss made one side of the face repulsive, while the other might have been modelled in marble. "Desperado" was written in large letters all over him. I almost repented of having sought his acquaintance. * * *

This man, known through the Territories and beyond them as "Rocky Mountain Jim," or, more briefly, as "Mountain Jim," is one of the famous scouts of the Plains, and is the original of some daring portraits in fiction concerning Indian frontier warfare. So far as I have at present heard, he is a man for whom there is now no room, for the time for blows and blood in this part of Colorado is past, and the fame of many daring exploits is sullied by crimes which are not easily forgiven here. He now has a "squatter's claim," but makes his living as a trapper, and is a complete child of the mountains. Of his genius and chivalry to women there does not appear to be any doubt; but he is a desperate character, and is subject to "ugly fits," when people think

---

6. I have not curtailed this description of the roughness of a Colorado settler's life, for, with the exceptions of the disrepair and the Puritanism, it is a type of the hard, unornamented existence with which I came almost universally in contact during my subsequent residence in the Territory [Bird's note].

7. A small beard beneath the lower lip.

it best to avoid him. It is here regarded as an evil that he has located himself at the mouth of the only entrance to the Park, for he is dangerous with his pistols, and it would be safer if he were not here. His besetting sin is indicated in the verdict pronounced on him by my host: "When he's sober Jim's a perfect gentleman; but when he's had liquor he's the most awful ruffian in Colorado." * * *

[Their acquaintance blossomed into friendship, and Mountain Jim took Bird to the summit of Long's Peak (14,700 feet), a serious climb and a grand adventure. Bird thrived on the outdoor life in Estes Park.]

* * * We were to have had a grand cattle-hunt yesterday, beginning at 6.30, but the horses were all lost. Often out of fifty horses all that are worth anything are marauding, and a day is lost in hunting for them in the canyons. However, before daylight this morning Evans called through my door, "Miss Bird, I say we've got to drive cattle fifteen miles, I wish you'd lend a hand; there's not enough of us; I'll give you a good horse."

The scene of the drive is at a height of 7500 feet, watered by two rapid rivers. On all sides mountains rise to an altitude of from 11,000 to 15,000 feet, their skirts shaggy with pitch-pine forests, and scarred by deep canyons, wooded and boulder-strewn, opening upon the mountain pasture previously mentioned. Two thousand head of half-wild Texan cattle are scattered in herds throughout the canyons, living on more or less suspicious terms with grizzly and brown bears, mountain lions, elk, mountain sheep, spotted deer, wolves, lynxes, wild cats, beavers, minks, skunks, chipmonks, eagles, rattlesnakes, and all the other two-legged, four-legged, vertebrate, and invertebrate inhabitants of this lonely and romantic region. On the whole, they show a tendency rather to the habits of wild than of domestic cattle. They march to water in Indian file, with the bulls leading, and when threatened, take strategic advantage of ridgy ground, slinking warily along in the hollows, the bulls acting as sentinels, and bringing up the rear in case of an attack from dogs. Cows have to be regularly broken in for milking, being as wild as buffaloes in their unbroken state; but, owing to the comparative dryness of the grasses, and the system of allowing the calf to have the milk during the daytime, a dairy of 200 cows does not produce as much butter as a Devonshire dairy of fifty. Some "necessary" cruelty is involved in the stockman's business, however humane he may be. The system is one of terrorism, and from the time that the calf is bullied into the branding-pen, and the hot iron burns into his shrinking flesh, to the day when the fatted ox is driven down from his boundless pastures to be slaughtered in Chicago, "the fear and dread of man" are upon him.

The herds are apt to penetrate the savage canyons which come down from the Snowy Range, when they incur a risk of being snowed up and starved, and it is necessary now and then to hunt them out and drive them down to the "park." On this occasion, the whole were driven down for a muster, and for the purpose of branding the calves.

After a 6.30 breakfast this morning, we started, the party being composed of my host, a hunter from the Snowy Range, two stockmen from the Plains, one of whom rode a violent buck-jumper, and was said by his comrade to be the "best rider in North Americay," and myself. We were all mounted on Mexican saddles, rode, as the custom is, with light snaffle bridles, leather guards over our feet, and broad wooden stirrups, and each carried his lunch in a pouch slung on the lassoing horn of his saddle. Four big, badly-trained dogs accompanied us. It was a ride of nearly thirty miles, and of many hours, one of the most splendid I ever took. We never got off our horses except to tighten the girths, we ate our lunch with our bridles knotted over our saddle-horns, started over the level at full gallop, leapt over trunks of trees, dashed madly down hillsides rugged with rocks or strewn with great stones, forded deep, rapid streams, saw lovely lakes and views of surpassing magnificence, startled a herd of elk with uncouth heads and monstrous antlers, and in the chase, which for some time was unsuccessful, rode to the very base of Long's Peak, over 14,000 feet high, where the bright waters of one of the affluents of the Platte burst from the eternal snows through a canyon of indescribable majesty. The sun was hot, but at a height of over 8000 feet the air was crisp and frosty, and the enjoyment of riding a good horse under such exhilarating circumstances was extreme. In one wild part of the ride we had to come down a steep hill, thickly wooded with pitch pines, to leap over the fallen timber, and steer between the dead and living trees to avoid being "snagged," or bringing down a heavy dead branch by an unwary touch.

Emerging from this, we caught sight of a thousand Texan cattle feeding in a valley below. The leaders scented us, and, taking fright, began to move off in the direction of the open "park," while we were about a mile from and above them. "Head them off, boys!" our leader shouted; "all aboard; hark away!" and with something of the "High, tally-ho in the morning!" away we all went at a hand-gallop down-hill. I could not hold my excited animal; down-hill, up-hill, leaping over rocks and timber, faster every moment the pace grew, and still the leader shouted, "Go it, boys!" and the horses dashed on at racing speed, passing and repassing each other, till my small but beautiful bay was keeping pace with the immense strides of the great buck-jumper ridden by "the finest rider in North Americay," and I was dizzied and breathless by the pace at which we were going. A shorter time than it takes to tell it brought us close to and abreast of the surge of cattle. The bovine waves were a grand sight: huge bulls, shaped like buffaloes, bellowed and roared, and with great oxen and cows with yearling calves, galloped like racers, and we galloped alongside of them, and shortly headed them, and in no time were placed as sentinels across the mouth of the valley. It seemed like infantry awaiting the shock of cavalry as we stood as still as our excited horses would allow. I almost quailed as the surge came on, but when it got close to us my comrades hooted fearfully, and we dashed forward with the dogs, and, with bellowing, roaring, and thunder of hoofs, the wave receded as it came. I rode up to our leader, who received me with much laughter. He said I was "a good cattleman," and that he had forgotten that a lady was of the party till he saw me "come leaping over the timber, and driving with the others."

It was not for two hours after this that the real business of driving began, and I was obliged to change my thoroughbred for a well-trained cattle-horse—a *broncho*, which could double like a hare, and go over any ground. I had not expected to work like a *vachero* [cowboy], but so it was, and my Hawaiian experience was very useful. We hunted the various canyons and known "camps," driving the herds out of them; and, until we had secured 850 head in the *corral* some hours afterwards, we scarcely saw each other to speak to. Our first difficulty was with a herd which got into some swampy ground, when a cow, which afterwards gave me an infinity of trouble, remained at bay for nearly an hour, tossing the dog three times, and resisting all efforts to dislodge her. She had a large yearling calf with her, and Evans told me that the attachment of a cow to her first calf is sometimes so great that she will kill her second that the first may have the milk. I got a herd of over a hundred out of a canyon by myself, and drove them down to the river with the aid of one badly-broken dog, which gave me more trouble than the cattle. The getting over was most troublesome; a few took to the water readily and went across, but others smelt it, and then, doubling back, ran in various directions; while some attacked the dog as he was swimming, and others, after crossing, headed back in search of some favourite companions which had been left behind, and one specially vicious cow attacked my horse over and over again. It took an hour and a half of time and much patience to gather them all on the other side.

It was getting late in the day, and a snowstorm was impending, before I was joined by the other drivers and herds, and as the former had diminished to three, with only three dogs, it was very difficult to keep the cattle together. You drive them as gently as possible, so as not to frighten or excite them, riding first on one side, then on the other, to guide them; and if they deliberately go in a wrong direction, you gallop in front and head them off. The great excitement is when one breaks away from the herd and gallops madly up and down hill, and you gallop after him anywhere, over and among rocks and trees, doubling when he doubles, and heading him till you get him back again. The bulls were quite easily managed, but the cows with calves, old or young, were most troublesome. By accident I rode between one cow and her calf in a narrow place, and the cow rushed at me and was just getting her big horns under the horse, when he reared, and spun dexterously aside. This kind of thing happened continually. * * * Just at dusk we reached the corral—an acre of grass enclosed by stout post-and-rail fences seven feet high, and by much patience and some subtlety lodged the whole herd within its shelter, without a blow, a shout, or even a crack of a whip, wild as the cattle were. It was fearfully cold. We galloped the last mile and a half in four and a half minutes, reached the cabin just as snow began to fall, and found strong, hot tea ready. * * *

October 19

Evans offers me six dollars a week if I will stay into the winter and do the cooking after Mrs. Edwards leaves! I think I should like playing at being a "hired girl" if it were not for the bread-making! But it would suit me better to ride after cattle.
1873   1878

Sir Henry Morton Stanley
1841–1904

Stanley was brought up in a Welsh workhouse; he ran away to sea, jumped ship in New Orleans, and served on both sides in the American Civil War. He became a foreign correspondent for the *New York Herald*, and in 1871 the paper had him organize an expedition to Central Africa to find the Scottish missionary David Livingstone, who had not been heard from in several years. Stanley battled through swamps, malaria, crocodiles, and local wars for nearly a year before delivering his famous line, "Dr. Livingstone, I presume?" In 1874 he returned to fill in the "blank spaces" on the map: this dramatic three-year journey across Africa, recounted in his best-seller *Through the Dark Continent* (1878), was hailed as the greatest feat of exploration of the century. Although half of his African crew and all three of his English companions died in the process, Stanley mapped the lakes of Central Africa, solved the mystery of the sources of the Nile, and became the first European to descend the Congo River to the Atlantic Ocean. His subsequent surveys of the Congo on behalf of King Leopold of Belgium opened the way both for Arab slave traders and for the European "Scramble" to divide up Africa. A speech by Stanley promoting King Leopold's enterprise can be found on page 2198 as a background to Joseph Conrad's *Heart of Darkness*.

from **Through the Dark Continent**

[By the end of 1876, when Stanley turned his attention to the Congo River—which he called the Livingstone—he had already been exploring Central Africa for two years, and his expedition had been ravaged by disease, hunger, and conflicts with African tribes. But, he wrote, "the object of the desperate journey is to flash a torch of light across the western half of the Dark Continent," so he pushed on toward his goal of finding a passage to the Atlantic Ocean.]

[ATTACKED FROM BOTH BANKS]

Dec. 26.— * * * The next day at dawn we embarked all the men, women, and children, 149 souls in all, and the riding-asses of the Expedition, and, telling Tippu-Tib[1] we should on the morrow pull up stream and descend the river close to the village of Vinya-Njara for a last farewell, we pulled across to the islet near the right bank, where we constructed a rude camp for the only night we should remain.

When I ascertained, after arrival, that every soul connected with the Expedition was present, my heart was filled with a sense of confidence and trust such as I had not enjoyed since leaving Zanzibar.[2]

In the evening, while sleep had fallen upon all save the watchful sentries in charge of the boat and canoes, Frank[3] and I spent a serious time.

Frank was at heart as sanguine as I that we should finally emerge somewhere, but, on account of the persistent course of the great river towards the north, a little uneasiness was evident in his remarks.

"Before we finally depart, sir," said he, "do you really believe, in your inmost soul, that we shall succeed? I ask this because there are such odds against us—not that I for a moment think it would be best to return, having proceeded so far."

"Believe? Yes, I do believe that we shall all emerge into light again some time. It is true that our prospects are as dark as this night. Even the Mississippi presented no such obstacles to De Soto[4] as this river will necessarily present to us. Possibly its islands and its forests possessed much of the same aspect, but here we are at an altitude of sixteen hundred and fifty feet above the sea. What conclusions can we arrive at? Either that this river penetrates a great distance north of the Equator, and taking a mighty sweep round, descends into the Congo—this, by the way, would lessen the chances of there being many cataracts in the river;—or that we shall shortly see it in the neighbourhood of the Equator, take a direct cut towards the Congo, and precipitate itself, like our Colorado river, through a deep cañon, or down great cataracts; or that it is either the Niger or the Nile. I believe it will prove to be the Congo; if the Congo, then there must be many cataracts. Let us only hope that the cataracts are all in a lump, close together.

"Any way, whether the Congo, the Niger, or the Nile, I am prepared, otherwise I should not be so confident. Though I love life as much as you do, or any other man does, yet on the success of this effort I am about to stake my life, my all. To prevent

1. A powerful Arab trader whose men had escorted Stanley's expedition for two months through hostile territory.
2. Stanley's journey had begun two years earlier in Zanzibar, an island off the eastern coast of Africa.
3. The cheerful Francis Pocock accompanied Stanley for

nearly three years. He later drowned in rapids on 3 June 1877, two months short of their goal. His brother, Edward, died earlier on the expedition.
4. Hernando de Soto (c. 1500–1542), Spanish explorer of North America.

its sacrifice foolishly I have devised numerous expedients with which to defy wild men, wild nature, and unknown terrors. There is an enormous risk, but you know the adage, 'Nothing risked, nothing won.'"

* * *

"Now look at this, the latest chart which Europeans have drawn of this region. It is a blank, perfectly white. We will draw two curves just to illustrate what I mean. One shows the river reaching the Equator and turning westward. Supposing there are no cataracts, we ought to reach 'Tuckey's Furthest' by the 15th of February; but if the river takes that wider sweep from 2° north of the Equator, we may hope to reach by the 15th of March, and, if we allow a month for cataracts or rapids, we have a right to think that we ought to see the ocean by either the middle or the end of April, 1877.[5]

"I assure you, Frank, this enormous void is about to be filled up. Blank as it is, it has a singular fascination for me. Never has white paper possessed such a charm for me as this has, and I have already mentally peopled it, filled it with most wonderful pictures of towns, villages, rivers, countries, and tribes—all in the imagination—and I am burning to see whether I am correct or not. *Believe?* I see us gliding down by tower and town, and my mind will not permit a shadow of doubt. Good-night, my boy! Good-night! and may happy dreams of the sea, and ships and pleasure, and comfort, and success attend you in your sleep! To-morrow, my lad, is the day we shall cry—'Victory or death!' " * * *

Dec. 29.— * * * Below Kaimba Island and its neighbour, the Livingstone assumes a breadth of 1800 yards. The banks are very populous: the villages of the left bank comprise the district of Luavala. We thought for some time we should be permitted to pass by quietly, but soon the great wooden drums, hollowed out of huge trees, thundered the signal along the river that there were strangers. In order to lessen all chances of a rupture between us, we sheered off to the middle of the river, and quietly lay on our paddles. But from both banks at once, in fierce concert, the natives, with their heads gaily feathered, and armed with broad black wooden shields and long spears, dashed out towards us.

Tippu-Tib before our departure had hired to me two young men of Ukusu—cannibals—as interpreters. These were now instructed to cry out the word "Sennenneh!" ("Peace!"), and to say that we were friends.

But they would not reply to our greeting, and in a bold peremptory manner told us to return.

"But we are doing no harm, friends. It is the river that takes us down, and the river will not stop, or go back."

"This is our river."

"Good. Tell it to take us back, and we will go."

"If you do not go back, we will fight you."

"No, don't; we are friends."

"We don't want you for our friends; we will eat you."

But we persisted in talking to them, and as their curiosity was so great they persisted in listening, and the consequence was that the current conveyed us near to the right bank; and in such near neighbourhood to another district, that our discourteous escort had to think of themselves, and began to skurry hastily up river, leaving us unattacked.

---

5. In fact, Stanley did not reach the Atlantic until 12 August 1877.

The villages on the right bank also maintained a tremendous drumming and blowing of war-horns, and their wild men hurried up with menace towards us, urging their sharp-prowed canoes so swiftly that they seemed to skim over the water like flying-fish. Unlike the Luavala villagers, they did not wait to be addressed, but as soon as they came within fifty or sixty yards they shot out their spears, crying out, "Meat! meat! Ah! ha! We shall have plenty of meat! Bo-bo-bo-bo, Bo-bo-bo-bo-o o!"

Undoubtedly these must be relatives of the terrible "Bo-bo-bo's" above, we thought, as with one mind we rose to respond to this rabid man-eating tribe. Anger we had none for them. It seemed to me so absurd to be angry with people who looked upon one only as an epicure would regard a fat capon. Sometimes also a faint suspicion came to my mind that this was all but a part of a hideous dream. Why was it that I should be haunted with the idea that there were human beings who regarded me and my friends only in the light of meat? Meat! *We?* Heavens! what an atrocious idea!

"Meat! Ah! we shall have meat to day. Meat! meat! meat!"

There was a fat-bodied wretch in a canoe, whom I allowed to crawl within spear-throw of me; who, while he swayed the spear with a vigour far from assuring to one who stood within reach of it, leered with such a clever hideousness of feature that I felt, if only within arm's length of him, I could have bestowed upon him a hearty thump on the back, and cried out applaudingly, "Bravo, old boy! You do it capitally!"

Yet not being able to reach him, I was rapidly being fascinated by him. The rapid movements of the swaying spear, the steady wide-mouthed grin, the big square teeth, the head poised on one side with the confident pose of a practised spear-thrower, the short brow and square face, hair short and thick. Shall I ever forget him? It appeared to me as if the spear partook of the same cruel inexorable look as the grinning savage. Finally, I saw him draw his right arm back, and his body incline backwards, with still that same grin on his face, and I felt myself begin to count, one, two, three, four— and *whizz!* The spear flew over my back, and hissed as it pierced the water. The spell was broken.

It was only five minutes' work clearing the river. * * *

Jan. 4. [1877]— * * * At 4 P.M. we came opposite a river about 200 yards wide, which I have called the Leopold River, in honour of his Majesty Leopold II., King of the Belgians, and which the natives called either the Kankora, Mikonju, or Munduku. Perhaps the natives were misleading me, or perhaps they really possessed a superfluity of names, but I think that whatever name they give it should be mentioned in connection with each stream.

Soon after passing by the confluence, the Livingstone, which above had been 2500 yards wide, perceptibly contracted, and turned sharply to the east-north-east, because of a hill which rose on the left bank about 300 feet above the river. Close to the elbow of the bend on the right bank we passed by some white granite rocks, from one to six feet above the water, and just below these we heard the roar of the First Cataract of the Stanley Falls series.

But louder than the noise of the falls rose the piercing yells of the savage Mwana Ntaba from both sides of the great river. We now found ourselves confronted by the inevitable necessity of putting into practice the resolution which we had formed before setting out on the wild voyage—to conquer or die. What should we do? Shall we turn and face the fierce cannibals, who with hideous noise drown the solemn roar of the cataract, or shall we cry out "Mambu Kwa Mungu"—"Our fate is in the hands of God"—and risk the cataract with its terrors!

Meanwhile, we are sliding smoothly to our destruction, and a decision must therefore be arrived at instantly. God knows, I and my fellows would rather have it not to do, because possibly it is only a choice of deaths, by cruel knives or drowning. If we do not choose the knives, which are already sharpened for our throats, death by drowning is certain. So finding ourselves face to face with the inevitable, we turn to the right bank upon the savages, who are in the woods and on the water. We drop our anchors and begin the fight, but after fifteen minutes of it find that we cannot force them away. We then pull up anchors and ascend stream again, until, arriving at the elbow above mentioned, we strike across the river and divide our forces. Manwa Sera[6] is to take four canoes and to continue up stream a little distance, and, while we occupy the attention of the savages in front, is to lead his men through the woods and set upon them in rear. At 5.30 P.M. we make the attempt, and keep them in play for a few minutes, and on hearing a shot in the woods dash at the shore, and under a shower of spears and arrows effect a landing. From tree to tree the fight is continued until sunset, when, having finally driven the enemy off, we have earned peace for the night.

Until about 10 P.M. we are busy constructing an impenetrable stockade or boma of brushwood, and then at length, we lay our sorely fatigued bodies down to rest, without comforts of any kind and without fires, but (I speak for myself only) with a feeling of gratitude to Him who had watched over us in our trouble, and a humble prayer that His protection may be extended to us, for the terrible days that may yet be to come. * * *

Feb. 1.— * * * We emerge out of the shelter of the deeply wooded banks in presence of a vast affluent, nearly 2000 yards across at the mouth. As soon as we have fairly entered its waters, we see a great concourse of canoes hovering about some islets, which stud the middle of the stream. The canoe-men, standing up, give a loud shout as they discern us, and blow their horns louder than ever. We pull briskly on to gain the right bank, and come in view of the right branch of the affluent, when, looking up stream, we see a sight that sends the blood tingling through every nerve and fibre of the body, arouses not only our most lively interest, but also our most lively apprehensions—a flotilla of gigantic canoes bearing down upon us, which both in size and numbers utterly eclipse anything encountered hitherto! Instead of aiming for the right bank, we form in line, and keep straight down river, the boat taking position behind. Yet after a moment's reflection, as I note the numbers of the savages, and the daring manner of the pursuit, and the desire of our canoes to abandon the steady compact line, I give the order to drop anchor. Four of our canoes affect not to listen, until I chase them, and threaten them with my guns. This compelled them to return to the line, which is formed of eleven double canoes, anchored 10 yards apart. The boat moves up to the front, and takes position 50 yards above them. The shields are next lifted by the non-combatants, men, women, and children, in the bows, and along the outer lines, as well as astern, and from behind these, the muskets and rifles are aimed.

We have sufficient time to take a view of the mighty force bearing down on us, and to count the number of the war-vessels which have been collected from the Livingstone and its great affluent. There are fifty-four of them! A monster canoe leads the way, with two rows of upstanding paddles, forty men on a side, their bodies bend-

---

6. Manwa Sera was a distinguished chief who had been with Stanley in 1871 when he went to assist Livingstone; he accompanied Stanley as one of his seconds-in-command on this expedition.

ing and swaying in unison as with a swelling barbarous chorus they drive her down towards us. In the bow, standing on what appears to be a platform, are ten prime young warriors, their heads gay with feathers of the parrot, crimson and grey: at the stern, eight men, with long paddles, whose tops are decorated with ivory balls, guide the monster vessel; and dancing up and down from stem to stern are ten men, who appear to be chiefs. All the paddles are headed with ivory balls, every head bears a feather crown, every arm shows gleaming white ivory armlets. From the bow of the canoe streams a thick fringe of the long white fibre of the Hyphene palm. The crashing sound of large drums, a hundred blasts from ivory horns, and a thrilling chant from two thousand human throats, do not tend to soothe our nerves or to increase our confidence. However, it is "neck or nothing." We have no time to pray, or to take sentimental looks at the savage world, or even to breathe a sad farewell to it. So many other things have to be done speedily and well.

As the foremost canoe comes rushing down, and its consorts on either side beating the water into foam, and raising their jets of water with their sharp prows, I turn to take a last look at our people, and say to them:—

"Boys, be firm as iron; wait until you see the first spear, and then take good aim. Don't fire all at once. Keep aiming until you are sure of your man. Don't think of running away, for only your guns can save you."

Frank is with the *Ocean* on the right flank, and has a choice crew, and a good bulwark of black wooden shields. Manwa Sera has the *London Town*—which he has taken in charge instead of the *Glasgow*[7]—on the left flank, the sides of the canoe bristling with guns, in the hands of tolerably steady men.

The monster canoe aims straight for my boat, as though it would run us down; but, when within fifty yards off, swerves aside, and, when nearly opposite, the warriors above the manned prow let fly their spears, and on either side there is a noise of rushing bodies. But every sound is soon lost in the ripping, crackling musketry. For five minutes we are so absorbed in firing that we take no note of anything else; but at the end of that time we are made aware that the enemy is reforming about 200 yards above us.

Our blood is up now. It is a murderous world, and we feel for the first time that we hate the filthy, vulturous ghouls who inhabit it. We therefore lift our anchors, and pursue them up-stream along the right bank, until rounding a point we see their villages. We make straight for the banks, and continue the fight in the village streets with those who have landed, hunt them out into the woods, and there only sound the retreat, having returned the daring cannibals the compliment of a visit.

While mustering my people for re-embarkation, one of the men came forward and said that in the principal village there was a "Meskiti," a "pembé"—a church, or temple, of ivory—and that ivory was "as abundant as fuel." In a few moments I stood before the ivory temple, which was merely a large circular roof supported by thirty-three tusks of ivory, erected over an idol 4 feet high, painted with camwood dye, a bright vermilion, with black eyes and beard and hair. The figure was very rude, still it was an unmistakable likeness of a man. The tusks being wanted by the Wangwana, they received permission to convey them into the canoes. One hundred other pieces of ivory were collected, in the shape of log wedges, long ivory war-horns, ivory pestles to pound cassava[8] into meal and herbs for spinach, ivory armlets and balls, and ivory mallets to beat the figbark into cloth. * * *

---

7. The *Ocean*, the *London Town*, and the *Glasgow* were the names of some of the expedition's canoes.

8. A tropical plant with fleshy edible roots.

[THE DREAD RIVER]

Mar. 15.—The wide wild land which, by means of the greatest river of Africa, we have pierced, is now about to be presented in a milder aspect than that which has filled the preceding pages with records of desperate conflicts and furious onslaughts of savage men. The people no longer resist our advance. Trade has tamed their natural ferocity, until they no longer resent our approach with the fury of beasts of prey.

It is the dread river itself of which we shall have now to complain. It is no longer the stately stream whose mystic beauty, noble grandeur, and gentle uninterrupted flow along a course of nearly nine hundred miles, ever fascinated us, despite the savagery of its peopled shores, but a furious river rushing down a steep bed obstructed by reefs of lava, projected barriers of rock, lines of immense boulders, winding in crooked course through deep chasms, and dropping down over terraces in a long series of falls, cataracts, and rapids. Our frequent contests with the savages culminated in tragic struggles with the mighty river as it rushed and roared through the deep, yawning pass that leads from the broad table-land down to the Atlantic Ocean. * * *

Mar. 16.— * * * Itsi of Ntamo[9] had informed us there were only three cataracts, which he called the "Child," the "Mother," and the "Father." The "Child" was a two hundred yards' stretch of broken water; and the "Mother," consisting of half a mile of dangerous rapids, we had succeeded in passing, and had pushed beyond it by crossing the upper branch of the Gordon-Bennett, which was an impetuous stream, 75 yards wide, with big cataracts of its own higher up. But the "Father" is the wildest stretch of river that I have ever seen. Take a strip of sea blown over by a hurricane, four miles in length and half a mile in breadth, and a pretty accurate conception of its leaping waves may be obtained. Some of the troughs were 100 yards in length, and from one to the other the mad river plunged. There was first a rush down into the bottom of an immense trough, and then, by its sheer force, the enormous volume would lift itself upward steeply until, gathering itself into a ridge, it suddenly hurled itself 20 or 30 feet straight upward, before rolling down into another trough. If I looked up or down along this angry scene, every interval of 50 or 100 yards of it was marked by wave-towers—their collapse into foam and spray, the mad clash of watery hills, bounding mounds and heaving billows, while the base of either bank, consisting of a long line of piled boulders of massive size, was buried in the tempestuous surf. The roar was tremendous and deafening. I can only compare it to the thunder of an express train through a rock tunnel. To speak to my neighbour, I had to bawl in his ear.

The most powerful ocean steamer, going at full speed on this portion of the river, would be as helpless as a cockle-boat. * * *

Mar. 21.— * * * The seventeen canoes now left to us were manned according to their capacity. As I was about to embark in my boat to lead the way, I turned to the people to give my last instructions—which were, to follow me, clinging to the right bank, and by no means to venture into mid-river into the current. While delivering my instructions, I observed Kalulu[1] in the *Crocodile*, which was made out of the *Bassia Parkii* tree, a hard heavy wood, but admirable for canoes. When I asked him

---

9. Chief of a village near Livingstone Falls.
1. Stanley was deeply attached to Kalulu, who had been with him since his previous expedition. Treating him as an adopted son, Stanley had taken Kalulu to England and the United States and sent him to school in London for 18 months.

what he wanted in the canoe, he replied, with a deprecating smile and an expostulating tone, "I can pull, sir; see!" "Ah, very well," I answered.

The boat-boys took their seats, and, skirting closely the cliffy shore, we rowed down stream, while I stood in the bow of the boat, guiding the coxswain, Uledi,[2] with my hand. The river was not more than 450 yards wide; but one cast of the sounding-lead close to the bank obtained a depth of 138 feet. The river was rapid, with certainly a 7-knot current, with a smooth greasy surface, now and then an eddy, a gurgle, and gentle heave, but not dangerous to people in possession of their wits. In a very few moments we had descended the mile stretch, and before us, 600 yards off, roared the furious falls since distinguished by the name "Kalulu."

With a little effort we succeeded in rounding the point and entering the bay above the falls, and reaching a pretty camping-place on a sandy beach. The first, second, and third canoes arrived soon after me, and I was beginning to congratulate myself on having completed a good day's work, when to my horror I saw the *Crocodile* in mid-river far below the point which we had rounded, gliding with the speed of an arrow towards the falls over the treacherous calm water. Human strength availed nothing now, and we watched it in agony, for I had three favorites in her—Kalulu, Mauredi, and Ferajji; and of the others, two, Rehani Makua and Wadi Jumah, were also very good men. It soon reached the island which cleft the falls, and was swept down the left branch. We saw it whirled round three or four times, then plunged down into the depths, out of which the stern presently emerged pointed upward, and we knew then that Kalulu and his canoe-mates were no more.

Fast upon this terrible catastrophe, before we could begin to bewail their loss, another canoe with two men in it darted past the point, borne by irresistibly on the placid but swift current to apparent, nay, almost certain destruction. I despatched my boat's crew up along the cliffs to warn the forgetful people that in mid-stream was certain death, and shouted out commands for the two men to strike for the left shore. The steersman by a strange chance shot his canoe over the falls, and, dexterously edging his canoe towards the left shore a mile below, he and his companion contrived to spring ashore and were saved. As we observed them clamber over the rocks to approach a point opposite us, and finally sit down, regarding us in silence across the river, our pity and love gushed strong towards them, but we could utter nothing of it. The roar of the falls completely mocked and overpowered the feeble human voice.

Before the boat's crew could well reach the descending canoes, the boulders being very large and offering great obstacles to rapid progress, a third canoe—but a small and light one—with only one man, the brave lad Soudi, who escaped from the spears of the Wanyaturu assassins in 1875, darted by, and cried out, as he perceived himself to be drifting helplessly towards the falls, "La il Allah, il Allah" (There is but one God), "I am lost, Master?" He was then seen to address himself to what fate had in store for him. We watched him for a few moments, and then saw him drop. Out of the shadow of the fall he presently emerged, dropping from terrace to terrace, precipitated down, then whirled round, caught by great heavy waves, which whisked him to right and left, and struck madly at him, and yet his canoe did not sink, but he and it were swept behind the lower end of the island, and then darkness fell upon the day of horror. Nine men lost in one afternoon!

1878

2. Stanley called Uledi, the steersman of his boat, the *Lady Alice*, "the best soldier, sailor, and artisan, and the most faithful servant, of the Expedition."

Mary Kingsley
1862–1900

Mary Kingsley—the niece of the controversial clergyman and author Charles Kingsley—was freed from her role as stay-at-home daughter by the deaths of her parents in 1892 when she was nearly thirty. Courageous and unconventional, she decided to go and explore the West African backcountry. With comic understatement and deadpan humor, she relates her adventures: trekking through uncharted swamps, trading with cannibal tribes, piloting a riverboat, and fending off nosy crocodiles. Back in England, Kingsley was an outspoken critic of British colonial policies in Africa and of missionary efforts to undermine local cultures. At the age of thirty-eight she died of fever in South Africa while nursing Boer prisoners.

from Travels in West Africa
[SETTING OUT]

It was in 1893 that, for the first time in my life, I found myself in possession of five or six months which were not heavily forestalled, and feeling like a boy with a new halfcrown, I lay about in my mind, as Mr Bunyan would say, as to what to do with them. "Go and learn your tropics," said Science. Where on earth am I to go, I wondered, for tropics are tropics wherever found, so I got down an atlas and saw that either South America or West Africa must be my destination, for the Malayan region was too far off and too expensive. Then I got Wallace's *Geographical Distribution* and after reading that master's article on the Ethiopian region I hardened my heart and closed with West Africa. I did this the more readily because while I knew nothing of the practical condition of it, I knew a good deal both by tradition and report of South East America, and remembered that Yellow Jack[1] was endemic, and that a certain naturalist, my superior physically and mentally, had come very near getting starved to death in the depressing society of an expedition slowly perishing of want and miscellaneous fevers up the Parana.

My ignorance regarding West Africa was soon removed. And although the vast cavity in my mind that it occupied is not even yet half filled up, there is a great deal of very curious information in its place. I use the word curious advisedly, for I think many seemed to translate my request for practical hints and advice into an advertisement that "Rubbish may be shot here." This same information is in a state of great confusion still, although I have made heroic efforts to codify it. I find, however, that it can almost all be got in under the following different headings, namely and to wit:—

The dangers of West Africa.
The disagreeables of West Africa.
The diseases of West Africa.
The things you must take to West Africa.
The things you find most handy in West Africa.
The worst possible things you can do in West Africa.

---

1. Yellow fever, an infectious tropical disease.

I inquired of all my friends as a beginning what they knew of West Africa. The majority knew nothing. A percentage said, "Oh, you can't possibly go there; that's where Sierra Leone is, the white man's grave, you know." If these were pressed further, one occasionally found that they had had relations who had gone out there after having been "sad trials," but, on consideration of their having left not only West Africa, but this world, were now forgiven and forgotten. One lady however kindly remembered a case of a gentleman who had resided some few years at Fernando Po, but when he returned an aged wreck of forty he shook so violently with ague as to dislodge a chandelier, thereby destroying a valuable tea-service and flattening the silver teapot in its midst.

No; there was no doubt about it, the place was not healthy, and although I had not been "a sad trial," yet neither had the chandelier-dislodging Fernando Po gentleman. So I next turned my attention to cross-examining the doctors. "Deadliest spot on earth," they said cheerfully, and showed me maps of the geographical distribution of disease. Now I do not say that a country looks inviting when it is coloured in Scheele's green or a bilious yellow, but these colours may arise from lack of artistic gift in the cartographer. There is no mistaking what he means by black, however, and black you'll find they colour West Africa from above Sierra Leone to below the Congo. * * *

It was the beginning of August '93 when I first left England for "the Coast." Preparations of quinine[2] with postage partially paid arrived up to the last moment, and a friend hastily sent two newspaper clippings, one entitled "A Week in a Palm-oil Tub," which was supposed to describe the sort of accommodation, companions, and fauna likely to be met with on a steamer going to West Africa, and on which I was to spend seven to *The Graphic* contributor's one; the other from *The Daily Telegraph,* reviewing a French book of "Phrases in common use" in Dahomey. The opening sentence in the latter was, "Help, I am drowning." Then came the inquiry, "If a man is not a thief?" and then another cry, "The boat is upset." "Get up, you lazy scamps," is the next exclamation, followed almost immediately by the question, "Why has not this man been buried?" "It is fetish[3] that has killed him, and he must lie here exposed with nothing on him until only the bones remain," is the cheerful answer. This sounded discouraging to a person whose occupation would necessitate going about considerably in boats, and whose fixed desire was to study fetish. So with a feeling of foreboding gloom I left London for Liverpool—none the more cheerful for the matter-of-fact manner in which the steamboat agents had informed me that they did not issue return tickets by the West African lines of steamers.

I will not go into the details of that voyage here, much as I am given to discursiveness. They are more amusing than instructive, for on my first voyage out I did not know the Coast, and the Coast did not know me, and we mutually terrified each other. I fully expected to get killed by the local nobility and gentry; they thought I was connected with the World's Women's Temperance Association, and collecting shocking details for subsequent magic-lantern lectures on the liquor traffic; so fearful misunderstandings arose, but we gradually educated each other, and I had the best of the affair; for all I had got to teach them was that I was only a beetle and fetish hunter, and so forth, while they had to teach me a new world, and a very fascinating course of study I found it. * * *

---

2. Preventative against malaria.
3. The word applies both to objects believed to have magical powers and to the rites of worship surrounding such objects.

[CROCODILES]

* * * Now a crocodile drifting down in deep water, or lying asleep with its jaws open on a sand-bank in the sun, is a picturesque adornment to the landscape when you are on the deck of a steamer, and you can write home about it and frighten your relations on your behalf; but when you are away among the swamps in a small dug-out canoe, and that crocodile and his relations are awake—a thing he makes a point of being at flood tide because of fish coming along—and when he has got his foot upon his native heath—that is to say, his tail within holding reach of his native mud—he is highly interesting, and you may not be able to write home about him— and you get frightened on your own behalf. For crocodiles can, and often do, in such places, grab at people in small canoes. I have known of several natives losing their lives in this way. * * * In addition to this unpleasantness you are liable—until you re-alise the danger from experience, or have native advice on the point—to get tide-trapped away in the swamps, the water falling round you when you are away in some deep pool or lagoon, and you find you cannot get back to the main river. For you can-not get out and drag your canoe across the stretches of mud that separate you from it, because the mud is of too unstable a nature and too deep, and sinking into it means staying in it, at any rate until some geologist of the remote future may come across you, in a fossilised state, when that mangrove swamp shall have become dry land. Of course if you really want a truly safe investment in Fame, and really care about Pos-terity, and Posterity's Science, you will jump over into the black batter-like, stinking slime, cheered by the thought of the terrific sensation you will produce 20,000 years hence, and the care you will be taken of then by your fellow-creatures, in a museum. But if you are a mere ordinary person of a retiring nature, like me, you stop in your la-goon until the tide rises again; most of your attention is directed to dealing with an "at home"[4] to crocodiles and mangrove flies, and with the fearful stench of the slime round you. What little time you have over you will employ in wondering why you came to West Africa, and why, after having reached this point of absurdity, you need have gone and painted the lily and adorned the rose, by being such a colossal ass as to come fooling about in mangrove swamps. Twice this chatty little incident, as Lady MacDonald[5] would call it, has happened to me, but never again if I can help it. On one occasion, the last, a mighty Silurian,[6] as *The Daily Telegraph* would call him, chose to get his front paws over the stern of my canoe, and endeavoured to improve our acquaintance. I had to retire to the bows, to keep the balance right,[7] and fetch him a clip on the snout with a paddle, when he withdrew, and I paddled into the very middle of the lagoon, hoping the water there was too deep for him or any of his friends to repeat the performance. Presumably it was, for no one did it again. I should think that crocodile was eight feet long; but don't go and say I measured him, or that this is my outside measurement for crocodiles. I have measured them when they have been killed by other people, fifteen, eighteen, and twenty-one feet odd. This was only a pushing young creature who had not learnt manners. * * *

4. Ladies would normally be "at home" to receive visitors once a week on a particular afternoon.
5. Lady Ethel MacDonald was the wife of Sir Claude MacDonald, governor of the Niger Coast Protectorate.
6. Crocodile. The Silurian period was part of the Paleo-zoic era, and suggests the crocodile's primitive and an-cient appearance. *The Daily Telegraph* was a popular Lon-don paper given to dramatic exaggeration.
7. It is no use saying because I was frightened, for this miserably understates the case [Kingsley's note].

[*After exploring the swamps, Kingsley traveled by steamer and canoe up the Ogowé River in the French Congo—now Gabon—then set out on foot through the jungle. She was accompanied by four Ajumba tribesmen, whom she called Gray Shirt, Singlet, Silence, and Pagan, and by three Fan tribesmen, Kiva, Fika, and Wiki. There was also Ngouta, an interpreter, and two more members of the party, whom she called the Duke and the Passenger.*]

[THE BLESSING OF A GOOD THICK SKIRT]

Our first day's march, though the longest, was the easiest, though, providentially I did not know this at the time. From my Woermann road walks[8] I judge it was well twenty-five miles. It was easiest however, from its lying for the greater part of the way through the gloomy type of forest. All day long we never saw the sky once. * * *

We had to hurry because Kiva, who was the only one among us who had been to Efoua, said that unless we did we should not reach Efoua that night. I said, "Why not stay for bush?" not having contracted any love for a night in a Fan town by the experience of M'fetta;[9] moreover the Fans were not sure that after all the whole party of us might not spend the evening at Efoua, when we did get there, simmering in its cooking-pots.

* * * I kept going, as it was my only chance, because I found I stiffened if I sat down, and they always carefully told me the direction to go in when they sat down; with their superior pace they soon caught me up, and then passed me, leaving me and Ngouta and sometimes Singlet and Pagan behind, we, in our turn, overtaking them, with this difference that they were sitting down when we did so.

About five o'clock I was off ahead and noticed a path which I had been told I should meet with, and, when met with, I must follow. The path was slightly indistinct, but by keeping my eye on it I could see it. Presently I came to a place where it went out, but appeared again on the other side of a clump of underbush fairly distinctly. I made a short cut for it and the next news was I was in a heap, on a lot of spikes, some fifteen feet or so below ground level, at the bottom of a bag-shaped game pit.

It is at these times you realise the blessing of a good thick skirt. Had I paid heed to the advice of many people in England, who ought to have known better, and did not do it themselves, and adopted masculine garments, I should have been spiked to the bone, and done for. Whereas, save for a good many bruises, here I was with the fulness of my skirt tucked under me, sitting on nine ebony spikes some twelve inches long, in comparative comfort, howling lustily to be hauled out. The Duke came along first, and looked down at me. I said, "Get a bush-rope, and haul me out." He grunted and sat down on a log. The Passenger came next, and he looked down. "You kill?" says he. "Not much," say I; "get a bush-rope and haul me out." "No fit," says he, and sat down on the log. Presently, however, Kiva and Wiki came up, and Wiki went and selected the one and only bush-rope suitable to haul an English lady, of my exact complexion, age, and size, out of that one particular pit. * * *

[*They reached at last the village of Efoua, where the chief offered her his hut to sleep in.*]

---

8. Woermann was a German trading company; the Woermann Road led from the company factory in Glass, French Congo, to the company farm, six miles away.
9. The Fans were a fierce tribe reputed to be cannibals; Kingsley had great admiration for their energy, courage, and resourcefulness. Kingsley had spent the previous night in M'fetta, Kiva's village, where she had been tormented by mosquitoes.

[AN UNPLEASANT DISCOVERY]

* * * Every hole in the side walls had a human eye in it, and I heard new holes being bored in all directions; so I deeply fear the chief, my host, must have found his palace sadly draughty. I felt perfectly safe and content, however, although Ngouta suggested the charming idea that "P'r'aps them M'fetta Fan done sell we." The only grave question I had to face was whether I should take off my boots or not; they were wet through, from wading swamps, &c., and my feet were very sore; but on the other hand, if I took those boots off, I felt confident that I should not be able to get them on again next morning, so I decided to lef 'em.

As soon as all my men had come in, and established themselves in the inner room for the night, I curled up among the boxes, with my head on the tobacco sack, and dozed.

* * * Waking up * * * I noticed the smell in the hut was violent, from being shut up I suppose, and it had an unmistakably organic origin. Knocking the ash end off the smouldering bush-light that lay burning on the floor, I investigated, and tracked it to those bags, so I took down the biggest one, and carefully noted exactly how the tie had been put round its mouth; for these things are important and often mean a lot. I then shook its contents out in my hat, for fear of losing anything of value. They were a human hand, three big toes, four eyes, two ears, and other portions of the human frame. The hand was fresh, the others only so so, and shrivelled.

Replacing them I tied the bag up, and hung it up again. I subsequently learnt that although the Fans will eat their fellow friendly tribesfolk, yet they like to keep a little something belonging to them as a memento. This touching trait in their character I learnt from Wiki; and, though it's to their credit, under the circumstances, still it's an unpleasant practice when they hang the remains in the bedroom you occupy, particularly if the bereavement in your host's family has been recent. I did not venture to prowl round Efoua; but slid the bark door aside and looked out to get a breath of fresh air. * * *

[After several more days of marching through jungle and swamp, they reached Agonjo, a trading post on the Rembwé river. From the stores of Mr. Glass, the M'pongwe agent for Hatton and Cookson's factory, Kingsley paid her Ajumba and Fan companions and said goodbye to them. Mr. Glass was anxious to help her find a canoe and crew to continue her journey downriver and back to the coast.]

[NOCTURNAL NAVIGATION]

At this point in the affair there entered a highly dramatic figure. He came on to the scene suddenly and with much uproar, in a way that would have made his fortune in a transpontine drama.[1] I shall always regret I have not got that man's portrait, for I cannot do him justice with ink. He dashed up on to the verandah, smote the frail form of Mr Glass between the shoulders, and flung his own massive one into a chair. His name was Obanjo, but he liked it pronounced Captain Johnson, and his profession was a bush and river trader on his own account. Every movement of the man was theatrical, and he used to look covertly at you every now and then to see if he had produced his impression, which was evidently intended to be that of a reckless,

---

1. Cheap melodrama performed in London on the Surrey side of the Thames.

rollicking skipper. There was a Hallo-my-Hearty atmosphere coming off him from the top of his hat to the soles of his feet, like the scent off a flower; but it did not require a genius in judging men to see that behind, and under this was a very different sort of man, and if I should ever want to engage in a wild and awful career up a West African river I shall start on it by engaging Captain Johnson. He struck me as being one of those men, of whom I know five, whom I could rely on, that if one of them and I went into the utter bush together, one of us at least would come out alive and have made something substantial by the venture. * * *

I left him and the refined Mr Glass together to talk over the palaver of shipping me, and they talked it at great length. Finally the price I was to pay Obanjo was settled and we proceeded to less important details. It seemed Obanjo, when up the river this time, had set about constructing a new and large trading canoe at one of his homes, in which he was just thinking of taking his goods down to Gaboon. The only drawback was this noble vessel was not finished; but that did not discourage any of us, except Mr Glass, who seemed to think the firm would debit me to his account if I got lost. However, next morning Obanjo with his vessel turned up, and saying farewell to my kind host, Mr Sanga Glass, I departed. * * *

We left Agonjo with as much bustle and shouting and general air of brisk seamanship as Obanjo could impart to the affair, and the hopeful mind might have expected to reach somewhere important by nightfall. I did not expect that; neither, on the other hand, did I expect that after we had gone a mile and only four, as the early ballad would say, that we should pull up and anchor against a small village for the night; but this we did, the captain going ashore to see for cargo, and to get some more crew.

There were grand times ashore that night, and the captain returned on board about 2 A.M. with some rubber and pissava and two new hands whose appearance fitted them to join our vessel; for a more villainous-looking set than our crew I never laid eye on. One enormously powerful fellow looked the incarnation of the horrid negro of buccaneer stories, and I admired Obanjo for the way he kept them in hand. We had now also acquired a small dug-out canoe as tender, and a large fishing-net.

About 4 A.M. in the moonlight we started to drop down river on the tail of the land breeze, and as I observed Obanjo wanted to sleep I offered to steer. After putting me through an examination in practical seamanship, and passing me, he gladly accepted my offer, handed over the tiller which stuck out across my bamboo staging, and went and curled himself up, falling sound asleep among the crew in less time than it takes to write. On the other nights we spent on this voyage I had no need to offer to steer; he handed over charge to me as a matter of course, and as I prefer night to day in Africa, I enjoyed it. Indeed, much as I have enjoyed life in Africa, I do not think I ever enjoyed it to the full as I did on those nights dropping down the Rembwé. The great, black, winding river with a pathway in its midst of frosted silver where the moonlight struck it: on each side the ink-black mangrove walls, and above them the band of star and moonlit heavens that the walls of mangrove allowed one to see. Forward rose the form of our sail, idealised from bedsheetdom to glory; and the little red glow of our cooking fire gave a single note of warm colour to the cold light of the moon. Three or four times during the second night, while I was steering along by the south bank, I found the mangrove wall thinner, and standing up, looked through the network of their roots and stems on to what seemed like plains, acres upon acres in extent, of polished silver—more specimens of those awful slime lagoons, one of which, before we reached Ndorko, had so very nearly collected me. I watched them, as we leisurely stole past, with a sort of fascination. On the second night, towards the dawn, I had the great joy of seeing Mount Okoneto, away to the S.W., first showing moonlit, and then taking the colours of the dawn before they reached us down below. Ah me! give me a West African river and a canoe for sheer good pleasure. Drawbacks, you say? Well, yes, but where are there not drawbacks? The only drawbacks on those Rembwé nights were the series of horrid frights I got by steering on to tree shadows and thinking they were mud banks, or trees themselves, so black and solid did they seem. I never roused the watch fortunately, but got her off the shadow gallantly single-handed every time, and called myself a fool instead of getting called one. My nautical friends carp at me for getting on shadows, but I beg them to consider before they judge me, whether they have ever steered at night down a river quite unknown to them an unhandy canoe, with a bed-sheet sail, by the light of the moon. And what with my having a theory of my own regarding the proper way to take a vessel round a corner, and what with having to keep the wind in the bed-sheet where the bed-sheet would hold it, it's a wonder to me I did not cast that vessel away, or go and damage Africa.

By daylight the Rembwé scenery was certainly not so lovely, and might be slept through without a pang. It had monotony, without having enough of it to amount to grandeur. Every now and again we came to villages, each of which was situated on a heap of clay and sandy soil, presumably the end of a spit of land running out into the mangrove swamp fringing the river. Every village we saw we went alongside and had a chat with, and tried to look up cargo in the proper way. One village in particular did we have a lively time at. Obanjo had a wife and home there, likewise a large herd of goats, some of which he was desirous of taking down with us to sell at Gaboon. It was a pleasant-looking village, with a clean yellow beach which most of the houses faced. But it had ramifications in the interior. I being very lazy, did not go ashore, but watched the pantomime from the bamboo staging. The whole flock of goats enter at right end of stage, and tear violently across the scene, disappearing at left. Two minutes elapse. Obanjo and his gallant crew enter at right hand of stage, leg it like lamplighters across front, and disappear at left. Fearful pow-wow behind the scenes. Five minutes elapse. Enter goats at right as before, followed by Obanjo and company as before, and so on *da capo* [from the beginning]. * * * It was a spirited performance I assure you and I and the inhabitants of the village, not personally interested in goat-catching, assumed the *rôle* of audience and cheered it to the echo. While engaged in shouting "Encore" to the third round, I received a considerable shock by hearing a well-modulated evidently educated voice saying in most perfect English:

"Most diverting spectacle, madam, is it not?"

Now you do not expect to hear things called "diverting spectacles" on the Rembwé; so I turned round and saw standing on the bank against which our canoe was moored, what appeared to me to be an English gentleman who had from some misfortune gone black all over and lost his trousers and been compelled to replace them with a highly ornamental table-cloth. The rest of his wardrobe was in exquisite condition, with the usual white jean coat, white shirt and collar, very neat tie, and felt hat affected by white gentlemen out here. Taking a large and powerful cigar from his lips with one hand, he raised his hat gracefully with the other and said:

"Pray excuse me, madam."

I said, "Oh, please go on smoking."

"May I?" he said, offering me a cigar-case.

"Oh, no thank you," I replied.

"Many ladies do now," he said, and asked me whether I "preferred Liverpool, London, or Paris."

I said, "Paris; but there were nice things in both the other cities."

"Indeed that is so," he said; "they have got many very decent works of art in the St. George's Hall."

I agreed, but said I thought the National Gallery preferable because there you got such fine representative series of works of the early Italian schools. I felt I had got to rise to this man whoever he was, somehow, and having regained my nerve, I was coming up hand over hand to the level of his culture when Obanjo and the crew arrived, carrying goats. Obanjo dropped his goat summarily into the hold, and took off his hat with his very best bow to my new acquaintance, who acknowledged the salute with a delicious air of condescension.

"Introduce me," said the gentleman.

"I cannot," said Obanjo.

"I regret, madam," said the gentleman, "I have not brought my card-case with me. One little expects in such a remote region to require one; my name is Prince Makaga."

I said I was similarly card-caseless for reasons identical with his own, but gave him my name and address, and Obanjo, having got all aboard, including a member of the crew, fetched by the leg, shoved off, and with many bows we and the black gentleman parted. As soon as we were out of earshot from shore "Who is he, Obanjo?" said I. Obanjo laughed, and said he was a M'pongwe gentleman who had at one time been agent for one of the big European firms at Gaboon, and had been several times to Europe. Thinking that he could make more money on his own account, he had left the firm and started trading all round this district. At first he made a great deal of money, but a lot of his trust had recently gone bad, and he was doubtless up here now looking after some such matter. Obanjo evidently thought him too much of a lavender-kid-glove gentleman to deal with bush trade, and held it was the usual way; a man got spoilt by going to Europe. I quite agree with him on general lines, but Prince Makaga had a fine polish on him without the obvious conceit usually found in men who have been home.

1897

Rudyard Kipling
1865–1936

This poem was addressed to Americans following their acquisition of Cuba and the Philippines in the Spanish-American War of 1898. With its emphasis on moral responsibility toward colonized peoples, the poem expresses an idealized Victorian notion of empire as a noble undertaking. Enormously popular, it has also been frequently vilified as hypocritical, paternalistic, and racist. The title phrase quickly entered the language as a euphemism for imperialism. Within a week of its publication, the American pacifist Ernest Crosby parodied it in the *New York Times*: "Take up the White Man's burden, / And teach the Philippines / What interest and taxes are / And what a mortgage means. / Give them electrocution chairs, / And prisons, too, galore, / And if they seem inclined to kick, / Then spill their heathen gore."

For more about Rudyard Kipling, see the principal listing on page 1858.

The White Man's Burden

Take up the White Man's burden—
    Send forth the best ye breed—
Go bind your sons to exile
    To serve your captives' need;
5   To wait in heavy harness
      On fluttered folk and wild—
Your new-caught, sullen peoples,
    Half-devil and half-child.

Take up the White Man's burden—
10   In patience to abide,
To veil the threat of terror
    And check the show of pride;
By open speech and simple,
    An hundred times made plain,
15   To seek another's profit,
    And work another's gain.

Take up the White Man's burden—
    The savage wars of peace—
Fill full the mouth of Famine
20   And bid the sickness cease;
And when your goal is nearest
    The end for others sought,
Watch Sloth and heathen Folly
    Bring all your hope to nought.

25 Take up the White Man's burden—
    No tawdry rule of kings,
But toil of serf and sweeper—
    The tale of common things.
The ports ye shall not enter,
30   The roads ye shall not tread,
Go make them with your living,
    And mark them with your dead!

Take up the White Man's burden—
    And reap his old reward:
35   The blame of those ye better,
      The hate of those ye guard—
The cry of hosts ye humour
    (Ah, slowly!) toward the light:—
"Why brought ye us from bondage,
40   Our loved Egyptian night?"[1]

1. When Moses led the Israelites out of bondage in Egypt, they complained about the rigors of the journey and regretted the familiar comforts of slavery (Exodus 16). Kipling thus sees colonial administrators not as Egyptian masters but as unappreciated liberators (from moral and spiritual darkness).

Take up the White Man's burden—
   Ye dare not stoop to less—
Nor call too loud on Freedom
   To cloak your weariness;
45 By all ye cry or whisper,
   By all ye leave or do,
The silent, sullen peoples
   Shall weigh your Gods and you.

Take up the White Man's burden—
50   Have done with childish days—
The lightly proffered laurel,
   The easy, ungrudged praise.
Comes now, to search your manhood
   Through all the thankless years,
55 Cold, edged with dear-bought wisdom,
   The judgment of your peers!

1899

━━✦ END OF PERSPECTIVES: TRAVEL AND EMPIRE ✦━━

━━✦✦✦✦━━

Robert Louis Stevenson
1850–1894

"I have drawed a man's *body*, shall I do his *soul* now?" the three-year-old Robert Louis Steven-son asked his mother. Belief in the duality of human nature, or what Stevenson later called—referring to Dr. Jekyll's transformations—"the war in the members," permeated every corner of the Stevensons' Calvinist household in Edinburgh. The very furniture served as a reminder of the battle between flesh and spirit, for the Stevensons took pride in owning a cabinet that had been made by a double personality, Deacon Brodie—upstanding citizen by day, infamous serial killer by night. The family atmosphere stressed the precarious position of the individual, poised between heaven and hell, torn between the obligation to be good and the seductiveness of evil. "I would fear to trust myself to slumber," Stevenson recalled, "lest I was not accepted [into heaven] and should slip, ere I awoke, into eternal ruin."

A sickly boy who later memorialized his childhood joys and anxieties in *A Child's Garden of Verses* (1885), Stevenson grew up surrounded by stories of crime and punishment for an-other reason: the city of Edinburgh itself possessed a dual personality. The Stevensons lived in the respectable New Town, a landmark district of graceful neoclassical Georgian architecture, but the area coexisted uneasily with the gothic Old Town of narrow alleyways, bars, and broth-els, where Deacon Brodie had prowled by night. In his student days Stevenson and his cousin Bob explored the dark side of town in defiance of his family. He further strained the relation-ship in 1873 when he announced that he was an agnostic and joined the Edinburgh University Skeptics Club, whose motto was "Disregard everything our parents have taught us."

But it was Stevenson's attention to the power of a good story, learned from his father and his nurse, "Cummy," that led him, after studying medicine and law, to became a fiction writer. And it was his Calvinistic background, with its sense of sin lurking beneath apparent virtue, that colored his theory of literature. In 1885, in a widely read literary debate with Henry James over the nature of the novel, Stevenson argued for fiction's difference from life. To James's assertion that a novel should produce the illusion of reality, Stevenson responded that the author should tell stories that express life's deeper meanings. Influenced by Hawthorne, Stevenson felt that the writer must create "romance" rather than realism, not merely to entertain readers but also to capture the underlying truths of the human condition, including the struggle between good and evil.

In what became the pattern for his adult life, Stevenson left Edinburgh in the later 1870s to travel abroad and recuperate his failing health while looking for new literary material. In France he met his future wife, Fanny, an American. She was ten years older than he, married, and a mother. But making a hazardous journey across the Atlantic and overland to San Francisco, he married her there when her divorce came through in 1880. They had a rustic honeymoon in a cabin in Napa Valley, recounted in Stevenson's *The Silverado Squatters* (1883). With Fanny's son Lloyd, the couple then returned to Britain, where Stevenson's father reconciled with his errant son, giving him a modest allowance so he could travel and write. In the 1880s Stevenson concentrated on short fiction, including many tales based on Scottish lore. Together with Kipling he helped make the short story, until then very much a French and American genre, a vital part of English literature. His first popular success, however, resulted from the map of an imaginary isle he was making with Lloyd. Written at top speed on a family vacation in Scotland, *Treasure Island* (1883) mingles a boy's adventure story with a voyage of self-discovery and growth; mesmerized by Long John Silver and tales of buried pirate treasure, the young Jim Hawkins must also realize what greed and gold do to people. The book's divided narrative, Jim's ambiguous role amid pirates and privateers, and the atmospheric description— all anticipate *Dr Jekyll and Mr Hyde* (1886). Stevenson confirmed his position as the leading "boy's writer" with *Kidnapped* (1886). He returned with his family to the United States in 1887, and then set out from San Francisco for the South Pacific, where they sailed from island to island, Stevenson writing all the time, finally settling in Samoa. Although the outdoor life had apparently restored Stevenson's health, he died suddenly in 1894, at the age of forty-four, while working on *The Weir of Hermiston* (1896).

The inspiration for *Dr Jekyll and Mr Hyde* came to the author in a frightening dream. "I had long been trying to write a story on this subject," said Stevenson, "to find a body, a vehicle, for that strong sense of man's double being which must at times come in upon and overwhelm the mind of every thinking creature." The dream produced Mr. Hyde and his sudden transformation, but Fanny felt that Stevenson's first draft did not do justice to the theme. So Stevenson burned the original manuscript and in three days produced the text as we now have it, "the most famous fable in the English language on the theme of the split personality," according to the critic Susan Wolfson. Like Mary Shelley's *Frankenstein* (1818) the story is (re)constructed by several narrators, and like Victor Frankenstein, Dr. Henry Jekyll makes a revolutionary scientific discovery that has fatal repercussions. But unlike Dr. Frankenstein, Dr. Jekyll has no noble aspirations to serve humanity: he deliberately intends to be bad. While some readers have found in both works a similar message about the dangers of tampering with nature, others have felt that morality and propriety are the true evils for Stevenson; what endangers Dr. Jekyll is the restrictive social code he lives by. The story's oppressive London setting is clearly based on the Edinburgh of Stevenson's childhood, where the fog and darkness signal the presence of sin and Satan, and the isolated lives of the narrators, all men without families, echo the lonely repression of Dr. Jekyll. Only Hyde's voice is missing from the narrative. But through him Stevenson hints at the scandalous idea that the darker side of human nature needs more room for self-expression.

From the moment *Dr Jekyll and Mr Hyde* was published the story generated great interest, rapidly achieving a classic status continually reinforced by the numerous theatrical and cinematic versions it has inspired. It was an instant hit on the London and New York stage, and life appeared to imitate art when the notorious Jack-the-Ripper murders, still unsolved, took place in London the year after the novel appeared. The universal appeal of *Dr Jekyll and Mr Hyde* seems based on a striking literary effect—most readers, Victorian as well as modern, identify with the "villain" of the piece. The critic J. A. Symonds protested to Stevenson, "it touches one too closely. Most of us at some epoch of our lives have been upon the verge of developing a Mr. Hyde." The poet and priest Gerard Manley Hopkins confessed to his friend Robert Bridges, who had questioned the realism of the story, "You are certainly wrong about Hyde being overdrawn: my Hyde is worse." For Victorians, to read the book was to yield a bit to the inner Hyde, to feel the temptations of Dr. Jekyll. As the reviewer for the London *Times* noted in 1886, by virtue of "a flash of intuitive psychological research" the reader feels "a curiosity that keeps on growing because it is never satisfied." Having become helplessly involved, "every connoisseur who reads the story once, must certainly read it twice."

For a selection of Stevenson's poetry, see page 1840.

The Strange Case of Dr Jekyll and Mr Hyde
Story of the Door

Mr Utterson the lawyer was a man of a rugged countenance, that was never lighted by a smile; cold, scanty and embarrassed in discourse; backward in sentiment; lean, long, dusty, dreary and yet somehow lovable. At friendly meetings, and when the wine was to his taste, something eminently human beaconed from his eye; something indeed which never found its way into his talk, but which spoke not only in these silent symbols of the after-dinner face, but more often and loudly in the acts of his life. He was austere with himself; drank gin when he was alone, to mortify a taste for vintages; and though he enjoyed the theatre, had not crossed the doors of one for twenty years. But he had an approved tolerance for others; sometimes wondering, almost with envy, at the high pressure of spirits involved in their misdeeds; and in any extremity inclined to help rather than to reprove. "I incline to Cain's heresy,"[1] he used to say quaintly: "I let my brother go to the devil in his own way." In this character, it was frequently his fortune to be the last reputable acquaintance and the last good influence in the lives of down-going men. And to such as these, so long as they came about his chambers, he never marked a shade of change in his demeanour.

No doubt the feat was easy to Mr Utterson; for he was undemonstrative at the best, and even his friendships seemed to be founded in a similar catholicity[2] of good-nature. It is the mark of a modest man to accept his friendly circle ready-made from the hands of opportunity; and that was the lawyer's way. His friends were those of his own blood or those whom he had known the longest; his affections, like ivy, were the growth of time, they implied no aptness in the object. Hence, no doubt, the bond that united him to Mr Richard Enfield, his distant kinsman, the well-known man about town. It was a nut to crack for many, what these two could see in each other or what subject they could find in common. It was reported by those who encountered them in their Sunday walks, that they said nothing, looked singularly dull, and would hail with obvious relief the appearance of a friend. For all that, the two men put the greatest store by these excursions, counted them the chief jewel of each week, and not only set aside occasions of pleasure, but even resisted the calls of business, that they might enjoy them uninterrupted.

---

1. In the Bible, Cain kills his brother Abel. When the Lord asks him where Abel is, Cain replies, "Am I my brother's keeper?" (Genesis 4).
2. Universality.

It chanced on one of these rambles that their way led them down a bystreet in a busy quarter of London. The street was small and what is called quiet, but it drove a thriving trade on the week-days. The inhabitants were all doing well, it seemed, and all emulously hoping to do better still, and laying out the surplus of their gains in coquetry; so that the shop fronts stood along that thoroughfare with an air of invitation, like rows of smiling saleswomen. Even on Sunday, when it veiled its more florid charms and lay comparatively empty of passage, the street shone out in contrast to its dingy neighbourhood, like a fire in a forest; and with its freshly painted shutters, well-polished brasses, and general cleanliness and gaiety of note, instantly caught and pleased the eye of the passenger.

Two doors from one corner, on the left hand going east, the line was broken by the entry of a court; and just at that point, a certain sinister block of building thrust forward its gable on the street. It was two storeys high; showed no window, nothing but a door on the lower storey and a blind forehead of discoloured wall on the upper; and bore in every feature, the marks of prolonged and sordid negligence. The door, which was equipped with neither bell nor knocker, was blistered and distained. Tramps slouched into the recess and struck matches on the panels; children kept shop upon the steps; the schoolboy had tried his knife on the mouldings; and for close on a generation, no one had appeared to drive away these random visitors or to repair their ravages.

Mr Enfield and the lawyer were on the other side of the bystreet; but when they came abreast of the entry, the former lifted up his cane and pointed.

"Did you ever remark that door?" he asked; and when his companion had replied in the affirmative, "It is connected in my mind," added he, "with a very odd story."

"Indeed?" said Mr Utterson, with a slight change of voice, "and what was that?"

"Well, it was this way," returned Mr Enfield: "I was coming home from some place at the end of the world, about three o'clock of a black winter morning, and my way lay through a part of town where there was literally nothing to be seen but lamps. Street after street, and all the folks asleep—street after street, all lighted up as if for a procession and all as empty as a church—till at last I got into that state of mind when a man listens and listens and begins to long for the sight of a policeman. All at once, I saw two figures: one a little man who was stumping along eastward at a good walk, and the other a girl of maybe eight or ten who was running as hard as she was able down a cross street. Well, sir, the two ran into one another naturally enough at the corner; and then came the horrible part of the thing; for the man trampled calmly over the child's body and left her screaming on the ground. It sounds nothing to hear, but it was hellish to see. It wasn't like a man; it was like some damned Juggernaut.[3] I gave a view halloa, took to my heels, collared my gentleman, and brought him back to where there was already quite a group about the screaming child. He was perfectly cool and made no resistance, but gave me one look, so ugly that it brought out the sweat on me like running. The people who had turned out were the girl's own family; and pretty soon, the doctor, for whom she had been sent, put in his appearance. Well, the child was not much the worse, more frightened, according to the Sawbones;[4] and there you might have supposed would be an end to it. But there was one curious circumstance. I had taken a loathing to my gentleman at first sight. So

3. An overwhelming, crushing force (from the Hindu god Jagannath; an idol of this deity was carried on a huge chariot before which devotees are said to have thrown themselves and been crushed to death).

4. Slang for doctor.

had the child's family, which was only natural. But the doctor's case was what struck me. He was the usual cut and dry apothecary, of no particular age and colour, with a strong Edinburgh accent, and about as emotional as a bagpipe. Well, sir, he was like the rest of us; every time he looked at my prisoner, I saw that Sawbones turn sick and white with the desire to kill him. I knew what was in his mind, just as he knew what was in mine; and killing being out of the question, we did the next best. We told the man we could and would make such a scandal out of this, as should make his name stink from one end of London to the other. If he had any friends or any credit, we undertook that he should lose them. And all the time, as we were pitching it in red hot, we were keeping the women off him as best we could, for they were as wild as harpies.[5] I never saw a circle of such hateful faces; and there was the man in the middle, with a kind of black, sneering coolness—frightened too, I could see that—but carrying it off, sir, really like Satan. 'If you choose to make capital out of this accident,' said he, 'I am naturally helpless. No gentleman but wishes to avoid a scene,' says he. 'Name your figure.' Well, we screwed him up to a hundred pounds for the child's family; he would have clearly liked to stick out; but there was something about the lot of us that meant mischief, and at last he struck. The next thing was to get the money, and where do you think he carried us but to that place with the door?—whipped out a key, went in, and presently came back with the matter of ten pounds in gold and a cheque for the balance on Coutts's,[6] drawn payable to bearer and signed with a name that I can't mention, though it's one of the points of my story, but it was a name at least very well known and often printed. The figure was stiff; but the signature was good for more than that, if it was only genuine. I took the liberty of pointing out to my gentleman that the whole business looked apocryphal, and that a man does not, in real life, walk into a cellar door at four in the morning and come out of it with another man's cheque for close upon a hundred pounds. But he was quite easy and sneering. 'Set your mind at rest,' says he, 'I will stay with you till the banks open and cash the cheque myself.' So we all set off, the doctor, and the child's father, and our friend and myself, and passed the rest of the night in my chambers; and next day, when we had breakfasted, went in a body to the bank. I gave in the cheque myself, and said I had every reason to believe it was a forgery. Not a bit of it. The cheque was genuine."

"Tut-tut," said Mr Utterson.

"I see you feel as I do," said Mr Enfield. "Yes, it's a bad story. For my man was a fellow that nobody could have to do with, a really damnable man; and the person that drew the cheque is the very pink of the proprieties, celebrated too, and (what makes it worse) one of your fellows who do what they call good. Black mail, I suppose; an honest man paying through the nose for some of the capers of his youth. Black Mail House is what I call that place with the door, in consequence. Though even that, you know, is far from explaining all," he added, and with the words fell into a vein of musing.

From this he was recalled by Mr Utterson asking rather suddenly: "And you don't know if the drawer of the cheque lives there?"

"A likely place isn't it?" returned Mr Enfield. "But I happen to have noticed his address; he lives in some square or other."

"And you never asked about—the place with the door?" said Mr Utterson.

---

5. Voracious mythical beasts with the head and torso of a woman and the tail, wings, and talons of a bird.   6. An English bank.

"No, sir: I had a delicacy," was the reply. "I feel very strongly about putting questions; it partakes too much of the style of the day of judgment. You start a question, and it's like starting a stone. You sit quietly on the top of a hill; and away the stone goes, starting others; and presently some bland old bird (the last you would have thought of) is knocked on the head in his own back garden and the family have to change their name. No, sir, I make it a rule of mine: the more it looks like Queer Street,[7] the less I ask."

"A very good rule, too," said the lawyer.

"But I have studied the place for myself," continued Mr Enfield. "It seems scarcely a house. There is no other door, and nobody goes in or out of that one but, once in a great while, the gentleman of my adventure. There are three windows looking on the court on the first floor; none below; the windows are always shut but they're clean. And then there is a chimney which is generally smoking; so somebody must live there. And yet it's not so sure; for the buildings are so packed together about that court, that it's hard to say where one ends and another begins."

The pair walked on again for a while in silence; and then "Enfield," said Mr Utterson, "that's a good rule of yours."

"Yes, I think it is," returned Enfield.

"But for all that," continued the lawyer, "there's one point I want to ask: I want to ask the name of that man who walked over the child."

"Well," said Mr Enfield, "I can't see what harm it would do. It was a man of the name of Hyde."

"Hm," said Mr Utterson. "What sort of a man is he to see?"

"He is not easy to describe. There is something wrong with his appearance; something displeasing, something downright detestable. I never saw a man I so disliked, and yet I scarce know why. He must be deformed somewhere; he gives a strong feeling of deformity, although I couldn't specify the point. He's an extraordinary looking man, and yet I really can name nothing out of the way. No, sir; I can make no hand of it; I can't describe him. And it's not want of memory; for I declare I can see him this moment."

Mr Utterson again walked some way in silence and obviously under a weight of consideration. "You are sure he used a key?" he inquired at last.

"My dear sir . . . " began Enfield, surprised out of himself.

"Yes, I know," said Utterson; "I know it must seem strange. The fact is, if I do not ask you the name of the other party, it is because I know it already. You see, Richard, your tale has gone home. If you have been inexact in any point, you had better correct it."

"I think you might have warned me," returned the other with a touch of sullenness. "But I have been pedantically exact, as you call it. The fellow had a key; and what's more, he has it still. I saw him use it, not a week ago."

Mr Utterson sighed deeply but said never a word; and the young man presently resumed. "Here is another lesson to say nothing," said he. "I am ashamed of my long tongue. Let us make a bargain never to refer to this again."

"With all my heart," said the lawyer. "I shake hands on that, Richard."

Search for Mr Hyde

That evening, Mr Utterson came home to his bachelor house in sombre spirits and sat down to dinner without relish. It was his custom of a Sunday, when this meal was over, to sit close by the fire, a volume of some dry divinity on his reading desk, until

7. A peculiar or suspicious situation, perhaps involving financial difficulties.

the clock of the neighbouring church rang out the hour of twelve, when he would go soberly and gratefully to bed. On this night, however, as soon as the cloth was taken away, he took up a candle and went into his business room. There he opened his safe, took from the most private part of it a document endorsed on the envelope as Dr Jekyll's Will, and sat down with a clouded brow to study its contents. The will was holograph,[8] for Mr Utterson, though he took charge of it now that it was made, had refused to lend the least assistance in the making of it; it provided not only that, in case of the decease of Henry Jekyll, M.D., D.C.L., LL.D., F.R.S., &c.,[9] all his possessions were to pass into the hands of his "friend and benefactor Edward Hyde," but that in case of Dr Jekyll's "disappearance or unexplained absence for any period exceeding three calendar months," the said Edward Hyde should step into the said Henry Jekyll's shoes without further delay and free from any burthen or obligation, beyond the payment of a few small sums to the members of the doctor's household. This document had long been the lawyer's eyesore. It offended him both as a lawyer and as a lover of the sane and customary sides of life, to whom the fanciful was the immodest. And hitherto it was his ignorance of Mr Hyde that had swelled his indignation; now, by a sudden turn, it was his knowledge. It was already bad enough when the name was but a name of which he could learn no more. It was worse when it began to be clothed upon with detestable attributes; and out of the shifting, insubstantial mists that had so long baffled his eye, there leaped up the sudden, definite presentment of a fiend.

"I thought it was madness," he said, as he replaced the obnoxious paper in the safe, "and now I begin to fear it is disgrace."

With that he blew out his candle, put on a great coat and set forth in the direction of Cavendish Square, that citadel of medicine where his friend, the great Dr Lanyon, had his house and received his crowding patients. "If anyone knows, it will be Lanyon," he had thought.

The solemn butler knew and welcomed him; he was subjected to no stage of delay, but ushered direct from the door to the dining-room where Dr Lanyon sat alone over his wine. This was a hearty, healthy, dapper, red-faced gentleman, with a shock of hair prematurely white, and a boisterous and decided manner. At sight of Mr Utterson, he sprang up from his chair and welcomed him with both hands. The geniality, as was the way of the man, was somewhat theatrical to the eye; but it reposed on genuine feeling. For these two were old friends, old mates both at school and college, both thorough respecters of themselves and of each other, and, what does not always follow, men who thoroughly enjoyed each other's company.

After a little rambling talk, the lawyer led up to the subject which so disagreeably preoccupied his mind.

"I suppose, Lanyon," said he, "you and I must be the two oldest friends that Henry Jekyll has?"

"I wish the friends were younger," chuckled Dr Lanyon. "But I suppose we are. And what of that? I see little of him now."

"Indeed?" said Utterson. "I thought you had a bond of common interest."

"We had," was the reply. "But it is more than ten years since Henry Jekyll became too fanciful for me. He began to go wrong, wrong in mind; and though of course I continue to take an interest in him for old sake's sake as they say, I see and I

8. A document in the handwriting of the person who has signed it.

9. Medical Doctor, Doctor of Civil Law, Doctor of Law, Fellow of the Royal Society.

have seen devilish little of the man. Such unscientific balderdash," added the doctor, flushing suddenly purple, "would have estranged Damon and Pythias."[1]

This little spirt of temper was somewhat of a relief to Mr Utterson. "They have only differed on some point of science," he thought; and being a man of no scientific passions (except in the matter of conveyancing[2]) he even added: "It is nothing worse than that!" He gave his friend a few seconds to recover his composure, and then approached the question he had come to put.

"Did you ever come across a protégé[3] of his—one Hyde?" he asked.

"Hyde?" repeated Lanyon. "No. Never heard of him. Since my time."

That was the amount of information that the lawyer carried back with him to the great, dark bed on which he tossed to and fro, until the small hours of the morning began to grow large. It was a night of little ease to his toiling mind, toiling in mere darkness and besieged by questions.

Six o'clock struck on the bells of the church that was so conveniently near to Mr Utterson's dwelling, and still he was digging at the problem. Hitherto it had touched him on the intellectual side alone; but now his imagination also was engaged or rather enslaved; and as he lay and tossed in the gross darkness of the night and the curtained room, Mr Enfield's tale went by before his mind in a scroll of lighted pictures. He would be aware of the great field of lamps of a nocturnal city; then of the figure of a man walking swiftly; then of a child running from the doctor's; and then these met, and that human Juggernaut trod the child down and passed on regardless of her screams. Or else he would see a room in a rich house, where his friend lay asleep, dreaming and smiling at his dreams; and then the door of that room would be opened, the curtains of the bed plucked apart, the sleeper recalled, and lo! there would stand by his side a figure to whom power was given, and even at that dead hour, he must rise and do its bidding.[4] The figure in these two phases haunted the lawyer all night; and if at any time he dozed over, it was but to see it glide more stealthily through sleeping houses, or move the more swiftly and still the more swiftly, even to dizziness, through wider labyrinths of lamplighted city, and at every street corner crush a child and leave her screaming. And still the figure had no face by which he might know it; even in his dreams, it had no face, or one that baffled him and melted before his eyes; and thus it was that there sprang up and grew apace in the lawyer's mind a singularly strong, almost an inordinate, curiosity to behold the features of the real Mr Hyde. If he could but once set eyes on him, he thought the mystery would lighten and perhaps roll altogether away, as was the habit of mysterious things when well examined. He might see a reason for his friend's strange preference or bondage (call it which you please) and even for the startling clauses of the will. And at least it would be a face worth seeing: the face of a man who was without bowels of mercy: a face which had but to show itself to raise up, in the mind of the unimpressionable Enfield, a spirit of enduring hatred.

From that time forward, Mr Utterson began to haunt the door in the bystreet of shops. In the morning before office hours, at noon when business was plenty and time scarce, at night under the face of the fogged city moon, by all lights and at all hours of solitude or concourse, the lawyer was to be found on his chosen post.

"If he be Mr Hyde," he had thought, "I shall be Mr Seek."

---

1. Legendary friends in ancient Greece.
2. The transfer of property.
3. A person whose career is aided by a more experienced

or influential person.
4. Cf. Mary Shelley's *Frankenstein* (ch. 4), where the monster stands over his sleeping creator.

And at last his patience was rewarded. It was a fine dry night; frost in the air; the streets as clean as a ballroom floor; the lamps, unshaken by any wind, drawing a regular pattern of light and shadow. By ten o'clock, when the shops were closed, the bystreet was very solitary and, in spite of the low growl of London from all round, very silent. Small sounds carried far; domestic sounds out of the houses were clearly audible on either side of the roadway; and the rumour of the approach of any passenger preceded him by a long time. Mr Utterson had been some minutes at his post, when he was aware of an odd, light footstep drawing near. In the course of his nightly patrols, he had long grown accustomed to the quaint effect with which the footfalls of a single person, while he is still a great way off, suddenly spring out distinct from the vast hum and clatter of the city. Yet his attention had never before been so sharply and decisively arrested; and it was with a strong, superstitious prevision of success that he withdrew into the entry of the court.

The steps drew swiftly nearer, and swelled out suddenly louder as they turned the end of the street. The lawyer, looking forth from the entry, could soon see what manner of man he had to deal with. He was small and very plainly dressed, and the look of him, even at that distance, went somehow strongly against the watcher's inclination. But he made straight for the door, crossing the roadway to save time; and as he came, he drew a key from his pocket like one approaching home.

Mr Utterson stepped out and touched him on the shoulder as he passed. "Mr Hyde, I think?"

Mr Hyde shrank back with a hissing intake of the breath. But his fear was only momentary; and though he did not look the lawyer in the face, he answered coolly enough: "That is my name. What do you want?"

"I see you are going in," returned the lawyer. "I am an old friend of Dr Jekyll's—Mr Utterson of Gaunt Street—you must have heard my name; and meeting you so conveniently, I thought you might admit me."

"You will not find Dr Jekyll; he is from home," replied Mr Hyde, blowing in the key. And then suddenly, but still without looking up, "How did you know me?" he asked.

"On your side," said Mr Utterson, "will you do me a favour?"

"With pleasure," replied the other. "What shall it be?"

"Will you let me see your face?" asked the lawyer.

Mr Hyde appeared to hesitate, and then, as if upon some sudden reflection, fronted about with an air of defiance; and the pair stared at each other pretty fixedly for a few seconds. "Now I shall know you again," said Mr Utterson. "It may be useful."

"Yes," returned Mr Hyde, "it is as well we have met; and *a propos*, you should have my address." And he gave a number of a street in Soho.

"Good God!" thought Mr Utterson, "can he too have been thinking of the will?" But he kept his feelings to himself and only grunted in acknowledgement of the address.

"And now," said the other, "how did you know me?"

"By description," was the reply.

"Whose description?"

"We have common friends," said Mr Utterson.

"Common friends?" echoed Mr Hyde, a little hoarsely. "Who are they?"

"Jekyll, for instance," said the lawyer.

"He never told you," cried Mr Hyde, with a flush of anger. "I did not think you would have lied."

"Come," said Mr Utterson, "that is not fitting language."

The other snarled aloud into a savage laugh; and the next moment with extraordinary quickness, he had unlocked the door and disappeared into the house.

The lawyer stood awhile when Mr Hyde had left him, the picture of disquietude. Then he began slowly to mount the street, pausing every step or two and putting his hand to his brow like a man in mental perplexity. The problem he was thus debating as he walked, was one of a class that is rarely solved. Mr Hyde was pale and dwarfish, he gave an impression of deformity without any nameable malformation, he had a displeasing smile, he had borne himself to the lawyer with a sort of murderous mixture of timidity and boldness, and he spoke with a husky, whispering and somewhat broken voice; all these were points against him, but not all of these together could explain the hitherto unknown disgust, loathing and fear with which Mr Utterson regarded him. "There must be something else," said the perplexed gentleman. "There *is* something more, if I could find a name for it. God bless me, the man seems hardly human! Something troglodytic,[5] shall we say? or can it be the old story of Dr Fell?[6] or is it the mere radiance of a foul soul that thus transpires through, and transfigures, its clay continent? The last, I think; for O my poor old Harry[7] Jekyll, if ever I read Satan's signature upon a face, it is on that of your new friend."

Round the corner from the bystreet, there was a square of ancient, handsome houses, now for the most part decayed from their high estate and let in flats and chambers to all sorts and conditions of men: map engravers, architects, shady lawyers and the agents of obscure enterprises. One house, however, second from the corner, was still occupied entire; and at the door of this, which wore a great air of wealth and comfort, though it was now plunged in darkness except for the fan-light, Mr Utterson stopped and knocked. A well-dressed, elderly servant opened the door.

"Is Dr Jekyll at home, Poole?" asked the lawyer.

"I will see, Mr Utterson," said Poole, admitting the visitor, as he spoke, into a large, low-roofed, comfortable hall, paved with flags, warmed (after the fashion of a country house) by a bright, open fire, and furnished with costly cabinets of oak. "Will you wait here by the fire, sir? or shall I give you a light in the dining-room?"

"Here, thank you," said the lawyer, and he drew near and leaned on the tall fender. This hall, in which he was now left alone, was a pet fancy of his friend the doctor's; and Utterson himself was wont to speak of it as the pleasantest room in London. But to-night there was a shudder in his blood; the face of Hyde sat heavy on his memory; he felt (what was rare with him) a nausea and distaste of life; and in the gloom of his spirits, he seemed to read a menace in the flickering of the firelight on the polished cabinets and the uneasy starting of the shadow on the roof. He was ashamed of his relief, when Poole presently returned to announce that Dr Jekyll was gone out.

"I saw Mr Hyde go in by the old dissecting room door, Poole," he said. "Is that right, when Dr Jekyll is from home?"

"Quite right, Mr Utterson, sir," replied the servant. "Mr Hyde has a key."

"Your master seems to repose a great deal of trust in that young man, Poole," resumed the other musingly.

"Yes, sir, he do indeed," said Poole. "We have all orders to obey him."

5. Primitive and brutish, like a cave dweller.
6. An allusion to Thomas Brown's famous rhyme about the Dean of Christ Church, Oxford, Dr. John Fell (1625–1686): "I do not love thee, Dr. Fell, / The reason why I cannot tell; / But this I know, and know full well, / I do not love thee, Dr. Fell."
7. "Old Harry" is slang for the devil.

"I do not think I ever met Mr Hyde?" asked Utterson.

"O, dear no, sir. He never *dines* here," replied the butler. "Indeed we see very lit-tle of him on this side of the house; he mostly comes and goes by the laboratory."

"Well, good night, Poole."

"Good night, Mr Utterson."

And the lawyer set out homeward with a very heavy heart. "Poor Harry Jekyll," he thought, "my mind misgives me he is in deep waters! He was wild when he was young; a long while ago to be sure; but in the law of God, there is no statute of limi-tations. Ay, it must be that; the ghost of some old sin, the cancer of some concealed disgrace: punishment coming, *pede claudo*,[8] years after memory has forgotten and self-love condoned the fault." And the lawyer, scared by the thought, brooded awhile on his own past, groping in all the corners of memory, lest by chance some Jack-in-the-Box of an old iniquity should leap to light there. His past was fairly blameless; few men could read the rolls of their life with less apprehension; yet he was humbled to the dust by the many ill things he had done, and raised up again into a sober and fear-ful gratitude by the many that he had come so near to doing, yet avoided. And then by a return on his former subject, he conceived a spark of hope. "This Master Hyde, if he were studied," thought he, "must have secrets of his own: black secrets, by the look of him; secrets compared to which poor Jekyll's worst would be like sunshine. Things cannot continue as they are. It turns me cold to think of this creature stealing like a thief to Harry's bedside; poor Harry, what a wakening! And the danger of it; for if this Hyde suspects the existence of the will, he may grow impatient to inherit. Ay, I must put my shoulder to the wheel—if Jekyll will but let me," he added, "if Jekyll will only let me." For once more he saw before his mind's eye, as clear as a trans-parency, the strange clauses of the will.

Dr Jekyll Was Quite at Ease

A fortnight later, by excellent good fortune, the doctor gave one of his pleasant din-ners to some five or six old cronies, all intelligent, reputable men and all judges of good wine; and Mr Utterson so contrived that he remained behind after the others had departed. This was no new arrangement, but a thing that had befallen many scores of times. Where Utterson was liked, he was liked well. Hosts loved to detain the dry lawyer, when the light-hearted and the loose-tongued had already their foot on the threshold; they liked to sit awhile in his unobtrusive company, practising for solitude, sobering their minds in the man's rich silence after the expense and strain of gaiety. To this rule, Dr Jekyll was no exception; and as he now sat on the opposite side of the fire—a large, well-made, smooth-faced man of fifty, with something of a slyish cast perhaps, but every mark of capacity and kindness—you could see by his looks that he cherished for Mr Utterson a sincere and warm affection.

"I have been wanting to speak to you, Jekyll," began the latter. "You know that will of yours?"

A close observer might have gathered that the topic was distasteful; but the doc-tor carried it off gaily. "My poor Utterson," said he, "you are unfortunate in such a client. I never saw a man so distressed as you were by my will; unless it were that hide-bound pedant, Lanyon, at what he called my scientific heresies. O, I know he's a good fellow—you needn't frown—an excellent fellow, and I always mean to see more

8. On halting foot (Latin); i.e. limping.

of him; but a hide-bound pedant for all that; an ignorant, blatant pedant. I was never more disappointed in any man than Lanyon."

"You know I never approved of it," pursued Utterson, ruthlessly disregarding the fresh topic.

"My will? Yes, certainly, I know that," said the doctor, a trifle sharply. "You have told me so."

"Well, I tell you so again," continued the lawyer. "I have been learning something of young Hyde."

The large handsome face of Dr Jekyll grew pale to the very lips, and there came a blackness about his eyes. "I do not care to hear more," said he. "This is a matter I thought we had agreed to drop."

"What I heard was abominable," said Utterson.

"It can make no change. You do not understand my position," returned the doctor, with certain incoherency of manner. "I am painfully situated, Utterson; my position is a very strange—a very strange one. It is one of those affairs that cannot be mended by talking."

"Jekyll," said Utterson, "you know me: I am a man to be trusted. Make a clean breast of this in confidence; and I make no doubt I can get you out of it."

"My good Utterson," said the doctor, "this is very good of you, this is downright good of you, and I cannot find words to thank you in. I believe you fully; I would trust you before any man alive, ay, before myself, if I could make the choice; but indeed it isn't what you fancy; it is not so bad as that; and just to put your good heart at rest, I will tell you one thing: the moment I choose, I can be rid of Mr Hyde. I give you my hand upon that; and I thank you again and again; and I will just add one little word, Utterson, that I'm sure you'll take in good part: this is a private matter, and I beg of you to let it sleep."

Utterson reflected a little looking in the fire.

"I have no doubt you are perfectly right," he said at last, getting to his feet.

"Well, but since we have touched upon this business, and for the last time I hope," continued the doctor, "there is one point I should like you to understand. I have really a very great interest in poor Hyde. I know you have seen him; he told me so; and I fear he was rude. But I do sincerely take a great, a very great interest in that young man; and if I am taken away, Utterson, I wish you to promise me that you will bear with him and get his rights for him. I think you would, if you knew all; and it would be a weight off my mind if you would promise."

"I can't pretend that I shall ever like him," said the lawyer.

"I don't ask that," pleaded Jekyll, laying his hand upon the other's arm; "I only ask for justice; I only ask you to help him for my sake, when I am no longer here."

Utterson heaved an irrepressible sigh. "Well," said he. "I promise."

The Carew Murder Case

Nearly a year later, in the month of October 18—, London was startled by a crime of singular ferocity and rendered all the more notable by the high position of the victim. The details were few and startling. A maid servant living alone in a house not far from the river, had gone upstairs to bed about eleven. Although a fog rolled over the city in the small hours, the early part of the night was cloudless, and the lane, which the maid's window overlooked, was brilliantly lit by the full moon. It seems she was romantically given, for she sat down upon her box, which stood immediately under the window, and fell into a dream of musing. Never (she used to say, with streaming tears, when she narrated that experience) never had she felt more at peace with all men or thought more kindly of the world. And as she so sat she became aware of an aged and beautiful gentleman with white hair, drawing near along the lane; and advancing to meet him, another and very small gentleman, to whom at first she paid less attention. When they had come within speech (which was just under the maid's eyes) the older man bowed and accosted the other with a very pretty manner of politeness. It did not seem as if the subject of his address were of great importance; indeed, from his pointing, it sometimes appeared as if he were only inquiring his way; but the moon shone on his face as he spoke, and the girl was pleased to watch it, it seemed to breathe such an innocent and old-world kindness of disposition, yet with something high too, as of a well-founded self-content. Presently her eye wandered to the other, and she was surprised to recognise in him a certain Mr Hyde, who had once visited her master and for whom she had conceived a dislike. He had in his hand a heavy cane, with which he was trifling; but he answered never a word, and seemed to listen with an ill-contained impatience. And then all of a sudden he broke out in a great flame of anger, stamping with his foot, brandishing the cane, and carrying on (as the maid described it) like a madman. The old gentleman took a step back, with the air of one very much surprised and a trifle hurt; and at that Mr Hyde broke out of all bounds and clubbed him to the earth. And next moment, with apelike fury, he was trampling his victim under foot, and hailing down a storm of blows, under which the bones were audibly shattered and the body jumped upon the roadway. At the horror of these sights and sounds, the maid fainted.

It was two o'clock when she came to herself and called for the police. The murderer was gone long ago; but there lay his victim in the middle of the lane, incredibly mangled. The stick with which the deed had been done, although it was of some rare and very tough and heavy wood, had broken in the middle under the stress of this insensate cruelty; and one splintered half had rolled in the neighbouring gutter—the other, without doubt, had been carried away by the murderer. A purse and a gold watch were found upon the victim; but no cards or papers, except a sealed and stamped envelope, which he had been probably carrying to the post, and which bore the name and address of Mr Utterson.

This was brought to the lawyer the next morning, before he was out of bed; and he had no sooner seen it, and been told the circumstances, than he shot out a solemn lip. "I shall say nothing till I have seen the body," said he; "this may be very serious. Have the kindness to wait while I dress." And with the same grave countenance he hurried through his breakfast and drove to the police station, whither the body had been carried. As soon as he came into the cell, he nodded.

"Yes," said he, "I recognise him. I am sorry to say that this is Sir Danvers Carew."

"Good God, sir," exclaimed the officer, "is it possible?" And the next moment his eye lighted up with professional ambition. "This will make a deal of noise," he said. "And perhaps you can help us to the man." And he briefly narrated what the maid had seen, and showed the broken stick.

Mr Utterson had already quailed at the name of Hyde; but when the stick was laid before him, he could doubt no longer: broken and battered as it was, he recognised it for one that he had himself presented many years before to Henry Jekyll.

"Is this Mr Hyde a person of small stature?" he inquired.

"Particularly small and particularly wicked-looking, is what the maid calls him," said the officer.

Mr Utterson reflected; and then, raising his head, "If you will come with me in my cab," he said, "I think I can take you to his house."

It was by this time about nine in the morning, and the first fog of the season. A great chocolate-coloured pall lowered over heaven, but the wind was continually charging and routing these embattled vapours; so that as the cab crawled from street to street, Mr Utterson beheld a marvellous number of degrees and hues of twilight; for here it would be dark like the back-end of evening; and there would be a glow of a rich, lurid brown, like the light of some strange conflagration; and here, for a moment, the fog would be quite broken up, and a haggard shaft of daylight would glance in between the swirling wreaths. The dismal quarter of Soho seen under these changing glimpses, with its muddy ways, and slatternly passengers, and its lamps, which had never been extinguished or had been kindled afresh to combat this mournful reinvasion of darkness, seemed, in the lawyer's eyes, like a district of some city in a nightmare. The thoughts of his mind, besides, were of the gloomiest dye; and when he glanced at the companion of his drive, he was conscious of some touch of that terror of the law and the law's officers, which may at times assail the most honest.

As the cab drew up before the address indicated, the fog lifted a little and showed him a dingy street, a gin palace, a low French eating house, a shop for the retail of penny numbers and twopenny salads, many ragged children huddled in the doorways, and many women of many different nationalities passing out, key in hand, to have a morning glass; and the next moment the fog settled down again upon that part, as brown as umber, and cut him off from his blackguardly surroundings. This was the home of Henry Jekyll's favourite; of a man who was heir to quarter of a million sterling.

An ivory-faced and silvery-haired old woman opened the door. She had an evil face, smoothed by hypocrisy; but her manners were excellent. Yes, she said, this was Mr Hyde's, but he was not at home; he had been in that night very late, but had gone away again in less than an hour; there was nothing strange in that; his habits were very irregular, and he was often absent; for instance, it was nearly two months since she had seen him till yesterday.

"Very well then, we wish to see his rooms," said the lawyer; and when the woman began to declare it was impossible, "I had better tell you who this person is," he added. "This is Inspector Newcomen of Scotland Yard."

A flash of odious joy appeared upon the woman's face. "Ah!" said she, "he is in trouble! What has he done?"

Mr Utterson and the inspector exchanged glances. "He don't seem a very popular character," observed the latter. "And now, my good woman, just let me and this gentleman have a look about us."

In the whole extent of the house, which but for the old woman remained otherwise empty, Mr Hyde had only used a couple of rooms; but these were furnished with luxury and good taste. A closet was filled with wine; the plate was of silver, the napery[9] elegant; a good picture hung upon the walls, a gift (as Utterson supposed) from Henry Jekyll, who was much of a connoisseur; and the carpets were of many plies and agreeable in colour. At this moment, however, the rooms bore every mark

9. Table linens.

of having been recently and hurriedly ransacked; clothes lay about the floor, with their pockets inside out; lockfast drawers stood open; and on the hearth there lay a pile of gray ashes, as though many papers had been burned. From these embers the inspector disinterred the butt end of a green cheque book, which had resisted the action of the fire; the other half of the stick was found behind the door; and as this clinched his suspicions, the officer declared himself delighted. A visit to the bank, where several thousand pounds were found to be lying to the murderer's credit, completed his gratification.

"You may depend upon it, sir," he told Mr Utterson: "I have him in my hand. He must have lost his head, or he never would have left the stick or, above all, burned the cheque book. Why, money's life to the man. We have nothing to do but wait for him at the bank, and get out the handbills."

This last, however, was not so easy of accomplishment; for Mr Hyde had numbered few familiars—even the master of the servant maid had only seen him twice; his family could nowhere be traced; he had never been photographed; and the few who could describe him differed widely, as common observers will. Only on one point, were they agreed; and that was the haunting sense of unexpressed deformity with which the fugitive impressed his beholders.

Incident of the Letter

It was late in the afternoon, when Mr Utterson found his way to Dr Jekyll's door, where he was at once admitted by Poole, and carried down by the kitchen offices and across a yard which had once been a garden, to the building which was indifferently known as the laboratory or the dissecting rooms. The doctor had bought the house from the heirs of a celebrated surgeon; and his own tastes being rather chemical than anatomical, had changed the destination of the block at the bottom of the garden. It was the first time that the lawyer had been received in that part of his friend's quarters; and he eyed the dingy windowless structure with curiosity, and gazed round with a distasteful sense of strangeness as he crossed the theatre, once crowded with eager students and now lying gaunt and silent, the tables laden with chemical apparatus, the floor strewn with crates and littered with packing straw, and the light falling dimly through the foggy cupola. At the further end, a flight of stairs mounted to a door covered with red baize; and through this, Mr Utterson was at last received into the doctor's cabinet. It was a large room, fitted round with glass presses, furnished, among other things, with a cheval-glass and a business table, and looking out upon the court by three dusty windows barred with iron. The fire burned in the grate; a lamp was set lighted on the chimney shelf, for even in the houses the fog began to lie thickly; and there, close up to the warmth, sat Dr Jekyll, looking deadly sick. He did not rise to meet his visitor, but held out a cold hand and bade him welcome in a changed voice.

"And now," said Mr Utterson, as soon as Poole had left them, "you have heard the news?"

The doctor shuddered. "They were crying it in the square," he said. "I heard them in my dining-room."

"One word," said the lawyer. "Carew was my client, but so are you, and I want to know what I am doing. You have not been mad enough to hide this fellow?"

"Utterson, I swear to God," cried the doctor, "I swear to God I will never set eyes on him again. I bind my honour to you that I am done with him in this world. It is all at an end. And indeed he does not want my help; you do not know him as I do; he is safe, he is quite safe; mark my words, he will never more be heard of."

The lawyer listened gloomily; he did not like his friend's feverish manner. "You seem pretty sure of him," said he; "and for your sake, I hope you may be right. If it came to a trial your name might appear."

"I am quite sure of him," replied Jekyll; "I have grounds for certainty that I cannot share with any one. But there is one thing on which you may advise me. I have— I have received a letter; and I am at a loss whether I should show it to the police. I should like to leave it in your hands, Utterson; you would judge wisely, I am sure; I have so great a trust in you."

"You fear, I suppose, that it might lead to his detection?" asked the lawyer.

"No," said the other. "I cannot say that I care what becomes of Hyde; I am quite done with him. I was thinking of my own character, which this hateful business has rather exposed."

Utterson ruminated awhile; he was surprised at his friend's selfishness, and yet relieved by it. "Well," said he at last, "let me see the letter."

The letter was written in an odd, upright hand and signed "Edward Hyde": and it signified, briefly enough, that the writer's benefactor, Dr Jekyll, whom he had long so unworthily repaid for a thousand generosities, need labour under no alarm for his safety, as he had means of escape on which he placed a sure dependence. The lawyer liked this letter well enough; it put a better colour on the intimacy than he had looked for; and he blamed himself for some of his past suspicions.

"Have you the envelope?" he asked.

"I burned it," replied Jekyll, "before I thought what I was about. But it bore no postmark. The note was handed in."

"Shall I keep this and sleep upon it?" asked Utterson.

"I wish you to judge for me entirely," was the reply. "I have lost confidence in myself."

"Well, I shall consider," returned the lawyer.—"And now one word more: it was Hyde who dictated the terms in your will about that disappearance?"

The doctor seemed seized with a qualm of faintness; he shut his mouth tight and nodded.

"I knew it," said Utterson. "He meant to murder you. You have had a fine escape."

"I have had what is far more to the purpose," returned the doctor solemnly: "I have had a lesson—O God, Utterson, what a lesson I have had!" And he covered his face for a moment with his hands.

On his way out, the lawyer stopped and had a word or two with Poole. "By the by," said he, "there was a letter handed in to-day: what was the messenger like?" But Poole was positive nothing had come except by post; "and only circulars by that," he added.

This news sent off the visitor with his fears renewed. Plainly the letter had come by the laboratory door; possibly indeed, it had been written in the cabinet; and if that were so, it must be differently judged, and handled with the more caution. The newsboys, as he went, were crying themselves hoarse along the footways: "Special edition. Shocking murder of an M.P."[1] That was the funeral oration of one friend and client; and he could not help a certain apprehension lest the good name

1. Member of Parliament.

of another should be sucked down in the eddy of the scandal. It was, at least, a tick-lish decision that he had to make; and, self-reliant as he was by habit, he began to cherish a longing for advice. It was not to be had directly; but perhaps, he thought, it might be fished for.

Presently after, he sat on one side of his own hearth, with Mr Guest, his head clerk, upon the other, and midway between, at a nicely calculated distance from the fire, a bottle of a particular old wine that had long dwelt unsunned in the foundations of his house. The fog still slept on the wing above the drowned city, where the lamps glimmered like carbuncles; and through the muffle and smother of these fallen clouds, the procession of the town's life was still rolling on through the great arteries with a sound as of a mighty wind. But the room was gay with firelight. In the bottle the acids were long ago resolved; the imperial dye had soft-ened with time, as the colour grows richer in stained windows; and the glow of hot autumn afternoons on hillside vineyards was ready to be set free and to disperse the fogs of London. Insensibly the lawyer melted. There was no man from whom he kept fewer secrets than Mr Guest; and he was not always sure that he kept as many as he meant. Guest had often been on business to the doctor's; he knew Poole; he could scarce have failed to hear of Mr Hyde's familiarity about the house; he might draw conclusions: was it not as well, then, that he should see a letter which put that mystery to rights? and above all since Guest, being a great student and critic of handwriting, would consider the step natural and obliging? The clerk, besides, was a man of counsel; he would scarce read so strange a docu-ment without dropping a remark; and by that remark Mr Utterson might shape his future course.

"This is a sad business about Sir Danvers," he said.

"Yes, sir, indeed. It has elicited a great deal of public feeling," returned Guest. "The man, of course, was mad."

"I should like to hear your views on that," replied Utterson. "I have a document here in his handwriting; it is between ourselves, for I scarce know what to do about it; it is an ugly business at the best. But there it is; quite in your way: a murderer's auto-graph."

Guest's eyes brightened, and he sat down at once and studied it with passion. "No, sir," he said; "not mad; but it is an odd hand."

"And by all accounts a very odd writer," added the lawyer.

Just then the servant entered with a note.

"Is that from Dr Jekyll, sir?" inquired the clerk. "I thought I knew the writing. Anything private, Mr Utterson?"

"Only an invitation to dinner. Why? do you want to see it?"

"One moment. I thank you, sir;" and the clerk laid the two sheets of paper along-side and sedulously compared their contents. "Thank you, sir," he said at last, return-ing both; "it's a very interesting autograph."

There was a pause, during which Mr Utterson struggled with himself. "Why did you compare them, Guest?" he inquired suddenly.

"Well, sir," returned the clerk, "there's a rather singular resemblance; the two hands are in many points identical: only differently sloped."

"Rather quaint," said Utterson.

"It is, as you say, rather quaint," returned Guest.

"I wouldn't speak of this note, you know," said the master.

"No, sir," said the clerk. "I understand."

But no sooner was Mr Utterson alone that night than he locked the note into his safe, where it reposed from that time forward. "What!" he thought. "Henry Jekyll forge for a murderer!" And his blood ran cold in his veins.

Remarkable Incident of Doctor Lanyon

Time ran on; thousands of pounds were offered in reward, for the death of Sir Danvers was resented as a public injury; but Mr Hyde had disappeared out of the ken of the police as though he had never existed. Much of his past was unearthed, indeed, and all disreputable: tales came out of the man's cruelty, at once so callous and violent, of his vile life, of his strange associates, of the hatred that seemed to have surrounded his career; but of his present whereabouts, not a whisper. From the time he had left the house in Soho on the morning of the murder, he was simply blotted out; and gradually, as time drew on, Mr Utterson began to recover from the hotness of his alarm, and to grow more at quiet with himself. The death of Sir Danvers was, to his way of thinking, more than paid for by the disappearance of Mr Hyde. Now that that evil influence had been withdrawn, a new life began for Dr Jekyll. He came out of his seclusion, renewed relations with his friends, became once more their familiar guest and entertainer; and whilst he had always been known for charities, he was now no less distinguished for religion. He was busy, he was much in the open air, he did good; his face seemed to open and brighten, as if with an inward consciousness of service; and for more than two months, the doctor was at peace.

On the 8th of January Utterson had dined at the doctor's with a small party; Lanyon had been there; and the face of the host had looked from one to the other as in the old days when the trio were inseparable friends. On the 12th, and again on the 14th, the door was shut against the lawyer. "The doctor was confined to the house," Poole said, "and saw no one." On the 15th, he tried again, and was again refused; and having now been used for the last two months to see his friend almost daily, he found this return of solitude to weigh upon his spirits. The fifth night, he had in Guest to dine with him; and the sixth he betook himself to Doctor Lanyon's.

There at least he was not denied admittance; but when he came in, he was shocked at the change which had taken place in the doctor's appearance. He had his death-warrant written legibly upon his face. The rosy man had grown pale; his flesh had fallen away; he was visibly balder and older; and yet it was not so much these tokens of a swift physical decay that arrested the lawyer's notice, as the look in the eye and quality of manner that seemed to testify to some deep-seated terror of the mind. It was unlikely that the doctor should fear death; and yet that was what Utterson was tempted to suspect. "Yes," he thought; "he is a doctor, he must know his own state and that his days are counted; and the knowledge is more than he can bear." And yet when Utterson remarked on his ill-looks, it was with an air of great firmness that Lanyon declared himself a doomed man.

"I have had a shock," he said, "and I shall never recover. It is a question of weeks. Well, life has been pleasant; I liked it; yes, sir, I used to like it. I sometimes think if we knew all we should be more glad to get away."

"Jekyll is ill, too," observed Utterson. "Have you seen him?"

But Lanyon's face changed, and he held up a trembling hand. "I wish to see or hear no more of Doctor Jekyll," he said in a loud, unsteady voice. I am quite done with that person; and I beg that you will spare me any allusion to one whom I regard as dead."

"Tut-tut," said Mr Utterson; and then after a considerable pause, "Can't I do anything?" he inquired. "We are three very old friends, Lanyon; we shall not live to make others."

"Nothing can be done," returned Lanyon; "ask himself."

"He will not see me," said the lawyer.

"I am not surprised at that," was the reply. "Some day, Utterson, after I am dead, you may perhaps come to learn the right and wrong of this. I cannot tell you. And in the meantime, if you can sit and talk with me of other things, for God's sake, stay and do so; but if you cannot keep clear of this accursed topic, then, in God's name, go, for I cannot bear it."

As soon as he got home, Utterson sat down and wrote to Jekyll, complaining of his exclusion from the house, and asking the cause of this unhappy break with Lanyon; and the next day brought him a long answer, often very pathetically worded, and sometimes darkly mysterious in drift. The quarrel with Lanyon was incurable. "I do not blame our old friend," Jekyll wrote, "but I share his view that we must never meet. I mean from henceforth to lead a life of extreme seclusion; you must not be surprised, nor must you doubt my friendship, if my door is often shut even to you. You must suffer me to go my own dark way. I have brought on myself a punishment and a danger that I cannot name. If I am the chief of sinners, I am the chief of sufferers also. I could not think that this earth contained a place for sufferings and terrors so unmanning; and you can do but one thing, Utterson, to lighten this destiny, and that is to respect my silence." Utterson was amazed; the dark influence of Hyde had been withdrawn, the doctor had returned to his old tasks and amities; a week ago, the prospect had smiled with every promise of a cheerful and an honoured age; and now in a moment, friendship, and peace of mind and the whole tenor of his life were wrecked. So great and unprepared a change pointed to madness; but in view of Lanyon's manner and words, there must lie for it some deeper ground.

A week afterwards Dr Lanyon took to his bed, and in something less than a fortnight he was dead. The night after the funeral, at which he had been sadly affected, Utterson locked the door of his business room, and sitting there by the light of a melancholy candle, drew out and set before him an envelope addressed by the hand and sealed with the seal of his dead friend. "PRIVATE: for the hands of J.G. Utterson ALONE and in case of his predecease *to be destroyed unread*," so it was emphatically superscribed; and the lawyer dreaded to behold the contents. "I have buried one friend to-day," he thought: "what if this should cost me another?" And then he condemned the fear as a disloyalty, and broke the seal. Within there was another enclosure, likewise sealed, and marked upon the cover as "not to be opened till the death or disappearance of Dr Henry Jekyll." Utterson could not trust his eyes. Yes, it was disappearance; here again, as in the mad will which he had long ago restored to its author, here again were the idea of a disappearance and the name of Henry Jekyll bracketed. But in the will, that idea had sprung from the sinister suggestion of the man Hyde; it was set there with a purpose all too plain and horrible. Written by the hand of Lanyon, what should it mean? A great curiosity came on the trustee, to disregard the prohibition and dive at once to the bottom of these mysteries; but professional honour and faith to his dead friend were stringent obligations; and the packet slept in the inmost corner of his private safe.

It is one thing to mortify curiosity, another to conquer it; and it may be doubted if, from that day forth, Utterson desired the society of his surviving friend with the same eagerness. He thought of him kindly; but his thoughts were disquieted and fearful. He went to call indeed; but he was perhaps relieved to be denied admittance; perhaps, in his heart, he preferred to speak with Poole upon the doorstep and surrounded by the air and sounds of the open city, rather than to be admitted into that house of voluntary bondage, and to sit and speak with its inscrutable recluse. Poole had, indeed, no very pleasant news to communicate. The doctor, it appeared, now more than ever confined himself to the cabinet over the laboratory, where he would sometimes even sleep; he was out of spirits, he had grown very silent, he did not read; it seemed as if he had something on his mind. Utterson became so used to the unvarying character of these reports, that he fell off little by little in the frequency of his visits.

Incident at the Window

It chanced on Sunday, when Mr Utterson was on his usual walk with Mr Enfield, that their way lay once again through the bystreet; and that when they came in front of the door, both stopped to gaze on it.

"Well," said Enfield, "that story's at an end at least. We shall never see more of Mr Hyde."

"I hope not," said Utterson. "Did I ever tell you that I once saw him, and shared your feeling of repulsion?"

"It was impossible to do the one without the other," returned Enfield. "And by the way what an ass you must have thought me, not to know that this was a back way to Dr Jekyll's! It was partly your own fault that I found it out, even when I did."

"So you found it out, did you?" said Utterson. "But if that be so, we may step into the court and take a look at the windows. To tell you the truth, I am uneasy about poor Jekyll; and even outside, I feel as if the presence of a friend might do him good."

The court was very cool and a little damp, and full of premature twilight, although the sky, high up overhead, was still bright with sunset. The middle one of the three windows was half way open; and sitting close beside it, taking the air with an infinite sadness of mien, like some disconsolate prisoner, Utterson saw Dr Jekyll.

"What! Jekyll!" he cried, "I trust you are better."

"I am very low, Utterson," replied the doctor drearily, "very low. It will not last long, thank God."

"You stay too much indoors," said the lawyer. "You should be out, whipping up the circulation like Mr Enfield and me. (This is my cousin—Mr Enfield—Dr Jekyll.) Come now; get your hat and take a quick turn with us."

"You are very good," sighed the other. "I should like to very much; but no, no, no, it is quite impossible; I dare not. But indeed, Utterson, I am very glad to see you; this is really a great pleasure; I would ask you and Mr Enfield up, but the place is really not fit."

"Why then," said the lawyer, good-naturedly, "the best thing we can do is to stay down here and speak with you from where we are."

"That is just what I was about to venture to propose," returned the doctor with a smile. But the words were hardly uttered, before the smile was struck out of his face and succeeded by an expression of such abject terror and despair, as froze the very blood of the two gentlemen below. They saw it but for a glimpse, for the window was instantly thrust down; but that glimpse had been sufficient, and they turned and left the court without a word. In silence, too, they traversed the bystreet; and it was not until they had come into a neighbouring thoroughfare, where even upon a Sunday there were still some stirrings of life, that Mr Utterson at last turned and looked at his companion. They were both pale; and there was an answering horror in their eyes.

"God forgive us, God forgive us," said Mr Utterson.

But Mr Enfield only nodded his head very seriously, and walked on once more in silence.

The Last Night

Mr Utterson was sitting by his fireside one evening after dinner, when he was surprised to receive a visit from Poole.

"Bless me, Poole, what brings you here?" he cried; and then taking a second look at him, "What ails you?" he added, "is the doctor ill?"

"Mr Utterson," said the man, "there is something wrong."

"Take a seat, and here is a glass of wine for you," said the lawyer. "Now, take your time, and tell me plainly what you want."

"You know the doctor's ways, sir," replied Poole, "and how he shuts himself up. Well, he's shut up again in the cabinet; and I don't like it, sir—I wish I may die if I like it. Mr Utterson, sir, I'm afraid."

"Now, my good man," said the lawyer, "be explicit. What are you afraid of?"

"I've been afraid for about a week," returned Poole, doggedly disregarding the question, "and I can bear it no more."

The man's appearance amply bore out his words; his manner was altered for the worse; and except for the moment when he had first announced his terror, he had not once looked the lawyer in the face. Even now, he sat with the glass of wine untasted on his knee, and his eyes directed to a corner of the floor. "I can bear it no more," he repeated.

"Come," said the lawyer, "I see you have some good reason, Poole; I see there is something seriously amiss. Try to tell me what it is."

"I think there's been foul play," said Poole, hoarsely.

"Foul play!" cried the lawyer, a good deal frightened and rather inclined to be irritated in consequence. "What foul play? What does the man mean?"

"I daren't say, sir," was the answer; "but will you come along with me and see for yourself?"

Mr Utterson's only answer was to rise and get his hat and great coat; but he observed with wonder the greatness of the relief that appeared upon the butler's face, and perhaps with no less, that the wine was still untasted when he set it down to follow.

It was a wild, cold, seasonable night of March, with a pale moon, lying on her back as though the wind had tilted her, and a flying wrack of the most diaphanous and lawny texture. The wind made talking difficult, and flecked the blood into the face. It seemed to have swept the streets unusually bare of passengers, besides; for Mr Utterson thought he had never seen that part of London so deserted. He could have wished it otherwise; never in his life had he been conscious of so sharp a wish to see and touch his fellow-creatures; for struggle as he might, there was borne in upon his mind a crushing anticipation of calamity. The square, when they got there, was all full of wind and dust, and the thin trees in the garden were lashing themselves along the railing. Poole, who had kept all the way a pace or two ahead, now pulled up in the middle of the pavement, and in spite of the biting weather, took off his hat and mopped his brow with a red pocket-handkerchief. But for all the hurry of his coming, these were not the dews of exertion that he wiped away, but the moisture of some strangling anguish; for his face was white and his voice, when he spoke, harsh and broken.

"Well, sir," he said, "here we are, and God grant there be nothing wrong."

"Amen, Poole," said the lawyer.

Thereupon the servant knocked in a very guarded manner; the door was opened on the chain; and a voice asked from within, "Is that you, Poole?"

"It's all right," said Poole. "Open the door."

The hall, when they entered it, was brightly lighted up; the fire was built high; and about the hearth the whole of the servants, men and women, stood huddled together like a flock of sheep. At the sight of Mr Utterson, the housemaid broke into hysterical whimpering; and the cook, crying out "Bless God! it's Mr Utterson," ran forward as if to take him in her arms.

"What, what? Are you all here?" said the lawyer peevishly. "Very irregular, very unseemly; your master would be far from pleased."

"They're all afraid," said Poole.

Blank silence followed, no one protesting; only the maid lifted up her voice and now wept loudly.

"Hold your tongue!" Poole said to her, with a ferocity of accent that testified to his own jangled nerves; and indeed, when the girl had so suddenly raised the note of her lamentation, they had all started and turned towards the inner door with faces of dreadful expectation. "And now," continued the butler, addressing the knife-boy, "reach me a candle, and we'll get this through hands at once." And then he begged Mr Utterson to follow him, and led the way to the back garden.

"Now, sir," said he, "you come as gently as you can. I want you to hear, and I don't want you to be heard. And see here, sir, if by any chance he was to ask you in, don't go."

Mr Utterson's nerves, at this unlooked-for termination, gave a jerk that nearly threw him from his balance; but he recollected his courage and followed the butler into the laboratory building and through the surgical theatre, with its lumber of crates and bottles, to the foot of the stair. Here Poole motioned him to stand on one side and listen; while he himself, setting down the candle and making a great and obvious call on his resolution, mounted the steps and knocked with a somewhat uncertain hand on the red baize of the cabinet door.

"Mr Utterson, sir, asking to see you," he called; and even as he did so, once more violently signed to the lawyer to give ear.

A voice answered from within: "Tell him I cannot see anyone," it said complainingly.

"Thank you, sir," said Poole, with a note of something like triumph in his voice; and taking up his candle, he led Mr Utterson back across the yard and into the great kitchen, where the fire was out and the beetles were leaping on the floor.

"Sir," he said, looking Mr Utterson in the eyes, "was that my master's voice?"

"It seems much changed," replied the lawyer, very pale, but giving look for look.

"Changed? Well, yes, I think so," said the butler. "Have I been twenty years in this man's house, to be deceived about his voice? No, sir; master's made away with; he was made away with, eight days ago, when we heard him cry out upon the name of God; and who's in there instead of him, and why it stays there, is a thing that cries to Heaven, Mr Utterson!"

"This is a very strange tale, Poole; this is rather a wild tale, my man," said Mr Utterson, biting his finger. "Suppose it were as you suppose, supposing Dr Jekyll to have been—well, murdered, what could induce the murderer to stay? That won't hold water; it doesn't commend itself to reason."

"Well, Mr Utterson, you are a hard man to satisfy, but I'll do it yet," said Poole. "All this last week (you must know) him, or it, or whatever it is that lives in that cabinet, has been crying night and day for some sort of medicine and cannot get it to his mind. It was sometimes his way—the master's, that is—to write his orders on a sheet of paper and throw it on the stair. We've had nothing else this week back; nothing but papers, and a closed door, and the very meals left there to be smuggled in when nobody was looking. Well, sir, every day, ay, and twice and thrice in the same day, there have been orders and complaints, and I have been sent flying to all the wholesale chemists in town. Every time I brought the stuff back, there would be another paper telling me to return it, because it was not pure, and another order to a different firm. This drug is wanted bitter bad, sir, whatever for."

"Have you any of these papers?" asked Mr Utterson.

Poole felt in his pocket and handed out a crumpled note, which the lawyer, bending nearer to the candle, carefully examined. Its contents ran thus: "Dr Jekyll presents his compliments to Messrs. Maw. He assures them that their last sample is impure and quite useless for his present purpose. In the year 18—; Dr J. purchased a somewhat large quantity from Messrs. M. He now begs them to search with the most sedulous care, and should any of the same quality be left, to forward it to him at once. Expense is no consideration. The importance of this to Dr J. can hardly be exaggerated." So far the letter had run composedly enough, but here with a sudden splutter of the pen, the writer's emotion had broken loose. "For God's sake," he had added, "find me some of the old."

"This is a strange note," said Mr Utterson; and then sharply, "How do you come to have it open?"

"The man at Maw's was main angry, sir, and he threw it back to me like so much dirt," returned Poole.

"This is unquestionably the doctor's hand, do you know?" resumed the lawyer.

"I thought it looked like it," said the servant rather sulkily; and then, with another voice, "But what matters hand of write," he said. "I've seen him!"

"Seen him?" repeated Mr Utterson. "Well?"

"That's it!" said Poole. "It was this way. I came suddenly into the theatre from the garden. It seems he had slipped out to look for this drug or whatever it is; for the cabinet door was open, and there he was at the far end of the room digging among the crates. He looked up when I came in, gave a kind of cry, and whipped upstairs into the cabinet. It was but for one minute that I saw him, but the hair stood upon my head like quills. Sir, if that was my master, why had he a mask upon his face? If it was my master, why did he cry out like a rat, and run from me? I have served him long enough. And then . . . " the man paused and passed his hand over his face.

"These are all very strange circumstances," said Mr Utterson, "but I think I begin to see daylight. Your master, Poole, is plainly seized with one of those maladies that both torture and deform the sufferer; hence, for aught I know, the alteration of his voice; hence the mask and his avoidance of his friends; hence his eagerness to find this drug, by means of which the poor soul retains some hope of ultimate recovery—God grant that he be not deceived! There is my explanation; it is sad enough, Poole, ay, and appalling to consider; but it is plain and natural, hangs well together and delivers us from all exorbitant alarms."

"Sir," said the butler, turning to a sort of mottled pallor, "that thing was not my master, and there's the truth. My master"—here he looked round him and began to whisper—"is a tall fine build of a man, and this was more of a dwarf." Utterson attempted to protest. "O, sir," cried Poole, "do you think I do not know my master after twenty years? do you think I do not know where his head comes to in the cabinet door, where I saw him every morning of my life? No, sir, that thing in the mask was never Doctor Jekyll—God knows what it was, but it was never Doctor Jekyll; and it is the belief of my heart that there was murder done."

"Poole," replied the lawyer, "if you say that, it will become my duty to make certain. Much as I desire to spare your master's feelings, much as I am puzzled by this note which seems to prove him to be still alive, I shall consider it my duty to break in that door."

"Ah, Mr Utterson, that's talking!" cried the butler.

"And now comes the second question," resumed Utterson: "Who is going to do it?"

"Why, you and me, sir," was the undaunted reply.

"That is very well said," returned the lawyer; "and whatever comes of it, I shall make it my business to see you are no loser."

"There is an axe in the theatre," continued Poole; "and you might take the kitchen poker for yourself."

The lawyer took that rude but weighty instrument into his hand, and balanced it. "Do you know Poole," he said, looking up, "that you and I are about to place ourselves in a position of some peril?"

"You may say so, sir, indeed," returned the butler.

"It is well, then, that we should be frank," said the other. "We both think more than we have said; let us make a clean breast. This masked figure that you saw, did you recognise it?"

"Well, sir, it went so quick, and the creature was so doubled up, that I could hardly swear to that," was the answer. "But if you mean, was it Mr Hyde?—why, yes, I think it was! You see, it was much of the same bigness; and it had the same quick light way with it; and then who else could have got in by the laboratory door? You have not forgot, sir, that at the time of the murder he had still the key with him? But that's not all. I don't know, Mr Utterson, if ever you met this Mr Hyde?"

"Yes," said the lawyer, "I once spoke with him."

"Then you must know as well as the rest of us that there was something queer about that gentleman—something that gave a man a turn—I don't know rightly how to say it, sir, beyond this: that you felt it in your marrow kind of cold and thin."

"I own I felt something of what you describe," said Mr Utterson.

"Quite so, sir," returned Poole. "Well, when that masked thing like a monkey jumped from among the chemicals and whipped into the cabinet, it went down my spine like ice. "O, I know it's not evidence, Mr Utterson; I'm book-learned enough for that; but a man has his feelings, and I give you my bible-word it was Mr Hyde!"

"Ay, ay," said the lawyer. "My fears incline to the same point. Evil, I fear, founded—evil was sure to come—of that connection. Ay, truly, I believe you; I believe poor Harry is killed; and I believe his murderer (for what purpose, God alone can tell) is still lurking in his victim's room. Well, let our name be vengeance. Call Bradshaw."

The footman came at the summons, very white and nervous.

"Pull yourself together, Bradshaw," said the lawyer. "This suspense, I know, is telling upon all of you; but it is now our intention to make an end of it. Poole, here, and I are going to force our way into the cabinet. If all is well, my shoulders are broad enough to bear the blame. Meanwhile, lest anything should really be amiss, or any malefactor seek to escape by the back, you and the boy must go round the corner with a pair of good sticks, and take your post at the laboratory door. We give you ten minutes, to get to your stations."

As Bradshaw left, the lawyer looked at his watch. "And now, Poole, let us get to ours," he said; and taking the poker under his arm, he led the way into the yard. The scud had banked over the moon, and it was now quite dark. The wind, which only broke in puffs and draughts into that deep well of building, tossed the light of the candle to and fro about their steps, until they came into the shelter of the theatre, where they sat down silently to wait. London hummed solemnly all around; but nearer at hand, the stillness was only broken by the sound of a footfall moving to and fro along the cabinet floor.

"So it will walk all day, sir," whispered Poole; "ay, and the better part of the night. Only when a new sample comes from the chemist, there's a bit of a break. Ah, it's an ill-conscience that's such an enemy to rest! Ah, sir, there's blood foully shed in every step of it! But hark again, a little closer—put your heart in your ears Mr Utterson, and tell me, is that the doctor's foot?"

The steps fell lightly and oddly, with a certain swing, for all they went so slowly; it was different indeed from the heavy creaking tread of Henry Jekyll. Utterson sighed. "Is there never anything else?" he asked.

Poole nodded. "Once," he said. "Once I heard it weeping!"

"Weeping? how that?" said the lawyer, conscious of a sudden chill of horror.

"Weeping like a woman or a lost soul," said the butler. "I came away with that upon my heart, that I could have wept too."

But now the ten minutes drew to an end. Poole disinterred the axe from under a stack of packing straw; the candle was set upon the nearest table to light them to the attack; and they drew near with bated breath to where that patient foot was still going up and down, up and down, in the quiet of the night.

"Jekyll," cried Utterson, with a loud voice, "I demand to see you." He paused a moment, but there came no reply. "I give you fair warning, our suspicions are aroused, and I must and shall see you," he resumed; "if not by fair means, then by foul—if not of your consent, they by brute force!"

"Utterson," said the voice, "for God's sake, have mercy!"

"Ah, that's not Jekyll's voice—it's Hyde's!" cried Utterson. "Down with the door, Poole."

Poole swung the axe over his shoulder; the blow shook the building, and the red baize door leaped against the lock and hinges. A dismal screech, as of mere animal terror, rang from the cabinet. Up went the axe again, and again the panels crashed and the frame bounded; four times the blow fell; but the wood was tough and the fittings were of excellent workmanship; and it was not until the fifth, that the lock burst in sunder and the wreck of the door fell inwards on the carpet.

The besiegers, appalled by their own riot and the stillness that had succeeded, stood back a little and peered in. There lay the cabinet before their eyes in the quiet lamplight, a good fire glowing and chattering on the hearth, the kettle singing its thin strain, a drawer or two open, papers neatly set forth on the business table, and nearer the fire, the things laid out for tea: the quietest room, you would have said, and, but for the glazed presses[2] full of chemicals, the most commonplace that night in London.

Right in the midst there lay the body of a man sorely contorted and still twitching. They drew near on tiptoe, turned it on its back and beheld the face of Edward Hyde. He was dressed in clothes far too large for him, clothes of the doctor's bigness; the cords of his face still moved with a semblance of life, but life was quite gone; and

---

2. Cabinets with glass doors.

by the crushed phial[3] in the hand and the strong smell of kernels that hung upon the air, Utterson knew that he was looking on the body of a self-destroyer.

"We have come too late," he said sternly, "whether to save or punish. Hyde is gone to his account; and it only remains for us to find the body of your master."

The far greater proportion of the building was occupied by the theatre, which filled almost the whole ground story and was lighted from above, and by the cabinet, which formed an upper story at one end and looked upon the court. A corridor joined the theatre to the door on the bystreet; and with this, the cabinet communicated separately by a second flight of stairs. There were besides a few dark closets and a spacious cellar. All these they now thoroughly examined. Each closet needed but a glance, for all were empty and all, by the dust that fell from their doors, had stood long unopened. The cellar, indeed, was filled with crazy lumber, mostly dating from the times of the surgeon who was Jekyll's predecessor; but even as they opened the door, they were advertised of the uselessness of further search, by the fall of a perfect mat of cobweb which had for years sealed up the entrance. Nowhere was there any trace of Henry Jekyll, dead or alive.

Poole stamped on the flags of the corridor. "He must be buried here," he said, hearkening to the sound.

"Or he may have fled," said Utterson, and he turned to examine the door in the bystreet. It was locked; and lying near by on the flags they found the key, already stained with rust.

"This does not look like use," observed the lawyer.

"Use!" echoed Poole. "Do you not see, sir, it is broken? much as if a man had stamped on it."

"Ay," continued Utterson, "and the fractures, too, are rusty." The two men looked at each other with a scare. "This is beyond me, Poole," said the lawyer. "Let us go back to the cabinet."

They mounted the stair in silence, and still with an occasional awestruck glance at the dead body, proceeded more thoroughly to examine the contents of the cabinet. At one table, there were traces of chemical work, various measured heaps of some white salt being laid on glass saucers, as though for an experiment in which the unhappy man had been prevented.

"That is the same drug that I was always bringing him," said Poole; and even as he spoke, the kettle with a startling noise boiled over.

This brought them to the fireside, where the easy chair was drawn cosily up, and the tea things stood ready to the sitter's elbow, the very sugar in the cup. There were several books on a shelf; one lay beside the tea things open, and Utterson was amazed to find it a copy of a pious work, for which Jekyll had several times expressed a great esteem, annotated, in his own hand, with startling blasphemies.

Next, in the course of their review of the chamber, the searchers came to the cheval glass,[4] into whose depths they looked with an involuntary horror. But it was so turned as to show them nothing but the rosy glow playing on the roof, the fire sparkling in a hundred repetitions along the glazed front of the presses, and their own pale and fearful countenances stooping to look in.

"This glass have seen some strange things, sir," whispered Poole.

"And surely none stranger than itself," echoed the lawyer in the same tones. "For what did Jekyll"—he caught himself up at the word with a start, and then conquering the weakness: "what could Jekyll want with it?" he said.

---

3. Vial, a small container for liquids.   4. A free-standing mirror mounted on swivels in a frame.

"You may say that!" said Poole.

Next they turned to the business table. On the desk among the neat array of papers, a large envelope was uppermost, and bore, in the doctor's hand, the name of Mr Utterson. The lawyer unsealed it, and several enclosures fell to the floor. The first was a will, drawn in the same eccentric terms as the one which he had returned six months before, to serve as a testament in case of death and as a deed of gift in case of disappearance; but in place of the name of Edward Hyde, the lawyer, with indescribable amazement, read the name of Gabriel John Utterson. He looked at Poole, and then back at the paper, and last of all at the dead malefactor stretched upon the carpet.

"My head goes round," he said. "He has been all these days in possession; he had no cause to like me; he must have raged to see himself displaced; and he has not destroyed this document."

He caught up the next paper; it was a brief note in the doctor's hand and dated at the top. "O Poole!" the lawyer cried, "he was alive and here this day. He cannot have been disposed of in so short a space, he must be still alive, he must have fled! And then, why fled? and how? and in that case, can we venture to declare this suicide? O, we must be careful. I foresee that we may yet involve your master in some dire catastrophe."

"Why don't you read it, sir?" asked Poole.

"Because I fear," replied the lawyer solemnly. "God grant I have no cause for it!" And with that he brought the paper to his eyes and read as follows.

"My dear Utterson,—When this shall fall into your hands, I shall have disappeared, under what circumstances I have not the penetration to foresee, but my instinct and all the circumstances of my nameless situation tell me that the end is sure and must be early. Go then, and first read the narrative which Lanyon warned me he was to place in your hands; and if you care to hear more, turn to the confession of

"Your unworthy and unhappy friend,

"HENRY JEKYLL"

"There was a third enclosure?" asked Utterson.

"Here, sir," said Poole, and gave into his hands a considerable packet sealed in several places.

The lawyer put it in his pocket. "I would say nothing of this paper. If your master has fled or is dead, we may at least save his credit. It is now ten; I must go home and read these documents in quiet; but I shall be back before midnight, when we shall send for the police."

They went out, locking the door of the theatre behind them; and Utterson, once more leaving the servants gathered about the fire in the hall, trudged back to his office to read the two narratives in which this mystery was now to be explained.

Doctor Lanyon's Narrative

On the ninth of January, now four days ago, I received by the evening delivery a registered envelope, addressed in the hand of my colleague and old school-companion, Henry Jekyll. I was a good deal surprised by this; for we were by no means in the habit of correspondence; I had seen the man, dined with him, indeed, the night before; and I could imagine nothing in our intercourse that should justify the formality of registration. The contents increased my wonder; for this is how the letter ran:

"10th December, 18—

"Dear Lanyon,—You are one of my oldest friends; and although we may have differed at times on scientific questions, I cannot remember, at least on my side, any break in our affection. There was never a day when, if you had said to me, 'Jekyll, my life, my honour, my reason depend upon you,' I would not have sacrificed my fortune or my left hand to help you. Lanyon, my life, my honour, my reason, are all at your mercy; if you fail me to-night, I am lost. You might suppose, after this preface, that I am going to ask you for something dishonourable to grant. Judge for yourself.

"I want you to postpone all other engagements for to-night—ay, even if you were summoned to the bedside of an emperor; to take a cab, unless your carriage should be actually at the door; and with this letter in your hand for consultation, to drive straight to my house. Poole, my butler, has his orders; you will find him waiting your arrival with a locksmith. The door of my cabinet is then to be forced; and you are to go in alone; to open the glazed press (letter E) on the left hand, breaking the lock if it be shut; and to draw out, *with all its contents as they stand,* the fourth drawer from the top or (which is the same thing) the third from the bottom. In my extreme distress of mind, I have a morbid fear of misdirecting you; but even if I am in error, you may know the right drawer by its contents: some powders, a phial and a paper book. This drawer I beg of you to carry back with you to Cavendish Square exactly as it stands.

"That is the first part of the service: now for the second. You should be back, if you set out at once on the receipt of this, long before midnight; but I will leave you that amount of margin, not only in the fear of one of those obstacles that can neither be prevented nor foreseen, but because an hour when your servants are in bed is to be preferred for what will then remain to do. At midnight, then, I have to ask you to be alone in your consulting room, to admit with your own hand into the house a man who will present himself in my name, and to place in his hands the drawer that you will have brought with you from my cabinet. Then you will have played your part and earned my gratitude completely. Five minutes, afterwards, if you insist upon an explanation, you will have understood that these arrangements are of capital importance; and that by the neglect of one of them, fantastic as they must appear, you might have charged your conscience with my death or the shipwreck of my reason.

"Confident as I am that you will not trifle with this appeal, my heart sinks and my hand trembles at the bare thought of such a possibility. Think of me at this hour, in a strange place, labouring under a blackness of distress that no fancy can exaggerate, and yet well aware that, if you will but punctually serve me, my troubles will roll away like a story that is told. Serve me, my dear Lanyon, and save

"Your friend,
"H.J.

"P.S. I had already sealed this up when a fresh terror struck upon my soul. It is possible that the post office may fail me, and this letter not come into your hands until to-morrow morning. In that case, dear Lanyon, do my errand when it shall be most convenient for you in the course of the day; and once more expect my messenger at midnight. It may then already be too late; and if that night passes without event, you will know that you have seen the last of Henry Jekyll."

Upon the reading of this letter, I made sure my colleague was insane; but till that was proved beyond the possibility of doubt, I felt bound to do as he requested. The less I understood of this farrago,[5] the less I was in a position to judge of its importance; and an appeal so worded could not be set aside without a grave responsibility. I rose accordingly from table, got into a hansom,[6] and drove straight to Jekyll's house. The butler was awaiting my arrival; he had received by the same post as mine a registered letter of instruction, and had sent at once for a locksmith and a carpenter. The tradesmen came while we were yet speaking; and we moved in a body to old Dr Denman's surgical theatre, from which (as you are doubtless aware) Jekyll's private cabinet[7] is most conveniently entered. The door was very strong, the lock excellent; the carpenter avowed he would have great trouble and have to do much damage, if force were to be used; and the locksmith was near despair. But this last was a handy fellow, and after two hours' work, the door stood open. The press marked E was unlocked; and I took out the drawer, had it filled up with straw and tied in a sheet, and returned with it to Cavendish Square.

Here I proceeded to examine its contents. The powders were neatly enough made up, but not with the nicety of the dispensing chemist; so that it was plain they were of Jekyll's private manufacture; and when I opened one of the wrappers, I found what seemed to me a simple, crystalline salt of a white colour. The phial, to which I next turned my attention, might have been about half-full of a blood-red liquor, which was highly pungent to the sense of smell and seemed to me to contain phosphorus and some volatile ether. At the other ingredients, I could make no guess. The book was an ordinary version book and contained little but a series of dates. These covered a period of many years, but I observed that the entries ceased nearly a year ago and quite abruptly. Here and there a brief remark was appended to a date, usually no more than a single word: "double" occurring perhaps six times in a total of several hundred entries; and once very early in the list and followed by several marks of exclamation, "total failure!!!" All this, though it whetted my curiosity, told me little that was definite. Here were a phial of some tincture,[8] a paper of some salt, and the record of a series of experiments that had led (like too many of Jekyll's investigations) to no end of practical usefulness. How could the presence of these articles in my house affect either the honour, the sanity, or the life of my flighty colleague? If his messenger could go to one place, why could he not go to another? And even granting some impediment, why was this gentleman to be received by me in secret? The more I reflected, the more convinced I grew that I was dealing with a case of cerebral disease; and though I dismissed my servants to bed, I loaded an old revolver that I might be found in some posture of self-defence.

Twelve o'clock had scarce rung out over London, ere the knocker sounded very gently on the door. I went myself at the summons, and found a small man crouching against the pillars of the portico.

"Are you come from Dr Jekyll?" I asked.

He told me "yes" by a constrained gesture; and when I had bidden him enter, he did not obey me without a searching backward glance into the darkness of the square. There was a policeman not far off, advancing with his bull's eye[9] open; and at the sight, I thought my visitor started and made greater haste.

These particulars struck me, I confess, disagreeably; and as I followed him into the bright light of the consulting room, I kept my hand ready on my weapon. Here, at last, I had a chance of clearly seeing him. I had never set eyes on him before, so much was certain. He was small, as I have said; I was struck besides with the shocking expression of his face, with his remarkable combination of great muscular activity and great

---

5. Hodgepodge.
6. Horse-drawn cab.
7. Office.

8. An alcohol solution; for example, tincture of iodine.
9. Policeman's lantern.

apparent debility of constitution, and—last but not least—with the odd, subjective disturbance caused by his neighbourhood. This bore some resemblance to incipient rigor, and was accompanied by a marked sinking of the pulse. At the time, I set it down to some idiosyncratic, personal distaste, and merely wondered at the acuteness of the symptoms; but I have since had reason to believe the cause to lie much deeper in the nature of man, and to turn on some nobler hinge than the principle of hatred.

This person (who had thus, from the first moment of his entrance, struck in me what I can only describe as a disgustful curiosity) was dressed in a fashion that would have made an ordinary person laughable: his clothes, that is to say, although they were of rich and sober fabric, were enormously too large for him in every measurement—the trousers hanging on his legs and rolled up to keep them from the ground, the waist of the coat below his haunches, and the collar sprawling wide upon his shoulders. Strange to relate, this ludicrous accoutrement was far from moving me to laughter. Rather, as there was something abnormal and misbegotten in the very essence of the creature that now faced me—something seizing, surprising and revolting—this fresh disparity seemed but to fit in with and to reinforce it; so that to my interest in the man's nature and character, there was added a curiosity as to his origin, his life, his fortune and status in the world.

These observations, though they have taken so great a space to be set down in, were yet the work of a few seconds. My visitor was, indeed, on fire with sombre excitement.

"Have you got it?" he cried. "Have you got it?" And so lively was his impatience that he even laid his hand upon my arm and sought to shake me.

I put him back, conscious at his touch of a certain icy pang along my blood. "Come, sir," said I. "You forget that I have not yet the pleasure of your acquaintance. Be seated, if you please." And I showed him an example, and sat down myself in my customary seat and with as fair an imitation of my ordinary manner to a patient, as the lateness of the hour, the nature of my preoccupations, and the horror I had of my visitor, would suffer me to muster.

"I beg your pardon, Dr Lanyon," he replied civilly enough. "What you say is very well founded; and my impatience has shown its heels to my politeness. I come here at the instance of your colleague, Dr Henry Jekyll, on a piece of business of some moment; and I understood . . . " he paused and put his hand to his throat, and I could see, in spite of his collected manner, that he was wrestling against the approaches of the hysteria—"I understood, a drawer . . . "

But here I took pity on my visitor's suspense, and some perhaps on my own growing curiosity.

"There it is, sir," said I, pointing to the drawer, where it lay on the floor behind a table and still covered with the sheet.

He sprang to it, and then paused, and laid his hand upon his heart; I could hear his teeth grate with the convulsive action of his jaws; and his face was so ghastly to see that I grew alarmed both for his life and reason.

"Compose yourself," said I.

He turned a dreadful smile to me, and as if with the decision of despair, plucked away the sheet. At sight of the contents, he uttered one loud sob of such immense relief that I sat petrified. And the next moment, in a voice that was already fairly well under control, "Have you a graduated glass?" he asked.

I rose from my place with something of an effort and gave him what he asked.

He thanked me with a smiling nod, measured out a few minims of the red tincture and added one of the powders. The mixture, which was at first of a reddish hue, began, in proportion as the crystals melted, to brighten in colour, to effervesce audibly, and to throw off small fumes of vapour. Suddenly and at the same moment, the ebullition ceased and the compound changed to a dark purple, which faded again more slowly to a watery green. My visitor, who had watched these metamorphoses with a keen eye, smiled, set down the glass upon the table, and then turned and looked upon me with an air of scrutiny.

"And now," said he, "to settle what remains. Will you be wise? will you be guided? will you suffer me to take this glass in my hand and to go forth from your house without further parley? or has the greed of curiosity too much command of you? Think before you answer, for it shall be done as you decide. As you decide, you shall be left as you were before, and neither richer nor wiser, unless the sense of service rendered to a man in mortal distress may be counted as a kind of riches of the soul. Or, if you shall so prefer to choose, a new province of knowledge and new avenues to fame and power shall be laid open to you, here, in this room, upon the instant; and your sight shall be blasted by a prodigy to stagger the unbelief of Satan."

"Sir," said I, affecting a coolness that I was far from truly possessing, "you speak enigmas, and you will perhaps not wonder that I hear you with no very strong impression of belief. But I have gone too far in the way of inexplicable services to pause before I see the end."

"It is well," replied my visitor. "Lanyon, you remember your vows: what follows is under the seal of our profession. And now, you who have so long been bound to the most narrow and material views, you who have denied the virtue of transcendental medicine, you who have derided your superiors—behold!"

He put the glass to his lips and drank at one gulp. A cry followed; he reeled, staggered, clutched at the table and held on, staring with injected eyes, gasping with open mouth; and as I looked there came, I thought, a change—he seemed to swell—his face became suddenly black and the features seemed to melt and alter—and the next moment, I had sprung to my feet and leaped back against the wall, my arm raised to shield me from that prodigy, my mind submerged in terror.

"O God!" I screamed, and "O God!" again and again; for there before my eyes—pale and shaken, and half fainting, and groping before him with his hands, like a man restored from death—there stood Henry Jekyll!

What he told me in the next hour, I cannot bring my mind to set on paper. I saw what I saw, I heard what I heard, and my soul sickened at it; and yet now when that sight has faded from my eyes, I ask myself if I believe it, and I cannot answer. My life is shaken to its roots; sleep has left me; the deadliest terror sits by me at all hours of the day and night; I feel that my days are numbered, and that I must die; and yet I shall die incredulous. As for the moral turpitude that man unveiled to me, even with tears of penitence, I cannot, even in memory, dwell on it without a start of horror. I will say but one thing, Utterson, and that (if you can bring your mind to credit it) will be more than enough. The creature who crept into my house that night was, on Jekyll's own confession, known by the name of Hyde and hunted for in every corner of the land as the murderer of Carew.

HASTIE LANYON

Henry Jekyll's Full Statement of the Case

I was born in the year 18— to a large fortune, endowed besides with excellent parts,[1] inclined by nature to industry, fond of the respect of the wise and good among my fellow-men, and thus, as might have been supposed, with every guarantee of an

---

1. Talents or abilities.

honourable and distinguished future. And indeed the worst of my faults was a certain impatient gaiety of disposition, such as has made the happiness of many, but such as I found it hard to reconcile with my imperious desire to carry my head high, and wear a more than commonly grave countenance before the public. Hence it came about that I concealed my pleasures; and that when I reached years of reflection, and began to look round me and take stock of my progress and position in the world, I stood already committed to a profound duplicity of life. Many a man would have even blazoned such irregularities as I was guilty of; but from the high views that I had set before me, I regarded and hid them with an almost morbid sense of shame. It was thus rather the exacting nature of my aspirations than any particular degradation in my faults, that made me what I was and, with even a deeper trench than in the majority of men, severed in me those provinces of good and ill which divide and compound man's dual nature. In this case, I was driven to reflect deeply and inveterately on that hard law of life, which lies at the root of religion and is one of the most plentiful springs of distress. Though so profound a double-dealer, I was in no sense a hypocrite; both sides of me were in dead earnest; I was no more myself when I laid aside restraint and plunged in shame, that when I laboured, in the eye of day, at the furtherance of knowledge or the relief of sorrow and suffering. And it chanced that the direction of my scientific studies, which led wholly towards the mystic and the transcendental, reacted and shed a strong light on this consciousness of the perennial war among my members. With every day, and from both sides of my intelligence, the moral and the intellectual, I thus drew steadily nearer to that truth, by whose partial discovery I have been doomed to such a dreadful shipwreck: that man is not truly one, but truly two. I say two, because the state of my own knowledge does not pass beyond that point. Others will follow, others will outstrip me on the same lines; and I hazard the guess that man will be ultimately known for a mere polity of multifarious, incongruous and independent denizens. I for my part, from the nature of my life, advanced infallibly in one direction and in one direction only. It was on the moral side, and in my own person, that I learned to recognise the thorough and primitive duality of man; I saw that, of the two natures that contended in the field of my consciousness, even if I could rightly be said to be either, it was only because I was radically both; and from an early date, even before the course of my scientific discoveries had begun to suggest the most naked possibility of such a miracle, I had learned to dwell with pleasure, as a beloved daydream, on the thought of the separation of these elements. If each, I told myself, could but be housed in separate identities, life would be relieved of all that was unbearable; the unjust might go his way, delivered from the aspirations and remorse of his more upright twin; and the just could walk steadfastly and securely on his upward path, doing the good things in which he found his pleasure, and no longer exposed to disgrace and penitence by the hands of this extraneous evil. It was the curse of mankind that these incongruous faggots were thus bound together—that in the agonised womb of consciousness, these polar twins should be continuously struggling. How, then, were they dissociated?

I was so far in my reflections when, as I have said, a side light began to shine upon the subject from the laboratory table. I began to perceive more deeply than it has ever yet been stated, the trembling immateriality, the mist-like transience, of this seemingly so solid body in which we walk attired. Certain agents I found to have the power to shake and to pluck back that fleshly vestment, even as a wind might toss the curtains of a pavillion. For two good reasons, I will not enter deeply into this scientific branch of my confession. First, because I have been made to learn that the doom and burthen of our life is bound forever on man's shoulders, and when the attempt is made to cast it off, it but returns upon us with more unfamiliar and more awful pressure. Second, because as my narrative will make alas! too evident, my discoveries were incomplete. Enough, then, that I not only recognised my natural body for the mere aura and effulgence of certain of the powers that made up my spirit, but managed to compound a drug by which these powers should be dethroned from their supremacy, and a second form and countenance substituted, none the less natural to me because they were the expression, and bore the stamp, of lower elements in my soul.

I hesitated long before I put this theory to the test of practice. I knew well that I risked death; for any drug that so potently controlled and shook the very fortress of identity, might by the least scruple of an over-dose or at the least inopportunity in the moment of exhibition, utterly blot out that immaterial tabernacle which I looked to it to change. But the temptation of a discovery so singular and profound, at last over-came the suggestions of alarm. I had long since prepared my tincture; I purchased at once, from a firm of wholesale chemists, a large quantity of a particular salt which I knew, from my experiments, to be the last ingredient required; and late one accursed night, I compounded the elements, watched them boil and smoke together in the glass, and when the ebullition had subsided, with a strong glow of courage, drank off the potion.

The most racking pangs succeeded: a grinding in the bones, deadly nausea, and a horror of the spirit that cannot be exceeded at the hour of birth or death. Then these agonies began swiftly to subside, and I came to myself as if out of a great sickness. There was something strange in my sensations, something indescribably new and, from its very novelty, incredibly sweet. I felt younger, lighter, happier in body; within I was conscious of a heady recklessness, a current of disordered sensual images running like a mill race[2] in my fancy, a solution of the bonds of obligation, an unknown but not an innocent freedom of the soul. I knew myself, at the first breath of this new life, to be more wicked, tenfold more wicked, sold a slave to my original evil; and the thought, in that moment, braced and delighted me like wine. I stretched out my hands, exulting in the freshness of these sensations; and in the act, I was suddenly aware that I had lost in stature.

There was no mirror, at that date, in my room; that which stands beside me as I write, was brought there later on and for the very purpose of these transformations. The night, however, was far gone into the morning—the morning, black as it was, was nearly ripe for the conception of the day—the inmates of my house were locked in the most rigorous hours of slumber; and I determined, flushed as I was with hope and triumph, to venture in my new shape as far as to my bedroom. I crossed the yard, wherein the constellations looked down upon me, I could have thought, with wonder, the first creature of that sort that their unsleeping vigilance had yet disclosed to them; I stole through the corridors, a stranger in my own house; and coming to my room, I saw for the first time the appearance of Edward Hyde.

I must here speak by theory alone, saying not that which I know, but that which I suppose to be most probable. The evil side of my nature, to which I had now transferred the stamping efficacy, was less robust and less developed than the good which I had just deposed. Again, in the course of my life, which had been, after all, nine

2. Forceful channel of water that turns a mill wheel.

tenths a life of effort, virtue and control, it had been much less exercised and much less exhausted. And hence, as I think, it came about that Edward Hyde was so much smaller, slighter and younger than Henry Jekyll. Even as good shone upon the countenance of the one, evil was written broadly and plainly on the face of the other. Evil besides (which I must still believe to be the lethal side of man) had left on that body an imprint of deformity and decay. And yet when I looked upon that ugly idol in the glass, I was conscious of no repugnance, rather of a leap of welcome. This, too, was myself. It seemed natural and human. In my eyes it bore a livelier image of the spirit, it seemed more express and single, than the imperfect and divided countenance, I had been hitherto accustomed to call mine. And in so far I was doubtless right. I have observed that when I wore the semblance of Edward Hyde, none could come near to me at first without a visible misgiving of the flesh. This, as I take it, was because all human beings, as we meet them, are commingled out of good and evil: and Edward Hyde, alone in the ranks of mankind, was pure evil.

I lingered but a moment at the mirror: the second and conclusive experiment had yet to be attempted; it yet remained to be seen if I had lost my identity beyond redemption and must flee before daylight from a house that was no longer mine; and hurrying back to my cabinet, I once more prepared and drank the cup, once more suffered the pangs of dissolution, and came to myself once more with the character, the stature and the face of Henry Jekyll.

That night I had come to the fatal cross roads. Had I approached my discovery in a more noble spirit, had I risked the experiment while under the empire of generous or pious aspirations, all must have been otherwise, and from these agonies of death and birth, I had come forth an angel instead of a fiend. The drug had no discriminating action; it was neither diabolical nor divine; it but shook the doors of the prison-house of my disposition; and like the captives of Philippi,[3] that which stood within ran forth. At that time my virtue slumbered; my evil, kept awake by ambition, was alert and swift to seize the occasion; and the thing that was projected was Edward Hyde. Hence, although I had now two characters as well as two appearances, one was wholly evil, and the other was still the old Henry Jekyll, that incongruous compound of whose reformation and improvement I had already learned to despair. The movement was thus wholly toward the worse.

Even at that time, I had not yet conquered my aversion to the dryness of a life of study. I would still be merrily disposed at times; and as my pleasures were (to say the least) undignified, and I was not only well known and highly considered, but growing towards the elderly man, this incoherency of my life was daily growing more unwelcome. It was on this side that my new power tempted me until I fell in slavery. I had but to drink the cup, to doff at once the body of the noted professor, and to assume, like a thick cloak, that of Edward Hyde. I smiled at the notion; it seemed to me at the time to be humorous; and I made my preparations with the most studious care. I took and furnished that house in Soho, to which Hyde was tracked by the police; and engaged as housekeeper a creature whom I well knew to be silent and unscrupulous. On the other side, I announced to my servants that a Mr Hyde (whom I described) was to have full liberty and power about my house in the square; and to parry mishaps, I even called and made myself a familiar object, in my second character. I next drew up that will to which you so much objected; so that if anything befell me in the person of Doctor Jekyll, I could enter on that of Edward Hyde without pecuniary loss. And

3. The apostle Paul and his followers are freed from a prison in Philippi by an earthquake (Acts 16).

thus fortified, as I supposed, on every side, I began to profit by the strange immunities of my position.

Men have before hired bravos to transact their crimes, while their own person and reputation sat under shelter. I was the first that ever did so for his pleasures. I was the first that could thus plod in the public eye with a load of genial respectability, and in a moment, like a schoolboy, strip off these lendings[4] and spring headlong into the sea of liberty. But for me, in my impenetrable mantle, the safety was complete. Think of it—I did not even exist! Let me but escape into my laboratory door, give me but a second or two to mix and swallow the draught that I had always standing ready; and whatever he had done, Edward Hyde would pass away like the stain of breath upon a mirror; and there in his stead, quietly at home, trimming the midnight lamp in his study, a man who could afford to laugh at suspicion, would be Henry Jekyll.

The pleasures which I made haste to seek in my disguise were, as I have said, undignified; I would scarce use a harder term. But in the hands of Edward Hyde, they soon began to turn towards the monstrous. When I would come back from these excursions, I was often plunged into a kind of wonder at my vicarious depravity. This familiar that I called out of my own soul, and sent forth alone to do his good pleasure, was a being inherently malign and villainous; his every act and thought centered on self; drinking pleasure with bestial avidity from any degree of torture to another; relentless like a man of stone. Henry Jekyll stood at times aghast before the acts of Edward Hyde; but the situation was apart from ordinary laws, and insidiously relaxed the grasp of conscience. It was Hyde, after all, and Hyde alone, that was guilty. Jekyll was no worse; he woke again to his good qualities seemingly unimpaired; he would even make haste, where it was possible, to undo the evil done by Hyde. And thus his conscience slumbered.

Into the details of the infamy at which I thus connived (for even now I can scarce grant that I committed it) I have no design of entering. I mean but to point out the warnings and the successive steps with which my chastisement approached. I met with one accident which, as it brought on no consequence, I shall no more than mention. An act of cruelty to a child aroused against me the anger of a passer by, whom I recognised the other day in the person of your kinsman; the doctor and the child's family joined him; there were moments when I feared for my life; and at last, in order to pacify their too just resentment, Edward Hyde had to bring them to the door, and pay them in a cheque drawn in the name of Henry Jekyll. But this danger was easily eliminated from the future, by opening an account at another bank in the name of Edward Hyde himself; and when, by sloping my own hand backward, I had supplied my double with a signature, I thought I sat beyond the reach of fate.

Some two months before the murder of Sir Danvers, I had been out for one of my adventures, had returned at a late hour, and woke the next day in bed with somewhat odd sensations. It was in vain I looked about me; in vain I saw the decent furniture and tall proportions of my room in the square; in vain that I recognised the pattern of the bed curtains and the design of the mahogany frame; something still kept insisting that I was not where I was, that I had not wakened where I seemed to be, but in the little room in Soho where I was accustomed to sleep in the body of Edward Hyde. I smiled to myself, and, in my psychological way, began lazily to inquire into the elements of this illusion, occasionally, even as I did so, dropping back into a comfortable

---

4. Clothes, and also the trappings of respectability. At the sight of the ragged beggar Poor Tom, King Lear tore off his clothes, crying "Off, off you lendings" (*King Lear* 3.4.112).

morning doze. I was still so engaged when, in one of my more wakeful moments, my eye fell upon my hand. Now the hand of Henry Jekyll (as you have often remarked) was professional in shape and size: it was large, firm, white and comely. But the hand which I now saw, clearly enough, in the yellow light of a mid-London morning, lying half shut on the bed clothes, was lean, corded, knuckly, of a dusky pallor and thickly shaded with a swart growth of hair. It was the hand of Edward Hyde.

I must have stared upon it for near half a minute, sunk as I was in the mere stupidity of wonder, before terror woke up in my breast as sudden and startling as the crash of cymbals; and bounding from my bed, I rushed to the mirror. At the sight that met my eyes, my blood was changed into something exquisitely thin and icy. Yes, I had gone to bed Henry Jekyll, I had awakened Edward Hyde. How was this to be explained? I asked myself; and then, with another bound of terror—how was it to be remedied? It was well on in the morning; the servants were up; all my drugs were in the cabinet—a long journey, down two pair of stairs, through the back passage, across the open court and through the anatomical theatre, from where I was then standing horror-struck. It might indeed be possible to cover my face; but of what use was that, when I was unable to conceal the alteration in my stature? And then with an overpowering sweetness of relief, it came back upon my mind that the servants were already used to the coming and going of my second self. I had soon dressed, as well as I was able, in clothes of my own size: had soon passed through the house, where Bradshaw stared and drew back at seeing Mr Hyde at such an hour and in such a strange array; and ten minutes later, Dr Jekyll had returned to his own shape and was sitting down, with a darkened brow, to make a feint of breakfasting.

Small indeed was my appetite. This inexplicable incident, this reversal of my previous experience, seemed, like the Babylonian finger on the wall, to be spelling out the letters of my judgment;[5] and I began to reflect more seriously than ever before on the issues and possibilities of my double existence. That part of me which I had the power of projecting, had lately been much exercised and nourished; it had seemed to me of late as though the body of Edward Hyde had grown in stature, as though (when I wore that form) I were conscious of a more generous tide of blood; and I began to spy a danger that, if this were much prolonged, the balance of my nature might be permanently overthrown, the power of voluntary change be forfeited, and the character of Edward Hyde become irrevocably mine. The power of the drug had not been always equally displayed. Once, very early in my career, it had totally failed me; since then I had been obliged on more than one occasion to double, and once, with infinite risk of death, to treble the amount; and these rare uncertainties had cast hitherto the sole shadow on my contentment. Now, however, and in the light of that morning's accident, I was led to remark that whereas, in the beginning, the difficulty had been to throw off the body of Jekyll, it had of late, gradually but decidedly transferred itself to the other side. All things therefore seemed to point to this: that I was slowly losing hold of my original and better self, and becoming slowly incorporated with my second and worse.

Between these two, I now felt I had to choose. My two natures had memory in common, but all other faculties were most unequally shared between them. Jekyll (who was composite) now with the most sensitive apprehensions, now with a greedy gusto, projected and shared in the pleasures and adventures of Hyde; but Hyde was

5. Belshazzar, king of Babylon, is shocked by the appearance of a divine hand writing mysterious words on the palace wall; the prophet Daniel interprets the words as foretelling the downfall of the king and his realm (Daniel 5).

indifferent to Jekyll, or but remembered him as the mountain bandit remembers the cavern in which he conceals himself from pursuit. Jekyll had more than a father's interest; Hyde had more than a son's indifference. To cast in my lot with Jekyll, was to die to those appetites which I had long secretly indulged and had of late begun to pamper. To cast it in with Hyde, was to die to a thousand interests and aspirations, and to become, at a blow and forever, despised and friendless. The bargain might appear unequal; but there was still another consideration in the scales; for while Jekyll would suffer smartingly in the fires of abstinence, Hyde would be not even conscious of all that he had lost. Strange as my circumstances were, the terms of this debate are as old and commonplace as man; much the same inducements and alarms cast the die for any tempted and trembling sinner; and it fell out with me, as it falls with so vast a majority of my fellows, that I chose the better part and was found wanting in the strength to keep to it.

Yes, I preferred the elderly and discontented doctor, surrounded by friends and cherishing honest hopes; and bade a resolute farewell to the liberty, the comparative youth, the light step, leaping pulses and secret pleasures, that I had enjoyed in the disguise of Hyde. I made this choice perhaps with some unconscious reservation, for I neither gave up the house in Soho, nor destroyed the clothes of Edward Hyde, which still lay ready in my cabinet. For two months, however, I was true to my determination; for two months, I led a life of such severity as I had never before attained to, and enjoyed the compensations of an approving conscience. But time began at last to obliterate the freshness of my alarm; the praises of conscience began to grow into a thing of course; I began to be tortured with throes and longings, as of Hyde struggling after freedom; and at last, in an hour of moral weakness, I once again compounded and swallowed the transforming draught.

I do not suppose that, when a drunkard reasons with himself upon his vice, he is once out of five hundred times affected by the dangers that he runs through his brutish, physical insensibility; neither had I, long as I had considered my position, made enough allowance for the complete moral insensibility and insensate readiness to evil, which were the leading characters of Edward Hyde. Yet it was by these that I was punished. My devil had been long caged, he came out roaring. I was conscious, even when I took the draught, of a more unbridled, a more furious propensity to ill. It must have been this, I suppose, that stirred in my soul that tempest of impatience with which I listened to the civilities of my unhappy victim; I declare at least, before God, no man morally sane could have been guilty of that crime upon so pitiful a provocation; and that I struck in no more reasonable spirit than that in which a sick child may break a plaything. But I had voluntarily stripped myself of all those balancing instincts, by which even the worst of us continues to walk with some degree of steadiness among temptations; and in my case, to be tempted, however slightly, was to fall.

Instantly the spirit of hell awoke in me and raged. With a transport of glee, I mauled the unresisting body, tasting delight from every blow; and it was not till weariness had begun to succeed, that I was suddenly, in the top fit of my delirium, struck through the heart by a cold thrill of terror. A mist dispersed; I saw my life to be forfeit; and fled from the scene of these excesses, at once glorying and trembling, my lust of evil gratified and stimulated, my love of life screwed to the topmost peg. I ran to the house in Soho, and (to make assurance doubly sure) destroyed my papers; thence I set out through the lamplit streets, in the same divided ecstasy of mind, gloating on my crime, light-headedly devising others in the future, and yet still hastening and still hearkening in my wake for the steps of the avenger. Hyde had a song upon his lips as he compounded the draught, and as he drank it, pledged the dead man. The pangs of transformation had not done tearing him, before Henry Jekyll, with streaming tears of gratitude and remorse, had fallen upon his knees and lifted his clasped hands to God. The veil of self-indulgence was rent from head to foot, I saw my life as a whole: I followed it up from the days of childhood, when I had walked with my father's hand, and through the self-denying toils of my professional life, to arrive again and again, with the same sense of unreality, at the damned horrors of the evening. I could have screamed aloud; I sought with tears and prayers to smother down the crowd of hideous images and sounds with which my memory swarmed against me; and still, between the petitions, the ugly face of my iniquity stared into my soul. As the acuteness of this remorse began to die away, it was succeeded by a sense of joy. The problem of my conduct was solved. Hyde was thenceforth impossible; whether I would or not, I was now confined to the better part of my existence; and O, how I rejoiced to think it! with what willing humility, I embraced anew the restrictions of natural life! with what sincere renunciation, I locked the door by which I had so often gone and come, and ground the key under my heel!

The next day, came the news that the murder had been overlooked, that the guilt of Hyde was patent to the world, and that the victim was a man high in public estimation. It was not only a crime, it had been a tragic folly. I think I was glad to know it; I think I was glad to have my better impulses thus buttressed and guarded by the terrors of the scaffold. Jekyll was now my city of refuge; let but Hyde peep out an instant, and the hands of all men would be raised to take and slay him.

I resolved in my future conduct to redeem the past; and I can say with honesty that my resolve was fruitful of some good. You know yourself how earnestly in the last months of last year, I laboured to relieve suffering; you know that much was done for others, and that the days passed quietly, almost happily for myself. Nor can I truly say that I wearied of this beneficent and innocent life; I think instead that I daily enjoyed it more completely; but I was still cursed with my duality of purpose; and as the first edge of my penitence wore off, the lower side of me, so long indulged, so recently chained down, began to growl for license. Not that I dreamed of resuscitating Hyde; the bare idea of that would startle me to frenzy: no, it was in my own person, that I was once more tempted to trifle with my conscience; and it was as an ordinary secret sinner, that I at last fell before the assaults of temptation.

There comes an end to all things; the most capacious measure is filled at last; and this brief condescension to my evil finally destroyed the balance of my soul. And yet I was not alarmed; the fall seemed natural, like a return to the old days before I had made my discovery. It was a fine, clear, January day, wet under foot where the frost had melted, but cloudless overhead; and the Regent's park was full of winter chirruppings and sweet with Spring odours. I sat in the sun on a bench; the animal within me licking the chops of memory; the spiritual side a little drowsed, promising subsequent penitence, but not yet moved to begin. After all, I reflected I was like my neighbours; and then I smiled, comparing myself with other men, comparing my active goodwill with the lazy cruelty of their neglect. And at the very moment of that vainglorious thought, a qualm came over me, a horrid nausea and the most deadly shuddering. These passed away, and left me faint; and then as in its turn the faintness subsided, I began to be aware of a change in the temper of my thoughts, a greater boldness, a contempt of danger, a solution of the bonds of obligation. I looked down; my clothes hung formlessly on my shrunken limbs; the hand that lay on my knee was corded and hairy. I was once more Edward Hyde. A moment before I had been safe of all men's respect, wealthy, beloved—the cloth laying for me in the dining room at home; and now I was the common quarry of mankind, hunted, houseless, a known murderer, thrall to the gallows.

My reason wavered, but it did not fail me utterly. I have more than once observed that, in my second character, my faculties seemed sharpened to a point and my spirits more tensely elastic; thus it came about that, where Jekyll perhaps might have succumbed, Hyde rose to the importance of the moment. My drugs were in one of the presses of my cabinet; how was I to reach them? That was the problem that (crushing my temples in my hands) I set myself to solve. The laboratory door I had closed. If I sought to enter by the house, my own servants would consign me to the gallows. I saw I must employ another hand, and thought of Lanyon. How was he to be reached? how persuaded? Supposing that I escaped capture in the streets, how was I to make my way into his presence? and how should I, an unknown and displeasing visitor, prevail on the famous physician to rifle the study of his colleague, Dr Jekyll? Then I remembered that of my original character, one part remained to me: I could write my own hand; and once I had conceived that kindling spark, the way that I must follow became lighted up from end to end.

Thereupon, I arranged my clothes as best I could, and summoning a passing hansom, drove to an hotel in Portland street, the name of which I chanced to remember. At my appearance (which was indeed comical enough, however tragic a fate these garments covered) the driver could not conceal his mirth. I gnashed my teeth upon him with a gust of devilish fury; and the smile withered from his face—happily for him—yet more happily for myself, for in another instant I had certainly dragged him from his perch. At the inn, as I entered, I looked about me with so black a countenance as made the attendants tremble; not a look did they exchange in my presence; but obsequiously took my orders, led me to a private room, and brought me wherewithal to write. Hyde in danger of his life was a creature new to me: shaken with inordinate anger, strung to the pitch of murder, lusting to inflict pain. Yet the creature was astute; mastered his fury with a great effort of the will; composed his two important letters, one to Lanyon and one to Poole; and that he might receive actual evidence of their being posted, sent them out with directions that they should be registered.

Thenceforward, he sat all day over the fire in the private room, gnawing his nails; there he dined, sitting alone with his fears, the waiter visibly quailing before his eye; and thence, when the night was fully come, he set forth in the corner of a closed cab, and was driven to and fro about the streets of the city. He, I say—I cannot say, I. That child of Hell had nothing human; nothing lived in him but fear and hatred. And when at last, thinking the driver had begun to grow suspicious, he discharged the cab and ventured on foot, attired in his misfitting clothes, an object marked out for observation, into the midst of the nocturnal passengers, these two base passions raged within him like a tempest. He walked fast, hunted by his fears, chattering to himself, skulking through the less frequented thoroughfares, counting the minutes that still divided him from midnight. Once a woman spoke to him, offering, I think, a box of lights.[6] He smote her in the face, and she fled.

When I came to myself at Lanyon's, the horror of my old friend perhaps affected me somewhat: I do not know; it was at least but a drop in the sea to the abhorrence with which I looked back upon these hours. A change had come over

6. Matches, also called lucifers.

me. It was no longer the fear of the gallows, it was the horror of being Hyde that racked me. I received Lanyon's condemnation partly in a dream; it was partly in a dream that I came home to my own house and got into bed. I slept after the prostration of the day, with a stringent and profound slumber which not even the nightmares that wrung me could avail to break. I awoke in the morning shaken, weakened, but refreshed. I still hated and feared the thought of the brute that slept within me, and I had not of course forgotten the appalling dangers of the day before; but I was once more at home, in my own house and close to my drugs; and gratitude for my escape shone so strong in my soul that it almost rivalled the brightness of hope.

I was stepping leisurely across the court after breakfast, drinking the chill of the air with pleasure, when I was seized again with those indescribable sensations that heralded the change; and I had but the time to gain the shelter of my cabinet, before I was once again raging and freezing with the passions of Hyde. It took on this occasion a double dose to recall me to myself; and alas, six hours after, as I sat looking sadly in the fire, the pangs returned, and the drug had to be re-administered. In short, from that day forth it seemed only by a great effort as of gymnastics, and only under the immediate stimulation of the drug, that I was able to wear the countenance of Jekyll. At all hours of the day and night, I would be taken with the premonitory shudder; above all, if I slept, or even dozed for a moment in my chair, it was always as Hyde that I awakened. Under the strain of this continually impending doom and by the sleeplessness to which I now condemned myself, ay, even beyond what I had thought possible to man, I became, in my own person, a creature eaten up and emptied by fever, languidly weak both in body and mind, and solely occupied by one thought: the horror of my other self. But when I slept, or when the virtue of the medicine wore off, I would leap almost without transition (for the pangs of transformation grew daily less marked) into the possession of a fancy brimming with images of terror, a soul boiling with causeless hatreds, and a body that seemed not strong enough to contain the raging energies of life. The powers of Hyde seemed to have grown with the sickliness of Jekyll. And certainly the hate that now divided them was equal on each side. With Jekyll, it was a thing of vital instinct. He had now seen the full deformity of that creature that shared with him some of the phenomena of consciousness, and was co-heir with him to death: and beyond these links of community, which in themselves made the most poignant part of his distress, he thought of Hyde, for all his energy of life, as of something not only hellish but inorganic. This was the shocking thing; that the slime of the pit seemed to utter cries and voices; that the amorphous dust gesticulated and sinned; that what was dead, and had no shape, should usurp the offices of life. And this again, that that insurgent horror was knit to him closer than a wife, closer than an eye; lay caged in his flesh, where he heard it mutter and felt it struggle to be born; and at every hour of weakness, and in the confidence of slumber, prevailed against him, and deposed him out of life. The hatred of Hyde for Jekyll, was of a different order. His terror of the gallows drove him continually to commit temporary suicide, and return to his subordinate station of a part instead of a person; but he loathed the necessity, he loathed the despondency into which Jekyll was now fallen, and he resented the dislike with which he was himself regarded. Hence the apelike tricks that he would play me, scrawling in my own hand blasphemies on the pages of my books, burning the letters and destroying the portrait of my father; and indeed, had it not been for his fear of death, he would long ago have ruined himself in order to involve me in the ruin. But his love of life is wonderful; I go further: I, who sicken and freeze at the mere thought of him, when I recall the abjection and passion of this attachment, and when I know how he fears my power to cut him off by suicide, I find it in my heart to pity him.

It is useless, and the time awfully fails me, to prolong this description; no one has ever suffered such torments, let that suffice; and yet even to these, habit brought— no, not alleviation—but a certain callousness of soul, a certain acquiescence of despair; and my punishment might have gone on for years, but for the last calamity which has now fallen, and which has finally severed me from my own face and nature. My provision of the salt, which had never been renewed since the date of the first experiment, began to run low. I sent out for a fresh supply, and mixed the draught; the ebullition followed, and the first change of colour, not the second; I drank it and it was without efficiency. You will learn from Poole how I have had London ransacked; it was in vain; and I am now persuaded that my first supply was impure, and that it was that unknown impurity which lent efficacy to the draught.

About a week has passed, and I am now finishing this statement under the influence of the last of the old powders. This, then, is the last time, short of a miracle, that Henry Jekyll can think his own thoughts or see his own face (now how sadly altered!) in the glass. Nor must I delay too long to bring my writing to an end; for if my narrative has hitherto escaped destruction, it has been by a combination of great prudence and great good luck. Should the throes of change take me in the act of writing it, Hyde will tear it in pieces; but if some time shall have elapsed after I have laid it by, his wonderful selfishness and circumscription to the moment will probably save it once again from the action of his apelike spite. And indeed the doom that is closing on us both, has already changed and crushed him. Half an hour from now, when I shall again and forever reindue that hated personality, I know how I shall sit shuddering and weeping in my chair, or continue, with the most strained and fearstruck ecstasy of listening, to pace up and down this room (my last earthly refuge) and give ear to every sound of menace. Will Hyde die upon the scaffold? or will he find the courage to release himself at the last moment? God knows; I am careless; this is my true hour of death, and what is to follow concerns another than myself. Here then, as I lay down the pen and proceed to seal up my confession, I bring the life of that unhappy Henry Jekyll to an end.

1886

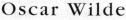

Oscar Wilde
1854–1900

"He hasn't a single redeeming vice." Oscar Wilde's witticism hardly applied to himself: his character was a quixotic mixture of brilliance and folly. Flamboyant, extravagant, outrageous, the most splendid playwright of the century lived his own life on center stage. Though his flagrant self-promotion irritated many, he was generous and good-natured, unable to imagine that the Victorian morality he satirized would finally bring about his own fall.

Wilde was born in Dublin, and although he spent much of his adult life in England, he never lost the sense of himself as a foreigner. His parents—Irish Protestants, ardent nationalists, and prolific writers—were notable figures in their own right: Sir William Robert Wilde was a famous surgeon, fathered three illegitimate children, and was sued by a former patient who claimed he had drugged and raped her. Lady Wilde, who changed her name from Jane Frances to Speranza Francesca, was a self-dramatizing and unconventional woman whom her son adored.

Wilde was educated in Ireland until 1874 when he won a scholarship to Oxford. Here he began to establish a reputation as an Aesthete and an admirer of Pre-Raphaelite poets such as Swinburne, Rossetti, and William Morris. He was also attracted to the contradictory artistic creeds of both John Ruskin and Walter Pater, Ruskin proclaiming that all good art is moral art, Pater preferring "poetic passion, the desire of beauty, the love of art for art's sake." Wilde dressed ostentatiously, wore his hair long, and decorated his rooms with lilies, a favorite symbol of the Aesthetes. His literary abilities won him both the Newdigate Prize for poetry and a double first (highest honors). But along with these academic awards he was celebrated for a remark which seemed to epitomize aestheticism: "I find it harder and harder every day to live up to my blue china."

Following his triumphs at Oxford, Wilde cast about for a career. His father had died leaving only a small inheritance, and Wilde's attempts to win a university fellowship failed. In London he set about making himself conspicuous, and soon he was the center of the social scene. Few could help being dazzled by his witty conversation. Yet some were skeptical, including an actress who said: "What has he done, this young man, that one meets him everywhere? Oh yes he talks well, but what has he done? He has written nothing, he does not sing or paint or act—he does nothing but talk."

Wilde's talk, however, was glorious and eventually would find lasting expression in his plays. Meanwhile, he played the dandy, and was satirized by Gilbert and Sullivan in *Patience* (1881) as the most illustrious Aesthete of the day, who had walked "down Piccadilly with a poppy or a lily in his medieval hand." Wilde reacted with good humor, observing that "To have done it was nothing, but to make people think one had done it was a triumph."

In the early 1880s Wilde began to refute the charge that he did nothing but talk. He wrote his first play, called *Vera; or, The Nihilists* (1880), about Russian czars and revolutionaries; the play's portrayal of an assassination attempt made it politically unacceptable, and the production was canceled. He privately published a book of poems in 1881, opening with the sonnet *Hélas!* They were praised by Matthew Arnold and by Swinburne, but elsewhere denounced as immoral.

Wilde's finances received an unexpected boost when the New York production of *Patience* led to an invitation to lecture in the United States. His arrival in New York in 1882 was a media event: he was mobbed by reporters, and his every utterance was quoted or misquoted in both the American and British press. He was reported to have been disappointed in the Atlantic—"It is not so majestic as I expected"—and to have told the customs officers, "I have nothing to declare except my genius." He stayed a full year, earned quite a lot of money, and returned home internationally famous.

Wilde followed up his conquest of America with a few months in Paris, where he met many leading painters and writers. Back in London, and short of money once again, his thoughts turned to marriage, and in 1884 he wed Constance Lloyd. She was well educated and well-off, and at first Wilde enjoyed the new roles of husband and then father to two sons, Cyril and Vyvyan. But he soon found married life a bore. Even during his honeymoon in Paris his thoughts were elsewhere: he became enamored of a book known as the Bible of decadence, *A Rebours* (1884) by Joris-Karl Huysmans. As his biographer Richard Ellmann has put it, this book "summoned him towards an underground life."

Wilde was a celebrity. He spent several years lecturing and reviewing, then entered the most inventive period of his life. Although he would later remark, "I have put only my talent into my works. I have put my genius into my life," the creative work of the early 1890s belies him. He articulated his theories on Art and Nature in two dialogues full of provocative paradoxes, *The Decay of Lying* (1888) and *The Critic as Artist* (1890). Then in his essay *The Soul of Man Under Socialism* (1891) he argued that the final goal of social evolution was joyous individualism. He continued his exploration of the relation of art to life in his only novel, *The Pic-*

Oscar Wilde and Lord Alfred
Douglas, 1893.

ture of Dorian Gray (1890), which tells of a promising golden boy fascinated by the seductively amoral ideas of a jaded cynic. Dorian makes a Faustian bargain: his corrupted soul will be mirrored, not in his own face—he remains eternally youthful—but in his portrait. Much influenced by *A Rebours, Dorian Gray* achieved instantaneous notoriety, not so much for its aestheticism as for its thinly veiled suggestions of homosexuality.

Lady Windermere's Fan (1891) met with the opposite reception: this sparkling comedy depicting a mother's secret sacrifice for her daughter was an immediate success. Inspired in part by the French symbolist poet, Stéphane Mallarmé, Wilde was also writing—in French—a very different play, *Salomé*, about the fatal perversity of love and desire. To Wilde's indignation, *Salomé* was banned in England. However, in 1894 he published an English translation, with dramatic and daring illustrations by Aubrey Beardsley.

Wilde wrote two more comedies, *A Woman of No Importance* and *An Ideal Husband*, followed by his masterpiece, *The Importance of Being Earnest* (1895). Its philosophy, Wilde said, is "That we should treat all trivial things very seriously, and all the serious things of life with sincere and studied triviality." The triumphant opening night of this delightfully sophisticated farce marked the culmination of Wilde's career.

Then, at the very crest of success, Wilde was brought down by catastrophe. Although homosexuality was a criminal offense in Britain, Wilde had made little effort to conceal his relations with younger men, particularly Lord Alfred Douglas. But if society turned a blind eye, Douglas's father, the Marquess of Queensberry, did not. He hounded his son's lover relentlessly, finally sending Wilde a ludicrously misspelled note calling him a "Somdomite." Egged on by Douglas, Wilde sued for libel. It was a fatal mistake. His private affairs were mercilessly exposed in court, and he lost the case. Wilde himself was then prosecuted for committing indecent acts, convicted, and sentenced to two years at hard labor.

His obsession with the young aristocrat—beautiful, vicious, and volatile—had been ruinous in every sense. Wilde was disgraced and bankrupted. So great was the collective repugnance for him that both of his currently running plays, *An Ideal Husband* and *The Importance of Being Earnest,* were obliged to close. But the nightmare was only beginning: following the public humiliation of the trials was the horror of prison. Confined in a small cell with a bare plank bed, revolting food, and no latrine, he suffered constantly from diarrhea. He was allowed only one twenty-minute visit every three months. No talking was permitted. Dreading that he might lose his sanity, Wilde pleaded in vain for early release.

He gave vent to his sufferings in a long letter to Douglas entitled *De Profundis.* It is a terrible indictment of Douglas's selfish behavior, but more than that it is an autobiography, the anguished confession of a soul coming face to face with itself. Painfully he reviews the events that led to his downfall, finding at last his own salvation in forgiveness: "I don't write this letter to put bitterness into your heart, but to pluck it out of mine. For my own sake I must forgive you." Wilde was allowed to take the letter with him when he left prison, but chose not to have it published until after his death.

Wilde emerged from the degradation of prison a broken and penniless man. He spent the remainder of his life in exile outside Britain. He was never again allowed to see his young sons, and their surname was changed to protect them from scandal. All but a few loyal friends shunned him. The man who had lavished champagne on his friends was reduced to scrounging drinks from strangers who pitied him. He was unable to resume his writing, except for *The Ballad of Reading Gaol* (1898), a long poem based upon his prison experience. He converted to Catholicism on his deathbed, in a Paris hotel, but continued bravely inventing witticisms to the end: "I am dying beyond my means."

Impression du Matin[1]

    The Thames nocturne of blue and gold
        Changed to a harmony in gray:[2]
        A barge with ochre-coloured hay
    Dropt° from the wharf: and chill and cold   *went downstream*

5   The yellow fog came creeping down
        The bridges, till the houses' walls
        Seemed changed to shadows and St. Paul's
    Loomed like a bubble o'er the town.

    Then suddenly arose the clang
10   Of waking life; the streets were stirred
        With country wagons: and a bird
    Flew to the glistening roofs and sang.

    But one pale woman all alone,
        The daylight kissing her wan hair,
15   Loitered beneath the gas lamps' flare,
    With lips of flame and heart of stone.

1877   1881

1. Impression of the morning (French). The title evokes the paintings of the French Impressionists and their attempts to show how light transforms the landscape. The group received its name in 1874 when a critic singled out Monet's *Impression: Sunrise* as representative.
2. The American James McNeill Whistler painted a series of Thames night scenes, called "nocturnes" (see Color Plate 18). He entitled some of his daytime scenes "harmonies." His close friendship with Wilde turned into a bitter rivalry by the mid-1880s; Whistler accused Wilde of plagiarizing his ideas.

RESPONSE
Lord Alfred Douglas: Impression de Nuit[1]
London

See what a mass of gems the city wears
Upon her broad live bosom! row on row
Rubies and emeralds and amethysts glow.
See! that huge circle like a necklace, stares
5   With thousands of bold eyes to heaven, and dares
The golden stars to dim the lamps below,
And in the mirror of the mire I know
The moon has left her image unawares.

That's the great town at night: I see her breasts,
10   Pricked out with lamps they stand like huge black towers.
I think they move! I hear her panting breath.
And that's her head where the tiara rests.
And in her brain, through lanes as dark as death,
Men creep like thoughts . . . The lamps are like pale flowers.

1894

The Harlot's House

We caught the tread of dancing feet,
We loitered down the moonlit street,
And stopped beneath the harlot's house.

Inside, above the din and fray,
5   We heard the loud musicians play
The "Treues Liebes Herz" of Strauss.[1]

Like strange mechanical grotesques,
Making fantastic arabesques,[2]
The shadows raced across the blind.

10   We watched the ghostly dancers spin
To sound of horn and violin,
Like black leaves wheeling in the wind.

---

1. Lord Alfred Douglas received not only Wilde's amorous attentions but also his literary encouragement. The sonnet *Impression de Nuit* ("impression of the night") complements Wilde's *Impression du Matin* (itself a reaction to Whistler's painting *Nocturne in Blue and Gold*) by enlarging and transforming Wilde's conventional final image of a prostitute beneath a streetlamp. In Douglas's poem, the city becomes a gigantic, panting woman, the streetlights her jewelry. Wilde builds his poem on a seemingly objective series of visual images that balances the natural and the artificial; Douglas elaborates a personal vision of urban life that invokes both the decadent fascination with the *femme fatale* and a gay man's quest for nocturnal sexual adventure. For more on Douglas, see page 2085.
1. "The Heart of True Love," a waltz by Viennese composer Johann Strauss (1825–1899).
2. "Arabesque" is a term both for a ballet posture and, in art, for patterns of interlaced lines.

Like wire-pulled automatons,
Slim silhouetted skeletons
15   Went sidling through the slow quadrille.[3]

They took each other by the hand,
And danced a stately saraband;
Their laughter echoed thin and shrill.

Sometimes a clockwork puppet pressed
20   A phantom lover to her breast,
Sometimes they seemed to try to sing.

Sometimes a horrible marionette
Came out, and smoked its cigarette
Upon the steps like a live thing.

25   Then, turning to my love, I said,
"The dead are dancing with the dead,
The dust is whirling with the dust."

But she—she heard the violin,
And left my side, and entered in:
30   Love passed into the house of Lust.

Then suddenly the tune went false,
The dancers wearied of the waltz,
The shadows ceased to wheel and whirl.

And down the long and silent street,
35   The dawn, with silver-sandalled feet,
Crept like a frightened girl.

1885, 1908

Symphony in Yellow[1]

An omnibus across the bridge
    Crawls like a yellow butterfly,
    And, here and there, a passer-by
Shows like a little restless midge.

5   Big barges full of yellow hay
    Are moored against the shadowy wharf,
    And, like a yellow silken scarf,
The thick fog hangs along the quay.

The yellow leaves begin to fade
10   And flutter from the Temple elms,[2]
    And at my feet the pale green Thames
Lies like a rod of rippled jade.

1889

3. Square dance for four couples. The saraband (line 17) is an old Spanish dance.
1. The title suggests Whistler's series of paintings that he called "symphonies" in various colors. The Aesthetic vogue for titles that mingle the arts originated with the French poet Théophile Gautier, who in 1852 named a poem *Symphony in White Major*. In the 1880s yellow—the color of sunflowers and paperback French novels—became associated with the Aesthetic movement.
2. The Middle Temple and Inner Temple form part of the Inns of Court; their garden runs down to the River Thames.

from **The Decay of Lying**[1]
An Observation

A dialogue. Persons: Cyril and Vivian.[2]

SCENE: *The library of a country house in Nottinghamshire.*

CYRIL (*coming in through the open window from the terrace*): My dear Vivian, don't coop yourself up all day in the library. It is a perfectly lovely afternoon. The air is exquisite. There is a mist upon the woods, like the purple bloom upon a plum. Let us go and lie on the grass, and smoke cigarettes, and enjoy Nature.

VIVIAN: Enjoy Nature! I am glad to say that I have entirely lost that faculty. People tell us that Art makes us love Nature more than we loved her before; that it reveals her secrets to us; and that after a careful study of Corot and Constable we see things in her that had escaped our observation. My own experience is that the more we study Art, the less we care for Nature. What Art really reveals to us is Nature's lack of design, her curious crudities, her extraordinary monotony, her absolutely unfinished condition. Nature has good intentions, of course, but, as Aristotle once said, she cannot carry them out.[3] When I look at a landscape I cannot help seeing all its defects. It is fortunate for us, however, that Nature is so imperfect, as otherwise we should have had no art at all. Art is our spirited protest, our gallant attempt to teach Nature her proper place. As for the infinite variety of Nature, that is a pure myth. It is not to be found in Nature herself. It resides in the imagination, or fancy, or cultivated blindness of the man who looks at her.

CYRIL: Well, you need not look at the landscape. You can lie on the grass and smoke and talk.

VIVIAN: But Nature is so uncomfortable. Grass is hard and lumpy and damp, and full of dreadful black insects. Why, even Morris' poorest workman[4] could make you a more comfortable seat than the whole of Nature can. Nature pales before the furniture of "the street which from Oxford has borrowed its name," as the poet you love so much once vilely phrased it.[5] I don't complain. If Nature had been comfortable, mankind would never have invented architecture, and I prefer houses to the open air. In a house we all feel of the proper proportions. Everything is subordinated to us, fashioned for our use and our pleasure. Egotism itself, which is so necessary to a proper sense of human dignity, is entirely the result of indoor life. Out of doors one becomes abstract and impersonal. One's individuality absolutely leaves one. And then Nature is so indifferent, so unappreciative. Whenever I am walking in the park here, I always feel that I am no more to her than the cattle that browse on the slope, or the burdock that blooms in the ditch. Nothing

1. Published in January 1889 in *The Nineteenth Century*, then revised and reprinted in Wilde's *Intentions* (1891). This essay adopts the form of a Platonic dialogue in order to reconsider Plato's famous assertion in *The Republic* that art is falsehood. Wilde agrees with Plato that the artist tells lies, but instead of finding this morally repugnant, he praises the artist's imaginative victory over nature and mere fact. Questioning Plato's claim that art is a shadowy reflection of real life, Wilde claims that art comes first: "life is the mirror, and art the reality." As he explores the paradoxes of his theory that life imitates art, Wilde seeks to shock his audience into revising its aesthetic values; he wittily subverts the Victorian reverence for nature, sincerity, moral teaching, and artistic verisimilitude.

2. Wilde's two sons, aged three and two at the time Wilde wrote this, were named Cyril and Vyvyan.

3. In the *Poetics*, Aristotle suggests that, through mimesis or imitation of life, the artist completes nature's work.

4. William Morris employed skilled craftsmen to produce handmade furniture and textiles.

5. The goods sold on Oxford Street in London outshine the products of Wordsworth's beloved Nature. The line in Wordsworth's *The Power of Music* actually reads: "In the street that from Oxford hath borrowed its name."

is more evident than that Nature hates Mind. Thinking is the most unhealthy thing in the world, and people die of it just as they die of any other disease. Fortunately, in England at any rate, thought is not catching. Our splendid physique as a people is entirely due to our national stupidity. I only hope we shall be able to keep this great historic bulwark of our happiness for many years to come; but I am afraid that we are beginning to be over-educated; at least everybody who is incapable of learning has taken to teaching—that is really what our enthusiasm for education has come to. In the meantime, you had better go back to your wearisome uncomfortable Nature, and leave me to correct my proofs.

CYRIL: Writing an article! That is not very consistent after what you have just said.

VIVIAN: Who wants to be consistent? The dullard and the doctrinaire, the tedious people who carry out their principles to the bitter end of action, to the *reductio ad absurdum* of practice. Not I. Like Emerson, I write over the door of my library the word "Whim."[6] Besides, my article is really a most salutary and valuable warning. If it is attended to, there may be a new Renaissance of Art.

CYRIL: What is the subject?

VIVIAN: I intend to call it "The Decay of Lying: A Protest."

CYRIL: Lying! I should have thought that our politicians kept up that habit.

VIVIAN: I assure you that they do not. They never rise beyond the level of misrepresentation, and actually condescend to prove, to discuss, to argue. How different from the temper of the true liar, with his frank, fearless statements, his superb irresponsibility, his healthy, natural disdain of proof of any kind! After all, what is a fine lie? Simply that which is its own evidence. If a man is sufficiently unimaginative to produce evidence in support of a lie, he might just as well speak the truth at once. No, the politicians won't do. Something may, perhaps, be urged on behalf of the Bar. The mantle of the Sophist[7] has fallen on its members. Their feigned ardours and unreal rhetoric are delightful. They can make the worse appear the better cause, as though they were fresh from Leontine schools,[8] and have been known to wrest from reluctant juries triumphant verdicts of acquittal for their clients, even when those clients, as often happens, were clearly and unmistakeably innocent. But they are briefed by the prosaic, and are not ashamed to appeal to precedent. In spite of their endeavours, the truth will out. Newspapers, even, have degenerated. They may now be absolutely relied upon. One feels it as one wades through their columns. It is always the unreadable that occurs. I am afraid that there is not much to be said in favour of either the lawyer or the journalist. Besides, what I am pleading for is Lying in art. Shall I read you what I have written? It might do you a great deal of good.

CYRIL: Certainly, if you give me a cigarette. Thanks. By the way, what magazine do you intend it for?

VIVIAN: For the *Retrospective Review*.[9] I think I told you that the elect had revived it.

CYRIL: Whom do you mean by "the elect"?

6. Ralph Waldo Emerson, the American essayist, wrote in *Self-Reliance* (1841): "I shun father and mother and wife and brother when my genius calls me. I would write on the lintels of the doorpost, *Whim*."

7. The Sophists were Greek philosophers who taught the art of rhetoric; the word now refers to a deceptive reasoner.

8. Leontini was a Greek colony in Sicily where the sophist and rhetorician Gorgias (c. 483–375 B.C.) was educated.

9. A periodical, published in the 1820s and again in the 1850s that promoted interest in earlier literature. It was not, in fact, revived in the 1890s.

VIVIAN: Oh, The Tired Hedonists of course.[1] It is a club to which I belong. We are supposed to wear faded roses in our button-holes when we meet, and to have a sort of cult for Domitian.[2] I am afraid you are not eligible. You are too fond of simple pleasures.

CYRIL: I should be black-balled on the ground of animal spirits, I suppose?

VIVIAN: Probably. Besides, you are a little too old. We don't admit anybody who is of the usual age.

CYRIL: Well, I should fancy you are all a good deal bored with each other.

VIVIAN: We are. That is one of the objects of the club. Now, if you promise not to interrupt too often, I will read you my article.

CYRIL: You will find me all attention.

VIVIAN (reading in a very clear, musical voice): "THE DECAY OF LYING: A PROTEST.— One of the chief causes that can be assigned for the curiously commonplace character of most of the literature of our age is undoubtedly the decay of Lying as an art, a science, and a social pleasure. The ancient historians gave us delightful fiction in the form of fact; the modern novelist presents us with dull facts under the guise of fiction. The Blue-Book[3] is rapidly becoming his ideal both for method and manner. He has his tedious 'document humain,'[4] his miserable little 'coin de la création,' into which he peers with his microscope. He is to be found at the Librairie Nationale, or at the British Museum, shamelessly reading up his subject. He has not even the courage of other people's ideas, but insists on going directly to life for everything, and ultimately, between encyclopaedias and personal experience, he comes to the ground, having drawn his types from the family circle or from the weekly washerwoman, and having acquired an amount of useful information from which never, even in his most meditative moments, can he thoroughly free himself.

"The loss that results to literature in general from this false ideal of our time can hardly be overestimated. People have a careless way of talking about a 'born liar,' just as they talk about a 'born poet.' But in both cases they are wrong. Lying and poetry are arts—arts, as Plato saw, not unconnected with each other—and they require the most careful study, the most disinterested devotion. Indeed, they have their technique, just as the more material arts of painting and sculpture have, their subtle secrets of form and colour, their craft-mysteries, their deliberate artistic methods. As one knows the poet by his fine music, so one can recognize the liar by his rich rhythmic utterance, and in neither case will the casual inspiration of the moment suffice. Here, as elsewhere, practice must precede perfection. But in modern days while the fashion of writing poetry has become far too common, and should, if possible, be discouraged, the fashion of lying has almost fallen into disrepute. Many a young man starts in life with a natural gift for exaggeration which, if nurtured in congenial and sympathetic surroundings, or by the imitation of the best models, might grow into something really great and wonderful. But, as a rule, he comes to nothing. He either falls into careless habits of accuracy—"

CYRIL: My dear fellow!

---

1. Hedonists believe that pleasure is the greatest good in life; a tired hedonist would be one exhausted by pleasure (a parody of Wilde's own image).

2. Emperor of Rome (A.D. 81–96), Domitian was famous for his cruelty.

3. Parliamentary reports. The whole passage is aimed at contemporary Realist and Naturalist novelists, such as George Gissing and Émile Zola, who sought to document everyday life, especially among the poor.

4. Human document, from the title of an essay by Zola, who wrote in What I Hate: "A work of art is a nook of creation ("un coin de la création") seen from the perspective of a temperament."

VIVIAN: Please don't interrupt in the middle of a sentence. "He either falls into careless habits of accuracy, or takes to frequenting the society of the aged and the well-informed. Both things are equally fatal to his imagination, as indeed they would be fatal to the imagination of anybody, and in a short time he develops a morbid and unhealthy faculty of truth-telling, begins to verify all statements made in his presence, has no hesitation in contradicting people who are much younger than himself, and often ends by writing novels which are so like life that no one can possibly believe in their probability. This is no isolated instance that we are giving. It is simply one example out of many; and if something cannot be done to check, or at least to modify, our monstrous worship of facts, Art will become sterile, and Beauty will pass away from the land." * * *

* * * Believe me, my dear Cyril, modernity of form and modernity of subject-matter are entirely and absolutely wrong. We have mistaken the common livery of the age for the vesture of the Muses, and spend our days in the sordid streets and hideous suburbs of our vile cities when we should be out on the hillside with Apollo. Certainly we are a degraded race, and have sold our birthright for a mess of facts.[5]

CYRIL: There is something in what you say, and there is no doubt that whatever amusement we may find in reading a purely modern novel, we have rarely any artistic pleasure in re-reading it. And this is perhaps the best rough test of what is literature and what is not. If one cannot enjoy reading a book over and over again, there is no use reading it at all. But what do you say about the return to Life and Nature? This is the panacea that is always being recommended to us.

VIVIAN: I will read you what I say on that subject. The passage comes later on in the article, but I may as well give it to you now:—

"The popular cry of our time is 'Let us return to Life and Nature; they will recreate Art for us, and send the red blood coursing through her veins; they will shoe her feet with swiftness and make her hand strong.' But, alas! we are mistaken in our amiable and well-meaning efforts. Nature is always behind the age. And as for Life, she is the solvent that breaks up Art, the enemy that lays waste her house."

CYRIL: What do you mean by saying that Nature is always behind the age?

VIVIAN: Well, perhaps that is rather cryptic. What I mean is this. If we take Nature to mean natural simple instinct as opposed to self-conscious culture, the work produced under this influence is always old-fashioned, antiquated, and out of date. One touch of Nature may make the whole world kin, but two touches of Nature will destroy any work of Art. If, on the other hand, we regard Nature as the collection of phenomena external to man, people only discover in her what they bring to her. She has no suggestions of her own. Wordsworth went to the lakes, but he was never a lake poet. He found in stones the sermons he had already hidden there.[6] He went moralizing about the district, but his good work was produced when he returned, not to Nature but to poetry. Poetry gave him "Laodamia," and the fine sonnets, and the great Ode,[7] such as it is. Nature gave him "Martha Ray" and "Peter Bell," and the address to Mr Wilkinson's spade.

---

5. When he was hungry, Esau sold his birthright to his brother Jacob for "a mess of pottage" (Genesis 25.30–34).
6. "And this our life, exempt from public haunt, / Finds tongues in trees, books in the running brooks, / Sermons in stones, and good in every thing" (*As You Like It* 2.1.15–17).
7. Presumably Wordsworth's Ode: *Intimations of Immortality*. Vivian next mentions several distinctly lesser poems.

CYRIL: I think that view might be questioned. I am rather inclined to believe in the "impulse from a vernal wood,"[8] though of course the artistic value of such an impulse depends entirely on the kind of temperament that receives it, so that the return to Nature would come to mean simply the advance to a great personality. You would agree with that, I fancy. However, proceed with your article.

VIVIAN (reading): "Art begins with abstract decoration, with purely imaginative and pleasurable work dealing with what is unreal and nonexistent. This is the first stage. Then Life becomes fascinated with this new wonder, and asks to be admitted into the charmed circle. Art takes life as part of her rough material, recreates it, and refashions it in fresh forms, is absolutely indifferent to fact, invents, imagines, dreams, and keeps between herself and reality the impenetrable barrier of beautiful style, of decorative or ideal treatment. The third stage is when Life gets the upper hand, and drives Art out into the wilderness. This is the true decadence, and it is from this that we are now suffering.

"Take the case of the English drama. At first in the hands of the monks Dramatic Art was abstract, decorative, and mythological. Then she enlisted Life in her service, and using some of life's external forms, she created an entirely new race of beings, whose sorrows were more terrible than any sorrow man has ever felt, whose joys were keener than lover's joys, who had the rage of the Titans[9] and the calm of the gods, who had monstrous and marvellous sins, monstrous and marvellous virtues. To them she gave a language different from that of actual use, a language full of resonant music and sweet rhythm, made stately by solemn cadence, or made delicate by fanciful rhyme, jewelled with wonderful words, and enriched with lofty diction. She clothed her children in strange raiment and gave them masks, and at her bidding the antique world rose from its marble tomb. A new Caesar stalked through the streets of risen Rome, and with purple sail and flute-led oars another Cleopatra passed up the river to Antioch.[1] Old myth and legend and dream took shape and substance. History was entirely re-written, and there was hardly one of the dramatists who did not recognize that the object of Art is not simple truth but complex beauty. In this they were perfectly right. Art itself is really a form of exaggeration; and selection, which is the very spirit of art, is nothing more than an intensified mode of over-emphasis.

"But Life soon shattered the perfection of the form. Even in Shakespeare we can see the beginning of the end. It shows itself by the gradual breaking up of the blank-verse in the later plays, by the predominance given to prose, and by the over-importance assigned to characterization. The passages in Shakespeare—and they are many—where the language is uncouth, vulgar, exaggerated, fantastic, obscene even, are entirely due to Life calling for an echo of her own voice, and rejecting the intervention of beautiful style, through which alone should Life be suffered to find expression. Shakespeare is not by any means a flawless artist. He is too fond of going directly to life, and borrowing life's natural utterance. He forgets that when Art surrenders her imaginative medium she surrenders everything. Goethe says, somewhere—

In der Beschränkung zeigt sich erst der Meister,[2]

---

8. "One impulse from a vernal wood / May teach you more of man / Of moral evil and of good / Than all the sages can." From Wordsworth's The Tables Turned.
9. Mythological giants who were overthrown by the gods.

1. References to Shakespeare's Julius Caesar and Antony and Cleopatra.
2. From Nature and Art by Johann Wolfgang von Goethe (1749–1832).

" 'It is in working within limits that the master reveals himself,' and the limitation, the very condition of any art is style. However, we need not linger any longer over Shakespeare's realism. *The Tempest* is the most perfect of palinodes.[3] All that we desired to point out was, that the magnificent work of the Elizabethan and Jacobean artists contained within itself the seeds of its own dissolution, and that, if it drew some of its strength from using life as rough material, it drew all its weakness from using life as an artistic method. As the inevitable result of this substitution of an imitative for a creative medium, this surrender of an imaginative form, we have the modern English melodrama. The characters in these plays talk on the stage exactly as they would talk off it; they have neither aspirations nor aspirates; they are taken directly from life and reproduce its vulgarity down to the smallest detail; they present the gait, manner, costume, and accent of real people; they would pass unnoticed in a third-class railway carriage. And yet how wearisome the plays are! They do not succeed in producing even that impression of reality at which they aim, and which is their only reason for existing. As a method, realism is a complete failure.

"What is true about the drama and the novel is no less true about those arts that we call the decorative arts. The whole history of these arts in Europe is the record of the struggle between Orientalism, with its frank rejection of imitation, its love of artistic convention, its dislike to the actual representation of any object in Nature, and our own imitative spirit. Wherever the former has been paramount, as in Byzantium, Sicily, and Spain, by actual contact, or in the rest of Europe by the influence of the Crusades, we have had beautiful and imaginative work in which the visible things of life are transmuted into artistic conventions, and the things that Life has not are invented and fashioned for her delight. But wherever we have returned to Life and Nature, our work has always become vulgar, common, and uninteresting. Modern tapestry, with its aërial effects, its elaborate perspective, its broad expanses of waste sky, its faithful and laborious realism, has no beauty whatsoever. The pictorial glass of Germany is absolutely detestable. We are beginning to weave possible carpets in England, but only because we have returned to the method and spirit of the East. Our rugs and carpets of twenty years ago, with their solemn depressing truths, their inane worship of Nature, their sordid reproductions of visible objects, have become, even to the Philistine,[4] a source of laughter. A cultured Mahomedan once remarked to us, "You Christians are so occupied in misinterpreting the fourth commandment that you have never thought of making an artistic application of the second."[5] He was perfectly right, and the whole truth of the matter is this: The proper school to learn art in is not Life but Art."

And now let me read you a passage which seems to me to settle the question very completely.

"It was not always thus. We need not say anything about the poets, for they, with the unfortunate exception of Mr Wordsworth, have been really faithful to their high mission, and are universally recognized as being absolutely unreliable. But in the works of Herodotus, who, in spite of the shallow and ungenerous at-

3. A retraction or recantation.
4. In *Culture and Anarchy* (1869), Matthew Arnold used this term to refer to the materialistic and uncultured middle classes.
5. The Fourth Commandment is "Remember the Sabbath day, to keep it holy"; the Second is "Thou shalt not make unto thee any graven image, or any likeness of any thing that is in heaven above, or that is in the earth beneath, or that is in the water underneath the earth" (Exodus 20.4–5). Islamic art is traditionally decorative rather than imitative, in observance of the second commandment.

tempts of modern sciolists[6] to verify his history, may justly be called the 'Father of Lies'; in the published speeches of Cicero and the biographies of Suetonius; in Tacitus at his best; in Pliny's *Natural History*; in Hanno's *Periplus*; in all the early chronicles; in the Lives of the Saints; in Froissart and Sir Thomas Mallory; in the travels of Marco Polo; in Olaus Magnus, and Aldrovandus, and Conrad Lycosthenes, with his magnificent *Prodigiorum et Ostentorum Chronicon*; in the autobiography of Benvenuto Cellini; in the memoirs of Casanuova; in Defoe's *History of the Plague*; in Boswell's *Life of Johnson*; in Napoleon's despatches, and in the works of our own Carlyle, whose *French Revolution* is one of the most fascinating historical novels ever written, facts are either kept in their proper subordinate position, or else entirely excluded on the general ground of dullness. Now, everything is changed. Facts are not merely finding a footing-place in history, but they are usurping the domain of Fancy, and have invaded the kingdom of Romance. Their chilling touch is over everything. They are vulgarizing mankind. The crude commercialism of America, its materializing spirit, its indifference to the poetical side of things, and its lack of imagination and of high unattainable ideals, are entirely due to that country having adopted for its national hero a man, who according to his own confession, was incapable of telling a lie, and it is not too much to say that the story of George Washington and the cherry-tree has done more harm, and in a shorter space of time, than any other moral tale in the whole of literature."

CYRIL: My dear boy!

VIVIAN: I assure you it is the case, and the amusing part of the whole thing is that the story of the cherry-tree is an absolute myth. However, you must not think that I am too despondent about the artistic future either of America or of our own country. Listen to this:—

"That some change will take place before this century has drawn to its close we have no doubt whatsoever. Bored by the tedious and improving conversation of those who have neither the wit to exaggerate nor the genius to romance, tired of the intelligent person whose reminiscences are always based upon memory, whose statements are invariably limited by probability, and who is at any time liable to be corroborated by the merest Philistine who happens to be present, Society sooner or later must return to its lost leader, the cultured and fascinating liar. Who he was who first, without ever having gone out to the rude chase, told the wondering cavemen at sunset how he had dragged the Megatherium[7] from the purple darkness of its jasper cave, or slain the Mammoth in single combat and brought back its gilded tusks, we cannot tell, and not one of our modern anthropologists, for all their much-boasted science, has had the ordinary courage to tell us. Whatever was his name or race, he certainly was the true founder of social intercourse. For the aim of the liar is simply to charm, to delight, to give pleasure. He is the very basis of civilized society, and without him a dinner party, even at the mansions of the great, is as dull as a lecture at the Royal Society, or a debate at the Incorporated Authors, or one of Mr Burnand's farcical comedies.[8]

"Nor will he be welcomed by society alone. Art, breaking from the prison-house of realism, will run to greet him, and will kiss his false, beautiful lips, knowing that he alone is in possession of the great secret of all her manifestations, the

---

6. Know-it-alls.
7. Large extinct animal.

8. Frances Cowley Burnand (1836–1917), editor of *Punch* and popular dramatist.

secret that Truth is entirely and absolutely a matter of style; while Life—poor, probable, uninteresting human life—tired of repeating herself for the benefit of Mr Herbert Spencer,[9] scientific historians, and the compilers of statistics in general, will follow meekly after him, and try to reproduce, in her own simple and untutored way, some of the marvels of which he talks.

"No doubt there will always be critics who, like a certain writer in the *Saturday Review*, will gravely censure the teller of fairy tales for his defective knowledge of natural history,[1] who will measure imaginative work by their own lack of any imaginative faculty, and will hold up their inkstained hands in horror if some honest gentleman, who has never been farther than the yew-trees of his own garden, pens a fascinating book of travels like Sir John Mandeville, or, like great Raleigh, writes a whole history of the world, without knowing anything whatsoever about the past.[2] To excuse themselves they will try and shelter under the shield of him[3] who made Prospero the magician, and gave him Caliban and Ariel as his servants, who heard the Tritons blowing their horns round the coral reefs of the Enchanted Isle, and the fairies singing to each other in a wood near Athens, who led the phantom kings in dim procession across the misty Scottish heath, and hid Hecate in a cave with the weird sisters. They will call upon Shakespeare—they always do—and will quote that hackneyed passage about Art holding the mirror up to Nature, forgetting that this unfortunate aphorism is deliberately said by Hamlet in order to convince the bystanders of his absolute insanity in all art-matters."[4]

CYRIL: Ahem! Another cigarette, please.

VIVIAN: My dear fellow, whatever you may say, it is merely a dramatic utterance, and no more represents Shakespeare's real views upon art than the speeches of Iago represent his real views upon morals.[5] But let me get to the end of the passage:

"Art finds her own perfection within, and not outside of, herself. She is not to be judged by any external standard of resemblance. She is a veil, rather than a mirror. She has flowers that no forests know of, birds that no woodland possesses. She makes and unmakes many worlds, and can draw the moon from heaven with a scarlet thread. Hers are the "forms more real than living man,"[6] and hers the great archetypes of which things that have existence are but unfinished copies. Nature has, in her eyes, no laws, no uniformity. She can work miracles at her will, and when she calls monsters from the deep they come. She can bid the almond tree blossom in winter, and send the snow upon the ripe cornfield. At her word the frost lays its silver finger on the burning mouth of June, and the winged lions creep out from the hollows of the Lydian hills. The dryads peer from the thicket as she passes by, and the brown fauns smile strangely at her when she comes near them. She has hawk-faced gods that worship her, and the centaurs gallop at her side."

9. English philosopher and theorist of evolution (1820–1903).

1. Wilde alludes to an anonymous review of his fairy tale, *The Happy Prince*.

2. Mandeville was the purported author of a highly fanciful medieval book of travels in the East; Sir Walter Raleigh published his *History of the World* in 1614.

3. I.e., Shakespeare. The sentence alludes to *The Tempest, A Midsummer Night's Dream*, and *Macbeth*.

4. Explaining why performers should not overact, Hamlet says: "For anything so o'erdone is [apart] from the purpose of playing, whose end, both at the first and now, was and is, to hold, as 't were, the mirror up to nature" (*Hamlet* 3.2.19–22).

5. Iago is the villain in Shakespeare's *Othello*.

6. Shelley, *Prometheus Unbound*, line 748.

CYRIL: I like that. I can see it. Is that the end?

VIVIAN: No. There is one more passage, but it is purely practical. It simply suggests some methods by which we could revive this lost art of Lying.

CYRIL: Well, before you read it to me, I should like to ask you a question. What do you mean by saying that life, "poor, probable, uninteresting human life," will try to reproduce the marvels of art? I can quite understand your objection to art being treated as a mirror. You think it would reduce genius to the position of a cracked looking-glass. But you don't mean to say that you seriously believe that Life imitates Art, that Life in fact is the mirror, and Art the reality?

VIVIAN: Certainly I do. Paradox though it may seem—and paradoxes are always dangerous things—it is none the less true that Life imitates art far more than Art imitates life. We have all seen in our own day in England how a certain curious and fascinating type of beauty, invented and emphasized by two imaginative painters,[7] has so influenced Life that whenever one goes to a private view or to an artistic salon one sees, here the mystic eyes of Rossetti's dream, the long ivory throat, the strange square-cut jaw, the loosened shadowy hair that he so ardently loved, there the sweet maidenhood of "The Golden Stair," the blossom-like mouth and weary loveliness of the "Laus Amoris," the passion-pale face of Andromeda, the thin hands and lithe beauty of the Vivien in "Merlin's Dream." And it has always been so. A great artist invents a type, and Life tries to copy it, to reproduce it in a popular form, like an enterprising publisher. Neither Holbein nor Vandyck[8] found in England what they have given us. They brought their types with them, and Life with her keen imitative faculty set herself to supply the master with models. The Greeks, with their quick artistic instinct, understood this, and set in the bride's chamber the statue of Hermes or of Apollo, that she might bear children as lovely as the works of art that she looked at in her rapture or her pain. They knew that Life gains from Art not merely spirituality, depth of thought and feeling, soul-turmoil or soul-peace, but that she can form herself on the very lines and colours of art, and can reproduce the dignity of Pheidias as well as the grace of Praxiteles.[9] Hence came their objection to realism. They disliked it on purely social grounds. They felt that it inevitably makes people ugly, and they were perfectly right. We try to improve the conditions of the race by means of good air, free sunlight, wholesome water, and hideous bare buildings for the better housing of the lower orders. But these things merely produce health, they do not produce beauty. For this, Art is required, and the true disciples of the great artist are not his studio-imitators, but those who become like his works of art, be they plastic as in Greek days, or pictorial as in modern times; in a word, Life is Art's best, Art's only pupil. * * *

* * * All that I desire to point out is the general principle that Life imitates Art far more than Art imitates Life, and I feel sure that if you think seriously about it you will find that it is true. Life holds the mirror up to Art, and either reproduces some strange type imagined by painter or sculptor, or realizes in fact what has been dreamed in fiction. Scientifically speaking, the basis of life—the energy of life, as

7. The Pre-Raphaelites Dante Gabriel Rossetti and Edward Burne-Jones; Wilde lists typical features of Rossetti's works, followed by the titles of three of Burne-Jones's paintings.
8. Hans Holbein the younger (c. 1497–1543) and Sir Anthony Van Dyke (1599–1641), Dutch portrait painters who greatly influenced English painters. Holbein became the court painter to Henry VIII, and Van Dyke became court painter under James I.
9. Ancient Greek sculptors.

Aristotle would call it[1]—is simply the desire for expression, and Art is always presenting various forms through which this expression can be attained. Life seizes on them and uses them, even if they be to her own hurt. Young men have committed suicide because Rolla did so, have died by their own hand because by his own hand Werther died.[2] Think of what we owe to the imitation of Christ, of what we owe to the imitation of Caesar.

CYRIL: The theory is certainly a very curious one, but to make it complete you must show that Nature, no less than Life, is an imitation of Art. Are you prepared to prove that?

VIVIAN: My dear fellow, I am prepared to prove anything.

CYRIL: Nature follows the landscape painter then, and takes her effects from him?

VIVIAN: Certainly. Where, if not from the Impressionists,[3] do we get those wonderful brown fogs that come creeping down our streets, blurring the gas-lamps and changing the houses into monstrous shadows? To whom, if not to them and their master, do we owe the lovely silver mists that brood over our river, and turn to faint forms of fading grace curved bridge and swaying barge? The extraordinary change that has taken place in the climate of London during the last ten years is entirely due to this particular school of Art. You smile. Consider the matter from a scientific or a metaphysical point of view, and you will find that I am right. For what is Nature? Nature is no great mother who has borne us. She is our creation. It is in our brain that she quickens to life. Things are because we see them, and what we see, and how we see it, depends on the Arts that have influenced us. To look at a thing is very different from seeing a thing. One does not see anything until one sees its beauty. Then, and then only, does it come into existence. At present, people see fogs, not because there are fogs, but because poets and painters have taught them the mysterious loveliness of such effects. There may have been fogs for centuries in London. I dare say there were. But no one saw them, and so we do not know anything about them. They did not exist till Art had invented them. Now, it must be admitted, fogs are carried to excess. They have become the mere mannerism of a clique, and the exaggerated realism of their method gives dull people bronchitis. Where the cultured catch an effect, the uncultured catch cold. And so, let us be humane, and invite Art to turn her wonderful eyes elsewhere. She has done so already, indeed. That white quivering sunlight that one sees now in France, with its strange blotches of mauve, and its restless violet shadows, is her latest fancy, and, on the whole, Nature reproduces it quite admirably. Where she used to give us Corots and Daubignys, she gives us now exquisite Monets and entrancing Pisaros.[4] Indeed there are moments, rare, it is true, but still to be observed from time to ime, when Nature becomes absolutely modern. Of course she is not always to be relied upon. The fact is that she is in this unfortunate position. Art creates an incomparable and unique effect, and, having done so, passes on to other things. Nature, upon the other hand, forgetting that imitation can be made the sincerest form of insult, keeps on repeating this effect until

---

1. In his *Physics*, Aristotle equates nature with energy.
2. Rolla is the Byronic hero of *Rolla* (1833), by the French poet Alfred de Musset; Werther is the romantic hero of Goethe's *The Sorrows of Young Werther* (1774).
3. French Impressionist painters such as Monet, Renoir, and Pissarro sought to capture the interplay of light, atmosphere, and the elements, but it was Whistler (probably the "master" alluded to in the next sentence) who discovered London fogs, barges, and misty bridges as artistic subjects.
4. Earlier in the century, Corot and Daubigny had painted muted landscapes; Wilde's contemporaries Claude Monet and Camille Pissarro produced bright, Impressionist canvases.

we all become absolutely wearied of it. Nobody of any real culture, for instance, ever talks nowadays about the beauty of a sunset. Sunsets are quite old-fashioned. They belong to the time when Turner was the last note in art.[5] To admire them is a distinct sign of provincialism of temperament. Upon the other hand they go on. Yesterday evening Mrs Arundel insisted on my going to the window, and looking at the glorious sky, as she called it. Of course I had to look at it. She is one of those absurdly pretty Philistines, to whom one can deny nothing. And what was it? It was simply a very second-rate Turner, a Turner of a bad period, with all the painter's worst faults exaggerated and over-emphasized. Of course, I am quite ready to admit that Life very often commits the same error. She produces her false Renés and her sham Vautrins, just as Nature gives us, on one day a doubtful Cuyp, and on another a more than questionable Rousseau.[6] Still, Nature irritates one more when she does things of that kind. It seems so stupid, so obvious, so unnecessary. A false Vautrin might be delightful. A doubtful Cuyp is unbearable. However, I don't want to be too hard on Nature. I wish the Channel, especially at Hastings, did not look quite so often like a Henry Moore,[7] grey pearl with yellow lights, but then, when Art is more varied, Nature will, no doubt, be more varied also. That she imitates Art, I don't think even her worst enemy would deny now. It is the one thing that keeps her in touch with civilized man. But have I proved my theory to your satisfaction?

CYRIL: You have proved it to my dissatisfaction, which is better. But even admitting this strange imitative instinct in Life and Nature, surely you would acknowledge that Art expresses the temper of its age, the spirit of its time, the moral and social conditions that surround it, and under whose influence it is produced.

VIVIAN: Certainly not! Art never expresses anything but itself. This is the principle of my new aesthetics; and it is this, more than that vital connection between form and substance, on which Mr Pater dwells,[8] that makes music the type of all the arts. Of course, nations and individuals, with that healthy natural vanity which is the secret of existence, are always under the impression that it is of them that the Muses are talking, always trying to find in the calm dignity of imaginative art some mirror of their own turbid passions, always forgetting that the singer of life is not Apollo, but Marsyas.[9] Remote from reality, and with her eyes turned away from the shadows of the cave,[1] Art reveals her own perfection, and the wondering crowd that watches the opening of the marvellous, many-petalled rose fancies that it is its own history that is being told to it, its own spirit that is finding expression in a new form. But it is not so. The highest art rejects the burden of the human spirit, and gains more from a new medium or a fresh material than she does from any enthusiasm for art, or from any lofty passion, or from any great awakening of the human consciousness. She develops purely on her own lines. She is not symbolic of any age. It is the ages that are her symbols.

5. The atmospheric landscape paintings of J. M. W. Turner (1775–1851) were much admired by Ruskin in *Modern Painters* (1843–1860).
6. François-René de Chateaubriand's *René* (1802) told the story of a superior but sorrowful young man who flees to the wilderness of America to seek solitude; Vautrin, villain of a series of novels by Honoré de Balzac (1799–1850); Albert Cuyp (1620–1691), Dutch painter of wintry pastoral landscapes; Théodore Rousseau (1812–1867), French painter of the Barbizon school.
7. English painter (1831–1895) who specialized in seascapes.
8. Walter Pater's views of art influenced Wilde; Vivian refers to Pater's *The School of Giorgione*, an essay added to *The Renaissance* in 1888, where Pater says, "All art constantly aspires towards the condition of music."
9. A flute player who challenged Apollo, the god of music, to a contest; he was defeated and flayed alive for his presumption.
1. In the *Republic*, Plato suggests that reality is to the absolute what shadows in a cave are to the objects which cast the shadows—i.e., dim and imperfect indications.

Even those who hold that Art is representative of time and place and people, cannot help admitting that the more imitative an art is, the less it represents to us the spirit of its age. The evil faces of the Roman emperors look out at us from the foul porphyry and spotted jasper in which the realistic artists of the day delighted to work, and we fancy that in those cruel lips and heavy sensual jaws we can find the secret of the ruin of the Empire. But it was not so. The vices of Tiberius could not destroy that supreme civilization, any more than the virtues of the Antonines could save it.[2] It fell for other, for less interesting reasons. The sibyls and prophets of the Sistine may indeed serve to interpret for some that new birth of the emancipated spirit that we call the Renaissance; but what do the drunken boors and brawling peasants of Dutch art tell us about the great soul of Holland? The more abstract, the more ideal an art is, the more it reveals to us the temper of its age. If we wish to understand a nation by means of its art, let us look at its architecture or its music.

CYRIL: I quite agree with you there. The spirit of an age may be best expressed in the abstract ideal arts, for the spirit itself is abstract and ideal. Upon the other hand, for the visible aspect of an age, for its look, as the phrase goes, we must of course go to the arts of imitation.

VIVIAN: I don't think so. After all, what the imitative arts really give us are merely the various styles of particular artists, or of certain schools of artists. Surely you don't imagine that the people of the Middle Ages bore any resemblance at all to the figures on mediaeval stained glass, or in mediaeval stone and wood carving, or on mediaeval metal-work, or tapestries, or illuminated MSS.[3] They were probably very ordinary-looking people, with nothing grotesque, or remarkable, or fantastic in their appearance. The Middle Ages, as we know them in art, are simply a definite form of style, and there is no reason at all why an artist with this style should not be produced in the nineteenth century. No great artist ever sees things as they really are. If he did, he would cease to be an artist. Take an example from our own day. I know that you are fond of Japanese things. Now, do you really imagine that the Japanese people, as they are presented to us in art, have any existence? If you do, you have never understood Japanese art at all. The Japanese people are the deliberate self-conscious creation of certain individual artists. If you set a picture by Hokusai, or Hokkei,[4] or any of the great native painters, beside a real Japanese gentleman or lady, you will see that there is not the slightest resemblance between them. The actual people who live in Japan are not unlike the general run of English people; that is to say, they are extremely commonplace, and have nothing curious or extraordinary about them. In fact the whole of Japan is a pure invention. There is no such country, there are no such people. One of our most charming painters[5] went recently to the Land of the Chrysanthemum in the foolish hope of seeing the Japanese. All he saw, all he had the chance of painting, were a few lanterns and some fans. He was quite unable to discover the inhabitants, as his delightful exhibition at Messrs Dowdeswell's Gallery showed only too well. He did not know that the Japanese people are, as I have said, simply a mode of style, an

---

2. Tiberius (44 B.C.–A.D. 37) was a cruel and lustful Roman emperor; Antoninus Pius and his son-in-law, the philosopher Marcus Aurelius, were later emperors noted for their wisdom and good character.
3. Manuscripts.

4. Katsushika Hokusai (1760–1849) and Hokkei (1780–1850), Japanese artists.
5. Mortimer Menpes, Australian artist and disciple of Whistler who gave a Japanese exhibition at Dowdeswell's Gallery in 1888.

exquisite fancy of art. And so, if you desire to see a Japanese effect, you will not behave like a tourist and go to Tokio. On the contrary, you will stay at home, and steep yourself in the work of certain Japanese artists, and then, when you have absorbed the spirit of their style, and caught their imaginative manner of vision, you will go some afternoon and sit in the Park or stroll down Piccadilly, and if you cannot see an absolutely Japanese effect there, you will not see it anywhere. Or, to return again to the past, take as another instance the ancient Greeks. Do you think that Greek art ever tells us what the Greek people were like? Do you believe that the Athenian women were like the stately dignified figures of the Parthenon frieze, or like those marvellous goddesses who sat in the triangular pediments of the same building? If you judge from the art, they certainly were so. But read an authority, like Aristophanes[6] for instance. You will find that the Athenian ladies laced tightly, wore high-heeled shoes, dyed their hair yellow, painted and rouged their faces, and were exactly like any silly fashionable or fallen creature of our own day. The fact is that we look back on the ages entirely through the medium of Art, and Art, very fortunately, has never once told us the truth.

CYRIL: But modern portraits by English painters, what of them? Surely they are like the people they pretend to represent?

VIVIAN: Quite so. They are so like them that a hundred years from now no one will believe in them. The only portraits in which one believes are portraits where there is very little of the sitter, and a very great deal of the artist. Holbein's drawings of the men and women of his time impress us with a sense of their absolute reality. But this is simply because Holbein compelled life to accept his conditions, to restrain itself within his limitations, to reproduce his type, and to appear as he wished it to appear. It is style that makes us believe in a thing—nothing but style. Most of our modern portrait painters are doomed to absolute oblivion. They never paint what they see. They paint what the public sees, and the public never sees anything.

CYRIL: Well, after that I think I should like to hear the end of your article.

VIVIAN: With pleasure. Whether it will do any good I really cannot say. Ours is certainly the dullest and most prosaic century possible. * * * However, I must read the end of my article:—

"What we have to do, what at any rate it is our duty to do, is to revive this old art of Lying. Much of course may be done, in the way of educating the public, by amateurs in the domestic circle, at literary lunches, and at afternoon teas. But this is merely the light and graceful side of lying, such as was probably heard at Cretan dinner parties. There are many other forms. Lying for the sake of gaining some immediate personal advantage, for instance—lying with a moral purpose, as it is usually called—though of late it has been rather looked down upon, was extremely popular with the antique world. Athena laughs when Odysseus tells her 'his words of sly devising,' as Mr William Morris phrases it,[7] and the glory of mendacity illumines the pale brow of the stainless hero of Euripidean tragedy,[8] and sets among the noble women of the past the young bride of one of Horace's most exquisite odes.[9] Later on, what at first had been merely a natural instinct

6. Athenian satiric dramatist (c. 448–c. 380 B.C.).
7. Wilde quotes Morris's translation of the *Odyssey* (bk. 13), where Odysseus lies to Athena, his patron goddess, when she appears to him in disguise.
8. In Euripides' *Ion* the hero lies about his parentage.
9. Horace tells how Hypermnestra saved her husband's life by warning him that her father, Danaus, was conspiring to kill him; thus she was "splendidly false / to her treacherous father" (Horace, *Odes*, 3.11.34–35; trans. by David Mulroy, 1994).

was elevated into a self-conscious science. Elaborate rules were laid down for the guidance of mankind, and an important school of literature grew up round the subject. Indeed, when one remembers the excellent philosophical treatise of Sanchez[1] on the whole question, one cannot help regretting that no one has ever thought of publishing a cheap and condensed edition of the works of that great casuist. A short primer, 'When to Lie and How,' if brought out in an attractive and not too expensive a form, would no doubt command a large sale, and would prove of real practical service to many earnest and deep-thinking people. Lying for the sake of the improvement of the young, which is the basis of home education, still lingers amongst us, and its advantages are so admirably set forth in the early books of Plato's *Republic*[2] that it is unnecessary to dwell upon them here. It is a mode of lying for which all good mothers have peculiar capabilities, but it is capable of still further development, and has been sadly overlooked by the School Board. Lying for the sake of a monthly salary is of course well known in Fleet Street, and the profession of a political leader-writer is not without its advantages. But it is said to be a somewhat dull occupation, and it certainly does not lead to much beyond a kind of ostentatious obscurity. The only form of lying that is absolutely beyond reproach is Lying for its own sake, and the highest development of this is, as we have already pointed out, Lying in Art. Just as those who do not love Plato more than Truth cannot pass beyond the threshold of the Academe,[3] so those who do not love Beauty more than Truth never know the inmost shrine of Art. The solid stolid British intellect lies in the desert sands like the Sphinx in Flaubert's marvellous tale,[4] and fantasy, *La Chimère*, dances round it, and calls to it with her false, flute-toned voice. It may not hear her now, but surely some day, when we are all bored to death with the commonplace character of modern fiction, it will hearken to her and try to borrow her wings.

"And when that day dawns, or sunset reddens, how joyous we shall all be! Facts will be regarded as discreditable, Truth will be found mourning over her fetters, and Romance, with her temper of wonder, will return to the land. The very aspect of the world will change to our startled eyes. Out of the sea will rise Behemoth and Leviathan,[5] and sail round the high-pooped galleys, as they do on the delightful maps of those ages when books on geography were actually readable. Dragons will wander about the waste places, and the phoenix will soar from her nest of fire into the air. We shall lay our hands upon the basilisk, and see the jewel in the toad's head. Champing his gilded oats, the Hippogriff will stand in our stalls, and over our heads will float the Blue Bird singing of beautiful and impossible things, of things that are lovely and that never happen, of things that are not and that should be. But before this comes to pass we must cultivate the lost art of Lying."

1. Fernando Sanchez, author of *A Treatise on the Noble and High Science of Nescience* [Ignorance] (1581).
2. In Books 2 and 3, which discuss the education of the future Guardians of the ideal republic, Plato advocates suppressing stories that evoke the terror of death or that portray the gods as undignified or immoral.
3. A gibe at Plato's coercive method of teaching. Wilde reverses Aristotle's remark, "Plato is dear to me, but dearer still is truth." Plato's school in Athens was called the Academy because he taught his students in an olive grove dedicated to the hero Academus.
4. *The Temptation of Saint Anthony* (1874) by French novelist Gustave Flaubert.
5. The hippopotamus and the whale in the Book of Job. The rest of the paragraph refers to fabulous mythical animals: the phoenix was a legendary bird that immolated itself on a pyre, then rose regenerated from the ashes; the basilisk was a reptile whose breath and glance were fatal; the hippogriff was part gryphon and part horse.

CYRIL: Then we must certainly cultivate it at once. But in order to avoid making any error I want you to tell me briefly the doctrines of the new aesthetics.

VIVIAN: Briefly, then, they are these. Art never expresses anything but itself. It has an independent life, just as Thought has, and develops purely on its own lines. It is not necessarily realistic in an age of realism, nor spiritual in an age of faith. So far from being the creation of its time, it is usually in direct opposition to it, and the only history that it preserves for us is the history of its own progress. Sometimes it returns upon its footsteps, and revives some antique form, as happened in the archaistic movement of late Greek Art, and in the pre-Raphaelite movement of our own day. At other times it entirely anticipates its age, and produces in one century work that it takes another century to understand, to appreciate, and to enjoy. In no case does it reproduce its age. To pass from the art of a time to the time itself is the great mistake that all historians commit.

The second doctrine is this. All bad art comes from returning to Life and Nature, and elevating them into ideals. Life and Nature may sometimes be used as part of Art's rough material, but before they are of any real service to art they must be translated into artistic conventions. The moment Art surrenders its imaginative medium it surrenders everything. As a method Realism is a complete failure, and the two things that every artist should avoid are modernity of form and modernity of subject-matter. To us, who live in the nineteenth century, any century is a suitable subject for art except our own. The only beautiful things are the things that do not concern us. It is, to have the pleasure of quoting myself, exactly because Hecuba is nothing to us that her sorrows are so suitable a motive for a tragedy.[6] Besides, it is only the modern that ever becomes old-fashioned. M. Zola sits down to give us a picture of the Second Empire.[7] Who cares for the Second Empire now? It is out of date. Life goes faster than Realism, but Romanticism is always in front of Life.

The third doctrine is that Life imitates Art far more than Art imitates Life. This results not merely from Life's imitative instinct, but from the fact that the self-conscious aim of Life is to find expression, and that Art offers it certain beautiful forms through which it may realize that energy. It is a theory that has never been put forward before, but it is extremely fruitful, and throws an entirely new light upon the history of Art.

It follows, as a corollary from this, that external Nature also imitates Art. The only effects that she can show us are effects that we have already seen through poetry, or in paintings. This is the secret of Nature's charm, as well as the explanation of Nature's weakness.

The final revelation is that Lying, the telling of beautiful untrue things, is the proper aim of Art. But of this I think I have spoken at sufficient length. And now let us go out on the terrace, where "droops the milk-white peacock like a ghost,"[8] while the evening star "washes the dusk with silver."[9] At twilight nature becomes a wonderfully suggestive effect, and is not without loveliness, though perhaps its chief use is to illustrate quotations from the poets. Come! We have talked long enough.

1889, 1891

6. Hecuba, queen of Troy, lost her sons and her husband when the Greeks defeated Troy. Wilde alludes to a scene in *Hamlet* where an actor recites a speech about her suffering and Hamlet asks himself, "What's Hecuba to him, or he to Hecuba, / That he should weep for her?"

(2.2.559–60).
7. In France, the period from 1852 to 1870.
8. From Tennyson's *The Princess* (1847); see page 1256.
9. From Blake's *To the Evening Star* (1783).

from The Soul of Man Under Socialism[1]

The chief advantage that would result from the establishment of Socialism is, undoubtedly, the fact that Socialism would relieve us from that sordid necessity of living for others which, in the present condition of things, presses so hardly upon almost everybody. In fact, scarcely anyone at all escapes.

Now and then, in the course of the century, a great man of science, like Darwin; a great poet, like Keats; a fine critical spirit, like M. Renan;[2] a supreme artist, like Flaubert, has been able to isolate himself, to keep himself out of reach of the clamorous claims of others, to stand "under the shelter of the wall," as Plato puts it, and so to realise the perfection of what was in him, to his own incomparable gain, and to the incomparable and lasting gain of the whole world. These, however, are exceptions. The majority of people spoil their lives by an unhealthy and exaggerated altruism—are forced, indeed, so to spoil them. They find themselves surrounded by hideous poverty, by hideous ugliness, by hideous starvation. It is inevitable that they should be strongly moved by all this. The emotions of man are stirred more quickly than man's intelligence; and, as I pointed out some time ago in an article on the function of criticism,[3] it is much more easy to have sympathy with suffering than it is to have sympathy with thought. Accordingly, with admirable though misdirected intentions, they very seriously and very sentimentally set themselves to the task of remedying the evils that they see. But their remedies do not cure the disease: they merely prolong it. Indeed, their remedies are part of the disease.

They try to solve the problem of poverty, for instance, by keeping the poor alive; or, in the case of a very advanced school, by amusing the poor.

But this is not a solution: it is an aggravation of the difficulty. *The proper aim is to try and reconstruct society on such a basis that poverty will be impossible.* And the altruistic virtues have really prevented the carrying out of this aim. Just as the worst slave-owners were those who were kind to their slaves, and so prevented the horror of the system being realised by those who suffered from it, and understood by those who contemplated it, so, in the present state of things in England, the people who do most harm are the people who try to do most good; and at last we have had the spectacle of men who have really studied the problem and know the life—educated men who live in the East-end[4]—coming forward and imploring the community to restrain its altruistic impulses of charity, benevolence, and the like. They do so on the ground that such charity degrades and demoralizes. They are perfectly right. Charity creates a multitude of sins.

There is also this to be said. It is immoral to use private property in order to alleviate the horrible evils that result from the institution of private property. It is both immoral and unfair.

1. Published in *The Fortnightly Review* in 1891, this essay had an important underground life during the next few decades; translated into many languages, it was also secretly printed and circulated in Tzarist Russia. In the 1880s and 1890s, socialism, which advocates collective ownership of property and the means of production, emerged as a strong nationwide movement in Britain, bolstered by trade unionism and such intellectual and feminist groups as the Fabian Society and the Ethical Socialists. Wilde had no formal connection to socialist groups, but was sympathetic to many of their concerns, and apparently wrote this essay after attending a meeting where Bernard Shaw was the chief speaker. Wilde's essay is remarkable in its claim that socialism—usually said to put the needs of society ahead of personal interests—will lead to the fulfillment of the individual. He wrote elsewhere: "to make men Socialists is nothing, but to make Socialism human is a great thing."

2. Ernest Renan, French scholar and essayist, author of *La Vie de Jésus* (1863; English trans. 1888).

3. Wilde's essay *The Critic as Artist* (1890) challenged Matthew Arnold's *The Function of Criticism at the Present Time* (1864) by arguing that good criticism is "creative and independent" and "more creative than creation" because it is further removed from life than the work of the writer or artist.

4. The poorest section of Victorian London.

Under Socialism all this will, of course, be altered. There will be no people living in fetid dens and fetid rags, and bringing up unhealthy, hunger-pinched children in the midst of impossible and absolutely repulsive surroundings. The security of society will not depend, as it does now, on the state of the weather. If a frost comes we shall not have a hundred thousand men out of work, tramping about the streets in a state of disgusting misery, or whining to their neighbours for alms, or crowding round the doors of loathsome shelters to try and secure a hunch of bread and a night's unclean lodging. Each member of the society will share in the general prosperity and happiness of the society, and if a frost comes no one will practically be anything the worse.

Upon the other hand, *Socialism itself will be of value simply because it will lead to Individualism.*

Socialism, Communism, or whatever one chooses to call it, by converting private property into public wealth, and substituting cooperation for competition, will restore society to its proper condition of a thoroughly healthy organism, and insure the material well-being of each member of the community. It will, in fact, give Life its proper basis and its proper environment. But for the full development of Life to its highest mode of perfection, something more is needed. What is needed is Individualism. If the Socialism is Authoritarian; if there are Governments armed with economic power as they are now with political power; if, in a word, we are to have Industrial Tyrannies, then the last state of man will be worse than the first. At present, in consequence of the existence of private property, a great many people are enabled to develop a certain very limited amount of Individualism. They are either under no necessity to work for their living, or are enabled to choose the sphere of activity that is really congenial to them, and gives them pleasure. These are the poets, the philosophers, the men of science, the men of culture—in a word, the real men, the men who have realised themselves, and in whom all Humanity gains a partial realisation. Upon the other hand, there are a great many people who, having no private property of their own, and being always on the brink of sheer starvation, are compelled to do the work of beasts of burden, to do work that is quite uncongenial to them, and to which they are forced by the peremptory, unreasonable, degrading Tyranny of want. These are the poor, and amongst them there is no grace of manner, or charm of speech, or civilization, or culture, or refinement in pleasures, or joy of life. From their collective force Humanity gains much in material prosperity. But it is only the material result that it gains, and the man who is poor is in himself absolutely of no importance. He is merely the infinitesimal atom of a force that, so far from regarding him, crushes him: indeed, prefers him crushed, as in that case he is far more obedient.

Of course, it might be said that the Individualism generated under conditions of private property is not always, or even as a rule, of a fine or wonderful type, and that the poor, if they have not culture and charm, have still many virtues. Both these statements would be quite true. The possession of private property is very often extremely demoralising, and that is, of course, one of the reasons why Socialism wants to get rid of the institution. In fact, property is really a nuisance. Some years ago people went about the country saying that property has duties. They said it so often and so tediously that, at last, the church has begun to say it. One hears it now from every pulpit. It is perfectly true. Property not merely has duties, but has so many duties that its possession to any large extent is a bore. It involves endless claims upon one, endless attention to business, endless bother. If property had simply pleasures, we could stand it; but its duties make it unbearable. In the interest of the rich we must get rid of it. The virtues of the poor may be readily admitted, and are much to be regretted. * * *

* * * Misery and poverty are so absolutely degrading, and exercise such a paralysing effect over the nature of men, that no class is ever really conscious of its own suffering. They have to be told of it by other people, and they often entirely disbelieve them. What is said by great employers of labour against agitators is unquestionably true. Agitators are a set of interfering, meddling people, who come down to some perfectly contented class of the community, and sow the seeds of discontent amongst them. That is the reason why agitators are so absolutely necessary. Without them, in our incomplete state, there would be no advance towards civilization. Slavery was put down in America, not in consequence of any action on the part of the slaves, or even any express desire on their part that they should be free. It was put down entirely through the grossly illegal conduct of certain agitators in Boston and elsewhere, who were not slaves themselves, nor owners of slaves, nor had anything to do with the question really. It was, undoubtedly, the Abolitionists who set the torch alight, who began the whole thing. And it is curious to note that from the slaves themselves they received, not merely very little assistance, but hardly any sympathy even; and when at the close of the war the slaves found themselves free, found themselves indeed so absolutely free that they were free to starve, many of them bitterly regretted the new state of things. To the thinker, the most tragic fact in the whole of the French Revolution is not that Marie Antoinette was killed for being a queen, but that the starved peasant of the Vendee voluntarily went out to die for the hideous cause of feudalism.[5]

It is clear, then, that no Authoritarian Socialism will do. For while under the present system a very large number of people can lead lives of a certain amount of freedom and expression and happiness, under an industrial-barrack system, or a system of economic tyranny, nobody would be able to have any such freedom at all. It is to be regretted that a portion of our community should be practically in slavery, but to propose to solve the problem by enslaving the entire community is childish. Every man must be left quite free to choose his own work. No form of compulsion must be exercised over him. * * *

Now as the State is not to govern, it may be asked what the State is to do. The State is to be a voluntary association that will organize labour, and be the manufacturer and distributor of necessary commodities. *The State is to make what is useful. The individual is to make what is beautiful.* And as I have mentioned the word labour, I cannot help saying that a great deal of nonsense is being written and talked nowadays about the dignity of manual labour. There is nothing necessarily dignified about manual labour at all, and most of it is absolutely degrading. It is mentally and morally injurious to man to do anything in which he does not find pleasure, and many forms of labour are quite pleasureless activities, and should be regarded as such. To sweep a slushy crossing for eight hours on a day when the east wind is blowing is a disgusting occupation. To sweep it with mental, moral, or physical dignity seems to me to be impossible. To sweep it with joy would be appalling. Man is made for something better than disturbing dirt. All work of that kind should be done by a machine.

And I have no doubt that it will be so. Up to the present, man has been, to a certain extent, the slave of machinery, and there is something tragic in the fact that as soon as man had invented a machine to do his work he began to starve. This,

5. Marie Antoinette, Queen of France, was beheaded in 1793 during the French Revolution; the Vendée was a center of counterrevolutionary activity.

however, is, of course, the result of our property system and our system of competition. One man owns a machine which does the work of five hundred men. Five hundred men are, in consequence, thrown out of employment, and having no work to do, become hungry and take to thieving. The one man secures the produce of the machine and keeps it, and has five hundred times as much as he should have, and probably, which is of much more importance, a great deal more than he really wants. Were that machine the property of all, every one would benefit by it. It would be an immense advantage to the community. All unintellectual labour, all monotonous, dull labour, all labour that deals with dreadful things, and involves unpleasant conditions, must be done by machinery. Machinery must work for us in coal mines, and do all sanitary services, and be the stoker of steamers, and clean the streets, and run messages on wet days, and do anything that is tedious or distressing. *At present machinery competes against man. Under proper conditions machinery will serve man.* There is no doubt at all that this is the future of machinery, and just as trees grow while the country gentleman is asleep, so while Humanity will be amusing itself, or enjoying cultivated leisure—which, and not labour, is the aim of man—or making beautiful things, or reading beautiful things, or simply contemplating the world with admiration and delight, machinery will be doing all the necessary and unpleasant work. The fact is, that civilization requires slaves. The Greeks were quite right there. Unless there are slaves to do the ugly, horrible, uninteresting work, culture and contemplation become almost impossible. Human slavery is wrong, insecure, and demoralising. On mechanical slavery, on the slavery of the machine, the future of the world depends. And when scientific men are no longer called upon to go down to a depressing Eastend and distribute bad cocoa and worse blankets to starving people, they will have delightful leisure in which to devise wonderful and marvellous things for their own joy and the joy of everyone else. There will be great storages of force for every city, and for every house if required, and this force man will convert into heat, light, or motion, according to his needs. Is this Utopian?[6] A map of the world that does not include Utopia is not worth even glancing at, for it leaves out the one country at which Humanity is always landing. And when Humanity lands there, it looks out, and, seeing a better country, sets sail. Progress is the realisation of Utopias. * * *

It is to be noted also that Individualism does not come to man with any sickly cant about duty, which merely means doing what other people want because they want it; or any hideous cant about self-sacrifice, which is merely a survival of savage mutilation. *In fact, it does not come to man with any claims upon him at all. It comes naturally and inevitably out of man.* It is the point to which all development tends. It is the differentiation to which all organisms grow. It is the perfection that is inherent in every mode of life, and towards which every mode of life quickens. And so Individualism exercises no compulsion over man. On the contrary it says to man that he should suffer no compulsion to be exercised over him. It does not try to force people to be good. It knows that people are good when they are let alone. Man will develop Individualism out of himself. Man is now so developing Individualism. To ask whether Individualism is practical is like asking whether Evolution is practical. *Evolution is the law of life, and there is no evolution except towards Individualism.* * * *

* * * Man has sought to live intensely, fully, perfectly. When he can do so without exercising restraint on others, or suffering it ever, and his activities are all pleasurable to him, he will be saner, healthier, more civilized, more himself. Pleasure is

6. I.e., impossibly idealistic. In *Utopia* (1516) Sir Thomas More described an imaginary island of that name as having a perfect social and political system.

Nature's test, her sign of approval. When man is happy, he is in harmony with himself and his environment. The new Individualism, for whose service Socialism, whether it wills it or not, is working, will be perfect harmony. It will be what the Greeks sought for, but could not, except in Thought, realise completely, because they had slaves, and fed them; it will be what the Renaissance sought for, but could not realise completely except in Art, because they had slaves, and starved them. It will be complete, and through it each man will attain to his perfection. The new Individualism is the new Hellenism.[7]

1891

Preface to *The Picture of Dorian Gray*[1]

The artist is the creator of beautiful things.

To reveal art and conceal the artist is art's aim.

The critic is he who can translate into another manner or a new material his impression of beautiful things.

The highest as the lowest form of criticism is a mode of autobiography.

Those who find ugly meanings in beautiful things are corrupt without being charming. This is a fault.

Those who find beautiful meanings in beautiful things are the cultivated. For these there is hope.

They are the elect to whom beautiful things mean only Beauty.

There is no such thing as a moral or an immoral book.

Books are well written, or badly written. That is all.

The nineteenth century dislike of Realism is the rage of Caliban[2] seeing his own face in a glass.

The nineteenth century dislike of Romanticism is the rage of Caliban not seeing his own face in a glass.

The moral life of man forms part of the subject-matter of the artist, but the morality of art consists in the perfect use of an imperfect medium.

No artist desires to prove anything. Even things that are true can be proved.

No artist has ethical sympathies. An ethical sympathy in an artist is an unpardonable mannerism of style.

No artist is ever morbid. The artist can express everything.

Thought and language are to the artist instruments of an art.

Vice and virtue are to the artist materials for an art.

From the point of view of form, the type of all the arts is the art of the musician. From the point of view of feeling, the actor's craft is the type.

All art is at once surface and symbol.

7. I.e., it embodies the ideals of ancient Greece, including a respect for the life of the mind and the love of beautiful things. Also an allusion to Matthew Arnold's argument in *Culture and Anarchy* (see page 1695) that a Hellenic cultivation of these values is what British society most desperately needs.
1. When Wilde's novel *Dorian Gray* first appeared in *Lippincott's Monthly Magazine* in July 1890, it scandalized readers with its portrayal of a cruelly hedonistic young man who remains unblemished by his crimes while his portrait ages hideously. Responding to his critics' charges

that the novel fostered immoral ideas, Wilde published the preface separately in *The Fortnightly Review* in March 1891. He then added it to the revised novel when it came out in book form a month later. In its defiant tone and "art for art's sake" insistence that literature has no moral content, Wilde's preface echoes Théophile Gautier's preface to *Mademoiselle de Maupin* (1835), a founding text of the Aesthetic movement.
2. In Shakespeare's *The Tempest*, the "monster" Caliban is the offspring of the witch Sycorax and is a native of Prospero's island.

Those who go beneath the surface do so at their peril.
Those who read the symbol do so at their peril.
It is the spectator, and not life, that art really mirrors.
Diversity of opinion about a work of art shows that the work is new, complex, and vital.
When critics disagree the artist is in accord with himself.
We can forgive a man for making a useful thing as long as he does not admire it. The only excuse for making a useless thing is that one admires it intensely.
All art is quite useless.

OSCAR WILDE

THE IMPORTANCE OF BEING EARNEST Wilde's last play, *The Importance of Being Earnest*, is one of the great comedies in the English language. Fast-paced and sparkling, the play opened on 14 February 1895, to widespread acclaim. But it was forced to close less than three months later, amidst the scandal surrounding Wilde's trials for sodomy in April 1895. Eventually, however, the play's reputation was firmly established, and Wilde's witty master-piece took its place in an Anglo-Irish tradition of classic comedies that includes Goldsmith's *She Stoops to Conquer*, Sheridan's *The Rivals*, and Synge's *Playboy of the Western World*. The title alludes to the Victorian obsession with earnestness as both character trait and moral ideal. The play's philosophy, Wilde claimed, was that "We should treat all the trivial things of life seriously, and all the serious things of life with sincere and studied triviality." In the dandified world of this drama, paying scrupulous attention to surfaces is an act of the deepest sincerity.

Wilde drafted the play in four acts, then at the request of the producer revised it to a tauter three-act version that has become the standard text for performance and reading. Formally, *The Importance of Being Earnest* shows the clever construction and neat resolution popular in nineteenth-century British and French drama. But it also fulfills the classical definition of comedy as beginning in error and confusion, and ending in knowledge, recognition, and self-discovery. Questioning social hierarchies based on birth, the plot turns on the mysteries of social and personal identity: "Would you kindly inform me who I am?" asks Jack Worthing at the play's climactic moment.

To explore the fictions of personality, Wilde meticulously sketches the trivialities that constitute social ritual and class distinction. From cucumber sandwiches at the start of the play to champagne and muffins in Act 3, the way Wilde's well-bred sophisticates consume food and drink becomes evidence of their character, emotional state, and social status. While the rigid conventions of this world apparently force young men like Jack and Algy to live double lives, they freely exploit their fictive selves as events dictate. Yet they are easily stage-managed by the women they love. Gwendolen and Cecily, who are more preoccupied with writing in their diaries than with the events they record in them, deploy their self-conscious sexual innocence to make life and love conform to the conventions of literature. *The Importance of Being Earnest* presents life as an aesthetic spectacle, in which the careful observation of outward form is the truest path toward an ironic authenticity and self-fulfillment.

"If I were asked of myself as a dramatist," Wilde mused, "I would say that my unique position was that I had taken the Drama, the most objective form known to art, and made it as personal a mode of expression as the Lyric or the Sonnet, while enlarging the characterization of the stage." Wilde refashioned the late-Victorian theater in his own image through the self-conscious brilliance of his language and the outrageousness of his comic invention. He delighted in artifice and exaggeration for their own sake. As he argued in *The Decay of Lying*, art is not an imitation of life but a more aesthetically satisfying restructuring of it. With droll wordplay, paradox, and ridiculous coincidence casting existential dilemmas into comic relief, *The Importance of Being Earnest* anticipates the modern Theater of the Absurd; it heralds the profound slapstick of Pirandello, Ionesco, Beckett, and Stoppard.

The Importance of Being Earnest
A Trivial Comedy for Serious People

FIRST ACT

SCENE: *Morning-room in Algernon's flat in Half Moon Street.*[1] *The room is luxuriously and artistically furnished. The sound of a piano is heard in the adjoining room.*

[*Lane is arranging afternoon tea on the table, and after the music has ceased, Algernon enters.*]

ALGERNON: Did you hear what I was playing, Lane?

LANE: I didn't think it polite to listen, sir.

ALGERNON: I'm sorry for that, for your sake. I don't play accurately—anyone can play accurately—but I play with wonderful expression. As far as the piano is concerned, sentiment is my forte. I keep science for Life.

LANE: Yes, sir.

ALGERNON: And, speaking of the science of Life, have you got the cucumber sandwiches cut for Lady Bracknell?

LANE: Yes, sir. [*Hands them on a salver.*]

ALGERNON [*inspects them, takes two, and sits down on the sofa*]: Oh! . . . by the way, Lane, I see from your book that on Thursday night, when Lord Shoreham and Mr Worthing were dining with me, eight bottles of champagne are entered as having been consumed.

LANE: Yes, sir; eight bottles and a pint.

ALGERNON: Why is it that at a bachelor's establishment the servants invariably drink the champagne? I ask merely for information.

LANE: I attribute it to the superior quality of the wine, sir. I have often observed that in married households the champagne is rarely of a first-rate brand.

ALGERNON: Good Heavens! Is marriage so demoralizing as that?

LANE: I believe it *is* a very pleasant state, sir. I have had very little experience of it myself up to the present. I have only been married once. That was in consequence of a misunderstanding between myself and a young person.

ALGERNON [*languidly*]: I don't know that I am much interested in your family life, Lane.

LANE: No, sir; it is not a very interesting subject. I never think of it myself.

ALGERNON: Very natural, I am sure. That will do, Lane, thank you.

LANE: Thank you, sir. [*Lane goes out.*]

ALGERNON: Lane's views on marriage seem somewhat lax. Really, if the lower orders don't set us a good example, what on earth is the use of them? They seem, as a class, to have absolutely no sense of moral responsibility.

[*Enter Lane.*]

LANE: Mr Ernest Worthing.

[*Enter Jack. Lane goes out.*]

ALGERNON: How are you, my dear Ernest? What brings you up to town?

JACK: Oh, pleasure, pleasure! What else should bring one anywhere? Eating as usual, I see, Algy!

---

1. A fashionable address in the West End of London.

ALGERNON [*stiffly*]: I believe it is customary in good society to take some slight refreshment at five o'clock. Where have you been since last Thursday?

JACK [*sitting down on the sofa*]: In the country.

ALGERNON: What on earth do you do there?

JACK [*pulling off his gloves*]: When one is in town one amuses oneself. When one is in the country one amuses other people. It is excessively boring.

ALGERNON: And who are the people you amuse?

JACK [*airily*]: Oh, neighbours, neighbours.

ALGERNON: Got nice neighbours in your part of Shropshire?[2]

JACK: Perfectly horrid! Never speak to one of them.

ALGERNON: How immensely you must amuse them! [*Goes over and takes sandwich.*] By the way, Shropshire is your county, is it not?

JACK: Eh? Shropshire? Yes, of course. Hallo! Why all these cups? Why cucumber sandwiches? Why such reckless extravagance in one so young? Who is coming to tea?

ALGERNON: Oh! merely Aunt Augusta and Gwendolen.

JACK: How perfectly delightful!

ALGERNON: Yes, that is all very well; but I am afraid Aunt Augusta won't quite approve of your being here.

JACK: May I ask why?

ALGERNON: My dear fellow, the way you flirt with Gwendolen is perfectly disgraceful. It is almost as bad as the way Gwendolen flirts with you.

JACK: I am in love with Gwendolen. I have come up to town expressly to propose to her.

ALGERNON: I thought you had come up for pleasure? . . . I call that business.

JACK: How utterly unromantic you are!

ALGERNON: I really don't see anything romantic in proposing. It is very romantic to be in love. But there is nothing romantic about a definite proposal. Why, one may be accepted. One usually is, I believe. Then the excitement is all over. The very essence of romance is uncertainty. If I ever get married, I'll certainly try to forget the fact.

JACK: I have no doubt about that, dear Algy. The Divorce Court was specially invented for people whose memories are so curiously constituted.

ALGERNON: Oh! there is no use speculating on that subject. Divorces are made in Heaven—[*Jack puts out his hand to take a sandwich. Algernon at once interferes.*] Please don't touch the cucumber sandwiches. They are ordered specially for Aunt Augusta. [*Takes one and eats it.*]

JACK: Well, you have been eating them all the time.

ALGERNON: That is quite a different matter. She is my aunt. [*Takes plate from below.*] Have some bread and butter. The bread and butter is for Gwendolen. Gwendolen is devoted to bread and butter.

JACK [*advancing to table and helping himself*]: And very good bread and butter it is too.

ALGERNON: Well, my dear fellow, you need not eat as if you were going to eat it all. You behave as if you were married to her already. You are not married to her already, and I don't think you ever will be.

---

2. Worthing's estate is actually in Hertfordshire, which is a long way from Shropshire.

JACK: Why on earth do you say that?

ALGERNON: Well, in the first place girls never marry the men they flirt with. Girls don't think it right.

JACK: Oh, that is nonsense!

ALGERNON: It isn't. It is a great truth. It accounts for the extraordinary number of bachelors that one sees all over the place. In the second place, I don't give my consent.

JACK: Your consent!

ALGERNON: My dear fellow, Gwendolen is my first cousin. And before I allow you to marry her, you will have to clear up the whole question of Cecily. [*Rings bell.*]

JACK: Cecily! What on earth do you mean? What do you mean, Algy, by Cecily? I don't know anyone of the name of Cecily.

[*Enter Lane.*]

ALGERNON: Bring me that cigarette case Mr Worthing left in the smoking-room the last time he dined here.

LANE: Yes, sir. [*Lane goes out.*]

JACK: Do you mean to say you have had my cigarette case all this time? I wish to goodness you had let me know. I have been writing frantic letters to Scotland Yard[3] about it. I was very nearly offering a large reward.

ALGERNON: Well, I wish you would offer one. I happen to be more than usually hard up.

JACK: There is no good offering a large reward now that the thing is found.

[*Enter Lane with the cigarette case on a salver. Algernon takes it at once. Lane goes out.*]

ALGERNON: I think that is rather mean of you, Ernest, I must say. [*Opens case and examines it.*] However, it makes no matter, for, now that I look at the inscription inside, I find that the thing isn't yours after all.

JACK: Of course it's mine. [*Moving to him.*] You have seen me with it a hundred times, and you have no right whatsoever to read what is written inside. It is a very ungentlemanly thing to read a private cigarette case.

ALGERNON: Oh! it is absurd to have a hard-and-fast rule about what one should read and what one shouldn't. More than half of modern culture depends on what one shouldn't read.

JACK: I am quite aware of the fact, and I don't propose to discuss modern culture. It isn't the sort of thing one should talk of in private. I simply want my cigarette case back.

ALGERNON: Yes; but this isn't your cigarette case. This cigarette case is a present from someone of the name of Cecily, and you said you didn't know anyone of that name.

JACK: Well, if you want to know, Cecily happens to be my aunt.

ALGERNON: Your aunt!

JACK: Yes. Charming old lady she is, too. Lives at Tunbridge Wells.[4] Just give it back to me, Algy.

3. London police headquarters.   4. A fashionable resort.

ALGERNON [*retreating to back of sofa*]: But why does she call herself little Cecily if she is your aunt and lives at Tunbridge Wells? [*Reading.*] "From little Cecily with her fondest love."

JACK [*moving to sofa and kneeling upon it*]: My dear fellow, what on earth is there in that? Some aunts are tall, some aunts are not tall. That is a matter that surely an aunt may be allowed to decide for herself. You seem to think that every aunt should be exactly like your aunt! That is absurd! For Heaven's sake give me back my cigarette case. [*Follows Algernon round the room.*]

ALGERNON: Yes. But why does your aunt call you her uncle? "From little Cecily, with her fondest love to her dear Uncle Jack." There is no objection, I admit, to an aunt being a small aunt, but why an aunt, no matter what her size may be, should call her own nephew her uncle, I can't quite make out. Besides, your name isn't Jack at all; it is Ernest.

JACK: It isn't Ernest; it's Jack.

ALGERNON: You have always told me it was Ernest. I have introduced you to everyone as Ernest. You answer to the name of Ernest. You look as if your name was Ernest. You are the most earnest looking person I ever saw in my life. It is perfectly absurd your saying that your name isn't Ernest. It's on your cards. Here is one of them. [*Taking it from case.*] "Mr Ernest Worthing, B. 4, The Albany." I'll keep this as a proof that your name is Ernest if ever you attempt to deny it to me, or to Gwendolen, or to anyone else. [*Puts the card in his pocket.*]

JACK: Well, my name is Ernest in town and Jack in the country, and the cigarette case was given to me in the country.

ALGERNON: Yes, but that does not account for the fact that your small Aunt Cecily, who lives at Tunbridge Wells, calls you her dear uncle. Come, old boy, you had much better have the thing out at once.

JACK: My dear Algy, you talk exactly as if you were a dentist. It is very vulgar to talk like a dentist when one isn't a dentist. It produces a false impression.

ALGERNON: Well, that is exactly what dentists always do. Now, go on! Tell me the whole thing. I may mention that I have always suspected you of being a confirmed and secret Bunburyist, and I am quite sure of it now.

JACK: Bunburyist? What on earth do you mean by a Bunburyist?

ALGERNON: I'll reveal to you the meaning of that incomparable expression as soon as you are kind enough to inform me why you are Ernest in town and Jack in the country.

JACK: Well, produce my cigarette case first.

ALGERNON: Here it is. [*Hands cigarette case.*] Now produce your explanation, and pray make it improbable. [*Sits on sofa.*]

JACK: My dear fellow, there is nothing improbable about my explanation at all. In fact it's perfectly ordinary. Old Mr Thomas Cardew, who adopted me when I was a little boy, made me in his will guardian to his granddaughter, Miss Cecily Cardew. Cecily who addresses me as her uncle from motives of respect that you could not possibly appreciate, lives at my place in the country under the charge of her admirable governess, Miss Prism.

ALGERNON: Where is that place in the country, by the way?

JACK: That is nothing to you, dear boy. You are not going to be invited. . . . I may tell you candidly that the place is not in Shropshire.

ALGERNON: I suspected that, my dear fellow! I have Bunburyed all over Shrop-shire on two separate occasions. Now, go on. Why are you Ernest in town and Jack in the country?

JACK: My dear Algy, I don't know whether you will be able to understand my real motives. You are hardly serious enough. When one is placed in the position of guardian, one has to adopt a very high moral tone on all subjects. It's one's duty to do so. And as a high moral tone can hardly be said to conduce very much to either one's health or one's happiness, in order to get up to town I have always pretended to have a younger brother of the name of Ernest, who lives in the Albany, and gets into the most dreadful scrapes. That, my dear Algy, is the whole truth pure and simple.

ALGERNON: The truth is rarely pure and never simple. Modern life would be very tedious if it were either, and modern literature a complete impossibility!

JACK: That wouldn't be at all a bad thing.

ALGERNON: Literary criticism is not your forte, my dear fellow. Don't try it. You should leave that to people who haven't been at a University. They do it so well in the daily papers. What you really are is a Bunburyist. I was quite right in saying you were a Bunburyist. You are one of the most advanced Bunburyists I know.

JACK: What on earth do you mean?

ALGERNON: You have invented a very useful younger brother called Ernest, in or-der that you may be able to come up to town as often as you like. I have invented an invaluable permanent invalid called Bunbury, in order that I may be able to go down into the country whenever I choose. Bunbury is perfectly invaluable. If it wasn't for Bunbury's extraordinary bad health, for instance, I wouldn't be able to dine with you at Willis's[5] tonight, for I have been really engaged[6] to Aunt Augusta for more than a week.

JACK: I haven't asked you to dine with me anywhere tonight.

ALGERNON: I know. You are absurdly careless about sending out invitations. It is very foolish of you. Nothing annoys people so much as not receiving invitations.

JACK: You had much better dine with your Aunt Augusta.

ALGERNON: I haven't the smallest intention of doing anything of the kind. To be-gin with, I dined there on Monday, and once a week is quite enough to dine with one's own relations. In the second place, whenever I do dine there I am always treated as a member of the family, and sent down[7] with either no woman at all, or two. In the third place, I know perfectly well whom she will place me next to, tonight. She will place me next Mary Farquhar, who always flirts with her own husband across the dinner-table. That is not very pleasant. Indeed, it is not even decent . . . and that sort of thing is enormously on the increase. The amount of women in London who flirt with their own husbands is perfectly scandalous. It looks so bad. It is simply washing one's clean linen in public. Besides, now that I know you to be a confirmed Bunburyist I naturally want to talk to you about Bun-burying. I want to tell you the rules.

JACK: I'm not a Bunburyist at all. If Gwendolen accepts me, I am going to kill my brother, indeed I think I'll kill him in any case. Cecily is a little too much inter-ested in him. It is rather a bore. So I am going to get rid of Ernest. And I strongly

---

5. An expensive London restaurant.
6. I.e., pledged to attend her dinner party.
7. Sent in to the dining room as someone's escort.

advise you to do the same with Mr . . . with your invalid friend who has the absurd name.

ALGERNON: Nothing will induce me to part with Bunbury, and if you ever get married, which seems to me extremely problematic, you will be very glad to know Bunbury. A man who marries without knowing Bunbury has a very tedious time of it.

JACK: That is nonsense. If I marry a charming girl like Gwendolen, and she is the only girl I ever saw in my life that I would marry, I certainly won't want to know Bunbury.

ALGERNON: Then your wife will. You don't seem to realize, that in married life three is company and two is none.

JACK [sententiously]: That, my dear young friend, is the theory that the corrupt French Drama[8] has been propounding for the last fifty years.

ALGERNON: Yes; and that the happy English home has proved in half the time.

JACK: For heaven's sake, don't try to be cynical. It's perfectly easy to be cynical.

ALGERNON: My dear fellow, it isn't easy to be anything nowadays. There's such a lot of beastly competition about. [The sound of an electric bell is heard.] Ah! that must be Aunt Augusta. Only relatives, or creditors, ever ring in that Wagnerian manner.[9] Now, if I get her out of the way for ten minutes, so that you can have an opportunity for proposing to Gwendolen, may I dine with you tonight at Willis's?

JACK: I suppose so, if you want to.

ALGERNON: Yes, but you must be serious about it. I hate people who are not serious about meals. It is so shallow of them.

[Enter Lane.]

LANE: Lady Bracknell and Miss Fairfax.

[Algernon goes forward to meet them. Enter Lady Bracknell and Gwendolen.]

LADY BRACKNELL: Good afternoon, dear Algernon, I hope you are behaving very well.

ALGERNON: I'm feeling very well, Aunt Augusta.

LADY BRACKNELL: That's not quite the same thing. In fact the two things rarely go together. [Sees Jack and bows to him with icy coldness.]

ALGERNON [to Gwendolen]: Dear me, you are smart![1]

GWENDOLEN: I am always smart! Aren't I, Mr Worthing?

JACK: You're quite perfect, Miss Fairfax.

GWENDOLEN: Oh! I hope I am not that. It would leave no room for developments, and I intend to develop in many directions. [Gwendolen and Jack sit down together in the corner.]

LADY BRACKNELL: I'm sorry if we are a little late, Algernon, but I was obliged to call on dear Lady Harbury. I hadn't been there since her poor husband's death. I never saw a woman so altered; she looks quite twenty years younger. And now I'll have a cup of tea, and one of those nice cucumber sandwiches you promised me.

ALGERNON: Certainly, Aunt Augusta. [Goes over to tea-table.]

LADY BRACKNELL: Won't you come and sit here, Gwendolen?

GWENDOLEN: Thanks, mamma, I'm quite comfortable where I am.

ALGERNON [picking up empty plate in horror]: Good heavens! Lane! Why are there no cucumber sandwiches? I ordered them specially.

8. Late 19th-century French plays frequently focused on marital infidelity.

9. I.e., loud and dramatic, like the grand operas of Richard Wagner (1813–1883).

1. Chic.

LANE [*gravely*]: There were no cucumbers in the market this morning, sir. I went down twice.

ALGERNON: No cucumbers!

LANE: No, sir. Not even for ready money.

ALGERNON: That will do, Lane, thank you.

LANE: Thank you, sir. [*Goes out.*]

ALGERNON: I am greatly distressed, Aunt Augusta, about there being no cucumbers, not even for ready money.

LADY BRACKNELL: It really makes no matter, Algernon. I had some crumpets with Lady Harbury, who seems to me to be living entirely for pleasure now.

ALGERNON: I hear her hair has turned quite gold from grief.

LADY BRACKNELL: It certainly has changed its colour. From what cause I, of course, cannot say. [*Algernon crosses and hands tea.*] Thank you. I've quite a treat for you tonight, Algernon. I am going to send you down with Mary Farquhar. She is such a nice woman, and so attentive to her husband. It's delightful to watch them.

ALGERNON: I am afraid, Aunt Augusta, I shall have to give up the pleasure of dining with you tonight after all.

LADY BRACKNELL [*frowning*]: I hope not, Algernon. It would put my table completely out. Your uncle would have to dine upstairs. Fortunately he is accustomed to that.

ALGERNON: It is a great bore, and, I need hardly say, a terrible disappointment to me, but the fact is I have just had a telegram to say that my poor friend Bunbury is very ill again. [*Exchanges glances with Jack.*] They seem to think I should be with him.

LADY BRACKNELL: It is very strange. This Mr Bunbury seems to suffer from curiously bad health.

ALGERNON: Yes; poor Bunbury is a dreadful invalid.

LADY BRACKNELL: Well, I must say, Algernon, that I think it is high time that Mr Bunbury made up his mind whether he was going to live or to die. This shilly-shallying with the question is absurd. Nor do I in any way approve of the modern sympathy with invalids. I consider it morbid. Illness of any kind is hardly a thing to be encouraged in others. Health is the primary duty of life. I am always telling that to your poor uncle, but he never seems to take much notice . . . as far as any improvement in his ailments goes. I should be much obliged if you would ask Mr Bunbury, from me, to be kind enough not to have a relapse on Saturday, for I rely on you to arrange my music for me. It is my last reception, and one wants something that will encourage conversation, particularly at the end of the season[2] when everyone has practically said whatever they had to say, which, in most cases, was probably not much.

ALGERNON: I'll speak to Bunbury, Aunt Augusta, if he is still conscious, and I think I can promise you he'll be all right by Saturday. Of course the music is a great difficulty. You see, if one plays good music, people don't listen, and if one plays bad music people don't talk. But I'll run over the programme I've drawn out, if you will kindly come into the next room for a moment.

LADY BRACKNELL: Thank you, Algernon. It is very thoughtful of you. [*Rising, and following Algernon.*] I'm sure the programme will be delightful, after a few expurgations. French songs I cannot possibly allow. People always seem to think that they are improper, and either look shocked, which is vulgar, or laugh, which is

---

2. Fashionable people left their country estates to spend the social season in London; it began in late spring and lasted through July.

worse. But German sounds a thoroughly respectable language, and indeed, I believe is so. Gwendolen, you will accompany me.

GWENDOLEN: Certainly, mamma.

[*Lady Bracknell and Algernon go into the music-room, Gwendolen remains behind.*]

JACK: Charming day it has been, Miss Fairfax.

GWENDOLEN: Pray don't talk to me about the weather, Mr Worthing. Whenever people talk to me about the weather, I always feel quite certain that they mean something else. And that makes me so nervous.

JACK: I do mean something else.

GWENDOLEN: I thought so. In fact, I am never wrong.

JACK: And I would like to be allowed to take advantage of Lady Bracknell's temporary absence . . .

GWENDOLEN: I would certainly advise you to do so. Mamma has a way of coming back suddenly into a room that I have often had to speak to her about.

JACK [*nervously*]: Miss Fairfax, ever since I met you I have admired you more than any girl . . . I have ever met since . . . I met you.

GWENDOLEN: Yes, I am quite aware of the fact. And I often wish that in public, at any rate, you had been more demonstrative. For me you have always had an irresistible fascination. Even before I met you I was far from indifferent to you. [*Jack looks at her in amazement.*] We live, as I hope you know, Mr Worthing, in an age of ideals. The fact is constantly mentioned in the more expensive monthly magazines, and has reached the provincial pulpits I am told: and my ideal has always been to love some one of the name of Ernest. There is something in that name that inspires absolute confidence. The moment Algernon first mentioned to me that he had a friend called Ernest, I knew I was destined to love you.

JACK: You really love me, Gwendolen?

GWENDOLEN: Passionately!

JACK: Darling! You don't know how happy you've made me.

GWENDOLEN: My own Ernest!

JACK: But you don't really mean to say that you couldn't love me if my name wasn't Ernest?

GWENDOLEN: But your name is Ernest.

JACK: Yes, I know it is. But supposing it was something else? Do you mean to say you couldn't love me then?

GWENDOLEN [*glibly*]: Ah! that is clearly a metaphysical speculation, and like most metaphysical speculations has very little reference at all to the actual facts of real life, as we know them.

JACK: Personally, darling, to speak quite candidly, I don't much care about the name of Ernest . . . I don't think the name suits me at all.

GWENDOLEN: It suits you perfectly. It is a divine name. It has a music of its own. It produces vibrations.

JACK: Well, really, Gwendolen, I must say that I think there are lots of other much nicer names. I think Jack, for instance, a charming name.

GWENDOLEN: Jack? . . . No, there is very little music in the name Jack, if any at all, indeed. It does not thrill. It produces absolutely no vibrations . . . I have known several Jacks, and they all, without exception, were more than usually plain. Besides, Jack is a notorious domesticity for John! And I pity any woman who is married to a man called John. She would probably never be allowed to know the entrancing pleasure of a single moment's solitude. The only really safe name is Ernest.

JACK: Gwendolen, I must get christened at once—I mean we must get married at once. There is no time to be lost.

GWENDOLEN: Married, Mr Worthing?[3]

JACK [*astounded*]: Well . . . surely. You know that I love you, and you led me to believe, Miss Fairfax, that you were not absolutely indifferent to me.

GWENDOLEN: I adore you. But you haven't proposed to me yet. Nothing has been said at all about marriage. The subject has not even been touched on.

JACK: Well . . . may I propose to you now?

GWENDOLEN: I think it would be an admirable opportunity. And to spare you any possible disappointment, Mr Worthing, I think it only fair to tell you quite frankly beforehand that I am fully determined to accept you.

JACK: Gwendolen!

GWENDOLEN: Yes, Mr Worthing, what have you got to say to me?

JACK: You know what I have got to say to you.

GWENDOLEN: Yes, but you don't say it.

JACK: Gwendolen, will you marry me? [*Goes on his knees.*]

GWENDOLEN: Of course I will, darling. How long you have been about it! I am afraid you have had very little experience in how to propose.

JACK: My own one, I have never loved anyone in the world but you.

GWENDOLEN: Yes, but men often propose for practice. I know my brother Gerald does. All my girl-friends tell me so. What wonderfully blue eyes you have, Ernest! They are quite, quite, blue. I hope you will always look at me just like that, especially when there are other people present.

  [*Enter Lady Bracknell.*]

LADY BRACKNELL: Mr Worthing! Rise, sir, from this semi-recumbent posture. It is most indecorous.

GWENDOLEN: Mamma! [*He tries to rise; she restrains him.*] I must beg you to retire. This is no place for you. Besides, Mr Worthing has not quite finished yet.

LADY BRACKNELL: Finished what, may I ask?

GWENDOLEN: I am engaged to Mr Worthing, mamma. [*They rise together.*]

LADY BRACKNELL: Pardon me, you are not engaged to anyone. When you do become engaged to some one, I, or your father, should his health permit him, will inform you of the fact. An engagement should come on a young girl as a surprise, pleasant or unpleasant, as the case may be. It is hardly a matter that she could be allowed to arrange for herself. . . . And now I have a few questions to put to you, Mr Worthing. While I am making these inquiries, you, Gwendolen, will wait for me below in the carriage.

GWENDOLEN [*reproachfully*]: Mamma!

LADY BRACKNELL: In the carriage, Gwendolen! [*Gwendolen goes to the door. She and Jack blow kisses to each other behind Lady Bracknell's back. Lady Bracknell looks vaguely about as if she could not understand what the noise was. Finally turns round.*] Gwendolen, the carriage!

GWENDOLEN: Yes, mamma. [*Goes out, looking back at Jack.*]

LADY BRACKNELL [*sitting down*]: You can take a seat, Mr Worthing.

3. Gwendolen reverts to using Jack's last name when she is reminded that he has not yet formally proposed.

[*Looking in her pocket for note-book and pencil.*]

JACK: Thank you, Lady Bracknell, I prefer standing.

LADY BRACKNELL [*pencil and note-book in hand*]: I feel bound to tell you that you are not down on my list of eligible young men, although I have the same list as the dear Duchess of Bolton has. We work together, in fact. However, I am quite ready to enter your name, should your answers be what a really affectionate mother requires. Do you smoke?

JACK: Well, yes, I must admit I smoke.

LADY BRACKNELL: I am glad to hear it. A man should always have an occupation of some kind. There are far too many idle men in London as it is. How old are you?

JACK: Twenty-nine.

LADY BRACKNELL: A very good age to be married at. I have always been of opinion that a man who desires to get married should know either everything or nothing. Which do you know?

JACK [*after some hesitation*]: I know nothing, Lady Bracknell.

LADY BRACKNELL: I am pleased to hear it. I do not approve of anything that tampers with natural ignorance. Ignorance is like a delicate exotic fruit; touch it and the bloom is gone. The whole theory of modern education is radically unsound. Fortunately in England, at any rate, education produces no effect whatsoever. If it did, it would prove a serious danger to the upper classes, and probably lead to acts of violence in Grosvenor Square.[4] What is your income?

JACK: Between seven and eight thousand a year.

LADY BRACKNELL [*makes a note in her book*]: In land, or in investments?

JACK: In investments, chiefly.

LADY BRACKNELL: That is satisfactory. What between the duties expected of one during one's lifetime, and the duties exacted from one after one's death,[5] land has ceased to be either a profit or a pleasure. It gives one position, and prevents one from keeping it up. That's all that can be said about land.

JACK: I have a country house with some land, of course, attached to it, about fifteen hundred acres, I believe; but I don't depend on that for my real income. In fact, as far as I can make out, the poachers are the only people who make anything out of it.

LADY BRACKNELL: A country house! How many bedrooms? Well, that point can be cleared up afterwards. You have a town house, I hope? A girl with a simple, unspoiled nature, like Gwendolen, could hardly be expected to reside in the country.

JACK: Well, I own a house in Belgrave Square,[6] but it is let by the year to Lady Bloxham. Of course, I can get it back whenever I like, at six months' notice.

LADY BRACKNELL: Lady Bloxham? I don't know her.

JACK: Oh, she goes about very little. She is a lady considerably advanced in years.

LADY BRACKNELL: Ah, nowadays that is no guarantee of respectability of character. What number in Belgrave Square?

JACK: 149.

LADY BRACKNELL [*shaking her head*]: The unfashionable side. I thought there was something. However, that could easily be altered.

JACK: Do you mean the fashion, or the side?

LADY BRACKNELL [*sternly*]: Both, if necessary, I presume. What are your politics?

---

4. A fashionable area in the West End of London.   6. A fashionable West End address in Belgravia.
5. "Death duties" are inheritance taxes.

JACK: Well, I am afraid I really have none. I am a Liberal Unionist.[7]

LADY BRACKNELL: Oh, they count as Tories. They dine with us. Or come in the evening, at any rate. Now to minor matters. Are your parents living?

JACK: I have lost both my parents.

LADY BRACKNELL: Both? To lose one parent may be regarded as a misfortune— to lose *both* seems like carelessness. Who was your father? He was evidently a man of some wealth. Was he born in what the Radical papers call the purple of commerce, or did he rise from the ranks of the aristocracy?

JACK: I am afraid I really don't know. The fact is, Lady Bracknell, I said I had lost my parents. It would be nearer the truth to say that my parents seem to have lost me . . . I don't actually know who I am by birth. I was . . . well, I was found.

LADY BRACKNELL: Found!

JACK: The late Mr Thomas Cardew, an old gentleman of a very charitable and kindly disposition, found me, and gave me the name of Worthing, because he happened to have a first-class ticket for Worthing in his pocket at the time. Worthing is a place in Sussex. It is a seaside resort.

LADY BRACKNELL: Where did the charitable gentleman who had a first-class ticket for this seaside resort find you?

JACK [*gravely*]: In a hand-bag.

LADY BRACKNELL: A hand-bag?

JACK [*very seriously*]: Yes, Lady Bracknell. I was in a hand-bag—a somewhat large, black leather hand-bag, with handles to it—an ordinary hand-bag in fact.

LADY BRACKNELL: In what locality did this Mr James, or Thomas, Cardew come across this ordinary hand-bag?

JACK: In the cloak-room at Victoria Station. It was given to him in mistake for his own.

LADY BRACKNELL: The cloak-room at Victoria Station?

JACK: Yes. The Brighton line.

LADY BRACKNELL: The line is immaterial. Mr Worthing, I confess I feel somewhat bewildered by what you have just told me. To be born, or at any rate bred, in a hand-bag, whether it had handles or not, seems to me to display a contempt for the ordinary decencies of family life that reminds one of the worst excesses of the French Revolution. And I presume you know what that unfortunate movement led to? As for the particular locality in which the hand-bag was found, a cloak-room at a railway station might serve to conceal a social indiscretion—has probably, indeed, been used for that purpose before now—but it could hardly be regarded as an assured basis for a recognized position in good society.

JACK: May I ask you then what you would advise me to do? I need hardly say I would do anything in the world to ensure Gwendolen's happiness.

LADY BRACKNELL: I would strongly advise you, Mr Worthing, to try and acquire some relations as soon as possible, and to make a definite effort to produce at any rate one parent, of either sex, before the season is quite over.

JACK: Well, I don't see how I could possibly manage to do that. I can produce the hand-bag at any moment. It is in my dressing-room at home. I really think that should satisfy you, Lady Bracknell.

---

7. In 1886 Liberal Unionists joined the Conservatives (the "Tories") in voting against the Liberal Prime Minister Gladstone's bill supporting Home Rule for Ireland.

LADY BRACKNELL: Me, sir! What has it to do with me? You can hardly imagine that I and Lord Bracknell would dream of allowing our only daughter—a girl brought up with the utmost care—to marry into a cloak-room, and form an alliance with a parcel? Good morning, Mr Worthing!

[Lady Bracknell sweeps out in majestic indignation.]

JACK: Good morning! [Algernon, from the other room, strikes up the Wedding March. Jack looks perfectly furious, and goes to the door.] For goodness' sake don't play that ghastly tune, Algy! How idiotic you are!

[The music stops, and Algernon enters cheerily.]

ALGERNON: Didn't it go off all right, old boy? You don't mean to say Gwendolen refused you? I know it is a way she has. She is always refusing people. I think it is most ill-natured of her.

JACK: Oh, Gwendolen is as right as a trivet.[8] As far as she is concerned, we are engaged. Her mother is perfectly unbearable. Never met such a Gorgon[9] . . . I don't really know what a Gorgon is like, but I am quite sure Lady Bracknell is one. In any case, she is a monster, without being a myth, which is rather unfair . . . I beg your pardon, Algy, I suppose I shouldn't talk about your own aunt in that way before you.

ALGERNON: My dear boy, I love hearing my relations abused. It is the only thing that makes me put up with them at all. Relations are simply a tedious pack of people, who haven't got the remotest knowledge of how to live, nor the smallest instinct about when to die.

JACK: Oh, that is nonsense!

ALGERNON: It isn't!

JACK: Well, I won't argue about the matter. You always want to argue about things.

ALGERNON: That is exactly what things were originally made for.

JACK: Upon my word, if I thought that, I'd shoot myself . . . [A pause.] You don't think there is any chance of Gwendolen becoming like her mother in about a hundred and fifty years, do you Algy?

ALGERNON: All women become like their mothers. That is their tragedy. No man does. That's his.

JACK: Is that clever?

ALGERNON: It is perfectly phrased! and quite as true as any observation in civilized life should be.

JACK: I am sick to death of cleverness. Everybody is clever nowadays. You can't go anywhere without meeting clever people. The thing has become an absolute public nuisance. I wish to goodness we had a few fools left.

ALGERNON: We have.

JACK: I should extremely like to meet them. What do they talk about?

ALGERNON: The fools? Oh! about the clever people, of course.

JACK: What fools!

ALGERNON: By the way, did you tell Gwendolen the truth about your being Ernest in town, and Jack in the country?

JACK [in a very patronizing manner]: My dear fellow, the truth isn't quite the sort of thing one tells to a nice sweet refined girl. What extraordinary ideas you have about the way to behave to a woman!

---

8. Reliable and steady, like a stand used to hold a pot over the fire.

9. A mythical female monster with snakes for hair.

ALGERNON: The only way to behave to a woman is to make love to her,[1] if she is pretty, and to someone else if she is plain.

JACK: Oh, that is nonsense.

ALGERNON: What about your brother? What about the profligate Ernest?

JACK: Oh, before the end of the week I shall have got rid of him. I'll say he died in Paris of apoplexy. Lots of people die of apoplexy, quite suddenly, don't they?

ALGERNON: Yes, but it's hereditary, my dear fellow. It's a sort of thing that runs in families. You had much better say a severe chill.

JACK: You are sure a severe chill isn't hereditary, or anything of that kind?

ALGERNON: Of course it isn't!

JACK: Very well, then. My poor brother Ernest is carried off suddenly in Paris, by a severe chill. That gets rid of him.

ALGERNON: But I thought you said that . . . Miss Cardew was a little too much interested in your poor brother Ernest? Won't she feel his loss a good deal?

JACK: Oh, that is all right. Cecily is not a silly romantic girl, I am glad to say. She has got a capital appetite, goes long walks, and pays no attention at all to her lessons.

ALGERNON: I would rather like to see Cecily.

JACK: I will take very good care you never do. She is excessively pretty, and she is only just eighteen.

ALGERNON: Have you told Gwendolen yet that you have an excessively pretty ward who is only just eighteen?

JACK: Oh! one doesn't blurt these things out to people. Cecily and Gwendolen are perfectly certain to be extremely great friends. I'll bet you anything you like that half an hour after they have met, they will be calling each other sister.

ALGERNON: Women only do that when they have called each other a lot of other things first. Now, my dear boy, if we want to get a good table at Willis's, we really must go and dress. Do you know it is nearly seven?

JACK [irritably]: Oh! it always is nearly seven.

ALGERNON: Well, I'm hungry.

JACK: I never knew you when you weren't. . . .

ALGERNON: What shall we do after dinner? Go to a theatre?

JACK: Oh no! I loathe listening.

ALGERNON: Well, let us go to the Club?

JACK: Oh, no! I hate talking.

ALGERNON: Well, we might trot round to the Empire[2] at ten?

JACK: Oh, no! I can't bear looking at things. It is so silly.

ALGERNON: Well, what shall we do?

JACK: Nothing!

ALGERNON: It is awfully hard work doing nothing. However, I don't mind hard work where there is no definite object of any kind.

[Enter Lane.]

LANE: Miss Fairfax.

[Enter Gwendolen. Lane goes out.]

ALGERNON: Gwendolen, upon my word!

---

1. I.e., to flirt with or court her.   2. A popular music hall.

GWENDOLEN: Algy, kindly turn your back. I have something very particular to say to Mr Worthing.

ALGERNON: Really, Gwendolen, I don't think I can allow this at all.

GWENDOLEN: Algy, you always adopt a strictly immoral attitude towards life. You are not quite old enough to do that.

[*Algernon retires to the fireplace.*]

JACK: My own darling!

GWENDOLEN: Ernest, we may never be married. From the expression on mamma's face I fear we never shall. Few parents nowadays pay any regard to what their children say to them. The old-fashioned respect for the young is fast dying out. Whatever influence I ever had over mamma, I lost at the age of three. But although she may prevent us from becoming man and wife, and I may marry someone else, and marry often, nothing that she can possibly do can alter my eternal devotion to you.

JACK: Dear Gwendolen!

GWENDOLEN: The story of your romantic origin, as related to me by mamma, with unpleasing comments, has naturally stirred the deeper fibres of my nature. Your Christian name has an irresistible fascination. The simplicity of your character makes you exquisitely incomprehensible to me. Your town address at the Albany I have. What is your address in the country?

JACK: The Manor House, Woolton, Hertfordshire.

[*Algernon, who has been carefully listening, smiles to himself, and writes the address on his shirt-cuff. Then picks up the Railway Guide.*]

GWENDOLEN: There is a good postal service, I suppose? It may be necessary to do something desperate. That of course will require serious consideration. I will communicate with you daily.

JACK: My own one!

GWENDOLEN: How long do you remain in town?

JACK: Till Monday.

GWENDOLEN: Good! Algy, you may turn round now.

ALGERNON: Thanks, I've turned round already.

GWENDOLEN: You may also ring the bell.

JACK: You will let me see you to your carriage, my own darling?

GWENDOLEN: Certainly.

JACK [*to Lane, who now enters*]: I will see Miss Fairfax out.

LANE: Yes, sir. [*Jack and Gwendolen go off.*]

[*Lane presents several letters on a salver to Algernon. It is to be surmised that they are bills, as Algernon, after looking at the envelopes, tears them up.*]

ALGERNON: A glass of sherry, Lane.

LANE: Yes, sir.

ALGERNON: Tomorrow, Lane, I'm going Bunburying.

LANE: Yes, sir.

ALGERNON: I shall probably not be back till Monday. You can put up my dress clothes, my smoking jacket, and all the Bunbury suits . . .

LANE: Yes, sir. [*Handing sherry.*]

ALGERNON: I hope tomorrow will be a fine day, Lane.

LANE: It never is, sir.

ALGERNON: Lane, you're a perfect pessimist.

LANE: I do my best to give satisfaction, sir.

[*Enter Jack. Lane goes off.*]

JACK: There's a sensible, intellectual girl! the only girl I ever cared for in my life. [*Algernon is laughing immoderately.*] What on earth are you so amused at?

ALGERNON: Oh, I'm a little anxious about poor Bunbury, that is all.

JACK: If you don't take care, your friend Bunbury will get you into a serious scrape some day.

ALGERNON: I love scrapes. They are the only things that are never serious.

JACK: Oh, that's nonsense, Algy. You never talk anything but nonsense.

ALGERNON: Nobody ever does.

[*Jack looks indignantly at him, and leaves the room. Algernon lights a cigarette, reads his shirt-cuff, and smiles.*]

ACT DROP

SECOND ACT

SCENE: *Garden at the Manor House. A flight of gray stone steps leads up to the house. The garden, an old-fashioned one, full of roses. Time of year, July. Basket chairs, and a table covered with books, are set under a large yew tree.*

[*Miss Prism discovered seated at the table. Cecily is at the back watering flowers.*]

MISS PRISM [*calling*]: Cecily, Cecily! Surely such a utilitarian occupation as the watering of flowers is rather Moulton's duty than yours? Especially at a moment when intellectual pleasures await you. Your German grammar is on the table. Pray open it at page fifteen. We will repeat yesterday's lesson.

CECILY [*coming over very slowly*]: But I don't like German. It isn't at all a becoming language. I know perfectly well that I look quite plain after my German lesson.

MISS PRISM: Child, you know how anxious your guardian is that you should improve yourself in every way. He laid particular stress on your German, as he was leaving for town yesterday. Indeed, he always lays stress on your German when he is leaving for town.

CECILY: Dear Uncle Jack is so very serious! Sometimes he is so serious that I think he cannot be quite well.

MISS PRISM [*drawing herself up*]: Your guardian enjoys the best of health, and his gravity of demeanour is especially to be commended in one so comparatively young as he is. I know no one who has a higher sense of duty and responsibility.

CECILY: I suppose that is why he often looks a little bored when we three are together.

MISS PRISM: Cecily! I am surprised at you. Mr Worthing has many troubles in his life. Idle merriment and triviality would be out of place in his conversation. You must remember his constant anxiety about that unfortunate young man his brother.

CECILY: I wish Uncle Jack would allow that unfortunate young man, his brother, to come down here sometimes. We might have a good influence over him, Miss Prism. I am sure you certainly would. You know German, and geology, and things of that kind influence a man very much. [*Cecily begins to write in her diary.*]

MISS PRISM [*shaking her head*]: I do not think that even I could produce any effect on a character that according to his own brother's admission is irretrievably weak and vacillating. Indeed I am not sure that I would desire to reclaim him. I am not in favour of this modern mania for turning bad people into good people at a moment's notice. As a man sows so let him reap.[3] You must put away your diary, Cecily. I really don't see why you should keep a diary at all.

3. "Be not deceived; God is not mocked: for whatsoever a man soweth, that shall he also reap" (Galatians 6.7).

CECILY: I keep a diary in order to enter the wonderful secrets of my life. If I didn't write them down I should probably forget all about them.

MISS PRISM: Memory, my dear Cecily, is the diary that we all carry about with us.

CECILY: Yes, but it usually chronicles the things that have never happened, and couldn't possibly have happened. I believe that Memory is responsible for nearly all the three-volume novels that Mudie sends us.[4]

MISS PRISM: Do not speak slightly of the three-volume novel, Cecily. I wrote one myself in earlier days.

CECILY: Did you really, Miss Prism? How wonderfully clever you are! I hope it did not end happily? I don't like novels that end happily. They depress me so much.

MISS PRISM: The good ended happily, and the bad unhappily. That is what Fiction means.

CECILY: I suppose so. But it seems very unfair. And was your novel ever published?

MISS PRISM: Alas! no. The manuscript unfortunately was abandoned. I use the word in the sense of lost or mislaid. To your work, child, these speculations are profitless.

CECILY [smiling]: But I see dear Dr Chasuble coming up through the garden.

MISS PRISM [rising and advancing]: Dr Chasuble! This is indeed a pleasure.
     [Enter Canon Chasuble.][5]

CHASUBLE: And how are we this morning? Miss Prism, you are, I trust, well?

CECILY: Miss Prism has just been complaining of a slight headache. I think it would do her so much good to have a short stroll with you in the Park, Dr Chasuble.

MISS PRISM: Cecily, I have not mentioned anything about a headache.

CECILY: No, dear Miss Prism, I know that, but I felt instinctively that you had a headache. Indeed I was thinking about that, and not about my German lesson, when the Rector came in.

CHASUBLE: I hope Cecily, you are not inattentive.

CECILY: Oh, I am afraid I am.

CHASUBLE: That is strange. Were I fortunate enough to be Miss Prism's pupil, I would hang upon her lips. [Miss Prism glares.] I spoke metaphorically.—My metaphor was drawn from bees. Ahem! Mr Worthing I suppose, has not returned from town yet?

MISS PRISM: We do not expect him till Monday afternoon.

CHASUBLE: Ah yes, he usually likes to spend his Sunday in London. He is not one of those whose sole aim is enjoyment, as, by all accounts, that unfortunate young man his brother seems to be. But I must not disturb Egeria[6] and her pupil any longer.

MISS PRISM: Egeria? My name is Laetitia, Doctor.

CHASUBLE [bowing]: A classical allusion merely, drawn from the Pagan authors. I shall see you both no doubt at Evensong?[7]

MISS PRISM: I think, dear Doctor, I will have a stroll with you. I find I have a headache after all, and a walk might do it good.

CHASUBLE: With pleasure, Miss Prism, with pleasure. We might go as far as the schools and back.

---

4. Mudie's Select Library lent novels to subscribers for a fee; at the time of this play, both Mudie's and the three-volume novel were becoming outmoded.
5. A canon is a cathedral clergyman; a chasuble is a vestment.
6. Roman goddess of fountains; her name was used for a woman who instructed other women.
7. Evening church services.

MISS PRISM: That would be delightful. Cecily, you will read your Political Economy in my absence. The chapter on the Fall of the Rupee you may omit.[8] It is somewhat too sensational. Even these metallic problems have their melodramatic side. [*Goes down the garden with Dr Chasuble.*]

CECILY [*picks up books and throws them back on table*]: Horrid Political Economy! Horrid Geography! Horrid, horrid German!

[*Enter Merriman with a card on a salver.*]

MERRIMAN: Mr Ernest Worthing has just driven over from the station. He has brought his luggage with him.

CECILY [*takes the card and reads it*]: "Mr Ernest Worthing, B.4 The Albany, W." Uncle Jack's brother! Did you tell him Mr Worthing was in town?

MERRIMAN: Yes, Miss. He seemed very much disappointed. I mentioned that you and Miss Prism were in the garden. He said he was anxious to speak to you privately for a moment.

CECILY: Ask Mr Ernest Worthing to come here. I suppose you had better talk to the housekeeper about a room for him.

MERRIMAN: Yes, Miss. [*Merriman goes off.*]

CECILY: I have never met any really wicked person before. I feel rather frightened. I am so afraid he will look just like everyone else.

[*Enter Algernon, very gay and debonair.*]

He does!

ALGERNON [*raising his hat*]: You are my little cousin Cecily, I'm sure.

CECILY: You are under some strange mistake. I am not little. In fact, I believe I am more than usually tall for my age. [*Algernon is rather taken aback.*] But I am your cousin Cecily. You, I see from your card, are Uncle Jack's brother, my cousin Ernest, my wicked cousin Ernest.

ALGERNON: Oh! I am not really wicked at all, cousin Cecily. You mustn't think that I am wicked.

CECILY: If you are not, then you have certainly been deceiving us all in a very inexcusable manner. I hope you have not been leading a double life, pretending to be wicked and being really good all the time. That would be hypocrisy.

ALGERNON [*looks at her in amazement*]: Oh! Of course I have been rather reckless.

CECILY: I am glad to hear it.

ALGERNON: In fact, now you mention the subject, I have been very bad in my own small way.

CECILY: I don't think you should be so proud of that, although I am sure it must have been very pleasant.

ALGERNON: It is much pleasanter being here with you.

CECILY: I can't understand how you are here at all. Uncle Jack won't be back till Monday afternoon.

ALGERNON: That is a great disappointment. I am obliged to go up by the first train on Monday morning. I have a business appointment that I am anxious . . . to miss.

CECILY: Couldn't you miss it anywhere but in London?

ALGERNON: No: the appointment is in London.

CECILY: Well, I know, of course, how important it is not to keep a business engagement, if one wants to retain any sense of the beauty of life, but still I think you had

---

8. The declining value of the Indian rupee would hurt British civil servants in India, who were paid in rupees.

better wait till Uncle Jack arrives. I know he wants to speak to you about your emigrating.

ALGERNON: About my what?

CECILY: Your emigrating. He has gone up to buy your outfit.

ALGERNON: I certainly wouldn't let Jack buy my outfit. He has no taste in neckties at all.

CECILY: I don't think you will require neckties. Uncle Jack is sending you to Australia.[9]

ALGERNON: Australia! I'd sooner die.

CECILY: Well, he said at dinner on Wednesday night, that you would have to choose between this world, the next world, and Australia.

ALGERNON: Oh, well! The accounts I have received of Australia and the next world are not particularly encouraging. This world is good enough for me, cousin Cecily.

CECILY: Yes, but are you good enough for it?

ALGERNON: I'm afraid I'm not that. That is why I want you to reform me. You might make that your mission, if you don't mind, cousin Cecily.

CECILY: I'm afraid I've no time, this afternoon.

ALGERNON: Well, would you mind my reforming myself this afternoon?

CECILY: It is rather Quixotic[1] of you. But I think you should try.

ALGERNON: I will. I feel better already.

CECILY: You are looking a little worse.

ALGERNON: That is because I am hungry.

CECILY: How thoughtless of me. I should have remembered that when one is going to lead an entirely new life, one requires regular and wholesome meals. Won't you come in?

ALGERNON: Thank you. Might I have a buttonhole[2] first? I never have any appetite unless I have a buttonhole first.

CECILY: A Maréchal Niel?[3] [Picks up scissors.]

ALGERNON: No, I'd sooner have a pink rose.

CECILY: Why? [Cuts a flower.]

ALGERNON: Because you are like a pink rose, Cousin Cecily.

CECILY: I don't think it can be right for you to talk to me like that. Miss Prism never says such things to me.

ALGERNON: Then Miss Prism is a short-sighted old lady. [Cecily puts the rose in his buttonhole.] You are the prettiest girl I ever saw.

CECILY: Miss Prism says that all good looks are a snare.

ALGERNON: They are a snare that every sensible man would like to be caught in.

CECILY: Oh! I don't think I would care to catch a sensible man. I shouldn't know what to talk to him about.

[They pass into the house. Miss Prism and Dr Chasuble return.]

MISS PRISM: You are too much alone, dear Dr Chasuble. You should get married. A misanthrope I can understand—a womanthrope, never!

---

9. Australia was no longer a penal colony, but it was still a place where families sent their ne'er-do-well sons.
1. Hopelessly idealistic, like Don Quixote.

2. A flower to wear in his lapel.
3. A yellow rose.

CHASUBLE [*with a scholar's shudder*][4]: Believe me, I do not deserve so neologistic a phrase. The precept as well as the practice of the Primitive Church was distinctly against matrimony.[5]

MISS PRISM [*sententiously*]: That is obviously the reason why the Primitive Church has not lasted up to the present day. And you do not seem to realize, dear Doctor, that by persistently remaining single, a man converts himself into a permanent public temptation. Men should be more careful; this very celibacy leads weaker vessels astray.

CHASUBLE: But is a man not equally attractive when married?

MISS PRISM: No married man is ever attractive except to his wife.

CHASUBLE: And often, I've been told, not even to her.

MISS PRISM: That depends on the intellectual sympathies of the woman. Maturity can always be depended on. Ripeness can be trusted. Young women are green. [*Dr Chasuble starts.*] I spoke horticulturally. My metaphor was drawn from fruits. But where is Cecily?

CHASUBLE: Perhaps she followed us to the schools.

[*Enter Jack slowly from the back of the garden. He is dressed in the deepest mourning, with crape hat-band and black gloves.*]

MISS PRISM: Mr Worthing!

CHASUBLE: Mr Worthing?

MISS PRISM: This is indeed a surprise. We did not look for you till Monday afternoon.

JACK [*shakes Miss Prism's hand in a tragic manner*]: I have returned sooner than I expected. Dr Chasuble, I hope you are well?

CHASUBLE: Dear Mr Worthing, I trust this garb of woe does not betoken some terrible calamity?

JACK: My brother.

MISS PRISM: More shameful debts and extravagance?

CHASUBLE: Still leading his life of pleasure?

JACK [*shaking his head*]: Dead!

CHASUBLE: Your brother Ernest dead?

JACK: Quite dead.

MISS PRISM: What a lesson for him! I trust he will profit by it.

CHASUBLE: Mr Worthing, I offer you my sincere condolence. You have at least the consolation of knowing that you were always the most generous and forgiving of brothers.

JACK: Poor Ernest! He had many faults, but it is a sad, sad blow.

CHASUBLE: Very sad indeed. Were you with him at the end?

JACK: No. He died abroad; in Paris, in fact. I had a telegram last night from the manager of the Grand Hotel.

CHASUBLE: Was the cause of death mentioned?

JACK: A severe chill, it seems.

MISS PRISM: As a man sows, so shall he reap.

CHASUBLE [*raising his hand*]: Charity, dear Miss Prism, charity! None of us are perfect. I myself am peculiarly susceptible to draughts. Will the interment take place here?

---

4. He shudders because Miss Prism has mangled the language by coining a word, "womanthrope," to describe someone who dislikes women, instead of using the correct term, "misogynist." A neologism is a newly invented word.

5. Protestant clergy are allowed to marry, but as a High Church Anglican, Chasuble is interested in preserving the rituals and practices of the early Catholic church.

JACK: No. He seemed to have expressed a desire to be buried in Paris.

CHASUBLE: In Paris! [*Shakes his head.*] I fear that hardly points to any very serious state of mind at the last. You would no doubt wish me to make some slight allusion to this tragic domestic affliction next Sunday. [*Jack presses his hand convulsively.*] My sermon on the meaning of the manna in the wilderness[6] can be adapted to almost any occasion, joyful, or, as in the present case, distressing. [*All sigh.*] I have preached it at harvest celebrations, christenings, confirmations, on days of humiliation and festal days. The last time I delivered it was in the Cathedral, as a charity sermon on behalf of the Society for the Prevention of Discontent among the Upper Orders. The Bishop, who was present, was much struck by some of the analogies I drew.

JACK: Ah! that reminds me, you mentioned christenings I think, Dr Chasuble? I suppose you know how to christen all right? [*Dr Chasuble looks astounded.*] I mean, of course, you are continually christening, aren't you?

MISS PRISM: It is, I regret to say, one of the Rector's most constant duties in this parish. I have often spoken to the poorer classes on the subject. But they don't seem to know what thrift is.

CHASUBLE: But is there any particular infant in whom you are interested, Mr Worthing? Your brother was, I believe, unmarried, was he not?

JACK: Oh, yes.

MISS PRISM [*bitterly*]: People who live entirely for pleasure usually are.

JACK: But it is not for any child, dear Doctor. I am very fond of children. No! the fact is, I would like to be christened myself, this afternoon, if you have nothing better to do.

CHASUBLE: But surely, Mr Worthing, you have been christened already?

JACK: I don't remember anything about it.

CHASUBLE: But have you any grave doubts on the subject?

JACK: I certainly intend to have. Of course I don't know if the thing would bother you in any way, or if you think I am a little too old now.

CHASUBLE: Not at all. The sprinkling, and, indeed, the immersion of adults is a perfectly canonical practice.

JACK: Immersion!

CHASUBLE: You need have no apprehensions. Sprinkling is all that is necessary, or indeed I think advisable. Our weather is so changeable. At what hour would you wish the ceremony performed?

JACK: Oh, I might trot round about five if that would suit you.

CHASUBLE: Perfectly, perfectly! In fact I have two similar ceremonies to perform at that time. A case of twins that occurred recently in one of the outlying cottages on your own estate. Poor Jenkins the carter, a most hard-working man.

JACK: Oh! I don't see much fun in being christened along with other babies. It would be childish. Would half-past five do?

CHASUBLE: Admirably! Admirably! [*Takes out watch.*] And now, dear Mr Worthing, I will not intrude any longer into a house of sorrow. I would merely beg you not to be too much bowed down by grief. What seem to us bitter trials are often blessings in disguise.

MISS PRISM: This seems to me a blessing of an extremely obvious kind.

---

6. Cf. Exodus 16.

[*Enter Cecily from the house.*]

CECILY: Uncle Jack! Oh, I am pleased to see you back. But what horrid clothes you have got on! Do go and change them.

MISS PRISM: Cecily!

CHASUBLE: My child! my child!

[*Cecily goes towards Jack; he kisses her brow in a melancholy manner.*]

CECILY: What is the matter, Uncle Jack? Do look happy! You look as if you had toothache, and I have got such a surprise for you. Who do you think is in the dining-room? Your brother!

JACK: Who?

CECILY: Your brother Ernest. He arrived about half an hour ago.

JACK: What nonsense! I haven't got a brother.

CECILY: Oh, don't say that. However badly he may have behaved to you in the past he is still your brother. You couldn't be so heartless as to disown him. I'll tell him to come out. And you will shake hands with him, won't you, Uncle Jack? [*Runs back into the house.*]

CHASUBLE: These are very joyful tidings.

MISS PRISM: After we had all been resigned to his loss, his sudden return seems to me peculiarly distressing.

JACK: My brother is in the dining-room? I don't know what it all means. I think it is perfectly absurd.

[*Enter Algernon and Cecily hand in hand. They come slowly up to Jack.*]

JACK: Good heavens! [*Motions Algernon away.*]

ALGERNON: Brother John, I have come down from town to tell you that I am very sorry for all the trouble I have given you, and that I intend to lead a better life in the future.

[*Jack glares at him and does not take his hand.*]

CECILY: Uncle Jack, you are not going to refuse your own brother's hand?

JACK: Nothing will induce me to take his hand. I think his coming down here disgraceful. He knows perfectly well why.

CECILY: Uncle Jack, do be nice. There is some good in everyone. Ernest has just been telling me about his poor invalid friend Mr Bunbury whom he goes to visit so often. And surely there must be much good in one who is kind to an invalid, and leaves the pleasures of London to sit by a bed of pain.

JACK: Oh! he has been talking about Bunbury has he?

CECILY: Yes, he has told me all about poor Mr Bunbury, and his terrible state of health.

JACK: Bunbury! Well, I won't have him talk to you about Bunbury or about anything else. It is enough to drive one perfectly frantic.

ALGERNON: Of course I admit that the faults were all on my side. But I must say that I think that Brother John's coldness to me is peculiarly painful. I expected a more enthusiastic welcome, especially considering it is the first time I have come here.

CECILY: Uncle Jack, if you don't shake hands with Ernest I will never forgive you.

JACK: Never forgive me?

CECILY: Never, never, never!

JACK: Well, this is the last time I shall ever do it. [*Shakes hands with Algernon and glares.*]

CHASUBLE: It's pleasant, is it not, to see so perfect a reconciliation? I think we might leave the two brothers together.

MISS PRISM: Cecily, you will come with us.

CECILY: Certainly, Miss Prism. My little task of reconciliation is over.

CHASUBLE: You have done a beautiful action today, dear child.

MISS PRISM: We must not be premature in our judgements.

CECILY: I feel very happy. [*They all go off.*]

JACK: You young scoundrel, Algy, you must get out of this place as soon as possible. I don't allow any Bunburying here.

    [*Enter Merriman.*]

MERRIMAN: I have put Mr Ernest's things in the room next to yours, sir. I suppose that is all right?

JACK: What?

MERRIMAN: Mr Ernest's luggage, sir. I have unpacked it and put it in the room next to your own.

JACK: His luggage?

MERRIMAN: Yes, sir. Three portmanteaus, a dressing-case, two hat-boxes, and a large luncheon-basket.

ALGERNON: I am afraid I can't stay more than a week this time.

JACK: Merriman, order the dog-cart[7] at once. Mr Ernest has been suddenly called back to town.

MERRIMAN: Yes, sir. [*Goes back into the house.*]

ALGERNON: What a fearful liar you are, Jack. I have not been called back to town at all.

JACK: Yes, you have.

ALGERNON: I haven't heard anyone call me.

JACK: Your duty as a gentleman calls you back.

ALGERNON: My duty as a gentleman has never interfered with my pleasures in the smallest degree.

JACK: I can quite understand that.

ALGERNON: Well, Cecily is a darling.

JACK: You are not to talk of Miss Cardew like that. I don't like it.

ALGERNON: Well, I don't like your clothes. You look perfectly ridiculous in them. Why on earth don't you go up and change? It is perfectly childish to be in deep mourning for a man who is actually staying for a whole week with you in your house as a guest. I call it grotesque.

JACK: You are certainly not staying with me for a whole week as a guest or anything else. You have got to leave . . . by the four-five train.

ALGERNON: I certainly won't leave you so long as you are in mourning. It would be most unfriendly. If I were in mourning you would stay with me, I suppose. I should think it very unkind if you didn't.

JACK: Well, will you go if I change my clothes?

ALGERNON: Yes, if you are not too long. I never saw anybody take so long to dress, and with such little result.

JACK: Well, at any rate, that is better than being always over-dressed as you are.

ALGERNON: If I am occasionally a little over-dressed, I make up for it by being always immensely over-educated.

JACK: Your vanity is ridiculous, your conduct an outrage, and your presence in my garden utterly absurd. However, you have got to catch the four-five, and I hope you will have a pleasant journey back to town. This Bunburying, as you call it, has not been a great success for you. [*Goes into the house.*]

---

7. A horse-drawn cart with seats, and a box for hunting dogs.

ALGERNON: I think it has been a great success. I'm in love with Cecily, and that is everything.

[*Enter Cecily at the back of the garden. She picks up the can and begins to water the flowers.*]

But I must see her before I go, and make arrangements for another Bunbury. Ah, there she is.

CECILY: Oh, I merely came back to water the roses. I thought you were with Uncle Jack.

ALGERNON: He's gone to order the dog-cart for me.

CECILY: Oh, is he going to take you for a nice drive?

ALGERNON: He's going to send me away.

CECILY: Then have we got to part?

ALGERNON: I am afraid so. It's a painful parting.

CECILY: It is always painful to part from people whom one has known for a very brief space of time. The absence of old friends one can endure with equanimity. But even a momentary separation from anyone to whom one has just been introduced is almost unbearable.

ALGERNON: Thank you.

[*Enter Merriman.*]

MERRIMAN: The dog-cart is at the door, sir.

[*Algernon looks appealingly at Cecily.*]

CECILY: It can wait, Merriman . . . for . . . five minutes.

MERRIMAN: Yes, Miss. [*Exit Merriman.*]

ALGERNON: I hope, Cecily, I shall not offend you if I state quite frankly and openly that you seem to me to be in every way the visible personification of absolute perfection.

CECILY: I think your frankness does you great credit, Ernest. If you will allow me I will copy your remarks into my diary. [*Goes over to table and begins writing in diary.*]

ALGERNON: Do you really keep a diary? I'd give anything to look at it. May I?

CECILY: Oh no. [*Puts her hand over it.*] You see, it is simply a very young girl's record of her own thoughts and impressions, and consequently meant for publication. When it appears in volume form I hope you will order a copy. But pray, Ernest, don't stop. I delight in taking down from dictation. I have reached "absolute perfection." You can go on. I am quite ready for more.

ALGERNON [*somewhat taken aback*]: Ahem! Ahem!

CECILY: Oh, don't cough, Ernest. When one is dictating one should speak fluently and not cough. Besides, I don't know how to spell a cough. [*Writes as Algernon speaks.*]

ALGERNON [*speaking very rapidly*]: Cecily, ever since I first looked upon your wonderful and incomparable beauty, I have dared to love you wildly, passionately, devotedly, hopelessly.

CECILY: I don't think that you should tell me that you love me wildly, passionately, devotedly, hopelessly. Hopelessly doesn't seem to make much sense, does it?

ALGERNON: Cecily!

[*Enter Merriman.*]

MERRIMAN: The dog-cart is waiting, sir.

ALGERNON: Tell it to come round next week, at the same hour.

MERRIMAN [*looks at Cecily, who makes no sign*]: Yes, sir. [*Merriman retires.*]

CECILY: Uncle Jack would be very much annoyed if he knew you were staying on till next week, at the same hour.

ALGERNON: Oh, I don't care about Jack. I don't care for anybody in the whole world but you. I love you, Cecily. You will marry me, won't you?

CECILY: You silly boy! Of course. Why, we have been engaged for the last three months.

ALGERNON: For the last three months?

CECILY: Yes, it will be exactly three months on Thursday.

ALGERNON: But how did we become engaged?

CECILY: Well, ever since dear Uncle Jack first confessed to us that he had a younger brother who was very wicked and bad, you of course have formed the chief topic of conversation between myself and Miss Prism. And of course a man who is much talked about is always very attractive. One feels there must be something in him after all. I daresay it was foolish of me, but I fell in love with you, Ernest.

ALGERNON: Darling! And when was the engagement actually settled?

CECILY: On the 14th of February last. Worn out by your entire ignorance of my existence, I determined to end the matter one way or the other, and after a long struggle with myself I accepted you under this dear old tree here. The next day I bought this little ring in your name, and this is the little bangle with the true lovers' knot I promised you always to wear.

ALGERNON: Did I give you this? It's very pretty, isn't it?

CECILY: Yes, you've wonderfully good taste, Ernest. It's the excuse I've always given for your leading such a bad life. And this is the box in which I keep all your dear letters. [Kneels at table, opens box, and produces letters tied up with blue ribbon.]

ALGERNON: My letters! But my own sweet Cecily, I have never written you any letters.

CECILY: You need hardly remind me of that, Ernest. I remember only too well that I was forced to write your letters for you. I wrote always three times a week, and sometimes oftener.

ALGERNON: Oh, do let me read them, Cecily?

CECILY: Oh, I couldn't possibly. They would make you far too conceited. [Replaces box.] The three you wrote me after I had broken off the engagement are so beautiful, and so badly spelled, that even now I can hardly read them without crying a little.

ALGERNON: But was our engagement ever broken off?

CECILY: Of course it was. On the 22nd of last March. You can see the entry if you like. [Shows diary.] "Today I broke off my engagement with Ernest. I feel it is better to do so. The weather still continues charming."

ALGERNON: But why on earth did you break it off? What had I done? I had done nothing at all. Cecily, I am very much hurt indeed to hear you broke it off. Particularly when the weather was so charming.

CECILY: It would hardly have been a really serious engagement if it hadn't been broken off at least once. But I forgave you before the week was out.

ALGERNON [crossing to her, and kneeling]: What a perfect angel you are, Cecily.

CECILY: You dear romantic boy. [He kisses her, she puts her fingers through his hair.] I hope your hair curls naturally, does it?

ALGERNON: Yes, darling, with a little help from others.

CECILY: I am so glad.

ALGERNON: You'll never break off our engagement again, Cecily?

CECILY: I don't think I could break it off now that I have actually met you. Besides, of course, there is the question of your name.

ALGERNON: Yes, of course. [*Nervously.*]

CECILY: You must not laugh at me, darling, but it had always been a girlish dream of mine to love some one whose name was Ernest. [*Algernon rises, Cecily also.*] There is something in that name that seems to inspire absolute confidence. I pity any poor married woman whose husband is not called Ernest.

ALGERNON: But, my dear child, do you mean to say you could not love me if I had some other name?

CECILY: But what name?

ALGERNON: Oh, any name you like—Algernon—for instance . . .

CECILY: But I don't like the name of Algernon.

ALGERNON: Well, my own dear, sweet, loving little darling, I really can't see why you should object to the name of Algernon. It is not at all a bad name. In fact, it is rather an aristocratic name. Half of the chaps who get into the Bankruptcy Court are called Algernon. But seriously, Cecily . . . [*moving to her*] . . . if my name was Algy, couldn't you love me?

CECILY [*rising*]: I might respect you, Ernest, I might admire your character, but I fear that I should not be able to give you my undivided attention.

ALGERNON: Ahem! Cecily! [*Picking up hat.*] Your Rector here is, I suppose, thoroughly experienced in the practice of all the rites and ceremonials of the Church?

CECILY: Oh yes. Dr Chasuble is a most learned man. He has never written a single book, so you can imagine how much he knows.

ALGERNON: I must see him at once on a most important christening—I mean on most important business.

CECILY: Oh!

ALGERNON: I shan't be away more than half an hour.

CECILY: Considering that we have been engaged since February the 14th, and that I only met you today for the first time, I think it is rather hard that you should leave me for so long a period as half an hour. Couldn't you make it twenty minutes?

ALGERNON: I'll be back in no time. [*Kisses her and rushes down the garden.*]

CECILY: What an impetuous boy he is! I like his hair so much. I must enter his proposal in my diary.

[*Enter Merriman.*]

MERRIMAN: A Miss Fairfax has just called to see Mr Worthing. On very important business Miss Fairfax states.

CECILY: Isn't Mr Worthing in his library?

MERRIMAN: Mr Worthing went over in the direction of the Rectory some time ago.

CECILY: Pray ask the lady to come out here; Mr Worthing is sure to be back soon. And you can bring tea.

MERRIMAN: Yes, Miss. [*Goes out.*]

CECILY: Miss Fairfax! I suppose one of the many good elderly women who are associated with Uncle Jack in some of his philanthropic work in London. I don't quite like women who are interested in philanthropic work. I think it is so forward of them.

[*Enter Merriman.*]

MERRIMAN: Miss Fairfax.

[*Enter Gwendolen. Exit Merriman.*]

CECILY [*advancing to meet her*]: Pray let me introduce myself to you. My name is Cecily Cardew.

GWENDOLEN: Cecily Cardew? [*Moving to her and shaking hands.*] What a very sweet name! Something tells me that we are going to be great friends. I like you already more than I can say. My first impressions of people are never wrong.

CECILY: How nice of you to like me so much after we have known each other such a comparatively short time. Pray sit down.

GWENDOLEN [*still standing up*]: I may call you Cecily, may I not?

CECILY: With pleasure!

GWENDOLEN: And you will always call me Gwendolen, won't you.

CECILY: If you wish.

GWENDOLEN: Then that is all quite settled, is it not?

CECILY: I hope so.

[*A pause. They both sit down together.*]

GWENDOLEN: Perhaps this might be a favourable opportunity for my mentioning who I am. My father is Lord Bracknell. You have never heard of papa, I suppose?

CECILY: I don't think so.

GWENDOLEN: Outside the family circle, papa, I am glad to say, is entirely unknown. I think that is quite as it should be. The home seems to me to be the proper sphere for the man. And certainly once a man begins to neglect his domestic duties he becomes painfully effeminate, does he not? And I don't like that. It makes men so very attractive. Cecily, mamma, whose views on education are remarkably strict, has brought me up to be extremely short-sighted; it is part of her system; so do you mind my looking at you through my glasses?

CECILY: Oh! not at all, Gwendolen. I am very fond of being looked at.

GWENDOLEN: [*after examining Cecily carefully through a lorgnette*]: You are here on a short visit I suppose.

CECILY: Oh no! I live here.

GWENDOLEN [*severely*]: Really? Your mother, no doubt, or some female relative of advanced years, resides here also?

CECILY: Oh no! I have no mother, nor, in fact, any relations.

GWENDOLEN: Indeed?

CECILY: My dear guardian, with the assistance of Miss Prism, has the arduous task of looking after me.

GWENDOLEN: Your guardian?

CECILY: Yes, I am Mr Worthing's ward.

GWENDOLEN: Oh! It is strange he never mentioned to me that he had a ward. How secretive of him! He grows more interesting hourly. I am not sure, however, that the news inspires me with feelings of unmixed delight. [*Rising and going to her.*] I am very fond of you, Cecily; I have liked you ever since I met you! But I am bound to state that now that I know that you are Mr Worthing's ward, I cannot help expressing a wish you were—well just a little older than you seem to be—and not quite so very alluring in appearance. In fact, if I may speak candidly—

CECILY: Pray do! I think that whenever one has anything unpleasant to say, one should always be quite candid.

GWENDOLEN: Well, to speak with perfect candour, Cecily, I wish that you were fully forty-two, and more than usually plain for your age. Ernest has a strong upright nature. He is the very soul of truth and honour. Disloyalty would be as impossible to him as deception. But even men of the noblest possible moral character are extremely susceptible to the influence of the physical charms of others. Modern, no less than Ancient History, supplies us with many most painful examples of what I refer to. If it were not so, indeed, History would be quite unreadable.

CECILY: I beg your pardon, Gwendolen, did you say Ernest?

GWENDOLEN: Yes.

CECILY: Oh, but it is not Mr Ernest Worthing who is my guardian. It is his brother—his elder brother.

GWENDOLEN [*sitting down again*]: Ernest never mentioned to me that he had a brother.

CECILY: I am sorry to say they have not been on good terms for a long time.

GWENDOLEN: Ah! that accounts for it. And now that I think of it I have never heard any man mention his brother. The subject seems distasteful to most men. Cecily, you have lifted a load from my mind. I was growing almost anxious. It would have been terrible if any cloud had come across a friendship like ours, would it not? Of course you are quite, quite sure that it is not Mr Ernest Worthing who is your guardian?

CECILY: Quite sure. [*A pause.*] In fact, I am going to be his.

GWENDOLEN [*enquiringly*]: I beg your pardon?

CECILY [*rather shy and confidingly*]: Dearest Gwendolen, there is no reason why I should make a secret of it to you. Our little county newspaper is sure to chronicle the fact next week. Mr Ernest Worthing and I are engaged to be married.

GWENDOLEN [*quite politely, rising*]: My darling Cecily, I think there must be some slight error. Mr Ernest Worthing is engaged to me. The announcement will appear in the "Morning Post" on Saturday at the latest.

CECILY [*very politely, rising*]: I am afraid you must be under some misconception. Ernest proposed to me exactly ten minutes ago. [*Shows diary.*]

GWENDOLEN [*examines diary through her lorgnette carefully*]: It is certainly very curious, for he asked me to be his wife yesterday afternoon at 5.30. If you would care to verify the incident, pray do so. [*Produces diary of her own.*] I never travel without my diary. One should always have something sensational to read in the train. I am so sorry, dear Cecily, if it is any disappointment to you, but I am afraid I have the prior claim.

CECILY: It would distress me more than I can tell you, dear Gwendolen, if it caused you any mental or physical anguish, but I feel bound to point out that since Ernest proposed to you he clearly has changed his mind.

GWENDOLEN [*meditatively*]: If the poor fellow has been entrapped into any foolish promise I shall consider it my duty to rescue him at once, and with a firm hand.

CECILY [*thoughtfully and sadly*]: Whatever unfortunate entanglement my dear boy may have got into, I will never reproach him with it after we are married.

GWENDOLEN: Do you allude to me, Miss Cardew, as an entanglement? You are presumptuous. On an occasion of this kind it becomes more than a moral duty to speak one's mind. It becomes a pleasure.

CECILY: Do you suggest, Miss Fairfax, that I entrapped Ernest into an engagement? How dare you? This is no time for wearing the shallow mask of manners. When I see a spade I call it a spade.

GWENDOLEN [*satirically*]: I am glad to say that I have never seen a spade. It is obvious that our social spheres have been widely different.

[*Enter Merriman, followed by the footman. He carries a salver, table cloth, and plate stand. Cecily is about to retort. The presence of the servants exercises a restraining influence, under which both girls chafe.*]

MERRIMAN: Shall I lay tea here as usual, Miss?

CECILY [*sternly, in a calm voice*]: Yes, as usual.

[*Merriman begins to clear table and lay cloth. A long pause. Cecily and Gwendolen glare at each other.*]

GWENDOLEN: Are there many interesting walks in the vicinity, Miss Cardew?

CECILY: Oh! yes! a great many. From the top of one of the hills quite close one can see five counties.

GWENDOLEN: Five counties! I don't think I should like that. I hate crowds.

CECILY [sweetly]: I suppose that is why you live in town?

[Gwendolen bites her lip, and beats her foot nervously with her parasol.]

GWENDOLEN [looking round]: Quite a well-kept garden this is, Miss Cardew.

CECILY: So glad you like it, Miss Fairfax.

GWENDOLEN: I had no idea there were any flowers in the country.

CECILY: Oh, flowers are as common here, Miss Fairfax, as people are in London.

GWENDOLEN: Personally, I cannot understand how anybody manages to exist in the country, if anybody who is anybody does. The country always bores me to death.

CECILY: Ah! This is what the newspapers call agricultural depression,[8] is it not? I believe the aristocracy are suffering very much from it just at present. It is almost an epidemic amongst them, I have been told. May I offer you some tea, Miss Fairfax?

GWENDOLEN [with elaborate politeness]: Thank you. [Aside.] Detestable girl! But I require tea!

CECILY [sweetly]: Sugar?

GWENDOLEN [superciliously]: No, thank you. Sugar is not fashionable any more.

[Cecily looks angrily at her, takes up the tongs and puts four lumps of sugar into the cup.]

CECILY [severely]: Cake or bread and butter?

GWENDOLEN [in a bored manner]: Bread and butter, please. Cake is rarely seen at the best houses nowadays.

CECILY [cuts a very large slice of cake, and puts it on the tray]: Hand that to Miss Fairfax.

[Merriman does so, and goes out with footman. Gwendolen drinks the tea and makes a grimace. Puts down cup at once, reaches out her hand to the bread and butter, looks at it, and finds it is cake. Rises in indignation.]

GWENDOLEN: You have filled my tea with lumps of sugar, and though I asked most distinctly for bread and butter, you have given me cake. I am known for the gentleness of my disposition, and the extraordinary sweetness of my nature, but I warn you, Miss Cardew, you may go too far.

CECILY [rising]: To save my poor, innocent, trusting boy from the machinations of any other girl there are no lengths to which I would not go.

GWENDOLEN: From the moment I saw you I distrusted you. I felt that you were false and deceitful. I am never deceived in such matters. My first impressions of people are invariably right.

CECILY: It seems to me, Miss Fairfax, that I am trespassing on your valuable time. No doubt you have many other calls of a similar character to make in the neighbourhood.

[Enter Jack.]

GWENDOLEN [catching sight of him]: Ernest! My own Ernest!

JACK: Gwendolen! Darling! [Offers to kiss her.]

GWENDOLEN [drawing back]: A moment! May I ask if you are engaged to be married to this young lady? [Points to Cecily.]

8. A pun on the word "depression"; beginning in the 1870s, British agriculture had been in a slump, causing losses and hardship among landowners.

JACK [*laughing*]: To dear little Cecily! Of course not! What could have put such an idea into your pretty little head?

GWENDOLEN: Thank you. You may! [*Offers her cheek.*]

CECILY [*very sweetly*]: I knew there must be some misunderstanding, Miss Fairfax. The gentleman whose arm is at present round your waist is my dear guardian, Mr John Worthing.

GWENDOLEN: I beg your pardon?

CECILY: This is Uncle Jack.

GWENDOLEN [*receding*]: Jack! Oh!
    [*Enter Algernon.*]

CECILY: Here is Ernest.

ALGERNON [*goes straight over to Cecily without noticing anyone else*]: My own love!
    [*Offers to kiss her.*]

CECILY [*drawing back*]: A moment, Ernest! May I ask you—are you engaged to be married to this young lady?

ALGERNON [*looking round*]: To what young lady? Good heavens! Gwendolen!

CECILY: Yes, to good heavens, Gwendolen, I mean to Gwendolen.

ALGERNON [*laughing*]: Of course not! What could have put such an idea into your pretty little head?

CECILY: Thank you. [*Presenting her cheek to be kissed.*] You may.
    [*Algernon kisses her.*]

GWENDOLEN: I felt there was some slight error, Miss Cardew. The gentleman who is now embracing you is my cousin, Mr Algernon Moncrieff.

CECILY [*breaking away from Algernon*]: Algernon Moncrieff! Oh!
    [*The two girls move towards each other and put their arms round each other's waists as if for protection.*]

CECILY: Are you called Algernon?

ALGERNON: I cannot deny it.

CECILY: Oh!

GWENDOLEN: Is your name really John?

JACK [*standing rather proudly*]: I could deny it if I liked. I could deny anything if I liked. But my name certainly is John. It has been John for years.

CECILY [*to Gwendolen*]: A gross deception has been practised on both of us.

GWENDOLEN: My poor wounded Cecily!

CECILY: My sweet wronged Gwendolen!

GWENDOLEN [*slowly and seriously*]: You will call me sister, will you not?
    [*They embrace. Jack and Algernon groan and walk up and down.*]

CECILY [*rather brightly*]: There is just one question I would like to be allowed to ask my guardian.

GWENDOLEN: An admirable idea! Mr Worthing, there is just one question I would like to be permitted to put to you. Where is your brother Ernest? We are both engaged to be married to your brother Ernest, so it is a matter of some importance to us to know where your brother Ernest is at present.

JACK [*slowly and hesitatingly*]: Gwendolen—Cecily—It is very painful for me to be forced to speak the truth. It is the first time in my life that I have ever been reduced to such a painful position, and I am really quite inexperienced in doing anything of the kind. However I will tell you quite frankly that I have no brother Ernest. I have no brother at all. I never had a brother in my life, and I certainly have not the smallest intention of ever having one in the future.

CECILY [*surprised*]: No brother at all?

JACK [*cheerily*]: None!

GWENDOLEN [*severely*]: Had you never a brother of any kind?

JACK [*pleasantly*]: Never. Not even of any kind.

GWENDOLEN: I am afraid it is quite clear, Cecily, that neither of us is engaged to be married to anyone.

CECILY: It is not a very pleasant position for a young girl suddenly to find herself in. Is it?

GWENDOLEN: Let us go into the house. They will hardly venture to come after us there.

CECILY: No, men are so cowardly, aren't they?

[*They retire into the house with scornful looks.*]

JACK: This ghastly state of things is what you call Bunburying, I suppose?

ALGERNON: Yes, and a perfectly wonderful Bunbury it is. The most wonderful Bunbury I have ever had in my life.

JACK: Well, you've no right whatsoever to Bunbury here.

ALGERNON: That is absurd. One has a right to Bunbury anywhere one chooses. Every serious Bunburyist knows that.

JACK: Serious Bunburyist! Good heavens!

ALGERNON: Well, one must be serious about something, if one wants to have any amusement in life. I happen to be serious about Bunburying. What on earth you are serious about I haven't got the remotest idea. About everything, I should fancy. You have such an absolutely trivial nature.

JACK: Well, the only small satisfaction I have in the whole of this wretched business is that your friend Bunbury is quite exploded. You won't be able to run down to the country quite so often as you used to do, dear Algy. And a very good thing too.

ALGERNON: Your brother is a little off colour, isn't he, dear Jack? You won't be able to disappear to London quite so frequently as your wicked custom was. And not a bad thing either.

JACK: As for your conduct towards Miss Cardew, I must say that your taking in a sweet, simple, innocent girl like that is quite inexcusable. To say nothing of the fact that she is my ward.

ALGERNON: I can see no possible defence at all for your deceiving a brilliant, clever, thoroughly experienced young lady like Miss Fairfax. To say nothing of the fact that she is my cousin.

JACK: I wanted to be engaged to Gwendolen, that is all. I love her.

ALGERNON: Well, I simply wanted to be engaged to Cecily. I adore her.

JACK: There is certainly no chance of your marrying Miss Cardew.

ALGERNON: I don't think there is much likelihood, Jack, of you and Miss Fairfax being united.

JACK: Well, that is no business of yours.

ALGERNON: If it was my business, I wouldn't talk about it. [*Begins to eat muffins.*] It is very vulgar to talk about one's business. Only people like stockbrokers do that, and then merely at dinner parties.

JACK: How you can sit there, calmly eating muffins when we are in this horrible trouble, I can't make out. You seem to me to be perfectly heartless.

ALGERNON: Well, I can't eat muffins in an agitated manner. The butter would probably get on my cuffs. One should always eat muffins quite calmly. It is the only way to eat them.

JACK: I say it's perfectly heartless your eating muffins at all, under the circumstances.

ALGERNON: When I am in trouble, eating is the only thing that consoles me. Indeed, when I am in really great trouble, as anyone who knows me intimately will tell you, I refuse everything except food and drink. At the present moment I am eating muffins because I am unhappy. Besides, I am particularly fond of muffins. [*Rising.*]

JACK [*rising*]: Well, that is no reason why you should eat them all in that greedy way.

[*Takes muffins from Algernon.*]

ALGERNON [*offering tea-cake*]: I wish you would have tea-cake instead. I don't like tea-cake.

JACK: Good heavens! I suppose a man may eat his own muffins in his own garden.

ALGERNON: But you have just said it was perfectly heartless to eat muffins.

JACK: I said it was perfectly heartless of you, under the circumstances. That is a very different thing.

ALGERNON: That may be. But the muffins are the same. [*He seizes the muffin-dish from Jack.*]

JACK: Algy, I wish to goodness you would go.

ALGERNON: You can't possibly ask me to go without having some dinner. It's absurd. I never go without my dinner. No one ever does, except vegetarians and people like that. Besides I have just made arrangements with Dr Chasuble to be christened at a quarter to six under the name of Ernest.

JACK: My dear fellow, the sooner you give up that nonsense the better. I made arrangements this morning with Dr Chasuble to be christened myself at 5.30, and I naturally will take the name of Ernest. Gwendolen would wish it. We can't both be christened Ernest. It's absurd. Besides, I have a perfect right to be christened if I like. There is no evidence at all that I ever have been christened by anybody. I should think it extremely probable I never was, and so does Dr Chasuble. It is entirely different in your case. You have been christened already.

ALGERNON: Yes, but I have not been christened for years.

JACK: Yes, but you have been christened. That is the important thing.

ALGERNON: Quite so. So I know my constitution can stand it. If you are not quite sure about your ever having been christened, I must say I think it rather dangerous your venturing on it now. It might make you very unwell. You can hardly have forgotten that someone very closely connected with you was very nearly carried off this week in Paris by a severe chill.

JACK: Yes, but you said yourself that a severe chill was not hereditary.

ALGERNON: It usen't to be, I know—but I daresay it is now. Science is always making wonderful improvements in things.

JACK [*picking up the muffin-dish*]: Oh, that is nonsense; you are always talking nonsense.

ALGERNON: Jack, you are at the muffins again! I wish you wouldn't. There are only two left. [*Takes them.*] I told you I was particularly fond of muffins.

JACK: But I hate tea-cake.

ALGERNON: Why on earth then do you allow tea-cake to be served up for your guests? What ideas you have of hospitality!

JACK: Algernon! I have already told you to go. I don't want you here. Why don't you go!

ALGERNON: I haven't quite finished my tea yet! and there is still one muffin left.

[*Jack groans, and sinks into a chair. Algernon still continues eating.*]   ACT DROP

THIRD ACT

SCENE: *Morning-room*[9] *at the Manor House.*

[*Gwendolen and Cecily are at the window, looking out into the garden.*]

GWENDOLEN: The fact that they did not follow us at once into the house, as anyone else would have done, seems to me to show that they have some sense of shame left.

CECILY: They have been eating muffins. That looks like repentance.

GWENDOLEN [*after a pause*]: They don't seem to notice us at all. Couldn't you cough?

CECILY: But I haven't got a cough.

GWENDOLEN: They're looking at us. What effrontery!

CECILY: They're approaching. That's very forward of them.

GWENDOLEN: Let us preserve a dignified silence.

CECILY: Certainly. It's the only thing to do now.
[*Enter Jack followed by Algernon. They whistle some dreadful popular air from a British Opera.*][1]

GWENDOLEN: This dignified silence seems to produce an unpleasant effect.

CECILY: A most distasteful one.

GWENDOLEN: But we will not be the first to speak.

CECILY: Certainly not.

GWENDOLEN: Mr Worthing, I have something very particular to ask you. Much depends on your reply.

CECILY: Gwendolen, your common sense is invaluable. Mr Moncrieff, kindly answer me the following question. Why did you pretend to be my guardian's brother?

ALGERNON: In order that I might have an opportunity of meeting you.

CECILY [*to Gwendolen*]: That certainly seems a satisfactory explanation, does it not?

GWENDOLEN: Yes, dear, if you can believe him.

CECILY: I don't. But that does not affect the wonderful beauty of his answer.

GWENDOLEN: True. In matters of grave importance, style, not sincerity is the vital thing. Mr Worthing, what explanation can you offer to me for pretending to have a brother? Was it in order that you might have an opportunity of coming up to town to see me as often as possible?

JACK: Can you doubt it, Miss Fairfax?

GWENDOLEN: I have the gravest doubts upon the subject. But I intend to crush them. This is not the moment for German scepticism.[2] [*Moving to Cecily.*] Their explanations appear to be quite satisfactory, especially Mr Worthing's. That seems to me to have the stamp of truth upon it.

CECILY: I am more than content with what Mr Moncrieff said. His voice alone inspires one with absolute credulity.

GWENDOLEN: Then you think we should forgive them?

CECILY: Yes. I mean no.

GWENDOLEN: True! I had forgotten. There are principles at stake that one cannot surrender. Which of us should tell them? The task is not a pleasant one.

CECILY: Could we not both speak at the same time?

---

9. An informal room for receiving morning calls from friends (afternoon visitors were received in the formal drawing room).
1. Probably a reference to Gilbert and Sullivan, who had made fun of Wilde and the Aesthetic movement in *Patience* (1881); see page 2062.
2. Many 19th-century German scholars were skeptical in their treatment of religious texts.

GWENDOLEN: An excellent idea! I nearly always speak at the same time as other people. Will you take the time from me?

CECILY: Certainly.

[*Gwendolen beats time with uplifted finger.*]

GWENDOLEN AND CECILY [*speaking together*]: Your Christian names are still an insuperable barrier. That is all!

JACK AND ALGERNON [*speaking together*]: Our Christian names! Is that all? But we are going to be christened this afternoon.

GWENDOLEN [*to Jack*]: For my sake you are prepared to do this terrible thing?

JACK: I am.

CECILY [*to Algernon*]: To please me you are ready to face this fearful ordeal?

ALGERNON: I am!

GWENDOLEN: How absurd to talk of the equality of the sexes! Where questions of self-sacrifice are concerned, men are infinitely beyond us.

JACK: We are. [*Clasps hands with Algernon.*]

CECILY: They have moments of physical courage of which we women know absolutely nothing.

GWENDOLEN [*to Jack*]: Darling!

ALGERNON [*to Cecily*]: Darling! [*They fall into each other's arms.*]

[*Enter Merriman. When he enters he coughs loudly, seeing the situation.*]

MERRIMAN: Ahem! Ahem! Lady Bracknell!

JACK: Good heavens!

[*Enter Lady Bracknell. The couples separate in alarm.*] [*Exit Merriman.*]

LADY BRACKNELL: Gwendolen! What does this mean?

GWENDOLEN: Merely that I am engaged to be married to Mr Worthing, mamma.

LADY BRACKNELL: Come here. Sit down. Sit down immediately. Hesitation of any kind is a sign of mental decay in the young, of physical weakness in the old. [*Turns to Jack.*] Apprised, sir, of my daughter's sudden flight by her trusty maid, whose confidence I purchased by means of a small coin, I followed her at once by a luggage train. Her unhappy father is, I am glad to say, under the impression that she is attending a more than usually lengthy lecture by the University Extension Scheme on the Influence of a permanent income on Thought. I do not propose to undeceive him. Indeed I have never undeceived him on any question. I would consider it wrong. But of course, you will clearly understand that all communication between yourself and my daughter must cease immediately from this moment. On this point, as indeed on all points, I am firm.

JACK: I am engaged to be married to Gwendolen, Lady Bracknell!

LADY BRACKNELL: You are nothing of the kind, sir. And now, as regards Algernon! . . . Algernon!

ALGERNON: Yes, Aunt Augusta.

LADY BRACKNELL: May I ask if it is in this house that your invalid friend Mr Bunbury resides?

ALGERNON [*stammering*]: Oh! No! Bunbury doesn't live here. Bunbury is somewhere else at present. In fact, Bunbury is dead.

LADY BRACKNELL: Dead! When did Mr Bunbury die? His death must have been extremely sudden.

ALGERNON [*airily*]: Oh! I killed Bunbury this afternoon. I mean poor Bunbury died this afternoon.

LADY BRACKNELL: What did he die of?

ALGERNON: Bunbury? Oh, he was quite exploded.

LADY BRACKNELL: Exploded! Was he the victim of a revolutionary outrage?³ I was not aware that Mr Bunbury was interested in social legislation. If so, he is well punished for his morbidity.

ALGERNON: My dear Aunt Augusta, I mean he was found out! The doctors found out that Bunbury could not live, that is what I mean—so Bunbury died.

LADY BRACKNELL: He seems to have had great confidence in the opinion of his physicians. I am glad, however, that he made up his mind at the last to some definite course of action, and acted under proper medical advice. And now that we have finally got rid of this Mr Bunbury, may I ask, Mr Worthing, who is that young person whose hand my nephew Algernon is now holding in what seems to me a peculiarly unnecessary manner?

JACK: That lady is Miss Cecily Cardew, my ward.

[*Lady Bracknell bows coldly to Cecily.*]

ALGERNON: I am engaged to be married to Cecily, Aunt Augusta.

LADY BRACKNELL: I beg your pardon?

CECILY: Mr Moncrieff and I are engaged to be married, Lady Bracknell.

LADY BRACKNELL [*with a shiver, crossing to the sofa and sitting down*]: I do not know whether there is anything peculiarly exciting in the air of this particular part of Hertfordshire, but the number of engagements that go on seems to me considerably above the proper average that statistics have laid down for our guidance. I think some preliminary enquiry on my part would not be out of place. Mr Worthing, is Miss Cardew at all connected with any of the larger railway stations in London? I merely desire information. Until yesterday I had no idea that there were any families or persons whose origins was a Terminus.⁴

[*Jack looks perfectly furious, but restrains himself.*]

JACK [*in a clear, cold voice*]: Miss Cardew is the granddaughter of the late Mr Thomas Cardew of 149, Belgrave Square, S.W.; Gervase Park, Dorking, Surrey; and the Sporran, Fifeshire, N.B.⁵

LADY BRACKNELL: That sounds not unsatisfactory. Three addresses always inspire confidence, even in tradesmen. But what proof have I of their authenticity?

JACK: I have carefully preserved the Court Guides⁶ of the period. They are open to your inspection, Lady Bracknell.

LADY BRACKNELL [*grimly*]: I have known strange errors in that publication.

JACK: Miss Cardew's family solicitors are Messrs Markby, Markby, and Markby.

LADY BRACKNELL: Markby, Markby, and Markby? A firm of the very highest position in their profession. Indeed I am told that one of the Mr Markbys is occasionally to be seen at dinner parties. So far I am satisfied.

JACK [*very irritably*]: How extremely kind of you, Lady Bracknell! I have also in my possession, you will be pleased to hear, certificates of Miss Cardew's birth, baptism, whooping cough, registration, vaccination, confirmation, and the measles; both the German and the English variety.

LADY BRACKNELL: Ah! A life crowded with incident, I see; though perhaps somewhat too exciting for a young girl. I am not myself in favour of premature ex-

---

3. Anarchy and political assassination were much in the news; Wilde's earliest drama, *Vera, or the Nihilists* (1881), dealt with the subject.
4. A railway station at the end of the line.

5. North Britain, i.e., Scotland.
6. Annual publications listing the names and London addresses of the upper classes.

periences. [*Rises, looks at her watch.*] Gwendolen! the time approaches for our departure. We have not a moment to lose. As a matter of form, Mr Worthing, I had better ask you if Miss Cardew has any little fortune?

JACK: Oh! about a hundred and thirty thousand pounds in the Funds.[7] That is all. Goodbye, Lady Bracknell. So pleased to have seen you.

LADY BRACKNELL [*sitting down again*]: A moment, Mr Worthing. A hundred and thirty thousand pounds! And in the Funds! Miss Cardew seems to me a most attractive young lady, now that I look at her. Few girls of the present day have any really solid qualities, any of the qualities that last, and improve with time. We live, I regret to say, in an age of surfaces. [*To Cecily.*] Come over here, dear. [*Cecily goes across.*] Pretty child! your dress is sadly simple, and your hair seems almost as Nature might have left it. But we can soon alter all that. A thoroughly experienced French maid produces a really marvellous result in a very brief space of time. I remember recommending one to young Lady Lancing, and after three months her own husband did not know her.

JACK [*aside*]: And after six months nobody knew her.

LADY BRACKNELL [*glares at Jack for a few moments. Then bends, with a practised smile, to Cecily.*]: Kindly turn round, sweet child. [*Cecily turns completely round.*] No, the side view is what I want. [*Cecily presents her profile.*] Yes, quite as I expected. There are distinct social possibilities in your profile. The two weak points in our age are its want of principle and its want of profile. The chin a little higher, dear. Style largely depends on the way the chin is worn. They are worn very high, just at present. Algernon!

ALGERNON: Yes, Aunt Augusta!

LADY BRACKNELL: There are distinct social possibilities in Miss Cardew's profile.

ALGERNON: Cecily is the sweetest, dearest, prettiest girl in the whole world. And I don't care twopence about social possibilities.

LADY BRACKNELL: Never speak disrespectfully of Society, Algernon. Only people who can't get into it do that. [*To Cecily.*] Dear child, of course you know that Algernon has nothing but his debts to depend upon. But I do not approve of mercenary marriages. When I married Lord Bracknell I had no fortune of any kind. But I never dreamed for a moment of allowing that to stand in my way. Well, I suppose I must give my consent.

ALGERNON: Thank you, Aunt Augusta.

LADY BRACKNELL: Cecily, you may kiss me!

CECILY [*kisses her*]: Thank you, Lady Bracknell.

LADY BRACKNELL: You may also address me as Aunt Augusta for the future.

CECILY: Thank you, Aunt Augusta.

LADY BRACKNELL: The marriage, I think, had better take place quite soon.

ALGERNON: Thank you, Aunt Augusta.

CECILY: Thank you, Aunt Augusta.

LADY BRACKNELL: To speak frankly, I am not in favour of long engagements. They give people the opportunity of finding out each other's character before marriage, which I think is never advisable.

JACK: I beg your pardon for interrupting you, Lady Bracknell, but this engagement is quite out of the question. I am Miss Cardew's guardian, and she cannot marry without my consent until she comes of age. That consent I absolutely decline to give.

7. The Consolidated Funds, reliable interest-bearing government bonds.

LADY BRACKNELL: Upon what grounds may I ask? Algernon is an extremely, I may almost say an ostentatiously, eligible young man. He has nothing, but he looks everything. What more can one desire?

JACK: It pains me very much to have to speak frankly to you, Lady Bracknell, about your nephew, but the fact is that I do not approve at all of his moral character. I suspect him of being untruthful.

[Algernon and Cecily look at him in indignant amazement.]

LADY BRACKNELL: Untruthful! My nephew Algernon? Impossible! He is an Oxonian.[8]

JACK: I fear there can be no possible doubt about the matter. This afternoon, during my temporary absence in London on an important question of romance, he obtained admission to my house by means of the false pretence of being my brother. Under an assumed name he drank, I've just been informed by my butler, an entire pint bottle of my Perrier-Jouet, Brut, '89; a wine I was specially reserving for myself. Continuing his disgraceful deception, he succeeded in the course of the afternoon in alienating the affections of my only ward. He subsequently stayed to tea, and devoured every single muffin. And what makes his conduct all the more heartless is, that he was perfectly well aware from the first that I have no brother, that I never had a brother, and that I don't intend to have a brother, not even of any kind. I distinctly told him so myself yesterday afternoon.

LADY BRACKNELL: Ahem! Mr Worthing, after careful consideration I have decided entirely to overlook my nephew's conduct to you.

JACK: That is very generous of you, Lady Bracknell. My own decision, however, is unalterable. I decline to give my consent.

LADY BRACKNELL [to Cecily]: Come here, sweet child. [Cecily goes over.] How old are you, dear?

CECILY: Well, I am really only eighteen, but I always admit to twenty when I go to evening parties.

LADY BRACKNELL: You are perfectly right in making some slight alteration. Indeed, no woman should ever be quite accurate about her age. It looks so calculating. . . . [In a meditative manner.] Eighteen, but admitting to twenty at evening parties. Well, it will not be very long before you are of age and free from the restraints of tutelage. So I don't think your guardian's consent is, after all, a matter of any importance.

JACK: Pray excuse me, Lady Bracknell, for interrupting you again, but it is only fair to tell you that according to the terms of her grandfather's will Miss Cardew does not come legally of age till she is thirty-five.

LADY BRACKNELL: That does not seem to me to be a grave objection. Thirty-five is a very attractive age. London society is full of women of the very highest birth who have, of their own free choice, remained thirty-five for years. Lady Dumbleton is an instance in point. To my own knowledge she has been thirty-five ever since she arrived at the age of forty, which was many years ago now. I see no reason why our dear Cecily should not be even still more attractive at the age you mention than she is at present. There will be a large accumulation of property.

CECILY: Algy, could you wait for me till I was thirty-five?

ALGERNON: Of course I could, Cecily. You know I could.

CECILY: Yes, I felt it instinctively, but I couldn't wait all that time. I hate waiting even five minutes for anybody. It always makes me rather cross. I am not punctual

8. I.e., he attended Oxford University.

myself, I know, but I do like punctuality in others, and waiting, even to be married, is quite out of the question.

ALGERNON: Then what is to be done, Cecily?

CECILY: I don't know, Mr Moncrieff.

LADY BRACKNELL: My dear Mr Worthing, as Miss Cardew states positively that she cannot wait till she is thirty-five—a remark which I am bound to say seems to me to show a somewhat impatient nature—I would beg of you to reconsider your decision.

JACK: But my dear Lady Bracknell, the matter is entirely in your own hands. The moment you consent to my marriage with Gwendolen, I will most gladly allow your nephew to form an alliance with my ward.

LADY BRACKNELL [*rising and drawing herself up*]: You must be quite aware that what you propose is out of the question.

JACK: Then a passionate celibacy is all that any of us can look forward to.

LADY BRACKNELL: That is not the destiny I propose for Gwendolen. Algernon, of course, can choose for himself. [*Pulls out her watch.*] Come, dear; [*Gwendolen rises.*] we have already missed five, if not six, trains. To miss any more might expose us to comment on the platform.

[*Enter Dr Chasuble.*]

CHASUBLE: Everything is quite ready for the christenings.

LADY BRACKNELL: The christenings, sir! Is not that somewhat premature?

CHASUBLE [*looking rather puzzled, and pointing to Jack and Algernon*]: Both these gentlemen have expressed a desire for immediate baptism.

LADY BRACKNELL: At their age? The idea is grotesque and irreligious! Algernon, I forbid you to be baptized. I will not hear of such excesses. Lord Bracknell would be highly displeased if he learned that that was the way in which you wasted your time and money.

CHASUBLE: Am I to understand then that there are to be no christenings at all this afternoon?

JACK: I don't think that, as things are now, it would be of much practical value to either of us, Dr Chasuble.

CHASUBLE: I am grieved to hear such sentiments from you, Mr Worthing. They savour of the heretical views of the Anabaptists,[9] views that I have completely refuted in four of my unpublished sermons. However, as your present mood seems to be one peculiarly secular, I will return to the church at once. Indeed, I have just been informed by the pew-opener[1] that for the last hour and a half Miss Prism has been waiting for me in the vestry.

LADY BRACKNELL [*starting*]: Miss Prism! Did I hear you mention a Miss Prism?

CHASUBLE: Yes, Lady Bracknell. I am on my way to join her.

LADY BRACKNELL: Pray allow me to detain you for a moment. This matter may prove to be one of vital importance to Lord Bracknell and myself. Is this Miss Prism a female of repellent aspect, remotely connected with education?

CHASUBLE [*somewhat indignantly*]: She is the most cultivated of ladies, and the very picture of respectability.

LADY BRACKNELL: It is obviously the same person. May I ask what position she holds in your household?

9. A 16th-century Protestant sect that believed in adult baptism.   1. Usher.

CHASUBLE [*severely*]: I am a celibate, madam.

JACK [*interposing*]: Miss Prism, Lady Bracknell, has been for the last three years Miss Cardew's esteemed governess and valued companion.

LADY BRACKNELL: In spite of what I hear of her, I must see her at once. Let her be sent for.

CHASUBLE [*looking off*]: She approaches; she is nigh.

[*Enter Miss Prism hurriedly.*]

MISS PRISM: I was told you expected me in the vestry, dear Canon. I have been waiting for you there for an hour and three quarters. [*Catches sight of Lady Bracknell who has fixed her with a stony glare. Miss Prism grows pale and quails. She looks anxiously round as if desirous to escape.*]

LADY BRACKNELL [*in a severe, judicial voice*]: Prism! [*Miss Prism bows her head in shame.*] Come here, Prism! [*Miss Prism approaches in a humble manner.*] Prism! Where is that baby? [*General consternation. The Canon starts back in horror. Algernon and Jack pretend to be anxious to shield Cecily and Gwendolen from hearing the details of a terrible public scandal.*] Twenty-eight years ago, Prism, you left Lord Bracknell's house, Number 104, Upper Grosvenor Street, in charge of a perambulator that contained a baby, of the male sex. You never returned. A few weeks later, through the elaborate investigations of the Metropolitan police, the perambulator was discovered at midnight, standing by itself in a remote corner of Bayswater.[2] It contained the manuscript of a three-volume novel of more than usually revolting sentimentality. [*Miss Prism starts in involuntary indignation.*] But the baby was not there! [*Everyone looks at Miss Prism.*] Prism! Where is that baby? [*A pause.*]

MISS PRISM: Lady Bracknell, I admit with shame that I do not know. I only wish I did. The plain facts of the case are these. On the morning of the day you mention, a day that is for ever branded on my memory, I prepared as usual to take the baby out in its perambulator. I had also with me a somewhat old, but capacious handbag in which I had intended to place the manuscript of a work of fiction that I had written during my few unoccupied hours. In a moment of mental abstraction, for which I never can forgive myself, I deposited the manuscript in the bassinette, and placed the baby in the hand-bag.

JACK [*who has been listening attentively*]: But where did you deposit the hand-bag?

MISS PRISM: Do not ask me, Mr Worthing.

JACK: Miss Prism, this is a matter of no small importance to me. I insist on knowing where you deposited the hand-bag that contained that infant.

MISS PRISM: I left it in the cloak-room of one of the larger railway stations in London.

JACK: What railway station?

MISS PRISM [*quite crushed*]: Victoria. The Brighton line. [*Sinks into a chair.*]

JACK: I must retire to my room for a moment. Gwendolen, wait here for me.

GWENDOLEN: If you are not too long, I will wait here for you all my life.

[*Exit Jack in great excitement.*]

CHASUBLE: What do you think this means, Lady Bracknell?

LADY BRACKNELL: I dare not even suspect, Dr Chasuble. I need hardly tell you that in families of high position strange coincidences are not supposed to occur. They are hardly considered the thing.

[*Noises heard overhead as if someone was throwing trunks about. Everyone looks up.*]

2. An area in the West End of London, near Kensington Gardens.

CECILY: Uncle Jack seems strangely agitated.

CHASUBLE: Your guardian has a very emotional nature.

LADY BRACKNELL: This noise is extremely unpleasant. It sounds as if he was having an argument. I dislike arguments of any kind. They are always vulgar, and often convincing.

CHASUBLE [*looking up*]: It has stopped now. [*The noise is redoubled.*]

LADY BRACKNELL: I wish he would arrive at some conclusion.

GWENDOLEN: This suspense is terrible. I hope it will last.

[*Enter Jack with a hand-bag of black leather in his hand.*]

JACK [*rushing over to Miss Prism*]: Is this the hand-bag, Miss Prism? Examine it carefully before you speak. The happiness of more than one life depends on your answer.

MISS PRISM [*calmly*]: It seems to be mine. Yes, here is the injury it received through the upsetting of a Gower Street omnibus in younger and happier days. Here is the stain on the lining caused by the explosion of a temperance beverage, an incident that occurred at Leamington. And here, on the lock, are my initials. I had forgotten that in an extravagant mood I had had them placed there. The bag is undoubtedly mine. I am delighted to have it so unexpectedly restored to me. It has been a great inconvenience being without it all these years.

JACK [*in a pathetic voice*]: Miss Prism, more is restored to you than this hand-bag. I was the baby you placed in it.

MISS PRISM [*amazed*]: You?

JACK [*embracing her*]: Yes . . . mother!

MISS PRISM [*recoiling in indignant astonishment*]: Mr Worthing! I am unmarried!

JACK: Unmarried! I do not deny that is a serious blow. But after all, who has the right to cast a stone against one who has suffered?[3] Cannot repentance wipe out an act of folly? Why should there be one law for men, and another for women? Mother, I forgive you. [*Tries to embrace her again.*]

MISS PRISM [*still more indignant*]: Mr Worthing, there is some error. [*Pointing to Lady Bracknell.*] There is the lady who can tell you who you really are.

JACK [*after a pause*]: Lady Bracknell, I hate to seem inquisitive, but would you kindly inform me who I am?

LADY BRACKNELL: I am afraid that the news I have to give you will not altogether please you. You are the son of my poor sister, Mrs Moncrieff, and consequently Algernon's elder brother.

JACK: Algy's elder brother! Then I have a brother after all. I knew I had a brother! I always said I had a brother! Cecily—how could you have ever doubted that I had a brother. [*Seizes hold of Algernon.*] Dr Chasuble, my unfortunate brother. Miss Prism, my unfortunate brother. Gwendolen, my unfortunate brother. Algy, you young scoundrel, you will have to treat me with more respect in the future. You have never behaved to me like a brother in all your life.

ALGERNON: Well, not till today, old boy, I admit. I did my best, however, though I was out of practice. [*Shakes hands.*]

GWENDOLEN [*to Jack*]: My own! But what own are you? What is your Christian name, now that you have become someone else?

JACK: Good heavens! . . . I had quite forgotten that point. Your decision on the subject of my name is irrevocable, I suppose?

---

3. Jesus saves a woman who is about to be stoned for committing adultery, saying, "He that is without sin among you, let him first cast a stone at her" (John 8.7).

GWENDOLEN: I never change, except in my affections.

CECILY: What a noble nature you have, Gwendolen!

JACK: Then the question had better be cleared up at once. Aunt Augusta, a moment. At the time when Miss Prism left me in the hand-bag, had I been christened already?

LADY BRACKNELL: Every luxury that money could buy, including christening, had been lavished on you by your fond and doting parents.

JACK: Then I was christened! That is settled. Now, what name was I given? Let me know the worst.

LADY BRACKNELL: Being the eldest son you were naturally christened after your father.

JACK [irritably]: Yes, but what was my father's Christian name?

LADY BRACKNELL [meditatively]: I cannot at the present moment recall what the General's Christian name was. But I have no doubt he had one. He was eccentric, I admit. But only in later years. And that was the result of the Indian climate, and marriage, and indigestion, and other things of that kind.

JACK: Algy! Can't you recollect what our father's Christian name was?

ALGERNON: My dear boy, we were never even on speaking terms. He died before I was a year old.

JACK: His name would appear in the Army Lists of the period, I suppose, Aunt Augusta?

LADY BRACKNELL: The General was essentially a man of peace, except in his domestic life. But I have no doubt his name would appear in any military directory.

JACK: The Army Lists of the last forty years are here. These delightful records should have been my constant study. [Rushes to bookcase and tears the books out.] M. Generals ... Mallam, Maxbohm,[4] Magley, what ghastly names they have— Markby, Migsby, Mobbs, Moncrieff! Lieutenant 1840, Captain, Lieutenant-Colonel, Colonel, General 1869, Christian names, Ernest John. [Puts book very quietly down and speaks quite calmly.] I always told you, Gwendolen, my name was Ernest, didn't I? Well, it is Ernest after all. I mean it naturally is Ernest.

LADY BRACKNELL: Yes, I remember now that the General was called Ernest. I knew I had some particular reason for disliking the name.

GWENDOLEN: Ernest! My own Ernest! I felt from the first that you could have no other name!

JACK: Gwendolen, it is a terrible thing for a man to find out suddenly that all his life he has been speaking nothing but the truth. Can you forgive me?

GWENDOLEN: I can. For I feel that you are sure to change.

JACK: My own one!

CHASUBLE [to Miss Prism]: Laetitia! [Embraces her.]

MISS PRISM [enthusiastically]: Frederick! At last!

ALGERNON: Cecily! [Embraces her.] At last!

JACK: Gwendolen! [Embraces her.] At last!

LADY BRACKNELL: My nephew, you seem to be displaying signs of triviality.

JACK: On the contrary, Aunt Augusta, I've now realized for the first time in my life the vital Importance of Being Earnest.

TABLEAU

1894, performed 1895

CURTAIN
1899

---

4. A pun on the name of Wilde's friend Max Beerbohm.

Aphorisms[1]

[On arriving in America] I have nothing to declare except my genius.

F. Harris, *Oscar Wilde*

We have really everything in common with America nowadays, except, of course, language.

The Canterville Ghost

A poet can survive everything but a misprint.

The Children of the Poets

Meredith is a prose Browning, and so is Browning. He used poetry as a medium for writing in prose.

The Critic as Artist

Anybody can make history. Only a great man can write it.

Ibid.

The one duty we owe to history is to rewrite it.

Ibid.

A little sincerity is a dangerous thing, and a great deal of it is absolutely fatal.

Ibid.

There is only one thing in the world worse than being talked about, and that is not being talked about.

The Picture of Dorian Gray

Being natural is simply a pose, and the most irritating pose I know.

Ibid.

A man cannot be too careful in the choice of his enemies.

Ibid.

American girls are as clever at concealing their parents, as English women are at concealing their past.

Ibid.

Perhaps, after all, America never has been discovered. I myself would say that it had merely been detected.

Ibid.

---

1. Wilde's aphorisms often cleverly invert a cliché in order to produce a seeming paradox; they are perhaps his most characteristic form of expression in his conversation and writing alike. Wilde kept track of his favorite maxims, sometimes revising them in later works. In addition to the epigrammatic preface to *Dorian Gray*, he published two selections: *A Few Maxims for the Instruction of the Over-Educated* appeared anonymously in the *Saturday Review* in November 1894; *Phrases and Philosophies for the Use of the Young* was published in *The Chameleon* in December 1894.

Women give to men the very gold of their lives. But they invariably want it back in such very small change.

Ibid.

I hate vulgar realism in literature. The man who could call a spade a spade should be compelled to use one. It is the only thing he is fit for.

Ibid.

It is better to be beautiful than to be good. But . . . it is better to be good than to be ugly.

Ibid.

I can resist everything except temptation.

Lady Windermere's Fan

It's most dangerous nowadays for a husband to pay any attention to his wife in public. It always makes people think that he beats her when they're alone.

Ibid.

We are all in the gutter, but some of us are looking at the stars.

Ibid.

In this world there are only two tragedies. One is not getting what one wants, and the other is getting it.

Ibid.

What is a cynic? A man who knows the price of everything and the value of nothing.

Ibid.

Experience is the name everyone gives to their mistakes.

Ibid.

Repentance is quite out of date. And besides, if a woman really repents, she has to go to a bad dressmaker, otherwise no one believes in her.

Ibid.

It is perfectly monstrous the way people go about, nowadays, saying things against one behind one's back that are absolutely and entirely true.

A Woman of No Importance

The youth of America is their oldest tradition. It has been going on now for three hundred years.

Ibid.

The English country gentleman galloping after a fox—the unspeakable in full pursuit of the uneatable.

Ibid.

Twenty years of romance make a woman look like a ruin; but twenty years of marriage make her look like a public building.

Ibid.

One should never trust a woman who tells one her real age. A woman who would tell one that, would tell one anything.

Ibid.

The first duty in life is to be as artificial as possible. What the second duty is no one has as yet discovered.

Phrases and Philosophies for the Use of the Young

To love oneself is the beginning of a lifelong romance.

Ibid.

My wallpaper and I are fighting a duel to the death. One or the other of us has to go.

Richard Ellmann, *Oscar Wilde*

from De Profundis[1]

[January–March 1897]

H.M. Prison, Reading

Dear Bosie, After long and fruitless waiting I have determined to write to you myself, as much for your sake as for mine, as I would not like to think that I had passed through two long years of imprisonment without ever having received a single line from you, or any news or message even, except such as gave me pain.

Our ill-fated and most lamentable friendship has ended in ruin and public infamy for me, yet the memory of our ancient affection is often with me, and the thought that loathing, bitterness and contempt should for ever take that place in my heart once held by love is very sad to me: and you yourself will, I think, feel in your heart that to write to me as I lie in the loneliness of prison-life is better than to publish my letters without my permission or to dedicate poems to me unasked, though the world will know nothing of whatever words of grief or passion, of remorse or indifference you may choose to send as your answer or your appeal.

I have no doubt that in this letter in which I have to write of your life and of mine, of the past and of the future, of sweet things changed to bitterness and of bitter things that may be turned into joy, there will be much that will wound your vanity to the quick. If it prove so, read the letter over and over again till it kills your vanity. If

---

1. "Out of the depths" [have I cried unto thee, O Lord] (Latin), the first words of Psalm 130. While imprisoned in Reading Gaol, Wilde was allowed pen and paper only to write letters. He thus composed a meditation on his life in the form of a long letter to Lord Alfred Douglas (nicknamed Bosie), written from January to March 1897. Wilde referred to the text as "Epistola: In Carcere et Vinculis" (Letter: In Prison and in Chains). When he was released, he gave the manuscript to his friend, Robert Ross ("Robbie"), who entitled it *De Profundis* and published an abridged version—omitting all mention of Douglas—in 1905, after Wilde's death. In 1949, when Douglas had died, Wilde's son Vyvyan published a fuller text, based on an unreliable typescript supplied by Ross. Only in 1962, when scholars were allowed to consult the original manuscript—given by Ross to the British Museum—did a complete version finally appear.

you find in it something of which you feel that you are unjustly accused, remember that one should be thankful that there is any fault of which one can be unjustly accused. If there be in it one single passage that brings tears to your eyes, weep as we weep in prison where the day no less than the night is set apart for tears. It is the only thing that can save you. If you go complaining to your mother, as you did with reference to the scorn of you I displayed in my letter to Robbie, so that she may flatter and soothe you back into self-complacency or conceit, you will be completely lost. If you find one false excuse for yourself, you will soon find a hundred, and be just what you were before. Do you still say, as you said to Robbie in your answer, that I "*attribute unworthy motives*" to you? Ah! you had no motives in life. You had appetites merely. A motive is an intellectual aim. That you were "*very young*" when our friendship began? Your defect was not that you knew so little about life, but that you knew so much. The morning dawn of boyhood with its delicate bloom, its clear pure light, its joy of innocence and expectation you had left far behind. With very swift and running feet you had passed from Romance to Realism. The gutter and the things that live in it had begun to fascinate you. That was the origin of the trouble in which you sought my aid, and I, so unwisely according to the wisdom of this world, out of pity and kindness gave it to you. You must read this letter right through, though each word may become to you as the fire or knife of the surgeon that makes the delicate flesh burn or bleed. Remember that the fool in the eyes of the gods and the fool in the eyes of man are very different. One who is entirely ignorant of the modes of Art in its revolution or the moods of thought in its progress, of the pomp of the Latin line or the richer music of the vowelled Greek, of Tuscan sculpture or Elizabethan song may yet be full of the very sweetest wisdom. The real fool, such as the gods mock or mar, is he who does not know himself. I was such a one too long. You have been such a one too long. Be so no more. Do not be afraid. The supreme vice is shallowness. Everything that is realised is right. Remember also that whatever is misery to you to read, is still greater misery to me to set down. To you the Unseen Powers have been very good. They have permitted you to see the strange and tragic shapes of Life as one sees shadows in a crystal. The head of Medusa that turns living men to stone,[2] you have been allowed to look at in a mirror merely. You yourself have walked free among the flowers. From me the beautiful world of colour and motion has been taken away.

I will begin by telling you that I blame myself terribly. As I sit here in this dark cell in convict clothes, a disgraced and ruined man, I blame myself. In the perturbed and fitful nights of anguish, in the long monotonous days of pain, it is myself I blame. I blame myself for allowing an unintellectual friendship, a friendship whose primary aim was not the creation and contemplation of beautiful things, to entirely dominate my life. From the very first there was too wide a gap between us. You had been idle at your school, worse than idle at your university. You did not realise that an artist, and especially such an artist as I am, one, that is to say, the quality of whose work depends on the intensification of personality, requires for the development of his art the companionship of ideas, and intellectual atmosphere, quiet, peace, and solitude. You admired my work when it was finished: you enjoyed the brilliant successes of my first nights, and the brilliant banquets that followed them: you were proud, and quite naturally so, of being the intimate friend of an artist so distinguished: but you could not understand the conditions requisite for the production of artistic work. I am not

2. Medusa was a snake-haired monster, so horrifying that anyone who looked at her turned to stone.

speaking in phrases of rhetorical exaggeration but in terms of absolute truth to actual fact when I remind you that during the whole time we were together I never wrote one single line. Whether at Torquay, Goring, London, Florence or elsewhere, my life, as long as you were by my side, was entirely sterile and uncreative. And with but few intervals you were, I regret to say, by my side always. * * *

You send me a very nice poem, of the undergraduate school of verse, for my approval: I reply by a letter of fantastic literary conceits:[3] I compare you to Hylas, or Hyacinth, Jonquil or Narcisse,[4] or someone whom the great god of Poetry favoured, and honoured with his love. The letter is like a passage from one of Shakespeare's sonnets, transposed to a minor key. It can only be understood by those who have read the *Symposium* of Plato, or caught the spirit of a certain grave mood made beautiful for us in Greek marbles. It was, let me say frankly, the sort of letter I would, in a happy if wilful moment, have written to any graceful young man of either University who had sent me a poem of his own making, certain that he would have sufficient wit or culture to interpret rightly its fantastic phrases. Look at the history of that letter! It passes from you into the hands of a loathsome companion: from him to a gang of blackmailers: copies of it are sent about London to my friends, and to the manager of the theatre where my work is being performed: every construction but the right one is put on it: Society is thrilled with the absurd rumours that I have had to pay a huge sum of money for having written an infamous letter to you: this forms the basis of your father's worst attack: I produce the original letter myself in Court to show what it really is: it is denounced by your father's Counsel as a revolting and insidious attempt to corrupt Innocence: ultimately it forms part of a criminal charge: the Crown takes it up: the Judge sums up on it with little learning and much morality: I go to prison for it at last. That is the result of writing you a charming letter. * * *

Other miserable men, when they are thrown into prison, if they are robbed of the beauty of the world, are at least safe, in some measure, from the world's most deadly slings, most awful arrows. They can hide in the darkness of their cells, and of their very disgrace make a mode of sanctuary. The world, having had its will, goes its way, and they are left to suffer undisturbed. With me it has been different. Sorrow after sorrow has come beating at the prison doors in search of me. They have opened the gates wide and let them in. Hardly, if at all, have my friends been suffered to see me. But my enemies have had full access to me always. Twice in my public appearances at the Bankruptcy Court, twice again in my public transferences from one prison to another, have I been shown under conditions of unspeakable humiliation to the gaze and mockery of men. The messenger of Death has brought me his tidings and gone his way,[5] and in entire solitude, and isolated from all that could give me comfort, or suggest relief, I have had to bear the intolerable burden of misery and remorse that the memory of my mother placed upon me, and places on me still. Hardly has that wound been dulled, not healed, by time, when violent and bitter and harsh

---

3. Douglas's poem, *In Praise of Shame*, appears on page 2086. Wilde's letter, written in January 1893, was eventually read aloud at his trial:

My own Boy,

    Your sonnet is quite lovely, and it is a marvel that those red rose-leaf lips of yours should have been made no less for the music of song than for madness of kisses. Your slim gilt soul walks between passion and poetry. I know Hyacinthus, whom Apollo loved so madly, was you in Greek days.

Why are you alone in London, and when do you go to Salisbury? Do go there to cool your hands in the grey twilight of Gothic things, and come here whenever you like. It is a lovely place—it only lacks you; but go to Salisbury first.

    Always, with undying love,

                    Yours, Oscar

4. Beautiful young men whom Apollo loved.
5. Wilde's mother died while he was in prison.

letters come to me from my wife through her solicitor. I am, at once, taunted and threatened with poverty. That I can bear. I can school myself to worse than that. But my two children are taken from me by legal procedure.[6] That is and always will remain to me a source of infinite distress, of infinite pain, of grief without end or limit. That the law should decide, and take upon itself to decide, that I am one unfit to be with my own children is something quite horrible to me. The disgrace of prison is as nothing compared to it. I envy the other men who tread the yard along with me. I am sure that their children wait for them, look for their coming, will be sweet to them.

The poor are wiser, more charitable, more kind, more sensitive than we are. In their eyes prison is a tragedy in a man's life, a misfortune, a casualty, something that calls for sympathy in others. They speak of one who is in prison as of one who is "*in trouble*" simply. It is the phrase they always use, and the expression has the perfect wisdom of Love in it. With people of our rank it is different. With us prison makes a man a pariah. I, and such as I am, have hardly any right to air and sun. Our presence taints the pleasures of others. We are unwelcome when we reappear. To revisit the glimpses of the moon is not for us.[7] Our very children are taken away. Those lovely links with humanity are broken. We are doomed to be solitary, while our sons still live. We are denied the one thing that might heal us and help us, that might bring balm to the bruised heart, and peace to the soul in pain.

And to all this has been added the hard, small fact that by your actions and by your silence, by what you have done and by what you have left undone,[8] you have made every day of my long imprisonment still more difficult for me to live through. The very bread and water of prison fare you have by your conduct changed. You have rendered the one bitter and the other brackish to me. The sorrow you should have shared you have doubled, the pain you should have sought to lighten you have quickened to anguish. I have no doubt that you did not mean to do so. I know that you did not mean to do so. It was simply that "one really fatal defect of your character, your entire lack of imagination."

And the end of it all is that I have got to forgive you. I must do so. I don't write this letter to put bitterness into your heart, but to pluck it out of mine. For my own sake I must forgive you. One cannot always keep an adder in one's breast to feed on one, nor rise up every night to sow thorns in the garden of one's soul. It will not be difficult at all for me to do so, if you help me a little. Whatever you did to me in old days I always readily forgave. It did you no good then. Only one whose life is without stain of any kind can forgive sins. But now when I sit in humiliation and disgrace it is different. My forgiveness should mean a great deal to you now. Some day you will realise it. Whether you do so early or late, soon or not at all, my way is clear before me. I cannot allow you to go through life bearing in your heart the burden of having ruined a man like me. The thought might make you callously indifferent, or morbidly sad. I must take the burden from you and put it on my own shoulders.

I must say to myself that neither you nor your father, multiplied a thousand times over, could possibly have ruined a man like me: that I ruined myself: and that nobody, great or small, can be ruined except by his own hand. I am quite ready to do so. I am trying to do so, though you may not think it at the present moment. If I have

---

6. In February 1897 Constance Wilde petitioned for custody of their children, Cyril and Vyvyan, whom Wilde never saw again. Their surname was changed to Holland.

7. Cf. *Hamlet* 1.4.51–53.

8. The Anglican rite of confession asks forgiveness "for what we have done and for what we have left undone."

brought this pitiless indictment against you, think what an indictment I bring without pity against myself. Terrible as what you did to me was, what I did to myself was far more terrible still.

I was a man who stood in symbolic relations to the art and culture of my age. I had realised this for myself at the very dawn of my manhood, and had forced my age to realise it afterwards. Few men hold such a position in their own lifetime and have it so acknowledged. It is usually discerned, if discerned at all, by the historian, or the critic, long after both the man and his age have passed away. With me it was different. I felt it myself, and made others feel it. Byron was a symbolic figure, but his relations were to the passion of his age and its weariness of passion. Mine were to something more noble, more permanent, of more vital issue, of larger scope.

The gods had given me almost everything. I had genius, a distinguished name, high social position, brilliancy, intellectual daring: I made art a philosophy, and philosophy an art: I altered the minds of men and the colours of things: there was nothing I said or did that did not make people wonder: I took the drama, the most objective form known to art, and made it as personal a mode of expression as the lyric or the sonnet, at the same time that I widened its range and enriched its characterisation: drama, novel, poem in rhyme, poem in prose, subtle or fantastic dialogue, whatever I touched I made beautiful in a new mode of beauty: to truth itself I gave what is false no less than what is true as its rightful province, and showed that the false and the true are merely forms of intellectual existence. I treated Art as the supreme reality, and life as a mere mode of fiction: I awoke the imagination of my century so that it created myth and legend around me: I summed up all systems in a phrase, and all existence in an epigram.

Along with these things, I had things that were different. I let myself be lured into long spells of senseless and sensual ease. I amused myself with being a *flâneur* [idle stroller], a dandy, a man of fashion. I surrounded myself with the smaller natures and the meaner minds. I became the spendthrift of my own genius, and to waste an eternal youth gave me a curious joy. Tired of being on the heights I deliberately went to the depths in the search for new sensations. What the paradox was to me in the sphere of thought, perversity became to me in the sphere of passion. Desire, at the end, was a malady, or a madness, or both. I grew careless of the lives of others. I took pleasure where it pleased me and passed on. I forgot that every little action of the common day makes or unmakes character, and that therefore what one has done in the secret chamber one has some day to cry aloud on the housetops. I ceased to be Lord over myself. I was no longer the Captain of my Soul, and did not know it. I allowed you to dominate me, and your father to frighten me. I ended in horrible disgrace. There is only one thing for me now, absolute Humility: just as there is only one thing for you, absolute Humility also. You had better come down into the dust and learn it beside me.

I have lain in prison for nearly two years. Out of my nature has come wild despair; an abandonment to grief that was piteous even to look at: terrible and impotent rage: bitterness and scorn: anguish that wept aloud: misery that could find no voice: sorrow that was dumb. I have passed through every possible mood of suffering. Better than Wordsworth himself I know what Wordsworth meant when he said:

> Suffering is permanent, obscure, and dark
> And has the nature of Infinity.[9]

9. From *The Borderers*, (act 3).

But while there were times when I rejoiced in the idea that my sufferings were to be endless, I could not bear them to be without meaning. Now I find hidden away in my nature something that tells me that nothing in the whole world is meaningless, and suffering least of all. That something hidden away in my nature, like a treasure in a field, is Humility.

It is the last thing left in me, and the best: the ultimate discovery at which I have arrived: the starting-point for a fresh development. It has come to me right out of myself, so I know that it has come at the proper time. It could not have come before, nor later. Had anyone told me of it, I would have rejected it. Had it been brought to me, I would have refused it. As I found it, I want to keep it. I must do so. It is the one thing that has in it the elements of life, of a new life, a *Vita Nuova*[1] for me. Of all things it is the strangest. One cannot give it away, and another may not give it to one. One cannot acquire it, except by surrendering everything that one has. It is only when one has lost all things, that one knows that one possesses it.

Now that I realise that it is in me, I see quite clearly what I have got to do, what, in fact, I must do. And when I use such a phrase as that, I need not tell you that I am not alluding to any external sanction or command. I admit none. I am far more of an individualist than I ever was. Nothing seems to me of the smallest value except what one gets out of oneself. My nature is seeking a fresh mode of self-realisation. That is all I am concerned with. And the first thing that I have got to do is to free myself from any possible bitterness of feeling against you.

I am completely penniless, and absolutely homeless. Yet there are worse things in the world than that. I am quite candid when I tell you that rather than go out from this prison with bitterness in my heart against you or against the world I would gladly and readily beg my bread from door to door. If I got nothing at the house of the rich, I would get something at the house of the poor. Those who have much are often greedy. Those who have little always share. I would not a bit mind sleeping in the cool grass in summer, and when winter came on sheltering myself by the warm close-thatched rick, or under the penthouse of a great barn, provided I had love in my heart. The external things of life seem to me now of no importance at all. You can see to what intensity of individualism I have arrived, or am arriving rather, for the journey is long, and "where I walk there are thorns."[2]

Of course I know that to ask for alms on the highway is not to be my lot, and that if ever I lie in the cool grass at night-time it will be to write sonnets to the Moon. When I go out of prison, Robbie will be waiting for me on the other side of the big iron-studded gate, and he is the symbol not merely of his own affection, but of the affection of many others besides. I believe I am to have enough to live on for about eighteen months at any rate, so that, if I may not write beautiful books, I may at least read beautiful books, and what joy can be greater? After that, I hope to be able to recreate my creative faculty. But were things different: had I not a friend left in the world: were there not a single house open to me even in pity: had I to accept the wallet and ragged cloak of sheer penury: still as long as I remained free from all resentment, hardness, and scorn, I would be able to face life with much more calm and confidence than I would were my body in purple and fine linen, and the soul within it sick with hate. And I shall really have no difficulty in forgiving you. But to make it a pleasure for me you must feel that you want it. When you really want it you will find it waiting for you.

1. New life (Italian); Dante's book of this name was one of the few books Wilde was able to have sent to him in prison.
2. From Wilde's play, *A Woman of No Importance* (act 4).

I need not say that my task does not end there. It would be comparatively easy if it did. There is much more before me. I have hills far steeper to climb, valleys much darker to pass through. And I have to get it all out of myself. Neither Religion, Morality, nor Reason can help me at all.

Morality does not help me. I am a born antinomian.[3] I am one of those who are made for exceptions, not for laws. But while I see that there is nothing wrong in what one does, I see that there is something wrong in what one becomes. It is well to have learned that.

Religion does not help me. The faith that others give to what is unseen, I give to what one can touch, and look at. My Gods dwell in temples made with hands, and within the circle of actual experience is my creed made perfect and complete: too complete it may be, for like many or all of those who have placed their Heaven in this earth, I have found in it not merely the beauty of Heaven, but the horror of Hell also. When I think about Religion at all, I feel as if I would like to found an order for those who cannot believe: the Confraternity of the Fatherless one might call it, where on an altar, on which no taper burned, a priest, in whose heart peace had no dwelling, might celebrate with unblessed bread and a chalice empty of wine. Everything to be true must become a religion. And agnosticism should have its ritual no less than faith. It has sown its martyrs, it should reap its saints, and praise God daily for having hidden Himself from man. But whether it be faith or agnosticism, it must be nothing external to me. Its symbols must be of my own creating. Only that is spiritual which makes its own form. If I may not find its secret within myself, I shall never find it. If I have not got it already, it will never come to me.

Reason does not help me. It tells me that the laws under which I am convicted are wrong and unjust laws, and the system under which I have suffered a wrong and unjust system. But, somehow, I have got to make both of these things just and right to me. And exactly as in Art one is only concerned with what a particular thing is at a particular moment to oneself, so it is also in the ethical evolution of one's character. I have got to make everything that has happened to me good for me. The plank-bed, the loathsome food, the hard ropes shredded into oakum[4] till one's fingertips grow dull with pain, the menial offices with which each day begins and finishes, the harsh orders that routine seems to necessitate, the dreadful dress that makes sorrow grotesque to look at, the silence, the solitude, the shame—each and all of these things I have to transform into a spiritual experience. There is not a single degradation of the body which I must not try and make into a spiritualising of the soul.

I want to get to the point when I shall be able to say, quite simply and without affectation, that the two great turning-points of my life were when my father sent me to Oxford, and when society sent me to prison. I will not say that it is the best thing that could have happened to me, for that phrase would savour of too great bitterness towards myself. I would sooner say, or hear it said of me, that I was so typical a child of my age that in my perversity, and for that perversity's sake, I turned the good things of my life to evil, and the evil things of my life to good. What is said, however, by myself or by others matters little. The important thing, the thing that lies before me, the thing that I have to do, or be for the brief remainder of my days one maimed, marred, and incomplete, is to absorb into my nature all that has been done to me, to

---

3. A person who rejects conventional morality.
4. Prisoners were often forced to pick oakum—i.e., to

shred used ropes into fibers.

make it part of me, to accept it without complaint, fear, or reluctance. The supreme vice is shallowness. Whatever is realised is right.

When first I was put into prison some people advised me to try and forget who I was. It was ruinous advice. It is only by realising what I am that I have found comfort of any kind. Now I am advised by others to try on my release to forget that I have ever been in a prison at all. I know that would be equally fatal. It would mean that I would be always haunted by an intolerable sense of disgrace, and that those things that are meant as much for me as for anyone else—the beauty of the sun and the moon, the pageant of the seasons, the music of daybreak and the silence of great nights, the rain falling through the leaves, or the dew creeping over the grass and making it silver—would all be tainted for me, and lose their healing power and their power of communicating joy. To reject one's own experiences is to arrest one's own development. To deny one's own experiences is to put a lie into the lips of one's own life. It is no less than a denial of the Soul.

<hr />

COMPANION READING
H. Montgomery Hyde: from *The Trials of Oscar Wilde*[1]

[THE FIRST TRIAL]

Queensberry's leading counsel[2] rose from his place in the front row of barristers' seats in the Old Bailey courtroom to begin his cross-examination of the prosecutor. As he faced his old college classmate in the witness box, the two figures on whom every eye in court was now fixed presented a striking contrast. There was Wilde, dressed in the height of fashion, a flower in the buttonhole of his frock coat, and exuding an air of easy confidence; opposite him stood Carson, tall, saturnine, and with the most determined expression on his lantern-jawed countenance. * * *

The opening question immediately revealed the cross-examiner's skill. * * *

"You stated that your age was thirty-nine. I think you are over forty. You were born on the 16th of October 1854?" Carson emphasized the point by holding up a copy of the witness's birth certificate.

Wilde appeared momentarily disconcerted, but he quickly recovered his composure. "I have no wish to pose as being young," he replied sweetly. "You have my certificate and that settles the matter."

"But," Carson persisted, "being born in 1854 makes you more than forty?"

"Ah! Very well," Wilde agreed with a sigh, as if to congratulate his opponent on a remarkable feat of mathematics.

It was a small point that Carson had scored in this duel of wits, but not without considerable importance. At the very outset Wilde had been detected in a stupid lie,

<hr />

1. After Lord Alfred Douglas's father, the Marquess of Queensberry, accused Wilde of sodomy, Wilde brought suit for libel. Wilde lost his case, and was in turn prosecuted, in two subsequent criminal trials, for committing indecent acts. He was found guilty and sentenced to two years in prison with hard labor. The three trials took place in 1895, in the Old Bailey in London, and were the focus of immense public curiosity; the sensational story was followed daily in almost every London newspaper.

The following excerpts are from H. Montgomery Hyde's *The Trials of Oscar Wilde* (1948); it should be noted that since no authoritative transcripts of the court proceedings exist, his book is a reconstruction of events based on contemporary press reports and personal reminiscences. 2. Edward Carson, a renowned barrister, had been a classmate of Wilde's at Trinity College, Dublin. He successfully defended Queensberry against Wilde's charge of libel in the first trial.

the effect of which was not lost upon the jury, particularly when Carson followed it up by contrasting Wilde's true age with that of Lord Alfred Douglas,[3] with whom Wilde admitted to having stayed at many places, including hotels, both in England and on the Continent. Furthermore, it appeared that Douglas had also contributed to *The Chameleon*,[4] namely two poems. Wilde was asked about these poems, which he admitted that he had seen. "I thought them exceedingly beautiful poems," he added. "One was 'In Praise of Shame' and the other 'Two Loves.'"[5]

"These loves," Carson asked, with a note of distaste in his voice. "They were two boys?"

"Yes."

"One boy calls his love 'true love,' and the other boy calls his love 'shame'?"

"Yes."

"Did you think they made any improper suggestion?"

"No, none whatever."

Carson passed on to "The Priest and the Acolyte," which Wilde admitted that he had read.

"You have no doubt whatever that that was an improper story?"

"From the literary point of view it was highly improper. It is impossible for a man of literature to judge it otherwise; by literature, meaning treatment, selection of subject, and the like. I thought the treatment rotten and the subject rotten."

"You are of opinion, I believe, that there is no such thing as an immoral book?"

"Yes."

"May I take it that you think 'The Priest and the Acolyte' was not immoral?"

"It was worse. It was badly written."[6]

"Was not the story that of a priest who fell in love with a boy who served him at the altar, and was discovered by the rector in the priest's room, and a scandal arose?"

"I have read it only once, last November, and nothing will induce me to read it again. I don't care for it. It doesn't interest me."

"Do you think the story blasphemous?"

"I think it violated every artistic canon of beauty."

"That is not an answer."

"It is the only one I can give."

"I want to see the position you pose in."

"I do not think you should say that."

"I have said nothing out of the way. I wish to know whether you thought the story blasphemous."

"The story filled me with disgust. The end was wrong."

"Answer the question, sir," Carson rapped out sharply. "Did you or did you not consider the story blasphemous?"

"I thought it disgusting."

Professing himself satisfied with this reply, Carson turned to a particular incident in the story. "You know that when the priest in the story administers poison to the boy, he uses the words of the sacrament of the Church of England?"

---

3. Douglas was 24 years old; Wilde was 40.
4. Edited by Jack Bloxam, an Oxford undergraduate, *The Chameleon* was a literary magazine with a homoerotic tone; it appeared only once, in 1894. Bloxam was the author of *The Priest and the Acolyte*. At Douglas's request, Wilde had submitted some of his aphorisms to the maga-

zine, and his legal opponents sought to make Wilde appear guilty by association with the allegedly immoral contributions of Douglas and Bloxam.
5. These poems appear on page 2086.
6. Wilde is paraphrasing his preface to *The Picture of Dorian Gray* (see page 2002).

"That I entirely forgot."

"Do you consider that blasphemous?"

"I think it is horrible. 'Blasphemous' is not a word of mine." When Carson put the passage in question to him and asked whether he approved of the words used by the author, Wilde repeated his previous opinion: "I think them disgusting, perfect twaddle."

"I think you will admit that anyone who would approve of such a story would pose as guilty of improper practices?"

"I do not think so in the person of another contributor to the magazine. It would show very bad literary taste. Anyhow I strongly objected to the whole story. * * * Of course, I am aware that *The Chameleon* may have circulated among the undergraduates of Oxford. But I do not believe that any book or work of art ever had any effect whatever on morality."

"Am I right in saying that you do not consider the effect in creating morality or immorality?"

"Certainly, I do not."

"So far as your works are concerned, you pose as not being concerned about morality or immorality?"

"I do not know whether you use the word 'pose' in any particular sense."

"Is it a favourite word of your own?"

"Is it? I have no pose in this matter. In writing a play or a book, I am concerned entirely with literature—that is, with art. I aim not at doing good or evil, but in trying to make a thing that will have some quality of beauty." * * *

Carson now turned to *The Picture of Dorian Gray*[7] * * *

"'There is no such thing as a moral or an immoral book. Books are well written or badly written.' That expresses your view?"

"My view on art, yes."

"Then I take it, no matter how immoral a book may be, if it is well written, it is, in your opinion, a good book?"

"Yes, if it were well written so as to produce a sense of beauty, which is the highest sense of which a human being can be capable. If it were badly written, it would produce a sense of disgust."

"Then a well-written book putting forward perverted moral views may be a good book?"

"No work of art ever puts forward views. Views belong to people who are not artists."

"A perverted novel might be a good book?" Carson persisted.

"I don't know what you mean by a 'perverted' novel," Wilde answered crisply.

This gave Carson the opening he sought. "Then I will suggest *Dorian Gray* is open to the interpretation of being such a novel?"

Wilde brushed aside the suggestion with contempt. "That could only be to brutes and illiterates," he said. "The views of Philistines on art are unaccountable."

"An illiterate person reading *Dorian Gray* might consider it such a novel?"

"The views of illiterates on art are unaccountable. I am concerned only with my own view of art. I don't care twopence what other people think of it."

---

7. Wilde's novel describes the passion felt by an artist, Basil Hallward, for a beautiful young man, Dorian Gray, whose portrait he paints.

"The majority of persons come under your definition of Philistines and illiterates?"

"I have found wonderful exceptions."

"Do you think that the majority of people live up to the position you are giving us?"

"I am afraid they are not cultivated enough."

"Not cultivated enough to draw the distinction between a good book and a bad book?" The note of sarcasm in Carson's voice was unmistakable.

"Certainly not," Wilde replied blandly.

"The affection and love of the artist of *Dorian Gray* might lead an ordinary individual to believe that it might have a certain tendency?"

"I have no knowledge of the views of ordinary individuals."

"You did not prevent the ordinary individual from buying your book?"

"I have never discouraged him!" * * *

Having covered Wilde's published writings, Carson passed on to the allegedly compromising letters Wilde had written to Lord Alfred Douglas. * * *

"Why should a man of your age address a boy nearly twenty years younger as 'My own Boy'?"[8]

"I was fond of him. I have always been fond of him."

"Do you adore him?"

"No, but I have always liked him." Wilde then went on to elaborate upon the letter. "I think it is a beautiful letter. It is a poem. I was not writing an ordinary letter. You might as well cross-examine me as to whether *King Lear* or a sonnet of Shakespeare was proper."

"Apart from art, Mr Wilde?"

"I cannot answer apart from art."

"Suppose a man who was not an artist had written this letter, would you say it was a proper letter?"

"A man who was not an artist could not have written that letter."

"Why?"

"Because nobody but an artist could write it. He certainly could not write the language unless he were a man of letters."

"I can suggest, for the sake of your reputation, that there is nothing very wonderful in this 'red rose-leaf lips of yours'?"

"A great deal depends on the way it is read."

"'Your slim gilt soul walks between passion and poetry,'" Carson continued. "Is that a beautiful phrase?"

"Not as you read it, Mr Carson. You read it very badly."

It was now Carson's turn to be nettled. "I do not profess to be an artist," he exclaimed, "and when I hear you give evidence, I am glad I am not."

These words immediately brought Sir Edward Clarke[9] to his feet. "I don't think my learned friend should talk like that," he observed. Then, turning towards his client in the witness box, he added: "Pray do not criticize my learned friend's reading again."

This clash caused a buzz of excitement in the courtroom. When it had died down, Carson went on with his cross-examination, indicating the document he was holding in his hand. "Is not that an exceptional letter?"

"It is unique, I should say." Wilde's answer produced loud laughter in court, which was still largely on the side of the witness.

8. For the text of this letter, a response to Douglas's poem *In Praise of Shame*, see page 2048, n. 3.   9. Clarke was Wilde's attorney in all three trials.

"Was that the ordinary way in which you carried on your correspondence?"

"No. But I have often written to Lord Alfred Douglas, though I never wrote to another young man in the same way."

"Have you often written letters in the same style as this?"

"I don't repeat myself in style."

Carson held out another sheet of paper. "Here is another letter which I believe you also wrote to Lord Alfred Douglas. Will you read it?"

Wilde refused this invitation. "I don't see why I should," he said.

"Then I will," retorted Carson.

> Savoy Hotel
> Victoria Embankment
> London
>
> Dearest of all Boys,
>
> Your letter was delightful, red and yellow wine to me; but I am sad and out of sorts. Bosie, you must not make scenes with me. They kill me, they wreck the loveliness of life. I cannot see you, so Greek and gracious, distorted with passion. I cannot listen to your curved lips saying hideous things to me. I would sooner—than have you bitter unjust, hating. . . .
>
> I must see you soon. You are the divine thing I want, the thing of grace and beauty; but I don't know how to do it. Shall I come to Salisbury? My bill here is £49 for a week. I have also got a new sitting-room. . . .
>
> Why are you not here, my dear, my wonderful boy? I fear I must leave—no money, no credit, and a heart of lead.
>
> Your own
> OSCAR

"Is that an ordinary letter?" Carson asked, when he had finished reading it.

"Everything I wrote is extraordinary," Wilde answered with a show of impatience. "I do not pose as being ordinary, great heavens! Ask me any question you like about it."

Carson had only one question to ask about this letter, but its effect was deadly. "Is it the kind of letter a man writes to another?"

[THE SECOND TRIAL]

"During 1893 and 1894 you were a great deal in the company of Lord Alfred Douglas?"

"Oh, yes."

"Did he read that poem to you?"[1]

"Yes."

"You can perhaps understand that such verses as these would not be acceptable to the reader with an ordinary balanced mind?"

"I am not prepared to say," Wilde answered. "It appears to me to be a question of taste, temperament, and individuality. I should say that one man's poetry is another man's poison!"

"I daresay!" commented Gill[2] dryly, when the laughter had subsided. "The next poem is one described as 'Two Loves.' * * * Was that poem explained to you?"

"I think that is clear."

---

1. Douglas's sonnet *In Praise of Shame* appears on page 2086.

2. Charles Gill was counsel for the prosecution during the second and third trial.

"There is no question as to what it means?"

"Most certainly not."

"Is it not clear that the love described relates to natural love and unnatural love?"

"No."

"What is the 'Love that dare not speak its name'?"[3] Gill now asked.

"'The love that dare not speak its name' in this century is such a great affection of an elder for a younger man as there was between David and Jonathan, such as Plato made the very basis of his philosophy, and such as you find in the sonnets of Michelangelo and Shakespeare.[4] It is that deep, spiritual affection that is as pure as it is perfect. It dictates and pervades great works of art like those of Shakespeare and Michelangelo, and those two letters of mine, such as they are. It is in this century misunderstood, so much misunderstood that it may be described as the 'Love that dare not speak its name,' and on account of it I am placed where I am now. It is beautiful, it is fine, it is the noblest form of affection. There is nothing unnatural about it. It is intellectual, and it repeatedly exists between an elder and a younger man, when the elder has intellect, and the younger man has all the joy, hope, and glamour of life before him. That it should be so, the world does not understand. The world mocks at it and sometimes puts one in the pillory for it."

Wilde's words produced a spontaneous outburst of applause from the public gallery, mingled with some hisses, which moved the judge to say he would have the Court cleared if there were any further manifestation of feeling.

∽∾∽

---

3. Cf. *Two Loves*, line 74, page 2088.
4. King David of Israel, and Jonathan, the son of King Saul, were inseparable friends. On Jonathan's death, David declared that "your love to me was wonderful, passing the love of women" (2 Samuel 1.26). Plato argued that the passion of an older man for a younger one could be translated into a contemplation of the ideal and the universal. Both Shakespeare and Michelangelo wrote sonnets that can be read as describing platonic and/or erotic love between men.

⇒ PERSPECTIVES ⇐

Aestheticism, Decadence, and the *Fin de Siècle*

"I belong to the Beardsley period," Max Beerbohm remarked audaciously in 1894, when he and Aubrey Beardsley were both just twenty-two. Time has proved him correct. The late-Victorian period, the age of Beardsley and Wilde, Kipling and Conan Doyle, has indeed come to be seen as a distinctive era in which the aesthetic and moral values of the nineteenth century were twisted or transmuted into the revolutionary forces of modernism, in a blaze of daring new styles, attitudes, and modes of behavior.

By the early 1880s most of the major mid-Victorian writers had died or were well past their prime. As the Empire reached its peak, Britain's self-confidence eroded under the strain of maintaining its military might and economic supremacy against competition from the United States and Germany. About 1890, the general sense of fatigue and anxiety found expression in the French phrase *fin de siècle*—the "end of the age." The term suggested that Victorian values and energies had become exhausted and that an unsettling, amoral, post-Darwinian world was emerging in which contradictory impulses vied for attention: exquisite delicacy in poetry and brutal realism in fiction, effete dandyism among some men and hearty imperialism among others, socialism and Catholicism. The proliferation of women in the workforce ran headlong into the diagnosis of inherent female debility by medical authorities. Meanwhile, discussion clubs formed where both sexes openly debated the merits of marriage and free love. It was the era of the Manly Woman and the Womanly Man, the moment when sexology was invented and words like "homosexual," "lesbian," and—belatedly—"heterosexual" were coined to regulate the mysteries of sexual identity.

Partly in flight from the devastated industrial landscape, partly in rebellion against middle-class mores and artistic norms, Aesthetes like Pater, Wilde, Whistler, Beardsley, and Symons sought to create a pure art of flawless formal design, divorced from moral concerns but open to hitherto unexplored subject matter—the often artificial beauties of cosmetics, music halls, gaslit faces, or city streets seen through mist and rain. By the 1870s, critics were giving the labels "impressionist" and "aesthetic" to paintings by Whistler and Dante Gabriel Rossetti, and to poems by Rossetti, Swinburne, and Morris. With the help of flamboyant personalities such as Whistler and Wilde, Aestheticism became known in the 1880s as an entire way of life, involving flowing dress for both men and women, medieval- or Japanese-style home furnishings, and ostentatious worship of the beautiful in all the arts. There was even a distinctive Aesthetic vocabulary: "Constantly yearning for the intense," said one observer, "the language of the Aesthetes is tinged with somewhat exaggerated metaphor, and their adjectives are usually superlative—as supreme, consummate, utter, quite too preciously sublime."

Though its excesses were easy to mock, Aestheticism took hold so forcefully because its various strands had been developing, abroad and at home, for several generations. In 1873 Tennyson complained with some reason that Aesthetes lived on "poisonous honey stolen from France." Swinburne was clearly influenced by the French poets Théophile Gautier and Charles Baudelaire when he declared in 1866: "Art for art's sake first of all," explaining that "her business is not to do good on other grounds, but to be good on her own." Yet Tennyson himself was a pivotal figure for the Aesthetes and their immediate predecessors, the Pre-Raphaelites; both groups were inspired by his medievalism and sonorous morbidity.

Aestheticism often shaded over into Decadence, a term that was confusingly applied not only to the deliberately mannered works of the late Victorians, but also to the scandalous or effeminate conduct of their creators. By the 1890s the word had become a vague and fashionable label of both moral censure and avant-garde respect. The naturalist fiction of George Gissing and Émile Zola was called decadent because of its tawdry subject matter and amoral attitudes; Wilde on the other hand claimed that decadent pleasures alone made life worth living. Depending on one's point of view, "decadent" could describe, with praise or blame, a dissipated

Aubrey Beardsley, "*J'ai baisé ta bouche, Iokanaan.*" Illustration for Oscar Wilde's *Salomé*, 1893. Wilde wrote his play *Salomé* in French, but its production on the English stage (starring Sarah Bernhardt) was banned because of its depiction of biblical characters. Beardsley's outrageous illustrations for the English translation (1894) instantly made the book a decadent *cause célèbre* and a classic of Art Nouveau design. Beardsley depicts the play's climatic scene, in which Salomé, who has demanded John the Baptist's head as a reward for her dancing, kisses the dead lips of the prophet who had scorned her love.

THE SIX-MARK TEA-POT.

Æsthetic Bridegroom. "IT IS QUITE CONSUMMATE, IS IT NOT?"
Intense Bride. "IT IS, INDEED! OH, ALGERNON, LET US LIVE UP TO IT!"

George Du Maurier, *The Six-Mark Tea-Pot*, from *Punch* magazine, 1880. Born in Paris, Du Maurier shuttled between London and Paris, and studies in art and science, until he settled on a career as a magazine illustrator, joining the staff of *Punch* in 1864. His wittily captioned cartoons of Aesthetes fixed the movement in the public imagination. Having established his reputation as a keen satirist of cultural trends, he achieved international fame with his novel *Trilby* (1894), which was based on his days with Whistler as an art student in Paris.

young man like Wilde's Dorian Gray, or a vigorous freethinking feminist like the heroine of Grant Allen's *The Woman Who Did* (1895). In most cases the word suggested an ultra-refined sophistication of taste allied with moral perversity; and many feared that decadent ideas and behavior heralded social collapse and apocalyptic change for Western culture. Max Nordau's 1895 best-seller *Degeneration* portrayed decadence as evidence of "a twilight mood" in Europe; "degeneration and hysteria," he felt, were "the convulsions and spasms of exhaustion" in Western civilization. Delighting in this anxiety, Wilde told Yeats that Pater's *Renaissance* "is the very flower of decadence; the last trumpet should have sounded the moment it was written."

Together, the *fin de siècle* writers helped free English literature of moral inhibition, producing a richly descriptive poetry and prose marked by deep learning, love of London, bold sensuality, spiritual intensity, and a new focus on images rather than events. The concept of Decadence depended on a Christian mentality haunted by notions of sin, forgiveness, and damnation. Dissatisfied with life and art, and tempted by drugs and drinking, opium and absinthe, some writers met early deaths from dissipation or suicide. The quest for absolution led many, including Beardsley and Wilde, to convert to Catholicism.

While they strove for a refined art purified of morality and narrative content, Aesthetes and Decadents made it clear that art had a definitely sexual if often elusive essence. Though "consummate" was a favorite word, much of their work expressed a frustrated longing for a fleeting taste of forbidden fruits. Often both male and female writers envisioned women as dangerous idols, worshipped at first as chaste images of noble art but finally revealed as seductive vampires who sap masculine energy with insatiable desire.

As the critic Elaine Showalter points out, "The decadent or aesthete was the masculine counterpart to the New Woman" lauded by feminist fiction writers of the 1890s. More prevalent in art than life, these two literary figures spurred fears of a sexual revolution and cast doubt on Britain's ability to procreate future generations of Empire rulers. The anxiety over the blurring of gender boundaries helps explain the strange conflux of misogynist, homoerotic, androgynous, utopianly healthy, and luridly diseased discourses of sexuality that surfaced at this time—culminating in Bram Stoker's *Dracula* (1897), which portrayed the New Woman as an insatiable sexual vampire poised to destroy British manhood. Even a radical advocate of socialist free love, Karl Marx's daughter Eleanor, denounced "the effeminate man and the masculine woman" as horrifyingly unnatural. With slight exaggeration, Max Beerbohm alluded to "that amalgamation of the sexes which is one of the chief planks in the decadent platform."

The heyday of Aestheticism and Decadence came to an end with the trials of Oscar Wilde. When Wilde was arrested for sodomy in 1895, newspapers reported that he carried the notorious decadent magazine, *The Yellow Book,* with him to jail (it was actually a yellow-backed French novel). Mobs stoned the publisher's office; Beardsley, its editor, was fired; the magazine failed. A savage conservative backlash suddenly ended the vogue of the bold New Woman and the languid Aesthete. But it was in the "degenerate" turmoil of the *fin de siècle* that modernism got its start: James, Gissing, Dowson, Yeats, Bennett, Wells, Shaw, Ford, and Conrad all published in *The Yellow Book* or its short-lived successor, *The Savoy.* Though the Aesthetic creed seemed like an underground current to many during the Victorian period, by the turn of the century belief in the autonomy of the artist was on the brink of becoming modernism's main stream.

W. S. Gilbert
1836–1911

William Schwenk Gilbert is best known for his lengthy partnership with the composer Arthur Sullivan. Together they wrote fourteen light operas from 1871 to 1896, immensely popular entertainments that continue to be performed throughout the world today. Known as the "Savoy Operas" because they debuted at the Savoy Theatre built by Richard D'Oyly Carte expressly for their production, Gilbert and Sullivan's works include *H.M.S. Pinafore* (1878), *The Pirates of Penzance* (1879), and *The Mikado* (1885). Typically, these comic operettas poke gentle fun at British institutions such as the law, Parliament, and the navy, while also mocking Victorian obsessions with topics such as social hierarchy or orphanhood. Although Gilbert's satirical librettos perfectly complement Sullivan's sprightly scores, they can be read on their own as nimble evocations of Victorian foibles and follies. *Patience* spoofed Aestheticism just as it reached the public consciousness in the early 1880s; in the process the opera helped to articulate and spread the ideas it mocked. A composite caricature of Whistler and Wilde, the "ultra-poetical, super-aesthetical" Bunthorne is made to confess that his exquisite refinement is just a pose meant to attract the ladies.

If You're Anxious for to Shine in the High Aesthetic Line

Am I alone,
And unobserved? I am!
Then let me own
I'm an aesthetic sham!
5   This air severe
Is but a mere
Veneer!
This cynic smile
Is but a wile
10   Of guile!
This costume chaste
Is but good taste
Misplaced!
Let me confess!
15   A languid love for lilies does *not* blight me!
Lank limbs and haggard cheeks do *not* delight me!
I do *not* care for dirty greens
By any means.
I do *not* long for all one sees
20   That's Japanese.
I am *not* fond of uttering platitudes
In stained-glass attitudes.
In short, my mediaevalism's affectation,
Born of a morbid love of admiration!¹

Song

25   If you're anxious for to shine in the high aesthetic line as a man of culture rare,
You must get up all the germs of the transcendental terms,² and plant them everywhere.
You must lie upon the daisies and discourse in novel phrases of your complicated state of mind,
The meaning doesn't matter if it's only idle chatter of a transcendental kind.
And every one will say,
30   As you walk your mystic way,
"If this young man expresses himself in terms too deep for *me*,
Why, what a very singularly deep young man this deep young man must be!"

1. Stereotypical Aesthetic behavior, combining traits of Rossetti, Whistler, and Wilde, particularly as they were spoofed by the cartoonist George Du Maurier. Lilies and languid yet soul-tormented lovers figure in the work of Rossetti, as do medieval subjects and stained glass; Whistler's paintings featuring Japanese props and perspective helped create a vogue for Japanese art, dress, and decoration; Wilde's elaborate clothing and ostentatious worship of beauty were said to be merely attention-getting poses.
2. Transcendental philosophy values individual visionary understanding over objective, materialist apprehension of the world. *The Germ* (1850) was a short-lived Pre-Raphaelite journal that sought to promote a more spiritual art and poetry in Britain.

Be eloquent in praise of the very dull old days which have long since
    passed away,
And convince 'em, if you can, that the reign of good Queen Anne[3] was
    Culture's palmiest day.

35   Of course you will pooh-pooh whatever's fresh and new, and declare it's
    crude and mean,
For Art stopped short in the cultivated court of the Empress Josephine.[4]
        And every one will say,
        As you walk your mystic way,
"If that's not good enough for him which is good enough for *me*,
40   Why, what a very cultivated kind of youth this kind of youth must be!"

Then a sentimental passion of a vegetable fashion must excite your languid
    spleen,[5]
An attachment *à la* Plato for a bashful young potato, or a not-too-French
    French bean!
Though the Philistines may jostle, you will rank as an apostle in the high
    aesthetic band,
If you walk down Piccadilly[6] with a poppy or a lily in your mediaeval hand.
45   And every one will say,
        As you walk your flowery way,
"If he's content with a vegetable love which would certainly not suit *me*,
Why, what a most particularly pure young man this pure young man must be!"
                           1881

James Abbott McNeill Whistler
1834–1903

An American artist who settled in London in the early 1860s, Whistler provided much of the intellectual energy that inspired the Aesthetic Movement in the 1880s. He studied art in Paris, where he became friends with Gustav Courbet and Henri Fantin-Latour, absorbed the aesthetic doctrine of Théophile Gautier and Charles Baudelaire, and later came to know and influence Claude Monet and the poet Stéphane Mallarmé. Although Whistler never fully abandoned a representational style, he insisted that viewers accept a painting as an arrangement of lines and colors on a flat canvas. "I care nothing for the past, present, or future of the black figure," he said about a shadowy human outline in one of his paintings; "it was placed there because black was wanted at that spot."

    Whistler's *Nocturne in Black and Gold: The Falling Rocket* (1875) (see Color Plate 18) earned the ire of Ruskin, who declared that he was an impudent coxcomb who was "flinging a pot of paint in the public's face." Whistler sued Ruskin for libel, and the ensuing trial of 1878 marked a turning point in English art and taste. Whistler won, and the Ruskinian notion of art

3. Queen of Great Britain from 1702–1714; the simplicity of the era's neoclassical architecture and design found favor with Aesthetes tired of Victorian ornateness.
4. Wife of Napoleon Bonaparte and empress of France 1804–1809.
5. I. e., shake you out of your melancholy. The Aesthetes

supposedly cherished an idealized, platonic love of such flowering "vegetable" entities as poppies and lilies; here Gilbert applies the concept literally.
6. A fashionable thoroughfare in London. Wilde, whose passion for lilies was well known, is said to have done this.

as a social and moral force yielded ground to Whistler's concept of art as an expression of the artist's subjective vision, something beyond common comprehension.

Whistler delivered the following lecture in London on February 20, 1885, to an invitation-only audience that included journalists, artists, writers, and society figures. He chose to deliver his "Ten O'Clock" lecture at 10 P.M. so that his fashionable audience would not have to rush dinner. It is the era's clearest manifesto of art for art's sake, setting the artist above and beyond his moment in history. The lecture and its fastidious presentation brought to a larger audience the essentials of Whistler's artistic platform: the attention-getting declaration of artistic independence, the sarcastic dismissals of other theories, and the aggressively elitist public posture that made him "The Master" for other Aesthetes. Mallarmé translated the essay into French in 1888; Whistler himself published it in English in 1890, in *The Gentle Art of Making Enemies*. Struck by one of Whistler's witticisms, Oscar Wilde once confessed that he wished *he* had uttered it himself. Whistler replied dryly, "You will, Oscar, you will."

from Mr. Whistler's "Ten O'Clock"

LADIES AND GENTLEMEN:

* * * Art is upon the Town!—to be chucked under the chin by the passing gallant—to be enticed within the gates of the householder—to be coaxed into company, as a proof of culture and refinement.

If familiarity can breed contempt, certainly Art—or what is currently taken for it—has been brought to its lowest stage of intimacy.

The people have been harassed with Art in every guise, and vexed with many methods as to its endurance. They have been told how they shall love Art, and live with it. Their homes have been invaded, their walls covered with paper, their very dress taken to task—until, roused at last, bewildered and filled with the doubts and discomforts of senseless suggestion, they resent such intrusion, and cast forth the false prophets, who have brought the very name of the beautiful into disrepute, and derision upon themselves.

Alas! ladies and gentlemen, Art has been maligned. She has naught in common with such practices. She is a goddess of dainty thought—reticent of habit, abjuring all obtrusiveness, purposing in no way to better others.

She is, withal, selfishly occupied with her own perfection only—having no desire to teach—seeking and finding the beautiful in all conditions and in all times, as did her high priest Rembrandt, when he saw picturesque grandeur and noble dignity in the Jews' quarter of Amsterdam, and lamented not that its inhabitants were not Greeks.[1]

As did Tintoret and Paul Veronese,[2] among the Venetians, while not halting to change the brocaded silks for the classic draperies of Athens.

As did, at the Court of Philip, Velasquez, whose Infantas, clad in inaesthetic hoops, are, as works of Art, of the same quality as the Elgin marbles.[3]

No reformers were these great men—no improvers of the way of others! Their productions alone were their occupation, and, filled with the poetry of their science,

---

1. Rembrandt (1606–1669) was an important influence on Whistler. The Dutch artist painted many contemporary subjects and even used the costume of his day when portraying classical subjects, as in *Aristotle Contemplating the Bust of Homer*.

2. Tintoretto and Paolo Veronese, Italian Renaissance painters.

3. Diego Rodrigo de Silva y Velasquez (1599–1660), painter at the court of Philip IV of Spain. The Infantas were daughters of the monarch; in their hooped skirts they seemed no less artistic to Whistler than classical Greek statuary.

they required not to alter their surroundings—for, as the laws of their Art were revealed to them they saw, in the development of their work, that real beauty which, to them, was as much a matter of certainty and triumph as is to the astronomer the verification of the result, foreseen with the light given to him alone. In all this, their world was completely severed from that of their fellow-creatures with whom sentiment is mistaken for poetry; and for whom there is no perfect work that shall not be explained by the benefit conferred upon themselves.

Humanity takes the place of Art, and God's creations are excused by their usefulness. Beauty is confounded with virtue, and, before a work of Art, it is asked: "What good shall it do?"

Hence it is that nobility of action, in this life, is hopelessly linked with the merit of the work that portrays it; and thus the people have acquired the habit of looking, as who should say, not *at* a picture, but *through* it, at some human fact, that shall, or shall not, from a social point of view, better their mental or moral state. So we have come to hear of the painting that elevates, and of the duty of the painter—of the picture that is full of thought, and of the panel that merely decorates.

A favourite faith, dear to those who teach, is that certain periods were especially artistic, and that nations, readily named, were notably lovers of Art.

So we are told that the Greeks were, as a people, worshippers of the beautiful, and that in the fifteenth century Art was engrained in the multitude.

That the great masters lived in common understanding with their patrons—that the early Italians were artists—all—and that the demand for the lovely thing produced it.

That we, of to-day, in gross contrast to this Arcadian[4] purity, call for the ungainly, and obtain the ugly. * * *

Listen! There never was an artistic period.

There never was an Art-loving nation.

In the beginning, man went forth each day—some to do battle, some to the chase; others, again, to dig and to delve in the field—all that they might gain and live, or lose and die. Until there was found among them one, differing from the rest, whose pursuits attracted him not, and so he stayed by the tents with the women, and traced strange devices with a burnt stick upon a gourd.

This man, who took no joy in the ways of his brethren—who cared not for conquest, and fretted in the field—this designer of quaint patterns—this deviser of the beautiful—who perceived in Nature about him curious curvings, as faces are seen in the fire—this dreamer apart, was the first artist.

And when, from the field and from afar, there came back the people, they took the gourd—and drank from out of it.

And presently there came to this man another—and, in time, others—of like nature, chosen by the Gods—and so they worked together; and soon they fashioned, from the moistened earth, forms resembling the gourd. And with the power of creation, the heirloom of the artist, presently they went beyond the slovenly suggestion of Nature, and the first vase was born, in beautiful proportion. * * *

And centuries passed in this using, and the world was flooded with all that was beautiful, until there arose a new class, who discovered the cheap, and foresaw fortune in the facture of the sham.

4. Simple, rustic.

Then sprang into existence the tawdry, the common, the gewgaw.

The taste of the tradesman supplanted the science of the artist, and what was born of the million went back to them, and charmed them, for it was after their own heart; and the great and the small, the statesman and the slave, took to themselves the abomination that was tendered, and preferred it—and have lived with it ever since!

And the artist's occupation was gone, and the manufacturer and the huckster took his place.

And now the heroes filled from the jugs and drank from the bowls—with understanding—noting the glare of their new bravery, and taking pride in its worth.

And the people—this time—had much to say in the matter—and all were satisfied. And Birmingham and Manchester[5] arose in their might—and Art was relegated to the curiosity shop.

Nature contains the elements, in colour and form, of all pictures, as the keyboard contains the notes of all music.

But the artist is born to pick, and choose, and group with science, these elements, that the result may be beautiful—as the musician gathers his notes, and forms his chords, until he bring forth from chaos glorious harmony.

To say to the painter, that Nature is to be taken as she is, is to say to the player, that he may sit on the piano.

That Nature is always right, is an assertion, artistically, as untrue, as it is one whose truth is universally taken for granted. Nature is very rarely right, to such an extent even, that it might almost be said that Nature is usually wrong: that is to say, the condition of things that shall bring about the perfection of harmony worthy a picture is rare, and not common at all.

This would seem, to even the most intelligent, a doctrine almost blasphemous. So incorporated with our education has the supposed aphorism become, that its belief is held to be part of our moral being, and the words themselves have, in our ear, the ring of religion. Still, seldom does Nature succeed in producing a picture.

The sun blares, the wind blows from the east, the sky is bereft of cloud, and without, all is of iron. The windows of the Crystal Palace[6] are seen from all points of London. The holiday-maker rejoices in the glorious day, and the painter turns aside to shut his eyes.

How little this is understood, and how dutifully the casual in Nature is accepted as sublime, may be gathered from the unlimited admiration daily produced by a very foolish sunset.

The dignity of the snow-capped mountain is lost in distinctness, but the joy of the tourist is to recognise the traveller on the top. The desire to see, for the sake of seeing, is, with the mass, alone the one to be gratified, hence the delight in detail.

And when the evening mist clothes the riverside with poetry, as with a veil, and the poor buildings lose themselves in the dim sky, and the tall chimneys become campanili,[7] and the warehouses are palaces in the night, and the whole city hangs in the heavens, and fairy-land is before us—then the wayfarer hastens home; the working man and the cultured one, the wise man and the one of pleasure, cease to understand, as they have ceased to see, and Nature, who, for once, has sung in tune, sings

---

5. Large manufacturing towns.
6. Built in Hyde Park, London, to house the Great Exhibition of 1851, the Crystal Palace was three times the size of St. Paul's Cathedral. Resembling a gigantic greenhouse, it was the world's first building of this size to be constructed of metal and glass, and was considered one of the wonders of the age. In 1855 it was re-erected in Sydenham, Southeast London.
7. Italian bell towers.

her exquisite song to the artist alone, her son and her master—her son in that he loves her, her master in that he knows her.

To him her secrets are unfolded, to him her lessons have become gradually clear. He looks at her flower, not with the enlarging lens, that he may gather facts for the botanist, but with the light of the one who sees in her choice selection of brilliant tones and delicate tints, suggestions of future harmonies.

He does not confine himself to purposeless copying, without thought, each blade of grass, as commended by the inconsequent, but, in the long curve of the narrow leaf, corrected by the straight tall stem, he learns how grace is wedded to dignity, how strength enhances sweetness, that elegance shall be the result. * * *

Why this lifting of the brow in deprecation of the present—this pathos in reference to the past?

If Art be rare to-day, it was seldom heretofore.

It is false, this teaching of decay.

The master stands in no relation to the moment at which he occurs—a monument of isolation—hinting at sadness—having no part in the progress of his fellow men.

He is also no more the product of civilisation than is the scientific truth asserted dependent upon the wisdom of a period. The assertion itself requires the *man* to make it. The truth was from the beginning.

So Art is limited to the infinite, and beginning there cannot progress. * * *

False again, the fabled link between the grandeur of Art and the glories and virtues of the State, for Art feeds not upon nations, and peoples may be wiped from the face of the earth, but Art *is*.

It is indeed high time that we cast aside the weary weight of responsibility and co-partnership, and know that, in no way, do our virtues minister to its worth, in no way do our vices impede its triumph!

How irksome! how hopeless! how superhuman the self-imposed task of the nation! How sublimely vain the belief that it shall live nobly or art perish.

Let us reassure ourselves, at our own option is our virtue. Art we in no way affect.

A whimsical goddess, and a capricious, her strong sense of joy tolerates no dulness, and, live we never so spotlessly, still may she turn her back upon us.

As, from time immemorial, she has done upon the Swiss in their mountains.

What more worthy people! Whose every Alpine gap yawns with tradition, and is stocked with noble story; yet, the perverse and scornful one will none of it, and the sons of patriots are left with the clock that turns the mill, and the sudden cuckoo, with difficulty restrained in its box!

For this was Tell a hero! For this did Gessler die![8]

Art, the cruel jade,[9] cares not, and hardens her heart, and hies her off to the East, to find, among the opium-eaters of Nankin,[1] a favourite with whom she lingers fondly—caressing his blue porcelain, and painting his coy maidens, and marking his plates with her six marks of choice—indifferent in her companionship with him, to all save the virtue of his refinement!

---

8. William Tell was a legendary 14th-century Swiss hero whose defiance of Gessler, an Austrian bailiff, led to his well-known punishment: shooting an apple off his son's head. In revenge, Tell killed Gessler and led a revolt to liberate his country from Austrian control.
9. Disreputable woman.
1. The Chinese city of Nanjing.

He it is who calls her—he who holds her!

And again to the West, that her next lover may bring together the Gallery at Madrid, and show to the world how the Master towers above all;[2] and in their intimacy they revel, he and she, in this knowledge; and he knows the happiness untasted by other mortal.

She is proud of her comrade, and promises that in after-years, others shall pass that way, and understand.

So in all time does this superb one cast about for the man worthy her love—and Art seeks the Artist alone. * * *

Therefore have we cause to be merry!—and to cast away all care—resolved that all is well—as it ever was—and that it is not meet that we should be cried at, and urged to take measures!

Enough have we endured of dulness! Surely are we weary of weeping, and our tears have been cozened from us falsely, for they have called out woe! when there was no grief—and, alas! where all is fair!

We have then but to wait—until, with the mark of the Gods upon him—there come among us again the chosen—who shall continue what has gone before. Satisfied that, even were he never to appear, the story of the beautiful is already complete—hewn in the marbles of the Parthenon—and broidered, with the birds, upon the fan of Hokusai—at the foot of Fusiyama.[3]

1885   1890

"Michael Field"

Katharine Bradley   and   Edith Cooper
1846–1914   1862–1913

"I have found a new poet," announced Robert Browning to a hushed dinner party in 1885. He had actually found two poets, both women. "Michael Field" was the pseudonym of Katharine Bradley and her niece Edith Cooper; they were hailed as "the double-headed nightingale" by admirers. Their long collaboration produced twenty-seven poetic dramas on historical themes, and eight volumes of lyric poetry. Their work was praised by Meredith, Swinburne, and Wilde; but the general public was unaware that in lauding "Mr. Field," they were speaking of an aunt who esteemed William Michael Rossetti (Dante and Christina's brother) and a niece nicknamed "Field." Bradley had helped rear Cooper, the child of her invalid sister. In 1878 they moved to Bristol, where they both attended University College, living together from then on in a close emotional and sexual relationship. Commenting on the fabled intimacy of Robert and Elizabeth Barrett Browning, Bradley noted in her diary *we are closer married.* Having independent means, they spent their time reading, writing, and visiting galleries; they dressed and decorated their rooms in Aesthetic style, and their journals record their acute impressions of the many artists and writers they met. In 1907 both converted to Catholicism, apparently

---

2. Philip II of Spain created the Prado Gallery in Madrid; its collection was substantially enlarged by Philip IV. The Prado contains many works by "the Master" Velasquez, whose art greatly influenced Whistler.

3. Katsushika Hokusai (1760–1849), Japanese artist; Fujiyama or Mount Fuji, the highest mountain in Japan and a frequent subject in Hokusai's works.

because of the death of their dog Whym Chow, a Dionysian presence who not only inspired a volume of love poems but also killed Kipling's pet rabbit during a visit.

"We have many things to say," they wrote to Browning, "that the world will not tolerate from a woman's lips. . . . We cannot be stifled in drawing-room conventionalities." Their first joint volume of poems, *Long Ago* (1889), dared to complete Sappho's fragments in modern lyrics that highlighted the lesbian nature of the Greek poems. In a poem they proclaimed they would remain "Poets and lovers evermore . . . Indifferent to heaven and hell." Despite the passionate paganism of their early career, they condemned what they saw as the depravity of Zola and Beardsley, and withdrew one of their poems from *The Yellow Book*. "From decadence, Good Lord deliver us!" they exclaimed in a diary entry in 1891. Their poetry is notable for its subtle music and technical improvisation, as well as their sympathetic rendering of the femme-fatale imagery common at the time. Exploring the nature of womanhood was both a personal mission and an artistic ideal: "We hold ourselves bound in life and in literature," Bradley wrote in her diary, "to reveal . . . the beauty of the high feminine standard of *the ought to be*."

La Gioconda[1]
Leonardo Da Vinci
THE LOUVRE

Historic, side-long, implicating eyes;
A smile of velvet's lustre on the cheek;
Calm lips the smile leads upward; hand that lies
Glowing and soft, the patience in its rest
5   Of cruelty that waits and doth not seek
For prey; a dusky forehead and a breast
Where twilight touches ripeness amorously:
Behind her, crystal rocks, a sea and skies
Of evanescent blue on cloud and creek;
10   Landscape that shines suppressive of its zest
For those vicissitudes by which men die.

1892

A Pen-Drawing of Leda[1]
Sodoma[2]
THE GRAND DUKE'S PALACE AT WEIMAR

'Tis Leda lovely, wild and free,
Drawing her gracious Swan down through the grass to see
   Certain round eggs without a speck:
One hand plunged in the reeds and one dinting the downy neck,
5   Although his hectoring bill
   Gapes toward her tresses,
She draws the fondled creature to her will.

1. Leonardo's painting (c. 1503), also known as the *Mona Lisa*, hangs in the Louvre in Paris. The authors would have known Pater's famous description of it in *The Renaissance*; see page 1781. This and the following poem appeared in their collection *Sight and Song* (1892), which sought "to translate into verse what the lines and colours of certain chosen pictures sing in themselves."

1. In Greek myth Zeus took the form of a swan to have sex with Leda, a mortal; she subsequently gave birth to Helen of Troy. Compare this view of Leda to Yeats's poem *Leda and the Swan*, page 2410.
2. Nickname of the Sienese artist Giovanni Antonio Bazzi (1477–1549).

She joys to bend in the live light
Her glistening body toward her love, how much more bright!
10   Though on her breast the sunshine lies
And spreads its affluence on the wide curves of her waist and thighs,
       To her meek, smitten gaze
       Where her hand presses
The Swan's white neck sink Heaven's concentred rays.

1892

"A Girl"

A girl,
    Her soul a deep-wave pearl
Dim, lucent of all lovely mysteries;
    A face flowered for heart's ease,
5   A brow's grace soft as seas
    Seen through faint forest-trees:
    A mouth, the lips apart,
Like aspen-leaflets trembling in the breeze
From her tempestuous heart.
10   Such: and our souls so knit,
    I leave a page half-writ—
    The work begun
Will be to heaven's conception done,
    If she come to it.

1893

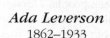

Ada Leverson
1862–1933

"You can't have got up, you must have sat up," said Oscar Wilde to his exquisitely dressed friend Ada Leverson when he was released from prison at an early hour. "How marvellous of you to know exactly the right hat to wear at seven o'clock in the morning to meet a friend who has been away!" Always perfectly attired, Leverson was a witty socialite whose genius for friendship and droll sense of humor put her at the center of *fin de siècle* literary life. Her friends wondered how someone so rich and beautiful could be indifferent to jewelry: "But it lasts so long," she said. Henry James was so struck by her remarks about his books that he called her the "incarnation" of the novelist's dream, "the Gentle Reader." Later she herself became a successful comic novelist, her best works being reissued as *The Little Ottleys* (1962). She wrote in bed, in a confusion of cigarettes, papers, and oranges. To escape parental control she married Ernest Leverson when she was only nineteen, he thirty-one. She soon regretted it but arranged to carry on quiet romances while he gambled or visited his mistress. The Leversons were united, however, in their emotional and financial support of Wilde after his troubles began; they sheltered Wilde secretly between his trials.

    It was Wilde who gave her the lasting nickname of "Sphinx" after she published a parody of his poem by that title in *Punch*. Leverson delighted in deflating Wilde's ego: when Wilde boasted that an Apache had become so devoted to him in Paris that he accompanied him everywhere with a knife in one hand, she replied, "I'm sure he had a fork in the other." She enjoyed exchanging wires with Wilde, claiming that she intended to edit *The Collected Telegrams of Oscar Wilde*. Her short story *Suggestion* was published in *The Yellow Book*, along with her portrait by Walter Sickert, in April 1895, the month when Wilde was arrested. From its provocative opening line to its immorally moral ending, *Suggestion* skewers Victorian patriarchy and double standards, even as it spoofs the New Woman, Aesthetes, and Wildean affectation. A parody of decadent gender confusion that appeared in *Punch* later that month may well have been aimed at Ada Leverson:

> Woman was woman, man was man,
> When Adam delved and Eve span.
> Now he can't dig and she won't spin
> Unless 'tis tales all slang and sin!

Suggestion

If Lady Winthrop had not spoken of me as "that intolerable, effeminate boy," she might have had some chance of marrying my father. She was a middle-aged widow; prosaic, fond of domineering, and an alarmingly excellent housekeeper; the serious work of her life was paying visits; in her lighter moments she collected autographs. She was highly suitable and altogether insupportable; and this unfortunate remark about me was, as people say, the last straw. Some encouragement from father Lady Winthrop must, I think, have received; for she took to calling at odd hours, asking my sister Marjorie sudden abrupt questions, and being generally impossible. A tradition existed that her advice was of use to our father in his household, and when, last year, he married his daughter's school-friend, a beautiful girl of twenty, it surprised every one except Marjorie and myself.

The whole thing was done, in fact, by suggestion. I shall never forget that summer evening when father first realised, with regard to Laura Egerton, the possible. He was giving a little dinner of eighteen people. *Through a mistake of Marjorie's* (my idea) Lady Winthrop did not receive her invitation till the very last minute. Of course she accepted—we knew she would—but unknowing that it was a dinner party, she came without putting on evening-dress.

Nothing could be more trying to the average woman than such a *contretemps*; and Lady Winthrop was not one to rise, sublimely, and laughing, above the situation. I can see her now, in a plaid blouse and a vile temper, displaying herself, mentally and physically, to the utmost disadvantage, while Marjorie apologised the whole evening, in pale blue crêpe-de-chine; and Laura, in yellow, with mauve orchids, sat—an adorable contrast—on my father's other side, with a slightly conscious air that was perfectly fascinating. It is quite extraordinary what trifles have their little effect in these matters. *I* had sent Laura the orchids, anonymously; I could not help it if she chose to think they were from my father. Also, I had hinted of his secret affection for her, and lent her Verlaine.[1] I said I had found it in his study, turned down at her favourite page. Laura has, like myself, the artistic temperament; she is cultured, rather romantic, and in search of the *au-delà* [the transcendent]. My father has at times—never to me—rather charming manners; also he is still handsome, with that

---

1. French decadent poet (1844–1896) whose subtle musicality was much admired by English Aesthetes.

look of having suffered that comes from enjoying oneself too much. That evening his really sham melancholy and apparently hollow gaiety were delightful for a son to witness, and appealed evidently to her heart. Yes, strange as it may seem, while the world said that pretty Miss Egerton married old Carington for his money, she was really in love, or thought herself in love, with our father. Poor girl! She little knew what an irritating, ill-tempered, absent-minded person he is in private life; and at times I have pangs of remorse.

A fortnight after the wedding, father forgot he was married, and began again treating Laura with a sort of *distrait* [absent-minded] gallantry as Marjorie's friend, or else ignoring her altogether. When, from time to time, he remembers she is his wife, he scolds her about the housekeeping in a fitful, perfunctory way, for he does not know that Marjorie does it still. Laura bears the rebukes like an angel; indeed, rather than take the slightest practical trouble she would prefer to listen to the strongest language in my father's vocabulary.

But she is sensitive; and when father, speedily resuming his bachelor manners, recommenced his visits to an old friend who lives in one of the little houses opposite the Oratory,[2] she seemed quite vexed. Father is horribly careless, and Laura found a letter. They had a rather serious explanation, and for a little time after, Laura seemed depressed. She soon tried to rouse herself, and is at times cheerful enough with Marjorie and myself, but I fear she has had a disillusion. They never quarrel now, and I think we all three dislike father about equally, though Laura never owns it, and is gracefully attentive to him in a gentle, filial sort of way.

We are fond of going to parties—not father—and Laura is a very nice chaperone for Marjorie. They are both perfectly devoted to me. "Cecil knows everything," they are always saying, and they do nothing—not even choosing a hat—without asking my advice.

Since I left Eton I am supposed to be reading with a tutor,[3] but as a matter of fact I have plenty of leisure; and am very glad to be of use to the girls, of whom I'm, by the way, quite proud. They are rather a sweet contrast; Marjorie has the sort of fresh rosy prettiness you see in the park and on the river. She is tall, and slim as a punt-pole,[4] and if she were not very careful how she dresses, she would look like a drawing by Pilotelle in the *Lady's Pictorial*.[5] She is practical and lively, she rides and drives and dances; skates, and goes to some mysterious haunt called *The Stores*,[6] and is, in her own way, quite a modern English type.

Laura has that exotic beauty so much admired by Philistines; dreamy dark eyes, and a wonderful white complexion. She loves music and poetry and pictures and admiration in a lofty sort of way; she has a morbid fondness for mental gymnastics, and a dislike to physical exertion, and never takes any exercise except waving her hair. Sometimes she looks bored, and I have heard her sigh.

"Cissy," Marjorie said, coming one day into my study, "I want to speak to you about Laura."

"Do you have pangs of conscience too?" I asked, lighting a cigarette.

---

2. The Brompton Oratory, in West London, is a Roman Catholic church where Cardinal Newman and other leading clerics preached.
3. In preparation for attending Oxford or Cambridge.
4. A long, thin pole used to propel a punt, a flat-bottomed boat.

5. Georges Labadie Pilotell (1844–1918), French illustrator and caricaturist.
6. Large department stores, relatively new at the time. In her athleticism and up-to-date practicality, Marjorie is a version of the New Woman—as opposed to Laura's languid Aestheticism.

2074 PERSPECTIVES: Aestheticism, Decadence, and the *Fin de Siècle*

"Dear, we took a great responsibility. Poor girl! Oh, couldn't we make Papa more—"

"Impossible," I said; "no one has any influence with him. He can't bear even me, though if he had a shade of decency he would dash away an unbidden tear every time I look at him with my mother's blue eyes."

My poor mother was a great beauty, and I am supposed to be her living image.

"Laura has no object in life," said Marjorie. "I have, all girls have, I suppose. By the way, Cissy, I am quite sure Charlie Winthrop is serious."

"How sweet of him! I am so glad. I got father off my hands last season."

"Must I really marry him, Cissy? He bores me."

"What has that to do with it? Certainly you must. You are not a beauty, and I doubt your ever having a better chance."

Marjorie rose and looked at herself in the long pier-glass that stands opposite my writing-table. I could not resist the temptation to go and stand beside her.

"I am just the style that is admired now," said Marjorie, dispassionately.

"So am I," I said reflectively. "But *you* will soon be out of date."

Every one says I am strangely like my mother. Her face was of that pure and perfect oval one so seldom sees, with delicate features, rosebud mouth, and soft flaxen hair. A blondness without insipidity, for the dark-blue eyes are fringed with dark lashes, and from their languorous depths looks out a soft mockery. I have a curious ideal devotion to my mother; she died when I was quite young—only two months old—and I often spend hours thinking of her, as I gaze at myself in the mirror.

"Do come down from the clouds," said Marjorie impatiently, for I had sunk into a reverie. "I came to ask you to think of something to amuse Laura—to interest her."

"We ought to make it up to her in some way. Haven't you tried anything?"

"Only palmistry; and Mrs. Wilkinson prophesied her all that she detests, and depressed her dreadfully."

"What do you think she really needs most?" I asked.

Our eyes met.

"Really, Cissy, you're too disgraceful," said Marjorie. There was a pause.

"And so I'm to accept Charlie?"

"What man do you like better?" I asked.

"I don't know what you mean," said Marjorie, colouring.

"*I* thought Adrian Grant would have been more sympathetic to Laura than to you. I have just had a note from him, asking me to tea at his studio to-day." I threw it to her. "He says I'm to bring you both. Would that amuse Laura?"

"Oh," cried Marjorie, enchanted, "of course we'll go. I wonder what he thinks of me," she added wistfully.

"He didn't say. He is going to send Laura his verses, 'Hearts-ease and Heliotrope.'"[7]

She sighed. Then she said, "Father was complaining again to-day of your laziness."

"I, lazy! Why, I've been swinging the censer in Laura's boudoir because she wants to encourage the religious temperament, and I've designed your dress for the Clives' fancy ball."

"Where's the design?"

---

7. Heartsease is a pansy; heliotrope is a plant with fragrant purple flowers; the title is typical of 1890s preciousness.

"In my head. You're not to wear white; Miss Clive must wear white."

"I wonder you don't marry her," said Marjorie, "you admire her so much."

"I never marry. Besides, I know she's pretty, but that furtive Slade-school[8] manner of hers gets on my nerves. You don't know how dreadfully I suffer from my nerves."

She lingered a little, asking me what I advised her to choose for a birthday present for herself—an American organ, a black poodle, or an *édition de luxe* of Browning. I advised the last, as being least noisy. Then I told her I felt sure that in spite of her admiration for Adrian, she was far too good natured to interfere with Laura's prospects. She said I was incorrigible, and left the room with a smile of resignation.

And I returned to my reading. On my last birthday—I was seventeen—my father—who has his gleams of dry humour—gave me *Robinson Crusoe!* I prefer Pierre Loti,[9] and intend to have an onyx-paved bath-room, with soft apricot-coloured light shimmering through the blue-lined green curtains in my chambers, as soon as I get Margery married, and Laura more—settled down.

I met Adrian Grant first at a luncheon party at the Clives. I seemed to amuse him; he came to see me, and became at once obviously enamoured of my step-mother. He is rather an impressionable impressionist, and a delightful creature, tall and graceful and beautiful, and altogether most interesting. Every one admits he's fascinating; he is very popular and very much disliked. He is by way of being a painter; he has a little money of his own—enough for his telegrams, but not enough for his buttonholes—and nothing could be more incongruous than the idea of his marrying. I have never seen Marjorie so much attracted. But she is a good loyal girl, and will accept Charlie Winthrop, who is a dear person, good-natured and ridiculously rich—just the sort of man for a brother-in-law. It will annoy my old enemy Lady Winthrop—he is her nephew, and she wants him to marry that little Miss Clive. Dorothy Clive has her failings, but she could not—to do her justice—be happy with Charlie Winthrop.

Adrian's gorgeous studio gives one the complex impression of being at once the calm retreat of a mediaeval saint and the luxurious abode of a modern Pagan. One feels that everything could be done there, everything from praying to flirting—everything except painting. The tea-party amused me, I was pretending to listen to a brown person who was talking absurd worn-out literary clichés—as that the New Humour is not funny, or that Bourget understood women,[1] when I overheard this fragment of conversation.

"But don't you like Society?" Adrian was saying.

"I get rather tired of it. People are so much alike. They all say the same things," said Laura.

"Of course they all say the same things to *you*," murmured Adrian, as he affected to point out a rather curious old silver crucifix.

"That," said Laura, "is one of the things they say."

About three weeks later I found myself dining alone with Adrian Grant, at one of the two restaurants in London. (The cooking is better at the other, this one is the more becoming.) I had lilies-of-the-valley in my button-hole, Adrian was wearing a

---

8. The Slade School of Art in London, founded 1871, had become more fashionable than the Royal Academy, whose teaching was regarded as dry and stuffy.
9. Pen name of French impressionist novelist Julien Viaud (1850–1923) who was drawn to exotic civilizations

and landscapes.
1. The "New Humor" is coined on the model of other 1890s trends, such as the New Woman, the New Journalism, and the New Drama; the French author Paul Bourget (1852–1935) wrote psychological novels.

red carnation. Several people glanced at us. Of course he is very well known in Society. Also, I was looking rather nice, and I could not help hoping, while Adrian gazed rather absently over my head, that the shaded candles were staining to a richer rose the waking wonder of my face.

Adrian was charming of course, but he seemed worried and a little preoccupied, and drank a good deal of champagne.

Towards the end of dinner, he said—almost abruptly for him—"Carington."

"Cecil," I interrupted. He smiled.

"Cissy . . . it seems an odd thing to say to you, but though you are so young, I think you know everything. I am sure you know everything. You know about me. I am in love. I am quite miserable. What on earth am I to do!" He drank more champagne. "Tell me," he said, "what to do." For a few minutes, while we listened to that interminable hackneyed *Intermezzo,* I reflected; asking myself by what strange phases I had risen to the extraordinary position of giving advice to Adrian on such a subject?

Laura was not happy with our father. From a selfish motive, Marjorie and I had practically arranged that monstrous marriage. That very day he had been disagreeable, asking me with a clumsy sarcasm to raise his allowance, so that he could afford my favourite cigarettes. If Adrian were free, Marjorie might refuse Charlie Winthrop. I don't want her to refuse him. Adrian has treated me as a friend. I like him—I like him enormously. I am quite devoted to him. And how can I rid myself of the feeling of responsibility, the sense that I owe some compensation to poor beautiful Laura?

We spoke of various matters. Just before we left the table, I said, with what seemed, but was not, irrelevance, "Dear Adrian, Mrs. Carington——"

"Go on, Cissy."

"She is one of those who must be appealed to, at first, by her imagination. She married our father because she thought he was lonely and misunderstood."

"*I* am lonely and misunderstood," said Adrian, his eyes flashing with delight.

"Ah, not twice! She doesn't like that now."

I finished my coffee slowly, and then I said,

"Go to the Clives' fancy-ball as Tristan."[2]

Adrian pressed my hand. . . .

At the door of the restaurant we parted, and I drove home through the cool April night, wondering, wondering. Suddenly I thought of my mother—my beautiful sainted mother, who would have loved me, I am convinced, had she lived, with an extraordinary devotion. What would she have said to all this? What would she have thought? I know not why, but a mad reaction seized me. I felt recklessly conscientious. My father! After all, he was my father. I was possessed by passionate scruples. If I went back now to Adrian—if I went back and implored him, supplicated him never to see Laura again!

I felt I could persuade him. I have sufficient personal magnetism to do that, if I make up my mind. After one glance in the looking-glass, I put up my stick and stopped the hansom. I had taken a resolution. I told the man to drive to Adrian's rooms.

He turned round with a sharp jerk. In another second a brougham[3] passed us—a swift little brougham that I knew. It slackened—it stopped—we passed it—I saw my father. He was getting out at one of the little houses opposite the Brompton Oratory.

"Turn round again," I shouted to the cabman. And he drove me straight home.

1895

---

2. A fancy dress ball is a costume ball; Tristan was a legendary knight in love with Isolde, his king's wife.

3. A one-horse closed carriage.

Arthur Symons
1865–1945

Born in Wales, the son of a Methodist minister, Arthur Symons devoted his life to becoming British literature's most decadent cosmopolitan. While his parents wanted him to be good, he recalled, "all I really wanted was to be clever." Under the influence of Walter Pater, who praised his early work, Symons set about capturing the transient pleasures of London in the 1890s. "If ever there was a religion of the eyes," Symons said, "I have devoutly practiced that religion. I noted every face that passed me on the pavement; I looked into the omnibuses, the cabs, always with the same eager hope of seeing . . . some gracious movement, a delicate expression. . . . My eyes ached with the effort, but I could not control them." Symons soon made his mark as an up-to-the-minute critic and poet: he belonged to the Rhymers' Club, whose members included Richard Le Gallienne, Lionel Johnson, and William Butler Yeats. He contributed to *The Yellow Book*, and when Beardsley was fired as the magazine's editor, he joined with him to edit its daring successor, *The Savoy*, in 1896. Nights spent carousing in music halls, bars, and brothels provided the radical new themes of his poetry, but Symons also had the discipline to craft his experiences into poetic forms that were equally scandalous. His deft depiction of fleeting moments, his acute emphasis on the visual details of modern life (such as the glow of a cigarette), and his refusal to moralize or explain, all make Symons something of a proto-Imagist, an important figure in the transition to modernism.

Symons enjoyed the uproar caused by his poems and brought out second editions of *Silhouettes* (1892; 1896) and *London Nights* (1895; 1897) with prefaces that eloquently defended his preference for artifice and "decadent" subject matter. "Symons," Yeats remarked, "studied the music halls as he might have studied the age of Chaucer." Under the spell of French writers, particularly Baudelaire, he traveled often to Paris, where he was an habitué of Mallarmé's literary circle and became good friends with Paul Verlaine. The self-appointed custodian of the Decadent movement, Symons took pride in his role as a literary missionary; he personally introduced many writers, including Yeats, to French poets and their works. In 1899 Symons published *The Symbolist Movement in Literature* (originally titled "The Decadent Movement"), which decisively influenced Yeats and T. S. Eliot.

Pastel[1]

The light of our cigarettes
   Went and came in the gloom:
   It was dark in the little room.

Dark, and then, in the dark,
5   Sudden, a flash, a glow,
   And a hand and a ring I know.

And then, through the dark, a flush
   Ruddy and vague, the grace—
   A rose—of her lyric face.

1892

---

1. An artwork done in chalklike pastels. The fresh, impromptu quality of pastels made them popular with 19th-century artists such as Degas and Whistler seeking to record contemporary life.

White Heliotrope[1]

The feverish room and that white bed,
    The tumbled skirts upon a chair,
    The novel flung half-open, where
Hat, hair-pins, puffs, and paints, are spread;

5   The mirror that has sucked your face
    Into its secret deep of deeps,
    And there mysteriously keeps
Forgotten memories of grace;

And you, half dressed and half awake,
10   Your slant eyes strangely watching me,
    And I, who watch you drowsily,
With eyes that, having slept not, ache;

This (need one dread? nay, dare one hope?)
    Will rise, a ghost of memory, if
15   Ever again my handkerchief
Is scented with White Heliotrope.

1895

from The Decadent Movement in Literature[1]

The latest movement in European literature has been called by many names, none of them quite exact or comprehensive—Decadence, Symbolism, Impressionism, for instance. It is easy to dispute over words, and we shall find that Verlaine objects to being called a Decadent, Maeterlinck to being called a Symbolist, Huysmans to being called an Impressionist.[2] These terms, as it happens, have been adopted as the badge of little separate cliques, noisy, brainsick young people who haunt the brasseries of the Boulevard Saint-Michel,[3] and exhaust their ingenuities in theorizing over the works they cannot write. But, taken frankly as epithets which express their own meaning, both Impressionism and Symbolism convey some notion of that new kind of literature which is perhaps more broadly characterized by the word Decadence. The most representative literature of the day—the writing which appeals to, which has done so much to form, the younger generation—is certainly not classic, nor has it any relation with that old antithesis of the Classic, the Romantic. After a fashion it is no doubt a decadence; it has all the qualities that mark the end of great periods, the qualities that we find in the Greek, the Latin, decadence: an intense self-consciousness, a restless curiosity in research, an over-subtilizing refinement upon refinement, a spiritual and moral perversity. If what we call the classic is indeed the supreme art—those qualities of perfect simplicity, perfect sanity,

---

1. The perfume made from heliotrope, a fragrant flowering plant.
1. Published in *Harper's New Monthly Magazine*, November 1893.
2. Paul Verlaine (1844–1896), French poet, who declared "I am the Empire at the end of its decadent era"; Count Maurice Maeterlinck (1862–1949), Belgian writer known for his symbolist dramas; Joris-Karl Huysmans

(1848–1907), French novelist whose highly impressionistic fantasy of the senses, *A Rebours* (*Against the Grain*, 1884), was regarded as "the Bible of Decadence." Symons suggests that these men reject the literary labels that their own works have helped define.
3. A street synonymous with literary life and intellectual fashion, on the Left Bank in Paris; a brasserie is a beer hall.

perfect proportion, the supreme qualities—then this representative literature of to-day, interesting, beautiful, novel as it is, is really a new and beautiful and interest-ing disease.

Healthy we cannot call it, and healthy it does not wish to be considered. The Goncourts,[4] in their prefaces, in their *Journal*, are always insisting on their own pet malady, *la névrose* [neurosis]. It is in their work, too, that Huysmans notes with de-light "le style tacheté et faisandé"—high-flavored and spotted with corruption—which he himself possesses in the highest degree. "Having desire without light, cu-riosity without wisdom, seeking God by strange ways, by ways traced by the hands of men; offering rash incense upon the high places to an unknown God, who is the God of darkness"—that is how Ernest Hello,[5] in one of his apocalyptic moments, characterizes the nineteenth century. And this unreason of the soul—of which Hello himself is so curious a victim—this unstable equilibrium, which has overbal-anced so many brilliant intelligences into one form or another of spiritual confu-sion, is but another form of the *maladie fin de siècle*. For its very disease of form, this literature is certainly typical of a civilization grown over-luxurious, over-inquiring, too languid for the relief of action, too uncertain for any emphasis in opinion or in conduct. It reflects all the moods, all the manners, of a sophisticated society; its very artificiality is a way of being true to nature: simplicity, sanity, proportion—the classic qualities—how much do we possess them in our life, our surroundings, that we should look to find them in our literature—so evidently the literature of a decadence?

Taking the word Decadence, then, as most precisely expressing the general sense of the newest movement in literature, we find that the terms Impressionism and Symbolism define correctly enough the two main branches of that movement. Now Impressionist and Symbolist have more in common than either supposes; both are re-ally working on the same hypothesis, applied in different directions. What both seek is not general truth merely, but *la vérité vraie*, the very essence of truth—the truth of appearances to the senses, of the visible world to the eyes that see it; and the truth of spiritual things to the spiritual vision. The Impressionist, in literature as in painting, would flash upon you in a new, sudden way so exact an image of what you have just seen, just as you have seen it, that you may say, as a young American sculptor, a pupil of Rodin,[6] said to me on seeing for the first time a picture of Whistler's, "Whistler seems to think his picture upon canvas—and there it is!" Or you may find, with Sainte-Beuve,[7] writing of Goncourt, the "soul of the landscape"—the soul of what-ever corner of the visible world has to be realized. The Symbolist, in this new, sudden way, would flash upon you the "soul" of that which can be apprehended only by the soul—the finer sense of things unseen, the deeper meaning of things evident. And naturally, necessarily, this endeavor after a perfect truth to one's impression, to one's intuition—perhaps an impossible endeavor—has brought with it, in its revolt from ready-made impressions and conclusions, a revolt from the ready-made of language, from the bondage of traditional form, of a form become rigid.

1893

---

4. Edmond (1822–1896) and Jules de Goncourt (1830–1870), French novelists and brothers who often wrote in collaboration; their *Journal* or diary forms a day-to-day record of literary life in Paris over the course of several decades.

5. Actual name of a French writer (1828–1885).
6. Auguste Rodin (1840–1917), French sculptor of such works as *The Thinker* and *The Kiss*.
7. Charles Augustin Sainte-Beuve (1804–1869), French critic and author.

from **Silhouettes**

from *Preface: Being a Word on Behalf of Patchouli*[1]

An ingenuous reviewer once described some verses of mine as "unwholesome," because, he said, they had "a faint smell of Patchouli about them." I am a little sorry he chose Patchouli, for that is not a particularly favourite scent with me. If he had only chosen Peau d'Espagne,[2] which has a subtle meaning, or Lily of the Valley,[3] with which I have associations! But Patchouli will serve. Let me ask, then, in republishing, with additions, a collection of little pieces, many of which have been objected to, at one time or another, as being somewhat deliberately frivolous, why art should not, if it please, concern itself with the artificially charming, which, I suppose, is what my critic means by Patchouli? All art, surely, is a form of artifice, and thus, to the truly devout mind, condemned already, if not as actively noxious, at all events as needless. That is a point of view which I quite understand, and its conclusion I hold to be absolutely logical. I have the utmost respect for the people who refuse to read a novel, to go to the theatre, or to learn dancing. That is to have convictions and to live up to them. I understand also the point of view from which a work of art is tolerated in so far as it is actually militant on behalf of a religious or a moral idea. But what I fail to understand are those delicate, invisible degrees by which a distinction is drawn between this form of art and that; the hesitations, and compromises, and timorous advances, and shocked retreats, of the Puritan conscience once emancipated, and yet afraid of liberty. However you may try to convince yourself to the contrary, a work of art can be judged only from two standpoints: the standpoint from which its art is measured entirely by its morality, and the standpoint from which its morality is measured entirely by its art. * * *

Patchouli! Well, why not Patchouli? Is there any "reason in nature" why we should write exclusively about the natural blush, if the delicately acquired blush of rouge has any attraction for us? Both exist; both, I think, are charming in their way; and the latter, as a subject, has, at all events, more novelty. If you prefer your "new-mown hay" in the hayfield, and I, it may be, in a scent-bottle, why may not my individual caprice be allowed to find expression as well as yours? Probably I enjoy the hayfield as much as you do; but I enjoy quite other scents and sensations as well, and I take the former for granted, and write my poem, for a change, about the latter. There is no necessary difference in artistic value between a good poem about a flower in the hedge and a good poem about the scent in a sachet. I am always charmed to read beautiful poems about nature in the country. Only, personally, I prefer town to country; and in the town we have to find for ourselves, as best we may, the *décor* which is the town equivalent of the great natural *décor* of fields and hills. Here it is that artificiality comes in; and if any one sees no beauty in the effects of artificial light, in all the variable, most human, and yet most factitious town landscape, I can only pity him, and go on my own way.

1896

---

1. A heavy perfume made from an East Indian plant.
3. Fresh floral scent.
2. Fragrance; the name is French for "skin of Spain."

Richard Le Gallienne
1866–1947

Richard Gallienne came from a middle-class background in Liverpool, where he apprenticed with an accounting firm. But by the early 1890s he had settled in London, made himself part of the literary scene, and added the distinctive "Le" to his name. He was at first a reader for publishers Elkin Mathews and John Lane, who selected his book of poems, *Volumes in Folio* (1889), to be the initial publication of their Bodley Head Press. The press soon went on to notoriety by producing *The Yellow Book* (1894–1897), to which Le Gallienne contributed regularly. Acquainted with Swinburne and Wilde, Le Gallienne also joined the celebrated Rhymers' Club, whose other members included Ernest Dowson, Lionel Johnson, John Davidson, Arthur Symons, and W. B. Yeats.

Unlike most of his fellow Rhymers, however, Le Gallienne was a popular writer and journalist, the author of fiction and essays as well as poetry. Although he cultivated a dandyish air in the 1890s, Le Gallienne was torn between acceptance and criticism of the aesthetic creed. Rather like Max Beerbohm, he trod a fine line between fully participating in the movement and parodying it. *A Ballad of London* (1895) thus maintains an ironic distance on its seductive subject. The poem is the period's classic statement of London's artificial, nocturnal allure, evoking the decadent delights of a great capital city too bent on pleasure to long endure. Le Gallienne emigrated to the United States in 1903.

A Ballad of London

Ah, London! London! our delight,
Great flower that opens but at night,
Great City of the Midnight Sun,
Whose day begins when day is done.

5   Lamp after lamp against the sky
Opens a sudden beaming eye,
Leaping alight on either hand,
The iron lilies of the Strand.

Like dragonflies, the hansoms° hover,   *horse-drawn cabs*
10   With jewelled eyes, to catch the lover;
The streets are full of lights and loves,
Soft gowns and flutter of soiled doves.°   *prostitutes*

The human moths about the light
Dash and cling close in dazed delight,
15   And burn and laugh, the world and wife,
For this is London, this is life!

Upon thy petals butterflies,
But at thy root, some say, there lies
A world of weeping trodden things,
20   Poor worms that have not eyes or wings.

From out corruption of their woe
Springs this bright flower that charms us so,

Men die and rot deep out of sight
To keep this jungle-flower bright.

25   Paris and London, World-Flowers twain
Wherewith the World-Tree[1] blooms again,
Since Time hath gathered Babylon,
And withered Rome still withers on.

Sidon and Tyre[2] were such as ye,
30   How bright they shone upon the Tree!
But Time hath gathered, both are gone,
And no man sails to Babylon.

Ah, London! London! our delight,
For thee, too, the eternal night,
35   And Circe[3] Paris hath no charm
To stay Time's unrelenting arm.

Time and his moths shall eat up all.
Your chiming towers proud and tall
He shall most utterly abase,
40   And set a desert in their place.

1895

✦ ☰◇☰ ✦

Lionel Johnson
1867–1902

"Life is ritual," Lionel Johnson was fond of telling his close friend William Butler Yeats, and in his poetry he sought to achieve the elegant simplicity and graceful, lasting form he associated with religious practice. Born in Kent, Johnson was educated in classics at Oxford, where Pater was his tutor, then moved to London in 1890 to work as a literary journalist. He converted to Roman Catholicism in 1891 and considered becoming a priest. In that year he also joined the Rhymers' Club, which met frequently to read and discuss poetry at a London pub, the Cheshire Cheese. Other members included Yeats, Arthur Symons, and his constant drinking companion, Ernest Dowson. Seeking a pure poetry, Johnson lived a celibate, bookish life, brightened by whiskey and conversation, during which he repeated verbatim imaginary conversations he had had with Cardinal Newman and Prime Minister Gladstone. Yeats, who greatly admired his work, remembered Johnson as representative of "The Tragic Generation" of the 1890s, whose unhappy lives and dissipation prevented them from realizing their talent. A sufferer from insomnia and alcoholism, Johnson died at thirty-five as a result of falling off a barstool.

Johnson was ambivalent about the idea of decadence as a literary style and deeply distressed about it as a code of behavior. Since the 1890s were "an age of afterthought," Johnson argued, the era encouraged poets to "careful meditation on life." But it also weakened them, he said, with "the vice of over-subtilty and of affectation, when thought thinks upon itself, and when emotions become entangled with the consciousness of them." His own poetry hovers be-

---

1. In Norse mythology, the mighty ash tree Yggdrasil was said to support the whole universe, connecting heaven, earth, and hell.

2. The chief cities of ancient Phoenicia.
3. The sorceress who enticed Odysseus's men, then transformed them into swine.

tween these virtues and vices: distinguished by learning, polish, and musicality, his lines pit an intensity of religious and sensual passion against the classical restraint of their form. *A Decadent's Lyric*, probably meant as a parody of Symons, shamelessly indulges in sexual synaesthesia. Two more revealing poems, *The Destroyer of a Soul* and *The Dark Angel*, bristle with hatred, guilt, remorse, and despair: the first is addressed to Oscar Wilde, who he thought had seduced his friend Lord Alfred Douglas; the second addresses Johnson's own fear of seduction.

The Destroyer of a Soul
To—.[1]

I hate you with a necessary hate.
First, I sought patience: passionate was she:
My patience turned in very scorn of me,
That I should dare forgive a sin so great,
As this, through which I sit disconsolate;
Mourning for that live soul, I used to see;
Soul of a saint, whose friend I used to be:
Till you came by! a cold, corrupting, fate.

Why come you now? You, whom I cannot cease
With pure and perfect hate to hate? Go, ring
The death-bell with a deep, triumphant toll!
Say you, my friend sits by me still? Ah, peace!
Call you this thing my friend? this nameless thing?
This living body, hiding its dead soul?

1892

The Dark Angel

Dark angel, with thine aching lust
To rid the world of penitence:
Malicious Angel, who still dost
My soul such subtile violence!

Because of thee, no thought, no thing,
Abides for me undesecrate:
Dark Angel, ever on the wing,
Who never reachest me too late!

When music sounds, then changest thou
Its silvery to a sultry fire:
Nor will thine envious heart allow
Delight untortured by desire.

Through thee, the gracious Muses turn
To Furies,[1] O mine Enemy!

1. Almost certainly Oscar Wilde; Johnson met Wilde at Oxford when the latter paid a visit to Johnson's tutor, Walter Pater. Johnson in turn introduced Wilde to his friend and fellow undergraduate Lord Alfred Douglas in June 1891, after having lent Douglas his copy of *The Pic-*

ture of Dorian Gray. Johnson's letters reveal he was successively enamored of all three men.
1. The Muses were the goddesses of literature and the arts; the Furies were the avengers of blood crimes.

15   And all the things of beauty burn
     With flames of evil ecstasy.

     Because of thee, the land of dreams
     Becomes a gathering place of fears:
     Until tormented slumber seems
20   One vehemence of useless tears.

     When sunlight glows upon the flowers,
     Or ripples down the dancing sea:
     Thou, with thy troop of passionate powers,
     Beleaguerest, bewilderest, me.

25   Within the breath of autumn woods,
     Within the winter silences:
     Thy venomous spirit stirs and broods,
     O Master of impieties!

     The ardour of red flame is thine,
30   And thine the steely soul of ice:
     Thou poisonest the fair design
     Of nature, with unfair device.

     Apples of ashes, golden bright;[2]
     Waters of bitterness, how sweet!
35   O banquet of a foul delight,
     Prepared by thee, dark Paraclete![3]

     Thou art the whisper in the gloom,
     The hinting tone, the haunting laugh:
     Thou art the adorner of my tomb,
40   The minstrel of mine epitaph.

     I fight thee, in the Holy Name!
     Yet, what thou dost, is what God saith:
     Tempter! should I escape thy flame,
     Thou wilt have helped my soul from Death:

45   The second Death, that never dies,
     That cannot die, when time is dead:
     Live Death, wherein the lost soul cries,
     Eternally uncomforted.[4]

     Dark Angel, with thine aching lust!
50   Of two defeats, of two despairs:
     Less dread, a change to drifting dust,
     Than thine eternity of cares.

2. The apples of Sodom grew in the ruins of Sodom and
Gomorrah; they were enticing in appearance, but turned
into smoke and ashes when plucked. See Milton, *Paradise
Lost* 10.560–66.
3. Advocate, i.e., the Holy Spirit. See John 14.16,26,
where Jesus characterizes the Holy Spirit as a Comforter
and Intercessor. The "dark Paraclete" satanically inter-

cedes to draw the speaker away from Christ.
4. I.e., if the speaker can successfully resist the Dark Angel, the struggle will have spared him the damning "second Death" which imprisons the soul in the dead body to
torment it eternally; see Augustine, *The City of God*
7.21.3.

Do what thou wilt, thou shalt not so,
Dark Angel! triumph over me:
55   *Lonely, unto the Lone I go,*
Divine, to the Divinity.[5]

1894

A Decadent's Lyric

Sometimes, in very joy of shame,
Our flesh becomes one living flame:
And she and I
Are no more separate, but the same.

5   Ardour and agony unite;
Desire, delirium, delight:
And I and she
Faint in the fierce and fevered night.

Her body music is: and ah,
10   The accords of lute and viola!
When she and I
Play on live limbs love's opera!

1897

Lord Alfred Douglas
1870–1945

Lord Alfred Douglas embodied the new sexual freedom of the early 1890s, both in his life and in his polished verses on erotic themes. He was the son of the pugnacious Marquess of Queensberry, who had established the rules of boxing but who violated almost every social code in his public antagonism toward his son. In 1891, while Douglas was still an undergraduate at Oxford, Lionel Johnson introduced him to Oscar Wilde, who encouraged both his affections and his writing. Their tempestuous relationship lasted until Wilde's death in 1900, despite Queensberry's constant efforts to disgrace them both. During Wilde's trials, provoked largely by the desire of father and son to injure each other, Douglas stayed safely in France, at Wilde's request. Their reunion after Wilde's imprisonment was marked by mutual recrimination; Wilde addressed to Douglas the bitter accusations detailed in *De Profundis*, and Douglas contended that he alone among Wilde's friends had remained true. In 1902 Douglas surprised everyone by secretly marrying the poet Olive Custance, whom he had met the year before. The marriage ended in 1913, by which time Douglas had converted to Catholicism and renounced his earlier homosexual activity. In his later life Douglas wrote much about his relationship with Wilde, including *Oscar Wilde and Myself* (1914) and *Oscar Wilde: A Summing Up* (1940). Like his father, he took pleasure in attacking the integrity of other people, and in 1923–1924 spent six months in prison for criminally libeling Winston Churchill.

---

5. According to the Neoplatonic philosopher Plotinus, the good life, unswayed by worldly pleasures, is "a flight of the alone to the alone" (*Enneads* 6.9).

Douglas's early career coincided with the period of sexual openness and homosexual activism that occurred between 1885 and 1895. The term "homosexuality" was invented in 1869, and entered English just as Parliament criminalized all homosexual activity in 1885; medical theories of homosexual "degeneration" soon followed. Yet this climate also inspired resistance among authors who lauded the spiritual and emotional rewards of same-sex relationships. Douglas, by contrast, explored the dangerous pleasures of all kinds of sexuality: he translated Wilde's *Salomé* (1894) from French to English, and his own *Impression de Nuit: London* combines the aesthetic preference for urban artifice with the decadent penchant for monstrously appetitive female bodies. (See Response to Wilde's "Impression du Matin," page 1981.) He also made two contributions—*In Praise of Shame* and *Two Loves*—to *The Chameleon* (1894), an Oxford magazine with a distinctly homoerotic slant. The prosecution read both poems at Wilde's second trial in an effort to make Wilde appear guilty by association. Already outraged by the exposure of male prostitution in the Cleveland Street Scandal of 1889, the jury and the public found confirmation in Douglas's poetry that a new threat to the nation had arisen, the "deviant" or "invert."

In Praise of Shame

Last night unto my bed methought there came
Our lady of strange dreams, and from an urn
She poured live fire, so that mine eyes did burn
At sight of it. Anon the floating flame
5   Took many shapes, and one cried: "I am Shame
That walks with Love, I am most wise to turn
Cold lips and limbs to fire; therefore discern
And see my loveliness, and praise my name."

And afterwards, in radiant garments dressed
10 With sound of flutes and laughing of glad lips,
A pomp of all the passions passed along
All the night through; till the white phantom ships
Of dawn sailed in. Whereat I said this song,
"Of all sweet passions Shame is loveliest."

                                                            1894

Two Loves

I dreamed I stood upon a little hill,
And at my feet there lay a ground that seemed
Like a waste garden, flowering at its will
With buds and blossoms. There were pools that dreamed
5   Black and unruffled; there were white lilies
A few, and crocuses, and violets,
        Purple or pale, snake-like fritillaries[1]
Scarce seen for the rank grass, and through green nets
Blue eyes of shy pervenche[2] winked in the sun.
10   And there were curious flowers, before unknown,
Flowers that were stained with moonlight, or with shades
        Of Nature's wilful moods; and here a one
That had drunk in the transitory tone

---

1. A flower similar to the lily.   2. Periwinkle, a small blue flower.

Of one brief moment in a sunset; blades
15   Of grass that in an hundred springs had been
Slowly but exquisitely nurtured by the stars,
And watered with the scented dew long cupped
In lilies, that for rays of sun had seen
Only God's glory, for never a sunrise mars
20 The luminous air of Heaven. Beyond, abrupt,
A grey stone wall, o'ergrown with velvet moss,
Uprose; and gazing I stood long, all mazed
To see a place so strange, so sweet, so fair.
And as I stood and marvelled, lo! across
25   The garden came a youth; one hand he raised
To shield him from the sun, his wind-tossed hair
Was twined with flowers, and in his hand he bore
A purple bunch of bursting grapes, his eyes
Were clear as crystal, naked all was he,
30   White as the snow on pathless mountains frore,°   frozen
Red were his lips as red wine-spilth that dyes
A marble floor, his brow chalcedony.°   quartz
And he came near me, with his lips uncurled
And kind, and caught my hand and kissed my mouth,
35 And gave me grapes to eat, and said, "Sweet friend,
Come, I will show thee shadows of the world
And images of life. See from the South
Comes the pale pageant that hath never an end."
And lo! within the garden of my dream
40 I saw two walking on a shining plain
Of golden light. The one did joyous seem
And fair and blooming, and a sweet refrain
Came from his lips; he sang of pretty maids
And joyous love of comely girl and boy;
45   His eyes were bright, and 'mid the dancing blades
Of golden grass his feet did trip for joy;
And in his hands he held an ivory lute
With strings of gold that were as maidens' hair,
And sang with voice as tuneful as a flute,
50 And round his neck three chains of roses were.
But he that was his comrade walked aside;
He was full sad and sweet, and his large eyes
Were strange with wondrous brightness, staring wide
With gazing; and he sighed with many sighs
55   That moved me, and his cheeks were wan and white
Like pallid lilies, and his lips were red
Like poppies, and his hands he clenchèd tight
And yet again unclenchèd, and his head
Was wreathed with moon-flowers[3] pale as lips of death.

3. A fragrant morning glory.

60   A purple robe he wore, o'erwrought in gold
        With the device of a great snake, whose breath
     Was like curved flame: which when I did behold
        I fell a-weeping, and I cried, "Sweet youth,
     Tell me why, sad and sighing, thou dost rove
65   These pleasant realms? I pray thee, speak me sooth,
     What is thy name?" He said, "My name is Love."
        Then straight the first did turn himself to me
     And cried: "He lieth, for his name is Shame,
        But I am Love, and I was wont to be
70   Alone in this fair garden, till he came
        Unasked by night; I am true Love, I fill
     The hearts of boy and girl with mutual flame."
        Then sighing, said the other: "Have thy will,
     I am the love that dare not speak its name."

                                              1894

Olive Custance (Lady Alfred Douglas)
1874–1944

In April 1895, *Punch* published a satiric poem by an "Angry Old Buffer" concerned about the masculine New Woman and the effeminate Decadent:

> . . . a new fear my bosom vexes;
> To-morrow there may be *no* sexes!
> Unless, as end to all pother,
> Each one in fact becomes the other.

Olive Custance contributed notably to the era's uncertainty about gender roles and the nature of romantic love. Coming from a well-to-do upper-class background, she fell in love at sixteen with the decadent poet John Gray, who was Oscar Wilde's lover at the time. Nothing came of this infatuation but poetry; by the age of twenty she was known in fashionable society as a beautiful young poet, friend to Aubrey Beardsley and contributor to the daring *Yellow Book* magazine. She called her first book *Opals* (1897), after the semiprecious stones that are said to bring the wearer bad luck; she liked to be called "Opal" herself, and sometimes "Wild Olive." Her poetry, like the long letters she wrote to friends, is remarkable for its intensity and emotional candor.

In 1901 she received a passionate fan letter from Natalie Clifford Barney, an American poet and heiress living in Paris. Custance replied with a daring poem:

> For I would dance to make you smile, and sing
> Of those who with some sweet mad sin have played,
> And how Love walks with delicate feet afraid
> 'Twixt maid and maid.

During their brief, stormy relationship, evoked in the poem *The White Witch*, Barney introduced Custance to the lesbian literary scene in Paris. By the time they traveled to Venice together in 1902, however, Custance was already in love with Wilde's friend Lord Alfred Douglas, to whom *she* had sent a fan letter in 1901. His imagined resemblance to a Roman statue inspired several poems, including the decadent classic, *Statues*, which revises the gender terms of the Pygmalion myth. Jilting an earl to whom she had just become engaged, Custance secretly married Douglas in March 1902. By the time the marriage ended in 1913, partially due to Douglas's conversion to Catholicism, Custance had stopped writing. After a reconciliation in 1932, they lived apart but saw each other almost every day until her death. Douglas wrote in his autobiography that "the very thing she loved in me was that which I was always trying to suppress and keep under: I mean the feminine part."

The Masquerade[1]

Masked dancers in the Dance of life
We move sedately . . . wearily together,
Afraid to show a sign of inward strife,
We hold our souls in tether.

5   We dance with proud and smiling lips,
With frank appealing eyes, with shy hands clinging.
We sing, and few will question if there slips
A sob into our singing.

Each has a certain step to learn;
10   Our prisoned feet move staidly in set paces,
And to and fro we pass, since life is stern,
Patiently, with masked faces.

Yet some there are who will not dance,
They sit apart most sorrowful and splendid,
15   But all the rest trip on as in a trance,
Until the Dance is ended.

1902

Statues

I have loved statues . . . spangled dawns have seen
Me bowed before their beauty . . . when the green
And silver world of Spring wears radiantly
The morning rainbows of an opal sky . . .
5   And I have chanted curious madrigals[1]
To charm their coldness, twined for coronals[2]
Blossoming branches, thinking thus to change
Their still contempt for mortal love, their bright
Proud scorn to something delicate and strange,
10   More sweet, more marvellous, than mere delight!

I have loved statues—passionately prone
My body worshipped the white form of stone!
And like a flower that lifts its chalice up
Towards the light—my soul became a cup
15   That over-brimming with enchanted wine
Of ecstasy—was raised to the divine
Indifferent lips of some young silent God

---

1. Cf. Wilde's *The Harlot's House*, page 1981.
1. Love poems, often sung by several unaccompanied   voices.
2. Wreathlike crowns.

Standing aloof from all our tears and strife,
Tranced in the paradise of dreams, he trod
20   In the untroubled summer of his life!

I have loved statues . . . at night the cold
Mysterious moon behind a mask of gold—
Or veiled in silver veils—has seen my pride
Utterly broken—seen the dream denied
25   For which I pleaded—heedless that for me
The miracle of joy could never be . . .
As in old legends beautiful and strange,
When bright gods loved fair mortals born to die,
And the frail daughters of despair and change
30   Become the brides of immortality?
c. 1902   1905

The White Witch

Her body is a dancing joy, a delicate delight,
Her hair a silver glamour in a net of golden light.

Her face is like the faces that a dreamer sometimes meets,
A face that Leonardo would have followed through the streets.

5   Her eyelids are like clouds that spread white wings across blue skies,
Like shadows in still water are the sorrows in her eyes.

How flower-like are the smiling lips so many have desired,
Curled lips that love's long kisses have left a little tired.
c. 1901   1902

━━◄✦►━━

Max Beerbohm
(1872–1956)

Max Beerbohm published his collected *Works* in 1896, at the ripe old age of twenty-four. In his preface he declared that he was retiring from literary production, leaving the field to "younger men, with months of activity before them." He broke this promise, but his stories continued to center on the 1890s; *Enoch Soames*, written in 1914, is a masterful recreation of *fin-de-siècle* London. It was a world in which Beerbohm played a prominent part. In 1894, still an Oxford under-graduate in his spare time, he burst on the London scene when his *In Defense of Cosmetics* appeared in the first issue of *The Yellow Book*. A sly parody of decadent life, the essay scandalized readers who saw it as idolizing languid young men who spent their days dressing up and putting on make-up. Oscar Wilde, though, saw the double-edged quality of Beerbohm's precocious writing: "You must take up literature," he advised him; "you have a style like a silver dagger."

Beerbohm had a genius for friendship, and a genius for caricaturing his contemporaries, visually as well as verbally. Some of the most vivid portraits of the era are found in his satiric illustrations of Beardsley and Wilde, of Kipling and Tennyson (see *Tennyson Reading "In Memoriam" to his Sovereign*, reproduced on page 1232). In 1895, during Wilde's sodomy trials, the London *World* paired Beerbohm with Aubrey Beardsley, in a satire of *The Yellow Book* based on Lewis Carroll's *Jabberwocky*:

> Beware the Yallerbock, my son!
>   The aims that rile, the art that racks
> Beware the Aub-Aub Bird, and shun
>   The stumious Beerbomax.

While Beerbohm was still an undergraduate, the artist William Rothenstein painted him for a book of portraits of prominent Oxford figures. Rothenstein became a lifelong friend, and has a walk-on role in *Enoch Soames*, whose comic mingling of fact and fiction reflects the interplay of artifice and reality, artistic rebellion and social climbing, in the London of the 1890s. The story is both the definitive send-up of the Decadent movement and also a clear-eyed memoir, with Beerbohm himself serving as narrator and guide to the world of his youth. "He plays with words as one plays with what one loves," Wilde remarked to their mutual friend Ada Leverson. "When you are alone with him," Wilde asked her, "does he take off his face and reveal his mask?"

Enoch Soames

When a book about the literature of the eighteen-nineties was given by Mr. Holbrook Jackson[1] to the world, I looked eagerly in the index for SOAMES, ENOCH. I had feared he would not be there. He was not there. But everybody else was. Many writers whom I had quite forgotten, or remembered but faintly, lived again for me, they and their work, in Mr. Holbrook Jackson's pages. The book was as thorough as it was brilliantly written. And thus the omission found by me was an all the deadlier record of poor Soames' failure to impress himself on his decade.

I daresay I am the only person who noticed the omission. Soames had failed so piteously as all that! Nor is there a counterpoise in the thought that if he had had some measure of success he might have passed, like those others, out of my mind, to return only at the historian's beck. It is true that had his gifts, such as they were, been acknowledged in his life-time, he would never have made the bargain I saw him make—that strange bargain whose results have kept him always in the foreground of my memory. But it is from those very results that the full piteousness of him glares out.

Not my compassion, however, impels me to write of him. For his sake, poor fellow, I should be inclined to keep my pen out of the ink. It is ill to deride the dead. And how can I write about Enoch Soames without making him ridiculous? Or rather, how am I to hush up the horrid fact that he *was* ridiculous? I shall not be able to do that. Yet, sooner or later, write about him I must. You will see, in due course, that I have no option. And I may as well get the thing done now.

In the Summer Term of '93 a bolt from the blue flashed down on Oxford. It drove deep, it hurtlingly embedded itself in the soil. Dons[2] and undergraduates stood around, rather pale, discussing nothing but it. Whence came it, this meteorite? From Paris. Its name? Will Rothenstein.[3] Its aim? To do a series of twenty-four portraits in lithograph. These were to be published from the Bodley Head, London.[4] The matter was urgent. Already the Warden of A, and the Master of B, and the Regius Professor of C, had meekly "sat." Dignified and doddering old men, who had never consented to sit to any one, could not withstand this dynamic little stranger. He did not sue: he invited; he did

1. Holbrook Jackson's *The Eighteen Nineties* (1913) is still one of the best books on the subject.
2. Professors.
3. William Rothenstein (1872–1945), British painter. He studied at the Slade School, was a close friend of Whistler, and specialized in portraits of celebrities.
4. Founded by John Lane and Elkin Mathews, the Bodley Head Press published many of the most important works of the 1890s, including the anthologies of the Rhymers' Club, the poems of Wilde, and *The Yellow Book* magazine, which Beardsley coedited with Henry Harland, the literary editor.

not invite: he commanded. He was twenty-one years old. He wore spectacles that flashed more than any other pair ever seen. He was a wit. He was brimful of ideas. He knew Whistler. He knew Edmond de Goncourt.[5] He knew every one in Paris. He knew them all by heart. He was Paris in Oxford. It was whispered that, so soon as he had polished off his selection of dons, he was going to include a few undergraduates. It was a proud day for me when I—I was included. I liked Rothenstein not less than I feared him; and there arose between us a friendship that has grown ever warmer, and been more and more valued by me, with every passing year.

At the end of Term he settled in—or rather, meteoritically into—London. It was to him I owed my first knowledge of that forever enchanting little world-in-itself, Chelsea, and my first acquaintance with Walter Sickert[6] and other august elders who dwelt there. It was Rothenstein that took me to see, in Cambridge Street, Pimlico, a young man whose drawings were already famous among the few—Aubrey Beardsley, by name. With Rothenstein I paid my first visit to the Bodley Head. By him I was inducted into another haunt of intellect and daring, the domino room of the Café Royal.[7]

There, on that October evening—there, in that exuberant vista of gilding and crimson velvet set amidst all those opposing mirrors and upholding caryatids, with fumes of tobacco ever rising to the painted and pagan ceiling, and with the hum of presumably cynical conversation broken into so sharply now and again by the clatter of dominoes shuffled on marble tables, I drew a deep breath, and "This indeed," said I to myself, "is life!"

It was the hour before dinner. We drank vermouth. Those who knew Rothenstein were pointing him out to those who knew him only by name. Men were constantly coming in through the swing-doors and wandering slowly up and down in search of vacant tables, or of tables occupied by friends. One of these rovers interested me because I was sure he wanted to catch Rothenstein's eye. He had twice passed our table, with a hesitating look; but Rothenstein, in the thick of a disquisition on Puvis de Chavannes,[8] had not seen him. He was a stooping, shambling person, rather tall, very pale, with longish and brownish hair. He had a thin vague beard—or rather, he had a chin on which a large number of hairs weakly curled and clustered to cover its retreat. He was an odd-looking person; but in the 'nineties odd apparitions were more frequent, I think, than they are now. The young writers of that era—and I was sure this man was a writer—strove earnestly to be distinct in aspect. This man had striven unsuccessfully. He wore a soft black hat of clerical kind but of Bohemian intention, and a grey waterproof cape which, perhaps because it was waterproof, failed to be romantic. I decided that "dim" was the *mot juste*[9] for him. I had already essayed to write, and was immensely keen on the *mot juste*, that Holy Grail of the period.

The dim man was now again approaching our table, and this time he made up his mind to pause in front of it. "You don't remember me," he said in a toneless voice.

5. Edmond de Goncourt (1822–1896) was the author, with his brother Jules, of a famous *Journal* describing Parisian cultural life.
6. English painter (1860–1942) known for his scenes of music halls and bohemian life in London. Sickert worked under Whistler in Paris.
7. During the 1890s, Wilde, Douglas, Symons, Beerbohm, and many other literary and artistic figures congregated at

the fashionable Café Royal on Regent Street; it was there that Wilde met with friends to plan his defense against the Marquess of Queensberry.
8. French painter (1824–1898) known for his pale, languid murals of pastoral subjects.
9. Perfect word or expression. The novelist Gustave Flaubert made the search for *le mot juste* an artistic duty.

Rothenstein brightly focussed him. "Yes, I do," he replied after a moment, with pride rather than effusion—pride in a retentive memory. "Edwin Soames."

"Enoch Soames," said Enoch.

"Enoch Soames," repeated Rothenstein in a tone implying that it was enough to have hit on the surname. "We met in Paris two or three times when you were living there. We met at the Café Groche."

"And I came to your studio once."

"Oh yes; I was sorry I was out."

"But you were in. You showed me some of your paintings, you know . . . I hear you're in Chelsea now."

"Yes."

I almost wondered that Mr. Soames did not, after this monosyllable, pass along. He stood patiently there, rather like a dumb animal, rather like a donkey looking over a gate. A sad figure, his. It occurred to me that "hungry" was perhaps the *mot juste* for him; but—hungry for what? He looked as if he had little appetite for anything. I was sorry for him; and Rothenstein, though he had not invited him to Chelsea, did ask him to sit down and have something to drink.

Seated, he was more self-assertive. He flung back the wings of his cape with a gesture which—had not those wings been waterproof—might have seemed to hurl defiance at things in general. And he ordered an absinthe. "*Je me tiens toujours fidèle,*" he told Rothenstein, "*à la sorcière glauque.*"[1]

"It is bad for you," said Rothenstein dryly.

"Nothing is bad for one," answered Soames. "*Dans ce monde il n'y a ni de bien ni de mal.*"[2]

"Nothing good and nothing bad? How do you mean?"

"I explained it all in the preface to 'Negations.'"

"'Negations'?"

"Yes; I gave you a copy of it."

"Oh yes, of course. But did you explain—for instance—that there was no such thing as bad or good grammar?"

"N–no," said Soames. "Of course in Art there is the good and the evil. But in Life—no." He was rolling a cigarette. He had weak white hands, not well washed, and with finger-tips much stained by nicotine. "In Life there are illusions of good and evil, but"—his voice trailed away to a murmur in which the words "vieux jeu"[3] and "rococo" were faintly audible. I think he felt he was not doing himself justice, and feared that Rothenstein was going to point out fallacies. Anyhow, he cleared his throat and said "*Parlons d'autre chose.*"[4]

It occurs to you that he was a fool? It didn't to me. I was young, and had not the clarity of judgment that Rothenstein already had. Soames was quite five or six years older than either of us. Also, he had written a book.

It was wonderful to have written a book.

If Rothenstein had not been there, I should have revered Soames. Even as it was, I respected him. And I was very near indeed to reverence when he said he had another book coming out soon. I asked if I might ask what kind of book it was to be.

---

1. I always keep myself faithful . . . to the green witch (French). Absinthe, a bitter, anise-flavored liqueur, is green until water is added to it, when it turns white.
2. In this world there is neither good nor evil.
3. Old game; rococo is an elaborate artistic style that flourished in the 18th century.
4. Let's talk about something else.

"My poems," he answered. Rothenstein asked if this was to be the title of the book. The poet meditated on this suggestion, but said he rather thought of giving the book no title at all. "If a book is good in itself—" he murmured, waving his cigarette.

Rothenstein objected that absence of title might be bad for the sale of a book. "If," he urged, "I went into a bookseller's and said simply 'Have you got?' or 'Have you a copy of?' how would they know what I wanted?"

"Oh, of course I should have my name on the cover," Soames answered earnestly. "And I rather want," he added, looking hard at Rothenstein, "to have a drawing of myself as frontispiece." Rothenstein admitted that this was a capital idea, and mentioned that he was going into the country and would be there for some time. He then looked at his watch, exclaimed at the hour, paid the waiter, and went away with me to dinner. Soames remained at his post of fidelity to the glaucous witch.

"Why were you so determined not to draw him?" I asked.

"Draw him? Him? How can one draw a man who doesn't exist?"

"He is dim," I admitted. But my *mot juste* fell flat. Rothenstein repeated that Soames was non-existent.

Still, Soames had written a book. I asked if Rothenstein had read "Negations." He said he had looked into it, "but," he added crisply, "I don't profess to know anything about writing." A reservation very characteristic of the period! Painters would not then allow that any one outside their own order had a right to any opinion about painting. This law (graven on the tablets brought down by Whistler from the summit of Fujiyama)[5] imposed certain limitations. If other arts than painting were not utterly unintelligible to all but the men who practised them, the law tottered—the Monroe Doctrine, as it were, did not hold good. Therefore no painter would offer an opinion of a book without warning you at any rate that his opinion was worthless. No one is a better judge of literature than Rothenstein; but it wouldn't have done to tell him so in those days; and I knew that I must form an unaided judgment on "Negations."

Not to buy a book of which I had met the author face to face would have been for me in those days an impossible act of self-denial. When I returned to Oxford for the Christmas Term I had duly secured "Negations." I used to keep it lying carelessly on the table in my room, and whenever a friend took it up and asked what it was about I would say "Oh, it's rather a remarkable book. It's by a man whom I know." Just "what it was about" I never was able to say. Head or tail was just what I hadn't made of that slim green volume. I found in the preface no clue to the exiguous labyrinth of contents, and in that labyrinth nothing to explain the preface.

> "Lean near to life. Lean very near—nearer.
> "Life is web, and therein nor warp nor woof is, but web only.
> "It is for this I am Catholick in church and in thought, yet do let swift Mood weave there what the shuttle of Mood wills."

These were the opening phrases of the preface, but those which followed were less easy to understand. Then came "Stark: *A Conte*," about a midinette who, so far as I could gather, murdered, or was about to murder, a mannequin.[6] It was rather like a story by Catulle Mendès[7] in which the translator had either skipped or cut out

---

5. See Mr. *Whistler's* "*Ten O'Clock*," page 2065. With a view to silencing his critics and keeping Wilde out of art criticism, Whistler insisted that only painters should make pronouncements about art.

6. A story about a shopgirl murdering a fashion model.
7. French poet, critic, and novelist (1841–1909), member of the aestheticist Parnassian School.

every alternate sentence. Next, a dialogue between Pan and St. Ursula[8]—lacking, I felt, in "snap." Next, some aphorisms (entitled ἀφορίσματα). Throughout, in fact, there was a great variety of form; and the forms had evidently been wrought with much care. It was rather the substance that eluded me. Was there, I wondered, any substance at all? It did now occur to me: suppose Enoch Soames was a fool! Up cropped a rival hypothesis: suppose I was! I inclined to give Soames the benefit of the doubt. I had read "L'Après-midi d'un Faune" without extracting a glimmer of meaning.[9] Yet Mallarmé—of course—was a Master. How was I to know that Soames wasn't another? There was a sort of music in his prose, not indeed arresting, but perhaps, I thought, haunting, and laden perhaps with meanings as deep as Mallarmé's own. I awaited his poems with an open mind.

And I looked forward to them with positive impatience after I had had a second meeting with him. This was on an evening in January. Going into the aforesaid domino room, I passed a table at which sat a pale man with an open book before him. He looked from his book to me, and I looked back over my shoulder with a vague sense that I ought to have recognised him. I returned to pay my respects. After exchanging a few words, I said with a glance to the open book, "I see I am interrupting you," and was about to pass on, but "I prefer," Soames replied in his toneless voice, "to be interrupted," and I obeyed his gesture that I should sit down.

I asked him if he often read here. "Yes; things of this kind I read here," he answered, indicating the title of his book—"The Poems of Shelley."

"Anything that you really"—and I was going to say "admire?" But I cautiously left my sentence unfinished, and was glad that I had done so, for he said, with unwonted emphasis, "Anything second-rate."

I had read little of Shelley, but "Of course," I murmured, "he's very uneven."

"I should have thought evenness was just what was wrong with him. A deadly evenness. That's why I read him here. The noise of this place breaks the rhythm. He's tolerable here." Soames took up the book and glanced through the pages. He laughed. Soames' laugh was a short, single and mirthless sound from the throat, unaccompanied by any movement of the face or brightening of the eyes. "What a period!" he uttered, laying the book down. And "What a country!" he added.

I asked rather nervously if he didn't think Keats had more or less held his own against the drawbacks of time and place. He admitted that there were "passages in Keats," but did not specify them. Of "the older men," as he called them, he seemed to like only Milton. "Milton," he said, "wasn't sentimental." Also, "Milton had a dark insight." And again, "I can always read Milton in the reading-room."

"The reading-room?"

"Of the British Museum. I go there every day."

"You do? I've only been there once. I'm afraid I found it rather a depressing place. It—it seemed to sap one's vitality."

"It does. That's why I go there. The lower one's vitality, the more sensitive one is to great art. I live near the Museum. I have rooms in Dyott Street."

"And you go round to the reading-room to read Milton?"

"Usually Milton." He looked at me. "It was Milton," he certificatively added, "who converted me to Diabolism."

---

8. Pan, the lusty Greek god of forests and pastures, was part man, part goat; St. Ursula was a 10th-century British saint and martyr associated with virginity.

9. *The Afternoon of a Faun* (c. 1865) by French poet Stéphane Mallarmé, famous for the suggestive obscurity of his symbolist style.

"Diabolism? Oh yes? Really?" said I, with that vague discomfort and that intense desire to be polite which one feels when a man speaks of his own religion. "You— worship the Devil?"

Soames shook his head. "It's not exactly worship," he qualified, sipping his absinthe. "It's more a matter of trusting and encouraging."

"Ah, yes . . . But I had rather gathered from the preface to 'Negations' that you were a—a Catholic."

"*Je l'étais à cette époque.*[1] Perhaps I still am. Yes, I'm a Catholic diabolist."

This profession he made in an almost cursory tone. I could see that what was uppermost in his mind was the fact that I had read "Negations." His pale eyes had for the first time gleamed. I felt as one who is about to be examined, *viva voce* [orally], on the very subject in which he is shakiest. I hastily asked him how soon his poems were to be published. "Next week," he told me.

"And are they to be published without a title?"

"No. I found a title, at last. But I shan't tell you what it is," as though I had been so impertinent as to inquire. "I am not sure that it wholly satisfies me. But it is the best I can find. It suggests something of the quality of the poems . . . Strange growths, natural and wild, yet exquisite," he added, "and many-hued, and full of poisons."

I asked him what he thought of Baudelaire. He uttered the snort that was his laugh, and "Baudelaire," he said, "was a *bourgeois malgré lui.*"[2] France had had only one poet: Villon;[3] "and two-thirds of Villon were sheer journalism." Verlaine was "an *épicier malgré lui.*"[4] Altogether, rather to my surprise, he rated French literature lower than English. There were "passages" in Villiers de l'Isle-Adam.[5] But "I," he summed up, "owe nothing to France." He nodded at me. "You'll see," he predicted.

I did not, when the time came, quite see that. I thought the author of "Fungoids" did—unconsciously, of course—owe something to the young Parisian décadents, or to the young English ones who owed something to *them.* I still think so. The little book—bought by me in Oxford—lies before me as I write. Its pale grey buckram cover and silver lettering have not worn well. Nor have its contents. Through these, with a melancholy interest, I have again been looking. They are not much. But at the time of their publication I had a vague suspicion that they *might* be. I suppose it is my capacity for faith, not poor Soames' work, that is weaker than it once was . . .

To a Young Woman

Thou art, who hast not been!
  Pale tunes irresolute
  And traceries of old sounds
  Blown from a rotted flute
Mingle with noise of cymbals rouged with rust,
  Nor not strange forms and epicene

1. I was at that time.
2. Middle-class despite himself. Charles Baudelaire (1821–1867), French poet and author of *Les Fleurs du Mal* (*The Flowers of Evil*), repeatedly attacked bourgeois complacency and morality.
3. François Villon, medieval French poet whose work was rediscovered in the 19th century.
4. A grocer despite himself. Paul Verlaine (1844–1896),

symbolist poet whose private life embodied decadence: he left his wife and children to have an affair with the poet Arthur Rimbaud, was imprisoned in England for shooting Rimbaud, and in later years divided his time among poetry, sex, and absinthe.
5. Comte Auguste de Villiers de l'Isle-Adam (1838–1889), French novelist and playwright who scorned the vulgarity of modern life.

> Lie bleeding in the dust,
>> Being wounded with wounds.
> For this it is
> That in thy counterpart
>> Of age-long mockeries
> *Thou hast not been nor art!*

There seemed to me a certain inconsistency as between the first and last lines of this. I tried, with bent brows, to resolve the discord. But I did not take my failure as wholly incompatible with a meaning in Soames' mind. Might it not rather indicate the depth of his meaning? As for the craftsmanship, "rouged with rust" seemed to me a fine stroke, and "nor not" instead of "and" had a curious felicity. I wondered who the Young Woman was, and what she had made of it all. I sadly suspect that Soames could not have made more of it than she. Yet, even now, if one doesn't try to make any sense at all of the poem, and reads it just for the sound, there is a certain grace of cadence. Soames was an artist—in so far as he was anything, poor fellow!

It seemed to me, when first I read "Fungoids," that, oddly enough, the Diabolistic side of him was the best. Diabolism seemed to be a cheerful, even a wholesome, influence in his life.

Nocturne[6]

> Round and round the shutter'd Square
> I stroll'd with the Devil's arm in mine.
> No sound but the scrape of his hoofs was there
> And the ring of his laughter and mine.
>> We had drunk black wine.
>
> *I scream'd, "I will race you, Master!"*
> *"What matter," he shriek'd, "to-night*
> *Which of us runs the faster?*
> *There is nothing to fear to-night*
>> *In the foul moon's light!"*
>
> Then I look'd him in the eyes,
> And I laugh'd full shrill at the lie he told
> And the gnawing fear he would fain disguise.
> It was true, what I'd time and again been told:
>> He was old—old.

There was, I felt, quite a swing about that first stanza—a joyous and rollicking note of comradeship. The second was slightly hysterical perhaps. But I liked the third: it was so bracingly unorthodox, even according to the tenets of Soames' peculiar sect in the faith. Not much "trusting and encouraging" here! Soames triumphantly exposing the Devil as a liar, and laughing "full shrill," cut a quite heartening figure, I thought—then! Now, in the light of what befell, none of his poems depresses me so much as "Nocturne."

---

6. Popularized by Whistler's series of paintings called *Nocturnes,* night scenes enjoyed great popularity among artists and poets during the 1880s and 1890s.

I looked out for what the metropolitan reviewers would have to say. They seemed to fall into two classes: those who had little to say and those who had nothing. The second class was the larger, and the words of the first were cold; insomuch that

Strikes a note of modernity throughout. . . . These tripping numbers.—*Preston Telegraph*

was the only lure offered in advertisements by Soames' publisher. I had hopes that when next I met the poet I could congratulate him on having made a stir; for I fancied he was not so sure of his intrinsic greatness as he seemed. I was but able to say, rather coarsely, when next I did see him, that I hoped "Fungoids" was "selling splendidly." He looked at me across his glass of absinthe and asked if I had bought a copy. His publisher had told him that three had been sold. I laughed, as at a jest.

"You don't suppose I *care,* do you?" he said, with something like a snarl. I disclaimed the notion. He added that he was not a tradesman. I said mildly that I wasn't, either, and murmured that an artist who gave truly new and great things to the world had always to wait long for recognition. He said he cared not a sou[7] for recognition. I agreed that the act of creation was its own reward.

His moroseness might have alienated me if I had regarded myself as a nobody. But ah! hadn't both John Lane and Aubrey Beardsley suggested that I should write an essay for the great new venture that was afoot—"The Yellow Book"? And hadn't Henry Harland, as editor, accepted my essay? And wasn't it to be in the very first number? At Oxford I was still *in statu pupillari* [a student]. In London I regarded myself as very much indeed a graduate now—one whom no Soames could ruffle. Partly to show off, partly in sheer good-will, I told Soames he ought to contribute to "The Yellow Book." He uttered from the throat a sound of scorn for that publication.

Nevertheless, I did, a day or two later, tentatively ask Harland if he knew anything of the work of a man called Enoch Soames. Harland paused in the midst of his characteristic stride around the room, threw up his hands towards the ceiling, and groaned aloud: he had often met "that absurd creature" in Paris, and this very morning had received some poems in manuscript from him.

"Has he *no* talent?" I asked.

"He has an income. He's all right." Harland was the most joyous of men and most generous of critics, and he hated to talk of anything about which he couldn't be enthusiastic. So I dropped the subject of Soames. The news that Soames had an income did take the edge off solicitude. I learned afterwards that he was the son of an unsuccessful and deceased bookseller in Preston, but had inherited an annuity of £300 from a married aunt, and had no surviving relatives of any kind. Materially, then, he was "all right." But there was still a spiritual pathos about him, sharpened for me now by the possibility that even the praises of *The Preston Telegraph* might not have been forthcoming had he not been the son of a Preston man. He had a sort of weak doggedness which I could not but admire. Neither he nor his work received the slightest encouragement; but he persisted in behaving as a personage: always he kept his dingy little flag flying. Wherever congregated the *jeunes féroces*[8] of the arts, in whatever Soho restaurant they had just discovered, in whatever music-hall they were most frequenting, there was Soames in the midst of them, or rather on the fringe of them, a dim but inevitable figure. He never sought to propitiate his fellow-writers, never bated a jot of his arrogance about his own work or of his contempt for theirs.

---

7. A penny. 8. Young Turks.

To the painters he was respectful, even humble; but for the poets and prosaists of "The Yellow Book," and later of "The Savoy," he had never a word but of scorn. He wasn't resented. It didn't occur to anybody that he or his Catholic Diabolism mattered. When, in the autumn of '96, he brought out (at his own expense, this time) a third book, his last book, nobody said a word for or against it. I meant, but forgot, to buy it. I never saw it, and am ashamed to say I don't even remember what it was called. But I did, at the time of its publication, say to Rothenstein that I thought poor old Soames was really a rather tragic figure, and that I believed he would literally die for want of recognition. Rothenstein scoffed. He said I was trying to get credit for a kind heart which I didn't possess; and perhaps this was so. But at the private view of the New English Art Club, a few weeks later, I beheld a pastel portrait of "Enoch Soames, Esq." It was very like him, and very like Rothenstein to have done it. Soames was standing near it, in his soft hat and his waterproof cape, all through the afternoon. Anybody who knew him would have recognised the portrait at a glance, but nobody who didn't know him would have recognised the portrait from its bystander: it "existed" so much more than he; it was bound to. Also, it had not that expression of faint happiness which on this day was discernible, yes, in Soames' countenance. Fame had breathed on him. Twice again in the course of the month I went to the New English, and on both occasions Soames himself was on view there. Looking back, I regard the close of that exhibition as having been virtually the close of his career. He had felt the breath of Fame against his cheek—so late, for such a little while; and at its withdrawal he gave in, gave up, gave out. He, who had never looked strong or well, looked ghastly now—a shadow of the shade he had once been. He still frequented the domino room, but, having lost all wish to excite curiosity, he no longer read books there. "You read only at the Museum now?" asked I, with attempted cheerfulness. He said he never went there now. "No absinthe there," he muttered. It was the sort of thing that in the old days he would have said for effect; but it carried conviction now. Absinthe, erst but a point in the "personality" he had striven so hard to build up, was solace and necessity now. He no longer called it "la sorcière glauque." He had shed away all his French phrases. He had become a plain, unvarnished, Preston man.

Failure, if it be a plain, unvarnished, complete failure, and even though it be a squalid failure, has always a certain dignity. I avoided Soames because he made me feel rather vulgar. John Lane had published, by this time, two little books of mine, and they had had a pleasant little success of esteem. I was a—slight but definite—"personality." Frank Harris had engaged me to kick up my heels in *The Saturday Review*, Alfred Harmsworth was letting me do likewise in *The Daily Mail*. I was just what Soames wasn't. And he shamed my gloss. Had I known that he really and firmly believed in the greatness of what he as an artist had achieved, I might not have shunned him. No man who hasn't lost his vanity can be held to have altogether failed. Soames' dignity was an illusion of mine. One day in the first week of June, 1897, that illusion went. But on the evening of that day Soames went too.

I had been out most of the morning, and, as it was too late to reach home in time for luncheon, I sought "the Vingtième." This little place—Restaurant du Vingtième Siècle,[9] to give it its full title—had been discovered in '96 by the poets and prosaists, but had now been more or less abandoned in favour of some later find. I don't think it

9. Restaurant of the Twentieth Century.

lived long enough to justify its name; but at that time there it still was, in Greek Street, a few doors from Soho Square, and almost opposite to that house where, in the first years of the century, a little girl, and with her a boy named De Quincey, made nightly encampment in darkness and hunger among dust and rats and old legal parchments.[1] The Vingtième was but a small whitewashed room, leading out into the street at one end and into a kitchen at the other. The proprietor and cook was a Frenchman, known to us as Monsieur Vingtième; the waiters were his two daughters, Rose and Berthe; and the food, according to faith, was good. The tables were so narrow, and were set so close together, that there was space for twelve of them, six jutting from either wall.

Only the two nearest to the door, as I went in, were occupied. On one side sat a tall, flashy, rather Mephistophelian[2] man whom I had seen from time to time in the domino room and elsewhere. On the other side sat Soames. They made a queer contrast in that sunlit room—Soames sitting haggard in that hat and cape which nowhere at any season had I seen him doff, and this other, this keenly vital man, at sight of whom I more than ever wondered whether he were a diamond merchant, a conjurer, or the head of a private detective agency. I was sure Soames didn't want my company; but I asked, as it would have seemed brutal not to, whether I might join him, and took the chair opposite to his. He was smoking a cigarette, with an untasted salmi of something on his plate and a half-empty bottle of Sauterne before him; and he was quite silent. I said that the preparations for the Jubilee made London impossible.[3] (I rather liked them, really.) I professed a wish to go right away till the whole thing was over. In vain did I attune myself to his gloom. He seemed not to hear me nor even to see me. I felt that his behaviour made me ridiculous in the eyes of the other man. The gangway between the two rows of tables at the Vingtième was hardly more than two feet wide (Rose and Berthe, in their ministrations, had always to edge past each other, quarrelling in whispers as they did so), and any one at the table abreast of yours was practically at yours. I thought our neighbour was amused at my failure to interest Soames, and so, as I could not explain to him that my insistence was merely charitable, I became silent. Without turning my head, I had him well within my range of vision. I hoped I looked less vulgar than he in contrast with Soames. I was sure he was not an Englishman, but what *was* his nationality? Though his jet-black hair was *en brosse* [crew-cut], I did not think he was French. To Berthe, who waited on him, he spoke French fluently, but with a hardly native idiom and accent. I gathered that this was his first visit to the Vingtième; but Berthe was off-hand in her manner to him: he had not made a good impression. His eyes were handsome, but—like the Vingtième's tables—too narrow and set too close together. His nose was predatory, and the points of his moustache, waxed up beyond his nostrils, gave a fixity to his smile. Decidedly, he was sinister. And my sense of discomfort in his presence was intensified by the scarlet waistcoat which tightly, and so unseasonably in June, sheathed his ample chest. This waistcoat wasn't wrong merely because of the heat, either. It was somehow all wrong in itself. It wouldn't have done on Christmas morning. It would have struck a

1. In his *Confessions of an English Opium Eater* (1821), Thomas De Quincey describes the poverty of his youth, when he lived with a young girl named Ann in the Soho area of London; see pages 1042–71.
2. Mephistopheles represents the Devil in the legend of Faust, a German scholar who sells his soul to the Devil in exchange for youth or knowledge. See Christopher Marlowe's *Doctor Faustus* (c. 1594) and Johann Wolfgang von Goethe's play *Faust* (1808; 1832).
3. In 1897 Queen Victoria celebrated her Diamond Jubilee, the sixtieth year of her reign.

jarring note at the first night of "Hernani."[4] I was trying to account for its wrongness when Soames suddenly and strangely broke silence. "A hundred years hence!" he murmured, as in a trance.

"We shall not be here!" I briskly but fatuously added.

"We shall not be here. No," he droned, "but the Museum will still be just where it is. And the reading-room, just where it is. And people will be able to go and read there." He inhaled sharply, and a spasm as of actual pain contorted his features.

I wondered what train of thought poor Soames had been following. He did not enlighten me when he said, after a long pause, "You think I haven't minded."

"Minded what, Soames?"

"Neglect. Failure."

"*Failure?*" I said heartily. "Failure?" I repeated vaguely. "Neglect—yes, perhaps; but that's quite another matter. Of course you haven't been—appreciated. But what then? Any artist who—who gives—" What I wanted to say was, "Any artist who gives truly new and great things to the world has always to wait long for recognition;" but the flattery would not out: in the face of his misery, a misery so genuine and so unmasked, my lips would not say the words.

And then—he said them for me. I flushed. "That's what you were going to say, isn't it?" he asked.

"How did you know?"

"It's what you said to me three years ago, when 'Fungoids' was published." I flushed the more. I need not have done so at all, for "It's the only important thing I ever heard you say," he continued. "And I've never forgotten it. It's a true thing. It's a horrible truth. But—d'you remember what I answered? I said 'I don't care a sou for recognition.' And you believed me. You've gone on believing I'm above that sort of thing. You're shallow. What should *you* know of the feelings of a man like me? You imagine that a great artist's faith in himself and in the verdict of posterity is enough to keep him happy. . . You've never guessed at the bitterness and loneliness, the"— his voice broke; but presently he resumed, speaking with a force that I had never known in him. "Posterity! What use is it to *me?* A dead man doesn't know that people are visiting his grave—visiting his birthplace—putting up tablets to him—unveiling statues of him. A dead man can't read the books that are written about him. A hundred years hence! Think of it! If I could come back to life *then*—just for a few hours—and go to the reading-room, and *read!* Or better still: if I could be projected, now, at this moment, into that future, into that reading-room, just for this one afternoon! I'd sell myself body and soul to the devil, for that! Think of the pages and pages in the catalogue: 'SOAMES, ENOCH' endlessly—endless editions, commentaries, prolegomena, biographies"—but here he was interrupted by a sudden loud creak of the chair at the next table. Our neighbour had half risen from his place. He was leaning towards us, apologetically intrusive.

"Excuse—permit me," he said softly. "I have been unable not to hear. Might I take a liberty? In this little restaurant-sans-façon"[5]—he spread wide his hands— "might I, as the phrase is, 'cut in'?"

I could but signify our acquiescence. Berthe had appeared at the kitchen door, thinking the stranger wanted his bill. He waved her away with his cigar, and in another moment had seated himself beside me, commanding a full view of Soames.

4. Play by Victor Hugo. The arch-aesthete Théophile Gautier made a sensation by wearing a bright pink vest to its opening in 1830.
5. Unpretentious.

"Though not an Englishman," he explained, "I know my London well, Mr Soames. Your name and fame—Mr Beerbohm's too—very known to me. Your point is: who am I?" He glanced quickly over his shoulder, and in a lowered voice said, "I am the Devil."

I couldn't help it: I laughed. I tried not to, I knew there was nothing to laugh at, my rudeness shamed me, but—I laughed with increasing volume. The Devil's quiet dignity, the surprise and disgust of his raised eyebrows, did but the more dissolve me. I rocked to and fro, I lay back aching. I behaved deplorably.

"I am a gentleman, and," he said with intense emphasis, "I thought I was in the company of *gentlemen*."

"Don't!" I gasped faintly. "Oh, don't!"

"Curious, *nicht wahr* [isn't it]?" I heard him say to Soames. "There is a type of person to whom the very mention of my name is—oh-so-awfully-funny! In your theatres the dullest comédien needs only to say 'The Devil!' and right away they give him 'the loud laugh that speaks the vacant mind.' Is it not so?"

I had now just breath enough to offer my apologies. He accepted them, but coldly, and re-addressed himself to Soames.

"I am a man of business," he said, "and always I would put things through 'right now,' as they say in the States. You are a poet. *Les affaires* [business dealings]—you detest them. So be it. But with me you will deal, eh? What you have said just now gives me furiously to hope."

Soames had not moved, except to light a fresh cigarette. He sat crouched forward, with his elbows squared on the table, and his head just above the level of his hands, staring up at the Devil. "Go on," he nodded. I had no remnant of laughter in me now.

"It will be the more pleasant, our little deal," the Devil went on, "because you are—I mistake not?—a Diabolist."

"A Catholic Diabolist," said Soames.

The Devil accepted the reservation genially. "You wish," he resumed, "to visit now—this afternoon as-ever-is—the reading-room of the British Museum, yes? but of a hundred years hence, yes? *Parfaitement*. Time—an illusion. Past and future—they are as ever-present as the present, or at any rate only what you call 'just-round-the-corner.' I switch you on to any date. I project you—pouf! You wish to be in the reading-room just as it will be on the afternoon of June 3, 1997? You wish to find yourself standing in that room, just past the swing-doors, this very minute, yes? and to stay there till closing time? Am I right?"

Soames nodded.

The Devil looked at his watch. "Ten past two," he said. "Closing time in summer same then as now: seven o'clock. That will give you almost five hours. At seven o'-clock—pouf!—you find yourself again here, sitting at this table. I am dining tonight *dans le monde—dans le higlif*.[6] That concludes my present visit to your great city. I come and fetch you here, Mr Soames, on my way home."

"Home?" I echoed.

"Be it never so humble!" said the Devil lightly.

"All right," said Soames.

"Soames!" I entreated. But my friend moved not a muscle.

The Devil had made as though to stretch forth his hand across the table and touch Soames' forearm; but he paused in his gesture.

6. In society—in the high-life.

"A hundred years hence, as now," he smiled, "no smoking allowed in the reading-room. You would better therefore——"

Soames removed the cigarette from his mouth and dropped it into his glass of Sauterne.

"Soames!" again I cried. "Can't you"—but the Devil had now stretched forth his hand across the table. He brought it slowly down on—the table-cloth. Soames' chair was empty. His cigarette floated sodden in his wine-glass. There was no other trace of him.

For a few moments the Devil let his hand rest where it lay, gazing at me out of the corners of his eyes, vulgarly triumphant.

A shudder shook me. With an effort I controlled myself and rose from my chair. "Very clever," I said condescendingly. "But—'The Time Machine' is a delightful book,[7] don't you think? So entirely original!"

"You are pleased to sneer," said the Devil, who had also risen, "but it is one thing to write about an impossible machine; it is a quite other thing to be a Supernatural Power." All the same, I had scored.

Berthe had come forth at the sound of our rising. I explained to her that Mr Soames had been called away, and that both he and I would be dining here. It was not until I was out in the open air that I began to feel giddy. I have but the haziest recollection of what I did, where I wandered, in the glaring sunshine of that endless afternoon. I remember the sound of carpenters' hammers all along Piccadilly, and the bare chaotic look of the half-erected "stands." Was it in the Green Park, or in Kensington Gardens, or where was it that I sat on a chair beneath a tree, trying to read an evening paper? There was a phrase in the leading article that went on repeating itself in my fagged mind—"Little is hidden from this august Lady full of the garnered wisdom of sixty years of Sovereignty." I remember wildly conceiving a letter (to reach Windsor by express messenger told to await answer):

> MADAM,—Well knowing that your Majesty is full of the garnered wisdom of sixty years of Sovereignty, I venture to ask your advice in the following delicate matter. Mr Enoch Soames, whose poems you may or may not know, . . .

Was there no way of helping him—saving him? A bargain was a bargain, and I was the last man to aid or abet any one in wriggling out of a reasonable obligation. I wouldn't have lifted a little finger to save Faust. But poor Soames!—doomed to pay without respite an eternal price for nothing but a fruitless search and a bitter disillusioning. . . .

Odd and uncanny it seemed to me that he, Soames, in the flesh, in the waterproof cape, was at this moment living in the last decade of the next century, poring over books not yet written, and seeing and seen by men not yet born. Uncannier and odder still, that to-night and evermore he would be in Hell. Assuredly, truth was stranger than fiction.

Endless that afternoon was. Almost I wished I had gone with Soames—not indeed to stay in the reading-room, but to sally forth for a brisk sight-seeing walk around a new London. I wandered restlessly out of the Park I had sat in. Vainly I tried to imagine myself an ardent tourist from the eighteenth century. Intolerable was the strain of the slow-passing and empty minutes. Long before seven o'clock I was back at the Vingtième.

---

7. H. G. Wells's pioneering work of science fiction had just appeared in 1895.

I sat there just where I had sat for luncheon. Air came in listlessly through the open door behind me. Now and again Rose or Berthe appeared for a moment. I had told them I would not order any dinner till Mr Soames came. A hurdy-gurdy began to play, abruptly drowning the noise of a quarrel between some Frenchmen further up the street. Whenever the tune was changed I heard the quarrel still raging. I had bought another evening paper on my way. I unfolded it. My eyes gazed ever away from it to the clock over the kitchen door. . . .

Five minutes, now, to the hour! I remembered that clocks in restaurants are kept five minutes fast. I concentrated my eyes on the paper. I vowed I would not look away from it again. I held it upright, at its full width, close to my face, so that I had no view of anything but it . . . Rather a tremulous sheet? Only because of the draught, I told myself.

My arms gradually became stiff; they ached; but I could not drop them—now. I had a suspicion, I had a certainty. Well, what then? . . . What else had I come for? Yet I held tight that barrier of newspaper. Only the sound of Berthe's brisk footstep from the kitchen enabled me, forced me, to drop it, and to utter:

"What shall we have to eat, Soames?"

"*Il est souffrant, ce pauvre Monsieur Soames?*"[8] asked Berthe.

"He's only—tired." I asked her to get some wine—Burgundy—and whatever food might be ready. Soames sat crouched forward against the table, exactly as when last I had seen him. It was as though he had never moved—he who had moved so unimaginably far. Once or twice in the afternoon it had for an instant occurred to me that perhaps his journey was not to be fruitless—that perhaps we had all been wrong in our estimate of the works of Enoch Soames. That we had been horribly right was horribly clear from the look of him. But "Don't be discouraged," I falteringly said. "Perhaps it's only that you—didn't leave enough time. Two, three centuries hence, perhaps—"

"Yes," his voice came. "I've thought of that."

"And now—now for the more immediate future! Where are you going to hide? How would it be if you caught the Paris express from Charing Cross? Almost an hour to spare. Don't go on to Paris. Stop at Calais. Live in Calais. He'd never think of looking for you in Calais."

"It's like my luck," he said, "to spend my last hours on earth with an ass." But I was not offended. "And a treacherous ass," he strangely added, tossing across to me a crumpled bit of paper which he had been holding in his hand. I glanced at the writing on it—some sort of gibberish, apparently. I laid it impatiently aside.

"Come, Soames! pull yourself together! This isn't a mere matter of life and death. It's a question of eternal torment, mind you! You don't mean to say you're going to wait limply here till the Devil comes to fetch you?"

"I can't do anything else. I've no choice."

"Come! This is 'trusting and encouraging' with a vengeance! This is Diabolism run mad!" I filled his glass with wine. "Surely, now that you've *seen* the brute——"

"It's no good abusing him."

"You must admit there's nothing Miltonic about him, Soames."

"I don't say he's not rather different from what I expected."

"He's a vulgarian, he's a swell-mobsman, he's the sort of man who hangs about the corridors of trains going to the Riviera and steals ladies' jewel-cases. Imagine eternal torment presided over by *him!*"

"You don't suppose I look forward to it, do you?"

8. Is poor Mr. Soames ill?

"Then why not slip quietly out of the way?"

Again and again I filled his glass, and always, mechanically, he emptied it; but the wine kindled no spark of enterprise in him. He did not eat, and I myself ate hardly at all. I did not in my heart believe that any dash for freedom could save him. The chase would be swift, the capture certain. But better anything than this passive, meek, miserable waiting. I told Soames that for the honour of the human race he ought to make some show of resistance. He asked what the human race had ever done for him. "Besides," he said, "can't you understand that I'm in his power? You saw him touch me, didn't you? There's an end of it. I've no will. I'm sealed."

I made a gesture of despair. He went on repeating the word "sealed." I began to realise that the wine had clouded his brain. No wonder! Foodless he had gone into futurity, foodless he still was. I urged him to eat at any rate some bread. It was maddening to think that he, who had so much to tell, might tell nothing. "How was it all," I asked, "yonder? Come! Tell me your adventures."

"They'd make first-rate 'copy,' wouldn't they?"

"I'm awfully sorry for you, Soames, and I make all possible allowances; but what earthly right have you to insinuate that I should make 'copy,' as you call it, out of you?"

The poor fellow pressed his hands to his forehead. "I don't know," he said. "I had some reason, I know . . . I'll try to remember."

"That's right. Try to remember everything. Eat a little more bread. What did the reading-room look like?"

"Much as usual," he at length muttered.

"Many people there?"

"Usual sort of number."

"What did they look like?"

Soames tried to visualise them. "They all," he presently remembered, "looked very like one another."

My mind took a fearsome leap. "All dressed in Jaeger?"[9]

"Yes. I think so. Greyish-yellowish stuff."

"A sort of uniform?" He nodded. "With a number on it, perhaps?—a number on a large disc of metal sewn on to the left sleeve? DKF 78,910—that sort of thing?" It was even so. "And all of them—men and women alike—looking very well-cared-for? very Utopian? and smelling rather strongly of carbolic? and all of them quite hairless?" I was right every time. Soames was only not sure whether the men and women were hairless or shorn. "I hadn't time to look at them very closely," he explained.

"No, of course not. But——"

"They stared at *me*, I can tell you. I attracted a great deal of attention." At last he had done that! "I think I rather scared them. They moved away whenever I came near. They followed me about at a distance, wherever I went. The men at the round desk in the middle seemed to have a sort of panic whenever I went to make inquiries."

"What did you do when you arrived?"

Well, he had gone straight to the catalogue, of course—to the S volumes, and had stood long before SN-SOF, unable to take this volume out of the shelf, because his heart was beating so. . . . At first, he said, he wasn't disappointed—he only thought there was some new arrangement. He went to the middle desk and

9. Dr. Gustav Jaeger advocated the use of wool clothing for health reasons; his ideas were taken up enthusiastically by Bernard Shaw, among others.

asked where the catalogue of *twentieth*-century books was kept. He gathered that there was still only one catalogue. Again he looked up his name, stared at the three little pasted slips he had known so well. Then he went and sat down for a long time. . . .

"And then," he droned, "I looked up the 'Dictionary of National Biography' and some encyclopaedias . . . I went back to the middle desk and asked what was the best modern book on late nineteenth-century literature. They told me Mr. T. K. Nupton's book was considered the best. I looked it up in the catalogue and filled in a form for it. It was brought to me. My name wasn't in the index, but—Yes!" he said with a sudden change of tone. "That's what I'd forgotten. Where's that bit of paper? Give it me back."

I, too, had forgotten that cryptic screed. I found it fallen on the floor, and handed it to him.

He smoothed it out, nodding and smiling at me disagreeably. "I found myself glancing through Nupton's book," he resumed. "Not very easy reading. Some sort of phonetic spelling . . . All the modern books I saw were phonetic."

"Then I don't want to hear any more, Soames, please."

"The proper names seemed all to be spelt in the old way. But for that, I mightn't have noticed my own name."

"Your own name? Really? Soames, I'm *very* glad."

"And yours."

"No!"

"I thought I should find you waiting here to-night. So I took the trouble to copy out the passage. Read it."

I snatched the paper. Soames' handwriting was characteristically dim. It, and the noisome spelling, and my excitement, made me all the slower to grasp what T. K. Nupton was driving at.

The document lies before me at this moment. Strange that the words I here copy out for you were copied out for me by poor Soames just seventy-eight years hence. . . .

From p. 234 of "Inglish Littracher 1890–1900" bi T. K. Nupton, publishd bi th Stait, 1992:

> Fr egzarmpl, a riter ov th time, naimd Max Beerbohm, hoo woz stil alive in th twentieth senchri, rote a stauri in wich e pautraid an immajnari karrakter kauld 'Enoch Soames'—a thurd-rait poit hoo beleevz imself a grate jeneus an maix a bargin with th Devvl in auder ter no wot posterriti thinx ov im! It iz a sumwot labud sattire but not without vallu az showing hou seriusli the yung men ov th aiteen-ninetiz took themselvz. Nou that the littreri profeshn haz bin auganized az a departmnt of publik servis, our riters hav found their levvl an hav lernt ter doo their duti without thort ov th morro. 'Th laibrer iz werthi ov hiz hire,' an that iz aul. Thank hevvn we hav no Enoch Soameses amung us to-dai!

I found that by murmuring the words aloud (a device which I commend to my reader) I was able to master them, little by little. The clearer they became, the greater was my bewilderment, my distress and horror. The whole thing was a nightmare. Afar, the great grisly background of what was in store for the poor dear art of letters; here, at the table, fixing on me a gaze that made me hot all over, the poor fellow whom—whom evidently . . . but no: whatever down-grade my character might take in coming years, I should never be such a brute as to—

Again I examined the screed. "Immajnari"—but here Soames was, no more imaginary, alas! than I. And "labud"—what on earth was that? (To this day, I have never made out that word.) "It's all very—baffling," I at length stammered.

Soames said nothing, but cruelly did not cease to look at me.

"Are you sure," I temporised, "quite sure you copied the thing out correctly?"

"Quite."

"Well, then it's this wretched Nupton who must have made—must be going to make—some idiotic mistake . . . Look here, Soames! you know me better than to suppose that I . . . After all, the name 'Max Beerbohm' is not at all an uncommon one, and there must be several Enoch Soameses running around—or rather, 'Enoch Soames' is a name that might occur to any one writing a story. And I don't write stories: I'm an essayist, an observer, a recorder . . . I admit that it's an extraordinary coincidence. But you must see——"

"I see the whole thing," said Soames quietly. And he added, with a touch of his old manner, but with more dignity than I had ever known in him, "*Parlons d'autre chose.*"

I accepted that suggestion very promptly. I returned straight to the more immediate future. I spent most of the long evening in renewed appeals to Soames to slip away and seek refuge somewhere. I remember saying at last that if indeed I was destined to write about him, the supposed "stauri" had better have at least a happy ending. Soames repeated those last three words in a tone of intense scorn. "In Life and in Art," he said, "all that matters is an *inevitable* ending."

"But," I urged, more hopefully than I felt, "an ending that can be avoided *isn't* inevitable."

"You aren't an artist," he rasped. "And you're so hopelessly not an artist that, so far from being able to imagine a thing and make it seem true, you're going to make even a true thing seem as if you'd made it up. You're a miserable bungler. And it's like my luck."

I protested that the miserable bungler was not I—was not going to be I—but T. K. Nupton; and we had a rather heated argument, in the thick of which it suddenly seemed to me that Soames saw he was in the wrong: he had quite physically cowered. But I wondered why—and now I guessed with a cold throb just why—he stared so, past me. The bringer of that "inevitable ending" filled the doorway.

I managed to turn in my chair and to say, not without a semblance of lightness, "Aha, come in!" Dread was indeed rather blunted in me by his looking so absurdly like a villain in a melodrama. The sheen of his tilted hat and of his shirt-front, the repeated twists he was giving to his moustache, and most of all the magnificence of his sneer, gave token that he was there only to be foiled.

He was at our table in a stride. "I am sorry," he sneered witheringly, "to break up your pleasant party, but——"

"You don't: you complete it," I assured him. "Mr Soames and I want to have a little talk with you. Won't you sit? Mr Soames got nothing—frankly nothing—by his journey this afternoon. We don't wish to say that the whole thing was a swindle—a common swindle. On the contrary, we believe you meant well. But of course the bargain, such as it was, is off."

The Devil gave no verbal answer. He merely looked at Soames and pointed with rigid forefinger to the door. Soames was wretchedly rising from his chair when, with a desperate quick gesture, I swept together two dinner-knives that were on the table, and laid their blades across each other. The Devil stepped sharp back against the table behind him, averting his face and shuddering.

"You are not superstitious!" he hissed.

"Not at all," I smiled.

"Soames!" he said as to an underling, but without turning his face, "put those knives straight!"

With an inhibitive gesture to my friend, "Mr Soames," I said emphatically to the Devil, "is a *Catholic* Diabolist"; but my poor friend did the Devil's bidding, not mine; and now, with his master's eyes again fixed on him, he arose, he shuffled past me. I tried to speak. It was he that spoke. "Try," was the prayer he threw back at me as the Devil pushed him roughly out through the door, "*try* to make them know that I did exist!"

In another instant I too was through that door. I stood staring all ways—up the street, across it, down it. There was moonlight and lamplight, but there was not Soames nor that other.

Dazed, I stood there. Dazed, I turned back, at length, into the little room; and I suppose I paid Berthe or Rose for my dinner and luncheon, and for Soames': I hope so, for I never went to the Vingtième again. Ever since that night I have avoided Greek Street altogether. And for years I did not set foot even in Soho Square, because on that same night it was there that I paced and loitered, long and long, with some such dull sense of hope as a man has in not straying far from the place where he has lost something. . . . "Round and round the shutter'd Square"—that line came back to me on my lonely beat, and with it the whole stanza, ringing in my brain and bearing in on me how tragically different from the happy scene imagined by him was the poet's actual experience of that prince in whom of all princes we should put not our trust.

But—strange how the mind of an essayist, be it never so stricken, roves and ranges!—I remember pausing before a wide doorstep and wondering if perchance it was on this very one that the young De Quincey lay ill and faint while poor Ann flew as fast as her feet would carry her to Oxford Street, the "stony-hearted step-mother" of them both, and came back bearing that "glass of port wine and spices" but for which he might, so he thought, actually have died. Was this the very doorstep that the old De Quincey used to revisit in homage? I pondered Ann's fate, the cause of her sudden vanishing from the ken of her boyfriend; and presently I blamed myself for letting the past override the present. Poor vanished Soames!

And for myself, too, I began to be troubled. What had I better do? Would there be a hue and cry—Mysterious Disappearance of an Author, and all that? He had last been seen lunching and dining in my company. Hadn't I better get a hansom and drive straight to Scotland Yard? . . . They would think I was a lunatic. After all, I re-assured myself, London was a very large place, and one very dim figure might easily drop out of it unobserved—now especially, in the blinding glare of the near Jubilee. Better say nothing at all, I thought.

And I was right. Soames' disappearance made no stir at all. He was utterly forgotten before any one, so far as I am aware, noticed that he was no longer hanging around. Now and again some poet or prosaist may have said to another, "What has become of that man Soames?" but I never heard any such question asked. The solicitor through whom he was paid his annuity may be presumed to have made inquiries, but no echo of these resounded. There was something rather ghastly to me in the general unconsciousness that Soames had existed, and more than once I caught myself wondering whether Nupton, that babe unborn, were going to be right in thinking him a figment of my brain.

In that extract from Nupton's repulsive book there is one point which perhaps puzzles you. How is it that the author, though I have here mentioned him by name and have quoted the exact words he is going to write, is not going to grasp the obvi-ous corollary that I have invented nothing? The answer can be only this: Nupton will not have read the later passages of this memoir. Such lack of thoroughness is a serious fault in any one who undertakes to do scholar's work. And I hope these words will meet the eye of some contemporary rival to Nupton and be the undoing of Nupton.

I like to think that some time between 1992 and 1997 somebody will have looked up this memoir, and will have forced on the world his inevitable and startling conclusions. And I have reasons for believing that this will be so. You realise that the reading-room into which Soames was projected by the Devil was in all respects precisely as it will be on the afternoon of June 3, 1997. You realise, therefore, that on that afternoon, when it comes round, there the self-same crowd will be, and there Soames too will be, punctually, he and they doing precisely what they did before. Recall now Soames' account of the sensation he made. You may say that the mere difference of his costume was enough to make him sensational in that uniformed crowd. You wouldn't say so if you had ever seen him. I assure you that in no period could Soames be anything but dim. The fact that people are going to stare at him, and follow him around, and seem afraid of him, can be explained only on the hypothesis that they will somehow have been prepared for his ghostly visitation. They will have been awfully waiting to see whether he really would come. And when he does come the effect will of course be—awful.

An authentic, guaranteed, proven ghost, but—only a ghost, alas! Only that. In his first visit, Soames was a creature of flesh and blood, whereas the creatures into whose midst he was projected were but ghosts, I take it—solid, palpable, vocal, but unconscious and automatic ghosts, in a building that was itself an illusion. Next time, that building and those creatures will be real. It is of Soames that there will be but the semblance. I wish I could think him destined to revisit the world actually, physically, consciously. I wish he had this one brief escape, this one small treat, to look forward to. I never forget him for long. He is where he is, and forever. The more rigid moralists among you may say he has only himself to blame. For my part, I think he has been very hardly used. It is well that vanity should be chastened; and Enoch Soames' vanity was, I admit, above the average, and called for special treatment. But there was no need for vindictiveness. You say he contracted to pay the price he is paying; yes; but I maintain that he was induced to do so by fraud. Well-informed in all things, the Devil must have known that my friend would gain nothing by his visit to futurity. The whole thing was a very shabby trick. The more I think of it, the more detestable the Devil seems to me.

Of him I have caught sight several times, here and there, since that day at the Vingtième. Only once, however, have I seen him at close quarters. This was in Paris. I was walking, one afternoon, along the Rue d'Antin, when I saw him advancing from the opposite direction—over-dressed as ever, and swinging an ebony cane, and altogether behaving as though the whole pavement belonged to him. At thought of Enoch Soames and the myriads of other sufferers eternally in this brute's dominion, a great cold wrath filled me, and I drew myself up to my full height. But—well, one is so used to nodding and smiling in the street to anybody whom one knows that the action becomes almost independent of oneself: to prevent it requires a very sharp effort and great presence of mind. I was miserably aware, as I passed the Devil, that I nodded and smiled to him. And my shame was the deeper and hotter because he, if you please, stared straight at me with the utmost haughtiness.

To be cut—deliberately cut—by *him!* I was, I still am, furious at having had that happen to me.

1914

LITERARY AND CULTURAL TERMS*

Absolutism. In criticism, the belief in irreducible, unchanging values of form and content that underlie the tastes of individuals and periods and arise from the stability of an absolute hierarchical order.

Accent. Stress or emphasis on a syllable, as opposed to the syllable's length of duration, its quantity. *Metrical accent* denotes the metrical pattern (⏑ –) to which writers fit and adjust accented words and rhetorical emphases, keeping the meter as they substitute word-accented feet and tune their rhetoric.

Accentual Verse. Verse with lines established by counting accents only, without regard to the number of unstressed syllables. This was the dominant form of verse in English until the time of Chaucer.

Acrostic. Words arranged, frequently in a poem or puzzle, to disclose a hidden word or message when the correct combination of letters is read in sequence.

Aestheticism. Devotion to beauty. The term applies particularly to a 19th-century literary and artistic movement celebrating beauty as independent from morality, and praising form above content; art for art's sake.

Aesthetics. The study of the beautiful; the branch of philosophy concerned with defining the nature of art and establishing criteria of judgment.

Alexandrine. A six-foot iambic pentameter line.

Allegorical Meaning. A secondary meaning of a narrative in addition to its primary meaning or literal meaning.

Allegory. A story that suggests another story. The first part of this word comes from the Greek *allos*, "other." An allegory is present in literature whenever it is clear that the author is saying, "By this I also mean that." In practice, allegory appears when a progression of events or images suggests a translation of them into conceptual language.

Alliteration. "Adding letters" (*Latin ad + littera*, "letter"). Two or more words, or accented syllables, chime on the same initial letter (*lost love alone; after apple-picking*) or repeat the same consonant.

Alliterative Verse. Verse using alliteration on stressed syllables for its fundamental structure.

Allusion. A meaningful reference, direct or indirect, as when William Butler Yeats writes, "Another Troy must rise and set," calling to mind the whole tragic history of Troy.

Amplification. A restatement of something more fully and in more detail, especially in oratory, poetry, and music.

Analogy. A comparison between things similar in a number of ways; frequently used to explain the unfamiliar by the familiar.

Anapest. A metrical foot: ⏑ ⏑ – .

Anaphora. The technique of beginning successive clauses or lines with the same word.

Anatomy. Greek for "a cutting up": a dissection, analysis, or systematic study. The term was popular in titles in the 16th and 17th centuries.

Anglo-Norman (Language). The language of upper-class England after the Norman Conquest in 1066.

Anglo-Saxon. The people, culture, and language of three neighboring tribes—Jutes, Angles, and Saxons—who invaded England, beginning in 449, from the lower part of Denmark's

---

*Adapted from *The Harper Handbook to Literature* by Northrop Frye, Sheridan Baker, George Perkins, and Barbara M. Perkins, 2d edition (Longman, 1997).

Jutland Peninsula. The Angles, settling along the eastern seaboard of central and northern England, developed the first literate culture of any Germanic people.

Antagonist. In Greek drama, the character who opposes the protagonist, or hero: therefore, any character who opposes another. In some works, the antagonist is clearly the villain (Iago in *Othello*), but in strict terminology an antagonist is merely an opponent and may be in the right.

Anthropomorphism. The practice of giving human attributes to animals, plants, rivers, winds, and the like, or to such entities as Grecian urns and abstract ideas.

Antithesis. (1) A direct contrast or opposition. (2) The second phase of dialectical argument, which considers the opposition—the three steps being *thesis, antithesis, synthesis*. (3) A rhetorical figure sharply contrasting ideas in balanced parallel structures.

Aphorism. A pithy saying of known authorship, as distinguished from a folk proverb.

Apology. A justification, as in Sir Philip Sidney's *The Apology for Poetry* (1595).

Apostrophe. (Greek, "a turning away"). An address to an absent or imaginary person, a thing, or a personified abstraction.

Archaism. An archaic or old-fashioned word or expression—for example, *o'er, ere*, or *darkling*.

Archetype. (1) The first of a genre, like Homer's *Iliad*, the first heroic epic. (2) A natural symbol imprinted in human consciousness by experience and literature, like dawn symbolizing hope or an awakening; night, death or repose.

Assonance. Repetition of middle vowel sounds: *fight, hive; pane, make*.

Aubade. Dawn song, from French *aube*, for dawn. The aubade originated in the Middle Ages as a song sung by a lover greeting the dawn, ordinarily expressing regret that morning means parting.

Avant-Garde. Experimental, innovative, at the forefront of a literary or artistic trend or movement. The term is French for *vanguard*, the advance unit of an army. It frequently suggests a struggle with tradition and convention.

Ballad. A narrative poem in short stanzas, with or without music. The term derives by way of French *ballade* from Latin *ballare*, "to dance," and once meant a simple song of any kind, lyric or narrative, especially one to accompany a dance.

Ballad Stanza. The name for common meter as found in ballads: a quatrain in iambic meter, alternating tetrameter and trimeter lines, usually rhyming *abcb*.

Bard. An ancient Celtic singer of the culture's lore in epic form; a poetic term for any poet.

Baroque. (1) A richly ornamented style in architecture and art. Founded in Rome by Frederigo Barocci about 1550, and characterized by swirling allegorical frescoes on ceilings and walls, it flourished throughout Europe until 1700. (2) A chromatic musical style with strict forms containing similar exuberant ornamentation, flourishing from 1600 to 1750. In literature, Richard Crashaw's bizarre imagery and the conceits and rhythms of John Donne and other metaphysical poets are sometimes called baroque, sometimes mannerist.

Bathos. (1) A sudden slippage from the sublime to the ridiculous. (2) Any anticlimax. (3) Sentimental pathos. (4) Triteness or dullness.

Blank Verse. Unrhymed iambic pentameter. *See also* Meter.

Bloomsbury Group. An informal social and intellectual group associated with Bloomsbury, a London residential district near the British Museum, from about 1904 until the outbreak of World War II. Virginia Woolf was a principal member. The group was loosely knit, but famed, especially in the 1920s, for its exclusiveness, aestheticism, and social and political freethinking.

Burden. (1) A refrain or set phrase repeated at intervals throughout a song or poem. (2) A bass accompaniment, the "load" carried by the melody, the origin of the term.

Burlesque. (1) A ridicule, especially on the stage, treating the lofty in low style, or the low in grandiose style. (2) A bawdy vaudeville, with obscene clowning and stripteasing.

Caesura. A pause in a metrical line, indicated by punctuation, momentarily suspending the beat (from Latin "a cutting off"). Caesuras are *masculine* at the end of a foot, and *feminine* in mid-foot.

Canon. The writings accepted as forming a part of the Bible, of the works of an author, or of a body of literature. Shakespeare's canon consists of works he wrote, which may be distinguished from works attributed to him but written by others. The word derives from Greek *kanon*, "rod" or "rule," and suggests authority. Canonical authors and texts are those taught most frequently, noncanonical are those rarely taught, and in between are disputed degrees of canonicity for authors considered minor or marginalized.

Canto. A major division in a long poem. The Italian expression is from Latin *cantus*, "song," a section singable in one sitting.

Caricature. Literary cartooning, depicting characters with exaggerated physical traits such as huge noses and bellies, short stature, squints, tics, humped backs, and so forth.

Catalog. In literature, an enumeration of ancestors, of ships, of warriors, of a woman's beauties, and the like; a standard feature of the classical epic.

Celtic Revival. In the 18th century, a groundswell of the Romantic movement in discovering the power in ancient, primitive poetry, particularly Welsh and Scottish Gaelic, as distinct from that of the classics.

Chiasmus. A rhetorical balance created by the inversion of one of two parallel phrases or clauses; from the Greek for a "placing crosswise," as in the Greek letter χ (chi).

Chronicle. A kind of history, with the emphasis on *time* (Greek *chronos*). Events are described in order as they occurred. The chronicles of the Middle Ages provided material for later writers and serve now as important sources of knowledge about the period.

Chronicle Play. A play dramatizing historical events, as from a chronicle.

Classical Literature. (1) The literature of ancient Greece and Rome. (2) Later literature reflecting the qualities of classical Greece or Rome. *See also*, Classicism; Neoclassicism. (3) The classic literature of any time or place, as, for example, classical American literature or classical Japanese literature.

Classicism. A principle in art and conduct reflecting the ethos of ancient Greece and Rome: balance, form, proportion, propriety, dignity, simplicity, objectivity, rationality, restraint, unity rather than diversity. In English literature, classicism emerged with Erasmus (1466–1536) and his fellow humanists. In the Restoration and 18th century, classicism, or neoclassicism, expressed society's deep need for balance and restraint after the shattering Civil War and Puritan commonwealth. Classicism continued in the 19th century, after the Romantic period, particularly in the work of Matthew Arnold. T. E. Hulme, Ezra Pound, and T. S. Eliot expressed it for the 20th century.

Cliché. An overused expression, once clever or metaphorical but now trite and timeworn.

Closed Couplet. The heroic couplet, especially when the thought and grammar are complete in the two iambic pentameter lines.

Closet Drama. A play written for reading in the "closet," or private study.

Cockney. A native of the East End of central London. The term originally meant "cocks' eggs," a rural term of contempt for city softies and fools. Cockneys are London's ingenious street peddlers, speaking a dialect rich with an inventive rhyming slang, dropping and adding aitches.

Comedy. One of the typical literary structures, originating as a form of drama and later extending into prose fiction and other genres as well. Comedy, as Susanne Langer says, is the image of Fortune; tragedy, the image of Fate.

Comedy of Humors. Comedy based on the ancient physiological theory that a predominance of one of the body's four fluids (humors) produces a comically unbalanced personality: (1) blood—sanguine, hearty, cheerful, amorous; (2) phlegm—phlegmatic, sluggish; (3) choler (yellow bile)—angry, touchy; (4) black bile—melancholic.

Comedy of Manners. Suave, witty, and risqué, satire of upper-class manners and immorals, particularly that of Restoration masters like George Etherege and William Congreve.

Common Meter. The ballad stanza as found in hymns and other poems: a quatrain (four-line stanza) in iambic meter, alternating tetrameter and trimeter, rhyming *abcb* or *abab*.

Complaint. A lyric poem, popular in the Middle Ages and the Renaissance, complaining of unrequited love, a personal situation, or the state of the world.

Conceit. Any fanciful, ingenious expression or idea, but especially one in the form of an extended metaphor.

Concordia Discors. "Discordant harmony," a phrase expressing for the 18th century the harmonious diversity of nature, a pleasing balance of opposites.

Concrete Poetry. Poetry that attempts a concrete embodiment of its idea, expressing itself physically apart from the meaning of the words. A recent relative of the much older *shaped poem*, the concrete poem places heavy emphasis on the picture and less on the words, so that the visual experience may be more interesting than the linguistic.

Connotation. The ideas, attitudes, or emotions associated with a word in the mind of speaker or listener, writer or reader. It is contrasted with the *denotation*, the thing the word stands for, the dictionary definition, an objective concept without emotional coloring.

Consonance. (1) Repetition of inner or end consonant sounds, as, for example, the *r* and *s* sounds from Gerard Manley Hopkins's *God's Grandeur:* "broods with warm breast." (2) In a broader sense, a generally pleasing combination of sounds or ideas.

Couplet. A pair of rhymed metrical lines, usually in iambic tetrameter or pentameter. Sometimes the two lines are of different length.

Cynghanedd. A complex medieval Welsh system of rhyme, alliteration, and consonance, to which Gerard Manley Hopkins alluded to describe his interplay of euphonious sounds, actually to be heard in any rich poet, as in the Welsh Dylan Thomas: "The force that through the green fuse drives the flower / Drives my green age."

Dactyl. A three-syllable metrical foot: $-\smile\smile$. It is the basic foot of dactylic hexameter, the six-foot line of Greek and Roman epic poetry.

Dactylic Hexameter. The classical or heroic line of the epic. A line based on six dactylic feet, with spondees substituted, and always ending $-\smile\smile \mid --$.

Dead Metaphor. A metaphor accepted without its figurative picture: "a jacket," for the paper around a book, with no mental picture of the human coat that prompted the original metaphor.

Decasyllabic. Having ten syllables. An iambic pentameter line is decasyllabic.

Deconstruction. The critical dissection of a literary text's statements, ambiguities, and structure to expose its hidden contradictions, implications, and fundamental instability of meaning. Jacques Derrida originated deconstruction in *Of Grammatology* (1967) and *Writing and Difference* (1967).

Decorum. Propriety, fitness, the quality of being appropriate.

Defamiliarization. Turning the familiar to the strange by disrupting habitual ways of perceiving things. Derived from the thought of Victor Shklovsky and other Russian formalists, the idea is that art forces us to see things differently as we view them through the artist's sensibility, not our own.

Deism. A rational philosophy of religion, beginning with the theories of Lord Herbert of Cherbury, the "Father of Deism," in his *De Veritate* (1624). Deists generally held that God, the supreme Artisan, created a perfect clock of a universe, withdrew, and left it running, not to return to intervene in its natural works or the life of humankind; that the Bible is a moral guide, but neither historically accurate nor divinely authentic; and that reason guides human beings to virtuous conduct.

Denotation. The thing that a word stands for, the dictionary definition, an objective concept without emotional coloring. It is contrasted with the *connotation*, ideas, attitudes, or emotions associated with the word in the mind of user or hearer.

Dénouement. French for "unknotting": the unraveling of plot threads toward the end of a play, novel, or other narrative.

Determinism. The philosophical belief that events are shaped by forces beyond the control of human beings.

Dialect. A variety of language belonging to a particular time, place, or social group, as, for example, an 18th-century cockney dialect, a New England dialect, or a coal miner's dialect. A language other than one's own is for the most part unintelligible without study or translation; a dialect other than one's own can generally be understood, although pronunciation, vocabulary, and syntax seem strange.

Dialogue. Conversation between two or more persons, as represented in prose fiction, drama, or essays, as opposed to *monologue*, the speech of one person.

Diatribe. Greek for "a wearing away": a bitter and abusive criticism or invective, often lengthy, directed against a person, institution, or work.

Diction. Word choice in speech or writing, an important element of style.

Didactic. Greek for "teaching": instructive, or having the qualities of a teacher. Literature intended primarily for instruction or containing an important moralistic element is didactic.

Dirge. A lamenting funeral song.

Discourse. (1) A formal discussion of a subject. (2) The conventions of communication associated with specific areas, in usages such as "poetic discourse," "the discourse of the novel," or "historical discourse."

Dissenter. A term arising in the 1640s for a member of the clergy or a follower who dissented from the forms of the established Anglican church, particularly Puritans. Dissenters generally came from the lower middle classes.

Dissonance. (1) Harsh and jarring sound; discord. It is frequently an intentional effect, as in the poems of Robert Browning. (2) Occasionally a term for half rhyme or slant rhyme.

Distich. A couplet, or pair of rhymed metrical lines.

Dithyramb. A frenzied choral song and dance to honor Dionysus, Greek god of wine and the power of fertility. Any irregular, impassioned poetry may be called *dithyrambic*.

Doggerel. (1) Trivial verse clumsily aiming at meter, usually tetrameter. (2) Any verse facetiously low and loose in meter and rhyme.

Domesday Book. The recorded census and survey of landholders that William the Conqueror ordered in 1085; from "Doomsday," the Last Judgment.

Dramatic Irony. A character in drama or fiction unknowingly says or does something in ironic contrast to what the audience or reader knows or will learn.

Dramatic Monologue. A monologue in verse. A speaker addresses a silent listener, revealing, in dramatic irony, things about himself or herself of which the speaker is unaware.

Eclogue. A short poem, usually a pastoral, and often in the form of a dialogue or soliloquy.

Edition. The form in which a book is published, including its physical qualities and its content. A *first edition* is the first form of a book, printed and bound; a *second edition* is a later form, usually with substantial changes in content.

Edwardian Period (1901–1914). From the death of Queen Victoria to the outbreak of World War I, named for the reign of Victoria's son, Edward VII (1901–1910), a period generally reacting against Victorian propriety and convention.

Elegiac Stanza. An iambic pentameter quatrain rhyming *abab*, taking its name from Thomas Gray's *Elegy Written in a Country Churchyard* (1751).

Elegy. Greek for "lament": a poem on death or on a serious loss; characteristically a sustained meditation expressing sorrow and, frequently, an explicit or implied consolation.

Elision. Latin for "striking out": the omission or slurring of an unstressed vowel at the end of a word to bring a line of poetry closer to a prescribed metrical pattern.

Elizabethan Drama. English drama of the reign of Elizabeth I (1558–1603). Strictly speaking, drama from the reign of James I (1603–1625) belongs to the Jacobean period and that from the reign of Charles I (1625–1642) to the Caroline period, but the term *Elizabethan* is sometimes extended to include works of later reigns, before the closing of the theaters in 1642.

Elizabethan Period (1558–1603). The years marked by the reign of Elizabeth I.

Ellipsis. The omission of words for rhetorical effect: "*Drop dead*" for "You drop dead."

Emblem. (1) A didactic pictorial and literary form consisting of a word or phrase (*mot* or *motto*), a symbolic woodcut or engraving, and a brief moralistic poem (*explicatio*). Collections of emblems in book form were popular in the 16th and 17th centuries. (2) A type or symbol.

Emendation. A change made in a literary text to remove faults that have appeared through tampering or by errors in reading, transcription, or printing from the manuscript.

Empathy. Greek for "feeling with": identification with the feelings or passions of another person, natural creature, or even an inanimate object conceived of as possessing human attributes.

Emphasis. Stress placed on words, phrases, or ideas to show their importance, by *italics*, **boldface,** and punctuation "!!!"; by figurative language, meter, and rhyme; or by strategies of rhetoric, like climactic order, contrast, repetition, and position.

Empiricism. Greek for "experience": the belief that all knowledge comes from experience, that human understanding of general truth can be founded only on observation of particulars. Empiricism is basic to the scientific method and to literary naturalism.

Enclosed Rhyme. A couplet, or pair of rhyming lines, enclosed in rhyming lines to give the pattern *abba*.

Encomium. Originally a Greek choral song in praise of a hero; later, any formal expression of praise, in verse or prose.

End Rhyme. Rhyme at the end of a line of verse (the usual placement), as distinguished from *initial rhyme*, at the beginning, or *internal rhyme*, within the line.

Enjambment. Run-on lines in which grammatical sense runs from one line of poetry to the next without pause or punctuation. The opposite of an end-stopped line.

Enlightenment. A philosophical movement in the 17th and 18th centuries, particularly in France, characterized by the conviction that reason could achieve all knowledge, supplant organized religion, and ensure progress toward happiness and perfection.

Envoy (or Envoi). A concluding stanza, generally shorter than the earlier stanzas of a poem, giving a brief summary of theme, address to a prince or patron, or return to a refrain.

Epic. A long narrative poem, typically a recounting of history or legend or of the deeds of a national hero. During the Renaissance, critical theory emphasized two assumptions: (1) the encyclopedic knowledge needed for major poetry, and (2) an aristocracy of genres, according to which epic and tragedy, because they deal with heroes and ruling-class figures, were reserved for major poets.

Epic Simile. Sometimes called a *Homeric simile:* an extended simile, comparing one thing with another by lengthy description of the second, often beginning with "as when" and concluding with "so" or "such."

Epicurean. Often meaning hedonistic (*see also* Hedonism), devoted to sensual pleasure and ease. Actually, Epicurus (c. 341–270 B.C.) was a kind of puritanical Stoic, recommending detachment from pleasure and pain to avoid life's inevitable suffering, hence advocating serenity as the highest happiness, intellect over the senses.

Epigram. (1) A brief poetic and witty couching of a home truth. (2) An equivalent statement in prose.

Epigraph. (1) An inscription on a monument or building. (2) A quotation or motto heading a book or chapter.

Epilogue. (1) A poetic address to the audience at the end of a play. (2) The actor performing the address. (3) Any similar appendage to a literary work, usually describing what happens to the characters in the future.

Epiphany. In religious tradition, the revelation of a divinity. James Joyce adapted the term to signify a moment of profound or spiritual revelation. For Joyce, art was an epiphany.

Episode. An incident in a play or novel; a continuous event in action and dialogue.

Episodic Structure. In narration, the incidental stringing of one episode upon another, with no necessary causal connection or plot.

Epistle. (1) A letter, usually a formal or artistic one, like Saint Paul's Epistles in the New Testament, or Horace's verse *Epistles,* widely imitated in the late 17th and 18th centuries, most notably by Alexander Pope. (2) A dedication in a prefatory epistle to a play or book.

Epitaph. (1) An inscription on a tombstone or monument memorializing the person, or persons, buried there. (2) A literary epigram or brief poem epitomizing the dead.

Epithalamium (or Epithalamion). A lyric ode honoring a bride and groom.

Epithet. A term characterizing a person or thing: e.g., *Richard the Lion-Hearted*.

Epitome. (1) A summary, an abridgment, an abstract. (2) One that supremely represents an entire class.

Essay. A literary composition on a single subject; usually short, in prose, and nonexhaustive. The word derives from French *essai* "an attempt," first used in the modern sense by Michel de Montaigne, whose *Essais* (1580–1588) are classics of the genre.

Estates. The "three estates of the realm," recognized from feudal times onward: the clergy (Lords Spiritual), the nobility (Lords Temporal), and the burghers (the Commons). The Fourth Estate is now the press and other media.

Eulogy. A speech or composition of praise, especially of a deceased person.

Euphemism. Greek for "good speech": an attractive substitute for a harsh or unpleasant word or concept; figurative language or circumlocution substituting an indirect or oblique reference for a direct one.

Euphony. Melodious sound, the opposite of cacophony. A major feature of verse, but also a consideration in prose, euphony results from smooth-flowing meter or sentence rhythm as well as attractive sounds.

Euphuism. An artificial, highly elaborate affected style that takes its name from John Lyly's *Euphues: The Anatomy of Wit* (1578). Euphuism is characterized by the heavy use of rhetorical devices such as balance and antithesis, by much attention to alliteration and other sound patterns, and by learned allusion.

Excursus. (1) A lengthy discussion of a point, appended to a literary work. (2) A long digression.

Exegesis. A detailed analysis, explanation, and interpretation of a difficult text, especially the Bible.

Exemplum. Latin for "example": a story used to illustrate a moral point. *Exempla* were a characteristic feature of medieval sermons.

Existentialism. A philosophy centered on individual existence as unique and unrepeatable, hence rejecting the past for present existence and its unique dilemmas. Existentialism rose to prominence in the 1930s and 1940s, particularly in France after World War II.

Expressionism. An early 20th-century movement in art and literature, best understood as a reaction against conventional realism and naturalism, and especially as a revolt against conventional society. The expressionist looked inward for images, expressing in paint, on stage, or in prose or verse a distorted, nightmarish version of reality.

Eye Rhyme. A rhyme of words that look but do not sound the same: *one, stone; word, lord; teak, break*.

Fable. (1) A short, allegorical story in verse or prose, frequently of animals, told to illustrate a moral. (2) The story line or plot of a narrative or drama. (3) Loosely, any legendary or fabulous account.

Falling Meter. A meter beginning with a stress, running from heavy to light.

Farce. A wildly comic play, mocking dramatic and social conventions.

Feminine Ending. An extra unstressed syllable at the end of a metrical line, usually iambic.

Feminine Rhyme. A rhyme of both the stressed and the unstressed syllables of one feminine ending with another.

Feudalism. The political and social system prevailing in Europe from the ninth century until the 1400s. It was a system of independent holdings (*feud* is Germanic for "estate") in which autonomous lords pledged fealty and service to those more powerful in exchange for protection, as did villagers to the neighboring lord of the manor.

Fiction. An imagined creation in verse, drama, or prose. Fiction is a thing made, an invention. It is distinguished from nonfiction by its essentially imaginative nature, but elements of fiction appear in fundamentally nonfictional constructions such as essays, biographies, autobiographies, and histories. Although any invented person, place, event, or condition is a fiction, the term is now most frequently used to mean "prose fiction," as distinct from verse or drama.

Figurative Language. Language that is not literal, being either metaphorical or rhetorically patterned.

Figure of Speech. An expression extending language beyond its literal meaning, either pictorially through metaphor, simile, allusion, and the like, or rhetorically through repetition, balance, antithesis, and the like. A figure of speech is also called a *trope*.

Fin de Siècle. "The end of the century," especially the last decade of the 19th. The term, acquired with the French influence of the symbolists Stéphane Mallarmé and Charles Baudelaire, connotes preciosity and decadence.

First-Person Narration. Narration by a character involved in a story.

Flyting. Scottish for "scolding": a form of invective, or violent verbal assault, in verse; traditional in Scottish literature, possibly Celtic in origin. Typically, two poets exchange scurrilous and often exhaustive abuse.

Folio. From Latin for "leaf." (1) A sheet of paper, folded once. (2) The largest of the book sizes, made from standard printing sheets, folded once before trimming and binding.

Folktale. A story forming part of the folklore of a community, generally less serious than the stories called *myths*.

Foot. The metrical unit; in English, an accented syllable with accompanying light syllable or syllables.

Formula. A plot outline or set of characteristic ingredients used in the construction of a literary work or applied to a portion of one.

Foul Copy. A manuscript that has been used for printing, bearing the marks of the proofreader, editor, and printer, as well as, frequently, the author's queries and comments.

Four Elements. In ancient and medieval cosmology, earth, air, fire, and water—the four ultimate, exclusive, and eternal constituents that, according to Empedocles (c. 493–c. 433 B.C.) made up the world.

Fourteeners. Lines of 14 syllables—7 iambic feet, popular with the Elizabethans.

Frame Narrative. A narrative enclosing one or more separate stories. Characteristically, the frame narrative is created as a vehicle for the stories it contains.

Free Verse. French *vers libre*; poetry free of traditional metrical and stanzaic patterns.

Genre. A term often applied loosely to the larger forms of literary convention, roughly analogous to "species" in biology. The Greeks spoke of three main genres of poetry—lyric, epic, and drama.

Georgian. (1) Pertaining to the reigns of the four Georges—1714–1830, particularly the reigns of the first three, up to the close of the 18th century. (2) The literature written during the early years (1910–1914) of the reign of George V.

Georgic. A poem about farming and annual rural labors, after Virgil's *Georgics*.

Gloss. An explanation (from Greek *glossa* "tongue, language"); originally, Latin synonyms in the margins of Greek manuscripts and vernacular synonyms in later manuscripts as scribes gave the reader some help.

Glossary. A list of words, with explanations or definitions.

Gothic. Originally, pertaining to the Goths, then to any Germanic people. Because the Goths began warring with the Roman empire in the 3rd century A.D., eventually sacking Rome itself, the term later became a synonym for "barbaric," which the 18th century next applied to anything medieval, of the Dark Ages.

Gothic Novel. A type of fiction introduced and named by Horace Walpole's *Castle of Otranto, A Gothic Story* (1764). Walpole introduced supernatural terror, with a huge mysterious helmet, portraits that walk abroad, and statues with nosebleeds. Mary Shelley's *Frankenstein* (1818) transformed the Gothic into moral science fiction.

Grotesque. Anything unnaturally distorted, ugly, ludicrous, fanciful, or bizarre; especially, in the 19th century, literature exploiting the abnormal.

Hedonism. A philosophy that sees pleasure as the highest good.

Hegelianism. The philosophy of G. W. F. Hegel (1770–1831), who developed the system of thought known as Hegelian dialectic, in which a given concept, or *thesis*, generates its opposite, or *antithesis*, and from the interaction of the two arises a *synthesis*.

Heroic Couplet. The closed and balanced iambic pentameter couplet typical of the heroic plays of John Dryden; hence, any closed couplet.

Heroic Quatrain. A stanza in four lines of iambic pentameter, rhyming *abab* (*see also* Meter). Also known as the *heroic stanza* and the *elegiac stanza*.

Hexameter. Six-foot lines.

Historicism. (1) Historical relativism. (2) An approach to literature that emphasizes its historical environment, the climate of ideas, belief, and literary conventions surrounding and influencing the writer.

Homily. A religious discourse or sermon, especially one emphasizing practical spiritual or moral advice.

Hubris. From Greek *hybris*, "pride": prideful arrogance or insolence of the kind that causes the tragic hero to ignore the warnings that might turn aside the action that leads to disaster.

Humors. The *cardinal humors* of ancient medical theory: blood, phlegm, yellow bile (choler), black bile (melancholy). From ancient times until the 19th century, the humors were believed largely responsible for health and disposition. In literature, especially during the early modern period, characters were portrayed according to the humors that dominated them, as in the comedy of humors.

Hyperbole. Overstatement to make a point, as when a parent tells a child "I've told you a thousand times."

Iambus (or Iamb). A metrical foot: ⌣ –.

Idealism. Literary idealism follows from philosophical precepts, emphasizing a world in which the most important reality is a spiritual or transcendent truth not always reflected in the world of sense perception.

Idyll. A short poem of rustic pastoral serenity.

Image. A concrete picture, either literally descriptive, as in "Red roses covered the white wall," or figurative, as in "She is a rose," each carrying a sensual and emotive connotation.

Impressionism. A literary style conveying subjective impressions rather than objective reality, taking its name from the movement in French painting in the mid–19th century.

Industrial Revolution. The accelerated change, beginning in the 1760s, from an agricultural-shopkeeping society, using hand tools, to an industrial-mechanized one.

Influence. The apparent effect of literary works on subsequent writers and their work, as in Robert Browning's influence on T. S. Eliot.

Innuendo. An indirect remark or gesture, especially one implying something derogatory; an insinuation.

Interlocking Rhyme. Rhyme between stanzas; a word unrhymed in one stanza is used as a rhyme for the next, as in terza rima: *aba bcb cdc* and so on.

Internal Rhyme. Rhyme within a line, rather than at the beginning (*initial rhyme*) or end (*end rhyme*); also, rhyme matching sounds in the middle of a line with sounds at the end.

Intertextuality. (1) The relations between one literary text and others it evokes through such means as quotation, paraphrase, allusion, parody, and revision. (2) More broadly, the relations between a given text and all other texts, the potentially infinite sum of knowledge within which any text has its meaning.

Inversion. A reversal of sequence or position, as when the normal order of elements within a sentence is inverted for poetic or rhetorical effect.

Irony. In general, irony is the perception of a clash between appearance and reality, between *seems* and *is*, or between *ought* and *is*. The myriad shadings of irony seem to fall into three categories: (1) *Verbal irony*—saying something contrary to what it means; the appearance is what the words say, the reality is their contrary meaning. (2) *Dramatic irony*—saying or doing something while unaware of its ironic contrast with the whole truth; named for its frequency in drama, dramatic irony is a verbal irony with the speaker's awareness erased. (3) *Situational irony*—events turning to the opposite of what is expected or what should be.

Italian Sonnet (or Petrarchan Sonnet). A sonnet composed of an octave and sestet, rhyming *abbaabba cdecde* (or *cdcdcd* or some variant, without a closing couplet).

Italic (or Italics). Type slanting upward to the right. *This sentence is italic.*

Jacobean Period (1603–1625). The reign of James I, *Jacobus* being the Latin for "James." A certain skepticism and even cynicism seeped into Elizabethan joy.

Jargon. (1) Language peculiar to a trade or calling, as, for example, the jargon of astronauts, lawyers, or literary critics. (2) Confused or confusing language.

Jeremiad. A lament or complaint, especially one enumerating transgressions and predicting destruction of a people, of the kind found in the Book of Jeremiah.

Juvenilia. Youthful literary products.

Kenning. A compound figurative metaphor, a circumlocution, in Old English and Old Norse poetry: "whale-road," for the sea.

Lament. A grieving poem, an elegy, in Anglo-Saxon or Renaissance times. *Deor's Lament* (c. 980) records the actual grief of a scop, or court poet, at being displaced in his lord's hall.

Lampoon. A satirical, personal ridicule in verse or prose.

Lay (or Lai). (1) A ballad or related metrical romance originating with the Breton lay of French Brittany and retaining some of its Celtic magic and folklore.

Lexicon. A word list, a vocabulary, a dictionary.

Libretto. "The little book" (Italian): the text of an opera, cantata, or other musical drama.

Litany. A prayer with phrases spoken or sung by a leader alternated with responses from congregation or choir.

Literal. According to the letter (of the alphabet): the precise, plain meaning of a word or phrase in its simplest, original sense, considered apart from its sense as a metaphor or other figure of speech. Literal language is the opposite of figurative language.

Literature. Strictly defined, anything written. Therefore the oral culture of a people—its folklore, folk songs, folktales, and so on—is not literature until it is written down. The movies are not literature except in their printed scripts. By the same strict meaning, historical records, telephone books, and the like are all literature because they are written in letters of the alphabet, although they are not taught as literature in schools. In contrast to this strict, literal meaning, literature has come to be equated with *creative writing* or works of the imagination: chiefly poetry, prose fiction, and drama.

Lollards. From Middle Dutch, literally, "mumblers": a derisive term applied to the followers of John Wyclif (c. 1328–1384), the reformer behind the Wyclif Bible (1385), the first in English. Lollards preached against the abuses of the medieval church, setting up a standard of poverty and individual service as against wealth and hierarchical privilege.

Lyric. A poem, brief and discontinuous, emphasizing sound and pictorial imagery rather than narrative or dramatic movement.

Macaronic Verse. (1) Strictly, verse mixing words in a writer's native language with endings, phrases, and syntax of another language, usually Latin or Greek, creating a comic or burlesque effect. (2) Loosely, any verse mingling two or more languages.

Mannerism, Mannerist. Literary or artistic affectation; a stylistic quality produced by excessively peculiar, ornamental, or ingenious devices.

Manners. Social behavior. In usages like comedy of manners and novel of manners, the term suggests an examination of the behavior, morals, and values of a particular time, place, or social class.

Manuscript. Literally, "written by hand": any handwritten document, as, for example, a letter or diary; also, a work submitted for publication.

Marginalia. Commentary, references, or other material written by a reader in the margins of a manuscript or book.

Masculine Ending. The usual iambic ending, on the accented foot: ⏑ –.

Masculine Rhyme. The most common rhyme in English, on the last syllable of a line.

Masque. An allegorical, poetic, and musical dramatic spectacle popular in the English courts and mansions of the 16th and early 17th centuries. Figures from mythology, history, and romance mingled in a pastoral fantasy with fairies, fauns, satyrs, and witches, as masked amateurs from the court (including kings and queens) participated in dances and scenes.

Materialism. In philosophy, an emphasis upon the material world as the ultimate reality. Its opposite is *idealism*.

Melodrama. A play with dire ingredients—the mortgage foreclosed, the daughter tied to the railroad tracks—but with a happy ending.

Menippean Satire. Satire on pedants, bigots, rapacious professional people, and other persons or institutions perceiving the world from a single framework. Typical ingredients include a rambling narrative; unusual settings; displays of erudition; and long digressions.

Metaphor. Greek for "transfer" (*meta* and *trans* meaning "across"; *phor* and *fer* meaning "carry"): to carry something across. Hence a metaphor treats something as if it were something else. Money becomes a *nest egg*; a sandwich, a *submarine*.

Metaphysical Poetry. Seventeenth-century poetry of wit and startling extended metaphor.

Meter. The measured pulse of poetry. English meters derive from four Greek and Roman quantitative meters (*see also* Quantitative Verse), which English stresses more sharply, although the patterns are the same. The unit of each pattern is the *foot*, containing one stressed syllable and one or two light ones. *Rising meter* goes from light to heavy; *falling meter*, from heavy to light. One meter—iambic—has dominated English poetry, with the three others lending an occasional foot, for variety, and producing a few poems.

Rising Meters

Iambic: ⏑ – (the iambus)
Anapestic: ⏑ ⏑ – (the anapest)

Falling Meters

Trochaic: – ⏑ (the trochee)
Dactylic: – ⏑ ⏑ (the dactyl)

The number of feet in a line also gives the verse a name:

1 foot: monometer
2 feet: dimeter
3 feet: trimeter
4 feet: tetrameter
5 feet: pentameter
6 feet: hexameter
7 feet: heptameter

All meters show some variations, and substitutions of other kinds of feet, but three variations in iambic writing are virtually standard:

Inverted foot: – ⏑ (a trochee)
Spondee: – –
Ionic double foot: – – ⏑ ⏑

The *pyrrhic foot* of classical meters, two light syllables (⌣⌣), lives in the English line only in the Ionic double foot, although some prosodists scan a relatively light iambus as pyrrhic.

Examples of meters and scansion:

Iambic Tetrameter
An-ni | hil-a- | ting all | that's made |
To a | green thought | in a | green shade |

> *Andrew Marvell, "The Garden"*

Iambic Tetrameter
(*with two inverted feet*)
Close to | the sun | in lone- | ly lands, |
Ringed with | the az- | ure world, | he stands |

> *Alfred, Lord Tennyson, "The Eagle"*

Iambic Pentameter
Love's not | time' fool, | though ros- | y lips | and cheeks |
Within | his bend- | ing sick- | le's com- | pass come |

> *William Shakespeare, Sonnet 116*

When to | the ses- | sions of | sweet si- | lent thought |

> *William Shakespeare, Sonnet 30*

Anapestic Tetrameter
(*trochees substituted*)
The pop- | lars are felled; | farewell | to the shade |
And the whis- | pering sound | of the cool | colonnade |

> *William Cowper, "The Popular Field"*

Trochaic Tetrameter
Tell me | not in | mournful | numbers |

> *Henry Wadsworth Longfellow, "A Psalm of Life"*

Dactylic Hexameter
This is the | forest prim- | eval. The | murmuring | pines and the | hemlocks |
Bearded with | moss. . . .

> *Henry Wadsworth Longfellow, "Evangeline"*

Metonymy. "Substitute naming." A figure of speech in which an associated idea stands in for the actual item: "The *pen* is mightier than the *sword*" for "Literature and propaganda accomplish more and survive longer than warfare."

Metrics. The analysis and description of meter; also called *prosody*.

Middle English. The language of England from the middle of the 12th century to approximately 1500. English began to lose its inflectional endings and accepted many French words into its vocabulary, especially terms associated with the new social, legal, and governmental structures (*baron, judge, jury, marshal, parliament, prince*), and those in common use by the French upper classes (*mansion, chamber, veal, beef*).

Mimesis. A term meaning "imitation." It has been central to literary criticism since Aristotle's *Poetics*. The ordinary meaning of *imitation* as creating a resemblance to something else is clearly involved in Aristotle's definition of dramatic plot as *mimesis praxeos*, the imitation of an action.

Miracle Play. A medieval play based on a saint's life or story from the Bible.

Miscellany. A collection of various things. A literary miscellany is therefore a book collecting varied works, usually poems by different authors, a kind of anthology.

Mock Epic. A poem in epic form and manner ludicrously elevating some trivial subject to epic grandeur.

Modernism. A collective term, generally associated with the first half of the 20th century, for various aesthetic and cultural attempts to place a "modern" face on experience. Modernism arose from a sense that the old ways were worn out.

Monodrama. (1) A play with one character. (2) A closet drama or dramatic monologue.

Monody. (1) A Greek ode for one voice. (2) An elegiac lament, a dirge, in poetic soliloquy.

Monologue. (1) A poem or story in the form of a soliloquy. (2) Any extended speech.

Motif (or Motive). (1) A recurrent thematic element—word, image, symbol, object, phrase, action. (2) A conventional incident, situation, or device like the unknown knight of mysterious origin and low degree in the romance, or the baffling riddle in fairy tales.

Muse. The inspirer of poetry, on whom the poet calls for assistance. In Greek mythology the Muses were the nine daughters of Zeus and Mnemosyne ("Memory") presiding over the arts and sciences.

Mystery Play. Medieval religious drama; eventually performed in elaborate cycles of plays acted on pageant wagons or stages throughout city streets, with different guilds of artisans and merchants responsible for each.

Mysticism. A spiritual discipline in which sensory experience is expunged and the mind is devoted to deep contemplation and the reaching of a transcendental union with God.

Myth. From Greek *mythos*, "plot" or "narrative." The verbal culture of most if not all human societies began with stories, and certain stories have achieved a distinctive importance as being connected with what the society feels it most needs to know: stories illustrating the society's religion, history, class structure, or the origin of peculiar features of the natural environment.

Narrative Poem. One that tells a story, particularly the epic, metrical romance, and shorter narratives, like the ballad.

Naturalism. (1) Broadly, according to nature. (2) More specifically, a literary movement of the late 19th century; an extension of realism, naturalism was a reaction against the restrictions inherent in the realistic emphasis on the ordinary, as naturalists insisted that the extraordinary is real, too.

Neoclassical Period. Generally, the span of time from the restoration of Charles II to his father's throne in 1660 until the publication of William Wordsworth and Samuel Taylor Coleridge's *Lyrical Ballads* (1798). Writers hoped to revive something like the classical Pax Romana, an era of peace and literary excellence.

Neologism. A word newly coined or introduced into a language, or a new meaning given to an old word.

New Criticism. An approach to criticism prominent in the United States after the publication of John Crowe Ransom's *New Criticism* (1941). Generally, the New Critics were agreed that a poem or story should be considered an organic unit, with each part working to support the whole. They worked by close analysis, considering the text as the final authority, and were distrustful, though not wholly neglectful, of considerations brought from outside the text, as, for example, from biography or history.

New Historicism. A cross-disciplinary approach fostered by the rise of feminist and multicultural studies as well as a renewed emphasis on historical perspective. Associated in particular with work on the early modern and the romantic periods in the United States and England, the approach emphasizes analysis of the relationship between history and literature, viewing writings in both fields as "texts" for study. New Historicism has tended to note political influences on literary and historical texts, to illuminate the role of the writer against the backdrop of social customs and assumptions, and to view history as changeable and interconnected instead of as a linear progressive evolution.

Nocturne. A night piece; writing evocative of evening or night.

Nominalism. In the Middle Ages, the belief that universals have no real being, but are only names, their existence limited to their presence in the minds and language of humans. This belief was opposed to the beliefs of medieval realists, who held that universals have an independent existence, at least in the mind of God.

Norman Conquest. The period of English history in which the Normans consolidated their hold on England after the defeat of the Saxon King Harold by William, Duke of Normandy, in 1066. French became the court language and Norman lords gained control of English lands, but Anglo-Saxon administrative and judicial systems remained largely in place.

Novel. The extended prose fiction that arose in the 18th century to become a major literary expression of the modern world. The term comes from the Italian *novella*, the short "new" tale of intrigue and moral comeuppance most eminently disseminated by Boccaccio's *Decameron* (1348–1353). The terms *novel* and *romance*, from the French *roman*, competed interchangeably for most of the 18th century.

Novella. (1) Originally, a short tale. (2) In modern usage, a term sometimes used interchangeably with short novel or for a fiction of middle length.

Octave. (1) The first unit in an Italian sonnet: eight lines of iambic pentameter, rhyming *abbaabba*. *See also* Meter. (2) A stanza in eight lines.

Octavo (Abbreviated 8vo). A book made from sheets folded to give signatures of eight leaves (16 pages), a book of average size.

Octet. An octastich or octave.

Octosyllabic. Eight-syllable.

Ode. A long, stately lyric poem in stanzas of varied metrical pattern.

Old English. The language brought to England, beginning in 449, by the Jute, Angle, and Saxon invaders from Denmark; the language base from which modern English evolved.

Omniscient Narrative. A narrative account untrammeled by constraints of time or space. An omniscient narrator perspective knows about the external and internal realities of characters as well as incidents unknown to them, and can interpret motivation and meaning.

Onomatopoeia. The use of words formed or sounding like what they signify—*buzz, crack, smack, whinny*—especially in an extensive capturing of sense by sound.

Orientalism. A term denoting Western portrayals of Oriental culture. In literature it refers to a varied body of work beginning in the 18th century that described for Western readers the history, language, politics, and culture of the area east of the Mediterranean.

Oxymoron. A pointed stupidity: *oxy*, "sharp," plus *moron*. One of the great ironic figures of speech—for example, "a fearful joy," or Milton's "darkness visible."

Paleography. The study and interpretation of ancient handwriting and manuscript styles.

Palimpsest. A piece of writing on secondhand vellum, parchment, or other surface carrying traces of erased previous writings.

Panegyric. A piece of writing in praise of a person, thing, or achievement.

Pantheism. A belief that God and the universe are identical, from the Greek words *pan* ("all") and *theos* ("god"). God is all; all is God.

Pantomime. A form of drama presented without words, in a dumb show.

Parable. (1) A short tale, such as those of Jesus in the gospels, encapsulating a moral or religious lesson. (2) Any saying, figure of speech, or narrative in which one thing is expressed in terms of another.

Paradox. An apparently untrue or self-contradictory statement or circumstance that proves true upon reflection or when examined in another light.

Paraphrase. A rendering in other words of the sense of a text or passage, as of a poem, essay, short story, or other writing.

Parody. As comedy, parody exaggerates or distorts the prominent features of style or content in a work. As criticism, it mimics the work, borrowing words or phrases or characteristic turns of thought in order to highlight weaknesses of conception or expression.

Passion Play. Originally a play based on Christ's Passion; later, one including both Passion and Resurrection.

Pastiche. A work created by assembling bits and pieces from other works.

Pastoral. From Latin *pastor*, a shepherd. The first pastoral poet was Theocritus, a Greek of the 3rd century B.C. The pastoral poem is not really about shepherds, but about the complex society the poet and readers inhabit.

Pathetic Fallacy. The attribution of animate or human characteristics to nature, as, for example, when rocks, trees, or weather are portrayed as reacting in sympathy to human feelings or events.

Pathos. The feeling of pity, sympathy, tenderness, compassion, or sorrow evoked by someone or something that is helpless.

Pedantry. Ostentatious book learning.

Pentameter. A line of five metrical feet. (*See* Meter.)

Peripeteia (or Peripetia, Peripety). A sudden change in situation in a drama or fiction, a reversal of luck for good or ill.

Periphrasis. The practice of talking around the point; a wordy restatement; a circumlocution.

Peroration. (1) The summative conclusion of a formal oration. (2) Loosely, a grandiloquent speech.

Persona. A mask (in Latin); in poetry and fiction, the projected speaker or narrator of the work—that is, a mask for the actual author.

Personification. The technique of treating abstractions, things, or animals as persons. A kind of metaphor, personification turns abstract ideas, like love, into a physical beauty named Venus, or conversely, makes dumb animals speak and act like humans.

Petrarchan Sonnet. Another name for an Italian sonnet.

Phoneme. In linguistics, the smallest distinguishable unit of sound. Different for each language, phonemes are defined by determining which differences in sound function to signal a difference in meaning.

Phonetics. (1) The study of speech sounds and their production, transmission, and reception. (2) The phonetic system of a particular language. (3) Symbols used to represent speech sounds.

Picaresque Novel. A novel chronicling the adventures of a rogue (Spanish: *picaro*), typically presented as an autobiography, episodic in structure and panoramic in its coverage of time and place.

Picturesque, The. A quality in landscape, and in idealized landscape painting, admired in the second half of the 18th century and featuring crags, a torrent or winding stream, ruins, and perhaps a quiet cottage and cart, with contrasting light and shadow.

Plagiarism. Literary kidnapping (Latin *plagiarius*, "kidnapper")—the seizing and presenting as one's own the ideas or writings of another.

Plain Style. The straightforward, unembellished style of preaching favored by 17th-century Puritans as well as by reformers within the Anglican church, as speaking God's word directly from the inspired heart as opposed to the high style of aristocratic oratory and courtliness, the vehicle of subterfuge. Plain style was simultaneously advocated for scientific accuracy by the Royal Society.

Platonism. Any reflection of Plato's philosophy, particularly the belief in the eternal reality of ideal forms, of which the diversities of the physical world are but transitory shadows.

Poetics. The theory, art, or science of poetry. Poetics is concerned with the nature and function of poetry and with identifying and explaining its types, forms, and techniques.

Poet Laureate. Since the 17th century, a title conferred by the monarch on English poets. At first, the laureate was required to write poems to commemorate special occasions, such as royal birthdays, national celebrations, and the like, but since the early 19th century the appointment has been for the most part honorary.

Poetry. Imaginatively intense language, usually in verse. Poetry is a form of fiction—"the supreme fiction," said Wallace Stevens. It is distinguished from other fictions by the compression resulting from its heavier use of figures of speech and allusion and, usually, by the music of its patterns of sounds.

Postmodernism. A term first used in relation to literature in the late 1940s by Randall Jarrell and John Berryman to proclaim a new sensibility arising to challenge the reigning assumptions and practices of modernism. Intruding into one's own fiction to ponder its powers became a hallmark of the 1960s and 1970s.

Poststructuralism. A mode of literary criticism and thought centered on Jacques Derrida's concept of deconstruction. Structuralists see language as the paradigm for all structures. Poststructuralists see language as based on differences—hence the analytical deconstruction of what seemed an immutable system. What language expresses is already absent. Poststructuralism invites interpretations through the spaces left by the way words operate.

Pragmatism. In philosophy, the idea that the value of a belief is best judged by the acts that follow from it—its practical results.

Preciosity. An affected or overingenious refinement of language.

Predestination. The belief that an omniscient God, at the Creation, destined all subsequent events, particularly, in Calvinist belief, the election for salvation and the damnation of individual souls.

Pre-Raphaelite. Characteristic of a small but influential group of mid-19th-century painters who hoped to recapture the spiritual vividness they saw in medieval painting before Raphael (1483–1520).

Presbyterianism. John Calvin's organization of ecclesiastical governance not by bishops representing the pope but by elders representing the congregation.

Proscenium. That part of the stage projecting in front of the curtain.

Prose. Ordinary writing patterned on speech, as distinct from verse.

Prose Poetry. Prose rich in cadenced and poetic effects like alliteration, assonance, consonance, and the like, and in imagery.

Prosody. The analysis and description of meters; metrics (*see also* Meter). Linguists apply the term to the study of patterns of accent in a language.

Protagonist. The leading character in a play or story; originally the leader of the chorus in the agon ("contest") of Greek drama, faced with the antagonist, the opposition.

Pseudonym. A fictitious name adopted by an author for public use.

Psychoanalytic Criticism. A form of criticism that uses the insights of Freudian psychology to illuminate a work.

Ptolemaic Universe. The universe as perceived by Ptolemy, a Greco-Egyptian astronomer of the 2nd century A.D., whose theories were dominant until the Renaissance produced the Copernican universe. In Ptolemy's system, the universe was world-centered, with the sun, moon, planets, and stars understood as rotating around the earth in a series of concentric spheres.

Puritanism. A Protestant movement arising in the mid-16th century with the Reformation in England. Theocracy—the individual and the congregation governed directly under God through Christ—became primary, reflected in the centrality of the Scriptures and their exposition, and the direct individual experience of God's grace.

Quadrivium. The more advanced four of the seven liberal arts as studied in medieval universities: arithmetic, geometry, astronomy, and music.

Quantitative Verse. Verse that takes account of the quantity of the syllables (whether they take a long or short time to pronounce) rather than their stress patterns.

Quarto (Abbreviated 4to, 4o). A book made from sheets folded twice, giving signatures of four leaves (eight pages).

Quatrain. A stanza of four lines, rhymed or unrhymed. With its many variations, it is the most common stanzaic form in English.

Rationalism. The theory that reason, rather than revelation or authority, provides knowledge, truth, the choice of good over evil, and an adequate understanding of God and the universe.

Reader-Response Theory. A form of criticism that arose during the 1970s; it postulates the essential active involvement of the reader with the text and focuses on the effect of the process of reading on the mind.

Realism (in literature). The faithful representation of life. Realism carries the conviction of true reports of phenomena observable by others.

Realism (in philosophy). (1) In the Middle Ages, the belief that universal concepts possess real existence apart from particular things and the human mind. Medieval realism was opposed to nominalism. (2) In later epistemology, the belief that things exist apart from our perception of them. In this sense, realism is opposed to idealism, which locates all reality in our minds.

Recension. The text produced as a result of reconciling variant readings.

Recto. The right-hand page of an open book; the front of a leaf as opposed to the *verso* or back of a leaf.

Redaction. (1) A revised version. (2) A rewriting or condensing of an older work.

Refrain. A set phrase, or chorus, recurring throughout a song or poem, usually at the end of a stanza or other regular interval.

Relativism. The philosophical belief that nothing is absolute, that values are relative to circumstances. In criticism, relativism is either personal or historical.

Reversal. The thrilling change of luck for the protagonist at the last moment in comedy or tragedy.

Rhetoric. From Greek *rhetor*, "orator": the art of persuasion in speaking or writing.

Rhetorical Figure. A figure of speech employing stylized patterns of word order or meaning for purposes of ornamentation or persuasion.

Rhetorical Question. A question posed for effect, usually with a self-evident answer.

Rhyme (sometimes Rime, an older spelling). The effect created by matching sounds at the ends of words. The functions of rhyme are essentially four: pleasurable, mnemonic, structural, and rhetorical. Like meter and figurative language, rhyme provides a pleasure derived from fulfillment of a basic human desire to see similarity in dissimilarity, likeness with a difference.

Rhyme Royal. A stanza of seven lines of iambic pentameter, rhyming *ababbcc* (*see also* Meter).

Rhythm. The measured flow of repeated sound patterns, as, for example, the heavy stresses of accentual verse, the long and short syllables of quantitative verse, the balanced syntactical arrangements of parallelism in either verse or prose.

Romance. A continuous narrative in which the emphasis is on what happens in the plot, rather than on what is reflected from ordinary life or experience. Thus a central element in romance is adventure.

Romanticism. A term describing qualities that colored most elements of European and American intellectual life in the late 18th and early 19th centuries, from literature, art, and music, through architecture, landscape gardening, philosophy, and politics. The Romantics stressed the separateness of the person, celebrated individual perception and imagination, and embraced nature as a model for harmony in society and art.

Roundheads. Adherents of the Parliamentary, or Puritan, party in the English Civil War, so called from their short haircuts, as opposed to the fashionable long wigs of the Cavaliers, supporters of King Charles I.

Rubric. A heading, marginal notation, or other section distinguished for special attention by being printed in red ink or in distinctive type.

Run-on Line. A line of poetry whose sense does not stop at the end, with punctuation, but runs on to the next line.

Satire. Poking corrective ridicule at persons, types, actions, follies, mores, and beliefs.

Scop. An Anglo-Saxon bard, or court poet, a kind of poet laureate.

Semiotics. In anthropology, sociology, and linguistics, the study of signs, including words, other sounds, gestures, facial expressions, music, pictures, and other signals used in communication.

Senecan Tragedy. The bloody and bombastic tragedies of revenge inspired by Seneca's nine closet dramas.

Sensibility. Sensitive feeling, emotion. The term arose early in the 18th century to denote the tender undercurrent of feeling in the neoclassical period.

Sequel. A literary work that explores later events in the lives of characters introduced elsewhere.

Serial. A narration presented in segments separated by time. Novels by Charles Dickens and other 19th-century writers were first serialized in magazines.

Shakespearean Sonnet (or English Sonnet). A sonnet in three quatrains and a couplet, rhyming *abab cdcd efef gg*.

Signified, Signifier. In structural linguistics, the *signified* is the idea in mind when a word is used, an entity separate from the *signifier*, the word itself.

Simile. A metaphor stating the comparison by use of *like*, *as*, or *as if*.

Slang. The special vocabulary of a class or group of people (as, for example, truck drivers, jazz musicians, salespeople, drug dealers), generally considered substandard, low, or offensive when measured against formal, educated usage.

Sonnet. A verse form of 14 lines, in English characteristically in iambic pentameter and most often in one of two rhyme schemes: the *Italian* (or *Petrarchan*) or *Shakespearean* (or *English*). An Italian sonnet is composed of an octave, rhyming *abbaabba*, and a sestet, rhyming *cdecde* or *cdcdcd*, or in some variant pattern, but with no closing couplet. A Shakespearean sonnet has three quatrains and a couplet, and rhymes *abab cdcd efef gg*. In both types, the content tends to follow the formal outline suggested by rhyme linkage, giving two divisions to the thought of an Italian sonnet and four to a Shakespearean one.

Sonnet Sequence. A group of sonnets thematically unified to create a longer work.

Spondee. A metrical foot of two long, or stressed, syllables: – –.

Sprung Rhythm. Gerard Manley Hopkins's term to describe his variations of iambic meter to avoid the "same and tame." His feet, he said, vary from one to four syllables, with one stress per foot, on the first syllable.

Stanza. A term derived from an Italian word for "room" or "stopping place" and used, loosely, to designate any grouping of lines in a separate unit in a poem: a verse paragraph. More strictly, a stanza is a grouping of a prescribed number of lines in a given meter, usually with a particular rhyme scheme, repeated as a unit of structure.

Stereotype. A character representing generalized racial or social traits repeated as typical from work to work, with no individualizing traits.

Stichomythia. Dialogue in alternate lines, favored in Greek tragedy and by Seneca and his imitators among the Elizabethans—including William Shakespeare.

Stock Characters. Familiar types repeated in literature to become symbolic of a particular genre, like the hard-boiled hero of the detective story.

Stoicism. (1) Generally, fortitude, repression of feeling, indifference to pleasure or pain. (2) Specifically, the philosophy of the Stoics, who, cultivating endurance and self-control, restrain passions such as joy and grief that place them in conflict with nature's dictates.

Stress. In poetry, the accent or emphasis given to certain syllables, indicated in scansion by a *macron* (–). In a trochee, for example, the stress falls on the first syllable: sŭmmĕr. *See also* Meter.

Structuralism. The study of social organizations and myths, of language, and of literature as structures. Each part is significant only as it relates to others in the total structure, with nothing meaningful by itself.

Structural Linguistics. Analysis and description of the grammatical structures of a spoken language.

Sublime. In literature, a quality attributed to lofty or noble ideas, grand or elevated expression, or (the ideal of sublimity) an inspiring combination of thought and language. In nature or art, it is a quality, as in a landscape or painting, that inspires awe or reverence.

Subplot. A sequence of events subordinate to the main story in a narrative or dramatic work.

Syllabic Verse. Poetry in which meter has been set aside and the line is controlled by a set number of syllables, regardless of stress.

Symbol. Something standing for its natural qualities in another context, with human meaning added: an eagle, standing for the soaring imperious dominance of Rome.

Symbolism. Any use of symbols, especially with a theoretical commitment, as when the French Symbolists of the 1880s and 1890s stressed, in Stéphane Mallarmé's words, not the thing but the effect, the subjective emotion implied by the surface rendering.

Syncopation. The effect produced in verse or music when two stress patterns play off against one another.

Synecdoche. The understanding of one thing by another—a kind of metaphor in which a part stands for the whole, or the whole for a part: *a hired hand* meaning "a laborer."

Synesthesia. Greek for "perceiving together": close association or confusion of sense impressions, as in common phrases like "blue note" and "cold eye."

Synonyms. Words in the same language denoting the same thing, usually with different connotations: *female, woman, lady, dame; male, masculine, macho.*

Synopsis. A summary of a play, a narrative, or an argument.

Tenor and Vehicle. I. A. Richards's terms for the two aspects of metaphor, *tenor* being the actual thing projected figuratively in the *vehicle*. "She [tenor] is a rose [vehicle]."

Tercet (or Triplet). A verse unit of three lines, sometimes rhymed, sometimes not.

Terza Rima. A verse form composed of tercets with interlocking rhyme (*aba bcb cdc*, and so on), usually in iambic pentameter. Invented by Dante for his *Divine Comedy*.

Third-Person Narration. A method of storytelling in which someone who is not involved in the story, but stands somewhere outside it in space and time, tells of the events.

Topos. A commonplace, from Greek *topos* (plural *topoi*), "place." A rhetorical device, similarly remembered as a commonplace.

Tragedy. Fundamentally, a serious fiction involving the downfall of a hero or heroine. As a literary form, a basic mode of drama. Tragedy often involves the theme of isolation, in which a hero, a character of greater than ordinary human importance, becomes isolated from the community.

Tragic Irony. The essence of tragedy, in which the most noble and most deserving person, because of the very grounds of his or her excellence, dies in defeat. *See also* Irony.

Tragicomedy. (1) A tragedy with happy ending, frequently with penitent villain and romantic setting, disguises, and discoveries.

Travesty. Literally a "cross-dressing": a literary work so clothed, or presented, as to appear ludicrous; a grotesque image or likeness.

Trivium. The first three of the seven liberal arts as studied in medieval universities: grammar, logic, and rhetoric (including oratory).

Trochee. A metrical foot going – ⌣ .

Trope. Greek *tropos* for "a turn": a word or phrase turned from its usual meaning to an unusual one; hence, a figure of speech, or an expression turned beyond its literal meaning.

Type. (1) A literary genre. (2) One of the type characters. (3) A symbol or emblem. (4) In theology and literary criticism, an event in early Scriptures or literatures that is seen as prefiguring an event in later Scriptures or in history or literature generally.

Type Characters. Individuals endowed with traits that mark them more distinctly as representatives of a type or class than as standing apart from a type: the typical doctor or rakish aristocrat, for example. Type characters are the opposite of individualized characters.

Typology. The study of types. Typology springs from a theory of literature or history that recognizes events as duplicated in time.

Utopia. A word from two Greek roots (*outopia*, meaning "no place," and *eutopia*, meaning "good place"), pointing to the idea that a utopia is a nonexistent land of social perfection.

Verisimilitude (*vraisemblance* in French). The appearance of actuality.

Verso. The left-hand page of an open book; the back of a leaf of paper.

Vice. A stock character from the medieval morality play, a mischief-making tempter.

Vignette. (1) A brief, subtle, and intimate literary portrait, named for *vignette* portraiture. (2) A short essay, sketch, or story, usually fewer than five hundred words.

Villanelle. One of the French verse forms, in five tercets, all rhyming *aba*, and a quatrain, rhyming *abaa*. The entire first and third lines are repeated alternately as the final lines of tercets 2, 3, 4, and 5, and together to conclude the quatrain.

Virgule. A "little rod"—the diagonal mark or slash used to indicate line ends in poetry printed continuously in running prose.

Vulgate. (1) A people's common vernacular language (Latin *vulgus*, "common people"). (2) The Vulgate Bible, translated by St. Jerome c. 383–405.

Wit and Humor. *Wit* is intellectual acuity; *humor*, an amused indulgence of human deficiencies. Wit now denotes the acuity that produces laughter. It originally meant mere understanding, then quickness of understanding, then, beginning in the 17th century, quick perception coupled with creative fancy. Humor (British *humour*, from the four bodily humors) was simply a disposition, usually eccentric. In the 18th century, *humour* came to mean a laughable eccentricity and then a kindly amusement at such eccentricity.

Zeugma. The technique of using one word to yoke two or more others for ironic or amusing effect, achieved when at least one of the yoked is a misfit, as in Alexander Pope's "lose her Heart, or Necklace, at a Ball."

BIBLIOGRAPHY
The Victorian Period

Bibliographies • Brahma Chaudhuri, ed., *Annual Bibliography of Victorian Studies*, 1976–. • Brahma Chaudhuri, ed., *A Comprehensive Bibliography of Victorian Studies, 1970–1984*, 3 vols. • *Modern Language Association International Bibliography*, online. • David Nicholls, *Nineteenth-Century Britain, 1815–1914*. 1978. • *Victorian Poetry*. Annual "Guide to the Year's Work on Victorian Poetry." 1963–. • *Studies in English Literature*. Annual review of "Recent Studies in the Nineteenth Century" (autumn issue), 1961–. • *Victorian Studies*. Annual "Victorian Bibliography" (summer issue), 1957–.

Cultural and Intellectual Background • Richard D. Altick, *Victorian People and Ideas*, 1973. • Asa Briggs, *Victorian People: A Reassessment of Persons and Themes 1851–67*, 1965. • Asa Briggs, *Victorian Things*, 1988. • Jerome H. Buckley, *The Victorian Temper: A Study in Literary Culture*, 1951. • Jerome H. Buckley, *The Triumph of Time: A Study of the Victorian Concepts of Time, History, Progress, and Decadence*, 1966. • David Cannadine, *The Decline and Fall of the British Aristocracy*, 1990. • A. Dwight Culler, *The Victorian Mirror of History*, 1985. • Philip Davis, *The Victorians: The Oxford English Literary History*, Vol. 8, 1830-1880, 2004. • David J. Delaura, *Hebrew and Hellene in Victorian England: Newman, Arnold, and Pater*, 1969. • Peter Gay, *The Bourgeois Experience: From Victoria to Freud*, 2 vols., 1984–1986. • Robin Gilmour, *The Victorian Period: The Intellectual and Cultural Context of English Literature, 1830–1890*, 1993. • Christopher Herbert, *Culture and Anomie: Ethnographic Imagination in the Nineteenth Century*, 1991. • Thomas William Heyck, *The Transformation of Intellectual Life in Victorian England*, 1982. • Walter E. Houghton, *The Victorian Frame of Mind, 1830–1870*, 1957. • Richard Jenkyns, *The Victorians and Ancient Greece*, 1980. • Steven Marcus, *The Other Victorians: A Study of Sexuality and Pornography in Mid-Nineteenth-Century England*, 1964. • Sally Mitchell, ed., *Victorian Britain: An Encyclopedia*, 1988. • E. Royston Pike, ed., *"Hard Times": Human Documents of the Industrial Revolution*, 1966; *"Golden Times": Human Documents of the Victorian Age*, 1967; *"Busy Times": Human Documents of the Age of the Forsytes*, 1969. • Mary Poovey, *Making a Social Body: British Cultural Formation, 1830–1864*, 1995. • Thomas Richards, *The Commodity Culture of Victorian England: Advertising and Spectacle, 1851–1914*, 1990. • Edward Said, *Orientalism*, 1978. • Richard L. Stein, *Victoria's Year: English Literature and Culture, 1837–1838*, 1987. • George W. Stocking, *Victorian Anthropology*, 1987. • Herbert Sussman, *Victorians and the Machine*, 1968. • David Trotter, *Cooking With Mud: The Idea of Mess in Nineteenth-Century Art and Fiction*, 2000. • Herbert F. Tucker, ed., *A Companion to Victorian Literature and Culture*, 1999. • Frank M. Turner, *Contesting Cultural Authority: Essays in Victorian Intellectual Life*, 1993. • Basil Willey, *Nineteenth Century Studies*, 1949. • Basil Willey, *More Nineteenth Century Studies*, 1956. • Raymond Williams, *Culture and Society 1780–1950*, 1958. • Janet Wolff and John Seed, eds., *The Culture of Capital: Art, Power and the Nineteenth-Century Middle Class*, 1988. • G. M. Young, *Victorian England: Portrait of an Age*, 1936.

Fiction • Richard D. Altick, *The Presence of the Present: Topics of the Day in the Victorian Novel*, 1991. • Nancy Armstrong, *Desire and Domestic Fiction: A Political History of the Novel*, 1987. • Joseph W. Childers, *Novel Possibilities: Fiction and the Formation of Early Victorian Culture*, 1995. • Deirdre David, ed., *The Cambridge Companion to the Victorian Novel*, 2001. • Peter Garrett, *The Victorian Multiplot Novel*, 1980. • Barbara Hardy, *Forms of Feeling in Victorian Fiction*, 1985. • E. A. Horsman, *The Victorian Novel*, 1991. • George Levine, *The Realistic Imagination: English Fiction from Frankenstein to Lady Chatterley*, 1981. • D. A. Miller, *The Novel and the Police*, 1988. • J. Hillis Miller, *The Form of Victorian Fiction*, 1968. • Ira B. Nadel and William E. Fredeman, eds., *Victorian Novelists Before 1885*, in *Dictionary of Literary Biography*, vol. 21, 1983. • Robert Polhemus, *Erotic Faith: Being in Love from Jane Austen to D. H. Lawrence*, 1990. • Barry Qualls, *The Secular Pilgrims of Victorian Fiction*, 1982. • Elaine Showalter, *A Literature of Their Own: British Women Novelists from Brontë to Lessing*, 1977. • Lionel Stevenson, *The English Novel: A Panorama*, 1960.

• Ronald R. Thomas, *Dreams of Authority: Freud and the Fictions of the Unconscious*, 1990.

Gender and Culture • Amanda Anderson, *Tainted Souls and Painted Faces: The Rhetoric of Fallenness in Victorian Culture*, 1993. • Nina Auerbach, *Romantic Imprisonment: Women and Other Glorified Outcasts*, 1985. • Nina Auerbach, *Woman and the Demon: The Life of a Victorian Myth*, 1982. • Francoise Basch, *Relative Creatures: Victorian Women in Society and the Novel*, 1974. • Susan Casteras and Linda H. Peterson, *A Struggle for Fame: Victorian Women Artists and Authors*, 1994. • Lloyd Davis, ed., *Virgin Sexuality and Textuality in Victorian Literature*, 1993. • Richard Dellamora, *Masculine Desire: The Sexual Politics of Victorian Aestheticism*, 1990. • Kristine Ottesen Garrigan, ed., *Victorian Scandals: Representations of Gender and Class*, 1992. • Sandra Gilbert and Susan Gubar, *The Madwoman in the Attic: The Woman Writer and the Nineteenth-Century Literary Imagination*, 1979. • A. James Hammerton, *Cruelty and Companionship: Conflict in Nineteenth-Century Married Life*, 1992. • Kathleen Hickok, *Representations of Women: Nineteenth-Century British Women's Poetry*, 1984. • Margaret Homans, *Bearing the Word: Language and Female Experience in Nineteenth-Century Women's Writing*, 1986. • Dorothy Mermin, *Godiva's Ride: Women of Letters in England, 1830–1880*, 1993. • Ellen Moers, *Literary Women*, 1976. • Deborah Epstein Nord, *Walking the Victorian Streets: Women Representation, and the City*, 1995. • Christopher Parker, ed., *Gender Roles and Sexuality in Victorian Literature*, 1995. • Eve Kosofsky Sedgwick, *Between Men: English Literature and Male Homosocial Desire*, 1985. • Alan Sinfield, *Cultural Politics—Queer Reading*, 1994.

History and Politics • Derek Beales, *From Castlereagh to Gladstone: 1815–1885*, 1970. • Patrick Brantlinger, *The Spirit of Reform: British Literature and Politics, 1832–1867*, 1977. • Asa Briggs, *A Social History of England*, 1983. • Barbara Dennis and David Skilton, eds., *Reform and Intellectual Debate in Victorian England*, 1987. • C. C. Eldridge, *Victorian Imperialism*, 1978. • E. J. Feuchtwanger, *Democracy and Empire: Britain, 1865–1914*, 1985. • Jose Harris, *Private Lives, Public Spirit: A Social History of Great Britain, 1870–1914*, 1993. • Patricia Jalland, *Women, Marriage, and Politics, 1860–1914*, 1987. • Patrick Joyce, *Visions of the People: Industrial England and the Question of Class, 1848–1914*, 1991. • J. P. Parry, *The Rise and Fall of Liberal Government in Victorian Britain*, 1994. • David Thomson, *England in the Nineteenth Century*, 1950. • E. P. Thompson, *The Making of the English Working Class*, 1963. • F. M. L. Thompson, *The Rise of Respectable Society: A Social History of Victorian Britain, 1830–1900*, 1988. • *Victorian Studies. Special Issue: Victorian Ethnographies*, vol. 41, no. 3, 1999.

Literature • William E. Buckler, *The Victorian Imagination: Essays in Aesthetic Exploration*, 1980. • Raymond Chapman, *The Sense of the Past in Victorian Literature*, 1986. • Alison Milbank, *Dante and the Victorians*, 1998. • J. Hillis Miller, *The Disappearance of God: Five Nineteenth Century Writers*, 1963. • J. Hillis Miller, *Victorian Subjects*, 1990. • David Morse, *High Victorian Culture*, 1993. • John R. Reed, *Victorian Conventions*, 1975 • Ruth Robbins and Julian Wolfreys, eds., *Victorian Identities: Social and Cultural Formations in Nineteenth-Century Literature*, 1996.

Nonfiction Prose • Andrea Broomfield and Sally Mitchell, eds., *Prose by Victorian Women: An Anthology*, 1996. • Jerome H. Buckley, *The Turning Key: Autobiography and the Subjective Impulse since 1800*, 1984. • A. O. J. Cockshut, *The Art of Autobiography in 19th and 20th Century England*, 1984. • Mary Jean Corbett, *Representing Femininity: Middle-Class Subjectivity in Victorian and Edwardian Women's Autobiographies*, 1992. • Avrom Fleishman, *Figures of Autobiography: The Language of Self-Writing in Victorian and Modern England*, 1983. • Regenia Gagnier, *Subjectivities: A History of Self-Representation in Britain, 1832–1920*, 1991. • Heather Henderson, *The Victorian Self: Autobiography and Biblical Narrative*, 1989. • John Holloway, *The Victorian Sage*, 1953. • George P. Landow, ed., *Approaches to Victorian Autobiography*, 1979. • A. L. Le Quesne, *Victorian Thinkers: Carlyle, Ruskin, Arnold, Morris*, 1993. • George Levine and William Madden, eds., *The Art of Victorian Prose*, 1968. • Laura Marcus, *Auto/biographical Discourses: Theory, Criticism, Practice*, 1995. • Thaïs E. Morgan, ed., *Victorian Sages and Cultural Discourse: Renegotiating Gender and Power*, 1991. • Linda Peterson, *Victorian Autobiography: The Tradition of Self-Interpretation*, 1986.

Poetry • Isobel Armstrong, *Victorian Poetry: Poetry, Poetics, and Politics*, 1993. • Douglas Bush, *Mythology and the Romantic Tradition in English Poetry*, 1937. • Carol T. Christ, *The Finer Optic: The Aesthetic of Particularity in Victorian Poetry*, 1975. • Carol T. Christ, *Victorian and Modern*

Poetics, 1984. • Thomas J. Collins, ed., *The Broadview Anthology of Victorian Poetry and Poetic Theory*, 1999. • William E. Fredeman and Ira B. Nadel, eds., *Victorian Poets After 1850*, in *Dictionary of Literary Biography*, vol. 35, 1985. • William E. Fredeman, and Ira B. Nadel, eds., *Victorian Poets Before 1850*, in *Dictionary of Literary Biography*, vol. 32, 1984. • Eric Griffiths, *The Printed Voice of Victorian Poetry*, 1989. • Antony H. Harrison, *Victorian Poets and Romantic Poems: Intertextuality and Ideology*, 1990. • E. D. H. Johnson, *The Alien Vision of Victorian Poetry*, 1952. • Robert Langbaum, *The Poetry of Experience: The Dramatic Monologue in Modern Literary Tradition*, 1957. • Angela Leighton, *Victorian Women Poets: Writing Against the Heart*, 1992. • Angela Leighton, ed., *Victorian Women Poets: A Critical Reader*, 1996. • Angela Leighton and Margaret Reynolds, eds., *Victorian Women Poets: An Anthology*, 1995. • Laurence W. Mazzeno, *Victorian Poetry: An Annotated Bibliography*, 1995. • W. David Shaw, *The Lucid Veil: Poetic Truth in the Victorian Age*, 1987.

Reading and Readership • Richard D. Altick, *The English Common Reader: A Social History of the Mass Reading Public 1800–1900*, 1957. • Richard D. Altick, *Writers, Readers, and Occasions*, 1989. • N. N. Feltes, *Modes of Production of Victorian Novels*, 1986. • Kate Flint, *The Woman Reader, 1837–1914*, 1993. • John O. Jordan and Robert L. Patten, eds., *Literature in the Marketplace: Nineteenth-Century British Publishing and Reading Practices*, 1995. • Judith Kennedy, ed., *Victorian Authors and Their Works: Revision, Motivations, and Modes*, 1991. • Q. D. Leavis, *Fiction and the Reading Public*, 1932. • Joanne Shattock and Michael Wolff, eds., *The Victorian Periodical Press*, 1982. • John Sutherland, *Victorian Fiction: Writers, Publishers, Readers*, 1995. • David Vincent, *Literacy and Popular Culture: England 1750–1914*, 1990.

Theater • Michael R. Booth, ed., *English Plays of the Nineteenth Century*, 5 vols., 1969–1976. • Michael R. Booth, *Theater in The Victorian Age*, 1991. • Michael R. Booth, ed., *The Lights o'London and other Victorian Plays*, 1995. • Tracy C. Davis, *Actresses as Working Women: Their Social Identity in Victorian Culture*, 1991. • Anthony Jenkins, *The Making of Victorian Drama*, 1991. • Joel H. Kaplan and Sheila Stowell, *Theatre and Fashion: Oscar Wilde to the Suffragettes*, 1994.

Visual Arts • Richard Altick, *Paintings from Books: Art and Literature in Britain, 1760–1900*, 1985.

• Tim Barringer, *Reading the Pre-Raphaelites*, 1999. • Kenneth Bendiner, *An Introduction to Victorian Painting*, 1985. Deborah Cherry, *Painting Women: Victorian Women Artists*, 1993. • Carol T. Christ and John O. Jordan, eds., *Victorian Literature and the Victorian Visual Imagination*, 1995. • Gerard Curtis, *Visual Words: Art and the Material Book in Victorian England*, 2000. • Linda Dowling, *The Vulgarization of Art: The Victorians and Aesthetic Democracy*, 1996. • William Gaunt, *The Pre-Raphaelite Dream*, 1966. • Helmut Gernsheim, *Julia Margaret Cameron: Her Life and Photographic Work*, 1975. • Heinz K. Henisch, *The Photographic Experience, 1839–1914*, 1994. • U. C. Knoepflmacher and G. B. Tennyson, eds., *Nature and the Victorian Imagination*, 1977. • Jeremy Maas, *Victorian Painters*, 1969. • Jan Marsh, *Pre-Raphaelite Sisterhood*, 1985. • Ira Bruce Nadel and F. S. Schwartzbach, eds., *Victorian Artists and the City*, 1980. • Pamela Gerrish Nunn, *Problem Pictures: Women and Men in Victorian Painting*, 1996. • Victoria Olsen, *From Life: Julia Margaret Cameron and Victorian Photography*, 2003. • Leslie Parris, ed., *The Pre-Raphaelites*, 1984. • Graham Reynolds, *Victorian Painting*, 1966; rev. 1987. • Lindsay Smith, *Victorian Photography, Painting, and Poetry: The Enigma of Visibility in Ruskin, Morris and the Pre-Raphaelites*, 1995. • Roy Strong, *And When Did You Last See Your Father?: The Victorian Painter and British History*, 1978. • Julian Treuherz, *Victorian Painting*, 1993. • Mike Weaver, *British Photography in the Nineteenth Century: The Fine Art Tradition*, 1989. • Christopher Wood, *The Pre-Raphaelites*, 1981.

World Wide Web Addresses. • *British Poetry 1780–1910: A Hypertext Archive of Scholarly Editions*: etext.lib.virginia.edu/britpo.html • *Northeast Victorian Studies Association*: www.stonehill.edu/nvsa/ [Maintains list of other Victorian web sites.] • *Victoria Research Web*: www.victorianresearch.org [Lists other Victorian web sites, and online Victorian journals and discussion groups.]. • *Victorian Literary Resources*: andromeda.rutgers.edu/~jlynch/Lit /victoria.html • *Victorian Studies on the Web*: www.victoriandatabase.com/ • George Landow's *Victorian Web*: www.victorianweb.org/ • *Victorian Women Writers Project*: www.indiana.edu/~letrs/vwwp/. • *Voice of the Shuttle*: vos.ucsb.edu/browse.asp?id=1156 [General resources in Victorian literature.].

Perspectives: Aestheticism, Decadence and the Fin de Siècle • *Anthologies.* Karl Beckson, ed., *Aesthetes and Decadents of the 1890s: An Anthology of British Poetry and Prose*, 1966; 1981. • Graham Hough and Eric Warner, eds., *Strangeness and Beauty: An Anthology of Aesthetic Criticism, 1840–1910*, 2 vols., 1983. • Sally Ledger and Roger Luckhurst, eds., *The Fin de Siècle: A Reader in Cultural History, c. 1880–1900*, 2000. • Ian Small, ed., *The Aesthetes: A Sourcebook*, 1979. • Derek Stanford, ed., *Poets of the 'Nineties: A Biographical Anthology*, 1965. • R. K. R. Thornton, ed., *Poetry of the Nineties*, 1970. • Stanley Weintraub, ed., *The Yellow Book: Quintessence of the Nineties*, 1964.

Criticism. • Karl Beckson, *London in the 1890s: A Cultural History*, 1992. • Gene H. Bell-Villada, *Art for Art's Sake and Literary Life: How Politics and Markets Helped Shape the Ideology and Culture of Aestheticism, 1790–1990*, 1996. • G. A. Cevasco, ed., *The 1890s: An Encyclopedia of British Literature, Art, and Culture*, 1993. • Richard Dellamora, *Masculine Desire: The Sexual Politics of Victorian Aestheticism*, 1990. • Linda C. Dowling, *Aestheticism and Decadence: A Selective Annotated Bibliography*, 1977. • Linda C. Dowling, *Hellenism and Homosexuality in Victorian Oxford*, 1994. • Linda C. Dowling, *Language and Decadence in the Victorian Fin de Siècle*, 1986. • Bram Dijkstra, *Idols of Perversity: Fantasies of Feminine Evil in Fin-de-Siècle Culture*, 1986. • Ian Fletcher, ed., *Decadence and the 1890s*, 1979. • Hilary Fraser, *Beauty and Belief: Aesthetics and Religion in Victorian Literature*, 1986. • William Gaunt, *The Aesthetic Adventure*, 1945. • Richard Gilman, *Decadence: The Strange Life of an Epithet*, 1979. • Walter Hamilton, *The Aesthetic Movement in England*, 1882. • Simon Houfe, *Fin de Siècle: The Illustrators of the 'Nineties*, 1992. • Graham Hough, *The Last Romantics*, 1947. • Holbrook Jackson, *The Eighteen Nineties*, 1913. • Sally Ledger and Scott McCracken, eds., *Cultural Politics at the Fin de Siècle*, 1995. • Patricia Marks, *Bicycles, Bangs, and Bloomers: The New Woman in the Popular Press*, 1990. • Linda Merrill, *A Pot of Paint: Aesthetics on Trial in "Whistler v. Ruskin,"* 1992. • John R. Reed, *Decadent Style*, 1985. • Elaine Showalter, *Sexual Anarchy: Gender and Culture at the Fin de Siècle*, 1990. • Chris Snodgrass, *Aubrey Beardsley: Dandy of the Grotesque*, 1995. • Robin Spencer, *The Aesthetic Movement: Theory and Practice*, 1972. • John Stokes, *In the Nineties*, 1989. • John Stokes, ed., *Fin de Siècle/Fin de Globe: Fears and Fantasies of the Late Nineteenth Century*, 1992. • Mikulas Teich and Roy Porter, eds., *Fin de Siècle and its Legacy*, 1990. • R. K. R. Thornton, *The Decadent Dilemma*, 1983.

Our Texts. • GILBERT: "If You're Anxious for to Shine" from *The Complete Plays of Gilbert and Sullivan*, 1941; WHISTLER: "Mr. Whistler's 'Ten O'Clock'" from *The Gentle Art of Making Enemies*, 2nd ed., 1892; "MICHAEL FIELD": "La Gioconda" and "A Pen-Drawing of Leda" from *Sight and Song*, 1892; "A Girl" from *Underneath the Bough*, 1893; LEVERSON: "Suggestion" from *The Yellow Book*, April 1895; SYMONS: "Pastel" and Preface from *Silhouettes*, 1896; "White Heliotrope" from *London Nights*, 2nd ed., 1897; "The Decadent Movement in Literature" from *Harper's New Monthly Magazine*, vol. 87 (Nov. 1893); LE GALLIENNE: "A Ballad of London" from *Robert Louis Stevenson: An Elegy and Other Poems*, 1895; JOHNSON: from *Complete Poems*, ed. Iain Fletcher, 1953; DOUGLAS: "Two Loves" from *Two Loves and Other Poems*, 1990; "Impression de nuit" from *The Collected Poems of Lord Alfred Douglas*, 1919; CUSTANCE: from *The Selected Poems of Olive Custance*, 1995; BEERBOHM: "Enoch Soames" from *Seven Men and Two Others*, 1950.

Perspectives: Imagining Childhood • *Anthologies.*
• Patricia Demers, ed., *A Garland from the Golden Age: An Anthology of Children's Literature from 1850 to 1900*, 1983. • E. Royston Pike, ed., *Human Documents of the Victorian Golden Age, 1850–1875*, 1967.

Criticism. • Philippe Ariès, *Centuries of Childhood*, trans. R. Baldick, 1986. • Jacqueline Banerjee, *Through the Northern Gate: Childhood and Growing Up in British Fiction, 1719–1901*, 1996. • Penny Brown, *The Captured World: The Child and Childhood in Nineteenth-Century Women's Writing in England*, 1993. • Humphrey Carpenter, *Secret Gardens: A Study of the Golden Age of Children's Literature*, 1985. • Peter Coveney, *The Image of Childhood*, 1967. • Charles Frey and John Griffith, *The Literary Heritage of Childhood: An Appraisal of Children's Classics in the Western Tradition*, 1987. • Mary Hilton, Morag Styles, and Victor Watson, eds., *Opening the Nursery Door: Reading, Writing and Childhood 1600–1900*, 1997. • Peter Hunt, ed., *Children's Literature: An Illustrated History*, 1995. • Thomas E. Jordan, *Victorian Childhood: Themes and Variations*, 1987. • U. C. Knoepflmacher, *Ventures into Childhood: Victorians, Fairy Tales, and Femininity*, 1998.

• Antony and Peter Miall, *The Victorian Nursery Book*, 1980. • Lance Salway, ed., *A Peculiar Gift: Nineteenth Century Writings on Books for Children*, 1976. • Sharon Smulders, "Sound, Sense, and Structure in Christina Rossetti's *Sing-Song*," *Children's Literature* 22, 1994. • Carole G. Silver, *Strange and Secret Peoples: Fairies and Victorian Consciousness*, 1999. • James Walvin, *A Child's World: A Social History of English Childhood, 1800–1914*, 1982. • Jackie Wullschläger, *Inventing Wonderland: The Lives and Fantasies of Lewis Carroll, Edward Lear, J. M. Barrie, Kenneth Grahame and A. A. Milne*, 1995.

Our Texts. • DARWIN, "A Biographical Sketch of an Infant," 1877 • COOK, *Eliza Cook's Journal*, 1849 • HOFFMANN, *The English Strewwelpeter*, 1848 • T. MILLER, *Original Poems for My Children*, 1850 • W. MILLER, *Whistle-Binkie*, 1841 • LEAR, Limericks: *A Book of Nonsense* 1861; "The Owl and the Pussy-Cat" and "The Jumblies" from *Nonsense Songs*, 1871; "How Pleasant to know Mr. Lear!" from *The Complete Nonsense Book*, edited by Lady Strachey, 1912. • ROSSETTI, *Poetical Works*, 1906 • STEVENSON, *A Child's Garden of Verses*, 1885 • BELLOC, *The Bad Child's Book of Beasts*, 1897; *Cautionary Tales for Children*, 1907 • POTTER, *The Tale of Peter Rabbit*, 1902 • ASHFORD, *The Young Visiters; or, Mr. Salteena's Plan*, 1919.

Perspectives: The Industrial Landscape
• *Anthologies.* • David J. Bradshaw and Suzanne Ozment, eds., *The Voice of Toil: Nineteenth-Century British Writings About Work*, 2000. • F. P. Donovon, *The Railroad in Literature: A Brief Survey of Railroad Fiction, Poetry, Songs, Biography, Essays, Travel, and Drama in the English Language*, 1940. • E. Royston Pike, *"Hard Times": Human Documents of the Industrial Revolution*, 1966. • Jeremy Warburg, ed., *The Industrial Muse: The Industrial Revolution in English Poetry*, 1958.

Criticism. • John Belchem, *Industrialization and the Working Class: The English Experience; 1750–1900*, 1990. • Asa Briggs, *Victorian Cities*, 1963. • D. S. L. Cardwell, *The Norton History of Technology*, 1994. • Alice Chandler, *A Dream of Order: The Medieval Ideal in Nineteenth-Century English Literature*, 1970. • S. G. Checkland, *The Rise of Industrial Society in England, 1815–1885*, 1964. • Kenneth Clark, *The Gothic Revival: An Essay in the History of Taste*, 1928. • Bruce I. Coleman, ed., *The Idea of the City in*

Nineteenth-Century Britain, 1973. • H. J. Dyos and Michael Wolff, eds., *The Victorian City: Images and Realities*, 2 vols., 1973. • Frank Ferneyhough, *The History of Railways in Britain*, 1975. • E. J. Hobsbawm, *Industry and Empire*, 1968. • Peter Keating, *The Working Classes in Victorian Fiction*, 1971. • David Levine, *The Making of an Industrial Society*, 1991. • Steven Marcus, *Engels, Manchester, and the Working Class*, 1974. • Ivan Melada, *The Captain of Industry in English Fiction, 1821–1871*, 1970. • Joel Mokyr, ed., *The British Industrial Revolution: An Economic Perspective*, 1993. • Joel Mokyr, ed., *The Economics of the Industrial Revolution*, 1986. • Deborah Epstein Nord, *Walking the Victorian Streets: Women, Representation, and the City*, 1995. • Ivy Pinchbeck, *Women Workers and the Industrial Revolution, 1750–1850*, 1930. • Sonya O. Rose, *Limited Livelihoods: Gender and Class in Nineteenth-Century England*, 1992. • Jack Simmons, *The Victorian Railway*, 1991. • Herbert Sussman, *Victorians and the Machine: The Literary Response to Technology*, 1968. • E. P. Thompson, *The Making of the English Working Class*, 1963. • Barrie Stewart Trinder, *The Making of the Industrial Landscape*, 1982. • Martha Vicinus, *The Industrial Muse: A Study of Nineteenth Century Working-Class Literature*, 1974. • James Walvin, *English Urban Life, 1776–1851*, 1984. • Raymond Williams, *The Country and the City*, 1973. • Edward A. Wrigley, *Continuity, Chance and Change: The Character of the Industrial Revolution in England*, 1989.

Our Texts. • "The Steam Loom Weaver" from Martha Vicinus, *The Industrial Muse*, 1974; KEMBLE: *Record of a Girlhood*, vol. 2, 1879; MACAULAY: "A Review of Southey's Colloquies" from *Edinburgh Review*, Jan. 1830; PARLIAMENTARY PAPERS: from *Victorian Women: A Documentary Account of Women's Lives*, eds. Hellerstein, Hume, and Offen, 1981; DICKENS: *Dombey and Son*, Charles Dickens Edition, 1867; *Hard Times*, 1854; DISRAELI: *Sybil* from *The Works of Benjamin Disraeli*, 1904; ENGELS: *The Condition of the Working Class in England*, 1845, trans. W. O. Henderson and W. H. Chaloner, 1958; MAYHEW: *London Labour and the London Poor*, vols. 1 and 2, 1861–1862; SMITH: "Glasgow" from *City Poems*, 1857.

Popular Short Fiction • *Anthologies.* • Nina Auerbach and U. C. Knoepflmacher, eds., *Forbidden Journeys: Fairy Tales and Fantasies by Victorian Women Writers*, 1992. • Everett F.

Bleiler, ed., *A Treasury of Victorian Detective Stories*, 1979. • Jonathan Cott, ed., *Beyond the Looking Glass: Extraordinary Works of Fairy Tale and Fantasy*, 1973. • Michael Cox, ed., *Victorian Detective Stories*, 1993. • Michael Cox and R. A. Gilbert, eds., *Victorian Ghost Stories*, 1991. • Richard Dalby, ed., *The Virago Book of Victorian Ghost Stories*, 1987. • Harold Orel, ed., *Victorian Short Stories: An Anthology*, 1987. • Harold Orel, ed., *Victorian Short Stories 2: The Trials of Love*, 1990. • Jack Zipes, ed., *Victorian Fairy Tales*, 1987.

Criticism. • Walter Allen, *The Short Story in English*, 1981. • Dean Baldwin, "The Tardy Evolution of the British Short Story," in *Studies in Short Fiction* 30 (1993). • Julia Briggs, *Night Visitors: The Rise and Fall of the English Ghost Story*, 1977. • Margaret Dalziel, *Popular Fiction 100 Years Ago*, 1958. • Alvar Ellegard, *The Readership of the Periodical Press in Mid-Victorian Britain*, 1957. • John R. Greenfield, ed., *British Short-Fiction Writers, 1800–1880*, in *Dictionary of Literary Biography*, vol. 159, 1996. • Clare Hanson, *Short Stories and Short Fictions, 1880–1980*, 1985. • Wendell V. Harris, *British Short Fiction in the Nineteenth Century: A Literary and Bibliographic Guide*, 1979. • Rosemary Jackson, *Fantasy: The Literature of Subversion*, 1981. • Peter Keating, *Working Class Stories of the 1890s*, 1972. • Lionel Madden and Diana Dixon, eds., *The Nineteenth-Century Periodical Press in Britain: A Bibliography of Modern Studies, 1901–1971*, 1976. • Harold Orel, *The Victorian Short Story: Development and Triumph of a Literary Genre*, 1986. • Peter Penzoldt, *The Supernatural in Fiction*, 1952. • Stephen Prickett, *Victorian Fantasy*, 1979. • David Punter, *The Literature of Terror: A History of Gothic Fictions from 1765 to the Present Day*, 1980. • Joanne Shattock and Michael Wolff, eds., *The Victorian Periodical Press: Samplings and Soundings*, 1982. • Valerie Shaw, *The Short Story: A Critical Introduction*, 1983. • Alvin Sullivan, ed., *British Literary Magazines*, Vol. 3: *The Victorian and Edwardian Age, 1837–1913*, 1984. • Jack Sullivan, *Elegant Nightmares: The English Ghost Story from Le Fanu to Blackwood*, 1978. • William B. Thesing, ed., *British Short-Fiction Writers, 1880–1914: The Realist Tradition*, in *Dictionary of Literary Biography*, vol. 135, 1995. • Marshall B. Tymn et al., eds., *Fantasy Literature: A Core Collection and Reference Guide*, 1979.

Perspectives: Religion and Science • *Anthologies.* • Tess Cosslett, ed., *Science and Religion in the Nineteenth Century*, 1984. • Richard J. Helm-stadter and Paul T. Phillips, eds., *Religion in Victorian Society: A Sourcebook of Documents*, 1985. • Gerald Parsons, ed., *Religion in Victorian Britain*, Vol. 3: *Sources*. 1988.

Criticism. • Peter Addinall, *Philosophy and Biblical Interpretation: A Study in Nineteenth-Century Conflict*, 1991. • D. W. Bebbington, *Evangelicalism in Modern Britain: A History from the 1730s to the 1980s*, 1989. • Gillian Beer, *Open Fields: Science in Cultural Encounter*, 1995. • P. J. Bowler, *Evolution: The History of an Idea*, 1984. • P. J. Bowler, *The Invention of Progress: The Victorians and the Past*, 1989. • Ian Bradley, *The Call to Seriousness*, 1976. • Douglas Bush, *Science and English Poetry, 1590–1950*, 1949. • Owen Chadwick, *The Victorian Church*, 2 vols., 1966, 1970. • Owen Chadwick, *The Secularisation of the European Mind in the Nineteenth Century*, 1975. • Tess Cosslett, *The 'Scientific Movement' and Victorian Literature*, 1982. • Sydney Eisen and Bernard V. Lightman, *Victorian Science and Religion: A Bibliography*, 1984. • Barbara T. Gates, *Kindred Nature: Victorian and Edwardian Women Embrace the Living World*, 1999. • Alan D. Gilbert, *Religion and Society in Industrial England: Church, Chapel and Social Change, 1740–1914*, 1976. • Stephen Jay Gould, *Time's Arrow, Time's Cycle*, 1987. • Richard J. Helmstadter and Bernard Lightman, eds., *Victorian Faith in Crisis: Essays on Continuity and Change in Nineteenth-Century Religious Belief*, 1990. • Elisabeth Jay, ed., *The Evangelical and Oxford Movements*, 1983. • Thomas W. Laqueur, *Religion and Respectability: Sunday Schools and Working Class Culture, 1780–1850*, 1975. • George Levine, *One Culture: Essays in Science and Literature*, 1987. • Peter Morton, *The Vital Science: Biology and the Literary Imagination, 1860–1900*, 1984. • James Paradis and George C. Williams, eds., *Evolution and Ethics: With New Essays on Its Victorian and Sociobiological Context*, 1989. • James Paradis and Thomas Postlewait, eds., *Victorian Science and Victorian Values: Literary Perspectives*, 1985. • G. Parsons, ed., *Religion in Victorian Britain*, 4 vols., 1988. • Bernard M. G. Reardon, *Religious Thought in the Victorian Age: A Survey from Coleridge to Gore*, 1995. • Martin J. S. Rudwick, *Scenes from Deep Time: Early Pictorial Representations of the Prehistoric World*, 1992. • James A. Secord, *Victorian Sensation: The Extraordinary Publication, Reception, and Secret Authorship of Vestiges of the Natural History of Creation*, 2000. • A. Symondson, ed., *The Victorian Crisis of Faith*, 1970. • W. R. Ward, *Religion and Society in England, 1790–1850*, 1972. • W. R.

Ward, *The Protestant Evangelical Awakening,* 1992. • Michael Wheeler, *Death and the Future Life in Victorian Literature and Theology,* 1990.

Our Texts. • MACAULAY: "Lord Bacon" from *Critical and Historical Essays,* vol. 2, 1865; DICKENS: *Sunday Under Three Heads,* 1836; STRAUSS: *The Life of Jesus Critically Examined,* 1846; BRONTE: *Jane Eyre,* 1848; CLOUGH: *The Poems of Arthur Hugh Clough,* ed. A. L. P. Norrington, 1968; COLENSO: *The Pentateuch and Book of Joshua Critically Examined,* 1863; NEWMAN: *Apologia Pro Vita Sua,* 1866; HUXLEY: *Evolution and Ethics,* 1894; GOSSE: *Father and Son,* 1907.

Perspectives: Travel and Empire • *Anthologies.* • Percy G. Adams, ed., *Travel Literature Through the Ages: An Anthology,* 1988. • Paul Fussell, ed., *The Norton Book of Travel,* 1987. • Leo Hamalian, ed., *Ladies on the Loose: Women Travellers of the 18th and 19th Centuries,* 1981. • Peter Kitson, ed., *Nineteenth-Century Travels, Explorations and Empires: Writings from the Era of Imperial Consolidation, 1835–1910,* 2003. • John Julius Norwich, ed., *A Taste for Travel: An Anthology,* 1987.

Criticism. • Patrick Brantlinger, *Rule of Darkness: British Literature and Imperialism, 1830–1914,* 1988. • Barbara Brothers and Julia Gergits, eds., *British Travel Writers, 1837–1875,* in *Dictionary of Literary Biography,* vol. 166, 1996. • James Michael Buzard, *Off the Beaten Track: European Tourism, Literature, and the Ways to Culture, 1800–1918,* 1993. • Deirdre David, *Rule Britannia: Women, Empire, and Victorian Writing,* 1995. • Shirley Foster, *Across New Worlds: Nineteenth-Century Women Travellers and their Writings,* 1990. • Maria H. Frawley, *A Wider Range: Travel Writing by Women in Victorian England,* 1994. • Martin Green, *Dreams of Adventure, Deeds of Adventure,* 1979. • Geoffrey Hindley, *Tourists, Travellers, and Pilgrims,* 1983. • Karen R. Lawrence, *Penelope Voyages: Women and Travel in British Literary Tradition,* 1994. • Dorothy Middleton, *Victorian Lady Travellers,* 1965. • Sara Mills, *Discourses of Difference: An Analysis of Women's Travel Writing and Colonialism,* 1991. • Christopher Mulvey, *Transatlantic Manners: Social Patterns in Nineteenth-Century Anglo-American Travel Literature,* 1990. • Ian Ousby, *The Englishman's England: Travel, Taste, and the Rise of Tourism,* 1990. • Mary Louise Pratt, *Imperial Eyes: Travel Writing and Transculturation,* 1992. • Mary Russell, *The Blessings of a Good Thick Skirt: Women Travellers and Their World,* 1988. • David Spurr, *The Rhetoric of Empire: Colonial Discourse in Journalism, Travel Writing, and Imperial Administration,* 1993. • Catherine Barnes Stevenson, *Victorian Women Travel Writers in Africa,* 1982.

Perspectives: Victorian Ladies and Gentlemen • *Anthologies.* • Susan Groag Bell and Karen M. Offen, *Woman, the Family, and Freedom: The Debate in Documents,* 2 vols., 1983. • Erna Olafson Hellerstein, Leslie Parker Hume, and Karen M. Offen, eds., *Victorian Women: A Documentary Account of Women's Lives,* 1981. • Elizabeth K. Helsinger, Robin Lauterbach Sheets, and William Veeder, eds., *The Woman Question: Society and Literature in Britain and America, 1837–1883,* 3 vols., 1983. • Janet Murray, *Strong-Minded Women and Other Lost Voices from Nineteenth-Century England,* 1982.

Criticism. • James Eli Adams, *Dandies and Desert Saints: Styles of Victorian Masculinity,* 1995. • Patricia Branca, *Silent Sisterhood: Middle-Class Women in the Victorian Home,* 1975. • Michael Brander, *The Victorian Gentleman,* 1975. • Joan N. Burstyn, *Victorian Education and the Ideal of Womanhood,* 1980. • David Castronovo, *The English Gentleman: Images and Ideals in Literature and Society,* 1987. • John Chandos, *Boys Together: English Public Schools, 1800–1864,* 1984. • Leonore Davidoff and Catherine Hall, *Family Fortunes: Men and Women of the English Middle Class, 1780–1850,* 1987. • Jonathan Gathorne-Hardy, *The Public School Phenomenon,* 1977. • Robin Gilmour, *The Idea of the Gentleman in the Victorian Novel,* 1981. • Mark Girouard, *The Return to Camelot: Chivalry and the English Gentleman,* 1981. • Deborah Gorham, *The Victorian Girl and the Feminine Ideal,* 1982. • Donald E. Hall, ed., *Muscular Christianity: Embodying the Victorian Age,* 1994. • Lee Holcombe, *Victorian Ladies at Work: Middle-Class Women in England and Wales, 1850–1914,* 1973. • Richard Holt, *Sport and the British: A Modern History,* 1989. • Margaret Homans, *Royal Representations: Queen Victoria and British Culture, 1837–1876,* 1998. • Margaret Homans and Adrienne Munich, eds., *Remaking Queen Victoria,* 1997. • J. R. de S. Honey, *Tom Brown's Universe: The Development of the English Public School in the Nineteenth Century,* 1977. • Kathryn Hughes, *The Victorian Governess,* 1993. • Elizabeth Langland, *Nobody's Angels: Middle-Class Women and Domestic Ideology in Victorian Culture,* 1995. • Anita Levy, *Other Women: The Writing of Class, Race, and Gender, 1832–1898,* 1991. • Elizabeth Longford, *Eminent Victorian Women,*

1981. • J. A. Mangan and James Walvin, eds., *Manliness and Masculinity: Middle-Class Masculinity in Britain and America, 1800–1940*, 1987. • Philip Mason, *The English Gentleman: The Rise and Fall of an Ideal*, 1982. • Claudia Nelson and Lynne Vallone, eds., *The Girl's Own: Cultural Histories of the Anglo-American Girl, 1830–1915*, 1994. • Mary Poovey, *Uneven Developments: The Ideological Work of Gender in Mid-Victorian England*, 1988. • Sonya O. Rose, *Limited Livelihoods: Gender and Class in Nineteenth-Century England*, 1992. • Brian Simon and Ian Bradley, eds., *The Victorian Public School: Studies in the Development of an Educational Institution*, 1975. • Herbert Sussman, *Victorian Masculinities: Manhood and Masculine Poetics in Early Victorian Literature and Art*, 1995. • Dorothy Thompson, *Queen Victoria: The Woman, the Monarchy, and the People*, 1990. • Lynne Vallone, *Becoming Victoria*, 2001. • Norman Vance, *The Sinews of the Spirit: The Ideal of Christian Manliness in Victorian Literature and Religious Thought*, 1985. • Martha Vicinus, ed., *Suffer and Be Still: Women in the Victorian Age*, 1972. • Martha Vicinus, ed., *A Widening Sphere: Changing Roles of Victorian Women*, 1977.

Our Texts. • COBBE: *Life of Frances Power Cobbe*, 1904; ELLIS: *The Women of England*, 1839; C. BRONTE: *The Brontës: Their Lives, Friendships, and Correspondence*, eds. Wise and Symington, Vol. 1, 1933; A. BRONTE: *Agnes Grey*, 1860; NEWMAN: *The Idea of a University*, 1873; NORTON: "A Letter to the Queen," 1855; HUGHES: *Tom Brown's School Days*, 1869; BEETON: *The Book of Household Management*, 1861; VICTORIA: see footnotes; KINGSLEY: *The Works of Charles Kingsley*, vol. 7, 1899; NEWBOLT: "Vitaï Lampada," *The Island Race*, 1898.

Matthew Arnold • *Editions.* • Kenneth Allott, ed., *Arnold: The Complete Poems*, 1965; 2nd ed., Miriam Allott, 1979. • Miriam Allott and R. H. Super, eds., *Matthew Arnold*, 1986 [annotated selection]. • Cecil Y. Lang, ed., *The Letters of Matthew Arnold*, 1996–. • Howard Foster Lowry, ed., *The Letters of Matthew Arnold to Arthur Hugh Clough*, 1968. • R. H. Super, ed., *The Complete Prose Works of Matthew Arnold*, 11 vols., 1960–1977.

Biography. • Ian Hamilton, *A Gift Imprisoned: The Poetic Life of Matthew Arnold*, 1999. • Park Honan, *Matthew Arnold: A Life*, 1981. • Nicholas Murray, *A Life of Matthew Arnold*, 1997.

Criticism. • Kenneth Allott, ed., *Matthew Arnold*, 1975. • Ruth Roberts, *Arnold and God*, 1983. • Harold Bloom, ed., *Matthew Arnold*, 1987. • William E. Buckler, *On the Poetry of Matthew Arnold*, 1982. • Douglas Bush, *Matthew Arnold: A Survey of His Poetry and Prose*, 1971. • Joseph Carroll, *The Cultural Theory of Matthew Arnold*, 1982. • Stefan Collini, *Arnold*, 1988. • Dwight Culler, *Imaginative Reason*, 1966. • Carl Dawson and John Pfordresher, eds., *Matthew Arnold, the Poetry: The Critical Heritage*, 1973; and *Matthew Arnold, Prose Writings: The Critical Heritage*, 1979. • T. S. Eliot, "Matthew Arnold," in his *The Use of Poetry and the Use of Criticism*, 1933. • T. S. Eliot, "Arnold and Pater," in his *Selected Essays*, 1932. • R. Giddings, ed., *Matthew Arnold: Between Two Worlds*, 1986. • Leon Gottfried, *Matthew Arnold and the Romantics*, 1983. • D. G. James, *Matthew Arnold and the Decline of English Romanticism*, 1961. • Edward D. H. Johnson, *The Alien Vision of Citorian Poetry*, 1952. • James C. Livingston, *Matthew Arnold and Christianity: His Religious Prose Writings*, 1986. • David G. Riede, *Matthew Arnold and the Betrayal of Language*, 1988. • Alan Roper, *Arnold's Poetic Landscapes*, 1969. • G. Robert Stange, *The Poet as Humanist*, 1967. • Lionel Trilling, *Matthew Arnold*, 1949.

Our Texts. • The poems in this anthology are from Allott, *Complete Poems*; our prose selections are from Super, *Complete Prose*.

Isabella Bird • Alexandra Allen, *Travelling Ladies*, 1980. • Evelyn Bach, "A Traveller in Skirts: Quest and Conquest in the Travel Narratives of Isabella Bird" in *Canadian Review of Comparative Literature*, 22 (1995). • Pat Barr, *A Curious Life for a Lady: The Story of Isabella Bird*, 1970. • Cicely Palser Havely, ed., *This Grand Beyond: The Travels of Isabella Bird Bishop*, 1985. • Evelyn Kaye, *Amazing Traveller: Isabella Bird*, 1994. • Dorothy Middleton, *Victorian Lady Travellers*, 1965. • Anna Stoddart, *The Life of Isabella Bird*, 1906.

Our Text. • G. P. Putnam's Sons, 1881.

Elizabeth Barrett Browning • *Editions.* • Cora Kaplan, ed., *Aurora Leigh and Other Poems*, 1978. • Philip Kelley and Ronald Hudson, eds., *The Brownings' Correspondence*, 1984–. • Elvan Kintner, ed., *The Letters of Robert Browning and Elizabeth Barrett Browning, 1845–1846*, 2 vols., 1969. • Charlotte Porter and Helen Clarke, eds., *Complete Works*, 6 vols., 1900. • Harriet Waters Preston, ed., *The Complete Poetical Works of Elizabeth Barrett Browning*, 1900; 1974. • Margaret Reynolds, ed., *Aurora Leigh*, 1992; 1996.

Biography. • Angela Leighton, *Elizabeth Barrett Browning*, 1986. • Gardner B. Taplin, *The Life of Elizabeth Barrett Browning*, 1957.

Criticism. • Warner Barnes, *A Bibliography of Elizabeth Barrett Browning*, 1968. • Kathleen Blake, "Elizabeth Barrett Browning and Wordsworth: The Romantic Poet as a Woman," *Victorian Poetry* 24 (1986). • Helen Cooper, *Elizabeth Barrett Browning, Woman and Artist*, 1988. • Deirdre David, *Intellectual Women and Victorian Patriarchy: Harriet Martineau, Elizabeth Barrett Browning, George Eliot*, 1987. • Sandra M. Gilbert, "From *Patria* to *Matria*: Elizabeth Barrett Browning's Risorgimento." *PMLA* 99 (1984); repr. *Victorian Women Poets*, ed. Angela Leighton, 1996. • Alethea Hayter, *Mrs. Browning: A Poet's Work and Its Setting*, 1962. • Dorothy Mermin, *Elizabeth Barrett Browning: The Origins of a New Poetry*, 1989. • Virginia L. Radley, *Elizabeth Barrett Browning*, 1972. • Dolores Rosenblum, "Face to Face: Elizabeth Barrett Browning's *Aurora Leigh* and Nineteenth-Century Poetry," *Victorian Studies* 26 (1983). • Glennis Stephenson, *Elizabeth Barrett Browning and the Poetry of Love*, 1989. • Marjorie Stone, *Elizabeth Barrett Browning*, 1995. • Virginia Woolf, "*Aurora Leigh*," in *The Second Common Reader*, 1932. • Joyce Zonana, "The Embodied Muse: Elizabeth Barrett Browning's *Aurora Leigh* and Feminist Poetics," *Tulsa Studies in Women's Literature* 8 (1989); repr. in *Victorian Women Poets*, ed. Angela Leighton, 1996.

Our Texts. • Charlotte Porter and Helen Clarke, eds., *Complete Works*, 6 vols., 1900.

Robert Browning • *Editions.* • *Poetical Works of Robert Browning*, 16 vols., 1888–1889. • Ian Jack, Margaret Smith, and Robert Inglesfield, eds., *The Poetical Works of Robert Browning*, 1983–. • Philip Kelley and Ronald Hudson, eds., *The Brownings' Correspondence*, 1984–. • John Pettigrew and Thomas J. Collins, eds., *The Poems*, 2 vols., 1981.

Biography. • William Irvine and Park Honan, *The Book, the Ring, and the Poet*, 1974. • John Maynard, *Browning's Youth*, 1977. • Mrs. Sutherland Orr, *Life and Letters of Robert Browning*, 1891; 1908. • Clyde de L. Ryals, *The Life of Robert Browning: A Critical Biography*, 1993.

Criticism. • Isobel Armstrong, ed., *Robert Browning*, 1974. • Walter Bagehot, "Wordsworth, Tennyson, and Browning," in *Literary Studies*, ed. R. H. Hutton, 1895. • Harold Bloom and Adrienne Munich, eds., *Robert Browning: A Collection of Critical Essays*, 1979. • Joseph Bristow, *Robert Browning*, 1991. • G. K. Chesterton, *Robert Browning*, 1903. • Norman B. Crowell, *A Reader's Guide to Robert Browning*, 1972. • William C. DeVane, *A Browning Handbook*, 1955. • Philip Drew, ed., *Robert Browning: A Collection of Critical Essays*, 1966. • Donald Hair, *Browning's Experiments with Genre*, 1972. • Ian Jack, *Browning's Major Poetry*, 1973. • Roma A. King Jr., *The Bow and the Lyre*, 1957. • Robert Langbaum, *The Poetry of Experience: The Dramatic Monologue in Modern Literary Tradition*, 1957. • Boyd Litzinger and K. L. Knickerbocker, eds., *The Browning Critics*, 1965. • Boyd Litzinger and Donald Smalley, eds., *Browning: The Critical Heritage*, 1970. • Loy Martin, *Browning's Dramatic Monologues and the Post-Romantic Subject*, 1985. • William S. Peterson, *Robert and Elizabeth Barrett Browning: An Annotated Bibliography*, 1951–1970, 1974. • W. O. Raymond, *The Infinite Moment*, 1965. • Herbert F. Tucker, *Browning's Beginnings: The Art of Disclosure*, 1980.

Our Texts. • From *Poetical Works of Robert Browning*, 16 vols., 1888–1889.

Richard Burton • Thomas J. Assad, *Three Victorian Travellers: Burton, Blunt, Doughty*, 1964. • Fawn M. Brodie, *The Devil Drives: A Life of Sir Richard Burton*, 1967. • Isabel Burton, *The Life of Captain Sir Richard F. Burton*, 2 vols., 1893. Mary S. Lovell, *A Rage to Live: A Biography of Richard and Isabel Burton*, 1998. • Frank McLynn, *Burton: Snow Upon the Desert*, 1990. • Edward Rice, *Captain Sir Richard Francis Burton*, 1990.

Our Text. • *Memorial Edition*, 1893.

Thomas Carlyle • *Editions.* • C. R. Sanders, K. J. Fielding, Clyde de L. Ryals, et al., eds., *The Collected Letters of Thomas and Jane Welsh Carlyle*, 1970–. • H. D. Traill, ed., *The Works of Thomas Carlyle*, 30 vols., 1896–1899.

Biography. • J. A. Froude, *Thomas Carlyle: A History of the First Forty Years of his Life*,

1795–1835, 2 vols., 1882; *Thomas Carlyle: A History of his Life in London, 1834–1881*, 2 vols., 1884. • Fred Kaplan, *Thomas Carlyle: A Biography*, 1983.

Criticism. • Ruth Roberts, *The Ancient Dialect: Thomas Carlyle and Comparative Religion*, 1988. • K. J. Fielding and Rodger L. Tarr, eds., *Carlyle Past and Present*, 1976. • Michael Goldberg, *Carlyle and Dickens*, 1972. • John Holloway, *The Victorian Sage*, 1953. • Albert J. LaValley, *Carlyle and the Idea of the Modern*, 1968. • George Levine, *The Boundaries of Fiction: Carlyle, Macaulay, Newman*, 1968. • Emery Neff, *Carlyle and Mill*, 1926. • Barry Qualls, *The Secular Pilgrims of Victorian Fiction*, 1983. • John D. Rosenberg, *Carlyle and the Burden of History*, 1985. • Philip Rosenberg, *The Seventh Hero: Thomas Carlyle and the Theory of Radical Activism*, 1974. • Jules Paul Seigel, ed., *Thomas Carlyle: The Critical Heritage*, 1971. • Rodger Tart, *Thomas Carlyle: A Descriptive Bibliography*, 1990. • G. B. Tennyson, *"Sartor" Called "Resartus,"* 1965. • G. B. Tennyson, "Thomas Carlyle," in *Victorian Prose: A Guide to Research*, ed. David J. DeLaura, 1973. • Chris Vanden Bossche, *Carlyle and the Search for Authority*, 1991. • Basil Willey, *Nineteenth Century Studies*, 1949.

Our Texts. • Texts cited from H. D. Traill.

Lewis Carroll • *Editions*. • Morton N. Cohen, ed., *The Letters of Lewis Carroll*, 1979. • Martin Gardner, ed., *The Annotated Alice*, 1960. • Donald J. Gray, ed., *Alice in Wonderland*, 2nd ed., 1992. • Roger Lancelyn Green, ed., *The Diaries of Lewis Carroll*, 1953–54.

Biography. • Morton N. Cohen, *Lewis Carroll: A Biography*, 1995. • Morton N. Cohen, ed., *Lewis Carroll: Interviews and Recollections*, 1989. • Derek Hudson, *Lewis Carroll: An Illustrated Biography*, 1976.

Criticism. • Harold Bloom, ed., *Lewis Carroll*, 1987. • Edward Guiliano, ed., *Lewis Carroll: A Celebration*, 1982. • Michael Hancher, *The Tenniel Illustrations to the 'Alice' Books*, 1985. • Jo Elwyn Jones, *The Alice Companion: A Guide to Lewis Carroll's Alice Books*, 1998. • Robert Phillips, ed., *Aspects of Alice*, 1974. • Catherine Robson, *Men in Wonderland: The Lost Girlhood of the Victorian Gentlemen*, 2001.

Our Text. • *The Complete Writings of Lewis Carroll*, 1939.

Charles Darwin • *Editions*. • Philip Appleman, ed., *Darwin*, 1970; 2nd ed., 1979. • Nora Barlow, ed., *The Autobiography of Charles Darwin, 1809–1882: With Original Omissions Restored*, 1958. • Paul H. Barrett and R. B. Freeman, eds., *The Works of Charles Darwin*, 29 vols., 1986. • Richard E. Leakey, abridged and introduced, *The Illustrated Origin of Species*, 1979; 1986.

Biography. • John Bowlby, *Charles Darwin: A New Life*, 1990. • Francis Darwin, ed., *The Life and Letters of Darwin*, 1887–1888. • Adrian Desmond and James Moore, *Darwin*, 1991.

Criticism. • Mea Allan, *Darwin and His Flowers: The Key to Natural Selection*, 1977. • Gillian Beer, *Darwin's Plots: Evolutionary Narrative in Darwin, George Eliot, and Nineteenth-Century Fiction*, 1983. • Peter Brent, *Charles Darwin: "A Man of Enlarged Curiosity,"* 1981. • Sir Gavin De Beer, *Charles Darwin: Evolution by Natural Selection*, 1964. • Loren Eiseley, *Darwin's Century: Evolution and the Men Who Discovered It*, 1958. • Michael T. Ghiselin, *The Triumph of the Darwinian Method*, 1984. • Stephen Jay Gould, *Ever Since Darwin*, 1977. • Stephen Jay Gould, *The Flamingo's Smile*, 1985. • David Kohn, ed., *The Darwinian Heritage*, 1985. • George Levine, *Darwin and the Novelists: Patterns of Science in Victorian Fiction*, 1988. • Jonathan Miller and Borin Van Loon, *Darwin for Beginners*, 1982. • John D. Rosenberg, "Mr. Darwin Collects Himself," in *Nineteenth-Century Lives*, ed. Laurence S. Lockridge et al., 1989. • Robert M. Young, *Darwin's Metaphor: Nature's Place in Victorian Culture*, 1985.

Our Texts. • *The Voyage of the Beagle*, 1860, repr. 1962, ed. Leonard Engel; *On the Origin of Species*, 1859, repr. 1968, ed. J. W. Burrow; *The Descent of Man*, 2 vols., 1871; *The Autobiography of Charles Darwin, 1809–1882: With Original Omissions Restored*, ed. Nora Barlow, 1958.

Charles Dickens • *Editions*. • Charles Dickens, *Works*. The Clarendon Edition. 1966–. • Michael Patrick Hearn, *The Annotated Christmas Carol*, 1976. • Madeline House, Graham Storey, Katherine Tillotson et al., eds., *The Letters of Charles Dickens*, 1965–. • Michael Slater, ed., *The Christmas Books*, 2 vols., 1971.

Biography. • Peter Ackroyd, *Dickens*, 1990. • John Forster, *The Life of Charles Dickens*,

1872–1874. • Edgar Johnson, *Charles Dickens: His Tragedy and Triumph*, 1952. • Fred Kaplan, *Dickens: A Biography*, 1988.

Criticism. • Peter Ackroyd, *Introduction to Dickens*, 1991. • Nicolas Bentley, Michael Slater, and Nina Buris, *The Dickens Index*, 1989. • G. K. Chesterton, *Charles Dickens*, 1906. • Philip Collins, *Dickens and Crime*, 1962. • Philip Collins, ed., *Dickens: The Critical Heritage*, 1971. • Philip Collins, ed., *Dickens: Interviews and Recollections*, 2 vols., 1981. • Paul Davis, *The Lives and Times of Ebenezer Scrooge*, 1990. • *The Dickensian*. 89.3. 1993. Special issue on *A Christmas Carol*. • George H. Ford, *Dickens and His Readers*, 1955. • Robert Garis, *The Dickens Theatre*, 1965. • George Gissing, *Charles Dickens: A Critical Study*, 1903. • Ruth F. Glancy, *Dickens's Christmas Books, Christmas Stories, and Other Short Fiction: An Annotated Bibliography*, 1985. • Michael Goldberg, *Carlyle and Dickens*, 1972. • Patricia Ingham, *Dickens, Women, and Language*, 1992. • John O. Jordan, ed. *Cambridge Companion to Charles Dickens*, 2001. • Steven Marcus, *Dickens: From Pickwick to Dombey*, 1965. • J. Hillis Miller, *Charles Dickens: The World of His Novels*, 1958. • George Orwell, "Charles Dickens," in his *A Collection of Essays*, 1954. • Robert Partlow, ed., *Dickens the Craftsman*, 1970. • Daniel Pool, *What Jane Austen Ate and Charles Dickens Knew: From Fox-Hunting to Whist: The Facts of Daily Life in Nineteenth-Century England*, 1993. • F. S. Schwarzbach, *Dickens and the City*, 1979. • Michael Slater, *Dickens and Women*, 1983. • Harry Stone, *Dickens and the Invisible World: Fairy Tales, Fantasy and Novel-Making*, 1979. • Angus Wilson, *The World of Charles Dickens*, 1970. • Edmund Wilson, "Dickens: The Two Scrooges," in his *The Wound and the Bow*, 1952.

Our Texts. • *The Christmas Books*, 2 vols., ed. Michael Slater, 1971; *Charles Dickens: A December Vision: His Social Journalism*, eds. Neil Philip and Victor Neuburg, 1986.

Arthur Conan Doyle • T. J. Binyon, *"Murder Will Out": The Detective in Fiction*, 1989. • John Dickson Carr, *The Life of Sir Arthur Conan Doyle*, 1949. • Dorothy Glover, *Victorian Detective Fiction*, 1966. • Richard Lancelyn Green, Introduction to *The Adventures of Sherlock Holmes*, 1993. • John A. Hodgson, ed., *Sherlock Holmes: The Major Stories with Contemporary Critical Essays*, 1994. • Rosemary Jann, *The Adventures of Sherlock Holmes: Detecting Social Order*, 1995. • Glenn W. Most, and William W.

Stowe, eds., *The Poetics of Murder: Detective Fiction and Literary Theory*, 1983. • Pierre Nordon, *Conan Doyle*, trans. Frances Partridge, 1966. • Harold Orel, ed., *Critical Essays on Sir Arthur Conan Doyle*, 1992. • Ian Ousby, *Bloodhounds of Heaven: The Detective in English Fiction from Godwin to Doyle*, 1976. • Dennis Porter, *The Pursuit of Crime: Art and Ideology in Detective Fiction*, 1981. • Daniel Stashower, *Teller of Tales: The Life of Arthur Conan Doyle*, 1999. • Julian Symons, *Conan Doyle*, 1979. • Julian Symons, *Mortal Consequences: A History—from the Detective Story to the Crime Novel* [*Bloody Murder*], 1972; rev. 1985.

Our Text. • *Strand Magazine*, July 1891

Edward Fitzgerald • *Editions.* • George Bentham, ed., *The Variorum and Definitive Edition of the Poetical and Prose Writings of Edward Fitzgerald*, 1902. • Christopher Decker, ed., *Edward FitzGerald, Rubaiyat of Omar Khayyam: A Critical Edition*, 1997. • Alfred McKinley Terhune and Annabelle Burdick Terhune, eds., *The Letters of Edward FitzGerald*, 4 vols., 1980.

Biography. • Robert Bernard Martin, *With Friends Possessed: A Life of Edward FitzGerald*, 1985. • Iran B. Hassani Jewett, *Edward Fitzgerald*, 1977. • Alfred McKinley Terhune, *The Life of Edward Fitzgerald*, 1947.

Our Text. • From Bentham, *The Rubáiyát of Omar Khayyám*, 5th Edition.

Elizabeth Gaskell • W. A. Craik, *Elizabeth Gaskell and the English Provincial Novel*, 1975. • Angus Easson, *Elizabeth Gaskell*, 1979. • Angus Easson, ed., *Elizabeth Gaskell: The Critical Heritage*, 1991. • Rowena Fowler, "Cranford: Cow in Grey Flannel or Lion Couchant?" *SEL* 24 (1984). • Winifred Gérin, *Elizabeth Gaskell*, 1980. • Rae Rosenthal, "Gaskell's Feminist Utopia: The Cranfordians and the Reign of Goodwill," in *Utopian and Science Fiction by Women: Worlds of Difference*, eds. Jane L. Donawerth and Carol A. Kolmerten, 1994. • Hilary M. Schor, *Scheherezade in the Market Place: Elizabeth Gaskell and the Victorian Novel*, 1992. • Patsy Stoneman, *Elizabeth Gaskell*, 1987. • Jenny Uglow, *Elizabeth Gaskell: A Habit of Stories*, 1993. • Patricia A. Wolfe, "Structure and Movement in *Cranford*," in *Nineteenth-Century Fiction*, vol. 23, 1968. • Terence Wright, *Elizabeth Gaskell: "We are not angels": Realism, Gender, Values*, 1995.

Our Text. • *The Works of Mrs. Gaskell,* Knutsford Edition, 8 vols., 1906–1920. Ed. A. W. Ward. 1906–1911.

Thomas Hardy • Kristin Brady, *The Short Stories of Thomas Hardy: Tales of Past and Present,* 1982. • Reginald G. Cox, *Hardy: The Critical Heritage,* 1970. • Simon Gatrell, *Hardy, The Creator: A Textual Biography,* 1989. • Robert Gittings, *Young Thomas Hardy,* 1975. • Simon Gatrell, *The Older Hardy* [*Thomas Hardy's later years*], 1978. • Margaret Higonnet, ed., *The Sense of Sex: Feminist Perspectives on Hardy,* 1993. • Romey Keys, "Hardy's Uncanny Narrative: A Reading of 'The Withered Arm.'" *Texas Studies in Literature and Language,* 27 (1985). • Kathryn R. King, Introduction to *Wessex Tales,* World's Classics, 1991. • Robert Langbaum, *Thomas Hardy in Our Time,* 1995. • Michael Millgate, *Thomas Hardy: A Biography,* 1982. • Norman Page, *Thomas Hardy,* 1977. • Martin Ray, *Thomas Hardy: A Textual Study of the Short Stories,* 1997.

Our Text. • *Blackwood's Edinburgh Magazine,* January 1888.

Gerard Manley Hopkins • *Editions.* • Claude C. Abbott, ed., *The Correspondence of Gerard Manley Hopkins and Richard Watson Dixon,* 2 vols., 1935; rev. 1955. • Claude C. Abbott, *Further Letters of Gerard Manley Hopkins,* 1938; 1956. • Claude C. Abbott, *The Letters of Gerard Manley Hopkins to Robert Bridges,* 1935; 1955. • Christopher Devlin, ed., *The Sermons and Devotional Writings of Gerard Manley Hopkins,* 1959. • Humphrey House and Graham Storey, eds., *Journals and Papers,* 1959. • Norman H. MacKenzie, ed., *The Poetical Works of Gerard Manley Hopkins,* 1990. • Catherine Phillips, ed., *Gerard Manley Hopkins,* 1986.

Biography. • Robert Bernard Martin, *Gerard Manley Hopkins: A Very Private Life,* 1991. • Norman White, *Hopkins: A Literary Biography,* 1992.

Criticism. • Tom Dunne, *Gerard Manley Hopkins: A Comprehensive Bibliography,* 1976 [annual updates in *Hopkins Quarterly*]. • William H. Gardner, *G. M. Hopkins: A Study of Poetic Idiosyncrasy in Relation to Poetic Tradition,* 2 vols., 1944; 1949. • Richard F. Giles, ed., *Hopkins Among the Poets: Studies in Modern Responses to Gerard Manley Hopkins,* 1985. • Daniel Harris, *Inspirations Unbidden: The "Terrible Sonnets" of Gerard Manley Hopkins,*

1982. • Norman H. MacKenzie, *A Reader's Guide to Gerard Manley Hopkins,* 1981. • Paul L. Mariani, *A Commentary on the Complete Poems of Gerard Manley Hopkins,* 1970. • Walter J. Ong, *Hopkins, the Self, and God,* 1986. • Alison Sulloway, *Gerard Manley Hopkins and the Victorian Temper,* 1972.

Our Texts. • W. H. Gardner, ed., *Poems of Gerard Manley Hopkins,* 1948; Humphrey House, and Graham Storey, eds., *Journals and Papers,* 1959; Claude C. Abbott, ed., *The Correspondence of Gerard Manley Hopkins and Richard Watson Dixon,* 2 vols., 1935; rev. 1955.

Alexander Kinglake • Benjamin Dunlap, "Kinglake's *Eothen*," *Studies in the Literary Imagination* 8 (1975). • Charisse Gendron, "*Eothen* Again." *Victorian Newsletter* 68 (1985). • Heather Henderson, "The Travel Writer and the Text: 'My Giant Goes with Me Wherever I Go' " in *Temperamental Journeys: Essays on the Modern Literature of Travel,* ed. Michael Kowalewski, 1992. • Iran B. Hassani Jewett, *Alexander William Kinglake,* 1981. • V. S. Pritchett, "*Kinglake's Eothen*: A Nineteenth-Century Travel Classic," *Prairie Schooner* 44 (1970).

Our Text. • Oxford University Press, 1906.

Mary Kingsley • Alison Blunt, *Travel, Gender, and Imperialism: Mary Kingsley and West Africa,* 1994. • Olwen Campbell, *Mary Kingsley: A Victorian in the Jungle,* 1957. • Katherine Frank, *A Voyager Out: The Life of Mary Kingsley,* 1986. • Stephen Gwynn, *The Life of Mary Kingsley,* 1933. • Robert D. Pearce, *Mary Kingsley: Light at the Heart of Darkness,* 1990. • Catherine Barnes Stevenson, *Victorian Women Travel Writers in Africa,* 1982.

Our Text. • 1897 Macmillan edition (first edition).

Rudyard Kipling • *Editions.* • *Works.* Sussex Edition, 35 vols., 1937–1939. • Thomas Pinney, ed., *The Letters of Rudyard Kipling, 1872–1910,* 1990–. • Thomas Pinney, ed., *Something of Myself,* 1937; 1990 [Kipling's autobiography]. • *Rudyard Kipling's Complete Verse: Definitive Edition,* 1940.

Biography. • Charles Carrington, *Rudyard Kipling: His Life and Work,* 1955; rev. 1978. • David Gilmour, *The Long Recessional: The Imperial Life of Rudyard Kipling,* 2002. • Philip Mason, *Kipling: The Glass, the Shadow, and the*

Fire, 1975. • Angus Wilson, *The Strange Ride of Rudyard Kipling: His Life and Works*, 1977.

Criticism. • Helen Pike Bauer, *Rudyard Kipling: A Study of the Short Fiction*, 1994. • Francelia Butler, Barbara Rosen, and Judith A. Plotz, eds., *Children's Literature*, 20. Special Kipling issue, 1992. • Louis Cornell, *Kipling in India*, 1966. • Elliot L. Gilbert, *The Good Kipling: Studies in the Short Story*, 1971. • Elliot L. Gilbert, ed., *Kipling and the Critics*, 1965. • Roger Lancelyn Green, *Kipling: The Critical Heritage*, 1971. • Peter Keating, *Kipling the Poet*, 1994. • Sandra Kemp, *Kipling's Hidden Narratives*, 1987. • Harold Orel, ed., *Critical Essays on Rudyard Kipling*, 1989. • Harold Orel, *Rudyard Kipling: Interviews and Recollections*, 2 vols., 1983. • Mark Paffard, *Kipling's Indian Fiction*, 1989. • Norman Page, *A Kipling Companion*, 1984. • Andrew Rutherford, ed., *Kipling's Mind and Art*, 1964. • Zohreh T. Sullivan, *Narratives of Empire: The Fictions of Rudyard Kipling*, 1993. • J. M. S. Tompkins, *The Art of Rudyard Kipling*, 1959.

Our Texts. • "Without Benefit of Clergy" from *Macmillan's Magazine*, 62 (June 1890); *Rudyard Kipling's Complete Verse: Definitive Edition*, 1940; *Just So Stories for Little Children*, 1912.

Thomas Babington Macaulay • John Clive, *Macaulay: The Shaping of the Historian*, 1973. • George Levine, *The Boundaries of Fiction*, 1968. • William Madden, "Macaulay's Style," in *The Art of Victorian Prose*, 1968. • Jane Millgate, *Macaulay*, 1973. • Thomas Pinney, *The Letters of Thomas Babington Macaulay*, 5 vols., 1974–81. • Sir G. O. Trevelyan, *Life and Letters of Lord Macaulay*, 1876. • Lady Trevelyan, ed. *The Works of Lord Macaulay*, 12 vols., 1898.

Our Text. • Macaulay, *Speeches: with his Minute on Indian Education*, 1935

John Stuart Mill • *Editions.* • John Robson et al., eds., *Collected Works*, 33 vols., 1963–1991. • Ann P. Robson and John M. Robson, eds., *Sexual Equality: Writings by John Stuart Mill, Harriet Taylor Mill, and Helen Taylor*, 1994. • David Spitz, ed., *On Liberty*, Norton critical edition, 1975.

Biography. • Alexander Bain, *John Stuart Mill*, 1882; 1969. • Michael St. J. Packe, *The Life of John Stuart Mill*, 1954.

Criticism. • Fred Berger, *Happiness, Justice, and Freedom*, 1984. • Janice Carlisle, *John Stuart Mill*

and the Writing of Character, 1991. • Maurice Cowling, *Mill and Liberalism*, 1963. • F. W. Garforth, *Educative Democracy: John Stuart Mill on Education in Society*, 1980. • Peter Glassman, *The Evolution of a Genius*, 1985. • John Gray and G. W. Smith, eds., *J. S. Mill: On Liberty in Focus*, 1991. • Joseph Hamburger, *Intellectuals in Politics*, 1985. • Michael Laine, *Bibliography of Writings on John Stuart Mill*, 1982. • Michael Laine, ed., *A Cultivated Mind: Essays on J.S. Mill Presented to John M. Robson*, 1991. • John M. Robson, *The Improvement of Mankind: The Social and Political Thought of J. S. Mill*, 1968. • Alan Ryan, *John Stuart Mill*, 1970. • J. B. Schneewind, ed., *Mill: A Collection of Critical Essays*, 1968. • F. Parvin Sharpless, *The Literary Criticism of John Stuart Mill*, 1967. • Lynn Zastoupil, *John Stuart Mill and India*, 1994.

Our Texts. • John Robson et al., eds., *Collected Works*, 33 vols., 1963–1991.

William Morris • *Editions.* • Norman Kelvin, *The Collected Letters of William Morris, 1848–1896*, 4 vols., 1984–1996. • May Morris, ed., *The Collected Works of William Morris*, 24 vols., 1910–1915.

Biography. • Philip Henderson, *William Morris, His Life, Work and Friends*, 1967. • Fiona MacCarthy, *William Morris: A Life for Our Time*, 1995. • J. W. Mackail, *The Life of William Morris*, 2 vols., 1899; repr. 1968. • May Morris, *William Morris, Artist, Writer, Socialist*, 2 vols., 1936.

Criticism. • Gary L. Aho, *William Morris: A Reference Guide*, 1985. • Elizabeth Cumming and Wendy Kaplan, *The Arts and Crafts Movement*, 1991. • Peter Faulkner, *Against the Age: An Introduction to William Morris*, 1980. • Peter Faulkner, ed., *William Morris: The Critical Heritage*, 1973. • William Peterson, *The Kelmscott Press: A History of William Morris's Typographical Adventure*, 1991. • Carole Silver, *The Romance of William Morris*, 1982. • Peter Stansky, *Redesigning the World: William Morris, the 1880s, and the Arts and Crafts*, 1985. • E. P. Thompson, *William Morris: Romantic to Revolutionary*, 1955; rev. 1977.

Our Texts. • May Morris, ed., *The Collected Works of William Morris*, 24 vols., 1910–1915.

Edith Nesbit • Julia Briggs, *A Woman of Passion: The Life of E. Nesbit, 1858–1924*, 1987. • Shirley Foster and Judy Simons, *What Katy Read: Feminist Re-Readings of "Classic" Stories* for Girls, 1995. • Gloria G. Fromm, "E. Nesbit and the Happy Moralist," Journal of Modern Literature 11 (1984). • U. C. Knoepflmacher, "Of Babylands and Babylons: E. Nesbit and the Reclamation of the Fairy Tale," Tulsa Studies in Women's Literature 6 (1987). • Doris Langley Moore, E. Nesbit: A Biography, 1933; rev. 1966. • Stephen Prickett, Victorian Fantasy, 1979. • Noel Streatfeild, Magic and Magicians: E. Nesbit and Her Children's Books, 1958. • Nancy A. Walker, The Disobedient Writer, 3 1995 [chapter on Nesbit and fairy tales].

Our Text. • Edith Nesbit, Nine Unlikely Tales for Children, 1901.

Florence Nightingale • Editions. • Michael D. Calabria and Janet A. Macrae, eds., Suggestions for Thought: Selections and Commentaries, 1994. • Mary Poovey, ed., Cassandra and Others Selections from Suggestions for Thought, 1992. • Myra Stark, ed., Cassandra, 1978. • Martha Vicinus and Bea Nergaard, eds., Ever Yours, Florence Nightingale: Selected Letters, 1990.

Biography. • Sir Edward Cook, The Life of Florence Nightingale, 2 vols., 1913. • Cecil Woodham-Smith, Florence Nightingale, 1820–1910, 1951.

Criticism. • Nancy Boyd, Josephine Butler, Octavia Hill, Florence Nightingale: Three Victorian Women Who Changed Their World, 1982. • Vern Bullough, Bonnie Bullough, and Marietta P. Stanton, eds., Florence Nightingale and Her Era: A Collection of New Scholarship, 1990. • Elizabeth Longford, Eminent Victorian Women, 1981. • Elaine Showalter, "Florence Nightingale's Feminist Complaint: Women, Religion, and Suggestions for Thought." Signs 6 (1981). • F. B. Smith, Florence Nightingale: Reputation and Power, 1982. • Katherine V. Snyder, "From Novel to Essay: Gender and Revision in Florence Nightingale's 'Cassandra.'" in The Politics of the Essay: Feminist Perspectives, eds. Ruth-Ellen Boetcher Joeres and Elizabeth Mittman, 1993. • Lytton Strachey, Eminent Victorians, 1918 [contains classic essay on Nightingale].

Our Text. • Florence Nightingale, Suggestions for Thought to Searchers After Religious Truth, vol. 2, 1860 [privately printed].

Walter Pater • Editions. • William E. Buckley, ed., Walter Pater: Three Major Texts [The Renaissance, Appreciations, Imaginary Portraits], 1986. • Lawrence Evans, ed., Letters of Walter Pater, 1970. • Walter Pater, Works, 10 vols., 1910; repr. 1967.

Biography. • Michael Levey The Case of Walter Pater, 1978.

Criticism. • Harold Bloom, ed., Walter Pater: Modern Critical Views, 1985. • Laurel Brake, Walter Pater, 1994. • Laurel Brake and Ian Small, eds., Pater in the 1990s, 1991. • William Buckler, Walter Pater: The Critic As Artist of Ideas, 1988. • Franklin Court, ed., Walter Pater: An Annotated Bibliography of Writing About Him, 1980. • D. J. DeLaura, Hebrew and Hellene in Victorian England: Newman, Arnold, and Pater, 1969. • Denis Donoghue, Walter Pater: Lover of Strange Souls, 1995. • T. S. Eliot, "Arnold and Pater," in his Selected Essays, 1930. • Graham Hough, The Last Romantics, 1949. • Wolfgang Iser, Walter Pater: The Aesthetic Moment, 1960; trans. 1987. • Francis Charles McGrath, The Sensible Spirit: Walter Pater and the Modernist Paradigm, 1986. • Gerald Monsman, Walter Pater's Art of Autobiography, 1980. • R. M. Seiler, ed., Walter Pater: The Critical Heritage, 1980. • Carolyn Williams, Transfigured World: Walter Pater's Aesthetic Historicism, 1989.

Our Texts. • Works, 1910; repr. 1967.

Christina Rossetti • Editions. • Rebecca W. Crump, ed., The Complete Poems of Christina Rossetti: A Variorum Edition, 3 vols., 1979–1990. • William M. Rossetti, ed., The Poetical Works of Christina Rossetti, 1904. • Rebecca W. Crump, ed., The Family Letters of Christina Georgina Rossetti. 1908; 1968.

Biography. • Kathleen Jones, Learning Not to Be First: The Life of Christina Rossetti, 1991. • Jan Marsh, Christina Rossetti: A Writer's Life, 1995.

Criticism. • Mary Arseneau, Antony H. Harrison, and Lorraine Janzen Kooistra, eds., The Culture of Christina Rossetti: Female Poetics and Victorian Contexts, 1999. • Georgina Battiscombe, Christina Rossetti: A Divided Life, 1981. • Kathleen Blake, Love and the Woman Question in Victorian Literature, 1983. • Edna Kotin Chatles, Christina Rossetti: Critical Perspectives, 1862–1982, 1985. • Rebecca W. Crump, Christina Rossetti: A Reference Guide, 1976. • Antony H. Harrison, Christina Rossetti in Context, 1988. • Antony H. Harrison, ed., Victorian Poetry: special issue on Christina

Rossetti, vol. 32, no. 3–4, 1994. • Elizabeth K. Helsinger, "Consumer Power and the Utopia of Desire: Christina Rossetti's Goblin Market." ELH 58 (1991). • David A. Kent, ed., *The Achievement of Christina Rossetti*, 1987. • Katherine J. Mayberry, *Christina Rossetti and the Poetry of Discovery*, 1989. • Jerome McGann, "Christina Rossetti's Poems: A New Edition and a Revaluation," *Victorian Studies* 23 (1980). • Jerome McGann, "The Religious Poetry of Christina Rossetti," *Critical Inquiry* 10 (1983). • Dorothy Mermin, "Heroic Sisterhood in *Goblin Market*," *Victorian Poetry* 21 (1983). • Dolores Rosenblum, *Christina Rossetti: The Poetry of Endurance*, 1986. • Sharon Smulders, *Christina Rossetti, Revisited*, 1996. • Virginia Woolf, "I Am Christina Rossetti," in *The Second Common Reader*, 1932.

Our Texts. • Rebecca W. Crump, ed., *The Complete Poems of Christina Rossetti: A Variorum Edition*, 3 vols., 1979–1990.

Dante Gabriel Rossetti • *Editions.* • Oswald Doughty and John R. Wahl, eds., *Letters of Dante Gabriel Rossetti*, 4 vols., 1965–1967 [incomplete]. • William Michael Rossetti, ed., *The Works of Dante Gabriel Rossetti*, 1911.

Biography. • Oswald Doughty, *A Victorian Romantic: Dante Gabriel Rossetti*, 1949; 1960.

Criticism. • Francis L. Fennell, ed., *Dante Gabriel Rossetti: An Annotated Bibliography*, 1982. • William E. Fredeman, ed., "Dante Gabriel Rossetti: An Issue Devoted to the Works," *Victorian Poetry.* 20 (1982). • Jan Marsh, *The Legend of Elizabeth Siddal*, 1989. • Jerome McGann, "The Complete Writings and Pictures of Dante Gabriel Rossetti: A Hypermedia Research Archive," *Victorian Literature and Culture* 22 (1994). • John Rees, *The Poetry of Dante Gabriel Rossetti*, 1981. • David G. Riede, *Dante Gabriel Rossetti and the Limits of Victorian Vision*, 1983. • David G. Riede, *Dante Gabriel Rossetti Revisited*, 1992. • James Sambrook, ed., *Pre-Raphaelitism: A Collection of Critical Essays*, 1974. • Derek Stanford, ed., *Pre-Raphaelite Writing: An Anthology*, 1973. • Richard L. Stein, *The Ritual of Interpretation: The Fine Arts as Literature in Ruskin, Rossetti, and Pater*, 1975. • Lionel Stevenson, *The Pre-Raphaelite Poets*, 1973. • Virginia Surtees, *Dante Gabriel Rossetti: 1828–1882. The Paintings and Drawings: A Catalogue Raisonné*, 2 vols., 1971.

Our Texts. • William Michael Rossetti, ed.,

The Works of Dante Gabriel Rossetti, 1911.

John Ruskin • *Editions.* • Harold Bloom, ed., *The Literary Criticism of John Ruskin*, 1965. • Van Akin Burd, ed., *The Ruskin Family Letters, 1801–1843*, 2 vols., 1973. • E. T. Cook and Alexander Wedderburn, eds., *The Works of John Ruskin*, 39 vols., 1903–1912. • John D. Rosenberg, ed., *The Genius of John Ruskin: Selections from His Writings*, 1963.

Biography. • Joan Abse, *John Ruskin: The Passionate Moralist*, 1980. • Timothy Hilton, *John Ruskin: The Early Years, 1819–1859*, 1985. • John Dixon Hunt, *The Wider Sea: A Life of John Ruskin*, 1982.

Criticism. • Linda M. Austin, *The Practical Ruskin: Economics and Audience in the Late Work*, 1991. • Michael W. Brooks, *John Ruskin and Victorian Architecture*, 1987. • Susan Casteras et al., *John Ruskin and the Victorian Eye*, 1993. • Raymond Fitch, *The Poison Sky: Myth and Apocalypse in Ruskin*, 1982. • Elizabeth Helsinger, *Ruskin and the Art of the Beholder*, 1982. • Robert Hewison, *John Ruskin: The Argument of the Eye*, 1976. • Robert Hewison, ed., *New Approaches to Ruskin: Thirteen Essays*, 1981. • George P. Landow, *The Aesthetic and Critical Theories of John Ruskin*, 1971. • George P. Landow, *Ruskin*, 1985. • Linda Merrill, *A Pot of Paint: Aesthetics on Trial in Whistler v. Ruskin*, 1992. • John D. Rosenberg, *The Darkening Glass: A Portrait of Ruskin's Genius*, 1961. • J. C. Sherburne, *John Ruskin, or the Ambiguities of Abundance: A Study in Social and Economic Criticism*, 1972.

Our Texts. • E. T. Cook and Alexander Wedderburn, eds., *The Works of John Ruskin*, 39 vols., 1903–1912.

Henry Morton Stanley • Norman R. Bennett, ed., *Stanley's Dispatches to the New York Herald*, 1970. • John Bierman, *Dark Safari: The Life Behind the Legend of Henry Morton Stanley*, 1990. • Richard Hall, *Stanley: An Adventurer Explored*, 1975. • Frank McLynn, *Stanley: The Making of an African Explorer*, 1990. • Dorothy Stanley, ed., *The Autobiography of Sir Henry M. Stanley*, 1909. • Richard Stanley and Alan Neame, eds., *The Exploration Diaries*, 1961. • Lytton Strachey, *Eminent Victorians*, 1918 [chapter on Stanley].

Our Text. • London edition, 1899.

Robert Louis Stevenson • *Editions*. • Bradford A. Booth and Ernest Mehew, *The Letters of Robert Louis Stevenson*, 1994. • Roger C. Lewis, ed., *The Collected Poems of Robert Louis Stevenson*, 2004.

Biography. • Graham Balfour, *The Life of Robert Louis Stevenson*, 1901. • Jenni Calder, *R L S: A Life Study*, 1980. • Philip Callow, *Louis: A Life of Robert Louis Stevenson*, 2001. • Frank J. McLynn, *Robert Louis Stevenson: A Biography*, 1993. • R. C. Terry, ed., *Robert Louis Stevenson: Interviews and Recollections*, 1996.

Criticism. • Jenni Calder, ed., *Stevenson and Victorian Scotland*, 1981. • Ed Cohen, "The Double Lives of Men: Narration and Identification in the Late Nineteenth-Century Representation of Ex-Centric Masculinities," *Victorian Studies* 36.3, 1993. • David Daiches, *Robert Louis Stevenson and His World*, 1973. • Edwin Eigner, *Robert Louis Stevenson and Romantic Tradition*, 1966. • Henry Geduld, ed., *The Definitive Dr. Jekyll and Mr. Hyde Companion*, 1983. • John R. Hammond, *A Robert Louis Stevenson Companion: A Guide to the Novels, Essays, and Short Stories*, 1984. • Robert Kiely, *Robert Louis Stevenson and the Fiction of Adventure*, 1964. • Paul Maixner, ed., *Robert Louis Stevenson: The Critical Heritage*, 1981. • Elaine Showalter, "Dr. Jekyll's Closet," in *The Haunted Mind: The Supernatural in Victorian Literature*, eds. Smith and Haas, 1999. • Judith Walkowitz, *City of Dreadful Night: Narratives of Sexual Danger in Victorian London*, 1992. • William Veeder and Gordon Hirsch, eds., *Dr. Jekyll and Mr. Hyde after One Hundred Years*, 1988.

Our Text. • *The Strange Case of Dr. Jekyll and Mr. Hyde*, 1886.

Algernon Charles Swinburne • *Editions*. • *The Poems of Algernon Charles Swinburne*, 6 vols., 1904–1905. • Edmund Gosse and Thomas J. Wise, eds. *The Complete Works of Algernon Charles Swinburne*, 1925–1927, 20 vols. [inaccurate and incomplete]. • Cecil Y. Lang, ed., *Letters of Algernon Charles Swinburne*, 6 vols., 1959–1962.

Biography. • Philip Henderson, *Swinburne: The Portrait of a Poet*, 1974. • Rikky Rooksby, *A. C. Swinburne: A Poet's Life*, 1997. • Donald Thomas, *Swinburne: The Poet in His World*, 1979.

Criticism. • Kirk H. Beetz, *Algernon Charles Swinburne: A Bibliography of Secondary Works, 1861–1980*, 1982. • Antony H. Harrison, *Swinburne's Medievalism: A Study in Victorian Love Poetry*, 1988. • Clyde K. Hyder, *Swinburne's Literary Career and Fame*, 1933. • Clyde K. Hyder, ed., *Swinburne: The Critical Heritage*, 1970. • Margot K. Louis, *Swinburne and His Gods: The Roots and Growth of an Agnostic Poetry*, 1990. • Jerome J. McGann, *Swinburne: An Experiment in Criticism*, 1972. • Harold Nicolson, *Swinburne*, 1926. • David G. Riede, *Swinburne: A Study of Romantic Mythmaking*, 1978. • Rikky Rooksby and Nicholas Shrimpton, eds., *The Whole Music of Passion: New Essays on Swinburne*, 1993. • John D. Rosenberg, "Swinburne," *Victorian Studies* 11 (1967). • *Victorian Poetry*, special Swinburne issue, 9 (1971).

Our Texts. • *The Poems of Algernon Charles Swinburne*, 6 vols., 1904–1905.

Alfred Tennyson • *Editions*. • Cecil Y. Lang and Edgar F. Shannon Jr., eds., *The Letters of Alfred, Lord Tennyson*, 3 vols., 1981–1990. • Christopher Ricks, ed., *Poems*, 3 vols., 1987. • Hallam Tennyson, ed., *Works*, 9 vols., 1907–1908.

Biography. • Robert B. Martin, *Tennyson: The Unquiet Heart*, 1980. • Hallam Tennyson, *Alfred, Lord Tennyson: A Memoir, by His Son*, 2 vols., 1897.

Criticism. • Daniel Albright, *Tennyson: The Muses' Tug-of-War*, 1986. • Kirk K. Beetz, *Tennyson: A Bibliography, 1827–1982*, 1984. • Jerome H. Buckley, *Tennyson: The Growth of a Poet*, 1960. • Philip Collins, ed., *Tennyson: Seven Essays*, 1993. • A. Dwight Culler, *The Poetry of Tennyson*, 1977. • Donald S. Hair, *Tennyson's Language*, 1991. • Arthur H. Hallam, "On Some Characteristics of Modern Poetry, and On the Lytical Poems of Alfred Tennyson," *Englishman's Magazine* (August 1831). • Gerhard Joseph, *Tennyson and the Text: The Weaver's Shuttle*, 1992. • John D. Jump, ed., *Tennyson: The Critical Heritage*, 1967. • John Killham, ed., *Critical Essays on the Poetry of Tennyson*, 1960. • James R. Kincaid, *Tennyson's Major Poems: The Comic and Ironic Patterns*, 1975. • Sir Harold Nicolson, *Tennyson: Aspects of His Life, Character, and Poetry*, 1923. • Norman Page, ed., *Tennyson: Interviews and Recollections*, 1983. • Timothy Peltason, *Reading In*

Memoriam, 1985. • F. E. L. Priestley, *Language and Structure in Tennyson's Poetry*, 1973. • Christopher Ricks, *Tennyson*, 1972. • John D. Rosenberg, *The Fall of Camelot: A Study of Tennyson's "Idylls of the King,"* 1973. • Matthew Rowlinson, *Tennyson's Fixations: Psychoanalysis and the Topics of the Early Poetry*, 1994. • Marion Shaw, *An Annotated Critical Bibliography of Alfred, Lord Tennyson*, 1989. • W. David Shaw, *Tennyson's Style*, 1976. • Alan Sinfield, *Alfred Tennyson*, 1986. • Herbert F. Tucker, *Tennyson and the Doom of Romanticism*, 1988. • Herbert F. Tucker, ed., *Critical Essays on Alfred Lord Tennyson*, 1993. • Paul Turner, *Tennyson*, 1976.

Our Texts. • Hallam Tennyson, ed., *Works*, 9 vols., 1907–1908.

Frances Trollope • Helen Heineman, *Frances Trollope*, 1984. • Helen Heineman, *Mrs. Trollope: The Triumphant Feminine in the 19th Century*, 1979. • Johanna Johnston, *The Life, Manners and Travels of Fanny Trollope: A Biography*, 1978. Pamela Neville-Sington, *Fanny Trollope: The Life and Adventures of a Clever Woman*, 1998. • Teresa Ransom, *Fanny Trollope*, 1995. • Frances Eleanor Trollope, *Frances Trollope: Her Life and Literary Work from George III to Victoria*, 2 vols., 1895.

Our Text. • Fifth edition, 1839.

Oscar Wilde • *Editions.* • Richard Ellmann, ed., *The Artist as Critic: Critical Writings of Oscar Wilde*, 1969. • Rupert Hart-Davis, ed., *Letters*, 1962. • Rupert Hart-Davis, *More Letters*, 1985. • Isobel Murray, ed., *The Complete Shorter Fiction of Oscar Wilde*, 1979. • Isobel Murray, ed., *The Writings of Oscar Wilde*, 1989. • Robert Ross, ed., *First Collected Edition*, 14 vols., 1908.

Biography. • Richard Ellmann, *Oscar Wilde*, 1987. • Vyvyan Holland, *Oscar Wilde, a Pictorial Biography*, 1960. • Melissa Knox, *Oscar Wilde: A Long and Lovely Suicide*, 1994.

Criticism. • Karl Beckson, ed., *Oscar Wilde: The Critical Heritage*, 1970. • Patricia Flanagan Behrendt, *Oscar Wilde: Eros and Aesthetics*, 1991. • Harold Bloom, ed., *Oscar Wilde: Modern Critical Views*, 1985. • Harold Bloom, ed., *Oscar Wilde's "The Importance of Being Earnest": Modern Critical Interpretations*, 1988. • Ed Cohen, *Talk on the Wilde Side: Toward a Geneology of a Discourse on Male Sexualities*, 1993. • Richard Ellmann, ed., *Oscar Wilde: A Collection of Critical Essays*, 1969. • Regenia Gagnier, ed., *Critical Essays on Oscar Wilde*, 1991. • Regenia Gagnier, *Idylls of the Marketplace: Oscar Wilde and the Victorian Public*, 1986. • Christopher S. Nassaar, *Into the Demon Universe: A Literary Exploration of Oscar Wilde*, 1974. • Kerry Powell, *Oscar Wilde and the Theatre of the 1890s*, 1991. • Peter Raby, *The Importance of Being Earnest: A Reader's Companion*, 1995. • Peter Raby, ed., *The Cambridge Companion to Oscar Wilde*, 1997. • Epifanio San Juan Jr., *The Art of Oscar Wilde*, 1967. • Rodney Shewan, *Oscar Wilde: Art and Egotism*, 1977. • John Stokes, *Oscar Wilde: Myths, Miracles, and Imitations*, 1996.

Our Texts. • Poems from *First Collected Edition*, ed. Robert Ross, 1908; "The Soul of Man under Socialism" from *Fortnightly Review* (February 1891); "The Decay of Lying," from the Preface to *The Picture of Dorian Gray*, and "The Importance of Being Earnest" from *The Writings of Oscar Wilde*, ed. Isobel Murray, 1989; "De Profundis" from *The Letters of Oscar Wilde*, ed. Rupert Hart-Davis, 1962.

INDEX